Swahili-English dictionary

A C. b. 1846 Madan

Nabu Public Domain Reprints:

You are holding a reproduction of an original work published before 1923 that is in the public domain in the United States of America, and possibly other countries. You may freely copy and distribute this work as no entity (individual or corporate) has a copyright on the body of the work. This book may contain prior copyright references, and library stamps (as most of these works were scanned from library copies). These have been scanned and retained as part of the historical artifact.

This book may have occasional imperfections such as missing or blurred pages, poor pictures, errant marks, etc. that were either part of the original artifact, or were introduced by the scanning process. We believe this work is culturally important, and despite the imperfections, have elected to bring it back into print as part of our continuing commitment to the preservation of printed works worldwide. We appreciate your understanding of the imperfections in the preservation process, and hope you enjoy this valuable book.

SWAHILI-ENGLISH DICTIONARY

BY

A. C. MADAN, M.A.
STUDENT OF CHRIST CHURCH, OXFORD

OXFORD
AT THE CLARENDON PRESS
1903

HENRY FROWDE, M.A.
PUBLISHER TO THE UNIVERSITY OF OXFORD
LONDON, EDINBURGH
NEW YORK

PREFACE

This Dictionary is an attempt to bring together in a convenient form materials for the study of the language most widely known throughout East and Central Africa, and to combine them in the light of a long, though in various ways limited, experience.

It would be more accurately described as an annotated vocabulary of the dialect of Swahili commonly spoken in Zanzibar city. It cannot lay claim to the formal completeness, especially in the treatment of verbs, which attaches to the idea of a dictionary, and it deals with a dialect which in respect of a large number of words is distinguished by the Swahilis themselves from the Swahili dialect of the coast. It is based on the lists of words, singularly accurate and relatively complete in themselves, furnished by Bishop Steere's *Handbook of Swahili* and scattered throughout his collections and translations, and on Krapf's *Dictionary of Swahili*—works issued more than twenty years ago. Later sources have also been drawn upon, especially Père Sacleux's *Dictionnaire français-swahili*, 1891, and the ever-increasing volume of Swahili literature (chiefly documents, letters, stories and poetry) due to the industry and scientific enthusiasm of German colonists and scholars. No work, however, at present exists (1903) which attempts the same object as the present. It was beyond the scope of Bishop Steere's plan to supply more than full lists of useful words. As to Krapf's monumental work, it may be enough to express a hope that it will never be re-edited. It remains indispensable to every student of Swahili, and has the permanent value and charm of genuine philological pioneer work by an honest and able researcher. It deals almost entirely with the dialect of Swahili used at Mombasa, and revision might make it more practically useful by the removal of inaccuracies and repetitions, and by modifying the spelling and arrangement, but such treatment would be analogous to re-writing Schliemann's Troy or Livingstone's Journals. The many first-hand explanations and examples are too precious, however, to be left unused, and it is especially on these that the present Editor has ventured freely to draw.

As to the use made of these and other materials, this Dictionary makes no claim to be encyclopaedic, or to include more than the commoner technical terms of arts, crafts and commerce, or to represent fully the flora or fauna of Zanzibar. Like other dictionaries, it presupposes an elementary acquaintance with the grammar of the dialect dealt with, in this case a very simple one. But (apart from imperfections due to ignorance or oversight) it will probably be found to provide sufficiently for the ordinary wants of officials, missionaries, travellers, teachers and translators, especially when used in connexion with the *English-Swahili Dictionary* (also published by the Oxford University Press, second edition, 1901) by the same Editor.

Reasons for attempting to provide a Dictionary of this kind may be briefly stated. The common language of Zanzibar has hitherto been the best known and most widely useful form of Swahili. And Swahili is still by far the most important member of the Bantu family of language, i. e. of the solid block of dialects, closely related among themselves and clearly differentiated from all others, which are spoken throughout about a third of the African continent, i. e. over nearly the whole of it from Nigeria and the Soudan on the north to the Hottentot region on the extreme south. Hence Swahili has been ranked not unreasonably among the twelve most important languages of the modern world, and the position of Zanzibar as till lately the undisputed commercial capital and chief political power of Eastern and Central Africa has determined the form of Swahili still most useful as the key to that entire region. It is not necessary to enlarge on its characteristics, but one special feature of it may be more fully referred to here.

The term Swahili represents, ethnologically as well as linguistically, the mixture of African and Arab elements on the East Coast of Africa. The proportions of the mixture in the race and the language vary indefinably, but its main characteristic is constant, viz. that the language remains always African, —and by African in this connexion is meant *Bantu*—in all its leading grammatical and phonetic features, however largely Arabic, and in a small degree other foreign elements figure in its vocabulary. How largely they figure appears in this book. The Editor is not well acquainted with Arabic, Hindustani, or indeed other dialects of Bantu, but he has made an attempt to discriminate between the Bantu and foreign element throughout. All words believed to be of non-Bantu origin are marked with an asterisk (*). Such words are mostly Arabic, or introduced through Arabic channels, and an Arabic scholar could no doubt add considerably to the number. As it is, a glance will show the numerical importance of the foreign element. A close study is needed to realize its full significance, to detect it (often strangely disguised) in all stages of phonetic and even grammatical assimilation, and to recognize its subtle power of permeation, even to the absolute displacement of some of the commonest Bantu words, and almost a monopoly of the connectives of words and sentences except in the simplest relations, and to unfold its historical significance as a record of successive invasions of Arab influence, warlike and peaceful, to which the East coast has been for centuries subjected. Here two or three results may be noted briefly. The Arabic element is so large and penetrating as seriously to diminish the value of the Swahili dialect for the purposes of comparison with other dialects of Bantu, simply from the displacement of Bantu roots elsewhere general. On the other hand, the very opportunity and power of assimilation is and has proved to be a most valuable one. It enables the African to draw on the rich resources of the Arabic vocabulary for the expression or better expression of new ideas, while providing an easy, and as it were, natural channel for the germinant seeds of culture, taste, and enlightenment of all kinds, wherever Swahili penetrates throughout the continent. There is a third consideration of practical importance. Bantu, and especially Swahili, is easy to pronounce and even to represent in writing with the ordinary alphabet, and the tendency of Swahili is to make Arabic also easy to pronounce and even (in a degree) to spell.

As to the always difficult subject of spelling and transcription of a language only lately reduced to writing, the present Editor is content to adopt generally the remarks made by Bishop Steere (in his Handbook, at the end of the Introduction and in the chapter on the alphabet), corroborated as they are in principle by Professor Max Müller in his little-known Introduction to the Outline Dictionary for Students of Language by John Bellows (now long out of print). He would also avow his own tendency to *Bantize* rather than *Arabize*, i. e. to simplify rather than refine upon Arabic sounds uncongenial to the African, so far as their representation in writing is concerned. There seems no ground for deliberately contributing to their perpetuation. The principle just referred to is, that it is a practical necessity in the transcription of languages to indicate sounds, not depict them, and that for this purpose the ordinary English alphabet should be used with as few modifications as possible. Happily in Swahili there are no sounds commonly heard which are not sufficiently indicated by Roman characters. The only real difficulty is one inherent in all phonetic transliteration, viz. actual or supposed differences in the pronunciation of the same word, whether locally or by individuals, and consequent impossibility of a spelling both accurate and uniform. Such differences are partly natural and universal, few individuals pronouncing the same word in exactly the same way. In Swahili they are aggravated by the disturbing effect of Arabic, leading to strange but common transpositions of vowels and inversions of consonants in the effort of the African to imitate or assimilate its difficult characteristic sounds, and also by varying dialectic tendencies among the Africans themselves. English achieves uniformity of spelling by resigning all pretence to phonetic accuracy. In Swahili phonetic exactness at present would make uniform spelling impossible. Hence in this Dictionary, words will be found given in various forms, representing the word as heard by different and differently qualified transcribers. The consequence may be sometimes baffling, but seems unavoidable.

Only students need attend to the brief notes appended in brackets to many of the articles. They are mainly meant to supply hints for further study, by bringing together under each word, others which seem to throw light upon it as to origin or meaning—especially cognate words from the same root, words worth noting from similarity of form, synonyms in the wide sense of similar in general or in a special meaning, also words illustrative by contrast and opposed meaning. There are but few notes on life and customs, &c., in Zanzibar. The fact appears to be that under the outward forms of a purely Mohammedan régime, only modified on the surface as yet by European civilization, and slightly disturbed in its depths by the leaven of Christianity, there exists a medley of tribal customs and superstitions, as varied and varying as the population itself, which do not admit of disentanglement on the spot, and could only be profitably studied in the places from which they are derived.

For Arabic words Steingass' Dictionary has been chiefly

relied on, and Palmer's and Tien's Grammars. As to the manifold imperfections of this book, competent critics may be trusted to recognize and perhaps to allow for them. Every one who has experience of Zanzibar will find words which seem wrongly inserted or omitted. The prefaces of Johnson and Murray catalogue the difficulties which beset more or less the making of even a small dictionary of any language. The lexicographer is no doubt rightly defined as a drudge, but perhaps doubtfully as 'a harmless drudge.' The present Editor knows the Swahili of Zanzibar well enough to know that he does not know it well. But his work may (it is hoped) help others to know it as well— and better.

A. C. MADAN.

OXFORD, *July*, 1903.

INTRODUCTION
TO THE USE OF THIS DICTIONARY

To find words and ascertain their meanings in a dictionary too limited in size to allow a full enumeration of either, attention is needed to the following directions.

1. To find words.

All Swahili verbs, many nouns and adjectives, and some particles vary at the beginning, and will not commonly be found under the letter (sound) which comes first. As a rule, verbs and adjectives are to be looked for under the first letter of the root, and nouns under the form of the singular number. The variable formative elements, as distinct from the radical, are called in this Dictionary prefixes (pfx.), and for convenience prefix is often arbitrarily used to include infix, and affix or suffix. Prefixes are usually agglutinative elements, but some have a limited use as independent words. A glance at the Tabular Conspectus of the noun and verb which follows the Introduction will be practically sufficient, with a knowledge of the elements of the simple Swahili Grammar, to enable the root to be distinguished. Thus:

(*a*) A Noun beginning with *wa-*, *mi-*, *vi-*, *ny-*, *ma-*, which are common plural prefixes, may be looked for under the corresponding singular form.

Obs. The declension of each noun (which colours grammatically the whole of a Swahili sentence) is as a rule shown by placing immediately after it the plural prefix in brackets. This method sufficiently distinguishes declensions 1 to 5. Declension 6 does not change in the plural, and is shown by the absence of a prefix following, or by (—). Nouns of declension 8 should be looked for under the letter following *ku*, i. e. the verb from which they are in almost all cases formed. The declensions are commonly referred to as D 1 (S), i.e. First Declension Singular Number, D 1 (P), i.e. First Declension Plural Number, D 2 (S), D 2 (P), and so on.

(*b*) An adjective beginning with any one of the common adjectival prefixes (see Conspectus II (*c*)) may be looked for under the letter (sound) following it. Variable adjectives are written with a (-) before the root, e. g. *-ema*, and the more important variations of forms corresponding to different declensions are appended to each.

(*c*) Conspectus I both illustrates the difficulty of finding the root of a Swahili verb and also supplies a key. Combinations of any of the six classes of prefix, which may precede a root, must be recognized and removed, and then the letter following will be the first letter of the root.

2. To ascertain meanings.

Nouns and verb-stems are so readily developed from a root in Swahili, by a regular and almost mechanical process, i. e. by the use of certain prefixes, that it is impossible to give more than a selection from them. Their meaning may, however, be gathered as a rule from the known meaning of the prefix, and the root when recognized will usually be found independently or in some cognate word. The rarer the combination, the more certain the meaning to be simply the normal meanings of root and prefix combined.

(*a*) The commonest formative noun-prefixes are *M-* (*Mw-*), *Ki-* (*Ch-*), *U-* (*W-*), at the beginning of a word, often with a variable but significant ending, *-o*, *-ji*, or *-zi*. The characteristic force of each of these elements may be gathered from the notes on them in their places in this Dictionary.

(*b*) The Swahili verb-root is capable of such a rich and varied development in the form of additional verb-stems, each with its complement of conjugations, moods, tenses, &c., that only a few have been fully treated in this Dictionary, hardly any completely. Shades of meaning are so numerous and their differences so delicate, that appropriate renderings in English suited to each particular case have to be left very largely to the student's appreciation of each form separately. Only examples and suggestions can be given within reasonable limits of space. But the following considerations may enable him better to infer for himself the meaning of verb-forms not stated under the verb itself. And if he is still inclined to complain of vagueness and inadequacy in their interpretation, it may be remembered that language unwritten (like Swahili) is the speech of a living person, and so carries its own simultaneous commentary of look, gesture, and tone, as well as sound—appealing thus to four senses in sympathetic and intelligent relation to the speaker, and not only to the eye interpreting a written character. The full meaning of any written statement has at best often to be guessed, and a Swahili, if he writes, writes as he speaks, assuming a hearer and not a reader.

Subject only to the limitations imposed by common sense (i.e. by the meaning of the root itself) and common usage, all Swahili verbs may exhibit, beside (1) a simple or primary form (Pr.), seven derived forms, here called—(2) Applied (Ap.), (3) Causal (Cs.), (4) Reciprocal (Rp.), (5) Reversive (Rv.), (6) Stative (St.), (7) Reflexive (Rf.), and (8) Reduplicated (Rd.)— each (under the above limitations) with Active, Passive, and Neuter Voices, and Positive and Negative Conjugations, and each of them with its complement of Moods, Tenses, as well as derived nouns and adjectives, beside an indefinite number of other forms or stems formed by combinations of those just enumerated.

The characteristics by which each main form may be recognized, and the chief meanings of each, from which choice must be made, are briefly as follows :

1. *Primary* (Pr.), in which the root is followed by *a*, the simplest form of the verb and conveying its simplest meaning, but generally capable of both transitive and intransitive construction. (Obs. verbs of non-Bantu origin may end also in *-u*, and *-i*.)

(*a*) The Passive Voice in this (*and in all the verb-forms following*) is distinguished by *w* before the final vowel, and (*b*) the Neuter by *k* (*ik, ek*). The Neuter has three common uses, indicating (1) the same as the passive, but with less definite reference to any agent or instrument, (2) what is usual, (3) what is practicable, e. g. *njia hii yaendeka* may mean (1) this road is as a fact passed over, (2) this road is a regular thoroughfare, (3) this road is passable, open, safe. Obs. meaning (3) is also regularly indicated by *-kana*, for *ka*, e. g. *yaendekana*, i. e. a combination of the Neuter and Reciprocal forms (see below, 4).

2. *Applied* (Ap.), in which *i* or *e* is inserted between the root and final *a*, and choice has to be made among all the meanings usually expressed in English by a preposition following a verb, e. g. from, to, at, by, with, in, out of, for, against, about, &c. Only the sympathetic interpretation referred to above can determine the choice rightly in many cases. Obs. the Passive of the Ap. form is often used as the Passive of the Pr. form.

3. *Causal* (Cs.), in which *z* (*sh, s*, and sometimes *y*) is inserted between the root and final *a*. The meaning conveyed is (1) Causal, (2) Intensive or Emphatic. But the Causal sense includes at least six varieties of causation, needing often delicate discrimination and totally different translation, according

INTRODUCTION

as it is (1) simple, a causing to do (or be), (2) compulsive, forcing to do, (3) permissive, allowing to do, (4) suasive, inducing to do, (5) passive, not interfering with doing, (6) consequential, resulting in (tending to) doing.

4. *Reciprocal* (Rp.), in which *an* is inserted before the final *a*. Here again the form expresses several distinct aspects of common action, e.g. (1) reciprocal, e.g. *pigana*, 'give and return blows'—action and reaction, (2) connected action, e.g. *lokana na*, 'come out of,' *fuatana na*, 'follow,' (3) combined (mutual, joint) action, e.g. *endana*, 'all go together,' *liana*, 'cry together,' (4) interaction, of what affects all parts or different parts of the same single object, e.g. *shikana*, 'hold together, be compact (firm),' *kazana*, 'be tight, be pressed together,' (5) in connexion with the Neuter sign *ka* (see above), *-kana* indicates commonly what is practicable, possible, probable, &c., e.g. *onekana*, 'be visible, be within the range of vision, come into sight.'

5. *Reflexive* (Rf.), in which the syllable *ji* is prefixed to the root itself. The many shades of meaning thus conveyed may be gathered from the article on *ji* in the Dictionary.

6. *Reduplicated* (Rd.), in which a verb-stem is repeated twice and used as a single stem to indicate emphasis, frequency, or continuance, e.g. *piga piga*, 'beat soundly,' or 'keep on beating.'

7. *Reversive* (Rv.), in which *u* (sometimes *o*) is inserted between the root and final *a*, indicating the reverse of the simple Pr. form, but also (when the general result is identical) sometimes the same. Cf. *pinda* and *pindua*, *kama* and *kamua*, *zima* and *zimua*.

8. *Stative* (St.), in which *am* is inserted before the final *a*, indicating a relatively fixed state or permanent condition. It occurs also combined with *an*, i.e. *-aman*, in verbs like *shikamana*, *andamana*. See under *-mana* in its place.

II. CONSPECTUS OF

Illustrating the usual Prefixes which distinguish the various Declensions and Numbers, and also the chief Verbal and Adjectival Prefixes and Pronoun Forms corresponding to each. There is no distinction of Gender in Swahili Nouns.

DECLEN-SION.	NOUN-PREFIX.	ROOT.	ADJECTIVAL PREFIX.	PRONOUN.	VERBAL PREFIX.
	(a)	(b)	(c)	(d)	(e)
1.	*Sing.* m *Plur.* wa	(*e.g.*) tu (*thing*)	m, mw wa, w	huyu, yule hawa, wao	1st. 2nd. 3rd. *Sing. Subj.* ni, u, a *Obj.* ni, ku, m *Plur. Subj.* tu, m, wa *Obj.* tu, wa, wa
	e.g. (a, b) mtu, *person*, (c) mwema, *good*, (d) huyu, *this*, (e) ampenda, *he loves him*.					
2.	*Sing.* m *Plur.* mi	(*e.g.*) ti (*tree*)	m, mw mi, m	huu, ule hii, ile	*Sing. Subj.* } u, w *Obj.* } *Plur. Subj.* } i, y *Obj.* }
	e.g. (a, b) mti, *tree*, (c) mdogo, *small*, (d) huu, *this*, (e) waota, *it grows*.					
3.	*Sing.* ki *Plur.* vi	(*e.g.*) tu (*thing*)	ki, ch vi, vy	hiki, kile hivi, vile	*Sing. Subj.* } ki, ch *Obj.* } *Plur. Subj.* } vi *Obj.* }
	e.g. (a, b) kitu, *thing*, (c) kizuri, *pretty*, (d) hiki, *this*, (e) chapendeza, *it pleases*.					
4.	*Sing.* u, w *Plur.* ny	(*e.g.*) imbo (*song*)	m, mw n (*with euphonic variants*)	huu, ule hizi, zile	*Sing. Subj.* } u, w *Obj.* } *Plur. Subj.* } zi *Obj.* }
	e.g. (a, b) uimbo, *song*, (c) mbaya, *bad*, (d) huu, *this*, (e) wachukiza, *it disgusts*.					

(ZANZIBAR) SWAHILI NOUN

1, is the usual Declension of living beings, 2, of plants. Diminutives belong to 3, Amplificatives to 5, Abstracts mostly to 4, Foreign words to 6, and in some cases 5, 7 is Local only, and 8, Verbal. The (so-called) Possessive Adjectives and a few others follow the Pronominal Prefixes.

DECLENSION.	NOUN-PREFIX.	ROOT.	ADJECTIVAL PREFIX.	PRONOUN.	VERBAL PREFIX.
	(a)	(b)	(c)	(d)	(e)
5.	Sing. — Plur. ma	(e.g.) kasha (box)	— ma, m	hili, lile haya, yale	Sing. Subj. } li, l Obj. } Plur. Subj. } ya Obj. }
	e.g. (a, b) kasha, *box*, (c) kubwa, *large*, (d) hili, *this*, (e) latosha, *it suffices*.				
6.	Sing. — Plur. —	(e.g.) kazi (work)	n (with euphonic variants)	hii, ile hizi, zile	Sing. Subj. } i, y Obj. } Plur. Subj. } zi Obj. }
	e.g. (a, b) kazi, *work*, (c) ngumu, *hard*, (d) hii, *this*, (e) yachosha, *it wearies*.				
7.	Sing. — Plur. —	mahali (*place*) (only noun in this declension.)	pa, p — —	hapa, pale — —	Sing. Subj. } Obj. } pa Plur. Subj. } Obj. }
	e.g. (a, b) mahali, *place*, (c) pembamba, *narrow*, (d) hapa, *this*, (e) pafaa, *it suits*.				
8.	Sing. — Plur. —	(e.g.) kufa (dying)	ku, kw — —	huku, kule — —	Sing. Subj. } Obj. } ku, kw Plur. Subj. } Obj. }
	e.g. (a, b) kufa, *dying*, (c) kutukufu, *glorious*, (d) huku, *this*, (e) kwasifiwa, *it is praised*.				

ABBREVIATIONS

EASILY recognized abbreviations are used for the common grammatical names of parts of speech and their varieties—conjugations, moods, tenses, &c.

The eight Declensions given in Conspectus II are distinguished as *D* 1 (*S*), i.e. First Declension Singular Number, *D* 1 (*P*), i.e. First Declension Plural Number, *D* 2 (*S*), *D* 2 (*P*), *D* 3 (*S*), and so on.

The eight principal forms of verb-stem are distinguished as *Pr*. Primary or Simple, *Ap*. Applied, *Cs*. Causal, *Rp*. Reciprocal, *St*. Stative, *Rv*. Reversive, *Rf*. Reflexive, *Rd*. Reduplicated. *Ps*. denotes Passive, *Act*. Active, *Nt*. Neuter, *Pos*. Positive, *Neg*. Negative.

Pfx. Prefix, includes (for convenience) infix, suffix, and affix—the same formative element being often medial or final as well as initial.

Kr. Krapf, *Sac*. Sacleux, *Str*. Steere, the principal authorities relied upon throughout, are only cited in connexion with particular words or statements.

The chief languages referred to are: *B*. Bantu, *Ar*. or *Arab*. Arabic, *Swa*. Swahili, *Z*. Zanzibar, *Hind*. Hindustani, *Pers*. Persian, *Fr*. French, *Eng*. English, *Germ*. German, *Port*. Portuguese. Obs. *Arab*., and not *Ar*., denotes *Arabic* words but little used or assimilated in the common talk of Zanzibar.

The following may also be noted:—

    a. = adjective.
    adv. = adverb.
  amplif. = amplificative, denoting large (relative) size.
   conj. = conjunction.
 conjug. = conjugation.
    cf. = compare.
   conn. = connect, connected.
   contr. = contrast, contrary in meaning.
   dim. = diminutive, denoting small (relative) size.
   dist. = distinguish, distinct in meaning.
   esp. = especially.
   fig. = figurative, in a figurative sense.
  follg. = a word or article immediately following.
   int. = interjection.
 intens. = intensive, with intensive force, emphatic.
   lit. = literally, in a literal sense.

ABBREVIATIONS

n. = noun.
obs. = observe
opp. = opposed to, of opposite meaning.
perh. = perhaps.
prec. = a word or article immediately preceding
prep. = preposition
pron. = pronoun.
pronom. = pronominal or possessive—of adjectives, &c.
syn. = synonymous, in a wide sense, illustrative of the general, or of a special, meaning of a word.
usu. = usual, usually.

A SWAHILI-ENGLISH DICTIONARY

(Words marked * appear not to be of *Bantu* origin.)

A.

A represents generally the broad sound of *a* in 'father.' It also includes (chiefly in non-accented syllables) the lighter sound of *a* in 'man.' And there is a modification of it which is noted under certain words of Arabic origin, being heard and written sometimes as *e*. See **Elfu, Hewa,** and **E.**

A is far the commonest vowel sound in Swahili, and with the consonants *k* and *m* gives a distinct phonetic colour to the spoken language as a whole. Though comparatively rare as an initial sound of Bantu roots, it is the regular terminal sound of most Swahili verb-forms, appears in many of the formative prefixes of the verb, in the plural prefixes of two declensions, and in most of the common conjunctions and prepositions.

Aa is used to represent a long *a* sound, which usually indicates (1) in the case of Bantu words, a really double syllable with an *l* or *r* sound slurred or elided between the *a*'s; (2) in the case of Arabic words, the Bantu effort to express the sounds of Alif, Ain, or combinations of them.

———

A as a simple uncombined sound is used:

(1) As an interjection, whose meaning depends on the mode of utterance and intonation. Thus:

(a) *A!* or *Ah!* or *Ahh!* expresses simply wonder, pleasure, pain, grief, &c.

(b) *A-aa* or *A-haa* (also *A-hee* and *E-hee*)—the sounds distinct, with rising intonation, and stress on the last, 'yes, just so, exactly, I understand,' i. e. assent, affirmation.

(c) *Aa-a* or *A-a-a*—the sounds distinct, with falling intonation, and stress on the first, 'no, oh no, not so, 'by no means,' i. e. dissent and negation.

(2) As a preposition, but only occasionally as a slurred or shortened form of the full prepositional *wa, ya,* &c., after a vowel preceding. (See below.)

(3) Not (like the other personal prefixes, *ni, u, tu, m, wa*) as a verb-form '(he, she) is,' its place being taken sometimes by *yu*, otherwise by the general verb-form *ni*, e.g. *mfalme yu* (or *ni*) *mwema*, the king is good.

A in verb-formation is:

(1) The Pers. Pfx. of 3 Sing. in all Tenses, agreeing with D 1 (S), e.g. *atapenda*, he will love.

(2) The Tense Pfx. of Pres. Indef., e.g. *wapenda* (*u-a-penda*), you love, and (coalescing or dispensing with the Pers. Pfx. wholly or in part) *napenda* (*ni-a-penda*), I love, *apenda* (*a-a-penda*), he loves.

(3) Part of one form of the Past Tense Pfx. *ali* (otherwise *li* only), e.g. *nalipenda* (*n-ali-penda*, otherwise *ni-li-penda*), I loved.

N. *A* in Prefixes, (1) when followed by *e*, disappears regularly in *ka, ma, wa, pa*, sometimes in *a, na, ta,* never in the Neg. Pfx. *ha*, e. g. *akenda* (*a-ka-enda*), and he went, *penpe* (*pa-epe*), a white place; (2) when followed by *i*, coalesces with it to form *e*, e. g. *aketa* (*a-ka-ita*), and he called, *wezi* (*wa-izi*), thieves, *mengi* (*ma-ingi*), many.

B

-a is the invariable element, which combined with a prefix forms the various prepositions *wa, ya, za, cha, la, pa, kwa, mwa*. In meaning these all correspond generally to the English 'of,' and (with the noun following) to the Genitive Case in the classical languages, and include all such adjectival relations as 'belonging to, proceeding from, consisting of, of the class or kind of, relating to, qualified by,' &c.

Each of the above forms will be found in the Dictionary, but here it may be noted that:

(1) With a noun following, they supply the lack of adjectives, and, with an adverb preceding, the lack of prepositions, in Swahili, e. g. *nyumba ya mawe*, a stone house, *sumu ya kufisha*, deadly poison, *baada ya haya*, after these things, *kando la mto*, beside the river.

(2) Where the reference is general, or the noun easily supplied, they are sometimes used without a noun preceding, e.g. *ya kwanza*, in the first place, *wa vita*, warriors, *cha kula*, food. And by a curious idiom the preposition is sometimes referred to the person concerned and not to the thing qualified, e.g. *alimpiga wa jicho*, and he struck him a blow in the eye, not (*pigo*) *la jicho*.

(3) After some common nouns the preposition is often omitted, e. g. *binti Ali*, the daughter of Ali, *mwana chuoni*, the schoolboy, *kina bibi*, ladies. And it is sometimes slurred, if not elided, after *a* preceding, e. g. *saa a tano*, or *saa tano* (*saa ya tano*), the fifth hour.

*Aali, a. superior, excellent, exalted. (Arab. Cf. *taala* and *Ali*. *Aa* here represents the combination Alif, Ain, Alif.)

*Aasi, v. See Asi. (Ar.)

*Abadán, adv. always, constantly, ever. *Mwanamke a. harithi*, a woman is never contented. (Arab., for common *siku zote, daima*.)

*Abedari, n. (—, or *ma-*) and Bedari, a large block or pulley used in hoisting the main-yard of a native sailing vessel. (? Ar. or Hind. Cf. for pulley, *kapi, gofia*.)

*Abiri, v. cross, cross over, pass over, esp. of river or sea. *A. kwa* (*katika*) *chombo*, cross in a vessel. Ps. *abir-iwa*. Nt. *-ika, -ikana*. *Mto waabirika*, the river can be crossed. Ap. *abir-ia, -iwa, -ika*. *Mtumbwi wa kuabiria*, a canoe to cross in. *Fetha ya kuabiria*, fare for passage across. Cs. *abir-isha, -ishwa, -ishana*, send over, put across, ferry over. (Ar. Cf. follg. and syn. B. *vuka, kiuka, pita*.)

*Abiria, n. (—, and *ma-*), person crossing (a river, sea, &c.), passenger (in a boat, vessel, &c.). (Ar. Cf. *abiri*.)

*Abudu, v. worship, adore, venerate, prop. of religious worship and service, both outward and inward. *A. Muungu* (*sanamu*), worship God (idols). *A. sala*, perform a service of prayer. Ps. *abudiwa*, be (in fact) worshipped. Nt. *abudika*, be an object (generally, or a proper object) of worship. Ap. *abud-ia, -iwa, -ika*, offer worship to, worship in (for, on account of, &c.). Cs. *abud-isha, -ishwa*, cause to worship, convert. (Ar. Cf. *ibada, mwabudu, maabudu*, and, of external worship, *sujudu*.)

Acha, v. the main idea is, ceasing or breaking off connexion with something, and may be rendered in many ways, with many shades of meaning, e. g. (1) 'leave, leave off, leave behind, let go, let pass, let be, go (part, depart) from; (2) abandon, desert, neglect; (3) acquit, release, pardon; (4) allow, permit, give leave; (5) separate from, divorce.' *Acha!* (imper.) Let go! Give over! Hands off! *Sikuachi*, I will not let you go. *Akamwacha akenda zake*, and he left him and went away. *A. mtumwa huru*, let a slave go free (set him at liberty). Colloquially, *a.* is used somewhat as an expletive, e.g. *Acha* (or, *wache*, for *waache*) *Wazungu watawale kwa nguvu*, let alone Europeans for strong government, i.e. trust them for it. *Acha mizinga ilie*, just let the cannons fire, i.e. the cannons *did* make a noise. Ps. *achwa*. Many derivative verb-stems are used, with their characteristic meanings. Ap. *ach-ia, -iwa, -ika, -iana*. Also *-ilia, -iliwa, -ilika, -iliana*. *Kuachia mtoto mali*, to bequeath property to a child. *Ameachiwa*, he has had money left him. *Kumwachilia makosa*, to pardon his offences. *Thambi hii inaachilika*, this sin is venial. *Watu waachiliao nyama*, human beings who are quite distinct from animals. Cs. *ach-isha* (sometimes *asha*), *-ishwa, -ishia, -ishika*. *Achisha mtoto* (with or without *maziwa*), wean a child. *Ulimwachisha mkewe*, you caused him to desert (divorce) his wife. Rp. *ach-ana, -ania, -anisha*, leave each other, part, diverge, be different, be inconsistent. *Wameachana*, they have taken leave of each other. *Njia zinaa.*, the paths diverge. *Maneno yamea.*, the statements do not agree. *Achana na*, part from. (Cf. *saza, bakisha*.)

***Achali**, n. pickle, sauce, relish; jam, preserve. Usually of an acid mixture, made of lemon juice, salt, pepper, &c., but also of sweet ones. (Hind.)

***Ada**, n. (—, and *ma-*), (1) custom, habit, manner, and esp. (2) customary present, commission, fee,—as to a doctor, teacher, or workman on beginning or ending a job, or at a wedding. Such gifts, whether in cash or kind, have various significant names, e.g. *ufito*, stick, *kilemba*, turban, *kinyosha mgongo*, back-straightener, *kifungua mlango*, door-opener, *kipa mkono*, handshaker, &c. *A. ya biashara*, custom of trade. *Nipe a. yangu*, give me my fee. *A. zilizompasia jumbe*, customs proper to be observed as to a chief. (Ar. Cf. syn. *desturi, mila*, and for presents generally *bakshishi*.)

***Adabu**, n. good manners, proper behaviour, politeness, courtesy, civility, etiquette. *A. yake Arabu nyingine kuliko Waswahili*, Arab etiquette is often different from Swahili. *Huna a.*, you do not know how to behave (a very insulting expression). *Tia a.*, teach good manners. *Fanya a.*, behave well, show courtesy. Often used, like many nouns in Swahili, as an adjectival predicate. *Mtu huyu a. sana*, this person behaves like a gentleman. (Ar. Cf. *adibu, taadabu*, and dist. *athabu*, punishment, sometimes written *adabu*.)

***Adamu**, n. Adam. *Mwana wa Ad., mwana Ad., bin Adamu*, are commonly used for 'member of human race, human being, man.' (Ar. Cf. *mtu, mlimwengu, mwana*, and *wanadamu*, i.e. *u-anad*.)

***Adawa**, n. enmity, hostility, strife, quarrel. (Arab. Cf. more common *wadui* (*u-adui*), and *adui*.)

***Aden**, n. and **Adan**, Aden, also Eden. *Bustani ya Aden*, Garden of Eden. (Ar.)

***Adi**, v. cause to pass, let pass on, allow a guest to depart,—esp. after courteously accompanying him to the door, or a short distance on his journey. *Wakatusindikiza hatta mtoni wakatuadi*, they accompanied us as far as the river, and took leave of us. (Arab.,—the B. *sindikiza* being commonly used.)

***Adibu**, v. teach manners to, educate. Ps. *adibiwa*. Nt. *adibika*. *Mtoto yale haadibiki*, that child will never learn to behave. Ap. *adibia, -iwa*. Cs. *adib-isha, -shwa*,—used in same sense as the Pr. *adibu*, and more commonly. (Ar. Cf. *adabu, taadabu*, and contr. *adabu*, right external behaviour, with *adili*, right moral conduct. Also B. *lea*, bring up, educate.)

***Adili**, n. right, right conduct,

morals, morality. — a. right, righteous, just. *Hukumu a.*, a right judgement. *Mfalme a.*, a just king. — v. behave rightly, act morally. Cs. *adil-isha, -ishwa*, teach right conduct to, give a moral training to. (Ar. Cf. *-adilifu*, and contr. *adibu, adabu*.)

*-adilifu, a. as *adili*, a. upright, honourable, respectable, moral. (Ar. Cf. *adili*.)

*Adui, n. (—, and *ma-*), enemy, foe, opponent. (Ar. Cf. *adawa, wadui*, and syn. B. *mtesi, mshindani*.)

A-ee, int. also A-hee, E-hee, with second syllable accented and on a higher note, expressing assent, affirmation, 'yes, just so, exactly.' (Cf. *a* as int. and note.)

*Afa, n. (*ma-*), person or thing causing fear, a terror, horror, bugbear, enemy. (Arab. Cf. *hofu, mwafa*, and B. *kioja, kitisho*.)

*Afathali, adv. better, rather, preferably, as the best course, more correctly. *A. uenende*, you had better proceed. *Hivi a.*, it is best so. (Ar. Cf. *fathili, (u)tafathali*.)

*Afia, n. See Afya. (Ar.)

*Afikana, v. See Afiki. (Ar.)

*Afiki, v. agree with, correspond to, be same as, fit. *Tarihi ya mwaka iliafiki hamstashara Desember*, the date corresponded to Dec. 15. The most used forms are the Rp. *afikana*, agree together, make an agreement (contract, bargain), come to an understanding, be reconciled, and Cs. *afikanisha*, bring to terms, reconcile, pacify. (Ar. as if *wafiki*. Cf. *maafikano, mwafaka*, and syn. B. *patana, lingana*.)

*Afiuni, n. opium. (Ar. Cf. syn. *kasumba*.)

*Afu, v. also Afua, save, deliver, preserve, cure, pardon, acquit. *Muungu amemwafu*, God has preserved him. — n. (*ma-*), preservation, pardon. (Arab. not common and deriv. stems rare. Cf. *afu*, n. and *afya*, also common B. syn. *ponya, okoa*.)

Afu, n. blossoms of the wild jasmine, *mwafu*, growing in Z. and valued for the perfume. (Cf. *yasmini*.)

*Afua, v. See Afu, v.

*Afya, n. also Afia, good health, sound condition, safety, preservation, and also 'general condition, state of health,' with qualifying adj. *Sina a.*, I am not in good health. *A. njema (mbaya)*, good (bad) health. *Bora a.* (also *borafya*), good health. (Ar. Cf. *afu*, v. and *hali*, also B. syn. *uzima*.)

Afya, v. cause to swear, put on oath. (Cs. from *apa*, v. = *apisha*. See *apa*, and for interchange of *p* and *f*, see under *F*.)

Aga, v. (1) agree (with), promise (to), engage; (2) say good-bye (to), take leave (of), dismiss, let go. *Aga (agana) buriani*, say a last farewell, take solemn final leave (of). Fig. of sunset, *jua linaaga miti*, the sun is taking leave of the trees. Ps. *agwa*. *Wameagwa*, they have been told (received permission) to go. Ap. *ag-ia, -iwa, -ilia, -iliana*. *Uliniagia kofia*, you promised me a cap. *Niagie babangu*, say good-bye to my father for me. *Maneno waliyoagiliana yeye na rafiki zake*, the terms which he and his friends agreed upon. Cs. *ag-iza, -izwa*, usually Intens., charge, commission, order, appoint, give strict injunctions. *Kuagiza ni kuweza?* Does ordering mean it can be done? Rp. *ag-ana, -ania, -anika, -anisha*, (1) make a mutual agreement, come to terms, conclude a bargain; (2) exchange farewells, say good-bye to each other. Cs. *aganisha*, bring to terms, reconcile. (Cf. *agizo, agano*, and syn. *wasia, ahidi*.)

Agano, n. (*ma-*), (1) agreement, promise, contract, mutual understanding; (2) leave-taking, farewell. (Usu. in plur. Cf. *aga*, and syn. *mapatano, maafikano, ahadi, mkataba*.)

Agizo, n. (*ma-*), charge, injunction, commission, order, appointment; (2) commission for executing orders, fee. (Cf. *aga, agano.*)

Agua, v. predict, foretell, prophesy, divine, presage. Ps. *aguliwa.* Nt. *agulika.* Ap. *agu-lia, -liwa, -lika.* Cs. *agu-za, -zwa,* and Intens. *Bao la kuagulia,* a divining board. (Cf. *mwaguzi, maaguzi,* and for various kinds of divination, *bao, ramli, feli.*)

Agua, v. treat medically, supply medicine, operate (on). *Killa auguaye, humwagua,* every one who was sick he treated with medicine. *Atuague uganga wa vita,* let him supply us with war-medicine. *Chukua ndimu aagulie mgongo wake,* take a lime, and let him apply it to his back. (Derivs., &c. as prec. Cf. *ugua.*)

Ahaa, int. yes, just so (see *A,* as interject. sound, and cf. *A-ee,* int. note).

*__Ahadi,__ n. (—), also __Wahadi,__ promise, engagement, agreement. *Toa (funga, -pa) a.,* make a promise. *Vunja a.,* break a promise. *Timiza (fikisha, shika) a.,* keep (fulfil, &c.) a promise. *Ahadi yetu, tupeleke mzigo Tabora,* our engagement is, to convey a load to Tabora. (Ar. Cf. *ahidi.*)

*__Ahali,__ n. (—), relations, kindred, kinsman. Used comprehensively, and often in contrast with near relatives. *Wazee na ndugu na a.,* parents, brothers, and relations. *Ndugu na a.,* brothers and (other) kinsmen. *Mtu katika a. zake,* one of his relations. (Ar. Cf. *akraba, jamaa, utani, ukoo.*)

*__Ahera,__ n. and __Akhera, Aheri,__ (1) that which is last (or behind, or beyond), the end, the last stage; (2) esp. the next world, future life, last day, grave (as end of present life). *Toka awali hatta aheri,* from first to last, from beginning to end. (Syn. B. *toka mwanzo hatta mwisho.*) *Huko ahera ni kuzuri,* it is nice over yonder. *Hatta Sultani atakwenda ahera* (or, *aherani*), even a king must die (will come to his end).

(Ar. Cf. *ahiri,* and syn. B. *mwisho, kikomo,* end, and *kuzimu,* spirit world.)

*__Ahi,__ n. See __Akhi.__

*__Ahiri,__ v. and __Akhiri,__ stand over, be behindhand, be put off (deferred, adjourned), remain behind. Ps. *ahiriwa* (as *ahiri*). Ap. *-ahir-ia, -iwa, -ika.* Cs. *ahir-isha, -ishwa,* postpone, delay, adjourn, defer, cause to wait. *Maneno haya yanaahirika,* this business can be adjourned (taken afterwards). (Arab. Cf. *ahera,* and syn. *usiri,* B. *ngoja.*)

*__Ahsante,__ and __Ahasanta, Asánt,__ used as an expression of thanks and gratitude, 'thank you, you are very kind.' (Ar. = 'you have done well,' cf. *hisani.* Usually a kindness or gift is acknowledged, if at all, by *vema,* or *ngema,* it is well, good.)

Aibu, n. (that which is a) disgrace, shame, scandal, reproach; infamy, dishonour, shame. — v. (Pr. not used). Ap. *aib-ia, -iwa, -ika,* be put to shame, be dishonoured, be disgraced, &c. Cs. *aib-isha, -ishwa,* disgrace, bring dishonour, &c. on. (Ar. Cf. syn. *fetheha, haya,* and contr. *heshima.*)

*__Aili,__ v. take on oneself, make oneself responsible for, incur a debt. *A. deni,* charge oneself with another person's debt. Ap. *ail-ia, -iwa, -ika.* Cs. *ail-isha, -ishwa,* put responsibility on, declare guilty, hold culpable, condemn. — a. responsible, guilty. *Huyu si a. ni yeye,* this one is not responsible, it is that one. (Arab. not common. Cf. syn. *diriki.*)

*__Aina,__ n. kind, class, sort, species. (Ar. Cf. syn. *ginsi, namna,* and follg.)

*__Aini,__ v. specify, define, point out, distinguish, show, classify. Ps. *ainiwa.* Nt. *ainika.* Ap. *ain-ia, -iwa, -ika.* Cs. *ain-isha, -ishwa.* (Ar. Cf. *aina.*)

*__Aitha,__ conj. further, moreover, next, then. (Arab. Cf. *kathalika, thama,* and common *tena.*)

*Ajabu, v. also **Taaj.** and **Staaj.**, wonder, be astonished, feel surprise. Ap. *ajab-ia, -iwa, -ika,* wonder at. Cs. *ajab-isha, -ishwa,* surprise, astonish, &c. — n. (—, and *ma-*), (1) wonder, amazement, admiration, astonishment; (2) a marvel, surprise, a wonder, &c. *Ona a.,* feel wonder. — adv. wonderfully, extraordinarily. *Kubwa a.,* marvellously great. Often used to strengthen *mno,* and *sana. Nyingi mno a.,* exceedingly many. (Ar. Cf. *shangaa* v., *toshewa* v., and syn. *mwujiza,* &c.)

*Ajali, n. fate, doom, destiny, appointed end, death. *Leo imetimia a. yako,* to-day your hour is come. *Kusalimika ajali,* to be finally delivered up, to meet one's fate, to come to the appointed end. (Ar.)

*Ajara, n. and **Ijara, Ujira,** hire, wages. (Ar. Cf. *ajiri,* and *ujira, mshahara.*)

*Ajazi, v. be weak, be slack, be remiss. (Arab. Cf. *ajizi,* and syn. B. *legea, choka.*)

*Ajili, n. cause, reason, commonly in the phrase *kwa ajili ya,* because of, on account of, for the sake of, by reason of. Also conj. and *kwa ajili,* because, in order to. (Ar. and cf. syn. *sababu, maana, hoja.*)

*Ajiri, v. hire, engage to work for wages. Ps. *ajiriwa.* Nt. *ajirika, -kana. Wanaajirika,* men can be hired, they are procurable for wages. Ap. *ajir-ia, -iwa, -ika.* Cs. *ajirisha, -ishwa,* cause to work for wages, get for hire. (Ar. Cf. *ajara, ujira,* and syn. *mshahara.*)

*Ajizi, n. weakness, slackness, remissness. (Arab. Cf. *ajazi,* and common B. *legea, choka.*)

*Ajjem, n. Persia. Also *Uajj.,* Persia. *Mwajj.* (*wa-*), a Persian. *Kiajj.,* the Persian language, in Persian style. (Ar.; the word meaning not Arab, barbarian, then Persian.)

Aka, v. sometimes also **Waka,** especially if a vowel precedes, 'build, construct with stones and mortar, work as a mason.' *Aka nyumba,* build a stone house (*jenga* being commonly used of native construction, i.e. with poles, sticks, and earth). Ps. *akwa.* Ap. *ak-ia, -iwa, -ika. vitu vya kuakia,* mason's tools (materials, &c.). *Akisha* (*asha*), cause to build, have mason's work done, order to be built. (Cf. *mwashi, uashi,* and contr. *jenga* and *unda.* In other dialects *aka* means 'build,' without reference to masonry.)

*Akali, n. and a., a few (of), some. *A. ya vitu, vitu a.,* a few things. (Arab. Cf. common *haba,* and B. *-chache.*) — also a verb-form, 'and he is, he being'—(*a,* Pfx. 3 Pers. S., *ka* connective, *li* = is, being, which see).

-ake, a. of pron. 3 Pers. S., his, hers, her, its, of him (her, it). Additional emphasis and precision is given by adding *yeye, mwenyewe,* or both, e. g. *kiti chake,* his chair, *kiti chake yeye, his* chair, *kiti chake mwenyewe,* his own chair, *kiti chake yeye mwenyewe,* his very own chair. The various prefixes, connecting *-ake* with different classes of nouns are *w-, y-, ch-, vy-, l-, z-, p-, kw-, mw-.*

*Akhi, n. brother. (Arab. for common B. *ndugu.*)

*Akiba, n. store, reserve, stock, what is laid by for future use. *Weka a.,* put by, store up. (Ar.)

*Akida, n. (*ma-*), leader, commander, esp. of soldiers, *ak. wa asikari,* captain. (Ar. with article prefixed?)

*Akidi, v. suffice (for), be enough (for). *Chakula hiki chaakidi watu waliopo,* this food is enough for those present. (Arab. for common B. *tosha.* Cf. *kifu.*)

*Akika, n. an Arab domestic feast, e. g. on first hair-cutting of a child. (Ar.)

*Akiki, n. a red stone, red coral, cornelian. (Ar.)

*Akili, n. (1) intellect, intelligence,

consciousness, understanding, reason, sense; (2) ability, cleverness, judgement, discretion; (3) a trick, ruse, clever plan, happy thought; (4) also used of what is abstract and immaterial, 'pure thought.' *Hana a.*, he is a fool (simpleton, madman). *A. zake chache*, he is dull-witted, deficient. *A. nyingi*, great intelligence, plenty of sense. *Fanya a.*, use the brains, exercise intelligence. *A. yako haikuongoka*, your device did not succeed. *Katika a. yangu*, according to my view, so far as I understand. *Jambo la a. tupu, si la kiwiliwili*, something wholly immaterial, not of the body. *Fuata a. yako*, follow your own judgement. (Ar. Cf. *busara, ufahamu, utambuzi, ujuzi, moyo, welekevu*.)

Akina. See Kina.

-ako, a. of pron. 2 Pers. S., your, yours, of you. (Cf. *-ake* for prefixes, and use of *wewe, mwenyewe*, for emphasis.)

*Akraba, n. kinsman, relation, connexion, family. *A. za kuumeni (kukeni)*, relatives on the father's (mother's) side. (Ar. Cf. *ahali, jamaa, utani*, B. *ukoo*.)

*Akram, a. also il akram, honoured, respected. (Ar. occurs only in letters opening in the Arabic style, with other *a*. Cf. *dibaji*.)

*Al (and El), the Arab. article, is not used independently, but is incorporated with various Arabic words in common use among Swahilis, e.g. *alhamisi*, Thursday, *assubuhi*, morning, *liwali*, governor, and sometimes as possessive, *ras il mali*, capital sum of money.

*Ala, n. (—, *ma-*, and *ny-*), sheath, scabbard, case of knife (sword, &c.). (Cf. syn. *uo*.)

*Alafu, n. and a., thousand. See Elfu. (Ar., plur. of *Alf*.)

*Alama, n. sign, mark, token, trace, indication, vestige, signal. *Tia a.*, put a mark on, mark. (Ar. Cf. *elimu*, &c., and syn. *ishara, dalili*.)

*Alasiri, n. afternoon, and esp. of one of the regular Mahommedan hours of prayer, about 3.30 p.m. (Ar. *al asr*. Cf. *alfajiri, athuuri*, &c., and note on *Al*.)

*Alfu, n. and a., thousand. See Elfu. (Ar.)

*Alfajiri, n. dawn, daybreak, and esp. of one of the Mahommedan hours of prayer, about 4 a.m. (Ar. *al fajr*. Cf. *alasiri* and note.)

*Alhamdu lillahi, a common reply to a salute among some Swahilis, 'praised be God.' (Arab. Cf. *al*, and *himidi*.)

*Alhamisi, n. Thursday. (Ar. *Al hams*, i.e. 'the fifth' day of the week, according to the old oriental reckoning preserved by the Arabs, which regards the Sabbath as the last and Sunday as the first day of the week, making Thursday thus the fifth day. The name has been taken over by the Swahilis, though *juma a tano*, also meaning 'the fifth day of the week,' is also regularly used, and this denotes the day before *Alhamisi*, i.e. Wednesday, because the fifth day from (but not including) *Ijumaa*, Friday, the Mahommedan Sunday.

Ali, (1) a verb-form, he (she) is, he (she) being (*a*, Pfx. of 3 Pers. S. agreeing with D 1 (S), and *li*, which see, and cf. relative forms, *ali-ye, ali-o*, &c.); (2) a common name, 'Ali.'

Ali-, sign of 3 Pers. S. of Past Tense of the Affirm. Conjug., e.g. *alipenda (a-li-penda)*, he (she) loved.

-ali- (also -li-), sign of Past Tense of the Affirm. Conjug., following or coalescing with Pers. Pfx., e.g. *nalipenda (ni-ali-penda)*, I loved, *twalipenda (tu-ali-penda)*, we loved.

*Alia, v. make a mark on, e.g. by a blow. *Bakora imemwalia mtoto*, the stick has made a mark on the boy. (Ar.)

Alika, v. (1) invite, summon, call, give injunctions to, and in particular of a doctor's orders, i.e. 'treat (a patient)'; (2) make a short sharp sound, click, snap, crack. Ps. *alikwa*, e.g. be treated medically. Ap. *alik-ia, -iwa, -ika*. Cs. *alikisha, alisha, -shwa*. (1) *A. mbele ya wali (kazini, kucheza ngoma)*, summon before the governor (to work, to a dance). *Humwalika kwenda kwake kula*, he used to invite him to dinner. *A. vita vikubwa*, summon (for) a great war. *Mwalikwa*, an invited guest. (2) *A.* is used of the crackling of roasted grains of Indian corn (*mbisi*). *Alisha vidole*, crack the finger-joints. *Alisha mtambo wa bunduki*, make the trigger of a gun click, cock the trigger.

***Aliki**, v. hang, hang up, suspend. (Arab. for common B. *tundika, tungika, angika*.)

***Allah**, n. God, seldom used except (1) in Arab. formulas; (2) as a common expletive, with or without other words. (1) *La ilahi illa Allah*, the first clause of the Mahommedan creed, 'there is no God but God'—sung as a monotonous chant at funerals. *Allah bilkheri*, a common salutation, 'God prosper you.' *Alhamdu billahi*, a common rejoinder, 'praised be God.' *Allah dlam*, God knows, i.e. I do not know. (2) *Allah*, expressing wonder, disgust, &c. *Allah allah*, in letters, to call special attention, 'remember, be careful to note.' And cf. *Inshallah, bismilla, ee walla, wallai.* (Arab. Cf. *Rabbi, Mola*, and common B. *Muungu*.)

***Almaria**, n. embroidery. (? Hind.)

***Almasi**, n. diamond. (Ar., used also as a proper name.)

***Ama**, conj. (1) either, or. *Ama —ama*, either—or. (2) (or is it not? and so), surely, moreover, however. *Wa ama*, and further, yet. *Ama sizo?* Or is it not so? Do you not admit it? (Ar. Cf. *ao*, and negat. *wala*.)

-**ama**, Stative termination of some verbs in Swahili, often denoting a (relatively) permanent condition or state, e.g. *simama*, be standing, *tuama*, settle down, *kingama*, lie across, and sometimes combined with Rp. termination, *-na*, i.e. *-mana*, e.g. *fungamana*.

***Amali**, n. (1) action, act, thing done; (2) practice, occupation, business. *Mtu wa a.*, a man of action, an energetic practical man. *A. yake kutega mitego*, his business was trapping. (Ar., plur. of *aml*. Cf. B. *tendo, mtendaji*.)

***Amana**, n. pledge, deposit, thing entrusted. *Weka a.*, make a deposit, pledge. (Ar. Cf. *amini, amani*, ? *imani*.)

***Amani**, n. peace, safety, security, confidence, trust. *Amani?* Is it peace? Is all quiet?—a common inquiry on meeting in a journey. (Ar. Cf. *amini*.)

Amba, v. speak against, denounce, slander, abuse. Ps. *ambwa*. Only the Pr. form in this sense. Ap. *ambia, -iwa*, the common word for 'say to, speak to.' See **Ambia**. *Amba* is used, but not commonly in Z., (1) with Rel. Pfx. added, in the sense of a simple Rel. Pron. 'who, which', being followed by a finite verb, sometimes with a *kwamba* inserted between, sometimes with the verb itself in the Relative form, e.g. *Vyakula ambavyo havimo katika ulimwengu*, (such) food as does not exist in the world. *Watoto ambao kwamba wataka kwenda*, children who wish to go. *Killa mtu na mzigo wake ambao umtoshao*, every man with a load which is sufficient for him. (2) as a conjunction = *kama*, that, saying that, e.g. *wakamsema amba amefanya mabaya*, and they accused him, saying that he committed crimes. Also in the Infinitive form *kwamba*, (saying) that, that is to say (*ya kwamba*, that, is also used), and *kwamba* also means 'if, though.' See **Kwamba**. (Cf. syn. *tukana, suta, sema, mwambi*, and *kama*, conj. *Amba* is used for 'say, speak' in poetical

Swahili, and in other B. dialects. Cf. *jambo*, i.e. *ji-ambo*.)

Amba, v. for **Wamba**, which see.

Ambaa, v. means passing near to, but without actual contact, and has various shades of meaning, according as such contact is or is not desirable. (1) pass by, pass along, pass without touching (without affecting); (2) avoid contact with, escape, not to salute (recognize, hurt, &c.); (3) miss contact with, fail to see (salute, recognize). *A. pwani* (or, *na pwani*), coast along, hug the shore. *A. na maovu*, escape evil. *Maovu yakuambae*, may evil not touch you. *Nalimwambaa*, I avoided seeing him (cut him), or, I failed to see him. Derivatives seem rare. Cs. *ambaza*, cause to pass near. *Ambaza chombo na pwani*, coast along the shore. (Cf. *mwambao*, and perh. for close juxtaposition and contact, *ambo, ambisha, ambika, wambiso, ambuka, ambata*, &c.)

*****Ambari**, n. ambergris, found at times off the east coast of Africa. (Ar.)

Ambata, v. be close to, come in contact with, stick (to), adhere (to), be attached (to), cling, clasp. Ps. *ambatwa*. Nt. *ambatika*. *A. inchi* (*na inchi, katika inchi*), come close to (strike on, cohere with) the ground. *Mayayi yameambata kikangoni*, the eggs have stuck to the frying-pan. *Jua linaambata katika inchi*, the sun beats fiercely on the ground. *Moto uliniambata*, the heat scorched me. *Fimbo zimemwambata*, the blows of the stick made him feel. Ap. *ambat-ia, -iwa, -ika*. Cs. *ambatisha, -ishwa*. Rp. *ambat-ana, -anisha*, &c. *Mbau mbili hizi zimeambatana, haziambuliki*, these two boards have stuck together, they cannot be pulled apart. (Cf. *ambaa, ambua, amba, ambika, wamba, wambiso*, and for the termination, *fumbata, kamata, vuata, kumbatia*. Also syn. *nata*.)

Ambia, v. Ap. of *amba*, but meaning 'say to, report to, tell to, inform by word of mouth, speak to'—always with an objective prefix, and the words of the communication expressed or implied. Not used for 'talk to, converse with.' Often followed by *kama, ya kuwa, ya kwamba*, that, with Oblique or Direct narration. *Akamwambia, njoo ukale*, and he said to him, Come and eat. Ps. *ambiwa*, e.g. *asiyejua maana, haambiwi maana*, he who does not know the meaning, will not be told it. Ap. *amb-ilia, -iliwa, -ilika*. *Mtu wa kuambilika*, an affable, courteous, meek person. *Mtoto huyu haambiliki*, this child cannot bear being spoken to. Cs. *amb-iana*. *Nyote ambianeni*, all of you tell each other. (Strictly the Ap. form of **Amba**, which see. Cf. *sema, nena*.)

Ambika, v. be brought into contact, hold together, be firm (tight, coherent). (Cf. *ambaa*, and follg.)

Ambisha, v. and **Ambisa**, cause to be in contact, bring (force) together, make cohere. Rp. *ambishana*, e.g. Intens. of things cohering or cemented together. (Cf. *ambaa*, and follg. Also *wambiso*.)

Ambo, n. (*ma-*), (1) any glutinous substance, gum, glue, i.e. something which causes coherence. *Ambo la mkuyu wa kufungia nyaraka*, gum made from the sycamore to fasten up letters with. (Cf. *ambaa*, and *chambo*, i.e. *ki-ambo*?) (2) the cording of a native bedstead (also *uambo, wambo*, which see, and cf. *wamba*).

Ambua, v. break contact, remove, separate, take off (something adhering), often of removing husk, peel, skin, i.e. peel, husk, clean, flay. Ps. *ambuliwa*. Nt. *ambuka*. *Ngozi imeambuka*, the skin has peeled off, after an illness, or cast by a snake. *Ngozi ya simba ikaanikwa hatta ikaambuliwa*, the skin of the lion was dried in the sun, and finally cleaned. Cs. *ambukiza, -izwa*, see follg. Ap. *ambulia, -uliwa, -ulika*. (Cf. *ambaa*, *ambo*, &c., and *chambua, menya, paa*, &c.)

Ambukiza, v. (1) cause to be peeled off (removed, cast), and so (2) 'give a disease to, infect, carry contagion to, be contagious,' peeling of the skin being an obvious effect of some diseases. (Cf. follg. and *ambaa, ambua*, &c.)

Ambukizo, n. (*ma*-), infection, that which causes infection. (Cf. prec.)

*****Amdelhán**, n. a particular fabric of fine silky texture. (? Hind. see *nguo*.)

*****Amerikani**, n. (*ma*-, *wa*-) and a., (1) America, (2) American. *Mafuta Am.*, common petroleum for lamps, stoves, &c. *Nguo Am.*, calico, esp. (3) stout, unbleached cotton cloth or calico, as largely introduced from America.

*****Ami**, n. See **Amu**. (Ar.)

*****Amili**, v. manage, effect, bring about, work at. (Arab. Cf. *amali, mwamale*, and B. syn. *tenda, fanyiza*.)

*****Amin**, and **Amina**, Be it so, Amen. (Arab. Cf. *amini, amani*.)

*****Amini**, v. believe, trust, have faith (in), put confidence in. Ps. *aminiwa*. Nt. *aminika*. *A. Muungu*, believe God, trust God. *A. kwa Muungu*, believe in God, have faith towards God. *Sultani akamwamini sana*, the Sultan had great confidence in him. *Amini mtu na kitu*, entrust a person with a thing. Ap. *amin-ia, -iwa, -ika. Aminiwa*, have a thing entrusted to. *Haaminiki*, he is not deserving of confidence, he is untrustworthy. Cs. *amin-isha, -ishwa, -ishia*, &c., (1) cause to believe, inspire faith (confidence, trust); (2) entrust to, commit to care of, entrust with. *Aminisha mtu mali*, entrust a man with money. (3) Intens., have trust (about), feel confidence. *Hakuaminisha kwenda kulala*, he did not venture to go to sleep. — n. fidelity, trustworthiness, honesty, integrity, faithfulness. (Cf. *uamini, uaminifu*.) — a. and -**amini**, faithful, honest, trustworthy, &c. Cf. **-aminifu**. (Ar. Cf. *amana, imani*.)

*****-aminifu**, a. same as **Amini**, a. (Ar. Cf. *uaminifu*.)

*****Amiri**, n. (*ma*-), commander, leader, officer, esp. of soldiers. (Arab. Cf. *amri, amuru*, and syn. *akida*.)

Am'ka, v. also **Amuka**, awake, rouse oneself, rise up from sleep, regain life (consciousness, strength, &c.). Ap. *amk-ia, -iwa*, (1) wake up at (in, for, &c.), (2) in particular, pay a morning visit to, make an early call, visit formally,—the customary duty of dependents to patrons and superiors, and of children to parents, (3) in general, greet, accòst, salute, address, pay respects to, also (4) fig. of the dawn, *jumaa mosi kwa usiku kuamkia jumaa pili*, on Saturday late in the night as it dawned on Sunday. Cs. *am-sha, -shwa*, awaken, rouse up (from sleep, lethargy, &c.). *Amsha kanwa*, take breakfast. Cf. *chamsha kanwa*. (Cf. *uka, muka*, v. rise up, &c., in other dialects. *Amkua*, Ps. *amkuwa*, is found in Swa. poetry = *amkia*, rouse, accost, visit. Cf. *maamkizi*, and *umka*, also, for evening visit *tuesha*.)

*****Amri**, n. (1) a command, order, rule, regulation, direction, (2) authority, supreme power, rule, government, law. *Mwenyi a.*, ruler, chief, responsible head. *A. ya Muungu*, the will of God, providence, chance. *Sina a. nayo*, I have no power (responsibility) in the matter, it is not my affair. *Toa a.*, issue an order. *Shika (fuata) a.*, obey (execute, carry out) an order. *A. nyingi*, strict discipline. (Ar. Cf. *amuru, amiri*.)

*****Amru, Amria, Amrisha**, &c., v. See **Amuru**.

*****Amu**, n. also **Ami**, father's brother, paternal uncle. (Arab. Cf. B. *baba mdogo, baba mkubwa*, and dist. *mjomba*.)

Amua, v. judge, be umpire, arbitrate, settle dispute (between). Ps. *amuliwa*. Nt. *amulika*. Ap. *amu-lia, -liwa*, e.g. act as judge for, arbitrate between, and *amuliwa*, have a case settled, be judged (decided). Cs. (rare) *amusha, -shwa*. (Cf. *mwamuzi, maamuzi*, and Ar. syn. *hukumu*.)

*****Amuru**, v. also **Amru** (and so commonly the derivatives), order, command, direct, exercise authority, be the supreme power. Ps. *amuriwa*. *Alimwamuru kwenda upesi* (or, *aende upesi*), he ordered him to go quickly. Ap. *amr-ia, -iwa*, give orders about (for, at, &c.). *Ameamriwa kazi*, he has had orders as to work. Cs. *amr-isha, -ishwa*, usu. intens., give strict orders, have orders issued. (Ar. Cf. B. syn. *agiza*, from *aga*.)

Ana, verb-form, he (she) has (*a*, Pfx. of 3 Pers. S. agreeing with D 1 (S), and *na*, which see).

Ana-, at the beginning of verbs, is the sign of 3 Pers. S. of the Present Definite, agreeing with D 1 (S), e.g. *anakwenda* (*a-na-kwenda*), he is going.

-ana, as a verbal termination, is the sign of the Reciprocal Conjugation, which includes a wide and subtle variety of meanings noted under different words, e.g. (1) reciprocity of act or feeling, action and reaction, e.g. *pendana*, love each other, *pigana*, beat each other, fight. (2) community, collective action, interaction, e.g. *liana*, weep together, as well as *lizana*, excite each other to weep, *lana*, eat together, (as well as) eat each other. *Tokana na mtu*, part with a person. *Tokana na damu*, lose blood. (3) practicability, conditionality. This may be noted esp. in the combination of *-ana* with the Nt. Pfx. *ka*, e.g. *tendekana*, be possible, be able (under conditions) to be done, *patikana*, be procurable, be to be had. (4) coherence, combination, perhaps underlies such uses as *kazana*, be hard (tight, close), *pindamana, fungamana*, &c. (Cf. uses of Prep. *na*. *-ana* is also a widespread root in Bantu dialects. Cf. *Mwana*.)

-anana, a. (*anana* with D 5 (S) and D 6 (S), *anana* or *nyanana* with D 6 (P)), soft, thin, gentle (in action or effect). *Upepo mwan.*, gentle breeze. *Maji maan.*, quiet, still, slowly moving water. *Nguo an.*, soft clothes (fabric). (Not common, restricted in meaning, of things rather than persons. Cf. syn. A. *laini*, B. *-ororo*.)

*****Anasa**, n. (1) pleasure, enjoyment, luxury, convenience, often (2) in bad sense, over-luxuriousness, self-indulgence, sensuality. *Killa a. imo*, it contains every luxury. *Kaa a.*, live in comfort (or, self-indulgently). (Ar. Cf. *anisi*, and syn. *raha, furaha*.)

Andaa, v. (1) prepare, provide, get ready, put in order, arrange; (2) esp. of cooking, prepare food. Ap. *anda-lia, -liwa, -lika*. *Andalia vita*, prepare for war. (Cf. *maandasi, maandalio*, and for the root perh. *andika, andama*.)

Andama, v. follow, accompany, go along with (or, after), follow up, come next to, succeed. *Mwezi umeandama*, the moon has followed on, i.e. the new month has begun. (Cf. *mwezi mwandamo*.) Ap. *andam-ia, -iwa, -ika*. *Andamia tembo*, follow up (pursue) an elephant. Cs. *andam-isa, -izwa*, cause to follow, &c. *Mvua hii itauandamiza mwezi*, this rain will bring in the new moon, i.e. will last till next month begins. Rp. *andamana*, follow one another, go all together, form a procession. *Andamana na*, associate with, take the side of, be companion to. *Siye mtu wa kuandamana naye*, he is not a proper person to associate with. (Cf. follg. and *mwandani*.)

Andamano, n. (*ma-*), a following (of people), train, procession, retinue. (Cf. prec. and *mwandamano*.)

Andamizi, n. (*ma-*), following. (See **Mwandamizi**, and cf. *andama*.)

-andamo, a. following, succeeding. *Mwezi mwa.*, moon (month) following, new moon. (Cf. prec. and *andama, mwandamo*.)

Andao, n. and **Mwandao**, preparation, arrangement. *A. la maiti*, preparation of corpse for burial, funeral arrangements. (Cf. *anda*, and *mazishi*.)

Andasi, n. usu. in plur. *maandasi*, confectionery, pastry, &c. (Cf. *andaa, maandasi*.)

Andika, v. (1) set in order, lay out, set straight, give definite arrangement to; (2) write (i.e. make an orderly arrangement of letters); (3) register, enrol, make an entry, put on paper; (4) (of a ship), steer, keep on a course, set the course; (5) (*andikia, andika huru*), register as free, give freedom (to). *A. meza*, arrange (lay, set) a table, prepare a meal. *A. barua (waraka)*, write a letter. *A. asikari (jeshi)*, enlist soldiers (a force). *A. chombo*, keep a vessel on a course. *A. tanga*, arrange a formal mourning. Ps. *andikwa. Limeandikwa (na Muungu)*, it is written (by God, and therefore finally settled, destined). *Liandikwalo halifutiki*, what is written cannot be wiped out. Ap. *andik-ia, -iwa, -ika, -iana*, write for (to, at, &c.). *Tafathali uniandikie barua*, please write a letter for me. *Andikia mtumwa*, set a slave free. *Andikiana*, correspond (by letter). Cs. *andikisha, -ishwa, -ishia*, &c., e.g. cause to write, dictate a letter to, inspire writing, have set in order, have a meal laid. *Nalimwandikishia chakula*, I had a meal laid for him. Rp. *andik-ana, -anya. Waliandikana wapagazi wote*, they all entered as porters together (by common consent). *Andikanya sahani*, set plates in rows (piles, one on the other), make a row (pile) of plates. Cf. *panganya*. (Cf. *andiko, mwandiko, mwandiki, mwandikaji, mwandishi, uandishi*, &c. Cf. also *andaa*, and derivs. and syn. in some senses *tandika* and *tengeneza*.)

Andiko, n. (*ma-*), something written, a writing, letter, book. *Sio andiko lake*, it is not his writing (written by him). (Cf. *andika, mwandiko*.)

Anga, n. (1) light, brightness, lustre; (2) upper air, sky, bright expanse of the atmosphere; (3) fig. enlightenment, illumination, inspiration. *Ndege za a.*, birds of the air. *A. la jua*, sunshine. *Mwezi waleta a.*, the moon brings light. (Chiefly of sun and moon. Otherwise **mwanga** and **wangafu**, which see. A root *ang-* or *nga* seems traceable in many words relating to light, sight, and sky, cf. *angaza, angalia, -angafu, mwanga, mwango, mwangaza, maangazi, wangafu*. Also cf. *ng'aa, ngariza*, and possibly *angaika, angama, angamia*. Also *anga, mwanga*, of witchcraft.)

Anga, v. use sorcery, bewitch, perform incantations, &c. *Watu wa Donge humwangia uchawi wao wakamua*, the people of Donge practised their enchantments upon him, and killed him. (Not often in Z., where *uganga, uchawi*, and *loga* are usual. Cf. *mwanga, wanga*.)

Angaa, v. See **Ng'aa**. (Cf. *angalia*.)

-angafu, a. (*angafu* with D 5 (S), D 6), (1) bright, shining, luminous, radiant, polished, emitting (transmitting, reflecting) light; (2) enlightened, intellectual, clever, quick-witted. *Maji maangafu*, gleaming (glassy, clear) water. (Cf. *anga* and derivs.)

Angaika, v. be in suspense (anxious, confused, distressed, excited, &c.). Cs. *angaisha, -shwa*, make anxious, &c. (Cf. *angana*, and perh.

angaa, anga, and syn. *fathaika, sumbuka, taharuki*.)

Angalia, v. (1) have the eyes open (to), pay attention (to), observe, notice; (2) be careful, beware (of), take care. *Angalia!* (Imperat.), see! observe! take care! *Haangalii*, he does not attend (is careless, is unobservant). Ps. *angaliwa*. Nt. *angalika*. Ap. *anga-lilia, -liliwa, -lilika*. Cs. (seldom) *angaliza, -izwa*. (Specialized from same root as *anga*, and its derivatives. Cf. *-angalifu, uangalizi*.)

-**angalifu**, a. careful, observant, attentive. (Cf. *angalia, uangalifu*.)

Angama, v. be in mid-air, be suspended, hang. *A. mnazimi*, be left hanging in a cocoanut tree. *A. juu ya mti*, be caught in the boughs of a tree, when falling. (A St. form, cf. Nt. *angika*, and Rv. *angua*, and poss. *anga*. Also follg.)

Angamia, v. be ruined, be lost, be utterly undone, perish. *Watu wengi wameangamia vitani*, many perished in war. *A. mwituni*, be lost (perish) in the forest. Nt. (seldom) *angamika*, e.g. *Mali yangu imeangamika*, my property is ruined. Cs. *angamiza, -izwa*, ruin, spoil, destroy. (Apparently Ap. of *angama*, which see, with generalized meaning; cf. *uangamizi*.)

Angaza, v. (1) be light, give light, be bright, shine, e.g. *macho ya kuangaza*, bright (sharp, observant) eyes. *Mwanga wa taa unaangaza nyumba yote*, the light of the lamp gives light to the whole house; (2) look intently (at), fix attention (on), sometimes with *macho*, e.g. *angaza macho*, keep the eyes open (lit. make the eyes bright). *Angaza mali yako*, keep a sharp eye on your property; (3) remain awake, keep watch at night. *Nimeangaza usiku kucha nisilale*, I have kept awake the whole night without sleeping; (4) fig. open the eyes of, enlighten, instruct. Ps. *angazwa*. Ap. *ang-azia, -aziwa,* *-azika*, e.g. *kwani kuniangazia macho?* Why look so intently at me? Cs. *ang-azisha, ishwa*. Rp. *angazana*. (Cs. of (*angaa*) *ng'aa*, also Intens., cf. *anga, angalia, ng'aa, mwangaza, -angafu*, &c. And cf. syn. common in Z., (1) *kaza macho, kodoa*, gaze, stare; (2) *mulika*, give light; (3) *kesha*, keep awake, and *kaa macho*.)

Angika, v. hang up, hang, suspend, esp. against a wall on a peg or hook or on a branch. Ps. *angikwa*. Ap. *ang-ikia, -ikiwa, -ikika*. Cs. *ang-ikisha, -ikishwa*. (Cf. *angama, angua, chango*, i.e. *ki-ango, mwango, ?anga*. Also syn. *tungika, tundika*, both Nt. forms with act. meaning, as *anika, funika*, &c.)

-**angu**, a. of pron. 1 Pers. S., my, mine, of me. (Cf. *-ake* for Pfx., and use of *mimi, mwenyewe* for emphasis.)

Angua, v. (1) let fall, drop, take down, throw down, e.g. fruit from trees; (2) let out suddenly, utter, vent, e.g. *a. embe (nazi*, &c.), throw down mangoes (cocoanuts, &c.). *Sultani akaangua kilio*, the Sultan gave vent to a cry. Also (3) hatch, e.g. *a. mayai*, hatch eggs, *a. waana*, hatch out young birds (not 'lay,' which is *zaa, taga*). Ps. *anguliwa*. Nt. *anguka*, which see. Ap. *angu-lia, -liwa, -lika*. Cs. *angu-sha, -shwa, -shia, -shiwa*, often intens., e.g. (1) make fall, throw down violently; (2) fig. bring to ruin, send as a blow (curse, disaster). *Muungu amemwangushia mabaya*, God has sent down evil upon him. (Rv. of root found in *angika, angama*, which see, also *anguka*, and syn. *shua, shusha*. Dist. *kwangua*.)

Anguka, v. (1) fall, fall down, drop, have a downward movement (direction, tendency); (2) fig. meet with disaster, be ruined; (3) happen, befall, fall out. Ap. *anguk-ia, -iwa*, (1) fall down into (on, before, &c.); (2) come upon, fall in with. *Wakamwangukia miguu*, and they fell down before his feet, they submitted to him. *Kuangukiwa na msiba*, to be the victim of a calamity. *Akaangukia mji mgeni*, and he lighted upon a strange city. *Ukaanguka msiba mkubwa mno*, and a very great mourning took place. (Nt. of *angua*, cf. *anguko*, also *angika*, *angama*, and notes.)

Anguko, n. (*ma-*), (1) a fall, drop (downward), a downward movement, &c.; (2) ruin, fall; (3) something fallen, a ruin. *Maanguko ya maji* (*ya mto*), waterfall (also *maporomoko*). (Cf. *anguka*, *maangamizi*, &c.)

*****Ania**, v. intend, resolve, set the mind on, desire. No deriv. common. (Arab. Cf. syn. *Kusudia*, *azimu*, and B. *taka*. *Nia* seems a different word.)

Anika, v. set out to dry, expose to sun (or air), air, dry. *A. nguo* (*mchele*, &c.), dry clothes (rice, &c.). Ps. *anikwa*. Ap. *anikia*, *-iwa*, dry for (at, with, &c.). *Kamba ya kuanikia nguo*, a clothes-line. Cs. *anik-isha*, *-ishwa*. (Cf. *anua*, and syn. *kausha*.)

*****Anisi**, v. please, give pleasure to, gratify the desires of. *Wanapiga ngoma kwa ajili kutuanisi*, they are drumming in order to please us. (Arab. Cf. *anasa*, and syn. *rithisha*. B. *pendeza*.)

*****Ankra**, n. invoice, account, bill of sale, reckoning. (Hind. used in commerce. Cf. Arab. *orotha*.)

*****Anna**, n. one-sixteenth of a rupee, value 12 pies, or 4 pice, i.e. one penny. (Hind.)

Anua, v. take out of the sun (or air, or rain), put under cover (in shade, in the house). Ps. *anuliwa*. Nt. *anuka*, (1) be taken out of the sun, be dry, have done airing; (2) (of weather) be dry, have done raining, clear up. *Kumeanuka*, it has cleared up, it is fine again. Ap. *anu-lia*, *-liwa*, &c. *Sina mtu wa kunianulia nguo*, I have no one to go and bring in the clothes for me. (Rv. of same root as *anika*.)

*****Anwani**, n. heading, title, address (of a letter), direction, general description. *Andika a. ya barua*, write the address of a letter. *Tunaingia katika anwani ya vyakula*, we are entering on the subject of dietetics. (Arab.)

Anza, v. begin, commence, start, be the beginning, be the first. *Anza kazi*, begin work. *Kazi yaanza*, work begins. *Anza kusema*, begin to speak. *Kwanza*, Infin., and *ya kwanza*, used as adv., 'first, firstly, in the first place, to begin with.' *-a kwanza*, first (ordinal of *mosi*, one). Ps. *anzwa*. *Nyumba imeanzwa kujenga*, or *imeanza kujengwa*, the house has begun to be built. Nt. *anzika*. Ap. *anz-ia*, *-iwa*. Also *anz-ilia*, *-iliwa*, *-ilika*, make a beginning of, make an attempt at. Cs. *anz-isha*, *-ishwa*, *-ishia*, &c., set on foot, institute, found, see put in hand, start. Also *anz-ilisha*, and *-iliza*, which can be used of special earnestness, effort, or occasion. (Cf. *mwanzo*, *kwanza*.)

*****Anzwani**, n. Johanna (island).

*****Ao**, conj. also *au*, or; *ao—ao*, either—or. (A. Cf. *ama*, and disjunct. *wala*.)

-ao, a. of pron. 3 Pers. P., their, theirs, of them. (Cf. *-ake* for prefixes, and use of *wao*, *wenyewe*, for emphasis.)

Apa, v. swear, take an oath, utter an oath. *A. Korani*, swear by the Coran. *Sisadiki, apa yamini*, I do not believe, swear by your right hand. Ps. *apwa*. Ap. *apia*, swear to (about, with, in, &c.). *Akaniapia na kiapo*, and he swore to me with a formal oath. Cs. (1) *apisha* (also *afya*), *-ishwa*, cause to swear, put on oath, administer an oath to, adjure, conjure; (2) *ap-iza*, *-izwa*, usually Intens. with special sense, swear at, imprecate against, denounce, curse, abjure. *Apizana*, curse each other. Rp. *apiana*, take an oath together, join in swearing. (Cf. *uapo, wapo, kiapo, apizo.*)

Api, or (attached to a word ending with -*a*) -**pi**, same as *wapi*, where? (which see).

Apizo, n. (*ma*-), curse, imprecation. (Cf. *apa*, and syn. *laana*.)

*****Arabuni**, n. (1) earnest-money, deposit, advance, payment to secure future service; (2) with -*ni* locative, in Arabia. (Ar. For *Uarabuni*, see *Mwarabu*.)

*****Ari**, n. scandal, shame, disgrace, dishonour. *Nikiona ari, ulimwengu wanichukiza*, if I feel dishonoured, everything is hateful to me. (Ar. Cf. *aibu, fetheha, haya.*)

*****Aria**, n. part, section, party, following. (? Hind.)

*****Arifu**, v. inform, report, let know, give instructions about, esp. in writing, by letter, e.g. *baada ya salaam, nakuarifu haya*, after good wishes, I proceed to inform you as follows. Ps. *arifiwa*. Ap. *arif-ia, -iwa*, &c. — a. well-informed, ingenious, knowing. (Ar. Cf. *maarifa, taarifu*, and syn. *hubiri*.)

*****Aroba**, n. and a., also **Ar'ba**, **Arbaa**, four. (Arab., used mainly in conjunction with some other Ar. numeral, as *aroba mia*, 400, *aroba ashirini*, 24; otherwise usually the B. syn. *nne, -nne*.)

*****Arobaini**, n. and a., forty. Used also in technical senses, irrespective of number, e.g. (1) of a chief's bodyguard, 15 young men armed; (2) of a ceremonial interval, sometimes of a week, each of the four weeks after a birth. *Alipotoka katika arobaini*, when he was four weeks old. -*a arobaini*, fortieth. (Ar. See *Aroba*. B. *makumi manne*.)

*****Arobatashara**, n. and a., fourteen. -*a arobatashara*, fourteenth. (Ar. Cf. *asharini*, and *aroba*. B. *kumi na 'nne*.)

*****Arthi**, n. (1) soil, ground, earth; (2) land, as contr. with sea; (3) land, region, country. (Arab. Cf. *udongo*, 'soil' as a substance, *barra*, as opp. to *bahari*, sea; *ulaya* and *wilaya*, of territorial divisions; *inchi*, the common B. syn.)

*****Arusi**, n. also **Harusi**, (1) the marriage ceremony, a wedding, nuptials; (2) the marriage feast; (3) bride, bridegroom. (*A. ni mambo yatendwayo, mume akipelekwa kwa mke, Arusi* is all that is done when a man is conducted to his wife. *Yule ni arusi, leo ataingia nyumbani*, yonder is the bridegroom, to-day he will enter the bride's house. *Tumemleta arusi kwa mumewe*, we have brought the bride to her husband. (Ar.—the initial *Ain* being often heard as a faint *h* in Swah. Cf. *nikaha*, and syn. B. *ndoa, maozi*.)

*****Asali**, n. sweet syrup of several kinds, (1) *a. ya nyuki*, from bees, 'honey'; (2) *a. ya mua*, from sugar-cane, 'treacle, molasses'; (3) *a. ya tembo*, made by boiling palm-wine. (Ar.)

Asha, v. (1) for *akisha*, Cs. of *aka*, build, which see; (2) for *achisha*, Cs. of *acha*, which see. (Also in Ar. a woman's name. Dist. *washa*, Cs. of *waka*, burn.)

*****Ashara**, n. and a., ten. (Arab. for the common B. *kumi*, ten. Appears in *edashara, thenashara, ushuru*, &c. and follg.)

*****Asharini**, n. and a., and **Ishirini**, twenty. -*a asharini*, twentieth. (Ar. Cf. *ashara*, and B. *makumi mawili*.)

*****Ashekali**, a. better (after sickness), improved in condition, fit, in form. *Fanya a.*, get better. *Mimi leo a.*, I am better to-day, I am feeling well. (Ar. for common B. *sijambo, hujambo*, &c.)

*****Asherati**, n. also **Hash.**, **Uash.**, dissipation, profligacy, debauchery, fornication, adultery. — a. also -**ash.**, dissipated, immoral. *Mtu huyu asherati sana*, this person leads a very immoral life. (Ar. Cf. *ufisiki, ufisada*, and B. *uzini*.)

*Ashiki, v. have a passion for, be enamoured of, be in love with. (Arab. Cf. *shauko*.)

*Ashiria, v. Ap. make signs to (with, for, &c.), signal (to), indicate by signs (to). Ps. *ashiriwa*. (Ar. Cf. *ishara*, and B. syn. *onya, onyesha*.)

*Asi, v. rebel (against), disobey, mutiny, neglect duty (towards), quarrel (with). *Asi Muungu* (*mfalme, mke*), fail in duty towards God (king, wife). Ps. *asiwa*. Ap. *asi-a, -wa, -ka*, rebel against (at, on account of, &c.). Cs. *asisha, -shwa*, cause to rebel, abet in disobedience, &c. *Asisha mume na mke*, make a man quarrel with his wife. — a. (also -asi), rebellious, quarrelsome, undutiful. (Ar. Cf. *uasi, maasi, halifu*.)

*Asikari, n. (—, *wa-*, and *ma-*) and Askari, soldier, policeman, guard, armed attendant. *Andika* (*tia, changa*) *asikari*, enlist soldiers. *Cheza a.*, be drilled. (Ar.)

*Asili, n. (1) origin, source, root, stock; (2) inborn temperament, nature; (3) essence, fundamental principle, ground; (4) ancestry, family. *Watu wa a.*, original inhabitants, aborigines. *A. ya fullani mtumwa*, such and such a man is by origin a (born) slave. *A. yake, atoka wapi?* Where is his original home? *A. ya mali*, capital (of money). *Huyu a. yake ni mjinga*, this man is a born fool. *Hana a. wala fasili*, he has neither root nor branches, i. e. ancestry or connexions, standing or prospects. *Hakufanya kwa a.*, he did not act rightly (according to principle, properly). — adv. originally, by nature, in old times. (Ar. Cf. syn. B. *mwanzo, chanzo*.)

Assubuhi, n. also Subuhi, Ussubui, morning (in general), time of morning, earlier part of the day. As adv., 'in the morning,' and often emphasized by *na mapema*. *Njoo assubuhi na mapema*, come in the morning early. (Ar. with Article prefixed. Cf. *sabalkheri*, and *alasiri, alfajiri, athuuri* and B. *kucha*.)

*Asusa, n. something sweet or pleasant, used to correct an unpleasant taste or effect, e.g. something taken and chewed after a drinking bout, a corrective, comfort, relief. (Ar. Cf. *faraja*.)

-ata, a verbal formative termination, seeming to convey an idea of close contact, holding firmly, clasping, compressing. Cf. *ambata, kamata*.

Atamia, v. sometimes *tamia*, ? *otamia*, sit on eggs, brood (of a hen). Cs. *atamisha mayai*, put eggs under a hen, get a hen to sit on eggs. (An Ap. verb-form, ? a variant of *otama*, sit on the heels, squat on the ground.)

*Athabu, n. punishment, torture, chastisement, correction. *Tia a. kali*, punish severely. (Ar. Cf. *athibu*, and dist. *adabu*, good behaviour.)

*Athama, n. (1) greatness, grandeur, glory, exaltation; (2) (also *azama*), nose-ring. (Arab. Cf. *athimu*, and B. *utukufu, ukuu*.)

*Athana, n. the cry of the muezzin, the Mahommedan call to prayers. (Arab. Cf. *athini, mwathini*.)

*Athibu, v. punish, torment, chastise, physically and otherwise. *Usijiathibu bilashi*, do not worry yourself for nothing (be a self-tormentor). Ps. *athibiwa*. Nt. *athibika*. Ap. *athib-ia, -iwa, -ika*. Cs. *athib-isha, ishwa*. Also intens. *Ath. vikali*, punish severely, inflict condign punishment. (Ar.)

*Athima, n. a charm, spell, incantation, e.g. against evil spirits, to bring back runaway slaves, &c. (Arab. Cf. follg. and *talasimu, hirizi, dawa*.)

Athimia, v. Ap. make a charm (spell, incantation) against (for, with, &c.). (Arab. Cf. prec. and dist. *Athimia*, Ap. of *Athimu*, exalt.)

*Athimu, v. honour, exalt, make much of, celebrate, glorify. Ps. *athi-

miwa. Nt. *athimika.* Ap. *athimia, -iwa, -ika. Siku ya kuathimika,* a day to be kept (celebrated), a memorable day. Cs. *athimisha,* cause to honour (be honoured), and intens., honour highly. (Arab. Cf. *athama*, and B. syn. *tukuza*.)

***Athini**, v. call to public prayers, of the muezzin, according to Mahommedan universal custom. *Ukisikia mwathini akiathini, njoo,* when you hear the muezzin calling to prayers, come. (Arab. Cf. *mwathini, athana.* In Z. the call is usu. from the steps at the door of the Mosque, or from the roof, as only one mosque has a minaret, and many are only thatched houses.)

***Athuuri**, n. noon, midday, one of the regular Mahommedan hours of prayer. (Ar., with Article prefixed. Cf. *alasiri, assubuhi,* &c., and B. syn. *jua kichwani, jua kati, saa sita mchana*.)

***Ati**, a common int. or expletive, expressing surprise, or calling attention, 'I say, come now, look here, you see.' *Unaniumiza ati,* you are hurting me, I tell you. *Ati wewe uliopo, u mtu gani?* I say, you there, what is your tribe?

***Atia**, n. also **Hatia**, present, free gift, and as adv. gratis, as a gift, for nothing. *Vitu hivi amempa mtoto wake atia,* these things he has given to his child as a free gift. (Arab., one of the less common words for 'present.' Cf. *bakshishi, zawadi,* and notes. In the form *hatia, h* represents *Ain*.)

Atua, v. split, crack, e.g. of splitting logs for firewood. Nt. *atuka. Inchi imeatuka kwa jua,* the ground is cracked by the heat of the sun. (Cf. *chanja, pasua, tema*.)

***Au,** conj., also **Ao**, or. *Au—au,* either—or. (Ar. Cf. *ama,* and the disjunct. *wala*.)

Aua, v. survey, view, examine, trace, track out. *A. shamba,* survey an estate. *A. nyayo,* follow up tracks of men or animals. Ps. *auliwa.* Nt. *auka. Shamba lote limeauka,* the whole plantation has been inspected. Ap. *au-lia, -liwa, -lika,* survey for (with, by, &c.). *Vipande vya kuaulia,* surveying instruments. Cs. *au-sha,* e. g. cause (employ, send) to survey, show about, show the sights of. (Cf. *kagua, angalia, tazamia. Aua* is sometimes used for **Eua**, which see.)

***Auni**, v. also **Awini**, assist, help. — n. assistance, help. (Ar. Cf. more usual *msaada, saidia*.)

***Aushi**, n. endurance, permanence, durability, wear, quality of lasting. *Kitu cha a.,* a tough lasting material or substance. *Yuna a.,* he has lived long, he lasts well. (Ar. Cf. *ishi, maisha,* and syn. *udumu*.)

***Awala**, n. See **Hawala**. (Ar.)

***Awali**, n. beginning, start, first place. Also a. first, and adv. (1) firstly, at first; (2) just, nearly, almost. *A. wa inchi,* border, boundary of a country. *Awali ni awali, awali mbovu hapana,* first is first, there is no bad first. *Toka awali hatta aheri,* from first to last, from start to finish. *Awali Muungu,* Here goes! Here's for luck!—a workman's rejoinder to the overseer's call *Kazi!* Work hard, or *Jembe!* Dig away. (Ar. for common B. *mwanzo, kwanza*.)

***Awaza**, v. distribute, allot, arrange, dispose. (Arab. for common B. *gawa, tengeneza.* Cf. *Mwawazi*.)

***Awesia**, n. one kind of native sailing vessel,—having perpendicular stem, high rudder head, and sharp stern. (? Ar. or Hind. Cf. *chombo,* and note.)

***Aya**, n. a short section or division of a book, esp. of the Coran. (Arab. Cf. *juzu*.)

***Ayari**, n. (1) impostor, impudent cheat, knave, rogue (Ar.); (2) naut., shroud, rope supporting the mast of a ship. (? Ar. or Hind.)

*Ayika, v. for yeyuka, which see.
Aza, v. for waza, which see.
*Azama, n. See Athama (2).
*Azima, v. also Ázima, and Azimu, resolve, purpose, propose, intend, decide on. *Akaazima safari kwenda barra*, and he determined on a journey up country. Ps. *azimwa*. Nt. *azimika*. Ap. *azim-ia, -iwa, -ika*, decide about (for, against, &c.). Cs. *azim-isha, -ishwa*. Also Intens. — n. resolve, purpose, plan, design, proposal. (Ar., and for n. cf. *mradi*, and *shauri*. Dist. *azima* for *athima*, and *azima*, as follg.)

*Azima, v. lend, borrow, in money or kind. Ps. *azimwa*. Ap. *azim-ia, -iwa, -ika*. Cs. *azim-isha, -ishwa*. Rp. *azimana*. — n. loan, debt, advance, money or credit. (? Hind. Dist. *azima* prec., and *athima*. Cf. *deni, kopa*.)

*Aziri, v. slander, bring into disrepute, disparage. (Arab. for common B. *singizia, chongea*, and cf. *izara*.)

*Azizi, n. a rarity, wonder, curiosity, treasure. *Azizi ni kitu kisichoenea watu, azizi* means something uncommon, not widely known. Also a., precious, rare, valuable. *Pameingia mjini kitu azizi*, a great curiosity has arrived in the town. (Arab. Cf. *tunu, ajabu*.)

*Azur, n. perjury. See Zuri. (Arab.)

B.

B represents the same sound as in English.

B in some words is not distinguished from *p* in common talk, e.g. *bofu* and *pofu*, *babua* and *papua*, *bogoa* and *pogoa*, *boromoka* and *poromoka*.

Words not found under *B* may therefore be looked for under *P*, and vice versa.

B in some words appears as *v* in kindred words (cf. interchange of *p* and *f*), e.g. *gomba* and *ugomvi*, *iba* and *uivi*, *omba* and *maomvi* or *maombi*, *jambia* and *jamvia*, *kumbi* and *kumvi*.

B as initial sound of a root, when preceded by an *n* prefix, causes a euphonic change of *n* into *m*, e.g. *ubavu*, plur. *mbavu* for *nbavu*, and *mbele* for *nbele* from *ubele*. Also when an *n* prefix precedes initial *w* of a root, *mb* takes the place of *nw*, e.g. *uwingu*, plur. *mbingu* for *nwingu*. (*n*, *b* and *w* appear to be alternative sounds in some words. Cf. *uwinda* and *ubinda*.)

*Baa, n. (1) evil, trouble, disaster, plague, nuisance; (2) a reprobate, villain, bore. *Baa pia hutokana na vijana na watumwa*, all troubles proceed from children and slaves. *Baa la kujitakia*, a self-caused evil. (Ar. Cf. *shari, msiba, ukorofi*.)

*Baada, adv. or Bada, Badu, after, afterwards,—of time, and only of space 'behind,' so far as it is sometimes involved in the idea of succession, following after, coming next to or behind. Contr. *nyuma*. Seldom used alone, but commonly (1) with *ya*, forming a preposition, after, in succession to, next to. *Baada ya salaam nakuarifu*, after good wishes, I beg to inform you,—a phrase introducing the substance of a letter after the formal complimentary opening; (2) with *yake*, often in combination, *baadaye*, and general reference, 'after it, thereafter, afterwards, then, next.' (Ar. Cf. *bado, wabadahu*.)

Baamwezi. See Mbalamwezi.

*Baathi, a. some, a portion of, generally with *ya*, e.g. *baathi ya watu*, some of the people,—like *watu wangine, nuss ya watu*. (Ar.)

*Bab, n. kind, sort, class,—used sometimes in commerce of goods, e.g. *bab ulaya*, European goods, i.e. for or from Europe. *Panga bab-bab* (or *babu-babu*), arrange in classes, according to kind. (Arab. Cf. *aina, namna, ginsi*.)

*Baba, n. (1) father; (2) uncle on father's side; (3) ancestor; (4) patron, protector, guardian. *Baba haswa* is used to denote and emphasize actual paternity. *Huyu ni baba yanga haswa*, this is my real father. Paternal uncles are distinguished as *mkubwa*, if older, and *mdogo*, if younger, than the father. *Nina baba wakubwa wawili na mmoja mdogo*, I have two uncles older than my father and one younger. *Baba wa kambo*, step-father. *Baba* is treated grammatically as D1, in respect of the agreement of verbs and of all adjectives except the Pronominal. These latter are used in the forms agreeing with D6, commonly in the sing., almost always in the plur. for the sake of distinctness, and these forms often coalesce with *baba*. *Baba mwema*, a kind father. *Baba hataki kwenda*, my father refuses to go. *Baba wake* (or *babake*), *baba yake* (or *babaye*), his father. But *baba zao* (or *babazo*), rather than the ambiguous *baba wao*, their fathers. *Baba ya watoto*, a kind of owl. (Cf. *babu*, and syn. *amu*, and dist. *mjomba*.)

Babaika, v. stutter, stammer, hesitate in speaking, talk as in sleep. (Cf. *gugumiza, payuka*.)

Babata, v. tap, strike lightly,—as a blacksmith on thin metal.

Babu, n. (1) grandfather; (2) ancestor, ancient. (For grammatical treatment cf. *baba*. Also cf. *bibi*, grandmother, and *mzee*, ancestor.)

*Badala, n. and Badili, (1) thing given in exchange, or for barter, a substitute, an equivalent, a swop; (2) a person filling the place or office of another, substitute, representative, successor. *Badala ya*, in place of, instead of. (Cf. *badili*, and *mahali pa*, in place of.)

*Badani, n. the front or back piece together forming the body of a native dress, *kanzu*,—also called *kimo*. (? Ar. or Hind. Cf. *kanzu*.)

*Badili, v. change, become changed, exchange (whether by giving or taking), interchange, alternate, act reciprocally, exhibit successive changes. Esp. of exchange of goods, i. e. barter. Used both act. and neut. *B. mali*, barter goods. *B. fetha*, change money, whether for other coin or its equivalent. *B. zamu*, relieve guard, take an appointed turn or spell of work, &c. *B. nguo*, change clothes, put on another suit. Ps. *badiliwa*. Nt. *badilika*, change, be changed, be capable of change, be fit for exchange, be liable to change, &c. Ap. *badil-ia, -iwa, -ika*. Cs. *badil-isha, -ishwa, -ishana*, e. g. *badilishana*, of several persons, cause each other to exchange, agree upon terms of barter, wrangle over a sale. Rp. *badiliana*, e. g. of several persons engaged in a matter of exchange or barter. Sometimes Redupl. *badili-badili*, of frequent, rapid, or vexatious change. (Ar. As contr. with B. *geuka, geuza*, &c., both imply change, alteration, and so far can often be used convertibly, but change in *badili* properly implies only *another* thing or state, in *geuka*, another and a *different* thing or state, i. e. a change of quality, condition or form,—alteration as well as substitution, succession, &c. Thus *badili nguo* would properly mean, put on another suit of clothes, *geuza nguo*, put on a suit of a different kind (in a different condition). *Badili mali*, exchange goods, *geuza mali*, make goods better or worse.) — n. (*ma-*), change, exchange, alternation, successive change, repetition. Usu. in plur. (Ar. Cf. *badala, -badilifu*, B. *geuka, -geuzi*, &c.)

*-badilifu, a. (1) changing, changeable, liable to change; (2) of character, whimsical, shifty, untrustworthy. (Ar. See Badili, v.)

*Bado, adv. (1) of time, succession, subsequence, ' yet, as yet, (not) yet'; (2) of accession, addition, 'still, still more, further, moreover, as well, to boot.' Very common after a negat. verb, and esp. in the deferred tense, e. g. *amekuja?* Has he come? Ans. *Hajaja b.*, he has not yet come, or merely *bado*, i. e. (not) yet. *Yuko?* Is he there? Ans. *Yuko b.*, He is still there, or *hayuko b.*, he is not there as yet. Often too with an infin. loosely, with negative force, *b. kujua*, there is no knowing as yet. *Vita b. kwisha*, the war is not yet over. *Bwana b. kuam'ka*, my master is not yet awake. *B. analala*, he is still asleep. *B. -ngine*, still (yet) another. *B. kidogo*, yet (still) a little, i. e. soon, presently, wait a bit. *Utapata b.*, you will get it presently. *Mtu jamaa yao na b. mtu wa serkali*, a kinsman of theirs and moreover a government official. (Ar. Cf. *baada*. *Bado* implies succession, futurity, and so, expectation, and by implication, negation, i. e. the not-present.)

Bafe, n. a venomous kind of snake. (Cf. *nyoka*.)

*Bafuta, n. also Báfuta, a thin kind of bleached calico, used esp. for lining a *kanzu* (which see). Different qualities are distinguished as *B. ingereza* (fine), *B. fransa* (thicker), *B. dondo* (dressed), *B. maradufu* (heavy), &c. (Hind. See Nguo.)

*Bagala, n. also Bágala, a kind of native sailing vessel, — large, square stern, high poop, and long prow, used esp. in trade with India. Sometimes double - masted. See Chombo. (? Hind.)

*Bághala, n. also Baghla, a mule. (Ar. Cf. B. *nyumbu*, used as syn. in Z.)

Bagua, v. separate, put apart, divide off. *B. yaliyo yako*, pick out what is yours. Nt. *baguka*, be separated, be at variance, quarrel. *Bagukana*, be in hostile parties, quarrel together. (Cf. the common *tenga*.)

*Bahari, n. (1) sea; (2) fig. of what is of vast extent. *B. kuu*, the high seas, ocean. *B. ya Sham*, Red Sea. *B. il ali*, Persian Gulf. *B. Rum*, Mediterranean, i. e. Sea of Constantinople. *Watu wanaozama katika bahari ya maneno*, people who plunge into the ocean of words, i. e. embark on etymological studies. (Ar. Cf. *baharia*. Also opp. *barra*, B. *inchi kavu*.)

*Baharia, n. (—, and *ma*-), sailor, one of ship's company. (Ar. Cf. *bahari*, and B. *mwana maji*.)

*Bahasha, n. (—, and *ma*-), case, satchel, bag, packet, paper box (or, cover). *Bahasha ya nguo*, a bundle of clothes. Sometimes used to describe an 'envelope.' (? Hind.)

*Bahati, n. (1) fortune, chance, luck; (2) esp. good fortune, good luck. *Kwa b.*, by chance, by good luck. *B. njema (mbaya)*, good (bad) fortune. *Ndio b. yake*, that is his good luck. *Tumia b.*, do a thing at random, take the chance, risk everything, make a plunge, speculate, trust to luck. (Ar. See follg. Cf. syn. *nasibu*.)

*Bahatisha, v. guess, make a venture, speculate, trust to luck. Ps. *bahatishwa*. (Ar. Cf. *bahati*, and syn. *kisi*.)

*Bahili, n. and a., also Bakhili, and -bahili, a miser, miserly, covetous, grasping, parsimonious, i. e. *mwenyi kuweka mali*, one who hoards his money. *Mali ya bahili huliwa na dudu*, a miser's wealth gets worm-eaten. (Ar. Cf. *ubahili*, -*kabithi*, and for the idea, *roho, choyo, tamaa*.)

*Baina, n. clearness, clear knowledge, certainty. *Hapana b.*, there is no certainty (clear evidence). (Ar. Cf. *baini*, follg. and *uthahiri, hakika*.)

*Baini, v. and Bayini, (1) see clearly, know, distinguish, recognize; (2) make clear, prove, show; (3) be clear, be manifest, be plainly shown,—

this sense more usual with the Nt. *bainika*. Ps. *bainiwa*. *Mwivi amebainiwa*, the thief has been detected. Nt. *bainika*, be shown, be made clear. Ap. *bain-ia, -iwa, -ika, -ikia, -ikana.* Cs. *bain-isha, -ishwa,* &c., intens. make very plain, clearly distinguish, demonstrate. — a. and -**bainifu**, clear, plain, demonstrable, evident, well-known, notorious. — n. also **Baina**, which see. — adv. See **Beina**. (Ar. Cf. *bayini, ubaini, bayana, mbayana, ubayana,* and syn. *thihiri, wazi.*)

***Bajia**, n. a small cake of ground beans and pepper (Str.). (? Hind.)

Bajuni, n. (*ma-*), native from coast north of Mombasa. See **Mgunya**.

***Baki**, v. remain over, be left, stay behind. Ap. *baki-a, -iwa*, remain over to (for, in, &c.). *Walibakiwa mali*, they had property remaining over to them. Cs. *baki-sha, -shwa, -shia,* or *bakiza*, leave behind, cause to remain. Rp. *bakiana*, of several persons or things, remain behind all together (by consent). — n. (—, and *ma-*, also *bakia* (*ma-*) and *-o*), (1) that which remains over, remainder, residue; (2) in Arithm., subtraction. *Baki ya vitwana*, the remainder of the men-servants. (Ar. Cf. B. syn. *saa* (*ma-*), *salio*, &c.)

Bakora, n. a walking-stick,—usually of a white wood (the best being *mtobwe*, which see) with top bent at an angle, and rather larger at the lower end. *Alipigwa b. kumi*, he got ten strokes with a stick. (Various kinds of sticks are *fimbo, ufito,* (*ki*)*gongo,* (*ki*)*barango, rungu, mkongojo, mpiko, mpweke, kipigi, mtobwe.*)

***Bakshishi**, n. gratuity, gift, present, beggar's dole, fee. (A great variety of words and expressions denoting 'gift' from different points of view will be found in this Dictionary. Some are of a general kind, e.g. *ada, atia, karama, bakshishi, majazi, thawabu, zawadi, kipaji, kipawa, hedaya, tuzo* (*tuza, tunzo*), others of special character, for various occasions of charity, congratulation, affection, bribery, &c., e.g. *hiba, kumbu-kumbu, kisalama, kipukusa, sadaka, hongo, mlungula, rushwa, kijiri, mpenyezo,* or taken from a common form of present, e.g. *ufito, kilemba, pesa,* or from the service rewarded, *uongozi, uchukuzi, makombozi, maokozi* (and many words of similar formation), or from the immediate effect in view, e.g. *kipa mkono, kinyosha mgongo, kifungua mlango,* and many others.)

****Bakuli**, n. (—, and *ma-*), a large, deep basin, dish, or pan of earthenware. Dim. *kibakuli*. (Ar.)

***Balaa**, n. sorrow. (Arab. for common *huzuni*, &c.)

Balamwezi, n. also **Baamwezi**, moonshine. See **Mbalamwezi**.

Balanga, n. a disease producing light-coloured patches on a dark skin, ? a form of leprosy.

***Balari**; n. a kind of chisel. (? Hind.)

***Balasi**, n. (*ma-*), a very large kind of jar (of stone or earthenware, with narrow mouth), used esp. for storing water. Said to come from the Persian Gulf. (? Pers. Cf. *kasiki*, which is smaller. *Balasi* also means 'leprosy' in Arab., and is used so in Z. Cf. *ukoma*.)

*****Balehi**, v. grow up, come to (sexual) maturity, become marriageable. *Amebalehi sasa, apewe mke*, he is now grown up, he should be given a wife. — n. also **Mbalehe** (*wa-*), boy or girl growing up, entering on manhood or womanhood, developed, marriageable. (Ar. Cf. syn. *komaa, pevuka* and *ubalehe, -pevu, -zima*.)

*****Bali**, conj. but, nay, rather, on the contrary. (Arab. Cf. more common *lakini*.)

*****Balozi**, n. (*ma-*), also **Barozi**, which see, and **Balyozi**, consul, political agent. (? Turkish. Cf. *ubarozi*.)

*Balungi, n. (ma-), citron—the fruit of *mbalungi*. (Hind.)

Bamba, n. (ma-), a flat thin piece (esp. of metal), a sheet, plate, or strip of metal. *Mabamba ya chuma*, hoop-iron. Also of card-board, millboard. Dim. *kibamba*. (Cf. *mbamba, -embamba*, and follg.)

Bambo, n. (1) an iron instrument grooved and pointed, used for drawing a sample from a sack of grain; (2) (ma-), long cord-like strip of plaited grass, used for making coarse mats and baskets, and for cording a native bedstead. (Cf. *shupatu*, also *ubambo, mbamba, bamba*.)

*Bamia, n. same as Binda, n. (which see).

Bamvua, n. (ma-), spring tide. (Cf. syn. *maji makuu*.)

Bana, v. hold as in a vice, press, squeeze, pinch. Also in neut. sense, stick fast, jam. Ps. *baniwa*. Nt. *banika*, be fixed, e.g. between two sticks, for roasting by a fire. Also used act., set to roast at fire. Ap. *ban-ia, -iwa, -ika*, press to (with, in, &c.). *Jibania nguo*, gird oneself tightly, fasten one's clothes tight, as for work, a journey, &c. Cs. *ban-iza, ban-za*. *Jibanza ukutani*, squeeze oneself up against a wall, to allow something to pass. Rp. *banana*. (Cf. *banua, bano, mbano, banzi, kibanzi*, and syn. *kaza, songa*, &c.)

*Banada, n. also Banaderi, the ports on the Somali coast north of Zanzibar, esp. Barawa, Marka, Magdesh, Warsheikh, &c., now in the Italian Protectorate (1902). (Ar. Cf. *bandari*.)

*Banagiri, n. (—, and ma-), also Banajili, armlet, bracelet, in Z. usually of silver—a broad band ornamented with blunt projecting points. (Hind. Cf. *kikuku*, and for such ornaments generally, *urembo*.)

Banda, n. (ma-), large shed, workshop, factory—covered, open at the sides. *B. la frasi*, stable. Dim. *kibanda*.

*Bandari, n. harbour, anchorage, roadstead, port. *B. ni mahali pa pwani watu washukapo, a bandari* is a place on the shore where people disembark. (Ar. Cf. *banada*.)

*Bandera, n. See Bendera.

Bandi, n. (ma-), stitching, a row of stitches, a stitch, esp. of the coarser kinds of sewing. *Fanya (piga, shona) bandi*, baste, tack, run (in sewing). (Cf. *ponta, shuhu*, and see Shona.)

Bandia, n. puppet, toy-figure, doll. *Mtoto wa bandia*, a doll, often made of plaited grass, stuffed with rice.

Bandika, v. put on, stick on, fasten on, apply, attach, esp. of causing something to adhere to a surface, also 'add, place in addition to.' Sometimes fig. and neut., e.g. *Amewabandika*, he has attached himself to them, he sticks to them, of an unpleasant companion. *B. dawa*, apply a plaster (in medicine). Ps. *bandikwa*. Ap. *bandik-ia, -iwa*. Cs. *bandik-isha, -ishwa, -iza, -izwa*. *Bandikisha vyombo*, put on an extra load, add to a load. (Cf. *kandika*, and follg., and n. *pandika, pandikiza*.)

Bandua, v. take off, detach, remove, strip off, peel off, relieve of. Nt. *banduka*. *Hawambanduki Mzungu*, they never leave (part company with) the European. *Unisugue hatta nibanduke maganda*, rub me, till my shell comes off—of a tortoise. (In form and sense a Rv. form of *Bandika*, but no deriv. or cogn. forms common. Cf. *mbanduko*.)

*Banduru, n. bilge, place in ship's hold from which water is baled out, ship's well.

*Bangi, n. bhang, leaf of *mbangi* or Indian hemp, often chewed and smoked, and used in various sweet preparations. A strong intoxicant. (Hind. Cf. *mbangi, paru, boza, majuni, afyuni*.)

*Baniani, n. (ma-), a Banyan. See Banyani.

*Baniya, n. the Caaba at Mecca. (Arab. a building.)

Banja, v. crack, break, e. g. a nut.

Bano, n. (*ma-*), a carpenter's tool for holding work in position, cramp, holdfast. (Cf. *bana, mbano*.)

Banua, v. loosen, unfasten, slacken pressure, e.g. open the jaws of a vice. Nt. *banuka*. *Ban-ulia, -uliwa*. (Rv. of *bana*.)

***Banyani**, n. (*ma-*), Banyan, heathen Indian, usually trader from Cutch.

Banzi, n. (—, and *ma-*), thin strip of wood, or split stick, used for holding fish, meat, &c., to toast by a fire. (Cf. *bana*, and dim. *kibanzi*.)

Bao, n. (*ma-*). See **Bau**.

Bapa, n. also **Ubapa**, used of a broad flat, or slightly rounded, surface, e.g. *b. la upanga*, the flat blade of a sword, the flat side as opp. to the sharp edge (*makali*). *B. la uso*, broad forehead or broad cheek (face). *B. la kisu*, knife blade. (Cf. *kengee*.)

***Bara**, n. See **Barra**.

***Bara-bara**, a. also **Baraba**, just as it should be, quite right, exact, proper, without a flaw. *Ndipo mambo yawe baraba*, so all may be well. *Fetha hii ni baraba*, this is the exact sum. *Athuuri baraba*, just noon. (Hind.)

***Barafu**, n. ice. *Tukakuta barafu juu ya meza imeganda*, and we found ice formed on the table. (Ar.)

Baragumu, n. (—, and *ma-*), 'horn' used as a musical instrument, 'trumpet, war-horn,' blown through a hole near the small end. (Cf. *panda, pembe, siwa*, for similar instruments.)

***Baraji**, n. rope attached to the after end of the yard-arm in a native vessel, halyard. (Cf. *hamarawi*, and *foromali*.)

***Baraka**, n. (—, and *ma-*), also **Mbaraka** (*mi-*), (1) a blessing, generally; (2) (special forms of blessing, such as) prosperity, progress, advantage, plenty of food, abundant harvest, &c.; (3) a favour, gift. *Tuna b. leo*, we are getting on well to-day. (Ar. Cf. *bariki, mbaraka*.)

***Barakoa**, n. a mask, covering the face down to the mouth, all but the eyes, worn in public by Arab and Mahommedan women generally of the upper class. (Ar.)

***Barathuli**, n. See **Barazuli**.

***Barawai**, n. a swallow.

***Baraza**, n. (1) place of public audience or reception. In Z. a stone seat in the entrance hall, or against the wall outside a house, or a raised platform with stone seats and sometimes roofed over in front of the house, for receiving strangers, holding audiences, and transacting business. Hence also (2) a meeting, reception, public audience, council; (3) members of a council, cabinet, committee. (Ar. Cf. *barizi*.)

***Barazuli**, n. a dull-witted heavy man, simpleton, dupe,—one who is made a butt of by his companions. (Ar. Cf. *mjinga, mzuzu*.)

***Baridi**, n. (1) cold, coldness, chill, dampness; (2) wind, air, draft; (3) coolness, refreshment, relief (from heat and exhaustion), comfort; (4) fig. coldness of manner, dullness, lack of interest, repelling aspect or tone. (Thus *baridi* may imply both pleasant and unpleasant sensations, but the verb *burudisha*, &c., is always used of what has a pleasant effect.) *B. nyingi*, high winds, or great cold. *Maji ya b.*, (1) cold water, opp. to *maji ya moto*, hot water; or (2) fresh water, as opp. to *maji ya chumvi* (*ya bahari*), salt (sea) water. (Cf. *maji ya mvua, maji matamu*, &c.) *B. yabis*, rheumatism. *Maneno ya b.*, platitudes, or chilling remarks. (Ar. Cf. *burudisha, buruda, ubaridi*.)

***Bariki**, v. (1) bless, consecrate; (2) grant wealth (favour, prosperity, &c.) to; (3) knock down to (a bidder), accept the bid of at an auction. Ps. *barikiwa*. Ap. *barik-ia, -iwa*, give a blessing to (for, with, &c.). Cs. *barik-isha*, Intens. load with favours. (Ar. Cf. *baraka, mbaraka, taburuku*, and the common name *Mabruki*.)

*Barizi, v. (1) hold a reception, give an audience, summon a council, receive guests, sit in state; (2) attend an audience, go to a council (meeting, reception, &c.); (3) sit out of doors, sit together in a garden, &c. See **Baraza**. *Sultani anabarizi leo*, the Sultan is holding a court to-day. *Twabarizi kwa Mzungu*, we attend meetings at a European's house. (Ar. Cf. *baraza*.)

*Barra, n. or Bara, (1) 'land' in general, as opp. to sea, *b. na bahari*, land and sea; (2) land as most known to Swahili, i. e. wild, uncultivated country, *b. tupu, b. nyeupe*, bare, unoccupied land; (3) the region of the coast, *b. ya Waswahili*, the Swahili coastland; and also (4) the hinterland as contr. with coast, *tangu pwani hatta b.*, from the coast to the interior. *B. il asili*, mainland, continent. *B. al Hindi*, India. *Barabara* is used descriptively of a bare open locality, of a broad road or clearing. *Barabarani*, out in the open, on the high road. (Ar. Cf. Zanzibar, i. e. *Zanji-bara*, negro coast.)

*Barua, n. written form, note, bill, ticket, letter, esp. of formal official communications, but also generally of ordinary correspondence, like *waraka*. (Ar. Cf. *waraka, cheti, hati*, and *kibarua*.)

*Baruti, n. gunpowder. (Ar. *barud*.)

*Basbasi, n. mace, the inner husk of nutmeg (*kungu manga*). (Ar. for fennel?)

*Bashiri, v. (1) bring tidings, report news, announce (esp. of first tidings, and so) (2) tell in advance, announce beforehand, predict, foretell. Ps. *bashiriwa*. Ap. *bashiria, -iwa*. Common in the expression *Bashiri heri!* May it be good news! *Umbashirie heri*, predict good luck for him. (Ar. Cf. *mbashiri*.)

*Bassi, Bass, (1) conj. very commonly used as a connective in narratives, often heading each succeeding paragraph in a story, 'Well, and so, accordingly, and then'; (2) interj. generally expressing contentment or resignation, 'It is enough, very well, that will do'; but also often an order or decision, 'Stop that! That's all! Have done with it.' (Hind. *Bassi* is one of the commonest and most characteristic interjections in Swahili, and capable of conveying very different shades of meaning according to the tone of voice and expression, from the highest gratification to the extreme of mortification and disgust. In fact, a whole series of distinct ideas may be conveyed by the same word, e.g. at the close of a bargain a dialogue may be heard carried on with it alone. *Bassi?* (interrogatively and doubtfully), Is that really all that you can give me, your lowest terms? *Bassi* (with decision), Those are my final terms. *Bassi* (with reluctant resignation), Well, I suppose I must accept it. *Bassi* (with an air of satisfaction), Very well; that settles the matter. *Bassi* (final consent), Be it so! Done! Agreed!

*Bastola, n. pistol (? same word, through Arab.).

*Bata, n. (*ma-*), a duck. *B. la Bukini*, a goose, lit. Madagascar duck. *B. la mzinga*, a turkey, perh. from its note. *Kwenda batabata*, walk like a duck, waddle. (Ar.)

*Batela, n. also Betela, a kind of sailing vessel common at Z., smaller than *bágala*, cut-water slightly curved like a boat, square stern and usually a small quarterdeck. See **Chombo**. (Ar.)

*-bathiri, -bathirifu, a. extravagant, prodigal. (Ar. Cf. *ubathirifu*, and *batili, ubatili*.)

*Bati, n. (1) tin, block tin, sheet tin. Also used of (2) corrugated iron sheeting (*ma-*). *Tia bati*, tin, v., i. e. cover a copper vessel with tin.

*Batili, v. make worthless, reduce to nothing, cancel, annul, abolish, treat as of no use, defy, transgress. Ps. *batiliwa*. Nt. *batilika*. Ap. *batilia, -iwa*. Cs. *batil-isha, -ishwa*, &c.

-batili, a. and -batilifu, worthless, invalid, of no use (force, or effect). *Hoja batili*, a futile argument. *Nikaha ile batili*, that marriage is null and void. (Ar. Cf. *ubatili*, and B. syn. *languka*, v.)

*Batli, n. log, in naut. sense, i. e. a ship's record or journal. (? Hind.)

Batobato, n. (1) open place where dancing takes place, dancing-yard (more commonly *kiwanja cha ngoma* in Z.); (2) markings, coloured spots or stripes, of animal or insect. Also adv. (as if *batabata*) of waddling, flat-footed gait. *Yule ana batobato*, he walks flat-footed. Also *kibatobato*, with various spots (markings). (Cf. *kipaku*, and *madoadoa*.)

Bau, n. (—, and *ma-*), also Bao, a board, and as contr. with *ubau* (*mbau*), a large board; usually of a board of special kind or for special purpose, e.g. a bench or table; and also (1) a playing-board, for chess, cards, but most commonly (2) for a favourite game called *Bao* simply, or *Bao la mtaji*, like a chess-board with 64 (sometimes 32) holes for squares, and seeds or pebbles for counters. *Cheza bao*, play the Bao game. Hence *bau* is also used of (3) a game, generally, or victory in a game. *Twaliwafunga* (or *twaliwatia*) *mabau sita*, we won six games. *Tia bau*, mark a game, win; (4) a diviner's board, esp. *bau la mchanga*, a board covered with sand, called also *ramli* (Ar. for sand) and (locally) *kibunzi*. *Piga bau*, use a divining board, take the omens. (Cf. *ubau*.)

*Baura, n. anchor of European pattern and make, with two flukes (*makombe*). Also called *nanga ya baura*. (Cf. syn. *nanga*.)

Bavuni, adv. loc., alongside, at the side. See **Ubavu**.

Bawa, n. (*ma-*), wing of bird or insect. Dim. *kibawa*. (Cf. *ubawa*, wing-feather.)

*Bawaba, n. (—, and *ma-*), hinge. (Hind. Cf. *patta*.)

*Bawabu, n. (*ma-*), door-keeper, house-porter, chamberlain, turnkey. *B. wa kifungo*, gaoler. (Ar. Cf. *mngoje mlango*.)

*Bawasiri, n. piles, haemorrhoids. (Ar.)

-baya, a. (*mbaya*, with D 4 (P), D 6, *baya* with D 5 (S)), bad, in the widest sense, i. e. possessing the quality of not approving itself or being acceptable, whether materially, morally, intellectually, or aesthetically, i. e. a quality which is offensive (in whatever degree or way) to feelings, conscience, reason, or taste. It may therefore be rendered in a great number of ways in English, e.g. painful, unpleasant, inconvenient, defective, ugly, erroneous, wrong, wicked. (Cf. *ubaya, -ovu, -bovu*, and the opp. *-ema, -zuri, -zima*.) These and other words in Swahili express qualities, the degrees and kinds of which are not differentiated or clearly recognized. It is impossible, therefore, to enumerate the rich variety of English words, which find their readiest and sometimes their only mode of rendering in them.

*Bayana, a. and **Beyana**. See **Baini**. (Ar.)

*Bayini, v. and a. See **Baini**. (Ar.)

*Bazazi, n. (*ma-*) and **Mbazazi** (*wa-*), trader, tradesman, shopkeeper. (Ar. Cf. *ubazazi, tajiri, mchuruzi*.)

Beba, v. carry on the back,—as native women do their children in a cloth. Ps. *bebwa*. Ap. *beb-ea, -ewa*, carry for (in, to, &c.). Cs. *beb-esha, -eshwa*, place (a child) on the back (of the mother). *Asiye na mtoto na abebe jiwe*, if any one has no child, let her even bring a stone on her back.

Bebera, n. (*ma-*), also **Beberu,** (1) he-goat; (2) a strong man. (Cf. *mbuzi*. *Beberu*, or *beru*, also means an extemporized sail, made of loincloth, handkerchiefs, &c.)

*****Bedari,** n. See **Abedari.**

*****Bedawi,** n. (*ma-*), a Bedouin, wanderer, outcast. *Mfano wao kama Mabedawi*, they looked like Bedouins. (Ar.)

*****Bedeni,** n. a kind of sailing vessel from Arabia—cut-water and mast perpendicular, sharp stern, and high rudder-head. See **Chombo.** (? Ar.)

*****Bee,** int. also **Ebbe,** for **Lebeka,** which see. — n. See **Bei.**

*****Beek,** int. for **Lebeka,** which see.

Bega, n. (*ma-*), shoulder—of man or animal. *Chukua mzigo begani* (*kwa bega, juu ya bega*), carry a load on the shoulder.

*****Behewa,** n. inner court — surrounded by buildings and open to the air, as in all large stone houses in Z. (Ar.)

*****Bei,** n. also **Bee,** trade, commerce, bargain, sale, business transaction. *Piga* (*pigana*) *bei*, drive a bargain. *Bei hiyari*, mortgage with option of realizing by sale. *Bei rehani*, mortgage with right to amount of debt only. (Ar. Cf. *biashara, ubazazi.*)

*****Beina,** adv. also **Baina,** in the midst, between. *Beina ya*, amongst, between. (Ar. for more usual *kati*.)

Bekua, v. keep off, ward off, parry, strike aside, divert, receive and return a ball (blow, &c.), defend oneself, counteract. *B. mainzi*, keep off flies. *B. mchele katika pishi*, knock off the overflowing rice in a full measure. Ps. *bekuliwa.* Nt. *bekulika.* Ap. *beku-lia, -liwa.* Cs. *beku-lisha, -lishwa.* Rp. *bekuana.* (Cf. *kinga, epa, linda.*)

*****Belghamu,** n. phlegm. (Arab. for B. *kohozi*, or *kipande cha kohozi*, i. e. expectorated matter.)

Bemba, v. wheedle, cajole, fawn on, coax, caress, solicit, try to influence, win the favour (consent) of. Ps. *bembwa.* Nt. *bembeka.* Ap. *bemb-ea, -ewa, -elea, -elewa, -eleza,* &c., usu. with Intens. force. *Chakula cha kubembelezea njaa,* food cooked to take the edge off the appetite. *Amenibembeleza nimfanyizie kazi,* he has coaxed me into making a job for him. *Bembeleza macho,* put on a coaxing expression. Hence *bembelezana.* Cs. *bemb-eza, -ezwa.* (Cf. *bembe, -bembe, ubembe, ubembelezi,* &c.)

Bembe, n. pastry, confectionery, sweetmeats, esp. of a lover's presents, dainty dishes sent during Ramathan, &c. (Cf. *bemba.*)

-bembe, a. enticing, coaxing, wheedling, coquettish. (Cf. *bemba, bembe, ubembe.*)

*****Bendera,** n. and **Bandera,** (1) flag; (2) (the Arabian flag being red), red cotton cloth, Turkey red calico. *B. maradufu,* red cotton drill or twill. *Tweka b.,* hoist a flag. *Shusha* (*tua*) *b.,* lower a flag. *Bendera hufuata pepo,* the flag goes with the wind. (Ar.)

Benua, v. cause to project, stick out, bulge, protrude, put forward, expose to view. Ps. *benuliwa.* Nt. *benuka,* bulge, stick out, be convex. (Cf. *mbinu,* and syn. *toa nje, tokeza.*)

*****Bereu,** n. a sticky black stuff, black paint. (? Hind.)

*****Beti,** n. (—, and *ma-*), (1) small pouch, pocket bag, case. *B. ya kiasi,* cartridge pouch. *Mabeti kiunoni,* cartridge belt round the waist (possibly from Eng. 'belt'); (2) verse or couplet of a poem. *Uimbo huu una beti tatu,* this song has three verses. (Ar.)

*****Betili,** n. and **Batili,** a kind of sailing vessel from the Persian gulf— long projecting prow, sharp stern, high rudder-head. (See **Chombo,** and dist. *batela.*)

*****Bi,** prep. by, with, in, &c. (Arab., used in a few phrases, e. g. *bi nafsi yake,* by himself, and appears in a few words such as *bilashi, bismilla*.)

Bia, n. used, with various verbs, of joint action, co-operation, partnership, association, in business or pleasure. *Fanya bia*, do in common, act as a company, go shares in. *Changa b.*, make a joint contribution. *Gawa b.*, divide into shares. *Safiri b.*, travel together, each paying his own expenses. *Kula b.*, dine together at the expense of all. *Nunua b.*, purchase jointly. (Cf. *shariki*, and contr. *kikoa*.)

Bia, n. (*ma-*), a large cooking pot. (Cf. *kibia*.)

*****Biashara,** n. buying and selling, trade, commerce. *Fanya b.*, engage in trade. *B. tele*, trade is brisk. *Mfanyi b.*, trader, merchant. (Ar. *bay wa shira*, sale and purchase. Cf. *bei*.)

*****Bibi,** n. (—, and *ma-*), term of respectful reference and address to women (1) in general, 'lady, my lady, Madam, Miss'; (2) used of the 'Mistress' of a household, by or in reference to its members, slaves and others, 'the mistress, my mistress'; (3) also grandmother, and (4) used of the 'wife,' by or in reference to the husband, more courteous than *mke, mke wangu*. When there are several ladies in a household, they are distinguished as *bibi mkubwa*, the mistress, and *bibi mdogo* of other ladies. Sometimes the phrase *kina bibi*, the lady folk, the ladies, is used with courteous vagueness of one or more ladies. (Hind. Cf. Arab. *sitti*, rarely heard.)

Bibo, n. (*ma-*), cashew apple, fruit of the *mbibo*. (Cf. *mbibo, korosho*, cashew nut.)

-bichi, a. (*mbichi* with D 6, D 4 (P)), (1) not full-grown, unripe, immature; (2) raw, fresh, newly gathered, e.g. of eggs, grass, meat, vegetables, &c. *Chokaa mbichi*, unslaked lime, fresh plaster. *Nyama mbichi*, raw flesh, underdone meat.

Majani mabichi, fresh, green grass. (Contr. *-bivu*, and cf. *ubichi*.)

*****Bidi,** v. put pressure on, make obligatory on, compel, oblige, esp. of moral pressure, duty, honour, privilege. *Akanibidi kuleta washahidi*, and he bound me to produce witnesses. Frequent as an impersonal verb. *Ikabidi*, it was necessary, there was an obligation. *Ikambidi kukatwa mkono*, he was compelled (sentenced) to have his hands cut off. *Imenibidi*, I feel bound to. Ps. *bidiwa*, be under obligation to. Ap. *bidia, -iwa*. Cs. *bidisha*, and Intens. *jibidisha*, take special pains. (Ar. Cf. follg. and *pasa, lazima, shurutisha*.)

*****Bidii,** n. effort, energy, exertion, exercise (of strength or will), moral force, willingness to work. *Fanya b.*, work hard, take pains, show energy (interest, earnestness). *Mtu wa b.*, a man of energy, willing worker. (Ar. Cf. *bidi*, and B. syn. *utendaji*.)

*****Bikari,** n. pair of compasses, compass for drawing. (Arab.)

*****Bikira,** n. (*ma-*), a virgin. (Ar. Cf. B. *mwanamwali*, and follg.)

*****Bikiri,** v. deprive of virginity, deflower. Ps. *bikiriwa*. (Ar. Cf. *bikira, ubikira*.)

*****Bila,** prep. and **Billa,** without, except by, apart from,—with a noun, or Infin. or *ya*. *Siwezi kukaa billa mke*, I cannot remain without a wife. *Billa yeye kutoa fikira*, without his disclosing his idea. *Billa uthuru*, without excuse. Also with *ya*, *b. ya amri*, except by order. *B. ya kujua maana*, without knowing the meaning. (Ar. Cf. B. syn. *pasipo*.)

*****Bilashi,** adv. without (getting) anything, for nothing, in vain, gratis, gratuitously. *Utarudi bilashi*, it will be no use your returning. (Ar. *bila shai*, for the commoner *burre*.)

*****Bilauri,** n. (1) crystal, glass; (2) any small drinking vessel of glass, a glass, tumbler, wine-glass. *Jiwe la b.*, rock crystal. *Kikombe cha b.*, a glass cup, tumbler. *Lete b.*, bring a glass. (Ar.)

*Bildi, n. plummet, sounding-lead, i. e. *lisasi ya kupimia maji*, lead for measuring (the depth of) water. *Tia b.*, plumb, sound. (Ar. Cf. *chubwi, timazi.*)

*Bilingani, n. (*ma-*), and Bilinganya (*ma-*), a dark purple vegetable of the tomato kind, fruit of the Mbilingani (which see), sometimes called 'mad apple.'

*Bilisi, n. (*ma-*), devil, the devil, Satan. (Arab. for common *shetani*. Cf. *ubilisi*.)

*Bilula, n. a tap, turncock.

*Bima, n. insurance against loss, accidents, &c. *Lipa b., toa b.*, pay (effect) insurance of goods in commerce. *Fanya masharti ya b.*, draw up a deed of insurance. Also as v., insure, effect insurance on. (Hind.)

*Bin, n. son (of). (Arab. for common B. *mwana*.)

*Binadamu, n. member of human race, human being, man. Hence *kibinadamu*, of a human kind, human, natural to man, and *ubinadamu*, human nature, humanity. (Ar. *bin Adamu*. Cf. B. *mtu*.)

Binda, n. an Indian vegetable, a kind of hibiscus—also known as *bamia*.

Bindo, n. (*ma-*), fold of the loincloth, used as a pocket, bag, receptacle for carrying things, pocket, purse. *Pesa largu nimelipiga b.*, I have fastened my farthing in my loincloth. *Kinga b.*, hold out a fold of the loin-cloth to receive something. *Iliyo bindoni*, what is in the pocket, safe, secure. (Cf. *pinda, upindo*, &c., which is perh. the same word,—also *uwinda, ubinda*, and for 'bag, bundle' cf. *furushi, bahasha.*)

Bingwa, a. and -bingwa, clever, knowing, shrewd, capable. *Fundi huyu mbingwa*, he is a good workman. (Cf. *ubingwa*, and syn. *-stadi, waria.*)

*Bini, v. = Buni, which see. (Ar.)

*Binti, n. daughter, young lady. When followed by the father's name, without preposition, forms the usual designation of all women in Zanzibar except of the lowest class—slaves, beggars, and freed slaves, e. g. *binti Ali, binti Abdallah, binti Sulemani*. Not used by itself in address, except in a familiar way to young persons, 'my daughter.' (Ar. Cf. *bin*, and B. syn. *mwana*.)

*Birika, n. (—, and *ma-*, according to size), (1) large metal vessel for holding water, large kettle; (2) cistern, tank, bath—of masonry, such as are found in all the better houses of Zanzibar, either for holding rainwater or for bathing purposes. Sometimes (3) of ordinary European bath. (Ar.)

*Birinzi, n. a particular dish of cooked food—meat, rice, pepper, &c. (Cf. *pilau*.)

*Bisbis, n. (—), and Bisibisi, screwdriver. (Hind. Dist. *bisi*.)

Bisha, v. (1) strike, knock, beat, hit against. *B. mlango*, knock at a door. *B. hodi*, knock and ask leave to enter by saying 'hodi,'—the rule of courtesy universal in Z. (2) Oppose, resist, strive against, argue with, quarrel with; (3) joke, jest (cf. *ubishi*); (4) (of a ship), beat, tack. *B. chombo*, work a ship to windward. (Cf. *bisho*.) Ps. *bishwa*. Ap. *bish-ia, -iwa, -iana*. *Mtu huyu amenibishia hatta tumeteta*, this man opposed me, till at last we quarrelled. Rp. *bish-ana, -ania, -anya*. *Bishana maneno* (or *kwa maneno*), joke together, argue together, wrangle. *Bishanya*, shake together, mix by shaking. (Cf. *bisho, -bishi, ubishi, mabishano*.)

-bishi, a. of one who is always opposing, whether (1) goodhumouredly, 'joking, jesting,' or more commonly (2) captious, argumentative, combative, contradictory, obstinate—one who *killa umwambialo hakubali,* finds fault with everything you say. (Cf. *bisha, ubishi, bisho.*)

Bisho, n. also **Mbisho,** working to windward, beating, tacking. *Upepo wa b.,* head wind. *Piga b.,* beat to windward. (Cf. *bisha, mbisho,* &c.)

***Bisi,** n. also **Mbisi,** parched grains of Indian corn, described as *mahindi yaliyokaangwa,* a favourite preparation, cried in the streets of Z. as *bisi moto,* hot *bisi.* There is also *bisi la mtama,* made of millet.

***Bitana,** n. lining. *Nguo ya bitana,* clothes made with two thicknesses of material. (Ar. Cf. *bafta,* used as lining, and *tabaka, maradufu.*)

***Bithaa,** n. goods (for trading), merchandise. *Fetha na bithaa,* cash and goods, money and kind.

-bivu, a. (*mbivu,* with D 6, D 4 (P)), matured, ripe, well cooked, opp. to *-bichi. Embe mbivu,* ripe mangoes. *Nyama mbivu,* well-done meat. (Cf. *iva, ubivu,* and the less common forms *-wivu,* or *-ivu, uivu,* but dist. *-wivu,* jealous.)

Biwi, n. (*ma-*), heap of plantation or garden rubbish, sweepings, refuse, leaves.

***Bizari,** n. small seed such as pepper, caraway, and other condiments used in making curries. Hence sometimes 'curry powder.' *B. nene,* anise. (Ar.)

***Bizimu,** n. a buckle, brooch, clasp, fastening. (Ar.)

***Bobari,** n. carpenter's rounded chisel, gouge, also known as *ngabu.*

Bofu, n. (*ma-*), a large bladder. (Also heard as variant of *pofu,* froth, and *-bovu,* rotten. Cf. *kibofu.*)

Boga, n. (*ma-*), pumpkin, gourd, the plant being *mboga.* (Dist. *mboga,* vegetables in general.)

***Bohari,** n. (—, and *ma-*), storehouse, warehouse, large shop, magazine, go-down, described as *nyumba ya mali (ya kuwekea vitu),* house for goods (for storing things). *Mabohari ya makuti,* thatched store-houses. (Cf. *ghala.*)

***Bohora,** n. (*ma-*), also **Bohra,** a member of one of the two chief sects or divisions of Mahommedan Hindoos in Z., the other being *Khoja.* Each sect has its own mosques, club, burying ground, &c.

***Boi,** n. (*ma-*), house servant, personal attendant, domestic. So *fanya boi,* be servant. *Taka boi,* apply for service. (From Eng. *boy.* Cf. *mtumishi, mwandishi,* and see **Manowari.**)

***Boko,** n. (*ma-*), hippopotamus, esp. of a large size, the dim. *kiboko* being the common name in Z.

Bokoboko, n. a particular dish of cooked food (Str.), and hence to describe other things of a soft, jelly-like consistency.

Boma, n. (*ma-*), any kind of raised structure for defensive purposes, (1) earthwork, outer wall, rampart, mound, palisade, stockade, fence, and hence (2) fort, redoubt, castle. (Cf. *bomoa,* and syn. *ngome,* fort, and dist. *ua,* fence of yard or garden, *ukuta,* wall of house, partition wall.)

***Bomba,** n. (1) pump. *Bomba ya kuvuta maji,* a pump for drawing water. Also used of (2) chimney of a steamer, or any large pipe. (? Portug.)

Bombwe, n. (*ma-*), cut figure, carved pattern, carving, sculpture. *Kata mabombwe,* carve figures (patterns). (Also *kibombwe* (*vi-*). Cf. more usual *choro, nakshi.*)

Bomoa, v. break down, break through, make a breach in, cause to fall down, esp. of a wall or fence, or other artificial structure. Ps. *bomolewa.* Nt. *bomoka,* fall down, be broken through, collapse. Ap. *bomo-lea, -lewa. Mtambo wa kubomolea,* a crowbar to break down a wall with. Cs. *bomo-sha, -shwa.* (Cf. *boma,* and *poromoka, poromosha,* sometimes heard as *pomosha* or *bomosha, bomoka.*)

Bomu, n. (*ma-*), boom, sound of a drum, esp. of the larger, deep-sounding kind, or of a cannon. *Bomu la gogo*, a long drum with low note.

Bonde, n. (—, and *ma-*), valley, hollow between hills, low-lying country. (Cf. *Bondei*, the country between the Usambara hills and the coast near Tanga and Pangani, German East Africa.)

Bonge, n. (*ma-*). See **Donge**.

Bongo, n. (*ma-*), brains, marrow. (Cf. *ubongo*.)

*****Bonth**, n. bridge,—rarely heard. (Cf. Fr. pont, and syn. *daraja, ulalo*.)

Bonyea, v. yield to pressure, give way, sink in, be crushed, e.g. of soft ground, ripe fruit, &c., and other inanimate objects. Nt. *bonyeka*. Cs. *bony-esha, -eza*, press in, make impression on, examine by feeling and pressing. (Cf. syn. *tomasa*, of animate objects, and *bopa*.)

Bopa, v. (1) be soft to the touch, soften, feel soft, as of ripe fruit, an abscess, &c.; (2) sink in, become hollow (concave). Ap. *bopea*. *Mashavu yake yamebopea*, his cheeks are sunken (hollow). Cs. *bop-esha, -eshwa* (and possibly *bobya, bofya*, cf. *apa, afya* for *apisha*), press with finger, make impression on, feel. (Cf. *bonyea, bonyesha* (which implies greater force and effect), *tomasa*, and follg.)

Bopo, n. (*ma-*), soft place, mudhole, pit. (Kr.)

*****Bora**, a. of special quality (importance, or value), fine, high class, first-rate, excellent, good, noble, &c., often with implied comparison, 'better, the better, best.' *Tumbako bora*, there is nothing like tobacco. *Asikari ndume bora*, magnificent fighting men. (Ar. Cf. *afathali*, better, superior, and *-ema, -zuri*.)

*****Bori**, n. (1) clay bowl of a tobacco pipe. See **Kiko, Tosa**. (2) Tusk of ivory. See **Buri**.

*****Boriti**, n. also **Borti**, pole of the kind used for rafters in East Africa. (These poles are still an important article of trade on the African and Arabian coasts. They are a kind of mangrove, straight, hard, and (if kept dry) very durable, and carry the heavy concrete ceilings and roofs of all stone houses, incidentally limiting the dimensions of rooms and arrangement of the whole.)

*****Borohoa**, n. a native dish, beans, &c., pounded into a paste or thick broth and flavoured.

Boromoka, Boromoko. See **Poromoka**, &c.

Boronga, v. make a mess, muddle, fuss, bungle, mix. *B. kazi*, do a job badly (in a muddling, unworkmanlike way). Sometimes Redupl. *boronga-boronga*. Ps. *borongwa*. (Cf. follg., also *buruga, vuruga*.)

Borongo, n. muddle, mess, bungle. *Kazi ya b.*, a badly done job.

Borotangi, n. See **Buratangi**.

Boruga, v. See **Buruga**.

-bovu, a. (*mbovu* with D 6, D 4 (P)), bad, chiefly of physical condition, i.e. rotten, unsound, unhealthy, spoilt, decomposed, putrid. *Matunda mabovu*, rotten, unsound fruit. *Samaki mbovu*, stale fish. Hence also (2) worthless, unfit for use or service. *Mtu mbovu*, an ill-conditioned, unsound, worthless man. (Cf. the more comprehensive word *-baya*, and note, and the apparently cognate word *-ovu*, which indicates usually bad moral condition. *Mtu mwovu*, an evilly disposed, unprincipled, bad-natured man. Contr. *-zima, -zuri, -ema*.)

Boza, n. an intoxicating preparation of bhang. (See **Bangi**.) Hence perh. *bozibozi*, idle, dull, incapable of work. (St.)

Bu, int. descriptive of the thud of a heavy blow or fall. *Anguka bu*, fall heavily. *Piga bu*, give a heavy blow.

Bua, n. (*ma-*), stalk, stem, of the larger grasses, e.g. of *mtama*, millet, or *muhindi*, Indian corn. Used for house walls, fencing, and firing. (Cf. *ubua*, of smaller kinds.)

Buba, n. a bad skin disease, of a persistent and contagious kind.

Bubu, n. (*ma-*), a dumb person, mute, dumb. *Sema kwa bibubu*, speak in dumb language, i. e. by signs.

Bubujika, v. bubble out, burst forth in a flood. *B. machozi*, burst into a flood of tears. *B. maneno*, come out with a torrent of words.

*Buddi, n. escape, way out, alternative, means of avoiding. Seldom used except with negative parts of *kuwa na*, to have, in such phrases as *hakuna b.*, necessarily, undoubtedly; it must be so; *sina b.*, I must, I cannot avoid it. *Haina b. kuniambia habari yako*, there is no escape from telling me about yourself. *Billa b.*, inevitably, surely. *Bassi mimi nina b. ya kulia?* What! Can I help crying? (Ar. Cf. *labuda*. *Buddi* is sometimes heard as *bundi*.)

Buhuri, n. incense. (Arab. Cf. *ubani*, *uvumba*, *uudi*, and *vukiza*.)

Bugu, n. (*ma-*), a thick kind of withy, used as cord for binding. (Cf. *mbugu*, *nbugu*.)

Buibui, n. (—, and *ma-*), (1) spider. *Tando la (utando wa) b.*, spider's web; (2) a kind of large veil, covering the whole figure entirely, worn by some women (Arab, Comoro, and others) in Z. when out of doors.

Buki, n. Madagascar. Often in loc. form, *Bukini*. Also -*buki*, a., of Madagascar, cf. *Mbuki*, a Malagasy. *Bata la Bukini*, a goose. A district of Ng'ambo in Z. is called *Kwa Wabuki*.

Buku, n. (*ma-*), the very large, long-tailed rat common in town and country, Z. (*Buku* is also sometimes used of 'a book,'—from the English. But cf. *kitabu*, *chuo*, *msahafu*.)

Bukua, v. hunt out a secret, discover, reveal. (Cf. *mbukulia*.)

*Bulangeni, a. used of coloured, striped, variegated objects, e. g. a vessel painted in two or more colours, a coloured wall, &c. (? Ar.)

*Bulangeti, n. also Burangiti, blanket, rug. *B. magongoni*, blankets at their backs,—of a soldier's kit. (From the Eng.)

*Buli, n. (—, and *ma-*), teapot. Also *b. ya kahawa*, coffee-pot,—which is commonly *mdila* or *deli*.

Bumba, n. (—, and *ma-*), also Pumba, lump. *B. la tumbako*, plug, or packet, of tobacco. *B. la udongo*, clod of earth. *B. la nyuki*, cluster of bees, when swarming. Dim. *kibumba*. (Cf. *bumbwi*, and *pumba*.)

Bumbuazi, n. utter perplexity, helpless amazement, confusion of senses. *Kupigwa (kushikwa) na b.*, to be dumbfounded, to lose one's senses.

Bumbwi, n. grain (rice, millet, &c.) pounded and mixed up with grated cocoanut.

*Bumia, n. beam forming sternpost of native vessel, fastened to the keel (*mkuku*), and carrying the rudder-post (*fashini*).

Bumunda, n. (—, and *ma-*), a kind of dumpling or soft cake. (Str.)

Bundi, n. (—, or *ma-*, according to size), an owl. (Dist. *bundi*, as a variant of *buddi*.)

Bundika, v. plait the hair,—used of a simple kind of plaiting in three parts. (Cf. *suka*, of more elaborate plaiting.)

*Bunduki, n. gun, rifle, musket. *Piga b.*, fire a gun. *Elekeza b.*, point (aim) a gun. *Piga bunduki-bunduki*, keep up a fusillade. Guns are described as *b. ya jiwe*, or *ya gumegume*, a flint gun; *b. ya mrao*, a matchlock gun; *b. ya kushindiliwa*, or *ya fataki*, a muzzle-loading gun; *b. ya kuvunja*, or *ya kukunja*, a sporting (hinged) gun (rifle). *B. ya viasi*, a breech-loading rifle. *B. ya midomo miwili*, or *ya kasiba mbili*, a double-barrelled gun. Common trade guns are sometimes called *bunduki ya kindoro*, or *ya makoa*. (Ar.)

*Bungala, n. Bengal. Used of a species of rice, and of banana. (Cf. *mchele, ndizi*.)

Bungo, n. (*ma-*), fruit of *mbungo*, a kind of medlar. (Cf. *mbungo*.)

Bungu, n. (*ma-*), (1) fruit of *mbungu*, an india-rubber producing plant (cf. *mbungu*); (2) a large earthenware dish. *B. la kupozea uji*, a dish to cool rice-gruel in. Dim. *kibungu*. (3) A kind of caterpillar.

*Buni, v. sometimes Bini, (1) construct, contrive, compose, invent, make for the first time; (2) fabricate, make up (what is false), imagine, write fiction, &c. Ps. *buniwa*. Nt. *bunika*. Ap. *bun-ia, -iwa, -ika, -ikana*. Cs. *bun-isha, -ishwa*, &c. *B. mji*, found a town. *B. kitabu*, be the author of a book. *B. kitu kisichotambulikana*, invent an unheard-of contrivance. *Maneno haya ya kubuniwa*, these are purely imaginary statements. *Alibuni neno asilotumwa*, he invented a message he was not charged with. (Ar. Cf. *zua, tunga, vumbua*.)

*Buni, n. (1) fruit of *mbuni* (which see), coffee berry, raw coffee. *B. ya kahawa*, coffee beans. *B. iliyotwangwa*, pounded (ground) coffee berries. (2) An ostrich. (Ar.)

Bunju, n. a poisonous fish of the Diodon (Globe-fish) kind.

Bunzi, n. (*ma-*), a large stinging fly, building a clay nest.

Bupu, n. (*ma-*). *Bupu la dafu*, used of the cocoanut, when full of milk, and just forming a soft layer of nutty substance in the shell. (Cf. *dafu*.)

Bupuru, n. (*ma-*), an empty shell (external case). *B. la kichwa*, skull. (Cf. *fuvu*.)

*Bura, n. a kind of Muscat cloth. See Nguo.

*Burai, v. make a peaceful settlement (with, about), give up claim to, resign, let off payment. *B. mahari*, not to claim a dowry. Ps. *buraiwa*. Ap. *bura-ia, -iwa*. Cs. *buraisha*. (Ar., not common. Cf. syn. *samehe, rithi*.)

*Buratangi, n. also Borotangi, Portangi, Burutangi, a toy kite of paper, Indian make, causing a whirring sound. (Cf. *shada*.)

*Buri, n. (*ma-*), and Bori, elephant's tusk, tusk of ivory, larger than *kalasha*. (Cf. *pembe, kalasha*.)

*Buriani, n. used of final arrangements, esp. on parting company, last words, farewells, &c. *Kuwapa rafiki yao b.*, to give their friends a farewell (send-off). *Takana (agana) b.*, exchange final farewells. (? Cf. Ar. *burai*.)

*Burre, adv. (1) gratis, gratuitously, for nothing, without payment; (2) uselessly, vainly, in vain, for no good cause or result, idly, fruitlessly. *Kazi burre*, labour for nothing, i. e. wasted, or unpaid. *Tukana watu burre*, abuse people without cause. Also as n. *maneno ya burre*, idle (frivolous, foolish) words. (Ar. of Oman.?)

*Buruda, n. prayers for sick and dying, Mahommedan 'Visitation of the Sick.' *Chuo cha buruda*, service for the sick. (Arab. Cf. *baridi, burudisha*, &c., and for other services *fatiha, hitima, soma*.)

*Burudi, v. be (get) cool, be cold, but usu. in the neut. form *burudika*, be cooled, refreshed, relieved, comforted. Ps. *burudiwa*. Ap. *burudia*. Cs. *burud-isha, -ishwa*, cool, refresh, &c. (Ar. Cf. *baridi, buruda*, and B. syn. *poa*, get cool.)

Buruga, v. (1) stir up, mix together, beat up together, e. g. in preparing food; (2) put into confusion, disorder, muddle; (3) stir the soil, prepare a bed for planting, by hoeing, removing weeds, &c. Ps. *burugiwa*. Nt. *burugika*. Ap. *burug-ia, -iwa*. Cs. *burug-isha, -ishwa*. Rp. *buruganya*, stir up together, mix together. (Cf. *boronga, mburugo*, and *koroga, vuruga*.)

*Buruji, n. fortress, fort, castle. (Arab. Cf. *ngome, boma*.)

Burura, v. pull, haul, drag along on the ground. Ps. *bururiwa*. Nt. *bururika*. Ap. *burur-ia, -iwa*. Cs. *burur-isha, -ishwa*, e. g. *bururisha ndoo kisimani*, haul a bucket up from a well. (Cf. *mbururo*, and syn. *kokota, vuta*.)

*Busara, n. (1) good sense, practical wisdom, prudence, sagacity, skill, &c.; (2) plan, device, stratagem. *Leia b.*, employ a device. (Ar. Cf. *akili*.)

*Busati, n. a kind of matting, made at Muscat. (Str.)

*Busha, n. gun-wad, tow (for cleaning gun or cannon).

*Bushashi, n. a kind of muslin. (Str.)

*Bushuti, n. thick woollen stuff, blanket. (Ar. Prop. of Arab burnous, black cloaks of woollen cloth or camel's hair.)

*Bustani, n. a garden. (Ar. or Pers.)

*Busu, v. kiss. Ps. *busiwa*. Nt. *busika*. Ap. *bus-ia, -iwa, -iana*. *Busiana mikono*, kiss each other's hands. Cs. *bus-isha, -ishwa*. Rp. *busana*. — n. (*ma-*), a kiss. (Ar.)

*Buthara, n. prodigality, lavish outlay. (Arab. Cf. *-bathirifu, gharama*, and B. syn. *upotevu wa mali*.)

Buu, n. (*ma-*), maggot, grub, larva. *B. la nyuki*, bee grub. *B. likamea mbawa*, the grub grew wings. (Cf. *jana*.)

Buyu, n. (*ma-*), fruit of the baobab tree (*mbuyu*, which see), calabash. The pith is edible, and the husk is used to draw water with. Hence *buyu* often means 'a native bucket, pail.'

Buzi, n. (*ma-*), very large goat, for usual *mbuzi*. Dim. *kibuzi*.

Bwaga, v. throw off, throw down, relieve oneself of (as to, with). *B. mzigo*, tip a load off one's shoulders, throw it on the ground. *B. nazi*, throw down cocoanuts (from a tree). *B. moyo*, rest the mind, be cheered. *B. uimbo*, give a lead in singing. *B. matukano*, let off a volley of abuse. Ps. *bwagwa*. Nt. *bwagika*. Ap. *bwag-ia, -iwa*. *Jibwagia moyo*, relieve one's mind. Cs. *bwag-iza, -aza*. *Jibwagaza*, throw oneself down, sprawl on the ground.

Bwana, n. (—, and *ma-*), used (1) in reference, 'master, owner, possessor' of slaves, house, plantation or other property, and generally 'great man, dignitary, worthy, personage'; (2) in address, 'Master, Mr., Sir.' Often *bwana mkubwa*, to show special respect, and contr. *bwana mdogo* of the next in rank, or inferior. *Bwana* is also used by women of and to their husbands, and in Z. is a common designation of the Sultan as supreme. (For the root *-ana*, cf. *mwana, dubwana*.)

Bweta, n. small box, such as a desk, work-box, cash-box, jewel-case, &c. (? Portug. or French, or Ar. dim. of *bet*. Cf. syn. *kasha, sanduku*.)

CH.

C is used only in combination with H, to represent the sound of *ch* in English or *ty*, i. e. a sound between *t* and *ch*, as in *nature*.

CH (1) represents the pfx. *ki-* (which see) (*a*) regularly before adjectives (including the Pronominal) and tense-signs beginning with a vowel, e. g. *kitu changu* (for *ki-angu*), my thing; *kisu chakata* (for *ki-a-kata*), the knife cuts; *kikao chema cho chote* (for *ki-ema ki-o ki-ote*), any good dwelling whatever; (*b*) sometimes before other than adjectival roots beginning with a vowel, e. g. *chango* (for *ki-ango*), *chuo* (for *ki-uo*), a book; *chombo* (for *ki-ombo*), a vessel; *chumba* (for *ki-umba*), room in a house.

In all these cases the corresponding plural pfx. is *vy-*.

(2) Is a vulgar pronunciation of *ki* often heard among the poorer class and slave population of Zanzibar, e.g. *chitu* for *kitu*, thing; *chende* for *tende*, dates.

(3) In the Zanzibar dialect often represents a *t* or *ty* at Mombasa, as *chupa* for *tupa*, bottle; *chungwa* for *tungwa*, orange; *inchi* for *nti*, country.

(4) Is practically often not distinguished from *sh* or *j*, except in words where the distinction is necessary to make the meaning clear.

Hence words not found under *Ch* may be looked for under *ki, j, t,* or *sh*.

Words beginning with *ch* are with very few exceptions of Bantu origin.

Ch-, (1) = *ki*. (See prec. and **Ki-**); (2) is the pfx. corresponding to D 3 (S) in all adjectives and tense-prefixes in verbs, when they begin with a vowel. (See prec.)

Cha, prep. form of *-a* (which see), agreeing with D 3 (S), meaning 'of.' &c., e.g. *kisu cha chuma*, a knife of iron; *chumba cha bwana*, the master's room; and with *kitu* understood, *cha kula*, food; *cha kuogea*, a bath.

Cha, v. (also *kucha* in some forms. For use of *ku* before monosyllabic verb-roots, see **Ku-**, 1 (*d*).) (1) fear, be apprehensive of, reverence. Not often heard in Z. except in reference to God. *Kumcha Muungu*, to fear God. Ps. *chewa. Jina lako lichewe*, may your name be feared. (**Cheka** is usually quite a different word, which see.) Ap. *chea, chelea, chelewa*, &c. *Mchea mwana kulia, hulia yeye*, he who fears for his child's crying, will cry himself. *Mchelea bahari si msafiri*, he who is nervous about the sea is no traveller. See also **Chelewa.** Cs. *chesha*. Rp. *chana*. (These derived forms must be distinguished from identical forms with different meaning, see (2) follg. Cf. *-cha, uchaji*, and syn. *hofu, oga,* *ogopa*). (2) Dawn, change to dawn, be morning. *Kunakucha*, it is dawning. *Kumekucha*, dawn has come. *Hajacha*, it is not yet dawn. *Killa kukicha*, also *killa uehao*, i.e. *ussubuhi*, every morning at dawn. *Kukacha mwanga*, and the light (of morning) dawned. *Usiku na uche hima*, I hope the night will soon be over (turn to dawn). The Infin. form *kucha* is regularly used as a n., dawn, morning. *Kucha kucha*, just dawn, early morning. Also commonly, with or without *usiku*, of the whole period of darkness ending with dawn. *Usiku kucha*, all night long, till dawn of day. *Hakulala kucha*, he had no sleep all night. Cf. Ps. form *kuchwa* follg., with which it is also combined, *kuchwa kucha*, all day and all night. *Kucha hatta kuchwa*, from morning till evening. (Cf. *mchana, jicho, macho,* i.e. *ya jua*, and for 'morning' *alfajiri, assubuhi, mapampazuko, weupe*, and for 'rising' of sun *panda, chomoza*.) Ps. *-chwa*, set (of the sun), end (of daylight). (The root idea connecting the Act. and Ps. is not yet clear.) *Kumekuchwa*, it is past sunset. *Mchana utakuchwa*, the day will come to an end. *Jua limekuchwa*, the sun is setting. *Kwachwa*, evening is coming on. Like *kucha* (see above) *kuchwa* is used as a n. for whole preceding period of the day. *Kuchwa*, a whole day. *Nimeshinda leo k.*, I have stopped all day to-day. *Robo k.*, a shilling a day. *Pesa ya k.*, a day's wages (for which *k*. alone can be used, e.g. *k. yake rupia moja*, his wages for the one day are one rupee). *Kuchwa kucha*, all day and all night. *Mchana kuchwa*, all day long. Ap. Act. *chea, chewa, chelea, chelewa, chelesha, chelewesha*, &c. *Jua limenichea*, the sun rose while I was still indoors, I was surprised (overtaken) by sunrise, I was caught in bed (asleep), also expressed by the Ps. form alone *nimechewa*, i.e. *na jua*.

Hence a form of respectful morning greeting, not often heard in Z. itself, *Kuchewa*, i. e. *habari ya kuchewa?* How does the morning find you? Are you well to-day? to which the reply is simply *Kuchewa*, I am well to-day. Hence also the common use of *chelewa*, be late, prop. of being belated, taken by surprise, shown to be late in getting up, and *chwelewa* in similar sense. See **Chelewa**. Ap. Ps. *chwea, chwewa, chwelea, chwelewa*, &c. *Jua limekuchwea njiani, lala*, the sun has set before your journey is over (while you are still on the road), so lie down. *Tulichwelewa*, we were belated. Cs. *chana*, e. g. *usiku unachana*, the night is turning to day. (Cf. *machwa, machweo*, i. e. *ya jua*, and for ' evening,' *jioni, usiku, magaribi*, and for 'setting' of sun, *shuka, tua*.)

-cha, a. fearing, having fear (awe, reverence), esp. of religious feeling. *Mcha Muungu*, a God-fearing, religious, devout person. *Muungu humkirimu mcha wake*, God is always bounteous to him who fears him. (Cf. *cha*, v. (1), *-chaji, uchaji*, and syn. *-oga, -hofu*.)

Cha, n. See **Chai**.

Chacha, v. (1) ferment, as dough, native beer, &c.'; (2) froth, foam, form a scum; (3) turn sour, go bad, spoil, as stale food, &c.; (4) fig. be sour in temper, cross, irritated. Ps. *chachwa*. Nt. *chachika*. Ap. *chach-ia, -iwa, -iana. Wamechachiana*, they are cross with each other. Cs. *chach-isha, -ishwa*, (1) make sour (sharp, acid); (2) provoke, exasperate. (Cf. *chachu, chachuka*. Dist. **Chachia** below.)

Chachaga, v. wash—used only of washing clothes by rubbing in the hands and dabbing on a board or stone. Ps. *chachagwa*. Nt. *chagika*. Ap. *chachag-ia, -iwa*. Cs. *chachagisha, -ishwa*. (Cf. *fua, osha*.)

-chache, n. (*chache* with D 4 (P), D 6), (1) few in number, small (little) in quantity, not much, not many, slight, deficient; (2) (few, and so) rare, not easily got, scarce, (and so) of value. *Siku chache*, a few days. *Watu wachache*, not many people. *Akili zake chache*, or *mchache wa akili*, he is deficient in sense. (Cf. syn. *haba*, and *kidogo*.)

Chachia, v. press on, hamper, perplex, involve in difficulties. Ps. *chachiwa*. (Perh. same as tatia, which see, and cf. syn. *songa, funga, lemea*.)

Chachu, n. substance producing fermentation, yeast, leaven, such as *pombe, unga wa mtama*. (Cf. *chacha, uchachu*.)

Chachuka, v. (1) turn sour, ferment; (2) foam, froth. *Wali umechachuka leo*, the rice has gone sour to-day. *Bahari inachachuka*, the sea is frothy (yeasty, churning). (Cf. *chacha, chachu*.)

Chafi, n. a kind of fish.

Chafu, n. (—, and *ma-*), also heard as **Chavu**, and commonly **Shavu**, which see.

-chafu, a. (*chafu* with D 4 (P), D 5 (S), D 6), dirty, filthy, unclean, impure, obscene. *Nguo chafu chafu*, very dirty clothes. *Maneno machafu*, obscene language. (Cf. *uchafu*, and with milder meaning *chafua, uchafuko*. Also syn. *taka, -najisi*, and contr. *safi, -eupe, -nathifu*.)

Chafua, v. (1) make dirty, soil, spoil; (2) make in a mess, disorder, disarrange, disturb; (3) of the sea, make rough. *Samaki amechafua maji*, the fish has made the water muddy. *Nyumba imechafuka, yataka kufagiwa*, the house is in a mess, it wants to be swept. Ps. *chafuliwa*. Nt. *chafuka*. *Bahari ilichafuka sana*, the sea was very rough. *Mambo yamechafuka-chafuka*, affairs are in utter confusion. *Alichafuka moyo (tumbo)*, his stomach was upset, he was sick. Ap. *chafu-lia, -iwa*. *Amenichafulia nguo*, he has dirtied my clothes for me. (Cf. *uchafu, -chafu, uchafuko*.)

Chafuo, n. a poisonous kind of fly.

Chafya, v. sneeze. Also n. (*ma-*), e. g. *piga ch.*, *enda ch.*, sneeze (the v.). *Paa akaenda chafya, che-e-e*, the gazelle had a fit of sneezing.

Chago, n. (1) part of bedstead on which the head rests. See **Kitanda**. (2) A kind of crab. (Cf. *kaa*, n.)

Chagua, v. (1) choose, select, pick out, make a choice; (2) of biassed or partial selection, garble, give a false colour to, be unfair. *Mchagua jembe si mkulima*, a man who is particular about his spade is not the man to use it. Ps. *chaguliwa*. Ap. *chagu-lia, -liwa, -lika*. Cs. *chagu-za, -zwa*, offer choice to, give an order (leave, right) to choose. Rp. *chaguana*. Rd. *chagua-chagua*, of dainty, critical selection. (Cf. *-chaguzi, mchaguo*, and syn. *teua*.)

-chaguzi, a. given to choosing, dainty, critical, &c. (Cf. prec. and syn. *-teuzi*, also *uchaguzi*.)

*****Chai**, n. also **Cha**, and **Chayi**, tea,—plant leaf and beverage. (Hind. and Ar.)

-chaji, a. having fear, apprehensive, reverential,—of a more fixed habit and characteristic than *-cha*. (Cf. *cha*, v., *uchaji*, and *-cha, -oga, -hofu*.)

Chaka, n. (*ma-*), (1) clump of trees, dense part of a forest, described as *gongo la mwitu*. Dim. *kichaka*. (2) Summer, the hot season, i. e. Dec. to Feb., but *musimu, kaskazi* are usual in Z.

Chakaa, v. get old, get worn, wear out, be used up (worn, faded), be past work,—of things and persons. *Nguo zimechakaa*, the clothes are worn out. Ap. *chaka-lia, -liwa*. Cs. *chaka-za, -zwa*, use up, wear out. (Cf. *-chakafu, -kukuu*, and syn. *fifia*.)

Chakacha, v. pound, break small, as seeds in a mortar. *Ch. menoni*, crunch with teeth. Ps. *chakachwa*. Nt. *chakachika*, be pounded, be fit for pounding. Ap. *chakach-ia, -iwa, -ika*. Cs. *chakach-isha, -ishwa*. *Chakacha-chakacha* is also used as adv. of a rustling crackling sound, as of a silk dress, cf. *utakaso*. (Cf. syn. *twanga, ponda, seta, vunja*, &c.)

-chakafu, a. (*chakafu* with D 4 (P), D 5 (S), D 6), worn-out, old. *Nguo ch.*, worn-out clothes. (Cf. *chakaa*, and syn. *-kukuu*.)

Chake, a. pron. of 3 Pers. S. agreeing with D 3 (S), his, hers, her, its, of him (her, it). See *-ake*.

*****Chaki**, n. chalk, whiting, putty powder.

Chako, a. pron. of 2 Pers. S. agreeing with D 3 (S), your, yours, of you. See *-ako*.

Chakogea, n. (*vy-*), a chamber bath, for *kitu* (*chombo*) *cha kuogea*, something (a vessel) to bathe in. (Cf. *oga*, v., and *chakula, chamshakinwa*.)

Chakula, n. (*vy-*, sometimes *zakula*), something to eat, food, victuals, provender, a meal, i. e. *kitu cha kula*. *Ch. cha assubuhi*, breakfast, i. e. *chamshakinwa*. *Ch. cha mchana* (*cha athuuri*), midday meal, lunch, tiffin. *Ch. cha jioni*, evening meal, dinner, supper. *Huna chakula cha kulisha mimi wala cha kula wewe*, you have no food to give me to eat or to eat yourself. (Cf. *-la*, v., and *makuli*.)

Chakura, v. scratch, e. g. the ground like a fowl. *Mwana wa kuku hafunzwi kachakura*, a chicken is not taught scratching. (Cf. *mchakuro* and *chokora*, and syn. *papura*.)

Chale, n. (also pl. of *uchale*), (1) cut, gash, incision,—made on purpose, whether as tribal mark, for ornamental tattooing, or for medical purposes, &c. *Ch. zetu za kuchanjiana hazijapona*, our gashes for making blood-friendship have not yet healed. *Mganga akamchanja chale thelathini na wembe*, the doctor made thirty cuts on him with a razor, e. g. to reduce inflammation. (2) A kind of fish. (Cf. syn. *tojo*, and *chanja, toja, kata, tema*.)

Chali, adv. on the back, i. e. of

the recumbent, supine position. *Lala chali*, lie on the back. Also *chali-chali*. (Cf. syn. *kitani, kwa tani, kwa chani, kingalingali, mgongoni*, and opp. *kifulifuli*, on the face.)

Chama, n. club, guild, society, association. *Waana chama*, members of a club. (Many such exist in Z., esp. among artisans of the same trade, a kind of trades union.)

Chamba, v. wash oneself (after calls of nature),—of ordinary and also ceremonial washing before Mahommedan prayers. (Cf. *nawa*, prop. of hands and face; *tawaza*, of feet, and dist *jamba*, &c.) — n. (*vy-*), that which adheres, esp. a film over the eye. *Jicho lina chamba*, the eye has a film over it,—also described as *kiini cheupe*, white pupil of the eye. (*Chamba* for *ki-amba*. Cf. *ambaa, ambika*, &c. and follg.)

Chambo, n. (*vy-*), bait for catching animals, fish, &c. *Ch. cha kuvulia samaki*, fish bait. *Ch. cha kutegea ndege*, bait for luring birds. *Tia chambo katika ndoana*, bait a hook. Cf. *shimbika*. (Cf. *ambaa, chamba*, n., *ambika*, &c.)

Chambua, v. sometimes heard as *iambua, shambua*, (1) clean, dress, pick over, prepare, esp. of appropriate preparation of various products for use, cooking, market, e.g. *ch. pamba*, clean cotton, by removing the seeds, dirt, leaves; *ch. mbaazi*, beans by shelling; *ch. garafuu*, cloves by picking off the stalks. Also used (2) more generally, clean up, give a finish to, improve appearance of; (3) fig. criticize, cross-examine, expose the faults of. Ps. *chambuliwa*. Nt. *chambulika*. Ap. *chambu-lia, -liwa*, &c. Cs. *chambu-lisha, -lishwa*. (Cf. *ambua, ambaa, chamba*, n., &c.)

Chamburo, n. plate used in wire-drawing (Str.).

Chamchela, n. in phrase *pepo ya chamchela*, (1) whirlwind; (2) spirits supposed to cause the whirlwind, and propitiated as such with offerings. (*Chamchela = ki-amchela*. Cf. *kinyamkela*, also *kimbunga, kizumbi*.)

Chamshakinwa, n. (= *kitu cha kuamsha kinwa*), first food in the morning, morning meal, breakfast. (For form cf. *chakula, chakuogea*, and syn. *chakula cha assubuhi*.)

Chana, v. also **Tana**, slit, separate, part, comb. *Ch. miyaa*, slit leaves for plaiting, so *ch. makuti*, of cocoanut fronds. *Ch. nyele*, comb hair. *Ch. kitambaa*, cut, or pull, in shreds. *Ch. kwa fimbo*, of a severe flogging with a stick. Ps. *chaniwa*. Nt. *chanika*. Ap. *chan-ia, -iwa, -ika*. Cs. *chan-isha, -ishwa*. Rd. *chana-chana*, cut into small bits (shreds). (Cf. *kitana, chanua, chanuo, shanuo, chanyata*, and dist. *chana*. Rp. of *-cha*, v. dawn.) — n. also **Tana**, (1) a bunchlet, fruit clustre, on the great fruit stem (*mkungu*) produced by the banana plant (*mgomba*), the single fruit being *dole*, and the fruit generally *ndizi*; (2) same as **Chane** (which see). (Cf. *ngomba, mkungu, tana, dole, ndizi*.)

Chanda, n. (*vy-*), finger, toe, —at Mombasa. *Kidole* is almost invariably used in Z. *Chanda na pete*, finger and ring,—proverb of close connexion, coherence, affection. (Cf. *wanda*.)

Chandalua, n. (*vy-*), awning, canopy, covering, mosquito-net,—of any material used for protection against sun, rain, insects, &c. Used with such verbs as *funga*, fasten; *tungika*, hang up; *tandaza*, spread out.

Chane, n. (—), also **Chani**, and **Chana**, a slip of leaf, made by slitting it up finely or coarsely, for use in plaiting mats, cord, &c. (Cf. *chana*, and *mwaa*.)

Changa, v. collect, gather together. Esp. *ch. asikari* (*watu wa vita*), muster soldiers, levy a force. *Ch. fetha*, collect money by way of voluntary contribution. *Kuchanga* *mali kulipa deni*, to collect money for payment of a debt. *Mali ya kuchangiwa*, money collected for a special (or charitable) purpose. *Kula kwa kuchanga*, hold a club-, or subscription-, feast, each person contributing. (Cf. *kula bia.*) Ps. *changwa*. Nt. *changika*. Ap. *chang-ia, -iwa*, and rp. *-iana*, i.e. join in making contributions. Cs. *chang-isha, -ishwa, -iza, -izana*, and *changanya* (which see). *Changizana*, join in getting contributions. Rp. *changana*, of volunteers mustering for war. (Except in the above and similar senses, the common word is kusanya, which see. Cf. *chango, mchango, changanya, changamana*, &c., and perh. *mchanga*. *Changa* is sometimes heard for chanja, v., which see.)

-changa, a. (*changa* with D 4 (P), D 5 (S), D 6), young, immature, undeveloped, unripe, in an early stage of growth or experience, both of animal and plant life. *Mtoto mchanga*, a young child. *Kitoto kichanga*, a baby, a very young child. *Embe changa*, half-grown mangoes. *Mahindi machanga*, maize not fully developed. *Asikari mchanga*, a raw recruit. Sometimes of things inanimate, *assubuhi changachanga*, very early morning. (Cf. syn. *-bichi, -changa*, denoting esp. stage of growth, *-bichi*, fitness for use, and contr. *-pevu, -zima, -bivu*.)

Changamana, v. also Tangamana, be in a mixed-up condition, often with *na*, (1) be mixed up with; (2) meddle, interfere in; (3) be adjoining (bordering on, next to). *Shamba limechangamana na pwani*, the estate is adjacent to the shore. (Cf. *changa, changanya*, and *-mana*.)

-changam'fu, a. agreeable, enlivening, good-humoured, cheerful. (Cf. follg.)

Changam'ka, v. become cheerful, look bright and happy, be in good spirits, be in a buoyant mood. *Amechangam'ka*, he has recovered his spirits, he is happy. Used of the sun coming out bright after cloud or rain. Also of scenery, *inchi inachangam'ka*, the view has become bright, clear to the eye. Cs. *changam'sha, -shwa*, cheer up, revive the spirits, gladden, exhilarate. (Cf. follg., also *am'ka*, and syn. *furahi*, be happy; *chekelea*, be smiling.)

Changam'ko, n. (*ma-*), entertainment, amusement, pastime, play—anything that raises the spirits. (Cf. *mchezo, mazungumzo*.)

Changanua, v. separate what is mixed, resolve into constituent parts, analyse, simplify what is compound. (Cf. *changa*, v., *changanya*, &c.)

Changanya, v. (1) collect together, mix, form into one mass; (2) make in a mess, muddle, confuse. *Ch. tembo na maji*, mix palm wine with water. Ps. *changanywa*. Nt. *changanyika*. Ap. *changany-ia, -iwa*. Cs. *changany-isha, iza*, (1) mix, adulterate; (2) cause confusion in, perplex. (Cf. *changa*, v., *changanua*, and syn. (1) *kusanya*, (2) *chafua*.)

Changarawe, n. grit, small stones, fine gravel, bits of stone in sand or rice. (Not so fine as *mchanga*, sand; finer than *vikokoto*, small stones. With termination *-we*, cf. *jiwe, mbwe*.)

Chango, n. (*ma-*), (1) contribution, subscription, esp. of money or food, for a common object. *Ch. la mchele*, a contribution of rice. *Killa nyumba ilete ch.*, let every house bring a contribution (for a sacrifice); (2) levy, muster. *Ch. la watu, wachanganao kwenda vitani*, a muster of men, who muster together to go to war. (Cf. *changa*, v., and notes; also *mchango*.) — n. plur. of uchango, which see, (1) smaller intestines; also (2) (sing. and plur.) *chango za tumbo*, round intestinal worms. Also *chango* (*ma-*) in similar sense; *ch. la uzazi*, the umbilical cord. —n. (*vy-*) = *ki-ango*, i.e. *kidude cha kuangikia vitu,* something to hang things on (from), i.e. peg, rail, hook, &c. *Akaenda changoni akauangua upanga,* and he went to the peg, and took down the sword. (Cf. *angika, angua,* and note,—also *mwango.*)

Changu, n. a small kind of fish, common in Z. market. — a. pron. of 1 Pers. S., agreeing with D 3 (S), my, mine, of me. (Cf. *angu, -ake.*)

Changua, v. take to pieces, disconnect,—used of dismembering and cutting up animals for food. (Rv. form of *changa,* which see.)

Chani, adv. also **Tani,** on the back (in a recumbent position). *Lala chani,* lie on the back. Also *chanichani.* (Cf. *chali,* and dist. *chane, chanë.*)

Chanikiwiti, a. green, grass green. (Perh. from *ki-(j)ani kiwiti,* for *kibichi,* i.e. fresh grass (leaves), and so of colour. Cf. syn. *rangi ya majani,* grass-colour.)

Chanja, v. also sometimes *changa,* and *shanga, ?chenja,* (1) cut into, make a cut (incision, gash) in. *Ch. uchale,* make an incision (with knife, razor, lancet). *Ch. mti,* make cuts in a tree (whether to obtain sap or remove bark). *Mzichanje tuzikaushe hizi nyama,* slice up this flesh, so that we may dry it. (2) Cut up, split in pieces, make by cutting up. *Ch. kuni,* split logs for firewood. Ps. *chanjwa.* Nt. *chanjika.* Ap. *chanj-ia, -iwa. Kuchanjiwa ndui,* be vaccinated. *Chanjiana,* make incisions together, i.e. in making blood-friendship. Cs. *chanj-isha, -ishwa,* &c. Rp. *chanjana, -anisha,* &c. (Cf. *chenga,* and syn. *pasua, tema, kata, toja,* and follg. *chanjo, mchanjo.*) — n. used (not often in Z.) of many objects made of wicker-work, interwoven twigs, osiers, wattles, e.g. a screen, a kind of hurdle, a crib for holding an animal's food, a kind of sieve or strainer, a wicker stand for storing grain safely in a house, an arbour or shelter made of interlacing branches, summer-house, a frame for smoking meat on over a fire, &c. *Ch. ya chuma,* a gridiron. *Ch. ya kuanikia nyama moshini,* a frame for drying meat on in the smoke. *Ingia nyumbani hatta mvunguni hatta juu ya ch.,* go inside the house, and look even under the bed and even on the store-shelf.

*****Chanjari,** adv. See **Sanjari,** and **Vinjari.** (? Ar.)

Chanjo, n. (*ma-*), gash, cut, incision. *Piga chanjo la mti,* make a cut in a tree. (Cf. *chanja, mchanjo,* also syn. *chale, tojo.*)

Chano, n. (*vy-*), flat round wooden platter, with a low rim. Sometimes with a stand in one piece, forming a low table. Used as (1) plate for food, *chano wanachotia chakula,* a platter on which they place food; (2) a board for carrying mortar on; (3) a washing-table.

Chanua, v. (1) put out leaves (of plants generally). (Cf. *chipuka.*) (2) Rv. of *chana,* comb (with similar meaning), uncomb, comb out. (Cf. follg.)

Chanuo, n. (*ma-*) and **Shanuo,** a large comb, often of wood, with long coarse teeth, but neatly carved. (Cf. *kitana,* comb of a smaller kind.)

Chanyata, v. slice up (of bananas, cassavas, and various kinds of food). (Cf. *chana,* v. and n., and *mchanyato.*)

Chanzo, n. (*vy-*), (1) the beginning of something, a start, a first step; (2) a first principle, ground, reason; (3) draught, outline, sketch. *Chanzo cha mali,* capital. Cf. *ras il mali.* (For *kianzo,* cf. *anza,* and the more general *mwanzo.*)

Chao, a. pron. of 3 Pers. P. agreeing with D 3 (S), their, theirs, of them. (Cf. *-ao,* and *-ake.*)

Chapa, v. beat, hit, strike,—for the more common *piga*). *Niaku chapa kwa ufito,* I will strike you with a stick. *Chapa miguu,* stamp on the ground, tramp, walk heavily. (Cf. *chapa,* follg., *chapua,* and *chapu.*) — n. (1) stroke, blow, but esp. (2) of the result of a blow, stamp, mark, and hence used of various objects,

e. g. postage stamp, stencil, printer's type. *Akawapiga killa mtu ch. mkononi*, he branded each man on the arm. *Pipa limeandikwa ch.*, the cask has a mark on it. *Piga ch. kitabu*, print a book. (Cf. prec.)

Chapeo, n. hat (of a European kind), helmet. (Cf. French *chapeau*, and *kofia*.)

Chapua, v. give a blow (to), strike (with). *Chapua miguu*, stamp, tramp, walk quickly. *Chapua* (and also the Cs. Intens. form *chapuliza*) *ngoma*, beat hard on (get more sound out of) a drum. (Rv. of *Chapa*, v., but with similar meaning.)

Chapu-chapu, adv. and int., Quick! Make haste! Hurry up! *Chapu-chapu ni mwendo wa haraka*, 'chap-chap' means 'quick march.' (Cf. *chapa*.)

Chapuo, n. (*vy-*), a small kind of drum. (Cf. *chapua, chapa*, and see **Ngoma**.)

Charaza, v. sometimes used for (1) 'play, dance, play on an instrument'; also (2) 'go a stroll, strut or saunter about the town,' but not usual in Z.

Chatu, n. a large snake rather common in Z., growing to over 12 feet in length,—python, boa-constrictor.

Chavu, n. (*ma-*). See **Shavu**, n.

Chawa, n. (1) a louse.; (2) a kind of fish. *Kidole kimoja hakivunji ch.*, a single finger does not kill a louse.

*****Chayi**, n. tea. See **Cha, Chai**.

Chaza, n. an oyster.

Chazo, n. a sucker fish.

Cheche, n. (1) (—) a small reddish-brown animal like a mungoos, common in Z.; (2) (*ma-*), a spark. (Cf. *kimetimeti*.)

Chechea, v. be lame, walk lamely. (Cf. *chechemea*, and *chopi*.)

Chechele, n. absence of mind, an absent-minded person. *Chukuliwa na chechele*, have a fit of absence.

Chechemea, v. be lame. (Cf. *chechea, chopi*.)

Chechesha, v. dandle, fondle, attend to, play with a child, help an invalid.

Chege, n. (*ma-*), bow-leg, bandy-leg. *Ana chege la miguu, ana machege*, he is bandy-legged. Hence perh. *chegea*, walk awkwardly, in a lame way (Str.). — a. moist, watery, e. g. *muhogo mchege*, i. e. not dry and floury. (Not often in Z. Cf. *chepe-chepe*.)

Chego, n. (*ma-*), also **Jego**, molar tooth, back tooth, grinder. (Cf. *jino*, and *kichego*.)

Cheka, v. (1) laugh, smile, grin; (2) laugh at, mock, ridicule. *Tulimcheka sana*, we laughed at him heartily. Ps. *chekwa*. Nt. *chekeka*. Ap. *chek-ea, -ewa*, also *chek-elea, -elewa*, smile, smile at. Cs. *chek-esha, -eshwa, chesha*, cause to laugh, amuse, excite ridicule (amazement). Rp. *chekana*. (Cf. *cheka, -cheshi, cheza, mchezo*.)

Cheko, n. (*ma-*), a laugh, laughter. *Piga macheko makubwa*, utter roars of laughter. (Cf. *cheka*, &c.)

Chelea, v. Ap. from (1) -*cha* (which see), set (of the sun). *Jua linatuchelea*, we are caught by sunset, belated; (2) -*cha*, fear. *Namchelea zaidi ya Sultani*, he inspires more awe in me than the Sultan does. (Cf. follg. and *chelewa, cheleza*.)

Cheleo, n. (*ma-*), (1) delay; (2) object of fear. See **Chelea, Chelewa**.

Chelewa, v. be late, be too late, remain an unusual or unexpected time. *Sikukawia wala sikuchelewa*, I did not delay and I was not late. *Ukuni huu umechelewa moto sana*, this stick of wood has kept hot a wonderful time. *Maji yachelewa kisimani*, there is still water left in the well. (See -*cha* and **Chelea**, of sunset, of which it is apparently the Ap. Ps. form,—the idea of oversleeping, and being overtaken by dawn generalized to mean 'lateness' of any kind, and 'overlong remaining.' Cf. *cheleo, cheleza*, and for delay, lateness, *kawia, ukawa, usiri*.)

Cheleza, v. cause to remain till

morning (i.e. all night), and so cause to remain an unusual time, keep (preserve, leave) for a purpose. *Wakamcheleza mtoto shimoni*, they let the child remain in the pit (for safety). Ps. *chelezwa*. Ap. *chelez-ea, -ewa*. *Nimekuchelezea wali hatta alfajiri*, I have left rice ready for you in the morning, i. e. saved it from the evening meal. Cs. *chelez-esha, -eshwa*, cause to put aside, preserve, &c. (Cf. *-cha, chelea, chelewa*, &c.)

Chelezo, n. (*vy-*), (1) a buoy, lifebuoy, anchor buoy, described as *kigogo kieleacho kuonyesha nanga*, a floating log of wood showing where the anchor is; (2) fisherman's float, to support net or line. (From *elea*, and cf. *ki-elezo* with a different meaning.) (3) Something causing delay (cf. *cheleo, chelewa*, &c.).

Chembe, n. a grain, a single grain, a minute separate part of a thing, a single small thing,—e. g. a grain of sand (*mchanga*), of corn (*nafaka*), of incense (*ubani*), a seed, a bead (= *ushanga mmoja*). *Chembe chembe*, in grains, grain by grain, granular. *Chembe* is sometimes heard with the meaning 'arrow-head, spear-head,' i. e. *ki-embe* (cf. *wembe* and perh. *jembe* for *ji-embe*). Also *chembe ya moyo*, the place where the throb of the heart is felt, pit of the stomach. (Cf. syn. *punje*, also *kichembe*.)

Chembeu, n. (*vy-*), a kind of blunt chisel used for caulking.

Chemchemi, n. a spring (of water). (Cf. *chem'ka*, or ? Ar. *zamzam*.)

Chem'ka, v. and **Chemuka**, bubble, and so of hot water, boil. *Maziwa yacheni'ka kwa kupata moto sana*, milk bubbles up when it gets very hot. *Mayai ya kuchem'ka*, boiled eggs. Cs. *chem-sha, -shwa*, cause to boil, boil.

Chemko, n. boiling, bubbling,— also *mchemko, uchemko*. (Cf. prec.)

Cheneo, n. See **Kieneo**.

Chenezo, n. (*vy-*), a measure, measuring-rod (line), anything to measure with (stick, strip of cloth, string, grass, &c.). Described as *kidude cha kuenezea kitu*, a thing for measuring anything. (For *kienezo*, cf. *chelezo*, and *enea*, and syn. *cheo, kipimo*.)

Chenga, v. cut, esp. of the lighter operations of cutting, e. g. brushwood for firing or fencing, stalks of ripe grain, ripe heads of grain, bunches of grapes, &c. Ps. *chengwa*. Ap. *cheng-ea, -ewa*. (Cf. *chanja, pasua, kata*, &c., *mchengo*.)

Chenga, n. (—), name of a large fish, ? skate, sunfish.

Chenge, n. (*vy-*), for *kienge*, dim. of *mwenge* (which see).

Chenge-chenge, n. small bits, chips, snippings. (Cf. *chenga*, and *chembe-chembe*.)

Chenu, a. pron. of 2 Pers. P., agreeing with D 3 (S), your, yours, of you. (Cf. *-ake*, and *-enu*.)

Chenza, n. (*ma-*), a large kind of Mandarin orange, fruit of the *mchenza*. Some are red or blood oranges. The best are called *chenza za kiajjemi*, i.e. Persian, and a small kind *kangaja*. (Cf. *mchenza, mchungwa, kangaja*.)

Cheo, n. (*vy-*), (1) measure, measurement, dimensions, size; (2) rank, degree, station. *Toa ch.*, fix the size. *Ch. cha kuanzia kitako cha kikapo*, measurement for beginning the bottom of the basket,—and so settling the size. *Kupita ch.*, beyond measure, excessively. *Hana ch.*, he is an ill-bred (low-born) person. *Ch. bora (kikubwa)*, high rank. (Cf. syn. *chenezo, kipimo*; also *daraja*, rank.)

Chepe chepe, a. wet, soaked, soppy, moist. (Cf. *maji maji, rutuba, lowa, loweka*.)

*****Cherehana**, n. used generally of small foreign machines in Z., esp. sewing machines, which are common. *Ch. ya kushona*, a sewing machine. *Kazi ya ch.*, machine sewing. (Cf. Pers. *karhana*, manufactory.)

*Cherehe, Cheree, n. a grindstone. (Cf. *kinoo*, and prec.)

Chetezo, n. (*vy-*), a vessel to burn incense in, often of earthenware,—described as *kidude cha kuvukizia manukato*, something to burn sweet smelling substances in, a censer, censing-pot. (For *ki-etezo*, or ? *ki-otezo*, cf. *ota, otesha*, of crouching over a fire or anything warm. Cf. *vukiza, kivukizo*.)

*Cheti, n. (*vy-*), small written note or memorandum, note, certificate, ticket, passport, &c. (? Hind. Cf. *hati, barua*.)

Chetu, a. pron. of 1 Pers. P., agreeing with D 3 (S), our, ours, of us. (Cf. *-etu*, and *-ake*.)

Cheua, v. ruminate, chew the cud (of ruminant animals). Nt. *cheuka*, have a rising in the throat. Cs. *cheusha*, e. g. cause eructation. (*Cheu*, and *mcheu*, n. seem to be used also of rumination and eructation. Cf. *kiungulia*.)

Chewa, n. a large kind of fish.

Cheza, v. (1) play, sport, take a holiday, have a game, make a move in a game; (2) idle, waste time, not be in earnest, trifle; (3) act, work, move,—esp. of the easy motion of machine running well, or a hinge, bolt, wheel, watch, &c.; (4) drill, be drilled (as soldiers). Ps. *chezwa*. Nt. *chezeka*. Ap. *chez-ea, -ewa*, play with (in, for, &c.), make sport of, mock. *Kidude cha kuchezea watoto*, a child's plaything, a toy. Cs. *chez-esha, -eshwa*, give a holiday (rest) to. *Chezesha unyago*, cause to take part in unyago (which see). *Chezesha frasi*, make a horse curvet (prance). *Ch. mtoto*, dandle a child. Rd. *cheza-cheza*. *Likachezacheza lile jabali*, and the rock swayed. (Cf. *mchezo, chezo*, and perh. *cheka*. Also of pastime, *ongea, zungumza*.)

Chezo, n. (*ma-*), sport, game, play, pastime. (Cf. *cheza, mchezo*.)

Chicha, n. the white nutty substance inside a ripe cocoanut, when it has been scraped or grated out with an *mbuzi*, and the oil (*tui*) strained out by passing water through it. It is generally considered refuse, used for cleaning the hands with, and thrown to the fowls. Described as *nazi iliyokunwa, iliyokamuliwa, iliyochujiwa*, i. e. cocoanut grated, squeezed and strained. Also used of the residuum or lees of other oil-producing seeds. (Dist. *mchicha*, a vegetable, and cf. *tui, kasimele*.)

Chichiri, n. (*vi-*), commonly *kijiri*, a bribe, i. e. *mali ya kumpa kathi*, money given to a judge (to secure his verdict). (Cf. *rushwa, hongo, mlungula*.)

Chigi, n. or **Chinki,** a small yellow bird.

Chikichi, n. (*ma-*), fruit of the palm-oil tree (*mchikichi*), containing small nuts called *kichikichi*.

Chimba, v. dig, make (get) by digging,—of excavation, not as *lima*, of cultivation. *Ch. shimo*, dig a pit, sink a shaft (mine), make a hole. *Ch. kaburi*, dig a grave. *Ch. udongo*, dig out soil. Ps. *chimbwa*. Nt. *chimbika*. Ap. *chimb-ia, -iwa*. *Mto huu umechimbiwa na Wafransa*, this canal was excavated by the French. Cs. *chimb-isha, -ishwa*. (Cf. *chimbua, chimbuka, chimbo*. Also cf. *fukua, lima*.)

Chimbo, n. (—, and *ma-*), digging place, place dug out, a digging, pit, mine. *Ch. ya mawe*, quarry. *Ch. ya udongo*, clay-pit. (Cf. prec.)

Chimbua, v. dig out, dig up, get by digging, as *udongo*, clay, soil; *unga*, flour (out of a barrel); *magogo*, stumps, &c. Nt. *chimbuka*, which see. (Rv. of *chimba*, but similar in result. Cf. *chanua, chana*.)

Chimbuka, v. used esp. of sun or moon, 'appear, begin to shine, rise,' whether from horizon or from clouds. Also *chimbuza*, Intens. in same sense, force its way out, make its appearance. (Cf. *chimbua*, *chimba*,—if thus used, as it seems, metaphorically. Also follg.)

Chimbuko, n. (*ma-*), a first start, a beginning, standpoint, basis, source, first principle. (Cf. syn. *chanzo, asili*.)

Chimvi, n. See **Timvi**.

Chini, adv. (1) down, below, beneath, under, at the bottom, on the ground, downstairs, underground; (2) in a lower place, on foot, at a lower part; (3) in a low (inferior, subject, humble) state (rank, condition, &c.). Often *kwa chini* in same senses. *-a chini* forms an adjective bearing any of the above meanings. *Yuko ch.*, he is downstairs. *Lala ch.*, lie on the ground. *Wangine wanakwenda ch.; wangine juu ya nyama*, some go on foot, some ride on animals. *Kitambi cha kuvaa ch.*, a cloth to wear on the loins. *Njia ya ch.*, a subterranean passage. *Chumba cha ch.*, the lower room, or a cellar. *Ch. ya Sultani*, in the Sultan's jurisdiction. *Chini kwa chini*, emphat., at the very bottom, wholly below, &c. (*-ni* appears to be locative, i.e. *chini*, on the ground. Cf. *inchi*, and opp. *juu*.)

Chinja, v. (1) slaughter, cut the throat of, kill,—esp. of killing animals for food; (2) of brutal indiscriminate killing of persons,—massacre, slaughter, murder. *Alimchinja adui*, he slaughtered his opponent. (It seems sometimes locally used as *kata*, i.e. cut. *Kuchinja kanzu*, to cut out a dress.) Ps. *chinjwa*. Nt. *chinjika*. Ap. *chinj-ia, -iwa*. Cs. *chinj-isha, -ishwa*. Rp. *chinjana*. (Cf. *chinjo*. Same word appears at Mombasa as *tinda*, also *matindo*, and poss. in Z. in *tindika*, and *mtindo*. For syn. cf. *ua, fisha*, also *chanja*.)

Chinjo, n. (act, place, operation of) slaughtering, slaughter-house, massacre, battlefield. (Cf. *chinja*.)

Chinusi, n. a kind of spirit, supposed to drag people under water and drown them, swimmer's cramp.

Chinyango, n. a piece of meat forming a native butcher's perquisite. (Perh. *ki-nyango*. Cf. *chango*.)

Chipuka, v. also **Chupuka**, sprout, shoot, spring up,—of any plant showing signs of life and growth. Ap. *chipuk-ia*. Cs. *chipukisha, chipuza*, and Intens. sprout vigorously. (Cf. follg., and syn. *ota, mea, chanua*.)

Chipukizi, n. (—, and *ma-*), also **Chipuko**, shoot, young plant. Dim. *kichipukizi*. (Cf. *chipuka*, and syn. *mche*.)

Chiririka, v. also **Tiririka** and **Chururika**, flow, trickle, run off, glide,—as water, or a snake. (Cf. *mchilizi*, and *tiririka, churuzika*, syn. *chuza*.)

-chirizi, a. *machozi machirizi*, trickling tears. (Cf. *churuzika*.)

Cho, -cho, -cho-, a. relat. agreeing with D 3 (S), i.e. *ki-o*, which. (For relat. see *-o*.)

Choa, n. (*vy-*), mark or discoloration of skin—whether (1) by disease, ringworm, &c., or (2) artificial—beauty spot. *Choa cheusi*, black (beauty) spot.

Chocha, v. poke, prod, stir up, e.g. an animal in a hole. Ap. *choch-ea, -ewa, -elea, -elewa, elezea, -elezewa*, poke at, stir up, as a fire or lamp. *Chochea kwa kijiti utambi wa taa*, poke at the wick of a lamp with a bit of stick. *Chuma cha kuchochelea moto*, a poker. Also in fig. sense, stir up, excite, provoke. *Alimchochelezea maneno ya fitina*, he stirred up discord against him. Cf. *vumbilia*. (Cf. *mchocho, mchocheo, kichocho*.)

Chochoro, n. (*ma-*), alley, passage, esp. of narrow passages between houses in a native town. (Cf. the commoner *mchochoro, kichochoro*.)

Choka, v. become tired, get weary, be fatigued (worn out, overdone). *Nimechoka*, I am tired. With noun of things, *ch. njia* (*jua, kazi*, &c.), be tired of travelling (weary with the heat, worn out by work). *Ch. na mtu*, be weary of a person's company. Ap. *chok-ea, -ewa, chokeana*. Cs. *chosha, choke-za, choke-sha, -shwa*. Rp. *chokana*, e. g. all be weary together.

Chokaa, n. (1) lime; (2) white plaster; (3) mortar, i. e. in Z. a mixture of lime with sand and red earth. Lime is also used for chewing with tobacco. See **Tambuu.**

Chokea, n. a sty (in the eye).

Choki-choki, n. fruit of the *mchoki-choki*—with a deep-red prickly rind, sweet white pulp, and large stone. See **Mchokichoki.**

Choko, n. *vyoko*, also **Chocho,** oven. (See **Joko,** cf. *oka.*)

Chokora, v. and **Chokoa,** pick at, poke, esp. of working at a hard substance with a pointed instrument, knife, or finger, e. g. clear out a hole, take up weeds. *Ch. meno*, clean the teeth (with a toothpick). See **Msuaki.** Ps. *chokolewa*. Ap. *choko-lea, -lewa, kijiti cha huchokolea meno*, a toothpick. ? Cs. *chokoza*, which see. (Cf. *chocha, mchokoo, chokoza*, and *chakura.*) — n. (*ma-*), dependent, follower, hanger-on.

Chokoza, v. tease, bully, annoy, vex. Ps. *chokozwa*. Ap. *chokoz-ea, -ewa*. (Cf. *chokora*, and syn. *sumbua, tesa, uthi.*)

Chole, n. a kind of bird, ? a jay.

Choma, v. (1) pierce, stab, prick, thrust (something into); (2) apply fire to, cook, set on fire, burn, brand, cauterize; (3) hurt the feelings (of), provoke, give pain to, excite. *Ch. mtu kisu*, stab a man with a knife. *Ch. moto*, apply fire. *Ch. nyumba moto* (or, *kwa moto*), set a house on fire. *Ch. samaki*, harpoon a fish. *Ch. mkuki*, run a spear into. Ps. *chomwa*. Nt. *chomeka*, i. e. be pierced (burnt, hurt, &c.), but also Act., e. g. *chomeka mkuki*, stick a spear in the ground. *Chomeka kisu kiunoni*, stick a knife into the waistband (girdle). Ap. *chom-ea, -eana,
-elea, -elewa*. *Chomea majani mfukoni*, stuff grass into a bag. *Chomelea*, stick pieces into, e. g. of repairing clothes by patches, a roof with new thatch, and in masonry of bringing a rough wall to a surface with mortar and small stones. (Cf. *tomea, ntomo.*) Cs. *chom-esha, -eshwa*, e. g. *chomesha mbwa*. set a dog on, make him angry. (Cf. *chomo, mchomo, chomeo, chomoa, chomoza*, also *ntomo, tomea*, &c., in which *t* represents *ty, ch.*)

Chombo, n. (*vy-*), (1) implement, instrument, utensil, tool, piece of furniture, movable, of any kind or description. *Vyombo* includes all personal belongings, chattels, household apparatus, baggage. *Chombo cha kufanyia kazi*, an instrument to work with. *Vyombo vya seramala*, a carpenter's tools. *Chukua vyombo vyangu ndani*, carry my things indoors. (2) A cooking pot being the most universal and necessary utensil, *Chombo*, by itself, commonly refers to a vessel for containing something, 'pot, pan, jug, jar, cup,' but still more universally in Z. means (3) 'a native sailing vessel, a dhow.' In this sense it includes a number of varieties, e. g. *mtepe, betela, batili, bágala, bedeni, awesia, ghangi*, but is distinguished from others of a smaller size, e. g. *dau, mtumbwi, galawa, mashua*—all of which may also carry sails, and from those of European build, commonly called *merikebu, jahazi, meli, manowari*, &c. (All coast and foreign trade being formerly carried on in these vessels, the dhow was at once the most remarkable 'instrument' and also 'containing vessel' known to the natives, whence prob. the use of *chombo* as its name. Hence also many of the words connected with the dhow and its parts are of non-Bantu origin.) *Panda* (*ingia*) *chomboni*, go on board (embark in) a vessel. *Shuka chomboni*, land, go ashore, disembark. (Cf. *jombo*, and syn. as above, also *chungu.*)

Chomeo, n. (*ma-*), gridiron, toasting-fork, or other similar instrument for cooking, anything used for pricking or piercing. (Cf. *choma*.)

Chomo, n. (1) a burn, stab, prick, &c. (Cf. *mchomo*.) (2) Burnt stuff, dross, slag. *Ch. la chuma*, iron slag, refuse of smelting furnace. (Cf. *choma*.)

Chomoa, v. draw out, take out, expose, bring to light. *Ch. mkuki*, take out a spear from a wounded animal. *Ch. mwiba*, extract a thorn. *Ch. kisu*, unsheathe (draw, draw out) a knife. (Rv. form of *choma*. Cf. *omoa, chomoza*.)

Chomoza, v. (1) make a way out, come out, appear, stick out. *Maua yanachomoza*, the flowers are beginning to appear. *Ras inachomoza*, the cape juts out (comes into sight). Esp. of the sun, *jua limachomoza*, the sun bursts out. Hence (2) of the sun, 'be hot, scorch' (as if *choma*). (Intens. form of *chomoa*. Cf. *choma*.)

Chonga, v. cut to a shape, shape with a cutting instrument, whence a variety of meanings according to the instrument used and shape produced, 'hack, chip, bevel, dress, square, point, smooth, carve, &c.' *Chonga mti*, trim (dress, square) a tree, ready for cutting into planks. *Ch. boriti*, trim (square) a pole (for a rafter). *Ch. kijiti*, cut a stick to a point. *Ch. kalama*, point a pen, make a pen. *Ch. mtumbwi*, cut out a canoe. Also, *ch. maneno*, invent (add to, modify) a story. *Ch. sanamu*, cut out figures. *Ch. mawe*, dress stones. *Akachonga mvinje sura kama bin Adamu*, and he roughly carved the log of cassiorina into a human figure. *Mti lililochongwa ncha kama mkuki*, a piece of wood which was cut to a point, like a spear. Ps. *chongwa*. Nt. *chongeka*. Ap. *chong-ea, -ewa, -eana*, (1) cut with (for, in, &c.). *Chongea panda la mnazi*, cut a piece off the flower-stem of a cocoanut tree, to increase the flow of sap. But also common in (2) fig. sense, tell tales about, inform against, betray, complain of, accuse (esp. unkindly or falsely), slander, discredit, and still more emphatically *chongelea* and Intens. *chongeleza*. *Amenichongea kwa maneno mabaya kwa wali*, he discredited me with a shameful story to the governor. *Mtu huchongewa na ulimi wake*, a man is betrayed by his own tongue. Cs. *chong-esha, -eza, -ezwa*. Rp. *chongana*. (Cf. *chongo, mchongo, chonge, chonjo, uchongezi, chongelezo, chongoa*—also *chanja, chenga, chinja*—all referring to cutting.)

Chonge, n. also ? *chongole*, a canine (pointed) tooth, cuspid. *Chonge za meno*, teeth filed to a point. (Cf. *chonga*, with pass. termination *-e*, and for teeth, *jino*.)

Chongelezo, n. (*ma-*), what is told to a person's discredit or disadvantage,—tales, unkind gossip, scandal, &c. (Cf. *chonga, uchongezi*, &c.)

Chongo, n. absence of one eye, loss of an eye. *Mwenyi chongo*, a one-eyed person. *Ana chongo*, he has lost an eye. (Cf. ? *chonga*.)

Chongoa, v. (1) cut to a shape, round off, cut to an angle (point), bring to a point, sharpen, point; (2) be of a pointed shape, be angular, be jagged. *Ch. kikango*, round off a cooking pot. Nt. *chongoka*, be sharp, jagged, e.g. of craggy, precipitous rocks. *Ras imech. kama sindano*, the cape is as sharp as a needle. (Rv. form of *chonga*, with similar meaning. Cf. *choma, chomoa*.)

Chongoe, n. (*vy-*), a large kind of fish.

Choo, n. (*vy-*), privy, water-closet, cess-pit, i.e. in Z. a circular pit, lined with stone at the sides, and closing gradually into a small aperture over the centre. Usually connected with the bath-room in large houses. *Enda chooni*, go to the closet, go to stool. *Wakampeleka chooni wakamwegesha*, they conducted him to a closet and gave him a bath. Also used (1) of the action of the bowels, &c. *Pata ch.*, have a motion of the bowels. *Funga ch.*, be constipated, have an obstruction of the bowels. *Ch. safi*, free action of the bowels. *Ch. kikubwa* is used of solid, *ch. kidogo* of liquid motions; (2) of (solid) excreta. *Haifai kutia mkojo ao choo katika maji*, it is a mistake to put the excreta of either kind in water.

Chooko, n. See **Choroko**.

Chopa, n. (*ma-*), handful, of what can be gathered and held in the fingers, as sticks, ropes, bits of wood, &c. (Cf. *konzi*, n., and *chopoa*. Cf. *chopa*, v., trade in a small way, hawk goods about the country,—not used in Z. Cf. syn. *churuza*.)

Chopi, adv., *enda chopi*, be lame on one side, walk lamely.

Chopoa, v. snatch from the hand, take away suddenly, seize by surprise, pluck away, filch. Ps. *chopolewa*. Nt. *chopoka* (and a variant *chupuka, churupuka*), slip from the grasp, be filched away, escape, extricate oneself, e.g. from a snare. *Sungura akachopoka mkononi mwa simba*, the hare slipped from under the lion's paw. Ap. *chopo-lea, -lewa*. (Cf. *chopa*, and syn. *ponyoka*.)

Choro, n. (—, and *ma-*), marks made with a tool, engraving, carving, scratch, scrawl, bad writing, hieroglyphics. Also *machorochoro*, carved patterns, writing. (Cf. *chora*, and *nakshi, bombwe*.)

Choroko, n. also **Chooko**, a small dark-green pea or bean, often mixed with rice and other grain for food. Considered inferior to *kunde*. *Hukushiba mikundeni, utashiba michorokoni?* If *kunde* did not satisfy you, will *choroko*? (Cf. *mchoroko*.)

Chosha, v. (Cs. of *choka*, i.e. for *chokesha*), make weary, be fatiguing. See **Choka**.

-choshi, a. (*choshi* with D 4 (P), D 5 (S), D 6), tiresome, tiring. (Cf. *choka, -chovu*.)

Chosho, n. and **Josho**, for *ki-osho, ji-osho*, washing, place for washing, bathing-place. *Mahali pa choshoni*, place for washing, e.g. of corpses, or clothes. (Cf. *oga, osha*, and *fua, fuo*.)

Chosi, n. and **Chozi**, includes two species of birds, one very fond of fresh cocoanut sap, *tembo*,—a *Nectarinia* (Sa.).

Chota, v. take up a little of, take a pinch of, take up by bits (pieces), pick up with the fingers. *Ch. maji*, fetch a little water at a time. *Ch. kuni*, fetch firewood. Ps. *chotwa*. Nt. *choteka*. Ap. *chot-ea, -ewa*. *Kazi yake kumchotea maji mwalimu*, his duty was to supply his teacher with water. Cs. *chot-esha, -eshwa*. (Cf. *choto, mchoto*, and *danga, dona, donoa*, also *chopa*.)

Choto, n. a small part (piece, bit, quantity, amount, a scrap, a pinch). (Cf. *chota, mchoto*.)

-chovu, a. (*chovu* with D 4 (P), D 5 (S), D 6), (1) weary, tired, fatigued, worn out, bored, exhausted; (2) tiresome, tiring, wearying. (Cf. *choka, -choshi*.)

Chovya, v. put (into), plunge (into), dip (into), make contact with, touch, finger. *Ch. kidole motoni*, put a finger in the fire. *Ch. nguo katika maji*, plunge clothes into water. *Ch. asali*, dip into (touch) honey. *Mchovya asali hachovyi marra moja*, he who dips his finger in honey, does not do it once. *Alimchovya haya*, he plunged him in confusion. Nt. *chovyeka*. Ap. *chovy-ea, -ewa*. Cs. *chovy-esha, -eshwa*. (Cf. *chovyo, mchovyo*.)

Chovyo, n. (*ma-*), a dip, touch, what is got by a dip (touching). (Cf. *chovya*.)

Choyo, n. avarice (shown either in getting or keeping), greediness, covetousness, a grasping nature, miserliness, &c. *Mwenyi ch.*, a grasping, niggardly person. *Kuwa na ch.*, to be covetous, to grudge. *Lia ch.*, cry for (disappointed) greediness. Also as a., *huyu ni ch. sana*, he is a dog in the manger. (Cf. *bahili, roho, tamaa.*)

Chozi, n. (*ma-*), (1) a tear, teardrop; (2) anything resembling a tear, gum on trees, &c. *Toka (lia) machozi*, shed tears. *Bubujika machozi*, burst into a flood of tears. *Machozi yalimchuruzika usoni*, tears trickled down his face. (Cf. *chuza.*) (3) One or two species of bird. See **Chosi**.

Chua, v. sometimes **Tua**, as at Mombasa, (1) rub, rub down, and so variously, grind, file, pound, pol'sh; (2) fig. of quarrelling, &c., jar, rub, make discord. *Kuchua si kwema*, friction is not good. *Chua meno*, clean the teeth. *Chua mafumba ya unga*, rub down the lumps in meal. *Chua-chua kitwa*, rub (chafe) an aching head. Ap. *chu-lia, -liwa, -lika*. *Chulika mafuta*, have oil rubbed in. *Jiwe la kuchulia*, a grindstone. Rp. *chuana*, e. g. of persons wrestling. (Cf. *saga, sugua*, more common in Z.)

Chub, int. (the *ch* being mainly heard), expressing contempt or impatience, 'sht! nonsense!'

Chubua, v. take the skin off, abrade, bruise badly, flog, give a hiding to. *Kiatu changu kimenichubua mguu*, my shoe has rubbed the skin off my foot. Ps. *chubuliwa*. Nt. *chubuka*. *Mgongo umechubuka*, my back is raw. Ap. *chubu-lia, -liwa*. *Alimkanyaga mtoto akamchubulia ngozi*, he trod on the child and rubbed the skin off. (Cf. follg.)

Chubuko, n. (*ma-*), bruise, abrasion, raw place. (Cf. prec.)

Chubwi, n. a plummet, a sinker,— attached to fishing line to assist the cast and sink the bait. (Cf. *bildi*, sounding lead, *timazi*, carpenter's plumb line.)

Chuchu, n. (—, and *ma-*), a small hard protuberance on the skin, wart, pimple, small tumour, a callosity. *Chuchu la ziwa*, teat. (Cf. *sugu*.)

Chuchumia, v. Ap. reach up (to), stretch up to, as by rising on tiptoe or hind-legs. *Mbuzi anachuchumia*, the goat is trying to get at (the leaves).

Chui, n. leopard.

Chuja, v. (1) filter, strain; (2) strain out, remove by filtering or straining; (3) cleanse, purify. *Ch. maji yaliyo na taka*, filter dirty water. *Ch. nazi kwa kifumbu kupata tui*, filter (grated) cocoanut in a bag to get the milky extract. *Mungu achuje taka za moyo wetu*, may God take away the impurities of our heart. Ps. *chujwa*. Nt. *chujika*. *Moyo uliochujika*, a purified heart. Ap. *chuj-ia, -iwa*. *Chombo cha kuchujia*, a filter (? *chujio, ma-*). Cs. *chujisha, -ishwa*. (Cf. *chujo, chujua*, and perh. *vuja*.)

Chujo, n. (—, and *ma-*), what is got by straining or filtering. *Chujo ya asali*, molasses, treacle. (Cf. prec.)

Chujua, v. Rv. form of *chuja*, implying an opposite result in, or by use of, a liquid, i.e. spoil with water, by washing or otherwise. *Amechujua uji wangu, una maji*, he has spoilt my gruel, it is too watery. Ps. *chujuliwa*. Nt. *chujuka*, e.g. *nguo hizi zimechujuka*, these clothes are spoilt (in colour) by washing. *Rangi hii haichujuki*, this colour does not wash out, it is a fast colour. Ap. *chujulia, -iwa*. (Cf. *chuja*.)

Chuki, n. ill humour, bad temper, dislike, resentment. *Mtu wa chuki* (or, *wa chukichuki*), one who is quick-tempered, easily put out, ready to take offence. *Yuna ch.*, he is offended, he is sulky. *Ona ch.*, be in a bad temper. *Tia ch.*, offend, vex, make angry. (Cf. follg.)

Chukia, v. hate, have ill feeling towards (e.g. anger, resentment, disgust, loathing, aversion), dislike, abhor. Ps. *chukiwa*, be hated, &c. Cs. *chuk-iza, -izwa*, e. g. cause dislike, offend, put out. Hence *chukiz-ia, -iwa*. But note that *chukia* is also used, Act. and Ps., as *chukiza*, i. e. cause *chuki* in, as well as, feel *chuki* towards. *Bwana amechukiwa na mtumwa wake, mtumwa wake alimchukiza*, the master was provoked by his slave, his slave provoked him. *Jichukiza*, grow angry of oneself, be angry gratuitously (without cause). *Chukizisha*, cause to be annoying, make offensive. *Chukizana*, provoke each other. Rp. *chukiana*, hate each other. (Cf. *chuki, machukio*.)

Chuku, n. cupping-horn. *Piga ch.*, make a false impression, exaggerate, tell an incredible story, draw the long-bow. (Cf. *umika, ndumiko*.)

Chukua, v. (1) carry, bear (a load), take on one's back (shoulders or head, or in one's hands), e. g. as a caravan porter (*mpagazi*) or town porter (*hamali, mchukuzi*). *Ch. mzigo begani*, carry a load on the shoulder,—such load being usually about 60 lbs. weight in a mainland journey. (2) Take, conduct, convey, lead. *Ch. mtoto huyu kwa babaye*, take this child to his father (cf. *peleka* in this sense). (3) Take away, carry off, remove, transport. *Ch. taka*, remove a mess (cf. *ondoa*). Also of the feelings, carry away, transport, overwhelm (of joy, sorrow, &c.). (4) Bear up under (passively), i.e. endure, put up with, take peaceably, be resigned to (cf. *vumilia, stahimili, shukuru*); (5) bear the weight (responsibility) of, support, maintain, sustain. *Anach. wazee wake*, he is supporting his parents (cf. *ponya, ruzukisha, saidia*). (6) Take (in capacity), contain, hold, have capacity for (of a vessel, measure, &c.), and fig. include, involve, allow of. *Chombo hiki kitach. pishi tatu*, this vessel will hold three *pishi* (cf. *weka*). (7) Take up, use up, require. *Safari ile ilich. siku nyingi*, that journey occupied many days. *Zawadi hizi zitach. nguo nyingi*, these presents will require a lot of cloth. *Chukua* has many applications, e. g. *neno hili lach. mambo mengi*, this word includes many things, i.e. has many meanings. *Ch. mimba*, be pregnant. *Nguo hizi zinakuch.*, these clothes set off your appearance, give you a fine air (carriage). Ps. *chukuliwa*. Nt. *chukulika* (rarely *chukuka*). Ap. *chuku-lia, -liwa*, &c., e. g. carry to (for, from, &c.), feel for (towards, about, &c.). *Nikuchukulie*, let me carry it for you. *Chukuliwa mashuku*, be an object of suspicion. *Inachukulika*, it is not too heavy to be carried, it is endurable. Hence *chukuliana*, be compatible, agree, tolerate each other's company. Cs. *chukuza, -zwa*, employ a person to carry, lay a burden on, &c. Rp. *chukuana*, e. g. carry in turns, give mutual support, endure each other, agree together. (Cf. *mchukuzi, uchukuzi*.)

Chuma, n. (—, and *vy-*), iron, a piece of iron. *Chuma pua* (or *pua* alone), steel. *Mabamba ya ch.*, iron of a flat kind, hoop iron, iron plate, &c. *Pau* (or *fito*) *za ch.*, iron rods, bar iron. (For *ki-uma*, so cf. perh. *uma, kiuma*.)

Chuma, v. (1) pluck, gather,—of fruit, flowers, &c.; (2) make a profit, esp. in trade or business, gain in trade, prosper, be well paid. *Watu huenda chuma barra*, people go to make money up country. Ps. *chumwa*. Nt. *chumika*. Ap. *chum-ia, -iwa*. Cs. *chum-isha, -ishwa*. (Cf. *chumo, uchumi*, and syn. Ar. *faidi, faida*.)

Chumba, n. (*vy-*), room, chamber, apartment, i.e. part of a *nyumba*, esp. of a store house. *Nyumba hii ina vyumba vingi*, this house has many rooms. *Ch. cha kulala*, bed room, dormitory. *Ch. cha kulia*, dining room, refectory. (Cf.

nyumba, jumba, mchumba, also *mkato.*)

Chumo, n. (*ma-*), (1) plucking, gathering. *Machumo ya zabibu,* grapes plucked, vintage. (2) Profit, gain, source of gain, employment. (Cf. *chuma,* v., and *uchumi.*)

Chumvi, n. (1) salt; (2) saltness, pungency (of flavour or quality). *Maji ya ch.,* salt water, brine, sea water (contr. *maji baridi, maji ya mvua, maji matamu, maji ya pepo,* fresh water). *Ch. ya haluli,* sulphate of magnesia, Epsom salts. *Maneno yake ch.,* his remarks were pungent, had a flavour.

Chuna, v. skin, flay, take the whole skin off. *Mmchune ngozi kwa vizuri, msikate wala msiloboe, wala msichune na nyama, mmchune vema,* take off the beast's hide properly, do not cut it or make holes in it, and do not take off flesh with it, skin it carefully. Also of stripping bark off a tree. *Chuna kamba,* get (strips of bark for) rope. Ps. *chunwa.* Nt. *chunika.* Ap. *chun-ia, -iwa.* (Cf. *chunua, chuni, mchuni,* also *chubua, ambua.*)

Chunga, v. (1) tend, take care of, act as guardian to, but esp. of animals, i. e. act as keeper or herdman of sheep, cattle, goats, &c., feed, take to pasture, graze, &c. (Cf. *mchunga (-ji), machunga,* and syn. *tunza, lisha.*) (2) Sift, separate fine and coarse particles, e. g. of flour for cooking, of lime for plaster, &c., by shaking and tossing in a flat basket. (Cf. *pepeta,* and *tunga. Chunga* (—) is sometimes n., siftings, husks, coarse particles, &c.)

Chungu, n. (1) (*vy-*), the commonest kind of cooking pot,—usually a round rather shallow vessel of baked earthenware, red or black in colour, of various sizes, and with a lid of same material. (Cf. *ungu, jungu, kijungu,* and for other household vessels, *bakuli, bungu, bia, chano, hero, waya, fua, kombe, kibungu, mkungu, kikungu, kango, kikombe, kikango,* and see **Mtungi,** Sufuria, and Chombo.) (2) (—, and of size, *ma-*), a heap, a quantity, a pile, a mass. *Chungu chungu,* in heaps, quantities. *Fetha zikawa nyingi, chungu zima,* the coins were numerous, a whole pile. (Cf. syn. *fungu, jamii.*) (3) An ant, of a common small kind, and so used more generically than other names of species (e. g. mchwa, siafu, maji ya moto, which see). Also used fig. of a poor, insignificant person. (4) (—) sometimes for *uchungu,* of some particular kind of smart, e. g. *naona chungu ya mwiba,* I feel the sharp prick of a thorn. Cf. follg.

-chungu, a. (*chungu* with D 4 (P), D 5 (S), D 6), (1) bitter, acrid, sour, sharp in taste, acid; (2) disagreeable, unpleasant. *Dawa chungu,* bitter, unpalatable medicine. (Cf. *uchungu,* n., also often used as a., and *utungu.*)

Chungulia, v. look at (down upon, into), esp. of furtive or critical and thorough examination, i. e. peep (at), pry (into), cast glance (at), inspect closely. Ps. *chunguliwa.* Nt. *chunguli-ka, -kana.* Ap. *chungulilia. Ufa wa kuch.,* a peephole. Cs. *chunguza,* e. g. Intens. look carefully (anxiously, thoroughly) into. (Cf. syn. *angalia, tazamia, kagua.*)

Chungwa, n. (*ma-*), the common sweet orange, fruit of **mchungwa** (which see), abundant for nine months in the year in Z. (Cf. for other varieties, *chenza, danzi, limau, kangaja, ndimu, balungi, furungu.*)

Chuni, n. usu. in pl. *machuni,* process of skinning, flaying an animal. (Cf. *chuna, mchuni.*)

Chunjua, n. a small hard protuberance on the skin, a wart. (Cf. *chuchu.*)

Chunua, v. scrape skin off, skin. *Alichunua uso wake,* he took the skin off his face. Ps. *chunuliwa.*

E

Nt. *chunuka.* Ap. *chunu-lia, -liwa.* Cs. *chunu-za, -zwa.* (Cf. *chuna, chubua,* and follg.)

Chunusi, n. (1) and **Chunuzi,** a bit of skin taken off, abrasion, raw place; (2) same as **Chinusi,** which see.

Chunyu, n. incrustation of salt, deposit from salt water. *Nimeoga maji ya pwani nafanya chunyu,* I have had a sea-water bath, and feel the salt on me. (Cf. *munyu, chumvi, nyunyo.*)

Chuo, n. (*vy-*), (1) book; (2) school. *Buni (tunga) chuo,* write a book, compose a book. *Chuo cha serkali,* a government school. *Mwana-chuoni,* or *-vyuoni,* (1) a (boy) scholar, one who attends school; (2) an educated, learned man, a scholar, a man of books. *Enda chuoni,* go to school. *Tiwa chuoni,* be sent to school. (For *ki-uo,* from the appearance of a bound book, cf. *uo,* and for 'book' Ar. syn. *msahafu, kitabu,* and for 'school' *madarasa, soma,* v.)

Chupa, v. 'get over' something by leap, step, hop, jump. *Chupa gogo,* step over a log. Ap. *chup-ia, -iwa,* and see follg. Cs. *chup-isha, -ishwa.* (Cf. syn. *kia, kiuka,* and *vuka.*) — n. (—, and *ma-*), a bottle. *Ch. la kutilia marashi,* a scent-bottle. *Ch. la mvinyo,* a spirit bottle. Also used of the 'womb,' e. g. *kuvunja chupa,* of first stage of childbirth. Dim. *kitupa* (preserving the *t,* as at Mombasa).

Chupia, v. move quickly, rush, dash, gallop. *Frasi mzoefu wa kuchupia,* a horse accustomed to going quickly. (Conn. with *chupa,* v.)

Chupuka, Chupuza, v. See **Chipuka,** and **Chopoka.**

Chura, n. (*vy-*), a frog.

Churua, n. or **Churuwa,** and **Shurua,** measles.

Chururika, v. See **Chiririka,** and **Churuzika.**

Churuza, v. and **Chuuza,** keep a small shop, do a retail business, hawk goods about, be a pedlar. (Cf. *mchuruzi.*)

Churuzika, v. and **Chururika,** trickle down, run of, be drained away, as water from roof, blood from wound, rain from a tree, &c. *Anach. damu,* he bleeds freely. Cs. *churuzisha, -ishwa,* drain off, carry off. (Cf. *chirizika, mchirizi, tiririka,* and also *chuza.*

Chusa, n. (*vy-*), a harpoon, used for large fish, such as *papa, nguru, chewa.*

Chuza, v. or **Chuuza, Churuza,** trickle, glide, run down. *Chozi la unyonge likichuuza,* as the tear of abject misery falls. *Kuvuja na kuchuza hakulingani na wazi,* oozing and trickling is not the same as open (flood-gates). (Cf. *chiririka, churuzika.*)

-chwa, v. Ps. from **-cha,** which see.

D.

D represents the same sound as in English.

D, as an initial in words of Arabic origin, is used for three Arabic letters, viz. *Dal,* and sometimes *Tah* and *Dhal.* See **T, Th.**

D takes the place of *l* and *r,* as the initial of a root, if a formative *n* is prefixed. Thus *kasha refu,* a long box; *kamba ndefu,* a long rope.

D in Z. sometimes represents a *j* or *dy* in the Mombasa dialect, and in some words is not clearly distinguished from *t.* Thus words not found under *D* may be looked for under *J* or *T.*

Words beginning with *D* are mostly of non-Bantu origin.

-dachi, a. commonly used for 'German.' *Mdachi (wa-), Dachi (ma-),* a German. *Kidachi,* the German language, of the German kind. *Udachi,* Germany, also *ulaya Dachi.* (From *deutsch;* cf. *jamani.*)

Dada, n. sister, esp. elder sister, a term of endearment among women.

***Dadisi,** v. pry, be inquisitive, be curious (about), ask unnecessary questions (of). *Nimemdadisi sana hatta aniambie*, I plied him with questions to get him to tell me. Ps. *dadisiwa*. Nt. *dadisika*. (? Ar. Cf. *mdadisi*, and syn. *hoji, chungulia, pekua*.)

***Dadu,** n. and **Dado,** game, toy, esp. of dice in Z. *Cheza d.,* play with dice. *Machezo ya d.,* games with dice. (Ar.).

***Dafina,** n. hidden treasure, treasure-trove, godsend. (Ar.)

***Daftari,** n. an account book, catalogue, list. (Ar. Cf. *worotha, hesabu ya mali*.)

Dafu, n. (*ma-*), a cocoanut in the stage when it is full of milk, further described as (1) *bupu la dafu, punje la dafu, dafu la kukomba, dafu la kulamba,* i. e. when just beginning to form a soft layer of nutty substance in the shell, which can be licked or easily scraped off, and (2) *tonga la dafu,* when the nutty substance has become thick and tough. *Maji ya dafu,* cocoanut milk. *Dafu* is also commonly used for the milk itself,—little cared for by natives. (Cf. *nazi*.)

Dagaa, n. (? plur. of *udagaa*), very small fish, fish in an early stage, small fry,—like whitebait, a favourite dish with natives.

***Dai,** v. (1) summons, prosecute, sue at law, accuse, charge; (2) claim in court, demand as a right, claim. *Nakudai,* I accuse you. *Nadai kwako haki yangu,* I claim from you my lawful rights. *Rupia amdaiyo Tuna,* the rupee which Tuna claims from him. *Jidai ukali,* claim for oneself martial spirit, boast of prowess. Ps. *daiwa*. Ap. *daia,* claim on behalf of (in reference to, for, from, &c.), act as solicitor for. Rp. *daiana,* of counter claims, cross-suit. — n. (*ma-*), legal process, suit, claim, for the more usual *da'wa*). (Ar. Cf. *mdai, da'wa,* and for 'claim' *haki*.)

***Daima,** adv. perpetually, permanently, constantly, continually, always. *Namwona d. akipita,* I see him constantly passing. *Dumu d.,* emphat., always, for ever and ever, never endingly, eternally. *-a daima,* a. continual, permanent, lasting. (Ar. Cf. *dumu,* and syn. *siku zote, marra kwa marra,* and for 'lasting' *ishi, aushi*.)

Daka, v. catch, snatch, seize, get hold of,—with a sudden, quick movement, e. g. catch a ball thrown in the air, pounce on a thief, appropriate food greedily. Also *daka maneno,* make a smart response (quick repartee, sharp reply). Ps. *dakwa*. Ap. *dak-ia, -iwa*. Cs. *dak-iza, -izwa,* e. g. object to, rebut, contradict. (? Cf. *dakizo, dakua, udaku, dakuliza,* and *nyaka, nyakua,* and for 'seize' *kamata, shika*.) — n. (*ma-*), recess, receptacle, niche in wall, cupboard. *D. la mlango,* a recess with a door, cupboard. Dim. *kidaka*. (Cf. *dakua,* and *dukiza,*—prob. the same root.)

***Dakawa,** n. towing line, tow-rope, i. e. *kamba ya kufungasia*.

***Dakika,** n. the smallest division of time, moment, minute, second. *Kwa d. moja,* in a twinkling, at once. (Ar.)

Dakizo, n. (*ma-*), objection, contradiction, demurrer. (Cf. *daka*.)

***Daku,** n. midnight meal taken by Mahommedans during Ramathan. (Ar. Cf. *Ramathani, futari*.)

Dakua, v. let out secrets, gossip at random, talk indiscreetly. Ps. *dakuliwa*. Ap. *daku-lia, -liwa,* talk foolishly to (for, about, against, &c.). Cs. *dakuliza,* used as 'contradict, protest against, object to, rebut.' (Rv. of *daka*. Cf. *dakizo, udaku*.)

***Dalali,** n. salesman, auctioneer, broker, cheap-jack. (Ar. Cf. *udalali,* and syn. *mnadi*.)

*Dalasini, n. cinnamon, from the tree *mdalasini*. (Ar.)

Dalia, n. a yellow mixture, used by women for personal adornment (cosmetic, scent, &c., and colour).

*Dalili, n. sign, token, mark, trace, indication, evidence, signal. *D. ya mvua ni mawingu*, the sign of rain is clouds. *D. ya mguu*, footstep (on the ground). With negatives, *si hatta dalili*, not at all, not a vestige, not in the least.

*Dama, n. a game, played on a board like chess, a kind of draughts.

*Damu, n. blood. *Nyama na d.*, flesh and blood. *Anatoka d.*, he is bleeding. Also of the menses, *ingia damuni*, menstruate. Cf. *hethi*. (Ar.)

Dandalo, n. a kind of dance. (Cf. *ngoma*.)

Danga, v. (1) take up little by little, get a little at a time, scoop up carefully (of water in a pit), i. e. *d. maji*. (Cf. *chota*.) Hence (2) fig. of enforced and tedious delay, wait, have to wait (but perh. this is tanga, which see).

Danganya, v. elude, delude, deceive, defraud, cheat, beguile, impose on, belie. Ps. *danganywa*. Nt. *danganyi-ka, -kana*. Ap. *danganyia, -iwa*. Cs. *danganyisha, -ishwa*. Rp. *danganyana*. (Cs. form ? conn. with *danga*, or Hind. *dagaa*. Cf. *-danganyifu, mdanganyi*, and syn. *punja, kalamkia, hadaa, kopa*, and dist. *changanya*.) — n. (*ma-*), trick, delusion, &c.

-danganyifu, a. (*dang*. with D 4 (P), D 5 (S), D 6), deceptive, delusive, cheating, &c.) (Cf. *danganya*.)

Danzi, n. (*ma-*), a bitter orange, fruit of mdanzi, which see (and for other varieties, *chungwa*.)

*Darabi, n. (*ma-*), rose-apple, fruit of *mdarabi*.

*Daraja, n. (*ma-*), (1) step, set of steps, stairs, staircase, bridge; (2) degree, rank, dignity, social station. *Akashuka katika d.*, he descended the staircase. *D. kubwa (bora)*, high rank. A district of Zanzibar city near the bridge is called *Darajani*. (Ar. Cf. *ngazi, ulalo*, and for 'rank' *cheo*.)

*Daraka, n. (*ma-*), an arrangement, appointment, obligation, duty, undertaking. *Madaraka ya nyumbani*, household arrangements, domestic economy. *Chukulia d.*, go bail for, answer for, bear the punishment of. (Ar. Cf. *diriki, tadaruki*.)

*Darasa, n. (*ma-*), class, meeting for reading or study. *Madarasa*, school, academy. (Ar. Cf. *durusi*, also *chuo, soma*.)

*Dari, n. upper floor, upper story, ceiling, roof,—roofs and upper floors in an Arab house being alike made of concrete laid on poles and rammed hard. *Darini, juu ya dari*, upstairs, on the roof. (Ar. Cf. *sakafu, brofa*.)

*Darizi, v. See Tarizi.

*Darumeti, n. inside woodwork of native vessel, joists carrying the deck, cross-beams, &c.

*Dasi, n. rope sewn into the edge of a sail for strength, and distinguished as *d. ya bara*, on the upper (yard) side, *d. ya chini*, on the lower, *d. ya goshini* and *ya demani*, on the narrower and broader ends.

Dasili, n. a powder made of the dried and pounded leaves of a tree *mkunazi*, used as a detergent (Str.) for a kind of skin disease.

*Dasturi, n. bowsprit,—also called *mlingote wa maji*. (Dist. *desturi*.)

Dau, n. (*ma-*), a large native-built boat, both ends sharp and projecting, and usually with a square matting sail. (Cf. *chombo, mtumbwi, mashua, kidau*.)

*Daulati, n. the ruling power, government, authorities. (Arab. for the common *serkali*.)

*Dawa, n. (—, and *ma-*), medicine, medicament, anything supplied by a doctor, including 'charm, talisman, &c.,' used by native doctors. *D. ya kuhara*, a purgative, aperient. *D. ya* *kutapisha*, an emetic. *D. ya kunywa*, medicine for internal use. *Dawa ya kutia* (*kupaka, kubandika, kujisugua*), medicine for external use. *Madawa ya uongo-uongo*, quack medicines. (Ar. Dist. follg.)

*Da'wa, n. or Daawa, and sometimes Mdawa (*mi-*), legal process, suit, litigation, legal claim, dispute. (Ar., the *aa* representing *ain*. Cf. *dai*, and dist. *dawa*, medicine.)

*Dawati, n. writing desk, writing case. Dim. *kidawati*. (Ar. for inkstand.)

*Dayima, adv. always. See Daima.

*Debe, n. (*ma-*), tin can,—commonly of the 4-5 gal. tin in which American petroleum has been imported, often used as a pail. *Nataka debe mafuta*, I want a tin of oil. *Nataka debe la mafuta*, I want an oil-tin. (Hind.)

*Debwani, n. a turban-cloth,—an Indian cloth, mostly of silk, with red or brown stripes, and worn on the head as a turban.

Dege, n. (1) infantile convulsions, fits (cf. *kifafa*); (2) a kind of moth.

*Deheni, n. a water-proofing mixture of lime and fat, used on the bottoms of native vessels. Also as v. of applying the mixture. (Ar.)

Deka, v. (1) give oneself airs, live in style, play the grandee; (2) show conceit, be arrogant, be unpleasant. Also *jideka*, e. g. of a vain woman's gait and bearing. (Cf. syn. *jivuna, jiona, piga kiburi, jifahirisha*, and *shaua*.)

*Delki, adv. See Telki. (Ar.)

Dema, n. a kind of fish-trap of open wicker-work. (Cf. *mtego*.)

*Demani, n. (1) sheet (rope) of mainsail of a native sailing vessel. Hence (2) lee side (in navigation), also called *upande wa demani* (*wa demanini*), *upande wa chini*. Contr. *goshi, goshini*. (3) Season of the year from end of August to beginning of November, when the south monsoon slackens and gradually dies away,—spring-time in Zanzibar. Also sometimes of the whole season of the south monsoon, from April to October. (Contr. *Musimu*, and see Mwaka.)

Denge, n. a mode of wearing the hair, a patch on the top of the head only. *Kata denge*, shave the whole head except the crown.

*Dengu, n. a kind of pea imported from India, and usually mixed with grain, &c. for food. (Cf. *choroko, mbaazi, kunde*.)

*Deni, n. (—, and *ma-*), a debt, loan, money obligation. *Fanya* (*ingia, jipasha*) *d.*, get into debt, borrow, lend. *Lipa d.*, discharge a debt, repay a loan. (Ar. Cf. *azimu*, also *wia, wiwa*.)

*Deraya, n. armour, coat of mail, cuirass, i.e. *vao la chuma*. (Cf. Arab. *adrâ*.)

*Desturi, n. or Dasturi, custom, usage, regular practice, routine. The usual word in Z. (Hind. Cf. Ar. *kawaida, ada, mila, mathehebu*. Dist. *dasturi*, bowsprit.)

*Deuli, n. waistband,—a silk shawl or scarf worn round the waist. (Cf. *mshipi, mahazamu*.)

*Devai, n. wine in general. (Perh. Fr. *du vin*. Cf. *mvinyo*, used mainly of spirits.)

*Dia, n. money paid for a life, fine for murder, ransom. *Killa mtu dia ya roho yake*, every man his ransom (to save his life). (? Ar. Cf. *fidia, fidi*.)

*Dibaji, n. used of the string of prefatory epithets and complimentary titles in Arab letter writing, and more generally 'elegant composition, good style, fine writing.' (Arab. 'painting, embroidery,' cf. *udibaji*. Such epithets are *jenab, muhebb, akram, nasihi, azizi,* hashamu, karamu, fathili*,—often in pure Arab form with the article *il* prefixed to each. Cf. *anwani, waraka*.)

Didimia, v. sink down, go to the bottom, penetrate. Ap. *didimik-ia*,

-iwa, bore into, e. g. of a tool. Cs. *didim-isha, -ishwa*, cause to sink down, force down (into, &c.). *Didimisha nguo mkobani*, stuff clothes into a wallet. (Cf. *tota, zama, zizimia*.)

Difu, n. See **Kilifu**.

*****Digali**, n. stem of the bowl of a native pipe. See **Kiko**.

*****Diki**, adv. See **Tiki**, and **Shiki**. (Ar.)

Diko, n. (*ma-*), landing place.

*****Dimu**, n. See **Ndimu**.

*****Dini**, n. religion, creed, worship. *Kushika chuo na kusali ndio dini*, to follow the Coran and perform the prayers is (Mahommedan) religion. (Ar.)

*****Dira**, n. mariner's compass, i. e. *kipande cha kusafiria chombo baharini*, an instrument for a ship to steer by on the sea. (Ar.)

*****Diriki**, v. in general, have power (will, time, opportunity, &c., for), and so (1) be able, be in time (for), reach, succeed, attain, manage, arrange; (2) venture, undertake, guarantee, incur responsibility (for). *Nalitaka kwenda, sikudiriki*, I wanted to go, but I could not manage it. *Sijadiriki kuisha kusema*, before I could finish speaking. (Ar. Cf. *daraka*.)

*****Dirisha**, n. (*ma-*), window. *D. la vibau*, a louvre window. *D. la kuchungulilia*, a window to peep through. (Hind. Cf. *mwangaza*.)

*****Diwani**, n. (*ma-*), councillor, public functionary, magnate. (Ar.)

Doa, n. (*ma-*), spot, blotch, mark, stain. *Doa la mafuta*, a grease spot. *Madoadoa*, used as a., spotted, variegated, of different colours, speckled.

Doana, n. hook, fish-hook. See **Ndoana**.

*****Dobi**, n. (*ma-*), one who washes clothes, as a trade,—always a man in Z. *Usinifanye punda wa dobi*, do not treat me as a washerman's donkey. Cf. *chombo hiki ki dobi*, this vessel is heavily loaded. (Hind.)

*****Dodi**, n. (*ma-*), also **Udodi**, **Ndodi**, (1) fine wire, whether brass or iron; (2) a bracelet of fine wire, hair, or thread.

*****Dodo**, n. a very large kind of mango is called *embe dodo*, or *dodo*. The word is also used of 'a woman's breast.' *Yuna dodo*, she has breasts, she is growing up. (Cf. *embe*.)

*****Dodoki**, n. (*ma-*), a long slender fruit, eaten as a vegetable, a kind of lufah. See **Mdodoki**.

-dogo, a. (*ndogo* with D 4 (P), D 6, *dogo* with D 5 (S)), little (in condition, quality or quantity), small, slight, unimportant, young. *Mtoto mdogo*, a small child. *Ndugu mdogo*, a younger brother. *Baba mdogo*, father's brother, uncle. *Mtu mdogo*, a poor man. Adv. *kidogo*, a little, rather, not very, not much, in small amount. Used as adj. to denote 'small in quantity.' *Watu kidogo*, a few people. But *watu wadogo*, poor, inferior people. *Maji kidogo*, a little water. With negat. '(not) at all, (not) in the least, (none) whatever'; esp. with *hatta*. *Sikupi hatta kidogo*, I will not give you a single bit, I will not think of giving you any. Sometimes redupl. for emphasis, *vitanda vidogodogo*, or *vidogo-vidogo*, very small bedsteads. (Cf. contr. *-kubwa, -kuu, -ingi*.)

*****Dohani**, n. chimney, smoke-stack, and in Z. esp. of (1) funnel, smoke-stack, of a steamer. Hence *merikebu ya d.* (or *ya moshi*, smoke), a steamer; (2) a tall narrow basket of sticks and cocoanut leaf-fronds, used for carrying fruit to market. (Ar.)

Dokeza, v. give a hint of, suggest, foreshadow, sketch. (Perh. *tokeza*, cause to come out, make appear. See **Toka**, **Toa**. But cf. *kidoko*.)

*****Dokra**, n. a cent, hundredth part of a dollar. (Cf. *reale*.)

Dole, n. (*ma-*), single banana fruit, i. e. one of a cluster (*chana*) on a large fruit stem (*mkungu*). (Cf. *udole, kidole,* and *ndizi*.)

Domo, n. (*ma-*), (1) large lip, large beak; (2) protuberance, projection, thing resembling a beak, overhanging crag, &c.; (3) brag, boasting, cant. *Piga domo*, let the tongue wag, brag, boast. (Cf. *mdomo, kidomo*, and for 'boasting' (*ji*)*semea*, (*ji*)*vuna*, (*ji*)*gamba*, (*ji*)*sifu*.)

Dona, v. peck, pick at, pick up bit by bit. *Dona mchele*, pick up rice. Ap. *don-ea, -ewa*. Cs. *donesha, -eza, -ezwa*. Ap. *donana*. *Kuku wanadonana*, the fowls are pecking each other. (Cf. *donoa, dondoa*, and of similar action *chota, danga*.)

Donda, n. (—, and *ma-*), large sore, ulcer,—so common an ailment as to be used as typical of sickness and disaster generally. *Muungu atakupa d.*, God will bring sickness upon you. *Donda juu ya donda*, blow on blow (i.e. calamity). *D. ndugu*, spreading, confluent ulcers. Dim. *kidonda*. (Cf. *donda*, v., *dondoa*, and for 'small sores' *upele*.)
— v. fall by drops, drip, fall in bits (bit by bit). (Cf. more common *tona*, also *dondoa, donda*, n.)

Dondo, n. (*ma-*), (1) large tiger-cowry shell, used by tailors for smoothing down seams to a good surface (cf. *kauri*). Hence perh. (2) dressing for cloth, starch, chalk, &c., used to give a good surface and appearance to inferior material. *Nguo ya dondo*, glossy calico. (3) Sometimes of 'twigs, chips, scraps' of wood, leaves, &c., e.g. for lighting fires. (Cf. *donda*, v.)

Dondoa, v. (1) pick up bit by bit, pick over grain by grain, &c.; (2) let fall bit by bit, drop, cause to drip; and so perh. (3) form sores, cause illness; (4) make selections (from), compile knowledge (by). *Ukimlisha samaki utamdondoa mwili*, if you let him eat fish, you will cause sores on his body. Nt. *dondoka*. *Mbegu zimenidondoka*, the seeds dropped one by one from my hand. (Rv. of *donda*, with similar meaning. Cf. *chonga, chongoa*, &c.; also *donda*, n., and follg.)

Dondoo, n. (*ma-*), selections, notes, extracts, quotations, choice bits, e.g. in an anthology. (Cf. *donda, dondoa*, &c., and for similar idea *okota, mateuzi*.)

Dondoro, n. a kind of antelope. (See **Paa**, for the only sort seen in Z.)

Donge, n. (—, and *ma-*), also **Tonge**, small rounded mass, ball, lump, e.g. of a mouthful of rice, rolled in the fingers and put in the mouth, —in this sense usually *Tonge*. *Kuviringa donge za wali na kutia kinwani*, to make a little ball of rice and put it in the mouth. *Donge la uzi*, a ball of thread. *Damu inafanya madonge*, the blood is forming clots. Dim. *kidonge*, e.g. a pill. (Cf. *bonge, tonge*, and perh. *udongo*.)

Donoa, v. peck, strike at (with beak or fangs), e.g. of fowls and snakes. *Nyoka ilimdonoa juu ya utosi*, the snake struck him on the crown of his head. (Cf. *dona, dondoa*, &c.)

*****Dopa**, n. (*ma-*), a sail-maker's palm, for coarse sewing.

Doria, n. used of 'white muslin' in trade. (Hind.)

*****Doti**, n. a piece of cloth suited for, and worn as, a loincloth, *shuka*, i.e. about 2 yards of full width, or 4 yards of narrow material. (Hind.)

Doya, v. go as spy, reconnoitre, spy out (but in Z. *peleleza* is usual).

*****Dua**, n. a prayer, special supplication, request made in prayer, addressed to God. *Omba dua*, offer a prayer, make a request, to God. (Ar. Cf. *omba, maombi*, and *sala*, —which suggests the outward ceremonial aspect of prayer.)

*****Duara**, n. used of (1) wheel, circle, rounded object, and (2) any machine of which the principal feature is a wheel, e.g. crane, windlass, capstan, &c. (Ar. Cf. *mduara, duru, mviringo*.)

Dubwana, n. (*ma-*), a person of

extraordinary size, a giant, a colossus. Also used as a. -dubwana, of anything gigantic,—animal, tree, or other object. *Mtu mdubwana*, a giant. (? Cf. *bwana*.)

Dude, n. (*ma-*), the vaguest and most general term for referring to any object, = *kitu usichokijina jina lake*, 'something of which you do not know the name, or have no word to describe, a thing, a what-do-you-call-it, an object. *Dude gani hili?* What in the world is this object? Dim. *kidude*.

Dudu, n. (*ma-*, of size), large insect. See **Mdudu**, which is commonly used. Dim. *kidudu*.

Duduka, v. be disfigured (by illness or disease). *Duduka uso*, have face pitted, marked with small-pox. Ps. *dudukwa*. *Nadudukwa na pele*, I am disfigured by an eruption. (Cf. *umbua*.)

Duduvule, n. a stinging insect, which bores in wood (Str.).

-dufu, a. (*dufu* with D 4 (P), D 5 (S), D 6), dull, insipid, tasteless, flat, uninteresting, good for nothing, —of persons and things. *Tumbako dufu*, mild, flavourless tobacco. *Mtu mdufu*, a stupid, dull person;—also *dufu la mtu*, in same meaning.

*Duka, n. (*ma-*), shop, stall. *Tembea madukani*, walk in the bazaar. *Weka duka*, open a place of business. *Vunja duka*, close a shop, give up business. (Cf. Ar. *dakkân*.)

*Dukiza, v. and Dukisa, intrude oneself, listen secretly, try to overhear. *Jidukiza*, play the eavesdropper, intrude where not wanted (offensively). (? Ar. *dakas*, and follg. Perh. same as *dakiza*.)

*Dukizi, n. (*ma-*), eavesdropping, scandal-mongering. (Cf. *dukiza, mdukizi*.)

Dumbwi, n. See **Kidimbwe**.

Dume, n. (*ma-*), a male, esp. of animals. *Frasi dume*, or *dume la frasi*, a stallion. *Bata dume*, a drake. See -ume.

*Dumia, Dumisha. See Dumu.

*Dumu, v. remain, continue, endure, last, abide. *Dumu daima*, last for ever,—used also as adv., for ever and ever. Ap. *dum-ia, -iwa*. *Dumia kazi*, remain at, persevere in work. Also, remain with, attend on,—of service. Cs. *dum-isha, -ishwa*. (Ar. Cf. *daima, udumu*.)

*Dumu, n. (*ma-*), also **Mdumu** (*mi-*), can, pot, jug, mug, esp. of metal. *Dumu la maji*, water-can.

Dundu, n. (*ma-*), large pumpkin, gourd, calabash, the shell used as a vessel to hold liquids.

Dunge, n. (*ma-*), a cashew apple in green, unripe stage,—fruit of *mbibo*. (Cf. *mbibo, korosho, bibo*.)

Dungu, n. (*ma-*), a stage or platform, raised from the ground and often roofed over, for a watchman guarding crops on a plantation. (Cf. *kilingo*.)

Dungudungu, n. used to describe anything of unusual shape or quality, 'a wonder, marvel, curiosity.' (Cf. *ajabu, kioja, tunu*.)

Dungumaro, n. (1) a kind of evil spirit; (2) a drum used in expelling such a spirit. (? *Mdungumaro*, a person possessed by this spirit.)

*Duni, a. inferior, low, mean, abject, worthless. *Mtu d.*, a nobody, an insignificant person. *Hali d.*, an abject condition. (Ar. Cf. *thaifu, -nyonge, hafifu, -dogo*.)

*Dunia, n. and Dunya, the world, universe, earth (as a whole). *Fariki d.*, depart from the world, die. *Mtu wa d.*, a worldly man. *Mambo ya d.*, or simply *dunia*, the way of the world, worldly affairs, the spirit of the age. (Ar. Cf. *ulimwengu*.)

*Durabini, n. and Darubini, telescope, microscope, or similar optical instrument. i. e. *kipande cha kutazamia*, an instrument for seeing with. *Piga d.*, use a glass. (Ar. or Pers. Cf. *miwani*, spectacles.)

*Duru, v. surround, be round, go round, put round. (Arab. for common B. *zunguka, zungusha*, &c. (Cf. *duara*.)

*__Durusi__, v. study a book, meet in class, attend school. (Arab. for common B. *soma, enda chuoni*. Cf. *darasa*.)

*__Dusumali__, n. a coloured handkerchief or scarf, often with green and red stripes, and of Persian manufacture, worn on the head by women. (Ar. or Pers. Cf. *utaji, shela*.)

__Duzi__, n. (*ma-*), eavesdropper, talebearer, gossip-monger, slanderer. (Cf. *dukizi*, and the commoner *mpelelezi*.)

E.

__E__ represents the sound of *a* in 'gate,' and (esp. when unaccented) the lighter sound of *e* in 'ten.' In some words of Arabic origin (1) it is used for a sound between *a* and *e* (cf. __Elfu, Hewa__, and __A__); (2) it is used in Zanzibar characteristically for what is heard in other dialects as *a*, e.g. *merikebu*, rather than *marikabu*, *sheria* for *sharia*, *shebaha* for *shabaha*; (3) it is not distinguished from *i*, not being so distinguished in Arab. writing or common pronunciation. (Cf. *elimu, ilmu*, &c.)

Thus words not found under *E* may be looked for under *A* or *I*.

When *a* in a prefix or formative syllable precedes an *e* or *i*, the two together are usually pronounced *e*; e.g. *akenda* for *akaenda*, he went; *kuweta* for *kuwaita*, to call them; *wezi* for *waizi*, thieves; *mengi* for *maingi*, many (things).

For *e* as an interjection see __Ee__ and __Ehee__. The same *e* is used and repeated at the end of a word intensively, esp. to express distance, e.g. *akaenda e-e-e*, and he went on a very long way; *kule-e-e*, far away yonder; *peupe-e-e*, a very white, clean surface, — in each case the intonation of *e* being raised higher in proportion to the intensity or distance indicated.

-__e__ is (1) the characteristic sign of the Subjunctive Mood, taking the place of the final *a* of a verb in the Indicative Mood; (2) a passive termination of some verbal nouns, e.g. *kiumbe, kombe, uteule, ushinde, utume*.

-__e__ (or -__ye__) (1) affixed to a noun, represents the pronom. a. *yake*, e.g. *nyumbae* or *nyumbaye* for *nyumba yake*, his house; (2) after a verb-form or tense-sign, represents *ye*, the form of relative corresponding to 1, 2, 3 Pers. S., e.g. *niliye*, I who am; *umpendaye*, you who love him, or, he whom you love; (3) in combination with the prep. *na* or *kwa*, represents the pronoun of 3 Pers. S. *yeye*, e.g. *nae* or *naye*, for *na yeye*, and *kwae* or *kwaye*, for *kwa yeye*; (4) is used as the final sound of a common contracted form of the Personal Pronouns, except the 3 Pers. P. *wao*, i.e. *mi(y)e* for *mimi*, *we(y)e* for *wewe*, *yee* for *yeye*, *si(y)e* for *sisi*, *nyi(y)e* for *ninyi*.

*__Ebbe__, int. also __Bee__, commonly used by slaves or inferiors in reply to a call, 'yes! coming! I hear!' (Ar. See __Lebeka__.)

__Ebu__, int. also __Ebuu__ and __Hebbu__, Well then! Come then!—often in expostulation or reproof.

*__Eda__, n. time of customary ceremonial mourning, or seclusion from company, e.g. of a woman after a death or divorce. *Kalia eda*, remain in mourning, or in seclusion. *Akakaa eda akavaa kaniki miezi minne*, she remained in seclusion and wore mourning four months. (Ar. Cf. *matanga*, under __Tanga__.)

*__Edashara__, n. and a., eleven. -*a edashara*, eleventh. (Ar. Cf. *wahedi*, and *áshara*, also B. syn. *kumi na moja*.)

__Ee__, int. Oh,—in invocation or assent. *Ee Muúngu*, O God. *Ee bwana*, O Sir. *Ee walla, Ee waa*, O yes! All right! Certainly, Sir! (literally, Yes, by God!).

__Egama__, v. be in a resting or reclining position,—not lying down, but propped on elbow or support. Also Rf. *jiegama*, place oneself in a resting position, recline, prop oneself (in a position). Ap. *egam-ia, -iwa*, rest on, lean on, recline on. *Ameegamia kifuani mwake*, he leaned upon his chest. Cs. *egam-isha, -ishwa*, cause to lean, prop, support. (Cf. follg., also *tegemea*.)

Egemea, v. (1) lean on, rest on, be supported by; (2) trust to, rely upon. Ps. *egemewa*, be leaned upon, be a support (to), be trusted (by). Cs. *egem-esha, -eza, -eshwa*, &c., e.g. (1) prop up; (2) confirm, help to establish, give support to, find ground for. Rp. *egemeana*. (Cf. *egama, egesha, tegemea*.)

Egemeo, n. (*ma-*), prop (e.g. handrail or balustrade of staircase), support, ground of belief or action. (Cf. prec. and *tegemeo*.)

Egesha, v. Cs. cause to rest, bring into close contact, make secure, &c. *Egesha chombo pwani*, bring a vessel to land, moor, make fast. *E. mashua ngazini*, secure a boat to the gangway of a ship. *Sikumwegesha naye*, I did not bring him into contact with him, introduce him to him, make him a friend of his. Ps. *egeshwa*. Ap. *egesh-ea, -ewa*, &c. Rp. *egeshana*, e.g. moor two vessels alongside, bring together, come into contact.

Ehee, int. of assent (spoken with rising intonation, and stress on last syllable), yes, just so, I quite understand. (Contr. *Ee-he, ee-e*, of dissent, and cf. *a-haa*.)

Ekerahi, n. or **Ikirahi**, aversion, disgust, horror, abhorrence, that which provokes aversion, &c. (Ar. Cf. *kirihi*,—the *e-* or *i-* representing *Alif*.)

-ekevu, a. having aptitude, having capacity,—of persons. (Cf. *wekevu*, and *-elekevu*, of which it is a shortened form, *-ekevu*, for *-eekevu, -elekevu*. See **Elekea**.)

Ekua, v. break, break up, break down, cause to give way. *Ekua dari*, break through a concrete ceiling. Nt. *ekuka*. *Maji yameekua ngazi*, the water has broken down the steps (by undermining them). *Mwizi ameekua mlango*, the thief broke down the door. *Boriti ya dari imeekuka*, a rafter of the ceiling has given way. Also of breaking up a road, or floor. (Perh. a variant of *wekua* and *tekua*, with same meaning. Cf. *egemea* and *tegemea*.)

-ekundu, a. (*nyekundu* with D 4 (P), D 6, *jekundu* with D 5 (S)), 'red' of all shades and varieties—scarlet, purple, pink, &c. Of European complexion 'fair, fresh, ruddy,' of native 'light-coloured, reddish yellow,' esp. of Arabs. (*-ekundu, -eupe*, white, and *-eusi*, black, are the only simple adjs. of colour in Swahili, others are supplied by reference to typical objects.)

***Ela**, conj. also **Illa, Ila**, except, unless, but. (Ar., 'if not.' See **Illa**.)

***Elafu**, n. and a., a thousand. (Ar. See **Elfu**.)

***-ele**, a. sick, ill, bed-ridden. (Ar. See **Mwele, Uele**.)

Elea, v. (1) float, be afloat, swim (of things), be on the surface. *Chombo chaelea*, the vessel is afloat. Cs. *ele-za, -zwa*, set afloat, swim. Cf. *chelezo*. (2) Of uncomfortable internal feeling, *moyo wanielea*, my heart palpitates, my stomach is upset, I feel sick, I am nervous. Cs. *eleza moyo*, nauseate, make nervous, affect the heart or stomach. (3) fig. be clear, be intelligible. *Maneno yake yamenielea*, his statement is intelligible to me, I understand what he says. Ps. *elewa*. *Sielewi maana*, I do not see the meaning. Cs. *ele-za, -zwa*, explain, make clear. *Ntakueleza habari*, I will explain the matter to you. Also Ap. *ele-zea, -zewa*, in same meaning. (Dist. eleka, and elekea, which see.)

***Eleka**, v. carry astride on the hip—as native women do their children, secured by the arm. *Mama*, *nieleke*, mother, please carry me. *Asio mwana na eleke jiwe hivi*, whoever has not a child, let her just bring a stone instead. Cs. form, *elekanya*, pile up one on another. (Ar. Cf. *beba*, and *mbeleko*.)

Elekea, v. Ap. also **Lekea,** (1) point to, be directed towards, incline to, tend to, be opposite, face, correspond to, agree with; (2) be rightly directed, be satisfactory, turn out well, succeed. *Anaelekea kwenda*, he is inclined to go. *Maneno haya yameelekea*, this matter has been satisfactory. Cs. *elek-eza, -ezwa*, point, direct, show the way to. *Sermala waria awalekeza waanafunzi bass*, the master carpenter merely gives directions to his apprentices. *El. chombo*, steer a ship. *El. bunduki*, aim a gun. *El. kidole*, point the finger. *El. njia*, show the right course. *El. nia*, direct attention. *Elekezana*, come to an agreement among themselves. Rp. *elekeana*, be directed towards each other, or to a common point, be facing one another, be opposite (contradictory), agree, correspond. Obs. also *elekana*, correspond. Cs. *eleke-anisha, -anishwa*. (Poss. conn. with **Elea**, which see, and cf. follg.)

-**elekevu,** a. also -**lekevu,** and -**ekevu,** handy, apt, having a capacity for or a knack of. *Mtu mwelekevu wa kazi*, a good capable workman. (Cf. *elekea*, &c.)

Elemea, v. See **Lemea**.

*****Elfeen,** n. and a., two thousand. (Ar. dual of *elfu*. Cf. syn. *elfu mbili*.)

*****Elfu,** n. (—, and *ma-*), also **Elf, Elafu,** and a., a thousand, thousands. Rd. *elfu elfu*, of enormous numbers, myriads. *-a elfu*, thousandth. (Ar. *alf*, pl. *alaf*. Cf. *elfeen*, and syn. *mia kumi*, and obs. *e* for *a*.)

*****Elimisha,** v. Cs. with variants *elem'sha, limusha*, impart knowledge to, instruct, teach, educate. Ps. *elemishwa*. (Ar. Cf. *elimu*.)

*****Elimu,** n. and **Ilmu,** knowledge, learning, wisdom, science, education, doctrine, teaching. *Elimu ndio mwanga uongozao*, knowledge is the guiding light. (Ar. Cf. *mwalimu, maalamu, mtaalamu, elimisha*, and syn. *hekima, busara, maarifa, akili*.)

-**ema,** a. (*njema* with D 4 (P), D 6, *jema* with D 5 (S)), good,—including goodness of all kinds and degrees, whatever commends itself to feelings, taste, reason, or conscience, and translatable in a corresponding variety of ways, 'pleasant, beautiful, sensible, right.' *Muungu ni mwema*, God is good. *Chakula chema*, nice food. *Kazi njema*, sound workmanship. *Uso mwema*, a handsome face. *Dawa njema lakini si njema*, the medicine is effective, but nasty. *Linalokuja kwa Muungu lote jema*, all is good that comes from God. *Vema*, adv., well, rightly, nicely, &c. A common rejoinder of assent is *vema*, also *njema, ngema*, very well, certainly. *Sema vema*, speak clearly. *Tengeneza vema*, arrange carefully. Sometimes without a noun, *mema na maovu ndio ulimwengu*, the world is a mixture of good and evil. (Cf. syn. (in some senses) *-zuri, -zima*, and contr. *-baya, -ovu, -bovu*. Occasionally *-ema*, like *-ote, -enyewe*, takes pronominal forms. *Jawabu lema*, a good answer. *Zema haziozi*, good things never go bad.)

-**embamba,** a. (*nyemb.* with D 4 (P), D 6, *jembamba* with D 5 (S)), narrow, thin, slim, pinched, confined; (2) fine, delicate, minute (in texture, fabric, grain). *Mtu mw.*, a thin, spare man. *Mlango mw.*, a narrow entrance, strait. *Mchanga mw.*, fine sand. *Hewa nyemb.*, all-penetrating, thin air. *Nguo nyemb.*, fine, thin calico, gauze. (Cf. *bamba, ubamba*, and contr. *-pana, -nene*.)

Embe, n. (—, and of size *ma-*), mango, the fruit of the *mwembe*, very plentiful for three months, Dec. to

Feb., in Z. Various kinds are known as *embe dodo*, very large; *sikio la punda*, long and narrow in shape; *embe boribo*, i.e. the Bourbon mango. (See **Mwembe**, and **Tunda**. Dist. *uembe*.)

Embwe, n. (*ma-*), a kind of gum or glue. *E. la mbuyu*, a sticky paste made from the fruit of the baobab tree (*mbuyu*).

Enda, v. go—including a wide range of meanings under the general idea of motion, such as (1) go, move forward, proceed, progress; (2) begin to go, start, set off; (3) go away, depart, withdraw; (4) go on, keep on, continue; (5) move, have motion, be in motion, act, work, operate; (6) make its way, occur, have a use, be possible. (Cf. *huenda, kwenda.*) *Enda*, go away, is commonly followed by a pronom. adj. with pfx. *z*, as if with *njia* in plur. understood. *Naenda zangu*, I am going away. *Enda zako*, go (you) away, also *zake, zetu, zenu, zao*. The Rf. form *jienda* is used of automatic, easy, or perpetual motion, e.g. *mashua inajienda*, the boat goes of itself. The Rd. form *enda enda* denotes continued motion, 'go on and on.' *Enda* is used in some phrases idiomatically without idea of movement, e.g. *enda chafya*, sneeze; *enda mwayo*, yawn; *enda wazimu*, be mad, act as a madman. *Enda* is also used as a semi-auxiliary with future meaning and often followed by an Infinitive Mood without the Infinitive sign *ku-*. *Maji yaenda letwa*, water is going to be brought, but usu. including the idea of some one going for it. *Watu walikwenda kwitwa*, the people were sent for. *Mwivi aenda hukumiwa*, the thief is going to be tried. (See also -**endapo**.) *Enda tembea*, go a walk. *Enda kwa miguu*, go on foot, walk. *Enda kwa frasi*, ride. *Enda kwa gari*, drive. Ap. (1) *end-ea, -ewa, -eka, -ekeza, -eana*, &c., go to (for, by, in, &c.). *Endea kuni*, go for (to fetch) firewood. *Jiendea*, go voluntarily, walk for pleasure, amuse oneself, stroll about. (Contr. *jienda* above.) *Endeka*, admit of going upon, be passable, be practicable, e.g. of a road. *Njia hii haiendeki*, this road is impassable. *Hakuendeki*, of the weather or circumstances generally, 'travelling is out of the question.' *Endekeza*, make able to go, and so 'adapt, fit, put in order, put to rights.' (2) *End-elea, -elewa, -eleka, -eleza*, &c., (*a*) move on, progress, advance, increase, often further defined by *mbele*, forward. *Endelea nyuma*, go back, recede, decrease, &c. (*b*) Continue indefinitely, have no end. (Cf. *mwendelezi, maendeleo*, &c.) *Endeleza*, cause to go on, prolong, keep working at, make progress with. *End. maneno*, make a long speech. *End. mkeka*, work at a mat. *End. waraka*, go on with a letter. *Endeleza* is also used of spelling, i.e. making the letters or words go on. *End. neno hili*, spell this word. Cs. *end-esha, -eshwa, -eshana*, cause to go, permit to go, assist to go, send, dispatch, pay passage of, show the way to, accompany, &c. *Endesha mtoto*, teach a child to walk. *Endesha kazi*, push on a job. Rp. *endana*, e.g. *magurudumu yake yanaendana vizuri*, its wheels all work together beautifully, e.g. of watchwork. (Cf. *nenda, enenda, mwendo, endeleo, mwendelezi, huenda, -endapo*, &c.)

-**endapo**, a verb-form used, with Pers. Pfx., and sometimes *endapo* only for all persons, as a conj. 'in case of, if, when it happens that,' e.g. *nendapo nikifa ao nikaugua*, suppose I died or was taken ill. (From *enda* with the generalized meaning 'happen, take place,' and -*po*, which see. Cf. *huenda*.)

Endeleo, n. (*ma-*), usually in plur. form, going on, progress, advance, success. (Cf. *enda, mwendelezi*, &c.)

Enea, v. be spread out (abroad, over), be extended over (among, in), be diffused in, permeate, cover whole extent (of), become generally known (among, to, in), be distributed (to), be coextensive (with), correspond (to), be suited (fitted, adapted, for), &c. *Muungu aenea dunia yote*, God pervades the whole world, God is omnipresent. *Maji yameenea inchi yote*, the water has inundated the whole country. *Amewagawanyia watu nguo, lakini haikuenea*, he distributed cloth to the people, but it did not go round. *Upanga amekuenea*, the sword is just your size. Ps. *enewa*. Cs. *ene-za, -zwa, -zea, -zana*, &c., (1) spread, extend, cause to cover, distribute, make coextensive with, adapt, suit; (2) compare, cause to fit, measure one thing with another, take measure of, judge. *Walienezana*, they compared themselves. *Alieneza mtoto wake*, he took his son's measure. (Cf. *enenza*.) *Muungu amemwenezea killa mtu riziki zake*, God has put the means of living in every man's hands. *Eneza habari*, publish news, divulge information, advertise. Rf. *jieneza*. *Alijieneza mwili mzima selaha*, he armed himself from head to foot. (Cf. *eneo, enezi, enenza*.)

Enenda, v. also **Nenda**, same as *enda* in the simple senses, 'go, move, proceed, go on,' but not used by natives indiscriminately, and not usually in any derived forms. *Wakaenenda mji mwingine*, and they went to another town. *Tumbo la kuenenda*, diarrhoea.

Enenza, v. and **Enza**, (1) examine, inspect, consider; (2) measure, take the measure of, compare by measurement. Rp. *enenzana*. (Cf. *eneza* (2), with which it appears identical, and *enezi*, but obs. *enenzi* follg., and *enenda*.)

Enenzi, n. (*ma-*), esp. in plur., going, walking, pace, gait, way of going on, behaviour. *Maenenzi ya polepole (ya haraka, ya upesi)*, slow (hasty, quick) going. (Cf. *enenda, enda, mwenendo*.)

Eneo, n. (*ma-*), extent, spread, range, reach, province, covering power, extent covered or affected, sphere of influence. *E. la Muungu*, omnipresence of God. *E. la marathi*, spread of sickness, affected area. (Cf. *enea*, and follg.)

Enezi, n. (*ma-*), spreading out, extension, distribution. Cf. *Muungu ni mwenezi*, God is the Great Giver. *Maenezi ya chakula*, dealing out of portions of food, making food go round. (Cf. *enea, enezi, eneo*, &c.)

Enga, v. (1) split up, slice up,—used of preparing cassava (*muhogo*) for cooking. Also (2) coddle, pet,—of treating a child with overcarefulness. Sometimes Rd. *enga-enga mtoto*, spoil a child (by petting). Ps. *engwa*. Ap. *eng-ea, -ewa*. (Cf. *engua*.)

Engua, v. skim, take scum off, remove froth, &c., as of fermenting liquor, or in cookery. Ap. *eng-ulia, -uliwa*. (Cf. prec.)

-enu, a. pronom. of 2 Pers. P., your, yours, of you. (For the prefixes, and use in combination with *ninyi* or *wenyewe*, or both, see **-ake**.)

-enyewe, a. (like *-enyi*, follows the rules of the pronominal adjectives, *-angu, -ako*, &c., as to agreement with nouns), used to express identity, distinctness, and (of persons) personality. *Mtu mwenyewe*, the man himself, the very person, the particular individual. *Kasha lenyewe*, the actual box. *Vitu vyenyewe*, the very things. Often with the personal pronouns, *mimi mwenyewe, wewe mwenyewe*, &c., I myself, you yourself, and sometimes with *nafsi* added, *nipo mimi mwenyewe nafsi yangu*, here I am, my own proper particular self. *Sitaki mwenyewe*, I utterly refuse, I will not have it,—a strong emphatic refusal. Also with *ji* in reflexive verbs, e.g. *alijiumiza mwenyewe*, he hurt himself. *Mali ya mwenyewe*, the property of the owner, i. e. of some one else, not mine or yours. (Cf. -enyi, and mwenyewe.)

Enyi, int. of 2 Pers. P., You there! I say, you! (For *ee ninyi*. Cf. *ewe* for *ee wewe*.)

-enyi, a. (also **-enye**, following the rules of pronominal adjectives, *-angu*, &c., as to agreement with nouns), having, possessing, with, in a state or condition of. Always followed by a noun or equivalent, defining the object, state, condition, &c. referred to. Largely used to supply the lack of adjectives in Swahili, admitting as it does of combination with (1) Nouns, e.g. *-enyi mali*, wealthy, *-e. mawe*, stony, *-e. uzuri*, beautiful, *-e. kuwa*, self-existent, *-e. enzi*, all-powerful, *-e. watu wengi*, populous, *-e. tumbo*, corpulent, *-e. mimba*, pregnant. (Cf. similar use of prep. -a.) (2) Verb-forms, not only Infinitive, *-enyi kutawala*, ruling, reigning, *-e. kwenda*, capable of movement, &c., but also finite forms and even sentences, e.g. *mwenyi ameiba*, the man who has stolen, the thief. *Mwenyi hawezi*, a sick man. *Nani mwenyi ataka kwenda?* Who wants to go? *Hao ndio wenyi hawakuwapo*, these are the absentees. *Penyi, kwenyi, mwenyi* are also commonly used for defining time, place, or circumstances. *Penyi mwitu*, in a forest. *Kwenyi Ijumaa*, on Friday. *Mwenyi hapo*, when he is absent, in his absence. (Cf. *-enyewe, mwenyeji, mwenyi, mwinyi*.)

Enza, v. See **Enenza**.

*__Enzi__, n. also **Ezi**, supreme power, sovereignty, dominion, rule. *Mwenyi ezi Mngu*, Almighty God. *Kiti cha enzi*, chair of state, throne. (Ar. Cf. syn. *mamlaka, utawala, nguvu*, &c.)

Epa, v. get out of the way of, avoid being hit by, swerve from, flinch, shirk, e. g. of avoiding a missile, a blow, or any danger of the sort. *Epa jiwe*, avoid a stone. Ps. *epwa*. Nt. *epeka*. Ap. *ep-ea, -ewa, -eka, -ekika*. *Epea* is also used for another point of view, viz. fail to hit, not be in the line of, miss a mark, i. e. of throwing a missile, &c. *Bunduki yaepea*, the gun misses, does not shoot straight. But *epeka*, be avoided, be avoidable. *Inaepeka*, it is avoidable, you can get out of the way of it. (Cs. *ep-esha, -eshwa*. Rp. *epana*. Cf. *epua*.)

-epesi, a. also sometimes **-pesi** (*nyepesi* with D 4 (P), D 6, *jepesi* with D 5 (S)), (1) quick, agile, swift, active, nimble, willing, energetic; (2) overquick, hasty, rash, impatient, fiery, quick-tempered; (3) light (in weight, importance, &c.), easily moved, light in texture, fine, thin, delicate, insignificant, of no weight or consequence. Adv. *upesi*. *Njoo upesi*, come at once. (Cf. *upesi*, also *rahisi*, light in weight, and contr. *-zito*, and as adv. *hima, marra moja, sasa hivi*.)

Epua, v. also **Ipua** (which see), put out of the way, move away, take off, remove. *Epua chungu motoni*, take the pot off the fire. (Cf. contr. *teleka*, put on.) Nt. *epuka* (see below). Ap. *epu-lia, -liwa, -lika*. *Chuma cha kuepulia sufuria*, an iron handle for lifting off a cooking-vessel. Hence *epu-liza, -lizwa*, cause to remove, allow to take away. Cs. *epu-sha, -shwa*, Intens., reject, put away, avoid, keep at a distance. *Nimepushwa*, I am kept from, forbidden to do (take, &c.). Rp. *epushana*, e. g. of people refusing to recognize each other in passing. Nt. *epuka*, used as independent verb, like *epa*, avoid, get out of the way of, abstain from, withdraw from, keep from. *Anaiepuka*, he avoids me, keeps out of my way,—also *anaepuka nami*. Ps. *epukwa*, be avoided. Ap. *epuk-ia, -iwa*. Cs. *epuk-isha, -ishwa*. Rp. *epukana*, be estranged, disunited, discordant, keep out of each other's way,—less pointed and deliberate than *epushana* above. (Cf. *epa*.)

-erevu, a. (*nyerevu* with D 4 (P), D 6, *jerevu* with D 5 (S)), shrewd, clever, cunning, resourceful, canny, crafty,—not often a term of praise, but not always in disparagement, as *-janja*. (Perh. cf. *elea, mwelewa*, and follg., and contr. *-jinga, -pumbafu*.)

Erevuka, v. become shrewd, be clever, have worldly wisdom, have the eyes open. Cs. *erevu-sha, -shwa*, make wise, teach prudence to, open the eyes of, initiate in the ways of the world. (Cf. prec.)

*Esha, n. also Isha, th latest Mahommedan hour of prayer. *Kusali esha*, to attend evening prayers. Used for period from 6.30 p.m. to 8.30 p.m. (Ar. See Sala.)

-etu, a. pronom. of 1 Pers. P., our, ours, of us. (For the prefixes and use in combination with *sisi*, or *wenyewe* or both, see -ake.)

Eua, v. (sometimes heard as *aua*, cf. *geuza, gauza*), make white, whiten, clean, cleanse, purify, perh. only used in a ceremonial sense, purification after defilement by the usual Mahommedan rites, or a sprinkling as a charm against disease. *Mwanamke ameeuliwa ujusi*, the woman has been purified of her uncleanness. (Cf. *-eupe, weuo*, and syn. *takasa, tohara*.)

-eupe, a. (*nyeupe* with D 4 (P), D 6, *jeupe* with D 5 (S)), (1) white, of any shade or kind, light-coloured, bright, clear, transparent; (2) clean, clear of all obstruction, open, unoccupied; (3) pure, righteous. *Watu weupe*, white people, Europeans, but it is also used of light-coloured Arabs, Indians, Abyssinians, &c. *Moyo mweupe*, a pure, honourable, upright character. *Inchi haina mwitu, nyeupe*, the country is open and treeless. *Peupe*, an open place, clearing in a forest, square in a town, unoccupied ground. *Kweupe*, dawn of day, morning light, fine weather. (Cf. opp. *-eusi*, also *-ekundu* and note, *eua*, &c., and for 'brightness' *weupe, nuru, uangafu, mwanga*.)

-eusi, a. (*nyeusi* with D 4 (P), D 6, *jeusi* with D 5 (S)), black (of any shade or kind), dark-coloured, gloomy, dim, dusky, dark, including dark shades of blue, green, red, &c., colours being mainly grouped according to relative lightness and darkness. *Watu weusi*, natives (in general), i.e. non-Europeans. (Cf. *weusi, giza*, and opp. *-eupe*, &c.)

Ewaa, int. or Eewaa, commonly used in assent, by inferiors or slaves, 'Yes, Sir! Certainly, Sir!' Also of approval, 'Just so, that is right.' (Ar. = *ee wallah*, Yes, by God. Cf. *Inshallah, wallai*, &c.)

Ewe, int. for *ee wewe*, You there! I say, you!—in calling attention or in remonstrance.

Ewedeka, v. See **Wewedeka**.

Eza, v. See **Enza** for **Enenza**.

Ezeka, v. thatch, cover with thatch, i.e. usually with grass, reeds, or cocoanut leaves, *makuti*. E. *paa*, cover a roof with thatch. E. *nyumba*, thatch a house. Ps. *ezekwa*. Ap. *ezekea*, of men or material, *sina mtu wa (mali ya) kuniezekea*, I have no one (no means) to do my thatching. (Cf. follg.)

Ezua, v. take thatch off, strip a roof, uncover the rafters,—as is done, e.g. in Z., when a fire is spreading. (Cf. prec.)

F.

F represents the same sound as in English.

F and *v* are not distinguished in Arabic, and in some Swahili words they are not clearly distinguishable, as in the adjectival termination *-fu* or *-vu*, e.g. in *-kamilifu, -vumilivu*, and in words like *futa* (*vuta*), *firinga* (*viringa*), *fukiza* (*vukiza*), *funda* (*vunja*), though a difference of meaning is often involved. Cf. *faa* and *vaa*, *fua* and *vua*, &c. Hence words not found under F may be looked for under V.

F before the causal formative *-y* sometimes represents *p* in the simple verb, e.g. *ogopa* has a Cs. form *ogofya* as well as *ogofisha*, and *apa* has *afya* as well as *apisha*, *apiza*. (Cf. similar change of *v* for *b* in *gomba, ugomvi, iba, mwivi*.)

Fa, v. (also *kufa* in some forms. For the use of *ku-* before monosyllabic verb-roots see **Ku-** 1 (*d*).) (1) die, perish, cease to be (live, act, work, feel); (2) lose strength, decay, fade, be benumbed; (3) come to an end. *Wengi walikufa vitani*, many died in war. *Kufa*, or *kufa kwa*, *marathi* (*njaa, maji, baridi,* &c.), to die by pestilence (famine, drowning, cold, &c.). *Njia imekufa*, the path is disused. *Sheria inakufa*, the law is falling into abeyance, becoming obsolete. Ap. *fia, fiwa*, esp. (1) in local sense, *fia barra* (*bakari*), die up country (at sea), and (2) in a pathetic sense, die to the loss or sorrow of, e.g. *amefia mamaye*, he has died to his mother's sorrow, he has died and left his mother to mourn him. *Maua yamenifia kwa jua*, the sun has killed my poor flowers. *Kufa jua* and *kufia jua* are used of sunstroke. Esp. common in the Ps., i.e. *fiwa*, have a death in one's family or among one's friends. *Kumefiwa*, there has been a death. *Alifiwa na mtoto*, he lost his child. *Nakimbia pafiwapo, nakimbilia paliwapo*, I run from a house of mourning, I run to a house of feasting. Cs. *fisha, fishwa, fishia, fishiwa, fishana*, cause to die, put to death. *Amemfishia kazi yake*, he has ruined his work. *Jifisha*, destroy oneself,— of suicide. (Cf. *-fu, ufu, kifo, fufua,* ? *fifia*.)

Faa, v. be of use, be good of its kind, help, be enough, do (i.e. suffice). *Zawadi yako ilinifaa sana*, your present was of great service to me. *Itafaa*, it will do. *Haifai*, it is of no use, nonsense, rubbish. *Maneno yasiyofaa*, improper language. *Kufaa hakuthuru*, being of use does no harm. Ps. *fawa* (not usual). Ap. *falia, faliwa, faliana*. Rp. *faana*, give mutual assistance, &c. (Cf. *mafaa, kifaa*. *Fana* is sometimes used for *faa*. Cf. *fanikia*.)

Fafanisha, v. also **Fafanusha**, liken, compare, explain (i.e. use comparison and illustration), make clear. *Nifafanishe na nini?* What shall I liken it to? *Fafanisha maneno*, explain a statement, make a clear statement. (Cf. *mfano, fanana*, and follg.)

Fafanua, v. (1) explain; also (2) recognize, understand, see clearly. Nt. *fafanuka*, be clear, be known, be intelligible. With Ap. *fafanukia*, be clear to. *Nyumba ya Sultani imefafanukia*, the Sultan's place is clearly in view. Ap. *fafanu-lia, -liwa*, make clear to. Cs. *fafanu-sha, -shwa*, make clear, explain. (Cf. *mfano, fanana, fafanisha*, and syn. *tambua, pambanua, eleza*.)

Fagia, v. sweep (with brush, broom, besom). Ps. *fagiwa*. Ap. *fagi-lia, -liwa*, sweep at, sweep away (for, with, in, &c.). *Sina ya kufagilia*, I have nothing to sweep with. *Pamefagiliwa vizuri*, the place is beautifully swept. (Cf. *fagio, ufagio*.)

Fagio, n. (*ma-*), a large brush, broom, besom,—for sweeping floors, &c. (Cf. common *ufagio*.)

*****Fahali**, n. (*ma-*), bull, seldom in Z. of other male animals. *Mafahali wawili hawakai zizi moja*, two bulls cannot live in the same farmyard. But used descriptively of men, of special manliness, vigour, courage, &c. (Ar. of male horse or camel.)

*****-fahamifu**, a. intelligent, acute, with quick comprehension, having a good memory. (Ar. Cf. *fahamu*.)

*****Fahamu**, v. (1) know, perceive,

comprehend, understand; (2) remember, recall to mind, bear in mind; (3) be conscious, have one's senses. Often in Imperat. as a kind of expletive. *Fahamu!* or merely *Faham!* Take notice! Observe! Lo and behold! I tell you! Ps. *fahamiwa*. Nt. *fahamika*. Ap. *faham-ia, -iwa*. Cs. *faham-isha, ishwa*, cause to know, inform, instruct, remind, put in mind. — n. sense, consciousness. *Kupata fahamu*, recover consciousness, come to one's senses. *Hana fahamu ya moyo*, he has lost consciousness. (Ar. Cf. *tambua, jua, sikia*, and for 'remember,' *kumbuka*; also *ufahamu, ufahamifu*.)

*Fahari, n. (1) grandeur, glory, pomp, sublimity, magnificence; (2) display, show, ostentation. *Sultani anakaa kwa fahari kubwa*, the Sultan lives in great state. *Piga fahari*, play the grandee, make a vulgar show of wealth. So *fanya f., jifanya f.* — v. Rf. *jifaharisha*, make a display, show off.

*Faida, n. and Fayida, profit, gain, advantage, interest. (Ar. Cf. *chumo, pato*.)

*Faidi, v. get profit (from), derive benefit (from, by), turn to good account, prosper. Ap. *faid-ia, -iwa*. Cs. *faidisha*. (Ar. Cf. syn. *chuma*.)

*Faitika, v. be delayed, be kept back, be hindered (from going, &c.). (Ar.)

*Fakiri, n. a poor person, beggar. (Ar. Cf. *fukara*, and syn. *maskini, mwombaji*.)

*Falaki, n. astronomy, astrology, esp. in the phrase *piga f.*, i. e. (1) take the omens, by observing the stars or other ways. Also (2) fig. take time to consider. (Ar. Cf. *piga bao, unajimu, ramli, ndege*, &c., and follg.)

*Fali, n. omen. (Arab.)

Fanana, v. be like, be similar, resemble,—with *na* of object compared. Cs. *fananisha*, make like, liken, compare. (Cf. *mfano*, and syn. *lingana*.)

Fanikia, v. turn out well for, succeed. Ps. *fanikiwa*, have (a thing) turn out well, succeed, prosper. Cs. *fanik-isha, -ishwa, -ishia, -ishiwa*. (Cf. *fanya*, and *fana, faa*.)

*Fanusi, n. lantern, lamp. (Ar.)

Fanya, v. make. One of the commonest verbs in Swahili, always implying some result, purpose, or object, beyond mere act, for which *tenda* is used. Its many applications may be distinguished as—(1) make, make to be, produce, manufacture. *F. kasha (njia, shamba)*, make a box (road, plantation). *Zifanywazo*, manufactured articles. *F. ndege*, make a (model of, picture of, an artificial) bird. (Cf. *umba*, and *huluku*, of actual creation.) *F. mayai*, produce eggs. *F. mali*, amass wealth. *F. shauri*, make a plan, consider. (2) Do, work at, engage in (of the operation rather than the result). *F. kazi*, work, labour. *F. biashara*, carry on trade. *F. shughuli*, attend to business. *Nifanyeni?* What steps am I to take? *F. vyovyote*, act recklessly, at random. (3) Bring about a result, cause, compel. *F. aende*, take steps to make him go, make him go. (This sense is usually expressed by the Causative form of verbs, or by another word of definite compulsion, e. g. *lazimu, shurutisha, juzu*.) (4) Bring into play, allow to happen, give spontaneous vent to, esp. of the feelings, 'feel, show.' *F. furaha*, rejoice. *F. hofu (hasira)*, be afraid (angry). *F. fahari*, give oneself airs, play the grandee. (5) Make in imagination, suppose, regard as. *Umenifanya mimi mgonjwa*, you thought (made out) that I was ill (when I was not). *Jifanya*, make oneself, pretend to be, disguise oneself as. *Usifanye mzaha*, do not suppose it is a joke, do not make fun of it. Ps. *fanywa*. Nt. *fanyika*, e. g. be done, be able to be done, be practicable. Hence *fanyikia, -ikiwa*, be done for (for the benefit of, &c.), turn out well for;

F

and also 'be favourable to, favour, give prosperity to.' *Nimefanyikiwa*, I have prospered, things have gone well with me. Ap. *fany-ia, -iwa, -iana*, e. g. do for (to, with, at, &c.). Cs. *fany-iza, -izwa*; also *fanza, fanzwa*. Hence *fany-izia, -iziwa, -izika, fanzia, fanziwa*, cause to make, cause a making of, cause to be made, repair, put in order, mend, have (a thing) done (by giving orders, personal attention, &c.), provide, get ready. *Nifanzie nyumba hii*, have this house put in order for me. *Ntafanyiza*, I will have it done (see to it). *Fanza chakula*, get a meal ready. Sometimes intensive, e. g. *wakamfanza killa namna*, they did all sorts of things to him (of ill-treatment). Rp. *fanyana*, of mutual, concerted action, co-operation, e. g. with *kazi*, work; *shauri*, deliberation; *biashara*, trade. (In some of the deriv. forms, the *y* sound is often not distinguishable, e. g. *faniza, fanika*, and cf. *fanikia*, v. Cf. *tenda*, which can sometimes be used convertibly with *fanya*.)

***Fara**, n. brim, brimful. *Pishi ya fara*, a full *pishi* (see **Pishi**), about 6 oz. weight. *Fara ya pishi* is also used for 12 *pishi*, i. e. *fara*, a dozen. Adv. *fara*, or *farafara*, e. g. *kujaa farafara*, to be full to the brim, be quite full. (Ar. Cf. *furifuri, furika*, and perh. *fura*.)

***Faragha**, n. privacy, seclusion, leisure, retirement, secrecy. *Sina f. leo*, I have no time to-day, I am engaged. *Faraghani*, in seclusion, in secrecy. *Kwa faragha*, and as adv. *faragha*, secretly, privately. (Ar. Cf. *siri, upweke, utawa, eda*.)

***Faraja**, n. comfort, relief, cessation of pain, ease, consolation. *Pata f.*, be relieved. (Ar. Cf. *fariji*, and follg., and syn. *baridi, utulizo*.)

***Farajika**, v. Nt. See **Fariji**. (Ar.)

***Faraka**, n. a comb-like instrument for keeping threads apart, part of a weaver's loom. (Ar. Cf. *fariki*.)

***Farakana**, v. become parted, be estranged, be separated. *Kufarakana hakuvunji kujuana*, separation is not the end of acquaintance. (Ar. Cf. *faraka, fariki*.)

***Faranga**, n. (*ma-*), young bird, nestling, and esp. chick, chicken. (? Ar. *faruj*. Cf. syn. *kinda, mtoto wa kuku*.)

-**faransa**, a. and **Fransa, Fárasa**, French. *Mfaransa*, a Frenchman. *Kifransa*, the French language, of the French kind. *Ufransa*, or *Fransa*, or *Ulaya Fransa*, France (from *Français*).

***Farasi**, n., commonly **Frasi**, horse. *Enda kwa frasi*, ride, go on horseback (contr. *enda kwa miguu*). *Mpanda frasi*, a horseman, trooper (in cavalry). *Panda frasi* (or, *juu ya frasi*), mount a horse. *Shuka juu ya frasi*, dismount. Also used in joinery,—cross-bar, tie-beam. (Ar.)

***Farathi**, n. (1) a matter of necessity, obligation, prescribed duty, esp. of religion. *Nina farathi ya kula*, I am bound to have some food (cf. *lazima, sharti*). (2) Place of resort, haunt, usual abode. *Chakula pale ulapo, ndio farathi yako*, where you take your meals, that is your abode. (Ar.)

***Fariji**, v. comfort, console, relieve, ease, bless. Ps. *farijiwa*. Nt. *farijika* (and *farajika*). *Hafarijiki kabisa*, she is quite inconsolable. Ap. *farij-ia, -iwa, -iana*. (Ar. Cf. *faraja, mfariji*, and syn. *burudisha, tuliza*.)

***Fariki**, v. (1) depart (from), part company (with), but esp. (2) die, decease. *Hawezi kumfariki mkewe*, he cannot bear to leave his wife. *Amefariki dunia*, he has departed this life (lit. from the world). Ap. *farik-ia, -iwa, -iana*. *Amefarikiwa na mumewe*, she has lost her husband (by death or desertion). Cs.

farik-isha, *-ishwa*, separate, set apart, put away. Rp. see **Farakana**. (Ar. Cf. *faraka*, and syn. *ondoka, tenga*, and for 'die,' *fa*.)

*****Faro**, n. See **Kifaro**.

*****Faroma**, n. or **Faruma**, a block or mould to put caps on after washing, to prevent shrinking and preserve shape. (Ar.)

*****Farumi**, n. ballast in a ship. *Chombo halina kitu, utie farumi kipate kuwa kizito*, the dhow is empty, put some ballast on board to give it weight. (Hind.)

*****Fashini**, n. a block of wood fastened to the stern post (*bumia*) in a native-built vessel, and carrying the rudder (*msukani*).

*****Fasihi**, a. correct, pure, elegant, lucid (in taste or style), esp. of utterance or writings. *Ni f. wa kusema*, he has a good style of speaking. (Ar. Cf. *ufasihi*, and syn. *swafi*.)

*****Fasiki**, n. an immoral, profligate, vicious person. (Ar. Cf. *ufasiki*, and syn. *asherati, mfisadi*.)

*****Fasili**, n. sprout, shoot. *Huna asili wala fasili*, you have neither root nor offshoot, i.e. family or connexions, position or prospects. (Arab.)

*****Fasiri**, v. explain, interpret, translate. Ps. *fasiriwa*. Nt. *fasirika*. Ap. *fasir-ia, -iwa*. Cs. *fasiri-sha, -shwa*. (Ar. Cf. *ufasiri, tafsiri*, and syn. *fafanua, eleza*.)

*****Fataki**, n. gun cap. Also used of crackers, and other small fireworks. (Ar.)

*****Fathaa**, n. and **Fazaa**, dismay, confusion, perplexity, trouble, disquiet, bustle, agitation. *Muungu hana fathaa, yuna saburi*, God is not hasty, but patient. *Shikwa na f.*, be thrown into confusion. (Ar. of fear. Cf. follg. and syn. *ghasia*, B. *mashaka, matata*.)

*****Fathaika**, v. be troubled, disturbed, confused, &c., see **Fathaa**. Cs. *fatha-isha, -ishwa*, abash, confound, startle. (Ar. Cf. *fathaa*, and syn. *angaika, stuka*.)

*****Fathili**, v. do a kindness (to), confer a favour (on), put under an obligation, esp. as the act of a superior. Ps. *fathiliwa*. Nt. *fathilika*, receive a favour. *Muungu hafathiliwi*, there is no such thing as doing God a favour. Cs. *fathilisha, -shwa*, put under an obligation. — n. also **Fathali**, favour, kindness, benefit, privilege. *Akili ni f. aliyofathiliwa bin Adamu*, intellect is a special privilege conferred on man. *Nimekula f. yao*, I have experienced kindness from them, I am under an obligation to them. *Hana* (or *hajui*) *f.*, he has no sense of favour, he is ungrateful. *Lipa f.*, return a kindness. (Ar. Cf. *afathali, tafathali*.)

*****Fatiha**, n. and **Fátiha**, a Mahommedan office, or form of service, usually a reading from the Coran, used at various ceremonies, e.g. marriage, a funeral, visiting a grave, occupying a new house, starting on an expedition. (Properly, but not only, of an opening or introductory service, cf. *hitima* similarly of a closing service.) *Soma f., toa f.*, perform a service, usually the office of a *mwalimu*. *Jumbe akawaombea fatiha wavuvi*, the chief had a dismissal service for the fishermen. (Ar. Cf. *sala, hitima, buruda, hutuba*, &c.)

*****Fatiishi**, v. prey, search, be inquisitive. (Ar. Cf. *tafiti*.)

*****Faulu**, v. (1) of a vessel, get round (a point), get past, weather, and hence (2) succeed, obtain one's wish. *Amefaulu*, he has made his point, he has scored. (Ar. Cf. syn. *pata, shinda, fanikiwa*.)

Feka, v. also **Fyeka**, clear away trees and brushwood, clear forest land. *Feka mwitu*, make a clearing in a forest.

Felefele, n. an inferior kind of millet (*mtama*).

*****Feleji**, n. or **Fereji**, steel of a

good quality. *Upanga wa f.*, a long straight double-edged sword, often carried by Arabs. (Ar. Cf. *pua.*)

***Feleti**, v. discharge, let go, release, procure release of, esp. of discharging an obligation or debt for some one. (Arab. Cf. *fungua, komboa.*)

***Feli**, n. act, deed, way of acting. *Ndio feli ya yule mtoto,* that is what the boy did, the way he went on. *Umrudi aache feli yake,* reprove him that he may leave off his (bad) ways. (Arab. Cf. syn. B. *tendo, kitendo, kazi.*)

***Fenessi**, n. (*ma-*), jack-fruit. See **Mfenessi**. *F. la kizungu* is used of both durian, and bread-fruit.

***Fereji**, n. (*ma-*), a large ditch, channel. Cf. more usual *mfereji*. (Ar. Cf. *handaki, shimo.*)

***Feruzi**, n. turquoise,—a common name among the lower classes, like *Almasi*, diamond. (Ar.)

***Fetaa**, v. commonly **Fetwa**, give a legal decision, judge a point (of Mahommedan) law, give judgement. Ps. *fetiwa*, be judged, be sentenced. (Arab. for usual *hukumu, amua.*)

***Fetha**, n. (1) silver; (2) money, coin, cash,—in general. *Mkufu wa f.*, silver neck-chain,—often of great length, as a convenient means of investing and storing money. *Ana f. nyingi,* he is very wealthy. *F. tayari* (or, *mkononi*), ready money, cash (cf. *taslimu, nakudi*). *F. ya kuchwa,* a day's pay. (Ar. Cf. for 'coin,' *sarafu, pesa.*)

***Fethaluka**, n. *marijani ya f.,* the true red coral. *Ushanga wa f.,* ? a shiny semi-transparent kind of bead. (Cf. *marijani,* and *akiki.*)

***Fetheha**, n. disgrace, a disgraceful thing, shame, scandal. (Ar. Cf. follg. and syn. *aibu, haya.*)

***Fethehe**, v. disgrace, bring shame on, dishonour, put to shame. Ps. *fethehewa*. Nt. *fetheheka*. Cs. *fetheh-esha, -eshwa*. (Ar. Cf. *aibisha, tahayarisha, tweza.*)

***Feuli**, n. baggage compartment, in stern of native vessel.

***Fi**, prep. on, with, in such phrases as *saba fi saba*, seven by seven, seven times seven; also expressed by *saba marra saba*, seven times seven. (Arab.)

Fia, v. Ap. See **Fa**.

Fiata, v. See **Fyata**.

Ficha, v. hide (from), conceal (from), disguise, take shelter (from), give shelter (to), cover. With double obj. *Amenificha habari*, he concealed the news from me. *Alimficha kofia*, he hid his cap from him. Ps. *fichwa*, (1) be hidden from (something); (2) be kept from seeing (knowing, hearing something). Nt. *fichika*. Ap. *fich-ia, -iwa*. *Alimfichia kofia*, he hid his cap for him (at his request), or from him, i.e. to his loss or sorrow, like the Pr. *ficha*. Cs. *fich-isha, -ishwa*. Rp. *fichana*, conceal (or, hide) from each other; *fichamana*, hide themselves away all together (or, by common consent). Rf. *jificha*, &c. *Kujificha mvua*, take shelter from rain. *Kihema cha kujifichia*, a tent to take refuge in. *Bandari hii imejificha kwa upepo mbaya*, this port is sheltered from dangerous winds. (Cf. *kificho, mfichifichi, mfichaji*, and syn. *setiri, funika.*)

Ficho, n. usually in plur., i.e. *maficho*, hiding-place, concealment, disguise. (Cf. *ficha.*)

***Fidi**, v. ransom, pay ransom for, deliver by payment. *Mali yake imemfidi katika kifungo*, his wealth got him out of prison. Ps. *fidiwa*. Ap. *fidia*. *Amemfidia babaye kwa reale mia*, he has paid ransom for his father with a thousand dollars. (Ar. Cf. *dia, fidia, kifidio*, and common syn. *komboa, ukombozi.*)

***Fidia**, n. ransom, fine, money paid as composition or reparation. *Huyu hawi fidia ya gidamu ya kiatu cha babangu*, he is not worth my father's shoe-lace. (Ar. Cf. *dia*, and prec.)

Fifia, v. be dying away, fade, pine, dribble away, disappear, e.g. of a flower, an ink spot, a scar, &c. Ps. *fifiwa*. Ap. *fifi-lia, -liwa*. *Rangi yake imefifilia mbali*, its colour has completely faded away. Cs. *fifi-liza, -lizwa*, e.g. *jua limefifiliza mwanga wa mwili*, the sun has taken all the gloss off the body. Also of money disappearing gradually, 'filch away.' (Cf. *fa*, die, and *fufua*.)

Figa, n. esp. in plur. *mafiga*, i.e. three stones used as a tripod to support a cooking pot over a fire. Also called *mafya* (see **Jifya**), but the common word in Z. town is *meko* (for *majiko*, see **Jiko**).

Figili, n. (*ma-*), and **Fijili**, a kind of radish, both root and leaves being used as vegetables. See **Mfigili**.

Figo, n. (*ma-*), kidney, but in Z. usually *nso*, which see.

Fika, v. arrive (at), reach, get to, come (to). *F. Unguja*, arrive at Zanzibar. *F. mji*, or *mjini*, arrive at a town. *F. kwake*, reach his home. Ap. *fik-ia, -iwa, -ika, -iana*. *Waraka wako umenifikia*, your letter has reached me. *Fikika*, be accessible, be approachable, be hospitable (cf. *jika, karibika*). Also *fik-ilia, -iliwa*. *Nimefikiliwa*, I have had an arrival of guests, I am engaged with visitors. *Fikiliza*, see below. Cs. *fik-isha, -ishwa, -iza, -izwa, -iliza, -ilizwa*, with further deriv. *fikishia, fikilizia*, &c. *Chakula hiki kitanifikisha kwetu*, this food will take me home. *Ntamfikisha mbele njiani*, I will conduct him some way on the road. *Alimfikishia mbele mzigo*, he carried his load ahead for him. *Fikiliza mabaya*, bring evil (on). *Fikiliza ahadi*, perform a promise, carry out an engagement. *Fikilishia matukano*, abuse. *Fikizana* and other Rp. forms, see below. Rp. *fikana*, arrive together. Hence *fikanisha*. *Fikiana*, meet together, arrive at same place. *Fikizana, fikilizana, fikiliana*. *Maneno haya yanafiki-liana*, these statements converge on the same point, come to the same thing, coincide. (Cf. *mfiko*, and syn. *ja* (*jia*), *pata* (*patia*), &c.)

*****Fikara**, n. and **Fikira**, thought, thoughtfulness, meditation, consideration, reflection, esp. in the plur. *Ana f. zake*, he is thoughtful. *Yuko katika f. zake*, he is buried in thought. *Wamepata f. ya kujenga*, they have got an idea of building. (Ar. Cf. *fikiri, ufikira*.)

Fikicha, v. crumble in the fingers, rub to pieces, e.g. of lumps in flour, clods of earth, and husking grain by rubbing. Ps. *fikichwa*. Nt. *fikichika, -kana*, be crumbly, easily crumbled, friable. Ap. *fiki-chia, -chiwa*.

*****Fikiri**, v. think (about), ponder (over), meditate (upon), consider, reflect (about). Also Rd. of deep or repeated thought. Ps. *fikiriwa*. Nt. *fikirika*. Ap. *fikiria, -iwa*. Cs. *fikir-isha, -ishwa*, cause to think, make thoughtful, sober. (Ar. Cf. *waza, tia moyoni*, and dist. *thani, nia*.)

Filia, v. Ap. from *fa, fia* (which see).

*****Filifili**, n. (—), a carpenter's square. (Hind.)

Filimbi, n. a kind of flute. *Mpiga filimbi*, a flute-player.

*****Filisi**, v. sell up, declare bankrupt, distrain on goods of, make bankrupt, ruin. *Wali alimfilisi Abdallah*, the governor sold up Abdallah. Ps. *filisiwa*. Nt. *filisika*,—of person or goods. *Abdallah amefilisika*, Abdallah is bankrupt, has lost all his money. Ap. *filis-ia, -iwa*. Cs. *filis-isha, -ishwa*. (Ar.)

Fimbo, n. a stick, esp. a light stick carried in the hand, a walking-stick, a switch. (Cf. *bakora* for various kinds of stick, and *ufito*.)

Finessi, n. See **Fenessi**.

Fingirika, v. (also occurs as *bingirika*, and so in deriv. forms), go by rolling (by turning round), roll round, be rolled along, as a log—not as a stationary revolving wheel (cf. *zunguka*), but implying movement, e.g. of a wounded snake. Cs. *fingirisha, -ishwa*, push along something round, roll (something) along. *Usichoweza kuchukua, ufingirishe*, what you cannot carry, move by rolling. (Cf. *viringa, viringika, mviringo*, where *v* seems a variant for *f*. Also cf. *zunguka*, &c. of circular motion, and *duara, duru*.)

Finya, v. (1) pinch, pinch up, press with fingers or nails, nip; (2) make (or, be) narrow (pinched, contracted). *Alinifinya nikalia*, he gave me a pinch, and I screamed. *F. jicho*, half close the eye, as in dozing. *F. uso*, wrinkle the face, frown. *Kiatu chanifinya*, the shoe is tight (pinches me). Rd. *finyafinya*, used of pinching up, or crumbling small, as food for children. (Cf. *vinya*.) Rp. *finyana*, (1) be pinched together, be wrinkled, be creased, be folded; (2) be narrowed, contracted, cramped, confined. *Uso umefinyana*, his face is frowning (wrinkled). *Mlango umefinyana*, the door is narrow. *Adui sharti afinyane*, the enemy must certainly shrivel up. (Cf. *finyo* and *finyanga*; and for pinching, *nyakua*, and for making folds or creases, *kunja, kunjamana*.)

Finyanza, v. also Finyanga, Finyanja, knead clay, with hands or feet, as potters do, and hence 'do potters' work, make vessels of clay,' i.e. *fanya vyombo vya udongo*. (Cf. *mfinyanzi*, and *finya*, of which *finyanza* seems to be a derivative, equivalent to *finyanisha*.)

Finyo, n. (*ma-*), crease, fold, narrow place, narrowness. *Mafinyo ya uso*, wrinkles on the face, whether of a frown or grimace. *Njia ya finyo*, a narrow road. (Cf. *finya*.)

Fira, v. commit sodomy, adultery, fornication. Rp. *firana*.

*Firaka, n. penis. (Arab. Cf. syn. B. *mboo*. Cf. *fariki*.)

Firigisi, n. gizzard.

*Firuzi, n. See Feruzi. (Ar.)

*Fisadi, n. (*ma-*), a corrupter, esp. a corrupter of women, a seducer, an immoral person. (Ar. Cf. *ufisadi, fisidi*, and syn. *fasiki, mtongozi*.)

Fisha, v. Cs. of fa, which see.

Fisi, n. the common kind of hyaena. (Cf. *kingubwa*.)

*Fisidi, v. also Fisadi, corrupt, seduce, esp. of corrupting women. (Ar. Cf. *fisadi*.)

*Fithuli, a. and -fithuli, arrogant, insulting, officious, self-asserting. (Ar. Cf. *ufithuli, mfithuli*, and follg.)

*Fithulika, v. be arrogant, bluster, use insulting language, swagger, be insolent. Ap. *fithuli-kia, -kiwa*, be insolent to. (Ar. Cf. *fithuli*, and *kiburi*.)

*Fitina, n. (1) discord, variance, antagonism, quarrelling, misunderstanding. *Fanya f., tia f.*, cause discord, slander, be cause of discord. (2) Tumult, mutiny, insurrection; (3) a source of discord, an agitator, a fire-brand. *Akatokea mtu mmoja fitina*, a certain mischief-worker appeared on the scene. (Ar. Cf. follg. and *ufitina, ugomvi, uasi*.)

*Fitini, v. cause discord (among), make mischief, set at variance, cause to quarrel, make mutinous. Ps. *fitiniwa*. Nt. *fitinika*. Ap. *fitin-ia, -iwa, -ika*. Cs. *fitin-isha, -ishwa*. Rp. *fitiniana*.

*Fitiri, n. alms and presents given at the end of Ramathan, the Mahommedan month of fasting. (Ar. Cf. *futari, futuru*.)

Fito, n. plur. of ufito, which see.

Fiwa, v. Ps. Ap. of fa, which see.

Fiwi, n. a kind of bean used as food in Z., Cape bean. (For others, cf. *kunde, choroko, mbaazi, dengu*.)

Fo-fo-fo, adv. *kufa fo-fo-fo*, to die outright, sudden death. (Cf. *fa, -fu, kifo, fifia, fufua*.)

FOROMALI 71 FUAWA

*Foromali, n. yard (of a ship), i.e. *mti wa kufungia tanga*, the spar that carries the sail. It is controlled by braces fore, *baraji*, and aft, *hamarawi*, and hoisted by the *henza*, which see, and cf. *tanga*.

*Forsadi, n. fruit of the mulberry tree (*mforsadi*).

*Fortha, n. and Forotha, customhouse. The locative form *forthani* is commonly used in Z. for the place, and also for the district (*mtaa*), in which it is situated. (Ar.)

*Frasi, n. also Farasi, horse, mare. (Ar. See Farasi.)

-fu, a. (rarely in any forms except *mfu, wafu, kifu, mafu*), dead. *Mfu*, a dead person. *Kifu*, a dead thing. *Maji mafu*, neap tides. (Cf. *fa, ufu, kifo, fifia, fufua*.)

Fua, n. (—, or of size *ma-*), (1) a round wooden tray with raised rim, used for washing clothes on, a shallow wooden bowl for hand-washing, &c. (cf. *fua*, v. and *chano*, and for other kinds *chungu*). (2) Only in the plural *mafua*, chest, chest complaint. (See Mafua, and cf. *kifua*, and *fua*, v.)

Fua, v. beat, strike, hammer, but usually limited to certain operations, viz. (1) of smith's work, work at (a metal), make (of a metal). *F. chuma* (*shaba, fetha*), work in iron (brass, silver), follow the trade of blacksmith (silversmith, &c.). *F. kisu* (*jembe*), make a knife-blade (hoe). Cf. *mfua* (*chuma, fetha*, &c.), and *mhunzi*. (2) Of laundry work, wash clothes in the native way, dashing them on a stone or board. *Mfua nguo*, a washerman—men only making a profession of washing—commonly called *dobi* in Z. (Cf. *dobi*, and *chachaga*.) (3) Of husking cocoanuts, by dashing them on a pointed stake. *Fua nazi*, clean a cocoanut. Ps. *fuliwa*. Nt. *fulika*. *Madini hii haifuliki*, this metal is unworkable. Ap. *fu-lia, -liwa, -liana*, e.g. work metal for (with, at, &c.), wash for. Cs. *fu-liza, -lizwa*, e.g. (1) set to work as smith or washerman, employ, have work done by them. Also (2) of the artisan, procure work. *Fuliza nguo*, get clothes for washing, i.e. take in washing. (3) Keep on at, hammer at, cause to hammer or keep on, continue doing,—in a general sense, for which see Fuliza. Rp. *fuana*, work together as smiths, &c., help each other, or actually 'beat (hammer) each other.' (Cf. *mfua, fuawa, fuawe, kifua, mfuo, ufuko, fuo*, and for striking, *piga, chapa, menya*, &c. Dist. *vua*.) — n. see Mafua, and cf. *kifua*.

Fuama, v. lie on the face—not often in Z. Cs. *fuamisha*. (Cf. *lala fulifuli*.)

Fuasa, v. copy, imitate, follow a pattern. Cs. *fuas-isha, -ishwa*. *Fuasisha sauti kwa kinanda* (in music), accompany singing on the piano. (Cf. *fuata* and *mfuasi*.)

Fuata, v. (1) follow, come next to, succeed, come behind, pursue; (2) imitate, copy, accompany (in music), do like, be like; (3) obey, keep to, abide by, be follower (adherent) of. *Fuata maji yaendako*, swim with the stream. *Bendera yafuata pepo*, the flag follows the wind. *Nitafuata mbio na pembe hizi ndogo*, I will accompany the tune with these little horns. Often *f. nyuma*, follow behind. *F. sheria*, keep the law. *F. Muhammadi*, be a Mahommedan. Ps. *fuatwa*. Ap. *fuat-ia, -iwa*. Cs. *fuat-isha, -ishwa*, often intens., copy carefully—also Fuasa, which see. Rp. *fuatana*, accompany, follow in a crowd. *Fuatanisha*, send (some one) to accompany. (Cf. *andama, mfuasi, mafuatano*.)

Fuatano, n. (*ma-*), a following, succession, esp. in plur., e.g. *mafuatano ya sauti*, a tune, melody. (Cf. *fuata*.)

Fuawa, v. be beaten, hammered, e.g. of a vessel aground, and exposed to the full force of the waves. (Seems seldom used. Perh. Ps. form of *fua*, v., cf. follg.)

Fuawe, n. anvil, i.e. something to be hammered upon. (Cf. *fua*, v., and *fuawa*.)

Fudifudi, adv. on the face, face downwards. *Lala fudifudi*, lie on the face. (Cf. *fulifuli*, and follg.)

Fudikiza, v. turn upside down (inside out, face downwards), turn over, e.g. of cards in playing. (Cf. *fudifudi*, and syn. *pindukiza*.)

Fufua, v. cause to revive, bring to life again, resuscitate, restore, revive. *F. maiti*, bring a dead man to life. *F. mgonjwa*, give strength to an invalid. *F. deni*, bring up a forgotten debt. Nt. *fufuka*. Ap. *fufu-lia, -liwa*. Cs. *fuful-iza, -izwa*. (Cf. *fa, fifia, ufufuo, ufufuko*, and syn. *huisha, amsha*.)

Fuga, v. (1) keep in confinement, rear, breed (of tame animals, stock, poultry, &c.); and (2) tame, domesticate, break in (of wild animals). *Fuga ng'ombe (mbuzi, kuku)*, keep cows (goats, fowls). Ps. *fugwa*. Nt. *fugika*. *Frasi huyu hafugiki*, this horse is not (or, cannot be) broken in. Ap. *fug-ia, -iwa*. Cs. *fugi-sha, -shwa*, e.g. of professional horse-breaking. (Cf. *fugo, mfugo*. Perh. cf. *funga*.)

Fugo, n. (*ma-*), breeding, rearing, domestication, &c., of animals. (Cf. *fuga*, and *mfugo*.)

Fuja, v. make a mess of, disarrange, bungle. *F. kazi*, bungle work. *F. mali*, squander money. (Cf. *fujo*, and syn. *boronga, chafua*. Dist. *vuja*.)

Fujo, n. disorder, mess, bungle, disturbance, uproar, tumult. *Nyumba ya f.*, a disorderly, much frequented house. *Kazi ya f.*, work badly finished. *Fujo-fujo*, an utter mess. (Cf. *fuja*.)

Fuka, v. (1) emit, throw out, smoke, &c. See **Vuka**. (2) Fill up (a hole). See **Fukia**. — n. a thin kind of porridge (of rice flour, with sugar, honey, spice, &c.), served to guests at an entertainment or festival.

***Fukara**, n. a poor man, beggar. *Fukara hahehohe*, of extreme destitution. (Ar. Cf. *fakiri, fukarika*, and syn. *maskini, mwombaji*.)

***Fukarika**, v. become poor. (Ar. Cf. *fukara*, and opp. *tajiri, tajirika*.)

Fuke, n. See **Vuke**. (Cf. *fuka, vuka*.)

Fukia, v. fill in (a hole, grave, &c.), dig in, cover in. *F. kaburi*, fill up a grave. *Akaifukia sakafu yote kwa mchanga*, and he filled up all (the holes in) the floor with sand. *Alifukia kitabu katika sanduku*, he covered up the book in the box. *Nyumba ilimfukia*, the house (when it fell) buried him. Ps. *fukiwa*. Nt. *fukika*. Ap. *fuk-ilia, -iliwa, -ilika*. *Tundu linafukilika kwa udongo*, the hole can be filled in with earth. Cs. *fuk-iza, -izwa, -isha, -ishwa*. Rp. *fukiana*. (Cf. *fuka*, which is seldom heard, and *fukua*, also *mfuko*.)

Fukiza, **Fukizo**. See **Vukiza**, **Vukizo**.

Fuko, n. (1) (*ma-*), a large bag or pocket, saddle-bag. (Cf. for various kinds, *mfuko*.) (2) Hole, place dug out. *Kuku achimba fuko*, the fowl is digging a hole. (3) ? A burrowing animal, mole. (Cf. *fuka*, v., *fukia, ufuko, mfuko*.)

Fukua, v. dig out, dig up, make a hole, burrow, get out of a hole. *Fisi amemfukua mtu*, a hyaena has dug up the (buried) man. *F. mawe*, get stones by digging. Ps. *fukuliwa*. Nt. *fukuka*, be dug out, be hollowed, be concave. Ap. *fukulia, -liwa*. Cs. *fuku-lisha, -lishwa*. Rp. *fukuana*. (Cf. *fuka, fukia*, and perh. *fukuza*. Also syn. *chimba*.)

Fukuta, **Fukuto**. See **Vukuta**, **Vukuto**.

Fukuza, v. (1) force out, drive out, esp. in hunting or war, and hence both (2) drive off, chase away, banish, and (3) go in pursuit of, hunt, try to catch. *Mbwa wakazifukuza nguruwe wakazipata*, the hounds chased the pigs and caught them. *Wamefukuzia mbali adui*, they have chased the enemy quite away. Ps. *fukuzwa*. Ap. *fukuz-ia, -iwa*. Cs. *fukuz-isha, -ishwa*. Rp. *fukuzana*, e.g. of children chasing one another. (Seems to be Cs. form of *fukua*, with intensive force, and specialized meaning. Cf. *fuka, fukia, fukua, mfukuzi*, and syn. *kimbiza, winda, fuata*.)

Fuli, n. lesser rainy season. See **Mvuli**.

Fulifuli, adv. (1) also **Fudi-fudi**, on the face, face downwards,—of position; (2) for *furifuri=farafara*, in plenty, in quantities, brimful. See **Fara**.

Fuliza, v. keep on at, keep going, keep doing, quicken, hasten. *F. miguu*, walk quickly. *F. mwendo*, go speedily. Also *fufuliza* and *fululiza*, an emphatic Rd. form. Ps. *fuli-zwa*. Ap. *fuli-zia, -ziwa*. Rp. *fulizana*. (Cf. *fua*, of which it is an Intens. form with generalized meaning, and *mfulizo, mfululizo*.)

*****Fullani**, n. such a one, a certain one, so and so, such and such (things), alluding indefinitely to persons or things, for reference only. *F. amesema*, somebody has said. *Nataka bithaa f.*, I want such and such goods. (Ar.)

Fuma, v. (1) weave, and also of connecting together, forming a fabric, by sewing, &c. Ps. *fumwa*. Nt. *fumika*. Ap. *fum-ia, -iwa*. *Sindano ya kufumia nguo*, a needle for sewing clothes. Cs. *fum-isha, -ishwa*. (Cf. *mfuma*, a weaver, *mfumo*, weaving.) (2) Shoot, pierce (with a sharp weapon). In Z. *choma* is usual. (Cf. *fumo*, and esp. *fumua*, which retains the more general sense of the root, and for weaving *mfumo*.)

Fumania, v. come on suddenly, take in the act, intrude in the house of, surprise. Ps. *fumaniwa*. Nt. *fumanika*. Cs. *fumaniza*, and Intens., e.g. *alimwua mwanaume aliyemfumaniza na mkewe*, he killed the man whom he surprised with his wife. (Cf. syn. *gundua*.)

Fumba, v. (1) shut, close, by bringing things, or parts, together. *F. macho*, close the eyes. *F. kinwa*, shut the mouth. *F. mkono*, close the hand. *F. mikono*, clasp the hands together. *F. miguu*, bring the legs together. (2) Mystify, make a mystery about, disguise, use in an obscure way. *F. maneno*, use unintelligible, difficult language. *Fumbo humfumba mjinga*, a parable mystifies a fool. Ps. *fumbwa*. Nt. *fumbika*. *Maua yanafumbika*, the flowers are closing. See also **Vumbika**. Ap. *fumb-ia, -iwa*, e.g. shut up in (for, by, &c.), talk darkly about, &c. Cs. *fumb-isha, -ishwa*. Rp. *fumbana*, e.g. *hatta macho yakafumbana*, till his eyes closed. Rf. *jifumba*, shut oneself up (in meditation, study, &c.). (Cf. *fumba, kifumba*, also *fumbo, fumbua, fumbata*, and ? *vumbika*.)

Fumba, n. (*ma-*), (1) a matting sleeping bag, a mat doubled lengthways and the ends sewn up, used sometimes for burying. *Hutiwa maiti katika fumba* (*mkeka wa fumba*), *hushonwa mithili ya mfuko*, the body is put in a *fumba*, and sewn up as in a bag. Also for drowning criminals. *Wakatiwa katika mafumba, wakatoswa baharini*, they were put in bags and thrown into the sea. (2) Lump, clod. *F. la unga uliogandamana*, a lump in flour which was caked. *F. ya mtama*, caked millet. (Cf. *pumba*, lump.) For *makuti ya fumba*, cf. *makuti ya kumba*. See **Kuti**.

Fumbama, v. lose one's senses, be dazed, light-headed, e.g. *huyu amefumbama akili yake*, this man is not in his right mind. (Cf. prec. and *-ma*.)

Fumbata, v. enclose with hands,

or arms), grasp, clutch, encompass. *Siwezi kuufumbata mti huu kwa mikono yangu*, my arms will not go round this tree. *Amefumbata fetha mkononi*, he has grasped the money with his hand. Ps. *fumbatwa*. Nt. *fumbatika*, e.g. *konzi ya maji haifumbatiki*, water cannot be grasped in the fist. Ap. *fumbat-ia, -iwa*. Cs. *fumbat-isha, -ishwa*. (Cf. *fumba*, and syn. *ambata, kumbatia, kamata*.)

Fumbo, n. (*ma-*), anything puzzling, hidden, mysterious, and so 'puzzle, problem, dark saying, hint, proverb, parable, riddle.' *Sema kwa mafumbo*, speak in an unintelligible, difficult way. *Maneno ya fumbo*, and *fumbo la maneno*, mysterious language. (Cf. *fumba*, also syn. *siri, methali, mfano, kitendawili, matata*.)

Fumbua, v. Rv. of *fumba*, unclose, open, lay open, reveal, disclose, by separating things or parts which were close together, e.g. *fumbua mkono*, open the closed hand, and so of the eyes, mouth, &c. *F. maana*, unfold the meaning. *F. majani*, make openings in high grass, for air or planting. Ps. *fumbuliwa*. Nt. *fumbuka*. Ap. *fumbu-lia, -lika*. Cs. *fumbu-lisha, -lishwa*. Rp. *fumbuana*. (Cf. *fumba, ufumbulio*, and for similar meaning *vumbua* (perh. same word); *funua*, uncover; *fungua*, unfasten; *fumua*, unravel; *fundua*, untie.)

Fumo, n. (*ma-*), (1) a spear; (2) a chief,—but seldom heard in Z. for the usual *mkuki, mfalme*. (Cf. *fuma*.)

Fumua, v. Rv. of *fuma*, undo (what is woven, matted, sewn, connected together), and so (1) unravel, unpick, take to pieces, unstitch, &c.; (2) reveal, disclose, make clear, explain. (Cf. *fumbua*.) *F. uzi*, unstitch. *F. nyele*, let down hair. *F. nguo*, rip (pull in pieces) calico. *F. moto*, pull a fire to pieces, take sticks out the fire. *F. makuti*, take out (decayed) thatch. *F. mali*, squander money, be prodigal. Also in Nt. sense, *mtama unafumua*, the millet is coming into ear. *Maua yafumua*, the flowers are coming out. *Mfumua maneno nje*, of a spy or tale-bearer. Ps. *fumuliwa*. Nt. *fumuka*, e.g. *nguo imefumuka, ushone*, my dress is come undone, sew it up. *Mashua inafumuka*, the boat opens at the seams, leaks, is coming to pieces. Rp. *fumukana*, e.g. of people separating after a meeting, 'disperse.' Ap. *fumul-ia, -iwa*. (See Fuma, and cf. *fumbua, funua, fungua*.)

Fumukano, n. (*ma-*), separation, breaking up, dispersal, e.g. of people after a meeting. (Cf. *fuma, fumua*.)

Funda, v. pound, bruise, triturate, pulverize, e.g. rice, pepper, ginger, &c., in a mortar (*kinu*), also 'pound up together, mix with other ingredients,' e.g. *ondokeni mfunde unga*, get up and mix the meal. Ps. *fundwa*. Nt. *fundika*, be pounded, be mixed, and also in act. sense. (Perh. a form of *vunja*, retained in this special sense in Z. For the operation cf. *ponda, twanga, saga, chakacha, paaza*. For a root *funda*, teach, and also make a knot, not itself used in Z., cf. *fundi* and *fundo*. But *funda*, n. seems different from all.) — n. (*ma-*), a large mouthful, of liquid or solid, distending the cheeks, cf. *funda la shavu*, esp. common of liquids. *Piga mafunda*, take large mouthfuls, gulps, draughts, either to be swallowed, or for rinsing the mouth out after a meal and to be ejected. (Perh. cf. *fundo*, a knot, as *fumba* and *fumbo*.)

Fundi, n. (*ma-*), a person skilled in any art, craft, or profession, and so able to instruct others in it, a skilled workman, one who has learnt his trade, a trained artisan or craftsman, e.g. mason, carpenter, tailor, smith, washerman, &c.,—*mwalimu* being commonly used of the higher professions, esp. teaching. (Cf. *fundisha, funza, mkufunzi, ? funda.*)

Fundika, v. make into a knot, tie up. Usually *piga fundo, funga.* See **Fundo**.

Fundisha, v. teach, instruct, educate,—the work of a *fundi* or *mwalimu*. Ps. *fundishwa*. Ap. *fundish-ia, -iwa*, e.g. *vitu vya kufundishia*, aids to teaching, school accessories. Rp. *fundishana*. Rf. *jifundisha*, learn. (An Intens. form, cf. *fundi, funza, mkufunzi*, and follg.)

Fundisho, n. (*ma-*), teaching, what is taught, instruction, doctrine. (Cf. *fundisha.*)

Fundo, n. (*ma-*), (1) knot, anything resembling a knot; (2) fig. a difficulty, grudge, esp. (3) ill feeling, resentment. *F. la mti (mua)*, a knot in wood or a tree. *F. la uzi*, knot in thread. *F. la nguo*, clothes tied in a knot. *F. la utepe*, a rosette. *F. la chombo*, cross-beam in a dhow (cf. *mwashiri*), securing the mast. *F. la ushanga*, consists of ten strings (*kete*) of beads. See **Kete**. Also (4) a purse, usually consisting of a knotted piece of the waist cloth. *Siku ya mashaka, fundo*, for the day of adversity, a purse. *F. la mguu*, the ankle, also *kifundo*. *Piga f.*, tie a knot. *Fundua f.*, untie a knot. *Maji yalinipiga fundo*, the water choked me. (Cf. *fundua, kifundo, fundika, ? funda.*)

Fundua, v. undo a knot, untie, unfasten, and fig. explain (a difficulty), get over a crisis. *F. chupa*, uncork a bottle. (Cf. *zibua.*) Ps. *funduliwa*. Nt. *? funduka*. Ap. *fundu-lia, -liwa*. Cs. *fund-usha, -ushwa, -uza*, e.g. *fundusha maua*, of a tree flowering. (Cf. *fundo*, and for similar words *fumbua, fumua, fungua, fumua.*)

Funga, v. (1) fasten, make fast, tie, bind, secure. *F. mzigo*, tie up a load, finish packing. *F. mlango*, shut close (fasten) the door. (Cf. *shindika mlango*, put to, close the door.) *F. waraka*, seal up a letter. *F. choo*, constipate, be constipated. *Funga kamba* (or, *na kamba*), fasten with a cord. (2) Shut in, enclose, imprison, put in fetters. *F. gerezani (minyororoni, kifungoni)*, put in prison (in chains, under arrest). (3) Overcome (in a game or contest), win, checkmate, put in difficulties, convict. *Tuliwafunga mabao sita*, we won six games against them. *Neno lake lilimfunga mwenyewe*, his own statement convicted him. (4) Decide on, embark on, begin, take decisive steps towards. *Funga biashara*, conclude a bargain. *F. vita*, begin operations in war. *F. shauri*, resolve on a plan. *F. safari*, set out on a journey. (5) *Funga* is also used as Nt. in various senses, e.g. fast. *Leo sisi tunafunga*, to-day we are fasting. *Ramathani ni mwezi wa kufunga*, Ramathan is the month of fasting. *Mvua inafunga*, it is a settled rain. Cf. *mfungo, mfunguo*. *Mito imefunga*, the rivers are impassable. Rf. *jifunga*, as above, and esp. (1) devote oneself, engage oneself, give special attention. *Jifunga kusoma*, apply oneself to study (*kwa kazi*, to work, *na adui*, with an opponent in strife). (2) Get oneself into a fix, contradict oneself, hamper oneself. *Amejifunga kwa ulimi wake*, he is convicted by his own tongue. (3) *Jifunga*, avoid childbearing. Ps. *fungwa*. *Huna buddi kufungwa na mti*, you must be tied to a tree. Nt. *fungika*. *Mlango haufungiki*, the door is not secured, or, the door will not shut. Ap. *fung-ia, -iwa, -iana*. *Unifungie nini? wanifungia kuonea?* What would you tie me up for? are you doing it just to tease me? *Akamfungia frasi na kamba*, and he fastened the horse to him by a cord. *Nimefungiwa nyumba*, I am locked out of the house. *Fungiwa deni*, be imprisoned for debt. Cs. *fung-isha, -ishwa, -iza*, &c., cause to fasten, cause to be fastened, and Intens. bind tight, confine, close. *Ntamfungisha*, I will have him put in prison. *Mvua inakufungisha ndani*, the rain keeps you indoors. *Fungisha mji (njia)*, blockade a town (road). (Cf. *mfungizo*. Cf. also *fungasa*.) Rp. *fungana*, (1) fasten together, or with *na*, fasten to; (2) be fastened together, e.g. of clouds, forest, 'be dense, be thick.' Also *funganya*, of a work of common interest and co-operation. *Funganya mizigo*, join in a general packing up of loads. Also *funganisha*, e.g. *jahazi na jiwe*, make fast a vessel to a rock. Cf. also *fungamana*. See **Fungama**. (Cf. *fungu, kifungo, fungua*, &c.)

Fungama, v. be in a fixed, tight, dense, &c. condition. Rp. *fungamana*, e.g. of interlacing branches. *Mwitu umefungamana kabisa*, the forest is hopelessly dense, impenetrable. *Hapa pamefungamana na miiba*, here is a dense mass of thorns. (Cf. *funga*, and for form, *-mana, andamana, changamana*.)

Fungate, n. honeymoon,—period of seven days after marriage, during which food is supplied by relations. (*Fungate* = seven, in some Bantu dialects.)

Fungo, n. (1) fast, period of fasting. (Cf. *funga, mfunguo*.) (2) A kind of speckled civet cat,—smaller than the *ngawa*.

Fungu, n. (*ma-*), (1) portion, part, piece, share, lot. *Fungu la nyama*, a portion of meat. *Fungu zima*, a large share. (Cf. *kipande, sehemu*.) (2) Heap, pile, and esp. of sandbanks, shoals, reefs, &c. in the sea. *Chombo kimepanda funguni*, the dhow has run on a sandbank. Also of pile of stones over a grave. *Vunja fungu*, used of customary visit to a grave after forty days, with a valedictory offering.

Fungua, v. Rv. of *funga*, (1) unfasten, undo, untie, unbind, let loose, release, set free, open, &c. *F. mlango*, unfasten a door (cf. *shindua mlango*, set a door open). *F. mkono*, open the hand (like *fumbua*), give a gift. *Jifungua*, give birth to a child, be confined. (2) Cease fasting. *Nipe kidogo nifungue kinwa*, give me a morsel to break my fast with. (So *funguka, funguza*.) Ps. *funguliwa*. Nt. *funguka*. *Shikiza mlango, usifunguke wala usifungike*, fix the door so that it will neither open nor shut. *Amefunguka mtoto*, she has given birth to a child. Ap. *fungu-lia, -liwa, -lika*. *Nifungulie mzigo*, relieve me of my load. *Fungulia mtumwa*, give a slave freedom. *F. ng'ombe*, turn out cattle to graze. Cs. *fung-uza, -uzwa*, e.g. force (induce, allow, &c.) to open, cause to undo, &c. *Akawafunguza wale watu*, and he had those people set free. Also 'give a meal to' after fasting. *Alitufunguza*, he caused us to break our fast. Rp. *Funguana*. (Cf. *funga, mfunguo, mafungulia, ufunguo*, also as similar *fumua, funua, fumbua, fundua*.)

Funguo, n. plur. of **Ufunguo**, which see. Also 'breaking of a fast,' but usu. *mfunguo*. (Cf. *funga, fungua*.)

Funika, v. (1) cover, cover up, put a covering on; (2) fig. conceal, disguise. *F. chungu*, put a lid on a pot. *F. kitabu*, close a book. *F. maneno*, speak obscurely. *F. inchi maji*, cover the land with water, make an inundation. *Jifunika mkeka*, cover oneself with a mat. Ps. *funikwa*. Nt. *funikika*. *Jua limefunikika na mawingu*, the sun is concealed by clouds. Ap. *funik-ia, -iwa*. Cs. *funik-isha, -ishwa, -iza*, cause to cover, cause to be covered. *Maji yamefunikisha inchi*, the water has flooded the country. Rp. *funikana*. (Cf. *funua, kifuniko*, and syn. *setiri, ficha*.)

Funua, v. (1) uncover, lay open, undo; (2) disclose, reveal, explain, show. *F. chungu*, take the lid off a pot. *F. chuo,* open a book. *F. mabawa,* spread wings. Ps. *funuliwa.* Nt. *funuka,* e. g. *maua yanafunuka,* the flowers are opening, coming out. *Mwitu unafunuka,* the forest is getting more open, is passable. Ap. *funu-lia. Akamfunulia maana,* and he explained to him the meaning. (Cf. *funika, ufunuo,* and similar *fungua, fumua, fumbua, fundua.*)

Funza, v. same as *fundisha,* teach, instruct, educate. *Jifunza kazi,* learn a trade,—from a *fundi.* Ps. *funzwa.* Nt. *funzika,* e. g. *mtoto huyu hafunziki,* this child is unteachable, is too stupid (or, obstinate) to learn. Ap. *funz-ia, -iwa.* Cs. *funz-isha, -ishwa.* Rp. *funzana.* (Cf. *fundi, fundisha,* and follg.) — n. *(ma-),* grub, maggot, worm.

Funzio, n. *(ma-),* teaching, instruction. (For more usual *fundisho* cf. *funza.*)

Fuo, n. (1) *(ma-),* washing-place, *mahali pa kufulia nguo,* for washing clothes. (Cf. *fua, oga, chosho, kiogeo.*) (2) Scum, froth, foam. (Cf. *ufuo, ufuko, fua,* and syn. *pofu.*)

Fupa, n. *(ma-),* a large bone. *F. la kichwa,* the skull. *F. jororo,* a (large) cartilage. (Cf. *mfupa, kifupa, ufupa.*)

-fupi, a. *(fupi* with D 4 (P), D 5 (S), D 6), (1) short, low (in stature, length, or height); (2) brief, concise, abridged. (Cf. follg. and opp. *-refu.*)

Fupika, v. be shortened, be lessened (in height, length, stature), be abbreviated, &c. Cs. *fup-isha, -ishwa, -iza,* shorten, abridge. (Cf. *-fupi.*)

*****Fura,** v. rise up, swell, be puffed up (in physical sense only). *Mimba ya mtama inafura,* the bud of the millet swells,—as it ripens, and finally bursts *(inapasuka).* Nt. *furika,* swell up, run over, boil over, overflow (over), make an inundation.

Cs. *furik-isha, -ishwa,* cause an overflow, inundate. *Maji yakafurikisha inchi,* the water overflowed the country. (Ar. Cf. *fara, furifuri, furiko,* and syn. 'flood,' *gharikisha.*)

*****Furaha,** n. joy, pleasure, happiness, bliss, delight, gladness, mirth, merriment. *Fanya f., ona f.,* be happy. *Pokea kwa f.,* welcome. Also adv. gladly, with joy. *Tukaenda furaha,* and we went joyfully. *Furahani,* in a state of happiness. (Ar., no B. syn. Cf. *furahi,* and Ar. *raha* (higher but more passive), bliss, and such words as *mcheso, mazungumzo, mapendezi.*)

*****Furahi,** v. rejoice, be glad, feel pleasure, be happy, be pleased, enjoy oneself. Ps. *furahiwa,* be pleased (with), be made happy (by), be rejoiced (at). *Tulifurahiwa sana na barua yako,* we were delighted at your letter. Ap. *furah-ia, -iana,* rejoice (at, in, for, &c.). Cs. *furah-isha, -ishwa, -ishana,* gladden, cheer, rejoice, delight. *Ametufurahisha sana,* he caused us great amusement. (Ar. Cf. *furaha.*)

*****-furahifu,** n. *(furahifu* with D 4 (P), D 5 (S), D 6), joyous, cheering, pleasant. (Ar. Cf. *furaha.*)

*****Furika,** v. See **Fura,** and cf. follg.

*****Furiko,** n. usu. in plur. *mafuriko,* overflowing, flood, inundation. (Ar. Cf. *gharika.*)

Furuga, Furugika. See **Vuruga, Vurujika.**

Furukombe, n. a large bird of prey, a kind of eagle or vulture.

Furukuta, v. move about, be restless, toss about on a bed,—as when ill, excited, unable to sleep,—also (e. g.) of a rat under a carpet.

*****Furumi,** n. **Furuma,** n. See **Farumi,** and **Faroma.**

*****Furungu,** n. *(ma-),* (1) shaddock, fruit of *mfurungu;* (2) anklet (usu. of silver). (Cf. *mtali,* and for other ornaments, *urembo.*)

Furushi, n. *(ma-),* bundle, packet, package. (Cf. *kifurushi, bahosha.*)

*Fusfus, n. and Fussus, gem, precious stone. (Arab. Cf. *kito*.)

Fusho, n. or Vusho, something used for fumigation, something to be burnt, as a charm, or sanitary medicine. (Cf. *mvuke, vukiza, vukizo*, &c.)

Fusi, n. rubbish. See Kifusi.

Fusia, v. lay down a bed of small stones and rubbish for a concrete floor or roof, or to fill up foundations. (Cf. *kifusi, ufusio*.)

Futa, v. (1) wipe, wipe out (away, off); (2) remove, obliterate, abolish, cause to be forgotten. *F. vumbi nguoni*, wipe dust off clothes. *F. vibaya vya waraka*, scratch out the mistakes in a letter. *F. kamasi*, wipe the nose. *Muungu anifute thambi zangu*, may God wipe away my sins. *Liandikwalo halifutiki*, what is written cannot be effaced. *-a kufuta* is often used of what is plain, common, of inferior quality, e.g. *mkeka wa kufuta*, a common white mat. *Kanzu ya kufuta*, a plain white *kanzu* without any ornamental stitching. Cf. *mfuto*. Ps. *futwa*. Nt. *futika*, e.g. *hii yafutika, hii haifutiki*, one thing is pardonable, another is not (but see Futika). Ap. *fut-ia*, e.g. *kitambaa cha kufutia*, a cloth to wipe with, duster. Cs. *fut-isha, -ishwa*, set to wipe, wipe hard. Rp. *futana*. (Cf. *pangusa, sugua, tua*. Also *futa*, as for vuta, which see, and as a rarely used sing. n. see Mafuta.)

*Futari, n. first meal in the evening after a day's fast, usually rice-gruel (*uji*). (Ar. Cf. *fitiri, futuru*. Dist. *futuri*.)

*Futhuli, n. See Fithuli. (Ar.)

Futika, v. put in the pocket, stick in waist-cloth, tuck into the girdle,—as a native does his knife, money, or any small article. Ps. *futikwa*. Ap. *futik-ia, -iwa*. Cs. *futik-isha*. (Cf. *futua*, and dist. *futika*, as Nt. of *futa*.)

Futua, v. (1) open out, undo a bundle (or girdle), take out (of a bundle, pocket, &c.), pluck out; (2) fig. bring to light, make known, expose. *F. manyoya ya kuku* (*ya ndevu*), pluck off the feathers of a fowl (hairs of the beard). *F. kibofu cha ng'ombe*, take out the bladder of an ox. Rf. *jifutua*, make a show of oneself, boast, brag. Ps. *futuliwa*. Nt. *futuka*, (1) be brought out, be brought to light; (2) be provoked, be angry. Ap. *futukia*, be in a passion with. Hence *futu-lia, -liwa*, and *futukisha*, provoke. Cs. *futusha, -shwa. Jua linafutusha mahindi*, the sun is making the maize open out. Rp. *futuana*. (Cf. *futika*.)

*Futuri, n. short span, as a measure, from tip of thumb to tip of forefinger,—as dist. from *shibiri*, full span from thumb to little finger. (Ar.)

*Futuru, v. take the first meal after a day's fast. Ap. *futur-ia, -iwa*. Cs. *futur-isha, -ishwa*, provide with first meal. (Ar. Cf. *fitiri, futari*. Dist. *futuri*.)

Fuu, n. (*ma-*), (1) a small, black berry, edible fruit of *mfuu*. (See Mfuu, dist. *kifuu*.) (2) *Fuu la kichwa*, skull (see Fuvu).

Fuvu, n. (*ma-*), also Fuu, empty shell, husk. *F. la kichwa*, skull. *F. la nazi*, shell of a cocoanut (but generally *kifuu*). *F. la yai*, eggshell (but generally *kaka*).

Fuzi, n. See Ufuzi, Mafuzi.

Fyata, v. put (or, hold) between the legs. *F. nguo*, tuck the loin-cloth between the legs (see Uwinda). *F. mikono*, grasp the hands between (i.e. by closing) the thighs. *F. mkia*, put the tail between the legs. (Cf. follg.)

Fyatua, v. and ? Fyua, let go suddenly, let off (of something which is holding, a spring, a trap, &c.). Nt. *fyatuka*. Ap. *fyatu-lia, -liwa*. Cs. *fyatusha, fyatuli-sha, -shwa*. (Cf. prec.)

Fyeka, v. also Feka, clear away,

clear off, make a clearing in,—of clearing away trees, grass, jungle. *F. mwitu*, make a clearing in the forest. Ps. *fyekwa.* Ap. *fyek-ea, -ewa.* Cs. *fyek-esha, -eshwa.* (Cf. follg. and *fyoa.*)

Fyeko, n. esp. in plur. *mafyeko*, clearing operations, thing cleared away, clearings.

Fyoa, v. (1) cut. *F. masuke ya mtama*, cut ears of millet; (2) fig. use cutting or abusive language, reply insolently. Ap. *fyo-lea, -lewa*, abuse, jibe. (Cf. *fyeka*, and follg. Also perh. *fyonya*, and *fyonza*.)

Fyonya, v. make a chirping sound with lips, expressive of contempt, or disgust. (Cf. *fyoa*, and follg.)

Fyonza, v. also **Fyonja, Fyonda**, suck, suck at, suck out. *F. sukali*, suck sugar. *F. ziwa la mama*, suck the mother's breast. *F. damu,* suck out blood. (Cf. *fyonya*, and *nyonya*.)

-fyozi, a. abusive, scornful. (Cf. *fyoa*, and *ufyozi*.)

G.

G represents the same sound as in English 'go.' This hard *g* is used in Swahili for the Arabic consonants *Jim* and *Qaf* in some words of Arabic origin (cf. *g* in Egyptian dialect for *j* elsewhere), and also sometimes as a variant of *j* and *k* in other words and (perh. through an intermediate *dy* sound) of *d*.

Hence words not found under *g* may be looked for under *j* or *k*, and sometimes under *d*.

Obs. that the sound written *ng'* in this Dictionary is heard and written sometimes as *gn*, esp. at Mombasa.

Gh is used to represent the sound of the Arabic *Ghain* in the few words in which it is commonly retained as a deep guttural. It is more often pronounced as a deep slightly rolled *r*, or as a harsh *h*, and is in some words slurred and hardly heard at all, or pronounced by Swahilis as *g*. (Cf. *ghali, hamu, orofa, gubari.*)

Gaagaa, v. also **Garagara**, (1) roll from side to side, turn restlessly, sprawl, as on board a ship, or a sick man in bed, or an animal wallowing on the ground; (2) fig. be lazy, listless, indifferent, have nothing to do, loll. Cs. *gaagaaza.* (Dist. *kaa-kaa.*)

*****Gadi**, n. (*ma-*), prop, shore, e.g. to keep a vessel upright, when stranded, or a tree inclined to fall. *Tia magadi*, shore up. (Cf. follg.)

*****Gadimu**, v. prop, shore up,—with *gadi*, which see. Ps. *gadimiwa*. Nt. *gadimika.* Ap. *gadim-ia, -iwa*, prop up with (for, on, &c.). Cs. *gadim-isha, -ishwa.* (Cf. syn. *tegemea*, cf. *nguzo*, and ? *shiku*.)

Gae, n. (*ma-*), a large potsherd, a large broken piece of metal, glass, earthenware, &c. Dim. *kigae*. *Jungu bovu limekuwa magae*, the cracked dish is all in pieces.

Gaga, n. (*ma-*). See **Kigaga**.

Galawa, n. sometimes **Ngalawa**, a small dug-out canoe, with outriggers (*matengo*) and sail, much used by fishermen. *Galawa juu, wimbi chini*, the canoe on the surface and waves beneath,—to describe a safe voyage. (Cf. *mtumbwi.*)

Galme, n. also **Kalme**, *mlingote wa galme*, small second mast aft in a large dhow, mizzen mast, carrying its own sail.

Gamba, v. only in the Rf. form *jigamba*, vaunt oneself, brag, boast. (Cf. *jivuna, jisifu, jiona*.)

Gamba, n. (*ma-*), scale (of a fish). Also sometimes of any small detached part of outer skin of an animal, e.g. of the tortoise, *hatta nibanduke maganda*, till my shell comes off. (Cf. *ngamba*, and *ganda, gando*.)

*****Gamti**, n. unbleached cotton cloth from India, Indian grey sheetings. (Cf. *nguo.*)

Gana, n. or **Kana**, rudder-handle, tiller. (Cf. *msukani, shikio.*)

Ganda, v. become hard (fixed, congealed, curdled, frozen), get thick, coagulate, of a liquid. *Maziwa yameganda*, the milk is curdled. *Mito imeganda kwa baridi*, the rivers were frozen with the cold. (2) Stick to, cleave to, embrace closely, clasp. *Alimganda shingoni*, he clasped him round the neck. Ps. *gandwa*. Nt. *gandika*. Ap. *gand-ia, -iwa*. Cs. *gandi-sha, -shwa*. (Cf. *gandama, gandamana*, and *ganda*, n.) — n. (*ma-*), husk, rind, shell, outer covering of trees, plants, fruits, &c. *G. la yai*, eggshell. *G. la mchungwa*, orange peel. *G. la mkate*, crust of bread. *Maganda ya maziwa*, curds of milk, flakes. *Maganda ya mahindi*, the sheath enclosing the cob of Indian corn. (Cf. *gamba*, also *gome, kaka, kifuu*, and (husk) *kapi, kumvi, kumbi.*)

Gandama, v. stick together, get stuck, get hard, set, freeze, curdle, coagulate. *Asali imegandama na chombo*, the treacle sticks to the vessel. *Chungu zimegandama samlini*, the ants are stuck in the ghee. Ps. *gandamwa*. *Naligandamwa na kupe*, I had ticks sticking to me. Nt. *gandamika*. Ap. *gandam-ia, -iwa*, stick to, adhere, cling to, be true to. *G. chungu*, stick to a cooking pot. *G. rafiki*, hold fast to a friend. Cs. *gandam-iza, -izwa*, e.g. *G. mtu chini*, pin a man to the ground. Also Intens. *gandamiza ulimwengu*, cling to, take to one's heart, the world. Rp. *gandam-ana, -anisha*, e.g. *maji imegandamana*, the water is frozen hard. (St. of *ganda*, cf. *simama, tuama*, &c., and for similar idea *shikamana, kazana, shupana, pindana.*)

Gando, n. (*ma-*), claw of lobster (*kamba*) and crab (*kaa*), (and perh. of the cuttlefish (*pweza*), but cf. *mnyiri*). *Kaa akiinua gando mambo yamekatika*, when the crab raises his claw, there is an end of the matter. (Cf. *ganda*, v., and of animals, *ukucha.*)

Gandua, v. Rv. of *ganda*, (1) unfasten, pull away, separate something adhering closely; (2) fig. rescue from danger, save in a crisis, get out of a scrape. Ps. *ganduliwa*. Nt. *ganduka*. Ap. *gandulia, -liwa*. (Cf. *banduka, ambuka.*)

Ganga, v. bind up, fasten together, splice, mend (what is injured or broken). Hence esp. of doctors' work generally, 'apply remedy, cure, heal.' *Ganga mguu*, put a leg in splints. *G. jeraha*, bandage a wound. *G. tumbo*, attend to the stomach. Ps. *gangwa*. Nt. *gangika*, i.e. be cured, be curable. Ap. *gang-ia, -iwa*. Cs. *gang-isha, -ishwa*. Rp. *gangana*. (Cf. *mganga, uganga, mgango, gango, kigango*, and of treatment, *alika, uguza*).

Gango, n. (*ma-*), appliance for holding together what is separate or severed, cramp, brace, splint, splice, joining, patch. Dim. *kigango*. (Cf. *ganga.*)

Gani, a. interrog. of what sort, what kind of, what?—never used without a noun preceding. *Kitu gani?* What is it? *Sababu gani?* Why? *Ginsi gani?* How? *Wakati gani?* When? *Mahali gani?* Where? *Habari gani?* What is the news? How are you? *Mtu gani* always suggests primarily 'a man of what tribe (place, or country).'

Ganzi, n. (—, and *ma-*), deadness, numbness. *Mguu imekufa g.*, my foot is asleep (benumbed). Often of the teeth, *tia (fanya) g. la meno*, set the teeth on edge. *Meno yafanya ganzi*, my teeth are set on edge.

*****Garafuu**, n. (also written *garofuu, karafuu*), cloves, the flower-bud of the *mgarafuu*,—the most valuable and abundant article of commerce in Zanzibar and Pemba (except cocoa-nuts). (Ar. *karamful.*)

Garagara, v. See **Gaagaa**.

*Gari, n. (*ma-*), any vehicle on wheels, cart, waggon, carriage, barrow, perambulator, bicycle. Also *g. la moshi*, locomotive (or other) steam-engine. *G. la pepo*, bicycle. (Hind.)

*Gasia, n. See Ghasia. (Ar.)

Gauka, Gauza, v. See Geuka, Geuza.

Gawa, v. place in parts (pieces, portions, shares), divide up, distribute, deal out. *G. chakula*, apportion food. *G. karata*, deal (playing) cards. Ps. *gawiwa*. Nt. *gawika*. Ap. *gaw-ia, -iwa*. Cs. *gaw-isha, -ishwa*. Rp. *gawana*, e.g. *utakachopata tutagawana sawasawa mimi nawe*, whatever you get, we will go halves in, you and I. Also gawanya, which see. (Cf. *gawio, mgawo*.)

Gawanya, v. place in parts, apportion, divide, share, distribute,— prop. of mutual arrangement or equal rights, *gawa* rather of the act of an official, superior, or benefactor, e.g. *tugawanye; gawa wee*, let us have a division; do you act as divider. Ps. *gawanywa*. Nt. *gawany-ika, -ikia, -ikiwa*, be divided, be divisible. Rp. *gawanyikana*. Ap. *gawany-ia, -iwa, -iana*. Cs. *gawany-isha, -ishwa, -ishia, -iza, -izana*. (Cf. *gawa, kigawanyo*, and *tenga*, put apart.)

Gawio, n. (*ma-*), division, apportionment, sharing. *Kuu ni magawioni*, the critical point is in the division (of spoils). (Cf. *gawa, gawanya, mgawo*.)

Gema, v. get palm-wine. Also *gema tembo, gema mnazi*, of cutting the growing flower stem of the cocoanut tree, from which the sap flows into a calabash fastened to it. Also used of getting india-rubber by cutting a plant or tree, *gema mpira*. A special knife is used (*kotama*). Ps. *gemwa*. Ap. *gem-ea, -ewa*. Cs. *gem-esha, -eshwa*, employ (allow, undertake, contract) to tap cocoanut trees. (Cf. *mgema, kotama, tembo*.

Krapf quotes a native description of the whole process.)

Genge, n. (*ma-*), cliff, precipice, ravine, deep ditch. *Ukifika gengeni, jihathari*, when you come to the steep place, be careful.

-geni, a. (*ngeni* with D 4 (P), D 6, *geni* with D 5 (S)), strange, foreign, novel, outlandish, extraordinary, queer, curious. *Jambo geni*, a strange occurrence. *Maneno ya kigeni*, a foreign language. (Cf. *mgeni, ugeni*, and syn. *-pya, ajabu*.)

*Gereza, n. prison, fort used as a prison, barrack. *Tia (weka, funga, peleka) gerezani*, put in prison. *Toa (fungua, ondoa) gerezani*, let out of prison. (? Portug. Cf. syn. *kifungo, minyororo*.)

*Gesla, n. also Gezla. See Jizla.

Geua, v. change, make different, alter. *Ndiye ajigeuaye nyoka*, it is he who changes himself into a snake. The Cs. *genza* (see below) is usual in Z. in this sense. Ps. *geuliwa*. Nt. *geuka*, (1) be changed, be changeable, be alterable, alter; (2) change position, turn oneself, turn round; (3) change in appearance, be transformed, be disguised. *Aligeuka akamwona*, he turned round and saw him. *Amegeuka mwngine*, he has become another person. Hence *geuk-ia, -iwa*, turn to (from, for, at, &c.). Ap. *geu-lia, -liwa*. Cs. *geu-za, -zwa, -zia, -ziwa, -zana*, cause to change, alter, make different, disguise, transform, pervert, turn round, &c. (For difference of *geuza* and *badili*, see Badili. Cf. *-geuzi, -geu, mageuzi*.)

-geugeu, a. changeable, fickle, wayward. *Mambo ya kigeugeu*, constant changes. (Cf. *geua*.)

Geuzi, n. esp. in plur. *mageuzi*, change, alteration, shifting, turn, transformation.

-geuzi, a. changeable, fickle, unsettled, always changing. (Cf. *geua, -geugeu*.)

*Gháfala, n. a sudden occurrence, suddenness, carelessness, thoughtlessness, inattention, haste. *Neno la gh.*, sudden, abrupt statement. *Marathi ya gh.*, sudden stroke of illness. *Usikae katika gh.*, do not be imprudent, careless,—advice to an invalid. Often as adv. and also *kwa ghafala*, suddenly, unexpectedly, (Ar. Cf. follg. and syn. *tháruba, haraka.*)

*Ghafalika, v. be hurried, be thoughtless (imprudent, neglectful, inattentive), &c. Ap. *ghafalik-ia, -iwa*, be careless (hasty, &c.) about. (Ar. Cf. *gháfala, tagháfali*, and follg.)

*Ghafalisha, v. Cs. (1) make hurry, distract, flurry, come on suddenly; (2) do hurriedly, hurry over, neglect, fail to attend to. *Gh. kazi*, hurry over work. (Ar. Cf. *gháfala*, and prec.)

*Ghairi, v. (1) do something unexpected, sudden, or surprising, change one's mind, alter plan, annul; (2) disappoint, offend, surprise. *Labuda roho yake itaghairi*, perhaps his mind will change. *Akaghairi kuolewa*, she suddenly refused to be married. — n. sudden change, surprise, disappointment. *Tia ghairi*, disappoint, surprise, offend. Also used with *ya*, as prep. *ghairi ya*, without, except, apart from, without regard to. (Ar., seldom used in deriv. forms.)

*Ghala, n. store-room, store-house, magazine, go-down. *Weka vyakula ghalani*, put away food in the larder. (Ar. Cf. *bohari*.)

*Ghali, a. often heard as *r-rhali*, (1) scarce, rare, hard to get; (2) dear, expensive, costly. *Nguruwe zimekuwa ghali sasa, zimekwenda mbali*, pigs are scarce now, they have made off to a distance. *Sitaki ghali, nataka rahisi*, I do not want an expensive one, I want a cheap one. (Ar. Cf. follg. and syn. 'scarce' *-chache, haba*, 'costly' *-a thamani*. Also *rahisi*, cheap.)

*Ghalibu, v. 'compete' in commerce. Rp. *ghalibiana*, carry on a commercial war. (Ar. Cf. *mghalaba*, and syn. *shindana.*)

*Ghalika, v. (1) be rare, occur infrequently, be an infrequent visitor; (2) be dear, be costly, rise in price. *Umeghalikasana siku hizi*, you seldom come to see us now. *Viazi vimeghalika*, i.e. *vimekuwa ghali*, potatoes are dear, have risen in price. (Ar. Cf. *ghali.*)

*Ghalisha, v. Cs. make valuable, make scarce, raise the price of. (Ar. Cf. *ghali*, syn. *pandisha bei, zidisha thamani*, and contr. *rahisisha.*)

*Ghammu, n. grief. See Hamu. (Ar. Cf. *ghumia.*)

*Ghangi, n. also Ghanji, Ghanja, and Gangi, a native vessel, like an Indian *bághala*, but not so high in the stern or long in the prow. (Cf. *chombo.*)

*Gharama, n. expense, outlay, payment. *Fanya gh., toa gh.*, lay out money, incur expense. (Ar. Cf. *gharimia.*)

*Gharika, n. flood, deluge, inundation. (Ar. Cf. *furiko*, and follg.)

*Gharikisha, v. cause a flood (over), make a flood (in), inundate. *Maji imegharikisha inchi*, the water has flooded the country. (Ar. Cf. *gharika*, and *furika.*)

*Gharimia, v. Ap. spend money, or, incur expense for. Ps. *gharimiwa*. Nt. *gharimika*. Cs. *gharim-isha, -ishwa*, cause expense to. (Ar. Cf. *gharama.*)

*Ghasia, n. (also commonly *gasia*), confusion, complication, bustle, hurry, medley, crowding, and used of various things involving these ideas, and of annoyances generally, e.g. *gh. nyingi leo*, a lot of troubles to-day; *pana gh. mjini*, there is a disturbance in the town, a street crowd or riot;—also of a royal progress or *cortège*, the rush of a wild animal, &c. *Gh. ya machezo*, a medley of amusements. *Nikakuta nyumba tupu hamna gh.*,

I found the house empty, there was no stir or hum of people inside. (Ar. Cf. syn. *mchafuko, mashaka*.)

*Ghathabika, v. be furious, be enraged, be in a passion. Cs. *ghathabi-sha, -shwa*, exasperate, enrage, provoke. (Ar. Cf. *ghathabu*, and syn. *kasirika*.)

*Ghathabu, n. rage, fury, passion, anger, exasperation, used with such verbs as *fanya, ona, ingia*, also *ingiwa (na), shikwa (na), putwa (na)*. *Ana gh. ya kwenda*, he goes at a furious rate. *Mwenyi gh. mbele yake amesimama shetani*, a man in a passion has a devil before him. (Ar. Cf. syn. *hasira, uchungu*.)

*Ghofira, n. (*ma-*), pardon, forgiveness of sins, absolution,—used only of God. *Ghofira ya thambi*, pardon of sins. (Ar. Cf. follg. and syn. in a more general sense, *usamehe, masamaha, ondoleo, maachilio*.)

*Ghofiri, v. forgive, pardon, absolve. See **Ghofira**. Ps. *ghofiriwa*. Nt. *ghofirika*. Ap. *ghofiria*, grant forgiveness to. *Muungu ameghofiria thambi zake*, God has absolved him from his sins. Cs. *ghofiri-sha, -shwa*. (Ar. Cf. *ghofira, setiri, samehe, achilia, fungulia, ondolea*.)

*Ghórofa, n. upper story, upper room. See **Orofa**. (Ar.)

*Ghoshi, v. adulterate, falsify, debase. *Ameghoshi fetha kwa kuichanganya na kitu kingine*, he has debased the silver by mixing it with something else,—a common practice in Z. Ps. *ghoshiwa*. *Kitu kilichoghoshiwa*, an adulterated article. (Ar. Cf. syn. *haribu, changanya*.)

*Ghubari, n. (*ma-*), rain cloud. *Ulimwengu una magubari*, the whole sky is cloudy, looks rainy. (Ar. Cf. *wingu*.)

*Ghubba, n. (*ma-*), a bay of the sea, also of the 'sweep, curve, bend' of a river,—the concave aspect. (Ar. Cf. for curve, *tao, pindi, mzingo*.)

*Ghumia, v. be overwhelming (to), be perplexed (at), be taken aback, lose presence of mind. Ps. *ghumiwa*, in same sense. *Ametokewa na watu ameghumiwa*, some people came on him suddenly, and he was taken aback. Cs. *ghum-isha, -ishwa*. (Ar. Cf. *ghammu*, or *hamu*, grief, and syn. *shangaa, tekewa*.)

*Ghururi, n. and **Ugh-**, arrogance, self-conceit, infatuation, folly, blindness. *Mtu huyu amepatwa na ghururi ya ulimwengu*, this man is the victim of worldly delusion. (Ar. Cf. syn. *kiburi, ufithuli*.)

*Ghururika, v. also **Ghurika**, be proud, be arrogant. (Ar. Cf. *ghururi*.)

*Ghusubu, v. deceive, cheat, swindle, betray. *Sultani alighusubu haki ya maskini*, the king betrayed the rights of the poor man. (Ar. Cf. common *danganya, kopa, punja*, &c.)

*Gidamu, n. small leather thong in a sandal, passing between the toes from sole to cross-piece, and holding it on the foot. (? Ar. Cf. *gadimu*.)

*Gilgilani, n. coriander seed,—used in curry powder. (Hind.)

*Ginsi, n. also **Jinsi**, and **Jisi**, kind, sort, quality, (1) often combined with *gani*, as a general interrogative. *Ginsi gani?* How? Why? What? What is the meaning of it? (2) Also often followed by *-vyo* introducing a dependent adverbial sentence, i.e. as a conjunction, 'the manner in which, the way in which, how, in what way.' *Alimwambia ginsi alivyofanya*, he told him what he had done, or, how he had acted. (3) Also often as an interj. with either *gani* or *-vyo*. *Ginsi ilivyo njema!* Oh, how good it is! *Njema ginsi gani*, it is wonderfully good. (4) *Ginsi gani* is also used without an adjective to denote what is wonderful, nondescript, ridiculous, extravagant. *Maneno haya hi ginsi gani*, these statements are quite absurd, there is nothing to be made of them.

(Ar. the Egyptian dialect, viz. *g* for *j*. Cf. syn. *namna, aina*.)

Gisi, v. guess, &c. See **Kisi**.

Giza, n. (used as D 5 and D 6, and also *kiza* as D 3), darkness, gloom, blackness (but not, like *weusi*, used of the colour black). *Tia giza*, darken. *Giza ya* (or, *la*) *usiku*, the darkness of night. *Macho yake yaona giza*, his eyes are dim. *Kiza kikubwa* (*kipevu*), deep darkness, utter darkness. (Cf. *kiza*, and syn. *weusi*.)

Goboa, v. also **Koboa**, break off with the hand, a cob (*kibunzi*) of Indian corn, pluck the ears of maize. Also of cleaning cotton, and of removing the stem of a clove bud, leaving the *kiini* or seed, i. e. *garafuu hugobolewa*. Ps. *gobolewa*. Ap. *gobo-lea, -lewa*. (Cf. *konyoa, chambua, pujua*, and *muhindi*.)

*****Godoro**, n. (*ma-*), a mattress.

Gofia, n. pulley, such as is attached to the rope (*henza*) which hoists the yard in a native sailing vessel. (Cf. *kapi, abedari*.)

-gofu, a. (*gofu* with D 4 (P), D 5 (S), D 6), emaciated, broken down, in ruins, skin and bone. *Kigofu*, in an emaciated, &c., state. *Nyama gofu* or *kigofu*, a wretched, starved animal. Also as n. in such phrases as *gofa la mtu*, an emaciated person; *gofu la nyumba*, a tumble-down, ruinous house. (Cf. follg.)

Gofua, v. emaciate, wear out the strength of, reduce to a skeleton (or, to ruins). Also Cs. *gofusha* in same sense. *Marathi imemgofusha*, illness has broken him down. (Cf. *-gofu*, and syn. *kondesha, konda*.)

Gogo, n. (*ma-*), (1) log, trunk of a tree when felled, e. g. *gogo la mnazi*, of a cocoanut tree. Also fig. *lala kigogo*, sleep (lie) like a log, i. e. motionless, in a dead sleep. Dim. *kigogo*. (2) Used of a large and long drum (*ngoma*).

Gogota, v. knock at, tap, hammer at. *G. mlango*, knock hard at a door. *G. vijiti*, hammer pegs (redupl.

form of **Gota**, which see. Cf. *gonga, bisha*.) — n. a kind of woodpecker. Also *kigogota*.

Gole, n. (*ma-*), small pellet of opium (*afiuni*) prepared for smoking. (Cf. *gole*, expectorated matter, Kr.)

Goma, n. (*ma-*), a large drum. (Cf. *ngoma, kigoma*.)

Gomba, v. (1) gainsay, contradict, forbid; (2) argue (with), quarrel (with), wrangle. *Anagomba na mkewe*, he is squabbling with his wife. Ap. *gomb-ea, -ewa, -eka*, argue (for, against, at, &c.), press a claim. *Gombea ngazi*, quarrel over the gangway. *Gombea daraja*, stand up for one's rank (position, status). *Alitukanwa kwa sababu wewe kukugombea*, he was abused, because he stood up for you. Cs. *gomb-eza, -ezwa, -ezika*, (1) strictly forbid; (2) make quarrel, make a quarrel, scold. *Gombezika*, be blameworthy, deserve scolding. *Tumegombezwa tusiende* (or, *kwenda*), we are forbidden to go. Rp. *gomb-ana*, quarrel with each other, squabble. (Cf. *ugomvi, -gomvi, ugombezi, mgombezi*, and syn. *teta, bisha, nenea*, and 'forbid' *kataza*.) — n. (*ma-*), leaf of the banana plant (*mgomba*), i. e. *jani la mgomba*. See **Mgomba**.

Gombo, n. (*ma-*), leaf (sheet) of a book,—*gombo la chuo*.

Gome, n. (*ma-*) and perh. **Kome**, the hard external covering of trees and some animals, bark, shell. *Ambua* (*toa*) *magome*, take off strips of bark. Used of shell of crustaceans,—lobster, &c., also of mollusca (cf. *kome*), and as a colloquial word for half rupee, or shilling, 'bob.' (Cf. *ganda*, generally of soft outer covering, *ngozi*, v., ? *kome*.)

Gonda, v. grow thin. See **Konda**.

Gonga, v. beat, strike, knock. *Gonga mlango*, knock at a door. Ps. *gongwa*. Ap. *gong-ea, -ewa, -eana*. *Kugongeana bilauri*, to strike glasses together in drinking healths. Cs.

gong-eza, *-ezwa*. Rp. *gong-ana*, *-anisha*. *Vyombo vinagongana*, the dhows are colliding. (Cf. *gongo*, *mgongo*, and syn. *gota*, *bisha*, *fua*, *piga*, *chapa*, &c.)

Gongo, n. (*ma-*), (1) a thick, heavy stick, cudgel, club, bludgeon (for other kinds, see **Bakora**). Also of other thick things, e. g. (2) seam (in a dress); (3) hump (of a camel), cf. *nundu*; (4) dense wood, thicket, *gongo la mwitu*, where trees are thickest in a forest. (Cf. *mgongo*, *gonga*.)

Gongoja, v. See **Kongoja**.

Gongomea, v. hammer, give blows to, drive with blows, as rivets, nails, pegs, stakes, &c., and so 'nail up.' Ps. *gongomewa*, fasten up. *Akazigongomea nguo katika bweta*, and he nailed up his clothes in a box.

-gonjwa, a. sick, ill, unwell, indisposed. *U mgonjwa ao mzima?* Are you ill or well? *Huyu ni mgonjwa sana*, this man is very ill, a great invalid. (Cf. *ugonjwa*, *gonjweza*, and cf. *-weli*.)

Gonjweza, v. Cs. cause to be ill, make ill or sick. *Jigonjweza*, pretend to be sick, sham sickness, behave as if sick. Ps. *gonjwezwa*. (Cf. follg.)

*****Gora,** n. (*ma-*), also **Jora**, and commonly **Jura**, a length of calico, calico in the piece (of about 30 to 35 yards).

Gorong'ondwa, n. a kind of lizard (Str.). Cf. *mjusi*. (There is perh. also a verb *gorong'onda*, work about with a zigzag movement.)

*****Goshi,** n. also **Joshi**, windward or weather side, in navigation; also called *upande wa juu*, upper side. Contr. *demani*, lee side. *Upande wa goshini*, weather side, windward. *Pindua (chombo) kwa goshini*, tack about, bout ship. *Enda goshi*, sail near the wind. *Goshi la tanga*, the lower, forward part of the sail in a native vessel. See **Tanga**. *Kalia goshi*, (1) be to windward of, and so (2) fig. have an advantage over, have the best position as to. *Huyu anakukalia goshi*, this man has the better position, menaces your safety.

Gota, v. knock, tap, rap, strike. *Gota mlango*, tap at a door. Also **Gotagota**, of drumming on an instrument, and **Gogota**, which see. Ps. *gotwa*. Nt. *goteka*. Ap. *got-ea*, *-ewa*. Cs. *got-eza*, *-ezwa*, cause to knock, e. g. *goteza maneno*, of ill-pronounced, broken speech, the opposite of fluent speaking. *Gotagota maneno*, of jumbling words of different dialects together. Rp. *gotana*, —like *gongana*, e. g. *vyombo vinagotana*, the dhows are knocking together. (Cf. *mgoto*, and syn. *gonga*, *piga*, *fua*, *bisha*, &c.)

Goti, n. (*ma-*), knee. *Piga magoti*, kneel down.

Govi, n. also **Ngovi**, but in Z. **Ngozi**, which see. *Govi mboo*, prepuce, condition of being uncircumcised.

Guba, n. (*ma-*), packet of aromatic leaves (of *mkadi*, and other kinds), sold for their perfume. Cf. *kiguba*. (Dist. *ghubba*, *kuba*.)

*****Gubari,** n. (*ma-*). See **Ghubari**, and **Wingu**.

*****Gubeti,** n. prow of a native vessel; head, figure-head, often projecting far in front, and ornamented with carving, &c., described as *kikono cha omo*, as being like a hand held out from the bow. (Cf. *omo*, *hanamu*, and contr. *shetri*, stern.)

Gubi, n. (*ma-*), leaf stalk of cocoanut tree (*mnazi*).

*****Gudi,** n. (*ma-*), dock for ships. (Cf. *gadi*, and *majahaba*, lit. supports, props.)

*****Gudulia,** n. (*ma-*), pitcher, porous water jar, water-cooler of earthenware. Dim. *kigudulia*. (Cf. *kuzi*, *mtungi*.)

Gugu, n. (*ma-*), weed, undergrowth, wild plant of no value. *Gugu mwitu*, a plant resembling corn, tare. *Lala maguguni*, sleep in the bush; used a'so as indeclin. adj. (like *mwitu*), wild, uncultivated, from the jungle. (Cf. *kigugu*.)

Gugumiza, v. gulp, gulp down, swallow with a gurgling sound, splutter in the water,—as a swimmer in rough water, or man out of his depth; also of defective utterance. *Mgonjwa amegumiza maji kwa shidda*, the sick man has swallowed some water with an effort. *Agugumiza maneno*, he talks in a jerky, spluttering way. (Cf. *goteza*.)

Guguna, v. (1) gnaw, bite at; (2) carp at, annoy, molest. *Panya ameguguna muhogo*, a rat has gnawed the cassava. Ps. *gugunwa*. *Mtu amegugunwa na fisi*, the man has been gnawed by a hyaena. Nt. *gugunika*. Ap. *gugun-ia, -iwa*. Cs. *gugun-iza, -izwa*. (Cf. *tafuna*, ? *guna*, and perh. a verb *gugunua*, carp at, annoy, molest.)

Gugurusha, v. also heard as *gurugusha*, of movement, producing a rustling or scraping sound, as of a rat, rustle about, shuffle along, rattle about. (Cf. syn. *piga mtakaso* and *furukuta*.)

Guguta, n. cob or ear of Indian corn, with the grains removed. (Cf. *muhindi* and *kigunzi*.)

Guia, v. and **Guya**, seize, catch, hold. *Guia nyama*, catch an animal in a trap. Ps. *guiwa*. Cs. *guiza, -zwa*. Rp. *gui-ana*. (Cf. *shika, nasa, kamata*, all more used in Z.)

Gumba, n. *kidole cha gumba*, thumb. (? *Mtu gumba*, a solitary, childless, or sterile person.)

Gumegume, n. *bunduki ya gumegume*, a flint-gun. (Cf. *bunduki*, and perh. *-gumu*.)

-gumu, a. (*ngumu* with D 4 (P), D 6, *gumu* with D 5 (S)), (1) hard, tough, firm, solid, strong. (Contr. *-ororo, laini, thaifu*.) *Boriti hii ngumu kama chuma*, this pole is as hard as iron. (2) Hard to deal with, difficult, laborious, puzzling. (Contr. *rahisi, -epesi*.) *Kazi ngumu*, hard work. (3) Brave, resolute, stout-hearted, courageous, obstinate, self-willed, fixed, unyielding. *Mbona wewe ngumu sana?* Why will you not change your mind? (cf. syn. *hodari, thabiti, -kali*). (4) Inexorable, cruel, hard-hearted. (Contr. *-ema, -pole, -a huruma*.)

Guna, v. (1) grunt, grumble, murmur; (2) express disapproval, indignation, contempt, 'protest, complain, sneer at.' *Baathi ya watu wanamguna*, some of the people sneer at him. (Cf. *mguno, guno, nung'unika*.)

Gunda, n. (*ma-*), a horn used for blowing. Dim. *kigunda*. (In Z. commonly *pembe, baragumu*.)

*****Gundi**, n. gum-arabic.

Gundua, v. come upon unexpectedly, take by surprise, catch unawares, startle, start (a wild animal from its lair). Ps. *gunduliwa*. Nt. *gunduka*. Ap. *gundu-lia*, steal upon, approach secretly, stalk (cf. *nyemelea*). Cs. *gundu-lisha, -lishwa, -liza*. Rp. *gunduana*. (Cf. *stusha, stuka*, and *fumania, nyemelea*.)

Gunga, v. use (native) medicine (*uganga, dawa*) to secure health, safety, well being. *Jigunga*, secure oneself, take precautions for safety—by charms, medicine, &c., i.e. native form of life insurance.

Gungu, n. (*ma-*), a mode of dancing, a figure in a dance, e.g. *gungu la kukwaa*, the stumbling figure; *gungu la kufunda*, the pounding figure.

*****Guni**, n. (*ma-*), (1) a matting bag used for dates. Dim. *kiguni*. Also used to describe unrhymed or blank verse, *mashairi yenyi guni*, as opp. to rhymed poetry, *mashairi yenyi vina*. (2) A carpenter's spokeshave. (Hind. *Guni* of poetry may come from the name of a famous Pemba poet, *Guni*.)

*****Gunia**, n. (*ma-*), (1) a coarse bag or sack used chiefly for rice imported from India, &c. Also (2) the material of which it is made, sackcloth.

Guno, n. (*ma-*), grunt, grumble,—sound expressive of indignation or contempt. (Cf. *guna, mguno.*)

Gunzi, n. (*ma-*), full-grown ear, or cob, of Indian corn (*muhindi*). (Cf. *higunzi*, and *kibunzi.*)

Guru, n. *Sukali guru*, a coarse unrefined kind of sugar made from the cane, as in Z., and sold in large dark-coloured lumps.

*****Gurudumu**, n. (—, and *ma-*), a wheel. Used in the plur. of any vehicle of which the wheels are conspicuous. (Cf. *gari.*) *Magurudumu ya mzinga*, a gun carriage.

Guruguru, n. (*ma-*), and **Mguruguru**, a large kind of burrowing lizard. (Cf. *mjusi, kenge.*)

Gurugusha, v. a variant of **Gugurusha**, which see.

Guruta, v. smooth with a press, put through the rollers of a mangling machine, mangle,—of clothes and linen generally. *Guruta nguo hizi vizuri*, mangle these clothes properly. Ps. *gurutwa*. Nt. *gurutika*. Ap. *gurut-ia, -iwa*. *Sina cha kugurutia*, I have no mangling machine. Cs. *gurut-isha, -ishwa*.

Gusa, v. touch, finger, handle with the fingers. Ps. *guswa*. Nt. *gusika*. Ap. *gus-ia, -iwa*. Rp. *gusana*. (Cf. *tomasa, papasa, bonyesha.*)

Guta, v. bawl, shout, cry out. Ap. *gut-ia, -iwa*. Cs. *gut-isha, -ishwa*. (Cf. syn. *lia, piga kelele.*)

Gutu, n. (*ma-*), stump, remainder. *G. la mkono*, stump of mutilated arm. (Cf. *kikono.*) *G. la mnazi*, trunk of cocoanut tree with the crown broken off. Also dim. *kigutu*. (Cf. *shiku, baki, salio.*)

Gutua, v. or **Kutua**, startle, frighten, surprise. Nt. *gutuka*. (Cf. the more common *stusha, stuka.*)

Guu, n. (*ma-*), used of any object resembling a leg (foot), or of a leg (foot) of large size, but in Z. *mguu* is always used of the leg (foot) of an animal or man. *Ubau wa maguu matatu*, a three-legged stool, tripod.

Gwanda, n. also **Bwanda**, a short kind of kanzu (which see), sometimes worn by men, reaching to the knees.

*****Gwaride**, n. (*ma-*), one of the words used in Z. for the 'native police,' and esp. their military band, called also *mdundo, matarumpeta*. *Kucheza gwaride*, to drill. (Cf. Engl. *guard.*)

H.

H represents generally the same sound as in English,—a sound which is of great importance in verb-forms in Swahili, as being the main characteristic of the negative conjugation.

In words of Arabic origin, this sound represents both forms of Arabic *H*, and also in most words the Arabic *Kh*. The tendency in Swahili is to soften down all gutturals to the point of disappearance, though they are learnt and retained in some words of comparatively recent introduction and by persons brought into close relations with Arabs. *H* also represents in a few words an initial *Alif* or *Ain* in the Arab original, and when an *h* sound in Arabic follows a vowel closely, the tendency in Swahili is to pronounce it before the vowel.

A word not found under *H* may therefore be looked for under *Kh*, or under the first vowel of the word.

H- (1) is the characteristic of the a. and adv. demonstrat. of nearness and of reference, 'this, this near me, this referred to, that,' which appears (followed always by the same vowel as occurs in the following syllable) in *huyu, hawa, huu, hii, hizi, hiki, hiri, hili, haya, huku, humu, hapa*, and the corresponding forms in *-o*, *huyo*, &c. (See esp. **Huko**, and **Huyu**, and cf. the other characteristic demonstr. letter *L*.) (2) As a negative prefix, is found only in the 2 and 3 Pers. S. of verb-forms. See **Ha-** and **Hu-**.

Ha, a verb-form, he (she) is not, negative prefix used in agreement with *Mtu*. *Yeye ha mwema*, he is not good. *Si* is usually preferred to *ha*.

Ha- is the characteristic negative prefix of all verb-forms, except (1) where *si* is used, i.e. in the 1 Pers. S. of the Indic. Mood, in the Subjunctive, and in verb-forms containing a relative, e.g. *si-pendi*, I do not like; *asiende*, that he may not go; *yasi-yopendeza*, things which do not please. (2) Where it becomes *h-* only, i.e. in the 2 and 3 Pers. S., e.g. *h-u-pendi* for *ha-upendi*, you do not like, and *h-a-pendi* for *ha-apendi*, he does not like; (3) when an additional sign of the negative is required, viz. the change of final *a* to *i*, in the Present Indicative only, e.g. *hawapendi*, they do not like. *Ha-*, as Negative Prefix, is always initial.

Ha- is also a contraction for *nika-*, the sign of the First Person Singular in the *ka* or Narrative Tense. *Hamwona* for *nikamwona*, and I saw him. (Confusion with the negative is barred by the change of final *a* to *i* in the Present Tense, see above, e.g. *hamwoni*, he does not see him, or you (plur.) do not see.)

*****Haba**, a. (1) little (in quantity), few; (2) rare, scarce; (3) not enough, deficient, too little, short (in amount). *Chakula h.*, not enough food. *Mtu h.*, a rare kind of man. *Siku h.*, a few days, insufficient time. *Maji h.*, shallow water, not enough water. Sometimes used as a n., 'a little' of anything. (Cf. *kidogo*.) *Haba na haba hujaza kibaba*, grain upon grain fills the measure. (Cf. Ar. *haba*, a grain, and syn. B. *-chache*, *kidogo*, *kitambo*.)

*****Habari**, n. and **Khabari**, (1) news, report, message, information; (2) events, matters, proceedings, things. Common in salutations, of persons meeting, e.g. *Habari?* or *Habari gani?* How are you? How are you getting on? or *Habari ya siku nyingi?* How have you been of late? *Niambie h. yake*, tell me about him. *Kwa h. ya jambo lile*, as to that matter. *H. zangu zilizonipata*, things that happened to me. *Ginsi gani kutufanya h. ile?* What did you treat us like that for? (Ar. Cf. *hubiri*, and syn. *maarifa*, *tarifu*, *jambo*.)

*****Habba**, n. (*ma-*), and **Hubba**, (1) love, fondness, affection; (2) love-token, souvenir, gift. Of natural affection of friends and relatives, as well as of the sexes. *Tia habbani*, take a fancy to. *Ana habba nami*, he is in love with me. *Hanifunulii habba*, he does not open his feelings to me. *Amenitoka habbani*, I have ceased to care for him. (Ar. Cf. common address in letters, *muhebbi*, and syn. *pendo*, *mapenzi*, *shauku*.)

Habeshia, n. (*ma-*), also **Mhabeshia**, **Habushia**, an Abyssinian. Used also of female domestic slaves of the *suria* class, of whatever race.

*****Hadaa**, v. cheat, deceive, outwit. Ps. *hadaiwa*. Nt. *hadaika*, be deceived. — n. deception, cunning, trickery, &c. (Ar. Cf. *danganya*, *punja*, *kalamkia*, &c., also *hila*, *ujanja*, *werevu*.)

*****Hadimu**, n. (*ma-*), servant, attendant, slave. In Z. usually **Mhadimu**, which see, i.e. one of the original inhabitants of the island. (Cf. *hudumu*, *Mhadimu*, and syn. *mtumishi*, *mtumwa*, *mngoje*.)

*****Hadithi**, v. narrate, tell stories, relate, describe, recount, report. Ps. *hadithiwa*. Ap. *hadith-ia*, *-iwa*, tell to (for, about, in, &c.); e.g. *pamehadithiwa vingi*, there are many stories told about the place. *Tumehadithiwa*, we have been told, history relates. — n. story, tale, account, report, history, legend, fiction. *Ni hadithi tu*, it is only a story, mere fiction. (Ar. Cf. *sumulia*, and *habari, kisa, ngano*.)

*Hafifu, a. trifling, insignificant, poor in quality, valueless, frivolous. *Mtu h.*, a person of no consequence. *Nguo h.*, calico of inferior quality. *Roho h.*, a light, flighty, wayward disposition. (Ar. Cf. syn. *-nyonge, duni, -dogo, rahisi*.)

*Hai, a. or Hayi, alive, living, having life, animate. *Yu hai*, he is alive. (Ar. Cf. *uhai, huika, huisha*, and syn. B. *-zima*.)

Hai, a verb-form, it is not, they are not,—Negat. Pfx. with Pers. Pfx. agreeing with D 2 (P) or D 6 (S). See Ha-.

*Haiba, n. beauty, adornment, decoration. *Mwanamke ana h. uso wake*, the woman has beautified her face. *H. inaingia sasa nyumbani*, the house is becoming decorated now. (Ar. Cf. syn. *uzuri, pambo, urembo*.)

Haina, verb-form, it has not (is not), they have not (are not),—the Negat. Pfx. with Pers. Pfx. agreeing with D 2 (P) and D 6 (S),—and *na*. See Ha-, Na.

*Haini, n. traitor, betrayer, deceiver. Also rarely as v., betray. (Ar. Cf. *hiana*, and for deceiving, see Danganya.)

*Haithuru, v. often used as, it does not matter, never mind, it is all the same. (See Thuru, and syn. *mamoja*.)

*Haj, n. pilgrimage to Mecca, —incumbent on all Mahommedans, where possible, and often undertaken from Z. *Kwenda haj*, to go as a pilgrim to Mecca. (Ar. See Haji.)

*Haja, n. (1) need, want, appeal for aid, request; (2) reason, cause, ground, excuse, claim, right; (3) what is needed, necessaries, belongings, engagements, calls of nature. *Toa h. kwa, taka h. kwa*, make a request to, request something of. *Sina h. naye*, I have no need of him, he is of no use to me. *Hana h.*, he is not wanted. *Haina h. ya kugombana*, there is no reason for quarrelling. *Mabaghala ya kupakia h. zake*, mules to carry his baggage. *Kwa h. ya kutembea*, for the sake of a walk. *Fanya h*, attend to the calls of nature. (Ar. Cf. *hitaji, hoji, hoja* or *huja*, and syn. for 'need,' &c. *mahitaji, maombi, ukosefu*,—for 'reason, &c.' *sababu, ajili, maana, sharti*,—for 'necessaries' *riziki, mafaa, vyombo*, &c.)

Hajambo, verb-form,—Negat. Pfx. of 3 Pers. S. combined with *jambo*, thing, affair, matter,—he is not (affected by) anything, there is nothing the matter with him. See Jambo.

*Haji, n. (1) also Haj, a pilgrimage to Mecca, see Haj; (2) (*ma-*), a pilgrim, one who is on his way to or has been to Mecca; and (3) more generally of an adherent of any religion. *Mahaji ya kizungu*, people who follow the European religion. — v. also Hiji, Heji, make a pilgrimage to Mecca. Ap. *haj-ia, -iwa*. *Atanihajia mahali pangu*, he will make the pilgrimage for me. Cs. *haj-isha, -ishwa*, send as a pilgrim, allow to go, provide means for, &c. (Ar. Cf. *haj*. Dist. *haji*, he does not come, i.e. from *ja*, v.)

*Hajiri, v. remove (from), leave, emigrate, move house. (Ar. for the common B. syn. *hama*.)

*Hakali, n. or Hikali, payment for privilege, e.g. *kushika hakali*, force to make a deposit, or pay footing, as a stranger intruding, &c. (Arab. *higâl*.)

*Haki, n. (1) justice, right, lawfulness. *Mtu wa h.*, a just man. *Hukumu h.*, or *kwa haki*, judge justly. *Shika* (or *fanya*) *h.*, be just, deal justly. (2) In general, absolute justice, righteousness. *Mwungu ni* mwenyi h., God is the Righteous One. (3) In particular, a claim, a right, a privilege, a just share. *Nipe h. yangu*, give me my wages, what I have a right to. *Killa myenyi h. amwiaye fullani*, any one who has a claim as creditor of so and so. *Enda hakini*, appeal to the law. *Nakuuliza kwa haki*, I have a right to ask you. (Ar.)

Haki, verb-form, it is not. (Cf. *hai*.)

*Hakika, n. certainty, reality, genuineness, fact, truth. *Mambo haya ni h.*, these are facts. *H. yako*, truth as to you, you certainly, e. g. *h. yako umekosa*, you are certainly wrong. *Sina h. nalo*, I am not sure about it. As adv. truly, certainly, really. (Ar. Cf. *hakiki, halisi, kweli*.)

*Hakiki, v. make sure about, ascertain, investigate, prove, know for certain. Ps. *hakikiwa*. Nt. *hakikika*, e. g. *haihakikiki*, certainty is unattainable. Ap. *hakik-ia, -iwa*, inquire into (about, for, at). Cs. *hakik-isha, -ishwa*, cause to investigate, make a strict inquiry, have a matter gone into. (Ar. Cf. *hakika*.)

*Hakimu, n. (*ma-*), judge, ruler, chief. *H. wetu anayetumiliki*, our chief who rules over us. *H. hapendelei mtu*, the judge favours no one. (Ar., not often used in Z., cf. *hukumu*, and ? *hekima*, and syn. *sultani, mfalme, jumbe, fumu, kathi*.)

*Hakiri, v. treat with contempt, despise, abase. Cs. *hakir-isha, -ishwa*, e. g. as Intens., vilify, scorn. (Arab. for common *tharau, tweza, thilisha*.)

Hako, verb-form, also Hayuko, he (she) is not there (is away, is absent), Negat. Pfx. of 3 Pers. S. *ha* agreeing with D 1 (S), and Locat. Pfx. *ko*. (So *hayuko, hapo, hamo*, &c.)

Haku-, as first part of a verb-form, is the Negat. Pfx. with *ku*, which in this combination may be (1) sign of Past Tense Negat., e.g. *hakupendeza*, he did not please, or (2) pfx. agreeing with Infin. Mood, e. g. *kulala hakupendezi*, lying down is not pleasant, or (3) pfx. of general reference, e. g. *hakupendezi*, the circumstances are unpleasant, or (4) Pers. Pfx. of 2 Pers. S. object, or P. object (with -*eni*), e. g. *hakupendi, hakupendeni*, he does not like you.

Hakuna, verb-form, often used as simple negative no, not so, it is not,—Negat. Pfx. *ha-*, with *ku* of general reference or agreeing with an Infin. Mood, and **na**, which see. (Cf. *hamna, hapana*, and for Negat. *la, siyo*.)

*Hal, n. Hal wáradi, otto of roses,—one of the favourite and most costly perfumes in Z. (Ar.)

*Halafu, adv. afterwards, presently, not yet, after a bit. Also commonly *halafu yake*, afterwards. Always of time. (Ar. Cf. *baada, baadaye, bado kidogo*, and *nyuma*.)

*Halali, n. lawful, permissible, allowed, rightful, optional, available, ceremonially clean. *Mke wake h.*, his lawful, wedded wife. *H. kwenda*, you may go if you like. *Kwiba si h.*, it is unlawful to steal. Also as a n., *h. yako*, it is right for you, you may. *Kichwa changu h. yako*, my head is at your mercy. (Ar. Cf. *halalisha*, and *hiyari*. Contr. *haramu*, and dist. verb-form *halali*, he does not lie down, from *lala*.)

*Halalisha, v. Cs. make lawful, legalize, declare right, free from legal or ceremonial objections or disabilities. *Muhammadi hakuhalalisha nyama ya nguruwe*, Mohammed did not sanction pork (as food). Ps. *halalishwa*. (Ar. Cf. *halali*.)

*Halasa, n. sailor's wages, i. e. *ujira wa waanamaji*.

*Hali, n. state, condition, circumstances, case. A common form of address is *Hali gani?* or *U hali gani?* How are you? (Cf. *Habari, Jambo, Salaam*.) *Kwa killa h.*, in any case. *H. moja na*, on same side as, of same views as, a follower of. *Yu h. yetu*, he is one of us. *H. ya kuwa ukiwa*, a state of desertion, desolation,—of a woman abandoned by her husband. (Ar. Cf. *mahali, pahali*.)

Hali, verb-form, it is not, Negat. agreeing with D 5 (S). Cf. *hai*. (Dist. *hali*, he does not eat, Negat. Present, from *la*.)

*Halifu, v. (1) oppose, contradict, rebel (against), disobey. *H. mfalme*, or *kwa mfalme*, rebel against the king. *H. sheria*, transgress the law. *Amenihalifu sana*, he violently opposed me. (2) Leave behind, esp. at death, i.e. bequeath. *Andika mali yote aliyohalifu fullani*, make an inventory of all property left by So-and-So. Ps. *halifiwa*. Ap. *halif-ia, -iwa, -iana*. Cs. *halif-isha, -ishwa*, e.g. incite to disobedience, &c. — a. rebellious, disobedient, headstrong. (Ar. Cf. for (1) *-halifu, uhalifu*, and syn. *asi, kaidi*, and B. *pinga, bisha, teta*, &c., for (2) *halafu*, and *acha, rithisha*.)

*Halili, Halilisha. See Halali, Halalisha.

*Halisi, a. real, genuine, true, exact, precise, accurate. *Myao halisi*, a true genuine Yao. *Ndio halisi nitakayo*, that is exactly what I want. Also adv., exactly, perfectly, really, just, just so. *Njema halisi*, of the very best quality. (Ar. Cf. syn. *haswa, sawasawa, kweli*.)

*Halua, n. a common sweetmeat, made of flour, eggs, sugar, ghee, &c., and often brought by Arabs from Muscat.

*Haluli, n. *Chumvi ya haluli*, sulphate of magnesia, Epsom salts.

Ham, verb-form, you (plur.) are not,—Negat. Pfx. with Pfx. of 2 Pers. P. object. (Cf. *ha*, and *m*.)

Hama, v. change habitation, emigrate, flit, remove (from, to). *H. nyumba (mji, inchi)*, move from (or, to) a house (town, country). Ap. *ham-ia, -iwa*. Cs. *ham-isha, -ishwa*, e.g. cause to remove, eject, banish, transport. (Cf. *-hame, -hamishi*.)

*Hamaki, v. be confounded, lose one's wits, act foolishly. (Ar. Cf. *shangaa, toshewa, pumbaza*. Dist. *tahamaki*.)

*Hamali, n. (*ma-*), porter, carrier, coolie,—the professional town carrier in Z. Cf. *mchukuzi*, any carrier of a parcel, or load; *mpagazi*, a caravan-porter. *Merikebu ya h.*, a freight vessel, merchant ship. *Gari la h.*, a trolley, goods-van. (Ar. Cf. *hamili, himili, stahimili*, and syn. *mpagazi, mchukuzi*.)

*Hamami, n. a public bath, bathing establishment. (Ar. Cf. for room bath, *birika ya kuogea, kiogeo*.)

*Hamarawi, n. rope attached to lower or forward end of the yard in a native vessel, to steady it and assist in shifting, when tacking,—a forebrace. See Foromali.

*Hamaya, n. protection, guardianship. Usually in formal documents, e.g. *fi hamayat al Ingereza*, under British protection, for the common *chini ya mkono wa*, or *mkononi mwa*, in the hands of. (Ar. Cf. syn. B. *ulinzi, tunza*.)

*Hamdu, n. praise—usually in Arab formal expressions, e.g. *Al hamdu illahi*, praise to God. (Cf. *himidi, hemdi*, and syn. *sifa*.)

-hame, a. deserted, abandoned,—of place, e.g. *mahame, pahame*, a deserted village. (Cf. *hama, -hamishi*, and syn. *-kiwa*.)

*Hami, v. protect, defend. (Arab. Cf. *hamaya*, and the common syn. *tunza, linda*.)

*Hamila, Hamili. See Himila, Himili.

*Hamira, n. leaven, yeast, made by mixing flour and water, and leaving it to turn sour. (St.) (Arab. for common syn. B. *chachu*.)

-hamishi, a. wandering, nomad, migratory, homeless. (Cf. *hama, -hame*.)

Hamna, verb-form, (1) there is not inside, there is not, no—same as *hakuna, hapana*, but with *m* of reference to interior, for *ku, pa*; (2) you (plur.) have not, in which *m* is the Pers. Pfx. of 2 P. subject. See Hakuna.

Hamo, verb-form, also Hayumo, he is not within—same as Hako (which see) with *mo*, locative of interior, for *ko*.

*Hamsi, n. and a., five. Rarely used alone, for the common B. *tano. Hamsi mia*, five hundred. (Arab. Cf. *hamsini, hamstashara, alhamisi*.)

*Hamsini, n. and a., fifty. -a *hamsini*, fiftieth. (Ar. Cf. *hamsi*.)

*Hamstashara, n. and a., fifteen. -a *hamstashara*, fifteenth. (Ar. Cf. *hamsi, ashara*, and syn. B. *kumi na tano*.)

*Hamu, n. grief, sorrow, distress. *Tia hamu*, grieve. *Fanya (ingiwa na) hamu*, he grieved. (Ar. Cf. *ghammu*, and syn. *huzuni, sikitiko, majonsi*, &c. Dist. *hamu*, haste, hurry,—not often heard, cf. *hima*. *Tuna hamu ya kwenda zetu*, we are in a hurry to go, &c.)

*Hana, v. also Hani, mourn (with), pay a visit of condolence (to), join in a formal mourning. Ap. *han-ia, -iwa*. Cs. *hani-sha, -shwa*. Rp. *haniana*. (Ar. Cf. *matanga*.)

Hana, verb-form, he (she) has not—Negat. Pfx. with na, which see. *Hana hitu*, he has nothing. *Hana kwao*, he has no home, he is a vagabond.

*Hanamu, a. oblique, aslant, sideways. *Kata h.*, cut obliquely. (Cf. syn. *mshathali, kombo, upande*.)

*Handaki, n. ditch, trench, channel (artificial). (Ar. Cf. *shimo, msingi*.)

*Hando, n. a copper vessel, similar to the earthenware *mtungi*, with narrow circular opening at the top, used chiefly for carrying and storing water. (For other metal vessels cf. *sufuria, kitasa, kalasia*.)

*Hangaika, v. See Angaika.

*Hani, v. also Hana, which see.

Hanikiza, v. Cs. talk down, bear down with loud talking, drown an opponent's voice, bluff, prevent hearing. Rp. *hanikizana*.

*Hanisi, a. impotent (sexually), effeminate, weak. (Ar.)

*Hanithi, a. ribald, foul, shameless. *Acha neno h. wee*, stop that bad language, will you? (Arab. for more usual -*najisi, -chafu, -baya*.)

*Hanzua, n. a kind of sword dance, commonly played after Ramathani.

Hao, a. pron. of reference, 3 Pers. P. agreeing with D 1 (P), those referred to, those there. See Huyu, and O.

Hapa, a. pron. of place, this place,—agreeing with D 7, seldom of time or circumstances, and generally used alone as pron. or locative adv. *H. pazuri*, this is a nice place. *Toka h. hatta mjini*, from here to the town. *Njoo h.*, come here. *H. pana watu*, here there are people. Sometimes *papa hapa*, just here, on this very spot (cf. *papa*). See Huyu, and cf. follg.

Hapale, a. pron. for *hapa-pale*, just there, at that very place. (Cf. *huyule, hivile*, &c., and see Huyu, Yule.)

Hapana, verb-form, there is not there, there is none, no—same as *hakuna, hamna*, but with *pa*, agreeing with D 7, of place. Commonly as a simple negation, like *hakuna, la, siyo*.

Hapo, a. pron. of reference, agreeing with D 7, and like *hapa* commonly used alone, but unlike *hapa*, of time as well as place, and also more generally of circumstances. *Toka hapo!* get out of that! go along! *H. kale*, in the days of old, once upon a time, often at the beginning of a story. *Tangu h., tokea h.*, from long ago, ever so long. *Hapo*, in that case, under the circumstances. *H. mbali*, that was a different case.

Also *papo hapo*, just there, at that very place (time, crisis). (Cf. *hapa, huyo, papa*.)

Hapo, verb-form, also Hayupo. he (she) is not here,—same as *huko, hamo*, with locative -*po* for -*ko*, -*mo*.

*Hara, v. have looseness of the bowels, suffer from frequent purging, have diarrhoea, &c. *H. damu*, have dysentery, pass blood with the stools. *Dawa ya kuhara* (also, *ya kuharisha*), an aperient medicine, a laxative, a purge. Cs. *har-isha, -ishwa*. *Chakula hiki chaniharisha*, this food gives me diarrhoea. (Ar.)

*Harabu, n. (—, and *ma*-), one who is destructive, a spoiler, a ruffian, a vandal. *Mwarabu h. usiende mrima*, the Arab is a destroyer, so do not go to the mainland. *Nazi mbovu h. ya nzima*, bad cocoanuts spoil the good ones. Also a. -*harabu*, destructive, violent. (Ar. Cf. *haribu, uharabu*.)

*Haradali, n. mustard. (Ar.)

*Haraja, n. cost, expense, outlay, payment. (Ar. Cf. *harijia*, and more common syn. *gharama*.)

*Haraka, n. haste, hurry, bustle, excitement, fun. *Fanya h.*, make haste. *Enda kwa h.*, be in a hurry. *Haraka, haraka, haina baraka*, hurry has no blessing. Also as adv., in a hurry, hastily, flurriedly. (Ar. Cf. *harikisha*, and for haste, syn. *hima, wepesi*, and for flurry, *angaika, chafuka*.)

*Harakisha, v. Cs. and Harikisha, cause haste (bustle, excitement, &c.). (Ar. Cf. *haraka, taharuki*, and syn. *himiza*.)

*Haramia, n. outlaw, pirate, brigand, bandit, highway robber. (Ar. Cf. follg. and syn. *mtoro, pakacha, mnyanganyi*.)

*Haramu, a. forbidden, unlawful, prohibited, i.e. by Mahommedan law or custom. *Mwana wa h.*, an illegitimate child, a bastard. (Ar. *harimu, harimisha*, and cf. *gombeza, marufuku*, and contr. *halali*.)

*Harara, n. heat, warmth, (1) of the body, high temperature, inflammation, prickly heat, rash produced by heat. *Ameshikwa na h.*, he is hot, feverish. *Yuna h. ya mapaja kwa jua na njia*, he has a rash on the thighs from the heat and walking. (2) fig. hot temper, rashness, precipitancy. *H. ya moyo, moyo wa h., moyo h.*, a passionate disposition, quick temper. (Ar. Cf. *hari*, and syn. *moto, uvukuto*.)

*Hari, n. heat in general, and esp. perspiration, sweat. *H. ya jua*, the heat of the sun. *Mwili wangu una h.*, my body is hot. *Toka h.*, perspire. *H. zanitona*, sweat drops off me. (Ar. Cf. *harara*, and syn. *moto, josho*.)

*-haribifu, a. (*haribifu* with D 4 (P), D 5 (S), D 6), destructive, wasteful, prodigal, doing harm, spoiling. *Mharibifu wa mali*, a spendthrift. (Cf. *haribu, harabu, uharabu*, and syn. -*potevu, -bathirifu*.)

*Haribu, v. injure, destroy, spoil, damage, ruin, demoralize. *H. kazi*, spoil work. *H. safari*, break up an expedition. *H. inchi*, devastate a country. *H. mimba*, cause miscarriage. *H. moyo*, pervert, corrupt. Ps. *haribiwa*. Nt. *haribika*, with several derived forms. Ap. *haribikia*, be ruined, in respect of, suffer loss of, and Ps. *haribikiwa*, be the victim of violence, be robbed of everything, be utterly ruined. Cs. *haribikisha, -ishwa*, inflict ruin on. Rp. *haribikana*, be liable to destruction. Ap. *harib-ia, -iwa, -iana*. Cs. *harib-isha, -ishwa*. (Ar. Cf. *harabu, -haribifu*, and syn. B. *vunja, angamiza, poteza*.)

*Harijia, v. Ap. spend money on, incur outlay for, make provision for, be liberal to. Ps. *harijiwa*. (Ar. Cf. *haraja*, and the more usual syn. *gharimia*, and cf. *kirimu, karama*.)

Harimu, v. make illegal, declare unlawful, forbid, ban, interdict, excommunicate. Ps. *harimiwa*. Ap. *harimia*, forbid to, declare wrong for, &c.   Cs. *harim-isha*, *-ishwa*, often Intens. and so instead of the Pr. *harimu*, declare illegal, according to Mahommedan law. *Harimisha mtu kitu*, interdict some one from something. *Tumeharimishwa kileo*, we are forbidden intoxicants.   — n. (*ma-*), person or thing forbidden. *Maharimu*, persons within the prohibited degrees of consanguinity and so forbidden to each other.   (Ar. Cf. *haramu, haramia*, and for forbidding, *gombeza, kataza, piga, marufuku*.)

*Hariri, n. silk. (Ar.)

*Harisha, v. Cs. cause free action of the bowels, produce diarrhoea. (Ar. See Hara, and cf. syn. *endesha choo*.)

*Harufu, n. (1) a letter (of the alphabet), a written character, figure. *H. za kiarabu*, Arabic writing characters.   (Ar. Cf. *tarakimu*.)   (2) Scent, smell, odour, of any kind, good or bad.   (Cf. *nuka, manukato, uvundo*.)

*Harusi, n. wedding. See Arusi. (Ar.—the *h* representing *Ain*.)

*Hasara, n. loss, damage, injury. *Pata h.*, lose. *Tia h.*, cause loss to. *Lipa h.*, pay damages, repay, make amends.   (Ar. Cf. *hasiri, thara, upotevu*.)

*Hasha, int. certainly not, by no means, impossible, God forbid,— a very emphatic negative.   (Ar. Other negatives are *la, sio, hakuna*.)

*Hasherati, n. profligacy, vice. See Asherati. (Ar.)

Hasho, n. a piece of wood used as a patch, let in or fixed on, to close a hole, &c.

*Hasi, v. castrate, geld. Ps. *hasiwa*. Also n. (*ma-*), a bullock, a gelding. (Ar. Cf. *mhasi, maksai*, and syn. *tawashi*.)

*Hasibu, v. also Hesabu, count, reckon up, calculate.   (Ar. For derivatives, &c., see Hesabu.)

*Hasidi, v. also Husudu, envy, grudge, be jealous of. *Unamhasidi nguo zake*, you envy him his clothes. (For derivatives, &c., see Husudu.) — n. (1) envy, jealousy, spite; (2) an envious, spiteful person, and in general, enemy, foe. *Tukaona huyu ndiye hasidi*, and we see that he was indeed our enemy. (Ar. Cf. *uhasidi, uhusuda*, and syn. B. *uwivu*.)

*Hasimu, n. antagonist, rival, opponent.   (Arab. Cf. *husuma*,—for common *adui*, and cf. *mdai, mtesi*, &c.)

*Hasira, n. anger, wrath, passion. *Kuwa na h.*, to be angry. *Kutia h.*, to enrage. Used with many verbs, e.g. *fanya, ona, piga, shikwa na, ingia, ingiwa, patwa na*, &c. (The common word in Z.   Cf. *kasirika*, and syn. *ghathabu, uchungu, chuki*. Dist. follg.)

*Hasiri, v. injure, damage, hurt, inflict loss on. *Paka anahasiri watu*, the cat is doing injury to people. *Mbau zimemhasiri*, the planks have been a loss to him. Ps. *hasiriwa*. Nt. *hasirika*. Ap. *hasir-ia, -iwa*. Cs. *hasir-isha, -ishwa*, and Intens. injure. Rp. *hasiriana*.   (Ar. Cf. *hasara*, and syn. *thara, shari*. Dist. *hasira*, anger.)

*Hassa, adv. also Haswa, exactly, wholly, completely, very much. (Ar. Cf. *halisi, barabba, kabisa, sana*.)

*Hatamu, n. bridle, i.e. *ugwe wa mdomoni*, the mouth strap, to guide or fasten an animal with.   (Ar. The bit is *lijamu*.)

*Hatari, n. danger, peril, risk, jeopardy. *Hatari kwenda*, it is dangerous to go. *Jitia hatarini*, run a risk, imperil oneself. (Cf. *hatirisha*, and dist. *hathari*. Cf. *mashaka*.)

*Hathari, v. exercise care, be cautious, act with prudence. *Hathari kwa adui*, be on guard against (be on the look-out for) an enemy. *Jihathari* is a common cry of warning, Mind yourself! Look out! Take care!—like *bismilla*. — n. caution, care, prudence. Common in such phrases as *kuwa na h.*, to be on one's guard; *kutia h.*, to put on one's guard, to caution. Also *fanya h.*, *jipasha h.*, *pata h.* (Ar. Cf. syn. *angalia, jilinda, kuwa macho.*)

*Hati, n. written note, memorandum, document, certificate, writing, esp. of an official or formal kind, e. g. *andikia hati*, emancipate, write a freedom-paper for. (Ar. Cf. *waraka*, a news letter, of ordinary correspondence, and *barua, cheti.*)

Hatia, n. See Hatiya, and Atia.

*Hatibu, n. (*ma-*), a preacher. *H. anapanda ndani ya mimbara apate kuhutubu*, the preacher is mounting the pulpit to give his address. (Ar. Cf. *hutubu, hotuba.*)

*Hatima, n. end, conclusion. *Akakaa raha hatta hatima*, and he lived happily to the day of his death. *Hatimaye*, for *hatima yake*, used as adv., finally. — adv. finally, at last, in the end, and sometimes as prep. after, e. g. *hatima kufa kwake*, after his death. (Ar. Cf. *hitima, hitimu*, and syn. B. *mwisho, kikomo.*)

*Hatirisha, v. Cs. put in danger, endanger, risk, imperil. *Amehatirisha mali katika chombo*, he has risked his goods on a dhow. Ps. *hatirishwa*. Rf. *jihatirisha*, risk oneself, i. e. *jitia hatarini*. (Ar. Cf. *hatari.*)

*Hatiya, n. and Hatia, (1) fault, transgression, crime, sin; (2) guilt, blame, culpability. *Tia hatiyani*, find fault with, accuse. *Kuwa na h. na (mtu)* may mean either to have done a wrong to, or, to have a charge against. (Ar. Cf. *thambi, kosa.*)

*Hatta, (1) prep. until, up to, as far as, as much as,—implying a point, object, degree, or condition in view. *Toka hapa h. huko*, from here to there. *Tangu assubuhi h. jioni*, from morning to evening. *Simpi h. moja*, I will not give him as much as one (even one). Often with *kidogo*, after a negative, i. e. not in the least, not even a little, not at all. Also without *kidogo*, but in same sense, *habari hii si kweli hatta*, this report is not true at all. Sometimes even with negative only implied, e. g. *Amekwenda? hatta*, Has he gone? Not he. (2) conj. (a) connective, so, then, next, often merely transitional and not requiring translation, *h. assubuhi*, so in the morning. *H. siku moja*, one day, once upon a time. (b) subordinative, so as to, even if, though. *Ntafanza akili gani, h. tugawe sawasawa?* What plan shall I follow, so that we may divide equally? *H. aje na mkuki, usikubali*, even if he come with a spear, do not consent. (3) adv. *H. ntampiga*, I will even beat him, I will go so far as to beat him. *Bahati yako h. nimekuja*, Thanks to your good luck, I have even come, I am positively here. (Ar.)

Hatu, verb-form, we are not,—Negat. Pfx. with Pfx. of 1 Pers. P. See Ha-, and Tu.

*Hatua, n. step, pace, in walking, also footstep, mark left by the foot. *Pima kwa h.*, measure by paces. *Vuta h. hapa na hapa*, go a step in either direction. *Safari h.*, a journey on foot. *H. mbili mbele*, two steps to the front. (Ar. Cf. *uayo.*)

Hau, verb-form, it is not, Negat. Pfx., and Pfx. agreeing with D 2 (S), and D 4 (S). See Ha-, and U.

Hauna, verb-form, it is not (does not exist), it has not,—Negat. Pfx., and Pfx. agreeing with D 2 (S), D 4 (S), and na (which see).

Havi, verb-form, they are not,—Negat. Pfx. and Pfx. agreeing with D 3 (P). See Ha-.

Havina, verb-form, they are not, they have not,—Negat. Pfx. and Pfx. agreeing with D 3 (P), and na (which see).

*Hawa, n. (1) longing, bias, strong inclination, lust, passion.

Huyu yuna h. ya moyo, this man is deeply in love. *Usifanye h. nafsi*, do not show bias, do not be partial. (Ar., with *ya* final. Cf. syn. *shauko, habba, mapenzi, ngoa, tamaa, roho, maelekeo, uchu.*) (2) Air, the air. *H. ya kule nzuri sana*, the air there is delightful. *Badili h.*, take a change of air. (Ar., with *alif* final. Cf. *anga, upepo, baridi, tabia*, climate. *Hawa* is also sometimes written *hewa*,—the first *a* having a light sound like a short *e*. Cf. *alfu, elfu, mwalimu, elimu*, &c., and *e.*) (3) Eve, the first woman. (Ar., not the same *h* as (1) and (2). (4) See follg.

Hawa, pron. these, plur. of *huyu*, agreeing with D 1 (P).

Hawa, verb-form, they are not,—Negat. Pfx. with Pfx. agreeing with D 1 (P).

*****Hawa, Hawaa, Hawai**, n. also **Hawara**, a paramour, a woman living with a man who is not her husband. (Cf. *suria, kinyumba, mwandani, kahaba.*)

*****Hawala**, n. also **Awala**, money order, cheque, draft, bill of exchange. (Ar. Cf. syn. *hundi, hati.*)

Hawana, verb-form, they are not (do not exist), they have not,—Negat. Pfx. and Pfx. agreeing with D 1 (P), and *na* (which see).

Hawezi, n. 3 Sing. Pres. Indic. Negat. of *weza*, he is unable, he has not strength, he is sick. So commonly applied to the condition of sickness, as to be sometimes used as an indeclinable adj., sick, ill, e. g. *nalikuwa hawezi*, for *siwezi*, I was ill. *Walikuta watu wengi hawezi*, they found many people sick. And even as verb, e. g. *amehawezi*, he has become sick, he is ill. See **Weza**, and **Siwezi**.

Hawi, v. 3 Pers. Sing. Pres. Indic. Negat. of *-wa* (*kuwa*), he is not, he does not exist. See **-wa**.

*****Hawili**, v. (1) change, transfer. *H. chombo*, change ship, trans-ship. Cs. *hawil-isha, -ishwa*. (2) Give security for, guarantee, undertake responsibility for. *H. deni*, become responsible for a debt. (Ar. Cf. *hawala*, and syn. (1) *badili*, (2) *diriki.*)

*****Haya**, n. (1) shame, modesty, bashfulness, shamefacedness; (2) cause of shame, disgrace; (3) humility, respect, reverence. *Tia h.*, make ashamed. *Fanya (ona) h.*, feel shame, be shy. *Hana h.*, he is a shameless (impudent, brazen) person. (Ar. Cf. syn. *aibu, fetheha, tahayari*. Dist. follg.)

Haya, (1) int. as call to action or effort, come on! now then! work away! step out! make haste! &c.; (2) a. these, plur. of *huyu*, agreeing with D 5 (P); (3) verb-form, they are not,—Negat. Pfx. and Pfx. agreeing with D 5 (P).

Hayale, a. for *haya-yale*, those very (things), agreeing with D 5 (P). (Cf. *huyule, huyu, yule.*)

*****Hayamkini**, v. it is impossible. See **Yamkini**. (Ar.)

Hayana, verb-form, they are not (do not exist), they have not,—Negat. Pfx. and Pfx. agreeing with D 5 (P), and *na* (which see).

*****Hayawani**, n. a brute, a beast, like a brute, and so of persons, fool, idiot, brute. (Ar. Cf. *uhayawani*, and syn. *mjinga, mpumbafu.*)

*****Hayi**, a. alive, living. See **Hai**. (Ar.)

Hayo, a. of reference, agreeing with D 5 (P), those referred to, those yonder, those. (Cf. *huyo.*)

Hayuko, verb-form, he (she) is not there,—Negat. Pfx., Pfx. *yu* agreeing with D 1 (S), and locative Pfx. *-ko*. (Cf. *ha-, -ko.*)

*****Hazama**, n. also **Azama**, or **Athama**, nose-ornament, pendant. (Ar.)

*****Hazamu**, n. (*ma-*), girdle. Commonly in the plur. (Ar. Cf. *mahazamu, mshipi, masombo.*)

Hazi, verb-form, they are not,—

Negat. Pfx., with Pfx. agreeing with D 4 (P), D 6. (Cf. *ha-*.)

*Hazina, n. treasure, deposit of money, exchequer, privy purse. *H. ya mali, nyumba ya h.*, treasury. (Ar. Cf. *dafina, mali, akiba*.)

Hazina, verb-form, they are not (do not exist), they have not,—Negat. Pfx., with Pfx. agreeing with D 4 (P), D 6, and *na* (which see).

*Hebbu, v. like, be pleased with, take a fancy to. *Baba aliuhebbu unyoya ule*, his father took a fancy to that feather. Ap. *hebb-ia, -iwa*. (Arab. seldom used. Cf. *habba, hiba*.)

*Hedaya, n. gift, present, usually of something rare, costly, or wonderful. *Kitu cha h.*, a costly thing. (Arab. Cf. *atia, zawadi, bakshishi, tunu*, &c.)

*Hekalu, n. (*ma-*), a large building, a palace, a temple, the temple at Jerusalem. (Ar. Cf. syn. B. *jumba*.)

*Hekima, n. wisdom, knowledge, judgement. (Ar. Cf. *hakimu, hukumu*, and syn. *elimu, busara, akili, maarifa*.)

*Hekimiza, v. Cs. cause to know, give instructions to, inform, direct. *Ametuhekimiza tukutunze*, he directed us to take care of you. Ps. *hekimizwa*. (Ar. Cf. prec.)

*Hema, n. (—, and *ma-*), a tent. *Piga (simikisha) h.*, pitch a tent. *Ondoa (ng'oa) h.*, strike a tent. (Ar.)

*Hemdi, n. also Himidi, praise, esp. in ascription to God. (Ar. Cf. *hamdu*, follg. and syn. *sifa*.)

*Hemidi, v. and Himidi, praise. Ps. *hemidiwa*. (Ar. Cf. *hamdu, hemdi*, and syn. *sifu*.)

*Henza, n. halyard,—the thick rope by which the heavy yard and sail of a native vessel is hoisted. It passes over a sheave at the masthead, and carries a double or treble pulley (*gofia*) connected with another (*abedari*) on deck by a smaller rope (*jirari*), giving the necessary purchase. (Cf. *tanga*.)

*Henzarani, n. a cane, canework.

*Heri, n. happiness, blessedness, good fortune, luck, success, advantage. *H. yako ni yetu*, your happiness is ours. *Mtu wa h.*, a fortunate (happy, enviable) man. *Kujaliwa h.*, to be granted good fortune. *Kufunuliwa h.*, to make a lucky guess, hit on a happy idea. Common in formula of leave-taking, *kwa heri*, good-bye, or *kwa heri ya kuonana*, good-bye till we meet again. Also *heri*, it is well, it is best (like *afathali*), e. g. *heri uende*, you had better go. (Ar. Cf. *subalkheri, masalkheri*, in which the *kh* is more distinctly heard as a guttural.)

Hero, n. a small wooden dish, sometimes on legs, used for serving food on. (Cf. *chungu*.)

*Hesabu, v. also Hasibu, Hisabu, count, calculate, reckon up. Ps. *hesabiwa*. Nt. *hesabika*. *Hazi-hesabiki*, they are not counted, or, they are not to be counted, i. e. worthless, or, they are past counting, i. e. numberless. Ap. *hesab-ia*, reckon with (to the credit of, against, &c.). Rp. *hesabiana*, settle accounts together. Cs. *hesab-isha, -ishwa*, e. g. *ntahesabisha*, I will have an account taken. — n. (1) reckoning, calculation, enumeration; (2) a bill, an account (of money, measure, value); (3) the art of counting, numeration, arithmetic. *Chuo cha h.*, an account book, like *daftari*. *Toa h.*, give an account. *Andika katika h.*, put down to an account. *Fanya h.*, reckon up, calculate. *Taka h.*, demand an account. (Ar. Cf. *idadi, pima, kadiri*.)

*Heshima, n. often Héshima, (1) as a quality or condition, honour, dignity, position, rank; (2) the correlative attitude in others, respect, reverence, awe, courtesy; (3) as shown in act, a present, acknowledgement, fee. *Hana h.*, he has no dignity, or, he is disrespectful. *Wekea (wekeana) h.*, treat (each other) with honour. *H. kwake tele*, he is full of due consideration for people. (Ar. Cf. follg. and syn. (1) *utukufu, daraja, cheo*; (2) *hofu, adabu*; (3) *bakshishi*, &c.)

*Heshimu, v. honour, pay respect to, treat with courtesy, give a present to. Ps. *heshimiwa*. Ap. *heshim-ia, -iana*. (Ar. Cf. *tukuza, jali, stahi, hashimu*.)

*Hessi, n. (—, and *ma-*), a screw. Also *msomari wa hessi*. (Cf. *parafujo, msomari*.)

*Hethi, n. menses, menstruation, —more commonly *mwezi* or *damu*. *Kuwa na h.*, to menstruate, also *ingia mwezini (damuni)*. (Ar.)

Hi-, as first syllable of a verbform, is (if not part of the root) a contraction for *niki-*, i.e. Pfx. of 1 Pers. Sing. of the Pres. Partic., e.g. *hipenda*, for *nikipenda*. (Cf. *ha* for *nika*, and see **Ki**.)

Hiana, a. sometimes -hiana, (1) tough, hard, strong. *Mti huu ni h.*, or *una h.*, this wood is hard. (2) Hard, unyielding, domineering, oppressive, arrogant. (Cf. *uhiana*, and syn. *-gumu*.) — n. (1) hardness; (2) oppression. *Mtu hamfanyi mwenziwe h.*, a man is not hard upon his friend. (*Hiana, uhiana*, is also sometimes used as a variant of *haini*, treacherous, deceitful.)

*Hiari, n. and Hiyari, choice, option, power of deciding, control. *Hiari yako*, just as you like. *Kichwa changu h. yako*, my life (head) is in your hands, you may kill me if you like. *Killa mtu ana h. katika nyumba yake*, every man is master in his own house. *Kazi ya h.*, voluntary labour. — v. choose, prefer. *Waanake wakahiyari kukabili risasi zetu*, the women deliberately faced our bullets. (Ar. Cf. *ikhtiari*, and syn. *chagua, fanya kwa moyo*.)

*Hiba, n. gift, present, keepsake, souvenir,—given as sign of affection, hence also bequest, legacy. (Ar. Cf. *habba, muhebbi, hebbu*, and for 'present' generally *bakshishi, ada, zawadi*, &c.)

Hicho, a. of reference, that, that yonder, agreeing with D 3 (S). (Cf. *huyo* and *-o*.)

*Hidima, n. also Huduma, service, employment, ministration. *Mzungu atia watu katika h. yake*, this white man takes people into his service. (Ar. Cf. *hudumu, mhadimu*, and syn. *utumwa, utumishi, kazi*.)

*Hifathi, v. sometimes Hafithi, preserve, keep, protect, save. *Muungu amhifathi*, may God keep him. Ps. *hifathiwa*. Nt. *hifathika*. Ap. *hifath-ia, -iana*. Cs. *hifath-isha, -ishwa*. (Ar. Cf. *linda, tunza, ponya, okoa*, &c.)

Hii, a. dem. this, there,—agreeing with D 2 (P), D 6 (S). (Cf. *huyu*.) Also *hiile* (of emphasis, i.e. *hii-ile*), that (those) very. (Cf. *huyule*.)

*Hikaya, n. and Hekaya, story, anecdote, remarkable incident. *Nna h.*, I have something to tell you. *Tumeona h. leo*, we have seen a strange thing to-day. (Ar. Cf. *kisa, ngano, hadithi, habari*.)

Hiki, a. dem. this,—agreeing with D 3 (S). Also *hikile* (of emphasis, i.e. *hiki lile*), that very. (Cf. *huyu, huyule*.)

*Hila, n. device, trick, stratagem, craft, cunning, deceit. *Fanya h.*, use cunning, try to circumvent. *Mtu wa h.*, a wily, sly man. (Ar. Cf. *hadaa, madanganya, werevu, ujanja*.)

Hili, a. dem. this, agreeing with D 5 (S). Also *hilile* (of emphasis, i.e. *hili lile*), this very. (Cf. *huyu, huyule*.) Similarly *hilo*, of reference, that, that yonder. (Cf. *huyo, -o*.)

Hima, adv. quick, quickly, hastily, in a hurry. *Fanya h.*, make haste. *Twende h.*, let us go quickly. *Hima! hima!* quick! quick! (Cf. *himiza, hamu*, and syn. *upesi, haraka, mbio*.)

*Himidi, v. praise, extol, magnify, esp. of praise to God. Ps. *himi-

diwa. — n. praise. (Ar. Cf. *hamdu, hemdi*, and syn. *sifu, sifa*.)

*Himila, n. (1) load, burden; (2) pregnancy. *Mke wangu ana h., amechukua mimba*, my wife is with child, she has conceived. (Ar. for the commoner (1) *mzigo*, (2) *mimba*. Cf. follg.)

*Himili, v. (1) bear, support, carry, take away; (2) bear, endure, accept, be equal to; (3) be pregnant. *Ruhusa kuhimili mizigo*, leave to carry the loads. *Himili jua*, endure the heat of the sun. Ps. *himiliwa*. Nt. *himilika*. Ap. *himil-ia, -iwa, -iana*. Cs. *himil-isha, -ishwa*. (Ar. Cf. *himila, hamali, stahimili*, and syn. *chukua, vumilia, k..wa na mimba*.)

Himiza, v. Cs. hasten, hurry, cause to be done (to go) quickly. *Himiza watu kazi*, make men work quickly. *Himiza chakula*, hurry on a meal. Ps. *himizwa*. Ap. *himiz-ia, -iwa*. Rp. *himizana*. (Cf. *hima*, and syn. *kimbiza, endesha, harakisha*.)

Hina, n. henna, prepared from the plant *mhina*, a very favourite red dye.

*Hindi, n. (*ma-*), (1) a single grain of Indian corn, a seed of the plant *muhindi*, which see; (2) India, also *Ulaya Hindi, Uhindi*. (Dist. *Mhindi*, a Hindoo.)

*Hini, v. refuse to give (to), withhold (from), keep back (from). *Amenihini fetha yangu*, he has kept back my money. *Hatanihini uganga*, he will not refuse me medicine. *Jihini chakula*, deny oneself food. Ps. *hiniwa*. Nt. *hinika*. Ap. *hin-ia, -iwa, -iana*. Cs. *hin-isha, -ishwa*. *Jihinisha*, practise self-denial. (Ar. Cf. syn. *nyima, katalia*.)

*Hirimu, n. (—, and *ma-*), (1) age, period of life, and esp. of youth, from 10 to 25; (2) one of the same age, a contemporary. *Vijana wa h. moja*, young people of the same age. *Mahirimu yake ya kijana*, the companions of his youth. (Ar. Cf. *umri*.)

*Hirizi, n. charm, amulet, i. e. *uganga wa kuvaa mwilini, uvaliwao*, medicine worn on the person, which is put on, round the neck or at the side. Often a small leather case, containing a sentence from the Coran. (Ar. Cf. *uganga, dawa, talasimu*.)

*Hisa, n. (1) part, portion, share (cf. *fungu, sehemu*); (2) ? indulgence, permission, pardon. (Ar.)

*Hisani, n. kindness, favour, goodness. *Kwa h. yako*, by your kindness. (Ar. Cf. *ahsante*, and syn. *fathili, wema*.)

*Hitaji, v. need, require, be in need of, lack, want, feel want of, desire. *Nahitaji chakula*, I need food. Often impersonal, e. g. *yahitaji mashahidi wawe watu wa kweli*, witnesses need to be truthful. *Yahitaji ule sana*, you should eat heartily. Sometimes 'be wanting, be wanted,' e. g. *vitu vinavyohitaji katika mazishi*, requisites for burial. Ps. *hitajiwa*. Nt. *hitajika*. Ap. *hitajia*, like *hitaji*, e. g. *ahitajia kupigwa*, he wants a beating. *Ahitajia kuwapo hapa*, he needs must be here. Rp. *hitajiana*. — n. (*ma-*), need, want, petition. (Ar. Cf. *haja, mhitaji*, and syn. *taka*.)

*Hitari, v. choose, select, prefer. Ps. *hitariwa*. *Kalamu iliyohitariwa*, a choice, selected pen. Cs. *hitarisha, -ishwa*, e. g. cause to choose, give choice (of). (Ar. Cf. follg., and the common syn. *chagua, teua*.)

*Hitiari, n. also Ihtiari, choice, selection, preference. *H. yako*, as you like, i. e. *upendavyo*. *Nathari na h. ni kwako*, the decision and choice lie with you. (Ar. Cf. *hitari*, and syn. *hiyari, nathari*.)

Hitilafu, n. also Ihtilafu, (1) difference, something out of the way (unusual, of special interest, critical); (2) defect, blemish. *Shauri lao moja wala hapana h.*, their design is the same and there is no difference. *Aka-*

ona h. kidogo, he noticed a small variation. (3) Difference, discord, variance, quarrel, quarrelsomeness,— of persons. Also of musical sounds. *Hana h.*, there is nothing wrong about him, he does not give trouble, cause discord. — v. be different, make a difference. Sometimes impers. *imehitilafu*, there is a difference. Rp. *hitilafiana*, be different, distinct from each other, e. g. *lugha hizi zimehitilafiana*, these languages (Swahili and Arabic) are quite distinct. (Ar. Cf. *tafauti, mbalimbali, achana.*)

*Hitima, n. a Mahommedan service, or office, in conclusion of some event, i.e. a reading of certain portions of the Coran, esp. (1) a funeral service ; (2) service at a housewarming; (3) a feast given at such a ceremony, e. g. *siku ya tatu hufanya h., yaani hupika wali*, after three days (of mourning, *matanga*) a feast is made, i.e. rice is cooked. *Kusoma h. katika kaburi*, to hold a service at a grave. (Ar. Cf. *hitimu, hatima*, and for other services, *buruda, fatiha.*)

*Hitimu, v. finish, end, come to an end, be completed. Most common in the special sense, 'finish education, complete a course of reading or instruction, end an apprenticeship, become a qualified teacher or workman,' equivalent to 'pass, take a degree, be out of time.' *Mwalimu amehitimisha chuo mtoto, naye mtoto amehitimu*, the teacher has taken his pupil through the whole course of reading, and the pupil has passed. Ap. *hitim-ia, -iwa*. Cs. *hitim-isha, -ishwa*. *Kulihitimisha jambo letu*, to complete our business. (Ar. Cf. *hitima, hatima*, and in general syn. *isha, maliza, timiza, kamilisha.*)

Hivi, a. dem. these,—agreeing with D 3 (P). Also commonly as adv., thus, in this manner, accordingly, so. *Sasa hivi*, at this very moment, immediately, on the spot. *Leo hivi*, this very day. Also *hivile*, for emphasis, i.e. *hivi vile*, those very (things).

Hivyo, a. dem. of reference, those, those yonder. Also adv., in that manner, in the manner described, so. Often *vivyo hivyo*, just so, exactly so. (Cf. *huyo, -vyo.*)

Hiyana, Hiyari. See Hiana, Hiari.

Hiyo, a. dem. of reference, that (those), that (those) yonder,—agreeing with D 2 (P), D 6 (S). (Cf. *huyo, -o.*)

*Hizi, v. disgrace, put to shame, dishonour, insult, inflict punishment on. *Mtoto amemhizi babaye*, the child has disgraced his father. Ps. *hiziwa*. Nt. *hizika*. Ap. *hiz-ia, -iwa*. (Ar. Cf. syn. *aibisha, fethehesha, tahayarisha, tweza.*)

Hizi, a. dem. these,—agreeing with D 4 (P), D 6 (P). *Siku hizi*, some days ago, lately, modern times, nowadays. Also *zizi hizi*, just these, these very. Also *hizile*, for emphasis, i.e. *hizi zile*, those very. *Hizo*, as the form of reference, those, those yonder. (Cf. *huyu, huyo.*)

*Hodari, a. (1) strong, firm, stable, solid ; (2) active, energetic, brave, earnest, strong-willed. Used of strength generally, in substance, construction, character, &c. *Boriti h.*, strong poles. *Ukuta h.*, a solid wall. *Mtu h. wa kazi (wa vita, wa maneno)*, an effective, able mechanic (soldier, orator). (Perh. Hind. Cf. *thabiti*, and syn. B. *-a nguvu, -gumu*. Contr. *thaifu.*)

*Hodi, n. used in Z. invariably and only as a polite inquiry before entering a private house or room, 'May I come in?' and, unless an answer is given,—usually the same word or *karibu*, come in,—good manners forbid entry. (Prob. a word introduced by Arabs from Muscat, meaning 'safety, well-being,' and so equivalent to *wokovu, salamu*. Hence as an interrogative, Is all well? all well? and the answer, 'all well,' by the same word,—or by **karibu**, which see.)

***Hofu**, n. (1) fear, apprehension, awe; (2) cause of fear, danger. *Kuwa na h.*, to be afraid. *Fanya (piga, ona, ingia, ingiwa, patwa na, shikwa na) h.*, be frightened, be seized with fear. Sometimes also adj. *-hofu*, timid, fearful. — v. feel fear, be afraid of. Ps. *hofiwa*. Nt. *hofika*. Ap. *hofia*, fear for (about, in, &c.). Cs. *hof-isha, -ishwa*, terrify, frighten. (Ar. Cf. *afa, mwafa*, and common syn. B. *ogopa, oga, kitisho, uchaji, -cha*.)

***Hogo**, n. (*ma-*), a very large root of cassava. See **Muhogo**.

***Hohe hahe**, n. a solitary, destitute, outcast person or state. Cf. such phrases as *maskini (fukara) hohe hahe*, utterly poor and destitute. *Ni hohe hahe tu*, he is quite forlorn.

***Hoho**. *Pilipili hoho*, red pepper, as dist. from *pilipili manga*, black pepper. *Mkate wa h.*, a cake flavoured with pepper.

***Hoja**, n. also **Huja**, (1) want, need, necessity; (2) what is urgent or pressing, business, concern; (3) urgent request, argument, logical demonstration. *Kwa h. ya*, on account of, for the sake of. *Kwa h. yangu*, at my need, at my earnest request, also, on my account, for my sake. *Hakuna h.*, there is no objection. *Jambo hili lina h. nyingi*, this is a very troublesome affair. *H. ya nguvu*, a powerful argument. *Hatta tuishe h. hii mimi nawe*, let us even wind up this matter together, you and I. (Ar. Cf. *haja*, and follg. Also *hitaji*.)

***Hoji**, v. and **Huji**, give trouble to, apply pressure to, urge, annoy, cross-question, examine, petition, ply with arguments. Sometimes Rd. *hojihoji*. *Amemhoji hatta mtu kusema neno alilo nalo*, he kept on asking, till the man said what he knew. Ps. *hojiwa*. Ap. *hoj-ia, -iwa*. Rp. *hojiana*. (Ar. Cf. *hoja, haja*, and *hitaji*. Also syn. *dadisi, uliza, tafuta, sumbua, lemea*.)

***Homa**, n. fever, esp. of malarial or ague-fever, described as *marathi ya baridi*, or *ya baridi*, or *ya kitapo cha baridi*, i.e. the chilly or shivering sickness. *Shikwa na homa*, have an attack of fever. *Homa ya vipindi*, intermittent fever. (Ar. Cf. *kidinga popo*, dengue fever, *mkunguru*.)

Honga, v. make a payment, not as of debt, but to secure an end, hence bribe, pay toll, pay one's way, pay a footing. *Mhonge ndio mpate kujenga*, give him a present, and so get leave to build. Ap. *hongea*, pay for, secure an end, advance a stage, get past a crisis, be acquitted, get cleared of a charge. Thus fig. of a woman after childbirth. *Leo nimehongea* (or, *hongela*), I was delivered to-day. Also of a stage of recovery after circumcision. Cs. *hong-eza, -ezwa*, (1) cause to pay toll, blackmail; (2) cause (help, allow) to advance a stage, or, to secure an end, e.g. procure acquittal. *Kiapo kinihongeze*, may the ordeal be favourable to me, let me escape. Also of congratulations after some event or crisis, e.g. after a journey, childbirth, &c. *Mtu akisafiri akirudi, huja watu kumhongeza*, when a man returns from a journey, people come to congratulate him. *Akamhongeza mtoto wake kuzaa*, he congratulated his daughter on her safe delivery. (Cf. *hongo*. These words seem little used in Z., being appropriate to mainland usages and ideas. For bribing cf. *rushwa, mhungula, kijiri, upenyezi*, and for congratulation *salimu, pukusa, -pa mkono, tunza, fichua*.)

Hongo, n.* toll, tribute, blackmail,—used of customary presents given to native chiefs for leave to pass through the country. (Cf. *honga*, and for presents generally *bakshishi*.)

*Hori, n. (1) creek, inlet, gulf, arm of the sea. (Ar. Cf. *gubba*.) (2) (*ma-*), a kind of canoe, with raised stem and stern, usually from India, and employed on the creek at Z.

*Horji, n. a thickly padded quilt, used as a saddle for donkeys. (Ar. Cf. *seruji*.)

*Hotuba, n. See Hutuba.

Hu, verb-form, you are not,—Negat. Pfx. combined with Pfx. of 2 Pers. Sing., i.e. *ha-u*, e.g. *hu mrefu*, you are not tall. (Cf. *ha-*, *u*.)

Hu-, (1) verbal pfx. denoting customary or repeated action, without distinction of tense, person, or number. *Huenda*, my (your, his, her, its, our, their) custom (habit, practice, usual plan) is (was, has been, will be, &c.) to go. In narrative often followed by -*ka*-, *hufikia pale uwanjani akalala*, he would arrive in the courtyard and go to sleep. Sometimes cynically, *vita huja*, wars *will* happen. (2) Negat. Pfx. of 2 Pers. Sing., e.g. *huendi*, you do not go. (3) A formative element in several pronominal advs. and adjs. See Huku.

Hua, n. a dove. (Cf. *pugi*, *ninga*, *njiwa*.)

*Hubba, n. affection, desire. See Habba. (Ar.)

*Hubiri, v. give information (to, about), inform, bring news (to, about), announce, report, relate. *Roho yake ikamhubiri kuwa ndiye nunda*, his heart told him that was the wild beast. *H. anjili*, preach the Gospel. Ps. *hubiriwa*. Ap. *hubir-ia, -iwa*. Cs. *hubir-isha, -ishwa*. — n. (*ma-*), that which is related, report, announcement, &c. (Ar. Cf. *habari*, cf. syn. *arifu*, *sumulia*, *eleza*.)

*Huduma, n. also Hudumu, Hidima, service, attendance, waiting on a person, ministration. (Ar. Cf. follg.)

*Hudumu, v. serve, wait (on), attend (on). *Mmhudumu kwa uzuri*, see that you wait on him properly. Ps. *hudumiwa*. Nt. *hudumika*. Ap. *hudum-ia, -iwa*, serve, be in attendance upon, serve for (at, with, &c.). Cs. *hudum-isha, -ishwa*. (Ar. Cf. *huduma*, *mhadimu*, *uhadimu*, and syn. *tumikia*, *ngojea*, *andikia*.)

Huenda, used as adv., sometimes Hwenda, it happens, sometimes, at times, and so 'possibly, perhaps, it may be, there is a chance.' (*Enda* with pfx. *hu-* of customary or repeated action. Cf. syn. *kwenda*, *huwa*, *labuda*, *yamkini*.)

*Hui, v. become alive, revive, rise from the dead. Ps. *huiwa*. Nt. *huika*. *Amehuiwa na Muungu, naye amehuika*, he was restored to life by God, so he revived. Cs. *hui-sha, -shwa*, restore to life, resuscitate, save, keep alive. *Hui* is also used in this act. sense. (Ar. Cf. *hai*, and *fufua*, *amka*, *ishi*.)

*Huja, Huji. See Hoja, Hoji. (But dist. *huja*, and *huji*, as parts of the verb -*ja*, come. See Hu-.)

Hujambo, v. are you well? you are well. The commonest form of salutation in Z. Often *jambo* only. See Jambo.

Huko, adv. dem. of general reference, in that case referred to, with those circumstances in view, in connexion with that environment, but commonly of place and time, 'from (to, at, in, &c.) that place (or, time), there, thither, thence, then, &c.' *H. na h.*, hither and thither, here and there. *H. uendako*, where you are going to, your destination. *H. utokako*, where you come from, your starting-point. *H. nyuma*, (1) yonder in the rear; (2) meanwhile. *Kuko huko*, just yonder, just there, under those precise circumstances. *Huko* is also used to suggest the world beyond, the other world, the world of spirits. (*Huko* includes three formative elements, *hu, ku,* and -*o,* for which see **Huku,** and -**o.** For similar adv. with meanings often hardly distinguishable cf. *humo, hapo, kule, pale.*) — verb-form, you are not there,—Negat. Pfx. of 2 Pers. Sing., with -*ko* (see **Huko,** with which it is sometimes used, e. g. *huko huko,* you are not there).

Huku, (1) adj. dem. this,—agreeing with D 8, e. g. *kufa huku kuzuri,* this (mode of) dying is admirable, or with a locative form in -*ni,* from, to, e. g. *nyumbani huku,* to (from) this house. (2) adv. usually of place, here, near, in this place, but also of environment generally. *H. kuzuri,* it is pleasant here (in our present circumstances). *H. na h.,* this way and that, hither and thither. *Kuku huku,* just here. (*Hu-* is a demonstrative prefix, in *huyu, huu, huku, humu,* and the corresponding forms ending in -*o,* agreeing with D 1 (S), D 2 (S), D 8, and locat. in -*ni,*— the *h* alone being the characteristic demonstrative element throughout, as *l* is of other demonstratives. See also **Ku.**)

Huku-, at the beginning of a verb-form may be (1) *hu* of customary action with *ku,* Pfx. of 2 Pers. Sing. objective, e. g. *hukupenda,* there is a general liking for you; (2) *hu* the Negat. Pfx. of 2 Pers. Sing. with *ku* of general reference, e. g. *hukupendi,* you do not like the place (circumstances); (3) *hu,* Negat. Pfx. as in (2), with *ku,* sign of Negat. Past Tense, e. g. *hukupenda,* you did not like.

*****Hukumu,** v. give an official (or, authoritative) pronouncement (on), judge, decide, pass sentence (on), exercise authority (over), be ruler. Regularly used of the characteristic action of a supreme power, or judge, and hence of other formal decisions, orders, &c. *Alimhukumu auawe,* he ordered him to be put to death, he passed sentence of death upon him. So of other verdicts, *apigwe, afungwe, alipe, auzwe,* &c., or *kupigwa,* &c. Ps. *hukumiwa.* Ap. *hukum-ia, -iwa,* give judgement, &c. on (for, at, &c.). Cs. *hukum-iza, -izwa.* — n. judgement, (1) (in general), jurisdiction, authority, supreme power; (2) legal process, trial; (3) sentence, verdict, decision, order. *Mwenyi hukumu,* the supreme ruler, sovereign. *Peleka hukumuni,* send for trial, cause to be tried in a law court, or before a chief. *Anasikia hukumu yako,* he obeys your order. *Hukumu ya kufa,* capital sentence. (Ar. Cf. *hakimu, hekima,* also syn. *amua,* and for ruling, *tawala, amuru.*)

*****Huluku,** v. create, usually of original creation, by act of God. Ps. *hulukiwa,* be created, be a creature (created being). Ap. *huluk-ia, -iwa.* (Ar. Cf. *mhuluku,* and syn. B. *umba.*)

Humo, (1) adv. dem. of reference to an interior, in that place (referred to), inside yonder, in there. *H. mwetu,* in our house yonder. *Mumo h.,* just in there, in that very place. (2) verb-form, you are not in (there). See **Huko,** and **Hu-, Mo-,** &c.

Humu, (1) adj. dem. this,—agreeing with locative forms in -*ni,* e. g. *nyumbani humu,* in this house. (2) adv. dem. in this place, inside here. *Mumu h.,* just in here, in this very place. See **Huku,** and **Mu-.**

Huna, verb-form, you have not,— Negat. Pfx. of 2 Pers. Sing., and *na* (which see).

*****Hundi,** n. draft, cheque, money order, bill of exchange. (Hind. Cf. *hawala.*)

Huo, a. dem. of reference, that there, that yonder, that referred to,— agreeing with D 2 (S), D 4 (S). See **H-, Huko,** and -**o.**

*****Huru,** n. (*ma-*), and a. (also -*huru*), a freedman, a freeman, free, not a slave, free born, emancipated. *Acha (weka, andika), huru,* set free, emancipate. (Ar. Cf. *uhuru*, and syn. *mngwana*, contr. *mtumwa*. *Huru* in card-playing means diamonds, Str.)

*Huruma, n. (1) sympathy, consideration, fellow-feeling, kindliness; (2) mercy, pity, compassion. *Mwenyi h.*, compassionate, sympathetic, kind. *Kuwa na h.*, to be kind (merciful, &c.). *Fanya h., ona h., ingia* (or, *ingiwa*) *h.*, have kindly feeling. (Cf. follg. and syn. *rehema*, of which *huruma* is perh. a form, by a common Swahili transposition of Arab. consonants. See Rehema.)

*Hurumia, v. Ap. pity, have pity (compassion, sympathy) for, have mercy on. Ps. *hurumiwa*. (Ar. Cf. *huruma*, and syn. *rehemu*.)

*Husu, v. (1) give a share (to), assign as a person's share (right, due, privilege, &c.). Esp. in Ap. *husia*, e.g. *alimhusia kadiri yake*, he assigned him his proper portion. (2) Be assigned as share, be closely (specially, exclusively) concerned with, be the privilege (right, monopoly, peculiar property, quality) of, belong to, be limited to, refer only to, concern, be specially connected with, be confined to. *Ada yetu aliyotuhusu*, the fee which is our special privilege, which specially belongs to us. *Maneno yasiyomhusu*, statements which do not apply to him. *Nduguye aliyemhusu*, his nearest relative. *Neno lililohusu bwana zao*, a peculiar privilege of their masters. Often used also in the Nt. *husika* in this sense. *Ni mhalifu kwa neno lililohusika*, he is rebellious as regards a special duty. *Jina la 'mwenyi thambi' limehusika kwa Mwenyezi Mngu tu*, the word 'sinner' implies special reference to Almighty God. *Neno hili lahusika na watu hawa tu*, this word applies only to these persons. (Ar. Cf. *hisa*.)

*Husudu, v. also Hasidi, envy, grudge, be jealous (of), treat spitefully. *Kumhusudu mali yake*, to grudge him his money. Ps. *husudiwa*. Ap. *husud-ia, -iana*. Cs. *husud-isha, -ishwa*. (Ar. Cf. *hasidi*, and syn. B. *uwivu, kijicho*.)

*Husumu, v. strive, contend. (Arab. Cf. *hasimu*, for common *shindana, teta*, &c.)

*Husuni, n. fortress, fort, castle. (Arab. for common *ngome, gereza, boma*. Dist. *huzuni*.)

*Husuru, v. reduce to straits, oppress, besiege. (Arab. for common *onea*, and for besieging cf. *funga, zunguka, mazingiwa*.)

*Huthuria, v. Ap. be present (at), be placed ready (for), attend a meeting, form an audience. *Enyi watu waliohuthuria*, opening words of a speech, address to an audience, All you who are present. *Mahali pale pakihuthuria chakula*, that place is prepared for food. (Ar. Cf. syn. B. *-wapo*, e.g. *enyi watu mliopo hapa*.)

*Huthurungi, n. a yellowish-brown calico, usually made in Arabia,—a favourite material for men's dress (*kanzu*) in Z. (Ar.)

*Hutuba, n. reading of the Coran, preaching in a mosque, sermon. *Funga h.*, lit. arrange a reading (or, service), and so of a betrothal or marriage service. (Ar. Cf. follg. and *hatibu*.)

*Hutubu, v. read the Coran publicly, preach, give an address. Ap. *hutub-ia, -iwa*, preach to (about, in, for, &c.). (Ar. Cf. prec.)

Huu, a. dem. this—agreeing with D 2 (S), D 4 (S). (Cf. *h-, huko*, and *huyu*.) Sometimes redupl. *huu huu*, this very one, this same.

Huule, a. dem. of emphasis, 'that, that very,' for *huu ule*. (Cf. prec. and *huyule*.)

Huwa, verb-form, it is (was, will be) customary, i.e. *hu* of customary action, and *-wa*, v. be. Commonly used as adv. (1) regularly, commonly, e.g. *killa siku huwa wanakwenda*, every day as a rule they go; (2) perhaps, it may be, possibly, sometimes. (Cf. syn. *labuda, huenda, kwenda*.)

Huyo, a. dem. of reference, that there, that yonder, that referred to,—agreeing with D 1 (S). *Huyo! huyo!* there he is! That is he!—in a hue and cry after a thief, or chase after animals. (Cf. *huyu*, and *-o*.)

Huyu, a. dem. this,—agreeing with D 1 (S). (It includes the characteristic letter *h*, with the variable vowel *u*, and *yu*. See **H** and **Yu**.) Also in the emphatic form *huyule*, for *huyu yule*, that very, that. See **Yule**.

*__Huzuni__, n. grief, sorrow, distress, mourning, calamity, disaster. *-enyi huzuni*, sorrowful, depressed, downcast. So *-a huzuni. Kuwa na h.*, to be sad, to be sorrowful. *Fanya (ona, ingia, shikwa na,* &c.) *h.*, feel sorrow, be distressed, &c. (Ar. Cf. follg. and syn. *hamu, majonsi, sikitiko, msiba*, and for formal mourning, *matanga, maombolezo*.)

*__Huzunia__, v. Ap. grieve at (for, about, in, &c.). Ps. *huzuniwa*, be grieved, be caused grief. Nt. *huzunika*. Cs. *huzun-isha, -ishwa*. (Ar. Cf. prec. and syn. *sikitikia, lilia*.)

I.

I represents the sound of *e* in *be*, and also that of *i* in *in*, i.e. of both vowels in *begin*.

It is often difficult, esp. in unaccented syllables, to decide whether *e* or *i* best represents the sound heard, esp. in words of Arabic origin, in which they are not distinguished, e.g. *elimu* or *ilimu, ela* or *ila, -enye* or *enyi, ekirahi* or *ikirahi, settini* or *sittini*, &c.

An *i* sound before a vowel is generally consonantal, heard and written as *y*.

I best represents the vowel sound of *n*, where there is a tendency to pronounce *n* as a distinct syllable.

Thus the pfx. of the 1 Pers. Sing. is either *n-* or *ni-*, e.g. *ninapenda* or *nnapenda, nitalala* or *ntalala*. The tendency is decidedly commoner in Z. than in the Coast Swahili, e.g. *ingia* not *ngia, ingine* not *ngine, inchi* not *nchi, wingi* not *ungi, inzi* not *nzi*.

Hence words not found under *I* may be looked for under *E*, or *Y*, or *N*.

The numeral *nne*, four, is a dissyllable beginning with a faint *i* sound, represented by a double *n*, and not wholly lost in the adjectival forms of the numeral. *I* has been used as the initial of *imbu*, mosquito, because in this word *m* does not seem to keep its usual affinity for a *u* sound.

The *a* in certain pfxs., chiefly *wa-, ma-,* and *ka-*, when followed by an *i*, as a rule coalesces with it to form an *e* sound, e.g. *waivi* becomes *wevi, maino meno, akaingia akengia* (but not in *pa-, ha-, -ta, -na, -nga*, &c.).

Final *i* always takes the place of final *a* of a verb in the Pres. Indic. Negat.

I, verb-form, is, are,—agreeing with D 2 (P), and D 6 (S).

I- is a Pers. Pfx., subjective and objective, of verbs, agreeing with D 2 (P), and D 6 (S). This pfx. is also often used for general reference, and supplying an impersonal form of the verb, e.g. *haifai*, it is no good, nonsense. *Imekuisha*, all is over.

I- (or **E-**) before the final *a* of a verb forms the characteristic of the so-called *applied* verb-stems, and gives the simple root-meaning of the verb a very varied range of applications usually expressed in English by different prepositions following.

Iba, v. steal, thieve, embezzle, kidnap, purloin, filch, &c. (*Kwiba* is used as the root-form in some tenses. See **Isha**.) Ps. *ibwa*, and *ibiwa*, be stolen. Nt. *ibika*, be stolen, be capable of being stolen. Ap.

ibia, steal from, rob, e. g. *amemwibia mali yake*, he has stolen his money from him,—*ibiwa*, be stolen, be stolen from, lose by theft. Thus *tumeibiwa* may mean 'we have been kidnapped,' or, 'we have been robbed.' *Ibiana*, steal from each other. Cs. *ib-isha, -ishwa*, e. g. cause to steal, incite to theft. (Cf. *uizi, mwizi, mwibaji*, and syn. *nyanganya*.)

*Ibada, n. (1) worship, divine service. *Ameacha i.*, he has left off attending the mosque. *I. ya sanamu*, idolatrous worship. (2) Practical religion, a religious life, religious practices. *Mtu wa i.*, a devout man. *Iblisi akamharibia i. yake*, the devil corrupted his religion. (Ar. Cf. *abudu, maabudu*, and syn. *dini, utawa, usufii*.)

*Iblisi, n. the devil, Satan. (Arab. for usual *shetani*.)

*Idadi, n. reckoning, counting, number, computation. *Billa i.*, without number, numberless. *Desturi za adabu nyingi, hazina i.*, rules of etiquette are numerous, in fact past counting. (Ar. Cf. syn. *hesabu, hasibu*.)

*Idi, Idili. See Ada, Adili.

Ifu-ifu, a. ash-coloured, grey. See Jifu, Kijifu.

Iga, v. (1) imitate, copy, but commonly (2) in the sense, ape, mock, counterfeit, mimic, caricature. *I. maneno ya kiswahili*, try to talk Swahili. *I. kwa maneno*, use mocking expressions to. *Hodari wa kuiga*, a clever mimic. Ps. *igwa*. Nt. *igika*. Ap. *ig-ia, -iwa*. Cs. *ig-iza, -izwa*, and Intens. of copying with effort, trying to imitate. (Cf. *mwigo, mwigaji, thihaka*, and syn. *fuata, fuasa*.)

*Ihtaji, Ihtiari, Ihtilafu, Ihtimu. See under Hitaji, &c.

*Ijara, n. pay, hire, salary, wages, rent. *Mtu wa i.*, a hired servant,—not a slave. (Ar. Cf. *ujira, ajiri*, and syn. *mshahara*, and rent, *kodi*.)

*Ikirihi, n. also Ekerahi. See Kirihi.

Ikiza, v. Cs. lay across, set in position (from side to side), spread over. *I. nyumba boriti*, set up the poles (or rafters) in a house, to carry a concrete floor or roof. Also *i. mawe, i. dari*, of same operation. Also used of cookery, *ikiza na sukari*, spread with sugar, and *kuku ya kuikiza*.

Iko, verb-form, it is (they are) there,—Pfx. agreeing with D 2 (P), D 6 (S), and locative -ko (which see).

*Ila, n. defect, blemish, drawback, disgrace, stain, blot. *Mtu mzuri lakini ana ila*, a good man but he has his faults. Also for conj. illa, which see. (Ar. Cf. syn. *kipunguo, hililafu, kosa, waa*. Dist. *hila*.)

Ile, a. dem. that, those,—agreeing with D 2 (P), D 6 (S). (See I and Yule. Dist. *ile* as 3 S. Subj. from *la*, eat.)

*Iliki, n. cardamom.

*Illa, conj. also Ela, Ila, except, unless, but. *Hana illa mke mmoja*, he has but one wife. *Havai kilemba illa amekwenda Makha*, he does not wear a turban, unless he has been to Mecca. (Ar. Cf. *illakini*.)

*Illakini, conj. but, nevertheless, notwithstanding. (Ar. Cf. *illa*, and *lakini*.)

*Illi, conj. in order that, that. Used with Subj. and Infin. Moods, e. g. *amekwenda mjini illi kununua* (or, *anunue*) *chakula*, he has gone to town to buy food. (Ar. Cf. *kusudi*.)

*Ilmu, n. See Elimu, knowledge, learning, &c. (Ar.)

*Ima, conj. See Ama.

Ima, v. be erect, straight, &c. — a. B. verb, rare in Z. (Cf. *simama, simika, mwima, mwimo, ima-ima*.)

Ima-ima, a. and adv., upright, erect, steep, perpendicular. (Cf. prec.)

*Imamu, n. the minister of a Mahommedan mosque, who conducts the prayers and gives an address on Fridays. (Ar. Cf. *muathini, mwalimu, kathi.*)

*Imani, n. (1) faith, trust, confidence, trustworthiness, uprightness. *Maskini hana i.*, a poor man cannot be relied upon. *Upanga wa i.*, a kind of double-handled sword. (2) Religious faith, belief, object of belief, creed. *Imani kwa Muungu*, faith towards God. (Ar. Cf. *amini, amani, amana*, &c., and for creed, *shahada.*)

*Imara, n. firmness, compactness, hardness, strength, stability, solidity, —material and moral. *Ukuta huu hauna i.*, this wall is not strong. *Mtu wa i.*, a resolute, brave, strong-willed man. — a. firm, strong, hard, unbreakable, solid, courageous, brave. (Cf. follg. and syn. *-gumu, thabiti, hodari.*)

*Imarika, v. Nt., be strong, be firm, be solid, &c. Cs. *imar-isha, -ishwa.* See prec.

Imba, v. sing, sing of. Ps. *imbwa.* Nt. *imbika.* Ap. *imb-ia, -iwa, -iana.* Cs. *imb-isha, -ishwa,* cause to sing, instruct in singing, lead in singing, strike up a song. (Cf. *uimbo, uimbaji,* &c.)

Imbu, n. a mosquito. (Also written *mbu*, but in this word *m* does not appear to have its usual affinity for a *u* sound, though sounded as a distinct syllable.)

Ina, verb-form, it has, they have,— Pfx. agreeing with D 2 (P), D 6 (S), and na, which see.

Inama, v. stoop, bend down, let down, lower, bow, slope, decline, sink, depress. Used Neut. and Act. *Ukuta huu umeinama*, this wall has sunk, or, slopes downwards. *Inama kichwa*, bow the head. *Mji wote umejiinama*, the whole city is depressed. Ap. *inam-ia, -iwa,* bow to, incline towards, be directed to, depend on. *Nyumba hii imeniinamia*, this whole house rests on me. Cs. *inam-isha, -ishwa.* (St. form of a root *ina*, cf. *inika, inua*, and cf. syn. *shusha, tua.*)

Inchi, n. (1) country, district, land, region. *I. yetu, inchi ya kwetu*, our country, fatherland. *I. za barra*, the regions of the continent. *I. za Ulaya*, the countries of Europe. (Cf. *ulaya, wilaya, upande.*) (2) Land, ground, dry land, i.e. *i. kavu*, as opp. to the sea, *bahari. Piga katika i.* (or *chini*), throw to the ground, dash down. *Chini ya i., ndani ya i.*, underground. *I. sawa*, level country, a plain. (Cf. *barra.*) (3) The earth, the inhabited world. *Pembe za i.*, the corners of the earth, i.e. remotest parts of the world. (Cf. *dunia, ulimwengu.*) (Cf. *chini.* Never of the actual substance or materials of the ground, i.e. soil, earth, which is *udongo.* Cf. *arthi.* Obs. *inchi* is sometimes heard for English 'inch,' as *futi* for a 'foot,' by measure.)

Inda, Inga. See Winda.

*Ingereza, n. and a., also Ingreza, Ingrezi, -ngereza, an Englishman, England, English. *Mfalme I.*, the king of England. *Barozi I.*, the British Consul. *Ulaya Ingereza, Uingeza, Ingreza*, England. *Wa-ngereza*, the English. *Kiingereza*, the English language. *Unaweza kusema kiingereza?* Can you speak English?

-ingi, a. sometimes -ngi (*nyingi* with D 4 (P), D 6 (P), *chingi* with D 3 (S), *jingi* with D 5 (S), *wengi* with D 1 (P), *pengi* with D 7)), many, much, large (in quantity), plentiful, abundant. Of persons, *-ingi* is used with *wa*, i.e. bountiful in respect of, giving (having, enjoying) in abundance. *Mwingi wa baraka*, giving many blessings. (Cf. *wingi,* and syn. *tele, marithawa.*)

Ingia, v. sometimes Ngia, (1) go in (to), come in (to), enter, get in, fall in; (2) share in, take part in, engage in; (3) penetrate, pass into (a condition, state, &c.); (4) be imported. E.g. *i. nyumbani* (or *nyumba*, or *katika nyumba*), go into a house. *I. chomboni*, go on board a vessel, embark (also *panda chomboni*). *I. safarini*, join an expedition, or, start on a journey. *I. baridi*, become cold. *I. kutu*, get rusty. Esp. common of the feelings, e.g. *i. hofu*, be affected by fear, feel fear, be alarmed, and so with *kiburi, furaha, hasira, hazuni, uchungu*, &c. The passive construction is common in same sense, *ingiwa na*, or *ingiwa*. Ps. *ingiwa*. Nt. *ingika*. Ap. *ing-ilia, -iliwa, -ilika, -iliza, -ilizwa, -iana, -ilizana*, esp. of entry with a purpose, e.g. go in for, pry into, &c. *Alimwingilia mwanamke*, he went in to see the woman,—hence live with, cohabit with. *Ingiliza kazini*, introduce to work, instal in office. *Waingiliani maneno haya?* What are you prying into these matters for? Cs. *ing-iza, -izwa, -isha, -ishwa*,—the latter forms being usu. intensive, i.e. *ingiza*, of causing, allowing, procuring entry, *ingisha*, of special effort or force in entry. *Vitu viingizwavyo*, imports. Hence *ingizana*. Rp. *ingiana*. (Cf. *enda ndani, -ja ndani, penya*.)

-ingine, a. (but with some pfxs. commonly *-ngine*. Thus with D 1 (S), D 2 (S), D 4 (S) *mwingine* or *mngine*, with D 1 (P) *wangine*, with D 4 (P), D 6 *nyingine* or *ngine* or *zingine*, with D 5 (S) *jingine* or *lingine*, with D 5 (P) *mangine*, with D 7 *pangine*, with D 8 *kwingine*), other, another, different, some, a second. *Wangine—wangine*, some—some, some—others. *-ingine-ingine*, of different kinds, assorted, miscellaneous, of all sorts. *Vingine*, as adv. variously, in another way. *Vingine-vingine*, in different ways (degrees, classes, sorts), in all sorts of ways. *Vinginevyo*, in some other way, in any other way, and so with relative affixed to other forms, e.g. *mtu mwingineo*, some other person, any one else.

Ini, n. (*ma-*), the liver. Sometimes fig. of inmost seat of feelings, like *moyo*, e.g. *maneno yale yalimkata maini*, those words cut him to the heart.

Inika, v. (1) give a downward direction to, lay over on one side, give a cant (tilt, downward bend or turn) to, let hang down, turn down at the edge, &c.; (2) fig. humble, bring low, depress. *I. chombo*, careen a vessel (for repairs). *Usiuinike mzigo*, do not let your load hang down. *I. kichwa, jiinika*, hang down the head (in grief or shame). Also *jiinika*, make a bow, bow oneself gracefully. *I. mti*, bend down a tree (to get at the fruit). *Nani awezaye kumwinika mfalme?* Who can humiliate a king? Ps. *inikwa*. Ap. *inik-ia, -iwa*. Cs. *inik-isha, -ishwa, -iza*, e.g. *mwalimu ameinikiza watu kwa kusali*, the minister taught the congregation to bow down at prayers. (Cf. *inama, inua*, and syn. *laza, laza upande*.)

*Inshallah, adv. Used as the commonest and most trivial form of assent, 'oh yes, certainly, of course.' (Ar. = if God wills, God willing. See **Allah**. Cf. syn. *vema, naam, ndio*.)

Inua, v. (1) set up, raise up, build up, pile up, lift up, raise, hoist; (2) fig. inspirit, cheer, restore, cure, set up. *I. mzigo*, raise a load (cf. *twika*). *I. mtoto*, lift up a child. *I. macho*, raise the eyes. *I. mgonjwa*, restore an invalid. Ps. *inuliwa*. Nt. *inuka*, e.g. *inchi yote imeinuka*, the whole country is elevated, is a table-land. Ap. *inu-lia, -liwa*. Cs. *inu-liza, -lizwa*, e.g. *inuliza mzigo*, help a man up with his load. (Cf. *inama, inika*, and syn. *pandisha, kweza*.)

Inzi, n. (*ma-*), a fly,—in general, the common house-fly.

Ipi, a. interr. which? what?—agreeing with D 2 (P), D 6 (S). See -pi. Also generally, *kama ipi?* of what sort? how? (Cf. *-pi, wapi*.)

Ipua, v. same as **Epua**, which

see. But this form seems in some degree specialized, as meaning 'take off the fire' (a cooking pot, &c.). Cf. *tweka* and *twika*.

*Irabu, n. a vowel sign in writing Arabic. (Arab.)

*Iriba, n. usury, money-lending. See Riba. (Ar.)

*Iriwa, n. also Chiriwa, Jiriwa, a (screw) vice.

*Isa, n. a proper name, not uncommon in Z. Also the only name for Jesus Christ known to Mahommedans,—often with the addition *bin Maryamu*.

Isha, v. end, come to an end, bring to an end, make an end of, finish, close, complete. (The infinitive form *kwisha* is frequently used after some tense pfxs. of the indic. mood, esp. *na*, *ta*, *me*, and after the relative in a verb-form, e.g. *amekwisha*, *alipokwisha*. On the other hand, the initial *i* of the root often coalesces with preceding *a* in other pfxs. and forms the usual *e* sound, e.g. *wakesha* for *wakaisha*, they finished, and with a preceding *i* is often hardly heard, as in *pumzi limenisha*, my breath has come to an end, and *akisha*, upon his finishing. It is preserved, however, after *li*, e.g. *aliisha*, not *alisha*. For similar use of the infin. form cf. *ita*, *iva*, *iba*, *oga*, *uza*.) *Maneno yamekwisha*, the debate has come to an end. *Akala akesha akaenda zake*, he ate and when he had done he went away. *Akapigana nao akawaisha*, he fought with them and killed them all. *Kwisha kazi*, to finish a job. *Isha* is constantly used as a semi-auxiliary of time, expressing completion more emphatically than the tense pfx. *me*. Thus used it is commonly followed by the root-form of the principal verb, without the Infinitive pfx. *ku*. *Amekwisha fanya*, he has already done it, he has completed it. *Alipokwisha kuja*, when he had actually arrived. *-a kwisha*, last, extreme, worst. Ps. *ishwa*. Nt. *ishika*. *Nimeishwa na fetha*, my money has come to an end. *Haiishiki*, it cannot be completed. Ap. *ish-ia*, *-iwa*. *Mke wangu ameniishia mali*, my wife has used up my money. *Nimeishiwa wali*, my dish of rice has come to an end. *Ngoje nikuishie maneno*, wait till I finish my message to you. Also a further Ap. form *ish-ilia*, *-iliwa*, *-iliza*, *-ilizwa*, marking completion for some special purpose or of a particular kind. *Wakaishiliza mwezi*, they waited for the month to come to an end. So of *mwaka*, *kazi*, *maneno*, when there is a particular object in view. (Cf. *ingilia*, *toshelea*, *pigilia*, &c.) Cs. *ishiza*, *ishisha* (seldom heard). (Cf. *mwisho*, and syn. *maliza*, *timiza*, *kamilisha*, *komesha*. Dist. *ishi*, in some forms identical, e.g. *haishi*.)

*Isha, n. See Esha.

*Ishara, n. sign, token, signal, mark, omen, indication, warning, hint, crucial case, remarkable fact, a wonder. *Tumeona i. mwaka huu*, we have seen a wonderful thing this year. *Tia i.*, put a mark on. *Toa i.*, make a signal. (Ar. Cf. *ashiria*, and syn. *dalili*, *alama*.)

*Ishi, v. last, endure, continue, live, remain. *Aishi milele*, may he live for ever. *Mti huu hauishi sana*, this wood does not last long. (Ar. Cf. *aushi*, *maisha*.)

Isivyo, verb-form, used as a general Negat. Conj., as (in a way that) is not,—corresponding to adverbial use of forms in *vi*, *vyo* (*hivi*, *vile*, *vivyo*, &c.).

*Islamu, n. (1) (*wa-* and *ma-*), a Mahommedan; (2) the Mahommedan religion, Islam. *Kiislamu*, (of the) Mahommedan (kind). (Cf. *Mwaslimu*, *Mwislamu*, *Msilimu*, also *salamu*, *salimu*, &c.) Also *-islamu*, a. Mahommedan.

*Istiska, n. dropsy. (Ar. Cf. syn. *safura*.)

Ita, v. call, call to, summon, invite, name. (For use of *kwita* &c. in some forms see notes on **Isha**.) *Amekwenda kumwita*, he has gone to call him. Ps. *itwa*. *Unakwitwa*, you are summoned, somebody wants you. *Amekwenda kwitwa*, some one has gone to call him. Nt. *itika*, be called, obey a summons, answer to a call, respond, acknowledge a salute, reply. *Alikwitwa akaitika*, he was called, and replied. *Nyote mwaitika Vuga*, you all accept the supremacy of Vuga. *Itika rathi*, give a favourable reply, assent. Hence *itik-ia, -iwa*, answer for, reply to, correspond to, and in music accompany, follow the lead of, chime in, and fig. correspond to, harmonize with, suit, agree with. *Itikiza*, cause to reply, teach harmony to, also Intens., assent to, give a reply. *Itikizana*, reply to each other, all shout together in response, acclaim, correspond, harmonize, sing (play) in harmony. Ap. *it-ia, -iwa*, call to, summon for (by, in, &c.). *Akataaye kuitwa, hukataa aitiwalo*, he who rejects a call, rejects what he is called for. Cs. *it-isha, -ishwa* (seldom used). Rp. *itana*. (Cf. *mwito*, and syn. *alika*. Also *laja*, name, mention by name.)

*Ita, v. cast in a mould (Str.). (? *Wita*. Cf. Ar. *subu*, and *kiwita*.)

*Italassi, n. satin. (Arab.)

*Ithini, v. sanction, allow, authorize, assent to. Ps. *ithiniwa*. Nt. *ithinika*. Ap. *ithin-ia, -iwa*. Cs. *ithin-isha, -ishwa*. — n. sanction, permission, authorization, leave. *Akataka i. ya hupanda juu*, he asked for leave to go upstairs. *Toa i.*, sanction, authorize. (Ar. Cf. syn. *ruhusu, ruksa, kubali, rithia, sahihisha*.)

Iva, v. also Wiva, (1) become ripe, get ripe, mature, become cooked (done, fit to eat), come to a head; (2) fig. come to a point, be ready for action (or, execution), be fully prepared. *Embe zinaiva*, the mangoes are ripening. *Nyama imeiva*, the meat is cooked. Ap. *ivia*. Cs. *iv-isha, -ishwa*. (Cf. *-bivu, -pevu*, and *tayari*.)

-ivu, a. also -wivu, jealous, envious. (Cf. *uwivu*, and *hasidi*. N. *-ivu* sometimes for *-bivu*, ripe, and dist. *ifu-ifu*.)

Iwapo, verb-form, when (where) it is, when (where) they are,—Pfx. *i-* agreeing with D 6 (S) and D 2 (P), *-wa*, from the verb *kuwa*, and relative *-po*, of place, time, or condition generally. Used as a conj. when, if, in case, supposing, even if, although. *Iwapo una akili, ukae*, if you have sense, wait. See -wa, v., and po.

Izara, n. slander, disparagement, backbiting. (Ar. Cf. *aziri*, for common *masingizio*, &c.)

J.

J represents (1) in words of Arabic origin the same sound as *j* in *jar*. As in different Arabic dialects, *J* and *G* are sometimes interchanged (cf. *ginsi, jinsi*). (2) In words of Bantu origin, a very similar sound in Zanzibar, which elsewhere may be better represented by *dy* (cf. *ch* for *ty*, and *t* at Mombasa), and is used for *d, y,* and *z*, in some words common in neighbouring dialects, and so partially current in Zanzibar.

The sound of *J* is often practically indistinguishable from that of *Ch*.

Hence words not found under *J* may be looked for under *Ch*, or *G*.

J-, for ji-, in nouns and adjectives, before roots beginning with a vowel. See Ji-.

Ja, v. (1) come; (2) of events, happen, turn out, result. As in other monosyllabic verb-roots the Infinitive form *kuja* is used as the root form in some tenses (see **Ku**-), and *yu* is commonly prefixed to 3 Pers. Sing. of Pres. Indic., i. e. *yuaja* for *aja*. The Imperative in this verb only is irregular, viz. *njoo, njooni*, for 2 Pers. Sing. and Plur. *Alikuja nyumbani*, he came to the house. *Naja kwako na barua hii*, I approach you with this letter. *Umekuja kushtakiwa*, some one has come to accuse you. *Atakuja kuuawa*, he will come to be killed, he will some day be killed. Ap. *jia, jiwa, jika, jiana*, come to (for, about, at, in, &c.). *Maneno tuliyojia kwako ni hayo*, that is the errand on which we came to you. *Siku uliyojia*, the day on which you came. *Mgeni amenijia leo*, a visitor has come to me to-day. The passive is used by itself of receiving visits, e. g. *nimejiwa*, I have had a visitor, I have a friend with me. *Jika*, be approachable, be accessible. *Mji huu haujiki*, this town is not to be entered. Rd. *jiajia*, and ? *jajia*, of repeated or troublesome arrivals. *Wananijiajia tu*, they keep on bothering me with visits. Also Rf. *jijia*, e. g. *nikawa kujijia zangu hatta chini*, and I just fell anyhow (helplessly) to the bottom. See Ji-. Hence a further Ap. *jilia, jiliwa, jiliana, jiliza*, come to (at, for, &c.) with a special purpose, in a special way. Cs. not in use. *Ja* (like *isha*, and *toa*) is occasionally used as a semi-auxiliary followed by a verb in its root-form, e. g. *amekuja twaa*, he has come to taking, he actually takes (or, has taken). *Atakuja ua watu*, he will come to killing people, he will positively commit murder. And it regularly furnishes the formative element *ja* in three forms of the Swahili verb-system, viz. (*a*) in the Deferred Tense, with a Negative Prefix preceding, e. g. *hajaja*, he has not yet come, and (*b*) in its Subjunctive form, e. g. *asijelala*, without his yet lying down. Obs. also *ja* for *je* sometimes in the latter case, e. g. *asijalala* for *asijelala*, *asijawa* for *asijekuwa* (cf. *nge-, nga-*). Also *ja* is traceable without a negative preceding, e. g. *ujaonapi?* where have you yet seen?

Also there is a semi-auxiliary use of *-sija, -sije*, e. g. *wasije kuthurika*, lest they come to be hurt. *Asije kuja mtu mwingine akatuthuru*, lest another man chance to come and hurt us. (*c*) In the 'tense of Possible Condition' (Str.), i. e. with the relative *-po*, of time, place, or condition, e. g. *nijapolala, siwezi kugeuka*, even if I lie down, I cannot turn over. *Wajapo kuja*, even if they come. *Wajapo hawaji*, though they do not come. And n. *ijapo*, and even *japo*, used as conjunctions simple, even if, supposing that, although. (Cf. *njia, ujia, majilio*, of arriving, *fika, wasili*, and contr. *enda*, go. *Ja* appears to be one of the few roots occurring very widely in Bantu from Uganda to Zululand, *and also in Arabic.*)

Jaa, v. (1) become full (of); (2) fill up a given space, be plentiful, abound, swarm. Used of any vessel or space, and of its contents. *Mtungi umejaa maji*, the pitcher is full of water. *Maji yamejaa mtungini*, the water fills the pitcher. *Inchi imejaa miti*, the country abounds in trees. *Nzige walijaa kotekote*, locusts swarmed everywhere. *Maji ya kujaa (ya kupwa)*, high (low) tide. Ps. *jawa*, be filled, be full, like Act. but esp. of what are not the natural, suitable, usual contents. *Jawa na hofu (wazimu, kiburi)*, be filled with fear (frenzy, conceit). Ap. *ja-lia, -liwa*, be full up to, *jalia hatta juu* (not usual; dist. *jalia* from *jali*). *Jaliza, -lizwa, -lizia, -liziwa*, fill up, cause to fill (or, be filled), make quite full. Cs. *jaza, jazwa*, make full, fill (the ordinary process, *jaliza* indicating a step further, a more complete (or additional) filling). (Cf. *ujalifu, ujazi*.)

*****Jaa**, n. rubbish heap, dunghill, place where dust and refuse are thrown. *Mkuu ni jaa*, ? a great man is a dust heap. (Ar.)

*****Jaa**, n. the north, i.e. point of the compass (Arab.). (The northward direction is in Z. *kaskazini, kibla*.)

***Jabali**, n. (*ma-*), (1) a rock, hill, cliff, mountain; (2) rock (as a substance), stone; (3) raised line of needlework across the back in a native dress, *kanzu*. (Ar. Cf. *mwamba, mlima, jiwe*.)

***Jabari**, n. Supreme Ruler, Mahommedan title of God. (Arab.)

***Jadiliana**, v. Rp. argue together, reason with each other. (Ar. Cf. syn. *hujiana, bishana, semezana*.)

***Jaha**, n. honour, glory, prosperity. *Mtu alioshushiwa j.*, a man who was granted good fortune. *Kilango cha j.*, the Gate of Paradise. (Ar.)

***Jahazi**, n. ship, vessel,—of any description. (Ar. Cf. *chombo, merikebu*.)

***Jahili**, a. reckless, foolish, rash, precipitate, unthinking. (Arab. Cf. *mjinga*.)

***Jalada**, n. and **Jelada**, (1) cover of a book, binding; (2) whip. (Arab. leather. Cf. *mjeledi, jelidi*.)

***Jali**, v. give honour to, heed, respect, reverence. (Ar. Cf. syn. *heshimu, sikia, hofu*.)

***Jalia**, v. Ap. grant (to), give power (opportunity) to, enable, be gracious (to), esp. of God's favour and help. *Muungu akinijalia*, if God helps me, God willing. Ps. *jaliwa. Ntakwenda nikijaliwa*, I will go, if I can (if I am allowed, if all is well, God willing). *Lijaliwalo kuwa, halina uzuio*, what is allowed to happen, there is no preventing. (Ar. Cf. *sayidia, bariki, wezesha*. Dist. *jalia* from *jaa*, v.)

***Jaluba**, n. small ornamental box of metal. (Ar. ? Turkish. Cf. *kijaluba*.)

***Jamaa**, n. a number of persons gathered or connected together, family, society, company, assembly, gathering, meeting. *Mtu wa j.*, member of a family, kinsman. *Enyi j. waliohuthuria hapa* (on addressing an audience), my friends here present. Also of a single person, one of a family, friend. *Huyu ni j.*, this person is a connexion (friend) of mine. — v. See **Jamii**. (Ar. Cf. *jamii, juma*, and syn. *ndugu, mkutano*.)

***Jamala**, n. courtesy, good manners, elegance, grace, gracious (kind, obliging) behaviour. *J. yako haikupotei*, you will not lose by your kindness. (Ar. Cf. syn. *adabu, madaha, fathili*.)

***Jamanda**, n. (*ma-*), a round basket of plaited grass, usually with a cover. Used as a blinker for camels, hence *macho yangu yametiwa majemanda, kama ngamia*, my eyes have got blinkers like a camel. (Cf. *kijamanda, kidoto*, and for baskets generally *kikapo*.)

Jamani, a. also **Jaman, Jerman**, German. See **Dachi**, which is more usual.

Jamba, v. break wind with noise. — n. (*ma-*), breaking wind. (Cf. *shuta, shuzi*.)

***Jambia**, n. also **Jamvia**, a curved broad-bladed dagger, worn in the belt by Arabs, often highly ornamented. *J. lameta kumoja*, the dagger is bright on one side. *J. kiunoni na bakora mkononi*, dagger at waist and stick in hand.

Jambo, n. (*mambo*), (1) matter, affair, circumstance, business, thing (never of a concrete kind, which is *kitu*); (2) matter of importance, difficulty, trouble; (3) for *sijambo, hujambo*, see below. *J. hili gumu sana*, this matter is a very difficult one. *Amenitenda killa j. la wema*, he has treated me with every possible kindness. *Mambo ya serkali*, political (public, official) affairs. *Ulimwengu una mambo*, the world is full of troubles. *Jambo* (sometimes *yambo*) is the commonest form of greeting for all classes in Z. 'How do you do?' and also the commonest form of reply, 'I am quite well.' *Jambo* thus used represents in the greeting *hu jambo* (or strictly *huna jambo*, though this is never heard), and *hujambo* is the more correct and respectful form, spoken interrogatively, i. e. You have nothing the matter with you? Nothing the matter? You are well? Similarly in the reply, *jambo* is for the more correct *sijambo*, i. e. *sina jambo*, I have nothing the matter, I am quite well. *Jambo* with the Negat. Pfx. of the Pres. Tense is used as a verb, with the special sense of being well or improving in health or general condition, both of persons and things, e. g. *sijambo*, I am well, I am better, matters are improving with me. *Inchi yote sasa haijambo*, the whole country is now in a good state. *Haijambo*, it (the weather) is fine. Cf. the corresponding use of the Negat. Pres. of *weza*, i. e. *siwezi*, *huwezi*, &c., I am ill. Sometimes *jambo* is thus used with other tense pfxs., e. g. *umemtoa nyoka, hukujambo lolote*, you got the snake out, but you were none the better for it. *Hajambo*, like *hawezi*, is sometimes used adjectivally, e. g. *nikapata hajambo*, I got well. *Tukawa sote hajambo*, and we were all getting on well. (Cf. *amba*, orig. speak, *ji-ambo*, *jambo*, a subject of speech, thing talked of, affair. Cf. *neno*, word, matter, thing. Contr. *kitu*, a concrete thing, substance.)

*Jamdani, n. white brocade. (Hind. See Nguo.)

*Jamii, v. (1) collect together, but commonly Cs. *jami-isha, -ishwa*, in same sense; (2) copulate. — n. and Jamia, a collection of objects, group, company, number, mass, body, total, sum. *J. ya watoto*, a lot of children. *J. ya mali*, the whole of a sum of money. *J. ya makathi*, bench of judges. *J. ya watu*, the mass of men, most people, the public. *J. ya maneno*, the words taken together, the whole sentence, context. Also as adv., in a mass, collectively, as a whole, all together. *Wote jamii*, all the lot, the whole lot. (Ar. Cf. *jamaa, juma*, and syn. *kusanya*.)

Jamvi, n. (*ma-*), a piece of floor-matting, of the common coarse kind, made of plaited strips of leaf, used in houses, mosques, shops, &c. *J. la kutandika chini nyumbani*, matting to spread on the floor in houses. (Cf. *mkeka, msala*.)

*Jamvia, n. See Jambia.

Jana, n. and adv., yesterday, day before the present, period preceding the present. *Siku ya jana*, yesterday. *Mwaka wa jana*, last year. (Cf. *juzi, leo*, &c.)

Jana, n. (*ma-*), (1) a fine, large child, e. g. *jana dume*, a very fine boy. (Cf. *mwana*.) (2) A youth, lad (cf. the common *kijana* in same sense). (3) Grub, larva, young (of an insect). *Majana ya nyuki*, bees in the grub stage (cf. *buu*). *Hamna asili, twajitafunia majana*, there is no honey (in the comb), we are just munching grubs. (From same root as mwana, which see.)

*Janaba, n. pollution, defilement, esp. ceremonial, according to Mahommedan rule. (Ar. Cf. *unajisi, ujusi, uchafu*.)

Jangwa, n. (*ma-*), desert, wilderness, waste, barren ground, bare (desolate) country. (For *ji-angwa* cf. *wangwa*, and syn. *nyika, poli, pululu*.)

Jani, n. (*ma-*), leaf, blade of grass. *Majani*, leaves, grass, herbage of any kind, green vegetables. *Rangi ya majani*, green,—as a colour. Dim. *kijani*.

Japo, conj. also Ijapo, even if, although. For *japo* as a tense sign, and auxiliary, see -ja. (Cf. syn. *iwapo, kwamba*.)

*Jarari, n. or Jerari, halliard,—a rope running through a pulley (*abedari*) on deck, and another (*gofia*) attached to the thicker rope (*henza*), by which the mainyard and sail of a native vessel are hoisted. See Tanga, and Kamba.

*Jaribu, v. (1) experience, make trial of, attempt, try, test, prove,— only incidentally with any idea of trying, in the sense of ' do one's best,' 'make an earnest endeavour' (for which see *jitahidi, kaza, fanya, bidii, shika*); (2) in moral sense, test, tempt. *Akajaribu kuutikisa mti*, he tried shaking the tree. *J. safari*, attempt a journey. *J. upanga*, make trial of a sword. Ps. *jaribiwa*. Nt. *jaribika*, be liable (open) to test (or, temptation). Ap. *jarib-ia, -iwa, -iana*, make an attempt on, have a try at (for, with, in, &c.) Cs. *jarib-isha*. — n. (*ma-*), (1) trial, proof, test, attempt; (2) that which tries (tests, proves the nature or mettle), a trial, trouble, difficulty. (Ar. Cf. syn. *onja, angalia, tazamia*.)

Jarifa, n. (*ma-*), drag-net, seine,— of European make. (Cf. *juya, kimia, wavu*.)

Jasho, n. (1) sweat, perspiration; (2) high temperature, sultriness, heat,—causing perspiration. *Hakulaliki nyumbani kwa j.*, it is too hot to sleep indoors. *Fanya (toka) j.*, perspire, sweat. (Cf. *hari, moto, mvuke*.)

*Jasi, n. (1) a kind of soft friable stone (chalk, gypsum, pumice) rubbed on the fingers when plaiting mats. (Ar. Cf. *chaki*.) (2) (*ma-*), ornament worn in the lower lobe of the ear, often a round silver plate. (Cf. *kipuli, kipini*, and for ornaments, *urembo*.)

*Jasiri, v. be bold, dare, venture, risk, make a brave (foolhardy, venturesome) effort. *Amejasiri njia peke yake*, he risked travelling alone. Ps. *jasiriwa*. Nt. *jasirika*. Ap. *jasiria*, venture on, make a try at. Cs. *jasir-isha, -ishwa*, and Intens. — a. brave, venturesome, foolhardy. (Ar. Cf. *ujasiri*, and syn. *thubutu, -gumu, shujaa, jahili*.)

Jawa, v. Ps. of Jaa, v., which see.

*Jawabu, n. (*ma-*), (1) answer, reply, cf. *jibu*; (2) affair, matter, concern, cf. *jambo*. *J. liwe lote*, be the matter what it may. *Amefanya j. kuu*, he has done a great thing. *J. la kesho huandaa leo*, the business of to-morrow one gets ready for to-day.

*Jaza, v. and Jazi, reward, make a present to, grant favour to, give maintenance (to), supply (to), requite, punish. *Muungu amemjaza mengi*, God has been bountiful to him. Ap. *jaz-ia, -iwa, -izilia, -iziliwa*. (Ar. Cf. *tuza, lipa, -pa thawabu*, &c.) — n. (*ma-*) and *jazi, jazo*, gift, reward. (Ar. Cf. *bakshishi, zawadi*.)

*Jaza, n. Cs. of Jaa, which see.

*Jazi, a. sufficient, plentiful, common. *Kitu hiki ni j. mjini*, this article is common in the town. *Vyombo vi j.*, the vessels are numerous. (Ar. Cf. syn. *-ingi, tele, marithawa*, &c.) — n. also Juza, which see, and Jazo.

Je, interr. particle, How? Well? What now? Answer me! Tell me! *Je, bwana, hujambo?* Well, sir, how are you? *Je? ni halali?* Tell me, is it lawful? Often affixed to verbs. *Amejibuje?* How did he answer? What is his reply? *Kumekuwaje huko?* How did matters go there? What happened? *Nifanyeje?* How am I to act? What shall I do? (Cf. *nini, ginsi gani*.)

*Jebu, n. (*ma-*), an ornament worn by women hanging under the chin, often from the veil. (Cf. *urembo*.)

Jego, n. See Chego.

*Jelidi, v. bind,—a book, esp. with leather. Ps. *jelidiwa*. (Ar. Cf. *jalada, mjeledi*.)

Jema, a. form of -ema, good (which see), agreeing with D 5 (S).

*Jemadari, n. (*ma-*), commanding officer (of soldiers), general. (? Hind. Cf. *amiri, afsa*.)

Jembe, n. (*ma-*), hoe, of native make, the common instrument of cultivation,—a flat pear-shaped piece of hammered iron with a spike (*msuka*) passing through, and fixing it to, a short stout wooden handle (*kipini*). *J. la kizungu*, a spade. *Piga j.*, hoe, use a hoe (or, strike with a hoe). Dim. *kijembe*. (Cf. *wembe*.)

*Jeneza, n. a bier, i. e. *kitanda cha kuchukulia mtu aliyekufa*, a bedstead for carrying a dead person (to the grave). It has handles and a frame to support a covering. Or an ordinary *kitanda* is used, turned upside down. (Ar. Cf. *machela, tusi*.)

Jenga, v. construct, build—a house in the native way, of poles, sticks, mud, grass, &c., not of masonry (see Aka, Uashi), but also extended to building in general. *J. nyumba ya miti na udongo*, build a house of poles and clay. Also *j. merikebu*, build a ship (but this is more usually *unda*). Ps. *jengwa*. Nt. *jengeka*. Ap. *jeng-ea, -ewa*, build for (with, in addition to, at, &c.). *Nyumba hii imejengewa*, this house has been added to, enlarged. Cs. *jeng-esha, -eshwa*, cause to build, have built. (Cf. *jengo, mjengo, jenzi, mjenzi, njenzi*, also *aka, unda*.)

Jengo, n. (*ma-*), a building, a building operation, material for building, a house, shed, enclosure. *Toa j.*, design, draw, make a plan of a building. *J. la mawe na chokaa*, a structure of stones and mortar. *Majengo*, building materials. (Cf. *jenga*.)

Jengua, v. Rv. of *Jenga*, take a building to pieces, demolish, pull down. (Cf. *jenga*, and the more usual syn. *bomoa, vunja*.)

Jenzi, n. (*ma*), building, mode of building. *Ndio majenzi yao Wadoe*, that is the way the Doe tribe builds. (Cf. *jenga, mjenzi*.)

*Jeraha, n. (—, and *ma-*), a wound, a sore, ulcer. Dim. *kijeraha*. *Tia j.*, wound. *Pata j.*, be wounded. (Ar. Cf. follg.)

*Jeruhi, v. be wounded. (Ar. Cf. *jeraha, majeruhi*.)

*Jeshi, n. (*ma-*), a great company, assemblage, host, troop, army. *J. la asikari*, an army,—usually a larger body than *kikosi*, or *kundi*. *Fanya (changa, kusanya) j.*, muster (levy, enrol) an army.

*Jesila, n. See Jizla.

Jetea, v. rely on, trust to, be confident in, be puffed up by. *Jetea ulimwengu*, rest the hopes on this world, of a worldly person (*mlimwengu*). Rf. *jijetea*, be self-confident, be self-reliant, be arrogant. *Mwanamke huyu anajetea ujana wake*, this woman relies on her youthfulness, as her stock-in-trade. (Cf. *tegemea, egemea, tumaini, jivuna*.)

*Jethamu, n. a kind of leprosy, or elephantiasis. (Arab.)

*Jeuri, n. violence, outrage, brutality, assault, injustice, oppression. *Mwenyi j.*, a tyrant, oppressor, ruffian. *Fanya (piga, toa) j.*, act in a violent (brutal, outrageous) way. — a. and -jeuri, violent, tyrannical, &c. (Ar. Cf. *ujeuri*, and syn. *uthalimu, thulumu, shari, ukorofi*, and opp. *upole, haki, adili*.)

Ji (before vowels often j-) a prefix used as 1. formative only, (*a*) initial, before roots of (1) nouns of D 5, when they would be otherwise monosyllabic in the Singular, e. g. *jiwe* (plur. *mawe*, not *majiwe*), *jicho* (plur. *macho*, not *majicho*), *jino* (plur. *meno*, for *ma-ino*, indicating an *i* in the root), *jiko* (plur. *meko*, for *maiko*). (2) Declinable adjectives, when the root is monosyllabic or begins with a vowel, to mark agreement with D 5 (S), e. g. *jipya, jingi, jike, jekundu, jororo, jema*, &c. (*b*) Medial, between *ki-* diminutive and the root of nouns, in both sing. and plur., esp. when confusion might otherwise arise with a different word, e. g. *kijitu*, dim. of *mtu* (not *kitu*, a thing), *kijiti*, dim. of *mti* (not *kiti*, a seat), *kijiko* (not *kiko*, a pipe), *kijiwe* (not *kiwe*), *kijibwa* (not *kibwa*). It also occurs in dim. of *neno*, *kijineno* for *kineno*. (3) Terminal, attached to nouns directly formed from a verb, and commonly conveying the notion of habitual, customary, general action or condition, e. g. from *iga*, imitate, *mwiga*, one who imitates, and *mwigaji*, a regular imitator, caricaturist, from *omba*, beg, *mwomba*, one who begs, prefers a request, *mwombaji*, a professional beggar. (Cf. *ulaji*, gluttony, as a quality, habit, and obs. such words as *kinywaji*, that which is drunk, a beverage, in contr. with *kinywa*, mouth, where *ji* is mainly distinctive). 2. Amplificative, i. e. denoting relative largeness, before any suitable monosyllabic noun, and some dissyllables, e. g. *jitu*, *jibwa*, *jisu*, *jiguu*, *jumba* (*ji-umba*, cf. *nyumba*), *jombo* (*ji-ombo*, cf. *chombo*), *jivuli*, *jinywa*. (Contr. *ki*, as corresponding diminutive prefix.) 3. Reflexive, in verbs (often strengthened by a *nafsi* following) and verbal nouns (e. g. *jisifu*, *majisifu*, *jivuna*, *majivuno*, &c.), and either (*a*) simple, *jiua*, commit suicide, *jificha*, hide oneself, *jihathari*, guard oneself, *jiweka vema*, behave oneself, or (*b*) with a range of meanings both wide and delicately shaded, mostly centring on such ideas as independence, wilfulness, selfishness, interested action, personal aims and objects, or again, carelessness, indifference, random or chance action, &c., and capable of conveying alike a gross insult, or a subtle inuendo. A few examples are:—*jienda*, of easy, automatic, perpetual motion. *Jiendea*, take a walk (for pleasure), run amuck (like a madman). *Jijia*, come on one's own concerns (independently), jog along. *Nikawa kujijia zangu chini*, so I simply fell helplessly to the bottom. *Jikohoza*, give a significant cough. *Jigonjweza*, feign sickness, sham. *Jiona*, be conceited. *Jikalia*, lead a life of ease and idleness. *Jupitia*, go about one's own devices. *Kizee ajipitie impendezavyo*, the old lady can go about her business as she likes. *Ji-* being a prefix of such common use and wide application, words not found under *ji-* may be looked for under the letter following *ji-*. (Obs. sometimes a simple objective person pfx. is used for the reflexive *ji-*, e. g. *nikanywa mvinyo nikanilevya*, and I drank wine, and made myself drunk. *Umekuepuka na rehema ya Muungu*, you have shut yourself out from God's mercy.)

Jia, v. Ap. of Ja, which see.

*Jibini, n. cheese. (Arab.)

*Jibu, v. answer, reply, respond, retort. Ps. *jibiwa*, be answered, receive in answer, &c. Nt. *jibika*, be answerable, admit of an answer, &c. (also *jibikana*, in same senses). Ap. *jib-ia, -iwa, -iana*, e. g. *jibiana kwa waraka*, correspond (by letter). Cs. *jib-iza, -izwa, -isha, -ishwa, -izana*. *Akamjibisha majibu*, and he compelled him to reply, or, and he caused an answer to be given to him (the other person). *Jibizana*, e. g. of a class conducted by method of question and answer. — n. (*ma-*), answer, reply, retort, response. Commonly in plur. *leta majibu*, bring an answer. *Pa (toa) j.*, give an answer. (Ar. Cf. *jawabu, majibu*, rarely *jibile, jibio*. Dist. *jipu*, and *wajibu*.)

Jibwa, n. (*ma-*), a very large dog. (Cf. *mbwa, kijibwa*.)

Jicho, n. (*macho*), (1) eye. *Fumba j.*, close the eye. *Fumbua j.*, open the eye. *Finya j.*, half close the eye. *Kaza j.*, look fixedly, rivet the eye. *Tupa j.*, cast a glance. *Ngariza j.*, glare, stare. *Pepesa (jicho)*, wink. *Macho* is often used of wakefulness, or being awake, and fig. of vigilance, as n., a., and adv. *Ana macho*, or *yu macho*, he is awake. *Kaa macho*, remain awake, keep watch at night (cf. *kesha*).

Walikuwa macho, they were awake. (2) Spring, place where water bubbles from the ground. *Jicho la maji*, a spring of water. (Cf. *chemchemi*.) (3) Bud of a flower, when just opening. (Cf. *tumba, chipukizi*.) *Macho ya mtama* (?), husks of millet. (Perh. cf. *-cha*, v. dawn, and, for conditions of the eye, *upogo, upofu, chongo, makengeza, chamba cha jicho*.)

Jifu, n. (*ma-*), usu. in plur. ashes,—of burnt material. (Perh. cf. *jifya*.) *-jifujifu*, sometimes used as 'grey, ash-coloured, ashy.' (Cf. *ifu-ifu*.)

Jifya, n. (*mafya*), cooking stone,—one of the three used to support a cooking-pot over the fire. Not usu. in Z. town. (Cf. *jifu*, and see *figa, jiko*.)

Jigamba, v. Rf. of *gamba* (which is not used), vaunt oneself, boast, brag, show off. Ap. *jigambia*. Other forms rare. (Cf. syn. *jisifu, jiona, jivuna*.)

Jijiri, n. or **chichiri**. See **Kijiri**.

Jika, v. go to stool,—in Z. *enda chooni*. See **Choo**.

Jike, n. (*ma-*), female—animal. *Punda j.*, an ass. *Bata j.*, a duck. (Cf. *-ke, kijike*, and contr. *ndume*.)

Jiko, n. (*meko*), fire-place, hearth, kitchen. Often in the locat. form, *jikoni*, the kitchen. *Mtoto wa jikoni*, under-cook, scullery boy. *Mkaa jikoni*, a stay-at-home. The plur. *meko* is used most commonly in Z. for the (three) stones which support a cooking-pot over the fire, i. e. *mawe yazuiayo chungu cha kupika katika moto*. (Cf. *figa*, and note, *jifya*, and *ji-*.)

Jilio, n. (*ma-*), coming, approach, advent, usu. in plural. (Cf. *jio, jilia*, Ap. form of *ja*.)

Jimbi, n. (*ma-*), (1) a male fowl, a cock. *J. lawika*, the cock crows. (Cf. syn. *jogoo, pora*.) (2) A plant, of which both leaves and roots are eaten (Colocasia edulis, Sac.). (Cf. *mayugwa*.)

Jimbo, n. (*ma-*), inhabited country, district, province. (Cf. *wilaya*, which is used of the administrative divisions of Zanzibar Island.)

Jina, n. (*ma-*), name, i. e. proper name. *J. lako nani?* What is your name? *J. la kupangwa*, nickname (borrowed name). *Tia (-pa) j.*, give a name (to). *Taja mtu j.*, mention a person by name.

Jinamisi, n. (*ma-*), (1) bending (oneself) down, bowing down, e. g. *mahali pa jinamisi*, a place where you must bend down. (2) fig. humility, self-humiliation. (3) Nightmare. *J. limenilemea*, I am oppressed by a nightmare. (Cf. *inama*, and *ji-*.)

Jingi, n. (*ma-*), one of the two upright posts of a native frame for rope-making, supporting a cross board (*bau la jingi*). Also a form of *-ingi*, agreeing with D 5 (S).

*****Jini**, n. (*ma-*), a spirit, genius—a supernatural (created) being, powerful and capricious, but not always like *shetani*, malignant. (Ar. See **Pepo**.)

Jino, n. (*meno*), (1) tooth; (2) various objects resembling a tooth, as projecting, gripping, catching, e. g. cog (of a wheel), ward (of a lock), strand (of a rope), plug (of tobacco), battlement (on a wall), &c. *Kamba ya meno matatu*, a rope of three strands. *J. zima la tumbako, si kipande*, a whole plug of tobacco, not a cutting. *Ota j.*, cut a tooth,—of a child. *Ng'oa j.*, extract a tooth, have a tooth out. *Nauma j.*, I have a tooth-ache, also *j. laniyma*. *J. la mbele*, incisor, front tooth. *J. la nyuma*, back tooth, molar. *Toa meno*, show the teeth. *Tafuna kwa meno*, gnaw, nibble, chew with the teeth. *-a meno-meno*, battlemented, jagged, serrated. (Cf. *chonge, chego, pembe, kibogoyo*.)

*****Jinsi**, n. sort, kind, quality, class,—also commonly **ginsi**, which see. (Ar.)

Jinywa, n. (*ma-*), a large mouth,

esp. as an insulting term, e. g. *ziba jinywa lako*, stop that great mouth of yours, shut up. (Cf. common *kinywa, kanwa,* and *nya.*)

Jio, n. (*ma-*), coming, approach. Seldom used. *Jio la usiku*, approach of night, evening. (Cf. follg. and *ujio, jilio, njia,*—also *jia*, Ap. form of *ja.*)

Jiona, Jipevua, Jipotoa. See **Ona, Pevua, Potoa,** and **Ji-**.

Jioni, loc. form of *jio* used as n. or adv., evening, in the evening. *Jioni hivi* (or, *hii*, or, *leo*), this evening. (Cf. *jio*, and syn. *kuchwa, mshuko wa jua, magaribi,* and contr. *assubuhi.*)

Jipu, n. (*ma-*), boil, abscess. *J. laiva*, the boil is coming to a head. *J. limetumbuka*, the boil has burst. *J. litatoka usaha*, the boil will discharge. (Cf. *upele, kidonda.*)

Jipunguza, Jipurukusha. See **Punguza, Purukusha,** and **Ji-**.

Jipya, n. new,—agreeing with D 5 (S). See **-pya**.

*****Jirani**, n. (*ma-*), (1) neighbour, one living near; (2) anything near, adjacent, adjoining, on the boundary. *Nyumba yangu ni j. ya nyumba yake*, my house is next to his. *Shamba j.*, adjacent estate. (Ar. Cf. *ujirani, mpaka mmoja, pakia.*)

*****Jiri**, v. come to pass, take place, take effect. *Haikujiri neno*, it has no effect. Cs. *jirisha*. *Mfalme akaijirisha sheria*, the king gave effect to the laws, enforced the law. (Ar. for common *tukia, tokea, ja, wa.*)

*****Jiriwa**, n. (*ma-*), also **Iriwa**, a screw vice.

Jisifu, v. Rf. of *sifu* (which see), boast, brag, vaunt oneself, sing one's own praises, advertise oneself. — n. usu. in plur. *majisifu*, self-praise, boasting. See **Ji**.

Jisingizia, v. Rf. of **Singizia** (which see).

Jisu, n. (*ma-*); a large knife. (Cf. *kisu, kijisu.*)

*****Jitahidi**, v. make an effort, exert oneself, try hard, strain at. Cs. *jitahidisha*, in intens. sense, make a great effort. — n. effort, endeavour, exertion. *Jitahidi haiondoi amri ya Muungu*, human effort is powerless against God's will. (Ar. *-ji* not reflexive, cf. *juhudi* from same root, and syn. *fanya bidii, kaza, shika.*)

Jiti, n. (*ma-*), a large tree, a trunk of a tree, a large piece of wood. *Unapoikamata ngoma, kamata jiti lake*, when you get hold of a drum, see you get hold of its wooden part. (Cf. *mti, kijiti,* and dist. *kiti.*)

*****Jitimai**, n. grief, sorrow, affliction.

Jito, n. (*ma-*), also **Juto**, as from a root *uto*,—large river, lake. Lake Nyassa is sometimes spoken of as *jito*. (Cf. *mto, kijito,* and *ziwa*, lake.)

Jitu, n. (*ma-*), a very big man. *Anakuwa j. zima*, he is becoming a perfect giant. (Cf. *mtu, kijitu,* and syn. *pande,* or *pandikizi, la mtu,* and dist. *kitu*, a thing.)

Jivi, n. (*ma-*); (1) a great (notorious, famous) thief. (Cf. *mwivi, iba*). (2) A wild hog (Str.).

Jivu, n. (1) (*ma-*), ash, also **Jifu**, which see; (2) wooden socket in which the handle of a native drill turns. (Cf. *keke.*)

Jivuli, n. (*ma-*), great shadow, shadow of large object. *Jivuli la mvumo*, shadow of borassus palm. (Cf. *mvuli, kivuli,* &c.)

Jiwa, v. Ps. ap. of *-ja*, be approached, be visited, have guests. See **-ja**.

Jiwe, n. (*mawe*, or to indicate large size *majiwe*), a stone, a large stone, a piece of stone, stone (as material). *Nyumba ya mawe*, a stone house. *J. la thamani*, a precious stone. *Mawe* is used as a contemptuous expletive, Rubbish! nonsense! humbug! I don't believe you! *J. la kusagia*, a mill-stone. *J. la manga* (see **Manga**), a hard close-grained stone, used as a whetstone (*kinoo*). *Piga*, or *pigia, mawe*, throw stones at, stone. *Mtupo wa jiwe*, a stone's throw. The stone of Zanzibar is coral limestone of different ages. (Cf. *mbwe, kawe, kibwe, kikawe, kijiwe*, and for different sizes of stone, *mwamba, jabali, kokoto, changarawi, mchanga*.)

*Jizla, n. also Jesila, Gesla, a measure of weight, viz. 10 *frasila* or 60 *pishi*, about 350-60 lb. (Ar.)

Jogoo, n. (*ma-*), a male fowl, a cock. *Jogoo lawika*, the cock crows. *J. la kwanza*, first cockcrow, about 2 a.m. *J. la pili*, second cockcrow, just before dawn, 4 p.m. *Majogoo ndio saa la shamba*, the cock is the clock in the country. (Cf. *jimbi, pora, kuku*.)

*Johari, n. a jewel, a gem, a precious stone, e. g. *zumaridi, yakuti, almasi, feruzi, lulu*. Also fig. *j. za mtu ni mbili, akili na haya*, the most precious qualities are these two, intelligence and modesty. (Ar. Cf. *kito*.)

*Joho, n. (—, and *ma-*), (1) woollen cloth; (2) a long loose cloth coat or cloak, open in front, and often richly embroidered, worn by Arabs and well-to-do people. (Ar. Cf. *kanzu*, and *nguo*.)

Joka, n. (*ma-*), a very large snake, in general,—a serpent. (Cf. *nyoka*, n. and v. Dist. *choka*.)

Joko, n. (*ma-*), oven, kiln, esp. of potter's work, a place for baking earthen vessels, i.e. *mahali pa kuokea vyungu*. (From *ji*, which see, and *oka*. Cf. *josho*, and *choko*.)

Jombo, n. (*ma-*), ampl. of *chombo*, i.e. *ji-ombo*, a large utensil, a large vessel or ship. (Cf. *chombo, kijombo*.)

Jongea, v. move (pass) on, make a move, move, approach. *Jongea uvulini*, move into shade. *Jongee huku, nipishe mimi*, move aside and let me pass. Ap. *jong-elea, -elewa, -eleza, -elezwa, -eleana*, move to, approach, go up to, &c. *Akanijongelea hatta nilipo*, and he came close up to where I was. Cs. *jong-eza, -ezwa, -ezana*. (Cf. *enda, pita, sogea*. Dist. *chongea*.)

Jongo, n. (*ma-*), (1) a large, high back, a ridge, high projection; (2) a seam,—in sewing. *J. nene*, a large, projecting seam. (For *ji-ongo* cf. *maongo*, or *maungo*, and *gongo, mgongo* (elsewhere *mongo*), back, dorsal ridge, *kijongo, kibiongo*.)

Jongoo, n. (*ma-*), a very large black millipede, common in Z. and destructive to crops. *Mtupa jongoo hutupa na mti wake*, he who throws away a millipede, throws away the stick it is on as well.

Jororo, a. soft,—form of -*ororo*, agreeing with D 5 (S). (See -ororo, and ji.)

Josho, n. (*ma-*), for *ji-osho*, or same as *chosho*, i.e. *ki-osho*, a bathing-place, a place for washing. (Cf. *oga, osha*, and see Chosho.)

Joto, n. (*ma-*), for *ji-oto*, or same as *choto*, i.e. *ki-oto*, great heat, inflammation, pyrexia. *Pata joto* (or *joto joto*), get hot. (Cf. *ota, moto*.)

Joya, n. a white spongy substance sometimes found filling the shell of a cocoanut, instead of being deposited as the usual lining of nutty hard substance on the inside,—also the nut thus filled. *Joya la nazi*, either the substance or the nut. *Hutazamwa nazi, kama imefanya joya ndani*, a cocoanut is examined to see if it is spongy inside. *Kama j.*, spongy, porous, full of holes. *Nyumba yangu ni j., atakaye huingia*, my house is like a spongy cocoanut, any one who likes goes into it. (Cf. *nazi*.)

*Jozi, n. (1) a walnut; (2) a pair, brace, couple,—of anything. (Ar. 'nut' in general. Cf. *lozi*. The consonants are transposed of the Ar. word for 'pair.')

Jua, n. (*ma-*), (1) the sun, sunshine, fine weather; (2) time of day (as judged by the position of the sun). *J. kali (jingi)*, hot sun, hot weather. *J. kichwani (vichwani)*, time of sun overhead, noonday. *J. kucha (kupanda, kutoka, kuchomoza)*, sunrise. *J. kuchwa (tua, shuka)*, sunset. *J.*

linanga miti, the sun is taking farewell of the trees, i.e. is setting. *Macho ya j.*, sunrise, the Orient, the East. *Machweo ya j.*, sunset, the West. *J. limekuwa alasiri (athuuri, magaribi,* &c.), the time of day is afternoon (noon, evening, &c.). *Katika j. saa moja*, at 7 a.m.

Jua, v. know, know about, understand, be acquainted with. *Najua jambo hili (mtu huyu)*, I know this affair (this person). *Sijui maneno ya kiunguja*, I do not know the Zanzibar language. *Najua kufua chuma*, I know smith's work. *Namjua aliko*, I know where he is. Ps. *juliwa.* Nt. *julika*, be known, be knowable, be intelligible, and *julikana*, in the latter sense. Ap. *juilia, -iliwa*, know about, &c. *Alimjuilia kama amekasirika*, he recognized that he was angry. Cs. (rarely *juza*), *ju-lisha, -lishwa, -lishana*, cause to know, make known, inform. Also *juvya, juvisha* (sometimes meaning 'make impertinent, provoke to or teach impertinence.' Cf. *-juvi*). Rp. *ju-ana, -ania, -anisha. Nimewajuanisha*, I have introduced them to each other. (Cf. *-juzi, -juvi, ujuzi*, &c., and syn. *fahamu, tambua*.)

*Juba, n. (—, or *ma-*), (1) a kind of coat, vest, or jacket, open in front, with collar and wide sleeves of cloth or (unlike the *joho*) of calico and linen. (Arab. Cf. *joho, kanzu, nguo.*) (2) A mortising chisel. (Cf. *patasi, chembeu.*)

*Juhudi, n. effort, exertion, strain, ardour, zeal, painful stress, agony. *Ana j. ya kazi*, he is a zealous worker. *Fanya j.*, take great pains. *J. si pato*, trying is not the same as succeeding. (Ar. Cf. *jitahidi*, and cf. syn. *bidii, kazi, nguvu.*)

*Jukum, n. trader's risk, payment for taking risk, insurance. *Lipa j.*, insure (goods, in trading). *Chukua j.*, take the risk, guarantee. (Hind., used in commerce, cf. syn. *bima.*)

*Jukwaa, n. (*ma-*), also Jukwari, scaffolding, staging, stage, scaffold. (Hind.)

*Juma, n. (1) also Jumaa, Friday, and more fully *Ijumaa*, i.e. the day of assembly, e.g. *Kwenyi (iwapo) Ijumaa*, on Friday; (2) (*ma-*), a week. *J. moja*, one week. *J. zima*, a whole week. The days following are named from it, i.e. *Jumaa* (for *Juma ya*) *mosi*, Saturday, *Jumaa pili*, Sunday, *Jumaa tatu*, Monday, *Jumaa 'nne*, Tuesday, *Jumaa tano*, Wednesday. But *Alhamisi*, Thursday. See **Alhamisi.** (Ar. Cf. *jamaa, jamii, jumla*, and see **Siku.** *Juma* seems also sometimes used for *njumu.*)

*Jumaa, n. See **Juma.** *Moskiti wa jumaa*, the mosque of the congregation. (Arab.)

Jumba, n. (*ma-*), a large house, mansion, palace. (For *ji-umba* Cf. *nyumba, chumba, kijumba*, &c.)

Jumbe, n. (*ma-*), king, chief, head man,—also called locally *diwani, shomvi, pasi*. (Perh. *ji-umbe*, from *umba*, cf. *kiumbe*, and syn. *sultani, mfalme, mwinyi, mkuu*, and dist. *mjumbe*.)

*Jumla, n. (1) the sum, total, a lot, all together; (2) in Arithm. addition. Also adv. wholesale, in lots. (Ar. Cf. *juma, jamaa*, and syn. *jamii, shelabela*.)

*Jumlisha, v. Cs. add up, sum up, put all together. Ps. *jumlishwa.* (Ar. Cf. *jumla*, and syn. *jamiisha, tia pamoja*.)

Jungu, n. (*ma-*), a large cooking pot, usually round, of red or black earthenware, and with a cover. (For *ji-ungu*, and cf. *kijungu, kichungu, ungu* with pl. *nyungu*, and for other vessels, see **Chungu, Chombo.**)

*Jura, n. (*ma-*), also Jora, Gora, a length of calico, calico in the piece (of 30 to 35 yards). (? Ar.)

Juta, v. regret, feel the loss of, miss, be sorry for, feel remorse for, referring to something past. *Najuta mimi nafsi yangu kufanya neno hili*, I am sorry myself for doing this thing. *Juta maovu*, feel remorse for wrongdoing. Ps. *jutwa*. Nt. *jutika*, whence *jutikana*. Ap. *jutia, -iwa*. Cs. *jut-isha, -ishwa*. Rp. *jutana*, join in regretting. (Cf. *juto*, also *toba, tubu*.)

Juto, n. (*ma-*), (1) regret, remorse, sorrow for what is past. *Fanya (ona, ingiwa na*, &c.) *majuto*, feel remorse. *Shikwa (patwa) na majuto*, have a fit of remorse. *Wakajuta sana majuto makuu*, they very bitterly regretted it. *Majuto ni mjukuu, mwishowe huja kinyume*, remorse is a grandchild, it comes at last. (2) A form of *jito*, a large river. (Cf. *juta, toto*, and *mto*.)

Juu, adv. and (with *ya*) prep., (1) of position,—above, high up, over, on, upon, up (to) above, from above, upstairs, on the top (of). *J. ya nyumba*, on the top of the house. *Aliyoko juu, mngojee chini*, wait below for the man who is above. *Panda j.*, go upstairs. *Shuka j. ya frasi*, dismount from a horse. *Angenda j., hafikilii mbinguni*, though he soars high, he does not get to the sky. Also of rank, dignity, &c. *Aliye j. ni j.*, i.e. a great man is out of reach. *Juu, iliyo juu, palipo juu, juu yake*, is used of 'the top' of a thing. *Hapa ndipo juu*, here is the top, the highest point. (2) Resting on, dependent on, obligatory on, morally binding on, the business of, the duty of, &c. *J. yako*, you are responsible, it depends upon you. *J. ya mfalme kutawala*, it is the king's business to rule. (3) Over and above, in addition to, beside. *J. ya mambo haya*, besides all this. *Umpe mpia j. ya mshahara wake*, give him a rupee in addition to his wages. (4) About, concerning, as to, in respect of, with regard to. *Mtoto hufanya adabu j. ya mwalimu wake*, a pupil treats his teacher with all respect. *Fanya shauri j. ya safari yako*, make plans for your journey. *Alisema mengi j. yake*, he talked a great deal about him. (5) Against, in opposition to, to the prejudice (harm, loss) of. *Huna nguvu j. yangu*, you have no power against (over) me. *Wakaleta vita j. ya adui*, they made war upon (against) their enemies. (6) In an excited, perplexed, fluttered, alarmed state or condition (of mind and feeling). *Moyo wake ni j., yuna moyo j.*, he is excited, has taken offence, is angry, has lost his head, &c. The Rd. form *juujuu* is also often used, with different shades of meaning, e.g. (1) high up, very high, exalted. *Tazama kijuujuu*, take a birdseye, synoptic, general view; (2) proud, arrogant, supercilious; (3) superficial, foolish, shallow, excited, perplexed, &c. *Wakaulizwa ya juujuu*, they were asked the usual formal (civil) questions. *Mambo ya juujuu*, indifferent matters, gossip, topic of the hour. *Tukasemezana juujuu*, we had a chat together. (Contr. *chini*.)

Juvisha, Juvya, v. Cs. See **Jua**, v.

Juya, n. (*ma-*), a seine, drag-net, made of native materials. (Cf. *jarifa, wavu, kimia*.)

Juza, v. Cs. See **Jua**, v.

Juzi, n. (*ma-*), the day before yesterday. *J. na jana si kama ya leo*, yesterday, and the day before, are not like matters of to-day. *Mwaka j.*, or *wa j.*, the year before last. Also used indefinitely, *juzi*, or *juzi juzi*, a few days ago, lately. *J. hivi*, the other day. *Tangu majuzi yale*, some time ago. *Mtu wa j.*, a new-comer, a young person. *Kushinda j.*, three days ago.

*****Juzu**, v. be permissible, be allowable, be suitable, be fitting for, be right for, be duty of. *Nguo hii haimjuzu*, these clothes do not suit him, are not proper for him. *Neno hili lajuzu nami*, this matter is right for me, is my duty. Ap. *juz-ia, -iwa*, be right for, be allowed to, be obligatory for. *Mwanamke huyu anijuzia kumwoa*, it is right for me to marry this woman. So *nimejuziwa kumwoa*. Also n. and a., of what is allowable, within one's duty, and so (often) morally binding, obligatory. (Ar. Cf. *pasa, wajibu*.)

*Juzu, n. (*ma-*), division, section, chapter of a book, esp. of the Coran. *Anasoma j. ya thelathini*, he is reading the thirtieth chapter. (Ar. Cf. *kilabu, chuo*.)

K.

K represents the same sound as in English. The two different *k* sounds in words of Arabic origin are not commonly distinguished in Swahili. For the sound of Arabic *kh* see remarks on Kh- below.

K is often pronounced *ch* in Zanzibar, esp. among the slave class and new-comers from mainland tribes.

K is one of the commonest sounds in Swahili speech, entering as it does into the formatives ka, ki, ko, and ku (which see), and the preps. kwa, katika.

Words not found under *K* may be looked for under *Kh*, *H*, or *Ch*. For words beginning with *ki-* see remarks on Ki-, below.

K-, before a vowel, sometimes represents ka or ki, which see.

Ka, 1. is a verbal connective prefix, except in the cases noted below. In general, it connects two or more verbs together in such a way as either (*a*) to carry on the construction (mood and tense) of the first verb to those following with *ka-*, or (*b*) to supply in those verbs the construction appropriate to the context. But most commonly it is used (1) to connect a verb in the Past (Narrative) Tense Indicative with others following, or else (2) to connect a verb in the Imperative Mood with another in the Subjunctive, or Imperative. Thus the typical form of a narrative in Swahili begins with a verb in the Past (*li-*) Tense, and proceeds with verbs having *ka* for *li*, e.g. *paliondokea sermala akaenda kuoa mke*, there was once a carpenter and he went and married a wife. *Palikuwa mtu akawa tajiri*, there was once a man and he became rich. Hence *ka-* may be said commonly to carry the force of 'and' before a Past (Narrative) Tense. Similarly, the common form of Imperative sentence with more than one verb is *njoo kaone*, or *njoo ukaone*, or *njoo kaona*, come and see. *Nenda kalete* (*ukalete, kaleta*), go and fetch (it).

Beside these uses, *ka* is regularly employed (1) with a single Imperative as a semi-connective, i.e. with reference to something implied or understood, e.g. *leta*, bring it ; *kaleta* (*kalete*), bring it then. So *kaseme ati!* speak then! Also *nikawete?* Am I to call them then? (2) Prefixed to a verb-root, without Pers. Pfx. with the force of the 3 Pers. Sing. Perf. Indic., e.g. *kafa*, he is dead. *Kenda zake*, he has gone away. *Alikwenda mjini kapanda punda*, he went to town on a donkey, i.e. *amepanda punda*. (3) Affixed to the sign of the Future *ta*, when *ta* would otherwise be required to bear the accent, as in relative forms, e.g. *atakapokwenda* for *atapokwenda*, when he shall go.

In (2) and (3) *ka* has no connective force.

There remain a number of cases in which *ka* is less commonly used, e.g. with a Present Tense, *nikali*, and I am; with or following the *hu* tense, *hufikia pale akala*, he used to go there and eat; *hutoka assubuhi hukarudi*, he used to go out in the morning and come back; with a Future Tense, *ntaenda nikapata baraka*, I will go and win a blessing; with a subordinate verb, *nimekwenda kwake nikamtazame*, I have been to his house to see him; introducing a supplement especially to negative expressions, e.g. *asije akafa*, that he may not first come and die, for *asije kufa* or *asijafa*, before he die; *usinipige ukajuta*, do not strike me and then regret it (i.e. or you will regret it); *tusiende tukarudi*, do not let us go and then have to come back again; *kwenda akaja leo*, perhaps he comes to-day.

Ka coalesces commonly with *e* or *o* following, e.g. *akenda*, *akoga*, and with *i* following forms *e*, as *akesha*, for *akaisha*. *Nika* is often contracted into *ha*.

2. is a Diminutive Prefix of nouns and adjectives, more emphatic than *ki*, e.g. *katoto*, a tiny child; *kajiwe*, a very small stone; *kagongo kafupi*, a very short little club; *paka kadogo*, a very small kitten. *Kadogo* is used, like *kidogo*, as adv., in a very small degree, infinitesimally, to a very small amount.

Kaa, v. (1) stay, stop, rest, remain, wait; (2) sit, sit down, take a seat; (3) dwell, live (in), inhabit, reside (at); (4) continue, last, endure. *Unakaa wapi? nakaa shamba (mjini)*, Where do you live? I live in the country (in the town). *Kaa kitako*, sit on the haunches, squat, sit down. *Nimekaa*, I am seated,—often a polite rejoinder (whether seated or not) to the invitation *karibu*, walk in. *Nguo hii imekaa sana*, this dress has lasted a long time, has worn well. *Inchi hii inakaa watu*, this country is inhabited, i.e. *imekaliwa na watu*. Ps. *kaliwa* (rarely *kawa*). Nt. *kalika*, and *kalikana*, be habitable, &c. Ap. *ka-lia*, *-lisha*, *-lishwa*, e.g. *-liana*, wait for (with, in, by, &c.). *Akamkalia nabii Musa njiani*, and he waited for the prophet Moses in the road. *Kumkalia mtu matanga*, to join in the mourning for a person. *Imemkalia tamu*, it has remained agreeable to him. *Akakalia nyele zake*, and he waited with (for) his hair, i.e. he let it go untrimmed. *Wakakaliana karibu*, and they settled near each other. Cs. *ka-lisha* (? *kaza*), *-lishwa*. (Cf. *ukao*, *kikao*, *makazi*, *mkaa*, &c., and syn. *keti*, *shinda*, *ngoja*, *ishi*, *dumu*.)

Kaa, n. (*ma-*), (1) a piece of charcoal, also extended to mean 'a lump of coal.' *Makaa*, charcoal, coal, embers. Mineral coal is sometimes distinguished as *makaa ya mawe*, stone coal. *Makaa ya moto*, live embers. *Makaa zimwe* (*ya zimwe*, *mazimwe*), slaked embers, cinders, dead (burnt out) coal. *Makaa moshi* (*ya moshi*), soot. (Cf. *masizi*.) *Choma* (*oka*, *pika*) *makaa*, make charcoal. (2) (—), a crab, the most generic term, including many varieties, e.g. *kaa makoko* (*ya pwani*), *chago*, *ngadu*, *mwanamizi*. (Dist. follg.)

Kaaka, n. also **Kaa**, the palate, also *kaa la kinwa*.

Kaanga, v. fry, braze, cook with fat, i.e. *oka*, *kwa samli* (or, *kwa mafuta*). *K. nyama*, cook meat with fat. *K. moto*, heat, warm. *Mayai ya kukaanga*, poached (fried) eggs. *K. ngoma*, warm a drum at a fire to tighten the skin. Hence *ngoma ya kukaanga*, fig. for delay, i.e. a pause in a dance. (Cf. *kaango*, *kikaango*, *ukaango*, and for cooking, *pika*.)

Kaango, n. (—, and *ma-*), a cooking pot,—of earthenware, properly for cooking with fat, a frying-pan. (Cf. *kaanga*.)

*****Kaba**, v. press tight, squeeze. *Nguo inamkaba mwili*, his clothes are too tight for him. *Kaba roho*, seize by the throat, throttle, choke. *Wakamkaba roho hatta akazimia*, they throttled him till he fainted. (? Ar. Cf. syn. *bana*, *songa*, *kaza*, *saki*, *shika*, *kamata*.)

*****Kaba**, n. or **Kaaba**, (1) lining of the *kanzu* on neck and shoulders. See **Kanzu**. Also (2) a kind of vest with sleeves. (Ar. Cf. *juba*.)

*****Kabari**, n. (—, and *ma-*), a wedge

(of wood or iron), e.g. to split logs with.

*Kabila, n. (*ma-*), tribe, clan,—a smaller division than *taifa*, and larger than *ufungu, jamaa*.

*Kabili, v. (1) be in front, be opposite, face (towards), front, point to, correspond to, be directed towards, be exposed to; (2) incline towards, tend to, be inclined to, be likely to, have a propensity for; (3) confront, brave, defy, oppose, be contradictory to. *Nikamkabili uso kwa uso*, I met him face to face. *Mahali palipokabili baridi*, a place exposed to the wind. *Hakabili kuuza*, he is not inclined (likely) to sell. *Ulimwengu unakabili mvua*, the weather portends rain. *Hatuwezi kukabili bahari ile*, we cannot steer for (navigate, face) that sea. *Wakakabili risasi zetu*, they boldly faced our bullets. Ps. *kabiliwa*. Nt. *kabilika*. Ap. *kabil-ia, -iana*, be opposite, face each other, have a mutual attraction, correspond. Cs. *kabil-isha, -ishwa*. *Ntakukabilisha na wali*, I will confront you with (present you to) the governor. *Kabilisha mtu*, send a man in a given direction. *Kabilisha barua*, dispatch a letter, forward a letter to its destination. *Kabilisha moyo*, set the heart on, resolve. (Ar. Cf. *kubali, kabla, kibula,* and syn. *tekea, simamia, -wa mbele ya, kutana na, shindana na, lingana na,* &c.)

Kabisa, adv. utterly, altogether, quite, wholly, exactly. *Njema kabisa*, as good as can be. *Sitaki kabisa*, I absolutely refuse. (Cf. syn. *kamwe, haswa, halisi*.)

*Kabithi, v. also Takabathi, (1) take in the hand, receive, hold, lay hands on, seize, keep. Also (2) Cs. (for *kabithisha*), cause to hold in the hand, put in the hand (of), deliver (to), hand over (to), give (to). *Amemkabithi mwenyi deni*, he has seized the debtor. *Kabithi mali*, hoard, economize. *Ulitakabathi thamani*, you received the price. *Unakabithi watoto mali yao*, hand over this property to the children. *Nikawakabithi fetha wale watumwa*, I gave the money to the slaves. Cs. *kabithiwa*. Ap. *kabith-ia, -iana*. Cs. *kabith-isha, -ishwa*, cause to receive, hand over (to), deliver (to). (Ar. Cf. follg. and syn. (1) *pokea, kamata, shika;* (2) *salimu, toa, pokeza, lipa*.)

*-kabithi, a. economical, grasping, close-fisted, miserly. (Ar. Cf. *kabithi, ukabithi*.)

*Kabla, conj. and (with *ya*) prep., before,—almost exclusively of time, previously, antecedently, in advance of. Followed by a verb in the negative, usu. the *ja* tense and often with *bado*, or else a relative. *K. hajaja bado*, before he arrived. *K. haikutiwa nanga*, before casting anchor. *K. atakapohuja (ajapo)*, before he shall come (comes). *K. ya kuja*, before arrival. *K. ya siku chache*, before long, or, a few days before. (Ar. See Kabili, and follg. Cf. *mbele*.)

*Kabla, n. purpose, object, tendency, direction. *Tukaona kabla yao*, we saw what they were going to do. (Arab. seldom used. Cf. *kabili, kibula, kibla*.)

*Kabuli, n. (1) acceptance, sanction. (Ar. Cf. the more common *kibali, ukubali*). (2) An Indian dish of rice, curry, &c. (Hind. Cf. *pilau*.)

*Kaburi, n. grave, tomb, sepulchre, place of burial. *Makaburi,* or *makaburini,* a cemetery. *Chungulia kaburini*, have one foot in the grave. (Ar. Cf. *siara, kuzimu*.)

*Kadamu, n. (*ma-*), also Mkadamu, foreman,—used of the third in authority of the men superintending work on an estate, the head man being *msimamizi*, the second *nokoa*. (Ar. Cf. *takadamu*, and follg.)

*Kadimisha, v. Cs. cause to go before, send in advance. (Ar. Cf. *kadamu*, and *tangulia*.)

*Kadiri, v. also Kadri, (1) estimate, reckon, calculate, fix the value of, put a limit on; (2) form an opinion on, consider, weigh, judge. *K. mali*, make a valuation of property. *Nakadiri maneno haya ni kweli*, I judge that this statement is true. Ps. *kadiriwa*. Nt. *kadirika*, e.g. be limited, be measurable, be moderate (in amount, behaviour, &c.), be finite. *Kufa ni farathi ya iliyokadiriwa*, death is a necessary condition of what is finite. *Anatakabari mno, hakadiriki*, he shows great arrogance, he has no moderation. *Maneno yasiyokadirika*, unmeasured (or, unintelligible) language. Ap. *kadir-ia, -iwa*. Cs. *kadir-isha, -ishwa*, e.g. put limit to, restrain, cause a valuation (estimate) to be made, &c. — n. (1) amount, measure, extent, capacity, value, rank; (2) moderation, self-control, temperance. *K. ya watu kumi wamekuja*, as many as ten people have come. *K. gani?* What amount? How much? *Kaa mahali pa k. yako*, remain in a place suited to your condition. — as adv. conj. and (with *ya*) prep. in various senses, (1) about, nearly, up to; (2) as much as, as long as, as often as, whilst, when, as; (3) moderately, on an average, in a certain degree, e.g. *k. utakapofanyiwa maovu uniite*, whenever you are badly treated, call me. *K. akitia, hukaza*, as soon as he places it, he fastens it. *K. ya kukaa kitako*, just when he was sitting down. Common also with *-vyo* following, e.g. *k. awezavyo*, as far as he can, to the best of his ability. (Ar. Cf. *ukadiri*, and syn. *giusi, kiasi*.)

Kadogo, a. invar. dim. of *-dogo*, and more emphatic than *kidogo*, exceedingly small, minute, infinitesimal, tiny. Also adv., in a very small degree. (Cf. *-dogo, ki-* and *ka-*.)

*Kafara, n. (*ma-*), an offering, a sacrifice, a charm,—to avert evil. *Toa k.*, make an offering, sacrifice. *Chinja k.*, kill (an animal) as an offering. (Ar. cover, atone. Cf. *kafiri, kufuru*, and syn. *sadaka, thabihu*.)

Kafi, n. (*ma-*), paddle, small steering oar. *Piga k.*, use a paddle, paddle. (Cf. *kasia*.)

*Káfila, n. a caravan. (Arab. rarely heard, for common *msafara, safari*.)

*Kafini, v. cover up, wrap. *Mtu aliyekufa hukafiniwa kwa sanda*, a dead man is wrapped in a shroud. (Ar. *kafani*, a pall; rarely heard, for common *funua, vika*.)

*Kafiri, n. (*ma-*), one who is not of the Mahommedan religion, an infidel, an unbeliever, an atheist, a pagan, an apostate. (Ar. Cf. *kufuru, ukafiri*.)

*Kafuri, n. camphor. (Arab.)

Kaga, v. protect by a charm, put a charm on (in, near, &c.), e.g. *kaga shamba (mwili, kaburi)*, protect by charm a plantation (person, grave). Cf. follg.

Kago, n. (*makago* and *mago*), a charm (for protection or preservation). *K. la fisi*, charm against a hyaena. (Cf. *kaga*, and syn. *kafara, dawa, hirizi, talasimu*.)

Kagua, v. inspect, survey, examine. *K. shamba*, inspect a plantation. *K. asikari*, inspect, hold a parade of, troops. Ps. *kaguliwa*. Nt. *kagulika*. Ap. *kagu-lia, -liwa*. (Cf. *mkaguzi*, and syn. *angalia, tazamia*.)

*Kahaba, n. (*ma-*), prostitute. (Ar. Cf. *ukahaba*.)

*Kahawa, n. coffee, i.e. the beverage,—the berry being *buni*, or *buni ya kahawa*, and the plant *mbuni*. (Ar. Cf. *mkahawani*.)

*Kahini, n. (*ma-*), also Kuhani, priest, soothsayer, and sometimes in bad sense, deceiver, swindler. (Ar. Cf. *mkohani*, and *kasisi*.)

*Káhira, n. Cairo. (Arab.)

*Kaida, n. fundamental rule, canon, pattern, standard, method,—same as kawaida, which see. (Ar. Cf. syn. *kanuni.*)

***Kaidi**, v. be obstinate, be headstrong, rebel, refuse to obey, contradict. *Usimkaidi baba akisema neno*, do not contradict (disobey) your father, if he says anything. Cs. *kaid-isha, -ishwa*, e. g. incite to disobedience. (Ar. Cf. follg. and syn. *halifu, asi.*)

*-**kaidi**, a. obstinate, refractory, disobedient, rebellious, &c. (Ar. Cf. prec.)

***Kaimu**, n. (*ma-*), superintendent, guardian, vicegerent, viceroy. *Hakimu atakuwa k. wa shughuli ile*, the chief will undertake that business. (Arab. Cf. *waziri, wakili.*)

Kajekaje, n. small cords used to fasten the sail to the yard, in a native vessel. (Cf. *chombo*, and *kamba.*)

Kajia, n. an extremely small path or passage. Dim. of *njia*. (Cf. *njia, ujia*, and *ka-.*)

Kaka, n. (*ma-*), (1) used occasionally of an empty shell, e.g. of an egg, or of the rind of a fruit, e. g. of an orange, *k. la yai, k. la chungwa*. (But *ganda* is more usual, cf. *fuvu, fuu.*) (2) Elder brother, generally used playfully or colloquially, as *dada*. (3) A disease affecting the hand.

Kaka-kaka, adv. in a hurry, in a rush (press, bustle). (Cf. *kikaka.*)

Kakamia, v. strain after, make a sudden or violent effort to do, or get something, e. g. *k. maji*, of a thirsty man. (Cf. follg.)

Kakam'ka, v. make a muscular effort, strain,—as in lifting a load, breaking a stone, or in travail. Obs. also Rf. *jikakamua*, in same sense.

Kakawana, v. be strong, athletic, well knit, muscular. (Cf. syn. *shupaa, -wa na maungo.*)

***Kaki**, n. a thin hard-baked biscuit or cake. (Cf. *mkate.*)

***Kalafati**, v. caulk (the seams of a wooden vessel),—the tool used being *chembeu*. Described as *tia pamba na mafuta yasingie maji*, apply cotton and grease to prevent water getting in. Ps. *kalafatiwa*. — n. caulking, material used for caulking. (Ar.)

Kalala, n. also **Karara, Ukalala**, the tough leathery sheath of the cocoanut flower stem.

Kalam'ka, v. be quick witted, be wide awake, be sharp (intelligent, on the alert), have one's eyes open. Ap. *kalamkia, -iwa*, (usually) be too sharp for, outwit, deceive, cheat. (Cf. *kalam'zi*, and *am'ka*, and syn. *danganya, punja, hadaa.*)

***Kalamu**, n. pen (made of reed). Also any pen. *Chonga k.*, point a pen, make a pen. *K. na wino*, pen and ink. (Ar.)

Kalam'zi, a. crafty, cunning, sharp. (Cf. *kalam'ka*, and syn. *-janja, -erevu, ayari.*)

***Kalasha**, n. tusk of ivory, smaller than *buri*. (Cf. *pembe, buri.*)

***Kalasia**, n. small brass vessel with narrow neck, often used for milk. (Hind. Cf. *kopo, sufuria*, for metal vessels.)

Kale, n. old times, antiquity, the past, former ages. *Watu wa k.*, the ancients, men of old. *Zamani za k.*, old times, past ages. *Hapo k.*, once upon a time, long ago. *Kikale*, of the old style, old-fashioned, antiquated. *-a k.*, old, ancient. *-a kikale*, antiquated. (Cf. *zamani*, and dist. *uzee*, old age.)

***Kalfati.** See **Kalafati**. (Ar.)

-**kali**, a. (1) sharp, having a sharp edge, cutting, e. g. *kisu kikali*, a sharp knife, *makali ya upanga*, the edge of a sword, opp. to *butu*; (2) sharp to the taste, acid, sour, bitter, e. g. *siki kali*, sour vinegar, opp. to *laini, tamu*, and cf. *chungu*; (3) sharp in temper, severe, stern, cross, cruel, fierce, e. g. *ng'ombe mkali*, a fierce cow, opp. to *-pole, -a huruma*; (4) keen, intense, vehement, brave, *jua kali, tembo kali*, strong palm-wine, scorching sun, *watu wakali*, warlike people, opp. to *-legevu, -vivu, -oga*. (Cf. *ukali*.)

-kali, verb-form, used with Person prefixes, *nikali, tukali*, &c., and I am (was), and we are (were), &c. (Cf. *ka*, and *li*.)

Kalia, Kalika, v. See **Kaa**, v.

*__Kalibu__, n. a mould, e.g. for bullets, i.e. *kidude cha kusubia lisasi*, a thing for casting bullets in. Also of that in which metal, &c. is heated, a heating pot or furnace. (Cf. *subu, ita, joko, tanuu*.)

*__Kalima__, n. word. (Arab. for common *neno*. Cf. *mkalimani*.)

*__Kalme__. See **Galme**.

Kama, v. squeeze, but e p. of milking, e.g. *kama ng'ombe maziwa*, milk a cow, or simply *kama*. Ps. *kamwa*. Nt. *kamika, kamikana*. Ap. *kam-ia, -iwa*. (Dist. *kamia*, threaten.) Cs. *kam-isha, -ishwa*, e.g. *kamisha ng'ombe za watu*, act as milkman, undertake milking. (Cf. *kamua, kamata*, and *songa, kaba, shika*.)

*__Kama__, conj. also **Kana**, (1) as a particle of comparison in general, (*a*) as, such as, like, as if, as though, e.g. *uwe kama mimi*, be like me. *Ruka k. ndege*, fly like a bird. *Mtu mfupi k. wewe*, a man as short as you. *K. hivi (vile)*, as thus, like this, in this way, for instance. With a noun, often supplies a lacking adjective, e.g. *k. maji*, like water, i.e. liquid, fluid, also fluent, easy. *K. majani*, green. With *nini*, forms an expletive or adv. of emphasis, e.g. *kubwa k. nini*, wonderfully great. *Zuri k. nini*, inexpressibly beautiful, or in the form *kamani! wonderful! marvellous!* With a verb, *kama* is commonly followed by *-vyo*, e.g. *k. upendavyo*, as you please, *k. ulivyosema*, as you said, but also *k. wapenda, k. ulisema*. (*b*) Like, as it were, almost, about, nearly, of vague comparison, e.g. of numbers, *asikari k. mia*, about a hundred soldiers. *Ny-ingi k. si nyingi*, a moderate number. (*c*) In the definite comparison of two or more objects, ' as compared with, rather than, and not ' (cf. *kuliko*), e.g. *afathali kuweka mali k. kutumia yote*, it is better to save money than to use it all up. *Yeye mkubwa k. wewe*, he is big as compared with you, i.e. bigger than you. *Heri kupotea nikafa k. kuwa hai*, better I should be lost and die than live. *Bora thahabu k. fetha*, gold is more valuable than silver. (2) As a subordinative particle, (*a*) that,—of reported speech, &c. *Nasema k. ndivyo*, I say that it is so. *Nimesikia k. hajui*, I understand that he does not know. *Aliamuru k. aende*, he ordered that he should go. (Cf. similar use of *ya kuwa, ya kwamba, kwamba*, and *kama kwamba*.) (*b*) If, supposing that, though, i.e. conditional, e.g. *k. una homa nenda kwa mganga*, if you have fever, go to the doctor. *K. hutaki, bassi*, if you do not want to, there is an end of it. Also often with Pres. Partic., *k. ukipenda*, if you like. *K. fetha ikipatikana, ntalipa*, if the money is forthcoming, I will pay. (*c*) Whether, if, e.g. *sijui k. yuko*, I do not know whether he is there. *Alimuliza k. ndivyo*, he asked me whether it was so. (Ar. For comparative use cf. *sawa na, mfano wa, mithili ya, kuliko*. For conditional use cf. *ikiwa, iwapo, endapo*, and the use of *-ki-* and *-sipo-* in verbs.)

*__Kamali__, n. a game played by chucking small coin into a hole (Str.).

Kamamanga, n. See **Komamanga**.

*__Kamani__, adv. wonderfully, strangely, exceedingly. (For *kama nini*? Like what! see **Kama**.)

Kamasi, n. (*ma-*), mucus from the nose, catarrh. *Siwezi k.*, I have a cold in my head. (Cf. *mafua, kifua*.) *Futa makamasi*, wipe the nose.

Kamata, v. take forcible hold of, catch hold of, seize with the hands (arms, claws, a trap, &c.), grasp, clasp, make a prisoner of, arrest. *Chui alimkamata kuku*, the leopard got hold of the fowl. Ps. *kamatwa*. Nt. *kamatika*, e.g. *maji hayakamatiki*, water cannot be grasped in the hand. Ap. *kamat-ia, -iwa*, e.g. seize with, grasp at, get a partial hold of, &c. Cs. *kamatisha*, also Intens. hold fast. Rp. *kamatana*, grapple, e.g. in wrestling. (Implies some effort, difficulty to overcome. Cf. *shika, kabithi, guia, nasa*. For the termination cf. *ambata, fumbata, nata, pata*.)

Kamati, n. ball of wheat flour, leavened with *tembo*, i.e. palm-wine (Str.).

Kamba, n. cord, rope,—the most generic term, properly of the native kind, but made of twisted cocoanut fibre (*makumbi*). Hence *k. ya kumbi, kamba ya nazi*, to distinguish it from *k. ulaiti*, European, hempen rope, and *k. ya miwaa*, rope of plaited leaf strips. See **Ukambaa**. *Ukukuu wa kamba si upya wa ukambaa*, in a rope old fibre is better than new leaf strips. *Piga (funga) k.*, tie with a rope, cord (a load), but also like *songa k., suka (sokota) k.*, make a rope by twisting or plaiting. The ropes of a native sailing vessel have various names, all of non-Bantu origin, e.g. *amari, baraji, hamarawi, dasi, henza, jarari, demani, goshi, dakawa, mjiari*, or *ujari*. Various materials for binding are *ubugu, ugomba, ung'ong'o, uuunu, ukindu*, and *miwaa*. (Cf. *ukambaa*, also *ugwe, kitani*.)

Kamba, n. a lobster, crayfish, prawn, shrimp, sometimes distinguished as *k. ya pwani, k. ya bahari*, also **mkamba**,—the common lobster, and *k. ya mtoni*, crayfish. (Cf. *m-kamba, uduvi, kaa*.)

Kambali, n. (*ma-*), also **Kambari**, freshwater cat fish, with broad flat head and fleshy feelers,—the only freshwater fish common in Z., and sometimes of large size (15 lb. to 20 lb.)

Kambi, n. (*ma-*), encampment,—usually on enclosure occupied at night in travelling on the mainland. (? Eng. *camp*. Cf. *kituo, boma*.)

Kambo, n. *baba (mama) wa kambo*, step-father (-mother), *mtoto wa kambo*, step-child. (Perh. cf. *kambo*, used (Kr.) for the shoot sprouting from the roots of the banana (*mgomba*), near but separate from the chief stem.)

Kame, n. (*ma-*), barren land, wilderness, desert, waste, uncultivated ground. (Cf. *nyika, jangwa, poli*.)

Kamia, v. reproach, threaten, dun (a debtor). *Amemkamia sana kumpiga*, he threatened to beat him. *Mkamia maji hayanywi*, he who finds fault with the water will not drink it. *Jikamia*, reproach oneself. Ps. *kamiwa*. Nt. *kamika*. Rp. *kamiana*. (Cf. *kamio*, and *ogofya, laumu*.)

*****Kamili**, v. complete, finish, make perfect, also be complete, be finished. But these meanings are usually taken by the Cs. and Nt. or Ps. forms. Ps. *kamiliwa*. Nt. *kamilika*. Ap. *kamil-ia, -iwa*, e.g. end off, finish off. *Alipokamilia nyumba ile*, when he finished off that house. Cs. *kamil-isha, -ishwa*, e.g. *nimekamilisha mwezi wangu*, I have completed my month. — a. complete, perfect, whole, entire, unimpaired. (Ar. Cf. *maliza, timia, timiliza, isha*.)

*****-kamilifu**, a. same as **Kamili**, a., which see.

Kamio, n. (*ma-*), a reproach, a threat. (Cf. prec.)

*****Kampani**, n. also **Kumpani**, a commercial house, a trading association, a company. (From Eng. *company*.)

Kamua, v. Rv. of *kama* with similar meaning, squeeze, wring, compress, squeeze out, e. g. *k. nguo*, wring wet clothes; *k. chungwa*, squeeze the juice out of an orange. *K. jipu*, make an abscess discharge. *K. mafuta*, extract oil by pressure. Ps. *kamuliwa*. Nt. *kamulika*. Ap. *kamu-lia, -liwa*, e. g. *akamkamulia ndimu mwilini*, and he squeezed lime juice over his body. Cs. *kamu-lisha, -lishwa*. (Cf. *kama*, v.)

Kamusi, n. a lexicon, a dictionary. (Arab. ' ocean.')

Kamwe, adv. always with a negative preceding, (not) at all, (not) in the least, (not) ever (i.e. never, by no means). *Si kitu kamwe*, it is nothing at all. *Sitaki kamwe*, I will have nothing to do with it. (Cf. *l abisa, halisi, hatta kidogo*.)

Kana, v. also **Kanya**, deny, negative, say 'no,' disown, refuse, e. g. *kwanza mwivi amekana, sasa aungama*, at first the thief denied it, now he confesses. *Baba alimkana mtoto*, the father disowned the child. Ps. *kaniwa*. Nt. *kan-ika, -ikana*, e. g. *amekaniwa na watu si mwivi*, it was denied by the people that he was a thief. *Haikanikani kabisa*, it is absolutely undeniable. Ap. *kan-ia, -iana*, forbid to, refuse to, deny to (about, for, on the part of, by, at, &c.). *Baba amemkania mtoto kuiba* (or, *asiibe*), the father had forbidden the child to steal. Cs. *kan-isha, -ishwa*, also *kan-usha, -yusha, -ushwa, -ishia, -ishiwa, -ishana*, also Intens. deny emphatically, e. g. *amenikanushia haki yangu*, he has wholly denied me my rights. *Mwanamke amekukanisha mtoto wako*, the woman has induced you to disown your child. (Cf. *kanyo, kikano, kataa, kataza*.)

Kana, n. rudder handle, tiller, i. e. *mkono wa usukani*.

Kana, conj. See **Kama**.

Kanadili, n. (*ma-*), a projection from quarter or stern of native vessel, used as a closet (*choo*),—also quarter gallery.

Kanda, v. knead with the hand, press and work with the fingers, shampoo. *K. unga*, knead flour (dough). *K. udongo*, knead clay,—as a potter. *K. mwili*, of a kind of massage, to give relief in pain or weariness, or merely as a luxury. Ps. *kandwa*. Nt. *kandika*. Ap. *kand-ia, -iwa*. Cs. *kand-isha, -ishwa*. (Cf. *kandika*.)

Kanda, n. (—, and *ma-*), (1) a bag of native (plaited) matting,—often used for grain, broader at the bottom than at the mouth. Dim. *kikanda*. (Cf. *kikapo*.) (2) Leather thong, strap,—also plur. of *ukanda*.

Kande, n. and **Kandi**, stores, supplies,—for a journey, &c., esp. provisions. Not usual in Z. (Cf. *masarufu, akiba, riziki*.)

***Kanderinya**, n. kettle, tea-kettle.

Kandika, v. of the operation of covering the wooden framework of a native hut with clay to form the walls. Women bring water, while men dig and knead the clay, and apply it in lumps with the hand, between the sticks and inside and out. *K. nyumba kwa udongo*, plaster a house with clay. Ps. *kandikwa*. (Cf. follg. and *kanda, kando, paka*, v.)

Kandiko, n. (*ma-*), material for native plastering, i. e. earth or clay. (Cf. prec. and *jengo*.)

***Kandili**, n. (*ma-*), lamp, candlestick, chandelier. (Ar. Cf. *fanusi, kinara, taa, meshmaa*.)

Kando, n. (—, and *ma-*), side, edge, margin, brink (esp. of river or sea), bank, coast. *K. ya* (or *la*) *mto*, the margin of the river. Used commonly as adv. and (with *la, ya*) prep., on one side, aside, by the side, on the verge or edge, e. g. *aliye kando, haangukiwi na mti*, he who is on one side is not fallen upon by a tree. *K. yetu*, in our neighbourhood, near us. *Sawasawa k.*, parallel. *Weka k.* (or, *kando-kando*) *ya*, put by the side of. *K. zote*, on all sides. (Cf. *ukingo, upande*, and *ukando*.)

K

Kanga, v. See Kaanga.

Kanga, n. (1) *kanga la mnazi*, the fruit stem or stalk bearing the nuts on a cocoanut tree, when stripped of the nuts, the bare stalk, dry stem. (The same when growing, and with nuts on it, is *utawi*, cf. *mnazi*.) (2) Common speckled guinea-fowl (cf. *kororo*). (3) In commerce, scarf,—piece of calico of all patterns and colours, worn by native women and men. Described as *leso ya upande mmoja*. (Cf. *shiti, kisuto, leso, nguo*.)

Kangaja, n. (*ma-*), (1) small mandarin orange, fruit of the *mkangaja*; (2) a sea-fish, with a disagreeable smell.

Kango, n. (*ma-*), a frying-pan. See Kaango.

*Kaniki, n. in commerce, blue shirtings,—a dark blue calico, worn by the poorer classes commonly as an undergarment, or at work. See Nguo.

*Kanisa, n. (*ma-*), synagogue, temple, church. (Arab. Cf. *msikiti, hekalu*.)

*Kanju, n. (*ma-*), fruit of the cashew tree, *mkanju*,—which in Z. is called *mbibo*. See Mbibo.

Kano, n. (*ma-*), large sinew or tendon (of animals). (Cf. *mkano*.)

*Kantara, n. a bridge. (Arab. Cf. *daraja, bonth, ulalo*.)

*Kanuni, n. that which is regular (necessary, indispensable), a fundamental rule, a necessary condition, a *sine qua non*. As adv. undoubtedly, certainly, truly. (Ar. Cf. *farathi, sharti, kawaida, hakika, yakini*.)

Kanusha, v. Cs. from Kana, which see. Other forms are *kanyusha* and *kanisha*.

Kanya, v. same as Kana (which see), refuse a proposal, give a negative answer.

Kanyo, n. (*ma-*), denial, refusal, contradiction, negative answer. (Cf. *kanya, kana, mkano*, and syn. *katao, katazo*.)

Kanwa, n. (*ma-*), also Kanywa, mouth (of man, and animals in general). *K. jumbe la maneno*, the month is ruler of speech. (Dim. from *nywa*, see -nya, and cf. *kinwa*, which is usual in Z.)

*Kanzi, n. what is kept in store, a treasure, a hoard, also treasury, store-room. *Aweke mali kanzini*, let him put his belongings in the store-room. (Ar. Cf. *tunu, hazina*, and *kandi, ghala, akiba*.)

Kanzu, n. the usual outer garment of men in Z., a long-sleeved calico gown, reaching from the neck to the ankles, usually plain white or yellowish-brown (*huthurungi*), with or without lines of silk stitch-work, red or white, on the neck, wrists, and front, and fastened with a small button or tassel at the throat. Worn over a loincloth, often with a light doublet, or under a coloured sleeveless open waistcoat (*kisibau*), or a cloth cloak (*joho*). Worn also by women, but then shorter, of coloured and varied materials, and with red binding. *Kanzu* are distinguished as *ya kufuta*, plain, common, *ya ziki*, with white cotton stitching at the neck, *ya kazi*, with ornamental stitching, and according to material, *ya bafta, ya huthurungi*, &c. (? Cf. Ar. *kasâ*, clothe. For parts, &c., of the *kanzu* see *badani, taharizi, sijafu, kikwapa, jabali, mhalbori, kaba, tiki, mrera, kiboko, kinara, tarizi, mjusi*, &c., and for tailoring, *shona, mshoni*.)

Kao, n. (*ma-*), place of residence, dwelling, habitation,—commonly in the plur. *makao*. Also of mode or act of remaining, residing, &c., situation, position, way of living, but thus more often *ukao, kikao*. (Cf. *kaa*, v., *ukao, kikao, ukazi, makazi*.)

*Kaoleni. See Kauli.

Kaomwa, n. and Kauma, calumba root,—mainly procured from East Africa. Described as 'the root of a creeping plant, like a sweet potatoe, a tonic of bitter taste' (Kr.).

Kapi, n. (—, and *ma-*), (1) a

pulley,—consisting of a sheave (*roda*), enclosed in a block (*makupa*). (For various sorts see **Gofia, Abedari**.) (2) Chaff, husks. (Cf. *kumvi, wishwa, kununu, macho ya mtama*.)

Kapo (*ma-*), and **Kapu**, a large basket (of plaited leaf-strips). See **Kikapo**.

***Karaha**, n. provocation, (giving) offence, (causing) aversion. *Mambo ya k.*, provocation, cause of ill-feeling, repulsion. (Ar. Cf. *kirihi*, also *ckerahi, ikirahi*.)

***Karakoli**, n. and **Karakoni**, prison. Not usual in Z. (? Turkish, introduced by Soudanese. Cf. *gereza, kifungo*.)

***Karama**, n. (1) an honour, privilege, valuable possession, gracious act, generous behaviour; (2) gracious gift, esp. a gift of God in answer to prayer. (Ar. Cf. *karimu* and follg., and for gifts generally *bakshishi*.)

***Karamu**, n. a feast, banquet, festive entertainment. (Ar. Cf. prec.)

***Karani**, n. (*ma-*), clerk, secretary, amanuensis, supercargo. (Ar.)

Karara, Karasia. See **Kalala, Kalasia**.

***Karata**, n. card, playing card. (? *charta*, card.)

***Karatasi**, n. paper, a piece of paper. (Ar.)

***Karatha**, n. money on loan, advance, credit. *K. ya fetha*, a cash advance. (Arab. Cf. follg.)

***Karathi**, v. and **Karithi**, (1) lend money, esp. make an advance for commercial purposes, accommodate with money or goods; (2) also as Cs. borrow, get an advance. Ps. *karathiwa*. (Ar. Cf. prec. and the commoner *kopa, kopesha*, and *azimu*.)

***Karibia**, v. Ap. come near (to), go near (to), approach, move close to, enter. Ps. *karibiwa*. Cs. *karib-isha, -ishwa*, bring near, move close, invite as guest, welcome, entertain. *Karibisha chakula* (*kiti*), invite to a meal (offer a seat to). *Tulikaribishwa vizuri*, we were hospitably treated. Rp. *karibiana*. (Ar. Cf. *karibu*, and *sogea*.)

***Karibu**, n. near relation, kinsman. *Watu hawa k. zangu*, these people are relations of mine. Also *mtu wa k.*, a relation. —adv. and (with *ya* and *na*) prep. (1) of space, near, close (to); (2) of time, presently, shortly, lately, recently; (3) in general, nearly, almost, about. *Hivi k.*, just lately. *Alikuja k.*, he came near, or, he arrived recently. *K. yangu*, near me. Common as reply to the inquiry *Hodi?* i.e. Come in, walk in, you are welcome. (Ar. Cf. *karibia*.)

***Karimu**, a. and -**karimu**, liberal, openhanded, generous. Also v. See **Kirimu**. (Ar. Cf. *karama, karamu*, and syn. -*paji*.)

Karipia, v. Ap. use harsh language to, reprimand, scold, chide. Ps. *karipiwa*. (Cf. *laumu, kemea, shutumu*. The Pr. form *karipa* is also used.)

***Kariri**, v. repeat, say over again and again, recite, rehearse. Ps. *karirwa*. Nt. *karirika*. Ap. *karir-ia*, say over to (for, at, &c.). Cs. *karir-isha, -ishwa*. (Ar. Cf. syn. B. *sema* (*soma*) *tena*, or *marra ya pili*, or *marra nyingi*).

Kasa, n. a sea turtle. (Cf. *ng'amba, kobe*.)

***Kasa**, adv. also **Kassa**, less, less by, short by, usually in connexion with *robo, themuni*, or similar words, e.g. *rupia mbili k. themuni*, two rupees less four annas; *saa sita k. robo*, a quarter to twelve o'clock (lit. six hours less a quarter). *K. robo*, three quarters (of a dollar), one rupee and a half. (Ar. Cf. *kasiri*, n. and *kasoro*.)

***Kasarani, Kasasi**, n. See **Kisirani, Kisasi**.

***Kasha**, n. (*ma-*), box, chest, cupboard, packing case. *Kasha la fetha*, (1) a silver box; (2) a money box, safe. (Cf. *sanduku, bweta,*—also Ital. *cassa*, Fr. *caisse*.)

*Kashabu, n. a wooden rod, which draws the threads of the web apart in native weaving. (? Ar. Cf. *mfumo, fuma*.)

*Kashifu, v. (1) reveal, disclose; (2) show up, discredit, disparage, tell stories of, slander. Ps. *kashifiwa*. (Ar. for more usual *chongea, singizia,* &c.)

Kasia, n. (*ma-*), an oar. *Piga* (*vuta*) *k.*, row. (Cf. *kafi*, a paddle.)

*Kasiba, n. barrel (of a gun). *Mdomo kama k.*, small round mouth, —a point of beauty. (Ar. 'reed.' Cf. *mwanzi, mdomo*.)

*Kasidi, n. Also Kusudi, which see. (Ar.)

*Kasiki, n. (—, and *ma-*), large earthen jar (for water, ghee, treacle, &c.). (Cf. *balasi*, which is larger.)

Kasimele, n. cocoanut cream, the thick oily juice squeezed from the grated nut by a strainer, before any water is mixed with it, i.e. *maji ya nazi yaliyokamuliwa mbele katika kifumbu,*—also called *tui la kasimele*, or *tui halisi*. The same nut, when mixed with water and strained again, produces *tui la nyuma, tui la kupopolea*, a white milky fluid. See Tui.

*Kasiri, v. cause to be angry, vex, provoke. *Hayo ndiyo maneno yaliyokukasiri*, these are the words which annoyed you. *Sultani alimkasiri mkewe*, the Sultan vexed his wife. But the Cs. is more common in this sense (see below). Ps. *kasiriwa*. Nt. *kasirika*, be angry, be excited, whence *kasirik-ia, -iwa*, be angry with. Ap. *kasir-ia, -iwa*. Cs. *kasir-isha, -ishwa*, enrage, provoke, exasperate, stir up violent feeling in, incite, inflame. Rp. *kasiri-ana*. (? Ar. Cf. *hasira*, and syn. *ghathabu, uchungu*. Dist. *hasara, hasiri* and also *kasiri*, n.)

*Kasiri, n. end. *Alasiri k.*, late afternoon, 5 p.m., i.e. *mwisho wa alasiri*. As adv. less. *K. ya, k. kuliko*, less than. (Arab., seldom heard. Cf. *kasa, kasoro*, and the commoner *hatima, mwisho*.)

*Kaskazi, n. (1) northerly wind, north monsoon. *K. inavuma*, the north wind is blowing. Cf. *kusi*, south wind, and *upepo*. (2) Season of the north monsoon, i.e. December to March, the hottest part of the year in Zanzibar, i.e. *wakati wa jasho na kukausha miti*, also called *musimu*, and sometimes *chaka*; (3) northerly direction, the north. Also called **Kibula Kibla**. *Kaskazini*, in the north, northwards. (Cf. *shemali*, the Ar. word for 'north,' and *jaa*.)

*Kasoro, adv. less (by), short (by). *Kasoro nussu*, less by a half. Sometimes as n., defect, blemish. (Ar. *kasr*. Cf. *kasa, kasiri*.)

*Kassa, adv. See Kasa.

*Kassi, adv. of intensity, used with verbs, much, very, with energy (vehemence, violence, &c.), e.g. *enda k.*, go with force, go quickly. *Mto unapita k.*, the river runs quickly, has a strong current. Also as a noun, *tia (piga) k.*, apply force, tighten. *Sokota kwa k.*, twist forcibly. (Prob. Ar. ? Cf. *kiasi*, or *kaza, kazi*.)

*Kastabini, n. a thimble. (Persian, for more common *subana*.)

*Kasumba, n. opium. (Hind. Cf. syn. Ar. *afiuni*.)

*Kata, v. (1) cut, cut off, cut away, cut short, cut up, or in pieces; (2) fig. divide, reduce, bring to an end, decide, frustrate. The noun following may define the thing cut, the nature of the cutting, the effect produced, or the instrument used. *K. miti*, cut down trees. *K. maji*, go up stream. *K. kisu* (or *kwa kisu*), cut with a knife. *K. nguo*, cut calico, often in the sense 'buy a piece of calico, order a new dress or suit. *K. nakshi*, carve (in wood or stone). *K. pesa*, reduce (or, withhold) a sum due. *K. maneno*, conclude (break off, decide, settle) a discussion.

K. hukumu, decide a suit, give sentence. *K. tamaa*, bring hopes to an end, despair, despond, be desperate. *K. kiu*, quench thirst. *K. shauri*, frustrate a plan. Ps. *katwa*, implying an agent, as present or prominent in the mind. Nt. *katika*, in which the fact rather than the agency is in view, e.g. *hukumu imekatwa*, the judge has decided the case. *Hukumu imekatika*, a verdict has been given. *Kusi imekatika*, the south wind is coming to an end. Hence, *katik-ia*, -*iwa*, &c. be cut off, &c. at (for, in, &c.), e.g. *muhogo ulikatikia mumo*, the cassava broke off where it stood. *Ugwe hukatikia pembamba*, cord breaks at the thinnest part. Also *katikana*, be capable of being cut, &c., be possibly cut. Ap. *kat-ia*, -*iwa*, -*iana*, cut at (into, off from, a part of, &c.), e.g. *katia hesabu*, cut off from (deduct from) an account. *Katia mti*, cut a piece from, chop at, make a cut in (not, cut down). *Katia njia*, cut into (strike on) a road. *Ni kiasi changu kama nalikatiwa mimi*, it fits me exactly, just as if it was made for me (or, I had been measured for it). *Tulikatiwa maneno*, we have had our matter settled. *Katiana*, settle accounts together, strike a balance, i.e. by striking out items on both sides. Cs. *kat-iza*, -*izwa*, -*izia*, -*iziwa*, -*izana*, cause to cut (be cut, &c.), or Intens. cut (end, decide) abruptly (vigorously, sharply, &c.). *Katiza maneno*, break off (interrupt, stop, apply closure to) a discussion. *Walikatiziwa vyakula*, their supplies were deliberately stopped. Rp. *katana*, e.g. *wanakatana kwa visu*, they are fighting with knives. Also Rf. *jikata, jikatia, jikatiza*, &c., and Rd. of emphasis, *katakata*, cut to pieces, make mincemeat of. (Ar. Cf. *mkata, mkato, kato, kata, mkatizo, mkate, mkataa*, and follg. Also syn. *tema, chanja, pasua, chonga, choma, vunja, maliza*.)

*Kata, n. also Kataa, a cutting, piece, part, portion, section, fraction, not of a literal cut or cutting, but fig., e.g. (a) part of a house, *k. ya nyumba*, a room, an apartment, one of the screened-off divisions in a native hut, or *k. ya chumba*, an alcove, recess, part of a room; (b) *k. ya kitabu*, part of a book, section, leaf, page (cf. *juzu, ukarasa*); also of a country, 'quarter, district,' *k. ya inchi* (? cf. *mtaa, kitaa*); (c) lengths of rope, string, silk, &c., as sold in shops, i.e. hank, skein, coil. (Ar. Cf. *kata*, v., and *kato, mkato*, &c.)

Kata, n. (*ma-*), (1) a ladle, dipper, scoop, used for drinking, or dipping water from a hole,—usually a coconut shell, with one end cut off, and fixed to the end of a stick. (Cf. *upawa*.) (2) A round pad, usually of leaves, grass, or a folded strip of cloth, worn on the head when carrying a load, water-jar, &c. (Dist. *mkata, ukata*.)

Kataa, v. refuse, reject, decline, say 'no.' Ps. *kataliwa*. Nt. *katalika*. Ap. *kata-lia*, -*liwa*, -*liana*, e.g. refuse, refuse credence to, decline acceptance from, say 'no' to, &c. Cs. *kata-za*, -*zwa*, -*zana*, prohibit, forbid, deter, cause to refuse, refuse peremptorily, &c. Also *kata-zia*, -*ziwa*, prohibit to (from, by, &c.). (Cf. *katazo, kana, gombeza, dakiza, teta, marufuku*.)

*Kataa, a. final, decisive, conclusive. *Neno hili k.*, this statement is decisive. (Ar. Cf. *kata, mkataa*.)

*Katabahu, lit. he wrote it,—usually at the end of letters, with the name of the writer, and sometimes *bijedihi*, by the hand of. (Arab. Cf. *kitabu, mkataba*.)

*Katani, n. also Kitani, flax, and what is made from it, linen, string, strong thread, twine. *Uzi wa k.*, thread made of flax or hemp, as dist. from *uzi wa pamba*, cotton thread. (Ar. Cf. *uzi, ugwe, kigwe, kamba*.)

Katazo, n. (*ma-*), prohibition, contradiction, objection. (Cf. *kataa*, and syn. *kindano, dakizo, teto*.)

*Kathalika, adv. in like manner, likewise, similarly, in the same way. (Ar. Cf. *aitha, thamma*, and follg., and syn. B. *vile vile, vivyo hivyo*.)

*Katháwakatha, a. and adv., thus and thus, and so on, et caetera, many other such, many more. *Watu k.*, lots of people. (Ar. Cf. *kathalika*.)

*Kathi, n. (*ma-*), judge, — the official term, magistrate appointed by the Sultan to decide questions of law. (Ar. Cf. *hakimu*, and *mwamuzi*.)

Kati, adv. and (with *ya*) prep., among, between, inside, in the middle of, amidst, surrounded by. *K. ya nyumba*, in the middle of the house. *Kata k.*, cut asunder (through the middle). Also as n., the middle, the centre, and -*a kati*, central, middle; *wakati wa k.*, the intervening period, interval; *pa k.*, the centre. Sometimes redupl. *katikati* (*ya*), between, among, in the very middle (of), also *kati na kati*. (Cf. *katika*, prep.)

*Katiba, n. ordinance, custom, natural (or original) constitution, destiny, doom,—from the idea of binding and permanent force of Mahommedan law as written in the Coran. (Ar. Cf. follg.)

Katibu, n. a writer, scribe, amanuensis, clerk. (Cf. *karani, mwandishi, katabahu*.) — v. write,—seldom used, e. g. in Rp. *tukatibiane*, let us draw up a written contract. (Cf. *mkataba, kitabu, kitaba*, and common syn. *andika*.)

Katika, prep. among, in, whether (*a*) of place,—in, at, to, towards, into, from (in), out of, away from; (*b*) of time,—in, at, during; (*c*) in general, —in, engaged in, to, in the direction of, from; (*d*) in the matter of, in reference to, concerning, as to, about. Very common in all senses. In local use, equivalent to -*ni*. Sometimes with *kwa*, when *kwa* with the word following indicates a single idea or object. *Kufika katika kwa mfalme*, to arrive in the king's court or presence. (Cf. *kati*, and the equally common *kwa*.)

Katikati, adv. and (with *ya*) prep. See Kati.

*Katili, n. a murderous person, a bloodthirsty man, a ruffian. (Arab. Cf. syn. B. *mwuaji*.)

*Kato, n. (*ma-*), a cutting, fragment, thing cut or broken off. (Cf. *kata, mkato*.)

*Katu, n. a kind of gum, imported to Z., and sold in small dark-red lumps chiefly for chewing with betel. See Tambuu, Uraibu.

Katua, v. polish, brighten, clean by rubbing. *K. bunduki*, clean rust, &c. off a gun. Ps. *katuliwa*. Nt. *katuka*. Ap. *katulia*. *Majifu ya kukatulia visu*, ashes to clean knives with.

Kauka, v. become dry, dry up, be parched. *Inchi imekauka*, the earth is parched. *Sauti imemkauka*, his voice is dried up, he is hoarse. Ap. *kauk-ia, -iwa*. *Sakafu imekaukia maji*, the water has dried off the roof. Cs. *kau-sha, -shwa*, dry, cause to dry up, parch. (Cf. -*kavu, yabis*, and of drying clothes by exposure to sun and air, *anika*.)

*Kauli, n. (1) sentence, expression; (2) expressed opinion, narrative, account. *K. tatu zilizosemwa*, three accounts were given. *Tufuase k. ya waalimu wetu*, let us follow the opinion of our teachers. *K. ile ikamuthi*, the expression vexed him. (Ar. for the common *neno*. Cf. *kalima* and *kauleni*, double tongued, untrustworthy, i. e. a man of two stories.)

Kauma, n. calumba root. See Kaomwa.

*Kauri, n. a cowry (shell). For various kinds cf. *dondo, kululu, kete*. *Kauri* is also used to describe china, *vitu vya kauri*, as opp. to earthenware, *vitu vya udongo*.

-kavu, a. (*kavu* with D 4 (P), D 5 (S), D 6), also **-kafu**, (1) dry, parched, waterless, barren. *Inchi k.*, dry land, *terra firma*, as opp. to *bahari*, sea. *Kuni k.*, dry firewood. *Nguo k.*, dry clothes. Prov. *maji mafu, mvuvi mkafu*, at neap tides the fisherman gets little. (2) Dry, humorous, satirical, amusing. *Mtu mkavu*, a witty person. *Maneno makavu*, witticisms. (3) Brave, fearless, unconcerned. Cf. the phrase *-kavu wa macho, -enyi macho makavu*, of a nonchalant, intrepid, dauntless look. (Cf. *kauka*.)

Kawa, v. be delayed, tarry, linger, delay, loiter, take a long time, be behind time, be late. Ap. *k wia*, same as *kawa*; also *kawilia*, delay for (on account of, at, about, &c.), and so *kaw-ilisha, -ilishwa*, cause to delay, keep back, make late. Cs. *kaw-isha, -ishwa*, put off, make stand over, adjourn, e.g. *kawisha kodi*, get in arrears for rent. (Cf. *usiri, ahiri, chelewa*, and ? cf. *kaa*.)

Kawa, n. (—, and of size *ma-*), (1) a dish cover, conical in shape, made of plaited grass. *Sahani isiyo na k.*, a dish without a cover. *Tulingane sawa sawa, kama sahani na k.*, let us suit each other (i.e. agree), like a dish and its cover. (2) Mildew, mould (Str.).

*****Kawadi**, n. (*ma-*), a procurer. (Arab.)

*****Kawaida**, n. also **Kaida**, regulative principle, fundamental rule, usage, custom, system, and so 'pattern, standard, maxim.' *K. kama sheria*, customary usage is like law. *Hatuna k. ya kuja mtu*, we are not used to a person coming, we do not allow it. (Ar. Cf. *desturi, kanuni*.)

Kawe, n. a very small stone, dim. of *jiwe, kijiwe.* (Cf. *jiwe, mbwe*, and *ka-*.)

Kawia, Kawilia, Kawisha, &c. See **Kawa**.

Kaya, n. (*ma-*), a kind of shellfish.

Kayamba, n. (1) a sieve; (2) a rattle resembling a sieve,—dry grain shaken inside a flat case of reeds.

Kaza, v. (1) fix, make fast, fasten, tighten; (2) grip, hold tight, fit tightly; (3) use force (in), exert energy, act with a will, emphasize, accentuate. *K. kamba*, make a rope fast. *K. mbio*, run hard. *K. kuimba*, sing with a will. *Nguo ya kukaza*, tight clothes. Ps. *kazwa*. Nt. *kazika*. Ap. *kaz-ia, -iwa*, e.g. *kazia macho*, rivet the gaze upon. Cs. *kaz-isha, -ishwa*. Rp. *kazana*, (1) hold each other, make a mutual effort; (2) hold together, be compact, be firm (stiff, hard). *Kazana na*, adhere to, stick to. (Cf. *kazi, kazo, mkazo*, and perh. *kaa*, v. Also similar Ar. words denoting effort, work, firmness.)

Kazi, n. (1) work, labour, employment, occupation, profession, business, function, a job; (2) hard work, toil, strain, effort, exertion; (3) normal action, regular duty, routine. *Mchezo huo ni k. burre*, a game like that is labour thrown away, —a native view of athletics. *Ndio k. yake*, that is what he always does, or, he is responsible for it. *Fanya (tenda) k.*, work, be a labourer. *Nguo hii ni k. ya Wahindi*, this stuff is made by Hindoos. *K. ya makataa*, contract work, task work. (Cf. *kaza*.)

Kazo, n. pressing tight, holding hard, grip. Also as a. *-kazo*, tight. (Cf. *kaza, mkazo*.)

Kazoakazoa, n. a term of abuse (perh. from *zoa* and *ka-*, which see), i.e. wretched gutter-scraper.

-ke, a. (1) (also *-a kike, jike*), of the female sex, female, feminine; (2) like a woman, timid, stupid. *Mke* (Pl. *wake*), *mtu mke* (Pl. *watu wake*), *mtu wa kike* (Pl. *watu wa kike*), and most commonly *mwana mke* (Pl. *waana wake*, or *waanake*), are all used of 'woman' generally, in respect of sex simply. In relation to the male sex, *mke* has the definite meaning 'wife, married woman,' and is then clearly distinguished from *mwanamke*, which denotes an irregular connexion, e.g. *mkewe waziri alikuwa mwanamke wake Abunuwasi*, the vizir's wife was Abunuwasi's paramour. *Mke ni nguo*, a wife means (the cost of her) dress. *Wake*, as a noun, plur. of *mke*, often takes for distinctness pronouns of the form in z-, i.e. *wake zake*, his wives, rather than *wake wake*. *Watoto waanake*, or *wa kike*, girls. *Bata jike*, a female duck. *Moyo wa kike*, a womanly (i.e. usually 'timid, stupid') character. (Cf. *jike, kike, kuke, uke*, and opp. *-ume*.)

Kefu, int. also **Kéfule**, expressing disgusted surprise, indignation, aversion. *K. mimi killa siku*, think of me (being so treated) every day. *Mtu hamfanyizii hiana mtu asioamini, kefu aliomwamini*, a man does not act treacherously towards one he distrusts, much less one he trusts.

Kefya-kefya, v. tease, annoy, nag at, depress, discourage, put out of heart. (Cf. *sumbua, tesa, chokoza, uthi*.)

Keke, n. a drilling tool, a drill, consisting of a steel bit (*kekee*), fitted into a wooden handle (*msuka, msukano*), which is turned in a wooden socket (*jivu*) by a bow and string (*uta*). Described generally as *kidude cha kuzulia mti*, a tool for boring wood.

Kekee, n. (1) a boring tool, see **Keke**; (2) a kind of silver bracelet, usually broad and flat, fastened by a clasp or bolt. (Cf. *kikuku, banagiri*, and *urembo*.)

Kekevu, n. hiccup. (Cf. *kikeukeu*, and more usu. in Z. *kwikwi*.)

Kelele, n. (*ma-*), a shout, shouting, uproar, noise. *Piga k.*, shout, give a shout. *Nena kwa k.*, or, *kikelele*, make a loud remark. *Makelele*, as an int. ordering silence, i.e. Too much noise! Be quiet! Silence! (Cf. *chub! huss! buu! nyamaza!* (or, Plur., *nyamazeni! kimya!* Also cf. *ukelele, kikelele*.)

***Kem**, interrog. adv. How much? How many? e.g. in inquiring price, *kem? wauzaje? kiasi gani?*—all meaning 'How much?' (Arab. Cf. *kima*.)

Kemea, v. scold, rebuke, speak loudly (roughly) to, snub. Ps. *kemewa*. (Cf. *karipia, laumu, nenea, ambilia*.)

Kenda, n. and a., nine. *-a kenda*, ninth. (Cf. syn. Ar. *tissia, tissa*, equally common.)

Kenda, v. for *kaenda*, he has gone. See **Ka-**. Also for Infin. *kwenda*, e.g. *kendapi?* for *kwenda wapi?* a general inquiry Where are you (he, they, &c.) going?

Kenge, n. a large water-lizard, common in Z. (For other kinds cf. *mjusi, guruguru*.)

Kengee, n. and **Ukengee**, the flat part of a cutting instrument, blade of knife, sword, spearhead, &c. (Cf. *bapa*, and contr. *makali*, edge, and *kipini*, handle, of such instruments.)

Kengele, n. (—, and of size *ma-*), a bell. *Piga k.*, ring a bell, ring. (Cf. *njuga*.)

Kera, v. worry, tease, annoy, vex. (Cf. *kero*, and syn. *kefya-kefya, sumbua, tesa*.)

Kereketa, n. cause an irritating sensation, esp. in tongue or throat, have a rough taste, cause a choking feeling. *Koho yangu yanikereketa kwa sababu ya kula tumbako*, my throat is irritated from chewing tobacco. *Tumbako yanikereketa*, the tobacco has a harsh taste to me. (Cf. syn. *washa*.)

Kereza, v. (1) saw into, cut into with a saw (rasp, file, &c.), make a cut or notch in; (2) cut in a lathe, turn. *Zikerezwazo*, turned articles, turnery. (Cf. follg.)

Kerezo, n. also **Keezo**, a machine for turning, a lathe.

***Kerimu**, v. See **Kirimu**.

Kering'ende, n. (1) a kind of dragon-fly; (2) a red-legged partridge (Str.); (3) ? a cricket.

Kero, n. trouble, annoyance, disturbance, vexatious conduct. (Cf. *kera*, and syn. *ghasia*, *masumbuo*, *uthia*.)

Kesha, v. remain awake, keep awake, stay up at night, not to sleep, watch, keep watch. *Ngoma ya vijana haikeshi*, a children's dance does not last all night. *Kesha kucha*, stay awake till the morning. Ap. *kesh-ea, -ewa*, stay up for, keep night watch with, nurse all night. Cs. *kesh-esha, -eshwa, -eza, -ezwa*, keep a person awake. Rp. *keshana*, remain awake together. (Cf. *kesha*, n. and *kesho*, and syn. *keti na macho, kaa macho*.)

Kesha, n. night watch, vigil. *Nna k. yangu usiku kucha*, I have my watch all night long. *Siku ya k. ya mwisho*, the last night of a formal mourning (*matanga*). (Cf. *kesha*, v., *kesho*, and dist. *kesha* for *kaisha*, he has finished.)

Kesho, n. and adv., to-morrow, the next day, the day after. *K. kuchwa*, the day after to-morrow. *K. yake*, the following day. *Kushinda kesho kuchwa*, the third day (also called *mtondo*).

Kete, n. (1) a small kind of cowry. Also a game played with these shells. *Meno kama k.*, teeth like cowries,—a point of beauty. (Cf. *kauri*.) (2) (*ma-*), a string (of beads, &c.). Two *makete* = one *timba*; ten *makete* = five *timba* = one *fundo*. (? Cf. *kata*, n.)

Keti, v. (1) (in poet. *keleti*), sit down, take a seat; (2) dwell, live, remain, stay, reside. *Tafathali uketi*, please take a seat (cf. *kaa kitako*, meaning strictly, squat in the native way). Ps. *ketiwa*. Ap. *ket-ia, -iwa*, e. g. *kidude cha kuketia*, something to sit upon. Cs. *ketisha, -shwa*, e. g. cause to remain, keep, preserve. (Cf. *kiti*, and syn. *kaa*.)

Kh-. Many Swahili words are taken from Arabic originals beginning with the sound of *Kh-*. These will be found under *H* in this Dictionary, representing the simple aspirate to which they all become assimilated in proportion as they become naturalized among Africans. On the other hand, the *Kh* sound is often more or less retained by persons imitating or influenced by Arabic pronunciation. Some of these words are:— *khabari, khadaa, khadimu, khafifu, khaini, khalifu, khamsi* (and derivatives), *khara, kharadali, khatari, khati, khatia, khatima, khazina, khema, kheri, kheza, khorji, khofu, khubiri, khutuba*.

*****Khoja**, n. a member of one of the two chief sects of Mahommedan Hindoos in Zanzibar, the other being **Bohora**, which see. (Hind.)

Ki, verb-form, (it) is, agreeing with D 3 (S), e. g. *kiti hiki ki ghali*, this chair is expensive.

Ki-, as an initial syllable, is in far the greater number of words a formative prefix, and one of the commonest formatives in the Swahili language,— so common that no attempt is made here to enumerate all the words beginning or regularly formed with *ki-*. Words not found under *ki-* may be looked for (1) under the letter immediately following *ki-*, or (2) under *Ch-*, since *ki-* usually (though not always) becomes *ch-* before a vowel (e. g. *chungu* for *ki-ungu*, but *kiungo*, not *chungo*), and moreover *ki-* in any word is often heard pronounced *chi-* among the lower classes in Zanzibar. *Ki* as a formative prefix is used (1) with verb-stems, to form verbal nouns denoting usually some concrete embodiment or special manifestation of the root-idea of a non-personal kind. (Contrast the characteristic use of *u-* in forming abstract, and of *m-* in forming personal derivative nouns.) When *ki* is prefixed, the verb-stem 'a' may retain its final -*a*. In this case, which is not common, the verbal noun is often followed by another noun depending directly on it, e. g. *kipa mkono*, *kifungua mlango* (denoting presents given on special occasions), also *kifa uwongo*, and cf. *kinywa*, mouth, *kidonda*, *kifaa*. (*b*) Changes final *a* to *o*, *si*, *zi*, or is followed by -*ji*, e. g. *kitendo*, *kifungo*, *kituo*, *kicheko*, *kiongozi*, *kikohozi*, *kinywaji*, *kipaji*. Obs. also *kiumbe*, and *chumba*. This form (*ki*- with a verbal root and termination -*o*) is not only common, but may practically be formed at pleasure from any suitable root. In some cases the word becomes specialized and limited in meaning (e. g. *kifuo*, a stake used for husking cocoanuts), but seldom loses altogether the power of including any of the following meanings,—act, process, time, place, method, instrument, instance or case, i. e. some particular embodiment of the idea conveyed by the root. Instances of all kinds follow in their place in the Dictionary, e. g. *kiango*, limited to a kind of lamp-stand; *kicho* including a feeling of fear, and an object feared; *kipendo*, meaning love, but strictly loving in connexion with some occasion or particular case either of the feeling or of the object; *kikao*, *kifungo*, with a wide range of meanings. *Ki*- is also used with other than verb-roots with the same general (concrete non-personal) meaning, e. g. *kitu* as comp. with *mtu*, *kivuli* with *mvuli* and *uvuli*, and even with reference to persons in such words as *kizee*, *kipofu*, *kiziwi*, *kibeti*, but see below (3). (2) To form diminutives with noun-stems, and as such may be used before any suitable noun whatever, often displacing an initial *m* or *u*, e. g. *kitoto*, *kipande*, *kivuli*, and sometimes followed by a *ji*- or *j*-, especially with monosyllabic roots, e. g. *kijiti*, *kijibwa*, *kijiji*, *kijana*, *kijumba*, *kijineno*. Obs. that *ki*- may convey the idea, not only (*a*) of relative smallness, but (*b*) of relative unimportance, e. g. *kishughuli*, a small trifling business; of endearment, e. g. *kipenzi*, darling; and of secrecy or contempt, e. g. *kishauri*, a plot, *kijumbe*, a secret (or private) messenger, *kijitu*, a mannikin. Obs. that relative degrees of size may be conveyed in the case of some words by placing them in different declensions, D 3, D 5, or D 6, e. g. *kipete*, a small ring; *pete*, a ring of ordinary size; *pete* (pl. *mapete*), a large ring. (3) With noun-stems and adjectives, to give them an adverbial use, and also a peculiar use as nouns, denoting the sort or kind which the noun itself expresses. E. g. *amevaa kizungu*, he is dressed in European fashion; *alilia kisimba*, he roared like a lion; *asema kigeni*, he talks in a foreign way, like a stranger. *Kaa kitako*, sit on the haunches. *Kiti cha kifalme*, a royal throne. *Mambo ya kisasa*, modern ways. *Vitu vya kikale*, antiquated, old-fashioned things (but *vitu vya kale*, antiquities, ancient things). When used independently, this form often denotes the language of a place or country, e. g. *kiunguja*, the language of Zanzibar. To this use may also be referred words like *kizee*, *kipofu*, *kilema*, &c., commonly used of persons, but meaning 'one of the old generation, one of the blind sort,' &c., and perhaps *kinyozi*, *kiongozi* (see above (1)). *Ki* is also used as follows:—(1) as the pfx. of all adjectives and verbs (both subjective and objective) corresponding to D 3 (S), e. g. *kitu kiki changu kizuri chakipendenza kitoto kile*, this pretty thing of mine pleases that little child. (2) In verbs, *ki* is (*a*) the characteristic of the Pres. Partic. corresponding to the Eng. Partic. in -*ing*, and may be translated according to the context by such words as, 'if, supposing, as, when, while, though, &c.' Obs. that *niki*- in this use is often contracted into *hi*, as *nika-* into *ha*. (*b*) Sometimes inserted before the root in Past Tense to denote an imperfect, or continuing action or state, e.g. *alipokisema*, while he was still talking; *alikingoja*, he was waiting. (*c*) Sometimes used for *ka* as a connective particle in narrative. So strongly is the *ki-* sound identified with its use as a prefix in Swahili, that even when it belongs to the root, as esp. in words of Arabic origin, it is constantly treated as a pfx., and changed to *vi-* in the Plur. of such nouns, e. g. in the case of *kitabu*, *kiasi*, *kilele*, *kiberiti*, and others.

Kia, n. (*via*), door bar. (Cf. *kiwi*, *pingo*, *komeo*.) Also as v., step over. (Seldom in Z. Cf. *kiuka*, *chupa*.)

*****Kiada**, adv. in an orderly, distinct, intelligible way. *Sema k.*, speak slowly and distinctly. *Nieleze k.*, explain to me distinctly. (Ar.)

Kialio, n. (*vi-*), stick laid across the bottom of a cooking pot inside, to prevent what is cooked from being burnt. Dim. of *walio*, or perh. for *kilalio*. (Cf. *ulalo*, *lala*.

Kiambaza, n. See **Kiwambaza**.

Kianga, n. (*vi-*), and sometimes **Kiangazi**, a burst of sunshine, ray of light, reflected brightness, interval of brightness, or fine weather. (Cf. *anga*, *mwanga*, *angalia*, &c.)

Kiango, n. (*vi-*), a small suspended stand, carrier, or support (for a lamp, &c.). Dim. of *mwango*. (Cf. *anga*, *angika*, and *chango*, a peg.)

Kiapo, n. (*vi-*), an oath, an ordeal, a trial by oath or ordeal, a thing sworn by, or used in ordeal. *Fanya* (*piga*, *shika*) *k.*, take an oath. *Tilia* (*pigisha*) *k.*, administer an oath. *Kula k.*, to submit to an ordeal. *Kama husadiki, tule kiapo*, if you do not believe, let us try ordeal. *Viapo thabiti*, binding oaths. *Peleka kiaponi*, compel to swear, require to undergo an ordeal. Various kinds of ordeal are *kiapo cha moto*, *cha mkate*, *cha sindano*, *cha mibano*, *cha mchele*, *cha kibao*, &c. (Cf. *apa*, *uapo*, *apiza*, also *yamini*, *zuru*.)

Kiarabu, n. and adv., the Arabic language, something of the Arabic kind, in the Arab way. (Cf. *Mwarabu*, and *ki-*.)

Kiasi, n. (*vi-*) and adv., also **Kassi**, (1) measure, quantity, amount (cf. *kadiri*, *kipimo*); (2) moderation, self-control, temperance (cf. *kadiri*, *kujizuia*); (3) a little, a small (moderate) amount (cf. *kidogo*); (4) the charge of a gun, cartridge. Common in inquiring price, *K. gani?* How much? What is the price? *Mtu wa k.*, a temperate person, a man of moderation. *Alimpa k.*, he gave him a little. As adv. of quantity, time, or space,—'a little,' e.g. *neno hili limeanza k.*, this business began some time ago. *Alikwenda k.*, he went a little way. (Ar., the radical *ki* being treated as formative, as in *kitabu*, &c. See **Ki**, and cf. *kidogo*.)

Kiatu, n. (*vi-*), native shoe, sandal, —and used of any kind known in Z. *K. cha ngozi*, leather sandal, flat sole with cross strap and small thong (*gidamu*) between the toes. (Cf. *kubazi*.) *K. cha mti*, a kind of wooden clog, worn indoors, and held on by a peg (*msuruaki*) between the toes. Known as *mtalawanda*, from the wood used. *K. cha kihindi* (*kizungu*), Indian (European) shoe. *Mshona viatu*, or *mshoni wa viatu*, a shoemaker.

Kiazi, n. (*vi-*), a sweet potatoe,— root of a kind of convolvulus. Different kinds are known as *kiazi sena* (white), *k. kindoro* (red). *K. cha kizungu*, the common (European) potatoe. *K. kikuu*, yam,—also *k. manga*.

Kibaba, n. (*vi-*), (1) a common dry measure, about a pint basin full, or a pound and a half of grain. A *kibaba* is half a *kisaga*, and a quarter of a *pishi*. *K. cha tele*, a full, heaped up measure. *K. cha mfuto*, a measure full to top only. (2) Dim. of *baba*.

*Kibakuli, n. (*vi-*), small basin. Also a kind of millet (*mtama*). (Ar. Cf. *bakuli*, and *chungu*.)

*Kibali, n. also Ikibali, Ukubali, acceptance, sanction, favour, assent. (Ar. Cf. *kubali*, and syn. *urathi, ithini*.).

Kibanda, n. (*vi-*), small hut, hovel, shed, workshop,—usu. covered, and open at the sides. Dim. of *banda*.

Kibano, n. (*vi-*), small forceps, split stick (for holding fish, &c. over a fire to roast). (Cf. follg.)

Kibanzi, n. (*vi-*) and Kibanji, splinter, chip. *K. cha ukuni chaliruka*, a chip from the firewood flew up. *Vibanzi vya shoka*, chips made by an axe. (Cf. *banzi, bana, kibano*.)

Kibao, n. See Kibau.

Kibapara, n. (*vi-*), a pauper, destitute person. Used in contempt. (Cf. *bupuru*, an empty shell, and syn. *maskini, fukara*.)

Kibara, n. dim. of *bara*, a small wilderness, a small patch of waste land, &c. See Bara.

Kibarango, n. dim. of *mbarango*, a short thick stick, cudgel, club. Also of a stumpy, thick-set person. (Cf. *bakora* for different kinds of stick.)

*Kibaraza, n. small seat, bench. See Baraza.

*Kibarua, n. (*vi-*), (1) a small written note, letter, ticket. Hence commonly (2) a day labourer of any kind,—from the ticket on presentation of which each is paid. Dim. of *barua*, which see.

Kibata, n. dim. of (1) *mbata*, which see; (2) *bata*, i.e. a duckling.

Kibau, n. (*vi-*), a small board, shelf, &c. *K. cha kuezekea*, roofing shingle. Dim. of *ubau*, which see.

Kibawa, n. (*vi-*), little wing, small feather, fin. Dim. of *bawa, ubawa*.

*Kiberiti, n. (*vi-*), sulphur, a match, a firework. *Washa kiberiti*, strike a match. *Rusha viberiti*, let off fireworks. (Ar. Cf. *fataki*.)

Kibete, n. (*vi-*), undersized creature (man, beast, bird), a dwarf, a bantam, &c. (Cf. *mbilikimo*.)

Kibia, n. (*vi-*), a small cooking pot or pan, or its lid, an earthenware cover. Seldom in Z. (Cf. *bia*, and *chungu*.)

Kibibi, n. (1) dim. of *bibi*, a little lady; (2) cramp (cf. *kiharusi*). *Mguu wangu umefanya kibibi*, I have cramp in the leg. (3) A name for the peacock (*tausi*).

Kibindo, n. mode of securing the loincloth round the waist,—by crossing the two upper (opposite) corners, and folding them back under the cloth itself. This is described as *piga (funga, kaza) kibindo*. *Futika kibindoni*, tuck into the fold of the waistcloth. (? Cf. *kipindo, pinda, pindo, upindo*, and dist. *ubinda, uwinda*.)

Kibinja, n. (*vi-*), a whistle (instrument). (Cf. *ubinja*.)

Kibiongo, n. (*vi-*), a person bent by age or infirmity, bowed, round-shouldered (Str.). (Cf. *jongo, maongo*.)

*Kibla, n. north. See Kibula. (Ar. Cf. *kabili*.)

Kibobwe, n. (*vi-*), a broad strip of calico, wound tightly round the waist for support during work or exercise, esp. by women.

Kibofu, n. (*vi-*), a bladder.

Kibogoshi, n. (*vi-*), a small bag made of a skin, a leather bag, used to carry miscellaneous articles on a journey, money, powder, &c.

Kibogoyo, n. a person who is toothless, or has but few teeth. (Cf. *jino*.)

Kiboko, n. (*vi-*), a hippopotamus, also Boko. *Viboko vya shingo*, small zigzag ornament embroidered in silk on a *kanzu* round the neck. See Kanzu.

Kibonde, n. (*vi-*), trench, deep furrow, hollow between ridges. Dim.

of *bonde*. *Kibondebonde*, uneven, undulating, rolling country.

Kibua, n. (*vi-*), a small kind of fish.

*****Kibula**, n. also **Kíbula**, and **Kibla, Kebla**, the direction of Mecca, the point to which Mahommedans turn in prayer, —in Zanzibar, the north. (Ar. Cf. *kabili*, and *kaskazi*.)

Kibumba, n. (*vi-*), also **Kipumba**, small packet, parcel, bunch, lump, cluster, e.g. of earth, tobacco, thread, flour. Dim. of *bumba*. Also adv., in lumps, in bunches, &c.

Kibungu, n. (*vi-*), small earthenware dish. Dim. of *bungu*. See **Chungu**.

Kibunzi, n. (*vi-*), a sanded board, used for predicting future events. (Cf. *ramli*.)

*****Kiburi**, n. pride, arrogance, conceit, haughtiness. *Piga (fanya) k.*, show off, be ostentatious, play the grandee. *Mtu asiye na k. na watu*, one who does not treat people in a discourteous (contemptuous, off-hand) way. (Ar. Cf. *takabari*, and *piga makuu, majivuno*.)

Kibuyu, n. (*vi-*), (1) a small calabash, nut of the tree *mbuyu*, used as a jug or bucket. Dim. of *buyu*. (2) A kind of fish.

Kibuzi, n. (*vi-*), a small goat, kid. Dim. of *mbuzi*.

Kibwana, n. (*vi-*), young master. Dim. of *bwana*.

Kibwe, n. (*vi-*), small pebble. Dim. of *mbwe*. (Cf. *kijiwe*.)

*****Kibweta**, n. (*vi-*), small box, small case, e.g. writing-desk, jewel-box, dressing-case. Dim. of *bweta*.

Kicha, n. (*vi-*), *k. cha ukindu*, a palm leaf as sold in bundles, before being slit into strips for plaiting. (Cf. *chana*, and *ukindu*.)

Kichaa, n. craziness, lunacy, madness. *Ana k.*, he is crazy. *Umasikini wake umemtia k.*, his poverty has driven him mad. (Cf. syn. *wazimu*.)

Kichaka, n. (*vi-*), small clump of trees, thicket, clump (or, heap) of brushwood, bundle of sticks. Dim. of *chaka*.

Kichala, n. (*vi-*), bunch, cluster of fruit. *K. cha mzabibu*, a bunch of grapes. (Cf. *uchala, chana, tana*.)

Kichalichali, adv. on the back, —of a supine position, i. e. *mgongoni*. See **Chali**.

Kichane, n. (*vi-*), small splinter of wood. See **Chana**, v.

Kichangam'ko, n. (*vi-*), display of gaiety, joyous outburst. (Cf. *changam'ka*.)

Kicheche, n. (*vi-*), dim. of *cheche*, which see.

Kichego, n. also **Kigego** and **Kijego** (which see).

Kicheko, n. (*vi-*), a laugh, smile, giggle, grin. (Cf. *cheka, cheko*.)

Kichembe, n. (*vi-*), (1) dim. of *chembe*, which see. *Kichembe cha moyo*, the pit of the stomach. Also (2) for *kitembe*, which see.

Kichikichi, n. (*vi-*), small nut or kernel contained in the fruit *chikichi* of the palm-oil tree (*mchikichi*).

Kichilema, n. (*vi-*), the heart of the growing part at the top of a cocoanut tree,—a soft nutty substance used as salad and also cooked. Called also *moyo wa mnazi, kilele cha mnazi*. See **Mnazi**.

Kichinjo, n. act (mode, operation, &c.) of slaughtering, or sacrificing an animal. *Kichinjo cha Ibrahimu*, Abraham's sacrifice (of Isaac). (Cf. *chinja, chinjo*.)

Kicho, n. (*vi-*), cause (feeling, act) of fear, danger, alarm, show of fear. *K. chake kikamponya*, his panic saved him. (Cf. *cha* v., *-cha, uchaji*. Dist. *jicho*.)

Kichocheo, n. (*vi-*), act, method, or instrument of stirring up, e.g. (1) a poker, making up a fire, stoking; (2) also fig. provocation, taunt, provocative speech, &c. (Cf. *chocha, chochea*, and follg.)

Kichocho, n. (*vi-*), sensation, excitement, stimulus. *Mwenyi k.*, in an excited state. (Cf. prec.)

Kichochoro, n. (*vi-*), a narrow alley or passage between native huts as in Zanzibar city, leaving room all round for the projecting eaves and for scaffolding if necessary. (Cf. *chochoro, mchochoro*.)

Kichomi, n. (*vi-*), stabbing pain, pricking sensation. (Cf. *choma*, and follg.)

Kichomo, n. (*vi-*), act (process, method, instrument, &c.) of stabbing, burning, &c. Used of cautery. (Cf. *choma, mchomo, kichomi*.)

Kichungu, a. bitter, of a bitter kind. *Majani kichungu*, bitter herbs. (Cf. *-chungu, uchungu*.)

Kichupa, n. (*vi-*) also **Kitupa**, small bottle, phial, flask. Dim. of *chupa*.

Kichwa, n. (*vi-*), also, but less commonly in Z., heard as *kitwa*, (1) the head; (2) the upper part, top; (3) principal thing, important part or person, prime mover, leader, author, beginning, chief point, source; (4) anything resembling a head; (5) pain in the head; (6) obstinacy, pride, headiness. *K. wazi*, bare head, bare headed. *Una k.? tufunge mgomba*, Have you a headache? let us apply a banana leaf. *Kuwa na k., kufanya k.*, to be headstrong (presumptuous, refractory). *K. kikubwa*, big head, swelled head, pride, arrogance, obstinacy. *Jipa k., pata k.*, be proud, &c. *Mwenyi k.*, a proud, obstinate person. *Kwa k. kikubwa*, in a presumptuous, headstrong way. *Kichwa kichwa*, topsy turvy, upside down.

Kichwa-ngomba, n. (*vi-*), turning head over heels, a somersault. (Cf. prec.)

Kidaka, n. (*vi-*), (1) a cocoanut in the first stage of growth on the flower stem, before it becomes *kitale* (see **Nazi**); (2) a recess in the wall of a house, a niche, cupboard (cf. *kishubaka*); (3) of the uvula,—called *kidaka tonge*. (Cf. *daka*, and similar name *kinywa mchuzi*, imperial.)

*****Kidamu**, n. front part of vessel, bow,—but more usual *omo, gubeti*, which see. — v. go before, go in front. (Ar. Cf. *takadamu, kadamu*.)

Kidanga, n. (*vi-*) and a., of fruit in a very early stage of formation, before it is even *changa*, e.g. *limau kidanga, embe k.*

Kidani, n. (*vi-*), a neck ornament, necklace, collar of gold or silver,—often chainwork, with large open links. (Cf. *mkufu*, and *urembo*.)

Kidari, n. (*vi-*), breast, chest,—of men and animals. (Cf. *kifua*, of man only.)

Kidau, n. (*vi-*), (1) a small kind of native boat (see **Dau**); (2) a small containing-vessel, pot, e.g. *kidau cha wino*, an ink-pot. (Also *kidawa* from Arab. *dawat*, ink-stand. Cf. *dawati*, and follg.)

*****Kidawati**, n. small box of writing materials, writing case. Dim. of *dawati* (which see, and prec.). (Ar.)

Kidevu, n. (*vi-*), chin. *Ndevu zamwota kidevuni*, a beard is growing on his chin. (Cf. *udevu*, and ? *-refu*.)

Kidimbwi, n. (*vi-*) also **Kidumbwi**, small pool, puddle, e.g. on the shore at low water.

Kidinga, n. *Kidinga popo*, dengue fever. (Cf. *homa*.)

Kidogo, from *-dogo*, which see. Very common as (1) n. a small piece, a morsel, a bit, a little. *Nipe k. cha mkate*, give me a morsel of bread. (2) adv. a little, in a small degree, on a small scale, moderately, not much, and of time 'presently, soon.' *Alifanya nguvu kidogo*, he exerted himself slightly. (3) a. in a small degree, in a small quantity, a few, a little, e.g. *watu kidogo*, a few people. *Mchele kidogo*, a little rice.

Kidoko, n. (*vi-*), also **Kidokezi**, (1) a click, smack. *Piga k.*, give a click with the tongue, smack the lips.

(2) A hint, sign, secret suggestion. (Cf. *dokeza*.)

Kidole, n. (*vi-*), one of the extremities of the hand or foot, a finger, a toe. Distinguished as *k. cha mguu*, a toe, and *k. cha mkono*, a finger; and these further as *k. cha gumba*, thumb; *k. cha shahada*, fore-finger; *k. cha kati* or *kikubwa*, middle finger; *k. cha kati ya kando*, fourth finger; *k. cha mwisho*, little finger. (Cf. *dole, udole*, rarely used in Z.)

Kidomo, n. (*vi-*), dim. of *mdomo*, (1) a little lip (beak, mouth); (2) daintiness in food. *Yuna kidomo*, he is dainty.

Kidonda, n. (*vi-*), dim. of *donda*, a small wound, sore, ulcer, breaking out. (Cf. *donda, ? dondoa*.)

Kidonge, n. (*vi-*) and **Kitonge**, a small round mass, a small lump, a little ball, a small mouthful (of food). *K. cha uzi*, a ball of cotton. *K. cha dawa*, a pill. Dim. of *donge*. (Cf. *donge, tonge*.)

Kidoto, n. (*vi-*), blinker,—a small patch or bandage of cloth, fastened over a camel's eyes while working a mill. *Funga vidoto*, blindfold. (Cf. *kijamanda*.)

Kidude, n. (*vi-*), dim. of *dude* (which see), a little what-do-you-call-it, a nondescript thing. *Kidude gani hiki?* What sort of a thing do you call this?

Kidudu, n. (*vi-*), dim. of *mdudu* (which see), a small insect.

Kidugu, n. and adv. (1) dim. of *ndugu*, little brother (cf. *kibuzi* and *mbuzi, kigao* and *ngao*); (2) in a fraternal way, like brothers. *Kupendana kidugu*, to love as brothers.

Kielezo, n. (*vi-*), act (process, manner, means) of showing or explaining, explanation, pattern, model, illustration, comment. *Fuasa k.*, copy a pattern. Dim. of *elezo*. (Cf. *elezo, chelezo, elea*.)

Kiembe, n. (*vi-*), arrow,—not often in Z. (Cf. *chembe* and note, and syn. *mshale*.)

Kiendeleo, n. (*vi-*), making a forward movement, progress, process. (Cf. *enda, endelea*, &c.)

Kieneo, n. (*vi-*), extending, extent, extension. (Cf. *enea, eneo*.)

Kienezo, n. (*vi-*), something to measure with, &c. See **Chenezo**.

Kienge, n. (*vi-*), dim. of *mwenge*, small torch, kindlings, any small thing burning or to burn.

Kifa, n. (1) (*vi-*), *kifa uwongo*, the sensitive plant,—lit. the death-shammer (cf. *fa*); (2) nipple of a gun, pan of a matchlock.

Kifaa, n. (*vi-*), a useful thing, a thing for use, personal belongings, household necessaries, utensil. (Cf. *faa*, v., and *faa, mafaa*, also *riziki, vyombo, pambo*.)

Kifafa, n. fits, convulsions, epilepsy. (Perh. cf. *-fa, kifa*, i.e. a sort of dying.)

Kifalme, n. and adv., also **Kifaume**, (1) (*vi-*), dim. of *mfalme*, a petty king; (2) royal state, of a royal sort, e.g. *kiti cha k., nguo za k.*, a royal seat, royal robes; (3) in a royal way, as a king.

Kifani, n. (*vi-*), and **Kifano**, a similar thing, that which matches, a fellow, a parallel, a match, an equal. *Haina kifani*, it is unique, it is unequalled. (Cf. *mfano, fanana*.)

Kifaranga, n. (*vi-*), young bird, chick, chicken. (Cf. syn. *kinda, kidege, mtoto*.)

Kifaro, n. (*vi-*), a rhinoceros,—*faro* being seldom heard. Also (1) a stick of thick hide, used to beat slaves with, and (2) a blow with such a stick, e.g. *ntamtia vifaro sita*, I will give him six cuts. (Cf. *kiboko*.)

Kifaume, n. (see **Kifalme**), royal state, regal dignity, &c. *Piga k.*, play the king.

Kificho, n. (*vi-*), act (process, manner, place, &c.) of hiding, place of concealment, a stealthy (underhand) manner. *Kwa kificho*, in a secret way. *Mambo ya kifichoficho*, intriguings, underhand ways. (Cf. *ficha, ficho,* and syn. *setiri, siri.*)

*Kifidio, n. (*vi-*), ransom, fine, redemption money. (Cf. *fidi, fidia,* and *dia, ukombozi.*)

Kifiko, n. act (time, manner, place, circumstances, &c.) of arriving, arrival, point arrived at, stage of journey, destination. (Cf. *fika.*)

Kifo, n. (*vi-*), act (circumstances, place, manner, &c.) of dying, death. *Hawakuona k. chake alikofia,* they did not see where his death took place. (Cf. *-fa, -fu, kifa, kifafa,* a thing dying, *kifu,* a dead thing, *ufu,* the state of being dead, and syn. *mauti.*)

*Kifu, v. be sufficient (for), suffice, satisfy. *Wanne hawakukifu,* four were not enough. Ap. *kif-ia, -iwa,* e. g. *amenikifia haja yangu,* he satisfied my wish. — n. a sufficient quantity, a full amount, abundance. (Ar. Cf. syn. *tosha, rithisha.*)

Kifu, n. and adv. (1) (*vi-*), a dead thing; (2) as if dead. (Cf. *-fa* and syn. *maiti.*)

Kifua, n. (*vi-*), (1) breast, bosom, chest, pulmonary region,—usu. of man only (cf. *kidari*); (2) any chest affection, cough, consumption, pleurisy, pneumonia. *Hawezi kifua,* he has a chest complaint. (3) A small round wooden platter,—used like *chano* for washing things on, and other purposes. (Cf. *fua,* beat, thump, and *mafua, pafu.*)

Kifudifudi, adv. on the face, face downwards,—of position. (Cf. *fudifudi, fudikiza, kifulifuli,* and contr. *kitanitani, kichalichali.*)

Kifuko, n. (*vi-*), dim. of *mfuko, fuko* (which see), small bag, pocket, purse.

Kifulifuli, adv. on the face, face downwards. (Cf. *kifudifudi.*)

Kifumba, n. (*vi-*), dim. of *fumba* (which see), a matting bag, sleeping sack. (Cf. follg.)

Kifumbu, n. (*vi-*), small round basket or bag used for squeezing grated cocoanut in, and straining out the juice (*tui*), a strainer. (Cf. *fumba, kifumba,* &c.)

Kifundo, n. (*vi-*), (1) a knot. *Piga k. cha nguo,* make a knot of a piece of calico, tie up in one's clothes. (2) Protuberance, joint,—as resembling a knot. *K. cha mguu,* the ankle. *K. cha mkono,* the wrist. *Mwili wa kifundo kifundo,* i.e. with small knot-like swellings on the body. (Cf. *fundo, fundua,* and perh. *funda,* and for ankle, wrist, *kiwiko.*)

Kifungo, n. (*vi-*), a fastening, act (process, method, &c.) of fastening, something which fastens. Hence a wide variety of meanings (see **Funga**), defined by the context, or by another word, e. g. (1) button, stud, brooch, buckle, clasp, chain, cord, or other contrivance for fastening; (2) prison, place of confinement, whether chain (*minyororo*), fetters (*pingu*), stocks (*mkatale*), enclosure or cell. *Peleka kifungoni,* send to prison. (3) fig. bond, charter, that which binds (seals, cements, &c.), e. g. Mahomet is called *k. cha dini,* i. e. the force which holds religion together, the corner stone of the faith. *Kifungo* may also mean (4) a puzzle, a poser, a dilemma; (5) an act of fasting, &c.; (6) bondage, slavery. (Cf. *funga,* and for binding materials *kamba.*)

Kifungu, n. (*vi-*), dim. of *fungu,* a small heap (portion, part, &c.). (Cf. *funga.*)

Kifungua, n. (*vi-*), an opener, an unfastener. A verbal noun governing the word following, e. g. *k. kopo,* a tin-opener. *K. mlango,* a present for opening a door. *K. kinwa,* breakfast. (Cf. *funga, fungua, mfunguo,* and follg.)

Kifunguo, n. (*vi-*), dim. of *ufunguo,* a small key (cf. prec.). Also of a private key, a thief's key, skeleton key (for which special meaning, see **Ki**).

Kifuniko, n. (*vi-*), anything which covers, (1) top, lid, cover, case, &c.; (2) fig. concealment, hiding. *K. cha siri*, concealment of a mystery. (Cf. *funika*.)

Kifunuo, n. (*vi-*), unfolding, uncovering, revealing, &c., that which unfolds, reveals, &c. (Cf. *funua*.)

Kifuo, n. a stake fixed in the ground with a pointed end for ripping off the husk of cocoanuts. Also dim. of *mfuo*, a small groove (line, mark, &c.). (Cf. *fua, ufuo, ufuko*.)

Kifupa, n. (*vi-*), dim. of *fupa*, a small bone.

Kifupi, adv. and n. of a short, abbreviated kind, in a brief way, a short piece. (Cf. *-fupi*.)

Kifurushi, n. (*vi-*), dim of *furushi*, a small parcel, packet, bundle.

Kifusi, n. rubbish, and esp. of old materials fit for further use, old stones and mortar, &c.,—not used like *mawe* in contempt. (Cf. *fusia*.)

Kifuu, n. (*vi-*), (1) an empty cocoanut shell; also (2) a cuttle-fish bone, i.e. *kifuu cha ngizi*. (Cf. *fuvu*, and *ufuu*.)

Kifya, n. (*vi-*), dim. form of *jifya*, which see.

Kigae, n. (*vi-*), piece of broken pottery, earthenware, china, glass, &c., potsherd. *K. cha paa*, used of a roofing tile. (Cf. *gae*.)

Kigaga, n. (*vi-*), dry hard scale, scurf, scab, &c. (Cf. *kikoko, ukoko*.)

Kiganda, n. (*vi-*), dim. of *ganda*. *K. cha mkate*, outside crust of bread (opp. to *nyama*, the crumb.)

Kigawanyo, n. that which divides, a divisor, distribution, division. So *kigawanyiko*, that which is divided or distributed, share, dividend. (Cf. *gawa, gawanya*.)

Kigego, n. See **Kijego**.

Kigelegele, n. (*vi-*), a peculiar high-pitched trill, shrill scream,—used by women esp. as a sign of joy or triumph, welcome on return, at a birth, &c. (Cf. *kelele*, and *shangwe*.)

Kigereng'enza, n. (*vi-*), a very small splinter, broken piece, fragment, chip. (Cf. *kigae*.)

Kigeugeu, n. a. and adv., changeable, fickle, unstable, wayward thing or person, of a changeable kind, in an uncertain fluctuating way. (Cf. *geuka*.)

Kigoe, n. (*vi-*), instrument for extraction, hooked stick, small hook, crook, claw. (Cf. *ng'oa, ugoe*.)

Kigogo, n. (*vi-*), dim. of *gogo*, a small log, a block of wood, a lump. Also adv. *lala k.*, sleep like a log.

Kigogota, n. (*vi-*), a woodpecker. (Cf. *gogota*.)

Kigoli, n. (*vi-*), a girl,—of one just growing up, almost marriageable; between *mtoto* and *mwali*. Not often heard in Z.

Kigomba, n. (*vi-*), dim. of *mgomba*, small banana plant, banana shoot.

Kigongo, n. (*vi-*), dim. of *mgongo* and *gongo*, (1) small club, cudgel; (2) hump, hunch, ridge, projection. Hence *kigongo*, or *mwenyi kigongo*, a hunchback, a deformed person. *Kigongo cha mlima*, mountain ridge. (3) A seam,—in sewing.

Kigosho, n. (*vi-*), bend, crook, curve, esp. when abnormal, a deformity. *Nimeteketea moto nikafanya k. cha mkono*, I burnt myself, and got a bent arm. *Mtu mwenyi k. (cha miguu)*, a knock-kneed man. *Fimbo hii ina k.*, this stick has a crook in it. (Cf. *kombo, kikombo, kipindi*.)

*****Kiguba**, n. (*vi-*), dim. of *guba* (which see), a small bunch of aromatic leaves, containing often *rihani* (sweet basil) sprinkled with *dalia* (a fragrant powder), and tied with a strip of *mkadi* leaf, i. e. from the *pandanus* tree (Str.).

Kigudulia, n. (*vi-*), dim. of *gudulia*, a small jar or pitcher, small water cooler of porous earthenware.

Kigugu, n. and adv. (1) a small weed or wild plant (cf. *gugu*); (2) like a weed, like weeds, in a wild uncultivated way, e. g. *nyumba hizi zimejengwa k.*, these houses are built like weeds,—all huddled together. *Panda k.*, plant too close together.

Kigugumizi, n. stammering, stuttering, speaking in jerks or gulps, &c., described as *kigugumizi cha maneno*, or *maneno ya kigugumizi*. (Cf. *gugumiza*.)

Kigunda, n. (*vi-*), dim. of *gunda*, horn, war-horn.

Kiguni, n. (*vi-*), dim. of *guni*, a small strong matting bag, often used for bringing dates to Z.

Kigutu, n. (*vi-*), stump of a tree, also of a human limb, injured or deformed. (Cf. *kikono, kiguu*.)

Kiguu, n. (*vi-*), dim. of *mguu*, (1) a leg or foot disabled or shortened by injury or disease, &c., a stump, a clubfoot; (2) a person so disabled or disfigured, one who is lame, crippled, unable to walk; (3) anything like a leg or leg-shaped, e. g. one of four 'little feet' or projections worked on either side of the *mjusi* (lizard-ornament) on the front of a native *kanzu*,—also called *kipaji*. See **Kanzu**. (*Kijiguu* is also dim. of *mguu*.)

Kiguzo, n. (*vi-*), dim. of *nguzo*, (1) small post, pillar, stake, palisade, prop; (2) anything serving a similar purpose, literally or fig.—support, prop, comfort, assurance, &c.

Kigwe, n. (*vi-*), dim. of *ugwe*, small cord, string, braid, piping on the edge of a dress, a rein. (Cf. *kitani, uzi, kamba*.)

Kihame, n. (*vi-*), a deserted house (village, district). (Cf. *hama, mahame, -e* being a passive termination.)

Kiherehere, n. (1) palpitation, confused movement, e. g. *k. cha moyo*, palpitation of the heart; (2) trepidation, bustle, anxiety.

***Kihindi**, n. and adv. (1) the Hindoo language, Hindostani; (2) of the Hindoo kind. *-a kihindi*, Indian. (Cf. *Mhindi*.)

***Kihori**, n. (*vi-*), dim. of *hori*, (1) small gulf, inlet; (2) small (Indian) canoe.

Kiinamizi, n. bending, stooping down,—as for work. *Nyama ya k.*, i. e. a butcher's perquisite of meat. (Cf. *inama, jinamizi*.)

Kiini, n. (*vi-*), innermost part of a thing, and so (1) kernel or stone of fruit, e.g. the inner part of a clove (*garafuu*), when the outer skin is removed after soaking in water; (2) the yolk of an egg, *kiini cha yai*; (3) the heart or hard core of a tree,—called also *moyo wa mti*, esp. if soft, nutty, or pithy; (4) pupil of the eye, cf. *mboni*. (Cf. *ini*, and syn. *moyo*.)

Kiini-macho, n. (*vi-*), also Mk., a conjurer, a conjurer's trick, sleight of hand, jugglery. Distinguished from *uganga*, e. g. *huyu si mganga, ni k.*, this man is not a real medicine man, but a juggler. *Mganga amefanya k.*, the medicine man used a juggler's trick. (Perh. cf. prec., also *inika* for root, and *jicho*.)

Kiinua, n. that which raises up,—verbal governing a word following, e.g. *kiinua mgongo*, that which raises the back, gratuity to one who has been bending over his work. (Cf. *kinyosha mgongo*, and *ki*.)

Kiisha, adv. for Ikiisha, also Kisha, this ended, afterwards, next, moreover, and besides, in fine, finally. *Huyu ni mbaya k. mchawi*, this man is a scoundrel and moreover a wizard. (From *isha*, v. Cf. *mwisho, hatima, baada*.)

Kiitiko, n. (*vi-*), and **Kiitikio**, response, musical refrain. (Cf. *ita*, v.)

Kijakazi, n. (*vi-*), a young slave girl, a poor slave woman. (Cf. *mjakazi*, and *mtumwa*.)

Kijaluba, n. (*vi-*), small narrow metal box, often used for aromatic substances, and carried on the breast by women.

Kijamanda, n. (*vi-*), small box

or basket of thick stiff plaited work, made of leaf-strips dyed various colours. Many come from Madagascar. (2) A small basket-work blinker, or cover fastened over the eyes of a camel while at work. (Cf. *kidoto* and *kinga*.)

Kijamba, n. (*vi-*), a small rock. Dim. of **mwamba**, which see.

Kijana, n. (*vi-*), dim. of *mwana*, meaning generally, a young person male or female, but also with special meanings, as youthfulness is viewed in reference to (1) age, (2) relationship, (3) physical development, (4) social position. (1) As to age, the *kijana* has ceased to be an *mtoto mchanga*, and is not yet *mtu mzima*, though still an *mtoto*. *Mtoto akipata miaka saba, amekuwa k. mwenyi akili*, when a child is seven years old, he is a *kijana* and come to years of discretion. *Amekuwa k., aweza kusema*, he is a *kijana*, he can speak for himself. *Wewe k., sisi watu wazima*, you are a *kijana*, we are grown-up people. (2) As to relationship, *kijana* means merely son or daughter. *Wakaomba kwa Muungu kupata k.*, and they prayed to God that they might have offspring (a child). *K. cha Sultani*, the Sultan's son. (3) As to physical development *k.* means any one in full vigour and capable of bearing arms, i.e. from boyhood till past the prime of life, as contr. with *mtoto* on one side, and *mzee* on the other, and practically synonymous with *mzima*. (4) As to social relations, *k.* means a dependent, servant, slave. It is also used of the 'master of the house' with reference to his own property (cf. use of *mwana* for 'mistress of the house,' i.e. perhaps heir of the house and so rightful owner). (Cf. *mwana*, *jana*, *bwana*.)

Kijego, n. (*vi-*), also **Kichego**, a child which develops its upper teeth first, and therefore considered unlucky, and often exposed or put to death by the relations. *Alikuwa k., alitanguliza kuota meno ya juu*, he was an unlucky child, his upper teeth grew first. (Cf. *chego*, and *jino*, also syn. *timvi*, *timfi*.)

Kijembe, n. (*vi-*), dim. of *jembe*, (1) small cutting instrument, penknife, lancet (cf. *kijisu*, and *jembe*, *kiembe*); (2) ? fig. of cutting, sarcastic, ironical language, i.e. *maneno ya kijembe*, *sema kijembe*.

Kijia, n. (*vi-*), also **Kinjia**, dim. of *njia*, little path, track, &c. (Cf. *njia*.)

Kijiboko, n. (*vi-*), dim. of *kiboko* (*boko* being seldom heard in Z.), a small hippopotamus.

Kijicho, n. (*vi-*), dim. of *jicho*, (1) a sly (sidelong, envious, malignant, evil) glance; (2) envy, malice, ill will. *Fanya k.*, be envious, be jealous. *Yuna k. rohoni*, he feels envious, he is jealous. *Hana k. nawe*, he bears you no malice. *Wangariza wana vijicho sana*, their eyes glare with envy and hate. (Cf. *uwivu*, *hasidi*, *roho*, *tamaa*.)

Kijichwa, n. (*vi-*), dim. of *kichwa*, a small head.

Kijiguu, n. (*vi-*), dim. of *mguu*, a small foot. (Dist. *kiguu*.)

Kijiji, n. (*vi-*), dim. of *mji*, a small town, village, hamlet. (Cf. syn. *kitongoji*.)

Kijike, n. (*vi-*), a young female, human or other. (Cf. *-ke*, and *jike*.)

Kijiko, n. (*vi-*), dim. of *mwiko*, (1) a small spoon; (2) a small stove, or fire-place. (Cf. *jiko*.)

Kijineno, n. (*vi-*), dim. of *neno*, a silly little speech, child's prattle.

*****Kijiri**, n. (*vi-*), also **Chichiri**, a bribe, hush-money. (? Ar. Cf. *ijara*, *ajiri*, and syn. *mlungula*, *rushwa*.)

Kijiti, n. (*vi-*), dim. of *mti*, a small tree, bush, shrub, small pole, piece of wood, peg, stick. (Cf. *mti*, and dist. *kiti*, a seat.)

Kijito, n. (*vi-*), dim. of *mto*, small river, brook, stream, rivulet.

(Cf. *mto, jito, juto*, and dist. *kito*, a jewel.)

Kijitu, n. (*vi-*), dim. of *mtu*, a little man. Also in contempt, mannikin, or in disgust, e. g. *Ewe kijitu kiovu*, Oh you wicked wretch. (Cf. *mtu, jitu,* and dist. *kitu*, a thing.)

Kijivi, n. (*vi-*), n. and adv., a thievish person, thief, brigand; and, in a thievish (sneaking, underhand) way. (Cf. *mwivi, iba,* and *jivi*.)

Kijiwe, n. and adv. (*vi-*), dim. of *jiwe*, a small stone, like a stone.

Kijogoo, n. (*vi-*), dim. of *jogoo*, (1) a small cock, a bantam cock; (2) a kind of shell-fish (Str.).

Kijoli, n. (*vi-*), set of slaves belonging to one master, establishment, domestic staff, domestics as a body. (Cf. *mjoli, ujoli,* and *mtumwa*.)

Kijombo, n. (*vi-*), dim. of *chombo*, a small sailing ship, a small vessel. (For *ki-ji-ombo, chombo* being for *ki-ombo*.)

Kijongo, n. (*vi-*), a hump-backed person, &c., like *kigongo*. (For *ki-ji-ongo*. Cf. *jongo, mgongo, kigongo, kibiongo*.)

Kijoyo, n. (*vi-*), dim. like *kimoyo*, small heart, slight inclination, hankering. (For *ki-ji-oyo, kimoyo*. Cf. *moyo* with plur. *mioyo*, and *nyoyo*, indicating a form *uoyo* for *moyo*.)

Kijukuu, n. (*vi-*), great-grand-child, dim. of *mjukuu*, which see.

Kijumba, n. (*vi-*), a small house, dim. of *jumba*. (For *ki-ji-umba*. Cf. *jumba, nyumba, chumba,* i. e. *ki-umba, kinyumba*.)

Kijumbe, n. (*vi-*), a special or secret messenger, a go-between, a matchmaker. (Cf. *mjumbe, jumbe, -e* being a passive termination. Cf. *mtume*.)

Kijungu, n. (*vi-*), a small cooking pot. (For *ki-ji-ungu*. Cf. *jungu, chungu,* &c.)

Kijusi, n. (*vi-*), an act (case, instance, &c.) of defilement, a particular (legal, ceremonial, physical) impurity. (Cf. *-jusi, ujusi*.)

Kijuto, n. (*vi-*), for usual *kijito*, dim. of *mto*, a small river. (For *ki-ji-uto*. Cf. *kijoyo*, for *kimoyo*.)

Kijuujuu, n. and adv. See **Juu**.

Kijuvi, n. (*vi-*), an impertinent child, a bit of impertinence, a saucy remark. (Cf. *-juvi, ujuvi, jua,* v.)

Kikaango, n. (*vi-*), small frying-pan. (Cf. *kaanga, kaango*.)

Kikaka, n. and adv. (*vi-*), (1) dim. of *kaka*, a bit of rind or peel; (2) hastiness, bustle, hurry, in a hurry. *Mbona wafanya k.?* Why are you in such a hurry? (Cf. *kaka*.)

Kikalasha, n. (*vi-*), dim. of *kalasha*, small tusk of ivory. (Cf. *pembe, bori*.)

Kikale, n. and adv., old style, antique fashion, an antiquated thing, out of date, of the past. *-a kikale*, old-fashioned. (Cf. *kale*, and contr. *kisasa*, up to date.)

Kikambo, n. the relation of step-parent and child, e. g. *baba ya kikambo*, step-father. (Cf. *kambo*.)

Kikao, n. (*vi-*), act (place, time, style, form) of sitting, dwelling, &c. See **Kaa**. Hence various meanings, e. g. (1) sitting, seat, dwelling-place, habitat (cf. *makao, makazi, masikani*); (2) stay, duration of residence, season of residence; (3) posture, position, office, dignity (cf. *mahali, cheo, daraja*); (4) style of living, social standing, place in society, conduct (cf. *maisha, mwenendo*); (5) society, club, mess, set (cf. *chama, jamaa*), e. g. *k. chake Unguja*, he lives in Zanzibar. *K. cha mizinga*, the place where cannon are kept, battery. *Katika k. chao walichokaa*, in their company, at their meeting. *Sipendi k. chake*, I do not like the way he goes on. (Cf. *kaa*, and syn. as above.)

Kikapo, n. (*vi-*), a wide-mouthed flexible basket of plaited leaf-strips or grass, with two small handles, used for all purposes in Z.,—made mostly by Sheheri Arabs. (Other kinds are *kapo, kanda, jamanda, tunga, dohani, pakacha, ungo, kiteo, kunguto, kifumbu,* and cf. *mfuko*.)

*Kikariri, n. and adv., repetition, repeated action, saying over and over again, repeatedly. (Cf. *kariri*, and for adv. *marra kwa marra, marra nyingi, tena na tena*.)

*Kikasiki, n. (*vi-*), dim. of *kasiki*, small pitcher.

Kikawe, n. (*vi-*), a very tiny stone. (Cf. *kijiwe, jiwe, kawe, mbwe*.)

Kikaza, n. (*vi-*), a thing which tightens, strengthens, holds together, but esp. of a board, pole, or beam over a window or doorway. (Cf. *kaza, kazo*.)

Kike, n. and adv. (seldom *vike* in plur., for usual *-a kike*, or *vijike*), a female of any kind, anything of feminine style, womanly behaviour (usually meaning weakness, timidity, foolishness), like a woman, in a feminine way, e. g. *watoto wa k.*, girls. *Mtu wa k.*, a womanish, weak, unmanly person. *Fanya k.*, act like a woman. *Sauti ya k.*, a shrill, treble voice. — a. from *-ke*, agreeing with D 3 (S), e.g. *kijana kike*, a young woman. (Cf. *-ke, jike, kuke, uke, kijike*, and contr. *-ume, kiume*.)

Kikebe, n. (*vi-*), dim. of *mkebe*, small pot, mug, canister.

Kikeukeu, n. convulsive sobbing, hiccup. (Cf. *kekeuu*, and *kwikwi*.)

Kikingo, n. (*vi-*), something to parry or defend oneself with, means of warding off, screen, defence, fender. (Cf. *kinga, ukingo*.)

Kikisa, v. speak in a hesitating, confused, broken way, be unintelligible or half-understood, puzzle, mystify. *Sema kwa kukikisa*, talk in a faltering uncertain way. *Maneno yake yamemkikisa*, he cannot get out his words clearly. *Jambo hili lakikisa*, this business is difficult, hard to get at. (Cf. *kigugumizi, gugumiza, gota, goteza*.)

Kiko, n. (*vi-*), tobacco pipe—of the sort common in Z., consisting of the *kiko* proper, i. e. a cocoanut shell partly filled with water, and two tubes of wood or reed (*digali, mdakali*), one leading from the bowl (*bori*) holding tobacco (*tumbako*) into the water, the other (*shilamu*) from the *kiko* to the mouthpiece through which the smoke is drawn. The bubbling of the water is called *malio ya kiko*. Other simpler pipes consist of a hollow reed and earthenware bowl only, e. g. *tosa*.

Kiko, verb-form, (it) is there,— agreeing with D 3 (S),—the pfx. *ki* and locative *-ko*, which see.

Kikoa, n. (*vi-*), (1) a meal eaten in common, provided by each of those who join in it by turns, a common table, a mess, boarding together. *Kula k.*, to have meals in common, also *kula chakula cha shirika*, as is done when food is scarce, weather unseasonable, &c. *Watu wala kikoa majira ya masika*, people mess together during the rainy season. *Leo k. changu*, it is my turn to provide the meal to-day. *Nikila k., ntalipa nini mkata mno?* If I join the mess, how shall I pay when I have not a penny? (Contr. *kula bia*, where each person provides a share at each meal.) (2) dim. of *koa*, small flat ring or band of metal,—used of the ornamentation of scabbards, also of anklets and bracelets. (Cf. *koa, ukoa*, and *pete, kikuku*.)

Kikofi, n. (*vi-*), the inside of the hand, what would lie on the upturned hand, a handful. (Cf. *kofi, ukofi*, also *chopa, konzi*.)

Kikohozi, n. (*vi-*), a cough, fit of coughing,—also of consumption, phthisis. (Cf. *kohoa, ukohozi, kohoo*.)

Kikoi, n. (*vi-*), white calico with coloured borders in cotton silk or both,—used for loincloths in great variety under many names. *K. cha Ulaya*, bordered shirtings,—in trade.

Kikoka, n. (*vi-*), blade or shoot of a grass used as forage. See *Ukoka*.

Kikoko, n (*vi-*), dim. of *koko, mkoko*, and *ukoko* (which see), a bit of hard, dried stuff, and so of a scab, or scurf. (Cf. *kiguga*.,

Kikomba, n. (1) *njaa ya kikomba*, or *ya kukomba*, ravenous hunger, that makes a man scrape up and sweep off everything (cf. *komba*). Also *kikomba cha njaa*, i. e. *makazo ya njaa*, intense hunger. (2) Dim. of *komba*, a small galago.

Kikombe, n. (*vi-*), dim. of *kombe*, a small dish, used commonly of a cup or basin, or mug of any material, *k. cha chai*, tea-cup. *K. cha bilauri*, tumbler, wine-glass, also *k. cha nuru*, i. e. transparent, bright, polished. *K. cha fetha*, silver goblet. (Cf. *komba, kombe*, i. e. a vessel scraped or hollowed out, *-e* being a passive termination, also *kopo, kikopo*, and for such vessels generally *chombo*.)

Kikombo, n. and adv., a small crooked, hook-shaped, or curved thing, e. g. a small curved gouge-shaped tool; also, a small bend, curve, irregularity, deflection, defect, fault, flaw. As adv., in a crooked, irregular way. (Cf. *komba*, v., *kombe, ukombo*, and syn. *pindo, mzingo, tao.*)

Kikomo, n. (*vi-*), (1) stop, stopping, stoppage, place or time of stopping, cessation, end; (2) *k. cha uso*, forehead, brow, i. e. *uso ulipokoma, pasipomea nyele, mbele ya uso, juu ya macho*, where the face ends, the hairless part in front over the eyes. (Cf. *koma, ukomo*, &c., and syn. *mwisho, kusimama*.)

Kikondoo, n. and adv. (1) a small sheep, lamb; (2) like a sheep, unresistingly, meekly, calmly. *Kufa kikondoo ndiko kufa kiungwana*, to die like a sheep is to die like a hero. (Cf. *kondoo*.)

Kikongwe, n. (*vi-*), a person bent and bowed with age, a very old person, esp. (like *kizee*) an old woman. Sometimes used, as intensive and descriptive, with *kizee*. (Cf. *konga, kongwe, kongwa*, and *kibiongo*.)

Kikono, n. (*vi-*), dim. of *mkono*, (1) small arm or hand, short or defective arm, stump of the arm, e. g. *ana k.*, she has lost a hand (arm) (cf. *kiguu*); (2) anything resembling a small hand, e. g. projecting prow of a vessel, guard of a sword-handle, small stalk or tendril of plants and flowers, tentacle or feeler of fish or insect.

Kikonyo, n. (*vi-*), like *kikono*, e. g. of a stalk, *vikonyo vya garafuu*, clove-stalks.

Kikope, n. (*vi-*), eyelid. (Cf. *ukope, kope, kopesa*.)

Kikopo, n. (*vi-*), dim. of *kopo*, small vessel, pot, jug, mug, esp. of metal. Used of spouts for carrying off water from a roof, &c.

Kikorombwe, n. (*vi-*), signal cry, call,—made by blowing into the hand or through the fingers.

Kikosi, n. (*vi-*), (1) the back of the neck, nape, i. e. *nyuma ya shingo*, below the *kishogo*, nape, and *kogo*, back of the head; (2) also *kikozi*, company, band, troop, esp. of soldiers or armed men. (Cf. *ukosi*.)

Kikotama, n. (*vi-*), dim. of *kotama*, small curved knife, garden- or pruning-knife. (Cf. *shembea*, and for knives generally *kisu*.)

Kikoto, n. (*vi-*), and **Chikoto**, (1) a whip of plaited grass, leaf-strips, or bark fibre, used by schoolmasters, overseers, &c. (cf. *mjeledi*); (2) plait of hair. *Piga (songa) vikoto*, plait.

Kikozi, n. (*vi-*), and **Kikosi**, company, band, troop, esp. of soldiers or armed men. (Cf. *jeshi*.)

Kikuba, n. (*vi-*), (1) see **Kiguba**; (2) dim. of *kuba*, small vault, dome, cupola, arched roof. Also as adv., like a dome, &c.

Kikucha, n. (*vi-*), also **Kikuchya, Kikuchia**, dim. of *ukucha*, a bit of the nail, a little projection of the nail, nail-paring.

Kikuku, n. (*vi-*), (1) ring, usually of metal, worn on arm or wrist, armlet, bracelet. Also used of an anklet of same kind. *K. cha kupandia frasi*, a stirrup. *K. cha pingu*, a handcuff. (Cf. *furungu, banagiri*, *kekee*, and *urembo*.) (2) Dim. of *kuku*, a small fowl, chicken, bantam.

Kikukuu, n. and adv., a thing old, worn out, past work, useless. *-a kikukuu*, worn out. See -Kukuu.

Kikulia, n. (*vi-*), a thing or person that has grown up at a place,—not born at a place, which is *kizalia*. (From *ki* and Ap. form of *kua*, *kulia*. Cf. *kimelea*.)

Kikumbatio, n. (*vi-*), embrace. (Cf. *kumbatia*, and syn. *ambiso*.)

Kikumbo, n. (*vi-*), thrust, shove, jostling. *Piga k.*, thrust away, shove aside, push by, nudge with the elbow. *Pigana vikumbo*, of rough hustling, horseplay. (Cf. *kumba*, and *songa*.)

Kikundi, n. (*vi-*), dim. of *kundi*, small company, group, knot, herd. (Cf. *kikosi*.)

Kikundu, n. (*vi-*), rump, dim. of *mkundu*.

Kikungu, n. (*vi-*), dim. of *mkungu*, small earthenware cooking pot, also the lid of such a pot. (Cf. *chombo, chungu*.)

Kikuta, n. (*vi-*), dim. of *ukuta*, small stone wall, parapet, masonry, partition.

Kikuti, n. (*vi-*), dim. of *kuti*, the tip of a cocoanut leaf, i.e. *ncha ya kuti*. See **Kuti**. (2) Chance, hap, luck, an incident, event, accident, occurrence. *Kikuti chema*, a happy chance. (Cf. *kuta*, v., and syn. *tukio, nasibu, bahati*.)

Kikwapa, n. (*vi-*), (1) armpit. Also various things connected with, or resembling the armpit; (2) the smell of the armpit; (3) the perspiration of the armpit; (4) the gore of a native dress (*kanzu*) under the armpit. Hence *kisibau cha k.*, an armpit tunic, i.e. sleeveless, stopping at the armpit. *Kikwapa cha tanga*, part of a sail.

Kikwata, n. and adv. (*vi-*), dim. of *kwata*, small hoof, damaged or maimed hoof. As adv. colloquially 'on foot.' *Enda k.*, go on foot. *Safari k.*, a journey on foot, i.e. *kwa miguu*.

Kilalo, n. (*vi-*), (1) camping- or sleeping-place on a journey (cf. *kituo, kambi*); (2) a sleeping-shelter, e.g. a few sticks resting on forked uprights, and carrying some grass as a covering. (Cf. *lala, ulalo*.)

Kilango, n. (*vi-*), dim. of *mlango*, a small door, narrow entrance, small opening, pass, strait. *K. cha bahari*, a strait. *K. cha jaha*, the strait gate of Paradise.

Kile, a. dem. that,—agreeing with D 3 (S). (Also Imperat. form of *-la*, e.g. *kitoto kile kikile kile kileji*, let that little child eat that cake.)

Kileji, n. (*vi-*), a round flat wheaten cake (Str.).

Kilele, n. (*vi-*), top, point, peak, pointed end, pinnacle, e.g. *k. cha mlima*, the top of the mountain. Also of plants and trees, *k. cha mnazi kikachanua*, the shoot of the cocoanut blossomed. (Dist. *kelele*.)

Kilema, n. (*vi-*), (1) a deformity, defect, blemish; (2) a deformed or disfigured person. *Si vema kucheka k.*, it is not well to mock at deformity. *K. wa jicho*, a one-eyed man, i.e. *chongo*. (Cf. *kiwete, kiziwi, kipofu, kibiongo*, &c.)

Kilemba, n. (*vi-*), (1) a cloth worn as a wrapper round the head, a turban,—the style of folding and wearing being according to the rank, dignity, &c. of the wearer, often of silk, and costly. *Piga k.*, wear a turban. (2) fig. gratuity at the end of a job, apprenticeship, course of teaching, &c. (cf. *ada, bakshishi, ufito*). (3) Crest, e.g. *k. cha jogoo*, cock's comb. (Cf. *shungi, kishungi*.)

Kilembwe, n. (*vi-*), great-great-grandchild. (Cf. *kiningina, kijukuu, mjukuu*.)

Kileo, n. (*vi-*), (1) state or case of intoxication, staggering, reeling, &c.; (2) anything intoxicating or narcotic, e.g. *pombe, mvinyo, tembo*, *bangi, kasumba,* &c. *K. kimempata,* he is under the influence of liquor. (Cf. *ulevi, levya.*)

Kilete, n. (*vi-*), (1) metal rowlock, crutch, for an oar (cf. *kishwara*); (2) stick used for twisting in native ropemaking. (Cf. *kisongo.*)

Kilicho, verb-form, which is,— agreeing with D 3 (S), i.e. pfx. *ki-, li,* is, and relative *cho,* agreeing with same.

Kilifu, n. (*vi-*), also sometimes **Kidifu,** and **Ndifu,** the cloth-like envelope of fibre binding the young leaves of the cocoanut round the growing stem. (Cf. *mnazi,* and *madifu.*)

Kilili, n. (*vi-*), dim. of *ulili,* a small bedstead. (Cf. *kitanda.*)

Kilima, n. (*vi-*), dim. of *mlima,* hill, eminence, rising ground, mound, ascent. Also name of a kind of evil spirit.

Kilimi, n. (*vi-*), dim. of *ulimi,* (1) a little tongue; (2) bad or abusive style of speaking, *-ki* being here depreciative as in *kidomo. Ana k.,* he uses abusive language. (Cf. *mlimi, mwambi.*)

Kilimia, n. the Pleiades (constellation). *K. ikizama kwa jua huzuka kwa mvua,* if the Pleiades set in fine weather, they rise in rain. (For stars cf. *nyota, sayari.*)

Kilimo, n. (*vi-*), (1) hoeing, and so the care of a plantation generally, i.e. cultivation, agriculture; (2) products of cultivation, produce, crop. *Mwaka huu watu wameongokewa na kilimo,* this year people have succeeded well in their cultivation. *Vilimo vinasongana,* the crops are too crowded, are planted too close. (Cf. *lima, mlima, mkulima,* &c.)

Kilinda, n. (*vi-*), verbal noun of *linda,* guard, protector, governing a noun follg., e.g. *kilinda chozi,* the tear-guard, i.e. the pendulous end of a cluster of banana fruits, with a pearly drop of moisture at the tip. (Cf. *linda, mlinzi,* and *kilindo.*)

Kilindi, n. (*vi-*), a place of deep water, a deep channel, a deep. (Cf. *lindi.*)

Kilindo, n. (*vi-*), (1) act (process, means, &c.) of guarding, protection, guard, charge, care. *Tu katika k. cha Muungu,* we are in God's keeping. (2) A watchman's platform in a plantation; (3) a shelter (from rain, sun, &c.). (Cf. *linda, mlinzi, lindo,* and Ar. syn. *hamaya.*)

Kilinge, n. (*vi-*), mystery, puzzle, trick. *Maneno ya k.,* dark, unintelligible utterances, i.e. *maneno ya fumbo,* or *ya mifano. K. cha mganga,* hocus pocus.

Kilingo, n. (*vi-*), (1) a notch cut as a mark, a blaze on trees to show the way; (2) (? for *kilindo*) a watchman's platform, a shelter; (3) a carpenter's shed for shaping timber, logs, &c. (Cf. *linga, ulingo.*)

Kilio, n. (*vi-*), (1) sounding, a sound, crying, weeping, mourning, a cry, scream, shout, dirge; (2) a subject for mourning, a sad thing. Also dim. in contrast with *mlio, lio,* i.e. *kilio kidogo. Nyamazisha k.,* put a stop to mourning. *Tia k.,* cause lamentation. *Amepeleka k. matangani,* he has contributed a wail to the mourning.

*****Killa,** a. also **Kulla,** every (as a rule with a singular noun only, and unlike all other adjs. in Swahili with its noun following it). *K. mtu,* every one. *K. siku,* daily, day by day. *K. aendako,* wherever he goes. *K. atakapo,* whenever he likes. Occasionally with Plur. *k. watu wakaenda zao,* all the people went away.

*****Kiluthu,** n. velvet.

Kima, n. a kind of monkey. (For other kinds cf. *nyani, tumbili, mbega, ndegele.*)

*****Kima,** n. (*vi-*), (1) price, value, e.g. *kima chake kadiri gani?* How much is it? and cf. *kem.* (2) Measure, stature, height, and cf. *kimo.* (Ar. Cf. (1) *kimo, kadiri, kiasi, thamani;* (2) *kipimo, urefu, ukubwa.*)

Kimacho, adv. wide awake, in a wakeful condition, on the watch. *Lala (kaa) k.*, lie (remain) awake. (Cf. *jicho, macho, kesha.*)

Kimaji, adv. and a., like water, wet, damp, watery, swampy. Also *-a kimaji*. (Cf. *maji, majimaji, rutuba.*)

Kimanda, n. (*vi-*), an omelette (of eggs, &c.). (Cf. *maandasi.*)

Kimandu, n. (*vi-*), a strip of wood, fixed inside a native doorframe at top and bottom, with holes in which the pivots of the door-valves turn.

Kimanga, n. and adv., something Arabian, of the Arab kind. Hence (1) the Arab language, (2) a particular kind of grain. *Sema (jua) k.*, speak (know) Arabic. *Jiwe la k.*, a hard stone used for sharpening tools on or grinding corn, &c., a whetstone, a grinding stone,—also *jiwe la manga*, and *kimango*. (See **Manga**, and cf. syn. *kiarabu.*)

Kimashamba, n. and adv., something of a country kind, rustic vulgar dialect, in a countryfied (rude, unpolished) way. *-a k.*, countryfied, vulgar. (Cf. *shamba.*)

Kimbia, v. run, run away, make haste, fly (from), escape (from). *Akimbiaye hawazi giza, wala haoni jua*, one who runs does not think of the darkness, or see the sunlight. *Adui walikimbia*, the enemy fled. *Mtoto amemkimbia simba*, the boy ran away from (escaped from) the lion. With *ji*, hide oneself away, be hidden, be out of view, e. g. *mji uliojikimbia*, a village concealed from view. Ps. *kimbiwa*, be run from, be escaped from. Nt. *kimbika*, e. g. allow of running (escape, &c.). Ap. *kimbilia*, run to (for, in, after, &c., but *not* as a rule, run away *from*), overtake, take refuge with, have recourse to, fall back upon, go on an errand for; e. g. *mbuzi hao watakimbia kukimbilia mama yao*, these kids will run off to find their dam. *Kimbilia roho*, run for (to save) one's life. *Kimbilia pesa*, run races for money. So Ps. *kimbiliwa*, be run to (for, after, &c.), be a refuge (asylum, resource), and Nt. *kimbilika*. With *ji*, e. g. *watu wakajikimbilia*, the people took to their heels,—of a promiscuous, shameful flight, every one for himself. Hence *kimbiliza, -izwa*, cause to run on, make go fast, hurry, hasten, do in a hurry, do rashly (precipitately, carelessly)— like *endeleza*, but more emphatic, e. g. *kimbiliza maneno*, talk too fast, talk recklessly (foolishly, at random, without thinking). *Kimbiliza jipu*, open an abscess too soon, treat it prematurely. *Kimbiliza udongo*, be quick with the clay, before it gets too dry and hard to use. *Kimbiliza kazi*, hurry on the work. Cs. *kimb-iza, -izwa*, cause (encourage, allow, &c.) to run, put to flight, allow to escape, help in escaping, drive away, pursue. *Alikimbiza roho yake*, he saved his life. *Akimbiza mtoto asije kuuawa*, he saves the child from being put to death. *Kimbiza punda*, run in front of a donkey, as a slave does before his Arab master, when riding. Hence *kimbiz-ia, -iwa*, e. g. *amenikimbizia watumwa wangu*, he has got all my slaves to run away from me. Also *kimbizana*, e. g. *watu wakakimbizana kuenenda*, the people encouraged each other to push on quickly. (Cf. *mbio*, on which *kimbia* appears to be formed, *mkimbizi, kimbilio.*)

Kimbio, n. and adv., at a running pace, with speed, at full speed, hastily, also *kimbiombio*. See **Mbio**, and **Kimbia**.

Kimbizi, n. and adv., similar to *kimbio*. *Maji ya kimbizi*, a swift current. (Cf. prec.)

Kimbunga, n. (*vi-*), typhoon, hurricane,—esp. the famous and exceptional typhoon at Zanzibar on April 15, 1872, often used as an epoch in reckoning time. *Kimbunga kikaang'usha minazi na mijumba* *yote*, the typhoon threw down all the cocoanut trees and houses. (Cf. *tháruba, tufane, chamchela*.)

Kimelea, n. (*vi-*), a plant which grows of itself, a self-sown plant, an indigenous plant, a parasitic plant (growing on to some other). *Jamii ya vimelea*, the whole flora (indigenous plant-life) of a place. (Cf. *mea, mmea*, also *kikulia, kizalia*.)

Kimeta, n. (*vi-*), also **Kimete**, sparkling, sparkle, glitter, lustre, shining. E. g. *k. cha jua*, sparkling radiance of the sun. *K. cha upanga*, the glitter of a sword. Also in the form *kimeti, kimetimeti, kimerimeti*, of anything sparkling, spangle, tinsel, and esp. of fire-flies, glow-worms. (Cf. *meta*, and *kimulimuli, kianga*.)

Kimia, n. (*vi-*), a circular casting net—of light fine twine. Also used to describe 'netting, network, lace, cambric,' &c., i.e. *nguo ya kimia*. *-a kimia*, of network, netted. (For nets cf. *wavu, jarifa*.)

Kimio, n. (*vi-*), something in the throat, and so (1) uvula; (2) a throat affection,—used to describe quinsy, croup, abscess in the throat, enlarged uvula or tonsils, &c.,—as *kifua*, of chest affections generally. (Cf. *umio*, and *roho, koo*.)

*****Kimo**, n. (*vi-*), (1) measure, stature, height, depth; (2) a measuring rod, tape, foot rule. *K. cha mtu*, a man's height. *Akupita k.*, he is taller than you. *Maji ya k.*, deep water. *K. cha mti*, a piece of wood to measure with. (Ar. Cf. *kima*, of which *kimo* is a modified form.— Dist. *kimo*, as verb-form, it is in (within, inside),—pfx. *ki* agreeing with D 3 (S), and locative -mo, which see.)

Kimoyo, n. also **Kimoyo-moyo**, something affecting the heart, e. g. (1) heart ailment, heart disease; (2) a feeling,—esp. fear, indignation, passion; (3) term of endearment, favourite, sweetheart (cf. *kipenzi, mchumba*). (Cf. *moyo*.)

Kimrima, n. the dialect of *Mrima*, i.e. the dialect of Swahili spoken on the coast adjacent to Z. (Cf. *Mrima*.)

Kimulimuli, n. (*vi-*), fire-fly, glow-worm. (Cf. *mulika*, and *kimeti*.)

Kimwa, v. become wearied, get cross, be disgusted, lose one's temper. *Kimwa kwa chakula (njia, kazi,* &c.), be put out by one's food (travelling, work, &c.). (Cf. syn. more usual, *kinai, choka, sumbuka, chukiwa*.)

Kimwitu, n. dim. of *mwitu*, small forest, patch of forest, jungle. (Cf. *mwitu, kichaka*.)

Kimwondo, n. (*vi-*), a shooting star, i.e. *nyota ya kuanguka*,—supposed to be fiery darts thrown by spirits of the air (*jini*) (Str.).

Kimya, n. and adv. (1) silence, stillness, absence of noise; (2) quietness, calm, reserve. As adv. silently, without noise. *K. kingi kina mshindo mkuu*, deep silence makes a loud noise. *Nyamaza k.*, hold one's tongue, be perfectly silent. *Sali k.*, pray in secret. *Mtu wa kimyakimya*, a very quiet, reserved person. *Akasikia k.*, and he heard no reply.

Kina, pfx. or n. used as pfx. (see note below) which with the noun following denotes a person or persons of a certain class, connected with another person by resemblance, dependence, or other social relation, or a person with others so connected with him. It is often heard as *akina* (see note), and in plur. form *wakina*. E.g. *kina sisi*, a kind of generalized plural,—'such as we, people like us, the lot of us, we.' *Akina nani huyu?* Who is this? implying 'What are his connexions?' whether as master or dependent. *Akina Abdallah* may mean (1) Abdallah's following generally, his people or dependents, or (2) Abdallah himself alone, or (3) Abdallah with his retinue. So *Akina bwana anakuja*, the master is coming. *Kina mwinyi mkuu*, the chief and his court. *Kina* is also used (with a noun) as a generalized mode of address, as well as reference, a polite substitute for direct mention of several or one, e.g. *akina bibi*, the lady-folk, the ladies, my ladies, my lady. So *akina bwana*, a slave's address to his master's son,—*akina baba*, a master's address half-playful to his slaves. It may also be used with contemptuous generality. *Wamekwitwa watu wale wakina Turi*, those people were known as Turi's lot. (Perh. generalized from Ar. *gan*, pl. *agina*, slave-born, a slave, or connected with the pfx. *ki*.)

Kina, n. (*vi-*), a rhyme, a terminal assonance, a similar final syllable. *Kuwa na vina*, to have rhymes,—of lines of poetry. *Tia vina*, make rhymes, rhyming endings. *Mashairi ya vina*, rhyming verses. (Cf. *guni*, for absence of rhyme, blank verse.)

Kina, n. *kina cha bahari*, a deep place in the sea. *Bahari ina k. sana*, the sea is very deep. (*Kilindi*, *lindi*, usual in Z.)

*****Kinai**, v. (1) be content, be self-satisfied, be independent, want no sympathy or help, be self-sufficient, be self-contained. Hence often (2) in a bad sense, of conceited, offensive, independent, or active dislike, i.e. be disgusted, be surfeited, dislike, have a loathing. E. g. of food, *amekinai*, he has had enough, he has had a full meal, (or of a sick man) he has no appetite, he revolts from food. *Jikinai*, feel quite satisfied or secure, be boastful, vaunt oneself. *Sultani ajikinai kwa nguvu*, the Sultan shows his pride of power. Cs. *kinaisha*, satisfy, surfeit, glut, disgust, nauseate, revolt. *Chakula hiki kinanikinaisha*, this food revolts me. *Atakukinaisha siku moja*, you will have enough of him in one day. *Kujikinaisha ubora*, to vaunt his perfections. (Ar. Cf. *-kinaifu*, *kinaya*, and syn. *shiba*, *shibisha*, *rithisha*, *chukiza*, and for boasting, *jisifu*, *jivuna*.)

*****-kinaifu**, a. one who has enough, does not desire or need anything, and so (1) moderate, self-controlled, sober, independent; or (2) self-sufficient, contemptuous, cold, supercilious, unsociable. (Cf. *kinai*, and *kiasi*, *upweke*, *baridi*.)

Kinamasi, n. mucilage, slime, slimy substance or fluid. *Mafuta ya-fanya k.*, the oil is getting thick and sticky. Also of a wet slippery soil (cf. *utope*).

Kinanda, n. (*vi-*), a stringed instrument of the kind commonest in E. Africa, a kind of banjo or guitar. Extended to include piano, organ, and almost any similar European instrument of music. *Piga k.*, play the banjo. (Cf. *ngoma* for other instruments.)

*****Kinara**, n. (*vi-*), dim. of *mnara*, (1) small pillar, column; (2) candlestick; (3) small ornament in the embroidery worked in silk on the collar of a native dress (*kanzu*), i.e. *vinara vya shingo*. (Ar. Cf. *mnara*.)

*****Kinaya**, n. self-content, independence, selfish isolation, a supercilious air, insolence. *Neno la k.*, a contemptuous remark. (Cf. *kinai*.)

Kinda, n. (*ma-*), young one, esp. of birds, a chick, but also of animals, e.g. *k. la frasi*, a foal, *k. kibwa*, a young dog, cub, whelp,—not of man. Sometimes a., e.g. *mnazi mkinda*, a young cocoanut tree.

Kinda, -**kindani**, **Kindano**. See **Kinza**, &c.

Kindu, n. (*ma-*), fruit of the palm *mkindu*, a kind of wild date. See also **Ukindu**.

Kinena, n. (*vi-*), middle of the body between the groins (*manena*).

Kinga, v. is used of the effect of what is interposed between two objects, and which acts offensively to the one and defensively as to the other. Hence (1) act as screen against, ward off, parry, check, stop, interpose, get in the way of, intercept, catch; and (2) fig. contradict, oppose, obstruct. Also (3) act as screen to, cover, be a defence to; (4) fig. help, assist, protect. *Kinga, jiwe hili litaanguka*, guard (yourself), or, ward it off, this stone is going to fall. *Nimekinga mwili wangu kwa ngao*, I interposed my body as a shield. *Muungu amenikinga*, God has protected me. *Kinga mvua (jua)*, keep off the rain (sun). Ps. *kingwa*, (1) be screened (warded) off; (2) be used as a screen; (3) be screened (protected). Nt. *kingika*. Ap. *king-ia, -iwa*, e. g. *ngao ya kukingia selaha*, a shield to keep off weapons. Cs. *kingiza*, usually protect, defend. *Kingiza na mvua*, protect from rain. *Jikingiza*, defend oneself. Rp. *kingana*, (1) protect each other; (2) oppose each other, with argument, force, &c. (Cf. follg.) — n. (—, and **Vinga**), something interposed, and which has different effects accordingly, e. g. (1) a check, a stopper, a fender, a fence, a guard, a screen, a shelter,—and so either (2) protection, defence, assistance, or (3) obstruction, difficulty, misfortune, limitation. E. g. *k. cha moto*, or *k.* only, a fireguard, i. e. commonly a firebrand, brand used as a guard, rather than 'a fender.' Cf. *kinga na kinga, ndipo moto uwakapo*, firebrands make the fire burn. *K. cha maji*, or *k.* alone, a long blade of grass or leaflet tied round the stem of a tree to collect the rain trickling down and direct it to a water jar. *K. ya jicho*, a blinker. Cf. *kidoto*, also *kijamanda*. (Cf. *kingama, mkingiko, kinda, pinga*, and *epusha, bekua*. For *kinga=kunga*, see **Kunga**.)

Kingaja, n. (*vi-*), armlet or bracelet of seeds, beads, &c. (Cf. *kekee, kikuku, banagiri*, and *urembo*.)

Kingalingali, n. on the back, face upwards. *Lala k.*, lie on the back. *Anguka k.*, fall backwards. (Cf. *kitanitani, kichali*.)

Kingama, v. (1) be interposed, lie across, be in the way, act as a screen; (2) obstruct, baffle, thwart. *Gogo limekingama njiani*, a log blocks the road. *Njia ngine inakingama njia ya mbele*, another path cuts across the road leading straight on. Ap. *kingam-ia, -iwa*, e. g. *nyoka amenikingamia njiani*, a snake stopped me on the road. Cs. *kingam-isha, -ishwa, -iza, -izwa*, intens. frustrate, stop altogether, block. Rp. *kingamana*, e. g. *tumekingamana mimi naye*, he and I had a (friendly or stormy) interview, we encountered each other. Hence *kingaman-isha, -ishwa*, cause to get in each other's way, make difficulties among. (St. form of *kinga*, i. e. be in an interposed position. Cf. *-ama, simama, tuama*, &c. Cf. *mkingamo*.)

Kingio, Kingo, n. screen, handscreen, shade, lamp-cover. (Cf. *kinga*.)

Kingoe, n. (*vi-*), dim. of *ngoe*, a small hook. See **Ngoe**.

Kingojezi, n. (*vi-*), similar to *kingojo*.

Kingojo, n. (*vi-*), act (time, place, &c.) of watching, watch, guard, guard-station, post, sentry-go, turn of watching. E. g. *linda k.*, keep watch. *Keti k.*, remain on watch. (Cf. *ngoja, kilindo, zamu*.)

Kingozi, n. the old dialect of Swahili, esp. as formerly spoken at Melindo, Patta, and the northward towns of the Zanzibar coast, now only poetical and hardly intelligible. Hence now used of 'difficult, half-understood speech.' *Maneno ya k.*, antiquated, meaningless terms.

Kingubwa, n. (*vi-*), spotted hyaena. (Cf. *fisi*.)

*****Kini, Kinika**, v. be sure, be certain, be ascertained,—apparently from Ar. **yakini** (which see), treated mistakenly by Swahilis as a form of a verb *kini*. E. g. *yamkinika* (or, *yamkini*) *Sultani kusafiri kesho*, it is certain as to the Sultan that he will set out to-morrow. (Ar. Cf. *yakini*, and dist. *yamkini*.)

Kining'ina, n. (*vi-*), great-great-grandchild. (Cf. *kijukuu*, *hilembwe*, and *ning'inia*, rock, dandle.)

Kinjurinjuri, n. a particular way of cutting the hair, leaving one long tuft, i. e. *kukata kinjurinjuri* (Str.).

Kinofu, n. (*vi-*), a scrap of meat. (Cf. *mnofu*.)

Kinono, n. (*vi-*), a fatted animal, a fatling. (Cf. *nona*, *-nono*, and *nenepa*.)

Kinoo, n. (*vi-*), a whetstone, i. e. *jiwe la kunolea*, a stone to sharpen things with. (Cf. *noa*, *noo*, *noleo*, and *cherehe*, a grindstone.)

Kinu, n. (*vi-*), a wooden mortar, made of a hard block of wood hollowed out in the centre, used for pounding and cleaning grain, and crushing and mixing vegetable food generally. Also for extracting oil. The wooden pestle is called *mche*, and the operation usually *kutwanga*. See **Mche**, **Twanga**. It is extended to metal mortars, e. g. *k. cha chuma*, an iron mortar, and also is used of a mill of any kind, e. g. *k. cha moshi*, a steam mill, *k. cha kushindikia*, a crushing mill, whether of oil seeds or sugar-cane. *K. cha mkono*, hand mill. *K. cha kusagia*, grinding (flour) mill.

Kinubi, n. (*vi-*) and adv. (1) a kind of harp, used in their dances by the *Wanubi*, i. e. Soudanese (or (Nubians) settled in Zanzibar. Also (2) the Soudanese language; (3) in the Soudanese style. *-a kinubi*, of the Soudanese kind.

Kinundu, n. (*vi-*), dim. of *nundu*, a little hump, knob, lump. Hence *kinundunundu*, to describe a rough, lumpy surface, as of plaster, &c.

Kinwa, n. (*vi-*), also **Kinywa** and **Kanwa**, the mouth (as organ of drinking) of man, animals, insects, &c. (of birds, usually *mdomo*). Also 'something to drink, a beverage,' but this is usually *kinwaji*. *K. mchuzi*, the hair on the under lip, the imperial, place where the imperial grows, lit. gravy drinker. *K. wazi*, open mouth, with open mouth, open mouthed. (Cf. *nya*, *kinwaji*, *kanwa*, and follg.)

Kinwaji, n. (*vi-*), also **Kinywaji**, and rarely **Kinweo**, **Kinwewa**, something to drink, a beverage, liquid for drinking purposes.

Kinweleo, n. (*vi-*), a pore (of the skin). (Cf. *nya*, *nyweleo*.)

Kinyaa, n. (*vi-*), excretum (liquid or solid), urine, excrement, dung, filth. (Cf. *nya*, *nyesi*, *kinyesi*, also *ukojo*, *mavi*.)

Kinyago, n. (*vi-*), anything used at an **unyago** (which see), but esp. a dressed-up grotesque figure, mock-ghost or scarecrow. *Cheza k.*, lit. play at *unyago*, play at ghosts, dress up,—of any kind of acting, theatricals, farce.

Kinyama, n. (*vi-*), dim. of *nyama*, small animals. *Vinyama vya mwitu wakaona kiu*, the lesser wild animals grew thirsty.

Kinyamkela, n. (*vi-*), (1) a kind of evil spirit, to be propitiated at crossways, a storm-devil; (2) of a whirlwind, i.e. *pepo za kinyamkela*. (Cf. *chamchela*.)

Kinyefu, n. (*vi-*), and **Kinyenyefu**, a tickling or tingling sensation, itching. (From *nyea*, cf. *nyegi*.)

Kinyegele, n. (*vi-*), name of a small animal, skunk (Str.).

Kinyemi, n. and a., something good, pleasing, acceptable. *Kipya kinyemi kingawa kidonda*, a novelty has its charms, even a new sore. (Cf. Ar. *neema*.)

Kinyesi, n. (*vi-*), excretum,—like *kinyaa*. Also in plur. *manyesi*. (From *nya*.)

Kinyonga, n. (*vi-*), (1) hip-complaint. (Cf. *kifua*, *kimio*, &c.).

(2) Chamelion. (Perh. both from *nyonga*, wriggle, twist.)

Kinyonge, n. and adv., from *-nyonge*, state of wretchedness, abject destitution, degradation, &c.

Kinyongo, n. (*vi-*), of a mental or moral twist, (1) fancy, scruple, fad; (2) ill-feeling, grudge, bitterness, spite, resentment. *Usifanye kazi kwa k.*, do not work unwillingly, as if against the grain. *Mpenzi hana k.*, a lover has no scruples (doubts, hesitation). *Mwenyi k.*, a hypochondriac. (Cf. *nyonga, kinyonga, unyonga*, also syn. *mfundo, kikombo, chuki, uchungu.*)

Kinyozi, n. (*vi-*), a barber, one who shaves. (From *nyoa.*)

Kinyuma, n. and adv. (also **Kinyume** commonly), the back part, the rear, behind, backwards, after time, late, in a contrary way. *Kwa kinyume*, backwards, to the rear. *Habari ya k.*, later, subsequent news. *Kinyume changu*, behind me. *Kuja k.*, to arrive late. *Maneno ya k.*, a kind of puzzle-language, the last syllable of each word being made the first. (Cf. *nyuma*, and *baada.*)

Kinyumba, n. (*vi-*), an unmarried woman, living with a man as his wife. (Cf. *nyumba, mchumba, suria, hawaa.*)

Kinyumbu, n. (*vi-*), dim. of *nyumbu*, a small mule.

Kinyunya, n. (*vi-*), a little cake, a bit of a cake, a sweetmeat. (Cf. *nyunyiza*, sprinkle, and *nyunyo.*)

Kinywa, Kinywaji, Kinyweleo. See **Kinwa, Kinwaji, Kinweleo.**

Kinza, v. object, contradict, deny, oppose, rebel. Rp. *kinzana*, object, stand in the way, oppose, contradict. *Kinzana na mtu*, dispute with a person. (Not often heard. Cf. follg. and *kinga, kingana, pingana.*)

-kinzani, n. refractory, combative, obstructive. (Cf. prec. and *ukinzani.*)

Kinzano, n. (*ma-*), objection, obstruction, contradiction. (Cf. prec. and *kinzana.*)

Kioja, n. (*vi-*), something that astonishes or terrifies, an oddity, a curiosity, a portent, a bugbear, a monster. (Cf. *kitisho, shani, ajabu, afa.*)

Kiokozi, n. (*vi-*), act (means, way, &c.) of recovering, and so, reward for finding something lost or in danger. Also of persons, one who saves, rescuer, preserver. (From *okoa*. Cf. *mwokozi, uokozi.*)

Kiolezo, n. (*vi-*), a pattern, sample. (Cf. *oleza*, and syn. *namna.*)

Kiongozi, n. (*vi-*), act (means, way, &c.) of directing; but usually, guide on a road, director, leader of a caravan. (Cf. *mkuu wa genzi.*) Also, reward for such service, guide's fee. (From *ongoa*. Cf. *mwongozi, uongozi.*)

Kiongwe, n. (*vi-*), a kind of donkey from the mainland,—mostly from the Unyamwezi country; used for carrying loads, i. e. *punda kiongwe*. (Also as a., obstinate, refractory (Kr.). Cf. *mbishi.*)

Kionja, verbal noun from *onja*, governing another noun, 'that which tastes.' *K. mchuzi*, the imperial, or under lip, i. e. gravy taster,—like *kinwa mchuzi*. (Cf. *onja*, and follg.)

Kionjo, n. (*vi-*), a little taste, a small sample, a trial. (Cf. *onja.*)

Kionyo, n. (*vi-*), secret warning, hint, suggestion. (Cf. *ona, onyo.*)

Kioo, n. (*vi-*), a piece of glass, looking-glass, mirror. *K. cheupe*, clear, white glass. *K. cha kuona*, transparent glass. *K. cha kutazamia uso*, a looking-glass. (Perh. conn. with *ona*, i.e. *kiono.*)

Kiopoo, n. (*vi-*), anything used for taking up, fishing up, as from a well or pit,—a pole, stick with fork, hook, gaff. (From *opoa.*)

Kiosha, verbal noun from *osha*, that which washes, e.g. *k. miguu*, that which washes the feet,—name of a wedding fee for particular service. (Cf. *kifungua mlango.*)

Kiosho, n. (*vi-*), act (place, means,

&c.) of washing. (Cf. *osha*, and *josho*.)

Kiota, n. (*vi-*), also **Kioto**, sitting-place of a bird, nest, roost, fowl's laying place. (Cf. *ota*, *oteo*, *moto*.)

Kioteo, n. (*vi-*), ambuscade, ambush, lurking-place. (Cf. *ota*, *otea*.)

Kiowe, n. (*vi-*), shout, cry for help. See **Kiyowe**.

Kioza, n. state of a putrid thing, putridity, gangrene. *Mtu huyu yuna k. ndani*, this man is rotten inside. (From *oza*.)

Kipa, n. verbal of *pa*, act of giving, that which gives, e. g. *k. mkono*, a fee given at a wedding for special attendance (cf. *kifungua mlango*, *kiosha miguu*). *K. imara*, that which gives strength. (Cf. *pa*, *kipaji*, *kipawa*.)

Kipaa, n. (*vi-*), dim. of *paa*, (1) a small roof, roof a shed, &c.; (2) one of the sides of the four-sided roof of a native hut, usually one of the smaller slopes, overlapped by the larger ones (*mapaa*). *K. cha mbele* (*cha nyuma*), the front (back) slope of a roof; (3) also **kipara**, which see.

Kipaji, n. (*vi-*), (1) a presentation, a present, donation, gift. *K. cha Muungu*, a gift of God. (From -*pa*, cf. *kipa*, *upaji*, -*paji*.) (2) Part of the forehead (*paji*), brow, eyebrow, e. g. *kunja vipaji vya uso*, knit the brows, frown. Also (3) a sweet-scented cosmetic, applied to the brows, an ornamental patch of colour, a brow ornament (cf. *urembo*). (4) A small projection on the side of the *mjusi* worked on the front of a native dress (*kanzu*), also called *kiguu*. See **Mjusi**.

Kipaka, n. (*vi-*), dim. of *paka*, a small cat, a poor cat, a kitten.

Kipakacha, n. (*vi-*), dim. of *pakacha*, a small kind of basket, of plaited cocoanut leaf-fronds. (For other kinds see **Kikapo**.)

Kipaku, n. (*vi-*), small spot, speck, patch of colour or coloured stuff, e. g. used of the mottled or speckled colouring of animals and birds. -*a k.*, or *k.* alone, mottled, speckled, e. g. *kuku k.*, a speckled fowl. Also *kipakupaku*, in same sense. (Cf. *paku*, and perh. *paka*, v., also *waa*, *doa*.)

Kipamba, n. (*vi-*), dim. from *pamba* (cotton), a small bit (tuft, plug, patch) of raw cotton (cotton wool, lint), e. g. for medical application.

Kipambo, n. (*vi-*), an ornament, ornamental work, a fitting, furniture of a house. *Nyumba hii haina k.*, this house is unfurnished, e. g. of a poor man's dwelling. (Cf. *pamba*, v., *pambo*, also syn. *kifaa*, *chombo*, *urembo*, *uzuri*.)

Kipande, n. (*vi-*), (1) a small bit, piece, slip, part, of anything (cf. *fungu*, *sehemu*, *kitambo*, *kidogo*, *kato*); (2) an instrument, tool, utensil (cf. *chombo*, *kitu*, *samani*). *K. cha nyama*, a scrap of meat. *K. cha mtu*, a diminutive man, a mannikin (contr. *pande la mtu*, *pandikizi*). *Vipande vya kupimia*, surveying instruments. (3) Used esp. of a light wooden rammer, used in hardening a concrete floor or roof. (Cf. *pande*, *upande*, *mpande*, *pandikizi*, ? all conn. with *panda*, v. plant,—the constant common occupation.)

Kipanga, n. (*vi-*), (1) dim. of *upanga*, a small sword; (2) a large bird of prey.

Kipango, n. (*vi-*), dim. of *pango*, a small cave, den, hole, mouse-hole. (Cf. *kitundu*, *kishimo*.)

Kipao, n. (*vi-*), act (means, way) of mounting up. (Cf. *paa*, v.)

Kipapatiko, n. (*vi-*), little flapping object, feathery waving end, e. g. of fin or feather. (Cf. *papatika*.)

Kipara, n. (*vi-*), and **Kipaa**, a clean-shaved patch, a bald place on the head, tonsure. *Mtu wa kikoa asilipe ana kipara cheupe*, a member of a mess, if he does not pay, has a bald patch, i. e. is a marked man. (Cf. *upaa*, *upara*, and ? *paa*, roof.)

Kipato, n. (*vi-*), dim. of *upato*, a small metal gong, usually of brass, with edges turned in, a metal tambourine, or dish of similar shape.

Kipawa, n. (*vi-*), (1) dim. of *pawa*, small ladle; (2) gift (but not so in Z.).

Kipele, n. (*vi-*), small pimple, pustule, sore, breaking-out. *Vipele*, skin eruption, erysipelas. (Cf. *upele*.)

Kipendi, n. (*vi-*), like *kipenzi*, a beloved object, a favourite, darling. (From *penda*.)

Kipendo, n (*vi-*), act (trait, manifestation, &c.) of affection, kindness, love. (Cf. *pendo, upendo*.)

Kipengee, n. (*vi-*), (1) side-path, by-way, way round, side-channel, out of the straight or usual course; (2) evasion, subterfuge, shift, indirect means of obtaining an object. *Maneno yake haya vipengee*, these statements of his are evasive (shuffling, deceitful). (Also *pengee*.)

Kipenu, n. (*vi-*), a shed or side-room built against the side of a wall or house outside, a lean-to, a cabin in a ship. (Cf. *upenu*.)

Kipenyo, n. (*vi-*), a hole through which something is passed, a thing which is passed through, e.g. the peg of a top, axis of a globe, &c. (Cf. *penya*.)

Kipeo, n. (*vi-*), (1) highest or furthest point, apex, top, end, culmination; (2) ideal, best example, standard of excellence, *chef-d'œuvre*. *K. cha macho*, furthest limit of vision, horizon. (Cf. *pea, upeo, pevuka*.)

Kipepeo, n. (*vi-*), (1) dim. of *pepeo*, a small fan; (2) a butterfly; (3) a kind of flat fish. (Cf. *upepo, pepea*.)

Kipete, n. (*vi-*), dim. of *pete*, a small ring, ferrule, circlet.

Kipeto, n. (*vi-*), bag (with flap or cover), case, receptacle, cover, parcel, packet. *K. cha barua*, letter case, envelope. (Cf. *peto, peta, pete*, and syn. *bahasha*.)

Kipi, n. (*vi-*), or **Kipia**, cock's spur, i.e. *kucha la* (or *mwiba wa*) *nyuma katika kisigino cha jogoo*, the spur behind at the cock's heel.

Kipigi, n. (*vi-*), also **Kipiki**, a little stick to beat with or throw. (Cf. *piga*, and follg.)

Kipigo, n. (*vi-*), stroke, blow, shot. *Tembo alianguka kwa kipigo cha heri*, the elephant fell by a lucky shot.

Kipila, n. (*vi-*), a curlew. (Also called *sululu*.)

Kipilipili, n. and adv., like black pepper-corns. *Nyele za k.*, hair of a short woolly kind, growing in small tufts. (Cf. *pilipili*, and *uele*.)

Kipimo, n. (*vi-*), thing for measuring, a measure, a weight, amount measured. (Cf. *pima*, and for measures *mkono, shibiri, wari, wakia, ratli, pishi, frasila, kibaba, kisaga*, &c.)

Kipinda, adv. *Kufa kipinda*, die a natural death. (Cf. *pinda*, n.)

Kipindi, n. (*vi-*), (1) a portion of time, period, e.g. *killa k., k. chote*, all times, at all times, constantly, always. *K. cha athuuri*, noon. *Kwa vipindi*, at times, periodically; also, by fits and starts, irregularly. *-a vipindi*, periodical, regular, irregular. *-a kipindi*, temporary. Also adv. *kipindi*, for a time, for a short time. (Cf. *kitambo, kidogo*, and *kipande*.) (2) A fixed time, a regular hour (cf. *saa*). *Tangu assubuhi hatta jioni ni vipindi kumi na mbili*, from morning to evening there are twelve hours. *Vipindi vya kusali*, the five regular Mahommedan hours of prayer. (Cf. *sala*.) (3) Fit, turn, attack, paroxysm of sickness, anger or emotion generally. *Homa ya vipindi*, recurrent (or, intermittent) fever. *K. cha hasira*, a fit of anger. (Cf. *pinda*, v., turn, and *pindi, upindi, kitambo, saa*.)

Kipindo, n. (*vi-*), a wrapper, esp. a folding cloth for a corpse before placing it in the shroud (*saanda*). Also, a fold (in a garment), pocket, purse, &c. (Cf. *pinda, upindo*, and *kipeto*.)

Kipindupindu, n. (*vi-*), descriptive of a violent seizure, convulsions, cholera, or other disease,—from its effect. (Cf. *pinda, kipindi*, and *wabba*.)

Kipingili, n. (*vi-*), ring marking a knot or joint in a plant, e. g. in sugar-cane. Also the part between two knots or joints, e. g. part of the leg between the knee and ankle, the shin. (Cf. *pingili*.)

Kipingo, n. (*vi-*), bar, pin, peg (keeping something in place), barrier, obstruction. (Cf. *pinga, kipingwa*, and follg.)

Kipingu, n. (*vi-*), dim. of *pingu*, a small fetter.

Kipingwa, n. (*vi-*), a door-bar, bolt. (Cf. *pinga*, and syn. *komeo, kiwi*.)

Kipini, n. (*vi-*), (1) handle, haft, holder,—of tools, knife, sword, &c. (cf. *mpini*, and for other handles *mkono, utambo*); (2) small stud or button-like ornament, worn on the nose or ear. (Cf. *kipuli, jasi*, and *urembo*.)

Kipipa, n. (*vi-*), dim. of *pipa*, small barrel, small cask. *Kipipa cha baruti*, barrel of gunpowder.

Kipira, n. (*vi-*), dim. of *mpira*, a small ball. Also? (2) a carpenter's moulding-plane, *k. cha mwiringo* (cf. *randa*), and (3) a projecting moulding.

Kipito, n. (*vi-*), a passing by or through, a way through, passage. (From *pita*, v.)

Kipofu, n. and adv. (1) blindness, a blind person, in a blind state or way, blindly. *Mtoto k., haoni, macho yake yamepofuka*, the child is blind, he does not see, his eyes are sightless. *K. wa macho*, bereft of sight, blind. *Mtu huyu ana k.*, this man is blind. Also (2) for *kibofu*, a bladder. (Cf. *-pofu, pofuka*, and *kiziwi, kilema*.)

Kipokee, adv. by turns, by taking turns, e. g. *chukua* (*twaa*) *kipokee*, of carrying a load, a corpse to the grave, &c. (From *pokea*.)

Kipolepole, n. (*vi-*) and adv. (1) a kind of butterfly; (2) from *-pole*, i. e. in a very slow (calm, gentle) way.

Kipondo, n. (*vi-*), dim. of *pondo*, small pole, esp. of pole for punting, propelling a canoe in shallow water. (Cf. *ponda, mpondo*, and follg.)

Kipondwe, n. (*vi-*), food consisting of something pounded or crushed, a mash, e. g. of cleaned grain and grated cocoanut mixed together in a mortar (*kinu*). (From *ponda*, with pass. termin. *-we*.)

Kiponya, n. (*vi-*), verbal of *ponya*, something which preserves or cures, a remedy. *K. cha njaa*, the remedy of hunger, i. e. food.

Kipooza, n. (*vi-*), verbal of *pooza*, paralysis, deadness, a paralysed person, a withered, dried-up thing. Also adv., in a withered (dead, helpless) state. (Cf. *mapooza*.)

Kipopo, n. (*vi-*), dim. of *popo*, a small bat (the animal).

Kipopoo, n. (*vi-*), dim. of *popoo*, a little ball, a round lump, e. g. of tobacco, sweets, bonbons, &c.

Kipora, n. (*vi-*), dim. of *pora*, a young cockerel.

Kipuku, Kipukupuku, adv. in showers, in numbers, wholesale, like leaves falling, e. g. of the effect of an epidemic in killing people, i. e. *marathi ya kipuku* (*pukupuku*). *Watu wanakufa kipuku*, people are dying like sheep. (Cf. *pukusa*, and follg.)

Kipukusa, n. (*vi-*), also **Kipukuba**, (1) something shed, cast, dropped, e. g. horns, but esp. of leaves or fruit self-detached or early shed. Also (2) dim. of *pukusa*, a small present, esp. of congratulation. (Cf. follg.)

Kipukute, n. and a. *Ndizi kipukute*, also *kipukusa*, a favourite species of banana. See **Ndizi**, and prec.

Kipuli, n. (*vi-*), a small trinket, often crescent-shaped, worn in the ear as a pendant, ear ornament. (Cf. also *jasi, shamili, kipini, puliki*, and for other ornaments *urembo*.)

Kipumba, n. (1) (*vi-*), also **Bumba**, dim. of *pumba* (*bumba*), a small clod, lump (perh. same as **kibumba**, which see); (2) n. and adv., a foolish act, a fool, folly. *Kuwa k.*, to be a fool. *Fanya k.*, to act as a fool. (Cf. *pumbaa, -pumbafu, upumbafu*, which are usual in Z.)

Kipumbu, n. (*vi-*), scrotum. (Cf. *pumba, pumbu*.)

Kipumziko, n. (*vi-*), act (place, time, means, &c.) of taking rest, resting-place, recreation time, refreshment, relief. (From *pumzika, pumuzi, pumu*. Cf. *baridi, maburudu*.)

Kipungu, n. name of a fish, and also of a bird of prey.

Kipunguo, n. (*vi-*), act (case, means, &c.) of lessening, diminution, defect, deficiency, short allowance. (From *pungua*. Cf. *-pungufu, upunguo*.)

Kipupa, n. and adv., unseemly haste, greediness, over-eagerness. *K. cha kula*, and *kula k.* (or *kwa k.*), voracious eating. (Cf. *pupa*.)

Kipupwe, n. the cold season, i.e. June, July, and August (when the barometer in Z. falls at nights to 75° or even 70°), cold weather. See **Mwaka** and **Pembe**.

Kipusa, n. (*vi-*), same as **kipukusa**, which see.

Kipwa, n. (*vi-*), rock, dry patch (left by receding tide), a shallow place. (Cf. *pwa, pwani, mapwaji*.)

*****Kirahi**, n. also **Ekerahi, Ikirahi**, being offended, disgust, aversion, causing offence, provocation, insult. (Ar. Cf. *kirihi*.)

Kiraka, n. and adv., a piece, spot, patch different from the rest or the surroundings, colour in spots or patches, e.g. *nguo ya k.*, patched, ragged clothes. *Mapwaji ya k.*, patches left by receding tide. *Kirakaraka*, anything variegated, mottled, dappled, speckled, spotted, e.g. of birds and animals. (Cf. *raka, doa, kipaku*.)

Kirembo, n. (*vi-*), anything ornamental, esp. of personal adornment. (Cf. *urembo, remba*, and *pamba*.)

*****Kiri**, v. acknowledge, admit, accept, assent, state formally, confess, allow, aver, ratify. Often in legal documents, e.g. *nimekiri nimekubali kwamba*, I do hereby formally acknowledge and agree that, &c. *K. makosa*, confess offences. *K. deni*, admit a debt. Ps. *kiriwa*. Nt. *kirika*. Ap. *kir-ia, -iwa*. Cs. *kir-isha, -ishwa*, e.g. obtain formal consent, extract confession, allow ratification, &c. Rp. *kiriana*. (Ar. Cf. *kubali, ithini, ungama*.)

*****Kiriba**, n. (*vi-*), water-skin, i.e. the skin of an animal made into a bag, and used for carrying water. (Ar., the *ki* belonging to the root, as in *kitabu*.)

*****Kirihi**, v. (1) loathe, hate, abominate, feel aversion (disgust, dislike, &c.); (2) give offence, provoke, insult, disgust, treat disrespectfully, &c. Ps. *kirihiwa*. Nt. *kirihika*. Cs. *kirih-isha, -ishwa*, e.g. offend, aggravate, exasperate. (Ar. Cf. *ekerahi, kirahi, makeruhu*, and syn. *chukia, chukiza, kasirisha*.)

Kirimba, n. (*vi-*), cage (for bird or animal). Also describes a meatsafe. (Cf. *kitundu, tundu, kizimba*.)

*****Kirimu**, v. also **Kerimu, Karimu**, treat hospitably, entertain, feast, give a present (to). *Tumkirimu mgeni*, let us entertain our guest. *Amemkirimu ng'ombe*, he has made him a present of an ox. Ps. *kirimiwa*. Nt. *kirimika*. Ap. *kirim-ia, -iwa*, e.g. make a present to, be generous to. Cs. *kirim-isha, -ishwa*. (Ar. Cf. *karamu, karama, -karimu*,—also *kariboisha, pokea*.)

Kiroboto, n. (*vi-*), flea. Formerly used as a nickname for irregular Arab soldiery at Z.

Kiroja, n. (*vi-*), same as **kioja**, which see.

Kirukanjia, n. (*vi-*), name of a kind of mouse. (Cf. *panya*.)

Kirukia, n. (*vi-*), name of a climbing plant.

Kirungu, n. (*vi-*), dim. of *rungu* (*lungu*), a small club, knob-kerry.

*****Kisa**, n. (*vi-*), (1) story, account, report, history, narrative; (2) statement of case, reason alleged, cause, explanation; (3) affair, matter, business, subject of report. E.g. *nipe k. chako*, tell me your story, i.e. all about yourself. *Visa vingi*, many stories, a complicated business, endless difficulties. *Hakumfanyiza k. hatta kimoja*, he did nothing whatever to hurt him. (Ar. Cf. *hadithi, habari, neno*.) Also (4) like *kiini*, the innermost part, e.g. *kisa cha koko*, the kernel inside a stone (of fruit).

Kisaga, n. (*vi-*), a dry measure of about a quart, equal to two *kibaba* or half a *pishi*. *Nimempimia kisaga cha mahindi*, I have measured him a quart of maize. (2) ? a weevil. (Cf. *saga*.)

*****Kisahani**, n. (*vi-*), dim. of *sahani*, a small dish, saucer. (Ar. Cf. *chombo, chungu*.)

Kisasa, n. and adv., a thing of the present day, a modern fashion, what is up to date. *Vao la k.*, fashionable dress; *maneno ya k.*, current phraseology. (Cf. *sasa*, and contr. *kikale, kale*.)

*****Kisasi**, n. (*vi-*), also **Kasasi**, vengeance, revenge, retaliation, requital, compensation for harm done, damages. *Toa* (*lipa*) *k.*, suffer vengeance, pay (for harm done). *Toza* (*lipiza, twaa*) *k.*, take revenge on, retaliate upon, extort compensation for. *Twaa k. cha ndugu*, avenge a brother.

*****Kisetiri**, n. (*vi-*), and **Kisitiri**, a cover, screen, screening wall, parapet, partition, hiding place, retiring place, closet. (Ar. Cf. *setiri, stara, kifuniko, kificho, kiwambaza*.)

Kisha, adv. and **Kiisha**, afterwards, moreover, in fine. See **Kiisha**, and **Isha**.

*****Kishada**, n. (*vi-*), dim. of *shada*, (1) tassel, bow, rosette; (2) a small cluster or bunch, e.g. of beads on strings, bunch of flowers, or fruit, nosegay, &c.; (3) a tailless kite. (Ar.)

Kishaufu, n. (*vi-*), anything showy, bit of finery, trinket, personal ornament. (Cf. *shaua, kipambo, kirembo*.)

Kishenzi, n. and adv., anything of a barbarous, rude, uncivilized kind, esp. barbarous language, up-country dialect. *-a k.*, barbarous, uncivilized. (Cf. *-shenzi, ushenzi*, and contr. *kiungwana*.)

Kishiku, n. (*vi-*), stump of a tree, log. (Cf. *shiku, kisiki, kigogo*.)

Kishimo, n. and adv. (*vi-*), dim. of *shimo*, a little pit, hole, underground passage, sudden fall, precipice. (Cf. *genge, tundu, chimbo*.)

Kishina, n. name of a dance (*ngoma*). Also dim. of *shina*.

Kishinda, n. (*vi-*), verbal from *shinda* (which see) in various senses, (1) that which conquers, baffles, is too much for another, e.g. *watu hawa ni vishinda waganga*, these people are a match for the medicine men. (2) A residue, a remainder, esp. of what is left in a vessel, dry or liquid, a quantity less than half of the content, e.g. *kishinda cha maji mtungini*, of a water-jar less than half full. Also a vague measure, a suitable amount for pounding in a mortar (*kinu*), e.g. *vishinda vingapi umetia?* How many measures have you put in? *Kinu tele ni kishinda kimoja*, one measure makes a full mortar, i.e. enough to pound at one time. (Cf. *shinda, shindika*. Perh. *kisinda* is the same word.)

Kishindo, n. and adv. (*vi-*), dim. of *shindo*, shock, blow, outburst, sudden noise, sound of steps (guns, blows, &c.), an agitation, a sensation. *Habari ina k.*, news always comes with a kind of shock. (Cf. *shinda, shindo, mshindo*.)

Kishogo, n. (*vi-*), nape of the neck, back of the head. *Kifo ni karibu, ni kishogoni mwako*, death is near, it is close behind you. *Aku-*

paye kishogo si mwenzio, he who turns his back on you is not your friend. (Cf. *kogo, kikosi.*)

Kishoka, n. (*vi-*), dim. of *shoka*, a small axe.

Kishoroba, n. (*vi-*), dim. of *shoroba* (which see).

*****Kishubaka**, n. (*vi-*), dim. of *shubaka*, a small recess, niche, pigeon-hole, loop-hole.

Kishungi, n. (*vi-*), dim. of *shungi*, (1) a small tuft of hair, crest of feathers, plume; (2) ends of a cloth, lappet, fringes. (Cf. *matamvua.*)

Kishwara, n. (*vi-*), a loop of rope, used to hold an oar (like a rowlock) in a boat, or to lift by. (Cf. *kitanzi*, and *shalaka.*)

Kisi, v. (1) also **Gisi**, consider critically, estimate, calculate, make a guess, form an opinion on, guess. *K. maneno*, weigh a statement. *K. mtama*, set a value on (judge the price of) millet (cf. *fikiri, kadiri, bahatisha, hesabu*). (2) As nautical term, shift, make a change in. *K. mtanga*, shift the sail over, tack, put about. (Cf. *pindua, bisha.*) Seldom in deriv. forms.

Kisibau, n. (*vi-*), a waistcoat, worn open in front. Described as *k. cha mikono*, i.e. sleeved; *k. cha kikwapa*, or *cha kwapa*, i.e. sleeveless,— the usual kind, *k. cha vitana*, i.e. lined; *k. cha kufuta*, i.e. in common plain style. Made of all kinds of materials and colours, and worn over the *kanzu*.

Kisigino, n. (*vi-*), heel, elbow, further distinguished as *k. cha mguu*, and *k. cha mkono*. (Cf. *kifundo, kiweko.*)

Kisiki, n. (*vi-*), log, stump, trunk of fallen tree. (Cf. *kishiku, gogo, shina.*)

Kisikusiku, adv. and n., at night, in the dark. (Cf. *usiku, siku.*)

Kisima, n. (*vi-*), well, water-hole, water-pit, place where water is drawn. (Perh. altered from Ar. *kathima.*)

Kisimi, n. (*vi-*), clitoris. (Cf. *simika.*)

Kisinda, n. (*vi-*), and ? **Kishinda, Kizinda**, hymen. *Weka k.*, preserve virginity. *Tomoa k.*, deprive of virginity. (Cf. *bikira.*)

Kisirani, n. also **Kisarani, Kasarani**, used of what is awkward, unpleasant, causing difficulty, &c., e.g. (1) mishap, unfortunate incident, hitch, awkward meeting, &c.; (2) ill-humour, awkward temper, grudging, rancour, caprice, spite, &c. *Piga k.*, make a hitch, cause a difficulty. *Sina k. moyoni mwangu*, I am quite agreeable. (Cf. *kifundo, hitilafu, kimoyo.*)

Kisiwa, n. (*vi-*), an island. (Cf. *siwa*, a large island.)

Kisombo, n. (*vi-*), a dish of beans, cassava, &c., beaten or mashed up into a thick soup or paste. (Cf. *kipondwe, kibumbwi, mseto.*)

Kisongo, n. (*vi-*), act (mode, means, &c.) of twisting, esp. an instrument for twisting, whether wood or metal, tourniquet,—also that used in rope-making, turned by the *kileti*, and itself attached to the rope. (Cf. *songa.*)

Kisonono, n. gonorrhoea,— various phases being distinguished as *k. cha mkojo* (urine), *k. cha usaha* (pus, matter), and *k. cha damu* (blood). (Cf. *sononeka.*)

Kisozi, n. (*vi-*), name of a small bird (Str.).

Kisu, n. (*vi-*), a knife, of any sort, often used with such verbs as *toa*, take out, draw, *tia*, apply, *noa*, sharpen, *futika*, stick in the girdle, put up, and *a. -kali*, sharp, *butu*, blunt, dull. *Wewe kisu, sisi nyama*, you are the knife, we are the victims, i.e. do what you will with us. *K. cha kukunja*, a pocket-knife, a clasp-knife. (Cf. *jisu, kijisu*, also *jambia, shembea, kotama, kijembe.*)

Kisua, n. (1) a kind of fine cloth, used as a turban, a kind of *kitambi*, also called *bura*. *Nimekwisha ku-*

jipamba kwa kisua na selaha, I have finished arraying myself with a turban and weapons. Also (2) to describe a person well dressed, of striking appearance, *yeye ni kisua kuwako duniani*, he is a fine figure, if there is one in the world.

Kisugulu, n. (*vi-*), mound, heap of earth. (Seldom heard, ? a Yao word for ant-hill.)

Kisuli, n. and adv., also **Kizuli**, giddiness. See **Kizuli**.

Kisusi, n. (*vi-*), one of the smaller slopes of a thatched roof, running up under the edge of the larger. (Cf. *paa, kipaa.*)

Kisusuli, n. (1) a kind of kite (cf. *shada, buratangi, tiara*); (2) anything whirling about, and dazing the eye, a whirling gust, a windmill. (Perh. a redupl. form = *kisulisuli*, and so cf. *kisuli, sulika, masua.*)

Kisutu, n. (*vi-*), a large piece of printed calico, forming a woman's dress in Z. In commerce, 'scarves,' of plain colour, red, blue, white, &c. *K. cha Mombee*, of Indian manufacture, *k. cha Ulaya*, of European. (Cf. *shiti* and *nguo.*)

Kitaa, n. (*vi-*), dim. of *mtaa*, district, quarter, parish. *K. cha imamu*, the district allotted to a Mahommedan minister.

***Kitabu**, n. (*vi-*), a book. (Ar., the *ki* being part of the root. Cf. *mkataba, katiba, katabahu*, and syn. *msahafu, chuo.*)

Kitakataka, n. (*vi-*), a particle of dust, a speck of dirt, a very small (trifling, worthless) thing, a mote. (From *taka*, n. Cf. *takasa, takatifu.*)

Kitakizo, n. end-piece, at head and foot of a native bedstead (*kitanda*, which see).

Kitako, n. and adv. (1) part of the body between the buttocks (*matako*), the fork of the legs; (2) as adv., on the base, or lower end, e.g. *weka pipa k.*, set the barrel on its end. *Kaa k.*, (1) sit down, take a seat, in the native way,—the usual expression, —also (2) remain settled, settle, reside. (Cf. *tako.*)

Kitale, n. (*vi-*), a young cocoanut in the second stage of development, between a *kidaka* and a *dafu*. See **Nazi**.

Kitalu, n. (*vi-*), a stone fence, walled enclosure, wall (of a yard, court, &c.).

Kitambaa, n. (*vi-*), a piece of cloth or calico, a strip or scrap of any kind of textile fabric for any use, a small cloth, e.g. napkin, towel, duster, handkerchief, bandage, tablecloth, —often with a defining phrase, *k. cha meza* (*cha kufutia mikono, cha kupangusia*, &c.). (Cf. *kitambi, utambi, tambi, kitambo, tambo, tambaa, utambaa, mtambo, tamba*, and others, which however do not seem referable to one root-meaning. See **Tamba**.)

Kitambi, n. (*vi-*), (1) a length or piece of cloth, usually of the kind used for head-wear, as a kind of turban,—defined as *k. cha kilemba*, —also worn round the waist, and as a loincloth. (2) *K. cha tambo*, the mesenteric membrane. (Cf. follg. and *kitambaa.*)

Kitambo, n. and adv. (1) a piece, a little—often of time, a short period, e.g. *alikaa k.* or *muda k.*, he remained a short time. *K. kidogo*, after a little, soon, presently (cf. *kipande, kidogo*, and *kitambaa*). (2) Also of stature, length, a certain length or height,—*mtu wa k.*, a man of some height, a tall man. (Cf. *tambo, pande.*)

Kitana, n. (*vi-*), a small comb. (Cf. *tana, chanuo, shanuo.*)

Kitanda, n. (*vi-*), a wooden frame for stretching something on, esp. a native bedstead, i.e. a frame consisting of two side-pieces (*mfumbati*), two end-pieces (*kitakizo*), resting on four legs (*tendegu, ma-*), and with cord of cocoanut fibre or plaited grass-strips interlaced across it. The head is called *mchago*, the space underneath (2 ft. to 3 ft. from the ground) *mvungu*. Usually a mat only (*mkeka*) is spread on it, sometimes a mattress (*godoro*) and pillows (*mto*). *Kitanda cha mfumi*, a weaver's frame, a loom, parts and instruments of which are *mdoshi, faraka* or *mfariki, marufaa, kashabu, mladi*. (Cf. *tanda, tandika*, and for other kinds of bedstead, *ulili, samadari*.)

Kitandiko, n. (*vi-*), a spreading, a thing spread, a mantle, anything worn as a covering. (Cf. *tanda, kitanda, tandiko*.)

Kitanga, n. (*vi-*), (1) a small piece of matting, usually circular, used as a praying mat (cf. *msala*), to lay out food on, or goods for sale. *Muungu hufufua nyama kitangani*, God saves even animals at the place of slaughter. (2) The palm of the hand, *k. cha mkono*. (3) The scale or pan of a balance, *k. cha mizani*. (4) A kind of dance, *k. cha pepo* (cf. *ngoma*). (Cf. *tanga*, n. and v.)

Kitango, n. (*vi-*), (1) gadding about, idling, loitering (cf. *tanga*, v.), e. g. *hana kitango*, he is no idler, he sticks to his work, he is steady. (2) Dim. of *tango*, a kind of small cucumber. (3) A bit of string, lace, shoelace, tuft on a mattress, used for fastening things up or together. (? Cf. *changa, mchango*.)

Kitanguo, n. (*vi-*), act (means, way, &c.) of abolishing, doing away, bringing to nothing. (Cf. *tangua, mtanguo*.)

*****Kitani**, n. flax, string, linen. (Ar. See **Katani**.)

Kitanitani, adv. on the back, backwards,—of position. (Cf. *tanua*, stretch out, spread out, and *kichali*.)

Kitanzi, n. (*vi-*), dim. of *tanzi*, small loop, noose, halter, snare, gin, e. g. loop for a button, snare for animals or birds. (Cf. *tanzi*.)

Kitao, n. (*vi-*), dim. of *tao* (which see), a small curved (arched, bent) thing. *K. cha pingu*, the ring of fetters.

Kitapo, n. shivering, shaking, trembling, quivering,—from cold, fear, illness, &c., e. g. the cold stage of fever, *kitapo cha homa*. (Cf. *tapa*, e. g. *mwili wanitapa*, my body shakes.)

Kitara, n. (*vi-*), a curved sword, scimitar. (Cf. *upanga, sime, jambia*.) (? Hind.)

Kitasa, n. (*vi-*), (1) a box-, door-, or cupboard-lock (cf. *kufuli*, a padlock), a buckle, fastening of a belt; (2) dim. of *tasa*, small metal pot.

Kitata, n. (*vi-*), (1) tangle, complication, mess (cf. *tata*); (2) a splint (for bandaging a broken limb, &c.). (Cf. *kigango*.)

Kitatange, n. a bright-coloured sea fish with spines, a sea porcupine (Str.).

Kitawa, n. and adv., devout life (act or character), in a religious way. *Nguo za k.*, dress of a devotee, habit of a monk, &c. *Fanya k.*, act as a devotee. *Kaa k.*, lead a secluded life. (Cf. *tawa, utawa*.)

Kitawi, n. dim. of *tawi*, a small branch, twig, cutting, bunch or cluster of fruit on a stem; (2) a kind of weed; (3) a tool used in weaving.

Kitaya, n. jaw (cf. *taya*). *Hatamu yatiwa kitayani*, the bridle is attached to the jaw.

Kite, n. (1) a cry of pain, a moan, a groan. *Piga kite*, give a groan. (2) Trust, liking, affection. *Hana kite naye*, he has no liking for him, he does not trust him.

Kitefutefu, n. also **Kitetefu**, sobbing, as before or after crying. (Cf. *kikeukeu*.)

Kiteku, n. an iron tool,—for breaking up floors, digging up stones, &c., a pickaxe. (Cf. *tekua*.)

Kitembe, n. and adv., a defect in speech, a lisp, thick utterance. *Piga (sema) kitembe*, speak with a lisp, in a thick indistinct way, as if there was something in the mouth. (Cf. *utembe*.)

Kitembwe, n. (*vi-*), a vegetable

fibre. (Cf. *utembwe*, also *uzi*, *mzizi*, *ugomba*, *unanasi*, &c.)

Kitendawili, n. (*vi-*), riddle, enigma, puzzle, charade, conundrum. The common word for propounding a riddle is *tega*, e.g. *Kitendawili!* Here's a riddle! *Tega!* Out with it! *Nyumba yangu kubwa, haina taa*, my house is large, but has no lamp. (Ans.) *Kaburi*, the grave. (? From *ki-tenda-wili*, i.e. *pili*, acting in two ways.)

Kitendo, n. (*vi-*), act, deed, exploit. (Cf. *tenda*, *tendo*, *utendaji*, &c.)

Kitengele, n. (*vi-*), also **Kichengele**, stripe, band of colour, &c. (Cf. more usual *mfuo*, *mlia*.)

Kitengenya, n. (*vi-*), ? name of a bird.

Kiteo, n. (*vi-*), dim. of *uteo*, a small flat basket used for sifting. (Cf. *ungo*, and *tunga*, more usual in Z.)

Kitete, n. (*vi-*), small hollow reed, small pipe. (Cf. *utete*.)

Kitetemo, n. (*vi-*), trembling, quivering, shaking, quaking. (Cf. *tetema*, and *kitapo*, *tikisika*.)

*__Kithiri__, v. get to be more, do in addition, cause to be more, increase, grow. *Mtende umekithiri kuzaa*, the date tree has borne more than ever. Ap. *kithir-ia*, *-iwa*, e.g. *kukithiriwa mapenzi*, to be loved more than others. Cs. *kithiri-sha*, *-shwa*, make more, increase, &c. (Ar. Cf. syn. *zidi*, more usual in Z.)

Kiti, n. (*vi-*), a native stool, seat. Hence a seat or chair of any kind. *K. cha kifalme*, a throne. *K. cha frasi*, a saddle (cf. *seruji*). (Cf. *keti*, and perh. *mti*, *kijiti*, *kiti*.)

Kitimbi, n. (*vi-*), also **Kitimfi**, a mischievous act, trick, artifice, stratagem. (Cf. *timfi*, and syn. *hila*.)

*__Kitimiri__, n. (1) name of the dog in the Seven Sleepers story; (2) name of an evil spirit. The consonants are sometimes written as a kind of charm on letters to ensure safe delivery. (Ar.)

Kitinda, n. (*vi-*), verbal of *tinda* (i.e. the root of *tindika*). *Kitinda mimba*, the last, youngest child, lit. the ending of conception.

Kitisho, n. (*vi-*), terrifying, something terrifying, a terror, a menace, a fearful thing, an overwhelming danger. (Cf. *tisha*, *tisho*, *utisho*, and syn. *afa*, *kioja*.)

Kititi, n. and adv. (1) dim. of *titi*, nipple (of the breast); (2) a small hare, leveret; (3) *kititi cha bahari*, the depths of the sea. As adv. (1) fully, wholly, altogether, all at once; (2) straight up, upright, in an erect position. *Genge limesimama k.*, the cliff rose up perpendicularly. *Mti umesimika k.*, the tree stood straight up, was perpendicular.

Kitiwanga, n. chicken-pox,—also called *titiwanga*, and *tete kwanga*. (Cf. *ndui*.)

Kito, n. (*vi-*), a precious stone, gem, jewel. (Cf. *johari*, *fusfus*.)

Kitobwe, n. (*vi-*), hole—e.g. one bored by an insect or tool, dimple on the chin. (Cf. *toboa*,—pass. form in *-e*, and syn. *kitundu*.)

Kitoma, n. (*vi-*), a small round pumpkin, the outer rind or shell of which is dried, hollowed out, and used as a vessel for liquids; (2) descriptive of orchitis, hydrocele. (Cf. *boga*, pumpkin,—usual in Z.)

Kitone, n. (*vi-*), dim. of *tone*, a small drop (of liquid), a small spot. *Kanga ni ndege wa vitone-tone*, the guinea-fowl is a speckled bird.

Kitongo, adv. sideways, obliquely. *Tazama kitongotongo*, look askance. (Cf. *tongoza*, *kitongoji*, and syn. *upande*, *mshathari*.)

Kitongoji, n. (*vi-*), small village, hamlet. *Wote walio nje mashamba vitongojini*, all who were out in the country villages. (Cf. *tongoza*, *kitongo*, and syn. *kijiji*.)

Kitoria, n. (*vi-*), edible fruit of the *mtoria* (a kind of Landolphia).

Kitoto, n. and adv. (*vi-*), dim. of *mtoto*, a small child, baby, like a child, foolishly.

Kitovu, n. (*vi-*), the navel, the umbilical cord.

Kitoweo, n. (*vi-*), and **Kitoeo**, anything eaten as a relish with other food,—meat, fish, curry, &c,—the third common ingredient being *mchuzi*, gravy. (Cf. *toweza*, and *kiungo*.)

Kitu, n. (*vi-*), (1) a thing, esp. a sensible, material object, but also what is an object to the mind; (2) substance, what a thing is made of, matter. *Mtu ni k., lakini si k.*, a man may be regarded as a thing, but he is not (only) a thing. *Pana k. hasira?* Is there such a thing as anger? *Si k.*, it is nothing, no matter (cf. *haithuru, mamoja*). *Hapana k.*, there is nothing, nothing at all, nought. *K. gani hicho?* What is that? *K. chake ni chuma*, its substance is iron. (Cf. *mtu*, and *utu*. The idea of 'substance' is often conveyed by the abstract forms beginning with -*u*, and *nyama* is also used, chiefly of organic substances.)

Kitua, n. (*vi-*), (1) a small tree, shrub, bush, branch; (2) shade of a tree, shaded spot. *Tuketi kituani*, let us sit in the shade. (Not usual in Z., cf. *kijiti, kivuli*, which are the common words.)

Kituko, n. (*vi-*), a feeling (object, cause, &c.) of fear, a terror, horror, fright, alarm. E.g. *inatia watu vituko vya hofu*, it causes people alarm. *Mtu yuna (ameingiwa na) kituko*, the man is frightened. *Vituko vikutishavyo*, terrors which alarm you. (Cf. *tukia, tukio*, of incident, accident, and so special sensational alarming occurrence. Or cf. *shtuka (stuka, situka), shtuko*, of what is startling, alarming. For syn. cf. *kitisho, kioja, afa*.)

Kitulizo, n. (*vi-*), a quieting influence, a soothing force, a comfort, relief, anodyne. (From *tua, tuliza*. Cf. *ututulivu, faraja, baridi*.)

Kitumba, n. (*vi-*), dim. of *mtumba, tumba*, (1) a small bag, case, cover; (2) a small bud. *Gunia ni k. cha Hindi*, a *gunia* is an Indian bag.

Kitumbo, n. and adv. (1) dim. of *tumbo*, small stomach, protuberance, swelling; (2) obesity, a large abnormal stomach (cf. *kikono, kiguu*, of malformation or maiming); (3) as an adv., *lala k.*, lie stomachwise, on the stomach. (Cf. *tumbua, mtumba, ? mtumbwi*.)

Kitumbua, n. (*vi-*), a small pancake, a fritter. (Cf. prec.)

Kitumwa, n. and adv. (*vi-*), (1) dim. of *mtumwa*, a little slave; (2) service, what is servile or degrading. *Fanya k.*, act as a slave. *-a k.*, of a slavish, servile kind. (Cf. *tuma, mtumwa*, &c.)

Kitunda, n. (*vi-*), (1) dim. of *tunda*, a small fruit; (2) a chess pawn (Str.).

Kitunga, n. (*vi-*), dim. of *tunga*, a small round flat basket.

Kitunguu, n. (*vi-*), an onion. *Kitunguu somu*, garlic. (*Sum* is Ar. for garlic.)

Kituo, n. (*vi-*), (1) stopping, resting, cessation, respite, remission, quiet; (2) a stopping-place, encampment, time for rest, stage in a journey; (3) a stop, a pause (e.g. in talking, music, &c.), a note of punctuation, end of a sentence. *Roho yake haina k.*, his spirit is always uneasy. *Hana k.*, he is always on the move (cf. opp. *kitango*). *Maneno yasiyo na k.*, talk without breaks or pauses. *Piga kituo*, form an encampment. *Kiswahili hakina k.*, the Swahili language has no fixed standard. (Cf. *tua, ututulivu, tuo*, and *simama, pumzika*.)

Kitupa, n. (*vi-*), dim. of (1) *tupa* (i.e. *chupa* in Z.), a small bottle, phial, flask; also of (2) *tupa*, a small file.

Kitwa, n. (*vi-*), usually in Z.

sounded more as **kichwa** (which see), head.

Kitwana, n. (*vi-*), a boy or youth of the slave class. Dim. of *mtwana*, and contr. *kijakazi*, a slave girl.

Kiu, n. absence of water, drought, want of water, thirstiness, thirst. *Kuwa na k.*, *kuona k:*, to be thirsty. *Komesha k.*, quench thirst. *K. ya maji*, lack of water.

Kiua, n. (*vi-*), (1) verbal from *ua*, v., that which kills; (2) dim. of *ua*, a small enclosure, or, a small flower. Also (3) name of a fish (perh. from (1)); (4) an eyelet-hole (Str.).

Kiuaji, n. (*vi-*), something that kills, a fatal, deadly thing, i.e. *kitu cha kufisha*, e.g. beast of prey, snake, poison, fire-arms. (Cf. *ua*, v.)

Kiuka, v. step over, get (leap, pass, jump) over, surmount. (Cf. *kia*, *chupa*, and more usual in Z. *ruka*, *vuka*.)

Kiuma, n. (*vi-*,—contr. *vyuma*, as plur. of *chuma*), (1) anything that bites, pierces, stings, hurts (cf. *k. mbuzi*, the goat-biter, as name of a kind of lizard; *k. inzi*, the fly-biter, name of an insect); (2) esp. a small pointed or pronged instrument, a fork, an insect's sting. (Cf. *uma*, n. and v.)

Kiumbe, n. (*vi-*), a created thing, a creature, but usually limited to the rational, or at least animate creation. E.g. *pana nyama wawili na k. kimoja*, there are two animals and one man. *Mti umeumbwa kuwa k., lakini si k., na nyama si k., mtu ni k.*, a tree is a creature like a *kiumbe*, but it is not strictly a *kiumbe*, nor is an animal a *kiumbe*, but only man. (Cf. *umba*, *umbo*, *maumbile*,—and pass. termin. -*e*.)

Kiumbizi, n. (*vi-*), name of a kind of dance with sticks. (Cf. *ngoma*.)

Kiume, n. and adv. (seldom *viume* in plur. for usual -*a kiume* and *ndume*), a male, something of the male kind, manly behaviour (bearing, fashion, way, proceeding, &c.), courage, strength, prudence, spirit, heroism. *Watoto wa k.*, boys. *Fanya k.*, act like a man, show spirit, be brave. *Sauti ya k.*, a bass, deep voice. *Vaa k.*, wear a man's clothes, dress as a man. — a. from -*ume*, agreeing with *kitu*, e.g. *kijana kiume*, a young man. (Cf. -*ume*, *kuume*, *ndume*, *ume*, and contr. *kike*.)

Kiunga, n. (*vi-*), (1) suburb of a town, suburban residence, outskirts, place adjacent. *Ana k. chake na nyumba yake mjini*, he has an estate (garden) in the suburbs, and a house in the town. *Akaa kiungoni*, he lives in the outskirts of the town. The *kiunga* is often an orchard, fruit or pleasure garden (contr. *shamba* which is general, and more in the country). (2) Name of a fish. (Cf. *unga*, *kiungo*.)

Kiungo, n. (*vi-*), (1) act (method, means, &c.) of joining, a joining, link, connecting part, connexion, amalgamation. Hence (2) a joint of the animal frame, a member of the body, i.e. *kiungo cha mwili*. *Viungo vimeachana*, the joints have come apart. Also *achana viungo*, loosen the joints, of a man lying at ease,—so too *jitupa viungo*, of a sprawling attitude. *Makuti ya kiungo*, or *ya viungo*, cocoanut leaves prepared for use as thatch. See **Kuti**. (3) Something which seasons, gives a taste or relish to, food, e.g. sauce, pickle, salt, vinegar, &c., i.e. *mchuzi*, *achali*, *chumvi*, *siki*. (Cf. *unga*, v.)

Kiunguja, n. and adv., the dialect of Swahili used in Zanzibar city and neighbourhood, as contrasted with the kindred dialects of the coast (*kimrima*), of Mombasa (*kimvita*), and Lamu (*kiamu*). *Kiunguja* is also used in contrast with *kiswahili*, with reference to points in which the Zanzibar use is different from all or most of the kindred dialects. (A native will often say *Kiswahili hilo, si kiunguja*, that word is Swahili, but it is not used in Zanzibar, e. g. the word *chaka* for 'hot season.') As adv., ' of the Zanzibar kind.' (Cf. *Unguja*, and the Preface to Sacleux, *Dictionnaire Français-Swahili.*)

Kiungulia, n. stomachic disorder causing eructation or belching, heartburn,—also *k. cha moyo*. (Cf. *ungua*, and for the symptoms, *cheuka*.)

Kiunguza, n. (*vi-*), and similarly **Kiunguzo**, something which burns, causes the sensation of burning,—as fire, acid, &c. (Cf. *ungua*.)

Kiungwana, adv. of a gentlemanly, civilized, educated kind (style, fashion, character, &c.), in a way becoming a free man. *Mwanamke wa k.*, a lady (by birth or manners). *-a kiungwana*, gentlemanly, courteous, &c. Cf. phrase *hajambo ya kiungwana*, i. e. he is quite well enough to work, if he chooses. (Cf. *-ungwana*.)

Kiuno, n. (*vi-*), loin, flank, waist, the part just above the hips (*nyonga*), and groin (*nena*). In building, an abutment. *Jambia kiunoni na bakora mkononi*, dagger at waist and stick in hand.

Kiunza, n. (*vi-*), a board laid over a corpse, when placed in a grave,—also called *mlango wa maiti*, the dead man's door. Sometimes bamboos or sticks are so used.

Kiunzi, n. (*vi-*), a wooden frame or structure, esp. of shipwrights' work, the hull of a vessel,—the chief native example of construction in wood. (Cf. *unda, mwunzi.*)

Kivi, n. (*vi-*), elbow. (Cf. *kisigino.*)

Kivimba, n. (*vi-*), and similarly **Kivimbe** (or -i), a swelling, a protuberance, girth, circumference, bigness of anything round. *K. cha mti*, girth of a tree. (Cf. *vimba*, and *mzingo.*)

Kivukizo, n. (*vi-*), act of burning incense, fumigation, substance used in fumigation. (Cf. *vukiza.*)

Kivuko, n. (*vi-*), act (place, time, means, &c.) of crossing (e. g. a river, marsh, &c.), crossing-place, ford, ferry; also, fee for crossing. *K. kikavu*, an isthmus connecting two pieces of land. (Cf. *vuka.*)

Kivuli, n. (*vi-*), (1) a shade, a shady place, a shadow; (2) a ghost. (Cf. *mvuli, uvuli, mwavuli.*)

Kivumbasi, n. a strong-smelling herb, used by the natives to keep off mosquitoes,—a kind of basil. (Cf. *rihani.*)

Kivumbi, n. and adv. (*vi-*), a particle of dust, like dust, dusty; also, a dust-cloud, sand-storm (?). (Cf. *vumbi.*)

Kivumi, n. (*vi-*), also similarly **Kivumo**, (1) a rumbling (humming, buzzing, or roaring) sound, rumble, hum, buzz, &c.; (2) a rumour, a report, bit of gossip, hearsay. (Cf. *vuma, uvumi.*)

Kivunjo, n. (*vi-*), act (means, way, &c.) of breaking. (Cf. *vunja, mvunjo*, &c.)

Kivuno, n. (*vi-*), a harvest, profit, something worth having. *Ganda la mua chungu kaona kivuno*, a bit of chewed sugar-cane the ant thought a prize. (Cf. *vuna*, and syn. *chumo, faida.*)

-kiwa, a. solitary, alone, desolate, abandoned, outcast (with pfx. *m-*, and *wa-*, of persons, *pa-* of place, and *u-* of things,—*nyumba ukiwa, shamba ukiwa*). (Cf. *ukiwa*, and *upweke, peke yake, -hame.*)

Kiwaa, n. (*vi-*), dim. of *waa*, small spot, blotch, patch, stain, blemish, blot. (Cf. *kipaku, ila.*)

Kiwamba, n. (*vi-*), a little frame, support, prop. *Watoto wanaotambaa na wanaokwendea viwamba*, children who crawl and who walk with something to hold to. (Cf. *wamba*, and follg.)

Kiwambaza, n. (*vi-*), also **Kiyambaza, Kiambaza**, a wall as made by natives, i.e. a screen of sticks fastened to upright poles and filled up with kneaded earth and stones. (Cf. *wamba, kiwambo*, and *ukuta*.)

Kiwambo, n. (*vi-*), also **Kiyambo, Kiambo**, the act (process, means, &c.) of making one thing cover another, and esp. of the thing which covers, overlays, or is stretched over another, e.g. the *k.* of a drum (*ngoma*) is the skin strained tightly over it, *ngozi iliyowambiwa ngoma. K. cha makuti*, a screen of cocoanut leaves. *K. cha kitanda*, the lacing of a bed-frame with cord. (Cf. *wamba, kiwambaza*.)

Kiwanda, n. (*vi-*), also **Kiwanja**, a plot of ground, used for occupation rather than cultivation, whether open or enclosed, i.e. a yard, premises, &c. uncovered or covered, i.e. a shed, a workshop, e.g. *unipatie k., nataka kujenga nyumba*, get me a piece of ground, I want to build a house. *Hii ilikuwa nyumba, imevunjika, sasa ni k. tu*, this was a house, but it was taken down, and now it is only a piece of ground. *Akatiwa kiwandani kushona nguo*, he was put in a workshop to learn tailoring. (Cf. *uwanda, uwanja*.)

Kiwango, n. (*vi-*), (1) number, a number (cf. *wanga*, and *cheo. Kiwango* is the B. word, but in Z. represented almost entirely by the Ar. *hesabu* and *daraja*.) (2) Importance, account, dignity, position; (3) behaviour or duties proper to a position, province, sphere of action. *Ni k. changu kusema*, it is my duty (it is proper for me) to speak thus. *K. cha mtumwa*, the position of a slave.

Kiwavi, n. (*vi-*), a nettle, sea nettle (Str.).

Kiwe, n. (*vi-*), pimple, vesicle, pustule,—as on the head after shaving the hair. (Cf. *upele*.)

Kiweko, n. (*vi-*), also **Kiwiko** (cf. *tweka*, and *twika*), (1) act, &c. of placing (see **Ki-** and **Weka**), place for putting, placing, resting, position; (2) pedestal, base, rest, socket. Used of wrist, *k. cha mkono*, and ankle, *k. cha mguu*. (Cf. *weko, kisigino, kifundo*.)

Kiwele, n. (*vi-*), milk-gland of a female animal, udder.

Kiwembe, n.(*vi-*), dim. of *uwembe*, a small razor, a knife. (Cf. *kisu, kijembe*.)

Kiweo, n. (*vi-*), thigh, ham, esp. of animals. (Cf. *paja*, more usual in Z.)

Kiwete, n. and adv. (1) lameness, crippled condition; (2) a crippled person, a cripple; (3) in a lame, halting, crippled way. *Kwenda k.*, walk lamely. *-a k.*, crippled. *Yu k., ana k.*, he is lame. (Cf. *kilema, kiguu, chechemea*.)

Kiwi, n. (*vi-*), (1) stout stick, bar of wood, set against a door, inside, as a fastening, &c. (cf. *komeo, pingo*); (2) state of being dazzled, dazed, unable to see clearly, i.e. *k. cha macho. Jua lafanya k. cha macho*, the sun blinds me, dazzles me. *Haoni usiku, ana k.*, he does not see at night, his sight is defective.

Kiwiko, n. (*vi-*). See **Kiweko**.

Kiwiliwili, n. and adv. (*vi-*), variously used as (1) the body in general, of man, animals, birds, &c., like *mwili*; (2) the main part of the body, the trunk, i.e. not with the head or limbs or both; (3) a part of the body, member, limb; (4) bulk, girth, size (cf. *kivimba, unene*). *Kuzikwa kwa fisi, si k. tu?* to be buried by a hyaena, is not that just leaving the body as it is, no grave at all? *Viwiliwili vyangu vyote vizima*, all my members are whole. *K. chake chapataje?* What does its bulk come to? What does it measure round? As adv., in a bodily form. (Cf. *mwili*. Dist. *-wili*, two, *kuwili*, &c.)

Kiwimawima, adv. in an erect position, upright, perpendicular, steep, e.g. of a steep hill, precipice. (Cf. *simama, ima, ? wima*.)

Kiwimbi, n. and adv. (*vi-*), dim. of *wimbi*, wavelet, ripple, eddy. As adv., like a wave. *Kama viwimbi*, undulating, with ridges, hillocks, &c.

Kiwingu, n. (*vi-*), dim. of *wingu*, a small cloud.

*****Kiyama**, n. the general resurrection of the dead, as conceived by Mahommedans, lit. standing up, rising up. (Ar. Cf. *ufufuo*.)

Kiyambasa, n. (*vi-*). See **Kiwambaza**.

Kiyoga, n. (*vi-*), a mushroom.

Kiyowe, n. (*vi-*), cry, shout, scream, esp. of a call for help. *Piga k.*, cry out for help. (Cf. *ukelele, kilio, kigelegele, shime*.)

Kiza, n. (*vi-*), more usually *giza* in Z., darkness, gloom, dimness, night. See **Giza**.

Kizalia, n. (*vi-*), that which is born in a given place, home-born, indigenous, native, e.g. of home-born slaves. *Huyu k. Unguja*, this man was born in Zanzibar. (Cf. *mzalia, zaa*, and *kikulia, kimelea*.)

Kizao, n. (*vi-*), a product, production, offspring. (Cf. *zaa, zao*.)

Kizazi, n. (*vi-*), any part or step in causing birth, or being born, procreation, generation. Usually (1) birth, production of offspring, being born. *Haya niliyoandika ya k. cha Buge*, this is my account of the circumstances of Buge's birth. *Ana k.*, he has birth, he is a man of family. (2) That which is born, a birth, offspring, whether individually 'a child, a young one,' or collectively 'a generation.' *K. hiki*, the present generation. (Cf. *zaa, uzazi, mzazi*.)

Kizee, n. (*vi-*) and adv., (1) an old person, or thing, esp. an old woman, crone, hag; (2) in antiquated style, old-fashioned. *-a kizee*, antique, old, old-fashioned (cf. *-a kikale*). *Enda kizee*, walk like an old person. (Cf. *-zee, mzee*, and perh. *zaa*.)

Kizembe, n. and adv. (*vi-*), idling, slack (remiss, negligent) conduct or act. (Cf. *-zembe, uvivu, ulegevu*.)

Kizibo, n. (*vi-*), (1) anything used to stop a hole or opening, a stopper, plug, cork, bung, &c., and (2) fig. of what is used merely for filling a hole, i.e. stop-gap, padding, temporary expedient. (Cf. *ziba, mziko*.)

Kizimba, n. (*vi-*), also **Kizimbi**, a cage with bars, coop for fowls, &c. (Cf. *kirimba, tundu*.)

Kizimwe, n. (*vi-*), also **Kizimwi**, (1) something dried up, dead, withered. *Nazi kizimwe*, a cocoanut without milk or nutty substance, dry and empty (cf. *zima* and *-zimwe*). (2) smut, blight (on cereals, &c.); (3) a fairy, an evil spirit. (Cf. *zimwi, mzimu*.)

Kizinga, n. (*vi-*), dim. of *mzinga*, which see.

Kizingiti, n. (*vi-*), top or bottom piece of the frame of a door or window, threshold, sill, lintel; (2) bar of a river, reef of rocks, natural dam, weir. *Mlango wa k.*, opening in a bar or reef, sluice, floodgate. (Cf. *mlango, kimandu, mwimo*.)

Kizingo, n. (*vi-*), turning, winding, curve, bend, e.g. of a river, road. *-a k.*, sinuous, winding, roundabout. Also *kizingozingo*. (Cf. *mzingo, zinga, zunguka*.)

Kizio, n. (*vi-*), a half of a cocoanut, i.e. *kizio cha nazi*, and of other fruit, cut in halves.

Kiziwi, n. (*vi-*), a deaf person. (Cf. *ukiziwi*, and possibly *ziba*. For form cf. *kipofu, kizee, kibiongo, kilema*, &c.)

Kizizi, n. (*vi-*), small stall, &c. Dim. of *zizi*, which see.

Kizua, n. See **Mazua**.

Kizuio, n. (*vi-*), and **Kizuizo** (and *-zi*), restraining, keeping back, restraint, obstruction, hindrance, stopper. (Cf. *zuio, zuia, pinga, mgogoro*.)

Kizuka, n. (*vi-*), (1) something which appears suddenly, thing seldom seen, an apparition, phantom, ghost, portent. Hence (2) fairy, evil spirit, ghost; (3) and also a widow living in seclusion after her husband's death. (Cf. *zuka, kizushi.*)

Kizuli, n. also **Kisuli**, giddiness, mental confusion. (Cf. *zulu, mazua, zulika.*)

Kizungu, n. and adv., a European language, in European style. *Sema k.*, speak a European language. *Vaa k.*, wear European dress. *-a k.*, European. (Cf. *mzungu* (*wa-* and *mi-*), and perh. *zunguka* and follg.)

Kizunguzungu, n. (*vi-*), giddiness, whirl, i.e. *kizunguzungu cha kichwa*, vertigo. *Mkondo wa k.*, an eddy, whirlpool. *Mzungu mambo yake ni kizunguzungu*, a European's ways makes one's head go round. (Cf. *kizua, mazua*, and *zunguka, mzungu.*)

Kizushi, n. (*vi-*), a person or thing suddenly appearing, i.e. (1) newcomer, intruder, heretic, revolutionist; (2) novelty, phenomenon, sensation, apparition. *Mwana wa mtu ni kizushi, akizuka zuka naye*, i.e. there is no knowing what a man may do, best follow all his movements. (Cf. *zua, zuka, kizuka, uzushi.*)

Kizuu, n. (*vi-*), a kind of evil spirit, capable of being employed to enter houses in the form of rats and kill people by devouring their livers. (? Cf. prec. and *zua*, also see **Uchawi**.)

-ko is a form of the Demonstr. Pfx. *ku*, the *o* (*a*) either denoting reference or relative distance, 'there'; (*b*) or else giving it the force of a relative pronoun, 'where' (see **Ku**). *Ko* (1) forms part of the Demonstr. adv. **huko** and **kuko**, which see; (2) affixed to *ndi-* and Pers. Pfx. and the verb *-wa* or its equivalents, has a demonstrative force usually local, 'there, thence, thither,' e.g. *yuko*, he is there. *Ndiko aliko*, that is where he is. (3) In verb-forms generally is the form of relative pronoun agreeing with the Infin. Mood, and nouns and pronouns, &c. with the Pfx. *ku*. *Huko anakokwenda*, there where he is going. *Kufa kulikompata*, the death which overtook him. *Ko* as a separate word only appears in such a phrase as *ko kote*, wherever, under whatever circumstances. (Cf. *huko, ku, mo, po.*)

Koa, n. (1) (*ma-*), a band of thin metal plate, esp. as worn for ornament on the neck or arm, e.g. *k. la fetha*, a silver armlet; *k. la shingo*, a neck ring (sometimes broadened into a crescent shape in front) (cf. *ukoa, kikoa*, also *furungu, kikuku*, and for ornaments generally *urembo*). (2) (—, and *ma-*), a snail, slug. *Ute wa k.*, the slime of a snail. (Cf. *konokono.*)

Kobe, n. (*ma-*), a land tortoise. (Cf. *kasa, ng'amba*. Dist. *mkobe*, a wallet.)

Koboa, v. See **Goboa**.

Kobwe, n. a kind of bean, like *kunde*, sold in Z.

Koche, n. (*ma-*), the edible fruit of a kind of palm. See **Mkochi**.

*****Kodi**, n. rent, tax, customs. (? Hind. Cf. Ar. *ushuru*.)

Kodoa, v. esp. with *macho*, open the eyes wide, stare, glare. Ap. *kodolea* (*macho*), *-ewa*, stare at, gaze at fixedly with eyes wide open. *Kwani kunikodolea macho?* Why are you staring at me? (Cf. *ngariza, kaza macho.*)

Kodwe, n. small stone, used as a marble in games,—as are *korosho* and *komwe*. (Cf. *jiwe, mbwe.*)

Kofi, n. (*ma-*), (1) flat of the hand, the palm extended or upturned; (2) a blow with the open hand, slap, box on the ears; (3) as much as can be held on the palm of the upturned hand. *Piga k.*, (1) slap, box on the ear, (2) clap the hands. (Cf. *mkono*, and for handfull *ukufi, kikofi, chopa, konzi.*)

*****Kofia**, n. Cap,—in Z. usually a fez of red cloth, or of white linen, often elaborately stitched. Used also of any foreign head-cover. *Vaa k.*, put on a cap. *Vua k.*, take off a cap. (Cf. *chapeo.*)

Koga, n. mould, blight, mustiness. *Fanya (ota) k.*, get mouldy (blighted). (Cf. *kutu, kizimwe,* and dist. *ukoga.*) Also v. for *kuoga,* bathe. See **Oga.**

Kogo, n. the part of the skull which projects at the back, the back of the head, occiput. (Cf. *kikosi, kishogo.*)

Kohoa, v. cough. Cs. *koko-za, -zwa. Jikohoza,* cough on purpose (as a sham, to attract attention, to deceive a person, &c.). (Cf. follg. and *koo.*)

Kohooi, n. (*ma-*) and **Kohozi,** expectoration, sputum, phlegm coughed up. (Cf. prec., and *ukohozi, kikohozi, belghamu.*)

Koikoi, n. (*ma-*), a kind of evil spirit. (Cf. *pepo.*)

Koja, n. (1) a neck ornament, a ring with disks or coins attached worn round the neck (cf. *koa,* and *urembo*); (2) a kind of metal pot (cf. *kopo, sufuria*); (3) see **Khoja.**

Kojoa, v. urinate, make water. Ap. *kojolea. Kopo (chombo, bakuli) la kukojolea,* chamber-pot. Cs. *kojosha,* e.g. *dawa ya kukojosha,* a diuretic. (Cf. follg. and *mkojo,* also *nya,* and Ar. *tabawali.*)

Kojozi, n. urine (for common *mkojo*). Also, that which causes micturition. (Cf. prec.)

Koka, v. set on fire (or ? heap up, e.g. *kokeni mabiwi ya moto,* of burning rubbish). Seldom in Z., for common *tia* (or, *choma*) *moto, washa.* Also *koka* for *kuoka,* bake (see **Oka,** and cf. *koga* for *kuoga*). (Perh. cf. *chocha,* and obs. *kokoa.*)

Koko, n. (—, and *ma-*), (1) stone of a fruit,—the kernel being *kiini* (cf. *kokwa*); (2) bush, underwood, jungle. *Mbwa koko,* a bush-dog, i.e. in a semi-wild state. *Kaa makoko,* small mud crabs (cf. *mkoko*). (Dist. *koko* for, or plur. of, *ukoko.*)

Kokoa, v. sweep up, collect together in a heap,—of dust, rubbish, &c., i.e. *k. matakataka.* Ps. *kokolewa,* e.g. *mchanga unakokolewa na maji,* the sand is swept away by the water. (Cf. *zoa, fagia.*)

Kokomoka, v. belch, vomit violently, and fig. blurt out, burst out with. (Cf. *bubujika,* and *tapika.*)

Kokota, v. drag, haul, tug at, pull along, draw. *K. gari,* draw a cart (carriage). *K. roho,* used of slow painful breathing. *K. maneno,* of slow dragging speech, difficult articulation. *K. kazi,* work slowly. *Jikokota,* move slowly (reluctantly, &c.). Ps. *kokotwa.* Nt. *kokoteka.* Ap. *kokot-ea, -ewa,* e.g. *kamba za kukokotea,* cords to draw with. Cs. *kokot-eza, -ezwa,* e.g. *kokoteza kazi,* work slowly (whether from care or laziness). (Contr. *kimbiza,* and cf. *endeleza.*) (Cf. *-kokotevu, kokoto,* and syn. *vuta.*)

-kokotevu, a. (same with D 5 (S), D 6), dragging, dilatory, slow. (Cf. prec.)

Kokoto, n. (*ma-*), usu. in plur. small stones, esp. with reference to use as material (e.g. *makokoto ya kupigilia,* for use in concrete, *m. ya kutomelea,* for use in plastering), and classed according to size, as compared with common fruits, e.g. *makokoto ya ndimu* (lime size), *m. ya malimau* (lemon size), *m. ya nazi* (cocoanut size). (Cf. *kokota.*)

Kokwa, n. (—, and *ma-*), stone— of a fruit. See **Koko** (with which it seems connected).

Kolea, v. (1) put something into food to give it a taste, season (with), flavour (with), give a relish to; (2) be properly seasoned, have a flavour; and (3) fig. have point (force, meaning). *K. samli katika chakula,* flavour food with ghee. *Ubishi wake haukukolea,* his joke fell flat. Obs. Cs. form in *koleza moto,* make up a fire, make it burn up (with oil, shavings, &c.) (? cf. *koka*). (Cf. follg., also syn. *unga, kiungo,* and *kitoweo.* Also cf. in Kr. *koleza,* v., seize person or property.)

Kolekole, n. name of a large fish, ? dolphin.

Koleo, n. (—, and *ma-*), a smith's tool for handling his work, i.e. *kidude cha kushikia chuma*, a pair of tongs, e.g. *kuzima koleo si mwisho wa uhunzi*, cooling the tongs is not the end of the job. Also (1) any similar instrument, pincers, &c.; (2) notch in an arrow (held on the string with the fingers). (Cf. prec.)

*****Koli**, n. and **Kol**, a ship's papers. (? Ar. *kul*.)

Koma, v. cease, come to an end, stop, decease. Also sometimes act., bring to an end, close. *Lisilo mkoma, hujikoma lilo*, what has no one to end it, ends of itself. *Walipokoma nussu ya njia*, when they ended half the journey. *Yalipokoma magrebi*, when evening set in. *Koma usije*, stop coming further. Cs. *kom-esha, -eshwa*, make stop, bring to an end, thwart, forbid, kill,—usually implying some force or abruptness. *Komesha maneno*, stop conversation, cut short a debate. (Cf. *kikomo, ukomo,* ? *ukoma*, and syn. *isha, nyamaa, tindika.*) — n. (*ma-*), the edible fruit of a kind of palm, *mkoma* (same as *koche*, a local name).

Komaa, v. (1) be fully ripe, be full grown (developed, matured), and so (2) be past the prime, fall off, begin to lose powers, decline, become demoralized. Cs. *komaza*, unduly stimulate, over-excite, make game of, mock. *Usinene nakukomaza*, do not say I am talking improperly with you. (Cf. *pevuka, balehi, -zima*.)

Komafi, n. (*ma-*), fruit of the tree **Mkomafi**, which see.

Komamanga, n. (*ma-*), pomegranate, the fruit of the *mkomamanga*. (Cf. *mkoma*, and *manga*.)

Komba, v. scrape out, hollow out, clean out. E.g. *k. ngoma*, make a drum (by hollowing it out). *K. dafu*, scrape out the nutty part of a cocoanut. Cf. *dafu la kukomba*, a cocoanut full of milk, but beginning to form the soft nutty substance inside. *K. chungu*, clean out a cooking pot. *K. taka (maji, vumbi)*, clean out dirt (water, dust). *K. mtu mali*, clear a man out of his money, ruin, impoverish. Ps. *kombwa*. Nt. *komoeka*, be cleaned or cleared out. Ap. *komb-ea, -cwa,*—also *komb-elea, -elcwa, -eleka, -elesha, -eleshwa*, e.g. *amekombeleka mali*, he has lost every penny he had. *Kombelesha mchuzi kwa wali*, sop up the gravy with the rice. Cs. *komb-esha, -eshwa*. (Cf. *ukombe, kombo, kombe, kikombe, komba, kikomba, kombeo, komboa,* and ? *kumba*.)

Komba, n. a small racoon-like animal, galago,—common in Z. and very destructive to cocoanuts. (Cf. prec.)

Kombamoyo, n. (*ma-*), a long thin straight pole. Used as rafters in constructing the roof of native huts, resting on the side poles (*nguzo*) and carrying the cross-pieces (*fito*) and thatch.

Kombe, n. (—, and *ma-*), (1) anything hollowed or scraped out, flat and slightly curved, and also (2) an instrument suited for scraping or hollowing. Hence various meanings, e.g. (1) a large dish, pan, or platter of earthenware, charger (cf. *kikombe*). (2) bivalve shell-fish and their shells, such as oysters, &c., *k. ya pwani* (cf. *kome, konokono, kauli*). (3) Shoulder blade, *k. la bega*, or *la mkono*, also of an empty skull, *k. la kichwa* (cf. *kichwa, bupuru, fuvu* or *fuu*). (4) Like *ukombe*, a gouge, scraper, e.g. *miiba na kombe za kunichoma*, thorns and sharp edges hurting me. Also of the fluke of an anchor, *baura ya makombe mawili*, a European anchor with two flukes. (Cf. *komba*, v. and note, and *ukombe*.)

Kombeo, n. (*ma-*), a sling—for throwing stones.

Kombo, n. (*ma-*), (1) a scrap, a scraping, a bit of food remaining over. (2) Like *kikombo* (which compare) (*a*) twist, turn, crook, crookedness, (*b*) deviation from the straight or standard, defect, fault, ill temper, awkwardness, difficulty, sticking point. *Mti huu ni kombo kombo*, or *una kombo*, this tree is all crooked. *Hapana k.*, there is no difficulty, it is all straightforward, plain sailing. *Mimi, ni k. nayo*, as for me, I just cannot do it. (3) Escape, acquittal, pardon, e.g. *omba k.*, ask for pardon, *-pa k.*, grant pardon. (Cf. *komboa*, and *komba*, v. and note.)

Komboa, v. (1) scrape out, and so (2) ransom, redeem, deliver, make compensation for, pay for. *Nitakomboa mtu aliyeuzwa*, I will redeem the man who was sold. *K. deni*, pay a debt, compensate a creditor. (3) Make crooked, warp, put out of the straight, or out of shape, give a turn (or twist) to, and so fig. cause difficulty to, thwart, hamper, give trouble to. Ps. *kombolewa*. Nt. *komboka*, e.g. (1) be crooked, (2) be redeemed. Ap. *kombo-lea, -leza, -lezwa*, e.g. *mali ya kukombolea*, money for a ransom. Cs. *kombo-za, -zwa*, (1) make crooked, (2) cause to ransom. (Cf. *komba*, v. and note,—also *mkombozi, ukombozi*.)

*****Kombora**, n. a bomb, a shell, also a mortar for throwing bombs. (Ar.)

Kombozi, n. (*ma-*), generally *ukombozi*, ransom, redemption-money, payment, compensation. (Cf. prec.)

Kome, n.(—, and *ma-*), also **Gome**, a kind of shell and shell-fish. *K. za pwani*, univalves. (Cf. *kombe*, and *gome*.)

Komea, v. bolt, bar, fasten with a *komeo*. Ps. *komewa*. Nt. *komeka*. Ap. *kome-lea, -lewa*, e.g. *ufunguo wa kukomelea*, a key to move a bolt. Cs. *kom-eza, -ezwa*, cause to fasten a door. (Cf. *komeo, komoa, kiwi, funga, pingo*.)

Komeo, n. (*ma-*), bar, bolt, latch (of wood), for fastening a door or window, a kind of native lock. (Cf. prec.)

Komoa, v. unbar, i.e. remove the *komeo*. Ps. *komolewa*. Ap. *komolea, -lewa*. (Cf. *komea*.)

Komwe, n. (*ma-*), seed of a plant *mkomwe*, used as counters in playing games.

Konda, v. also **Gonda**, grow thin, become lean, be emaciated, get into low condition of health or body, pine. Cs. *kond-esha, -eshwa*, cause to get thin, wear out, dispirit, cause to pine (languish). *Jikondesha*, worry oneself by brooding, taking a matter too much to heart.

Kondavi, n. (*ma-*), a broad belt of beads worked in patterns,—worn by women. (Cf. *ushanga, utunda*.)

Konde, n. (*ma-*), (1) fist, closed hand. *Piga k.*, strike with the fist (knuckles of the closed hand), i.e. *kwa nyuma ya vidole*. *Piga moyo k.*, take courage, cheer up, make a bold resolve (cf. *ngumi, konzi*). (2) A field, clearing, cultivated piece of ground. *Lima k.*, till a plot of land. (Cf. *shamba*.)

Kondo, n. *Kondo ya nyuma*, after-birth. (Cf. *mkondo*. *Kondo*, war, is not used in Z.)

Kondoo, n. (—, and *ma-*), a sheep. *Chunga k.*, keep sheep, act as shepherd. *Manyoya ya k.*, wool, fleece. *K. mume* (or, *ndume*), a ram. *K. jike*, ewe. (Cf. *kikondoo*. Sheep, mostly of the fat-tailed kind, are imported to Z., but not kept or bred there.)

Konga, v. grow old, get feeble with age. *Mzee huyu amekonga, hawezi kufanya kazi*, this old man is weak with age, he cannot work. Cs. *kong-esha, -eshwa*, make old, add to the age of, wear out, e.g. with nagging or abuse. (Cf. *-kongwe, kongoja*.)

Konge, n. plur. of *ukonge*, fibres of a kind of Sansevieria (*mkonge*), used for making string and cord. See **Mkonge**.

Kongo, n. also **Koongo**. See **Korongo**.

Kongoa, v. draw out, cut out,

extract, disengage. *K. mismari*, draw a nail. *K. jino*, extract a tooth (commonly *ng'oa jino*). *Walikongoa pembe*, they cut out the (elephant's) tusks. *K. unyele*, draw out a hair. Ap. *kongo-lea, -lewa*, take to pieces, break up, e. g. a frame of any sort, a box, a boat. *Mashua yote ilikongolewa vipande*, the whole boat was taken to pieces. *Kongolea sanduku*, open a case,—by extracting the nails, &c. (Cf. *ng'oa, kongomana*.)

Kongoja, v. walk feebly (with difficulty), totter, stagger. Ap. *kongoj-ea, -ewa*, e. g. *fimbo la kukongojea*, a stick to steady one's steps with. *Jikongojea*, prop oneself, steady oneself,—as with a stick. *Nipe gongo langu mkongojo nipate kujikongojea*, give me my staff that I walk with, so that I may steady myself. (Cf. *konga, -kongwe, mkongojo*.)

Kongomana, v. meet together, be united, be joined, be assembled, be heaped (gathered, piled) together. Cs. *kongomanisha*, gather, assemble, unite, weld, heap together, agglomerate. (Cf. *mkongomano, kongoa*, and the more common *kuta, kutana, kutanisha, kusanya*, &c.)

Kongomea, v. fasten up, nail up, put together. *Akazikongomea nguo zangu katika bweta*, and he nailed up all my clothes in a trunk. (Cf. prec.)

Kongomeo, n. (*ma-*), a fastening, also ? larynx, Adam's apple. (Cf. prec.)

Kongwa, n. (*ma-*), a forked stick, a slave stick, i. e. a stick or pole with a forked end in which the slave is secured by the neck with an iron cross-pin. (Cf. *mpanda, panda la mti*.)

Kongwe, n. a lead in singing. *Toa k.*, start a song, give a lead, lead off. (Cf. *bwaga wimbo*.)

-kongwe, a. old, worn-out, aged, past work. *Mzee mkongwe*, a feeble old man. (Cf. *konga, kikongwe, ukongwe*.)

Konka, v. take a sip of, get a drop of,—used of water enough to allay, not quench, thirst, i. e. *konka maji*. (Cf. *onja*.)

Kono, n. (*ma-*), something that projects, sticks out, e. g. a handle, a shoot or sprig of a plant. (Cf. *mkono, kikono, ukono*.)

Konoa, v. See **Konyoa**.

Konokono, n. (*ma-*), a snail. (Cf. *koa*.)

Konyeza, v. make a covert sign to, i. e. in order to attract notice, to warn, to give a hint to, e. g. *k. kwa macho*, raise the eyebrows, wink; *k. kwa mkono*, make a significant gesture. Ap. *konye-zea, -zewa*. (Cf. follg. and *ashiria, onya*. Kr. has *konya*, deceive, hoodwink,—not usual in Z.)

Konyezo, n. (*ma-*), a sign, hint, suggestion, warning. (Cf. prec.)

Konyoa, v. break off, pluck off, tear off, esp. with some instrument, e. g. of removing the grains from a cob of maize, by pounding, i. e. *k. mahindi*. *K. embe*, peel a mango with a knife. Also *k. maungo*, dismember, quarter. Ps. *konyolewa*. Nt. *konyoka*. Ap. *konyo-lea, -lewa*.

Konzi, n. (—, and *ma-*), (1) closed fist. *Piga k.*, rap with the knuckles, with the back of the hand. (2) A fistful, as much as can be taken up in the closed fingers, i. e. *vidole vilivyofumbwa*, e. g. *teka konzi mbili za mchele*, take two fistfuls of rice. (Cf. *konde, ngumi*, also *kofi, chopa*.)

Konzo, n. (*ma-*), large stick, stake, or pole,—with the end pointed and hardened with fire, used as weapon, hunting-spear, or in pitfalls set for large animals. (Cf. *mkonzo, mkuki*.)

Koo, n. (*ma-*), (1) throat; (*a*) ailment of the throat; (*b*) mucus from throat, expectoration (cf. *kohoa*, as if *kohoo* and *kohozi*). (2) Of a breeding animal or bird, e. g. *k. la kuku*, a breeding fowl. *K. la mbuzi*, a breeding goat (an idiomatic inversion of *kuku wa koo*, cf. *pandikizi la mtu*,

N

&c.). (Dist. *mkoo, ukoo,* and cf. *umio, roho.*)

Kopa, n. (*ma-*), a slice of dried cassava (*mhogo*). (Cf. *mhogo, ubale.*)

Kopa, v. (1) get food or money on credit, borrow for trading purposes, i.e. on promise to account for according to agreement, negotiate a loan on credit. *K. mali* (*nguo, fetha*), borrow goods (cloth, cash). (2) Swindle, cheat, defraud, get on false pretences. Ps. *kopwa,* i. e. (1) (of things) be borrowed; (2) (of persons) be swindled. Ap. *kop-ea, -ewa,* borrow from (for, with, &c.), cheat by (for, with, &c.), e.g. *nimekukopea nguo kwa Baniani kwa reale mbili, kwa muda wa miezi miwili,* I have borrowed cloth for you from the Banian for two dollars on a credit of two months. Cs. *kop-esha,-eshwa,-eshea, -eshewa,* lend, supply goods on credit (to), advance as a loan, e. g. *mlipe mtu kadiri akukopesheavyo,* pay him as much as he advances to you. (Cf. Ar. *azimu, karithi.*)

Kope, n. (—, and *ma-*), (1) burnt end of the wick of candle or lamp, snuff, i. e. *kope la taa, kope la utambi*; (2) eye-lid, e. g. *nje ya kope chozi likichuuza,* outside the eye-lid a tear was trickling. *Kwa kope la juu na chini,* in the twinkling of an eye. (Cf. *ukope, kikope, kopesa.*)

Kopesa, v. *kopesa macho,* wink. (Cf. *kope, pepesa macho, finya macho.*)

Kopo, n. (—, and *ma-*), used very generally of any vessel of metal (esp. of tin, zinc, sheet iron), can, mug, pot, jug, cup, &c.,—the size being relatively indicated by the declension, e. g. *kikopo,* a small jug, *makopo,* very large jugs. Used also of other metal articles, e. g. *kopo la maji,* a gutter, rain spout. (Cf. *tasa, sufuria,* and for other vessels generally *chombo, chungu.*)

*__Kora,__ v. please, satisfy, be on good (comfortable, confidential) terms with, be loved by. *Chakula hiki kimenikora,* this food has satisfied me. Ps. *korwa,* e. g. be loved by, have one's wishes met by, be pleased with. (Ar. Cf. syn. *pendeza, rithisha.*)

*__Korani,__ n. the Coran, the Mahommedan Bible. (Cf. *sura,* chapter; *juzu, aya,* short section; *soma* and *hitima* for reading.)

*__Korija,__ n. and __Korja,__ a score, a lot of twenty, twenty together. Used in selling poles, strings of beads, lengths of cloth, &c.

*__Korodani,__ n. sheave of a pulley. (? Ar. Cf. *roda.*)

-korofi, a. (same with D 4 (P), D 5 (S), D 6), (1) evil-minded, tyrannical, destructive, malignant, brutal, savage; (2) inauspicious, of ill omen, unlucky. *Mkorofi sana huyu,* he is a monster of cruelty. *Ndege korofi,* an evil (inauspicious, unlucky) omen. (Cf. follg. and *ukorofi.*)

Korofika, v. be treated brutally, be ruined. Also Cs. *korof-isha, -ishwa,* treat with cruelty, bring to ruin. (Cf. prec., and syn. *haribika, angamia.*)

Koroga, v. stir, stir up, mix by stirring (of liquids). *K. maji,* make water muddy by stirring. Ps. *korogwa.* Ap. *korog-ea, -ewa,* stir with (in, for, &c.). Cs. *korogesha, -eshwa.* (Cf. *buruga, vuruga, pigisha, mkorogo.*)

Koroma, v. snore, snort, groan, —and of similar sounds. *Amesikia wamekoroma,* he has heard them snoring. — n. (*ma-*), (1) a snore, snoring, snort (cf. *mkoromo, mkoromaji, msono*). (2) A cocoanut just becoming ripe, the milk drying, the nutty part formed and hardening, between the stages of *dafu* and *nazi.* See Nazi.

Korongo, n. (*ma-*), (1) a hole dibbled or dug in the ground for planting or sowing. *Mamlaka ya kupiga makorongo na kupiga mrabba,* the office of making the holes and marking out the plots. (2) Name of a crane, and so fig. used of a lean, lanky person.

Kororo, n. (*ma-*), a crested guinea-fowl,—the common sort being *kanga*.

Korosho, n. (*ma-*), a cashew nut, produced by the tree *mbibo* or *m-kanju*. (Cf. *bibo, dunge.*)

Koru, n. also **Kuro**, a water-buck.

Kosa, v. (1) make a mistake (as to), do wrong (to), offend (against), go astray (in), blunder, err; (2) fail to get (hit, find, attain), miss (a mark), fall short, be deficient, be defective; (3) lack, be without, lose, suffer loss of. E. g. *nimekosa*, I have failed, done wrong, sinned. *Hamkunikosa neno hatta sik: moja*, you never treated me badly (failed in duty to me) in any particular. *Mtu akikosa mali hawi mtu mbele ya watu*, a man without money is not a man in the sight of men. *Amemkosa nduguye*, he has lost his brother. *K. njia*, miss the road. *K. nyama*, miss (shooting) an animal. *K. shabaha*, miss the mark. *Kosakosa*, make a series of blunders. Ps. *koswa*. Nt. *koseka*, e. g. be done wrongly,—with Rp. *kosekana*, e.g. be missed, be wanting, be not to be had, fail. *Muungu hakosekani wala hafi*, God never fails (is absent) or dies. *Neno hili limekoseka*, this affair has been bungled. Ap. *kosea, -ewa*, offend (against, about, &c.). *Kosea sheria*, commit a legal offence. Cs. *kos-esha, -eshwa*, cause to do wrong, mislead. Rp. *kosana*, e. g. miss each other, quarrel, treat each other badly, disagree. (Cf. *-kosefu, ukosefu, ukosekano.*) — n. (*ma-*), mistake, a miss, error, fault, failing, failure, defect, wrongdoing, sin. *Si kosa lake*, it is not his fault. *Tia kosani*, blame, accuse. *Sahihisha makosa*, correct mistakes.

-kosefu, a. (same with D 4 (P), D 5 (S), D 6), full of (given to, liable to) mistakes, erroneous, defective, &c. (Cf. prec.)

Kosi, n. or **Kozi**, (1) name of a large bird of prey, vulture, eagle (cf. *tai, furukombe*); (2) like *kikosi*, back of the neck, nape, i. e. *nyuma ya shingo*. *Vunja kosi*, break the neck. (Cf. *kogo, kishogo.*)

Kota, n. (*ma-*), (1) a crook, bend, crooked condition, e. g. *k. la miguu*, crooked legs (cf. more usual *kombo*); (2) sweet stalks of a kind of millet, chewed like sugar-cane (cf. *bua*, and *mtama*).

Kota, v. *kota moto*, warm oneself by the fire. (See **Ota**, with Infin. *kuota, kota*, and *m-oto.*)

Kotama, n. a thin curved broad-bladed knife, used in getting palm wine (*tembo*), esp. for cutting a thin slice from the growing shoot to enable the sap to flow more freely. (Cf. *gema*, and for knives, *kikotama, kisu, jambia, kijembe.*)

Kote, a. form of *-ote*, all,—agreeing with D 8. As adv. *kote, kotekote*, under all circumstances, everywhere, on all sides.

Kovu, n. (—, and *ma-*), scar, mark of a wound or injury.

Ku (also *kw-* before a vowel, and sometimes *k* before *o* and *u*, e. g. *kwenda, koga, kote*), beside its independent use, is a pfx. used in verbs, adjectives, a few nouns, and in the prep. *kwa* (*ku-a*). (See follg.) Used independently, *ku* means 'is, are,' either with purely general reference to circumstances or environment, i. e. ' it is, there is,' or referring to an Infinitive or noun beginning with *ku-*, e. g. *ku kwema leo*, it is nice to-day; *kufa ku rahisi*, dying is easy.

Ku-, 1. in verbs, *ku-* is used as a Pers. Pfx., and as a sign of mood, and of tense. (*a*) As a Pers. Pfx., *ku* (1) may have a purely general reference, e. g. *kunani* (*kuna nini*)? What is there? What is the matter? *Kumetanda*, it is overcast (a dull day). *Kutoke watu wazima waenende*, let the grown-up people start to go. *Kulikuwa mtu*, there was a man. *Kuna safari leo*, there is a journey to-day. (2) May refer to an Infinitive or noun beginning with *ku-*, e.g. *kusafiri kumekwisha*, travelling is over. (3) Is the objective Pfx. of 2 Pers. Sing., e.g. *nakupenda*, I love you. *Kwenda huko kulikufaa*, going there did you good. And, with *-eni* following, the root *ku* supplies one form of the objective Pfx. of 2 Pers. Plur. *Nakuambieni*, I tell you (people). (*b*) As a sign of tense, *ku*, with the Negat. Pers. Pfx. preceding it, is the sign of the Past Tense of the Negat. Conjug., e.g. *sikujua*, I did not know. *Hazikupendwa*, they have not been liked. *Kuja huku hakukukukumbusha*, coming here did not remind you. (*c*) *Ku* is the sign of the Infin. Mood in all verbs, e.g. *kuwa, kwenda, kupenda*, &c. (*d*) *Ku* is inserted, without specific meaning, before the root of all monosyllabic verbs (i.e. *-fa, -cha, -la, -pa, -nya, -ja, -wa*), and of some disyllabic verbs occasionally (e.g. *isha, uza, oga, ota*), after all tense signs, except *a, ja, ka, ki, ku, nga* (which alone are capable of bearing an accent), e.g. *alikufa, amekufa, atapuja*, not *alifa, amepa, ataja*. Obs. *ku* as Infinitive sign is sometimes dropped, esp. when a verb preceding and governing the Infinitive is a semi-auxiliary, e.g. *nimekwisha pata* (for *kupata*), I have got. *Ataka fanya*, he wants to do it. *Aenda tafuta*, he goes to search. 2. In adjectives, *ku-* is the pfx. agreeing (*a*) with D 8; (*b*) like *pangu* and *mwangu*, with nouns of the Locative form, ending in *-ni*, e.g. *kukwaa kwake nyumbani kwangu*, his sojourn in my house. 3. *Ku* is also used, but only in connexion with a few roots, to form (*a*) nouns, e.g. *kuzimu*, the world of spirits, the state or place of departed souls, *kumoja*, one kind, e.g. *kazi zetu hazina kumoja*, our work is not all of one kind; *kushoto*, the left-hand, as indicating position generally; *kuume*, the right-hand position, also, the male sex, *kuke*, the female sex, e.g. *jamaa ya kukeni*, a relation, in the female line, or, on the mother's side. Also n. *kule*, that place (case, condition, &c.), *huku*, and *kwetu*, our country, home, as virtual nouns. (*b*) Adverbs, e.g. *upanga unakata kuwili*, the sword cuts on both sides, is double-edged. *Kaa kushoto*, sit on the left. Also *kule*, there, *huku*, here, *kuku huku*, just here. It is in these advs. and in its use as a person-pfx., that a positive demonstrative meaning of *ku* appears, viz. as an element denoting general reference to circumstances, condition, state, but esp. to locality, i.e. indicating 'circumstances under which' or 'place where' something occurs. (*c*) The prep. *kwa*, i.e. *ku-a*. See *-a*. (Cf. *ko*, also *pa, po*, and *mu, mo*.)

Kua, v. grow, grow up, get large, increase, become great,—used of the growth of men and animals (but *ota, mea*, usual of plants, and similar growths). *Mtoto umleavyo ndivyo akuavyo*, as you bring a child up, so he grows up. Ap. *ku-lia, -liwa*, e.g. (1) grow up in (at, by, for, &c.). E.g. *mtoto huyu amekulia hapa*, this child has grown up here (cf. *kikulia*). Also apparently (2) be (too) great for, be heavy to, burden, be hard for, e.g. *amekuliwa kufanya kazi hii*, he has found the job too hard for him. *Neno hili limemkulia, kubwa, zito*, the thing is too much for him, it is big and weighty (cf. *-kulifu*). Cs. *kuza, kuzwa*, make great, enlarge, magnify, increase, glorify. E.g. *kuza Sultani*, make the Sultan powerful. *Muungu amekuza umri wake*, God has prolonged your life. (Cf. *-kuu, -kubwa, tukuka, tukuza, kikulia, ukulifu*.)

Kuaheri, Kuaherini, good-bye, adieu!—for *kwa heri*. See **Heri**.

*****Kuba**, n. vaulted roof, arched

structure, cupola, dome. Dim. and adv. *kikuba*. (Ar. Cf. *zege*. *Kuba* is sometimes used for *kubwa*, great. Dist. *guba*, *ghubba*.)

*Kubali, v. accept, approve, acknowledge, assent (to), agree (to), welcome. Ps. *kubaliwa*. Nt. *kubalika*, e.g. be acceptable, be capable of acceptance. Nt. *kubalia*, -*iwa*, accept from (about, at, &c.). Cs. *kubali-sha*, -*shwa*, force to accept, procure acceptance by, win over, persuade, &c. Rp. *kubaliana*, e.g. be on good terms. (Cf. *kibali*, *ukubali*, and syn. *kiri*, *rithia*, *ithini*.)

Kubazi, n. (*ma-*), a plain kind of sandal with no ornamental work. (Cf. *kiatu*, *mtalawanda*.)

-kubwa, a. (*kubwa* with D 4 (P), D 5 (S), D 6),—sometimes pronounced *kuba*, (1) great, big, large, spacious, extensive, e.g. *nyumba k.*, a large house; *shamba k.*, an extensive estate, large garden. *Kisu kikubwa*, a large knife. (2) Great in power (influence, rank, importance, &c.), important, significant. *Bwana mkubwa*, *bibi mkubwa*, is a usual term of respectful address or reference. *Neno limekuwa kubwa*, *halikataliki*, the matter has become urgent, it cannot be met with a negative. *Asiosikia mkubwa*, *huona makubwa*, he who disregards a superior, generally finds serious consequences. (3) Elder, oldest. *Ndugu yangu mkubwa*, my elder brother. (4) -*kubwa* is used with a noun or another adjective simply to intensify its meaning, as having a quality in a marked way or high degree, like the adv. *sana*, e.g. *mwivi mkubwa*, a regular thief. *Mtu huyu ni mlevi mkubwa*, this fellow is an utter drunkard. Obs. *mkubwa* (*wa-*) is often used as a noun,—superior, chief, manager, master, director, &c. (Cf. -*kuu* and note on the comparative meaning, also *kua*, *tukuza*, &c.)

Kucha, v. (1) Infin. Act. of -*cha*, (*a*) fear, (*b*) dawn. See -**cha**. (2) Verbal n. of *cha*, the dawn, morning, all the night. See -**cha**. (3) Plur. of *ukucha*, nails, claws, and sometimes sing. *kucha* (*ma-*), of size.

Kuchewa, Kuchwa, Ps. forms from *kucha*. See -**cha**, v.

*Kufuli, n. (—, and *ma-*), a padlock. (Ar. Cf. *kitasa*.)

*Kufuru, v. (1) treat with mockery or contempt, revile, curse, and esp. (2) with reference to religion, become an unbeliever, apostatize, blaspheme, commit sacrilege, renounce God. Ps. *kufuriwa*. Nt. *kufurika*. Ap. *kufur-ia*, -*iwa*. Cs. *kufur-isha*, -*ishwa*, make (consider, treat as, force to be, urge to be, &c.) an unbeliever, cause to blaspheme. (Ar. Cf. *ukufuru*, *ukafiri*, -*kafiri*.)

Kuguni, n. a hartebeest.

*Kuhani, n. (*ma-*). See Kahini, Mkohani. (Ar.)

Kuke, n. and Kuuke (from -*ke*,—like *uke* and *kike*, of sex,—but more generalized), the female kind, feminine status or condition,—used only in a few adjectival phrases. *Mkono wa kuke*, the left hand, as the (usually) weaker, also *wa kike*,—but commonly *wa kushoto*. Opp. to *mkono wa kuume*. *Kukeni*, on the female side, by the mother. *Ujamaa wa kukeni*, relatives on the mother's side, in the female line. Contr. *ujamaa wa kike*, female relatives. (Cf. -*ke*, and *ku*.)

Kuko, (1) n. a. and adv. that there, that, there, e.g. *kuko ni kuzuri*, that is nice there. *Kupika kuko kwapendeza*, that way of cooking is satisfactory. *Kwenda kuko*, to go yonder. So *kwa kuko*, -*a kuko*. *Kuko huko*, just there, on that spot. (A Rd. form from *ku*, the *ko* being the form of reference. Cf. *kuku*, *huko*, and *mumo*, *papo*, &c.) (2) Verb-form, there is there, there is, it is there.

Kuku, (1) n. a fowl, a hen. *Mtoto wa* (*mwana wa*, *kinda la*) *k.*, a chicken,—also *faranga*, *kifaranga*.

Koo la k., a breeding fowl. (Cf. *posa, jogoo, jimbi.* Dist. *mkuku*, keel.) (2) n. a. and adv., this here, this, here, e. g. in the phrase *kuku huku*, just here, in this very place. (Cf. *kuko*, and *ku-*.)

-kukuu, a. (same with D 4 (P), D 5 (S), D 6), also -kuukuu, worn out, old, past work, useless from age or wear. (Cf. *-kongwe, -chakafu, -bovu.*)

*Kulabu, n. a hook, hooked instrument, grapple,—of various kinds. Used for holding work in position, e. g. by a tailor, blacksmith, and on ship board, for fastening clothes, &c. *Akapeleka k. yake chini*, he let down his hook. *Ulimi wangu umetiwa k., hauwezi kunena*, my tongue has had a hook put in it, it cannot speak. (Ar. Cf. *ndoana, kiopoo, upembo, ngoe.*)

Kule, used as (1) n. 'that' used indefinitely, *kule ni mbali*, that is a long way off. (2) A form of *-le*, agreeing with Infin. or noun in *ku-*. (3) adv. there, in (from, to) that position, &c. Sometimes reduplicated *kule kule*, just there. Also pronounced *kule-e-e-*,—the final vowel raised in pitch and prolonged in proportion to the distance indicated. (Cf. *ku, yule*, and *kuku, kuko*, &c.)

Kulia, v. be great (too great) for, be hard to, weigh on, depress, overwhelm, &c. (Prob. appl. form of kua, which see, and follg.)

-kulifu, a. (1) in Ps. sense, of one who is easily tired, discouraged, beaten, one who lacks grit (spirit, perseverance), i.e. remiss, weak-kneed, poor-spirited, &c. (Cf. *kulia, kua*, and syn. *-legevu, -zembe.*) But also (2) in Act. sense, oppressive, burdensome, tiresome, fatiguing. (Cf. *ukulifu*, and *ukalifu.*)

Kuliko, relative verb-form, (1) that which is, which is, referring to D 8, e. g. *kufa kuliko bora*, the mode of dying which is noble; (2) where there is,—the *ku* of general reference (see ku), e. g. *peponi kuliko raha*, in Paradise where there is rest; but (3) esp. common in comparisons, 'than' after an adjective, 'where there is' being equivalent to 'as compared with,' e. g. *yeye mkubwa kuliko nduguye*, he is bigger (taller, older) than his brother; also (4) in the general sense, 'as to, as regards,' e.g. *kuliko bei ya watumwa*, as regards the slave traffic. (See Ku, Li, Ko.)

*Kulla, a. every,—always preceding its noun. (Ar. See Killa.)

Kululu, n. (*ma-*), a large kind of cowry, a tiger-cowry. So little valued by the native that *kupata kululu* means 'to get nothing worth having.'

Kulungu, n. a species of antelope.

Kuma, n. vagina. (Cf. *uke.*)

Kumba, v. (1) push, shove, press against, jostle. Ps. *kumbwa*. Nt. *kumbika*. Ap. *kumb-ia, -iwa*. Cs. *kumb-iza, -izwa, -izia*, e. g. push off on to, transfer to. *Adamu alimkumbizia mkewe*, Adam put it off on his wife. Rp. *kumbana*, jostle each other, hustle (cf. *piga kikumbo*, and *sukuma*). (2) Clear out, take away all, make a clean sweep (of), glean. Same derivatives as above. E.g. *walikumba biashara yote ya tumbako*, they monopolized the whole traffic in tobacco. *Mwivi amenikumbia mali*, a thief has carried off everything I had. *Kumba maji*, bale out water. (Cf. *komba*, and follg.)

Kumba, n. (1) -*a kumba kumba*, miscellaneous, promiscuous, of all and any sort. *Safari ya kumbakumba*, a caravan of any who could be got together (a scratch lot) (cf. *kumba*, v.). (2) *Kuti la kumba*, a whole cocoanut leaf with the fronds plaited all along each side of the central rib. Used for light fences, and enclosures, back yards, &c. See Kuti.

Kumbatia, v. clasp in the arms, embrace. Ps. *kumbatiwa*. Nt. *kumbatika*. Cs. *kumbat-isha, -ishwa.*

Rp. *kumbatiana*, embrace each other. (Cf. *shika, kamata, pambaja*.)

Kumbe, adv. expressing astonishment, pleasant or unpleasant surprise, Lo and behold! What do you think? For a wonder, all of a sudden.

Kumbi, n. (*ma-*), also **Kumvi, Kumfi**, the fibrous husk or sheath of various plants, esp. of the cocoa-nut, areca-nut, &c. *Kumbi* is used collectively (i. e. of the material generally), but the plur. is commonly used. Single fibres are called *uzi* (pl. *nyuzi*). The husks are commonly buried in pits on the shore or in a wet place, till the fibres are loosened. They are then taken up, beaten out, and cleaned, and called *makumbi ya usumba*. (Cf. *kumvi, ukumvi*, prob. the same word,—like *jambia*, and *jamvia*, &c.)

Kumbi, n. plur. of *ukumbi*, which see.

Kumbikumbi, n. white ants in the flying stage, when they first issue in swarms from the ground. Used as food. (Cf. *mchwa*.)

Kumbo, n. devastation, depopulation, wholesale destruction. (Cf. *kumba, mkumbo*.)

-kumbufu, a. having a good memory, thoughtful. (Cf. *kumbuka*, and *-fahamifu*.)

Kumbuka, v. call to mind, remember, think of, bear in mind, brood over, i. e. mental attention directed usually to the past, or a subject connected with it. *Nakumbuka ulimwengu*, I am considering the situation. Ps. *kumbukwa*. Ap. *kumbuk-ia, -iwa*, direct the memory (or, attention) to. *Sikumbukii*, I do not recall it. *Amenikumbukia chuo changu*, he recollected my book for me, reminded me of it. Cs. *kumbusha, -shwa*, remind, put in mind (of). (Cf. *fahamu*, of memory, and *tambua*, of recognition. Also, *kumbukumbu, ukumbusho, -kumbufu*.)

Kumbukumbu, n. (*ma-*), mention, remembrance, memorial, parting gift, souvenir,—anything that recalls another thing to mind. (Cf. prec.)

Kumbusho, Kumbuu. See **Ukumbusho, Ukumbuu.**

Kumbwaya, n. a kind of drum standing on feet. (Cf. *ngoma*.)

Kumbwe, n. (*ma-*), a snack, a mouthful of food,—colloquial, *kumbwe na kinywco*, something to eat and drink. (A pass. form in *e-*, from *kumba*.)

Kumi, n. and a. (pl. *ma-*), ten,—the highest simple numeral of B. origin used in Swahili. Used of the three divisions of a month, a decade. *kumi la kwanza (la kati, la kwisha)*, the first (middle, last) decade. *-a kumi*, tenth. (Cf. Ar. *ashara*.)

Kumoja, n. one kind. *Kazi zetu hazina k.*, our occupations are not all of one kind. (Cf. *umoja*, and for *ku, kuzimu, kushoto, kuke*, &c.) — a. form of *-moja*, agreeing with D 8. — adv. on one side, from one point of view, i. e. *kwa upande mmoja. -kali kumoja*, with one sharp edge.

Kumunta, Kumunto, n.—in Z. more usually **kung'uta, kung'uto**, which see.

Kumvi, n. (*ma-*, also plur. of *ukumvi*), husk or sheath of various vegetable products, of maize, rice, &c., i. e. *k. la muhindi* (enclosing the ear, *suke*), *k. za mpunga*. (Cf. *kapi, wishwa, kununu*.)

Kuna, v. scratch. Used of allaying irritation rather than of laceration or wounding (cf. *papura, piga makucha*), e. g. *k. kichwa*, scratch the head; *k. ngazi*, scratch the skin. Also of coarse grating, e. g. *kuna nazi*, grate a cocoanut, i. e. extract the nutty part from the shell with the instrument called *mbuzi*. Ps. *kunwa* (dist. *kunywa*, to drink). Nt. *kunika*. Ap. *kun-ia, -iwa*, e. g. *mbuzi ya kunia nazi*, a cocoa-nut grater. Cs. *kun-isha, -ishwa*. Rp. *kunana*. (Cf. *mkuno, kuno, piga mtai, papura*.)

Kuna, verb-form, (1) there is, there are (*ku* of general reference, cf. *ku, mna, pana*); (2) it has, they have,—*ku* agreeing with D 8. The negative form *hakuna* is one of the commonest expressions for a simple negative, 'there is not, nothing, no.' *Kuna nini* (or *kunani*)? What is there? What is the matter? *Kunako*, there is (there), that is so,—in reference to the query *kuna*? *Kufa kuna maumivu*, death involves suffering. *Kuna* supplies one way of expressing abstract existence. *Kuna muungu*? Is there a God? Does God exist? *Kunaye*, He exists. Also *kunaye* may mean 'it depends on him (it is with him).' (See **Ku** and **Na**.)

Kunazi, n. (*ma-*), the small edible fruit of the tree *mkunazi*, which see.

Kunda, n. (*ma-*), a green vegetable like spinach (Str.).

Kundaa, v. be short, stunted, small of stature. (Cf. *via*.)

Kunde, n. plur. of *ukunde*, a kind of bean, produced by the plant *mkunde*, which see.

Kundi, n. (*ma-*), a number of things (usually living things) together, crowd, troop, group, flock, herd, swarm, &c. *Makundi makundi*, in troops, in large bodies, in masses.

Kunga, v. used of various processes of sewing, hem, make a border, trim, embroider, e. g. *kunga mshono*, make a stitched seam on band; *k. nguo*, put a border, trimming, or stitched edge to a cloth. *K. utepe*, with similar meaning. Ps. *kungwa*. Ap. *kung-ia, -iwa*. (Cf. *shona, pinda*.)

Kunga, n. sometimes **Kinga**, (1) a secret, wile, subterfuge, trick, device, e. g. *k. za moyo*, secret thoughts, private reflections. *Mtumi wa k. haambiwi maana*, he who conveys a secret message is not told its meaning. *Kazi haifai illa kwa k.*, work is no good, unless you have been taught the art. (2) Esp. of confidential and private instruction on matters unfit for open mention, e. g. sexual subjects,—called sometimes *malango*, rudiments, or *kunga za mwituni* (*za nyumbani, za jandoni*, and *ngungwi, ? nkungwi*). Hence (3) shameful things, what causes shame. (Cf. *mkunga, somo, siri, msiri*, and perh. *kunja*.)

Kungu, n. (1) also **Ukungu**, mist, fog, haze (cf. *ukungu, uwande, wingu*). (2) An edible stone-fruit from the tree *mkungu*. The stone contains a kernel, of which children are fond (cf. *mkungu*). *Kungu manga*, nutmeg, lit. the Arabian *kungu* (cf. *manga*),—fruit of the *mkungu manga*. (3) Confidential adviser, esp. an older friend who gives advice to unmarried women, and makes all arrangements for them at the time of marriage, receiving various fees and presents from the bridegroom for so doing. (Cf. *kunga, mkungwa, kungwe*.)

Kunguni, n. a bug.

Kunguru, n. (*ma-*), (1) a carrion crow,—black, with white on the neck and shoulders; (2) a kind of calico, made at Cutch.

Kung'uta, v. (1) shake out, shake off, sift, winnow; (2) test severely, scrutinize, examine. E. g. *k. mavumbi* (*mvua*), shake off dust (rain). *Jikung'uta*, shake oneself. *K. mabawa*, shake out the feathers,—of a bird basking in the sun. *Wakalipeleka jamvi uani wakaikung'uta*, they took the carpet to the yard, and gave it a shaking. Ps. *kung'-utwa*. Nt. *kungutika*. Ap. *kungut-ia, -iwa*. Cs. *kung'ut-isha, -ishwa*. (Cf. *kung'uto, chunga, pepeta*. The word *kumunta* is also heard, but not usual in Z., and *kumutika*, fig. be shaken, be alert, expectant, agitated, e. g. *roho yake inamkumutika*.)

Kung'uto, n. (*ma-*), a basket used as a sieve, strainer, or for tossing and winnowing grain. (Cf. *kikapo*, and *kiteo, tunga*.)

Kungwe, n. (*ma-*). See **Mkunga**.

Kuni, n. plur. of *ukuni*, firewood. (See **Ukuni**, and cf. *kuna*.)

Kunja, v. fold, wrap up, crease, wrinkle, tumble, make a mess of. E. g. *k. uzi*, wind up thread. *Kunja-kunja uzi*, tangle the thread. *K. uso*, knit the brow, frown. *K. mabawa*, fold the wings. *Jikunja*, shrink, cower, flinch (cf. *kunyata*). *Kisu cha kukunja*, a clasp-knife. Ps. *kunjwa*. Nt. *kunjika*, e.g. be folded, be easy to fold, admit of folding. Ap. *kunj-ia*, *-iwa*, e.g. wrap up for (with, in, &c.). Cs. *kunj-isha*, *-ishwa*. Rp. *kunjana*, e.g. *nguo imekunjana kwa upepo*, the calico (which was laid out smooth) has been ruffled up by the wind. (Cf. follg. and *kunjua*, *finya*, and perh. *kunga*.)

Kunjamana, v. be folded, wrinkled, creased. E. g. *k. uso*, knit the brows, frown,—so *uso umekunjamana*. (Cf. prec. and *-mana*.)

Kunjo, n. (*ma-*), fold, wrinkle, crease. E.g. *makunjo ya mshipi*, the folds of a fishing-line. (Cf. *kunja*, and *pindi*.)

Kunjua, v. Rv. of *kunja*, unfold, unwrap, smooth out, spread open. *K. nguo*, lay out clothes. *K. miguu*, stretch the legs out. *K. uso*, smooth the brow, smile, look pleased. *Jikunjua*, be cordial, be open. Ps. *kunjuliwa*. Nt. *kunjuka*. Ap. *kunju-lia*. (Cf. *-kunja*, *-kunjufu*.)

-kunjufu, a. (same with D 4 (P), D 5 (S), D 6), open, serene, unclouded, genial, amiable, merry. *Mtu mkunjufu*, a genial man. So with *uso* (face), *moyo* (temper). (Cf. *kunjua*, *kunja*, *ukunjufu*.)

Kuno, n. (*ma-*), what is produced by scraping, a scraping, scrap. *Makuno ya nazi*, grated cocoanut. (Cf. *kuna* v., *mkuno*.)

Kunrathi, v. a common phrase of polite apology,—pardon me, excuse me, by your leave, no offence meant. Often strengthened by *sana*. *Kunrathi sana*, with your kind permission, I humbly beg pardon. (Arab. Imperat. *kun rathi*, be content, but in common use. Cf. equivalent *uwe* (or *mwe*) *rathi*, and *rathi*, *rithi*, *utafathali*.)

Kununu, n. (*ma-*), *kununu la mawele*, an empty husk or spike of a kind of millet. (Cf. *kumvi*, *kapi*, *wishwa*.)

Kunyata, v. draw together, cause to shrink, compress. Seldom occurs except with Rf. *ji*, in the sense, cower, shrink together, esp. as an attitude of fear, pain, or supplication. *Jikunyata kama maskini*, humble oneself like a beggar. *Jik. kwa baridi*, be doubled up with cold. *Jik. uso*, have an offended, disgusted look. (Cf. *kunja uso*.)

Kunyua, v. (1) scratch at, give a scratch to, e.g. to hurt, or to attract notice; (2) call by a secret sign, give a private hint to, &c. *K. kidole*, hurt the finger by a scratch,—implying more than the simple *kuna*, scratch. Ps. *kunyuliwa*. Nt. *kunyuka*, e.g. *kunyuka na mti*, get scratched by a tree in passing by it. (Cf. *kuna*, *papura*, *piga mtai*.)

Kuo, n. (*ma-*), (1) furrow, trench, hollow, hole, i.e. made by hollowing out. *Makuo ya kauku*, holes scratched by fowls. Usually (2) a bed or row of seedlings, &c. (3) A plot of ground marked out by a furrow or line drawn on the ground, and given to a man to cultivate (cf. *ngwe*, same marked by a cord). Hence *nyosha k.*, mark out a piece of ground; *ongeza* (*punguza*) *k.*, enlarge (reduce) a plantation. (Cf. *mkuo*, and syn. *shimo*, *handaki*, *mfuo*.)

Kupaa, n. (*ma-*), also **Kupa**, (1) one of the two side-pieces forming a pulley (*kapi*, *gofia*) enclosing the sheave (*roda*) (cf. *korodani*); (2) ? cheek-bone, cheek-piece.

Kupe, n. a tick,—on cattle, dogs, &c. *Kama kupe na mkia wa ng'ombe*, like a tick and a cow's tail,—

of things adhering closely. (Cf. *kama pete na kidole*, like a ring and a finger.)

Kupua, v. shake out, shake off, throw off, let fall, drop on the ground (by a push, jerk, &c.). E.g. *k. nguo*, throw off clothes. *K. imbu*, drive off mosquitoes. Ps. *kupuliwa*. Nt. *kupuka*, e.g. fig. be cast off, be a fugitive (outcast). Hence *kupukia*. Ap. *kupu-lia, -liwa*. Cs. *kupu-sha, -shwa*. (Cf. *kung'uta, mkupuo*.)

*****Kura**, n. a lot, i.e. as in casting lots. *Piga kura*, cast lots. (Ar.)

Kuro, n. also **Koru**, **Kuru**, a water-buck.

*****Kurubia, Kurubisha,** v. See **Karibia, Karibisha**.

Kusa, v. Cs. of *kuta*, i.e. *kutisha* or *kusha, kusa*, cause to meet, bring on. *Nimemkusa mashaka*, I have got him into trouble. See **Kuta**.

Kusanya, v. collect, gather together, bring together, assemble, amass, make a pile or heap of. E.g. *k. watu*, collect people. *K. jeshi*, form an army. *K. mali*, amass wealth. Ps. *kusanywa*. Nt. *kusanyika*. Ap. *kusany-ia, -iwa*. Rp. *kusanyana*, e.g. meet together by common consent. (Cf. *kusanyiko, mkusanyo, kuta, kusa*.)

Kushoto, n. and adv., the left side, the left-hand position. *Mkono wa k.*, the left-hand, as opp. to *mkono wa kuume (wa kulia)*. *Kaa kushotoni*, sit on the left side. (Cf. *ku*, and *kumoja, kuzimu, kuke*, &c.)

Kusi, n. southerly wind, south monsoon,—prevailing at Z. from May to Oct. Hence also of the season, and of the southerly direction. *Kusini*, the south quarter, to (from, in) the south. *-a kusini*, of the south, southerly. Contr. *kaskazi*, the north wind, &c. (Cf. Ar. *suheli*, coast, used of Africa, i.e. south of Arabia, and hence 'south.')

*****Kusudi**, v. also **Kasidi**, intend, purpose, propose, design, aim at, usually in the Ap. form *kusudia*, with same sense. *Kusudia safari*, resolve on an expedition. *K. kwenda*, intend to go. Ps. *kusudiwa*. Nt. *kusudika*. Cs. *kusudisha, -ishwa*. — n. (*ma-*), intention, purpose, aim, object, end. *Kwa k.*, on purpose, intentionally, deliberately, wilfully (cf. *kwa moyo, kwa nafsi*). Also as adv., *kusudi*, and *makusudi*, like *kwa kusudi*. And as conj. with Infin. or Subjunct., 'on purpose to, in order that (to), with the object of,' e.g. *akaondoka kusudi aende* (or, *kwenda*) *Ulaya*, he started with the intention of going to Europe. (Cf. syn. *shauri, maana, nia, mradi*.)

Kuta, v. come upon, meet (with), chance on, hit on, find. *Nalimkuta hawezi (hayuko)*, I found him ill (absent). *Kuta mashaka*, meet with (experience) difficulties. Ps. *kutwa*. Nt. *kutika*. Ap. *kut-ia, -iwa*, e.g. *mauti imemkutia*, death came upon him, or *amekutiwa na mauti*. Cs. *kutisha*, or *kusha, kusa*, cause to come on, bring upon, involve in. Hence *kut-ishia, -ishiwa, kushia*, &c. Rp. *kutana*, meet together, assemble, gather, collect, hold a meeting, be crowded (cf. *kusanya, songa, barizi*). *Jeshi limekutana*, the crowd is dense. Hence *kutanika*, be assembled, meet. Also *kutan-ia, -iwa*, meet for (at, by, in, &c.). Cs. *kutanisha*, cause to meet, hold a meeting (of). (Cf. *mkutano*.)

Kuta, n. plur. of *ukuta* (which see), walls.

Kuti, n. (*ma-*), (1) a cocoanut leaf, whether green or dry; (2) a cocoanut leaf prepared for use in different ways, e.g. (*a*) *kuti la kumba* (and *fumba*), the whole leaf, with the fronds on either side simply plaited together, used in forming light fences, enclosures, shelters of any kind; (*b*) *kuti la pande*, with the fronds all plaited together on one side, similarly used; (*c*) *kuti la viungo*, lengths of the leaf-rib (*upongoo*) (or of stick) about three feet long with all the fronds attached to it and brought to one side. These form the usual roofing material of native houses in Z., and are a regular article of sale. (Cf. *mnazi*, and *kikuti*, *ukuti*.)

Kutu, n. rust,—or anything resembling it, a discoloration, &c. *K. ya shaba*, verdigris. *K. ya mwezi*, the shaded or darker parts of the moon.

Kutua, v. give a jerk to, pull suddenly, cause a shock to. *K. kamba*, jerk a rope. Nt. *kutuka*, e.g. fig. be shaken, startled, frightened, shocked, &c. Cs. *kutu-sha*, *-shwa*, startle, frighten, &c. (Cf. *kupua*, also *situka*, *tuka*, &c.)

-kuu, a. (same with D 4 (P), D 5 (S), D 6), great. Seldom simply 'big,' i.e. of merely physical size or material greatness, but implying some moral or sentimental element of pre-eminence, authority, and excellence. *-kubwa*, on the other hand, means 'big, large, extensive,' though also used to include and denote the natural effects of great size, i.e. authority, weight, influence, impressiveness. Thus (1) 'great, powerful, having natural or representative authority,' &c. *Wakuu kwa vijana* is a common contrast, 'old and young, great and small' (also *wakubwa kwa wadogo*). Cf. *mkuu* as n., chief, master, king (as also *mkubwa*, n., and in African stories the rabbit (*sungura*) is called the *mkuu wa nyama*, or *nyama mkuu*, king of beasts, while the elephant would be described as the *nyama mkubwa*, largest of animals. *Bustani kuu*, a great (grand, fine) garden. Obs. *kiazi kikuu*, yam,—often of great size in East Africa. (2) 'Noble, pre-eminent, high-class, excellent, influential.' (3) 'Over-great, presuming on greatness, excessive, unnatural, outrageous, beyond the proper bounds of decorum (self-control, human nature).' E.g. *maneno makuu*, presumptuous, boastful words. *Taka makuu*, aim too high, be over-ambitious. *Piga makuu*, give oneself airs, be arrogant, make a great show. *Hana makuu*, he is an unassuming, civil spoken, humble person,—sometimes in contrast to *-kuu* in other senses, e.g. *makuu mengi lakini hana makuu*, he has many great qualities, but he never makes too much of them. (Cf. *-kubwa*, *kua*, *kuza*, &c.)

Kuume, n. (from *-me*, like *ume*, and *kiume*, of sex, but more generalized), (1) the male kind (status, condition); (2) right-hand side, right-hand. Used (like *kuke*) only in a few adjectival and adverbial phrases. *Mtu huyu ni ndugu yangu wa kuumeni nami*, this man is a relation of mine on the father's side. *Mkono wa kuume*, the right-hand (also *mkono wa kulia*, the hand used in eating, opp. to *mkono wa kushoto*). *Kaa kuumeni*, sit on the right-hand side. *Wa kuume haukati wa kushoto*, the right hand does not cut the left. (Cf. *ku*, and *kushoto*, *kumoja*, *kuzimu*, and follg.)

Kuvuli, n. *mkono wa kuvuli*, the right-hand,—for *mkono wa kuume*, which is usual in Z. (Cf. prec.)

Kuwa, v. Infin. of *wa*, be (which see), to be, being, existence. Can be used of pure existence (cf. *Mwenyi kuwa*, as a title of God, the Existing One, the Self-existing.)

Kuwili, n. and adv., the double kind, in a double way, in two ways. *Kisu kikali kuwili*, a knife with two edges. *Anatajwa kuwili*, he has two names. (Cf. *ku*, and *kumoja*, *kuume*, &c.)

Kuyu, n. See **Mkuyu**.

Kuza, v. Infin. (1) Cs. of *kua*, make great. (2) *Uza*, sell, for *kuuza*. (3) *Uza* for *uliza*, ask.

-kuza, a. (same with D 4 (P), D 5 (S), and D 6), well-grown, fine, big of its kind,—of things capable of growth. *Yule paka mkuza sana*, that is a very fine cat. (Cf. *kua*, *-kubwa*, *-kuu*.)

Kuzi, n. (*ma*)-, also **Kusi,** an earthenware pitcher or jug, larger than *gudulia*, with handle or handles and narrow neck. (Cf. *mtungi, chombo.*)

Kuzimu, n. state (place, condition) of departed spirits of the dead, the grave, the lower world. *Enda kuzimuni,* die and be buried. *Chungulia k.,* look into the other world, i.e. be at death's door, have one foot in the grave. *K. kuna mambo,* the world of spirits has its wonders. (Cf. *mzimu,* and perh. *wazimu,* also *zima, zimwe,* and for the form *ku,* and syn. *ahera, peponi, huko.*)

Kw-, as a pfx. before vowels, is for **ku-,** which see.

Kwa, prep. (*ku* combined with the variable prepositional element -*a*, which see). This is the most common and comprehensive of the few Swahili prepositions,—so comprehensive as to cover most of the meanings of the other common prepositions, i.e. -*a*, *na*, and *katika*. Subject to the few limitations characteristic of each of these (see -a, Na, Katika), *kwa* can be represented according to the context by 'to, in, at, from, by, for, with, on account of, in respect of, as to,' and indeed almost any preposition denoting relations of time, place, motion, object, instrument, and condition generally. *Kwa* is seldom used, however, of the *Agent* proper, or of comparative nearness or distance (see Na), nor of relations which may be called adjectival (see -a). E.g. *toka kwa,* come from (or, out of); *kaa kwa,* remain at; *enda kwa,* go to. *Ua kwa mkuki,* kill with a spear. *Kwa nini?* For what? Why? *Kwa sababu ya,* because of, by reason of. *Kwa habari hizi,* at (about, on account of) these news. *Wali kwa mchuzi,* rice with gravy. *Mia kwa tano,* five per cent. *Wangwana kwa watumwa,* gentry, slaves and all. *Andika kwa kiswahili,* write in Swahili. *Kwa haraka,* in haste, hastily. *Kwa hivi,* thus. *Kwa* with a noun, commonly a name, following, often denotes a single object or idea, e.g. *kwa Mponda,* Mponda's town. *Kwa mfalme,* the chief's house. Hence *katika* is sometimes used with it, e.g. *katika kwa nduguye,* from (at, to) his brother's house. *Kwa* is rarely used with Personal Pronouns, the corresponding form of the adjective, i.e. *kwangu, kwako, kwake,* &c., being substituted, unless some special meaning is intended, e.g. *asiyeona kwa yeye, akionywa haoni,* he who does not see of himself does not see if he is shown. (Cf. -*a, katika, na.*)

Kwa, form of the prep. -*a* (which see) agreeing (1) with D 8, (2) with locatives ending in -*ni*, e.g. *nyumbani kwa nduguye,* in (to, from) his brother's house.

Kwaa, v. (1) strike the foot (against an object), stumble, knock, be stopped by a sudden obstacle; (2) fig. falter, hesitate, be brought to a stop or check, get into a difficulty. *K. na jiwe,* or *jiweni,* knock the foot against a stone. *Heri kukwaa kidole kuliko kukwaa ulimi,* better to stumble with the toe than the tongue. Ap. *kwalia, kwaia,* rarely heard. *Mkwaia nyoka, aonapo ukuti hushituka,* a man who has stumbled over a snake, starts if he sees a switch (cocoanut frond). Cs. *kwa-za, -zwa,* cause to stumble, make difficulties for, &c. Also intens. *dau limekwaza maweni,* the boat struck hard on the rocks. (But ? cf. *kwaza* for *kwaruza.*) Rp. *kwazana,* knock against each other. (Cf. *kwaza, kwama, kwao* or *kwayo, kwazo.*)

Kwaje, adv. interrog. (*kwa je?*) How? In what way? By what means? What do you mean? *Kwaje hufanya hivi?* How is it you do this? i.e. why, or in what way.

Kwake, (1) n. (*ku-ake*) his (hers, its) circumstances (position, house,

&c.). (2) adv. idiomatic equivalent of *kwa yeye*, to (from, at, with) him (her, it), to his house, &c. (3) Form of a. *-ake*, agreeing with D 8 and locatives in *-ni*. (Cf. *ku, -ake,* and *kwangu.*)

Kwako, n. adv. and adj., same as *kwake*, but relating to 2 Pers. Sing., i. e. *wewe*, you. (Cf. *-ako.*)

Kwale, n. partridge,—including several species.

Kwama, v. St. of *kwaa*, (1) become jammed, stick fast, come to a deadlock, be gripped, be squeezed; (2) fig. be in a fix, get into a difficulty. Ap. *kwam-ia, -iwa.* Cs. *kwam-isha, -ishwa,* cause to jam, make stick fast, put in a difficulty, &c. *Mti huu umenikwamisha mkono*, this tree has got my hand fixed in it. (Cf. *kwaa, kwaza, kwamua,* and syn. *shikika, fungwa, naswa, kamatwa.*)

Kwamba, conj. (*ku-amba*, saying), of very general meaning, and translatable according to the context defining the particular sense of 'saying,' intended, e. g. (1) (stating) that, so to say,—also *ya kwamba;* (2) (supposing) if, as if, suppose, even if; (3) (objecting) though. It is also used, though not commonly in Z., after the relative formed with *amba,* e. g. *ambaye kwamba*, who,—of a person, *ambalo kwamba,* which, &c., and with similar indefinite meaning in the phrase *Kwambaje?* How is it? *Kwambaje kwako?* How are you? (Cf. *kama, ya kuwa,* and see **Amba, Ambia.**)

Kwamua, v. Rv. of *kwama, kwaa,* get out of a tight place, set free, disengage, clear, loose. Ap. *kwamu-lia, -liwa.* (Cf. *kwama, kwaa,* and cf. *fungua, nanua, tatua.*)

Kwangu, (1) n. (*ku-angu*), my circumstances (condition, affairs, locality), my house. *Kwangu kuzuri,* my condition is prosperous, my surroundings are beautiful, &c. (2) adv. (for *kwa mimi*), to (with, from, &c.) me, at (in, to, from, &c.) my house. *Twende kwangu,* let us go to my house. (3) a. agreeing with D 8, and locatives in *-ni*. *Kufa kwangu,* my dying. *Nyumbani kwangu,* to my house. (So *kwako, kwake, kwetu, kwenu, kwao.*)

Kwangua, v. scrape, remove a coating, crust, or anything adhering (solid or liquid), e. g. *k. matope*, clean mud off (boots, &c.). *K. chungu,* scrape the burnt rice off the bottom of a cooking pot. *K. kucha,* pare the nails. *K. maji*, scrape up a remnant of water in a pit. Ap. *kwangu-lia, -liwa.* (No v. *kwanga* in use. Cf. *komba, paruza.*)

Kwani, (1) adv. interrog. for *Kwa nini?* What for? Why? For what reason? (cf. *mbona, kwaje*). (2) conj. for, because (cf. *kwa sababu, kwa maana, kwa ajili, kwa kuwa.*)

Kwanua, v. and **Kwanyua**, tear down, rip (split, strip) off, e. g. of branches, leaves, fruit. Ps. *kwanu-liwa.* Nt. *kwanyuka,* e. g. *panda ya mti imekwanyuka kwa mtu mzito,* the fork of the tree was split down by a heavy man. Ap. *kwanyu-lia, -liwa.* (Cf. *nyakua, pasua, rarua, ambua.*)

Kwanza, Infin. of *anza* (*ku-anza*), but often as adv., at the beginning, at first, firstly, in the first place. Also *ya k.,* often followed by *ya pili,* secondly, *ya tatu,* thirdly. *-a k.,* first, best. *Ngoja k.,* wait first (before acting), wait a bit. (Cf. *anza, mwanzo, chanzo,* and syn. Ar. *awali.*)

Kwao, (1) n. (*ku-ao*), their circumstances, their place (country, home), &c. *Mwanamke huyu ana-waza kwao,* this woman is thinking about her native country, is homesick. (2) adv. to (from, with) them. *Mfu-kuzwa kwao hana pa kwenda,* an outcast from his own people has nowhere to go. (3) a. their,—form of *-ao,* agreeing with D 8 and locatives in *-ni.* (Cf. *kwangu,* and *ku, wao.*)

Kwao, n. (*ma-*), also **Kwayo**,

stumbling-block, obstruction to the feet, difficulty. *Njia ya kwao*, a rough road, stony path. (Cf. *kwaa, mgogoro, zuio, kwaruza.*)

Kwapa, n. (*ma-*), armpit. *Futika (chukua) kwapani*, tuck (carry) under the arm. *Kisibau cha kwapa*, a sleeveless waistcoat. (Cf. *kikwapa.*)

Kwaruza, v. (1) scrape, grate, whether of action, movement (scrape along, move with difficulty), or sound (be harsh, be grating); (2) grate, be of a coarse, gritty, rough kind. E. g. *chombo kimekwaruza mwamba*, the vessel has grazed a rock. *Mchele huu unakwaruza watu*, this rice is gritty to the taste. *Njia ya kukwaruza*, a rough, stony road. (Cf. *mkwaruzo, paruza, para, kwangua*, and perh. *kwaa, kwaza*, and contr. *lainika, laini. Kwaza* appears sometimes to be a short form of *kwaruza*, with *kwazana* for *kwaruzana*, e. g. *madau yanakwazana*, the boats are colliding, scraping against each other.)

-kwasi, a. rich, wealthy, opulent. (Cf. *ukwasi*, and syn. *tajiri, mwenyi mali*, contr. *maskini, fukara*.)

Kwata, n. and **Kwato, Ukwato**, hoof. *Piga k.*, kick,—of an animal. (Cf. *piga teke.*)

Kwayo, n. (*ma-*). See **Kwao**, n.

Kwaza, v. Cs. of *kwaa*, and ? for **kwaruza** (which see).

Kwea, v. go up, get on the top of, mount, climb, ascend, rise, e. g. *k. mnazi*, or *mnazini*, climb a cocoanut tree; *k. mlima (frasi)*, mount a hill (a horse); *k. chombo*, get on board a vessel. Ps. *kwelewa*. Nt. *kweleka*. Ap. *kwelea*, e. g. *kamba ya kukwelea*, a cord to climb with. So *kwel-eza, -ezwa*. Cs. *kweza*, cause to go up, set up, raise, put one thing on another. *Kweza mashua*, haul a boat high on the beach. *Kweza bei*, raise the price of an article. *Vitu vimekwezwa*, things have been raised in price. *Kweza maturuma ya duara*, set the spokes in a wheel. *Kweza nguo*, lift the dress. *Jikweza*, boast, vaunt oneself. Hence *kwezana*. Rp. *kweana*. (Cf. *-kwezi, ukwezi*, and follg., and syn. *panda*, also *inua, simamisha.*)

Kwelea, n. *kwelea ya mawimbi, mawimbi ya kwelea*, a swell, rolling waves, as dist. from breakers. (Cf. *kwea*, and *wimbi*.)

Kweli, n. and adv., truth, truthfulness, reality, genuineness, certainty. *Kwa kweli si kwa ubishi*, seriously, not in fun. *Kweli iliyo uchungu si uwongo ulio tamu*, an unpleasing truth is better than a pleasing falsehood. *-a kweli*, true, truthful, genuine. As adv., truly, really, certainly, genuinely (cf. *hakika, yakini, halisi*).

Kweme, n. seed of a plant *mkweme*, very rich in oil.

Kwenda, (1) v. Infin. of *enda (ku-enda)*, to go; (2) used as adv., perhaps, possibly, I dare say, it may be. *Kwenda akaja leo*, perhaps he comes to-day. (Cf. *enda, huenda*, and syn. *labuda, yamkini.*)

Kwenu, (1) n. (*ku-enu*), your circumstances, place, country, home. (2) adv. (for *kwa ninyi*), to you, to your house. (3) a.—form of *-enu*, agreeing with *kupenda* and nouns in *-ni.* (Cf. *kwangu*, and *ku, -enu.*)

Kwenyi, form of *-enyi*, which see. Often used as equivalent of *kwa*, e. g. of time, *kwenyi Ijumaa*, on Friday. (So *mwenyi, penyi.*)

Kwetu, n. adv. and a., in same uses as *kwenu*, and *kwangu*, i.e. our circumstances, to us, our. The common expression for 'my (our) country, my home.' (Cf. *kwangu, ku, -etu.*)

Kweu, n. sometimes for the usual *kweupe*, clearness, dawn, light. *Mbele kweu na nyuma kweu*, brightness before and behind. (Cf. follg.)

Kweupe, n. (*ku-eupe*), brightness, whiteness, clearness, dawn, light, clear space, fine weather. *Kuna kweupe*, it is dawn, it is fine. (Cf. *-eupe, eua, weupe*, and *kweu*, and syn. *kucha*, dawn, contr. *kweusi, giza, usiku.*)

-**kwezi**, a. creeping, climbing, e. g. of a plant. (Cf. *kwea, ukwezi*, also *tambaa, -tambaazi.*)

Kwikwe, n. hiccup. *Kwikwe wa kulia*, convulsive sobbing (cf. *kitefutefu, kikeukeu*).

Kwisha, Infin. of *isha*, used as (1) n. ending, the end, extreme; (2) adv. finally, at last, in the end. *-a kwisha*, last, extreme, best, worst. (Cf. *mwisho, isha, kiisha*, and similar use of *kwanza*. Syn. for end, *kikomo, hatima, aheri.*)

L.

L represents the same sound as in English.

This sound is interchangeable in most Swahili words of Bantu origin with that of a smooth untrilled *r*, and often in words from Arab sources.

Hence words not found under *L* may be looked for under *R*.

On the other hand, the indiscriminate use of *l* and *r* makes many words of different meanings indistinguishable, and in some cases is carefully avoided, e. g. in the case of the initial sound of any word, and especially of *l-, la, li* as a formative syllable or prefix, and the dem. a. *-le*.

The *l* sound is generally latent in the long sound denoted by a vowel written twice, and sometimes heard (as in kindred dialects). In some words it is evanescent, e. g. *mlango* or *mwango*, a door; *ufalme* or *ufaume*, dominion.

After a formative *n, l* (and *r*) are represented by *d*, as in *ndefu*, for *nlefu (nrefu).*

L- (1) as a pfx. of verbs and pronom. adjs. agrees with D 5 (S), e. g. *kasha lililo lake li zito*, his box is heavy; (2) is the characteristic letter of the common demonstrative of distance, *yule*, &c. (Cf. *-le*, and *H.*)

La, v. (1) eat, consume,—of food generally (cf. *chakula*); (2) use, use up, require for use or efficiency (as material, time, &c., cf. *tumia, chukua*); (3) wear away, diminish, spend (materials, means, money). (The Infinitive form *kula* is used as the root form in certain tenses, as is the case with other monosyllabic verb-roots. See ku, 1. (*d*) and ja.) *Mlaji ni mla leo, mla jana kalani?* The eater of to-day is the man who eats, the eater of yesterday,—what has he eaten? Rarely *la* is used as the imperative, e. g. *vyakula hivi la*, eat this food. *Itakula fetha (saa nzima, siku nyingi)*, it will take money (a whole hour, several days). Ps. *liwa*, be eaten, &c. Nt. *lika*, be eaten, &c., be eatable, be fit for food. *Jiwe limeliwa na kamba*, the stone has been worn away by the rope. *Kitu hiki hakiliki*, this substance is not edible. *Chuma inalika*, iron rusts away. Ap. *lia, liana*, eat, &c. for (with, in, &c.), e. g. *mkono wa kulia*, the eating hand, the right hand. *Chumba cha kulia*, a dining room, refectory. *Kijiko cha kulia*, a spoon to eat with. *Amemlia mwenzi wali wake*, he has eaten up his friend's rice for him. *Jilia*, eat selfishly (for his own purposes, &c.), e. g. *mwana amejilia mali ya babaye*, the son has wasted his father's goods (like a fool, wilfully). *Tumeliana siku zote*, we have always had our meals together. Rp. *lana*, e. g. eat each other, all join in eating. Cs. *lisha, lishwa*, e. g. (1) cause to eat, feed, keep (animals, &c.), graze, pasture, i. e. *lisha kuku (ng'ombe, mbuzi)*, keep fowls (cows, goats). *Lisha ng'ombe majani*, feed cows on grass. *Lisha upanga viungo*, glut the sword with (dead men's) limbs. *Wanalisha miwa kinuni*, they feed the sugar-cane into the mill. (2) Eat, browse, feed on, e. g. *kulungu alisha majani*, the antelope browses on grass (cf. *malisha, malisho, chunga*). Hence *lishi-sha, -shwa*, make to eat, feed with, e. g. *lishisha sumu*, administer poison to. (Cf. *mlo, mla, mlaji, ulaji, mlafi, ulafi.*)

*La, int. no, not so, by no means. (Ar. Cf. *la ilaha illa Allah*, no God but the God, and syn. *sio, sivyo, hakuna, hapana, hasha*.)

-la, a. eating, feeding on, consuming,—verbal a. of *la*, v.

*Laana, n. (*ma-*), a curse, imprecation, oath. (Ar. Cf. *uapo, kiapo, apizo*.)

*Laani, v. curse, swear (at), damn. Ps. *laaniwa*. Nt. *laanika*. Cs. *laani-sha, -shwa*, cause to curse, get cursed, bring a curse on. (Ar. Cf. *-laanifu, laana, apa*.)

*-laanifu, a. (same with D 4 (P), D 5 (S), D 6), (1) given to cursing; (2) accursed. (Ar. Cf. *ulaanifu, laana, maleuni*.)

*Labeka, int. See Lebeka.

*Labuda, adv. often *lábuda, labda*, perhaps, it seems so, no doubt, probably, possibly. (Ar. *la-buddi*, there is no escape. Cf. *buddi*, and syn. *yamkini, yawezekana, huenda, kwenda*.)

*Ladu, n. a sweetmeat made up in balls, consisting of flour or fine grain mixed with treacle, ginger, pepper, &c.

Laika, n. (*ma-*), also Ulaika, a short, downy hair, as on the hands and human body generally. Also 'down' of birds. (Cf. *uele, unyoya*, and dist. Ar. *malaika*, an angel.)

*Laini, a. and -lainifu, (1) of things, smooth, supple, soft, pliable, of delicate texture, thin, delicate, fine (cf. *-ororo, -embamba*). (2) Of persons, facile, gentle, good-humoured (cf. *-pole, taratibu*). *Nguo l.*, smooth, fine cloth. *Mchanga l.*, fine sand. (Ar. Also as v., smoothen, but usu. as follg.)

*Lainika, v. (1) be smoothed, be made smooth; (2) fig. be softened, be appeased. Ps. *lainiwa*. Cs. *laini-sha, -shwa*, make smooth, &c. (Ar. Cf. *laini*.)

*Laiti, int. Oh that, if only, would that,—esp. of regret for what is past or impossible, and then used with verbs in the Past or Conditional Tenses. But also of hope, with the Present. E. g. *laiti safari ingalikwisha!* would that the journey had come to an end! *Laiti (kwamba) twalifika jana!* would that we had arrived yesterday! (Ar.)

Lake, a. form of *-ake*, his, hers, her, its,—agreeing with D 5 (S). Sometimes in the form *-le* affixed to a noun, e. g. *nenole*, his word.

*Laki, v. meet, go to meet, esp. in a friendly, complimentary, way. (Ar. Cf. *pokea, kuta*.)

*Lakini, conj. but, yet, however, nevertheless. (Ar. Cf. *walakini*.)

*Lakki, n. and a., a hundred thousand, a lac. (Ar.)

Lako, a. form of *-ako*, your, yours,—agreeing with D 5 (S). Sometimes in the form *-lo* affixed to a noun, e. g. *jinalo*, your name.

Lala, v. (1) lie, lie down, go to bed; (2) sleep, go to sleep; (3) settle down, fall, collapse; (4) lie flat, be spread out, be horizontal. Also *lala usingizi*, go to sleep. *Nyumba imelala chini*, the house has fallen down. *Inchi yote yalala sawasawa*, the whole country is a flat plain. *Jilala*, rest oneself, take a siesta. *Chumba chake cha kulala* (or *alicholala*), his bed-room. Ap. *lalia, laliwa, lalika, laliana*. *Lalia matanga*, sleep in the house of mourning. *Hakulaliki nyumbani kwa hari*, there is no sleeping indoors from the heat. *Mtu wa kulalia nyumba*, a night-watchman, a caretaker. *Mkeka mpya usiolaliwa*, a new mat which has never been slept upon. Hence *lalisha, lalishwa*. Cs. *laza, lazwa, lazia*. E. g. cause to lie down, put to bed, lay flat or horizontal. Rp. *lalana*, sleep at each other's houses, be on familiar terms. *Lala* (with objective pfxs., i. e. as act.), *laza*, and *lalana* are used of sexual intercourse. (Cf. for sleep, *sinzia*; for rest, *pumzika, jinyosha*.)

Lalama, v. ask for mercy (of),

make an appeal (to), cry out. *M-wivi amlalama wali apate kupona nafsi yake*, the thief throws himself on the governor's mercy to save his life. Ps. *lalam-iwa*. Nt. *lalamika*, be made to appeal for mercy, be reduced to submission, be beaten, —and so, beg for mercy, cry out for quarter. Ap. *lalamia*, e.g. *mdeni alimlalamia mwenyi mali*, the debtor threw himself on the mercy of the money-lender. Cs. *lalam-isha, -ishwa*, make cry out, bring to terms, force to confess. (Cf. *omba, kiri, ungama.*)

Lamba, v. also **Ramba**, lick, lick up with the tongue. *L. makombo ya sahani*, lick up the scraps on the plate. Ps. *lambwa*. *Haulambwi mkono mtupu*, an empty hand is not licked. Nt. *lambika*. Ap. *lamb-ia, -iwa*. *Lambiwa damu mkononi*, have the blood licked off the hand. Cs. *lamb-isha, -ishwa*. Rp. *lambana*. (Cf. *ulambilambi.*)

*****Lami**, n. pitch, tar.

Lango, n. (*ma-*), (1) city gate, large gate, gateway; (2) *malango* is used of secret instruction given to girls and boys on growing up. (Cf. *mlango, kilango*, and *kunga*.)

Langu, a. form of -*angu*, my, mine,—agreeing with D 5 (S). (Cf. *l-* and -*angu*.)

Lao, a. form of -*ao*, their, theirs,—agreeing with D 5 (S). (Cf. *l-*, and -*ao*.)

Lapa, v. finish off hastily, eat up ravenously, dismiss promptly. (Not common in Z. Cf. *hula kwa pupa*.)

*****Laumu**, v. reproach, find fault with, reprove, upbraid, blame, charge with a crime, accuse. Ps. *laum-iwa*. Nt. *laumika*. Ap. *laum-ia, -iwa*. Cs. *laum-isha, -ishwa*, intens. scold, rebuke sharply. Rp. *laumiana*. — n. (*ma-*), reproach, charge, blame, reproof. (Ar. Cf. *karipia, kemea, suta, nenea, rudi.*)

*****Lazimu**, v. be obligatory (on), be a necessity (to), be binding (on), bind, make responsible, put pressure on. *Sheria imemlazimu mfalme*, the law has bound (condemned) the king. *Tunakulazimu wee*, we make you responsible. Ps. *lazimiwa*, be bound, be under obligation, be responsible, &c. Ap. *lazim-ia, -iwa*. Cs. *lazim-isha, -ishwa*, intens. put strong pressure on, force, compel. *Jilazimisha na*, devote oneself to, accept full responsibility for. — n. also **Lázima, Lázim**, necessity, obligation, engagement, surety, bail, responsibility. E.g. *chukua l.*, bail, go bail. *Ni l. juu yako*, it is obligatory on you. *Si l.*, commonly means an absolute prohibition, i.e. it is imperative (obligatory, &c.) not to. *Si l. kuingia ndani, usipopiga hodi*, you must never enter a house without saying 'hodi.' (Ar. Cf. *sharti, farathi, bidi, juzu*.)

-le, final, (1) characteristic of a. demonstr. 'that' (see **Yule**); (2) sometimes a contraction for *lake*, e.g. *jinale*, his name (cf. *-lo* for *iako*); (3) subjunct. mood of *-la*, v. eat.

Lea, v. bring up, rear, nurse, educate. *Mtoto umleavyo, ndivyo akuavyo*, as you bring up a child, so he grows up. Ps. *lewa*, e.g. *amelewa vema*, he has been well brought up. (Cf. *mlezi, malezi*, and dist. *lewa*, be drunk.)

*****Lebasi**, n. and **Libasi**, clothes, raiment, wearing apparel. *Killa lebasi ya kiarabu*, all kinds of Arab clothes. (Arab. Cf. *nguo, mavazi.*)

*****Lebeka**, int. and **Labeka**, At your service, Yes, sir (madam)!—in answer to a call, Coming! I am here! A common reply of a slave or inferior to a master's call, and often pronounced *ebbe*, or simply *bee*. (Ar. phrase 'Here I am at your service.' Cf. *inshallah, eewalla, bismilla*, &c.)

Legea, v. **Regea** is also common, (1) be loose (slack, relaxed, soft, pliable); (2) be faint (weak, remiss), flag, yield, give in. E.g. of the body, effect of illness, hunger, exhaustion, &c.—or of a rope, &c. Cs. *leg-eza, -ezwa, -ezea,* loosen, slacken, exhaust, cause to yield, &c. (Cf. *-legefu, mlegeo, fungua, thoofika,* and dist. Ar. *regea* or *rejea,* return,—unless *legea* is orig. go back.)

-legefu, a. (same with D 4 (P), D 5 (S), D 6), slack, relaxed, weak, soft, yielding, remiss, inattentive, idle. (Cf. *legea, ulegefu,* and cf. *thaifu, -zembe, -vivu.*)

*Lehemu, v. solder, apply solder, repair with solder. Ps. *lehemiwa.* Nt. *lehemika.* Ap. *lehem-ia, -iwa.* Cs. *lehem-isha, -ishwa.* — n. also Lihamu, solder. *Tia l.,* apply solder. (Ar.)

Lekea, v. also Elekea, which see,—also for derivatives, *lekeza, lekeana,* &c.

Lema, n. (1) a variant of *dema,* a wicker fish-trap (see Dema). (2) a. occasional form of *-ema,* good,—agreeing with D 5 (S), i.e. following the analogy of the pronominal adjectives (like *-ote, -enye,* and a few other adjectives).

Lemaa, n. defect, deformity, disfigurement, blemish, mutilation. *-enyi lemaa,* deformed, maimed, crippled, &c. (Cf. follg. and *kilema.*)

Lemaza, v. Cs. maim, mutilate, disfigure, &c. (Cf. *lemaa, kilema.*)

Lemea, v. sometimes Elemea (cf. *lekea, elekea*), (1) press forward, go on steadily, push on; (2) press upon, rest heavily on, lie on the top of; (3) oppress, be burdensome, discommode. E.g. *tuzidi kulemea mbele,* let us press on faster. *Mzigo unamlemea,* his load is a heavy one. *Kasha lililemea juu ya kasha,* one box rested on another. *Nalilemea njia,* I pressed hard on the road, i.e. I walked fast. Ps. *lemewa,* be burdened, be oppressed, &c. Cs. *lem-eza, -ezwa,* e.g. pile up, place a load on, and so, oppress, burden. Hence *lemezana.* Rp. *lemeana,* lie on (lean on, rest against, press) each other. (Cf. *pagaa.*)

Lenga, v. *Lenga muhogo,* cut cassava in slices.

Lengelenge, n. (*ma-*), a blister. *Fanya (toka, tokwa na) malengelenge,* to get blistered.

Lenu, a. form of *-enu,* your, yours (plur.),—agreeing with D 5 (S). (Cf. *-l* and *-enu.*)

Leo, n. and adv., to-day, this day, the present time. Also *siku ya leo,* to-day. *Leo hivi,* this very day. *Si leo,* not to-day, long ago. *Si -a leo,* old, out of date.

Lepe, n. (*ma-*), or Leppe, Lepee, drowsiness, faintness, a heavy slumberous condition. *L. la usingizi,* sleepiness, drowsiness. *Fanya l.,* be drowsy. *Huyu ni lepee,* this man is drowsy, hard to rouse.

Leso, n. (—, and *ma-*), handkerchief,—of printed calico, often worn round the neck or on the head. *L. ya upande mmoja,* the 'scarf' of commerce, one piece forming a *kanga,* i.e. a woman's dress. *L. ya kushona,* handkerchief,—two pieces of three handkerchiefs each being sewn together to make a *kanga.*

Leta, v. bring, fetch, supply, cause to come to where a person is,—thus supplying a Cs. of *-ja,* come. Ps. *letwa.* Nt. rarely heard, *leteka.* Ap. *let-ea, -ewa, -eana.* Letewa, have (a thing) brought to. *Waliletewa chakula,* they were brought food. *Leteana barua,* exchange letters, correspond. Cs. *let-esha, -eshwa, -eza, -ezwa.* Rp. *letana.* (Cf. *chukua, peleka.*)

Letu, a. form of *-etu,* our, ours,—agreeing with D 5 (S). (Cf. *l* and *-enu.*)

-levi, a. drunken, intoxicated, given to drinking. (Cf. *levya, lewa, levuka, ulevi, kileo,* and *-lafi* from *-la.*)

Levuka, v. get sober, become

sober, become steady—in manner, gait, &c.—a Rv. Nt. form. (Cf. prec. and *lewa*.)

Levya, v. make drunk, intoxicate, cause to reel, make stagger, make giddy. *Jilevya*, make oneself drunk, get intoxicated. Also Rd. *levya-levya*—a Cs. form in *-ya*, cf. *ponya*. (Cf. prec.)

Lewa, v. be drunk (giddy, intoxicated), stagger, sway, reel, wave to and fro. *Lewa kwa pombe*, be drunk on native beer. *Lewa kwa bahari*, of the effects of sea-sickness,—be giddy. *Dau lalewa*, of a boat on a rough sea,—roll and pitch. Also Rd. *lewa-lewa*, reel and stagger. (Cf. *levya*, *levuka*, *-levi*, *ulevi*, *kileo*, and dist. *lewa*, Ps. of *lea*, rear, educate.)

Li, verb-form, (it) is,—agreeing with D 5 (S), e.g. *kasha li zito*, the box is heavy.

Li-, -li, (1) verb- and pron. a. pfx.,—agreeing with D 5 (S), e.g. *ulichukue kasha lile*, carry that box. (2) sign of Past Tense Affirmative, and also with *a-*, i.e. *-ali-*, and forms part of the Past Conditional Tense sign, *-ngali-*. (3) verb-form representing sometimes (and in some other Bantu dialects regularly) the present Tense of *wa*, be, with or without *a* prefixed, but not used to denote absolute existence, e.g. *nili* (*nali*), I am, *nikali*, and I am. *Ali*, he is. It is regularly used in connexion with the relative, i.e. *aliye*, he who is, not *awaye*; *walio*, they who are, not *wawao*; *lililo*, that which is, not *liwalo*.

Lia, v. (1) sound, make a sound (the most general word for sound of any kind, in animate or inanimate nature); (2) utter a cry, cry out (for joy, sorrow, pain, &c.); (3) mourn, weep. *Chuma yalia*, iron has a ring. *Panalia wazi*, the place sounds hollow. *Ndege analia*, the bird is singing. *Bunduki zalia*, guns are going off (sounding). *Lia machozi*, shed tears, cry. *Lia ng'oa* (*uwivu*), cry from passion (jealousy). Ap. *lilia, liliwa*, cry to (for, at, with, &c.), sound in harmony with, &c. *Liliwa*, be mourned for, &c. *Jililia*, bewail oneself. Cs. *liza, lizwa, lizana*, cause to sound, make cry, cause (or, be the occasion of) crying. *Lizana*, weep together, weep over each other. *Liza bunduki*, fire off a gun. *Jiliza*, pretend to cry, sham sorrow, shed mock tears. Rp. *liana*, e.g. of harmonious, concerted sounds, or general mourning, &c. (Cf. *mlio, kilio*, and *sauti, vuma, imba, nguruma*, &c.)

***Libasi**, n. See Lebasi. (Arab.)

Licha, conj. and *licha ya*, prep. let alone, not to say, much more (less). E.g. *sikupata robo moja, licha reale*, I did not get a shilling, not to mention (much less) a dollar. *Licha ya haya, hatta mangine mabaya*, apart from these, there are other bad points. *Licha tawi lilioiva, hatta bichi liko*, not to mention ripe bunches, there are unripe too. *Licha ya ndege moja, hatta wote ntakupa*, one bird is nothing, I will give you all of them.

***Lihamu**, n. solder. See Lehemu. (Ar.)

***Lijamu**, n. bit (of a horse). *Seruji na lijamu na vigwe*, saddle, bit, and reins. (Ar.)

Lika, v. Nt. of la, eat (which see).

Likiza, v. (1) give leave (respite, relief, holiday) to, release, let go; (2) dismiss, send away, make go, not allow to stay. Thus *likiza mtoto* may mean (1) give a boy a holiday, or (2) wean a child (cf. *achisha*). Ps. *likizwa*. Ap. *likiz-ia, -iwa*. Cs. *likiz-isha, -ishwa*. Rp. *likizana*. (Cf. *ondosha, ruhusu, achisha, chezesha*.)

Lima, v. Hoe,—the only native mode of cultivation, hence generally 'cultivate, work land.' Ps. *limwa*. Nt. *limika*, e.g. be fit for cultivation, arable. Ap. *lim-ia, -iwa*, e.g. *jembe la kulimia*, a hoe to dig with.

Cs. *lim-isha, -ishwa, -ishia,* &c., e.g. of the overseer (*msimamizi*), get hoeing done, or of the Mahommedan minister (*mwalimu*), give permission to begin hoeing. (Cf. follg. and *mlimo, mkulima, kilimo.*)

-limaji, a. engaged in agriculture. *Mlimaji,* same as *mkulima.* (Cf. *lima.*)

Limatia, v. be delayed, remain behind, be late, be too long. *Safari inalimatia,* the expedition is delayed. Ps. *limatiwa.* Cs. *limat-isha,-ishwa.* (Seldom in Z. Cf. syn. *kawia, chelewa, siri.*)

Limau, n. (*ma-*), a lemon, fruit of the *mlimau.*

Limbika, v. (1) allow time for, wait for; (2) keep from, let remain, reserve, economize, put aside (in store); (3) bear with, be patient to, show consideration for. E.g. *limbika maji,* wait for water,—at an exhausted or slow-running well. *L. ndizi (buni),* wait for bananas (coffee) to ripen. *L. nyele,* let the hair grow. *L. maneno,* to answer slowly, deliberately. *L. watu,* not to overwork people, treat with consideration. Ps. *limbikwa,* e.g. *nazi hulimbikwa juu ya mnazi hatta zikakauka,* the cocoanuts are left on the tree till quite dry, i.e. when wanted for seed. Ap. *limbik-ia,-iwa,* e.g. *amelimbikia watoto mali,* he has reserved (laid up) money for his children. (Cf. follg.)

Limbiko, n. (*ma-*), anything reserved, put away in store, hoard, reserve. (Cf. *limbika,* and follg., and syn. *akiba.*)

Limbuka, v. come to an end of waiting for, get the result of waiting (care, consideration, prudence), enjoy a looked-for advantage, have a first taste of pleasure deferred, enjoy the first-fruits, get the benefit of, use for the first time. E.g. *watu wanalimbuka leo vitu vya mwaka,* people are now beginning to enjoy the year's produce. *Kwenda kulimbuka katika shamba lake,* go to enjoy the first-fruits of his estate. Ps. *limbukwa.* Ap. *limbuk-ia,-iwa.* Cs. *limbu-sha, -shwa,* e.g. reward waiting, give a foretaste of, satisfy hope deferred, yield the wished-for result, answer expectations. (Cf. *limbika,* and follg.)

Limbuko, n. (*ma-*), first-fruits, reward of waiting, fulfilment of hope, foretaste of reward. (Cf. prec.)

-limi, a. talkative, chatting, long-winded. (Cf. *ulimi,* tongue, and *mwenyi domo.*)

Linda, v. (1) defend, protect; guard, watch, keep safe; (2) keep off, fend off, guard against, watch for. E.g. *angeuawa, lakini Muungu amemlinda,* he would have been killed, but God protected him. *Jilinde, nami ntakulinda,* defend yourself and I will defend you. *Linda kingojo ndege wasile matunda,* keep watch lest birds eat the fruit. *Mlinzi hulinda ndege,* the watchman watches against the birds. *Mke mzuri halindwi,* a pretty woman is not driven away, or, is not (easily) kept safe. Ps. *lindwa.* Nt. *lindika.* Ap. *lind-ia, -iwa,* e.g. *nimemlindia shamba lake,* I have guarded his plantation for him. Cs. *lind-isha,-ishwa.* Rp. *lindana.* (Cf. *mlinzi, lindo, ulinzi.*)

Lindi, n. (*ma-*), a deep place, deep channel, hole,—esp. in water, the sea. Also *l. la choo,* cesspool. (There is a town called *Lindi* on the coast south of Zanzibar, another *Malindi* (or *Melindi*) north, and a district of Zanzibar city is also called *Malindi.*)

Lindo, n. (*ma-*), a watching-place, station, post (to guard). (Cf. *linda,* and *kingojo.*)

Linga, v. (1) make equal, put side by side, match, compare, suit, level, smooth, straighten, harmonize; (2) be equal, be like, suit, harmonize, fit. *L. bunduki,* level a gun, take aim (cf. *elekeza*). *L. nguo,* try on clothes, be measured for clothes. *L. kichwa,* of a movement in dancing,—bending the head forward and sweeping round. *Watu pia wamelinga kiatu hiki*, every one has tried on this shoe,—of Cinderella's slipper. Ps. *lingwa*. Nt. *lingika*. Ap. *ling-ia, -iwa*. Rp. *lingana*, e.g. match, be like, be level, harmonize,—also, make a suitable reply. Also *linganya, linganisha*, ? *linganyua*. (Cf. *-linganifu*.)

-linganifu, a. (same with D 4 (P), D 5 (S), D 6), agreeing, matched, similar, suitable, harmonious, regular. (Cf. *linga, ulinganifu*.)

Linganya, v. Cs. of Linga (which see), e.g. suit, match, harmonize, tune (an instrument).

Lini, adv. interrog., When? At what time? (Cf. syn. *wakati gani? saa ngapi? siku ipi?*)

Lio, n. (*ma-*), sound, loud cry, shout, roar, loud wailing. *Malio ya kiko*, the bubbling sound of a native pipe (with a water-bowl). (Cf. *lia, mlio, kilio*.)

Lipa, v. (1) pay, give in payment, repay, make a return for, recompense, compensate, reward; (2) have to pay, suffer (for). *Lipa deni*, pay a debt. *Nikulipe mema yako uliyonitendea*, let me pay back your kindness to me. *Lipa kisasi*, suffer vengeance, —also, take vengeance, i.e. pay back. Ps. *lipwa*. Nt. *lipika*. Ap. *lip-ia, -iwa*, pay to (for, on behalf of, &c.), avenge. Cs. *lip-isha, -ishwa, -iza, -izwa, -izana*, make pay, exact a return from, &c. *Lipiza kisasi*, take vengeance on. *Jilipiza*, pay oneself by force, take as one's due, and with *kisasi*, avenge oneself on. (Cf. *lipo, lipizi*.)

Lipizi, n. (*ma-*), forced payment, exaction, vengeance. (Cf. *lipa, lipo*.)

Lipo, n. (*ma-*), payment, recompense, revenge. (Cf. *lipa*.)

*Lisani, n. tongue, flap,—used of the flap under the opening of a *kanzu* in front. (Ar.)

*Lisasi, n. (—, and *ma-*), also Risasi, (1) lead (the metal); (2) a bullet. (Cf. *malisaa, popoo*.)

Liwa, n. sweet-scented wood brought from Madagascar, like sandal-wood. It is grated, mixed with water, and used as a perfume. (Cf. *sandali, mliwa*.)

*Liwali, n. (*ma-*), also Wali, governor, headman, i.e. the Arab official representing the Sultan of Zanzibar, or supreme government. (Ar. *il wali*, changed to *liwali*, cf. *tawala*.)

Liza, v. (1) cause to buy, induce to buy, sell to, e.g. *mbona watu unawaliza?* Why are you getting people to buy? (seems to be conn. with *uza*, sell, as if for *uliza*, see *uza*). (2) Cs. of *lia*, cause to sound, make cry.

Liza, n. (—), door chain. See Riza.

Lo, a. relative, agreeing with D 5 (S), 'which, that.' Seldom used independently except in such a phrase as *kasha lo lote*, any box whatsoever. *Hakufanya (neno) lo lote*, he did nothing at all. (Cf. *l*, and *-o*.)

-lo, a. (1) short form of *lako*, appended sometimes to D 5 (S), e.g. *jinalo*, your name, i.e. *jina lako*. Also (2) in verbs, 'which, that,' agreeing with D 5 (S), *neno alilolinena*, the word which he spoke.

Lo, Loo, int. of pleasure, wonder, horror, &c.,—the intensity of feeling being represented by the indefinite prolongation of the vowel sound.

Loa, -loefu. See Lowa, -lowefu.

Loga, v. bewitch, use enchantment on, place under a spell or charm. Ps. *logwa*. (Cf. *uganga, uchawi, mwanga*, and *pagaza*.)

Loo, int. See Lo.

Lowa, v. and Loa, get wet, be soaked (drenched, saturated), be damp. Nt. *loweka*, (1) get wet,— same as *lowa*, and (2) make wet, drench, souse, e.g. *loweka nguo*, put clothes to soak. Ps. *lowekwa*, be wetted, drenched, soaked, &c. Cs. *low-esha, -eshwa*. Rp. *lowana*, i. e. all get wet together. (Both the *l* and *w* sounds are evanescent, and so *oa, oeka, oana* may be heard. Cf. follg. and *tia maji, rutubisha, chovya*.)

Lowama, v. be in a wet condition, be soaked, &c., and Ap. *lowamia*. Cs. *lowamisha*. (A St. form. Cf. *lowa*, and follg.)

-lowefu, a. and -loefu (same with D 4 (P), D 5 (S), D 6), wet, moist, damp, soaking. *Fanya gundi iloweke katika maji hatta ilowame*, let the gum be steeped in water, till it is thoroughly soaked. (Cf. *lowa*, and syn. *maji maji, chepe chepe, -a rutuba*.)

*Lozi, n. (*ma-*), an almond,—from the tree *mlozi*.

Luba, n. a leech. See Mruba.

*Lugha, n. language, speech. *L. ya kiunguja na kimvita ni mbali kidogo*, the language of Zanzibar and Mombasa differ slightly. (Ar. Cf. syn. *maneno*, and use of *ki-*.)

Lulu, n. a pearl. *Kuzamia l.*, to dive for pearls. *Bora kama l.*, as beautiful as a pearl. As a type of perfection, *l.* is playfully used in salutation. *Hujambo kama lulu?* Are you as well, as a pearl (is beautiful)? (Cf. for gems, *kito, almasi, firuzi*, &c.)

Lungu, n. (*ma-*). See Rungu.

Lungula, v. and Rungula, treat with violence, extort money from, blackmail, threaten, rob. Not often heard in Z. (Cf. *mlungula, hongo, nyang'anya*.)

*Luththa, n. taste, flavour, savour. (Ar. Cf. *utamu*.)

M.

M represents the same sound as in English. But beside this purely consonantal sound, it includes also a semi-vowel sound, very common in Swahili, capable of bearing an accent and so of being treated as a distinct syllable. This semi-vowel sound might be represented in many words by writing *m* with a *u* preceding or following, i. e. *mu-, um-*. But the vocalization of *m* is in Zanzibar so slight, and yet so characteristic, that *mw-* is best written for *mu-* before a vowel, and *m* written *m'*, when it is necessary to indicate its distinct syllabic character,—a necessity, however, which does not occur very often in practice. Thus the *m* is strictly the same in *mtoto* and *mtu, mtini* and *mti*, but as in Swahili the accent always falls on the last syllable but one, the *m* in *mtoto* and *mtini* has little more than a consonantal force, and the words may be scanned as disyllables, while in *mtu, mti, m* has a distinct syllabic force sufficiently shown by the form of the word and ordinary rules of Swahili pronunciation. On the other hand, *m* may well be written *m'* in words like *am'ka, alim'pa*, &c., and *mu* in words like *muhogo, muhindi* (which see).

M (like *k*, and the vowel *a*) is one of the commonest and most characteristic sounds of the Swahili language, owing to its wide use as a formative in Swahili generally, and also in Arabic words adopted and adapted for Swahili use, and though somewhat un-English it is not difficult for a foreigner to become accustomed to. In the Arabic words common in Swahili, *m, mu*, and *ma* generally point to verbal nouns of time, place, &c. or to the participles formed with *m*,—their accidental similarity to common Bantu forms helping to their adoption and adaptation, even when the original force of the Arab. formative is disregarded. E. g. the names *Muhamadi* (or *Mhamadi*), *Mabruki*, and *mathbuha, mathbahu*, &c. It is so common as a formative of verbal nouns, that it is impossible to give in this Dictionary all such nouns, actual or potential, in Swahili.

Many must therefore be looked for, if not found under *m*, *mw-* (or the other common pfxs. *ma-*, *mb-*), under the letter next following, where at least the root-meaning may be indicated.

M, as a simple independent syllable, is a verb-form '(you) are,' used like other person prefixes for *ni*, agreeing with the Pronoun of 2 Pers. Plur. e.g. *ninyi m watu wazuri*, you are fine people.

M (or *mw-* before a vowel, and in some words *mu-*) is, as a formative A. of nouns, (1) the characteristic initial sound (properly semi-vocal, but often practically consonantal, as noticed above) of D 1 (S), D 2 (S), and of adjectives agreeing with them other than pronominal (which as a rule begin with *w*, i.e. *u*, not *mu*, e.g. *mtu wangu*, *mti wenyewe*). The omission of *m* before words of these declensions has the effect of transferring them to D 5, usually giving them an amplificative meaning. (2) a formative of verbal nouns, prefixed at pleasure to any verbal stem, act. or pass., and forms a noun denoting 1. a personal agent (or patient) and (*a*) if the final vowel of the verb stem is unchanged, the noun is so completely verbal as usually to govern a noun following, e.g. *mla watu*, a cannibal,—but (*b*) if such final vowel is changed to -*e*, -*i*, or has -*ji* affixed, the noun is a true noun, -*e* often indicating a passive force, -*ji* an habitual agent, e.g. *mneni*, *mchungaji*, *mkate*. 2. If the final vowel is -*o*, the noun denotes an action or thing acting, not a personal agent. Cf. *mshindo*, *mwanzo*, *mzunguko*, &c.

B. In adjectives, a prefix agreeing (1) with D 2 (S), D 4 (S), e.g. *mtu mwema*, *mti mzuri* (but obs. that in the pronom. adj. *angu*, -*ako*, &c., *w* (for *u*) takes the place of *mw*, e.g. *mtu wangu*, and also in the adj. -*ote*, -*enyi*, -*enyewe*, in agreement with D 2 (S), D 4 (S), e.g. *mti wenyewe*), and (2) with nouns ending with the locative -*ni*, when indicating place or circumstances within which something happens, e.g. *nyumbani mwangu*, in my house. It is also prefixed to adjectives (3) with the same general force as *ku*, e.g. *mzuri humo*, like *kuzuri huko*, it is nice there. *Mwenyi* (or *kwenyi*) *saa moja*, at one (seven) o'clock, in one hour.

C. In verbs, (1) subjective pfx. of the 2 Pers. Plur., and occasionally, with -*ni* affixed to the verb, objective of the same, e.g. *mwapenda*, you love, *ampendani*, he loves you, (2) objective pfx. of 3 Pers. S. agreeing with D 1 (S), and also (3) subjective of the same, when the reference is to environment generally or place in particular, like *ku* and *pa*, e.g. *mnamo*, there is (in) there, and *mna*, there is (in) there. *Mnanuka humo*, there is a smell in there.

Obs. adjectives are as a rule in this Dictionary placed under the first letter of their root. But a number of adjectives practically confined by their meaning to D 1 are also for convenience given under *m*, as their most common singular form, and as often used of persons without any noun, and so practically nouns themselves. (Cf. *mo*, *mu*, *mwa*, and *ku*, *pa*.)

Ma-, as an initial syllable—1. is in most words of Arabic origin the Arabic formative of verbal nouns and participles, but from its identity of form it is sometimes treated by Swahili instinct as the B. formative of the plur. of D 5 (cf. same tendency as to the formative *ki*, e.g. *kitabu*, plur. *vitabu*). 2. as a formative proper in Swahili, *ma-* is (*a*) the plur. pfx. of D 5 and of adjectives agreeing with them (other than pronominal adjectives, these having *y*- for *ma-*). (*b*) a plur. pfx. denoting what is large of its kind. Thus many nouns have practically two plurals, expressing different degrees of size or importance, e.g. *pete*, as D 6, is a ring of moderate or ordinary size, plur. *pete*; but *pete*, plur. *mapete*, rings of unusual size (cf. the dim. *kipete*, a small ring, plur. *vipete*). (*c*) the plur. pfx. of most foreign words, even when the singular is treated as D 1, e.g. *sultani*, plur. *masultani*. (*d*) used with some adjectival roots with the meaning usually conveyed by the prefix *u*, e. g. *makali ya upanga*, the sharpness (or, edge) of a sword; *mapana ya mti*, the thickness (girth, diameter) of a tree; *makuu*, pride; and cf. *usumbuo*, (active) annoyance; *masumbuo*, annoying acts, and, when these are regarded collectively, 'annoyance' in general, like the sing. (*e*) as the plur. pfx. of nouns, which in the sing. usually occur as D 4, and some of these nouns have accordingly two plurals. In this case, *ma-* (1) often denotes concrete instances of what is in the sing. usually abstract, e. g. *uamkizi*, visiting in general; *maamkizi*, particular visits. (2) as a plur. pfx. of verbal nouns from an act. or pass. stem, e.g. *masifu, masifiwa, matakwa*, but the corresponding sing. is not used. It may also (3) refer to relative size, cf. (*b*) above. Obs. (1) the prefix *ma-* when followed by *e, i*, or *o*, coalesces with it to form an *e* sound, e.g. *makasha meupe* (*ma-eupe*), *mengi* (*ma-ingi*), *meroro* (*ma-eroro*). (2) the words given under *ma-* in this Dictionary are mainly either (*a*) of Arabic origin and form, or (*b*) used only or mostly in the plur., or (*c*) used in plur. with a meaning somewhat different from that of the sing., or (*d*) of unusual meaning. Words beginning with *ma-*, not found under *ma-*, may be looked for under the letter following *ma-*, or under *u* followed by that letter.

-ma (*-ama*) is the characteristic termination of what may be called the Stative form or conjugation of the Swahili verb, denoting a relatively permanent state or condition, e. g. *kwama, simama, fumbana, tuama*, &c. See also *-mana, -ama*.

*Maabudu, n. an object (objects) of worship. (Ar. Cf. *abudu, ibada*.)

*Maádam, conj. (1) when, while, since; (2) since, if, seeing that, because. E. g. *maddam amtaka*, when (as long as) he wants him. *Maddam ya kufika wewe huku*, since your arrival here. (Arab., not often heard. Cf. *wakati wa*, and *-po*.)

*Maafikano, n. plur. (1) agreement, contract, bargain, settlement; (2) mutual understanding (respect, esteem). *Nina maafikano naye*, I am on good terms with him. (Cf. *afiki, mwafaka*, and syn. *maagano, mkataba*.)

*Maakuli, n., and Makuli, victuals, food. (Arab. Cf. syn. *chakula*.)

*Maalum, a. well-known, recognized, true. (Arab. Cf. *elimu*.)

Maamkio, Maamkizi, n. plur., visits, acts of visiting. (Cf. *am'ka, zuru*.)

*Maamuma, n. an utter fool, blockhead, simpleton, ignoramus. (? Ar. Cf. syn. *mjinga, mshenzi, kafiri*.)

Maamuzi, n. plur., and Maam'zi, judgement, arbitration, verdict. (Cf. *amua, mwamuzi*, and syn. *hukumu*.)

*Maana, n. (1) cause, reason, sake, consideration; (2) meaning, import, purpose, intention; (3) reasonableness, sobriety, sense. E. g. *kwa maana (ya)*, because (of), on account of, for the sake of, considering (that). *Tia maanani*, keep in mind, ponder, reflect on. *Maneno ya m.*, statements of importance. *Waume wenyi m.*, manly, sensible persons. *Asiojua maana, haambiwi maana*, he who does not know the meaning will not be told it. Often (4) as conj., because, in order to (that).

Maandalio, n. plur., preparation, esp. of food, cooking and serving a meal. (Cf. *andaa, uandao, maandasi*.)

Maandamano, Maandamizi, n.

plur., a following, train, procession. (Cf. *andamana*.)

Maandasi, n. plur., used of any kind of confectionery, and sweet cooked dishes, e.g. pastry, pies, tarts, puddings, jams, cakes, buns, &c. Various kinds are *bumunda, ladu, kitumbua, mkate wa kumimina (wa kusonga, wa sinia, wa tambi, wa mofa), nyang'amba*, &c. *M. ya mayai*, an omelette. *Sinia ya maandasi*, a tray for sweetmeats. (Cf. *andaa*, and prec.)

Maandikio, n. plur., place (time, manner, &c.) of putting ready, preparation, arrangement, esp. of serving up meals. (Cf. *andika, mwandishi*, &c., and follg.)

Maandiko, n. plur., (1) setting in order, arranging, putting ready; (2) things set in order, arrangements, &c.; (3) esp. things written, writings, report, description. (Cf. *andika, mwandiko*, and *mkono*.)

Maandishi, n. plur., like *maandiko*, but esp. of preparing and serving food, food served, &c. Also of writing, handwriting. (Cf. prec.)

Maanga, a. *Maji maanga*, clear, transparent water. (Cf. *-angafu, anga*, &c.)

Maangalizi, n. plur., careful attention. (Cf. *angalia*.)

Maangamizi, n. plur., utter ruin, destruction, collapse. *M. ya kesho*, ruin in the next world, eternal damnation. (Cf. *angamia*.)

Maanguko, n. plur., fall, collapse, fallen remains, ruins. *M. ya maji*, cataract, cascade, waterfall. (Cf. *anguka*.)

Maao, n. plur., and **Maawio**. *Maao ya jua* (i.e. *mawao*, cf. *waa*), sunrise, the orient, east (cf. *macho ya jua*). (In Z. *mashariki* is usual.)

Maapizo, n. plur., imprecations, curses, denunciations. (Cf. *apa, apiza*.)

*__Maarifa__, n. knowledge, information, intelligence, news. *Mambo ni maarifa, si nguvu*, the world is ruled by knowledge, not by force. (Ar. Cf. *arifu, taarifu*, and follg., and syn. *elimu, busara, akili*.)

*__Maarufu__, a. known, celebrated, famous. (Ar. Cf. prec.)

*__Maasi__, n. any repudiation of obligation (duty, right), i.e. disobedience, rebellion, mutiny, disloyalty, apostasy, desertion of wife or children, &c. (Cf. *asi, uasi*, and syn. *halifu, thulumu*.)

Maawio, n. plur. See **Maao**.

*__Maazimu__, n. a loan, a debt. (Ar. Cf. *azimu, kopa*, and syn. *deni, karatha*.)

*__Mabruki__, n. a common Swahili name,—meaning blessed. (Ar. Cf. *bariki, mbaraka*.)

*__Maburudisho__, **Maburudu**, n. recreation, refreshment, relief. (Ar. Cf. *baridi, burudisha*.)

*__Machela__, n. litter, palanquin, sling or hammock for carrying a person. (Cf. *tusi*.)

Macheleo, n. plur. objects of fear (reverence, awe). (Cf. *cha*, v., fear, and *afa*.)

Macheo, n. plur. for *machweo*. *Macheo ya jua*, sunset, the west. (In Z. *magaribi* is usual. Cf. *cha*, v., and *machwa*.)

Machinjo, n. plur. slaughter, massacre, place of slaughter. Also *machinjio*, slaughter-house. (Cf. *chinja*.)

Macho, n. plur. (1) eyes (sing. *jicho*, which see), and as a. awake, on the alert; (2) *macho ya jua*, sunrise, east. (Cf. *cha*, v., dawn, and *maao*.)

Machubwichubwi, n. pl. mumps.

Machukio, n. plur., (1) objects of hate, abomination, offence; (2) and **Machukizo**, feeling of hate, hatred, disgust, aversion, loathing. *Namchukia machukio makuu*, I utterly detest him. (Cf. *chuki, chukia*.)

Machunga, n. plur. pasturage, pastures, feeding-places for animals. (Cf. *chunga*, and *malisha, lisha*.)

Machwa, n. plur. *Machwa ya*

jua, sunset, west. (Cf. *cha*, v., and *macheo* for *machweo*, follg.)

Machweo, n. plur. *Machweo ya jua*, as *machwa*.

Madadi, n. a preparation of opium, made up in pellets for smoking. (Cf. *afyuni, kasumba, bangi*.)

*__Madaha__, n. plur. airs, graces, fascinating manners. *Fanya (piga) m.*, show off, make a display,—of personal attractions.

Madai, n. plur. occupation or profession of an advocate. Also lawsuit, legal claims. (Cf. *dai, dawa*.)

Madanganya, n. plur. tricks, imposture, deception, illusion, cheating. (Cf. *danganya, hila, ujanja, werevu*.)

Madaraka, n. plur. arrangements, responsible management, care, direction. *M. ya nyumba*, house-keeping. (Cf. *diriki*, and syn. *matengenezo, maandiko*.)

Madende, n. plur. *Sauti ya madende*, an affected style of singing, with trills, quavers, protracted notes, &c.

Madevu, n. plur. beard, beard-like appendage or growth, e. g. of plants, maize, &c. (Cf. *udevu*, plur. *ndevu, kidevu*.)

Madifu, the fibrous envelope which binds the young cocoanut leaf to the parent stem. (Cf. *kilifu*.)

*__Madini__, n. metal,—of any kind. (Ar. For metals known in Z. cf. *chuma*, iron; *shaba*, copper, brass; *bati*, tin; *risasi*, lead; *thahabu*, gold; *fetha*, silver.)

Madoadoa, n. used as a., spotted, speckled. (Cf. *doa*, and *marakaraka*.)

Maelezi, n. plur. floating, being afloat, anchorage, roadstead, moderately deep water. (Cf. *elea, chelezo*, and follg.)

Maelezo, n. plur. explanations, descriptions, comment. (Cf. *elea, eleza*, and prec.)

Mafa, n. plur. place of burial, cemetery. (Cf. *fa*. In Z. *makaburi, maziara* are usual.)

Mafaa, n. use, utility, profit, advantage, e. g. *ng'ombe hizi hazina mafaa*, these oxen are no good. (Cf. *faa, vifaa, faida*, and syn. *uchumi*.)

Maficho, n. plur. concealment, place of concealment, hiding-place. *Amefanya kwa maficho*, he has acted secretly, i. e. *kificho ficho*. (Cf. *ficha*.)

Mafu, n. death, dead things. Also as adj., *maji mafu*, neap tide. (Cf. *fa, kifo, ufu, -fu*. In Z. *mauti* (Ar.) is usual for death.)

Mafua, n. plur. chest symptoms, chest complaint (cold in the chest, bronchitis, pneumonia, phthisis, &c.). (Cf. *kifua, pafu*.)

Mafungulia, n. plur. unfastening, —esp. *mafungulia ng'ombe*, as a mark of time, grazing time, about 8–9 a.m., when the dew is gone, and sun not too hot. (Cf. *fungua*.)

Mafusho, n. See **Mavusho**.

Mafuta, n. plur. oil, fat, grease (of any kind). *M. ya nyama*, fat, lard, dripping (also *shahamu*, animal fat. Butter is commonly distinguished as *siagi*, or *samli*, ghee). *Mafuta ya taa (ya kizungu, amerikano)*, common petroleum. Vegetable oils are *mafuta ya uta*, semsem oil; *m. ya mbárika*, castor oil; *m. ya nazi*, cocoanut oil. (Cf. *futa, ufuta, ?uta*.)

Mafuu, n. plur. craziness, silliness, half-witted state. (Cf. *kichaa, wazimu*.)

Mafya, n. plur. (sing. *jifya*), stones used to support a pot or kettle in cooking. (Cf. *mafiga, meko*.) Also name of an island (Momfia), S. of Zanzibar.

*__Magadi__, n. soda. Also plur. of *gadi* (which see).

*__Magaribi__, n. also **Mangaribi, Magrebi**, (1) time of sunset, Mahommedan evening prayers or vespers; (2) place of sunset, the west; (3) Morocco (as the western land). (Ar. Cf. *mashariki*.)

Mageuzi, n. plur. change, changes,

changeableness. Also *mageuzo*, i.e. changings,—the process rather than the fact or effect, and cf. *geua*.

Mago, n. plur. of *kago* (which see).

Magombezi, n. plur. quarrel, opposition, prohibition. Also *magombezo*, quarrellings,—of the action, rather than the fact or effect. (Cf. *gomba, gombeza, ugomvi*.)

*****Mahabba**, n. affection, fondness, love. (Ar. Cf. *habba, muhebbi*.)

*****Mahali**, n. also **Mahala**, cf. *pahali, pahala*, (1) place, position, situation, and fig. place of honour; (2) region, district, country (cf. *inchi*); (3) room, space, interval (cf. *nafasi*). *Mahali (pahali)* is the only noun in Swahili meaning 'place,' the only word with which the pfx. *p-* (*pa-, po*) in reference to space is regularly associated, and as a rule means 'place, position,' only. E.g. *mahali hapa*, this place. *M. hapo* (*pale*), that place. *M. pote*, every place, everywhere. *Mahali pa*, in the place of, instead of. *Wakamwendea pale pahali pake*, and they went to him at his place there. *Aniweka mahali*, he puts me in a place, i.e. treats me with distinction. (Ar. Cf. *pahali*,—a form assimilated to the B. pfx. of place. Dist. *mahari*, dowry.)

*****Maharazi**, n. a shoemaker's awl,—for stitching leather. (Arab.)

*****Mahari**, n. a marriage settlement, money or property paid to the wife's relations, or settled on the wife. *Tumepatana na mahari yake rupia sittini*, we have agreed as to her dowry, viz. sixty rupees. (Ar. Dist. *mahali*.)

*****Mahati**, n. a carpenter's gauge for marking lines. Also, a marking cord, ruddle. (Hind.)

*****Mahazamu**, n. a shawl or wrapper worn round the waist as a girdle. (Ar. Cf. *mshipi, masombo, utumbuu*.)

Mahindi, n. plur. single grains of Indian corn, maize, i.e. seeds of the plant *muhindi*. (Cf. *hindi, muhindi*.)

*****Mahiri**, a. and **Maheli**, skilful, clever, quick. *Fundi mahiri*, a clever craftsman. (Ar. Cf. *umahiri*, and syn. *mbingwa, mstadi, waria*, &c.)

Mahoka, n. plur. (1) (a kind of) evil spirits; (2) frenzy, mania, madness. (Cf. *shetani, pepo*.)

*****Maisha**, n. (1) continuance, duration, permanence; (2) life (in respect of length and duration), period of living, mode of life. E.g. *mti huu una m. sana*, this wood is very durable. *M. maovu*, evil living. *M. mengi*, long life. Also as adv., *maisha na milele*, for life and for ever, i.e. for ever and ever. *Utufunge maisha yetu*, imprison us for life. *Mpaka maisha*, till life ends, the whole life long. (*Maisha* is treated sometimes as D 6, sometimes as D 5, though there is no sing. *isha*. While *maisha mengi* means (see above) 'long life,' *maisha nyingi* would rather mean 'many lives,' i.e. life-periods. *Maisha* is life in respect of length and content; *umri*, time of life, age; *uzima*, life as manifest in the living condition, state of living; *roho*, the life-principle, soul, spirit. (Ar. Cf. *ishi, aushi, uzima, roho, umri*.)

*****Maiti**, n. a dead body, corpse,—usually human only. Also, a dead person, i.e. *mtu maiti*. *Hukuta maiti za Wawemba*, we kept coming on the bodies of dead Wawemba. (Ar. Cf. *mauti*, also *mzoga, pinda*.)

*****Majahaba**, n. a dock—for ships. (Cf. *gudi*.)

Majaliwa, n. what is granted, aid, help, favour, grace of God. (Cf. *jali, jalia*.)

Majani, n. plur. grass, leaves,—in general. See **Jani**.

*****Majeruhi**, a. wounded. (Ar. Cf. *jeraha, jeruhi*.)

Maji, n. water, or what resembles water, (1) in general,—liquid, fluid, moisture, damp; (2) in particular,—

secretion, juice, sap, &c. Usually treated as D 5 (P), no singular. E.g. *teka m.*, draw water (from a well, water-hole, &c.). *M. baridi* (*matamu, ya pepo, ya mvua*), fresh water. *M. ya chumvi (ya bahari)*, salt water. *M. bamvua (makuu)*, spring tide. *M. mafu*, neap tide. *M. ya moto*, (1) hot water, (2) a kind of light red or yellow ant. *Kama maji,* (1) fluid, liquid, (2) fluent, flowing,—of ready speech. Used also in virtual compounds, *mja maji*, one who arrives by sea, a stranger, newcomer. *Mwana maji*, a sailor, sea-faring man. *M. ya shahada*, water poured (by Mahommedans) into a small hole at the head of a grave, when filled in. Also as a., *maji, majimaji*, wet, damp. (Cf. Ar. *mâ*, water, *maj*, bitter, salt, briny, or better perh. *uji*, rice gruel, and ? *ja*, v. Other Bantu dialects have *madzi, amanzi, matsi, mezi, medi, mesi, mashi,* &c.)

*Majibizano, n. teaching by question and answer, catechetical instruction. (Cf. *jibu.*)

*Majibu, n. an answer, reply, response, also as a plur. form, answers. (Ar. Cf. *jibu, jawabu.*)

Majilio, n. plur. time (place, manner, &c.) of coming (to), approach, arrival, advent. (Cf. *ja, jilia.*)

Majilipa, n. also Majilipo, Majilip-izi, -izo, -isho, repayment, requital, revenge. (Cf. *lipa, malipo*, and syn. *kisasi.*)

*Majira, n. time, period, season. *Kwa m. haya*, at this time. *M. ya mvua*, rainy season. As conj. 'when, while,' e.g. *m. akilinda shamba*, while (he is) watching the plantation. (Ar. Cf. *wakiti, pindi.*)

*Májira, n. course of a ship,—in navigation. *Twaa májira*, get bearings, find the course. (Ar.)

Majisifu, n. plur. self-praise, boasting, brag, conceit. (From Rf. of *sifu*, cf. follg.)

Majivuno, n. plur. boasting, bragging, self-laudation. (From Rf. of *vuna*, cf. prec. and *kujiona.*)

Majonsi, n. sorrow, grief, mourning, sadness. *Fanya (ona) m.*, be sorrowful, sad. (Cf. *hamu, huzuni, simanzi, sikitiko,* &c.)

*Majuni, n. a preparation of opium, Indian hemp, &c., with sugar and other ingredients made up into a sweetmeat,—strongly intoxicating. (Cf. *madadi.*)

Majuto, n. plur. and Majutio, regret, repentance, remorse. *Majuto ni mjukuu*, remorse is like a grandchild, i.e. comes at last. (Cf. *juta*, and *toba.*)

Makaa, n. plur. coal, charcoal. See Kaa.

Makalalao, n. nickname of the Madagascar settlers in Zanzibar. (M. means cockroaches,—in Z. commonly *mende.*)

Makali, n. the sharp part, edge, point, of a thing, e.g. *makali ya upanga*, the edge of a sword, as contr. with *bapa*, the flat. (Cf. *-kali, ukali*, and *mapana.*)

*Makani, n. dwelling, dwelling-place, residence, home. (Ar. Cf. *masikani, makazi, kao, makao.*)

*Makasi, n. a pair of scissors,—sometimes *mkasi*, also treated as D 5 (P). (Ar.)

*Makataa, n. binding agreement, contract, final settlement, engagement. (Ar. Cf. *kata, kataa, mkataa*, and syn. *mkataba, sharti.*)

Makatazo, n. plur. prohibition, objection, refutation. (Cf. *kataa, kataza.*)

Makazi, n. plur. dwelling, dwelling-place, mode of dwelling. (Cf. *kaa*, v., *kao*, &c., and syn. *makani, masikani.*)

Makengeza, n. plur. squinting, a squint, i.e. *m. ya macho. Mwenyi m.*, one who squints. *Kuwa na m.*, to have a squint,—so *angalia kwa m.* (Cf. *upogo, kitongo.*)

*Makeruhi, a. offensive, in bad

taste, wrong. (Ar. Cf. *kirihi, ikirahi*, and syn. *machukizo*.)

***Maki**, n. thickness, stoutness. *Nguo za m.*, thick clothes. *Ukuta una m.*, the wall is thick. (Ar. *amag*, deep, depth, and cf. *unene, urefu, upana*.)

***Makini**, n. quiet, docile, amenable, well behaved, gentle, composed. *Roho makini*, a quiet disposition, e.g. of a child who stays at home, and does what it is told. (Ar. Cf. *-pole, -tulivu*.)

***Makiri**, n. a cleat on the side of a native vessel, for fastening a rope (Str.).

Makosekano, n. plur. failure, lack, defect, deficiency, want. *M. ya imani*, want of faith. *M. ya bithaa*, no supply of goods. (Cf. *kosa, kosekana*, and syn. *upungufu*.)

***Maksai**, n. a castrated animal, bullock, gelding. *Ng'ombe maksai*, a bullock. (Ar. Cf. *hasi*, and *towashi*.)

***Makubazi**, n. plur. a pair of leather sandals with ornamentation. (Cf. *kiatu, ndara, mlalawanda*.)

***Makufuru**, n. infidelity, sacrilege, blasphemy. (Ar. Cf. *kafiri, kufuru*.)

***Makuli**, n. and **Maakuli**, food, victuals, provisions. (Ar. Cf. *chakula, riziki, nafuu*.)

Makulima, n. plur. implements or operations of agriculture, agriculture, tillage. (Cf. *lima, mkulima, kilimo*.)

Makungu, n. plur. signs of dawn, daybreak. (Cf. *ukungu*.)

Makupaa, n. plur. See **Kupa**.

Makupwa, n. plur. shore, rocks, &c., left uncovered at low tide. (Cf. *pwa, pwani, kipwa*.)

Makusanyiko, n. plur. gathered people or things, a gathering, crowd, concourse, meeting, assembly, collection. (Cf. *kusanya, kutana*, and syn. *mkutano, makutano, jamii*.)

***Makusudi**, n. plur. and **Makasidi**, purposes, intentions, objects.

Also as adv., on purpose, intentionally, voluntarily, and as conj. that, in order that, to. (Ar. Cf. *kusudi*, and conj. *illi*.)

Makutano, n. plur. gathered people or things, a gathering, assemblage, meeting, crowd, collection. (Cf. *kuta, mkutano*, and syn. *makusanyiko, jamii*.)

Makuti, n. plur. used commonly of cocoanut leaves prepared for use as thatch in Zanzibar. See **Kuti**.

Makuu, n. (strictly plur. of a. *-kuu*), (1) pride, ambition, ostentation, show (cf. *fahari, kiburi, majisifu*). Also (2) presumption, which ignores human conditions of dependence and limitation, defiance of divine law, blasphemy, sacrilege (cf. *makufuru*). (Cf. *-kuu*.)

Makwa, n. plur. notches,—cut in the top of an upright post, to carry a cross-piece.

***Malaika**, n. (1) a messenger, an angel; (2) a baby (cf. *kitoto, mchanga*). (Ar., and dist. *malaika*, down, from *laika*.)

Malaji, n. plur. greediness, gluttony, voracity (as shown in acts or habits, while *ulaji* is rather of the quality or character in general). (Cf. *la, chakula, ulaji*.)

Malalo, n. plur. sleeping things, i.e. place, arrangements, bedding, things to lie on. (Cf. *lala, ulalo*, and follg.)

Malazi, n. plur. also **Malazo**, (1) things to sleep on, bedding,—like *malalo*, e.g. *nguo njema na malazi mema*, fine clothes and fine things to sleep on; (2) marriage bed, sexual intercourse. (Cf. *laza, lala*.)

Malele, n. orchilla weed, used as a dye, and a regular article of commerce in East Africa.

Malelezi, n. plur. the season of uncertain and changing winds, between the monsoons and during the rains, i.e. about April and November in Z. Also called *tanga mbili*. (Cf. *musimu, kusi, kaskazi*,

Malenga, n. a professional singer, employed to lead the singing in dances, concerts, &c. (Perhaps at first the name of a well-known singer.)

*****Maleuni,** a. accursed. (Arab. Cf. *laana, -laanifu.*)

Malevi, n. plur. of *ulevi,* drunkenness, i. e. drunken habits, acts, &c., -*ulevi,* rather of the quality or condition. (Cf. *lewa, levya,* and *malafi.*)

Malezi, n. plur. of *ulezi,* rearing, bringing up, both of nurture generally, and of education, training. *Malezi mazuri,* good breeding, good education. (Cf. *lea, ulezi.*)

*****Mali,** n. (treated indiscriminately as D 6 or D 5 (P)), property, goods, wealth, riches, possession. Thus *mali yake nyingi, mali mengi, mali zake chache. Ni mali ya,* it is the property of. *Mali ya watu* (or *ya mwenyewe*), it is some one else's property, it is not mine. There is a game called *mali ya ndimu,* guessing at an unseen striker. (Ar.)

Malidadi, n. one who makes a show, esp. of dress, a showily dressed person, fop, dandy, coxcomb. (Cf. *umalidadi, urembo, mlimbwende.*)

*****Maliki,** v. make a beginning of, set to work on, start a job, e. g. of construction, cultivation, &c. *M. nyumba,* begin to build a house. *M. shamba,* begin to clear, or hoe, a plantation. *M. kuunda chombo,* begin to construct a ship. Ps. *malikiwa.* Ap. *malik-ia, -iwa.* Cs. *malik-isha, -ishwa.* (? Ar. Cf. *miliki,* and syn. *anza, shika.*)

*****Maliki,** n. See **Malki.**

Malimwengu, n. i. e. *mambo ya ulimwengu,* worldly matters, mundane affairs, the concerns of men. (Cf. *ulimwengu, mlimwengu.*)

Malindi, n. (1) plur. of *lindi,* deep places, channels; (2) a district of Zanzibar city; (3) an ancient town on the coast north of Mombasa; (4) (Str.) the flap or small apron of beads worn by a string round the loins by native women on the mainland (but ? in Z.).

Malipizi, n. plur. causing to pay, retaliation, revenge, dunning for debts, distraint, extortion. *Malipizo* (and -*isho*), what is exacted, extorted, and so vengeance, fine, &c., but also as *malipizi.* (Cf. *lipa,* and follg.,—also *kisasi.*)

Malipo, n. plur. payment, reward, atonement, vengeance suffered or inflicted. (Cf. *lipa,* and prec.)

*****Malisaa,** n. shot, i. e. small shot, for firearms, &c. (Cf. *lisasi,* bullet, and *kiasi,* cartridge.)

Malisha, n. and **Malisho,** pasturage, grazing ground, paddock, forage, food for cattle, &c. (Cf. *la, lisha,* and *machunga.*)

Maliza, v. (1) complete, finish off, bring to end, conclude, wind up; (2) abolish, kill, destroy. *M. kazi,* finish a job. *M. deni,* pay off a debt. *M. adui,* annihilate an enemy. Ps. *malizwa.* Nt. *malizika.* Ap. *maliz-ia, -iwa.* Cs. *maliz-isha, -ishwa.* Rp. *malizana.* (Ar. Cf. *timiliza,* and syn. *kamilisha, isha.*)

Malizano, n. plur. mourning of many together, a general wailing. (Cf. *lia,* and Cs. *liza, lizana.*)

Malizi, n. plur. things causing a sound, things rustling, making a noise. E. g. *nasikia malizi nyasini,* I hear things rustling in the rushes. (Cf. *lia,* and prec.)

Malki, n. also **Maliki,** a king, ruler, sovereign. (Arab., not usual in Z. Cf. follg. and *miliki,* also syn. *sultani, mfalme, jumbe.*)

Malkia, n. (*ma-*), queen, female sovereign. (Cf. prec.)

Mama, n. mother, female ancestor or parent,—of all kinds. *Mama wa kambo,* step-mother. *Mama mkubwa* (*mdogo*), mother's elder (younger) sister. *Mama wee,* an African's most natural cry in pain, sorrow, or surprise. Kr. quotes *Mama ni Muungu wa pili*, one's mother comes next to God. *Mama* is treated grammatically like **Baba**, which see. *Mwana* is used in polite reference or address to one's own mother (cf. *mwana*, *bibi*).

Mamba, n. (1) a crocodile; (2) a name of a very dangerous kind of snake.

Mambo, n. plur. of **Jambo**, which see. Used independently *mambo* often means, affairs of importance, difficulties, problems, hardships, e. g. *ulimwengu una mambo*, the world is full of wonders (or, strange things, mysteries, difficulties). *Mambo mengi*, like *visa vingi*, complications, puzzles, perplexities. So used as int., i.e. wonderful! very awkward! a poser!

*****Mamlaka**, n. (1) authority, dominion, rule, rights of ownership; (2) property, possession, dominions. In the latter sense, *milki* is more usual. *Sina m. na kitu hicho*, I have no right to (power over) that thing. (Ar. Cf. *malki*, *miliki*, *milki*, and syn. *enzi*, *amri*, *hukumu*, *nguvu*, *uwezo*.)

Mamoja, a. form of -*moja*, agreeing with D 5 (P), i. e. of one kind, treated as one. Often used independently, e. g. *mamoja kwangu*, it is all one (all the same) to me, I do not care, I have no choice. *Mamoja*, as you like. (Cf. -*moja*, and syn. *haithuru*.)

-**mana**, as a termination of verbs is a combination of the Stative and Reciprocal suffixes, *ma-na*, e. g. *fungamana*, *shikamana*, *ungamana*. (Cf. *ma-(e)*.)

Manane, n. only in the phrase *usiku wa manane*, the dead of night, midnight. *Usiku huu umekuwa wa manane*, it is midnight. (Cf. *nane*, eight,—of which *manane* is perh. a plural. Thus *usiku wa manane* means 'the night at about 2 a.m.' See **Saa**, and syn. *kati ya usiku*, *usiku wa kati*.)

Mandasi, n. plur. See **Maandasi**, and **Andaa**.

*****Manemane**, n. myrrh.

Manena, n. groin, — between thigh and belly. (Cf. *kinena*.)

Manga, n. a name of Arabia, esp. the region of Muscat in the Persian Gulf. It is used to describe various objects connected with or derived from Arabia, e. g. *pilipili manga*, black pepper. *Mkoma manga*, pomegranate tree. *Njiwa manga*, a variety of pigeon. *Jiwe la manga*, a kind of whetstone (but cf. *mango*). (Cf. *mwarabu*, *Arabuni*.)

Mangi, Mangine, a. same as **Mengi, Mengine**, many, more,—formed from -*ngi*, -*ngine*, instead of -*ingi*, -*ingine*,—these latter being rather more usual in Z. (Cf. *I*.)

*****Mangili**, n. a kind of cat-head or cross-piece, for securing a cable, anchor, or rope at the bow of a native vessel.

Mango, n. a hard, black, rounded stone used for pounding, smoothing, and polishing.

Mangwaji, n. plur. finery, foppery, showy dress or appearance, foolish display. (Cf. syn. *umalidadi*, *ulimbwende*.)

Mani, n. semen. (Ar. syn. *shahawa*.)

Manjano, n. turmeric,—used as a yellow colouring material for ornament, and also in curry powder,—an East Indian vegetable product. *Rangi ya m.*, yellow colour.

Manowari, n. a man-of-war,—one of the earliest and most established adaptations of an English word in Swahili. (Others are more or less commonly known, e. g. *boi*, *kala*, *shati*, *koti*, *fulana*, *sitoki*, *kabati*, *bira*, *burashi*, *daktari*, *stima*, *meli*, *afsa*, *dazin*, *inche*, *spitali*, *posta*, *afisi*.)

*****Mansuli**, n. a kind of woollen material, used for dress and as a coverlet.

Manuka, n. plur. smell, scent

odour. (Cf. *nuka*, and follg., also syn. *harufu*.)

Manukato, n. plur. sweet scent, perfume, sweet-smelling substance. (Many such are used in Z., as liquids, in powders, for fumigation, &c. E. g. *marashi* (a general term for liquid scents), *meski, hal waridi, sandali, dasili, undi, ubani, dalia, maguba, rihani, garafuu, garafuu maiti, uvumba, liwa, buhuri, libu, kivumbasi, afu,* &c. Cf. *nuka*, and *-to*, which is not common as a suffix in Z. except in this word.)

*Manuku, n. a copy, transcript, translation, imitation. (Ar. Cf. *nakili*.)

Manyiga, n. a kind of hornet (Str.).

Manyoya, n. plur. of **unyoya** (which see).

Manyunyo, n. plur. showers, sprinkling, drizzle, light rain. (Cf. *nyunyiza*.)

Maokozi, n. plur. saving, rescue, means of saving. (Cf. *okoa, mwokozi*.)

Maombi, n. plur. also **Maomvi**. (cf. *iba, mwivi*), prayers, entreaties, requests, intercessions. (Cf. *omba*, and syn. *haja, dua, sala*.)

Maombolezo, n. plur. loud wailing, lamentations, mourning, dirges. (Cf. *omba, omboleza, malio*.)

Maondokeo, n. plur. (1) departure, going away, taking leave; (2) rising up, respectful salute. (Cf. *ondoka, ondokea*.)

Maondoleo, n. plur. taking away, removal. *M. ya thambi*, remission (forgiveness) of sin. (Cf. *ondoa, ondolea*.)

Maongezi, n. plur. talk, conversation, gossip, amusement, pastime. *Weka m.*, prepare for a long chat. (Cf. *ongea*, and syn. *mazungumzo*.)

Maongezo, n. plur. addition, increase, supplement. (Cf. *ongeza* and *nyongeza*, and syn. *mazidisho*.)

Maongo, n. plur. back (of men or animals), but in Z. usually *mgongo* (which see).

Maongozi, n. plur. direction, superintendence, management, administration, arrangements. *M. ya Muungu*, Providence, divine dispensation. (Cf. *ongoa*, and syn. *madaraka, matengeneo*.)

Maonji, n. plur. tasting, testing, trial, experiment. *Maonji ya mtambo*, testing a machine, to see if it works. (Cf. *onja*, and *maombi* from *omba*, and syn. *jaribu*.)

Maozi, n. giving in marriage, arrangements for bringing about a marriage. (Cf. *oa, oza*, and *mazishi*.)

Mapaji, n. present, gift. (Cf. *pa, -paji, upaji, mpaji*, and dist. *paji la uso*, forehead.)

Mapakizi, n. (1) arrangements connected with shipping and dispatch of goods, conveyance on board, payment of freightage, &c. Also (2) goods shipped, cargo, freight. Similarly *mapakio*. (Cf. *pakia*.)

Mapalilio, n. plur. also **Mapalilo**, **Mapalio**, time (place, process, &c.) of hoeing, i.e. not the first hoeing (*lima*), but the cross-hoeing, cleaning the ground among trees or crops already planted. (Cf. *paa, palia, palilia*.)

Mapambano, n. plur. contact, comparisons, collisions. (Cf. *pambana*.)

Mapana, n. plur. the wide or broad part of a thing, flat side, breadth, width, diameter. *Meza hii ina mapana*, this table is broad. *Njia mapana thaifu*, a road of insignificant width. (Cf. *-pana, upana*, and *-nene*, and for the form *makali*.)

Mapatano, n. plur. agreement, contract, understanding, conspiracy, alliance. (Cf. *pata, patana*, and syn. *maafikano, mkataa*.)

Mapema, adv. in good time, early, soon. *Assubuhi na mapema*, early in the morning.

Mapenda, n. plur. loving another, love. Other nouns of similar form from *penda* may be enumerated here, but most of them will be found also under a sing. form beginning with *u* or *p*, i.e. as D 5 or D 6. See also **Penda.** *Mapendano* (sing. *u-*), mutual love. *Mapendefu*, love, from the side of its object, i.e. being loved, love as experienced. *Mapendelefu*, *mapendeleo*, favour, bias, self-ingratiation, from the side of recipient or giver. *Mapendezi*, things that please, engaging manners, amiability, affectionateness. *Mapendo*, acts of love, loving-kindness. *Mapenzi*, love, liking, inclination, desire, will, wish, purpose. E.g. *afuata mapenzi ya moyo wako*, he follows his own caprices (whims, fancies, ideas, &c.). *Mapenzi hayana macho*, love is blind.

Mapepeta, n. plur. a preparation of immature rice (*pepeta za mpunga*). (Cf. *pepeta*.)

Mapinduzi, n. plur. turning things upside down, revolution, disorder. (Cf. *pinda, pindua*.)

Mapishi, n. plur. things (materials, utensils, &c.) for cooking. (Cf. *pika*.)

Mapiswa, n. unmeaning nonsense, drivel, silliness.

Mapokeo, n. plur. things received, traditions. See **Pokea**.

Maponea, n. plur. means of subsistence, livelihood, food. (Cf. *pona*, and follg. Also syn. *riziki, nafuu, vifaa*.)

Maponyea, n. plur. means of curing (rescuing, &c.). *Matikiti na matango ndio maponyea njaa*, water melons and cucumbers are what save from starvation, i.e. as the last resource in drought. (Cf. *pona, ponya*.)

Maponyo, n. plur. (1) healing things, drugs, medicines, means of saving, (2) getting well, a cure, rescue, preservation. (Cf. *pona, mapoza*.)

Mapooza, n. plur. and **Mapoza**, things withered, undeveloped, not matured, useless, e.g. of fruit dropped in an unripe green stage. (Cf. *pooza*.)

Maposo, n. plur. proposals or arrangements for marrying, wooing. (Cf. *posa*.)

Mapoza, n. plur. remedies, means or appliances for healing. (Cf. *poa, pona, poza*, and syn. *dawa*.)

Mapwaji, n. plur. coast, foreshore, part affected by tides. In Z. usually *pwani*. (Cf. *pwa, kipwa*.)

***Maradufu**, a. double, extra thick, of two thicknesses. (Ar. *radaf*, or ? *daaf*.)

***Marahaba**, int. used as a common rejoinder to the salute of an inferior, or on receipt of a present or favour, —thank you, very well. (Ar. 'it is welcome, I am pleased.' Cf. *ahsante*.)

***Marakaraka**, a. with patches, stripes, spots,—and so of colour, mottled, speckled, variegated, &c. (Cf. *raka, kiraka*, and syn. *madoadoa*.)

***Marasharasha**, n. sprinklings, showers, drizzle,—of rain, sprinkled perfume, &c. (Ar. Cf. *mrashi, marashi*.)

***Marashi**, n. scent, liquid perfume. *Marashi mawaridi*, rose water. (Ar. Cf. prec. and *tibu, manukato*.)

***Marathi**, n. sickness, disease,—in general. (Ar. Cf. syn. *uwele*, and B. *ugonjwa*. For particular diseases, cf. *homa, ndui, safura, shuruwa, titiwanga, ukoma, baridi yabis, sekeneko, kisonono*, &c.)

***Marathi**, a. also **Murathi, Matarithi**, well-content, acquiescent, agreeable, willing. (Ar. Cf. *rathi, rithika, urathi*.)

***Mardudi**, n. repudiation, rejection. (Arab.)

***Maregeo**, n. and **Marejeo**, coming back, return, and fig. reference, recurrence. (Ar. Cf. *rejea*.)

Marehemu, n. and a., one who has found mercy,—used as a euphemistic term of reference to a deceased person, the late, the departed, the defunct. (Ar. Cf. *rehema*.)

P

*Marejeo, n. See Maregeo, and Rejea. (Ar.)

Marembo, n. plur. ornaments,—personal, architectural, &c. articles of finery, carved work, bas-relief. (Cf. *urembo, remba,* and syn. *pambo, nakski, choro.*)

*Marhamu, n. ointment, unguent, plaster,—scented, medicated, &c. (Ar. Cf. *lehemu, lihamu,* and syn. *mafuta, bandiko.*)

*Marigeli, n. a large metal caldron,—chiefly for cooking rice in great quantities. (Ar. Cf. *chombo, chungu, sufuria,* &c., for vessels of different kinds.)

*Marijani, n. coral,—but in Z. not of the stone, or coral rock (cf. *tumbawi*), but of the red coral imported and used as ornament. Called also *marijani ya fethaluka.*

Marika, n. plur. of *rika,* contemporaries, of same age, i.e. *umri sawa.* (Cf. *hirimu* and *rika.* There is a town called *Márika,* or *Marka,* on the Somali coast, north of Z.)

*Marikebu, n. ship. See Merikebu. (Ar. Cf. *rekebu,* and syn. *jahazi,* and B. *chombo.*)

Marindi, n. See Malindi.

*Marini, a. pleasing in appearance, bright, smart, blooming. *Vijana marini,* fine young people. (Cf. syn. *-zuri.*)

*Marisaa, n. also Malisaa, shot,—i.e. for firearms. (Cf. *risasi, kiasi.*)

*Marithawa, a. in abundance, plenty, sufficient. (Ar. 'to one's heart's content, as much as one would wish.' Cf. *rithi, rathi,* and syn. *-ingi, tele.*)

*Marra, n. and adv. (1) a time, a single time, a turn, an occasion, an occurrence; (2) at once, immediately. *M. moja,* (1) once, (2) at once, immediately. *M. mbili,* twice. *M. ya kwanza,* the first time. *M. nyingi,* often, repeatedly. *Marra kwa marra,* time after time, often. *Marra marra,* at intervals, at times, occasionally. *M. hii,* at once, on the spot. *Marra chako, marra changu,* now yours, now mine,—a riddle to which the answer is *mali,* wealth. (Ar. Cf. *safari, zamu,* which are sometimes syn.)

*Marudi, n. plur. also Marudio, (1) a return, a recompense, a paying back; (2) punishment, discipline, correction. (Ar. Cf. *rejea,* and *malipo, athabu, zuio.*)

*Marufaa, n. plur. part of a native loom,—small boards between which the warp is stretched. See Kitanda cha mfumi.

*Marufuku, a. forbidden, prohibited. *Piga m.* (or *rufaka*), give public notice of prohibition, proclaim as forbidden, forbid officially. (Ar. Cf. *mfaka,* and syn. *kataza.*)

Marugurugu, n. and a., small swellings, lumps, e.g. *mtu akijikuna, hufanya m. ya mwili,* if a man scratches himself (as when stung), he raises swellings on his body.

Masaa, n. See Masalio, Masazo.

*Masafi, n. purity, cleanness, correctness. (Ar. Cf. *safi, usafi,* which is seldom used, *utakatifu, ufasaha, tohara.*)

*Masahaba, n. plur. the special friends and companions of Mahommed. (Ar. Cf. *sahibu.*)

*Masaibu, n. accident, calamity. (Ar. Cf. *msiba,* from same root.)

Masalio, n. plur. also Masalia, Masaa, remains, remnant, what is left over. (Cf. *salia, sazo, baki.*)

*Masalkheri, the common Arabic evening salutation, good evening,—as *subulkheri* for the morning. (Ar. *masaa,* evening, and *heri.*)

Masango, n. wire, esp. thick brass wire,—one of the commonest articles of exchange and barter in East Africa. Called also *seng'enge, masoka,* and a fine kind *udodi.* Different kinds of material are distinguished as *m. ya chuma, ya shaba nyeupe, ya shaba nyekundu, ya fetha,* i.e. iron, brass, copper, silver wire.

*Masarifu, n. also Masurufu,

Masruf, supplies for an expedition or journey, provisions, outfit, goods and money. (Ar. expenses, outlay. Cf. *sarifu, gharama*.)

***Mashairi**, n. plur. of *shairi*, verses, a poem, poetry. *Tunga mashairi*, compose poetry. (Ar.)

***Mashaka**, n. plur. of *shaka*, doubts, trouble, difficulties, danger. (Ar.)

Mashapo, n. plur. dregs, lees, sediment, e.g. of squeezed fruits, grains, herbs, &c. (Str.). (Cf. *masira, masalio*.)

***Mashariki**, n. the East. *-a mashariki*, eastern, easterly, oriental. (Ar. Cf. *magaribi*, and syn. *natlai, matokea (macho, maao) ya jua*.)

Mashendea, n. plur. rice cooked as a kind of pudding, used for invalids,—not dry like *wali*, nor gruel like *uji*. *Mashindea ya mchele*, rice-pudding. Also *m. ya mtama*.

Mashindano, n. plur. contest, race, competition, struggle, athletic sports. *M. ya mbio*, racing; *m. ya kuruka*, jumping competition; *m. ya kushikana mbavu*, wrestling. (Cf. *shinda, mshindani*.)

Mashtaka, n. plur. (seldom in sing. *shtaka*, cf. *mshtaka*), charges, accusations, reproaches. See **Shtaki**.

Mashua, n. boat, boats,—built of boards, &c., not hollowed out in native fashion. *M. ya moshi*, a steam launch. (Cf. *shua*, and *dau*.)

***Mashuuri**, a. famous, renowned, celebrated, well-known, notorious. (Ar. Cf. syn. *maarufu, -enyi sifa, -bayani*.)

Mashuzi, n. plur. breaking wind,—without noise. (Cf. *shuta, ushuzi*, and *jamba*.)

***Masia**, n. walking, a walk, gait. *Enda masia*, go out walking. (Arab., for usual *tembea, matembezi*.)

*****Masifiwa**, n. plur. things praised, recommended, advertised. (Verb. noun passive from *sifu*, cf. follg. and similar noun *mapendwa*, &c.)

*****Masifu**, n. plur. praises, congratulations. (For more usual *sifa*, cf. *sifu*, v.)

*-**masihiya**, a. Christian. (Cf. Ar. *masiha*, Christ, and *masiya*.)

Masika, n. the season of the greater rains (*majira ya mvua nyingi*) in Zanzibar, i.e. March, April, and May, when the hot north monsoon gives way to the cooler south. Corresponds to autumn in northern latitudes. (For seasons generally see **Mwaka**.)

*****Masikani**, n. dwelling place, abode. (Ar. Cf. *makani*, and syn. B. *kao*.)

*****Masikini**, n. (1) a poor man, beggar,—used descriptively, and also (2) in pity or contempt, a hapless, luckless, miserable individual. (3) a freed slave, who has no protector, home or belongings, i.e. *m. wa Muungu*, one who picks up a living as he can. (Ar. Cf. *fukara, mwombaji, mnyonge*.)

Masimango, n. plur. ill-natured remarks, reproaches,—of a patronizing contemptuous kind. (Cf. *simanga*, and *mashutumu, masuto, matusi*.)

Masingizio, n. plur. (1) slander, calumny, false insinuation, misrepresentation. Hence (2) pretence, disguise, make-believe, belying facts. (Cf. *singizia, nenea, sengenya, amba*.)

Masiwa, n. large islands,—used to describe the Comoro, or Seychelles islands. (Cf. *kisiwa, usiwa*.)

*****Masiya**, n. (*ma-*), the Anointed One, Christ. (Ar. *masiha*.)

Masizi, n. plur. soot, grime, i.e. *masizi ya moshi meusi yaliyogandamia chungu*, the black smoky grime that forms on a cooking pot. (Dist. *misizi*, rootlets, and *mazizi*, cattle-pens.)

Masoka, n. thick iron or brass wire. (Cf. *masango*, and *usoka*.)

Masombo, n. girdle,—consisting of a long piece of cloth wound round the waist, like (Ar.) *mahazamu*. (Cf. *ukumbuu*, which is shorter, and *mshipi*.)

Masongo, n. plur. plaits,—e. g. of hair, tresses, wreaths of flowers, garlands. (Cf. *msokoto*, and *suka*, *songa*.)

*****Masri,** n. and **Misri,** Egypt.

Masua, n. plur. and **Mazua,** giddiness. (Cf. *zulu*, *zulika*, *kizuli*, and syn. *kizunguzungu*.)

Masuguo, n. plur. rubbing, something to rub with, a whetstone, knife-board. (Cf. *sugua*, *noa*, *kinoo*.)

Masuko, n. plur. and commonly **Masukosuko,** (1) shaking, wagging, tossing, moving to and fro quickly,—and so generally (2) agitation, disturbance, a restless state of affairs. Used of the rolling or pitching of a vessel at sea. (Cf. *suka*, and *mramma*.)

*****Masuluhu,** n. reconciliation, peace after quarrelling. (Ar. Cf. *suluhisha*, *selehisha*.)

Masumbuo, n. plur. acts of annoyance, annoying habits or character. *Kijana kidogo kina masumbuo*, a small child is a nuisance. (Cf. *sumbua*, *-sumbufu*, *usumbuo*.)

Masuto, n. plur. reproaches, accusations, critical remarks, fault-finding, sarcasms. (Cf. *suta*, and syn. *laumu*, *shutumu*, *shtaka*.)

Mata, n. plur. of *uta*, native shooting weapon, bow and arrows. (Cf. *upindi*, *mshale*.)

*****Mataajabu,** n. plur. wonders, marvels, surprises. Also of wonder, as felt, e.g. *ona m.*, feel astonishment, wonder. (Ar. Cf. *ajabu*, *staajabu*, and syn. *mwujiza*, *shani*.)

Matabwatabwa, n. plur. rice cooked with a great deal of water, rice gruel, called *matabwatabwa ya wali*, *wali ulio mashendea membamba sana*, i.e. a thin porridge, *uji mwepesi*, *uji wa majimaji*, a very thin watery gruel. (Cf. *wali*, *utabwa*, *uji*.)

Matafuni, n. plur. chewings, nibblings, things chewed. (Cf. *tafuna*.)

Matagataga, adv. *enda m.*, walk with long striding steps, straddle along. (Cf. *taga* or *tagaa*.)

Mataka, n. plur. wantings, desires, inclination. (Cf. *taka*, v., *matakwa*, and syn. *haja*, *maelekeo*. Dist. *matakataka*.)

Matakata, n. plur. (1) cleansings, sweepings, scrapings, offscourings, and so (2) refuse, rubbish. (Cf. *takata*, *taka*, and follg.)

Matakataka, n. plur. dirt, filth, refuse, rubbish. (Cf. *taka*, n., *kitakataka*, *takata*, *kifusi*.)

Matakatifu, n. plur. pure living, holy life, holiness (i.e. perh. holiness not only considered as an attribute (*utakatifu*) but exemplified in acts. See **Ma-,** 2 (*d*) (1). (Cf. *-takata*, *-takatifu*, *utakatifu*.)

Matakwa, n. plur. (1) things wanted, needs, desires, requests; (2) being wanted, being in request, e.g. *matakwa yangu kuwa mtumishi killa mtu ayajna*, every one knows how I was wanted as a servant, how my services were in request.

*****Matana,** n. used sometimes of a form of leprous disease. (Cf. *balanga*, *ukoma*.)

Matanga, n. plur. of *tanga* (which see).

Matangamano, n. plur. a mixed crowd, medley, miscellaneous assemblage, promiscuous collection. (Cf. *tangamana*, also syn. *makutano*, *jamii*.)

Matata, n. plur. tangle, complication, complex affair, troubles, difficulties, &c. *Tia m.*, complicate, involve. (Cf. *tatiza*.)

Mate, n. plur. of *ute* (cf. *uta*, *mata*), spitting, spittle, saliva. *Matemate*, light spitting rain, drizzle (cf. *manyunyo*). *Tema mate*, spit, expectorate.

Mateka, n. plur. (1) booty, prey, plunder, and esp. (2) captive in war, slave,—used as sing. and plur. (Cf. *teka, v.*)

Matembezi, n. plur. (1) a walk taken for pleasure or business, a ramble, a tour, a round; (2) also idle strolling, street walking. *Nalikwenda kule matembezi,* I went there for a walk. (Cf. *tembea, masia.*)

*****Mathabahu**, n. and **Mathbahu**, place of sacrifice, altar. (Ar. Cf. *mathabuha, thabihu.*)

*****Mathabuha**, n. and **Mathbuha**, thing sacrificed, victim, offering. (Cf. prec.)

*****Mathahabu**, n. and **Mathehebu**, (1) customs, ideas, tenets, usages; (2) sect, denomination, party, persuasion. *M. ya maneno,* uses of words, formularies, idioms. *M. ya mambo,* usages, ceremonies, rites. (Ar. Cf. *desturi, kawaida, kanuni.* Dist. *thahabu.*)

*****Mathali**, conj. also **Máthal**, **Methali**, **Mithili**, **Mizli**, as, like. (Ar. See **Methali**, and cf. *kama.*)

*****Mathubuti**, n. and a., also **Mathubutu**, (1) evidence, proof, confirmation, support (cf. *ushahidi*); (2) trustworthy, honest, reliable, effective, decisive. E.g. *makarani si m.,* the clerks are not to be trusted. *Hoja m.,* a strong, conclusive argument. (Ar. Cf. *thubutu, thabiti,* and syn. *imara.*)

Matiko, n. hardening or tempering metal. *Tia m.,* harden, temper. *Fundi ametilia m. shoka langu,* the smith has tempered my axe. So *tilika (pata, ingia) matiko,*—of the metal. (? Cf. *utiko.*)

*****Matilaba**, n. desire, wish, purpose. *Matilaba na mradi,* desire and intention. (Arab., not often in Z. Cf. *tamaa, matamani, matakwa, shauri, shauko.*)

Matilo, n. and **Mantilo**, a rope from the after-part of the yard to the masthead, to give greater security in a high wind.

Matimutimu, n. *nyele za m.,* dishevelled, disordered hair.

Matindi, n. half-grown Indian corn (*muhindi.*).

Matiti, n. *enda m.,* trot, go at a trot,—of an animal. (Cf. *telki, mbio,* and dist. *titi, kititi.*)

*****Matlaa**, n. and **Matlai**, sunrise, the east, east wind, morning wind. (Ar. Cf. *mashariki.*)

Matongo, n. discharge from the eyes. *Mwenyi m. ya macho,* a person whose eyes run from weakness or disease. (Cf. *utongo, tongo,* and perh. *chongo.*)

Matukano, n. plur. insulting words, abuse, bad language, insults. (Cf. *tukana,* and syn. *matusi, masuto.*)

Matumbawe, n. plur. coral stone in the intermediate stage, between actual formation and complete fossilization,—a white, light, compact stone, used esp. on account of its lightness in concrete roofs; and, being comparatively soft, it is also cut to form a projecting support for plaster string-courses.

Matumishi, n. plur. service, a servant's work. (Cf. follg. and *mtumishi.*)

Matumizi, n. plur. (1) acts of using, use, using, employment; (2) things used, requisites, conveniences, e.g. food, clothes, firing, &c. E.g. *hana m. nayo,* he has no use for them. *Sina m. leo,* I am quite destitute at present. (Cf. *tumia,* and syn. *riziki, vifaa.*)

Maumbile, n. plur. created state, original condition, natural constitution (Kr.),—but *umbo* is usual in Z. (Cf. *umba, kiumbe.*)

Maungo, n. plur. of **ungo** (which see).

Maunzi, n. plur. a structure, frame, framework, esp. one of wood and of shipbuilding, i.e. the hull or framing of a vessel. (Cf. *unda, mwunzi.*)

Mauthiko, n. plur. annoyances, (feeling of) annoyance. *Kwa uchungu na m.,* from resentment and irritation. (Cf. *uthi, uthia,* and syn. *masumbuo.*)

*Mauti, n. death. *Patiwa na (kutiwa na, patikana na) mauti*, die. (Ar. Cf. *maiti*, and syn. B. *ufu, kifo*.)

Mavi, n. plur. (no sing.), (1) dung, excrement; (2) dross (of metal), scoria, e.g. *m. ya chuma*, iron-worker's refuse; *m. ya nyota*, star droppings,—used of bright, metallic, sparkling stone, mica, &c. (3) a coarse term of abuse and contempt, like *mawe*, rot, humbug, nonsense, trash.

Mavunde, n. plur., and Mavundevunde, broken, scattered, ragged clouds, a cloudy overcast sky. (Cf. *vunja*, and pass. termin. -*e*.)

Mavune, n. plur. that which is harvested or reaped. Sometimes used fig. of outcome, result, consequences, effect. (Cf. *vuna*, and pass. termin. -*e*, also follg.)

Mavuno, n. plur. (1) time (place, process, results, &c.) of harvesting, reaping crops; (2) fig. generally profit, gain, exploitation. *M. ya nyuki*, bee harvest, i.e. honey. (Cf. *vuna*, and prec., and for profit, *faida, uchumi*.)

Mavusho, n. plur. (like *mavukizo*), fumes, exhalations, fumigation, &c. (Cf. *vukizo, vukiza*.)

Mawe, n. plur. of *jiwe* (which see). Often used contemptuously of things common or worthless,—rubbish, nonsense, trash.

Mawele, n. plur. a very small species of grain, a kind of millet (*Penicillaria spicata*, Sac.).

*Mayiti, n. See Maiti.

Mayugwa, n. plur. leaves of the plant *jimbi*, a green vegetable like spinach when cooked.

Mazao, n. plur. natural produce, products, offspring, fruit. (Cf. *zaa, zao*.)

*Maziada, Mazidi, Mazidio, Mazidisho. See Ziada, &c. (Ar. Cf. *zidi*.)

Maziko, n. plur. process (time, place, &c.) of burial, funeral, interment. (Cf. *zika, mzishi, mazishi, kaburi*.)

Mazinga-ombwe, n. juggling tricks, conjuring, puzzles. (Cf. *kiini-macho, mizungu*, and follg.)

Mazingazinga, n. plur. going round, revolutions, rounds, e.g. of a patrol, police, &c. (Cf. *zinga, zunguka, mzinga*.)

Mazishi, n. plur. preparations for burying, attendance at a funeral, things used at a burial (e.g. *sanda, kiunza, pamba, ubani*, &c.). (Cf. *zika, maziko, mzishi*.)

Maziwa, n. (1) as a collective noun, milk of man or animal; (2) plur. of *ziwa*, i.e. (*a*) breasts, suckling organs; (*b*) pools, lakes. *M. mabivu*, curdled milk. (Cf. *mtindi*, butter-milk.) *M. ya watu wawili*, dragon's blood (sap of a tree).

Mazoea, n. plur. habituation, practice, familiarity, use, habit, custom. *Sina m. ya kusema naye*, I am not used to talking with him. *Fanya m.*, settle down, become sociable, get contented. (Cf. follg.)

Mazoezo, n. plur. and Mazoezi, habits, customs, usages, practice, wont. (Cf. *zoea, -zoefu*, and syn. *desturi*.)

Mazu, n. local name for a kind of banana, not in Z. (Cf. *ndizi, mgomba*.)

Mazua, n. plur. and Masua, giddiness, confusion. (Cf. *zulu, zulika*.)

Mazuka, n. plur. apparitions, ghosts, spirits. (Cf. *zuka, kizuka*, and syn. *kivuli, pepo*.)

Mazungumzo, n. plur. social intercourse, conversation, amusement. (Cf. *zungumza*, and syn. *maongezi, mchezo*.)

Mb-, a common plural prefix of nouns beginning with *u, w, uw, ub* in Singular, usually representing a euphonic change from original *n* sound. Words not found under *Mb* may therefore be looked for under *U, Uw, W, Ub*.

Mba, n. a kind of skin disease, causing irritation and subsequently scaling. (Cf. *choa, dasi, rupia, uwati*.)

Mbaamwezi, n. See **Mbalamwezi**.

Mbaazi, n. (*mi-*), (1) a shrub bearing a yellow laburnum-like blossom, and pods containing an edible pea or bean; (2) the beans of this shrub,—? Angola pea (*Cajanus Indicus*, Sac.). *Tundu la mibaazi*, a cage made of twigs of the *mbaazi*.

*****Mbaharia**, n. (*wa-*), commonly **Baharia** (*ma-*), a sailor. (Cf. *bahari*, and syn. *mwana maji*.)

*****Mbahili**, n. (*wa-*), a miser. (Ar. Cf. *bahili, ubahili, mkabithi*.)

Mbalamwezi, n. also **Mbaamwezi, Balamwezi**, moonshine, bright moonlight. (*Mbala-* is perh. a plur. form connected with *waa*, v., shine, i.e. *u(w)a(l)a, ua(l)a-, mba(l)a-*, combined with *mwezi*, moon.)

Mbalanga, n. also **Balanga**, a form of leprosy. (Cf. *ukoma, balasi*.)

*****Mbalehe**, n. (*wa-*) and a., boy or girl growing up, developed, marriageable. (Ar. Cf. *balehe*, and syn. *mzima, mpevu*.)

Mbali, adv. (1) far, far off, distant (in place or time), long ago, long after; (2) distinct, separate, different, contrary, opposite; (3) with the Ap. form of verb, 'altogether, completely, quite.' E. g. *walio mbali kwa mbali huonana kwa nyaraka*, people who are far apart meet by means of letters. *Weka m.*, put aside (apart). *Safari ya mbali*, a long journey. *Hakuja m. sana*, it is not very long since he came. Sometimes Rd. *rangi mbali mbali*, (of) different colours, many-coloured, variegated. *Mambo haya mbali mbali kabisa*, these things are diametrically opposed. With verbs, *ulia mbali*, kill outright. *Potetea mbali*, perish utterly,—a common imprecation, 'go and be hanged.' *Tupia mbali*, throw quite away. With *ya* or *na*, *mbali* is used as a prep., far from, distant from,—in time, space, or quality. (Cf. *ubali*, of which *mbali* is a plur. form, as *mbele* of *ubele*. Opp. *karibu, kando*.)

*****Mbalungi**, n. (*mi-*), a citron tree, its fruit being *balungi*. (For other varieties of orange see **Mchungwa**.)

Mbamba, n. (*mi-*), (1) thin, flat piece (of stone, metal, or other material), plate, layer, sheet, strip, chip, &c. *Mbamba wa jiwe, jiwe la mbamba*, a flat stone. Also (2) a plant, a kind of Euphorbia. (Cf. *bamba, bambo, -embamba*.)

Mbandiko, n. (*mi-*), a sticking on, application (e. g. of a plaster, &c.) (Cf. *bandika*.)

Mbanduko, n. (*mi-*), a taking off, removing (e. g. of a plaster, covering, clothes), a stripping off. (Cf. *bandua*.)

Mbangi, n. (*mi-*), the Indian hemp plant, from which the intoxicant *bangi* is made. (Cf. *afiuni, majuni, bangi*.)

Mbango, n. a kind of wild pig with projecting tusks. Hence of a person with projecting teeth. (Seldom in Z. Cf. *ngiri, nguruwe*.)

Mbano, n. an instrument for grasping and holding, forceps, pincers, a hand-vice, stick partly split. (Cf. *bano, bana, banzi, kibano*.)

*****Mbaraka**, n. (*mi-*), also **Baraka**, a blessing,—in Z. more usual form than *baraka*. *Shauri ni m.*, taking counsel brings a blessing. (Ar. Cf. *bariki*.)

Mbarango,* n. (*mi-*), also **Barango**, stout club, cudgel. Dim. *kibarango*. (Cf. *bakora, fimbo*.)

Mbárika, n. (*mi-*), the castor-oil plant,—elsewhere on the coast called *mbono*. *Mafuta ya mbárika*, castor-oil.

Mbaruti, n. (*mi-*), a thistle-like weed.

*****Mbashiri**, n. (*wa-*), one who brings news, one who foretells, a prophet. (Ar. Cf. *bashiri*.)

Mbasua, n. or **Mbazua**, giddiness, craziness. (Cf. *mazua, kizua, zulika*.)

Mbata, n. a cocoanut in the final state of ripeness and dryness, when the nutty part inside gets loose from the shell. Commonly used for copra. (Cf. *nazi, mnazi*.)

Mbati, n. (perh. plur. from a sing. *uwati*), the poles laid along the top of a wall, or of side posts, supporting the rafters on which the roof rests.

Mbatili, n. (*wa-*), prodigal, spendthrift, gambler. (Cf. *batili*, and *bathiri*, and syn. *mharibifu*, or *mpotevu, wa mali*.)

Mbau, n. (*mi-*), (1) a plank, a board. Also (2) plur. of *ubau*, a plank, i. e. timber generally, sawn wood.

Mbavuni, adv. by the side (of), alongside, on the sides (skirts, flanks). *Mbavuni mwa mlima*, on the flanks of the mountains. *Alimganda mbavuni*, he stuck to his side,—kept close to him. (Plur. of *ubavu*, with locative suffix *-ni*. Cf. *kando, upande*.)

Mbawa, n. plur. of *ubawa* (which see).

*****Mbayani**, n. (*wa-*), a well-known, notorious person. (Ar. Also baini, which see.)

*****Mbazazi**, n. (*wa-*), trader, dealer, pedlar. (Ar. trader in calico, draper. Cf. *ubazazi*, and syn. *tajiri, mchuruzi*.)

Mbega, n. a monkey with long black silky hair, white on the shoulders. (Cf. *kima*.)

Mbegu, n. (1) seed, germ, that from which a plant grows; (2) breed, race, stock. A wider term than *chembe, punje* (a single grain, a separate small thing), and including what is planted and set to grow, i. e. bulbs, roots, seedlings, cuttings, &c. Fig. of the germ of a disease.

*****Mbeja**, n. (*wa-*), a person who is neat, smart, well dressed, careful of personal appearance. *Mbeja wa kano*, a fine muscular man, athlete. (? Ar. *bahaj*. Cf. *umbuji*.)

Mbeko, n. perh. the same as mbeleko (which see).

Mbele, adv. and n. (1) of place,— before, in front, on the near side, on the far side, forward, beyond; (2) of time,—long ago, previously, in the past, in the future, hereafter; (3) fig. in the front, in a prominent place (as to rank, quality, value, &c.). *Mbele* is often used with *ya* or *za* (never *na*) in the above senses, and also (4) in the presence (of), in view of, and so, as compared with. E. g. as a noun, 'something before,' *huna mbele huna nyuma*, you have nothing before or behind you, no prospects or resources, you are utterly destitute. *Neno hili ntakuelezea mbele*, I will explain this matter to you presently. *Tuendelee mbele*, let us go forward. *Alikuja mbele*, he arrived previously. *Hawi mumewe mbele ya sheria*, he is not her husband in the eye of the law. *Dunia si kitu mbele ya jua*, the world (earth) is nothing compared with the sun. *Akiba ya mbeleni*, a provision for the future. (*Mbele* is a plur. form from *ubele*, or *wele*. Henceits prepositional use with *za*, as well as *ya*. The seeming vagueness of *mbele*, as meaning 'on the near side' and 'on the further side,' and also 'before' and 'after' in time, is generally removed by the context suggesting the point of view. If the idea of movement onward, progression, is suggested by the circumstances or only present in the mind, then *mbele* is usually 'on the further side, further on, after,' e. g. *mbele ya mlima*, beyond the mountain, *mbele ya siku kuu*, after the festival. Otherwise *mbele* may equally well mean 'in front of, before.' *Alisimama mbele ya mlima*, he stopped on this side of the mountain, in front of it. *Hufunga mbele ya siku kuu,* there is a general fast before the feast. (Cf. *kabla, nyuma, baada.*)

Mbeleko, n. also **Mbeko** and **Ubeleko,** a piece of calico used by women for carrying a child on the back while at work or walking. Such a cloth is a usual wedding present, made to the bride's mother. *Ondoa (vunja) mbeko,* put to shame. (Cf. *eleka.*)

Mbembe, n. (*wa-*), a coaxing, insinuating, flattering person, a coquette, a flirt. Also, a procurer. (Cf. *bembeleza, ubembe, bembe,* and follg.)

Mbembezi, n. (*wa-*), similar to **Mbembe.** (Cf. *ubembezi.*)

Mbibo, n. (*mi-*), the cashew-nut tree (also known as *mkanju*), bearing the cashew apple (*bibo*) with the attached nut (*korosho*). (Cf. *dunge, kanju.*)

Mbigili, n. (*mi-*), a thorny brier-like shrub.

Mbili, a. two, the form of *-wili* agreeing with D 4 (P), D 6 (P). (Cf. *pili, -wili.*)

Mbilikimo, n. (*wa-*), a name by which the pigmy races of the central African forest region are known on the coast, a dwarf.

Mbilingani, n. and **Mbilinganya,** a plant producing the edible vegetable *bilingani* (of the tomato class), sometimes called the mad-apple or egg-plant.

Mbingu, n. plur. of *uwingu,* the skies, the heavens, heaven.

Mbinja, n. plur. of *uwinja,* whistling. *Piga m.,* give a whistle. *Endeleza m.,* make a long whistle. (Cf. *ubinja, ubinda,* and ? *winda,* i.e. of hunting-calls, imitation of birds, &c. Also *miunzi, msonyo.*)

Mbinu, n. (—), roundness, plumpness, protuberance, a curve. *M. ya mkono,* a plump, well-shaped arm. (Cf. *benuka.*)

Mbio, n. and adv., act of running, running, with speed, fast. *Piga m.,* run,—like *kimbia. Enda m.,* go quickly. Rd. *mbio-mbio,* at full speed. (Cf. *kimbia,* and syn. *upesi, hima.*)

Mbirambi, used only in the semi-Arab. expression of condolence to a mourner, or bereaved person, or after any great personal loss, viz. *mbirambi zako.* Also in the form *bi rabbi zako,* e.g. *hunena bi rabbi zako. Hujibu, zimepita,* the usual words are 'thy (sorrows) be with the Lord,' and the usual reply, 'they are over.' (For *rambi* and *rabbi* cf. *bundi* and *buddi.*)

Mbisho, n. (*mi-*), (1) act of striking, knocking against; (2) opposition, contradiction; (3) in navigation,—beating to windward, tacking. *Mbisho wa pepo,* the winds being contrary. (Cf. *bisha, bisho, ubishi.*)

Mbisi, n. also **bisi** (which see), parched Indian corn. (Dist. *mbizi,* diving.)

Mbiu, n. (1) a buffalo's horn,— sometimes beaten as a musical instrument; (2) also blown to call public attention, and so meaning a proclamation. *Piga m.,* give public notice, announce. *Ilipokwisha m.,* when the proclamation had been made. (For horn cf. *pembe,*—for proclamation *hubiri, tangaza habari.*)

Mbizi, n. a dive, diving. *Piga (enda) m.,* dive. *Hodari sana kwenda m.,* a first-rate diver. (*Mbizi* is used mainly of the plunge itself. Professional diving is described by *zama,* which see.)

Mboga, n. (1) (*mi-*), the plant which produces the *boga,* pumpkin. E.g. *ukaota mboga, ukazaa maboga mengi,* and the plant grew and produced a number of pumpkins. (2) when treated as D 6, is a general term for garden produce, edible vegetables of all kinds,—including the above. *Mboga ya pwani,* an edible plant growing like a weed in creeks near Z. city,—*Sesuvium portulacastrum* (Sac.), purslane. (Various other vegetables are *dodoki, nyanya, mumunye, figili, bilinganya, jimbi,* *kiazi, tango, uwatu, mchicha, yugwa,* and several described as *majani.*)

Mboleo, n. manure, dung. (Cf. syn. *samadi.*)

Mbomoshi, n. (*wa-*), one who throws down (demolishes, destroys, ruins, &c.), a destroyer, a revolutionist. (Cf. *bomoa, bomosha.*)

Mbona, adv. interrog., why? what for? for what reason? (Cf. syn. *kwa nini, kwa sababu gani.*)

Mboni, n. *mboni ya jicho,* the seeing part of the eye, i.e. the apple or pupil of the eye, also described as *mwana wa mboni.* (Cf. *ona.*)

Mbono, n. (*mi-*), (1) the castor-oil plant,—known usually in Z. as *mbárika,* also (2) plur. of *ubono,* the seed of this plant.

Mboo, n. (*mi-*), penis. (Syn. Arab. *firaka.*)

Mbu, n. also imbu in Z. (rather than *umbu*), mosquito.

Mbuai, a. invar. savage, wild, rapacious. *Nyama mbuai,* beasts of prey. (Cf. *ua, mwuaji.* Perh. for *mbuaji.* Cf. syn. *-kali, -a mwitu.*)

Mbugu, n. (*mi-*), a creeper, creeping plant. (Cf. *ubugu, bugu,* and *mbungo.*)

Mbukulia, n. (*wa-*), one who gets hold of and tells secrets, a gossip, scandal-monger, tell-tale. (Cf. *bukua,* and syn. *mdaku, mdakizi.*)

Mbungo, n. (*mi-*), a creeping plant, bearing an edible fruit resembling a medlar (*bungo*), and producing india-rubber,—a kind of Landolphia. (Cf. *mtoria,* and *mbugu.*)

Mbuni, n. (1) (*wa-*), an ostrich; (2) (*wa-*), verbal noun of *buni,* i.e. an inventor, author, originator, deviser, e.g. *mbuni kitabu* (or, *wa kitabu*), the author of a book; (3) (*mi-*), a coffee plant, the berries being *buni,* or *buni za kahawa,* whence the beverage coffee (*kahawa*).

Mburugo, n. (*mi-*), and **Mvurugo,** a stirring up, a mixing, a muddling, disorder, mess. (Cf. *buruga.*)

Mbururo, n. (*mi-*), (1) a pulling, hauling, dragging; (2) track or marks made by pulling something along. (Cf. *burura,* and *mkokoto.*)

Mbuyu, n. (*mi-*), the baobab or calabash tree,—often of enormous girth in proportion to the height, producing a large nut (*buyu*), the hard shell of which is used for drawing water, and the kernel (*ubuyu,* a dry biscuit-like substance with an acid taste) for flavouring food. *Siogopi unene wa mbuyu,* I am not afraid of a baobab's size, i.e. appearance of strength without reality, the wood being soft and unworkable.

Mbuzi, n. (—), and **Mabuzi,** of size, (1) a goat; (2) an instrument for grating cocoanut, i.e. *mbuzi ya kukunia nazi,*—a piece of iron with serrated edge fixed in a board. (Cf. *kibuzi.* Next to fowls, goats are the usual and often the only feasible investment for a native. The next is a cow, or slave.)

Mbwa, n. (—), a dog,—an unclean animal to Mahommedans. *M. wa mwitu,* a jackal, or wild dog. *M. koko,* a bush-dog, the common pariah or half-wild dog of Zanzibar, of a reddish fox-like kind, living in the plantations near the town in a semi-domesticated state and invading it in troops at night. (Cf. *jibwa.*)

Mbwai. See **Mbuai.**

Mbwe, n. (—), small stone, pebble, shingle,—larger than *changarawe.* (Cf. *jiwe, kijiwe, kibwe.*)

Mbweha, n. (—), a fox, jackal.

Mbweu, n. (—), also **Mbweo,** belching, eructation. *Piga* (*enda*) *mbweu,* belch. (Cf. syn. Ar. *riyahi.*)

Mchafuko, n. (*mi-*), disorder, disturbance, chaos, confusion, mess. *M. wa watu,* riot, tumult. (Cf. *chafua,* and syn. *ghasia.*)

Mchago, n. (*mi-*), the end of a bedstead, where the head rests. (Cf. *kitanda.*)

Mchakacho, n. (1) a crushing, a pounding, and so (2) a crackling, rustling sound, e.g. of feet on dry grass and leaves. (Cf. *chakacha*, and perh. *mtakaso*.)

Mchakuro, n. (1) a scratching; (2) the sound of scratching. (Cf. *chakura*.)

Mchana, n. (no plur.), day as opposed to night (*usiku*), daytime, daylight. *Mchana* and *usiku* together make one day, or period of twenty-four hours. The *mchana* or period of daylight at Zanzibar varies little more than an hour in the course of the year,—so little that sunset, whenever it occurs, is taken as 6 p.m., the point from which the next twenty-four hours are to be reckoned. An evening salutation is *Za mchana?* i.e. *Habari za mchana?* How have you been to-day?—with the invariable response, *njema*, quite well. Also used in Z. as a kind of challenge word, e.g. *Mchana usiku?* Are you friend or foe? (lit. day or night). *Mchana kuchwa*, the whole day long, like *usiku kucha*, the whole night long. *Mchana* is also used in a more limited sense, midday, noon, also *mchana mkuu*, i.e. the height of day (and commonly *athuuri*, and *jua kichwani*). *Mchana mdogo*, the period before and after the midday hours. *Chakula cha mchana*, the midday meal, lunch, tiffin. The commonest divisions of daytime are *alfajiri*, when the first signs of it appear; *kucha*, dawn; *assubuhi*, forenoon (including *mafungulia njombe*, between 8 a.m. and 9 a.m.); *athuuri*, noon; *alasiri*, afternoon, about 3 p.m.; *jioni*, evening, till dark. (Perhaps conn. with *cha*, v. and *kucha*, *kuchwa*. Cf. *saa, siku, usiku*.)

Mchanga, n. (no plur.), sand. *M. nunene*, coarse sand. *M. mwembamba*, fine sand. *M. mtifu*, loose, dry, dust-like sand. *Chembe ya mchanga*, a grain of sand, and perh. *uchanga*. (? Cf. *-changa*, a., i.e. in a small undeveloped stage, or follg.)

Mchanganyiko, Mchanganyo, n. (*mi-*), mixture, promiscuous mingling, adulteration. (The two forms only differ in voice, Act. and Nt. 'a mixing, a being mixed,' both being covered by 'mixture.' Cf. *changanya*.)

Mchango, n. (*mi-*), (1) collecting, getting together, joining in an undertaking, contribution, e.g. *m. wa asikari*, mustering soldiers; *m. wa mali*, raising funds from different sources. (2) Intestinal worms, *m. wa tumbo*. (Cf. *changa, chango, uchango*.)

Mchanjo, n. (*mi-*), a cutting, a lopping, &c. (Cf. *chanja, chanjo*.)

Mchanyato, n. a native dish,—bananas, cassava, &c., sliced up and boiled with fish. (Cf. *chanyata*.)

Mchawi, n. (*wa-*), a wizard, a witch, one of either sex who practises the black arts, a sorcerer, a magician. Contr. *mganga*, whose art is in the main under the control of, and allowed by, the community. E.g. *huyu ni mganga, kisha ni mchawi, wala hawezekani*, he's a medicine-man, and what's more, a wizard, and we cannot put up with him. (Perh. conn with *cha*, v., fear, as a passive form, 'a dreaded one.' For syn. cf. *mwanga, mwangaji, mlozi*, i.e. *mlogaji*.)

Mche, n. (*mi-*), seedling, slip, shoot, cutting, young plant. E.g. *Mche huu ni mti gani?* What tree is this a cutting of? (Dist. *mchi, mchu*.)

Mchekeshaji, n. (*wa-*), an amusing droll person, a wag, a clown, a merry smiling person. (Cf. *cheka*, and follg.)

Mchekeshi, n. (*wa-*), and **Mcheshi**, like *mchekeshaji*.

Mcheko, n. (*mi-*), act (manner, circumstances) of laughing, &c. (Cf. *cheka*, and prec.)

Mchele, n. (*mi-*), rice,—collectively, the grain as gathered and cleaned of the husk. Plural seldom heard, e.g.

wakala michele pia, they ate up all the rice. *Mchele* has also a wider sense, i.e. 'cleaned grain' in general, hence *michele wa mtama*, millet grain, and *mchele wa mpunga* defining it as 'rice-grain.' Different sorts of rice are known as *sena, bungala, shindano, garafuu, kapwai, kifungo, madevu, mwanga, sifara, uchukwi*. (Dist. *mpunga*, the rice-plant, growing rice, and the various kinds of cooked rice, *wali, uji, ubwabwa*.)

Mchengo, n. (*mi-*), a cutting, esp. of wood, trees, bushes, stalks, &c. (Cf. *chenga, chanja*, and *kata*.)

Mchenza, n. (*mi-*), a tree bearing a large mandarin orange (*chenza*). (For other kinds cf. *mchungwa*.)

Mcheshi, n. (*wa-*), a merry, laughing, genial, amusing person. (Cf. *cheka, mchekeshi*.)

Mchezi, n. (*wa-*), one who plays, a gay sportive person, a player, an actor. (Cf. *cheza*, and follg.)

Mchezo, n. (*mi-*), game, pastime, amusement, sport. (Cf. *cheza*, and prec., and syn. *maongezi, mazungumzo*. For games cf. *tinge, bao, sataranji, karata, tiabu, dama, kishada*.)

Mchi, n. (*mi-*), a pestle, a pole of hard wood used for pounding grain &c. in a wooden mortar (*kinu*).

Mchicha, n. (*mi-*), a common plant with edible leaves, used as a vegetable, like spinach. (Dist. *chicha*.)

Mchikichi, n. (*mi-*), the palm-oil tree, bearing the fruit *chikichi*. (For other palms see *mnazi*.)

Mchinjaji, n. (*wa-*), a butcher, a slaughterer. (Cf. *chinja*, and follg.)

Mchinjo, n. (*mi-*), act (place, manner, &c.) of slaying, slaughter, butchery, massacre. (Cf. *chinja*.)

Mchirizi, n. (*mi-*), anything for collecting or draining away water, a gutter, a channel, a stick or leaflet or blade of grass for leading rain-water from the trunk of a tree to a pail. Also, the eaves of a house, from which rain drips or trickles. (Cf. *churuzika*.)

Mchiro, n. (*wa-*), but better *ng'chiro*, a mungoos.

Mchocheo, Mchocho, n. (*mi-*), a poking up, a rousing, stimulation, —from *chocha* (which see).

Mchochoro, n. (*mi-*), a narrow alley, or passage between houses. (Cf. *kichochoro*.)

Mchokichoki, n. (*mi-*), and **Mchokochoko**, a tree bearing the fruit *chokichoki* (which see) (*Nephelium Litschi*, Sac.).

Mchomo, n. act or process of burning, &c. See Choma, Chomo. Also irritation, smart, pricking, stabbing, &c.,—and of cooking. (Cf. *mkaango, mtokoso, mwoko*, &c.)

Mchonge, a. *mchonge wa jicho*, a one-eyed person, i.e. *mwenyi chongo*. (Cf. follg.)

Mchongo, n. (*mi-*), a cutting, act of cutting, making a cut,—with axe, knife, &c. *Mchongo wa kalamu*, cutting a pen. (Cf. *chonga, chonge, chongo*.)

Mchongoma, n. (*mi-*), a thorny shrub, with white flowers, and a small black edible fruit (Str.). Used for fences. Also ? a kind of Euphorbia.

Mchoro, n. (*mi-*), carving, engraving, making a scratch or scrawl. (Cf. *chora*, and follg.)

Mchorochoro, n. (*wa-*), a scrawler, scribbler, bad writer. (Cf. *chora*, and prec.)

Mchoroko, n. (*mi-*), the plant which produces the edible bean *choroko* (which see).

Mchoto, n. (*mi-*), a small bit, a scrap, a sample, a taste, e.g. of a delicacy or sweetmeat, sent as a present. (Cf. *chota, choto*.)

Mchovyo, n. (*mi-*), a dipping, plunging in a liquid,—and so used of tempering metals, process of plating or coating with a substance or colour. (Cf. *chovya*.)

Mchu, n. (*mi-*), a kind of mangrove, with tough whitish wood. (Dist. *mche, mchi.*)

Mchukuzi, n. (*wa-*), a bearer, carrier, porter. (Cf. *chukua*, and *mpagazi, hamali.*)

Mchumba, n. (*wa-*), one who seeks or is sought in marriage, suitor, lover, sweetheart, fiancée. (Cf. *chumba, kinyumba.*)

Mchunga, n. (*wa-*), one who has the care of animals, shepherd, herdsman, groom, &c.,—with or without a preposition. *M. (wa) ng'ombe*, a cowherd. *Mbuzi wasio m.*, goats without a goatherd. Also *m. wa gari*, coachman, driver. (Cf. *chunga, lisha.*)

Mchungaji, n. same as **Mchunga** (which see),—the *ji* suffix denoting a professional or habitual occupation, shepherd, &c.

Mchungwa, n. (*mi-*), an orange tree, bearing a sweet orange (*chungwa*) of the common kind, plentiful during nine months of the year in Z. (Cf. *chungwa*, and for other varieties *mchenza, mlimau, mbalungi, mndimu, mkangaja, mdanzi, mfurungu.*)

Mchuruzi, n. (*wa-*), small trader, shopman, retail-dealer, pedlar, stall-keeper. (Cf. *churuza*, and syn. *mbazazi, mfanyi biashara, mwenyi duka.*)

Mchuzi, n. (*mi-*), any kind of gravy, soup, sauce, broth,—esp. as used to flavour a dish of rice or other cooked grain. Prov. *mchuzi ni maji*, gravy means water,—of something indispensable. (Cf. *chuza*, and *kitoweo, kiungo.*)

Mchwa, n. (——), white ants,—of a small but destructive kind in Z. (For other varieties cf. *chungu, siafu, maji ya moto, sisimisi, kumbi.*)

Mda, n. (*mi-*), also **Muda** (which see), a space of time, period.

Mdaa, n. (*mi-*), a plant used for producing a black dye.

***Mdadisi**, n. (*wa-*), one who questions, an inquisitive, curious, prying person. (Ar. Cf. *dadisi.*)

Mdago, n. (*mi-*), a kind of weed.

***Mdai**, n. (*wa-*), a claimant, plaintiff, prosecutor, creditor. (Ar. Cf. *dai, dawa, mdawa*, and *mwii.*)

Mdakizi, n. (*wa-*), similar to **Mdaku**, and **Mdukizi** (which see), eavesdropper, gossip-monger, &c.

Mdaku, n. (*wa-*), one who catches up news, slanderer, tale-bearer, &c. (Cf. prec. and *daka.*)

Mdalasini, n. (*mi-*), a cinnamon tree, also the bark.

Mdanzi, n. (*mi-*), the tree bearing the *danzi*, or bitter orange. (For other kinds cf. *mchungwa.*)

***Mdarabi**, n. (*mi-*), also **Mtarabe**, the rose-apple tree, bearing the fruit *darabi*.

***Mdawa**, n. (1) (*wa-*), claimant, accuser, prosecutor, opponent, assailant. Sometimes (2) (*mi-*), a claim, suit, legal proceedings. (Ar. Like *mdai*, cf. *dai, da'wa*, and *mshtaki, mtesi.*)

***Mdeki**, n. (*mi-*), a ramrod. *Shindilia bunduki kwa mdeki*, to load a gun with a ramrod. (Ar.)

***Mdengu**, n. (*mi-*), a plant producing the small edible bean or pea, *dengu* (which see).

***Mdeni**, n. (*wa-*), a debtor, a person in debt. (Ar. Cf. *deni*, and *mwii, wia, wiwa.*)

***Mdila**, n. (*mi-*), a coffee-pot. (Ar. Cf. *buli*, teapot.)

Mdimu, n. (*mi-*). See **Mndimu**, the tree which bears the lime fruit *ndimu*.

Mdiria, n. (*wa-*), a kingfisher.

Mdodoki, n. (*mi-*), the climbing plant producing the edible vegetable *dodoki*, a kind of lufah.

Mdomo, n. (*mi-*), with variants *mlomo, muomo, mwomo*, (1) a lip; (2) beak, bill (of a bird); (3) fig. anything lip-like, i.e. a similar organ, a projection, overhanging part. *M. wa pande*, a hare-lip. *Piga m.*, pout,—also, make a long speech, be garrulous,—but usually *domo* in this sense. (Cf. *domo*, and *omo.*)

Mdoshi, n. (*mi-*), a kind of pedal

or treadle, working the part of a native loom which raises the threads of the warp alternately. (Cf. *mfumi, fuma, kitanda*.)

*Mduara, n. (*mi-*), and Duara, a circular thing, circle, round heap, wheel,—like *duara* (which see). (Ar. Cf. *mviringo, gurudumu*.)

*Mdudu, n. (*wa-*), the most general word for 'insect,' including ants, flies, fleas, grubs, worms, and all small creeping and flying creatures. Also used of various diseases caused by, or attributed by the natives to, parasites and other insects in the body. (Ar. Cf. *dudu, kidudu,* and dist. *dude*.)

Mdukizi, n. (*wa-*), eavesdropper, gossip-monger, slanderer. (Perh. the same as *mdakizi*, cf. *daka, mdaku, dakiza, dukiza*.)

Mdukuo, n. (*mi-*), a tap, push, poke, thrust,—given with stick, finger, or open hand, e.g. *mtie mdukuo wa jicho*, poke him in the eye. So *pigo la kidole*.

Mdumu, n. (*mi-*), commonly dumu (which see), pot, mug.

Mdundo, n. (*mi-*), used of a rolling, rumbling sound, as of drums or a band. (? Hind. *dund*. Cf. *vuma, mvumo*.)

Me-, (1) as a tense-sign, marks the completion of an action or process, or the consequent state and condition, and so supplies a Perfect and Pluperfect Tense. This form of the verb also often supplies the place of a Past Participle. It can never be combined with a relative-pfx.,—the necessary forms being supplied by the -*li*- (Past) Tense. It is rarely used with a negative pers.-pfx., *simekwambia?* Have I not told you?—its place being supplied by the Past Tense Negative with *ku-*. E.g. *amefika amechoka*, he has arrived in a tired state. *Tukamkuta amekufa*, we found him dead. *Amevaa nguo nzuri*, he is wearing fine clothes. (2) as an initial syllable, sometimes represents *ma-* combined with an -*i*-, *e-*, or *-o* following, e.g. *makasha mengine mengi*, for *ma-ingine, ma-ingi*, many other boxes; *mavazi meroro*, for *ma-ororo*, soft clothes. See A, E, I.

Mea, v. 'grow' as a vegetable or plant,—of plant life, but also of parts of the animal organization, which resemble plants in growth, i.e. hair, teeth, nails, &c. Also in a quasi-active sense, e.g. *buu likamea mbawa*, the grub grew wings. Ap. *melea*, grow in (on, by, &c.), grow as a parasite of, and also in a quasi-passive sense, be grown over, be overgrown, e.g. *shamba langu linamelea*, my plantation is overgrown (with weeds, &c.). Cs. *meza*, cause to grow, e.g. *Muungu amenimeza meno*, God has caused my teeth to grow. (Dist. *meza*, swallow.) (Cf. *mmea, umea, mmelea, kimelea,* and syn. *ota, kua*.)

Mega, v. break off a piece, take a bit, esp. with fingers or teeth,—of taking a share of food, a help from a common plate or dainty. Ps. *megwa*. Nt. *megeka*. Ap. *meg-ea, -ewa*. Cs. *megesha*, e.g. invite to take a bite, ask to help himself. Rp. *megana*, of general consent or common action. (Cf. follg. and *tonge, mmego*.)

Mego, n. (*wa-*), a piece, a bit, a morsel, a bite, a helping, esp. of food. (Cf. *mega*.)

Meka-meka, v. a variant of *metameta, merimeta, memeteka*, sparkle, glitter, shine, be bright, fiery, &c. (And cf. *mulimuli*.)

Meko, n. plur. of *jiko* (i.e. *majiko, maiko, meko*) (which see), and cf. *figa, jifya*, stones for supporting a cooking-pot over the fire.

Memeteka v. also Memetuka, sparkle, shine. (Cf. *metameta*.)

Mende, n. (—), a cockroach. Also a slang term for a rupee.

Mengi, a form of -*ingi* agreeing with D 5 (P), i.e. *maingi, mengi*. So *mengine*, from -*ingine*.

Meno, n. plur. of *jino* (i.e. *majino, maino, meno*), teeth. *Meno meno*, battlements, usually arched or pointed in Z. See **Jino**.

Menya, v. (1) shell, husk, peel, e. g. sugar-cane; (2) beat, pound (not usual in Z.). (Cf. *ambua, chambua, paa*, v.)

*****Merikebu**, n. (—), also **Marikebu, Marekabu**, a ship, esp. of foreign construction, as contr. with the native vessel *chombo*. Various kinds are distinguished as *merikebu ya matanga*, sailing vessel; *m. ya moshi*, steamer—also *ya dohani*; *m. ya kazi* or *ya serkali*, a freight vessel, as contr. with *meli* for passenger traffic; *m. ya milingote miwili* (*miwili u mussu, mitatu*), a brig or schooner (a barque, a full-rigged ship). *Ingia* (*panda*) *merikebuni*, go on board a vessel. *Shuka merikebuni*, disembark. (Ar. Cf. *jahazi, chombo*.)

Merimeta, v. sparkle, shine (cf. *metameta*).

*****Meshmaa**, n. (—), a candle. (Ar. *shamaa*,—sometimes changed to *mshumaa* (*mi-*).)

*****Meski**, n. and **Miski**, musk. Also similar scents. (Cf. *marashi, harufu*.)

*****Meskiti**, n. also **Msikiti, Moskiti**, a mosque. (Ar. changed from *mesgidi, masjidi*, cf. *sujudu*.)

Meta, v. also **Metameta**, shine, sparkle, glitter, be bright, &c., e. g. of polished metal, fireflies, stars, &c. Nt. *meteka*, e. g. *upanga humeteka kotekote*, the sword is bright all over. Cs. *metesha*, make shine, polish. (Cf. *merimeta, memeteka, memetuka, mekameka*,—all perh. variants of similar sound. Also *mulimuli, mulika*, and (of steady light) *ng'aa, anga*.)

*****Methali**, n. and conj., also in several other forms, *mathali, mathal, methili, mithili, mizli*, (1) a likeness, resemblance, emblem, similitude, parable, proverb, allegory. Often *methali ya*, like, resembling, a likeness of, in the likeness of, and so (2) as, like, just as if, for instance,—same as the commoner *kama*. *Mithili ni kuwa ameua mtu*, as for instance (it is as if) he has committed a murder. (Ar. Cf. syn. B. *mfano*, and conj. *kama*.)

Meza, v. (1) swallow, swallow up (perh. a Cs. of *mega* (which see), i. e. *megesha, meza*; (2) Cs. of *mea*, cause to grow.

*****Meza**, n. (—), a table, raised wooden bench, school form. *Mezani*, (of Europeans) at a meal, at dinner,—also a dining-room, mess-room, i. e. *chumba cha kulia*. (Portug. Cf. Lat. *mensa*.)

Mfaa, n. (*mi-*), centre-piece of native door, fixed to one valve, the other closing against it. (Cf. *mlango*.)

Mfalme, n. (*wa-*), king, chief, ruler, sultan. (Cf. *ufalme*, and syn. *jumbe, sultani, mkuu*.)

Mfano, n. (*mi-*), likeness, resemblance, similitude, emblem, sample, pattern, parable. *Mfano wa maneno*, an allegory, parable. *Kwa mfano wa*, or only *mfano na*, like. Also *mfano* alone, as conj. *ndio mfano nguo ya pili*, it acts as another garment. (Cf. *fanana, kifano*, and syn. Ar. *methali*, and conj. *kama*.)

Mfanyi, n. (*wa-*), a doer, a maker, one who practises,—usually as a verbal noun governing another noun, e. g. *mfanyi biashara*, a trader, a merchant; *mfanyi viatu*, a shoemaker. (From *fanya*.)

*****Mfaransa**, n. (*wa-*), also **Mfransa, Mfárasa**, a Frenchman. (From *Français*. Cf. *-faransa*.)

*****Mfariji**, n. (*wa-*), one who comforts, a comforter, a consoler. (Ar. Cf. *fariji*.)

*****Mfarika**, n. (*wa-*), a young animal, —goat, sheep, &c., grown but not yet breeding. (Ar. Cf. *fariki* and follg.)

*****Mfariki**, n. a divider, esp. a comb-like instrument used in weaving. Same as **faraka** (which see).

*****Mfasiri**, n. (*wa-*), an expounder,

interpreter, translator. (Ar. Cf. *fasiri*, and *mkalimani*.)

Mfathili, n. (*wa-*), a benefactor, helper, a kind, liberal, generous person. (Ar. Cf. *fathili*.)

Mfenessi, n. (*mi-*), a jack-fruit tree, a single fruit of which often weighs over 20 lb. (Cf. *fenessi*.)

Mfichaji, Mfichifichi, n. (*wa-*), one who habitually conceals, a very reserved or retiring person. (Cf. *ficha*, and *-nyamafu*.)

Mfigili, n. (*mi-*), and **Mfijili**, a kind of radish-plant, with an edible root, *figili*.

Mfiko, n. (*mi-*), arrival, reach, range. *Mfiko wa lisasi*, range of a bullet (gunshot, rifle). (Cf. *fika*.)

Mfilisi, n. (*wa-*), one who forces another into ruin, bankruptcy, &c., a distrainer, defrauder, embezzler. (Cf. *filisi*, and follg.)

Mfilisika, n. (*wa-*), a ruined person, bankrupt. (Cf. prec.)

Mfinessi, n. See **Mfenessi**.

Mfinyangi, n. (*wa-*), also **Mfinyanzi** (and *-ji*), a worker in clay, a potter. *Mfinyanzi hulia gae*, a potter eats off a potsherd, i. e. is no millionaire. (Cf. *finyanza, finya, ufinyanzi*.)

Mfisha, Mfishaji, n. (*wa-*), one who kills, a slaughterer. (Cf. *fa*, *fisha*.)

Mfithuli, n. (*wa-*), an insolent, rude, overbearing, insulting person. (Ar. Cf. *fithuli, ufithuli*, and syn. *mjeuri*.)

Mfitini, n. (*wa-*), one who causes discord, a quarrelsome person, brawler, agitator, disturber of peace, mutineer, conspirator. (Ar. Cf. *fitina, fitini*.)

Mfiwi, n. (*mi-*), plant producing the *fiwi*, Cape bean.

Mfo, n. (*mi-*), torrent, rain-fed stream, flood, also the channel or bed of a torrent. *Mfo mkavu*, dry bed,—of a torrent. *Leo kumeshuka mfo, hakupitiki*, to-day a flood has come down, it is impossible to cross. *Mto alikuwa na mfo*, the river was in flood. (Cf. *furiko*, and *mto*.)

Mforsadi, n. (*mi-*), a mulberry tree, bearing the fruit *forsadi*.

Mfu, n. (*wa-*), a dead person. (See *-fu*. Cf. *fa*, v., *kifo, ufu*, and syn. *maiti*.)

Mfua, (1) (*wa-*), one who beats, esp. of one who works in metal with hammer, &c., a smith. A verbal-noun from *fua*, governing a noun following, e.g. *mfua chuma* (*thahabu, fetha*, &c.), a blacksmith (goldsmith, silversmith, &c.). *Mfua nguo*, one who washes clothes, a washerman (commonly *dobi* in Z.). (2) (*mi-*), *mifua* (or *mifuo*), bellows. *Vukuta mifua*, blow bellows. (Cf. *fua, mvukuto*.)

Mfuasi, n. (*wa-*), (1) a follower, adherent, retainer, disciple; (2) a pursuer, tracker. (Cf. *fuata*.)

Mfufuzi, n. (*wa-*), one who raises from the dead, restorer of life. (Cf. *fufua*.)

Mfugo, n. (*mi-*), taming, breeding, rearing of birds or animals. *M. wa nyama*, cattle breeding. *M. wa frasi*, keeping a stable, breaking-in horses. *Nina mifugo mingi*, I rear many kinds of animals. (Cf. *fuga*.)

Mfuko, n. (*mi-*), a bag, a pocket,—a general term, with dim. *kifuko*, and *fuko* (*ma-*), a large bag, travelling bag, saddle-bag. (Cf. *fukia, fukua*. Various kinds of bags are *fumba, kifumba, gunia, kiguni, kanda, kikanda, mbatu, mkoba, mtumba*, &c.)

Mfukuzi, n. (*wa-*), (1) from *fukuza*, pursuer, persecutor; (2) from *fukua*, digger, miner, pitman.

Mfulizo, n. (*mi-*), causing to go on, giving an energetic impetus, a pull, tug, haul, thrust, shove, &c. *Kwa mfulizo mmoja*, all pulling together. (Cf. *fua, fuliza*, and follg.)

Mfululizo, n. (*mi-*), also **Mfufulizo**, a Rd. form of *mfulizo*, a going on and on, a regular progression, series, succession. *Siku tano ya mfululizo*, five consecutive days. (Cf. prec.)

Mfuma, Mfumaji, Mfumi, n.

(*wa-*), one who weaves, a weaver. *Mfuma nguo*, a weaver of cloth. *Kitanda cha mfumi*, a weaver's loom. *Mfumaji wa hariri*, a silk weaver. (Cf. *fuma*, and *kitanda*.)

Mfumbati, n. (*mi-*), side-piece of the frame of a native bedstead. See **Kitanda**.

Mfumi, n. See **Mfuma**.

Mfumo, n. (*mi-*), (1) art (act, process, &c.) of weaving; (2) texture, fabric. *Mfumo wake mzuri*, it is a well-woven stuff. (Cf. *fuma*, *mfumi*, *kitanda cha mfumi*, *mtande* (warp), *mshindio* (woof).)

Mfungizo, n. (*mi-*), a fastening up, an investment, blockade, siege. (Cf. *funga*, *fungiza*, and *mazingiwa*.)

Mfungo, n. (*mi-*), (1) a fastening, shutting, closing, tying, &c. (see **Funga**), and (2) esp. fasting,—used both of such fasts as the month Ramathan and of the carnival immediately preceding it. *Mfungo wa Ulaya*, European mode of fastening. (Cf. *funga*, *kifungo*, and follg.)

Mfunguo, n. (*mi-*), unfastening, untying, loosing, releasing, &c. (see **Fungua**). Used to describe the nine months following the month of fasting, Ramathan, viz. *mfunguo wa mosi*, *wa pili*, *wa tatu*, &c.,—the remaining three being called by the Arabic names Rajabu, Shaabani, Ramathani. (Cf. *fungua*, and prec.)

Mfunza, **Mfunzaji**, **Mfunzi**, n. (*wa-*), a teacher, instructor, tutor. (Cf. *funza*, *fundisha*, and syn. *mwalimu*, *mkufunzi*, *fundi*. Dist. *funza*, maggot.)

Mfuo, n. (*mi-*), (1) a beating, hammering, &c.,—verbal of *fua*, v.; (2) a groove, crease, mark made by drawing a line, stripe, band of colour, &c. E.g. *karatasi ya mifuo*, ruled paper. *Nguo ya mifuo*, striped cloth, tartan. (3) *Mifuo*, or *mifua*, bellows; (4) *mfuo wa mawinbi*, the beating of waves on the shore, and also, the beach, shore of the sea. (Cf. *ufuo*, *ufuko*, and *fua*.)

Mfupa, n. (*mi-*), a bone. *Mifupa*, a skeleton. *Mifupa mitupu*, a mere skeleton, i.e. very emaciated. Dim. *kifupa*. (Cf. *ufupa*, *fupa*.)

*****Mfuria**, n. also *kanzu ya mfuria*, an Arab garment, a sort of loose cloth coat, with a collar, but no sleeves. (Perh. Ar., meaning fur coat.)

Mfurungu, n. (*mi-*), the tree which bears the shaddock, *furungu*. (Cf. *mchungwa*.)

Mfuto, n. (*mi-*), (1) a wiping, sweeping, clearing off, erasing, abolition, absolution; (2) used to denote a common, plain, rough, inferior article of any kind, e.g. *mlango wa mfuto*, a plain door, without carving or ornamentation. *Mkeka wa mfuto*, a plain, cheap mat. (Cf. *futa*.)

Mfuu, n. (*mi-*), a tree bearing a small black edible berry (*fuu*).

Mfyozi, n. (*wa-*), an abusive, scornful, insolent person. (Cf. *fyoa*, and syn. *mfithuli*.)

Mganda, n. (*mi-*), (1) a bundle, a sheaf, e.g. of rice or other crop; (2) a kind of drum (cf. *ngoma*). (Cf. *ganda*, and follg.)

Mgandisho, n. (*mi-*), causing to coagulate (set, curdle, thicken), coagulation. (Cf. *ganda*, and follg.)

Mgando, n. (*mi-*). *Mgando wa chuma*, iron smelted and run out to cool, pig iron (cf. *mkuo*). *Piga chuma mgando*, make wrought iron. (Cf. *ganda*, and prec.)

Mganga, n. (*wa-*), a native doctor, medicine man,—the recognized representative of superior knowledge on all subjects mysterious to the native mind, and regarded with respect, fear, or toleration accordingly. The *mchawi* is, on the other hand, not recognized or tolerated as a rule by the community, however useful his services may be to individuals. *Mganga mkuu*, *mganga sana*, a famous medicine man. (Cf. *ganga*, *uganga*, and *mchawi*.)

Mgango, n. *mi-*, a binding up,

splicing, mending. (Cf. *ganga, gango, kigango.*)

Mgawanya, Mgawanyi, n. (*wa-*), a divider, a distributor. (Cf. *gawa, gawanya,* and follg., also *mwenezi.*)

Mgawo, n. (*mi-*), and **Mgao,** a dividing, division, distribution, partition. So also **Mgawanyo.** (Cf. *gawa,* and prec.)

Mgema, n. (*wa-*), and **Mgemi,** a man who climbs and taps cocoanut trees to get palm-wine (*tembo*). This business (*mgemo, kugema*) is a regular profession, and in Zanzibar is often carried on by Digo men from the coastland a little north of Z. Cf. Prov. *mgemi akisifiwa tembo hulitia maji,* if the tapper hears his tap praised he waters it. (Cf. *gema,* and *tembo.*)

Mgemo, n. See **Mgema.**

Mgeni, n. (*wa-*), (1) a stranger, new-comer, foreigner; (2) a guest. *Mgeni na aje mwenyeji apone,* let the foreigner come that the native may be the better off. (Cf. *-geni.*)

Mgereza, n. See **Mwingereza.**

*****Mghalaba,** n. competition, rivalry. *Bei ni mghalaba,* commerce is competition. (Ar. Cf. *ghalibu,* and syn. B. *shindana.*)

Mgogoro, n. (*mi-*), (1) an obstacle, obstruction, e.g. a stone or tree in a road; (2) a difficulty, nuisance, trouble, worry. (Cf. syn. *zuizo, tatizo, kwao.*)

Mgoja, n. See **Mngoja.**

Mgomba, n. (1) (*mi-*), the banana plant, plantain tree, bearing the fruit *ndizi* (which see), and producing a strong fibre (*ugomba*); (2) (*wa-*), verbal noun of gomba (which see, and cf. follg.).

Mgombwe, n. (*mi-*), bull's-mouth shell (*Cassis rubra,* Str.).

Mgomvi, n. (*wa-*), a quarrelsome person, brawler. (Cf. *gomba, ugomvi,* and *mfitini.*)

Mgongo, n. (*mi-*), (1) the back, back part, back-bone,—of man or animal; (2) of things resembling the back, anything raised, ridge, hump, edge. *Geuka* (*elekeza, pa*) *m.,* turn the back,—in fear, contempt, &c. (Cf. *pa kishogo*). *Lala mgongoni,* lie on the back (cf. *kichalichali, kitanitani*). *M. wa nyumba,* ridge of a roof. *Nyumba ya m.,* a house with ridge-roof (cf. *paa*). *Njia ya m.,* a raised path, causeway. *M. wa mwitu,* a thick line of trees, a forest ridge. *Kinyosha m.,* a back-straightener, i. e. a gratuity after a hard job. (Cf. *jongo, kijongo, kibiongo, maongo,*—all of which point to *ongo,* a form not used in Z. but occurring in *mongo, mwongo,* a back, —in other dialects. *Gongo,* a thick stick, is different, cf. *gonga,* strike, beat.)

Mgonjwa, n. (*wa-*), a sick person, an invalid,—used of any bodily ailment, serious or slight. Cf. *mwele,* bedridden, crippled,—of more serious illness, disablement, e. g. *mgonjwa aweza kutembea kidogo, mwele amekazwa na marathi, hawezi kutembea,* a *mgonjwa* can (at least) just move about, a *mwele* is gripped by his malady and cannot move. (Cf. *-gonjwa, gonjweza, ugonjwa,* and use of *hawezi,* as a semi-noun, and contr. *mzima,* sound, in good health.)

Mgoto, n. (*mi-*), (1) act of beating, knocking together, blows, strokes, clashing, sudden meeting, conflict, and (2) commonly of the sound of such beating, e. g. *m. wa makasia,* the beat of oars,—both act and sound; *m. wa maji,* the sound of meeting or falling water. (Cf. *gota,* and *pigo, shindo, mbisho.*)

Mgunga, n. (*mi-*), a kind of acacia (Sac.).

Mguno, n. (*mi-*), a grumbling, grunting, murmuring, complaining, discontent. (Cf. *guna, nung'unika.*)

Mgunya, n. (*wa-*), a native of a coast district between Mombasa and the river Juba. They use the sailing vessel called *tepe.*

Mguruguru, n. (*wa-*), a large kind of lizard, living in holes and feeding on insects. (For other varieties cf. *mjusi, kenge.*)

Mguu, n. (*mi-*), (1) the leg,—of man or any kind of living creature, and esp. the lower part of it, the foot; (2) anything resembling a leg, in shape or function. *Enda kwa miguu,* go on foot, walk. *Shika miguu (ya),* make obeisance (to), become a subject or dependent (of). *Panua (tanua) miguu,* take long strides. (Cf. *guu, kiguu.*)

***Mhabeshi,** n. (*wa-*), an Abyssinian,—esp. of the female, valued as a slave from the light complexion. (Cf. *Habeshia.*)

***Mhadimu,** n. (*wa-*), a *Hadimu,* —one of the earlier inhabitants of the island of Zanzibar, living mostly on the east and south of the island, retaining their own dialect and customs, and till latterly some independence. Mostly fishermen. (Ar. Cf. *hadimu, hudumu.*)

***Mhajiri,** n. (*wa-*), an emigrant, settler, colonist,—also one who travels to Mecca as a pilgrim. (Ar. Cf. *hajiri,* and *haj.*)

***Mhalbori,** n. a strip of lining under the ornamental silk stitching down the front of a *kanzu* (Str.).

Mhamishi, n. (*wa-*), a wandering, unsettled, homeless person, a nomad, pilgrim, tramp, vagrant. (Cf. *hama, mahame.*)

***Mharabu,** n. (*wa-*), a destructive person, a destroyer, a vandal. (Cf. *haribu,* and syn. *mwangamizi, mwuaji.*)

***Mhashiri,** n. (*mi-*), or **Mwashiri,** a strong beam, by which the mast is secured in position in a native vessel. (Cf. *mlingoti.*)

***Mhassi,** n. (*wa-*), a castrated man or animal, a eunuch. (Ar. Cf. *maksai,* and syn. *tawashi.*)

***Mhenzerani,** n. (*mi-*), a plant producing a small kind of cane, *henzerani.*

***Mhimili,** n. (1) (*mi-*), that which carries (bears, supports), a beam, girdle, post, prop, bearing. Also (2) (*wa-*), a patient, enduring person. (Ar. Cf. *himili, hamali, himila, stahimili,* and for 'patient' *mvumilivu.*)

Mhina, n. (*mi-*), the henna plant, the leaves of which steeped in water produce a red dye, much used for ornamental staining of fingers, feet, and often donkeys. (Cf. *hina.*)

***Mhindi,** n. (1) (*wa-*), also commonly **Muhindi,** a native of India, but in Z. usually restricted to the Mahommedan Hindoos, who are divided into two chief sects, the Bohoras and Khojas, each with their own mosques, burial grounds, clubs, &c. The heathen Hindoos are called *Baniani* (*ma-*). (Cf. *Hindi, kihindi.*) (2) (*mi-*), also commonly **Muhindi,** the plant bearing maize, or Indian corn—also called *Muhindi,* in its natural state and collectively. Single cobs are called *gunzi, kigunzi,* and the grains when separated *mahindi.* (Cf. *hindi, gunzi, bisi, kumvi, ganda.*)

***Mhitaji,** n. (*wa-*), (1) a person who wants (needs something), a candidate, applicant, petitioner. (2) one who is needy, in want, poor. E.g. *mimi si mhitaji nawe* (or *kwako*), I want nothing from you. *Bwana alikuwa tajiri, sasa mhitaji,* my master was once rich, now he is poor. (Ar. Cf. *hitaji, uhitaji, haja,* and syn. *masikini.*)

Mhogo, n. (*mi-*), also commonly **Muhogo,** the cassava or manioc plant, producing the edible roots, also called in their natural state and collectively *mhogo, muhogo.* Very large roots are called *hogo, mahogo.* The roots are cut in strips (cf. *kopa, ubale*) and dried; then, when wanted, pounded and boiled. There are several varieties, *m. wa bungala* and *m. mweusi,* with reddish stems, sweet and eatable without cooking; *m. wa kindoro, m. nangwa,* *m. mchungu*, with green stems, bitter, and requiring (excepting in one variety) to be dried before eaten. E. g. *siuchezei mhogo mchungu*, I do not play with bitter cassava. *Enga muhogo*, cut cassava in slices for cooking.

Mhunzi, n. (*wa-*), a worker in metals, or stone, a smith, a stone-cutter. Usually defined by a word following, e.g. *m. wa chuma (fetha, bati)*, a blacksmith (silversmith, tin-worker). *M. wa mawe*, a stone-cutter, carver in stone. (Cf. *mfua*, and *fundi*.)

Mi-, Plur. Pfx. of D 2, e.g. *mti*, a tree, *miti*, trees.

***Mia**, n. and a., a hundred, one hundred. *-a mia*, hundredth. *Mia kwa moja*, one per cent. *Mia mia*, hundreds, in hundreds,—of a large indefinite quantity. (Ar. Cf. dual from *miteen*.)

Miaa, n. plur. also **Miyaa**. See **Mwaa**.

Mikambe, n. *Piga m.*, in bathing, duck down and throw one leg over so as to strike the water with it.

***Mila**, n. (—), custom, habit, propensity, usage. (Ar. Cf. *desturi, tabia, ada*.)

***Milele**, n. and adv., eternity, perpetuity. *-a milele*, continual, never ending, everlasting. As adv., always, perpetually, for ever. *Maisha na milele*, for life and for ever, for ever and ever. Also **Umilele**. (Ar. Cf. syn. *daima, siku zote*.)

Milhoi, n. one kind of evil spirit. (Cf. *pepo*.)

Milia, n. plur. of *mlia*, but used as a., striped. *Punda milia*, zebra. (Cf. *mlia*.)

***Miliki**, v. possess, be owner (ruler, king) of, rule, exercise authority over. Ps. *milikiwa*. Ap. *milik-ia*, e.g. hold in trust for, be regent for, rule in (for, with, &c.). Cs. *milik-isha, -ishwa*, put in possession, make king or ruler. (Ar. Cf. *maliki, malkia, mamlaka*, and follg. Also syn. *tawala*.)

***Milki**, n. (—), sometimes also **Mulki**, and treated as if D 2, possession, property, dominion, kingdom. (Ar. Cf. prec.)

Mimba, n. (—), conception, pregnancy, embryo. *Shika (chukua, tunga,-wana) mimba*, be (or, become) pregnant, conceive. *Tia m.*, cause to be pregnant. *Haribu m.*, cause miscarriage, miscarry. Also of plants, *mtama unafanya mimba*, the millet is just forming the ear. (Cf. *himila, uzito*.)

***Mimbara**, n. (—), pulpit,—in a mosque. (Ar.)

Mimi, pron. of 1 Pers. S., I, me. Also often *miye*. *Mimi mwenyewe, mimi nafsi yangu* or *bi nafsi yangu*, I myself. *-angu mimi*, my own. (All the personal pronouns are reduplicated forms, except the third plural, *mimi, wewe, yeye, sisi, ninyi, wao*.)

Mimina, v. (1) pour out, pour, spill,—of anything in a fluid state, and so (2) run into a mould, cast. *Ameniminia samli chomboni mwangu*, he has poured me out some ghee in my vessel. *Mkate wa kuminina*, a kind of confectionery. Ps. *miminiwa*. Nt. *miminika*, e.g. be poured out, overflow. Ap. *miminia, -iwa*. Cs. *mimin-isha, -ishwa*. (Cf. follg., and *mwaga*, pour away, *subu*, cast.)

Miminiko, n. (*ma-*), something poured out, a casting. (Cf. prec.)

Minya, v. press, squeeze, squeeze out. Rp. *minyana*. (Cf. *finya*, and syn. *kama, kamua*.)

Mio, n. plur of umio (which see), (2) (*ma-*), amplif. form of *umio* (cf. *kimio*), e.g. *mio la mnyama*, the throat-passage of an animal.

Miongoni, plur. locat. form from *mwongo* (which see), number, account, reckoning. Used in *miongoni mwa*, as a prepositional phrase, in the number of, among, from among, on the side of, in the party of, i. e. *katika hesabu ya. Hawa si miongoni mwangu*, these are not among my people, in my service.

*Mirathi, n. inheritance, heritage, —for more usual *urithi*. (Ar. Cf. *rithi*.)

*Miski, n. and Meski, musk, or similar perfume.

*Misko, n. Moscow, and used for Russia.

*Misri, n. Egypt. (Ar.)

*Miteen, n. and a., two hundred. *-a miteen*, two-hundredth. (Ar. dual of *mia*, i. e. *mia mbili*.)

*Mithili, n. likeness, resemblance, similitude,—same as Methali (which see). Usually (1) in prepositional phrase *mithili ya*, like, just as,—or only *mithili*. (2) as conj., for (or with *kama*), as, like, like as. *Nataka kasha mithili ya hii*, I want a box of this pattern. *Wakaonana mithili kama auwali*, and they met like as at first. (Ar. Cf. *methali, kama*.)

Miunzi, n. plur. of *mwunzi*, which is seldom used, whistling, a whistle. *Piga miunzi*, whistle. (Cf. *ubinja, mbinja, msonyo*.)

Miwa, n. plur. of *muwa*, or *mwa*, sugar-cane.

Miwaa, n. plur. of *mwaa* (which see).

*Miwani, n. a pair of spectacles, eye-glasses. Commonly described as *macho mawili*, double eyes. (Ar.)

Miye, pron. 1 Pers. S., same as Mimi, I, me. (Cf. *weye, yeye, siye*.)

*Mizani, n. (1) weighing machine, balances, scales. The pan is called *kitanga*, and the beam of the scales *mtange*. Also (2) the pendulum, or balance, regulating a machine, clock, watch, &c. (Ar. Cf. *uzani, uthani*.)

Mja, n. (*wa-*), verbal of *ja*, one who comes, and so (1) a new-comer, foreigner,—also *mja na maji*, or *mja maji*; (2) a slave,—not usual in Z.,

for *mtumwa*. *Ada ya mja, hunena; mngwana ni kitendo*, a slave talks, but a free man acts.

Mjakazi, n. (*wa-*), a female slave. (Cf. *kijakazi*, and *mtumwa*. Perh. *mja*, and *kazi*, work, but *kazi, mkazi*, in some dialects means a woman.)

Mjane, n. (*wa-*), a widowed, bereaved person, male or female, a widow, a widower. (Cf. *ujane*.)

Mjanja, n. (*wa-*), cheat, impostor, knave, sharper. (Cf. *-janja, ujanja*, and syn. *ayari, mkopi*.)

Mjeledi, n. (*mi-*), whip (of leather), thong, strap. *Piga (tia) mijeledi*, beat with a whip. (Ar. leather. Cf. *jelidi, jalada*, and *ukanda*.)

Mjengo, n. (*mi-*), (1) act (process, style, method) of building, architecture, also (2) thing built, erection, structure, e. g. encampment, hut. (Cf. *jenga, jengo, mjenzi*.)

Mjenzi, n. (*wa-*), a builder, esp. in native style, i. e. of wooden structures. (Cf. *mwashi*, of stone work.) *Kwenyi miti hakuna mjenzi*, where the trees are, there is no one to use them. (Cf. *jenga*, and prec.)

Mji, n. (*mi-*), (1) village, hamlet, town, city, i. e. a collection of human dwellings irrespective of number, 5 or 5,000. (Cf. *kijiji, kitongoji*.) Used with and without preps. *Toka (ondoka, &c.) katika mji*, or *mjini*, or *mji* only. So *enda (fika, &c.) katika mji*, or *mjini*, or *mji*. (2) middle of a piece of cloth; (3) after-birth, placenta, and sometimes of the womb itself. (*Mji* is traceable in other Bantu dialects, some distant, as also *maji*, water.)

*Mjiari, n. (*mi-*), tiller-rope (Str.). Also *ujari*. (Cf. *kamba* for other ropes.)

*Mjibu, n. an affable, pleasant, accessible person. (Arab., not common, cf. *wajibu*.)

*Mjiguu, n. (*wa-*), a large foot, a long leg, a person with large feet (or long-legged). (Cf *kijiguu, mguu*.)

Mjiko, n. (*mi-*), lower bowel, rectum (Kr.). (Cf. *jika*.)

Mjima, n. (*wa-*), one who cooperates, or gives friendly help, an assistant. (Cf. *ujima*.)

Mjinga, n. (*wa-*), a fool, simpleton, ignoramus, dupe, and esp. of innocent ignorance, inexperience, and so, new-comer, raw slave, greenhorn, tenderfoot. *Akawa mjinga, kama mbuzi illa kasoro*, he was a fool, like a goat and even worse. *Mjinga ni mtu, usinene ni ng'ombe*, a simpleton is a human being, do not call him a cow,—a native type of silliness. (Cf. *mpumbafu, barazuli, mzuzu*.)

Mjio, n. (*mi-*), coming, arrival. Verbal of *ja*, v. (Cf. *majilio, jioni*.)

Mjoli, n. (*wa-*), fellow slave, member of same establishment, fellow servant. (Cf. *mtumwa*.)

Mjomba, n. (*wa-*), (1) uncle, nephew,—the term being used by each of the other. But *mjomba* also is used especially of the uncle on the mother's side, who is also called *baba mkubwa* or *mdogo* (according as he is older or younger than the father). Contr. *amu* (Ar.), uncle on the father's side. (2) a native name for a Swahili,—the Swahili region being called *Ujomba*, and language *kijomba*.

Mjukuu, n. (*wa-*), grandchild, or other relation of the second generation, grand-nephew (or -niece), second cousin (male or female). Fig. as in *majuto ni mjukuu*, remorse is a grandchild, i.e. comes at length. (Cf. *kijukuu, kilembwe, kining'ina*.)

Mjumbe, n. (*wa-*), messenger, go-between, deputed person, ambassador, delegate, representative. *Mjumbe hauawi*, a messenger's person is sacred. (Cf. *jumbe, kijumbe, ujumbe*.)

Mjume, n. (*wa-*), a skilled workman who executes ornamental work, engraving, inlaying, &c. on weapons, and personal ornaments. *M. wa visu*, a high-class cutler. (Cf. *ujume, mjumu*.)

Mjumu, n. or **Njumu**, inlaid work, ornamental decoration with various materials.

Mjusi, n. (*wa-*), (1) a lizard,—of the smaller sort, of which there are many varieties. (For larger kinds cf. *guruguru, kenge*.) (2) a lizard-shaped ornament worked in silk stitches on the front of a *kanzu* (which see).

Mjuu, n. used of wind,—as blowing above or overhead. (Cf. *juu*.)

Mjuvi, n. (*wa-*), a saucy, impudent, inquisitive, prying, intruding person. (Cf. *jua, ujuvi*, and follg.)

Mjuzi, n. (*wa-*), one who knows, a well-informed, large-minded, sagacious, wise person. *Mwenyezi Mngu ni msikizi na mjuzi wa killa kitu*, Almighty God hears and knows everything. (Cf. *jua, ujuzi*, and prec.)

Mkaa, n. (1) (*wa-*), one who sits, remains, lives, &c., an inhabitant, a resident, an occupant. *Mkaa jikoni*, a kitchen maid, a Cinderella. (Cf. *kaa*, and follg.) (2) (*mi-*), a tree, the bark of which is used medicinally as an astringent.

Mkaaji, **Mkaazi**, n. (*wa-*), an inhabitant, regular occupant, a stay-at-home, not a traveller, contr. to *mpitaji, mhamishi*. *Ukiwa mkaazi, jenga*, if you are come to stay, build a house. (Cf. *kaa*, v. and prec.)

*****Mkabala**, **Mkabil**, adv. mostly in prepositional phrase, *mkabala wa*, in front of, facing, opposite, corresponding to, fronting. Also, in front, future. (Ar. Cf. *kabili, kabla, kibula*, &c., and *lekea*.)

*****Mkabithi**, n. (*wa-*), verbal of *kabithi*, one who holds, keeps, &c., and so (1) a trustee, one who holds property or money; (2) a miser, an economizer, a thrifty person. (Cf. *kabithi*, and *bahili*.)

*Mkadamu, n. (*wa-*), and Mukadamu. See Kadamu.

Mkadi, n. (*mi-*), a pandanus tree, with strongly scented leaves used in perfumes, and large fruits like pineapples.

Mkaguo, n. (*mi-*), inspection, visitation, review. (Cf. *kagua*, and follg., also *angalia, tazamia*.)

Mkaguzi, n. (*wa-*), an inspector, examiner, reviewer. (Cf. *kagua*, and prec.)

Mkahaba, n. (*wa-*), also Kahaba (*ma-*), prostitute.

*Mkahawa, n. (*mi-*), coffee-house, restaurant, café. A square containing several of these in Z. is known as *Mkahawani*. (Cf. *kahawa*.)

Mkaja, n. (*mi-*), cloth worn by women round the body, esp. after child-birth,—one of the presents usually made to the bride's mother at marriage. (Cf. *mbeleko*, and follg.)

*Mkalimani, n. (*wa-*), interpreter, i. e. in a professional sense, one who is employed to translate into and from an unknown tongue. (Ar. *kalima*, a word, cf. syn. *mfasiri*. *Mkalimu* is also used for teacher.)

Mkalio, n. (*mi-*), a customary wedding fee, one of several given to the bride's attendants, lit. sitting by,—like *kiosha miguu, kipa mkono, kifungua mlango*, &c.

Mkamba, n. (*mi-*), a larger species of sea crab. (Cf. *kamba*, and *kaa*.)

Mkamshe, n. (*mi-*), a kind of wooden spoon (Str.). (Cf. *mwiko*.)

Mkana, n. (*wa-*), verbal of *kana*, one who denies, repudiates, &c. *Mkana Muungu*, an atheist. (Cf. *kana, mkanushi, ukanyo, ukani*, &c.)

Mkandaa, n. (*mi-*), a kind of mangrove, growing abundantly on the coast in East Africa. The bark is used for tanning, and furnishes a red dye. The hard straight trunks supply largely the *boriti* of commerce, i. e. poles used for carrying concrete roofs in house-building. (Cf. *mkoko*, and *mui*.)

Mkangaja, n. (*mi-*), a tree bearing a small kind of mandarin orange (*kangaja*) in thick clusters of bright orange-red colour. (Cf. *mchungwa*, for other varieties.)

Mkanju, n. (*mi-*), a cashew-nut tree,—known in Z. usually as mbibo (which see).

Mkano, n. (*mi-*), tendon, sinew, muscle,—of cattle and animals generally. (Cf. *kano, ukano*, and *mshipa*.)

*Mkasama, n. (1) division, part, portion; (2) in mathematics, division. (Arab. Cf. *mgawo*.)

Mkasasi, n. (*mi-*), a fine tree, useless for timber (Str., who quotes a couplet, *uzuri wa mkasasi ukipata maji basi*, the *mkasasi* is a fine tree, but all it yields is sap).

Mkasiri, n. (*mi-*), a tree, the bark of which is used to dye nets black (Str.).

Mkata, n. (*wa-*), (1) one who cuts,—verbal of *kata*, v. (cf. *mkate, mkati*); (2) a poor man,—seldom heard in Z. city. *Ni mkata, sina mbele wala nyuma*, I am a poor man, with nothing before or behind me. *Mkata hana kinyongo*, a poor man cannot afford fancies. (Cf. *ukata*, and syn. *masikini, fukara*.)

*Mkataa, n. and adv., also Makataa, (1) what is settled, final decision, end of an affair; (2) in a fixed, firm, decided, final way, e. g. *m. neno hili, sitakwenda*, this is my final word, I will not go. *Tumeafikana m.*, we made a final contract. *Sema kwa m.*, make a final statement. (Ar. Cf. *kata*.)

*Mkataba, n. (*mi-*), what is written, book, statute, contract, engagement. (Ar. Cf. *kitabu*, and syn. *hati, sharti, maagano*.)

Mkatale, n. (*mi-*), stocks, instrument for confining a prisoner by the feet, i. e. *mti uliochongwa ukazuliwa tundu*, a piece of wood shaped and with holes bored in it. (Cf. *kifungo, mnyororo, pingu*.)

*Mkate, n. (*mi-*), something cut,

and so, (1) any kind of lump, or separate piece, *m. wa tumbako*, a plug or cake of tobacco, *m. wa nyuki*, a piece of honey-comb, but esp. (2) a loaf, cake, bun, biscuit, or anything similar, and used commonly of European bread. Various kinds are distinguished as *m. wa ngano*, bread made of wheat flour; *m. wa mofa*, or *mofa* only, a cake of millet meal baked in an oven; *m. wa kumimina*, a cake of batter, fritter; *m. wa kusonga*, &c. When *mkate* is used of ordinary bread, the crust (*ganda la mkate*) is distinguished from the crumb (*nyama ya mkate*). (Ar. Cf. *kata*, v., and follg.)

Mkati, n. (*wa-*), one who cuts, cuts up, cuts out, cuts down, &c. (Cf. *kata*, v., *mkate*, *mkato*.)

*****Mkato**, n. (*mi-*), (1) a cutting, incision, amputation, cut; (2) effect of cutting, a slit, crack, crevice; (3) a fraction, piece, esp. a separate part of a native house, a division, apartment, room,—made by a partition or screen only, *kiwambaza*; (4) fig. a cutting down or away, cutting short, reduction, retrenchment; (5) a short, abrupt, decisive act or method. *Fanya kwa mkato*, like *mkataa*, act quickly, decisively, at a word. (Ar. Cf. *kata*, and prec.)

Mkazi, n. (*wa-*), (1) for **Mkaazi** (which see), an inhabitant; (2) *Muungu ni mkazi wa ulimwengu*, i. e. perh. from *kaza*, upholder, firm supporter. (Cf. follg.)

Mkazo, n. (*mi-*), using force, tension, effort, energy, pressure, exertion. (Cf. *kaza*, *kazi*, and syn. *bidii*, *nguvu*.)

Mke, n. (*wa-*) for *mtu mke*, a woman, a female, also *mwanamke*. Used alone, *mke* means distinctively 'wife,' in contrast with *mwanamke*. *Mume ni kazi, mke ni nguo*, the husband works, the wife dresses. See -ke. (Cf. *mume*.)

Mkebe, n. (*mi-*), pot, canister, mug (for drinking and other purposes). *Mkebe wa ubani*, a pot for keeping or burning incense in. (For other kinds cf. *chungu, chombo*.)

Mkeka, n. (*mi-*), a mat (usually of the kind used for sleeping on). Hence *kama kitanda kupata mkeka*, like a bedstead getting a mat, i.e. of natural completion, the final touch. These mats are oblong, made of certain leaves (*ukindu*), slit into strips, plaited, and stained various colours. The strips (*ukili*) are sewn together, and bound round the edge. The commonest in Z. are plain white, or with transverse stripes of colour. Their manufacture is the ordinary occupation of women when not engaged in cookery or other household work. *Mikeka* are described as *ya kulalia*, for sleeping on; *ya rangi*, with coloured stripes; *ya kufuta*, of common cheap make; *ya kazi*, plaited in patterns. (For other kinds cf. *jamvi, msala, kitanga, randa*.)

Mkereza, n. (*wa-*), one who turns with a lathe, a turner. (Cf. *kereza*.)

Mkewe, n. for *mke wake*, his wife. So *mkewo, mkeo*, your wife, i. e. *mke wako*.

Mkia, n. (*mi-*), a tail. *Suka m.*, wag the tail. *M. wa mjusi*, lines of silk stitching running up the front of a *kanzu* from the ornament called *mjusi*.

Mkilemba, n. (*wa-*), one who has earned a turban, i.e. by completing a job or a course of instruction, and so denotes a successful candidate, prizeman, graduate. (Cf. *kitemba*.)

Mkimbizi, n. (*wa-*), (1) one who runs, e.g. the slave who runs in front of his master's donkey, but also (2) one who runs away,—fugitive, runaway, deserter, truant; (3) one who causes to run, pursuer, hunter, persecutor,—also a robber, a highwayman (cf. *mtoro*). (Cf. *kimbia, mbio*.)

Mkindu, n. (*mi-*), the wild date palm,—producing an edible fruit (*ki-*

ndu), and leaves which furnish material (*ukindu*) for weaving fine mats, and a fibre used for string. (For other palms cf. *mnazi*.)

Mkinga, n. (*mi-*), anything that stops, obstructs, or diverts something else, e.g. *mkinga maji*, a strip of leaf or stick used to catch the water running down a tree, also *mchilizi*. (Cf. *kinga*, v., and follg.)

Mkingamo, n. (*mi-*), a crossing, being athwart, obstructing, in the way. *Njia ya mkingamo*, a cross-road. (Cf. *kinga*, *kingama*, and follg.)

Mkingiko, n. (*mi-*), a cross-pole laid on the top of upright posts to carry the lower ends of the rafters in building a native house. (Cf. *kinga*, and prec.)

Mkiwa, n. (*wa-*), a solitary, destitute, friendless person, a poor man. (Cf. *-kiwa*, *ukiwa*.)

Mkizi, n. (*wa-*), a kind of fish.

Mkoba, n. (*mi-*), bag, pouch, wallet,—sometimes made of the entire skin of a small animal. *Wimbi la mkoba*, bag-like waves, i.e. smooth swelling waves, not like breakers. (For various kinds of bag, &c. cf. *mfuko*, *kikapo*.)

Mkoche, n. (*mi-*), one name of a kind of palm (Hyphaene), known also as *mkoma*, but in Z. commonly as *mwaa*, or *mnyaa* (which see).

*****Mkohani**, n. (*wa-*), and **Mkuhani**, **Kuhani**, **Kahini**, priest; soothsayer, magician. (Ar. Cf. *kahini*, *kasisi*.)

Mkojo, n. (*mi-*), micturition, urine,—also *choo cha mbele*, *choo kidogo*. (Cf. *kojoa*, and follg., also *nya*, *choo*.)

Mkojozi, n. (*wa-*), one who cannot or does not control his urine, one who wets his bed. (Cf. *kojoa*, and prec.)

Mkoko, n. (*mi-*), a kind of mangrove, much used as firewood in Z., with a red bark used for dyeing. (Other kinds are *mkandaa*, and *mui*.)

Mkokoto, n. (*mi-*), (1) a dragging, a hauling, a pull; (2) the mark or trail of something dragged along. (Cf. *kokota*, and dist. *makokoto*.)

Mkoma, n. (1) (*wa-*), verbal of *koma* (which see), one who stops, ceases, comes to an end; (2) (*wa-*), a leper, one suffering from **ukoma** (which see); (3) (*mi-*), one of the names by which the Hyphaene palm is known on the East Coast,—others being *mkoche*, *mwaa* (which see).

Mkomafi, n. (*mi-*), name of a tree (*Carapa moluccensis*, Sac.). The wood is red, and was formerly much used in Z.

Mkombozi, n. (*wa-*), one who ransoms (buys back, gets out of pawn, recovers a deposit), a redeemer. (Cf. *komboa*, *ukombozi*.)

Mkomwe, n. (*mi-*), a kind of climbing plant,—the seeds of which are used as counters in playing various games. (Cf. *komwe*.)

Mkondo, n. (*mi-*), current, flow, rush, passage, run, e.g. of water in a river or poured on the ground; of air through a door or window, i.e. draft; of the wake of a ship, of an animal, i.e. track, run. Cf. *mkondo wa nyasi*, a track through rushes, showing where people have passed. (Cf. *kondo*.)

Mkonga, n. (*mi-*), trunk of an elephant,—in Z. commonly *mkono wa tembo*.

Mkongo, n. (*mi-*), (1) a fibre-producing plant, a kind of hemp or Sansevieria, i.e. *shubiri la kufanyia kitani*, the fibre being called *ukonge*, or *uzi wa mkonge*; (2) a kind of fish.

Mkongojo, n. (*mi-*), a staff used as a prop or crutch, for an old or weakly person. (Cf. *kongoja*, *ukongojo*, and for sticks *bakora*, *fimbo*.)

Mkongwe, n. (*wa-*), an aged, feeble, infirm person. (Cf. *konga*, *kikongwe*, and syn. *mzee*.)

Mkono, n. (*mi-*), (1) the arm of a human being, esp. of the lower arm, and the hand, e.g. *mkono hukatwa kati ya kisigino na mkono*, his arm is cut off between the elbow and hand.

Mkono wake watoa sana, his hand gives freely. *Pelekea mkono*, lay hands on, arrest. Then (2) of a corresponding member in animals, front paw. *Simba akamkamata mkononi*, the lion seized him with its paw. (Cf. *mkono wa tembo*, an elephant's trunk, and *mkono* (or *kikono, kono*), of the tendrils of a plant.) (3) of what resembles an arm, e.g. as projecting, *mkono wa sufuria*, the handle of a European saucepan,—as spreading, *mikono ya mto* (*bahari*), branches of a river, creeks of the sea,—as grasping, &c. (4) as a convenient measure, from finger tips to elbow, a cubit, same as (Ar.) *thiraa*, 18 inches, i.e. double of a span, and half a yard. Also in various figurative senses, e.g. *mwenyi mkono mrefu*, a thieving, mischievous, cunning person, a rogue. *Mkono wake mzuri*, he is a liberal, open-handed person. *Chuo cha mkono*, a handy book, manual. *Kupa mkono*, to give the hand, i.e. greet, congratulate, condole with, assist, take leave, take an oath, &c. *Mkono wa msiba*, condolence in grief. (Cf. *kono, kikono.*)

Mkonzo, n. (*mi-*). See **Konzo**.

Mkoo, n. (*wa-*), a slut, slattern, a dirty untidy person, male or female. (Cf. syn. *mchafu*, and dist. *ukoo, koo.*)

Mkopeshi, n. (*wa-*), one who supplies goods or capital on credit for commercial purposes, a lender, a usurer. (Cf. *kopa*, v., and follg.)

Mkópi, n. (*wa-*), (1) one who borrows goods or money, e.g. to trade with on the mainland; (2) a swindler, impostor, knave. (Cf. *kopa, ukopi*, and prec.)

Mkopo, n. (*mi-*), act (process, method, &c.) of borrowing, swindling, &c. (Cf. *kopa, ukopi*, and prec.)

Mkorofi, n. (*wa-*), an evil-minded, malignant, brutal, tyrannical person, a monster, a brute. (Cf. -*korofi, ukorofi.*)

Mkoroga, n. (*wa-*), a stirrer, i.e. (1) a maker of discord, an agitator, firebrand; (2) a blunderer, bungler. (Cf. *koroga*, and follg., and syn. *mfitini.*)

Mkorogo, n. (*mi-*), (1) a stirring, mashing, mixing of ingredients, &c.; (2) a causing discord, agitation, disturbance of peace, blundering, bungling. (Cf. *koroga*, and prec., also syn. *fitina, sukosuko.*)

Mkoromaji, n. (*wa-*), a regular snorer. (Cf. *koroma*, and prec.)

Mkoromo, n. (*mi-*), a snoring, snorting, or similar sound. (Cf. *koroma*, and follg., and *msono.*)

Mkubwa, n. (*wa-*), (1) a great man (in wealth, dignity, power, &c.); (2) chief, director, responsible head, master, owner. *Huyu ni mkubwa wetu*, here is our master. (Cf. -*kubwa*, and syn. *mkuu, msimamizi, bwana.*)

Mkuchyo, n. name of a town on the Somali coast, north of Mombasa, also called Mukdisha, and commonly Makdesh or Magadoxa.

Mkufu, n. (*mi-*), a chain, usually metal, of a light kind, worn as an ornament. (Contr. *muyororo*, and for ornaments cf. *urembo.*)

Mkufunzi, n. (*wa-*), a teacher,— more usual form for *mfunzi*. (Cf. *mfundishi, mwalimu*, and for the insertion of *ku* cf. *mkulima.*)

Mkuki, n. (*mi-*), a spear. *Chomeka mkuki*, to stick a spear in the ground. (For the iron head cf. *chembe, kengee*, for the shaft *mti, uti*, for the butt end *tako.*)

Mkuku, n. (*mi-*), the keel,—of a boat or ship. (Dist. *kuku*, a fowl.)

Mkule, n. (*wa-*), a garfish (Str.).

Mkulima, n. (*wa-*), a tiller of the ground, cultivator, agriculturist, field labourer, peasant. (Cf. *lima, mlimaji*, and for the form *mkufunzi*,— the *ku* being inserted perh. to distinguish from *mlima*, a hill.)

Mkumbizi, n. (*wa-*), one who clears up, makes a sweep of anything, a gleaner. (Cf. *kumba*, and follg.)

Mkumbo, n. (*mi-*), a complete

clearing out, a clean sweep, a thorough removal, wholesale devastation. (Cf. *kumba*.)

Mkunazi, n. (*mi-*), the jujube tree, bearing a small edible stonefruit like a cherry, *kunazi*.

Mkunde, n. (*mi-*), the shrub, which produces the common bean *ukunde*, much used in Z.

Mkundu, n. (*mi-*), the anus, orifice of the bowel.

Mkunga, n. (*wa-*), (1) a midwife, but in Z. commonly *mzalishi* (cf. *kunga*, *ukunga*, *kungu*); (2) a kind of eel, or sea-snake.

Mkungu, n. (*mi-*), (1) a large tree bearing a fruit (*kungu*) resembling a small apple, but with a large stone and kernel; (2) the fruit-stem or pedicel of a banana plant carrying the whole head of fruit; (3) an earthenware dish, used for cooking, and also its lid, *mkungu wa kufunikia*. (For other vessels cf. *chungu, chombo*.)

Mkunguru, n. also **Ukunguru**, the fever which attacks a new-comer at a place, after a change of residence and diet, sickness of acclimatization.

Mkung'uto, n. (*mi-*), a straining off, a shaking off, a wiping off, a sifting. (Cf. *kunguta, kunguto*.)

Mkunjo, n. a folding, a creasing, a turning over, a fold. (Cf. *kunja*.)

Mkuno, n. (*mi-*), a scratching, a grating. (Cf. *kuna*.)

Mkuo, n. (*mi-*), an ingot, lump or bar of cast or unwrought metal, pig (of iron), rough casting. (Cf. *mgando*, and ? *mtapo*.)

Mkupuo, n. (*mi-*), a shaking or pushing off, a getting rid of, a letting drop. (Cf. *kupua*, and *kung'uta*.)

Mkusanyi, n. (*wa-*), also **Mkusanya**, a collector, a gatherer together, convener. (Cf. follg.)

Mkusanyo, n. (*mi-*), a collecting, gathering, &c. (Cf. *kusanya*.)

Mkutano, n. (*mi-*), (1) meeting, gathering, assemblage, council, committee; (2) confluence, concurrence, coincidence. *M. wa watu*, a meeting. *M. wa mito*, junction of rivers. (Cf. *kuta, kutana, makutano*.)

Mkuto, n. (*mi-*), (1) a meeting with, a lighting upon, a finding; (2) ? a fold, like *kunjo*. *Kunja nguo mkuto*, fold up a dress. (Cf. *kuta*.)

Mkuu, n. (*wa-*), (1) a great person (in wealth, position, power, &c.), a grandee; (2) ruler, head, master, governor, &c. *Mkuu wa genzi*, leader of a caravan. (Cf. -*kuu*, -*kubwa*, and syn. *bwana, msimamizi*.)

Mkuyu, n. (*mi-*), the sycamore of the east, fig-mulberry tree, producing the fruit *kuyu*.

Mkwaju, n. (*mi-*), the tamarind tree, bearing the fruit *ukwaju*.

Mkwamba, n. (*mi-*), a kind of thorny shrub.

Mkwaruzo, n. (*mi-*), (1) a scraping, a grating; (2) track or trail of something scraping along, e.g. *mkwaruzo wa nyoka*, the trail of a serpent. (Cf. *kwaruza*.)

Mkwasi, n. (*wa-*), a rich man, a well-to-do opulent person. (Cf. -*kwasi, ukwasi*.)

Mkwe, n. (*wakwe*), used of near connexions by marriage, father (or mother) in law, son (or daughter) in law. (Cf. *mwamu, wifi*.)

Mkweme, n. (*mi-*), a species of climbing plant.

Mkweo, n. (1) (*mi-*), a climbing, a mounting up or upon (cf. *kwea*); (2) for *mkwe wako*, see **Mkwe**.

Mkwezi, n. (*wa-*), one who climbs, ascends, mounts up. (Cf. *kwea*.)

Mkwiro, n. (*mi-*), a drumstick, used with some kinds of native drum.

Mla, n. (*wala*), an eater, consumer, devourer,—verbal of *la*, governing a noun. *Mla watu*, a cannibal. *Mla leo ni mlaji*, the man who eats to-day (here and now) is the real eater. (Cf. *la*, v., *mlo, ulafi, ulaji, mlaji*.)

Mlaanizi, n. one who curses, swears, uses bad language. (Cf. *laana*, -*laanifu*.)

Mladi, n. (*mi-*), a thin piece of

wood,—used by a weaver (*mfumi*), with which the woof is tightened after each thread is inserted. Also called *upanga*. (Cf. *kitanda cha mfumi*.)

Mlafi, **Mlaji**, n. (*wa-*), an eater, a consumer, and esp. a voracious eater, glutton, gormandizer. *Mlafi* is always an uncomplimentary term. (Cf. *la*, v., *mla*, *mlo*, *ulafi*, *ulaji*.)

Mlala, n. (*mi-*), one of the names by which a Hyphaene palm, or a species of it, is known. Also the leaf which furnishes strips for making mats on for tying. *Kisu cha kuchania milala*, a knife for slitting palm leaves. (Cf. *mwaa*, *mkoche*, *mkindu*.)

Mlamba, n. (*wa-*), (1) name of a bird; (2) verbal of *lamba*, one who licks.

Mlango, n. (*mi-*), (1) door, doorway, gate; (2) entrance, means of access, fee for entrance; (3) anything resembling a door, e. g. a pass (in hills and mountains), a channel (across a bar), a strait, estuary, mouth of a river; (4) fig. of a man's relation to his family or friends, social attitude, circle of acquaintances, branch of a family. *Mlango wake mzuri*, he is a kind, hospitable, sociable person. *Wote walioko katika mlango wetu*, all who belong to our circle. *Penyi wimbi na mlango ni papo*, the channel and the breaker are close together, i. e. safety and danger. (Cf. *lango*, *kilango*.) Native doors are commonly of two kinds, (1) a single door made of pieces of *mwale* (i. e. mid-rib of a large raphia-palm leaf) set side by side with two cross-pieces passed through them, making a light screen, tied or propped in the doorway; or (2) a double or folding door of two boards (*ubau*) turning inwards on projecting tongues of wood fitting in socket holes in the top and bottom of the frame. One board carries a centre strip (*mfaa*) to cover the space between the valves when closed.

The frame consists of side-pieces (*mwimo*) and top and bottom pieces (*kizingiti*). Doors in Z. are often richly carved, and adorned with large brass studs.

*****Mlariba**, n. (*wa-*), a usurer, a money-lender. (Ar. Cf. *riba*, usury, interest, and syn. *faida*. The first syllable is perh. *mla*, one who eats, consumes.)

Mlazi, n. (*wa-*), bed-attendant, bed-fellow. (Cf. *lala*.)

Mle, (1) adv. there within,—like *kule*, *pale*; (2) form of the pronominal adj. *-le*, 'that,' agreeing with a noun in the locative form, e. g. *nyumbani mle*, in that house (cf. *yule*); (3) subjunct. 2 Pers. P. of *la*, (that) you may eat.

Mleo, n. (*mi-*), reeling, staggering, unsteady gait. Also **Mleoleo**, of uncertain wavering movement. (Cf. *lea*, and follg.)

Mlevi, n. (*wa-*), a drunkard, a drunken person. (Cf. *lea*, *levya*, and prec.)

Mlezi, n. (*wa-*), one engaged in the rearing or training of children, a nurse, governess, tutor. Also name of a disease, scrofula (Sac.).

Mlezo, n. for **Mwelezo**. (See *Chelezo*, and cf. *elea*.)

Mlia, n. (*mi-*), a stripe (line, band) of colouring. Used in plur. as adj. *Punda milia*, zebra.

Mlilana, n. (*mi-*), name of a shrub.

Mlima, n. (*mi-*), a mountain, high hill, long steep ascent. *Milima*, *milima mingi*, a mountain range. *Mlima mrefu* (*mkubwa*), a high mountain. (Cf. *kilima*, and *Mrima*, the name of the coast district opposite and south of Zanzibar.)

Mlimaji, n. (*wa-*), for the usual *mkulima*, cultivator, tiller of the ground. (Cf. *lima*.)

Mlimau, n. (*mi-*), the tree bearing lemons (*malimau*). (Cf. for other varieties *mchungwa*.)

Mlimbiko, n. (*mi-*), (1) a waiting for something, taking turns, a turn (in waiting); (2) a store, stock, reserve, treasure. *Mlimbiko wa fetha*, a reserve of funds. (Cf. *limbika*, and syn. *mngojo, zamu*.)

Mlimi, n. (*wa-*), a fluent, babbling, talkative person. (Cf. *ulimi*, and syn. *msemi, mwenyi domo*.)

Mlimo, n. (*mi-*), (1) tillage, husbandry, agriculture, cultivation; (2) results of cultivation, i.e. crops, produce. (Cf. *lima, mkulima, kilimo*.)

Mlimwengu, n. (*wa-*), (1) an inhabitant of the world, and (2) esp. a man of the world, a worldly man. *Mlimwengu ni mwanawe*, a man's hopes (chief worldly interest) are his child. (Cf. *ulimwengu, malimwengu*.)

Mlingoti, n. (*mi-*), mast,—of a vessel. *M. wa maji*, bowsprit. *M. wa mbele*, foremast,—also *wa omoni*. *M. wa kalme*, mizzen-mast. The mast rests on the false keel (*msitamu*) and is fixed by a crossbeam (*fundo*) and two longitudinal timbers (*mwashiri*). (Cf. *chombo*.)

Mlinzi, n. (*wa-*), guardian, protector, keeper, guard, watchman, sentinel, &c. (Cf. *linda, ulinzi*.)

Mlio, n. (*mi-*), a sound,—in the widest sense, a cry, a note, weeping. Used of all kinds of objects, animate and inanimate, yielding a sound. *M. wa mtoto*, a child's crying. *M. wa simba*, a lion's roar. *M. wa bunduki*, the report of a gun. *M. wa ndege*, a bird's singing. *Ngoma ya milio saba*, a drum with seven notes. (Cf. *lia, lio, kilio*.)

Mlipizi, n. (*wa-*), one who pays, one who causes to pay. *Mlipizi kisasi*, an avenger. (Cf. *lipa, malipo*.)

Mlisha, Mlishi, n. (*wa-*), one who feeds or has the care of animals or other creatures. (Cf. *la, lisha, malisha*, and follg.)

Mlisho, n. (*mi-*), (1) a feeding, giving food, rearing, supporting. *M. wa samaki*, baiting for fish. *M. wa mshipi*, putting bait on the fishing-line, bait. (2) native name for the month called in Arab. *Shaaban*, i.e. the month before Ramathan. (Cf. *la, lisha*, and prec.)

Mliwa, n. (*mi-*), a tree with fragrant aromatic wood. (Cf. *liwa, sandali*.)

*****Mlizamu**, n. (*mi-*), a spout for carrying water off a house-top, or eaves. Commonly called *kopo*.

Mlizi, n. (*wa-*), one who cries or makes a noise, a child who is always crying, a ranter, a loud-mouthed orator. (Cf. *lia, ulizi*.)

Mlomo, n. (*mi-*), a variant of *mdomo* (which see).

Mlongo, n. (*mi-*), a variant of *mwongo* (which see).

*****Mlozi**, n. (1) (*mi-*), an almond tree, producing the almond nut, *lozi*. (Ar.) (2) (*wa-*), wizard, sorcerer, for the more usual *mchawi*. (Cf. *loga, ulozi*.)

Mlungula, n. (*wa-*), a blackmailer, an extortioner, a robber. Also, blackmail, bribe extorted. (Cf. *hongo, rushwa*.)

Mmea, n. (*mi-*), anything possessing vegetable life, or growth resembling it, plant, shoot, sucker, sprout, &c. *Mimea*, vegetation,—in general. (Cf. *mea*, and syn. *ota, kua, mmelea*).

Mmego, n. (*mi-*), act of breaking off a piece or portion of food, with fingers or teeth. (Cf. *mega, mego*.)

Mmelea, n. (*mi-*), that which grows at (in, on) some place or thing, a creeper, a parasite shrub. (Cf. *mea, kimelea*.)

*****Mmnadi**, n. (*wa-*), also **Mnadi**, an auctioneer, salesman, broker, hawker of goods for sale, public crier. (Ar. Cf. *mnada, dalali*.)

Mmoja, n. One man, a man, a person, a certain man. See -*moja*.

Mmumunye, n. (*mi-*), the plant producing a kind of gourd (*mumunye*), like a vegetable marrow. The outer rind, when dry and hard, is used as a vessel for fluids. (Cf. *boga, buyu*.)

*Mmunina, n. (wa-), a true believer, i.e. a Mahommedan. (Ar. Cf. *imani, amini, mwamini.*)

Mmvita, n. (wa-), an inhabitant of *Mvita*, i.e. Mombasa.

Mna, verb-form, (1) there is (within) (cf. *m, na,* and *mna, pana*); (2) you (plur.) have. (Cf. *nina, una,* &c.)

*Mnada, n. (—), an auction, sale, public notice. *Mnadani,* a sale-room, place of auction. *Tia mnadani,* put up for sale. *Mnada wa Sultani unanadiwa,* a proclamation of the Sultan is being made. (Ar. Cf. follg.)

*Mnadi, v. also Nadi, sell by auction, put up for sale, hawk about the streets. Ps. *mnadiwa.* (Ar. Cf. *tembeza.*)

*Mnafiki, n. (wa-), a hypocrite, pretender, impostor, liar. (Ar. Cf. *unafiki,* and cf. *mwongo, mjanja, ayari.*)

*Mnajimu, n. (wa-), an astrologer. (Ar. Cf. *unajimu.*)

*Mnajisi, n. (wa-), an unclean, foul person, one who is profane in conduct or speech. (Ar. Cf. *unajisi, najisi,* and syn. *mchafu.*)

Mnana, n. (wa-), (1) a small yellowish bird, building in colonies on cocoanuts and other palms; (2) a substance used as a yellow dye for the leaf strips (*ukili*) used for plaiting mats.

*Mnanaa, n. (mi-), mint. (Ar. Cf. *nanaa.*)

*Mnanasi, n. (mi-), the pineapple plant,—the fruit being *nanasi.* (Hind.)

*Mnasara, n. (wa-) and Mnasarani, Nazarene,—used of Christians by Mahommedans. (Cf. -*masihiya.*)

Mnaso, n. (mi-), (1) a catching, holding, hampering; (2) difficulty, hitch, trap, impediment. (Cf. *nasa, mgogoro, kizuizo, mtego.*)

Mnazi, n. (mi-), cocoanut tree,—which grows in great numbers in Zanzibar, and the adjacent islands and coast, and next to cloves is the most important commercial product, as well as the most useful for local purposes. The tree-stem is little used, except for stout posts or props, but when cut down the soft nutty substance at the top, from which the leaves and blossoms grow, is eaten as a delicacy (*moyo wa mnazi, kilele* or *kichelema cha mnazi*). The other principal parts and products are the leaf *kuti,* fruit *nazi,* fibre *kumvi,* and sap called *tembo.* (See kuti, &c.) The trees are distinguished as *mkinda,* i.e. young, not yet bearing, *mume* male, and *mke* female. (See further under the words mentioned above. Various kinds of palm are *mkindu, mwaa, mpopoo, mvumo, mchikichi, mtende, mwale.*)

Mnena, n. (wa-), one who speaks, or who has the power of speech. (Cf. follg.)

Mnenaji, Mneni, n. (wa-), a speaker, a professional orator, an eloquent person. (Cf. *nena,* and *msemaji, msemi.*)

Mnenea, n. (wa-), (1) a pleader, interceder, one who speaks for or to the advantage of another; (2) a critic, opponent, one who speaks against or in rebuke of another. (Cf. *nena,* and prec.)

Mnevu, n. See Mnyefu.

Mng'ao, n. (mi-), (1) brightness, blaze, lustre, glare; (2) fig. clearness, perspicuity. *Mng'ao wa maneno,* lucidity of statement. (Cf. *ng'aa,* and follg.)

Mng'ariza, n. (wa-), with or without *macho,*—one who has glowing, glaring eyes, and so to the native mind one suspected of sorcery, malignity, evil intent. So also *mng'arizo,* gleaming, glaring, glitter. (Cf. *ngariza.*)

Mng'arizo, n. (mi-), like mng'ao, glitter, gleam, glare, radiance, &c. *M. wa macho,* glowing, radiant look, or, glaring, gleaming eyes. (Cf. *ng'aa.*)

Mngazija, n. (*wa-*), a native of the Great Comoro Island. (*Anzwani, Moalli, Maotwe* are other islands in the group.)

Mng'oaji, n. (*wa-*), one who digs out, roots up, extracts, &c. *Mng'oaji wa meno,* a dentist. (Cf. *ng'oa.*)

Mngoja, n. (*wa-*), also **Mngoje,** and **Mgoja, -e,** one who waits at a place (occupies a station, is on guard), sentinel, guard, keeper. *Mngoja mlango,* hall-porter, door-boy, gate-keeper. (Cf. *ngoja,* and follg., and syn. *mlinzi.*)

Mngojezi, n. (*wa-*), keeper, caretaker, guardian, watchman. (Cf. *ngoja,* and prec.)

Mng'ongo, n. (*mi-*), name of a tree.

Mnguri, n. (*mi-*), a shoemaker's mallet. (Cf. *mshoni.*)

Mngurumizi, n. (*wa-*), one who grumbles, growls. (Cf. *nguruma.*)

Mngwana, n. (*wa-*), one who is not a slave, a free (civilized, educated) person, gentleman, lady. *Mngwana ni kitendo,* a free man can act (while a slave can only talk). (Cf. *ungwana, kiungwana,* and contr. *mtumwa.*)

Mnjugu, n. (*mi-*), the plant producing the ground-nut *njugu.* (Also *njugu,* of the plant.)

Mno, adv. very much, too much, excessively, exceedingly, beyond measure. Sometimes combined with other adverbs of similar meaning, *sana mno, mno ajabu,* very exceedingly, wonderfully much.

Mnofu, n. flesh, meat, fleshy part, as opp. to bone, i. e. *nyama tupu,* all meat.

Mnong'onezi, Mnong'oni, n. (*wa-*), a whisperer. (Cf. follg.)

Mnong'ono, n. (*mi-*), whispering, a whisper. (Cf. *nong'ona.*)

Mnuna, Mnunaji, Mnuni, n. (*wa-*), a grumbler, one who complains (sulks, is discontented). (Cf. follg.)

Mnunda, n. (*mi-*), a semi-wild town cat. (Cf. *paka.*)

Mnuno, n. (*mi-*), grumbling, discontent, complaint, sulkiness. (Cf. *nuna,* and prec.)

Mnunuzi, n. (*wa-*), a buyer, customer, purchaser. (Cf. *nunua, ununuzi.*)

Mnyaa, n. (*mi-*), one of the names by which the Hyphaene palm is known,—commonly *mwaa* (which see).

Mnyakuzi, n. (*wa-*), a snatcher, pilferer, thief, shop-lifter, pickpocket. (Cf. *nyakua,* and syn. *mwizi.*)

Mnyama, n. (*wa-*), (1) an animal, a beast. Also fig. (2) having the characteristics of an animal, a stupid fool, a brute, a beast. But commonly *nyama* is used in both senses. (Cf. *nyama, ndama. Mnyama,* a riddle, is seldom used in Z.)

Mnyampara, n. (*wa-*), head of a body of men (caravan, expedition, army), or of a part of it, headman,—whether of porters or armed guard. (Cf. *mkuu wa genzi, msimamizi.*)

Mnyamwezi, n. (*wa-*), one of the Nyamwezi tribe, living on the mainland west of Zanzibar, and largely used as porters to and from the coast. Used as a term of contempt by coast people.

Mnyang'anyi, n. (*wa-*), robber, thief, highwayman, burglar. Commonly implies a larger scale of action than *mwizi,* which includes mere petty thieving or pilfering. (Cf. *nyang'anya, unyang'anyi,* and *mwizi.*)

Mnyanya, n. (*mi-*), the plant bearing the tomato (*nyanya*).

Mnyefu, n. (*mi-*), and **Mnefu,** damp, wet, moisture, dampness. (Cf. *nya, -nyefu,* and syn. *rutuba, maji, uloefu, chepechepe.*)

Mnyenyekeŏ, n. deference, a humble attitude, reverence, &c. (Cf. *nyenyekea.*)

Mnyeo, n. (*mi-*), a tickling, pricking, itching sensation, a creeping feeling, craving. *Mnyeo wa njaa,* the pricks, pangs of hunger. Also of prurience. (Cf. *nyea*, and *kinyefu, nyegi*.)

Mnyimo, n. (*mi-*), a withholding, refusal, prohibition. (Cf. *nyima*.)

Mnyiri, n. (*mi-*), also **Mnyiriri**, and **Mng'iri**, arm, tentacle, feeler, of the cuttle-fish *pweza* (and similar creatures?). Commonly *mkono wa pweza*.

Mnyofu, n. (*wa-*), a straightforward, honest, upright, trustworthy person. See -nyofu, Unyofu.

Mnyonge, n. (*wa-*), a humble, abject, low, debased person. *Mnyonge msonge*, name of a kind of musical entertainment or concert, in which the performers are women, forming a kind of club. (Cf. *-nyonge, unyonge*.)

Mnyororo, n. (*mi-*), also **Mnyoro**, **Mnyoo**, (1) a chain, used commonly for securing prisoners, slaves, &c., hence (2) fetters, prison, confinement, gaol. *Tia mnyororo*, or *mnyororoni*, imprison, put under arrest. Sometimes (3) intestinal worm, but commonly *chango*. (Cf. *kifungo, pingu, mti kati, mkatale*, and contr. *mkufu*, light ornamental chain.)

Mnyozi, n. (*wa-*), a barber, commonly kinyozi (which see).

Mnyunyo, n. (*mi-*), a sprinkling,—of liquid, scent, &c. (Cf. *nyunyiza, manyunyo*, and *marashi*.)

Mnywa, Mnywaji, n. (*wa-*), verbal of *nywa* (see **Nya**), one who drinks, a drinker, i.e. of any fluid. *Mnywa maji*, a water-drinker. *Mnywa pombe*, a beer-drinker. (Cf. *nya, kinwa, kinywaji*.)

-mo is the same element as *mu, m*,—the *o* either denoting reference or relative distance, 'in there,' or else giving it the force of a relative pronoun, 'in which.' (See **Mu, M,** and **-o**.) *Mo* (1) forms part of the demonstr. adv. humo, and mumo (which see); (2) affixed to *ndi-* and person-prefixes, and the verb *-wa* or its equivalents, has a demonstrative force, with general or usually local reference, 'in there, to (or, from) inside there,' e. g. *yumo*, he is in there. *Ndimo alimo*, that is where he is (in). *Mimi simo*, I am not in it, i. e. I have nothing to do with it. (3) in verb-forms generally is the form of relative pronoun referring to 'place within which,' e. g. *ndimo akaamo*, that is the place he lives in. *Hamna! hamna! ndimo mliwamo*, Nothing in that! nothing in that! that's where there is something (to be) eaten. *Mo* as a separate word only appears in such a phrase as *mo mote*, in whatever place, wherever. (Cf. *mu, mwa, humo, mumo*.)

Moalli, n. the island Mohilla in the Comoro group.

*****Mofa**, n. (1) a small, hard, round cake of millet (*mtama*) meal; (2) a cooking oven of burnt clay.

Moga, n. (*waoga*), coward, for muoga, mwoga (which see). (Cf. *oga, ogopa*.)

Moja, n., also **Moji, Mosi, Moya**, (the number) one, one as an abstract. *Kumi na moja*, ten and one, eleven. *Moja kwa moja*, straight on, continuously, without a break. *Njia inakwenda moja kwa moja*, the road goes straight on. *Barra na poli moja kwa moja*, desert and forest without a break. *Mia kwa moja*, one per cent.

-moja, a. (same with D 5 (S), D 6), (1) one, a single, a certain, an individual; (2) one in kind, similar, identical; (3) one in feeling, agreeing, harmonious, of one mind. *Mtu mmoja*, an individual, a certain man. *Nguo moja*, the same kind of cloth. *Moyo mmoja*, concord, harmony,—so *hali moja, shauri moja*. *Namna moja na kile*, the same pattern as that one. Various plural forms occur, e. g. *vitu vingi vimoja*, many single, separate, single things; *watu si wamoja*, people are not all alike. *Mtu na mwanawe, watu wamoja maskini*, a man and his son, both equally poor. *Mamoja*, often with *yote* or *pia* added, all one, all the same, all alike, to express indifference. *Mamoja kwangu*, it's all one to me, I do not care, never mind. (Cf. *haithuru*.) *-mojawapo*, any one whatever. *-moja-moja*, one by one, singly, individually, — so *vimoja*. *Pamoja* is used as an adv., all together, with one voice, unanimously, at one time (or, place). (Cf. *mosi*, and Ar. *wahedi*, which is also commonly used in counting.)

Mola, n. a title of God, 'Lord.' (Ar. Cf. *Muungu*, *Rabbi*.)

*****Mombasa**, n. the Arab name of the island and town of Mombasa, about 120 miles north of Zanzibar. The native name is *Mvita*. (There is also a village called Mombasa in Zanzibar near the town.)

Mombee, n. Bombay.

Morís, n. Mauritius.

Moshi, n. (*mi-*), (1) smoke, steam; (2) soot, lamp-black. *Moshi wa moto*, the smoke of a fire. *Moshi unasimama*, the smoke rises straight up. *Merikebu ya moshi*, a steamship. (Cf. *ota, moto,* and syn. *mvuke, masizi*.)

Mosi, n. (the number) one. *-a mosi*, first, but *-a kwanza* is usual. *Jumaa mosi* (*Juma ya mosi*), Saturday,—as being the first day after Friday, which is observed by the Mahommedans as Sunday. See **Juma**. (Cf. *moja*, and Ar. *wahedi*.)

Moskiti, n. also **Meskiti**, **Msikiti**, a mosque, the Mahommedan place of worship. (There are great numbers in Zanzibar city and island,—many being merely native houses of sticks, mud, and thatch, with a barrel or large vessel of water near the door. In the city they are mostly of stone, plain in architecture and ornamentation, only one with a minaret, and only one of large size. Each has its *mwalimu*, or official teacher, and *mwathini*, or crier, a cistern for ablutions, and for the most part a distinct congregation of members of the same nation, sect, or class. *Moskiti* is a form of *masgidi, mesjidi*, cf. *sujudu*.)

Mote, a. and **Mwote**, form of *-ote*, all,—agreeing with nouns having the locative termination *-ni*, e. g. *mjini mote*, in the whole town. (Cf. *-ote, kote, pote*.)

Moto, n. (*mioto*), (1) fire, flame, a fire, a conflagration; (2) heat, warmth, inflammation, temperature; (3) fig. zeal, ardour, energy, vehemence, martial spirit, fierceness. *Fanya m.*, make a fire. *Washa m.*, light a fire. *Pekecha m.*, light a fire by means of firesticks. *Pata m.*, get hot. *Ota* (*kota*) *m.*, sit by a fire, warm oneself. *Choma* (*pasha*) *m.*, or *kwa m.*, set fire to, heat, cook with fire. *Chochea m.*, stir the fire. *Zima* (*zimisha*) *m.*, put out the fire. Prov. *dawa ya moto ni moto*, fire must be met with fire. *Akajisifu moto*, he boasted of his martial prowess. *-a moto*, hot, warm, energetic, fiery, &c. *Kazi moto*, strenuous, eager work. *Maji ya moto*, (1) hot water; (2) a large red ant, living in trees, is so called. (Cf. *ota, moshi*. Firesticks are seldom seen in Z.,—matches being very cheap, and embers easily obtainable.)

Moyo, n. (*mioyo*, also *nyoyo* as if from *uoyo*), (1) the heart (the physical organ); (2) the heart, feelings, soul, mind, will, self; (3) inmost part, core, pith, centre; (4) courage, resolution, presence of mind; (5) special favourite, chief delight. *Unichinje utauona moyo wangu*, kill me and you will find my heart. *Jipa m., piga m. konde*, take heart, pluck up courage. *Tia* (*simika, kuza*) *m.*, encourage, cheer, hearten. *Shuka m.*, be depressed. *M. mchache*, lack of courage, a faint heart. *Mimi moyo wangu nataka*, I really desire it. *M. wa jipu*, the core of an abscess. *Moyo wa mnazi*, the soft nutty core at the top of a cocoanut tree, from which leaves and blossoms grow,—eaten as a delicacy. *Moyo wa kanzu*, the part of a *kanzu* over the chest. *Huyu ndiye moyo wake*, this is his great pet. *-a moyo*, voluntary, willing. *Sema (fanya) kwa moyo*, speak (act) voluntarily, readily. Also *sema kwa moyo*, say by rote, repeat without a book or reminder. (Cf. *roho, nafsi*, and *mtima*.)

Mpagazi, n. (*wa-*), carrier, bearer, caravan-porter. *Nikawapa wapagazi upagazi wao*, I gave the porters their wages. (Cf. *pagaa, upagazi*, and syn. *mchukuzi, hamali*.)

Mpaji, n. (*wa-*), donor, giver, benefactor, a generous, liberal person. But esp. of God, e. g. *mpaji wa kupa ni Muungu*, the real (only) Giver is God,—also called *mpaji asiyepewa*, He who always gives and never receives. (Cf. *pa, upaji, kipaji*, and *-karimu*. Dist. *paji, kipaji*, forehead, temple.)

Mpaka, n. (*mi-*), boundary, limit, border, term. *Piga (weka) m.*, fix a boundary, lay down a limit. *Ruka m.*, trespass, break bounds. *Mpaka mmoja*, adjacent, bordering, adjoining. Also used as prep., up to, to, as far as, till, until, to the time of,—like *hatta*. *Akafika mpaka kwetu*, he came as far as our country. *Nikae mpaka lini?* How long am I to stay? (Cf. *paka*, v., *pakana*, also *upeo*. Dist. *paka*, with other meanings.)

Mpaka, Mpaki, n. (*wa-*), verbal of *paka*, a plasterer, a painter; also *mpaka chokaa, mpaka rangi*.

Mpakato, n. (*mi-*), something applied, stuck on, e. g. a patch, a bandage. (Cf. *pakata, paka*, v.)

Mpakizi, n. (*wa-*), a shipper, a stevedore, one who sees goods or freight put on board. (Cf. *pakia*.)

Mpako, n. (*mi-*), a plastering, plaster. *Mpako wa rangi*, applying paint, painting. (Cf. *paka*.)

Mpalio, n. (*mi-*), (1) a rising in the throat or nostril, a choke; (2) a hoeing up the soil among growing crops. (Cf. *paa, palia*.)

Mpamba, n. (*mi-*), (1) the plant producing cotton, *pamba*; (2) (*wa-*), verbal of *pamba*, one who adorns. (Cf. *pamba*, and follg.)

Mpambaji, n. (*wa-*), an undertaker, one of the professional attendants who with the *mwosha* prepares a dead body for burial,—using such things as *pamba, dalia, manukato, mavukizo, sanda, mkeka wa pamba*. (Cf. *pamba*.)

Mpambano, n. (*mi-*), a meeting, colliding, confronting, an encounter. (Cf. *pambana*.)

Mpambe, n. (*wa-*), a person dressed up, bedecked with ornaments, in a showy costume, esp. of a female attendant on a chief at certain ceremonials, maid-of-honour. (Cf. follg.)

Mpambi, n. (*wa-*), a decorator,—of house, person, &c., e. g. a lady's maid. (Cf. *pamba*, v.)

Mpanda, n. (*wa-*), verbal of *panda*, (1) one who climbs, a climber; (2) one who plants, a planter. Also **Mpandaji, Mpandi**. Also (3) (*mi-*), a forked branch or stick,—such as is used for a slave-stick. See **Kongwa**.

Mpande, n. (*mi-*), piece, part, side. Rarely used. (Cf. *upande, kipande, pande*.)

Mpando, n. (*mi-*), (1) a climbing, mounting up, ascent. *Inchi ya mpando*, rising ground. (2) act (process, method, &c.) of planting, time or season of planting. Also of a row or line of plants, cuttings, seeds, &c., e. g. *mipando kumi ya muhindi*, ten rows of Indian corn. (Cf. *panda, mpanzi*.)

Mpango, n. (*mi-*), (1) act (process, manner, time, &c.) of arranging, setting in order, placing in line, marshalling (cf. *panga*, and syn. *andika*. Dist. *pango*). (2) act (terms, method, &c.) of hiring, renting, letting, &c. (Cf. *panga, kuchisha*.)

Mpanzi, n. (*wa-*), a planter, a

sower. (Cf. *panda, mpando*. Dist. *panzi*, grasshopper.)

Mpapai, n. (*mi-*), the tree which bears papaw-fruit (*papai*). The leaves and juices rubbed on meat make it tender, and are so used by cooks. Digestive preparations are now made from it.

Mpapatiko, n. (*mi-*), fluttering, throbbing. (Cf. *papatika*.)

Mpapuro, n. (*mi-*), a scratching, a scratch, esp. with nails or claws. (Cf. *papura*, and *mtai, mfuo, mkuno*.)

Mparamuzi, n. (*mi-*), name of a tree difficult to climb. *Mti pia umepanda, huu ndio mparamuzi*, you have climbed every kind of tree, but this is a puzzler (? *Bombax Ceiba*).

Mparuzi, n. (*wa-*), one who does not work smoothly, a bungler. (Cf. *paruza*.)

Mparuzo, n. (*mi-*), a scraping, rough work, bungling, &c. (Cf. prec.)

Mpasi, n. (*wa-*), one who gets, one who makes money, a rising ambitious man, a prosperous merchant. (Cf. *pata, pato*, and syn. *tajiri, mkwasi*.)

Mpatanishi, n. (*wa-*), a peace-maker, reconciler, one who brings people to terms, settles quarrels and difficulties, a negotiator. (Cf. *patana*, and *msuluhishi*.)

Mpato, n. (*mi-*), (1) verbal of *pata*, a getting, a procuring, &c.; (2) a float used for showing the position of a fishing-net, and keeping it extended; (3) ? lattice, trellis-work (Str.).

Mpekecho, n. (*mi-*), (1) a twirling, a stirring; (2) a disturbance, agitation, fomenting of discord. (Cf. *pekecha, upekecho*.)

Mpekuzi, n. (*wa-*), one who picks and scratches (like a fowl), an inquisitive person. (Cf. *pekua*.)

Mpelekwa, n. (*wa-*), a person sent, a messenger. (Cf. *peleka*, and syn. *tume*.)

Mpelelezi, n. (*wa-*), (1) one who investigates, reconnoitres, examines, &c.; (2) a spy, scout, tracker, eaves-dropper. (Cf. *peleleza*.)

Mpenda, Mpendi, n. (*wa-*), verbals of *penda*, one who loves, likes, intends, &c., a lover. *Mpendwa* (*wa-*), one who is loved. (Cf. *penda, mapenda, mpenzi, upendo*.)

Mpenyezi, n. (*wa-*), (1) one who introduces, causes to enter or penetrate, brings in, and esp. in an underhand secret way, hence (2) a traitor, smuggler, illicit trader, secret agent, one who gives bribes. *Mpenyezo*, a bribe. (Cf. *penya, upenyezi*.)

Mpenzi, n. (*wa-*), (1) one who is beloved, a dear favourite person; (2) one who loves, a lover, as *mpendi*. Cf. *mapenzi*, active love, inclination, will, and see Mapenda. *Mpenzi hana kinyongo*, (1) the object of affection has no defect, causes no scruples; (2) a lover sees no defects. (Cf. *penda, upenzi*.)

Mpepea, n. (*mi-*), a light breeze, a zephyr, i.e. *upepo mpepea*, a breeze that fans. (Cf. *pepea, upepo, pepeo*.)

Mpepetaji, n. (*wa-*), also **Mpetaji**, one who sifts or winnows grain, &c. (Cf. *pepeta*.)

Mpera, n. (*mi-*), the tree that bears the guava fruit, *pera*. *Mpera wa kizungu*, the rose-apple tree. Another variety is the *mtofaa*.

Mpetaji, n. (*wa-*), for *mpepetaji*.

Mpevushi, n. (*wa-*), a corrupter of morals, esp. of the young, lit. one who ripens, brings to maturity, forces growth. (Cf. *pevua, -pevu*, and *komaa*.)

Mpiga, n. (*wa-*), verbal of *piga*, in all its manifold uses, one who strikes, &c. See **Piga**.

Mpiganisho, n. (*mi-*), collision, encounter, conflict. (Cf. *piga, upigano*.)

Mpigo, n. (*mi-*), act (mode, &c.) of striking. (Cf. *pigo*.)

Mpikaji, n. (*wa-*), a cook, a professional cook, head cook. (Cf. *pika, mpishi*, and follg.)

Mpiko, n. (*mi-*), (1) stick or pole to carry or sling loads on; (2) act (process, method, &c.) of cooking,—including *mkaango, mchomo, mtokoso, mwoko*. See Pika.

Mpilipili, n. (*mi-*), the plant producing capsicums (*pilipili*), the red-pepper plant. (Cf. *pilipili*.)

Mpimo, n. (*mi-*), (1) act (mode, means, &c.) of measuring; (2) payment for measuring. (Cf. *pima, kipimo*.)

Mpindani, n. (*wa-*), a person bent or crooked by stiffness or disease. (Cf. *pinda*, and follg.)

Mpindano, n. (*mi-*), a bending together, a stiffening. *Mp. wa mshipa*, cramp. (Cf. *pinda*, and syn. *kiharusi*.)

Mpinduzi, n. (*wa-*), one who turns things upside down, a revolutionist, a disturber of peace. (Cf. *pinda, pindua*.)

Mpingani, n. (*wa-*), an obstructor, a stubborn opponent. (Cf. *pinga*.)

Mpingo, n. (*mi-*), the ebony tree.

Mpini, n. (*mi-*), a handle, haft,—of an instrument, such as knife, sword, tool. (Cf. *kipini*. Other kinds are called (1) *mkono*, e.g. projecting handle of a saucepan; (2) *utambo*, e.g. handle of a bucket.)

Mpira, n. (*mi-*), (1) a tree producing india-rubber; (2) the substance india-rubber; (3) a ball of india-rubber, and hence a ball of any material,—used of a cricket- or foot-ball, and extended to any games of ball. *Gema mpira*, draw off the sap from an india-rubber tree. *Mpira wa kuponda*, india-rubber got by boiling the roots of trees. The natives make up the sap into balls of about three inches diam. for sale. (Cf. *mbungo, mtoria*.)

Mpishi, n. (*wa-*), a cook. (Cf. *pika, pikisha, upishi*. Dist. *pisha*, Cs. of *pita*, and *pishi*, a measure.)

Mpofu, n. (*wa-*), an eland. Also (from *-pofu*), a blind person, blind, i.e. *mtu mpofu wa macho*. (Cf. *-pofu, pofua*. And for various antelopes cf. *paa*, n.)

Mpokezi, n. (*wa-*), one who receives, a receiver, recipient. (Cf. *pokea*, and *mkabithi*.)

Mponda, n. (*wa-*), verbal of *ponda*, one who crushes, breaks to pieces. *Mponda mali*, a spendthrift, prodigal.

Mpondo, n. (*mi-*), a pole for pushing a vessel in shallow water, a punting-pole. (Cf. *ponda*, also *pondo, kipondo*.)

Mpopoo, n. (*mi-*), the areca palm, bearing the betel-nut, *popoo*, which is always in great request for chewing. See Popoo, Tambuu, Uraibu.

Mposa, n. (*wa-*), a suitor, one who makes proposals of marriage to parents. (Cf. *posa*, and follg.)

Mposo, n. (*mi-*), proposal of marriage, wooing. (Cf. *posa*, and prec.)

Mpotezi, n. (*wa-*), one who spoils, ruins, corrupts, misleads, destroys, perverts, &c. (Cf. *potea, -potevu*, and follg., and syn. *mwangamizi*.)

Mpoto, n. (*wa-*), and more commonly **Mpotofu, Mpotoe**, wrong-headed, wilful, perverse, wayward, headstrong, unprincipled,—contr. of *mwongofu*, and described as *mtu asiyeongoka*, a man who does not go the right way; *asiyeshika akili za mtu mwingine*, one who never listens to others. (Cf. *potoa*, and *potea*.)

Mpozi, n. (*wa-*), one who cures, a physician,—a title which is usually ascribed to God. *Mpozi ni Muungu*, God is the real physician. Doctors are usually called *mganga, tabibu, daktari*. (Cf. *poa, pona, poza*.)

Mpumbafu, n. (*wa-*), a fool, a dupe, described as *mtu aseyiweza kufanyiza kazi ya nafsi yake*, a man who has not the wits to do what he sets himself to do. (Cf. *pumbaa, -pumbafu*, and syn. *mjinga, barathuli*.)

Mpunga, n. (*mi-*), the rice plant, and rice while still growing or in the husk. (When husked it is called *mchele*, when cooked in the ordinary way *wali*.)

Mpungate, n. (*mi-*), a kind of cactus (Str.).

Mpuzi, n. (*wa-*), one who is foolish, flippant, careless, loose,—in conduct, conversation, &c., a gossip, flirt, babbler, gad-about. (Cf. *-puzi, upuzi, puza*.)

Mpwa, n. (*wa-*), sister's child, nephew, niece, and ? cousin. (Not often in Z.)

Mpweke, n. (*mi-*), (1) a short thick stick, cudgel, bludgeon (cf. *kibarango*, and for other sticks *bakora, fimbo*). (2) a. See *-pweke*.

Mpya, a. See *-pya*.

***Mraba**, n. (*mi-*) and **Mrabba**, what is fourfold, square, a square, a rectangle, a right angle. Also of squares laid out for planting, garden beds. *-a miraba minne*, rectangular. *Mtu wa miraba minne*, a square-built, stout man. *Piga miraba katika shamba*, lay out beds for cultivation on an estate. (Ar. Cf. *robo, ároba*. Also in Ar. *mraba* means 'jam, preserve.')

***Mrabaha**, n. (*mi-*), royalty, fee paid to a chief by a trader for right of trading in a place. (Ar. Cf. *rabbi*.)

***Mradi**, n. (*mi-*), intention, plan, resolve. (Ar. Cf. *nia, shauri, azima, kusudi*.)

***Mrama**, n. also **Mramma, Mramaa**, pitching, tossing, rolling,—the motion of a ship at sea, e.g. *m. wa chombo. Enda m.*, roll, toss, pitch, &c.,—of a ship. (Ar. Cf. *sukosuko*.)

Mrao, n. (*mi-*), fuse for a gun, match for lighting the powder in a matchlock,—a small twisted bit of combustible fibre from a suitable tree. *Bunduki ya mrao*, a matchlock gun. (Cf. *utambi*.)

***Mrashi**, n. (*mi-*), a long-necked glass or metal bottle or flask, used for sprinkling scent. (Ar. Cf. *marathi*.)

***Mrejaa**, n. and **Mregaa**. *Bei ya mrejaa*, trading by commission, i.e. with goods lent for sale, and returnable if not sold. (Ar., lit. 'returning.' Cf. *rejea*, and *kopa, ukopi*.)

Mrenaha, n. (*mi-*), the thorn-apple tree (Str.).

Mreno, n. (*wa-*), a Portuguese. (Cf. *-reno*.)

Mrera, n. lines of ornamental stitching on the collar of a *kanzu*, usually of red silk. See **Kanzu**.

***Mrihani**, n. basil (the aromatic herb). (Ar. Cf. *rihani, manukato*.)

Mrija, n. (*mi-*), a small kind of reed,—often used as a pipe (for drinking with, musical, &c.), and so (2) a pipe, tube, piping.

Mrima, n. and **Merima**, name of the strip of coastland opposite and south of Zanzibar, with its own dialect of Swahili called Kimrima. The people also are described as Wamrima. (Perh. cf. *mlima*, i.e. the hill-country, rising from the coast inland.)

***Mrithi**, n. (*wa-*), an heir, legatee, inheritor. (Ar. Cf. *rithi, urithi, warithi*.)

***Mrithia**, n. (*wa-*), a pleasant, affable, amiable person. (Ar. Cf. *rathi, urathi*.)

Mrithishi, n. (*wa-*), an executor,—of a will. (Ar. Cf. *mrithi*.)

Mruba, n. (*mi-*), a leech.

***Mrututu**, n. sulphate of copper, blue-stone, blue vitriol,—often used as a caustic for sores, &c.

***Msaada**, n. (*mi-*), help, aid, assistance, support. (Ar. Cf. *saidia*, and syn. *auni, tegemeo, shime*.)

***Msafa**, n. (*mi-*), a line, row, series,—more commonly *safu* (which see). *Msafa wa milima*, a chain of mountains, mountain-range, i.e. *imefungamana, kama kilima kimoja kwa kimoja*, they are joined together like a continuous series of hills. (Ar. Cf. *mstari, -mpango*, and *safu*.)

*Msafara, n. (*mi-*), a travelling company, caravan, expedition,—for trading, war, &c. *Andika (tengeneza, panga) msafara*, organize an expedition. (Ar. Cf. *safiri, safari*, and follg.)

*Msafiri, n. (*wa-*), a traveller (by sea or land), wayfarer, voyager. (Ar. Cf. prec., and syn. *mpitaji, mtembezi, abiria*.)

*Msahafu, n. (*mi-*), a book (blank, written, or printed), esp. the Coran, the Book, the Mahommedan Bible. Also page or leaf of a book, i.e. *karatasi ya chuo kitupu, kisichoandikwa*, page of a blank book not written in. (Ar. *sahifat*, a page, layer. Cf. *kitabu, chuo*.)

*Msahau, n. (*wa-*), one who forgets, a forgetful person. (Ar. Cf. *sahau, -sahaulifu*.)

*Msaji, n. (*mi-*), the teak tree, teak wood,—imported to Zanzibar, resists the attacks of white ants.

Msakaji, n. (*wa-*), one who hunts, i.e. *msakaji nyama*, a hunter of game. (Cf. follg. and *mwinda, mwindaji*.)

Msako, n. (*mi-*), hunting, a hunt. (Cf. *saka*, and syn. *winda, mwindo*.)

*Msala, n. (*mi-*), (1) a praying mat,—usually oval, and hence of oval or round mats in general. Also (2) a private place, bath, closet,—like *faraghani*. *Yuko msalani*, he is engaged. *Akapelekwa msalani akaenda akaoga*, he was conducted to the bathroom and went and had a bath. (Ar. Cf. *sala, sali*, and for mats *mkeka, kitanga*. Also cf. *choo*.)

Msalaba, n. (*mi-*), (1) a cross, anything in the form of a cross. Also (2) instrument of torture, used for *mkatale*, stocks. (Ar. Cf. *sulubu*.)

*Msalata, n. (*wa-*), a harsh, overbearing, unfeeling, provoking person. (Ar. Cf. *saliti*, and syn. *mgomvi, msumbufu*, &c.)

Msalimina, Msalimu, n. (*wa-*), variants of *Mwislamu, Msilimu*, a Mahommedan, a Moslem.

*Msaliti, n. (*wa-*). See Msalata.

*Msamaha, n. (*mi-*) also Msameha, pardon, forgiveness, forbearance, respite. *Nataka msamaha kwako*, I beg your forgiveness. (Ar. Cf. *samehe*, and follg., and syn. *achilio, ghofira*.)

*Msamehe, n. (*wa-*), a forgiving, merciful person. (Ar. Cf. prec.)

Msamilo, n. (*mi-*), wooden headrest, used by natives as a pillow.

*Msanaa, n. (*wa-*), also Msani, one skilled in an art, artist, artisan. (Ar. Cf. *sanaa, -sanifu*. In Z. commoner syn. are *fundi, waria, mstadi, mbingwa*.)

*Msandali, n. (*mi-*), the tree producing the aromatic sandal-wood.

*Msandarusi, n. (*mi-*), the gum-copal tree. (Cf. *sandarusi*.)

Msangao, n. (*mi-*), also Mshangao (which see).

Msapata, n. (*mi-*), a kind of native dance. (Cf. *ngoma*.)

Msasa, n. (*mi-*), (1) a plant or shrub with rough leaves, used for smoothing wood. Hence (2) sandpaper, emery paper.

Msazo, n. (*mi-*), what is left over, leavings, remnant, remainder. (Cf. *salia, saza, sazo, salio*, and syn. *baki*.)

Msekeneko, n. syphilis. (Cf. *sekeneka*.)

*Mselehisha, n. (*wa-*), also -ishi, a reconciler, a peacemaker. (Ar. Cf. *suluhi, selehisha*, and syn. *mpatanishi*.)

Msema, n. (*wa-*), verbal of *sema*, one who says, speaks, has the power of speech. (Cf. *sema, nena*, and follg.)

Msemi, Msemaji, n. (*wa-*), (1) a speaker, a narrator; (2) an eloquent person, an orator, a fluent, talkative person. *Msemaji wa habari*, one who tells news, a narrator, an historian. (Cf. *sema*, and prec., *usemi, usemaji*.)

Msemo, n. (*mi-*), act (kind, style, &c.) of speaking, utterance, speech. *Kilichowafunga ni msemo wao we-*

nyewe, what convicted them was their own speech. (Cf. *sema*, and prec.)

Msetiri, n. (*wa-*). See **Mstiri**.

Mseto, n. (*mi-*), and **Msheto**, a mixture of grains and other ingredients cooked for food, a mash, e. g. *mtama, choroko, kunde, viazi*. (Cf. *seta*.)

Msewe, n. (*mi-*), a sort of rattle, fastened to the leg, to make a jingle in dancing. (Cf. *njuga*.)

*****Mshabaha**, n. (*mi-*), likeness, resemblance, similitude. Used also like *methali* (*mithili*) and *mfano* as a conj. 'in the likeness (of), like,'—for the common *kama, sawa* (*na*). *Mshabaha mmoja*, alike. (Ar. Cf. *shabaha*.)

*****Mshahara**, n. (*mi-*), monthly wages, regular salary. (Ar. *shahr*, a month. Cf. *ujira*.)

*****Mshairi**, n. (*wa-*), a composer of verses, a rhymer, a poet. (Ar. Cf. *shairi*.)

*****Mshakiki**, n. (*mi-*), (1) spit, skewer; (2) a bit of meat, toasted over embers on a skewer. (Ar. *sikkat*, and cf. syn. *kijiti, kibanzi*.)

Mshale, n. (*mi-*), an arrow. For various parts cf. *chembe* (iron head), *wano* (shaft), *manyoya* (feathers), *koleo* (notch). Dim. *kishale*. (Other common weapons are *mkuki, upanga, kisu, rungu*.)

Mshangao, n. (*mi-*), also **Msangao**, thrilling excitement, deep sensation, admiration, wonder, perplexity, amazement, bewilderment, stupefaction. *Ona* (*fanya, shikwa na, ingia*), be seized with wonder, &c. (Cf. *shangaa*, and *ajabu, bumbuazi, toshea*.)

*****Mshari**, n. (*wa-*), an evil person, one who brings ruin, strife, ill luck, destruction, &c. Opp. of *heri*. (Ar. Cf. syn. *mgomvi, mtesi, mkorofi, mchokozi, mpotezi*.)

*****Msharika**, n. (*wa-*), also **Mshiriki**, partner, participator, sharer, associate, equal,—but *msharika* may imply the closest possible identification of interests, communion of life, nature, and feeling. (Ar. Cf. *shariki, shiriki*, and syn. *mwenyi, rafiki*.)

*****Mshathali**, a. and adv., also **Mshethali**, and sometimes heard as **Msitara**, crooked, slanting, oblique, out of the straight or level, sloping, on one side. (? Ar., and cf. syn. *upande, kikombo, kipogo*.)

*****Mshauri**, n. (*wa-*), adviser, friend, counsellor. (Ar. Cf. *shauri*.)

*****Msheheri**, n. (*wa-*), an Arab from Sheher in South Arabia, usu. of a low class, engaged in manual trades and labour. (Ar.)

*****Mshemali**, n. (*wa-*), a northern Arab, i. e. one who comes from Muscat and the Persian Gulf. (Ar.)

Mshenzi, n. (*wa-*), a barbarian, savage, one of the aborigines, a person untouched by civilization. Often used contemptuously by the coast Swahilis of those who come from the interior. (Cf. *ushenzi, mjinga*.)

Msheto, n. (*mi-*). See **Mseto**.

Mshika, Mshiki, n. (*wa-*), one who holds, takes hold of, grasps. *Mshiki shikio* (or, *msukani*), pilot, steersman. (Cf. *shika*.)

Mshikilizo, n. (*mi-*), lit. a causing to hold on to, or together,—used of tacking or basting materials ready for sewing.

Mshinda, n. (*wa-*), verbal of *shinda*, one who remains, conquers, &c. (See the various meanings of *shinda*, and follg.)

Mshindaji, n. (*wa-*), a conqueror, victor, successful competitor or candidate. (Differs from *Mshinda, Mshindi*, only so far as the termination *ji* implies that the action is characteristic, repeated, or professional. Cf. *shinda, mshindi, mshindwa, mshinde, mshindo*, and follg.)

Mshindani, n. (*wa-*), (1) an opponent, rival, antagonist, competitor; (2) a contentious, obstructive, captious person. (Cf. *shinda, mashindano, ushindani*, and syn. *mbishi, mpingamizi, mtesi, adui*.

Mshinde, n. (*wa-*), one who is conquered. (From *shinda*, with pass. termin. *-e*. Not often used.)

Mshindi, n. (*wa-*), a conqueror, winner, prize-taker, victor. (Cf. *shinda, mshindi, mshindaji,* and prec.)

Mshindilio, n. (*mi-*), a pushing, a pressing, application of force. Used of (1) loading a gun, ramming the charge home. Also of (2) the charge or cartridge itself. (Cf. *shinda, shindilia,* and *kiasi.*)

Mshindio, n. (*mi-*), (1) the working of the woof or weft across the warp (*mtande*) in weaving; (2) the woof itself. Used also of the interlacing of plaited leaf strips (*mashupatu*) to form a bedstead (*kitanda*),—*mshindio wa mashupatu*. (Cf. *shinda,* and prec., also *mfumo* for weaving.)

Mshindo, n. (*mi-*), used to describe any act (process, effect), characterized by suddenness, force, violence, &c., and so translated variously as 'shock, blow, stroke, explosion, noise, bang, sensation, burst, thump, crash, outbreak, tumult, uproar,' &c. *Mshindo wa ngurumo,* peal of thunder. *Ngoma ya mishindo saba,* a drum with seven notes. *Ikawa mshindo mkubwa katika inchi,* there was a general rising throughout the land. Also of a report, rumour, news of a thrilling or sensational kind. *Mshindo wa miguu,* tramp of feet. (Cf. *shinda,* and prec., and dim. *kishindo.*)

Mshipa, n. (*mi-*), used rather vaguely of minor organs of the body not commonly distinguished by natives, blood-vessel, nerve, vein, artery, and of any pain, ache, disease or affection of them,—ache, swelling, throbbing, fullness of blood. E.g. *mshipa unampiga fundo,* there is a knot (obstruction, clot) in his vein,— of aneurism, &c. *Marathi ya mshipa,* neuralgic pain, sciatica, and similar pains. *Mshipa unamtambaa mwilini,* of creeping shooting pains in different parts of the body. *M. inapiga (inapuma, inatukutika),* the vein, or pulse, beats (throbs, is irregular). *Kanda mshipa,* feel the pulse.

Mshipi, n. (*mi-*), (1) a narrow strip of stuff (cloth, webbing, &c.), used as a belt, girdle, waist-band, halter,— also used of braces, suspenders; (2) a fishing-line, a fishing-net.

*****Mshitiri**, n. (*wa-*), customer, buyer. (Arab., for the common *mnunuzi.*)

Mshituko, n. (*mi-*). See **Mshtuko**.

Mshona, Mshoni, n. (*wa-*), one who sews,—always a man in Z., a tailor. *Mshona viatu, mshoni wa viatu,* a sandal-maker, a shoemaker. (Cf. *shona,* and follg.)

Mshono, n. (*mi-*), sewing, seam, suture. *Kunga mshono,* sew a seam. (Cf. *shona, ushoni,* prec., and *kunga.*)

*****Mshtaka**, n. (*mi-*), charge, accusation, complaint. *Fanya mshtaka,* prosecute. (Cf. *shtaki,* and follg., and *da'wa.*)

*****Mshtaki**, n. (*wa-*), accuser, prosecutor, plaintiff. (See **Shtaki**, and prec., and cf. *dai.*)

*****Mshubiri**, n. (*mi-*), an aloe. (Cf. also *subiri, sibiri.*)

Mshuko, n. (*mi-*), (1) descent, coming down, an incline; (2) coming to end, conclusion. Used of the time of coming away from the mosque after any of the usual prayers. *Mshuko wa jua (wa magaribi),* time of twilight, just after sunset, 6 to 6.30 p.m. (Cf. *shuka.*)

*****Mshumaa**, n. (*mi-*), candle. See **Meshmaa**. (Ar.)

*****Mshurutisho**, n. (*mi-*), a compelling, a compulsion, moral pressure. (Ar. Cf. *sharti, shuruti.*)

*****Msiba**, n. (*mi-*), (1) calamity, misfortune, untoward accident, disaster; (2) sorrow, distress of mind, grief; (3) formal mourning, outward signs of sorrow, &c. Used of war, famine, sickness, and minor calamities. *Msiba mkuu (mkubwa, mgumu),* a great disaster. *Fanya (ona, ingia, pata,* &c.), *m.,* take to heart, grieve (over). *Muungu hushusha msiba* *kwao watenda maovu,* God sends down calamities on evil-doers. *Kwenda kupa mkono wa msiba,* go and make a visit of condolence, offer sympathy, inquire after,—after a funeral, misfortune, &c. *Akakaa msiba wa mamaye,* he observed the usual mourning for his mother. *Ikiwa jumbe amekufa, ukaanguka msiba mkubwa mno wa ajabu,* when a chief dies, it means the occurrence of a very great and exceptional demonstration of sorrow. (Ar. Cf. *masaibu, sibu,* and follg.)

***Msibu**, n. (*wa-*), one who causes trouble, distress, &c. (Ar. Cf. *sibu,* and prec.)

***Msifu**, n. (*wa-*), verbal of *sifu,* one who praises, recommends, flatters. *Msifu mno,* a gross flatterer, toady, parasite. (Cf. *sifu, sifa.*)

Msijana, n. (*wa-*), young unmarried person of either sex, from ten to twenty-five years of age. (Not usual in Z. Cf. *kijana.* Perh. *m-si-jana,* i.e. one who is not a child. Cf. *msikwao.*)

***Msikiti**, n. mosque. See **Moskiti**. (Ar.)

Msikizi, n. (*wa-*), one who hears, heeds, obeys, and so (1) an auditor, hearer, listener, one who attends a class or meeting; (2) a follower, disciple, adherent, a teachable, obedient person, good pupil, good servant. *Mwenyezi Mngu ni msikizi na mjuzi wa killa kitu,* Almighty God sees and hears everything. *Natafuta watu wasikizi,* I am looking for people to listen to my case. (Cf. *-sikia, -sikifu, sikio.*)

Msikwao, n. (*wa-*), one who has no home, a vagrant, a wanderer (*si kwao*). (Cf. *mkiwa.*)

Msilimu, n. (*wa-*). See **Mwislamu**.

Msimamizi, n. (*wa-*), lit. one who causes to stand, or stands over, i.e. an overseer, overlooker,—esp. the headman of a plantation, or of a caravan. Also generally, responsible head, director, manager, superintendent, steward, foreman. (Cf. *simama,* and also *nokoa, kadamu.*)

Msimulizi, n. (*wa-*), one who reports, narrates, gives an account, tells a story, recounts news, newsman. (Cf. *sumulia.*)

Msindikizo, n. (*mi-*), act of escorting, escort, *cortège,* retinue. (Cf. *sindikiza, sindika.*)

***Msingefuri**, n. (*mi-*), the anatta plant. (Cf. *singefuri.*)

Msinji, n. (*mi-*), also **Msingi**, a trench, ditch, cutting made in the ground, e.g. round a house for carrying off water, &c., but esp. of the foundation for a stone house. *Piga (weka) msinji,* lay a foundation. (Perh. *mzingi,* and conn. with *zinga, zunguka,* &c.)

***Msiri**, n. (*wa-*), a confidential (intimate, bosom) friend, confidential agent (adviser, counsellor). (Ar. Cf. *siri,* and *mshauri, mkunga.*)

Msisimizi, n. See **Mzizimizi**.

Msisimuko, n. (*mi-*), and **Mzizim'ko**, a startling, nervous excitement, irritation, stimulation. (Cf. *sisima, zizimua,* and syn. *mshtuko.*)

Msitamu, n. (*mi-*), keelson or inner keel, to which the foot of the mast and ribs of a vessel are secured. (Cf. *mkuku,* keel, and *chombo.*)

Msitiri, n. (*mi-*), and **Msetiri**. See **Mstiri**.

Msitu, n. (—, and ? *mi-*), land covered with thick bushes, undergrowth, small trees. Sometimes *msitu wa miti,* forest, but *mwitu* is usual in this sense.

Msizi, n. (*mi-*), a plant from which a black dye or ink is made. (Cf. *masizi.* Dist. *mzizi,* a rootlet.)

***Msomari**, n. (*mi-*), also **Msumari, Mismari**, a nail, large pin, or anything similar in appearance or use. *Msomari wa parafujo,* a screw. (Ar.)

Msomeshi, n. (*wa-*), a teacher, instructor, reader, esp. one who teaches and leads Mahommedan devotions. (Cf. *soma*, and follg. Also *mwalimu, mkufunzi*.)

Msomo, n. (*mi-*), (1) reading, the act (method, means, &c.) of reading, repeating a lesson; (2) study, subject of study, lesson, lesson-book. (Cf. *soma, somo*.)

Msonde, n. (*mi-*), a kind of drum, long and of large size,—also called *gogo*. (Cf. *ngoma*.)

Msonge, n. and adv. (something) stirred, twisted, compressed, muddled, jumbled. *Maneno haya ni msongesonge*, these words are all jumbled together, confused. For *mnyonge msonge* see **Mnyonge**. (Cf. *songa*, and follg. The *-e* is a passive ending.)

Msongi, n. (*wa-*), one who stirs, twists, presses, &c. *Msongi wa nyele*, a hairdresser, who arranges the hair in folds (cf. *msusi wa nyele*, one who plaits the hair). (Cf. *songa*, and prec.)

Msongo, n. (*mi-*), a stirring, twisting, plaiting, compressing, muddling, &c. (Cf. *songa, kisongo*, and prec., and syn. *msuko*.)

Msonyo, n. (*mi-*), and **Msono**, a whistling sound, made with the teeth as well as the lip, to attract notice or express contempt. *Piga (vuta) msonyo*, give a whistle. (Cf. *sonya*, and *fyonya*, also *mwunzi, ubinja*, and *koroma*.)

Mstadi, n. (*wa-*), a skilled workman, one who knows his trade. (Cf. *fundi, waria, mbingwa*.)

*****Mstafeli**, n. (*mi-*), a fruit tree commonly called *mtopetope*, and sometimes *mtomoko*, custard-apple tree. There are several varieties known in Z., e.g. *mstafeli wa kizungu*, bearing the fruit called 'sour-sop,' *mst. wa Ajjemi*, bearing the 'bullock's heart.' There is also an *mst. wa mwitu*, or 'wild custard-apple.' (Cf. *topetope*.)

*****Mstaki**, n. (*wa-*). See **Mshtaki**.

*****Mstamu**, n. (*mi-*). See **Msitamu**.

*****Mstarehe**, n. state of rest, repose, calm,—esp. in the phrase *raha mstarehe*, i.e. absolute, complete repose. (Cf. *starehe, -starehefu, raha, utulivu, kimya*, and *mstiri*.)

*****Mstari**, n. (*mi-*), a line, an extended stroke, a line ruled or marked, a row. *Piga mstari*, draw a line. (Ar. Cf. *safu, mfuo, alama*.)

*****Mstiri**, n. (*wa-*), (1) for *mshtiri*, a customer, a buyer (Arab.). (2) (with variants *msetiri, msitiri*), one who conceals, a hider, one who covers, veils, disguises. (Ar. Cf. *stiri, ficha*.)

*****Msuaki**, n. (*mi-*), a twig of a fibrous shrub, the end of which is chewed and used for rubbing and cleaning the teeth, a tooth-stick, a tooth-brush. Often a twig of the *mzambarau*. (Ar. tooth-pick.)

*****Msufi**, n. (*mi-*), the cotton-tree (*Eriodendron anfractuosum*). (Cf. *sufi*, and dist. *mpamba*, the cotton plant, a small shrub.)

Msuka, n. (1) (*wa-*), verbal of *suka*, one who plaits, &c.; (2) (*mi-*), the spike of a native hoe (*jembe*),—the part of the iron head which passes through and is fixed in the handle (*kipini*). See **Jembe**.

*****Msukani**, n. (*mi-*), also **Sukani, Usukani**, rudder, and steering gear in general, of a boat or ship. The tiller or handle is called *kana*; the tiller-rope, rudder-line, *ujari* (plur. *njari*); the steersman, *mshiki msukani* or *rubani*; a steering wheel, *cherehe* (or *gurudumu*) *ya msukani*. (Hind. Cf. *shikio*.)

Msukano, n. (*mi-*) and **Msukawano**, part of the drill (*keke*) used for boring hard woods by native carpenters, viz. the shaft and barrel carrying the iron bit or boring tool. See **Keke**.

Msuki, n. (*wa-*), also **Msusi**, one who plaits, &c. See **Suka**. *M. wa nyele*, a professional or skilled hairdresser. *M. wa vikapo*, a basket maker.

Msuko, n. (*mi-*), act (process, style, &c.) of plaiting, a plait. Also of shaking, e.g. of a ship at sea. (Verbal of *suka*, in all its meanings.)

*****Msuluhishi**, n. (*wa-*), a peacemaker, a reconciler, one who brings to terms, arranges a bargain, ends a quarrel, &c. (Ar. Cf. *suluhisha*, *-suluhifu*, and syn. *mpatanishi*.)

Msumeno, n. (*mi-*), a sawing tool, a saw. *Piga m.*, use a saw. *Kata kwa m.*, cut with a saw, i.e. *pasua*. Various kinds are *m. wa kitanda*, frame-saw,—large ones being used as pit-saws, and for plank cutting. *M. wa kamba*, a fret-saw. *M. wa jambeni*, a saw with two saw edges. (Cf. Ar. *jambe*, two-sided. Also *ki-su*, *ji-su*, whence perh. *m-su* with *meno*, i.e. a toothed or serrated knife.)

*****Msunobari**, n. (*mi-*), pine-tree, fir-tree, deal,—timber imported in quantities to Z. chiefly from Norway. It is rapidly destroyed by white ants. (Ar. and Hind.)

Msuruaki, n. (*mi-*), the wooden peg on a kind of clog (*mtalawanda*) used by women indoors, passing between the toes and so holding the clog on the foot.

Msusi, n. (*wa*) for **Msuki** (which see). (Dist. *mzuzi*.)

Msusu, n. (*mi-*), name of a tree.

Msuto, n. (*mi-*) and **Msutu**, a large piece of coloured calico, often used as a screen or partition in a native house,—more commonly *kisutu*, a piece of coloured calico worn as a woman's dress. (Cf. *nguo*, *kisutu*.)

Msuzo, n. (*mi-*) and **Msuso**, handle of wood by which the upper stone is turned, in grinding grain between two stones.

*****Mtaa**, n. (*mi-*), division of a town, quarter, district, parish. *Kaa mtaa mmoja*, live in the same district, be neighbours. (Cf. syn. *fungu*, *sehemu*, *upande*.)

*****Mtaala**, n. study, practice, reading. (Ar. Cf. *taali*, and *soma*.)

*****Mtaalamu**, n. (*wa-*), an educated, learned, well-instructed person, a scholar, a sage. (Ar. Cf. *elimu*, and syn. *mwana vyuo*.)

*****Mtabiri**, n. (*wa-*), one who announces or foretells events, a prophet, a soothsayer. (Ar. Cf. *tabiri*, *hubiri*, and *nabii*.)

Mtafara, n. (*mi-*), crupper,—the cord used to fasten the saddle to the tail (Sac.).

Mtai, n. (*mi-*), a scratch, a slight cut. *Piga mtai*, make a scratch, scarify. (Cf. *papura*, *chora*, *toja*, *piga*, *ukucha*, also *mfuo*.)

Mtaimbo, n. (*mi-*), also **Mtalimbo**, an iron crowbar, lever, bar.

Mtajiri, n. (*wa-*). See **Tajiri**.

Mtaka, n. (*wa-*), one who wants, asks, begs, needs, &c. See **Taka**, v. *Mtaka yote hukora yote*, he who begs for everything gets nothing. (Cf. *mtashi*, *mwombaji*.)

Mtakaso, n. cleansing, a thing cleaned (cf. *takasa*). Also ? a rustling, rustle,—perh. a variant of *mchakacho* (which see).

Mtalawanda, n. (*mi-*), also **Mtaawanda**, (1) a tree supplying a light wood, from which clogs are made in Z. Hence also (2) a wooden clog, i.e. *kiatu cha mti*. (Cf. *kiatu*.)

Mtali, n. (*mi-*), an anklet, bangle. (Cf. *furungu*, and for other ornaments *urembo*.)

Mtama, n. (*mi-*), millet, Kaffir corn, sorghum,—a food staple in many districts near Z. *Mtama mtindi*, young half-grown millet. *Mtama tete*, millet with grain formed but not fully ripe. The stalk is *bua* (*ma-*), and of a sweet kind *kota* (*ma-*). Various kinds are known as *felefele*, *kipaje*, *kibakuli*, *fumbu*, &c. (Ar. *taam*, food, corn of any kind. For other kinds cf. *uwele*, *ulezi*, *uwimbi*, *ngano*, *shayiri*, *kimanga*, *mchele*.)

Mtamba, n. (*wa-*), a female animal that has not yet borne young. *Mt. wa ng'ombe*, a heifer. (Cf. *mfarika*.)

Mtambaazi, n. (*wa-*), any crawling creature, insect or reptile. (Cf. *-tambaa, -tambaazi, utambaazi,* and *tiririka,*—used of the gliding of snakes, i.e. without feet.)

Mtambo, n. (*mi-*), a trap with a spring-action. Hence of any similar contrivance or machine with movement. *Mtambo wa bunduki*, the lock (or, action) of a gun. *Tega mtambo*, set a trap. *Mtambo wa taa*, a clock (or, watch) spring. (Cf. *tamba, tambo, kitambo, utambo, tambi, tambaa,* &c.,—differing in meaning, but perh. with same root.)

Mtambuu, n. (*mi-*), the shrub which produces the betel-leaf,—in great request for chewing at Z. See **Tambuu, Uraibu**.

Mtambuzi, n. (*wa-*), a knowing, clever, well-informed, intelligent person. (Cf. *tambua, utambuzi,* and *tamba*.)

Mtanda, n. (*wa-*), verbal of *tanda*, one who spreads, &c. See **Tanda**, and follg.

Mtande, n. (*mi-*), lit. something spread or stretched out. Hence used of (1) a frame of sticks, or a line on which clothes, &c. are hung to dry. Also of a weaver's loom, more accurately called *kitanda cha mfumi*. (2) strip of flesh, or fish, hung up to dry in the sun or by the fire. Also of the threads of the warp in a loom,—the woof being *mshindio*. (Cf. *tanda*, and follg.)

Mtando, n. (*mi-*), a spreading, a stretching out, &c. Also of what is spread out. (Cf. *tanda*, and prec.)

Mtanga, n. (*wa-*), one who wanders idly and aimlessly about, an idler, loafer, common tourist, vagabond, tramp. So also **Mtangatanga**. (Cf. *tanga, mtango, kitanga,* and syn. *mtembezi, mpuzi*.)

Mtangazi, n. (*wa-*), one who makes generally known, proclaims, divulges. (Cf. *tangaa*.)

Mtango, n. (*mi-*), (1) a loitering, strolling about, idling (see **Tanga**, and prec.). (2) the plant producing the *tango*, a kind of cucumber used as a vegetable.

Mtangulizi, n. (*wa-*), one who goes before, leads the way, is preeminent or first in anything, and so a leader, ringleader, herald, forerunner, predecessor. (Cf. *tangulia*, and syn. *takadamu*.)

Mtani, n. (*wa-*), one of a family, clan, or tribe, a kinsman, a relation,—but not nearer than a cousin on the father's side. (Cf. *utani*.)

Mtapo, n. (*mi-*), name of a plant, a kind of Cycad. Also verbal n. of *tapa*, shivering.

Mtasbihi, n. (*mi-*), a kind of reed.

Mtashi, n. (*wa-*), an earnest, importunate suppliant, one whose mind is set on an object, an urgent pleader. (Cf. *taka*, v., and syn. *mwombaji*.)

Mtata, n. (*mi-*), name of a plant.

Mtatago, n. (*mi-*), a tree placed so as to bridge or dam a stream, i.e. *mti wa kukingamisha magogo mtoni*. (Cf. *ulalo*.)

Mtatio, Mtatizo, n. (*mi-*), a coiling (of cord), winding (of thread), an entanglement. (Cf. *tata, tatiza*.)

*****Mta'wa**, n. (*wa-*), (1) one who stays at home, keeps indoors, and so (2) one who leads a moral self-controlled life, a recluse, a devout religious person. (? Ar. Cf. *tawa*, close up, *utawa*. In (2) sense, the sound of *a* seems prolonged, and is written sometimes *mtaawa, mtaowa, mta'wa*.)

Mtawanya, n. (*wa-*), one who scatters, and so, one who spends freely, an open-handed, liberal person. (Cf. *tawanya*, and syn. *karimu, mpaji*.)

Mtazamo, n. (*mi-*), looking, gazing. See **Tazama**.

Mtego, n. (*mi-*), a trap, snare, gin,—used of all kinds of devices for snaring animals and birds. *Tega mtego*, set a trap. (Cf. *-tega*.)

Mtema, Mtemi, n. (*wa-*), verbal

of *tema*, one who spits, one who cuts. See **Tema**, and **Mtemo**.

Mtembezi, n. (*wa-*), (1) from *tembea*, one who walks about for pleasure or exercise rather than business, an idler, a pleasure-seeker, a tourist, &c., e.g. *mtembezi ala miguu yake*, one who travels for pleasure, lives off his own feet; (2) from *tembeza*, e.g. *mtembezi wa bithaa*, one who hawks goods about for sale, a pedlar, a commercial traveller. (Cf. *tembea, tanga, zunguka*.)

Mtemo, n. (*mi-*), (1) cutting; (2) spitting, i.e. *mtemo wa mate*. See **Tema**.

Mtendaji, n. (*wa-*), an active (energetic, enterprising, pushing) person. (Cf. *tenda, kitendo, utendaji*, &c.)

Mtende, n. (*mi-*), a date-palm, producing the fruit *tende*. Not numerous in Z., dates being imported from Arabia.

Mtendo, n. (*mi-*), a doing, mode of acting, performing, accomplishing. (Cf. *tenda, kitendo, utendaji*.)

Mtenga, n. (*wa-*), verbal of **tenga** (which see), one who separates, &c.

Mtengo, n. (*mi-*), a separating, a dividing off, &c. See **Tenga**.

Mtengwa, n. (*wa-*), one who is divided off, separated, put aside, set apart, devoted (to a work or occupation. (Cf. *tenga*.)

Mtenzi, n. (*wa-*), one who does things, carries on work, follows a trade or occupation, &c. *M. wa mashairi (wa maneno)*, one who makes poetry (stories), a poet, an author. *M. wa kazi*, an active, hard-working person. (Cf. *tenda, utenzi*.)

Mtepe, n. (*mi-*), a native sailing vessel, with a very long projecting prow, upright mast, and square matting sail. Constructed with wooden pegs and cord, at coast towns north of Mombasa,—Patta, Lamu, &c., and used by the Wagunyu in their trading voyages. (Cf. *chombo, dau*.)

Mtepetevu, n. (*wa-*), a slack, remiss, do-nothing person. (Cf. *-tepetevu, utepetevu*.)

Mteremezi, n. (*wa-*), a kindly, genial, friendly person, who sets others at their ease. (Cf. *terema*, and follg., *-kunjufu, changam'ka*.)

Mteremo, n. (*mi-*), cheerfulness, happiness, comfort, relief from trouble. (Cf. *terema*, and prec.)

Mtesi, n. (*wa-*), one who causes trouble or annoyance, a persecutor, opponent, enemy, a quarrelsome or litigious person. (Cf. *tesa, teso*.)

Mtete, n. (*mi-*), a reed. (Cf. *kitete, unyasi, mwanzi, bua*.)

Mtetemo, n. (*mi-*), shaking, trembling, shuddering, shivering, quaking. *Mtetemo wa inchi*, earthquake. *Mt. wa meno*, chattering of the teeth. (Cf. *tetema, tetemeko*, and syn. *mtikiso, msuko*.)

Mteua, n. (*wa-*), verbal of *teua*, one who chooses, criticizes, picks and chooses. *Mteua mno huangukia mbovu*, the dainty person is sure to find (his food) bad. (Cf. *teua*, and follg.)

Mteule, n. (*wa-*), one who is chosen, selected, picked out, and so choice, of high quality or character. (Cf. *teua, -teule, mteuzi*, and prec.)

Mteuzi, n. (*wa-*), like **Mteua**, a dainty person, a critic, an eclectic, a connoisseur, e.g. *mteuzi haachi tamaa*, i.e. a critic is never satisfied. (Cf. *teua*, and prec., and syn. *mchaguzi*.)

*****Mthalimu**, n. (*wa-*), an unjust, tyrannical person, an oppressor, despot, persecutor, defrauder, &c. (Ar. Cf. *thalimu, uthalimu, thulumu*.)

*****Mthamini**, n. (*wa-*), a surety, trustee, one who goes bail for another, a hostage, guarantor. (Ar. Cf. *thamini, thamana*.)

Mti, n. (*mi-*), (1) a tree,—of any kind and in any state; (2) tree-material, i.e. wood, timber; (3) a tree, or part of a tree, prepared for use,—pole, post, palisade. *Merikebu ya mti*, a wooden ship. *Nyumba ya* *mti*, a house of timber, a wooden house. *Nyumba ya miti*, a house built with poles. *Mti kati*, a post to which a prisoner is secured by fetters on his feet. (Cf. *mkatale*.) (Cf. *kijiti, uti*, and *ubau*, plank, sawn timber, *nguzo, boriti*. Lists of trees may be found in Sacleux, *Dictionnaire Franç.-Swahili*, Appendix, and for British Central Africa in Johnston's *British Central Africa*, p. 227, first ed.)

Mti, n. (—). *Marathi ya mti, uwele wa mti*, denotes sores of a scrofulous or gangrenous kind.

*****Mtii**, n. (*wa-*), an obedient (submissive, docile) person. (Ar. Cf. *tii, utii, ta'a*.)

Mtikiti, n. (*mi-*), the plant producing the water-melon, *tikiti*.

Mtima, n. (*mi-*), heart,—seldom used in modern Swahili, for *moyo*.

Mtindi, n. (—), buttermilk,—also described as *mtindi wa maziwa*, or *maziwa ya mtindi*. (Cf. *-tindi*.)

Mtindo, n. (*mi-*), (1) sort, shape, size, pattern, cut; (2) a special sort, a good kind, extra quality; (3) conclusion, end. *Nguo hii ya m.*, this is a special (unusual, superfine) calico (dress, fabric). *Mwanangu ni m. wa yule*, my son is just like him. *M. wa kusi*, the end of the (season of the) south wind. (Cf. *kitinda, tindika*. Perh. same as *chinja, mchinjo*, i.e. (1) a cutting; (2) cut, shape; (3) cutting off, end.)

*****Mtini**, n. (*mi-*), a fig-tree, the fruit being *tini*. (The wild fig is *mvumo*.)

Mtipitipi, n. (*mi-*), name of a climbing plant, or creeper. (Dist. *tipitipi*, a bird.)

Mto, n. (*mito*), (1) a river, small or large, rivulet, brook, stream, &c.; (2) creek, inlet, estuary, arm of the sea, i.e. *mto wa bahari*; (2) a cushion, pillow. *Mto wa kono*, a branching river, delta. *Mto mkavu*, a river bed, dry channel. *Mkono wa mto*, affluent, branch of a river. *Mto waenda kassi*, the river runs swiftly. *Vuka mto*, cross a river. *Kata mto*, go upstream. *Fuata mto*, go down-stream. *Mto haupitiki*, the river is impassable. (Cf. *jito, kijito*, also *juto*, and *uto, mfo*.)

Mtoa, Mtoaji, n. (*wa-*), verbal of *toa*, in all its senses, one who gives, removes, &c. See **Toa**. *Mtoaji kahawa*, one who serves coffee.

Mtobwe, n. (*mi-*), a tree from which a favourite kind of walking-stick is made,—white, and possessing the quality of bending and keeping any curve it is bent to, like lead. (Cf. *bakora, fimbo*.)

Mtofaa, n. (*mi-*), a fruit-tree, with an apple-like fruit, *tofaa* (*Jambosa Malaccensis*, Sac.), jamrack.

Mtoki, n. (—), painful swelling in the groin, usually accompanied by fever.

Mtokoso, n. (*mi-*), (1) act (condition) of boiling; (2) rice boiled and dried,—so sold in shops. (Cf. *chemka*.)

Mtombo, n. (*mi-*), and ? **Mtembo**, (1) the heart or centre of the sprouting shoot of a palm-tree, cocoanut or other (cf. *kilele, moyo*). (2) painful cracks and sores caused by the *buba* disease, esp. on the soles of the feet.

Mtomo, n. (*mi-*), solidity (firmness, strength, good workmanship) in building (Str.). (Cf. *tomea*, and syn. *imara, uthabiti*.)

Mtomoko, n. (*mi-*), a fruit-tree of the same class as the custard-apple (*mtopetope*).

Mtomondo, n. (*mi-*), a fruit-tree of the same class as the *mtofaa*,—a Baringtonia, bearing the fruit *tomondo*.

Mtondo, n. (*mi-*), the third day following,—the series being *leo*, to-day, *kesho*, to-morrow, *kesho kuchwa*, the day after to-morrow, then *mtondo*, the third day. The fourth day is called *mtondo goo*, or *kushinda mtondo*.

Mtondoo, n. (*mi-*), a large tree,

bearing the fruit *tondoo*, with a seed rich in oil,—*Calophyllum Inophyllum*.

Mtongozi, n. (*wa*-), one who tries to attract (allure, seduce), e.g. by words, signs, dress, &c., a seducer. (Cf. *tongoza, kitongo, utongozi*.)

Mtopetope, n. (*mi*-), the small tree which bears the custard-apple, *topetope*. Another variety is *mtopetope-mwitu*.

Mtoria, n. (*mi*-), a kind of Landolphia, producing india-rubber, and an edible fruit (*kitoria*). (Cf. *mbungo*.)

Mtoro, n. (*wa*-), (1) a runaway slave, a truant; (2) highwayman, robber, bandit. (Cf. *toroka*.)

Mtoto, n. (*wa*-), implies generally what is (A) in an early stage of development, or (B) in a subordinate position, and includes the following meanings. A. child, young person, offspring, offshoot, descendant. E. g. *m. mwanaume* (*mume, wa kiume*), male child, son, boy. *M. mwanamke* (*wakike, mke*), a female child, daughter, girl. An *mtoto* remains so till the age of about 7 years, or about 15 years,—next becoming a *kijana* (see **Kijana**). *M. mchanga*, a very young child, a baby. The offspring of any animal is called *mtoto*, e.g. *m. wa ng'ombe*, a calf; *m. wa mbuzi*, a kid; *m. wa kuku*, a chicken. For offshoot of plants cf. *watoto wa mgomba*, the young shoots springing from the roots of a banana. *Mtoto* is also used of morbid growths, e.g. *mtoto wa jicho*, of a growth near the eye. But cf. B. B. (1) dependant, subordinate, follower, servant, ward, member of a household in relation to its head. This sense is quite irrespective of age. (2) *Mtoto* is also extended to inanimate objects of all sorts, whose function is of a subordinate kind, but in this case it is sometimes treated as a *mi*- noun, i.e. with plur. *mitoto*, e.g. *m. wa meza*, the drawer of a table; *m. wa kasha*, a shelf or inner compartment in a box; *m. wa kitasa*, a ward of a lock; *m. wa mto*, tributary of a river; *m. wa parafujo*, the worm (thread) of a screw; *m. wa randa*, the iron used to stiffen the cutting-iron in a plane. (Cf. *kitoto, toto, kijana*, and syn. *mwana*.)

Mtoza, n. (*wa*-), verbal of *toa* (*toza*), one who causes to pay, an exactor, &c. *Mtoza ushuru*, a collector of taxes.

Mtu, n. (*wa*-), (1) a person, a human being, an individual, one of the human race, a man; (2) a dependant, servant, slave, follower, adherent. E.g. *mtu mume* (or *m'me*), a male, *mtu mke*, a female,—more commonly *mwanaume, mwanamke*. *Mtu wangu*, one of my servants (slaves). *Mtu wa nani?* Who does he belong to? *Mtu gani?* Of what tribe is he? *Si mtu*, not a man, no one. *Hakuna mtu*, there is no one, nobody. *Mtu* and *watu* are used to point a number of contrasts, each illustrating the content of the idea. Thus (1) *mtu, si watu*, one person, not many persons. (2) *mtu, si nyama*, a human being, not a beast. (3) *mtu, si kitu*, a living personality, not a chattel. (4) *mtu*, a mere man, a man as isolated and helpless. *Nimekuwa mtu tu*, of one conscious of his own existence only, ignorant of all his surroundings, 'I was a simple nonentity.' (5) *mtu*, a man as possessed of intrinsic worth, e.g. *sisi hatukuwa watu mbele yao*, we did not count as men in their eyes. (6) *mtu*, in an emphatic sense, a person of rank, importance and consideration, e.g. *mtoto wa watu*, a well-born (well-connected) child, a child of people of position. (7) *watu*, people in general, the average man; *mimi mtu kama watu*, I am a common man. (8) *watu*, other people, as distinct from the self, esp. as to ownership, e.g. *kwenda kwiba tango* *la watu,* to go and steal other people's cucumbers. *Fetha hii ya watu,* this money is not mine. (9) *watu,* public opinion, society. *Watu husema hivi,* it is a common (popular, general) opinion. (10) *mtu* is often used to denote the possession of a certain attribute, or condition, e. g. *tukawa watu wa kufa tu,* we were as good as dead (entirely at the mercy of an enemy, or mortally wounded). *Si mtu wa kwenda naye,* he is not a man to go with, a fit companion. (Cf. *utu, kitu, jitu, kijitu,* and syn. *mwana Adamu, bin Adamu.*)

Mtulinga, n. (*mi-*), the collarbone, i. e. *mfupa wa bega.*

Mtumba, n. (*mi-*), also **Tumba**, (1) a bale, bag, or bundle, e. g. of cloth or other goods, made up as a load for a caravan-porter, and so (2) in general, a load, a man's burden. (Cf. *tumba, tumbo,* ? *tumbi,* syn. *mzigo, mfuko, robota.*)

Mtumbuizi, n. (*wa-*), one who soothes (consoles, cheers) the pain or sorrow of another, esp. by singing. (Cf. *tumbuiza,* and syn. *fariji, tuliza.*)

Mtumbwi, n. (*mi-*), a native canoe, made all in one piece of a dug-out tree-trunk, often a hollowed log of the mango tree, without outriggers, but sometimes with a small mast and sail. (Cf. *tumbua, tumbo, tumba,* and for other kinds of boat *galawa, dau, mashua.*)

Mtume, n. (*wa-*), one who is employed or sent, a messenger, an emissary. But in Z. especially of Mahomet, i. e. the Apostle, and also of the chief characters of the Old Testament, Moses, Job, and others. *Tume* is used in the more general sense. (Cf. *tuma, tume, utume, utumwa,* and follg.)

Mtumishi, n. (*wa-*), a paid servant, hired domestic, house-servant,—not so general as *tume,* or so limited as *mtumwa.* (Cf. *tuma,* and prec., and syn. *boi, mwandishi.*)

Mtumwa, n. (*wa-*), one who is employed or sent, but usually in the special sense a bond-servant, slave, one who is the property of another. Contr. *bwana,* the master, owner of slaves, and *mngwana,* a freedman, or one who has never been a slave (see **Utumwa**). E. g. *mtumwa mwema nakawa hesabu yake nguo mbili na bunduki moja,* a stout, good-looking slave cost two lengths of calico and a gun,—i. e. an average price in the interior in past years. *Mtumwa wa shamba,* a plantation slave, mostly engaged in cultivation. *Mtumwa wa nyumbani,* a domestic slave, employed in his master's house. For various descriptions of slave see *mbwana, kitwana, mjakazi, kijakazi, suria, mzalia, mtoro, mjoli, kijoli, teka, mjinga, mstaarabu.* (Cf. *tuma, tume, mtume, mtumishi mtumwaji, utumwa.*)

Mtumwaji, n. (*wa-*), one who is regularly employed, or sent, an agent, a messenger, i. e. *mtumwa,* without the limitation to slaves. (Cf. *tuma,* and prec.)

Mtunduizi, n. (*wa-*), a spy, a scout. (Cf. *tunduia,* and syn. *mpelelezi.*)

Mtungi, n. (*mi-*), an earthen pitcher,—the commonest kind of water-jar in Z. of this baked earthenware, mostly plain and made by hand in the island, but also imported with colour and ornamentation. Water-jars of various shapes and kinds are *balasi, kasiki, kuzi, gudulia.* (Cf. *tunga, tungi,* and follg. Also *chombo.*)

Mtungo, n. (*mi-*), a putting together, arranging in a row (and in other senses of *tunga,* v.), also of things put together in a row. Used esp. of fish, *mtungo wa samaki,* or *mtungo* only, a string or stick of fish, i. e. fish on a string or stick. *Mtungo mkubwa,* a great lot (haul, catch) of fish. (Cf. *tunga, utungo,* also *tanda, panga.*)

Mtunguja, n. (*mi-*), name of a shrub, a kind of *Solanum*, with an edible fruit.

Mtupa, n. (*mi-*), a kind of Euphorbia, very poisonous. (Cf. *utupa*.) Also verbal n. of *tupa*, one who throws.

Mtutumo, n. (*mi-*), a low distant roll or rumbling sound, as of thunder, an earthquake, waterfall, boiling water, &c. (Cf. *tutuma*, and perh. *tetema*.)

Mtwaa, n. (*wa-*), one who takes, or carries off. *Ndiye mtwaa watu*, it is he who carries off people, i.e. the angel of death. (Verbal of *twaa*.)

Mtwango, n. (*mi-*), act (place, or manner, &c.) of pounding with pestle and mortar. Also the pounding instrument, a wooden pestle, usually *mchi*. (Cf. *twanga*.)

Mtweto, n. (*mi-*), panting, gasping. (Cf. *tweta*.)

Mu-, (1) is a prefix appearing in a few demonstrative adverbs, *humu*, *mumu*, *mumo*, *mle* (for *mule*), with the meaning 'in here, in there,' and corresponds generally to *ku* in similar uses. (See **Ku**, 3. (2).) It is more common in the relative form *mo*, which is also a demonstrative of reference or relative distance. (See **Mo**, and **-o**.) It is also identical with *m* in forms like *mna*, *mnamo*, there is (in there) (see **M-**), i.e. a demonstrative pfx. of general reference with the special idea of interiority, or being inside. (2) is used in some cases for the noun-pfx. m (which see), especially before a *u* following, as *Muungu*, *muumishi*, or before another *m* in *mume*, though the change represents no important difference of sound. Some foreign inhabitants of Zanzibar, however, e.g. the Goanese, regularly pronounce the *m*-pfx. as *mu*, e.g. *mutu*, *muti*, for *mtu*, *mti*. (3) appears as *mw* in *mwa*, as *kw* for *ku* in *kwa*. See **-a**.

Mua, n. (1) (*miwa*), sugar-cane,— better muwa (which see); (2) (*waua*), verbal form from *ua*, v., one who kills,—better mwua (which see), or muua.

Muaa, n. (*miaa*, *miyaa*). See **Mwaa**.

*****Muda**, n. (no plur. used), space of time, period, set term, fixed interval. *M. wa*, for the space of, during. *M. kitambo*, a short time. *M. mzima*, a considerable time, full time. *Baniani amempa muda miezi mitatu amlipe*, the Banian gave him a term of three months for payment. (Ar. Cf. follg. and syn. *muhulla*, *wakati*, *majira*, *nafasi*.)

*****Mudu**, v. stretch, extend. Seldom except in Rf. form *jimudu*, stretch oneself, move one's limbs,—as a sick person recovering or for relief. (Ar. Cf. *muda*, of time, and syn. *ji-nyosha*.)

*****Muhashamu**, a. a complimentary title in the Arabic fashion of beginning a letter, honoured. (Ar. Cf. *heshimu*, *heshima*, and see **Dibaji**.)

*****Muhebbi**, n. and a., also **Muhebu**, **Mohebb**, beloved friend, dear, affectionate,—used like **Muhashamu**. (Ar. Cf. *habba*, and prec.)

Muhindi, n. (1) (*Wahindi*), a native of India, but in Z. especially a Mahommedan from East India (as distinct from the non-Mahommedan Hindoos called Banians); (2) (*mi-*), Indian corn plant. See **Mhindi**.

Muhogo, n. (*mihogo*), the cassava plant. See **Mhogo**.

*****Muhtasari**, n. (—), abridgement, abstract, summary, list of contents, précis. (Ar.)

*****Muhulla**, n. (—), space of time, period, interval. (Ar. Cf. syn. *muda*.)

*****Muhuri**, n. (—), seal, signet, crest, armorial bearing. *Tia m.*, seal, set seal to, confirm, sign. (Ar.)

Mui, n. better muwi, miwi (which see).

Mukadisha, **Mukdesha**, n. a town on the Somali coast, north of Zanzibar, formerly (with *Barawa, Merka, Warsheikh*) under the Sultan, now in the Italian sphere.

Mulika, v. shine, gleam, throw (make, show) a light. *Akumulikaye mchana, hukunguza usiku,* who lights you by day, sets fire to you by night. Ap. *mulik-ia, -iwa,* bring a light for, make a light with, help with a light. E. g. *nimulikie chini,* light me downstairs. Cs. *mulik-isha, -ishwa.* (Cf. *kimulimuli.*)

Mume, n. (*waume*), for *mtu mume, mwanaume,* a male, a man. Used alone *mume* means distinctively husband, in contrast with *mwanaume.* (See -ume, and cf. *mke.*)

*****Mumiani,** n. (*ma-*), a mummy, (used in native medicine, &c.). (Ar.)

Mumo, adv. demonstr. of reference, also *mumo humo.* See **Mumu.**

Mumu, adv. demonstr., usually with *humu,* i. e. *mumu humu,* just inside this very place (in these circumstances), just in here. (See **Mu,** and cf. *mumo,* and adv. *kuku, papa.*)

Mumunya, v. also **Mung'unya,** and **Munya,** break in small pieces, —esp. in the mouth, i. e. mumble, munch, prepare for swallowing, e. g. like a toothless person or donkey. Nt. *mumunyika,* (1) be broken up, munched, crumble away; (2) be friable, easily crumbled or triturated, e. g. like bad mortar.

Mumunye, n. (*ma-*), a kind of gourd resembling a vegetable marrow, used as a vegetable. The rind when hard and dry is used as a vessel to hold fluids,—like the *boga, buyu.* The plant is *mmumunye.*

Munda, n. (*miunda*) (1) a harpoon, for spearing large fish, i. e. *wa kuchomea samaki kubwa.* Also (2) a piece of planking, used in wooden construction. (Cf. *unda.*)

Mundu, n. (*miundu*), a sickle, billhook, chopper.

Mungu, n. (*miungu*). See **Muungu.**

Mung'unya, Munya, Munya- munya, v., same meaning as mumunya (which see).

Munyi, n. a variant of *mwenyi,* used in the sing. as a title, chief. See **Mwenyi.**

Munyu, n. (no plur.), salt, incrustation. (Cf. *chunyu, chumvi, nyunyo.*)

Muo, n. (*miuo*), (1) a great killing, a slaughter, a massacre (cf. *ua,* v.). Also (2) a wooden stake used to dig up stones &c. with, or as a lever, often with an iron point. (Cf. *mtaimbo, mchokoo.*)

Muomo, Mwomo, n. (*miomo*), variants of *mdomo,* lip, which is usual in Z. *Ndevu za muomo,* or only *muomo,* moustache. (Cf. *mdomo, omo.*)

*****Musimu,** n. (no plur.), northerly wind, time of the north monsoon at Z., i. e. Dec. to Feb., but extended sometimes to the whole season from and to the period of southerly winds, i. e. from October to May. (Ar. For other seasons cf. *masika,* and *mwaka.*)

Muu-. See words under **Mwu-.**

Muuaji, Muuguzi, n. See **Mwuaji, Mwuguzi.**

Muumba, n. (*waumba*), one who creates, makes, fashions, esp. as a title of God in Z., the Creator of the world, i. e. *Muumba yote.* (Cf. *umba, kiumbe,* and syn. Ar. *huluku.*)

Muumishi, n. (*waumishi*), a professional cupper. (Cf. *umika.*)

Muundi, n. (*miundi*). *Muundi wa mguu,* the shin, shin bone, between knee and ankle.

Muungo, n. (*miungo*), a fastening, thing which fastens, esp. a tie, tie-beam, in wooden construction. (Cf. *unga, kiungo.*)

Muungu, n. (*miungu,*—the sing. being treated as D 1, the plur. as D 2). Also may be written *Mwungu, Mungu, Mngu,* (1) God, a god; (2) providence, luck, accident,—used to describe anything unaccountable or unexpected. Words commonly connected with *Muungu* are, *Mwenyezi Mngu*, i.e. *mwenyi enzi Muungu*, Almighty God. *Omba M.*, pray to God, also *omba kwa M.*,—*ombea* being usually 'pray for, intercede.' *Shukuru M.*, be resigned, accept the inevitable, submit,—seldom of felt or active gratitude. *Shiriki Muungu*, be wholly given to God,—the strongest expression for a religious life (cf. *shiriki*), and when pressed to its extreme, i.e. union or sharing the nature, repudiated by Mahommedans, as impious and inconceivable (cf. *shiba M.*). *Kumbuka M.*, meditate on God. *Ngoja M.*, trust in Providence. *Muungu akijalia*, God willing,—for the common Ar. *inshallah*. *Muungu akuweke*, may God provide for you (bless you), is often used by the lower classes,—also *M. akubariki*. *Mbaraka wa M.*, God's blessing. *Maskini wa Muungu*, a destitute person, esp. of a poor freed-slave, deprived by freedom of all claim to human (i.e. his master's) protection and support. (*Muungu* in various forms, *Mulungu*, *Muluku*, &c., occurs in most Bantu dialects on or near the East Coast. Swahilis sometimes use *Mola*, but seldom *Allah*, as an equivalent. The ideas conveyed are vague, but in Z. principally Mahommedan,—whence perhaps the anomalous plur. (of the inferior *mi*-class), to avoid encroachment on the unity of the Godhead. Cf. *Allah*, *Mola*, *Rabbi*, and various titles of God. Also *uungu*, and *umuungu*.)

Muwa, n. (*miwa*), also **Mua**, the sugar-cane. Less cultivated in Z. than formerly. There are still a few mills, producing treacle and a coarse brown sugar (*sukari guru*).

Muzimu, n. See **Mzimu**.

Mvi, n. (no plur., sing. is treated as D 4 and also D 6), grey hair. *Mwenyi mvi*, a grey-haired old man. So *ndevu za mvi*, grey beard. *Nywele za mvi*, grey hairs. *Mvi mweupe* or *nyeupe*. (Cf. *unyele*.)

Mviko, n. (*mi*-), act (style, &c.) of dressing, clothing, a garment, dress. (Cf. *vika*, and syn. *uvao*, *vazi*, *nguo*.)

Mvinje, n. (*mi*-), the cassiorina tree, a kind of fir growing freely on rocky ground near the seashore in Z.

*****Mvinyo**, n. (no plur., sing. is treated as D 4 and also D 6), wine, spirits, esp. the latter in Z. (Portuguese. Cf. *devai*, *tembo*, *pombe*.)

Mviringo, n. (*mi*-), roundness, a round shape, anything round, a circle, a curve, a ring, a washer. (Cf. *viringa*, *fingirisha*, and syn. *duara*, *duru*, *mduara*, *mzingo*, *pete*.)

Mvita, n. the Swahili name for the town and island of Mombasa. Also for *Mmvita*, an inhabitant of Mombasa.

Mvua, n. (1) (—), rain. *Mvua nyingi (kubwa)*, heavy rain. *Mvua ya mwaka*, a slight rainfall usually in August. *Alikwenda na mvua yake*, he went in the rain. Also (2) (*wa*-), verbal of *vua*, in all its senses, *mvua samaki*, a man fishing, *mvua nguo*, &c. (For the rainy seasons in Z. cf. *masika*, and *mvule*, and for light rain *manyunyo*.)

Mvuje, n. a fetid gum, asafoetida.

Mvuke, n. (*mi*-), vapour produced by heat, steam, perspiration. (Cf. *vukiza*, and follg. Also syn. *moshi*, *hari*, *jasho*.)

Mvukuto, n. (*mi*-), bellows,—as used by native smiths, i.e. two leather bags alternately inflated and deflated by hand. (Cf. *mfua* (*mi*-) and prec.)

Mvulana, n. (*wa*-), a young unmarried man, a bachelor. (Cf. *uvulana*, and syn. *kijana*.)

Mvule, n. also **Mvuli**, and **Vuli**, the lesser rains, the short rainy season, i.e. November in Z., when the north wind begins to set in. (Cf. *masika* and follg., and for the seasons *mwaka*. Perh. conn. with *uvuli*, shade, i.e. clouds after clear weather, or with *mvua*.)

Mvuli, n. (*mi-*), a shady place, shade of a tree, &c. (Cf. *kivuli*, a patch of shade, a shadow, &c., and *uvuli*, shade in general, gloom, darkness.)

Mvuma, n. (*wa-*) and **Mvumi**, verbal of *vuma*, one who mutters, hums, &c. See **Vuma** and follg. *Mvuma titi*, name of a bird.

Mvumo, n. (*mi-*), (1) a rumbling, muttering sound; (2) a report, rumour (see **Uvumi**); (3) a rubber (in cards, Str.); (4) the *Borassus* palm, not common in Z. island. (Cf. *vuma*, and for palms *mnazi*.)

Mvunaji, n. See **Mvuni**.

Mvungu, n. (*mi-*), a hollowed-out place, a hollow, hole, empty space, cavity,—e. g. a hole in a tree, the space under a bedstead, i. e. *mvungu wa kitanda*. *Mtaka cha mvunguni huinama*, he who wants what is under a bed must stoop for it. (Cf. *uvungu*.)

Mvuni, n. (*wa-*) and **Mvunaji**, one who gathers in a crop, a reaper, &c. (Cf. *vuna*.)

Mvunja, n. (*wa-*), verbal of **vunja** (which see), one who breaks, destroys, &c.

Mvunjo, n. (*mi-*), act (time, manner, &c.) of breaking. (See **Vunja** and prec., also *kivunjo*, *uvunjo*.)

Mvuo, n. (*mi-*), act (time, manner, place, &c.) of fishing, fishing ground, catch of fish. Also in other senses of **vua** (which see).

Mvurugo, n. (*mi-*), (1) messing, muddling, mixing up, mixture, and so (2) of unripe fruit in a squashy, messy condition, — squash, jam. (Cf. *vuruga*.)

Mvushi, n. (*wa-*), (1) a ferryman, (2) a preserver. See **Vuka**.

Mvuto, n. (*mi-*), act (manner, &c.) of drawing. Also in other senses of *vuta* (which see),—pulling, influence, persuasion, perversion, &c. *Mvuto wa maji* (*wa upepo*), current of water (air). (Cf. *mkondo*.)

Mvuvi, n. (*wa-*), a professional fisherman. Proverbially quarrelsome over their fish, and so *nyumba ya wavuvi*, a noisy, quarrelsome household. (Cf. *vua, mvuo*.)

Mw-, as a pfx. See **Mu**, and **M**.

Mwa, prep. form agreeing with the locative form of nouns in *-ni*, of (i. e. *mu-a*, see **Mu**, -a), e. g. *nyumbani mwa Mzungu*, in the house of the European.

Mwaa, n. also **Muaa**, **Mnyaa**, **Myaa**, with the plur. *miwaa*, also *miyaa*, *miaa*, (1) the Hyphaene, or Dwarf, palm, also commonly known as *mkoche* and *mkoma*, furnishing the leaves, which are generally used as material for mats, bags, baskets, coarse cord, and string, (2) a leaf-blade of this palm. The blade is divided into two parts, *chane*, and each part slit into three, the central piece being the finest material for plaiting, the outsides for coarser kinds. (Cf. *ung'ong'o, utangule, ukindu, ukili, chana, suka*.)

*****Mwafa**, n. (*miafa*), anything causing fear, danger, a terror, horror, bugbear, enemy. (Ar. Cf. *hofu, afa*, and syn. *kioja, kitisho*.)

*****Mwafaka**, n. (*miafaka*), agreement, bargain, conspiracy, plot. (Ar. Cf. *afiki*, and syn. *mapatano*.)

Mwafu, n. (*miafu*), wild jasmine. (Cf. *afu, yasmini*.)

Mwaga, v. pour out, pour away, spill, waste, empty out. Ps. *mwagwa*. Nt. *mwagika*. Hence *mwagikia, -iwa*. *Maji yaliyomwagika hayazoeleki*, spilt water cannot be picked up. Ap. *mwag-ia, -iwa*, pour out on (for, &c.). (Cf. *mimina*.)

Mwaka, n. (*miaka*), a year. Two ways of reckoning years are in use in Z., (1) the lunar year of twelve lunar months,—Ramathan being counted as the first month,—and about 355 days. This is the Arab official and religious year, and beginning ten days earlier each year has no correspondence with the seasons. (2) the solar year, with 365 days, the first day of the year being called *siku ya mwaka*, and kept as a popular festival, the last *kigunzi*, and the days being reckoned by decades (*miongo*). It is of Persian origin, and used for nautical and agricultural purposes. *Mwaka wa jana*, last year. *Mw. wa juzi*, the year before last. *Mw. wa kesho* (or *ujao*), next year. *Mwaka kwa mwaka, killa mwaka*, year by year, annually. *Mwakani*, in a year's time,—but often indefinitely, some day or other, sooner or later. *Mvua ya mwaka*, light rains which fall usually in August, between the two rainy seasons. The seasons in Zanzibar are regular and well defined. The island lying about 7° south of the equator, the sun is overhead about October 21 and February 21. These dates are followed by periods of calm, light variable winds, and rains,—the greater rains called *masika*, chiefly in April, the lesser rains *mvuli* in November. When the sun is in the south, the north wind blows, and the heat is greatest, i.e. in December, January, and February. This is called *kaskazi*, or *musimu*. When the sun is in the north, the south wind blows, and the heat is less, i.e. from June to October. This is called *kusi*, and includes the *kipupwe* or cool period in June and July, following the heavy rains, and the *demani* in September and October. The times of calms and light winds are called *malelezi*, or *tanga mbili*. The thermometer in the shade in Zanzibar city is seldom above 85° or below 75° night or day. For other divisions of time see **Mwezi** and **Siku**. (Perh. cf. *waka*, and *chaka*, the hot season,—the latter seldom heard in Z.)

Mwake, Mwako, a. forms of *-ake, -ako* agreeing with locative nouns in *-ni*, his (hers, its), your, e.g. *nyumbani mwake*, in his house.

Mwako, n. (*miwako*), blaze, flame, blazing, burning. *Mwako wa moto (jua)*, blaze of a fire (the sun). (Cf. *waka*.)

***Mwalamu**, n. (*mialamu*), a stripe, band, line of colour, esp. in a dress-material. (Cf. *mlia, utepe*.)

Mwali, n. (1) (*miwali*), a Raphia palm,—not common in Zanzibar island. The mid-rib of the leaves is very long (20 feet to 30 feet), strong and light, and is much used for doors (see **Mlango**), ladders, and other purposes. (2) (*wali*, for *waali*), a maiden, a virgin; usually with *mwana*, i.e. *mwana mwali*, plur. *waana wali*. (Cf. *bikira*.)

***Mwali**, n. (*nyali*), flame, tongue of fire. (Arab. Cf. *ulimi wa moto*.)

Mwaliko, n. (*mial-*), (1) a cracking sound, click, clap. (2) an invitation, summons, call. (Cf. *alika*, and *mwito*.)

***Mwalimu**, n. a learned man, a teacher, a schoolmaster, esp. the Mahommedan official teacher attached to a mosque. (Ar. Cf. *elimu, alama, mtaalamu*.)

Mwalishi, n. (*waal-*), one who calls, summons, invites, e.g. to a feast, wedding, &c. (Cf. *alika, mwaliko*.)

Mwamba, n. (*miamba*), (1) a rock, a mass of rock, a very large stone, a reef. (2) in building, a ridge pole or wall-plate, i.e. a transverse pole, resting on the top of poles forming the side or roof of a native house. (Dim. *kijamba*.)

Mwambao, n. (*miambao*), (1) a passing near to, grazing past, not touching, missing contact with; (2) passing along a shore (in a boat); (3) coast-line, coast, edge of the sea. *Safari ya mwambao*, a coasting voyage. *Safiri (vuta) mwambao*, make a coasting voyage. (Cf. *ambaa*.)

Mwambi, n. (*waambi*), one who speaks against another, a slanderer, a critic, a tale-bearer, a gossip. (Cf. *amba.*)

Mwamu, n. (*waamu*), brother-in-law, sister-in-law. (Cf. *wifi.*)

Mwamua, Mwamuzi, n. (*waam.*) a judge, arbitrator, umpire, mediator. (Cf. *amua, maamuzi,* and syn. *kathi,* which marks office rather than function, and *hakimu.*)

Mwana, n. (*waana, wana*), (1) specifically, child, son, daughter, dependent,—of relationship as such, without reference to age (cf. *mtoto,* which often connotes age). *Huyu ni mwanangu,* this is my child. *Akaoa akazaa mwana,* he married and begot a son. *Mwana (wa) Adamu,* a child (or descendant) of Adam, a human being, one of the human race. *Mwana mwali,* a maid, a virgin. (2) in general, without reference to relationship, a person, one of a class. E. g. *Mwana mume (mke),* a man (woman). *Mwana maji,* a sailor. *Mwanafunzi,* an apprentice, disciple, *Mwana sheria,* a lawyer. *Mwana vyuo,* a scholar. *Wanakuwa waana wazima,* they are becoming grown-up people (adults). *Marra nikaona waana wanakuja,* presently I saw people coming. Sometimes with *mtoto,* e. g. *akakaa hatta mwana mtoto asipate,* he lived on but did not get a child. *Mwana* has also various special senses, e. g. (*a*) lady of the house, mistress,—and in addressing such a one, madam,—like *bibi, bibi mkubwa.* Younger ladies of the house are called *wa kina mwana,* or *mamwana.* (*b*) used in polite reference or address to one's own mother,—madam. (*c*) a recess in a grave, closed by the *kiunza,* is called *mwana wa ndani* (cf. use of *mtoto,* of appendages of various kinds). (Cf. *jana* n., *kijana,* and the same root *-ana* is perh. seen in *bwana, mtwana,* for *mtu mwana, msijana, mvulana.*)

Mwanamizi, n. (*waan.*), a kind of crab, a hermit crab.

Mwandamano, n. (*miand.*), a following, procession, retinue. (Cf. *andama,* and follg.)

Mwandamizi, n. (*waand.*), (1) a follower, an attendant; (2) a successor, one who comes next after. (Cf. follg.)

Mwandamo, n. (*miand.*), act (time, manner, &c.) of following, a coming after, a procession. *Mwandamo wa mwezi,* the following of the moon, the beginning of a month,—also *mwezi mwandama,* the moon succeeding or following, i. e. the new moon. (Cf. *andama,* and prec.)

Mwandani, n. (*waand.*), companion, associate, friend. (Perh. for *mwandamani.* Cf. *andama,* and prec., also syn. *mwenzi, rafiki.*)

Mwandazi, n. (*waand.*), one who prepares food, cook, confectioner, pastry cook. (Cf. *andaa, maandasi,* and *mpishi.*)

Mwandikaji, n. (*waand.*), also **Mwandiki**, (1) one who arranges, serves, waits at table, a waiter, a server; (2) a writer, copyist, amanuensis, clerk. (Cf. *andika, mwandishi,* and follg. Also *karani.*)

Mwandiko, n. (*miand.*), (1) act (style, &c.) of writing, handwriting, (2) what is written, manuscript,—also what is printed, a writing, a book; (3) arrangement, careful treatment, manipulation, e. g. of a doctor. (Cf. *andika, andiko (ma-),* and prec.)

Mwandishi, n. (*waand.*), (1) one who serves (waits at table), waiter, house-servant (cf. *mtumishi, boi*); (2) a writer, clerk, secretary, amanuensis (cf. *karani*). (Cf. *andika,* and prec.)

Mwanga, n. (*mianga*), (1) a light, shining, that which gives light, e. g. *mwango wa jua (taa, moto),* the light of the sun (lamp, fire); (2) fig. (*wa-*), a very wise, enlightened person; and esp. (3) a wizard, sorcerer, supposed to go about at night, sometimes in the form of a rat, and frighten people; (4) name of a kind of rice. See **Mchele**. (Cf. *anga,* and follg.)

Mwangafu, n. (*waang.*), a clever, enlightened, intellectual, bright-witted person. (Cf. *anga, -angafu, uangafu,* and prec.)

Mwangalizi, n. (*waang.*), an overseer, manager, superintendent, director, administrator. (Cf. *angalia,* and syn. *msimamizi.*)

Mwangamizi, n. (*waang.*), one who ruins, a destroyer. (Cf. *angamia, maangamizi.*)

Mwangaza, n. (*miang.*), that which makes light, or enlightens, and so (1) light, brightness, clearness, radiance, daylight. *Mw. wa alfajiri,* the first streaks of dawn, twilight. *Weupe na mw.*, brightness and light. *Mwangazani,* in broad daylight, in full view. (2) a hole admitting light and air, as in stone houses in Z., an aperture, small window, loophole. *Akaona tundu dogo, aona mwangaza mbali sana,* and he saw a little hole, a light-hole a long way off. (3) fig. enlightenment, lucidity, shrewdness, prudence. (4) publicity, making known, showing, advertising, touting. *Jambo hili ni katika mwangaza,* this matter is open to all, public property. *Nifanyie mwangaza, nikione kitu hiki,* give me a chance of seeing, that I may examine the article. *Miangaza mingi,* much showing off (of goods). (5) way of escape, way out of a difficulty, a solution, a bright idea, a ruse, e.g. *nyangaza* (as from *uang.*) *mbili, mmoja humponya,* twofold chance of escape, one saves him. (Cf. *anga,* and follg.)

Mwangazi, n. (*waang.*), a clever, shrewd, clear-headed, well-informed person. (Cf. *anga, mwangafu, mwanga,* and prec.)

Mwango, n. (*miango*), (1) a frame hung against a wall to carry a native lamp,—and so, lamp-stand, lamp-holder, lamp-suspender (cf. *anga, mwanga*); (2) for *mlango,* door (which see).

Mwangu, n. form of *-angu* agreeing with a locative in *ni*, e.g. *shambani mwangu,* in my estate. See **Mu-** and **-angu.**

Mwanguzi, Mwangushi, n. (*waang.*), one who throws down, or causes to fall, one who overthrows (destroys, &c.). *Mw. wa nazi,* a professional cocoanut picker,—also *mkwezi,* who charges one (or two) pice per tree. (Cf. *angua.*)

Mwangwi, n. (*miangwi*), an echo. (Perh. cf. *mwanga,* wizard, mysterious person.)

*****Mwani**, n. (*miani*), (1) seaweed (in general) ; (2) an eye-glass. See **Miwani.** (Ar.)

Mwanya, n. (*mianya*), a gap, breach, hole, notch, narrow pass, small opening, cleft, crevice. *Mw. wa mguu,* a cloven foot. *Mw. wa udevu,* a forked beard. *Mlima wenyi mwanya,* a hill with a cleft, a double-peaked hill. (Cf. *pengo, ufa.*)

Mwanzi, n. (*mianzi*), a bamboo. Hence of other kinds of reed and cane, and things resembling them in appearance or use, e.g. a pipe or tube of any kind, an ear-trumpet, a musical pipe, flageolet, flute, telescope, a stick used for hanging things on. *Mwanzi wa pua,* the nostril. *Kalamu ya mwanzi,* a reed pen.

Mwanzo, n. (*mianzo*), (1) act (time, method, &c.) of beginning, a start, commencement, first stage ; (2) origin, primary principle. (Cf. *anza, chanzo,* and syn. Ar. *asili.*)

Mwao, n. (*miao*), (1) a piece of wood used as a support, prop, or strut (cf. *walio*). Also (2) trouble, effort, bother (Str.).

Mwao, a. form of *-ao,* agreeing with a locative in *-ni,* e.g. *mjini mwao,* in their town.

*****Mwarabu**, n. (*Waarabu*), an Arab. One from the south coast of Arabia is known as *Msheheri,* from the north, i.e. the Persian Gulf, *mshemali.* (Ar. Cf. *Uarabu, kiarabu, manga, Arabuni.*)

*****Mwáridi**, n. (*miwáridi*), a rose-tree, the flower being *wáridi.* (Ar. Cf. *wáridi.*)

Mwashi, n. (*waashi*), a mason, one who builds with stones and mortar. (Cf. *aka*, *nashi*, and contr. *mjenzi*.)

Mwashiri, n. (*miash.*), one of the longitudinal timbers which support the mast (*mlingote*) in a native vessel. See **Mlingote**, and **Chombo**.

***Mwathini**, n. (*waath.*), one who calls Mahommedans to prayer at the mosque at the regular hours, a muezzin. (Ar. Cf. *athini*, *athana*.)

Mwavuli, n. (*miavuli*), an umbrella, sunshade. (Cf. *mvuli*, *uvuli*, *kivuli*, and *tapa*.)

***Mwawazi**, n. (*waawazi*), disposer of events,—a title of God. (Ar. Cf. *awaza*.)

Mwayo, n. (*miayo*), a yawn. *Piga mwayo*, *enda mwayo*, yawn.

Mwaza, **Mwazi**, n. (*wawaza*), one who thinks (supposes, fancies, &c.). See **Waza**. (Dist. *wazi*, a.)

***Mwazimo**, n. (*miaz.*), a borrowing, a lending, accommodation, advance, loan. (Cf. *azima*, v.)

Mweko, n. (*miweko*), a putting aside (off, down, away, &c.). See **Weka**, also **Mwiko**.

***Mwele**, n. (1) (*waele*), a sick person, a bedridden patient, an invalid, a cripple. (Ar. Cf. *uwele*, and syn. *mgonjwa*.) (2) (*miele*), the plant bearing *mawele* or *uwele*, i.e. a kind of millet with an ear of very small edible seed (cf. *mawele*).

Mweleko, n. (*mieleko*), used of a leather sling for a gun. (Dist. *mbeleko*, *ubeleko*.)

Mwelewa, n. (*wael.*), one who understands, who is intelligent, takes a thing in. (Cf. *elea*, and follg., and perh. *mwerevu*, i.e. *mwelefu*, and syn. *mtambuzi*, *mwangafu*, &c.)

Mwelezo, n. (*miel.*), explanation, sign, indication, exposition, programme. (Cf. *elea*, and *elezo*, and prec. Also syn. *mafafanusi*.)

Mwembe, n. (*miembe*), a mango tree, bearing the fruit *embe*. Mangoes and cocoanuts are the commonest trees in Z. Canoes are made from the hollowed trunk of the mango. (See **Embe**, and dist. *uembe*, a razor.)

Mwenda, n. (*waenda*), verbal of *enda* (which see), one who goes. *Nyati ni mwenda pekee*, the (Indian) buffalo is a solitary beast. *Mwenda nguu*, one who despairs. (Cf. *nguu*.) See **Enda**.

Mwendeleo, n. (*miend.*), progress, advance, movement. (Cf. *enda*, and *mwendo*.)

Mwendelezi, n. (*waend.*), one who causes to go on, one who carries on or forward, and so in various senses of *endeleza* (see **Enda**). E. g. (1) a persistent, persevering, progressive person; (2) one who copies, one who spells words.

Mwendo, n. (*miendo*), a going, moving, motion, proceeding, progress, way (manner, style) of going, gait, behaviour, course, &c. E. g. *mwendo wa siku tatu*, a three days' journey. *Vunja mwendo*, prevent progress. *Mwendo wa jua*, the sun's course, orbit. (Cf. *enda*, *mwenendo*, and *mwendeleo*.)

Mwenea, n. (*waenea*), one who spreads out (pervades, extends),—esp. as a title of God, as omnipresent, i. e. *mwenea pote*. (Cf. *enea*, *mwenezi*.)

Mwenendo, n. (*mien-*), going on, moving, &c., like *mwendo*, but often fig. proceedings, behaviour, conduct. (Cf. *enda*, *enenda*.)

Mwenenzi, n. (*waen-*), (1) one who measures (surveys, compares, &c.) (cf. *enenza*); (2) one who goes, a traveller. (Cf. *enenda*.)

Mweneza, n. (*waen-*), one who allots (distributes, gives out), esp. as a title of God, the Giver of good to all. (Cf. *enea*, *eneza*.)

Mwenge, n. (*mienge*), a torch, a fire-brand, a wisp of straw or grass for carrying fire or a light.

Mwenyeji, n. (*wenyeji*), lit. the regular possessor (cf. *-enyi*, and the formative *-ji*). Hence (1) master of a house, householder, owner, occupant, citizen, inhabitant of a town, native (of a place); (2) host, in relation to guests (*wageni*), e. g. *kutumwe mwenyeji wetu aende kwa jumbe*, let our host be sent to go to the chief.

Mwenyewe, n. (*wenyewe*). See -enyewe. Sometimes used as *mwenyeji*, or *mwenyi*, e. g. *yule simba ndiye mwenyewe* (perh. for *mwenyi wake*) *asali*, that lion is the owner of the honey.

Mwenyezi, n. i. e. *mwenyi enzi*, usually a title of God, the Possessor of might, the Almighty, i. e. *mweza yote*. The commonest Swahili term in speaking of God is *Mwenyezi Mngu*. (Cf. -enyi.)

Mwenyi, n. (*wenyi*), one who possesses, an owner, an independent person. See -enyi. Not commonly used as a noun, except as a title, whether complimentary or official, and then sometimes *mwinyi*, and *munyi*. On the mainland *mwenyi mkuu* and *mwenyi mkubwa* sometimes denote the second and third official under a chief,—the first being *shehe* or *waziri*. Sometimes also a term of respectful reference or address, 'sir,' like *bwana*.

Mwenzi, n. (*wenzi*), (1) a friend, companion, associate, acquaintance; (2) of things as well as persons, fellow, counterpart, match, double, something resembling or corresponding to another. E. g. *hakuna msiba usio na mwenziwe*, no disaster but has another like it. (Cf. *enza*, a causal form of *enda*, i. e. cause to go, accompany, share the actions of, and syn. *rafiki*.)

Mwetu, a. form of *-etu*,—agreeing with locatives in *-ni*, our. E. g. *mjini mwetu*, in our town.

Mwewe, n. (*miewe*), a bird of prey, a kind of kite or hawk, which carries off chickens, &c.

Mweza, n. (*waweza*), verbal of *weza*, one who is able, possessed of power over (or, to do), a ruler. *Mweza inchi*, the ruler of a country. *Mweza mwenyewe*, his own master, an independent power. *Mweza yote*, supreme over all things, Almighty,— a title of God,—also *mweza kwetu*, ruler of our world. (Cf. *mwenyezi*.)

Mwezekaji, n. (*waez-*), a professional thatcher of houses. (Cf. *ezeka*, and follg.)

Mwezeko, n. (*miez-*), act (operation, style) of roofing a native house, thatching (with grass, &c.). (Cf. *ezeka*, and prec.)

Mwezi, n. (*miezi*), (1) the moon; (2) a month, i. e. a lunar month; (3) menses (also *damu*, and *hethi*, which see). (1) *Mwezi mkubwa* (*mpevu, kamili, duara, wa mviringo*), full moon. *Mwezi mdogo* (*mchanga, mpya, mwandama*), new moon. *Mwanga* (*mwangaza*) *wa mwezi*, moonshine, also *mbaamwezi*. *Mwezi wapasua wingu, wachimbuka, waleta anga*, the moon pierces the cloud, it bursts forth, it sheds light. (2) Each month begins when the new moon is first seen, or after 30 days from the last new moon. *Mwezi mwandamo, mwandamo wa mwezi*, new moon, the beginning of the month. *M. mpungufu*, a month of 29 days. *M. kamili*, a full month of 30 days. The month beginning when *Ramathani* ends is considered the first month, and called *Mfunguo mosi*, i. e. the first non-fasting month. The next are called (*Mfunguo*) *pili* (or *wa pili*), *tatu* (*wa tatu*), &c. to *kenda* (*wa kenda*), the ninth month —the remaining three having the Arab names *Rajabu, Shaabani* (or *Mlisho*), *Ramathani* (*mwezi wa Mfungo*). The other Arab names are used in letters, and in giving dates, but are not commonly known. The month is divided variously into (1) weeks, or quarters, i. e. four sets of seven days, *juma* (*ma-*). *Mwezi ni majuma manne*, the month is four weeks. But the weeks are reckoned independently of the months, the week and the month not necessarily beginning together. (2) decades, *kumi* (*ma-*) or *mwongo* (*miongo*), i. e. three sets of ten days, called *kumi la kwanza, la kati,* and *la kwisha,* the days in each being counted as *mwezi mosi,* the first day of the month, *mwezi pili,* the second day, and so on,—also *mwezi wa mosi, wa pili,* &c. Occasionally *mwezi mmoja* is used, e. g. *killa mwezi mmoja ukiandama,* on each succeeding first of the month. *Mwezi ngapi,* or *siku ya mwezi ngapi* (or *wa ngapi*)? What day of the month is it? (3) halves,—the full moon being the middle point, the first half being called *mwezi nje,* or *mwanga mkubwa,* the second *mwezi ndani* (*mchimbu*) or *giza.* (4) in letters, documents, agreements, &c. the days are usually reckoned straight on from one to thirty, and are commonly designated by the number only, e. g. *ishirini Shaabani,* the 20th of Shaabani, *mosi Ramathani,* the first of Ramathani. See also **Mwaka,** **Siku, Tarihi.**

Mwia, n. (*wawia*), a creditor, one who demands payment of a debt, a dun. (Cf. *wa,* v., *wia,* and *mdeni, mkopeshi.*)

Mwiba, n. (*miiba*), (1) any small sharp-pointed thing, e. g. a thorn, prickle, spur, sting, fish-bone, spine, sharp splinter, nail,—defined by context or qualifying word, as *mwiba wa nyuki,* a bee's sting, *mw. wa samaki, wa nge,* &c. (2) verbal of *iba,* one who steals (cf. follg.)

Mwibaji, n. (*waibaji*), a thievish person, a regular thief. (Cf. *iba, mwivi,* and prec.)

Mwiga, Mwigaji, n. (*waiga,* &c.), one who imitates (or, copies), —but commonly, a mocker, mimic, caricaturist. (Cf. *iga,* and follg.)

Mwigo, n. (*miigo*), (1) imitation, copying; (2) mimicry, mockery, counterfeit, forgery, caricature (cf. *iga,* and prec.); (3) (*waigo*), a large kind of pigeon or dove. (Cf. *njiwa, hua.*)

Mwiko, n. (*miiko*), (1) a spoon, or instrument resembling it, e. g. a mason's trowel (cf. *mkamshe, upawa,* and *kijiko*); (2) something put aside, esp. food left over from a meal, put away from evening to morning, &c., i. e. *chakula cha mwiko.* Also (3) something deliberately abstained from, by order of a doctor, or considerations of health, &c. *M. wa nyama,* abstention from meat. *M. wa vileo,* teetotalism. *Shika m.,* live by rule, diet oneself. *Mshike miiko, msionane na wake wenu,* keep the rules, and do not be seen by your wives. (Perh. cf. *weka,* at least for (2), and for the change of consonant cf. *tweka, twika.*)

Mwili, n. (*miili*), a body, human or animal, and usually a living body, a whole body, including head and limbs. Also the trunk of the body, without the head. (Cf. *kiwiliwili,* esp. of the trunk only, without head or limbs, and *maiti, pinda,* of dead bodies. Obs. *m-wili* is a possible form of *-wili,* twofold, double, two, and so perh. of the body as characterized by pairs of limbs and symmetrical sides.)

Mwima, n. (*waima*), one who stands erect (or, stands still). (Seldom in Z. Cf. *ima.*)

Mwimbaji, n. (*waimb.*), a singer, songster, chorister. (Cf. *imba,* and follg.)

Mwimbishi, n. (*waimb.*), one who teaches, or leads singing, a singing master, a conductor. (Cf. *imba,* and prec.)

Mwimo, n. (*miimo*), an upright or side-piece of a door-frame. (See **Mlango,** and cf. *ima.*)

Mwinamishi, n. (*wain.*), one who causes to bend (stoop). (Cf. *inama,* and follg.)

Mwinamo, n. (*miin.*), a stooping, a bending down. (Cf. *inama,* and prec.)

Mwinda, Mwindaji, n. (*wa-*

winda), a huntsman, one who hunts, —of any kind of game. (Cf. *winda, mwinzi, windo*, and syn. *saka*.)

Mwinyi, n. used as a title. See **Mwenyi**.

Mwinzi, n. (*wawinzi*), sometimes used for *mwinda, mwindaji* (which see, and cf. *winda*).

Mwisho, n. (*miisho*), act (time, place, manner, means) of ending, bringing to an end, end, result, conclusion, final step, extreme limit, consummation, annihilation, death. Often as adv., finally, lastly (cf. *hatima*). *-a mwisho*, final, last, extreme. (Cf. *isha*, and syn. *ukomo, upeo, mpaka*, and contr. *mwanzo*.)

***Mwislamu**, n. (*Waislamu*), a Mahommedan. Also **Msilimu, Mwaslimu** (which see).

Mwita, Mwitaji, n. (*waita*), one who calls (summons, invites). (Cf. *ita*, and *alika*.)

Mwito, n. (*miito*), act (time, manner, &c.) of calling, a summons, an invitation, a call. *Akataaye mwito, kukataa aitiwalo*, he who declines a call, declines what he is called for. (Cf. *ita*, and prec.)

Mwitu, n. (—, and *miitu*), forest, implying large trees and close together. *Mwitu mnene*, a thick, dense forest. *-a mwitu*, wild, savage, untamed. *Nyama ya mwitu*, a wild animal. *Gugu mwitu*, a weed. (Cf. *msitu*, thick underwood, jungle, *nyika*, open grassy forest sparsely covered with trees, also *poli, pululu*.)

Mwivi, n. (*wevi*), **Mwizi** (*wezi*), a thief, robber, kidnapper, swindler. *Mwivi hushikwa na mwivi mwenziwe*, a thief is caught by his fellow-thief. (Cf. *iba, mwibaji, uizi*, and syn. *mnyang'anyi, mkopi, pakacha, mlungula*.)

Mwoga, n. (*waoga*), (1) a coward, a timid person (cf. *oga, ogopa*, and syn. *mhofu*); (2) a bather (from *oga*, bathe, cf. *osha*).

Mwogofyo, n. (*miog.*), threatening, denunciation. (Cf. *ogofya*.)

Mwoko, n. (*mioko*), act (process, &c.) of baking, roasting. (Cf. *oga, joko*.)

Mwokotaji, n. (*waok.*), and **Mwokosi**, one who picks up, one who finds by chance. (Cf. *okota*.)

Mwokozi, n. (*waok.*), one who saves, a saviour, rescuer, preserver, deliverer. (Cf. *okoa, wokovu*.)

Mwomba, n. (*waomba*), one who asks (begs, prays),—verbal of *omba*, governing a noun following. *M. pesa*, one who asks for money. *M. dua*, one who makes a special petition. *M. Muungu*, a man of prayer, a devout person. (Cf. *omba*, and follg.)

Mwombaji, n. (*waomb.*), a beggar, a professional beggar, a mendicant. (Cf. *omba, mwomba, mwombi*, and follg.)

Mwombezi, n. (*waomb.*), one who begs on behalf of (or, against) another, an intercessor, pleader, advocate,—also, opponent. (Cf. *omba*, and follg.)

Mwombi, n. (*waombi*), one who makes a petition (or, prayer), a petitioner, a suppliant. (Cf. *omba, muomba, mwombaji*.)

Mwomo, n. (*miomo*), lip,—for usual *mdomo* (which see).

Mwongezi, n. (*waong.*) also **Mwongea**, one who talks (gossips, passes the time, amuses, &c.). *Mwongezi haongezwi*, one who amuses is not amused. (Cf. *ongea*.)

Mwongo, n. (*waongo*), a liar, impostor, inventor of falsehoods, deceiver, perverter of truth. (Cf. *uongo, -ongo*, and dist. follg.)

Mwongo, n. (*miongo*), (1) number, reckoning, rank. Usually in plur. *hamo katika miongo yao*, he is not one of them, and in the phrase *miongoni mwa*, used prepositionally, among the number of, on the side of, from among; (2) a period of time, esp. a decade, sometimes used as a division of the Swahili month. (See Mwezi, and syn. *kumi*. Dist. prec.)

Mwongofu, n. (*waong.*), one who is directed, guided, instructed, put in the right way,—and so in religion, i. e. *mwongofu wa dini*, a convert, a proselyte. *Mwongofu wa kazi*, a proficient in an art, a good workman. (Cf. *ongoa, uongofu*, and follg.).

Mwongozi, n.(*waong.*), also **Mwongoshi**, one who shows the right way (guides, leads), and so, a skilled workman who can show others how to work (cf. *fundi*), or a guide, pilot (cf. the usual *kiongozi*). (Cf. *ongoa*.)

Mwonjo, n. (*mionjo*), a tasting, a trial. (Cf. *onja*.)

Mwosha, n. (*waosha*), also **Mosha**, (1) one who washes,—in general, but also (2) esp. of one who is engaged to wash a corpse, and prepare it for burial, an undertaker,—sometimes one of three, who each take a part. *Mwosha naye huoshwa*, the washer of corpses is himself one day a corpse. (Cf. *osha, oga*, and also *fua, dobi*.)

Mwosho, n. (*miosho*), act (place, manner, &c.) of washing. (Cf. *osha, josho*, and prec.)

Mwozi, n. (*waozi*), one who has to do with marrying or causing to marry,—whether bridegroom, parent, or official. (Cf. *oa, oza, maozi*, &c.)

Mwua, n. (*waua*), also **Mua**, verbal of *ua*, one who kills, murders, puts to death.

Mwuaji, n. (*wauaji*), also **Muaji**, a slayer, murderer, assassin, destroyer of life. (Cf. *ua, uuaji*, and prec. Also *mchinjaji, mfishaji*.)

Mwuguzi, n. (*waug.*), one who tends or has the care of the sick, medical attendant, nurse. (Cf. *ugua*, and syn. *mlezi*.)

Mwujiza, n.(*miuj.*), anything wonderful, extraordinary, supernatural, a wonder, a surprise, a miracle. (Cf. syn. *ajabu, mzungu, shani*, and perh. *kioja*.)

Mwumba, n. (*waumba*), also **Muumba**, one who creates, esp. the Creator of all things,—God. *Mwumba ndiye Mwumbua*, the Maker is the Destroyer. (Cf. *umba, Muumba*, and follg.)

Mwumbaji, n. (*waumb.*), one who creates, usually of God only, the Creator. (Cf. *umba*, and prec.)

*****Mwumini**, n. (*waumini*), a believer, i. e. a Mahommedan. (Ar. Cf. *amini, mmunina*.)

Mwumishi, n. (*waum.*), a professional cupper. (Cf. *umika*.)

Mwumizi, n. (*waum.*), one who hurts, causes pain. (Cf. *uma, umizi*.)

Mwunda, n. (*wa-*), one who constructs, esp. of woodwork. Also *mwundi* (*wa chombo*, &c.), a shipwright, who does the work. *Mwundisha*, the person who orders, arranges, or contracts for the work. *Mwundiwa*, the person to whose order or for whose trade the work is done. (Cf. *unda, mwunzi*.)

Mwungama, n. (*waung.*), one who acknowledges (admits, confesses) wrongdoing. Used as a title of Mahommed. (Cf. *ungama*.)

Mwungamishi, n. (*waung.*), one who invites (receives, extorts) confession, &c. (Cf. *ungama*.)

Mwungamo, n. (*miung.*), (1) acknowledgment of obligation, confession, admission of guilt (cf. *ungama*, and prec.); (2) a plant, which produces *ungamo*, a yellow dye for matting. (Cf. *manjano*.)

Mwungo, n. (*miungo*), also **Muungo**, a joining together, a joint, e. g. *mwungo wa kufuli*, to describe a dovetail joint, lit. a lock-joining. (Cf. *unga* v., and the more usual *ungo, kiungo*.)

Mwunzi, n. (*waunzi*), also **Mwunda, Mwundi**, one who constructs (frames, builds), esp. of a carpenter's and shipwright's work. *Mwunzi wa chombo*, a shipbuilder. (Cf. *unda*, and see **Mwunda**.)

Mwunzi, n. usually in the plur., i.e. **miunzi**, whistling (which see).

Mwuza, n. (*wauza*), verbal of *uza*, one who sells. *Mwuza nguo*, a draper. *Mwuza samaki*, a fishmonger, &c. Also *mwuzazi*, a professional seller, a dealer, a salesman. Contr. *mnunuzi*, a buyer, a customer. (Cf. *uza*.)

Mzaa, n. (*wa-*), verbal of *zaa*, governing the word following, one who begets, or gives birth to. *Mzaa bibi*, great-grandmother. (Cf. *zaa, mzazi, kizazi, mzao*.)

***Mzabibu**, n. (*mi-*), a vine,—the fruit being *zabibu*. *Tawi la mz.*, a bunch of grapes. (Ar. *zabib*, raisin.)

***Mzabuni**, n. (*wa-*), a buyer, a bidder at a sale. (Ar. Cf. *zabuni*, and the common B. syn. *mnunuzi*.)

***Mzaha**, n. (*mi-*), fun, joke, ridicule, derision. *Jina la m.*, nickname. *Fanya m.*, do in fun. *Fanyizia m.*, make fun of. (Ar. Cf. *thihaka, ubishi, mchezo*.)

Mzalia, n. (*wa-*), with Ps. sense, one born at (or, in a place), a native (of a given spot), and esp. a home-born slave, one born in the house or country of his master. Such slaves rank above the raw slave (*mjinga*) from the interior. (Cf. *zaa*, and follg., and see **Mtumwa**.)

Mzalisha, Mzalishi, n. (*wa-*), a midwife. (Cf. *zaa*, and prec.)

Mzaliwa, n. (*wa-*), one born (at), e.g. *mzaliwa huko* (or, *wa huko*), one born there, a native.

Mzama, n. (*wa-*), verbal of *zama*, one who sinks, or dives in water. Also **Mzamaji** (*wa-*), a diver, but commonly *mzamia* (*lulu*), one who dives for (pearls). (Cf. *zama*, and *mzamishi*.)

***Mzambarau**, n. (*mi-*), a kind of Eugenia, a large fruit-tree, bearing a kind of damson or sloe, *zambarau*.

Mzamishi, n. (*wa-*), one who employs divers. Also **Mzamisho**, causing to sink, plunging in water, employment of divers. (Cf. *zama, zamisha*, and *mzama*.)

Mzamo, n. (*mi-*), diving, plunging (in liquid), drowning. (Cf. prec., and *zama*.)

***Mzandiki**, n. (*wa-*), a hypocrite, liar. (Ar. Cf. *mnafiki, mwongo*.)

Mzao, n. (*wa-*), child, offspring, descendant. (Cf. *zaa, mzazi*. Perh. for *mzawo*.)

Mzawa, n. Ps. verbal of *zaa*,—see **Mzaliwa**, which is the form commonly used.

Mzazi, n. (*wa-*), one who begets, or bears offspring, a parent (male or female). Used also of (1) a woman recently delivered, and (2) a prolific parent. (Cf. *zaa*, and -*zazi, uzazi, kizazi*.)

Mzee, n. (*wa-*), (1) an old person, an elder, (2) a parent, (3) an ancestor. *Mzee mmoja mzee sana*, one old man was very old. An old woman is usually *kizee*. (Cf. perh. *zaa*, also *uzee, kizee*.)

Mzibo, n. (*mi-*), (1) a stopping up, closing a hole (path, passage, &c.), a plug, a stopper, bung, &c. Also (2) fig. a check, a stop, a dead-lock. (Cf. *ziba, kizibo*.)

Mzigo, n. (*mi-*), a load, a burden,—esp. of such a load as a caravan porter (*mpagazi*) carries on his head in East Africa, i.e. about 60 lb. weight. Also fig. of a sorrow, bereavement, infirmity. *Mizigo ya kutafuta*, odd jobs of porterage. *Twika m.*, shoulder a load (i.e. usually, place on the head). *Tua* (*panga*) *m.*, lay down a load. *Funga mizigo*, prepare for a journey, pack, make preparations (for any undertaking). *Bwaga m.*, throw a load on the ground. (Cf. *mtumba, mpagazi*.)

Mziko, n. (*mi-*), act (manner, &c.) of burial. (Cf. *zika*, and the more usual *maziko*.)

Mzima, n. (*wa-*), (1) a person in good health, in sound condition of mind and body, whole; (2) a full-grown person, an adult. (Cf. -*zima*, a. *Mzima* is also verbal n. from *zima*, v., one who extinguishes, puts out a light, fire, &c.)

Mzimu, n. (*mi-*), a native place of worship, i. e. where offerings and prayers are made to spirits, whether of ancestors or others. In Z. it is usually a rock, cave, tree, or ruin, and the offerings are rags of calico, cooking pots, and occasionally small coin. *Peleka kitu mzimuni*, go and make an offering. (Cf. *kuzimu*, the state after death, the world of disembodied spirits, death (as a state), the grave. Also *zimwe*, a spirit, ghost, demon, and *wazimu*, madness, lit. spirits. Perh. also cf. *zimu, zimua, zimuka*, meaning 'to become cold, be extinguished, put out.' Contr. the *m* of *mzimu* of 'place within which,' with the more general *ku* of *kuzimu*, the whole environment, general condition.)

Mzinduko, n. (*mi-*), (1) opening ceremony, inauguration; (2) awakening suddenly from sleep. (Cf. *zinduka*.)

Mzinga, n. (*mi-*), anything of a cylindrical shape,—a round hollowed log, a native beehive (usually a hollowed section of a tree, and fixed in a tree), a cannon (from its shape). *Piga mzinga*, fire a cannon. *Mizinga ya salaam*, a salute (by cannon). (Cf. *zinga, mzingo, zunguka*, &c.)

Mzingile, n. (*mi-*). *Mzingile mwambiji*, a labyrinth, a maze, a puzzle (Str.). (Cf. *zinga*, and follg.)

Mzingo, n. (*mi-*), in general, a rounding, curving, bending, and so used to denote (1) circuit, bend, winding (e. g. of a river), turn; (2) working on a curve, making a bevel, making a round mat or basket; (3) circumference, distance round; (4) environment, neighbourhood, margin of a pool or stream, what is around one. Hence used prepositionally, *mzingo wa*, around, on all sides of. -*a mzingo*, around, enclosing, surrounding. *Shona mzingo*, sew in a curve. *Mzingo ni mzunguko wa mviringo, mzingo* means going round in a circle. (Cf. *zinga, mzinga, zunguka*.)

*****Mzinzi**, n. (*wa-*), an adulterer, a fornicator, a debauchee. (Ar. Cf. *zini, uzini, zinifa*.)

Mzishi, n. (*wa-*), one who has to do with a burial, and so (1) an undertaker, who manages it, or grave-digger; (2) a friend who attends it, esp. a trusted, intimate, bosom friend, as being relied on for securing decent burial. (Cf. *zika, mazishi*.)

Mzizi, n. (*mi-*), (1) a root, rootlet, i. e. *kishina kidogo cha mtini chini*, the small root-fibres of a tree beneath the ground; (2) perh. from the use of roots in native medicine, 'a doctor's prescription, dose, medicine,' described according to the way it is to be used, e. g. *wa kuchoma*, to be heated; *wa kusaga*, to be pulverized; *wa kuchanjia*, for inoculation; *wa kutafuna*, to be chewed; *wa kuchemsha*, to be boiled, &c. (Cf. *mwiko* and *shina*.)

Mzizimizi, n. (*wa-*), one who sinks, goes to the bottom, disappears suddenly and completely. Hence, an adventurer, stranger, swindler, who suddenly vanishes leaving no traces. (Cf. *zizimia*.)

Mzo, n. (*mizo*)—also **Mso**, a measure of weight or dry measure, viz. 10 *frasila*, or 60 *pishi*, i. e. about 350-360 lb.,—equivalent to *jizla*. (Ar.)

Mzoea, n. (*wa-*), verbal of *zoea*, one who is used, accustomed (to), practised (in), familiar (with). *Mimi mzoea sana naye*, I am on quite familiar terms with him. (Cf. *zoea, -zoefu*.)

Mzofafa, adv. on tiptoe, with a strut, proudly. (Ar. *zaf*,—for *mzafzaf*.)

Mzoga, n. (*mi-*), carcass, dead body, carrion,—not usually of a human body, corpse, i. e. *maiti*. (Cf. *mwili, pinda*.)

*****Mzomari**, n. a kind of scent,

? rosewater. (Dist. *msomari*, a nail, and *zomari*, a pipe, flute.)

Mzomeo, n. (*mi-*), derisive, sarcastic, insulting noises or speech. (Cf. *zomea*.)

Mzuka, n. (*wa-*), one who appears suddenly, — and so, an apparition, ghost, spirit, goblin. (Cf. *zua, zuka, kizuka, mzushi*.)

Mzungu, n. (1) (*wa-*), a European. *Mzungu mweusi*, a Europeanized native (cf. *kizungu, Uzungu*). (2) (*mi-*), something wonderful, startling, surprising, ingenuity, cleverness, a feat, a trick, a wonderful device. *Wazungu wana mizungu*, or *mizungu kwa Wazungu*, i.e. Europeans are always astonishing. (Cf. *-zungu*, and perh. conn. with *zunguka, kizunguzungu*.)

Mzunguko, n. (*mi-*), in general, a going round, a being round, a surrounding, and so (1) revolving, circular motion, turning, whirling, &c.; (2) eddy, whirlpool, circular course, orbit, circuit; (3) enclosing, surrounding, besieging (cf. *mazingiwa*); (4) sauntering, idling, shilly-shallying (cf. *zunguka*). (Cf. *zunguka, zunguko*, and *mzingo, zinga*.)

Mzungusho, n. (*mi-*), a causing to go round, a surrounding, an enclosing or placing round, &c. Also **Mzungushi** (*wa-*), one who causes to go (or, be) round. (Cf. *mzunguko*, and *zunguka, zungusha*.)

Mzushi, n. (*wa-*), also **Mzuzi**, one who causes to penetrate through and so emerge, who causes something to appear suddenly. Hence (1) an innovator, inventor, reformer, revolutionist, heretic, &c.; (2) tell-tale, slanderer, gossip-monger, &c. (Cf. *uzushi, zua, zuka, mzuka*.)

Mzuzu, n. (1) (*wa*), one who is inexperienced, at a loss what to do, and so 'a simpleton, a new-comer (greenhorn, tender-foot), an ignoramus. Also (2) name of a kind of banana (see **Ndizi**). (Cf. *zuzua*, and syn. *mjinga, mgeni, barathuli*.)

N.

N represents the same sound as in English. This sound involves more difficulties than any other in learning Swahili,—its grammatical function, together with its peculiar phonetic affinities, producing the only forms of words which can be called exceptional or irregular.

It may be considered A. as a sound, B. as a formative prefix.

A. The sound *n* is either (1) purely consonantal, or (2) semi-vocal.

(1) As a pure consonant, *n* can be combined with any vowel, but only five consonants, viz. *d, g, j, y*, and *z*, e.g. *ndio, ngoja, njaa, nyumba, nzuri*.

When its function as a prefix (see below) would require its use in combination with other consonants, the effect is as follows:—

Before *b*, *n* becomes *m*, e.g. *mbaya* for *nbaya*.

Before *w*, *n* becomes *m*, but the *w* following is also changed into *b*, e.g. *mbili* for *nwili*, *mbingu* for *nwingu*.

Before *r* (or its convertible sound *l*), *n* is retained, but the *r* (or *l*) is changed into *d*, e.g. *ndefu* for *nrefu*, *ndimi*, plur. of *ulimi*. Cf. also *nd*, in words like *ndume, ndoa, ndoto*, &c. (perh. indicating a lost *l* in the root).

Before *k, p, t*, *n* is represented, if at all, by giving an explosive force to those consonants, e.g. *pepo* as the plur. of *upepo*.

Before *ch, f, h, m, s*, and *v*, *n* does not appear, i.e. cannot be pronounced as a pure consonant.

(2) As a semi-vowel, or semi-independent syllable, *n* is limited, with few exceptions, to use before *g, ch, j, z, d, t, s* or another *n*. Thus it sometimes represents the prefix *ni* in verbs, as in *nnapenda, ntakwenda*, for *ninapenda, nitakwenda*, and appears in the words *nge, nje, nta, ncha, -ngi, -ngine, -nso, -nzi, nne*,—in which

n inclines to the sound of *in*, especially in the dialect of Zanzibar and in the words -*ingine*, -*ingi*, *inzi*. This faintly vocalized use of *n* is sometimes indicated by writing it '*n* or *n*', and accounts for the sound *ny*- which it often assumes before vowels, e.g. *nyumba*, *nyekundu*, *nyingi*.

(For further remarks on the *n* sound, see **Ny-**, **Ng'**, **Nya**, and **Njoo**.)

B. As a prefix, *n* is

(1) In verbs a shortened form of *ni*, i.e. the Pers. Pfx. subjective and objective of the 1 Pers. S. *nnapenda*, I love, *amenita*, he has called me. Cf. also *ndi* (for *ni*) in *ndio*, *ndiwe*, &c. See **Ndi-**, and obs. the irreg. Imperat. *n-joo*, from *ja*.

(2) In nouns, *n* or *ny*- (before a vowel) is a common initial of D 6 and the Plur. Pfx. characteristic of D 4, with various euphonic variants (see above).

(3) In adjectives, *n* or *ny*- is the Pfx. agreeing with D 4 (P), D 6, subject to the euphonic limitations given above, and excepting the pronominal and a few other adjectives. Obs. however, the two common irregular forms *njema* (and *ngema*) for *nyema*, and *mpya* (for the inadmissible monosyllable *pya*), also *nd* for *n-* (*ny-*) in *ndoto*, *ndume*, *ndoa*, *ndio*, *ndui*, and *nduma*, as plur. of *uma* (perh. to characterize the *n* as prefix, and not part of the root).

Na is a B. particle, used as a conj., prep., and with a verbal signification, with the general idea of connexion, association, or the opposites. Like *kwa* and *katika* it is one of the commonest particles in Swahili.

1. As a conjunction. (*a*) *na*, simply connective, 'and,' but connective mainly of nouns, pronouns, or their equivalents, not commonly of sentences, or adjectives, which in Swahili usually follow each other without a separate connective particle, e.g. *mimi na wewe*, I and you, *baba na mama*, father and mother; e.g. *wapikieni na nyama wapeni wale washibe walale*, cook for them, and give them meat, so that they may eat and be satisfied, and go to sleep. (The common connectives of paragraphs are *hatta* and *bassi*.) Even when beginning a paragraph, *na* is as a rule in close connexion with a noun. When used to connect two verbs, when the verbs are quite distinct in mood, tense, &c., e.g. *omba, na utapewa*, ask and you will receive, &c., the latter verb is commonly in the Infinitive (i. e. noun) form, the force of the inflections of the first verb, mood, tense, person, &c., being, however, carried on to the second, e. g. *moyo wangu waniambia, Soma na kusali*, my heart says to me, Read and pray. Even when connecting two adjectival ideas, the second is often in noun form, e. g. *inchi kubwa na uzuri*, an extensive and beautiful country,—otherwise *inchi kubwa nzuri*. (*b*) *na* qualifies, and corrects, 'and yet, withal, even,'—connexion suggesting some difference,—whether with nouns or verbs. *Na tungoje bassi*, let us even wait then. *Akala na nguruwe*, he ate even pork. *Na* is thus commonly used with pronouns, after a verb, with an idiomatic force qualifying the verb rather than the pronoun, e. g. *njoo nawe*, do come along, I wish you would come, lit. come even you. *Atakaja naye*, he is sure to come, lit. even he will come. *Kafa naye*, he is actually dead.

2. As a preposition, the main idea of *na* is connexion or association, i. e. 'with,' whether in thought, place, or time, but is inclusive of many correlative ideas, e. g. disconnexion, distance as well as nearness, reciprocation, separation as well as union, subtraction as well as addition, i. e. 'from' as well as 'with, by, to.' E. g. *alikwenda na baba yake*, he went with his father (also, 'he went and (so did) his father,' or 'his father went also,'

or 'even his father went'). Thus (*a*) *na* is the characteristic preposition of the *Agent* with a passive verb, *aliuawa na adui*, he was killed by his enemy,—the instrument being denoted by *kwa*. But *na* may be used of any active force, and also of the instrument. *Alishikwa na homa*, he was seized with fever. *Alipigwa na fimbo*, he was beaten with a stick,—also *kwa fimbo*, or *fimbo* alone. Also in other passive constructions, e. g. *alitokwa na damu*, he bled. (*b*) *na* is used with adjectives and adverbs in consonance with its main idea, e. g. *sawa na*, equal to; *mbali na* (or *ya*), distant from, different from; *karibu na* (or *ya*), near to; *pamoja na*, together with. (*c*) *na* is frequently connected with the Rp. form of verbs (which appears to be formed with it), *shindana na*, contend with, *agana na*, take leave of, *tengana na*, be divided from, *achana na*, depart from.

3. *Na* has a very common and important use in connexion, and in combination, with the verb *-wa*, be, and those other forms, including the person-prefixes, which are regularly used with the meaning of *-wa* (see **-wa**), especially *li* with the relative, and the person-prefixes, *ni, u, a, o, i, li, zi, ma, ya, pa, ku*, &c. With all these *na* is used (and too commonly to need illustration) to express (*a*) having, (*b*) being, existing. Thus (*a*) *-wa na*, &c., have, lit. be with, e. g. *alikuwa na mali*, he had property. *Kitabu alicho nacho*, the book which he has. *Sina nguvu*, I have no strength. *Yuna afya? anayo*, Has he health? he has (it). (*b*) *-wa na*, be, exist. *Palikuwa na mtu*, there was a man. *Kuna nini?* What is there? What is the matter? *Hakuna kitu*, there is nothing. In some negative phrases *na* seems to lose all trace of its connective meaning and prepositional force, and to represent itself the force of a verb, e. g. *hakuna*, there is not. (*Kuna* (*ina, pana*, &c.), 'there is,' is not used alone, but with a noun or pronoun following, or another element in combination, e. g. *kunako, zinazo*.) In all uses *na* is very commonly compounded with the pronouns (*nami, nawe, naye, nasui*, &c.), and with the relative forms of other prefixes (e. g. *nayo, nalo, nazo, napo, nako*, &c.).

-na, as a tense-prefix, is the sign of the Pres. Indef., e. g. *anakuja*, he is coming. The forms of this tense are constantly used in the sense of the Pres. Partic. (as the forms of the *me* tense are for the Past Partic.), e. g. *akamwona anakuja*, he saw him coming. (For *-na* combined with person-prefixes, e. g. *nina, zina, hamna, kuna*, &c., see **Na**, 3.)

***Naam**, a common affirmative particle, Yes, Certainly, I understand, It is so. (Ar. Cf. *neema*, and syn. *ndio, vema, a-hee*.)

***Nabii**, n. (*ma-*), a prophet, a preacher of righteousness, one who foretells the future. Used of Adam, Noah, Abraham, Jesus Christ, and others, as well as of Mahomet. (Ar. Cf. *bashiri, tabiri*.)

***Nadi**, v. (1) call, summon, announce publicly, proclaim. *Mnada wa Sultani unanadiwa*, the Sultan's proclamation is being made. *Akotokea Bilali akanadia kusali*, Bilali appeared and called to prayers. (2) hold a sale (or public auction). *Watu wananadi vitu kwa makelele*, people are having a noisy sale. *Mtu anadiye nguo*, a man who sells clothes by auction. (Ar. Cf. *mnada, mnadi*, and *dalali*.)

***Nafaka**, n. corn, grain,—in general, including rice, maize, millet, &c. (Ar.)

***Nafasi**, n. (1) breathing time, space, room, opportunity, leisure, relief, spare time; (2) means, money, wealth. *Sina nafasi*, I have no time, I am too busy. (Ar. Cf. *nafsi, nafusi*, and syn. *pumuzi, pumuzika*.)

*Nafisi, v. usually *nafisisha*, accommodate with money, relieve, put in easy circumstances. Rf. *jinafisisha*, make oneself comfortable. Nt. *nafisika*, get out of poverty, become well off, be relieved. (Ar. Cf. prec. and *tanafusi*.)

*Nafsi, n. (—), also Nafusi, vital spirit, breath, soul, self, person, individuality, essence. Generally used to emphasize personality, e. g. *mimi nafsi yangu* (or *bi nafsi yangu*), I myself. *Wakachukizwa nafsi zao*, they were deeply offended. (Ar. Cf. *nafasi*.)

*Nafuu, n. (—), profit, advantage, gain, progress, equipment, assistance, e. g. in money or food, for a journey; esp. of improvement in health, convalescence. *Amepata nafuu*, he has got better (like *hajambo*). (Ar. Cf. syn. *riziki, vifaa, faida*.)

*Nahau, n. (—), explanation, unfolding of meaning, and so (1) grammar, syntax; (2) excuse, quibble, subterfuge. *N. ya maneno*, an evasive statement. *Killa neno lina n. yake*, every word has its meaning. (Ar. for the more common *maana, tafsiri, elezo*. Also for 'grammar,' cf. *sarufi*.)

*Nahotha, n. (*ma*-), also Nakhotha, Nahoza, captain,—of a vessel. (Ar.)

*Najisi, -najisi, a. unclean, dirty, impure, profane. — v. also Najisisha, defile, contaminate, pollute, profane. (Ar. Cf. *unajisi, chafua*, and syn. B. *-chafu, -a takataka*.)

*Nakawa, a. clear, good-looking, in sound condition, of fine quality,— of persons and things. *Pembe n.*, good sound ivory. *Mtumwa mwema n.*, a fine good-looking slave. (Ar. Cf. *-ema, -zima, -zuri*.)

*Nakili, n. also Nakli, Nakulu, a copy, an imitation, a translation, duplicate. *Nakili ya waraka*, copy of a letter. — v. copy, transcribe, translate. Ps. *nakiliwa*. Nt. *nakilika*. Ap. *nakil-ia, -iwa*. Cs. *nakil-isha, -ishwa*. (Ar. Cf. *fuatisha, iga*, and *manuku*. Dist. *nakili*, for *nakiri*, Arab. not often used, reject, disapprove.)

Nako, for *na huko*, and there.

*Nakshi, n. and Nakishi, carving, carved ornament, fine chisel-work, engraving,—and used of any ornamentation of similar appearance, e. g. embroidery, painting. *Piga (kata) nakshi*, carve, adorn with carving (embroidery, &c.). — v. carve, adorn with carving, &c. Ps. *nakishiwa*. Ap. *nakish-ia, -iwa*. (Ar. Cf. *chora, pamba*.)

*Nakudi, n. cash, ready money, a trifle. *Nunua kwa nakudi*, buy off-hand, buy on the spot, i. e. *mkono kwa mkono*. (Ar. Cf. *sarifu*.)

*Nakulu, n. See Nakili.

Nama, v. bend down. See Inama.

*Nambari, n. a (single) number, e. g. the number which marks an object, person, &c. (Eng. *number*.)

Nami, for *na mimi*, and I, even me. See Na.

*Namna, n. (—), also Namuna, (1) example, sample, pattern, model, sort, kind; (2) special sort, perfect example, model, a rarity, choice article. *Wataka namna gani?* What sort do you want? *Nguo hii ya namna*, this calico is the best. (Hind. Cf. Ar. *ginsi, aina*.)

Namua, v. draw away, disengage, get out of a difficulty, take out of a trap, set free. (Not common in Z.)

*Nana, n. and Nanaa, mint. (Ar.)

*Nanasi, n. (*ma*-), pine-apple, the fruit of the *mnanasi*. Common in Zanzibar, in two principal varieties. Yields a fibre, used as string. (Ar. Cf. *unanasi*.)

Nane, -nane, n. and a., eight. *-a nane*, eighth. (Cf. Ar. *themani*, which is rarely used, and perh. *nne*, four.)

Nanga, n. an anchor,—properly, of the four-fluked pattern commonly used,—a European two-fluked anchor being *baura*. *Tia (puliza) nanga*, cast (let go) anchor. *Ng'oa nanga*, weigh anchor. (Cf. *baura*, *kombe*, fluke, also *amari*, cable.)

Nani, pron. interrog., What person (persons)? Who? *Jina lako nani?* What is your name? *-a nani*, Whose? (Cf. *nini*, *lini*, and *-pi*.)

Nao, for *na hao*, or *na wao*, and these, and they. **Napo**, for *na hapo*, and there. (See **Na**.)

Nasa, v. get hold of, catch in a trap, hold fast. Ps. *naswa*. Nt. *nasika*. Ap. *nas-ia*, *-iwa*. Cs. *nas-isha*, *-ishwa*. (Cf. *tega*, *guia*, *kamata*, and perh. *nata*.)

*__Nasaba__, n. pedigree, genealogy, lineage. (Arab.)

*__Nasibu__, n. chance, fortune, luck, accident. *Kwa nasibu*, accidentally, not on purpose, by chance. (Ar. Cf. *bahati*.)

Nasihi, v. give good advice (to), counsel wisely. Also n. a sincere friend, faithful counsellor, wise adviser. (Ar. Cf. *mshauri*.)

Nata, v. be sticky, adhere, stick. *Utomvu wafenessi wanata sana*, the sap of the jack-fruit is very sticky. Ap. *natana*, stick together. (Cf. *ambata*, *ganda*.)

*__Nathari__, n. (1) look, glance; (2) attention, consideration; (3) choice, discretion, judgement. *Nathari yako* (or, *kwako*), it is for you to choose. *Sina n.*, I have no choice. (Ar. Cf. *hitiari*.)

*__Nathifu__, a. also **Nadifu**, clean, neat, well-kept. *Nyumba yake nathifu sana*, his house was in very good order. (Ar. Cf. *safi*, *safidi*.)

*__Nathiri__, n. vow, solemn promise, dedication of something to God. *Weka n.*, make a vow. *Ondoa n.*, fulfil (perform) a vow. (Ar.)

*__Nauli__, n. fare, charge for freight (or, conveyance), passage-money. Also v. hire, pay fare for passage (carriage, &c.). Cs. *naulisha*, let for freight (carriage, conveyance), charter, be a ship's broker. (Ar.)

Nawa, v. wash ceremonially, perform ablutions, according to the prescribed Mahommedan custom, esp. wash the hands and face,—*tawaza* being used of the feet, *chamba* of other parts of the body. Sometimes *nawa mikono* (*uso*, *miguu*). Ps. *nawiwa*. Nt. *nawika*. Ap. *naw-ia*, wash with (at, by, &c.). *Maji ya kunawia*, water for ablutions. Cs. *nawisha*, e.g. *nawisha watu mikono*, i.e. bring people water to wash with. (Cf. also *oga*, *fua*, and *tohara*.)

Naye, for *na yeye*, and he, even him. *Mjinga ni mtu naye*, a fool is after all a fellow man. (See **Na**.)

Nazi, n. (—), the ripe fruit of the cocoanut-palm (*mnazi*), which is very plentiful in Z. (as well as the neighbouring islands and coast) and one of the most important commercial products. *Nazi* is the most general descriptive name, but seven stages in its development are distinguished under the names (which see): (1) *upunga*, the first forming of the fruit on the flower stem; (2) *kitale*, a young nut; (3) *kidaka*, half-grown; (4) *dafu*, full-grown and full of milk (*maji*), also cf. *uramberambe*, and *tonga*; (5) *koroma*, when the milk is decreasing, and nutty part forming; (6) *nazi*, fully ripe, no milk, and nut hardening; (7) *nazi kavu*, the nutty part dry and separating from the shell. Cf. *mbata*. Also *joya*, a nut full of a white spongy nut-substance; *kizimwi*, without milk or nut; *makumbi*, the fibrous husk; *kifuu*, the hard inner shell (dist. *kifuo*, a stake used for ripping off the husk); *ufuu*, the nutty part inside it; *kizio*, half a nut (when broken in two). As a rule, *nazi* only are gathered, i.e. fully ripe fruit, and the nutty part used for cooking (cf. *tui*, *chicha*, *mbuzi*) or dried and sold as copra. *Mafuta ya nazi*, cocoanut oil. Prov. *nazi mbovu harabu ya nzima*, a bad cocoanut spoils good ones. (See also *mnazi, tembo, gema, kuti*.)

Ncha, n. (—), also **Incha**, tip, point, end, extremity, e. g. of a knife, branch, cord, &c. *Hakuna refu lisilo ncha*, nothing so long that it has no end. *Habari ya uwongo ina ncha saba*, a false story has seven endings, i. e. can be told in many ways. (Cf. *kikomo, mwisho, mpaka*, and dist. *nta*, wax.)

Nchi, n. See **Inchi**.

Nd-, as an initial sound, cf. *N.* (See **N**, A (1), and **Ndi-**.)

Ndama, n. (—), the young of cattle, esp. a calf, but also distinguished as *ndama ya ng'ombe*, calf; *nd. ya mbuzi*, kid; *nd. ya kondoo*, lamb. (Cf. *nyama, mtamba*.)

Ndani, adv. within, inside, in the heart. Contr. *nje*. *Ndani ya*, prep. inside of, within. *-a ndani*, internal, inner, secret, heartfelt. *Kwa ndani*, internally, in the inside, in the heart, secretly.

Ndara, n. (—), a plain leather sandal. (Cf. *kiatu, makubazi*.)

Ndefu, (1) a. form of *-refu*, long, —agreeing with D 4 (P), D 6; (2) n. See **Ndevu**.

Ndege, n. (—), (1) a bird; (2) an omen. *N. za anga*, birds of the air. *N. njema (mbaya)*, a good (bad) omen. *N. akaruka juu*, the bird flew upward. *Tusimtilie n.*, do not let us obstruct him (by anything which might be a bad omen). Dim. *kidege*. (Cf. *nyuni*, rarely heard in Z.)

Ndevu, n. plur. of *udevu*, the hair of the face, beard, whiskers. Also *ndevu za mashavuni*, whiskers. *Ndevu za mdomo wa juu (wa chini)*, moustache (imperial). (Cf. *kidevu, udevu, sharabu*, and perh. *-refu*.)

Ndewe, n. (—), a hole pierced in the lobe of the ear, i. e. *ndewe ya sikio*, to hold an ornament, sometimes of great size. (Cf. *toja*.)

Ndezi, n. name of a kind of rat.

Ndi- is used as a pfx. of emphasis (perh. a strengthened and so emphatic form of *ni*, and see also **N**), in combination with (1) personal pronouns, *ndimi* (for *ni mimi*), *ndiwe, ndiye, ndiswi, ndinyi, ndio*, i. e. it is I, yes I, yes me, &c. (2) with the demonstratives ending in *-o*, i. e. *ndio (ni wao), ndiyo (ni hiyo), ndizo (ni hizo)*, &c., it is they, that is it, &c., and the adverbs of the same form, *ndiko, ndipo, ndimo*, there, it is there. *Ndiko atokako*, that is where he comes from. Often strengthened by repeating the demonstrative after it, *ndivyo hivyo*, it is just so, exactly so. *Ndiyo hiyo*, that is the very thing. *Ndio* is constantly in use as a simple affirmative, 'yes, it is so' (cf. *naam*). (Cf. n, A. (1), *nd-*, and perhaps the irregular form *njoo*, Imperat. of *ja*, come.)

Ndifu, n. (—), also **Kidifu**, and **Kilifu** (which see). (Perh. a plur. n. from *ulifu*, i. e. *nlifu, ndifu*.)

Ndilo, emphat. for *ni hilo*, that is it. See **Ndi-**.

Ndimi, (1) plur. of *ulimi*, a tongue; (2) emphat. for *ni mimi*, it it I. See **Ndi-**.

Ndimo, emphat. for *ni humo*, it is in there. (Cf. prec.)

Ndimu, n. (—), and sometimes **Dimu**, a lime, the fruit of the lime-tree, *mndimu, mdimu*. There are at least two varieties in Z., *ndimu kali*, the bitter lime, *ndimu tamu*, the sweet lime. (For kindred varieties see **Mchungwa**.)

Ndio, Ndipo, Ndiswi, Ndinyi, Ndivyo, &c. See **Ndi-**. *Ndio* is one of the commonest forms of simple affirmation, 'yes, it is so.' (Cf. Ar. *naam*.)

Ndizi, n. (—), banana, plantain, the fruit of the *mgomba*. The fruit-stalk with the whole head of fruit is called *mkungu*, a cluster or bunchlet on it *chana (tana)*, a single fruit *dole*. There are many varieties in Z.,—green, yellow, and deep red, known as *kisukari, kipukusa, mzuzu, mchenga, mkono wa tembo, bungala, paka, kiguruwe, kizungu*, &c.

Ndoa, n. (—), marrying, marriage,—often treated as a plur. noun, *ndoa zangu*, my marriage. (Cf. *oa, maozi*, and for the form *ndoto, ndume*, and see **Nd-**. Also cf. *harusi, nikaha*.)

Ndofu, n. (—, and *wa-*), also **Ndovu**, an elephant. (Rarely in Z., where *tembo* is used.)

Ndole, Ndomo, n. plur. of *udole, uomo* (i. e. *ulomo*). See **Kidole, Mdomo**.

Ndonya, n. (—), ring or round ornament worn in the upper l.p, esp. by women from Nyasaland (where it is also called *pelele*).

Ndoto, n. (—), a dream, dreaming. (Cf. *ota*.)

Ndugu, n. (—), brother, sister, cousin, relation, fellow-tribesman (-citizen, -countryman). Further defined as *n. mume*, brother, *n. mke*, sister. *N. baba mmoja mama mmoja*, full brother, with the same father and mother. *N. tumbo moja*, brother with the same mother, half-brother (at least). *N. kunyonya*, foster-brother. *Donda n.*, a malignant kind of ulcer. (Cf. *udugu, kidugu*, and *umbu, mtani, jamaa*.)

Ndui, n. plur. small-pox (*udui*, a single pustule). (Perh. from *ua*, cf. *nduli*, from its fatal effects.)

Nduli, n. and a., a savage person, a killer, murderous, blood-shedding.

Ndume, n. and a., a plur. form from *uume* (i. e. *ulume*), used as both sing. and plur.,(1) a male animal, as contr. with man; (2) a man, in respect of manly character and qualities, rather than of sex or individuality. *Punda ndume*, a male ass. *Bata ndume*, a drake. *Askari ndume bora*, warlike heroes. *Ndume za mpunga*, hard grains of rice which resist pounding. (Cf. *-ume*, and opp. *jike*.)

Ndumiko, n. cupping instrument, usually a horn, i. e. *pembe ya kuumikia*, with which the cupping is done. (Cf. *umika*, and *chuku*.)

***Neema**, n. (1) ease, affluence, comfort; (2) bounty, favour, help, grace. Esp. of providential blessings, plenty, a good harvest, abundance of food. *Inchi ile ina neema nyingi*, that is a favoured country, a good one to live in. *Imemshukia neema kubwa kwa Muungu*, a great mercy had descended on him from God. (Ar. Cf. *naam*, and follg., and syn. *mbaraka*.)

*-**neemefu**, a. plentiful, abundant. (Ar. Cf. follg.)

***Neemeka**, v. live at ease, have plenty, be in comfortable circumstances, possess property, get good profits. Cs. *neemesha*, make rich, provide well for. (Ar. Cf. *neema, uneemefu*.)

***Nejisi**, a. See **Najisi**. (Ar.)

***Neli**, n. a tube, a pipe,—the word commonly used being *mwanzi*. (Hind. *nal*. Cf. Ar. *kasiba*.)

***Nema**, v. bend, give way, yield. Nt. *nem'ka*, e. g. of graceful dancing. Cs. *nem-esha, -eshwa*, cause to bend. (Ar. Cf. *nepa*, and *inama*.)

Nembo, n. (—), a tribal mark,—usually a kind of tattoo. (Cf. syn. *chale, chanjo*, and *toja*. Prob. a Yao word.)

Nena, v. (1) speak, have the gift of rational speech, articulate, utter, say; (2) speak of, mention, name, declare. *Kinenacho na kisichonena*, that which speaks and that which does not,—a common way of contrasting people and things, the rational and irrational. Ps. *nena*. Nt. *neneka*, (1) be spoken, be mentioned; (2) be utterable, be such as can be expressed in words, be fit for mention, &c. *Mambo yasiyoneneka*, unutterable, indescribable things. *Neno hilo halineneki*, that word is not in use, is not a possible word. Ap. *nen-ea, -ewa*, e. g. speak against (for, to, with, &c.), but in common usage *ambia* regularly takes its place for 'speak to, say to,' and *nenea* (when not defined by the context) is used for 'speak against, rebuke, scold,' more commonly than 'speak for, intercede for, recommend, praise.' Hence *neneana*. Cs. *nen-esha, -eshwa, -eza, -ezwa*, e.g. cause (provoke) to speak. E.g. *wakanenezana kwa maneno mabaya*, they exasperated each other by abuse. Rp. *nenana*, speak of each other, and so commonly, quarrel, abuse each other. (Cf. *neno, uneni, mneni, mnena, mnenaji, mnenea*, &c. Also *sema*, and *ambia*. *Sema* is used exactly like *nena* of rational speech, and in most other senses. But (1) with a person-object, *nena* means mention, *sema*, speak against, rebuke, abuse (like *amba*). (2) *sema* has often the meaning ' talk, converse,' *nena* rarely. *Ambia* with a person-object regularly takes the place of both *nena* and *sema*, when the meaning is simply, speak to, say to.)

Nenda, v. See **Enenda**.

-nene, a. (*nene* with D 4 (P), D 5 (S), D 6), (1) thick, stout, fat, plump, broad; (2) full, whole, complete. (Cf. *nenepa, unene*, and *nono, nona, -pana, -zima*.)

Nenepa, v. become fat (stout, corpulent)—of persons, but *nona*, of animals. Cs. *nenepesha*, make stout, &c. (Cf. *-nene, nona*.)

Neno, n. (*ma-*), (1) a word, utterance, expression, message; (2) assertion, objection, argument, plea, point; (3) thing, fact, matter, affair, cause, case; (4) a serious matter, difficulty, danger, trouble. The plur. *maneno* is also used for (1) language, speech,—in general, and (2) consultation, discussion, argument, trial, debate. E.g. *sikufanya n.*, I did nothing. *Ukiona n., usinene n.; ukinena n., litakujia n.*, if you see anything, do not say anything; if you say anything, something will happen to you. *Fanya maneno*, hold a discussion, argue, debate. *Mtu wa maneno mengi*, a talkative, argumentative person. *Maneno ya kiunguja*, the Zanzibar dialect. *Hana n.*, he has nothing to say. *Mnisaidie, nisione neno njiani*, help me that I may not find difficulty in my way. (Cf. *nena*, and *jambo*.)

Nenyekea, v. See **Nyenyekea**.

Nepa, v. incline downwards, bend down, dip, drop (of a rope), sag. Cs. *nepesha*, cause to bend, bend (by pressure, &c.). *Bakora hii inanepa sana*, this stick bends very much. *Kisu chanepa*, the knife (blade) bends. (Cf. Ar. *nema*. Also *inama, pinda*.)

Ng', thus written, is used to represent the only sound in Swahili not easy to pronounce, viz. a close combination of *n* and *g* which does not pass on to the vowel following, though forming one syllable with it. Thus *yang'oa*, it plucks up, is pronounced quite differently from *ya ngoa*, of desire, in which *ngoa* is only a nasalized *goa*. The sound is not common, and only in a few words initial. (It is sometimes heard and written as *gn*, but Str. argues that words beginning with it are treated grammatically as of the *N* (i.e. D 6) declension, and that with pfxs. (e.g. *ki-* or *ma-*) the *g* is retained even if the *n* is dropped.)

-nga- and **-nge-**, as a pfx., is the sign of the Pres. Condit. Tense,—as *ngali* of the Past, e.g. *ningapenda*, I would love. See **Ngali-**.

Ng'aa, v. be bright, glitter, gleam, shine. Cs. *ng'aza*, make shine. (Cf. *anga, ng'ara*, &c.)

*****Ngabu**, n. (—), a gouge,—a carpenter's tool, same as *Bobari*.

Ngadu, n. a kind of crab. (Cf. *kaa*.)

Ngalawa, n. (—), commonly *galawa* (which see) in Z., a small dug-out canoe with outriggers.

-ngali-, as a pfx., is the sign of the Past Condit. Tense, e.g. *ningali-*

penda, I would have loved. Obs. in narrative *ngali* and *nga* are used with the person-pfxs. of actual facts, past or present, e. g. *angali anakwenda*, he was going; *kungali na mapema bado*, it was still early. *Mvua ingalikinya na tufane imekaza*, the rain was falling, and the storm at its height.

Ngama, n. (—), the hold of a vessel, i. e. in a native vessel amidships. Prov. *aendaye tezi na omo, hurudi ngamani*, he who goes to the stern or stem comes back to the hold. (Cf. *chombo*, and *banduru, tumbo*.)

Ng'amba, n. a kind of hawk's-head turtle, from which tortoise shell is procured. *Piga* (*pindua*) *n*. is used to describe pouncing on a harmless person and robbing him. *Chuma cha n.*, the shell. (Cf. *kasa*.)

Ng'ambo, n. one of two opposite sides or positions, the other side, the farther side, e. g. of a river or creek. *Ng'ambo ya huku*, the near side, this side. *Ng'. ya pili*, the other, further side. (In Zanzibar city *Ng'ambo* is the general name for all that part of it, including several minor districts (*mitaa*), which has grown up in the last 40 years on the land side of the creek which used to bound it.) (Cf. *Unguja*, and perh. Ar. *jamb*, side (of the body).)

Ngamia, n. (—), a camel. Also, a common term of abuse, like *ng'ombe, mbuzi*, i. e. idiot, fool,—the camel being regarded as a type of stupidity. (Camels are used in Z. only for turning oil-mills, and imported for the purpose.)

Ng'anda, n. (—), a handful, as much as can be held with the fingers, esp. of something clinging or sticking together,—as *ugali*. (Cf. ? *ganda*, or *chanda*, and dist. *kofi, konzi, chopa*.)

Ngano, n. (—), (1) a story, a tale, narrative, fable (cf. *kisa, hadithi*); (2) wheat, i. e. the grain. Prov. *amekula ngano*, he has eaten wheat, i. e. (?) he has committed a fatal error, he has done for himself. (Cf. *kisa, hadithi*, and for grain *nafaka*.)

Ngao, n. (—), (1) shield, buckler (2) face, or front, of a house. Also of the rear, *n. ya nyuma*. *Kifua cha n.*, a bosom like a shield,—a point of beauty. (Cf. *kigao*.)

Ngara, n. (—), blossom (male) of the Indian corn-plant (Sac.).

Ng'ara, v. also **Ng'ala, Ng'aa,** and **Angaa**, shine, glitter, be bright. (Cf. Cs. *ngariza*, and *anga*.)

Ngariba, n. (—), one who circumcises, a professional circumciser. (Cf. *tahiri, ukumbi*.)

Ng'ariza, v. Cs. of *ng'ara*, i. e. make bright, cause to shine, &c. *Ng'ariza macho*, glare with the eyes. Ap. *ng'arizia*, e. g. glare on (at, with, &c.). Cs. *ng'arizisha*, e. g. make glare, glare fiercely. (Cf. *anga, ng'aa, ng'aza*.)

Ngawa, n. (—), civet cat, i. e. *paka wa zabadi*. One of the few wild animals left in Z. (with the pig, monkey, and serval or leopard). *Umekaa kama ngawa*, you live like a wild creature. (Cf. *fungo, zabadi*.)

-ngawa, used with person-pfxs. to express 'though,' e. g. *ningawa*, though I am (was); *ingawa*, though it is (was). *Wangawa walikwenda*, though they went. (Pres. Condit. of *-wa*, v. Cf. *-nga-, -japo, kwamba*.)

Ngazi, n. (—), a ladder, set of steps, stairs, i. e. *ngazi ya kukwelea*. (Cf. *kwea, daraja*.)

Ngazija, n. the Great Comoro Island. Hence *Mngazija*, a Comoro man. *Kingazija*, the Comoro language.

Ng'chiro, n. (—), also **Mchiro,** a mangouste, mungoos.

-nge-, sign of the Pres. Condit. Tense. See -nga-.

Nge, n. (—), or **Inge**, a scorpion.

Ngedele, n. a small black monkey,—also called *tumbili, kitumbili*. (Cf. *kima*.)

Ngema, a. often used in Z. for *njema*, i.e. (1) the form of *-ema* agreeing with D 4 (P), D 6; (2) without a noun, as common expression of assent, good, very well, certainly,—like *inshallah, ewalla.* (Cf. *-ema.*)

Ngeu, n. (—), a line used by carpenters for marking work, a ruddle,—so called from the red chalky earth applied to make the mark.

Ngi, -ngi, n. and a., variants of *ungi; wingi, -ingi,* which are usual in Z. See **Ingi,** &c.

Ngia, -ngine. See **Ingia, -ingine.**

Ngiri, n. (—), wild boar,—commonly *nguruwe wa mwitu.*

Ngizi, n. (—), a kind of cuttle-fish. *Wino wa n.,* the dark fluid emitted. *Kifuu cha n.,* cuttle-fish bone.

Ng'oa, v. root up, dig out, tear out, pull up. *Ng'oa mti,* root up a tree. *Ng'oa jino,* extract a tooth. *Ng'oa macho,* gouge out the eyes. *Ng'oa hema,* strike a tent. *Ng'oa safari,* start on a journey. Ps. *ng'olewa.* Nt. *ng'oka,* e.g. *moyo umening'oka,* my heart jumped into my mouth. Ap. *ngo-lea.* (Cf. *fukua, toa, ondoa.*)

Ngoa, n. desire, passion, lust. *Timiza n.,* satisfy the passions. *Tia n.,* weep for jealousy. (Cf. *ha'wa, shauko.*)

Ng'oe, n. (—), a forked stick or pole, e.g. for gathering fruit, &c. (Cf. *ng'oa* and *kiopoe.*)

Ng'ofu, n. (—), roe of a fish.

Ngoja, v. wait, wait for, await, stay for, remain. *Ngoja mlango,* wait at a door, act as door-keeper. *Ningoje,* wait for me,—also *ningojee.* Ap. *ngoj-ea, -ewa,* wait for (at, with, &c.), be patient with, &c., e.g. *mngojee bwana aje,* wait for your master to come. Cs. *ngoj-eza, -ezwa,* e.g. keep waiting, delay, adjourn. Rp. *ngojana,* e.g. wait for each other, wait all together. (Cf. *mngoje, ngojo, kingojo, mngojezi.* The *n* sound is sometimes neglected, e.g. *mgoja mlango,* a door-keeper.)

Ngojo, n. (—), waiting-place, station, post, period of waiting, watch. (Cf. *ngoja, kingojo,* and *zamu, lindo.*)

Ngoma, n. a drum. As the one universal accompaniment of all merry-making, and ceremonial, *ngoma* is extended to include (1) any kind of dance, (2) music in general. *Piga (chapua) n.,* beat a drum. *Cheza (ingia) n.,* join in a dance. *N. ya kucheza,* dancing for amusement. *N. ya kupunga (pepo),* dance for the exorcizing of a spirit. *Ngoma ikilia sana, haikawii kupasuka,* when a drum sounds loud, it will soon break. (Drums are of many sizes and patterns, and these as well as the accompanying dances and modes of beating vary with every tribe, and with the different occasions of their use. Cf. *goma, kigoma,* and see *tari, msapata, dandalo, kiumbizi, msondo, vumi, chapuo, kumbwaya, kitanga, kishina, msoma, mganda.* And for musical instruments. *kinanda, santuri, kinubi, zeze, zomari, toazi, upato, kayamba, panda, baragumu, filimbi.*)

Ng'ombe, n. (—), ox, cow, bull, cattle. Defined as *n. ndume* (or, *maksai*), ox, bullock; *n. jike,* cow; *n. fahali* (or *fahali* only), bull. *Ndama ya n.,* a calf. *Kukama n.,* to milk a cow. Prov. *wawili hula ng'ombe,* two can manage an ox. Dim. *king'ombe.* Also used as a term of insult, idiot, blockhead, like *ngamia, mbuzi.* (Cf. *fahali, mtamba.*)

Ngome, n. (—), fort, fortress, stronghold, castle. (Cf. syn. *gereza, boma.*)

Ng'onda, v. cure,—of meat, fish, &c., e.g. by cutting in strips, and drying in the sun. Ps. *ng'ondwa.* (There seems also to be a n. *ng'onda, king'onda,* i.e. a strip or slice of dried meat, fruit, &c.)

Ng'ong'o, n. plur. of *ung'ong'o* (which see).

Ngono, n. (—), and plur. of *ugono,* (1) sleeping time, and so, night; (2)

sleeping-turn, a wife's turn or time for sleeping with her husband. (*Gona* in cognate dialects means sleep, v., but is not used in Z. Cf. *sinzia, lala*.)

Ng'oo, int. also **Nyoo**, expressing utter contempt, a contemptuous refusal.

Ngozi, n. and **Ngovi**, skin,—of any animal, hide, leather. *Chuna n.*, take off the skin, skin, flay. *Tengeneza (fanyiza) n.*, tan hides. (*Govi* also occurs, but in Z. in restricted sense, in relation to circumcision, *tohara*.)

Ngumi, n. fist. *Piga n.*, strike with the fist, give a cuff to. (Cf. syn. *konde*.)

Ngungwi, n. plur. or **Nkungwi**, songs taught to boys, when circumcised; also called *malango*. (Perh. cf. *kunga, kungwi*.)

Nguo, n. (—), (1) cloth, as material, i. e. any woven fabric, of cotton, flax, silk, &c., but commonly cotton cloth, calico; (2) a cloth, a piece of cloth, for whatever purpose, e. g. *nguo ya meza*, a tablecloth; *nguo za kitanda*, bed clothes; *nguo za kuugulia*, mourning; (3) clothes, a garment of any kind. *Vaa n.*, put on clothes, dress oneself. *Vika n.*, clothe (another). *Vua n.*, take off clothes, undress. *Fuma n.*, weave cloth. *Tanda n.*, prepare the web in weaving. *Sifa ya nguo ni pindo*, the merit of a cloth is the (coloured, embroidered) border. (Perh. cf. *uo, chuo*. Various kinds of cloth are known as *nguo asili*, in commerce 'grey sheeting,' *nguo maradufu*, grey drilling. *Amerikani, kaniki, bendera, bafta, huthurungi, satini, gamti, joho, ulaiti, hariri, shashi*, &c. For articles of dress cf. (1) for men, *kikoi, kanzu, kisibau, fulana, kitambi, kilemba, kofia, shuka, gwamba, joho, soruali, mfuria*. (2) for women, *shiti, kisuto, kanga, leso, kanzu, soruali, dusamali, barakoa, ukaya, shela*, &c.)

Nguri, n. a shoemaker's tool (Str.).

Nguru, n. (—), name of a fish,— of good quality for eating and often of large size. (Cf. *samaki*.)

Nguruma, v. make a rumbling or roaring noise,—of any loud and deep sound, e. g. roar of a lion, thunder, roar, growl, rumble. (Cf. follg. and *vuma*.)

Ngurumo, n. (—), a loud roaring, rumbling sound, growl. *Leo kunapiga ngurumo*, it is thundering to-day. *Mshindo wa ngurumo*, a clap of thunder, i. e. *radi*. (Cf. prec.)

Nguruwe, n. (—), also **Nguuwe**, **Nguwe**, a pig, hog, swine. *N. wa mwitu*, a wild pig. *N. jike*, a sow. *Nguruwe aendealo, ndilo atendalo*, what a pig goes for, that he does. Also of a loose, immoral character, *yule nguruwe aliyetaka kufisidi nyumba*, that vile wretch, who wanted to violate a home.

Nguruzi, n. See **Nguzi**.

Nguu, n. in the phrase *mwenda nguu*. *Kilio cha mwenda nguu*, the cry of one who utterly despairs,—of some irreparable calamity.

Nguva, n. (—), a dugong, manatee.

Nguvu, n. force, strength, power, —in general. Thus (1) strength of body, muscular physical power, strength of mind, or character, ability, energy, vehemence, or mere mechanical strength, force, impetus, momentum, solidity, stability, pressure; (2) authority, supremacy, influence, importance, weight, earnestness; (3) exercise of force, compulsion. *Tia (pa) n.*, strengthen, consolidate, establish. *Fanya (toa) n.*, use (put forth, exert) strength, exercise authority. *Neno la n.*, an effective, forcible statement, command. *Kwa nguvu*, (1) by force (strength, ability, energy, &c.), (2) in a high degree, strongly, earnestly, (3) reluctantly, under compulsion, against the will, e. g. *alikubali kwa nguvu*, he consented under pressure. (Cf. *bidii, uwezo*.)

Nguzi, n. also **Nguruzi**, a hole in the bottom of a boat or vessel, for letting water out, i.e. *tundu katika mkuku*.

Nguzo, n. (—), (1) pillar, supporting column, post, prop, buttress, palisade, pale, pole; (2) fig. assistance, support, evidence, fundamental principles. Forms of prayer are called *nguzo ya sala*. *Nguzo ya imani*, articles (pillars) of faith, creed. In house-building *nguzo* are the poles forming the sides and supporting the roof. (Cf. *kiguzo*, and *tegemeo*.)

-ngwana, a. (same with D 4 (P), D 5 (S), D 6), (1) of or belonging to the status of a free man, as contrasted with a slave (*mtumwa*), and so of a relatively high social grade, and (2) civilized, educated, gentlemanly, well-mannered. (Cf. *ungwana*.)

Ngwe, n. (perh. plur. of *ugwe*), a measured plot, or patch of ground, whether (1) a bed or row, of young plants, &c., or (2) an allotment, ground assigned for cultivation, or for a task. (Cf. *kuo*, and perh. *ugwe*, of the line used in measuring.)

Ni is used simply as a copula, without distinction of person or number, or definite indication of time, though usually equivalent to the present tense of the verb *wa*, i.e. I am (was), you are (were), he (she, it) is (was), we (you, they) are (were), e.g. *yeye ni mwema*, he is a good man. *Ni hivi tu*, it is just so. *Nyumba ni tupu*, the house is empty.

Ni-, -ni, -ni-, as a formative prefix (1) in verbs, is the pfx. of the 1 Pers. Sing. subjective and objective, I, me. When subjective, it is sometimes *n*, or omitted altogether, e.g. *ninapenda*, I love; *nnaona*, I see; *takwenda*, I will go. (2) in nouns, is suffixed to form a locative case, meaning 'in, at, to, from, into, near, by,' and used with the prep. *mwa, pa, kwa* (and *mw-, p-, kw-*, as the prefix of the pronom. adj. agreeing with nouns in the locative case), according as the reference is to (*a*) inside position, (*b*) place simply, (*c*) environment generally, e.g. *nyumbani mwangu*, in my house; *shambani pangu*, at my estate; *kuangukani kwangu*, in my fall, as I fell. (3) *-ni*, is subjoined to verbs as a contracted form of (*a*) *nini*? What? e.g. *kunani*? for *kuna nini*? What is the matter? or (*b*) of *ninyi*, e.g. *kwaherini*, good-bye all of you; *twende zetuni*, come along all of you; *amekupeni vingi*, he has given you many things.

*****Nia**, n. (—), intention, purpose, resolve,—but extended to any mental activity, and can be translated 'thought, idea, opinion, mind, conscience, heart, character,' &c. *Nia haikuwa moja, ndio usipate jambo*, your mind was not made up, so you did not succeed. *N. njema (swafi)*, a good disposition. *N. mbovu (batili)*, bad thoughts (character, conscience). — v. have in mind, think of, purpose, intend. (Ar. Cf. *nuia*, and syn. *kusudi, wazo, moyo, thamiri, mradi*.)

*****Nikahi**, n. (—), and **Nikaha**, marriage,—esp. with reference to formalities, ceremonial, &c., betrothal, espousals, marriage settlement, e.g. *humfungia nikaha humwoza*, he makes a match for her, and gives her in marriage. *Akamwoa kwa nikaha*, and he married her in due form. *Fungisha n.*, perform the marriage ceremony for. *Sikiliza (shuhudia) n.*, attend (attest) a marriage,—said of the congregation present at the mosque. (Ar. Cf. *ndoa, harusi, maozi*.)

Nikali, Nili, verb-forms, and I am (was), *-ni*, pfx. of 1 Pers. Sing., *ka* connective, *li* in the sense of *-wa*, v. *Nikali nikienda*, and I was on the move. See *-li*.

*****Nili**, n. (—), indigo, and esp. blue, as used in washing. (Ar.)

Nina, n. (1) mother,—only in poetry, and a few phrases in Z. (cf. *mama*). (2) verb-form, I have. See **Na**.

Ninga, n. (—), a kind of green dove. Used also as a woman's name. *Akakaa na Molawe, kama ninga na utawi*, and he rested with his God, like a dove on a branch.

Ning'inia, v. or **Nying'inia**, sway, swing, wave to and fro, dandle (a child), rock, e. g. of trees, *matawi yaning'inia*, the bunches (of fruit) swing to and fro on the tree. Cs. *ning'in-isha, -ishwa*. (Cf. *kining'ina*, and syn. *wayawaya, yumba-yumba*.)

Nini, pron. interrog. what?—often subjoined to verbs in the contracted form *-ni. Wataka nini?* What do you want? *Ya nini, kwa nini?* Why? What for? *Kunani?* for *kuna nini?* What is the matter? *Hujambo nini?* Are you well, (or) what? (Cf. *nani, lini*.)

Ninyi, pron. of 3 Pers. Plur., also **Nyinyi**, you, ye. Often subjoined to verbs in the unreduplicated form *-ni*, e. g. *njooni*, come (ye). *Kwaherini*, good-bye all of you. *Ntakupigeni*, I will beat you. (Cf. *-enu*, your, as containing the same element.)

Nipe, for *unipe*, give me,—2 Pers. Sing. Imperative (or Subjunctive) of *-pa*, v.

Nipo, verb-form, I am here,—*ni*, person-pfx. of 1 Pers. Sing., and *-po*, adverbial of place. (Cf. *hapo*.)

*****Nira**, n. (—), a yoke (for oxen). (Ar.)

*****Nisha**, n. (—), or **Nashaa**, starch. (Ar. Cf. syn. *uwanga*.)

*****Njaa**, n. (—), hunger, craving for food, lack of food, famine. *Nina (naona) n.*, I am hungry. *Shindisha kwa n.*, starve. *N. inauma*, I feel the pangs of hunger. *Njaa ya leo ni shiba ya kesho*, hunger to-day means (i. e. hopes for) plenty to-morrow. (Ar. Dist. *jaa*, dust-heap).

Nje, adv. outside,—opp. to *ndani*. *-a nje*, external, outside, outer, outward. *Nje ya*, outside of, on the surface of. *Kwa nje*, outwardly, on the outside.

Njema, a. also **Ngema**, an irregular form of *-ema*, good, agreeing with D 4 (P), D 6, for *ny-ema*. Often as an adv. in rejoinders, like *vema*, Good! Very well! Certainly! (Cf. *-ema, ngema*.)

Njia, n. plur. used as sing. (—), (1) path, road, way, track; (2) way (or means) of proceeding, method, means; (3) progress, effect, influence. *N. kuu*, highway. *N. panda*, a parting of roads, cross-ways. *N. ya kukata*, a short cut. *Maneno yenyi njia*, forcible (effective, practical) suggestions. *Njia ya mwongo fupi*, a liar's career is short. *Njia mbili zaumiza*, double courses bring pain. (Cf. *ja*, v., and the Ap. form *-jia*, also *ujia, kijia*.)

Njiwa, n. (—), a pigeon. *N. wa mwitu*, a wild pigeon. *N. manga*, a tame pigeon, i. e. brought from Arabia and domesticated. See **Manga**.

Njombo, n. (—), name of a fish, barred with black and yellow (Str.).

Njoo, Njooni, v., 2 Pers. Sing. and Plur. Imperat. of *-ja*, come,—perhaps the only really irregular forms which are invariably used in Swahili. Other monosyllabic verbs as a rule use for Imperat. the Subjunct. form, or else the Infin. form, and sometimes *e* for *a* in the plur., e. g. *kula*, eat, is used as an Imperat., and *leni*, eat, plur. So *kunywa*, and *nyweni*.

Njozi, n. (—), vision, apparition. (Cf. *ndoto, ota*.)

Njuga, n. (—), a small bell, worn as an ornament, and at dances. (Cf. *kengele*.)

Njugu, n. (—), ground nut. Two varieties are (1) *njugu mawe*, which are hard, and (2) *njugu nyasa*, soft.

*****Njumu**, n., used of ornamental work, done by inlaying, or studding with metal, brass nails, &c. *Kasha kubwa la njumu*, a large chest ornamented with metal. (Hind.)

Nne, n. and a., four. As a n. always a disyllable, and pronounced almost as *inne*; but as an a. with prefixes commonly heard as *-ne* only, e.g. *watoto wanne* or *wane*. *Nne* with D 4 (P), D 6. *-a nne*, fourth. *Kumi na nne*, fourteen. (Cf. Ar. syn. *ároba*, also often used.)

Noa, v. sharpen, make sharp, whet, give an edge to,—of metal tools, weapons, knives, &c. Ps. *nolewa*. Nt. *noleka*, e.g. take an edge, be capable of taking an edge. Ap. *nolea*, e.g. *jiwe la kunolea*, a whetstone. Cs. *no-lesha, -leshwa*. Rp. *noana*. (Cf. *kinoo, noleo, noo*, and dist. *nyoa*.)

-nofu, a., nofu with D 4 (P), D 5 (S), D 6, lean, (of meat) i.e. all flesh, no fat or bone, i.e. *nyama tupu*. (Cf. *mnofu*.)

Nokoa, n. (*ma*-), the second man in authority over a plantation, under the *msimamizi*, and over the *kadamu*, sub-overseer, assistant.

Noleo, n. (*ma*-), (1) any instrument for sharpening, i.e. a whetstone, grindstone, strop, knife-sharpener, i.e. *kitu cha kunolea* (cf. *kinoo, noa*); (2) a ferrule, metal ring round the haft of a tool. (Cf. *pete*.)

Nona, v. get fat, usually of animals (*nenepa* of man). Cs. *nonesha, -eshwa*. (Cf. *-nono, unono*, and *-nene*.)

Nondo, n. and **Noondo**, (1) a kind of moth or grub; (2) a kind of serpent.

Nong'ona, v. whisper, speak under one's breath (in a low tone). Cs. *nong'on-eza, -ezwa*, address in a whisper, whisper to, e.g. *mnong'oneze baba yangu*, whisper to my father. Rp. *nong'onana, nong'onezana*, whisper to each other. (Cf. *mnongonezi, mnongono, unong'onezi*.)

-nono, a. (*nono* with D 4 (P), D 5 (S), D 6, fat, sleek, plump, well fed,—of animals, &c. (-*nene* properly of human beings) and things, e.g. *maisha nono*, a life of luxury. *Ng'ombe wanono*, fat cattle. *Kinono*, a fatling. (Cf. *nona, unono*.)

Noo, n. (*ma*-), a large whetstone, grindstone. See **Noa**, **Kinoo**.

Nso, n. (—), and **Inso**, a kidney. (*Figo* also sometimes used.)

Nta, n. (—), and **Inta**, wax, beeswax,—collected by natives from *mizinga* (see **Mzinga**) and brought to the coast.

*****Nuia**, v. also **Nuya**, have in mind, consider, purpose, intend, form a resolution. Ps. *nuiwa*. Ap. *nui-lia, -liwa*, e.g. resolve as to, form a good resolution about. Cs. *nui-za, -zwa*, cause to have in mind, remind, instruct. (Ar. Cf. *nia*.)

Nuka, v. (1) give out a smell, have a smell, smell, but esp. (when used alone) of a bad smell, stink; (2) take into the nostrils, e.g. as snuff. *N. vizuri* (*vema*), have a pleasant smell. *N. vibaya* (or *nuka* alone), have a bad smell. But *nuka* is also used of a sweet smell, like *nukia*, e.g. *akinuka meski na ambari*, (a person) smelling of musk and ambergris, and with an objective pers.-pfx., *inaninuka ambari*, I smell ambergris. *Tumbako ya kunuka*, snuff. *Nuka* (usually *nusa*) *tumbako*, take snuff, or, smell of tobacco. Ap. *nukia*, have a sweet smell. Also *nuk-ilia, nuk-iliza*, smell out, follow by scent, e.g. *mbwa hodari wa kunukiliza*, excellent sporting dogs, dogs with a good sense of smell. Cs. *nusa, nukiza*, use the sense of smell, smell, smell out, and so of dogs hunting, scent, follow by scent,—and of taking snuff. (Cf. follg. and *harufu, uvundo*.)

Nukato, n. (*ma*-), anything having a sweet smell, odour, perfume, scent. (Cf. *nuka*, and see *-to*.)

*****Nukta**, n. a dot, point, mark, spot, vowel sign (in Arabic writing), mark of punctuation (comma, stop, &c.) (Ar.)

*****Nuku**, v. for **Nukulu**, copy, transcribe. — n. (*ma*-), a copy, duplicate. (Ar. Cf. *nakili, nakulu*.)

Nuna, v. grumble, show discontent, complain, be sullen, sulk. *Nuna uso*, look discontented (sulky). Ap. *nun-ia, -iwa*, be sulky about, complain of (to, &c.). Cs. *nun-isha, -ishwa*, put in a bad temper, cause to grumble, &c. Rp. *nunana*, sulk together, complain of each other. (Cf. *nung'unika, guna, mnunaji, mnuno*.)

Nunda, n. a fierce animal, beast of prey,—used also to describe a cruel bloodthirsty man. The semi-wild town cats are sometimes called *nunda (ma-)*, or *mnunda (mi-)*.

Nundu, n. a hump, protuberance, boss, lump, bump, esp. of the hump of native cattle, which is considered a delicacy. *Achinjaye ng'ombe, atoa nundu, akampa jumbe*, when a man kills a bullock, he takes the hump and presents it to the chief. *Nundunundu*, or *kinundunundu*, humpy, lumpy. (Cf. *kigongo*.)

Nungunungu, n. (*ma-*), a porcupine.

Nung'unika, v. murmur, grumble, show discontent, complain. Ap. *nung'unikia*, grumble at (about, to, &c.). (Cf. follg. and *guna*.)

Nung'uniko, n. (*ma-*), grumbling, murmuring, complaint. (Cf. prec.)

Nunua, v. buy, purchase, bargain about, make a bid for. Ps. *nunuliwa*. Nt. *nunulika*. Ap. *nunulia, -liwa*, buy for (with, at, &c.). *Amenunuliwa shamba*, he has had an estate bought for him. Cs. *nunu-za, -zwa*, e.g. cause (press, invite, persuade) to buy. *Nunua bia* (or *shirika*), buy jointly, combine to buy. (Cf. *mnunuzi*, and Ar. syn. *zabuni*.)

*****Nurisha**, v. Cs., cause to shine, make bright, give light to. (Ar. Cf. *nuru*, and *angaza, ngariza*.)

*****Nuru**, n. (—), light, brightness, illumination. *Tia n.*, brighten, illuminate, make bright (clear, intelligible). *Toa n.*, give out light, shine. Used of a bright expression or complexion, e.g. *nuru za uso zikampotea*, he lost his happy expression. *Waanake hao nuru zao sawasawa*, these two women are equally good-looking. (Ar. Cf. *mwanga, weupe*.)

Nusa, v. Cs. of **Nuka** (which see).

*****Nussu**, n. (—), and **Nuss**, a half, a part, a portion, a bit. *Nussu* may denote any fraction of a whole. *Nussu kidogo*, a little bit. *Kata nussu nussu*, cut in halves (pieces, bits). *Gawa nussu kwa nussu*, divide in halves. *Nussu . . . nussu*, partly . . . partly. (Cf. Ar. *nisf*, middle, half.)

*****Núsura**, n. (—), and **Nusra**, (1) aid, assistance, help; (2) as an adv., almost, nearly, within a little, e.g. *amenitukana núsura kunipiga*, he abused me almost to the point of striking me. (Ar. Cf. follg.)

*****Núsuru**, v. help, assist, defend, preserve,—esp. of God's help. *Muungu ameninusuru*, God has helped me. *Tunusuru watumwa wako*, help us your servants. (Ar. Cf. *saidia*.)

Nwa, Nweleo, Nwewa, Nwesha. See **Nywa, Nyweleo**, &c.

Nwele, n. plur. of **Unywele** (which see), hair.

Ny- represents the sound of *ni* in the word *companion*, but slightly thicker and more nasal (Str.),—the sound taken by *n* when a pfx. before a vowel (see **N**, B. (2), (3)), and also occurring in many Swahili words. See follg.

Nya, v. As in other monosyllabic verbs, the infinitive form, i.e. *kunya*, is used in forming certain tenses. See **Ku**, 1. (*d*). 1. Act., meaning 'discharge, emit, let fall, drop,' of something fluid or semi-fluid, but restricted almost entirely to the passage of excreta, and, when used alone, of urine. The only other common use is as a neuter, of rain, 'fall, be discharged.' Thus *kunya mavi* (*damu*), pass faeces (blood). *Kume-*

kunya sana leo, it has rained a great deal to-day. *Mvua yanya*, rain is falling. *Inakunya*, it is raining. Ps. *nywa* (see below). Ap. *nyea*, e.g. *aisifuye mvua, imemnyea*, he who praises rain has had it. Cs. *nyesha*, (1) of rain, *Muungu amenyesha mvua nyingi*, God has caused much rain to fall. (2) e.g. *nyesha mtoto*, attend to a child at stool. 2. Pass. The passive form *-nywa* is the common word for 'drink, absorb, suck up, exhaust, consume,' either of liquids or figuratively of other things,—corresponding to *-la*, eat. (*Nywa* only retains a trace of the vowel sound of *y*, and is often heard and written as *nwa*.) Having an active meaning, *nywa* has its own passive and derivative verb-stems, viz. Ps. *nywewa*, be drunk up, be absorbed, dwindle, pine away, be consumed, dissolve away, evaporate, vanish. Nt. *nyweka*, e.g. (1) be drunk up, &c.; (2) be capable of (fit for) being drunk, be good for drinking purposes. Ap. *nywea*, drink at (with, for, to, &c.), e.g. *kopo la kunywea*, a mug to drink with. *Nywea salamu*, drink to the health of. Sometimes also *nywea* for *nywewa*, e.g. *killa siku mkewe huzidi kunywea*, every day his wife got thinner. *Nyama imenywea*, the meat has dried up (in cooking). Cs. *nywesha, nyweshwa*, cause to drink, furnish drink to, supply with water, &c. (Cf. *kinywa, kinywaji, manyesi, manyunyo, nyweleo*, and for 'pour out' (a liquid), *mimina, mwaga*.)

Nyafua, v. snatch off, tear off, bite off, snap up, e.g. *simba amemnyafua ng'ombe nyama*, the lion has torn off a piece of the bullock's flesh. (Cf. follg., of which *nyafua* is perh. a variant.)

Nyaka, Nyakua, v. catch in the hands, snatch up, tweak, pluck with the fingers, twitch,—also filch, pilfer. Derivatives not commonly used. (With *nyaka*, which is seldom used, cf. *daka*, catch, e.g. a ball in play.)

Nyala, Nyali, Nyalio, plurals from *ala* (? *u-ala*), *wali*, rice, and *walio* (which see).

Nyama, n. (—, but see **Mnyama**), (1) an animal, beast, brute,—mostly of the larger animals; (2) flesh, meat; (3) body, substance, matter, chief constituent, e.g. *nyama ya mkate*, crumb as opp. to crust (of bread), *nyama ya embe*, the flesh of a mango-fruit, *nyama ya roho*, the material part of the soul; (4) fig. of a brutal, stupid, degraded person. *N. ya mwitu*, a wild animal. *N. mkali* (*mbuai*), a ferocious beast. *Wewe kisu, sisi nyama*, you are the knife, we are the animal, i.e. at your mercy. In concords *nyama* is treated as D 1 or D 6, e.g. *wakaenda nyama zote*, all the animals went. (Cf. *mnyama*, which seems only used when there is special reason for distinguishing an animal as a living creature. Also perh. cf. *ndama*.)

***Nyamaa**, v. be silent, stop talking, hold one's tongue, be (become) quiet, die away, cease, be still,—used not only of talking and noise, but of anything violent, troublesome, or painful, e.g. of wind, bodily suffering, &c., e.g. *kichwa chaliniuma, sasa himenyamaa*, my head was aching, now it does not ache. Ap. *nyamalia*, e.g. be quiet to (for, in, &c.). Cs. *nyamaza*, usually Intens., i.e. keep quiet, refrain from noise, repress oneself, and in the Imperat., Silence! Hold your tongue! Hence *nyamazia*, e.g. *mama amemnyamazia mtoto*, the mother made the child quiet, and a derived Cs. *nyamaz-isha, -ishwa*, reduce to silence, make quiet, calm, still. (Ar. *namas*, cf. follg. and *kimya, tulia* from *tua*.)

-nyamafu, a. same with D 4 (P), D 5 (S), D 6, silent, quiet, still, reticent, reserved. *Mtu mnyamafu*, a man who says very little, keeps to himself. *Panyumafu*, a quiet spot. (Cf. *nyamaa*, and *-lulivu*.)

Nyambua, v. pull in pieces, tear into bits, take off in strips, peel off. Ps. *nyambuliwa*. Nt. *nyambuka*, come to pieces, fall into bits, be peeled off, e.g. of over-ripe fruit, over-cooked meat. (Cf. *ambua*, and *nyumbua, nyafua*.)

Nyamgumi, n. (—), a whale.

-nyangálika, a. used as an evasive or contemptuous epithet of what is difficult, impossible, or unfit to describe, a sort of a —, a what-do-you-call-it, a nondescript. *Kitu kinyangalika*, a nondescript thing. *Mnyangalika gani huyu?* What sort of a wretch is this?

Nyang'amba, n. a sweetmeat.

Nyanganya, v. take by force, steal, plunder, rob,—with the thing stolen, or person robbed, as object. *Amemnyanganya mali*, he has robbed him of money. *Alinyanganya yule mtoto*, he kidnapped that child, or, he robbed that child. Ps. *nyanganywa*. Nt. *nyanganyika*. Ap. *nyangany-ia, -iwa*. Cs. *nyanganyisha, -ishwa*. Rp. *nyanganyana*. (Cf. *mnyanganyi*, and *iba, pokonya*.)

Nyangwa, n. plur. of *wangwa*.

Nyani, n. (—), an ape, a baboon. (Cf. *kima*.)

Nyanya, v. cause to be prominent, protrude, put out, raise up. *Akanyanya mkono, akachukua upanga mmoja*, and he put out his hand, and took one sword. — n. (*ma-*), tomato, fruit of the *mnyanya*. (Cf. *nyanyuka*, and *nyanyasa*.)

Nyanyasa, v. or **Nyanyaza**, tease, annoy, molest, treat disrespectfully or rudely, hurt the feelings of. (Not a common word, perh. Cs. of *nyanya*, cf. syn. *sumbua, uthi, chokoza*.)

Nyanyuka, v. be prominent, rise above the rest, stick up, stick out. Also perh. a variant of **nyambuka** (which see). (Cf. *inua, tokeza, onekana, nyanya*.)

Nyara, n. plur. (1) booty, spoils, plunder,—persons or things, taken by war or violence. *Teka nyara*, take captive. (2) for *nyala*, plur. of *ala* (which see). (Cf. *teka, mateka*, and perh. Arab. *ghara*, raid, plunder.)

Nyasi, n. (*ma-*), a reed, long coarse grass. Also plur. of *unyasi*.

Nyata, v. go silently (quietly, stealthily), steal along, slink, skulk, sneak, e.g. of a wild beast's stealthy walk, or of a hunter stalking game. Ap. *nyat-ia, -iwa*, creep up to, steal upon, stalk (of a hunter). (Cf. *nyemelea, tambalia, gundulia*.)

Nyati, n. (—), the African buffalo, and in Z. used of the Indian.

Nyauka, v. dry up, be withered, shrivel,—with heat, or drought. (Cf. the more common *kauka, anika, anuka*.)

Nyayo, n. plur. of *uayo* (which see).

Nyea, v. cause a tickling or itching sensation, tickle, itch. *Upele unaninyea*, the eruption itches. Ps. *nyewa*, be made to itch, be irritated, tickled. (Cf. *mnyeo, nyega, nyegi, kinyefu*, and syn. *washa*.)

-nyefu, a. (same with D 4 (P), D 5 (S), D 6), moist, wet, damp, humid, marshy, watery. Also *-nyefunyefu*. (Cf. *nya, nywa, mnyefu*, and syn. *rútuba, maji, uloefu, chepechepe*.)

Nyega, v. cause to itch or tickle, excite prurient desire. Cs. (intens.) *nyeg-esha, -eshwa*, and Rp. *nyegeshana*. (Cf. *nyea*, and folig.)

Nyegi, n. itching, tickling, irritation, esp. of sexual excitement, prurient desire; and in animals, heat. (Cf. prec.)

Nyele, n. plur. of *unyele* (which see).

Nyeleo, n. (*ma-*), also *unyeleo*, pore (of the skin). (Cf. *nya*, v., and *tokeo*.)

Nyemelea, v. go quietly up to, steal up to, creep upon, stalk (a wild animal or bird), surprise. Ps. *nyemelewa*, e.g. be approached by stealth, be taken by surprise. (? Cf. *nyamalia, nyamaa.*)

Nyenje, n. a kind of cricket.

Nyenya, v. talk a person into telling, talk over, extort an admission from, extract news, pump with questions. Ps. *nyenyewa.* Nt. *nyenyeka,* be talked over, give way to pressure, submit. See **Nyenyekea.** Ap. *nyenyelea,* get at a secret, &c., whence *nyenyeleza,* introduce quietly, slip in secretly. Cs. *nyenyesha,* intens. Rp. *nyenyana.* (Cf. follg.)

Nyenyekea, v. (strictly the Ap. form of Nt. of *nyenya*), act with submission (humility, reverence, respect) towards, be polite (obsequious, cringing, &c.) to, be humble, defer to. E.g. *kijana amenenyekea babaye,* the young man treated his father with due deference. Ps. *nyenyekewa.* Cs. *nyenyek-esha, -eshwa,* e. g. teach humility to, humiliate, &c. (Cf. *nyenya, mnyenyekeo,* and follg.)

Nyenzo, n. plur. of *uenzo, wenzo* (which see).

Nyesi, n. (*ma-*), excrement, dung, urine, filth. (Cf. *nya, kinyaa,* and syn. *mavi, ukojo.*)

Nyeta, v. be teasing (tiresome, hard to please, unsatisfied, never content), be ill-mannered (disrespectful, arrogant), swagger. Ap. *nyet-ea, -ewa,* e. g. be disrespectful to (about, &c.). Cs. *nyet-esha, -eshwa,* e. g. cause to be troublesome, impertinent, &c.

Nyie, pron. for *ninyi-ye,* you (plur.), you there. (Cf. *miye, weye,* and *ye.*)

Nyiga, n. (*ma-*), a large wasp, a hornet.

Nyika, n. (*ma-*), open, bare, treeless wilderness, open forest with high grass, a barren, desolate region, contr. with *mwitu,* e.g. *tukaenda wee mwitu na nyika, mwitu na nyika,* we went on and on, through woods and wastes, forest and field. (Cf. *poli, pululu, jangwa.*)

Nyima, v. withhold (from), keep back (from), deprive, refuse, not give,—esp. of what is due, a person's right, e. g. wages, a debt. E. g. *yuna haki ya kupewa, lakini amemnyima kasidi,* he has a right to be paid, but the other has kept it back purposely. *Muungu hapi kwa mvua, hanyimi kwa jua kali,* God does not give by rain, or withhold by heat. Ps. *nyimwa.* (Other deriv. rare.) (Cf. follg.)

Nyimi-nyimi, adv. in little bits, by beggarly scraps, with a grudging hand. (Cf. prec.)

Nyingi, Nyingine, a. forms of *-ingi, -ingine,*—agreeing with D 4 (P), D 6.

Nying'inia, v. See **Ning'inia.**

Nyinyi, pron., same as *ninyi* (which see), you (plur.).

Nyinyoro, n. a bulbous plant which throws up a large head of red flowers (Str.).

Nyoa, v. shave off,—of hair only. Ps. *nyolewa.* Ap. *nyo-lea, -lewa,* e. g. *uembe wa kunyolea nyele,* a razor to shave with. (Cf. *kinyozi,* and perh. *unyele,* and *nya, nyonyoa.*)

-nyofu, a. (same with D 4 (P), D 5 (S), D 6), (1) straight, extended, stretched out; (2) usually fig. straightforward, honest, upright, trustworthy, e. g. *mtu mnyofu,* an honourable man. *Maneno manyofu,* plain, direct statement. (Cf. *nyoka,* n. and v., *nyosha.*)

Nyoka, v. (1) become straight (extended, laid out in a straight line), be straightened; (2) fig. be straightforward, be honest (practical, steadfast, effective), e. g. *maneno ya kunyoka.* Cs. *nyosha* (which see). (Cf. *-nyofu,* and follg.)

Nyoka, n. a serpent or snake of any kind. There are not many poisonous varieties in Z. Pythons (*chatu*) are comparatively common. (Cf. prec.)

Nyonda, n. plur. trial, testing, proof, experiment. In Z. *nyonja* (from *onja*) would be more usual. (Cf. *onja, jaribu*.)

Nyondo, n. See **Nondo, Nyundo**.

Nyonga, v. (1) twist, twist the neck of, strangle, throttle; (2) vex, harass, worry; (3) as a neut., twist, wriggle, move from side to side. Ps. *nyongwa*. Ap. *nyong-ea, -ewa*. Cs. *nyong-esha, -eshwa*. (Cf. follg.)

Nyonga, n. plur. of *unyonga*, but also used as a sing. n. (—), the hip,—the part where the thigh (*paji*) and flank (*kiuno*) meet. *Uchungu wa mtoto u katika nyonga ya mamaye*, the trouble with a child is on the mother's hip,—native women often carrying a child astride on the hip. (Cf. *nyonga*, v.)

-nyonge, a. (same with D 4 (P), D 5 (S), D 6), of a low order (degree or kind), low, mean, base, degraded, servile, insignificant, vile. *Lia kinyonge*, cry in a feeble helpless way. (Cf. *nyonga, unyonge*, and syn. *hafifu, duni, -baya, thaifu*.)

Nyongeza, n. plur. of *uongeza*, addition, appendix, supplement. (Cf. *ongeza*.)

Nyongo, n. bile. Also sometimes as irreg. plur. of *mwongo*, as if *uongo*, e.g. *nyongoni mwa siku*, in course of time. (Cf. *mwongo, miongo*, number, reckoning, decade.)

Nyongoa, v. straighten, stretch, untwist. *Jinyongoa*, straighten oneself, stiffen oneself,—used of convulsive stretching. (*-oa* here seems Rv., like *-ua*. Cf. *nyonga*, and follg.)

Nyongonyea, v. be languid, be weary, get slack and weak. (Cf. *nyonga*,—the termination perh. giving the idea of being untwisted, loosened, relaxed. Cf. syn. *legea*.)

Nyonya, v. suck the breast,—of a child or animal. *Nyonya titi la mama*, suck the mother's teat. *Ndugu wa kunyonya*, foster-brother (or -sister). *Mtoto mnyonya*, a babe, suckling. Cs. *nyony-esha, -eshwa*, suckle, give suck to, put to the breast.

Nyonyoa, v. pluck out hair (feathers, wool, &c.), pluck a bird, shave unskilfully (pulling instead of cutting). *Mninyonyoeni manyoya*, pluck out my feathers. Ps. *nyonyolewa*, e.g. *ngozi ya kondoo, isiyonyonyolewa malaika*, a sheepskin with the wool on. Nt. *nyonyoka*, e.g. *kima amenyonyoka manyoya pia*, the monkey had all its hair plucked off. Ap. *nyonyo-lea, -lewa*. Cs. *nyonyosha*, used fig. nag, constantly harass, worry, tease. (Cf. *unyoya*, and *nyoa*.)

Nyonyota. See **Nyota**.

Nyoo, int. See **Ngoo**.

Nyosha, v. Cs. Cf. *nyoka*, v., make straight, straighten, stretch, extend, elongate. Ps. *nyoshwa*. Ap. *nyosh-ea, -ewa*. Rp. *nyoshana*. *Nyosha mkono*, put out the hand. *Nyosha kamba*, haul a rope tight. *Jinyosha*, stretch oneself, take one's ease, enjoy oneself, rest. So *nyosha ngongo*, straighten the back, on completion of a job. (Cf. *nyoka, -nyofu*.)

Nyota, n. (—), a star. *Nyota haionekani mchana*, a star is not visible in daylight. *Nyota-nyota*, or *nyonyota*, is used of a drizzling rain, lit. drops, droppings (cf. *manyunyo*). In poetry *nyota* means 'thirst, drought,' i.e. *kiu*. (? Cf. *ota*.)

Nyote, a common contraction for *ninyi nyote*, you all, all of you. Cf. *sote*, for *sisi sote*. *Ninyi wote*, commonly for 'both of you (two).' See *-ote*.

Nyoya, n. (*ma-*), also plur. of **Unyoya** (which see), a hair, a single feather, a piece of wool, an animal's hair. *Manyoya* is used generally of the external covering,—wool, hair, feathers,—of the bodies of birds and animals,—more particularly of the smaller body feathers of birds (contr. *ubawa, mbawa*, of the wing feathers),

U

and of short hair in animals (cf. *singa* of long hair),—down, both of birds and animals, being *malaika*. *Nyele*, *nyele za singa*, is regularly used of human hair. (Cf. *nyoa, unyoya, uoya, unyele*.)

Nyoyo, n. plur. See **Moyo**.

Nyua, n. plur. of **ua** (which see).

Nyuki, n. (—), a bee. *Asali ya nyuki*, honey. *Nyuki huenda na maua yake*, the bee goes with its flowers. *Fathili za nyuki ni moto*, a bee's thanks is fire, i.e. all the thanks it gets.

Nyuma, adv. after, behind, (1) of place,—behind, at the back of, whether (*a*) on the further side of, beyond, or (*b*) after, in the rear of; (2) of time, (*a*) hereafter, in the future, (*b*) behind, in the past. For the apparent vagueness of meaning cf. *mbele*, in which also the meaning is decided by the context and implied mental attitude. *Watu wabaya wataondoka nyuma yangu*, may mean 'bad people will rise up after me' (when I am gone, in the future, —if of time; or behind me, in my rear,—if of place). *Mambo ya nyuma*, may mean (1) the future, *mambo ya baadaye*, *mambo ya mbele*, or (2) the past, *mambo yaliyopita, yaliyokwisha zamani, yaliyokuwa mbele*. Cf. *baada ya nyie hakuna wangine nyuma yenu*, after you there are none coming after you, i.e. of greater consequence than you, which might also be expressed by *mbele yenu*. *Rudi n.*, go back. *Kaa n.*, sit behind. *Huko n.*, often means 'meanwhile, to resume,'—of returning to a point in a story. *-a nyuma*, behind, in the rear, in the past, in the future. *Nyuma ya*, after, behind, in the rear of, beyond. (Cf. *kinyume, mbele, baada, kabla*.)

Nyuma, n. plur. of **uma** (which see).

Nyumba, n. (—), (1) a house,—properly of a native house, made of poles, sticks, wattles, earth, grass, &c., and called *n. ya miti, ya udongo, ya makuti, ya majani*, &c., but extended also to a house of any kind, as of masonry, *n. ya mawe*, or of corrugated iron, *n. ya mabati*, &c.,—also called *jumba (ma-)*. Also sometimes of structures made by animals, birds' nests, lairs, burrows,—more commonly called *tundu, kitundu*; and fig. of objects resembling a house, e.g. *nyumba ya randa*, the stock of a plane. (2) household,—but this is more commonly *watu wa nyumbani*, or simply *nyumbani*, as in the polite inquiry, *Hujambo (u hali gani) nyumbani?* I hope your family are well? Prov. *nyumba kuu haina nafasi*, a great house has little room. *Nyumba ya udongo haihimili kishindo*, a house of earth cannot stand a shock. (For words connected with house-building, &c., cf. *jenga, aka,* (materials) *mti, udongo, kombamoyo, ufito, kamba, nguzo, mwamba, bati, jiwe, chokaa, tufali,* (roof, roofing) *paa, kipaa, kuti, jani, ezeka.* And with *nyumba*, cf. *jumba, kijumba, chumba, mchumba, kinyumba*, and *umba*.)

Nyumbo, Nyumba, n. (—), name of an antelope (wildebeest, or gnu, Str.). Used in Z. of the mule, also called **bághala** (which see).

Nyumbua, v. used of handling a flexible, elastic, adhesive substance, —bend, draw out, stretch, manipulate without breaking. Nt. *nyumbuka*, be flexible (elastic, bend, yield to pressure) without breaking. (Cf. *pinda, kunja*.)

Nyundo, n. (—), a hammer. (Cf. *unda, mwunzi*.)

Nyungu-nyungu, n. ulcerous cracks or sores on the feet, between the toes, &c. *Miguu yangu imefanya nyungu-nyungu kwa jasho*, my feet are ulcerated with the heat. Also a name of a worm.

Nyunyiza, v. sprinkle. Ps. *nyunyizwa*. Ap. *nyunyiz-ia, -iwa*. Cs. *nyunyiz-isha, -ishwa*. Rp.

nyunyizana. (Cf. *manyunyo,* and perh. *chunyu, nya.* Also *mimina, mwaga, rashi.*)

Nyunyo, n. mostly used in plur. form *manyunyo,* sprinkled liquid, sprinklings, drizzle, light rain. (Cf. prec. and *marashi.*)

Nyushi, Nyuta, n. See **Ushi, Uta.**

Nywa, Nywea, Nywesha, v. See **Nya.**

Nyweleo, n. (*ma-*), also **Nyeleo,** pore,—of the skin. (Cf. *nya, nywa,* and *kinweleo.*)

Nzi, n. (*mainzi*), a fly (insect). See **Inzi.**

Nzige, n. (—), a locust.

O.

O, A. As a sound, *O* represents the open vowel *o* sound, as in Italian and other continental languages, which would be written *aw* in English, or *or* with the *r* smooth, not trilled. The English closed vowel sound, as in *no,* is hardly pronounceable by a native.

When unaccented, the *o* retains the same difference in a less degree. The short *o* sound in English *not* would be represented by a Swahili as *nart,* not as *nort.* The *o* in Swahili words must always be uttered with the lips open, never with a *w* sound at the end, i.e. like *owe.*

O and *U* are often not clearly distinguished in Swahili, especially when unaccented, and in words of Arab or foreign origin, perhaps partly under the influence of Arabic, which has one vowel sign for both. In some words *o* and *u* coalesce. Thus *ao* and *au* represent equally well common pronunciations of the adverb meaning 'or.' *Kuoga, kuota* become *kwoga, kwota,* and *koga, kota; ku-ote* becomes *kwote* and *kote;* and *uoga, woga* and *oga.*

Comparatively few Swahili words begin with *o.*

B. (1) In prefixes, and also alone, as a suffix, *-o* is the sound characteristic of the relative pronoun, 'who, which.' It is used in combination with the appropriate declension prefix of the noun referred to, e.g. *wo, yo, lo, zo, cho, vyo, po, ko, mo,* but the simple *-o* is capable of being substituted for any of these, except in the few phrases when these relative forms are used as separate words, not affixed to a verb-form, e.g. *lo lote, vyo vyote,* &c., e.g. *kiwe cho chote.* The only exception is that *e* or *ye* is almost always used for *o,* to agree with the Personal Pronouns in the singular number, and with D 1 (S), e.g. *mtu aliye mwema,* a man who is good; *mimi nipendaye ndizi,* I who am fond of bananas.

The above relative forms cannot as a rule bear the accent, and therefore in verbs can only follow tense signs capable of bearing an accent (i.e. *na, ja, li, -ka,* not *ta, me,* &c.).

These forms are sometimes affixed to the adj. *-ingine,* somewhat generalizing the meaning, e.g. *vitu vinginevyo,* any other sorts of things, *panginepo,* elsewhere, in some (any) other place (cf. *-mojawapo*).

An independent (uncombined) relative form is made, regularly in Mombasa and elsewhere, but seldom in Z., by affixing the above forms to the root *amba,* with or without *kwamba* following, e.g. *kitu ambacho* (or, *ambacho kwamba*) *nakipenda,* a thing which I like, and so *ambaye, ambazo, ambalo,* &c. See **Amba.**

(2) Connected with the *o* of relation is the *o* of reference, which occurs (*a*) in one form of demonstrative adjective, viz. *huyo, huo, hiyo, hicho, hao,* &c., i.e. the pronoun of relative nearness or reference, 'that there, that already mentioned or referred to, that in question,' and in adverbs, &c., formed from it, *huko, hapo;* (*b*) in combination with *na,* when it may be regarded as a shortened form of the above demonstrative adjective of re-

ference, e. g. *yunaye* for *yu na yeye*, he is, *zinazo* for *zi na hizo*, they are, &c.

(3) *-o* is subjoined to nouns sometimes as an abbreviated form of *wao*, *wako*, e. g. *wenzio* for *wenzi wao*, their companions.

Oa, v. take a wife, marry a wife,— of the man only. Ps. *oawa* (seldom used), be married,—of the man only. Also Ps. *olewa*, be married,—of the woman only. Nt. *oleka*, of the woman only,—be married, be marriageable. Ap. *olea*, *olewa*, marry with (for, at, in, &c.), e.g. of gifts, accessories, place, &c. for marrying. Cs. *oza* (also *oaza*), *ozwa*, cause (persuade, allow) to marry, perform the ceremony of marriage. Used of parents, friends concerned, persons assisting, the official, &c., and even of the bridegroom, ' get for wife, take in marriage' (cf. *zika, zisha*). Hence Ap. *ozea, ozewa*, and *ozelea*, marry to (with, at, &c.). Hence *ozesha, ozeshwa*, e. g. *uniozeshe mtoto wako*, allow me to marry your daughter. Rp. *oana*, of the couple marrying, and of intermarriage generally, of families, tribes, &c. (Cf. *ndoa, harusi*, and *posa, poza*, and dist. *oza*, v.)

***Ofsa**, n. (*ma*-), also *obsa, hobsa, afsa*, officer, i. e. the English word as pronounced by a native. So *ófis*, for office.

Oga, (1) v. bathe, wash the whole body, take a bath. *Koga* is often used as the root (i. e. *ku-oga*, see **Ku-**), and distinguishes the verb from *oga*, fear. Ap. *ogea, ogewa*, e. g. *maji ya kuogea*, water to bathe with, and cf. *pakuogea*, a bathing-place, a bath-room, *chakuogea*, a vessel to bathe in, a bath, i.e. of the European kind,—otherwise *kiogeo, birika* (and cf. *hamamu*). Hence a further Ap. *ogelea, ogelewa, ogeleka*, used esp. of swimming, with a Cs. *ogel-eza, -esha, -ezwa*, make (cause, teach) to swim. *Ogelesha vyombo*, swim boats,—as children do. Sometimes *olesha*. *Hapaogeleki*, you cannot swim here. *Mwogeleshe punda*, make the donkey swim across. Cs. *ogesha, ogeshwa*, e. g. take (send, order) to bathe, and *osha, oshwa* (which see). Rp. *ogana*, e.g. all bathe together.

Oga, (2) v. fear, be afraid, be timid, be cowardly. Derivative stems *ogwa, ogeka, ogea, ogewa, ogesha, ogana*, seldom if ever heard,—their place being supplied by *ogopa, ogofya*, &c. (See follg., and cf. *hofu, tisha, shuka, -cha*, v. As contrasted with *hofu*, *oga* refers more to the character and disposition, the mental attitude, *hofu*, to its direction and object, esp. apprehension of the future.)

-**oga**, a. cowardly, timid, nervous, easily frightened. Sometimes also as n. for **woga** (**uoga**) (which see). (Cf. *oga*, v. fear, and follg.)

Ogofisha, Ogofya, v. both used as Cs. of *ogopa* (which see), frighten, terrify, alarm, threaten, menace. *Ogofya, ogofyo* (and *mwogofyo, uogofyo*), is also a n. generally used in the plur. *maogofya*, menace, threat, denunciation. (Cf. *oga, ogopa*, and syn. *kamia, hofisha, tisha*.)

Ogopa, v. be afraid (of), fear, feel fear. Ps. *ogopwa*. Ap. *ogop-ea, -ewa*, e. g. *akuta unyonge kwa kuogopea roho*, he gets disgrace because of being afraid for his life. Cs. *ogof-isha, -ishwa, ogofya*, i.e. frighten, terrify, threaten, menace. (For interchange of *f* and *p* see **F**, and cf. *gomba, ugomvi, iba, mwivi*. For *ya*, as a Cs. form, cf. *pona, ponya*, and *ya*. Also cf. *oga* (2), and note.)

Oka, v. roast, toast, bake, i. e. prepare by applying fire only, not with water. Of pottery, burn, bake. Ps. *okwa*. Nt. *okeka*. Ap. *okea, okewa*, and *okelea*. Cs. *okesha, okeshwa*. (Cf. *joko*, and for cooking *pika, choma, kaanga*.)

Okoa, v. save, rescue, deliver, preserve. Ps. *okolewa*. Nt. *okoka*. Ap. *oko-lea, -lewa*. Cs. *oko-za, -zwa*, intens. e. g. exert oneself to save, rescue, &c. Rp. *okoana*. (Cf.

wokovu, mwokozi, maokozi, also *opoa, pona.* Kr. connects it with *oka,* as a Rv. take off the fire, i. e. at the right time, keep safe and sound.)

Okota, v. (1) pick up, take up with fingers, hand, &c.; (2) light upon, come across, find by chance, get without exertion or anticipation. E. g. of fishing, *wakiokota nguva, hugawana,* if they come across a dugong, they divide it. Ps. *okotwa.* Nt. *okoteka,* e. g. *maji ikimwagika haiokoteki,* spilt water cannot be picked up. Ap. *okot-ea, -ewa.* Cs. *okot-esha, -eshwa.* Rp. *okotana.* (Cf. syn. *zoa, kuta, vumbua, pata,* and perh. *okoa.*)

Ole, n. (no plur., but treated as D 4 (S), *wole,* i. e. *uole*), usually with a pron. adj. as an exclamation of woe or pity, i. e. *ole wangu!* woe is me! *ole wao!* how sad for them! Also *mwenyi ole,* a melancholy, sad, despondent person.

Olesha, v. also **Oleza,** shortened Cs. of *oga,* for *ogelesha.* See **Oga** (1).

Olewa, v. Ps. of *oa* (which see), be married.

Oleza, v. and **Oleleza,** make straight (even, level) with,—and so, follow a pattern, copy, imitate. *Oleza kitu na kitu kingine,* make one thing like another. (Cf. *kiolezo.* Not a usual word in Z. Cf. *fuatisha, linganisha, sawazisha, iga.*)

Omba, v. beg (of), be a beggar, pray (to), request, ask (of),—with either person asked, or thing asked, as object, or both. Thus *omba mtu,* ask a person. *Omba mtu kitu,* ask a person for a thing. Also *omba kitu kwa mtu,* ask a thing of a person, e. g. *nimeomba nguo kwa bwana,* I asked my master for clothes (cf. *ombea*). *Ndivyo tuombavyo,* so we pray,—a common rejoinder on hearing good news. Ps. *ombwa.* Nt. *ombeka,* e. g. be asked, be a proper request. Ap. *omb-ea, -ewa,* usually in a restricted sense, e. g. ask on behalf of, plead for, intercede for, or petition against, rather than ask for (i. e. to have) or ask of (i. e. from). Thus *kumwombea kwa Muungu,* to intercede for him with God, is more usual than *kuombea baraka za Muungu,* ask for God's blessing, or simply *kuombea Muungu,* pray to God. Cs. *omb-esha (ombeza), -eshwa,* e. g. cause to beg, instruct in prayers, &c. Rp. *ombana.* (Cf. *mwombi, mwombaji, maombi, mwombezi, uombezi,* also syn. *sali, sihi, uliza.* In *sali (sala),* however, the outward form (ceremonial, ritual) of praying is the prominent idea, in *omba,* the object in view, in *sihi,* the praying itself as an expression of felt need, an urgent appeal. *Uliza,* is 'inquire of, or for').

Omboleza, v. bewail, lament,—in a ceremonial way. Used of formal chanting of dirges, &c. (Cf. *maomboleza, matanga,* and perh. *omba.*)

Omo, n. (*ma-*), forepart of ship, bows, prow,—also called *gubeti.* *Pepo za omo,* winds that carry forward, a wind astern, a fair wind. (Cf. *mdomo, mwomo, domo.*)

Omoa, v. (1) dig up, dig out, break up, e. g. of breaking up soil with crowbars, &c.; (2) fig. disturb, weaken, cause trouble in, make confusion; (3) bring to light, reveal, show, begin, set on foot. E. g. *omoa udongo,* break up earth. *Omoa vita,* bring about a war. Ps. *omolewa,* e. g. *mti huomolewa na tunda zake,* if a tree is dug up, so are its fruits. Nt. *omoka.* Ap. *omo-lea, -lewa.* Cs. *omo-sha, -shwa.* Rp. *omoana.* (Not often heard in Z. Cf. *chimbua, fukua, tekua, vumbua,* and perh. *umua.*)

Ona, v. used of any mode of perception by the senses or the mind, and hence with a wide range of meanings, viz. 1. of the senses. (1) of sight. *Ona* alone and unqualified by context usually means, see with the eyes, as contr. with other senses, e. g. *kusikia si kuona,* hearing is not the same as seeing. *Ona* (Imperat.), look, use your eyes (contr. *tazama*, fix your gaze upon, contemplate, *angalia*, observe, attend to). By a curious inversion, *ona* also is used for 'be transparent,' e. g. *nguo hii inaona*, this calico is transparent, i. e. one can see through it, it sees. (2) of the other senses, e. g. *naona kishindo*, I hear a noise. *Naona harufu*, I smell a smell. *Naona mti huu mgumu*, I feel this wood is hard. *Naona utamu wake*, I taste its flavour. *Naona kiu (njaa)*, I am thirsty (hungry). (3) get to see, come on, find (cf. follg.). 2. of mental perception, of all kinds. (1) of feelings, very commonly with a defining noun, e. g. *ona kiburi (huruma, hasira, uwivu, furaha, haya, mashaka, huzuni,* &c.), I feel pride (pity, anger, jealousy, joy, shame, doubt, sorrow, &c.). (2) of other mental faculties,—observe, think, be of opinion, notice, discern, judge, consider, expect, fancy, imagine. E.g. *naona*,—very commonly alone,—I think so, certainly, probably, possibly, it is likely, perhaps. *Naona nyani kusema*, I observe an ape speaking. *Naona utaona ajabu kuona barua hii*, I think you will feel surprise at seeing this letter. Ps. *onwa*, of all the senses of the Act. Nt. *oneka*, e. g. (1) be seen, &c.; (2) be perceptible (visible, audible, tangible, &c.). So *onekana*, i. e. come into view, become visible, be apparent, be perceptible, appear, appear like, (as if), seem to be. Rf. *jiona*, (1) feel oneself, e. g. *najiona nipo kwetu*, I feel myself quite at home, I am quite at my ease; (2) commonly of affectation, self-conscious pride, &c., i. e. be conceited (arrogant, ostentatious, affected), e. g. *anajiona*, he is conceited, proud of himself, showing off. Ap. *on-ea, -ewa*, e. g. (1) see, feel, &c. with (for, at, by, in, against, &c.), e. g. *nataka kujionea*, I want to see for myself. *Namwonea chuki*, I am offended with him. *Usimwonee makosa*, do not visit his errors upon him. (2) commonly used alone in the restricted sense of an active expression of ill-feeling against, i. e. ill-treat, harass, persecute, oppress. *Wale ndugu wakamwonea Siyalela*, the sisters were hard on Cinderella. So also in Ps. *onewa*, be ill-treated, persecuted. Hence also a Rp. *oneana*, tease each other, as well as 'feel towards each other,' and a further Ap. verb-stem *one-lea, -lewa*, in the simpler sense 'feel towards.' Cs. (a) *onya*, Ps. *onywa*, (1) cause to see, show, display, e. g. *nalimwonya njia*, I showed him the road; (2) warn, admonish, reprove, *nikamwonya asiende*, I warned him not to go. *Onya-onya kwa mikono*, gesticulate. Hence *onyeka*, and *onyekea*, e. g. *nimemwonya, lakini hakuoneka*, I warned him, but he was incapable of taking a warning. (b) *ony-esha, -eshwa*, show, point out, demonstrate, make clear (for the simple *onesha*, which seems never used,—though formed from *onya*). Hence *onyesh-ea, -ewa*, e. g. (pass.) have a thing shown to one. Also *onyana*, of mutual warning. Rp. *onana*, see each other,—often of friendly meetings, cf. *onana uso kwa uso*, meet face to face; *kwaheri ya kuonana*, good-bye till we meet again. (Cf. *tazama, sikia, angalia,* and *mboni, oneo, onefu.*)

Ondoa, v. (1) start off, set going off; (2) take (put, send, move) away, remove, take out of the way, set aside, dismiss; (3) do away with, abolish, finish off, conclude. *Uniondoe nisimame*, start me (help me) to get up. *Akili nyingi huondoa maarifa*. Over-cleverness overrides prudence, wits are not wisdom. *Daraka ya kuondoa na kuweka*, responsibility for removing or establishing. *Ondoa nathari (ahadi)*, fulfil a vow, discharge a promise. *Ondoa matanga*, bring funeral ceremonies to an end. *Ondoa thambi*, remit sin. Ps. *ondo-*

lewa. Nt. *ondoka*, e.g. (1) go away, make a move, get out of the way, start off, set out (on a journey), depart, withdraw, retire; (2) rise up, get up, stand upright (as the first step to going off, &c.), e.g. often in beginning a story, *paliondoka* (or *paliondokea*) *mtu*, a man went (began, made a start). *Ondoka mbele yangu*, get out of my way. *Ondoka katika ulimwengu*, depart from this world, die. *Alikuwa amelala, akaondoka anaketi*, he was lying prostrate, but he rose (made a move) and sits up. Hence *ondok-ea, -ewa*, (1) make a move for (against, at, with, &c.), get out of the way of, esp. of rising up before, as a sign of respect, e.g. *haondokewi*, no respect is shown him; also (2) rise up, swell, protrude, stand out, become prominent, e.g. *maziwa yaanza kumwondokea*, her breasts begin to swell. Hence a further Ap. form *ondokel-ea, -ewa*, e.g. rise up and leave a place, and *ondokeana*. Ap. *ondo-lea, -lewa*, e.g. send (take, put) away for (by, with, at, &c.), i.e. remove from, deprive of, rid of, condone, forgive, &c. *Ondolea heshima*, disgrace, degrade. *Ond. mashaka*, rid of difficulties. *Ond. huzuni*, comfort, cheer. *Ond. thambi*, absolve from sin. *Ond. hatiya*, acquit, &c. Rp. *ondoleana, ondoana*. Cs. *ondo-sha, -shwa*, intens. send off, despatch, dismiss, cause to go away, do away with. *Ondosha nanga*, get up an anchor (commonly *ng'oa*). *Ondosha mtumishi*, dismiss a servant, or despatch on an errand. (Cf. *toa, weka, twaa*, in various senses, and *maondokeo, maondoleo*, and follg.)

Ondokeo, n. (*ma-*), departure, &c. More usual in plur. (Cf. prec.)

Ondoleo, n. (*ma-*), removal, &c. More usual in plur. (Cf. *ondoa*.)

Onefu, n. (*ma-*), ill-feeling, unkindness. (Cf. *ona, onea*.)

Oneo, n. (*ma-*), unkind treatment, persecution.

Ongea, n. only used in Z. in the sense, spend time, talk, gossip, idle, converse, pass time, waste time. No derivative stems in use. (Cf. *maongezi, ongeza*, and syn. *zungumza, semezana, pisha wakati*.)

Ongeza, v. Cs. increase, add to, make greater, multiply, magnify, enlarge. *Ongeza maneno*, make a lengthy (or, additional) speech. *Ong. urefu*, lengthen. Ps. *ongezwa*. Nt. *ongezeka*, e.g. be added to, increase, multiply. Ap. *ongezea, -ewa*, e.g. *tumeongezewa mizigo*, we have had our loads added to. Rp. *ongezana*. (Cf. *maongezo, nyongeza*, and equally common Ar. syn. *zidisha, zidi*.)

Ongezo, n. (*ma-*). See more common (plur.) **Maongezo**.

Ongo, n. (*ma-*), only in plur. *maongo*, sometimes used for 'the back, back part' (of man or animals). (Cf. more usu. *mgongo*, and *ungo, maungo*.)

-ongo, a. lying, false, pretended, sham, deceitful,—but *-a uongo* is the form commonly used of things. (Cf. *mwongo* of persons, *uongo*, and perh. follg.)

Ongoa, v. cause to go right, guide, lead, set right, reform, correct, convert, make successful, prosper. *Ongoa mtoto*, give a child a good training. *Useme naye hatta umwongoe*, talk to him till you convert him. *Ongoa mbele*, lead forward. *Ongoa njia*, make the road straight, take a straight course on. *Uongo hauongoi*, a lie does not pay. Ps. *ongolewa*. Nt. *ongoka*, e.g. become straight, be set right, be well taught, prosper, be reformed, be converted, &c. E.g. *vilimo havikuongoka*, their plantings did not turn out well. *Ongoka moyo*, become a reformed character. *Mti umeongoka*, the pole has become straight, is straight. Hence *ongok-ea, -ewa*, e.g. *mwaka huu watu wameongokewa*, this year people have been prosperous (cf. *fanikiwa*). *Ongokea Muungu*, be turned (directed) to God. Ap. *ongo-lea, -lewa, ongoea,* e.g. *ongolea mtoto,* get a child to be tractable. *Muungu amemwongolea kazi,* God has granted success to his labours. Cs. *ongo-za, -zwa,* intens. make go right, drive forward, carry on vigorously. *Ongoza kazi,* do good work. *Ongoza maneno,* give a good turn to a discussion, clear up a statement. *Ongoza kuku,* drive fowls along a road. Hence *ongozana,* e.g. *ng'ombe zimeongozana,* the cattle have worked their way on. Rp. *ongoana.* (Cf. *mwongozi, kiongozi, -ongofu,* and perh. *ongea,* and even *-ongo,* of which *ongoa* is possibly Rv., i.e. turn from wrong.

-ongofu, a. one who is set right, reformed, converted, well-conducted, well-trained, successful. (Cf. prec.)

Onja, v. (1) taste, take a taste of; (2) try, test, examine. E.g. *onja uone,* taste and see,—if a thing is good. *Onja mitego,* inspect traps. Ps. *onjwa.* Nt. *onjeka.* Ap. *onj-ea, -ewa,* e.g. *mwiko wa kuonjea asali,* a spoon to taste the honey with. Cs. *onj-esha, -eshwa.* Rp. *onjana.* (Cf. *maonji, mwonjo, kionja, nyonda,* and *jaribu.*)

Opoa, v. (1) take (fetch, pull, draw) out; (2) fig. save, rescue, deliver. E.g. *opoa ndoo kisimani,* fish up a bucket out of a well. *Opoa sumu,* get poison out of the system,—by medicine. Ps. *opolewa.* Nt. *opoka,* e.g. be saved (rescued, cured). Ap. *opo-lea, -lewa,* e.g. *chuma cha kuopolea,* an iron hook (to pull with). Hence *opol-eza, -ezwa.* Cs. *opo-sha, -shwa.* Rp. *opoana.* (Cf. *kiopoo,* and *okoa, toa, pona.*)

*Orofa, n. (—, and *ma-*), also Ghórofa, upper room, upper floor (story, flat) of a house. *Nyumba ya orofa tatu,* a house with three upper rooms (or, stories). (Arab. *ghórofa,* cf. *chumba, dari, tabaka, juu.*)

-ororo, a. (*nyororo* with D 4 (P), D 6, *jororo* with D 5 (S)), soft, smooth, velvety, tender. *Nguo nyororo,* a soft fabric. *Godoro jororo,* a soft mattress. *Mwili mwororo,* soft flesh. (Cf. *laini, -anana,* contr. *-gumu,* hard.)

Osha, v. Cs. of *oga* (see Oga, Ogesha), wash,—the most general term for washing anything, but for special kinds of washing see Fua ('beat,' of clothes), Nawa, Tawaza. *Osha nguo,* wash clothes (cf. *josho, mwosho*). *Osha mwili (maiti),* wash the body (a dead body). Ps. *oshwa.* Nt. *osheka,* e.g. be washed, be washable, stand washing. *Nguo za kuosheka,* a good washing stuff. Ap. *oshea, oshewa,* e.g. *unioshee nguo,* wash my clothes for me. *Mahali pa kuoshewa maiti,* a place for washing corpses. Cs. *osheza, oshezwa.* Rp. *oshana.* (Cf. *oga,* &c., and see above.)

*Osia, v. also Usia, and Wosia (which see). (Ar.)

Ota, v. There appear to be three distinct verbs in this form, all common in restricted senses, and each with similar derived stems, viz. 1. grow, sprout, spring up,—usually of vegetable life, or of growth resembling it, e.g. of nails, hair, &c. (So also *mea,* but of animal growth usually *kua.*) E.g. *mihindi inaota,* the maize is springing up. *Simba huota nyele za shingo,* lions grow manes,—i.e. *ota,* in a semi-active sense. Hence Ap. *otea,* Cs. *otesha, oteshwa,* e.g. cherish, tend, rear. (Cf. *otea,* and ? *woto,* vegetation, plant-life.) 2. (*a*) dream, have a dream; (*b*) be in a dreamy, dozing state, be half awake, be silly,—often with *ndoto* following. Derivs. as above. Rp. *otana,* dream about each other (cf. *ndoto*). 3. sit by (in, for), squat down at, often with *jua,* i.e. bask in the sun, or *moto,* sit close to a fire, warm oneself. Ap. *otea, otewa,* like *ota,* and also esp. lie in wait, form an ambush, look out for. (Cf. ? *oteo,* an ambush, and *otama,* and perh. *moto.*

For sitting generally, *kaa kitako, keti*.)

Otama, v. squat, sit. (Seldom in Z. Cf. *ota*, 3, and perh. *atamia*.)

-ote, a. all, all the, the whole (of). Like the a. *-enyi, -enyewe, -ingine*, and sometimes *-ema, -ote* follows the so-called pronominal and demonstrative adjectives as to forms of agreement with nouns, i.e. *wote, yote, zote, chote, pote*, &c. (cf. *huyu*, and *-angu*), except that *yote* is the form agreeing with D 1 (S). *-ote* also takes the forms *sote, nyote* when associated with the pronouns *sisi, ninyi*. *Nyumba yote*, all the house, the whole house. *Nyumba zote*, all the houses. *-ote* is generalized by combination with a corresponding separate relative form, e.g. *mtu ye yote*, any man whatever. *Watu wo wote, neno lo lote*, &c. (cf. *awaye yote, kiwacho chote*). 'All,' in the sense of 'every individual,' is denoted by *-ote -moja-moja*, e.g. *vitu vyote kimoja-kimoja*, everything singly. (Cf. *killa*.)

Oteo, n. (*ma-*), (1) growth, shoot, sprout (cf. *ota*, 1); (2) ? ambush, lying in wait (cf. *ota*, 3).

-ovu, a. bad,—usually in a moral sense, wrong, unprincipled, wicked, evil. If required to agree with nouns not of D 1, then usually *-a uovu*, e.g. *nyumba za uovu*, wicked houses, not *nyumba ovu*. *Mema na maovu ndio ulimwengu*, the world is a mixture of good and bad. Contr. *-bovu*, apparently from the same root, but of physical condition, e.g. *nyumba mbovu*, dilapidated houses. Also cf. *-baya*, which includes the meanings of *-ovu* and *-bovu*. (Cf. *uovu*, and perh. *oza, ovyo*.)

Ovyo, n. and adv., trash, useless articles, rubbish, what is common and valueless. As adv. anyhow, recklessly, haphazard, at random, extravagantly, foolishly. *Mpanda ovyo hula ovyo*, he who sows rubbish gets rubbish to eat. (Perh. cf. *ovu*.)

Owama, Oweka, -owefu, v. See **Lowa, Lowama, Loweka, -lowefu**.

Oza, v. (1) go bad, rot, putrefy, spoil, be corrupt. *Tia dawa isioze*, use medicaments to prevent putrefaction, use antiseptics, embalm (a corpse). *Samaki moja akioza, wote wameoza*, if one fish is bad, all are. Ap. *oz-ea, -ewa*. Cs. *oz-esha, -eshwa*. (Cf. *-ovu, -bovu*, and *pooza*.) (2) Cs. of *oa* (which see), marry, and obs. in *oa* also a kindred form *posa, poza*).

P.

P represents the same sound as in English. At the beginning of some Swahili words it may be heard pronounced in an emphatic semi-explosive way (as *t* is in some words), which probably reflects a vanishing *n* sound before the *p*, as in *pepo*, plur. of *upepo*, for *npepo*. This difference is, however, never important and seldom noticeable in Z.

P before *y* is changed to *f* in some words, e.g. *ogofya*, Cs. of *ogopa*, fear, and *afya*, a Cs. of *apa*, swear.

P and *B* are hard to distinguish in some words as commonly pronounced, e.g. *poromoka, pofu*, and others. (Obs. these sounds are not distinguished in Arab.)

P- sometimes represents the pfx. *pa-* before an *e* or *a*. See **Pa-**.

Pa, (1) is the form of the preposition *-a*, of, agreeing with D 7, i.e. *mahali* (*pahali*), place, or with a noun with the locative termination *-ni*, e.g. *mahali pa mawe*, a stony place, or, stony places. *Mjini pa mgeni*, in the foreigner's town. (2) used alone (not as a preposition) after *mahali*, represents (like the other pers. pfxs.) the verb-form *ni*, is, e.g. *mahali hapa pa pema*, this place is a good one. (3) is a verb-root, meaning 'give.' See **Pa**, v.

Pa-, P-, is the pers.-pfx. (1) of verbs and adjectives agreeing with D 7, i.e. *mahali* (*pahali*), place.

(2) and of adjectives agreeing with nouns which have the locative ending -*ni*, indicating position. (*Ku-, kw-,* and *m-, mw-* are also used with nouns in *ni,* but *pa-* is more general than *m-,* into, within, from within, and less general than *ku-,* which includes the whole environment, not position only.) (3) *pa* is also used of time, i. e. position in time, esp. in the relative form *-po,* and in the adv. *hapa, pale,* in which 'here, on the spot' and 'now, at once,' are often blended. See Po. (4) *pa* is also prefixed to verbs in a general sense, without definite reference to place, e. g. *pana (palikuwa) mtu,* there is (was) a man. *Hapana,* there is not, no. *Palikwenda asikari,* a soldier went. (5) for this pfx. combined with the relative *-o* see Po. Cf. also *papa, papo, hapa, hapo.* E. g. *mahali pake pema pampendeza,* his good position pleases him. *Shambani pangu,* at my plantation. *Mahali pale pazuri ndipo palipokuwapo mamba,* that beautiful spot is where there were crocodiles. *Pa-* becomes *p-* in verbs before *a,* when a tense-sign, and in adjectives before *-a, -e,* and *-o,* e. g. *p-angu, p-ema, p-ote,* and coalesces with an *i* following to form *-e,* e. g. *pengi* for *paingi.*

Pa, v. give to, bestow on, present with. As a rule, the simple stem *pa* is combined with an objective pfx. denoting a person, not a thing, i. e. it occurs only as *nipa, kupa, mpa, tupa, wapa, jipa.* Thus it may be regarded grammatically as a dissyllabic root with varying initial syllable, and so does not follow the rule of monosyllabic verb-roots, as to the formation of tenses with *ku-,* i. e. the Infinitive form. See **-fa,** and **Ku-**. This restriction of the use of *pa* leads to the use of *toa* in its place, when all reference to a *person* as object is omitted, i. e. in the sense 'give, give away, bestow, distribute, present.' But *toa* is vague, and means 'take away' as well as 'give,' e. g. *aliitoa nguo,* he presented the garment, or, he removed, took away the garment. *Ilitolewa,* it was given, or, it was withdrawn. See **Toa.** (Exceptions to the above rule are rare, e. g. *Muungu hapi kwa mvua,* God does not give (i. e. bless) by rain (only). *Kitu kilichopewa na mtu,* a thing which was given by some one.) *Pa* is often contr. with *nyima,* e. g. *alionipa mimi, ndio aliokunyima wee,* what he gave to me is what he took from you. *-pa mgongo,* turn the back on. *-pa uso,* face. *-pa radhi,* content, satisfy. *-pa mkono,* congratulate, condole with. *-pa salamu,* salute. *Jipa* varies with the idea attached to the Rf., e. g. *jipa ujinga,* play the fool, be purposely silly. *Jipa mali,* pretend to be rich. *Jipa makuu,* be a grandee, make a foolish show. *Jipa moyo,* take heart, gain courage. *Jipa salamu,* consider oneself safe. *Jipa ubwana,* domineer, tyrannize,—and so on. See **Ji.** Ps. *pewa,* and sometimes *pawa,* with a personal subject only,—be given, be presented with, receive as a gift, e. g. *nimepewa,* I have had a present. Nt. *peka,* seldom used. Ap. *-pea, -pia* (and there is a Nt. *palika* as if from *pa-lia*), give to, &c. *Sumu umenipiani?* What, have you given me poison? Hence *peana, piana,* e. g. *peana mikono (salamu),* conclude a bargain, exchange greetings. Cs. (none in use). Rp. *pana,* e. g. *ahadi (mikono, zawadi),* make mutual promises (engagements, presents). (Cf. *mpaji, kipaji, kipawa,* and *toa.*)

Paa, v. (1) go up, ascend, mount, rise,—like *panda,* which is more common, and cf. *kwea.* Ps. *pawa,* Nt. *palika.* Ap. *palia, palika, paliwa,* e. g. *maji yanipalia rohoni,* phlegm rises in my throat, or *nimepaliwa na maji.* Cs. *paza, paliza,* *pazwa*, raise, cause to rise. *Paza (paliza) sauti*, lift up the voice, speak in a loud tone. *Paza pumuzi*, draw the breath in, inhale (*shusha pumuzi*, exhale). (Cf. *panda, kwea, inua*.) (2) (also *para*), scrape, scrape off, scrape up, e.g. *paa samaki* or *magamba ya samaki*, clean a fish for cooking by scraping off the scales. So of potatoes, gum copal, &c. *Paa moto*, convey fire, by getting a live ember on a sherd, i.e. *twaa moto kwa kigai*. *Paa inchi*, scrape, paw the ground, e.g. as a horse. *Paa karata*, clear off the cards, i.e. win a game (cf. *para, paruza*). Ps. *pawa*. Nt. *palika*. Ap. *palia, palika, paliwa, palilia, palililiwa*, (1) as above, e.g. *unipalie samaki*, clean the fish for me. (2) also esp. of cleaning ground under cultivation, i.e. which has been once hoed, i.e. 'collect weeds off, hoe the surface of the ground.' And *palilia* is used of the subsequent operations, piling grass (rubbish, weeds) in heaps, or round the roots of trees or plants, &c. *Palil-iza, -izwa*, employ in cleaning-work. (3) fig. raise up for (against), stir up feeling, e.g. *paliliza ugomvi*, raise a quarrel (cf. *chochelea, vumbilia*). Cs. *paaza, paazwa*. Used of coarse grinding of grain, or pounding with a pestle and mortar (as contr. with *saga*, fine grinding between mill stones). Rp. *paana*. (Cf. *para, paruza*, and *kuna, komba*.)

Paa, n. (1) (—), a gazelle, esp. one of the very small species which alone exists in Zanzibar and the neighbouring islands, and so represents 'antelope' there, though there is no such generic name. (Names of antelopes, which reach Z. from the mainland, are *kuru, mpofu (pofu), kulungu, kongoni (kuguni), mbawala (mbala), nyumbu*, &c.) (2) (*ma-*), (*a*) the sloping thatched side of a native roof,—the smaller sides or ends being *kipaa*, (*b*) the roof of a hut (in general). Thus *paa la makuti*, a roof of cocoanut-leaf thatch. *Paa la mgongo*, a gable roof. *Mapaa manne*, a four-sided roof. (? Cf. *paa*, v., and *panda*, mount up, or follg.) (3) (*ma-*), bald part of the head, i.e. *paa* (or *para*) *la kichwa*. (Cf. *upaa*, and perh. *paa*, v. scrape.)

Paanda, Paango, n. See **Panda, Pango.**

Paaza, v. grind coarsely,—of grain. (Prob. Cs. i.e. intensive form of **paa** (*para*), scrape (which see). (Cf. also *paruza*.)

Pacha, n. (—, and *ma-*), (1) a twin, one of twins; (2) something resembling another, counterpart. *Zaa (zaliwa) pacha*, bear (be born) twins. *Pacha-pacha*, like twins, similar, e.g. *nyumba hizi ni pacha-pacha*, these houses are a pair, exactly alike.

Pachika, v. secure in a particular position, fix, stick, e.g. *p. mshale*, adjust an arrow to the bowstring. *P. kisu mshipini (kiunoni)*, stick a knife into the girdle (at the waist). *Shada la maua la kujipachika sikioni*, a nosegay to wear over the ear. Also *jipachika*, sit astride of, bestride. Ps. *pachikwa*. Other derivs. seldom occur, e.g. Nt. *pachikia*. Cs. *pachikisha*. (Cf. *futika, chomeka*, and obs. Nt. termination with Act. meaning.)

*****Padre**, n. (*ma-*), a clergyman, a priest. (Portug. Cf. Ar. *kasisi, kuhani*.)

Pafu, n. (*ma-*), a lung,—esp. of a dead animal, i.e. a butcher's or doctor's term. (Cf. *kifua*, and *pumu*, of the living organ.)

Pagaa, v. (1) carry,—esp. as a load, on head or shoulders, but also more generally, e.g. of charms worn on the neck; (2) used of the influence or power of an evil spirit over a man, possess (i.e. perh. carry along against his will). Ps. *pagawa*, e.g. *amepagawa na pepo*, he is possessed by a spirit. Cs. *paga-za, -zwa*, e.g. (1) cause to carry a load, engage as a porter; (2) bring evil on, i.e. illness, calamity, an evil spirit. (Cf. *mpagazi, upagazi*, and follg., and syn. *chukua*, the common word for 'carry' in Z.,—*pagaa* being only used in restricted senses as above.)

Pagao, n. a charm (against possession by a spirit, or other calamity). (Cf. prec. and *upagazi, hirizi, talasimu*.)

Pagua, v. lop, prune, strip off, e.g. boughs, leaves, stalks, fibres,—of trees. Ps. *paguliwa*. Ap. *pagu-lia, -liwa*. (Cf. *pogoa*,—prob. a variant of the above.)

*****Pahali**, n. (—), place, spot, position, situation, locality. (Ar. *mahall*, whence the common *mahali*, —altered to *pahali* to suit the B. locative prefix *pa*.)

Paja, n. (*ma-*), thigh, ham, of human beings,—*kiweo* usually of animals. Also plur. of *upaja*, with same sense.

Paji, n. (*ma-*). *P. la uso*, forehead. Also called *kikomo cha uso*, and *kipaji*. (Dist. follg.)

-paji, a. liberal, generous, open-handed. (Cf. *pa, kipaji, upaji, mpaji*, and syn. *-karimu*.)

Paka, n. (—, or *ma-*, according to size), a cat. *Paka ndume*, a tomcat. A half-wild cat in a town is sometimes called *mnunda*. Dim. *kipaka*.

Paka, v. (1) also **Pakaa**, apply, lay (on), spread (on), usually of some greasy or adhesive substance, i.e. daub, smear, anoint, paint on, e.g. *paka mtoto mafuta*, smear a child with oil (ointment). *P. rangi*, paint. *P. chokaa*, plaster. *P. udongo*, plaster with mud (clay, earth). Ps. *pakwa*. Ap. *pakia*, e.g. of an instrument used for painting, &c. (but dist. *pakia*, put on board ship). Cs. *paka-za, -zwa*, intens. smear, rub on, e.g. *hupakaza mtoto dawa mwili mzima*, they smear the child's whole body with medicaments. (Perh. cf. *kipaku*, a patch, spot, smear, and ? *pakua*.) (2) mark the boundary of, fix the bounds of. *Paka shamba*, mark the bounds of an estate. No Ps. or other deriv. stems seem in use, except Rp. *pakana*, have a common boundary, be adjacent, adjoin, be next to each other,—with a Cs. *pakanisha*, lay out side by side, cause to adjoin. Other parts are supplied by *mpaka* with various verbs. (Cf. *mpaka*.)

Pakacha, n. (*ma-*), (1) a light basket,—used for carrying fish or fruit, &c., made by plaiting part of a cocoanut leaf. (Cf. *kikapo*.) (2) night-robber, one who waylays passers-by. (Cf. *mwivi, mnyanganyi*.)

Pakanya, n. rue (Str.).

Pakata, v. hold a child on the knee, lap, or shoulder. Ps. *pakatwa*. Nt. *pakatika*, e.g. *mtoto huyu hapakatiki, afurukuta*, there is no holding this child, he is so restless. Ap. *pakat-ia, -iwa*. Cs. *pakat-isha, -ishwa*. (Perh. cf. *paka*, v., and for the termination *-ta, ambata, fumbata, kamata*, &c.)

Pake, a. form of *-ake*, his, her, its,—agreeing with D 7 (*mahali*), and locatives in *-ni*.

Pakia, v. put (take) on board a vessel,—of passengers or cargo, ship, load a ship with, embark, have on board, stow, pile up. *Wakafanya merikebu, ikapakia vyakula*, they built a vessel, and it was loaded with provisions. Ps. *pakiwa*, be loaded, have on board. Ap. *paki-lia, -liwa*, (1) ship goods (a cargo, passengers, &c.) to (for, in, by, &c.). Also *pakili-za, -zwa*, ship, have shipped, see to the shipping of, contract for freight for, &c. (2) also, lay upon, charge up, lay to the charge of, put on the shoulders of, and more generally, pile up, make heaps of. Hence *pakiliana*, (1) load one on the top of another, pile up in heaps, and (2) of mutual recrimination, countercharges, &c. Cs. *paki-za, -zwa*, get freight stowed on board, see to shipping, contract for freight, with either the vessel (cart, vehicle, boat, &c.) loaded, or the cargo (load, freight), as object. *Pakiza gari*, load a cart. *Pakiza nazi*, ship cocoanuts. *Vitu vipakizwavyo*, exports. *Jipakiza*, take on one's own conscience, charge oneself with, undertake, be responsible for. *Pakiana*, get themselves on board, huddle together on board. (Cf. *upakizi, upakio, pakua*, and perh. *paka*, v.)

Pako, a. form of *-ako*, your, yours, —agreeing with D 7 (*mahali*) and locatives in *-ni*. (Cf. *pa-, -ako*.)

Paku, n. (*ma-*), usually in the dim. form kipaku (which see), a patch, spot, smear, &c. (Cf. *paka*, v.)

Pakua, v. Rv. of *pakia*, take out, take off, unload, e.g. *tukapakua vitu katika mashua*, and we unloaded the luggage from the boat. Commonly of taking cooked food off the fire,—dish up, serve up, bring on the table. Ps. *pakuliwa*. Nt. *pakulika*, e.g. be fit for serving up. Ap. *pakul-ia, -iwa*. Cs. *paku-lisha, -lishwa, -liza*. Rp. *pakuana*. (Cf. *pakia*.)

Pakuogea, n. i.e. *mahali p.*, a place to wash in, bathroom. (So *pakuingilia*, entrance, access; *pakutokea*, outlet, exit.

Palama, v. be unproductive, be unprofitable, e.g. of a tree, which does not bear well, or a town where trade is bad. (Not common, and no common derivatives.)

Pale, a. form of the demonstr. *-le*,—agreeing with D 7 (*mahali*) and locatives in *-ni*, that, that yonder. As an adv. there, in that spot, then, at that time. So *pale-pale*, on the spot, at once, just then, just there. *Pale* indicates distance, and great distance is indicated by prolonging the last vowel and raising the pitch of the voice proportionately, i.e. *palé-é-é*. (Cf. *mle, kule, papa, hapa, hapo*.)

Palia, Palilia, Paliza, &c. See **Paa**, v.

Palikuwa, v. Past Tense of *-wa*, v. be, with pfx. *pa*, of place. Often with *na* in narrative, e.g. *palikuwa na mtu*, there was once a man. (Cf. *pana*, there is, and *na*.)

Palu, n. (*ma-*), also **Paru**, a sweetmeat made of bhang, or opium, with sugar, &c.

Pamba, n. (—), (1) cotton, the produce of the cotton plant, *mpamba*. *Nguo ya pamba*, cotton cloth, calico. (Cf. *sufi*, tree cotton.) (2) sometimes for the common *pambo* (which see), ornament, furniture, fittings. (Cf. follg.)

Pamba, v. adorn, deck out, decorate, embellish,—and of a house, furnish, fit for occupation. *Pamba maiti*, prepare a corpse for burial. *Jipamba*, put on a gay dress (ornaments, &c.). Ps. *pambwa*. Nt. *pambika*. Ap. *pamb-ia, -iwa*, e.g. give a finishing touch to, finish off, e.g. a dish of food for the table. Cs. *pamb-isha, -ishwa*, e.g. undertake to decorate, furnish, &c. Rp. *pambana* (but see **Pambana**). (Cf. *pambo, mpambe, mpambi, mpambaji*, and syn. *rembesha, urembo*.)

Pambaja, v. embrace, clasp in the arms. (Not often in deriv. stems. Cf. *kumbatia*.) n. (—), embrace. *Piga p.*, embrace, v.

Pambana, v. come together, get into contact,—whether pleasant or otherwise,—thus of ships (1) go abreast, lie alongside, or (2) collide, fall foul of each other, jostle together. Ap. *pamban-ia, -iwa*. Cs. *pamban-isha, -ishwa*, e.g. (1) set side by side, bring together, exhibit, compare; (2) set in contrast, cause conflict (opposition, contradiction, confusion) in (or, among), e.g. *pambanisha maneno*, make conflicting statements, show to be contradictory, &c., and of persons, make trouble between, set at variance. Also *pambanya*, of persons and things, browbeat, talk down, discredit, shake the evidence of, &c. (Seems to have no connexion with *pamba*, v. Cf. *mpambano*, and follg.)

Pambanua, v. Rv. of *pambana*, draw apart, pick out, separate from others, and so, discriminate, distinguish, select, clear up, explain. Ps. *pambanuliwa*. Nt. *pambanuka*. Ap. *pambanu-lia*, *-liwa*. (Cf. syn. *eleza*, *fafanua*, and follg.)

Pambaua, Pambauka, Pambauko. See **Pambazua**, &c.

Pambazua, v. seems to be an irreg. Cs. connected with *pambanua*, make clear, explain, e. g. *p. maneno*, speak plainly, make a case clear. Nt. *pambazuka* is chiefly used in a purely physical sense, of the dawn,— become clear, get light, be daytime. *Kumepambazuka*, morning has come. Hence *pambazukia*, dawn upon, e. g. *tumepambazukiwa*, dawn has risen upon us, it has found us asleep, we are late in getting up. (For dawn, cf. *cha*, v., and follg.)

Pambazuko, n. (*ma-*), dawn, light of morning. (Cf prec., also *weupe*, *assubuhi*, *alfajiri*.)

-pambe, a. adorned, dressed up, decorated, e. g. *mnara mpambe*, a decorated tower. (Cf. *pamba*, and *mpambe*.)

Pambo, n. (*ma-*), ornament, decoration, embellishment,—and so of a house, fittings, furniture,—of dress, finery, jewellery, fine clothes, &c. (Includes any kind of personal and other adornment. Cf. *urembo*, for various kinds, and syn. *uzuri*; also *valia* from *vaa*, v., *pamba*, and follg.)

Pambua, v. Rv. of *pamba*, remove adornment, disfigure, disfurnish, &c. Ps. *pambuliwa*. Nt. *pambulika*. Ap. *pambu-lia*, *-liwa*. Cs. *pambulisha*, *-lishwa*. (Cf. *pamba*, and *umbua*.)

Pamoja, a. form of *-moja*,—agreeing with D 7 (*mahali*), and locatives in *-ni*, one, the same. Also as adv., at one place, at one time, all together, unanimously. *Pamoja na*, together with, at the same place (time) as, in company of. (Cf. *-moja*, *mamoja*.)

Pana, verb-form,—agreeing with D 7 (*mahali*), there is, it has. (Cf. *kuna*, *mna*, and see **Pa-**, **Na**.)

-pana, v. Rp. of *-pa*, v. (which see).

-pana, a. (same with D 4 (P), D 5 (S), D 6), broad, wide, flat, level. *Inchi panapana*, a flat country, a plain (cf. *sawa*). *Bahari panapana*, broad, open sea. *Mapana* is used as a n., breadth, broad (flat) side. *Kwa mapana*, breadth-wise, across. (Cf. *upana*, *panua*, and dist. *-nene*, thick, i. e. of measurement through an object, while *-pana* is rather of measurement of a surface, across an object.)

Panapo, verb-form, like *kunako*, *mnamo*, where there is (are, was, were), or, there is (are, was, were) there,—according as *-po* represents the relative or demonstrative. (Cf. *pa*, *na*, *pana*, *po*.)

Panda, v. A. (1) go up, ascend, climb, mount, get upon, ride upon (cf. *kwea*); (2) fig. rise (of price), increase (in number, weight, quantity, &c.) (cf. *zidi*); (3) cover (of a male animal). *Panda chomboni*, go on board a vessel (also *ingia*). *Chombo kimepanda pwani* (*mwamba*), the vessel has run ashore (on a rock). *Panda frasi* (*juu ya frasi*), mount a horse, get on horseback. *Mpanda frasi wawili, hujishuka miguu miwili*, he who mounts on two horses comes down with his two feet. *Atampanda huyu shetani*, this evil spirit will come out of him. *Panda mti* (*juu ya mti*), climb up a tree. Ps. *pandwa*. Nt. *pandika*. Ap. *pand-ia*, *-iwa*, e. g. get up with (to, by, &c.). *Ngazi ya kupandia*, a ladder to get up by. Cs. *pandisha*, *-ishwa*, also *panza*, e. g. cause to go up, raise, hoist, increase. *Panza mtambo* (*na bunduki*), cock the trigger (of a gun). *Amekipanza* *chombo mwamba*, he ran the vessel on a rock. Rp. *pandana*, get on one another, and so (e. g.) overlap, cross each other, lie across each other. (Cf. *pitana, kingamana, paliana*.) Hence *pandan-isha, -ishwa*. (Cf. *pandio, paa, kwea*.) B. sow, plant, set in the ground (whether seed or plant). Obs. *pandikiwa*, be grafted. *Pandik-iza, -izwa*, graft, e. g. *pandikiza chipukizi la mchungwa*, graft a cutting from an orange tree. But possibly this should be *bandikiza*, see **Bandika**. (Other derived stems as above. Cf. *mpanzi, mpandi, mpandaji, mpando, pando*.)

Panda, n. (1) (—, and *wa*-), parting, division, fork, bifurcation, e. g. *njia ya p.*, or *njia p.*, the place where a road divides, or where roads meet, cross-ways. *Panda za mto*, branches (arms) of a river. *Panda za mti*, arms of a tree. *Kijiti cha panda*, a forked stick, for getting down fruit from a tree. (2) a crosspiece, e. g. short arm of a cross (transept of a church). (3) a trumpet. *Piga panda*, blow a trumpet.

Pande, n. (1) (*ma-*), a big piece (part, side), block, mass, lump, e. g. *p. la chuma*, a bar (or lump) of iron; *p. la mti*, a block of wood; *p. la jitu*, a huge giant. (2) plur. of **upande** (which see). (Cf. *kipande*, and prec.)

Pandio, n. (*ma-*), means (act, method) of climbing, e. g. steps cut in a cocoanut stem.

Panga, v. (1) set in a line, put in order, arrange. E. g. *panga mizigo*, set down loads in a row. *Panga asikari*, draw up soldiers in line. Ps. *pangwa*. Nt. *pangika*. Ap. *pang-ia, -iwa*, e. g. arrange for (at, in, with, &c.). Hence *pangil-ia, -iwa*, set rows upon rows, i. e. interpose, intersperse, put in between rows, put in alternate places, e. g. *pangilia mapando*, plant crops in regular rotation, arrange a succession of crops. Also *pangiliana*, succeed in regular order, or rotation. Cs. *pangisha*, often intens., e. g. *pangisha watu karamuni*, see that guests are duly arranged at a feast. Rp. *pangana*, e. g. of people arranging themselves in rows, as soldiers, guests, &c. Also *pangana safu*, fall into line, dress,—of soldiers. (2) hire, rent, take for use on hire. *P. nyumba*, hire a house. *P. moto*, borrow a light for a fire. *Panga* also seems used to mean, let on hire,—the same transaction from another point of view, see below. Ps. *pangwa*, be let on hire, e. g. a house. And sometimes of the person hiring, get on hire. Nt. *pangika*. Ap. *pang-ia, -iwa*. Cs. *pang-isha, -ishwa*, e. g. get a person to let, hire, or, get a person to hire, allow to hire, let to a person. *Nimempangisha nyumba*, I have let a house to him, or, I have rented a house from him. *Unipangishe*, allow me to hire. (Cf. *mpango, kodi, kodisha, ajiri*.)

Panga, n. (*ma-*), a kind of shellfish, bivalve with broad, flat, sharp-edged shell. (Cf. *upanga*, a sword, but dist. its plur. *panga*.)

Pangilio, n. (*ma-*), interposition, succession, alternation, rotation, e. g. *mapangilio la mapando*, rotation of crops. Also of a vein, or lode, of metal, &c. enclosed in rock. (Cf. *panga*, v.)

Pangine, Panginepo, a. and adv., also **Pengine**, form of *-ngine, -ingine*,—agreeing with D 7 (*mahali*) or locatives in *-ni*. Also as adv. elsewhere, anywhere. (Cf. *-ngine, -ingine*, and *pa-*.)

Pango, n. (—, and of size, *ma-*), a hollowed-out place, natural recess, cave, grotto, den, hole, lair of an animal, esp. of a large one. Dim. *kipango*, e. g. of a rat hole. (Cf. *shimo, tundu*.)

Pangu, a. form of *-angu*,—agreeing with D 7 (*mahali*), and locatives in *-ni*. (Cf. *-angu*, and *pa-*.)

Pangua, v. cut off at a single stroke, slash off, remove with one sweep of the arm. (Cf. *upanga*.)

Pangusa, v. wipe, brush, rub clean, dust, e.g. with a brush or cloth. *Pangusa vumbi katika vyombo hivi*, wipe the dust off these articles. Ps. *panguswa*. Nt. *pangusika*. Ap. *pangus-ia, -iwa*. Cs. *pangus-isha, -ishwa*. (Cf. *futa, sugua*.)

Panja, n. (*ma-*), forelock, from which the hair is brushed away on both sides. (Cf. *shungi*.)

Panua, v. also sometimes **Panya**, make broad, broaden, widen, spread apart, open out. *Panua miguu*, sit with legs apart,—also, take long strides. *Panya mwanya*, make a wide gap—between teeth, for beauty. Ps. *panuliwa*. Nt. *panuka*. Ap. *panu-lia, -liwa*. (Cf. *-pana, namua*.)

Panya, n. (—, and of size, *ma-*), a rat,—of any common kind. Dim. *kipanya*, a young rat, a mouse. *Paka akiondoka, panya hutawala*, when the cat is away, the rat is king. (Cf. *buku*, the very large Zanzibar rat. Dist. *panya*, Cs. form for *panua*.)

Panza, v. Cs. of *panda*, for *pand-isha*.

Panzi, n. (*ma-*), (1) a grasshopper; (2) a flying-fish; (3) *panzi ya nazi*, the thin brown rind of the kernel of the cocoanut (Str.). Cf. *panda*, v.

Pao, n. (*ma-*), (1) long thin pole used in making the roof of a native hut, laid across the larger poles (*kombamoyo*) used as rafters, and carrying the thatch; (2) long thin pieces of iron, whether flat or round, e.g. *pao za chuma*, rod iron, iron bars; (3) clubs (in cards, Str.). (Cf. *upao, paua*, and *ufito*.)

Pao, a. form of *-ao*, their, theirs, agreeing with D 7 (*mahali*) and locatives in *-ni*. (Cf. *-ao, pa-*.)

Papa, v. A. (1) tremble, palpitate, flutter, e.g. of the heart,—and so (2) be agitated, doubtful, anxious. *Papa roho*, have a throbbing of the heart, e.g. after running, or a fright. (Cf. *papatika*, and syn. *puma, pigapiga, tekineka*.) B. allow exudation, be porous, let through (a liquid). (In Z. *chuja, vuja* are usual.)

Papa, n. (—), a shark. (Sac. gives twenty names of different varieties. Though common in the surrounding waters, large sharks very rarely visit the roadstead of Z. Dried shark, *papa kavu*, is a favourite relish, and largely imported from the north.)

Papa, adv. Used to strengthen *hapa* (which see), to which it is prefixed. Thus *papa hapa*, just here, at this very place, at this very time, now, on the spot. (Cf. *mumu humu, kuku huku*, and *pa-*.)

Papai, n. (*ma-*), a papaw, fruit of the papaw tree, *mpapai*,—one of the commonest fruits of Z.

Papasa, v. (1) stroke with the hand, touch gently, rub lightly; (2) grope about, feel about, feel one's way in the dark with hands spread out. Ps. *papaswa*. Nt. *papasika*. Ap. *papas-ia, -iwa*. Cs. *papas-isha, -ishwa*. Rp. *papasana*.

Papasi, n. (*ma-*), a kind of tick. (Cf. *kupe*.)

Papatika, v. flutter, move convulsively, flap the wings wildly, e.g. of a fowl. (Cf. *papa*, v.)

Papatua, v. remove the husk or shell (of a vegetable or fruit), e.g. *papatua maganda ya mbaazi*, shell beans. Nt. *papatuka*. (Cf. *ambua, pua, menya, fua*.)

Papayuka, v. be delirious, talk nonsense, chatter foolishly (unintelligibly). Cs. *papayu-sha, -shwa*. (A Rd. form of *payuka*, which see.)

Papi, n. plur. of *upapi* (which see).

Papia, v. eat voraciously, greedily, without regarding or waiting for others. (Cf. syn. *kula kwa pupa*, and *pupa*, from which *papia* seems formed, ? *pupia*.)

Papo, adv. related to *papa*, adv. (which see), as *mumo* to *mumu*, *kuko* to *kuku*,—with *hapo* following, i.e. *papo hapo*, also *papo kwa papo*, in that place or time referred to, there, then.

Papo, n. (*ma-*), a throb, flutter, palpitation, e.g. of the heart, *papo la moyo*. (Cf. *papa*, v. and *papatiko*.)

Papua, Papura, v. tear, claw, scratch, lacerate, rend in pieces, e.g. of wild beasts, birds of prey, thorns, combatants. *Papura uso kwa makucha*, scratch the face with the nails. Also fig. of quarrels, abus , &c. Ps. *papuriwa*. Nt. *papurika*. Ap. *papur-ia, -iwa*, whence *papuriana*. Cs. *papur-isha, -ishwa*.

Papuri, n. (*ma-*), thin cakes flavoured with asafoetida (Str.).

Para, v. also **Paa**, v. (which see), scrape. Rd. *parapara*, e.g. of a horse pawing the ground. — n. (1) (—), a scraping, sliding, gliding (cf. *mpáruzo*); (2) (*ma-*), cake of semsem (Str.); (3) baldness, a bald patch on the head. (Cf. *paa*, n.) *Para la kichwa*, a bald, or shaved, head.

*****Parafujo**, n. a screw, i.e. nail with a spiral groove, — also *msomari wa parafujo*.

Paraga, v. swarm up a tree, climb by grasping with arms and legs, i.e. *kwea kwa mikono na miguu*. (Perh. the idea is 'scrape up' a tree, and so cf. *paa*, *para*, v. and *paruga*.)

Paru, n. (*ma-*). See **Palu**.

Paruga, Paruza, v. (1) be rough, be grating, graze, grate, grind coarsely; (2) fig. be harsh (to), be unfeeling (towards). *Paruza kiberiti*, strike a match. Ps. *paruzwa*. Ap. *paruz-ia, -iwa*. Rp. *paruzana*, e.g. of boats scraping against each other. (Cf. *paa*, *para*, v. and *paraga*.)

Paruparu, adv. roughly, coarsely, —used of rough, untidy work, wanting care and finish. (Cf. *paruza*, *mparuzo*, and *buruga*.)

Pasa, v. concern, befit, be due (to), behove, be a duty, be binding, be of obligation,—including all degrees of moral obligation. Often used in an impersonal way, e.g. *yapasa, imepasa*, it is right, it is a duty, it is proper. Also *imenipasa*, it is my duty, I am bound. *Imekupasaje?* How does it concern you? Ps. *paswa*, e.g. *tumepaswa kwenda*, it is our duty to go. Ap. *pasia, pasiwa*, e.g. *ada zilizompasia jumbe*, the customary privileges of the chief. *Jamaa zake waliompasia*, the relations who had a claim on him. *Killa neno tililompasia maiti*, every proper attention to the corpse. *Pasiwa athabu*, be liable to punishment. Cs. *pas-isha, -ishwa*, e.g. *pasisha huhumu*, pass sentence on, give judgement on, condemn. Rp. *pasana*, be bound to each other, be under mutual obligations, belong to each other. (Cf. for moral obligation, *bidi, juzu, wajibu, wia, funga*.)

Pasha, v. Cs. of *pata* (which see).

*****Pasi**, n. (—, or *ma-*), an iron, —for ironing clothes. *Piga pasi nguo*, iron clothes. (Hind.)

-pasi, a. money-making, avaricious, ambitious, pushing. (Cf. *pata*, *pato*.)

Pasipo, verb-form (person-pfx. of place *pa-*, negative sign *si*, relative of place or time *-po*), 'where there is not,' used most frequently in a prepositional sense, 'without.' *Pasipo hofu*, without fear, fearless, safe. *Pasipo nguo*, without clothes. (Cf. *kuliko*,—used as 'than' in comparisons, and syn. Ar. *billa*.)

Pasiwe, verb-form, negat. subjunct. of *wa*, v., be, agreeing with D 7, i.e. may there not be, that there may not be, without there being.

Pasua, v. cleave, split, tear, rend, burst, blow into pieces, saw in two, make a cut in. Ps. *pasuliwa*. Nt. *pasuka*. Ap. *pasu-lia, -liwa*. (Cf. *kata, raruo, chenga, chanja, tema*.)

Pata, v. The general meaning is

'get,' with a wide range of application to persons and things. Thus (1) get, obtain, find, catch, get hold of, seize, secure, attain; (2) get to be, get at, get to, reach, find means to effect a purpose, succeed in doing; (3) happen to, come upon; (4) be the victim of, suffer, experience. E. g. *p. mali*, get rich; *p. faida*, get profit; *p. hasara*, suffer loss; *pata nguvu*, get strong; *p. homa*, get fever,—thus *nimepata homa*, I have got fever, or *homa imenipata*, fever has seized me, or *nimepatwa na homa*, I am seized with fever. *P. inchi*, reach a country, arrive at land. *Jiwe likampata mtoto*, the stone hit the child. *Kisu chapata*, the knife cuts. *Shoka hili' halipati*, this axe does not cut. *Nikapata kijana wa miaka miwili*, I became a child of two years old. Of time, *hawakupata mwezi mmoja, illa walisikia Sultani amefariki*, they did not pass a month before they heard the Sultan was dead. *Haukupata mwaka*, before a year passed. Sometimes *kupata* is used absolutely as a kind of conjunction. *Kupata njiani mwenzetu akakamatwa na simba*, as it happened, on the way our companion was seized by a lion. *Pata* is specially common in connexion with another verb, in a semi-auxiliary sense, like *kwisha*, the other verb sometimes following without the Infinitive prefix, e. g. *pata kujua*, or merely *pata jua*, get to know, find out. *Nimepata kufanya*, I have succeeded in doing it, I have done it. And in the Subjunctive, it often has the force of a final conjunction, 'in order to, so as to, to get to, so that.' *Akaenda apate kuona*, and he went in order to see. Ps. *patwa*, e. g. be got, be seized, be a victim, suffer, esp. of a calamity, illness, &c. E. g. *patwa na homa*, be attacked by fever; *patwa na hasira*, be seized with fury; *patwa na msiba*, be the victim of a misfortune. Also used of an eclipse, *mwezi umepatwa*, the moon is got hold of, i. e. eclipsed. Nt. *patika*, e. g. (1) be got; (2) be getable, be to be had, be procurable, be obtainable,—but this is commonly *patikana*. *Patika kosani*, be caught in a fault. Ap. *pat-ia, -iwa*, e. g. get for (by, with, in, &c.),—also often, get up to, overtake, attain to. Hence several further derivatives, with specialized meanings, —*patil-ia, -iwa*, e. g. *patilia hasira*, get angry with; *patil-iza, -izwa*, without a noun, cause to get,—usually of some unpleasant consequence, i. e. visit something upon, take vengeance on, remember something against, punish. *Muungu alimpatilizia Farao maovu yake*, God visited Pharaoh for his iniquities. And a further Rp. *patilizana*, of angry recrimination, each trying to inflict something on the other. Cs. *pasha* (or *patisha*), cause to get, cause to have, &c. *Pasha moto*, make warm, heat. *Pasha fetha*, give (lend) money to. *Baridi imekupasha homa*, cold has given you fever. *Ntampasha habari*, I will inform him (cause him to have the news). Rp. *patana*, get each other,—commonly used as 'come to terms, strike a bargain, agree, be reconciled, work harmoniously, harmonize, correspond.' (Cf. *mapatano*, and syn. *lingana, suluhi, afiki*.) Also Cs. *patan-isha, -ishwa*, reconcile, arrange terms between, make peace among. (Cf. -*pasi, pato, upatilizo.*)

Pata, n., or **Patta**, a hinge. (Probably a foreign word, cf. *bawaba*.)

*****Patasi**, n. (—), a chisel. (Cf. *juba, chembeu*.)

*****Pati**, n. name of a kind of coloured cloth.

Patiliza, v. Cs. See **Pata**.

Pato, n. (*ma-*), (1) something got, an acquisition; usu. in plur. *mapato*, gains, receipts, profits, income, revenue (cf. *pata*, v.); (2) a large flat gong of metal, commonly brass. (Cf. *upato*.)

Paua, v. used of preparing the

roof of a native hut, viz. fixing the cross-sticks (*pao*) to which the thatch is fastened. *Paua nyumba*, roof a house. Ps. *pauliwa*. Nt. *pauka*. Ap. *pau-lia, -liwa*, e. g. *ufito wa kupaulia nyumba*, a stick suitable for roofing. (Cf. *pao, upao,* and *paa*, a roof.)

Páuni, n. a pound,—weight or value. (From the English 'pound.')

Pawa, n. plur. of *upawa*, ladle. Dim. *kipawa* (which, however, also means 'present, a thing given,' but not in Z.).

Payo, n. (*ma-*), foolish talk, chatter, nonsense, gossip, blabbing; also of wandering of the mind, del'rium. *Mwenyi payo*, a talkative, gossiping person. *Ana payo*, he is always talking, lets out secrets, does not control his tongue. So *sema mapayo*, talk idly, mischievously, &c. (Cf. *payuka, papayuka, mpayo*.)

Payuka, v. talk foolishly (idly, indiscreetly, unintelligibly, &c.), talk nonsense, blurt out secrets, blab, be delirious. Cs. *payu-sha, -shwa*, e.g. *tembo limempausha*, palm-wine has loosed his tongue. *Homa inampausha*, fever makes him delirious. (Cf. prec.)

Pazia, n. (*ma-*), a curtain, screen (of calico, &c.), awning. (Cf. *chandalua*.)

Pea, v. become fully grown, be completely developed, attain to the highest point (limit, acme of perfection). *Tutazame hatta tende zitakapopea*, let us watch till the dates are fully ripe. (In Z. the Nt. form *pevuka* is commonly used, or the syn. *sitawi*. Cf. *upeo, kipeo, -pevu*.)

Peke, a word used in Z. only with a possessive adjective following, of the form agreeing with D 6 (S), and attaching to an object, state, or action, the attribute of singleness, loneliness, uniqueness. E. g. *mimi peke yangu*, I alone, I only, I by myself. *Nguo hii ni peke yake*, this calico is the only one of the kind. *Wakaa peke yako*, you live alone. So *peke yetu (yenu, yao)*. *-a peke yake*, or *-a pekee*, single, alone, unique, sui generis. *Mtu wa peke yake*, a unique individual, one who has no rival. *Jambo la peke yake*, an extraordinary, unprecedented circumstance. (Cf. *pekee, upweke,* and *ukiwa*.)

Pekecha, v. produce, or affect, by turning something with the hands, and so (1) bore a hole, drill, i. e. *pekecha tundu*,—with a pointed knife, drill, &c. (cf. *zua, tumbua, toboa*); (2) produce fire, i. e. *pekecha moto*, e. g. *wakapekecha moto wakawasha*, they used the firesticks, and lighted a fire, by rapidly twirling a pointed stick (*upekecho*) in a hole in another stick; (3) fig. excite bad feeling, bore, exasperate, e. g. by abuse, noise, or sorcery, &c.; and (4) make a mess of, spoil, e. g. *pekecha kazi*, bungle a job (cf. *boruga, chafua, fujo*). (Cf. *upekecho*. Sometimes *peka* is heard for *pekecha*, and *upeko*.)

Pekee, n. (in Z. usually *upweke, upekee*), being single, singular, alone, lonely, isolated, unique, different from everything else. *Mtu wa pekee*, a solitary man. *Mwenda pekee*, a solitary (and so) dangerous animal. (Cf. *peke, upweke. Pekee* perh. represents *peke yake*.)

Peketeka, v. be arrogant, be scornful, be high and mighty. Ap. *peketek-ea, -ewa*, treat with scorn, be insulting (or, contemptuous) to. (Poss. fig. from *pekecha, peketa*, be stirred up, inflated, conceited. Cf. follg.)

-peketevu, a. scornful, provoking, making discord. (Cf. prec. and *pekecha*.)

Pekua, v. (1) scratch up, scratch about, e. g. like a hen; (2) fig. be curious, inquisitive, prying. Ps. *pekuliwa*. Nt. *pekulika*. Ap. *pekulia*, e.g. hunt for, pry into. (Cf. follg. and *upekuzi*.)

-pekuzi, a. curious, inquisitive, prying. (Cf. prec. and *dadisi*.)

Pele, n. plur. of *upele* (which see), sores.

Peleka, v. sometimes *peeka, peka,* cause to go, send, take, convey, conduct, transmit, move, &c., both of persons and things. Dist. *tuma,* employ, use, send, which is limited (in the simple form) to the use of personal service, though *tumia* is used of an instrument. Thus *nataluma mtu kupeleka mzigo kwako,* I will employ a man to convey the load to your house. *Ntapeleka mtu na mzigo,* I will send a man with the load. *Baniani amepeleka mali kwa kutuma watu wawili,* the Banian has sent the money by employing two men. *Peleka mkono,* move the hand in a given direction, apply the hand, set to work. Ps. *pelekwa.* Ap. *pelek-ea, -ewa,* e.g. send to (for, by, in, &c.). Hence *pelekeana.* Rp. *pelekana,* e.g. accompany each other, all go together. (Cf. *mpelekwa,* and *tuma.*)

Peleleza, v. spy out, reconnoitre, secretly examine, pry into, be curious (or, inquisitive) about. *Peleleza inchi,* spy out a country. *Pel. siri,* pry into secrets. Ps. *pelelezwa.* Ap. *pelelez-ea, -ewa.* (Cf. *mpelelezi,* and syn. *chungulia, tazamia, pekua, dadisi.*)

Pemba, n. an island near Zanzibar, famous for its cloves. (*Wapemba,* the people of Pemba. *Kipemba,* the dialect of Pemba.)

Pemba, v. (1) grasp with a hook, grapple, hook down, e.g. of fruit, *pemba embe,* get mangoes down with a hook; (2) fig. take by a device, outwit, entrap, catch. (Cf. *upembo.*)

Pembe, n. (—), (1) horn, of an animal,—also the substance generally. *Pembe ya nyoka,* snake's horn,—a small white one, considered a valuable medicine (Str.). (2) tusk of an elephant, also ivory generally (cf. *kalasha, buri,* for tusks of different sizes,—*buri,* the larger). (3) a projection, angle, corner. (4) various articles of horn, esp. powder-flask, *tukamvulia pembe tukampa,* we took off his powder-horn, and gave it to him. *Pembeni,* in a corner. *-a pembe, -enyi pembe, pembepembe,* with many angles (corners, projections). *Pembe za inchi,* the uttermost parts of the land, quarters of the globe. *Pembe za mwaka,* the seasons of the year. (Cf. *mwaka.*)

Pembea, v. swing, sway, rock, balance, oscillate. Cs. *pembe-za, -zwa,* set swinging, rock to and fro. (Cf. *ning'inia, wayawaya, yumbayumba.*) — n. swing, see-saw, a European balance. *Funga pembea;* put up a swing. *Kiti cha pembea,* a rocking-chair.

Pembo, n. plur. of **upembo** (which see). (Cf. *pemba,* v.)

Penda, v. like, love, choose, wish, will. Ps. *pendwa.* Nt. *pendeka,* e.g. be loved, be lovable, be popular. Cs. *pendekeza,* cause to be loved, excite affection for. *Jipendekeza,* make oneself pleasant; ingratiate oneself. Ap. *pendea,* e.g. love for (on account of, with, in, &c.), whence *pendewa,* e.g. *pendewa uzuri,* be loved for beauty, and *pendelea,* have a special liking (predilection, bias, propensity) for, be partial to, favour, with Ps. *pendelewa.* Also *pendeleka, pendel-eza, -ezwa,* cause to favour, commend to favour, prepossess in favour (of), recommend, with further deriv. *pendelez-ea, -ewa, -eka.* Cs. *pendeza,* please, be pleasing (popular, attractive, amiable, &c.), cause to like (love, prefer). Hence *pendezwa, pendezea,* e.g. please with (for, in, &c.), and *pendezewa,* be pleased with (something), be pleased. Also *pendeze-sha, -shwa,* e.g. cause to please, make popular, &c. Also *pendezana,* be mutually agreeable, and *pendezan-isha, -ishwa.* Ap. *pendana,* love each other, whence *pendan-isha, -ishwa,* cause to be friends, reconcile. (Cf., among other derivatives, *pendo,* *upendo, penzi, upenzi, upendezi, upendeleo, upendano, -penzi, -penda, -pendwa, -pendelefu*, &c., and as syn. *taka, nia, azimu, kusudia, elekea*, &c. There seems no clear differentiation of meaning between many of the derivatives of *penda*,—the natural resources of the language being in advance of the power to utilize them.)

-**penda**, a. loving—with n. following, e. g. *mtoto mpenda sukali*, a child who likes sugar. (Cf. *penda*, v.)

-**pendefu**, -**pendelefu**, a. kind, loving, inclined to favour, sympathetic. (Cf. *penda*.)

Pendo, n. (—, and *ma-*), love, liking. Also plur. of *upendo*. (Cf. *penda, upendo, penzi*.)

Pengee, n. (—), (1) by-path, roundabout way, and (2) fig. dodge, device, wile. (Cf. *kipengee*.)

Pengi, a. form of -*ingi*, agreeing with D 7 (*mahali*) and locatives in -*ni* (i. e. *pa-ingi*), many.

Pengo, n. (—, and *ma-*), (1) gap, notch, hole, vacant space; (2) fig. defect, flaw. E. g. of a gap between teeth, i. e. *mwanya wa meno*. *Ana pengo*, he has lost a tooth. *Huwinda pazima ili kupatia pengo*, he hunts for a sound part in order to introduce a blemish in it.

Penu, a. form of -*enu*, your (plur.), agreeing with D 7 (*mahali*) and locatives in -*ni*.

Penu, n. (1) plur. of *upenu* (cf. *kipenu*). Also (2) aperture of urinal duct (Kr.). (Cf. follg.)

Penya, v. penetrate, make a way into, get inside, enter, pass into,—like *ingia*, but implying more effort, or purpose, difficulties in the way. *Ameingia mlangoni kwa kupenya, hakupata nafasi*, he got into the door by forcing his way, as there was not room enough. *Penya mwituni*, make one's way through a forest. Ps. *penyewa*. Nt. *penyeka*. Ap. *peny-ea, -ewa*, e. g. *tundu la kupenyea*, a hole to get in by. Cs. *peny-esha, -eshwa, -eza, -ezwa*, cause to go into, force into, insinuate, introduce (by stealth, force, stratagem, &c.). Hence, of slipping money into the hand of another, putting an idea into the mind of another, and so of bribery, undue influence, &c. Hence *penyez-ea, -ewa*. (Cf. *kipenya, mpenyezi*, and follg., and syn. *ingia*.)

Penyenye, n. (—), way (means) of getting in, access, hole, secret plan. (Cf. *mlango, tundu*, and *penya*, v.)

Penyewe, a. form of -*enyewe* (which see, and pa-), agreeing with D 7.

Penyi, a. form of -*enyi*, possessing, with, having,—agreeing with D 7 (*mahali*) and locatives in -*ni*. Also used as a prep. of place, at, in, near, e. g. *penyi mtende*, at the date-tree,—and with a noun to express a single idea, e. g. *penyi miti*, a wooded place, a forest, thicket, *penyi kuchimba mawe*, a quarry.

Penzi, n. (*ma-*), (1) love, liking, pleasure, wish, will; (2) that which is loved, liked, &c. *Mapenzi*, wishes, will, resolve. (Cf. *upenzi, penda*, &c.)

Pèpa, v. reel, stagger, totter, e. g. from weakness, drunkenness, &c. (Cf. *levya, sita, kongoja*, and perh. *pepea*.)

Pepe, n. (*ma-*), empty husk of grain, empty (barren) ear. (Cf. *tete, chembe*.)

Pepea, v. make a current of air, fan, wave (like a fan), wave about in the air. E. g. *wajakazi wamfuata jumbe wampepea*, female slaves follow the chief fanning him. *Pepea mainzi Sultani*, keep the flies off the Sultan with fans. P. *bendera*, wave a flag about. P. *vitambaa*, flourish handkerchiefs. P. *moto kwa kipepeo*, blow up a fire with a fan. Ps. *pepewa*, e. g. be fanned, wafted about, &c. Ap. *pepe-lea, -lewa*, e. g. *kupepelea mwana wali, ufate kupoa*, fan the child's rice for him, to make it cool.

(Cf. *upepo, pepesa*, and perh. *pepa*,— also follg.)

Pepeo, n. (*ma-*), a large fan, punkah. Also to describe a winnowing machine, vane on a tower, &c. (Cf. follg. and *pepea, kipepeo, upepeo*.)

Peperuka, v. be carried by a current of air, blown away, wafted, fly off, soar up. E.g. *nguo itapeperuka kwa pepo*, the dress will be carried away by the wind. Cs. *peperu-sha, -shwa*, blow away. (Apparently, like *pepesuka*, one of the very few compound Bantu words in Swahili, from *upepo*, wind, and *ruka*, fly. Cf. *pepea, pepesuka*.)

Pepesa, v. and **Pepeza**, wink,—the eye,—perh. really a Cs. form of *pepea*, i. e. clear, fan the eye by moving the eyelids, described as *ukope wa juu na chini*, eyelid up and down. Hence also, keep the eye clear (or, steady)— in taking aim, i. e. *pepesa jicho kushika shebaha*. (Cf. *kopesa, ukope, pepea*.)

Pepesuka, v. be shaken in the air, wind-tossed, caused to fly away, caused to wave about, shake, totter. (Perh. from *upepo*, wind, and *suka*, wave, like **peperuka** (which see).)

Pepeta, v. winnow, sift, separate husks, chaff, &c. from grain by shaking and tossing in the air with a flat basket. E.g. *pepeta mchele, wishwa zitoke*, sift rice to get out the husks. Ps. *pepetwa*. Nt. *pepeteka*. Ap. *pepet-ea, -ewa*. (Cf. *chunga, upepo, pepea*.)

Pepeta, n. (—). *P. za mpunga*, grains of rice heated, and then pounded.

Pepetua, v. break open (Str.). (Cf. *popotoa*, perh. a variant.)

Pepo, n. has the meaning of both (1) wind, and (2) spirit. (1) (—), wind. In this meaning *pepo* is used (*a*) as plur. of *upepo*, a wind (which see), and (*b*) as a sing. noun meaning much wind, a high (strong, violent) wind. *Pepo za chamchela*, a whirlwind. *Maji ya pepo*, rain water, fresh water. See **Maji**. *Pepo nyingi*, high winds, so *pepo ya nguvu*. (For chief winds see **Kusi, Kaskazi, Matlai**.) (2) (—), (*a*) a spirit, and esp. an evil spirit, i. e. *pepo mbaya*, or *shetani*. *Pagawa na p.*, be possessed by a spirit. *Punga p.*, exorcize, expel a spirit, by native methods, i. e. dancing, ceremonies, &c. *Mwenyi p.*, a possessed person. *Pepo yule atapanda*, that spirit will come forth,— from a person possessed. (For various names of kinds of spirits cf. *jini, shetani, milhoi, kinyamkela, kilima, dungamaro, mahoka, koikoi, kitimiri, kizuu, kizuka, kizimwe, mwana maua*.) (*b*) the region of spirits, spirit world, unseen world, place of departed spirits, paradise. *P. ya kesho*, the world to come, the life beyond the grave. *P. ya leo*, this world's rest (such as it is),—*pepo* not properly applying to it. *Peponi*, paradise, in paradise, at rest (cf. *rahani, baridini*). *Kama ameingia peponi*, (a man) as happy as if in paradise. (*c*) spirit, essence, strength, life, e. g. of a mild tobacco, *tumbako hii imekufa pepo*, this tobacco has lost its strength. (Cf. *upepo, pepea*.)

Pepua, v. sift, winnow,—like **pepea** (which see).

Pera, n. (*ma-*), guava, fruit of the tree *mpera*.

Perema, n. a disease producing a swelling of the whole cheek (? mumps, cf. *kichubwichubwi*).

*****Pesa**, n. (—, and *ma-*), (1) a pice, the Indian quarter anna, or 3-pie piece, a farthing. The two plurals differ a little in use, like pence (*pesa*) and pennies (*mapesa*). Though the *rupia* is equal to 16 annas, i.e. 64 pice, the actual number of pice obtainable for a rupee varies with the exchange from 64 to 70. (2) money,— in general, where small sums are alluded to (otherwise commonly *fetha*, silver). *Hana pesa*, he is a poor man. *Pesa hapana*, I have no money. *Robo pesa*, a pie, i.e. one-third of a pice. (For other coins cf. *rupia, reale, robo, themuni, robo pesa*.)

Pesi, n. (*ma-*), also **Pezi** (which see).

-pesi, a. quick, light. See *-epesi*.

Peta, v. bend round, bend, bow, curve, fold over, wrap up, make like a ring. *P. ufito,* bend a switch into a bow. *P. mguu,* bend the leg. *P. soruali,* turn up the trousers. *P. nguo,* roll up clothes. *P. uso,* put on an angry look, bend the brows. Ps. *petwa*. Nt. *peteka*. Ap. *pet-ea, -ewa*. Cs. *pet-esha, -eshwa,* e. g. bend round, make into a ring. Rp. *petana*, e.g. be bent round, be bowed, form a ring (a circle, a hoop) (Cf. *pete, petemana, peto, kipeto,* and syn. *kunja, pinda*. Dist. *peta* sometimes used for *pepeta* (which see).)

Pete, n. (—, and for large size *ma-*), a ring, hoop, staple, circle. *Kama pete na kidole,* like ring and finger,—of close contact and attachment. *Pete ya sikio,* ear-ring. Dim. *kipete*. (Cf. *duara, mviringo,* and follg.)

Petemana, v. be bent round, form a ring, be made into a hoop, or circle. Cs. *petamanisha*, make into a hoop (circle), bend round, give a curve to. E.g. *petamanisha fimbo hatta kugotana ncha zake,* bend a stick till its ends knock together. (For the form cf. *-mana, shikamana, fungamana, andamana*.)

Peto, n. (—, and of large size *ma-*), a bag, matting-sack, e.g. used for carrying stones and sand. (Cf. *kipeto, peta,* and for different kinds *kikapo*.)

Petu, a. form of *-etu*, our, ours,—agreeing with D 7 (*mahali*), and locatives in *-ni*. (Cf. *-etu, pa-*.)

Petua, v. turn round, turn over (bottom upwards, upside down), upset, capsize, e.g. *petua chombo,* turn a vessel over. Ps. *petuliwa*. Nt. *petuka*. Ap. *petu-lia, -liwa*. Cs. *petu-sha, -shwa, petuza*. (Cf. *peta,* and syn. *pindua, geuza*.)

-pevu, a. (*pevu* with D 4 (P), D 5 (S), D 6), full-grown, ripe, adult,—of plant or animal growth. *Mwili mpevu,* sound, healthy, well-developed body. *Tende pevu,* ripe dates. (Cf. *pea, pevua,* and syn. *-zima, -bivu*.)

Pevua, v. (1) develop fully, ripen, bring to perfection, hasten the maturity of. Hence (2) over-stimulate, excite unduly, pervert, teach bad ways to, corrupt. *Jipevua,* make a man of oneself, behave like a grown-up person or big man, swagger, be conceited, brag. Nt. *pevuka*. Cs. *pevu-sha, -shwa,* intens., as *pevua*. (Cf. *pea, -pevu,* and syn. *komaa, -iva*.)

Pewa, v. Ps. of *-pa,* give, i.e. be given, be the recipient, have a thing given to one, be presented with, receive. See **Pa**.

Pezi, n. (*ma-*), also **Pesi,** fin,—of a fish.

-pi, in combination with pers.-pfx. forms an interrog. adj., who? which? what? e.g. *mtu yupi?* which person? *mti upi?* which tree? *kitu kipi?* which thing? &c. Also (1) subjoined to verbs, with the meaning 'how? in what way?' e.g. *ntawezapi,* how shall I be able? And (2) contracted for *wapi,* e.g. *kendapi,* where (are you) going? i.e. *unakwenda wapi?* (Cf. *wapi, ngapi*.)

Pia, a. and adv., all, the whole, complete, quite, altogether. Often with *-ote,* giving it emphasis, e.g. *watu wote pia,* all the people without exception. *Ntakupa pia yote,* I will give you the whole lot. As an adv. often in rejoinders (1) all of it, that too, that as well; (2) exactly so, just so. *Nitwae hizi? Pia,* Am I to take these? Yes, all of them, or, those as well. (Cf. *-ote, killa*.)

Pia, n. (—), (1) a top, i.e. the toy, a child's plaything, a humming-top, a whipping-top; (2) *pia ya mguu,* the knee-cap.

Piga, v. strike, beat, hit, give a

blow. This is the common *definite* meaning of *piga*. But *piga* in the simple act. form has also an *indefinite* use, which is at once one of the commonest and most characteristic features of the Swahili language, and also difficult to describe. It is used with a great number and variety of nouns to express the act, action, or effect, which the noun itself most naturally suggests; and even when another verb exists conveying this meaning, *piga* is nevertheless often substituted for it with a peculiar significance and flavour of its own. This is no doubt connected with the original idea of *striking*, but 'striking' in different aspects,—sometimes suggesting its mode, i. e. the suddenness, forcibleness, effectiveness of a stroke, and sometimes the effect on the mind or senses, of what is striking, sensational, moving. It is impossible to enumerate all the nouns with which *piga* is commonly, or may be, used, or the most appropriate renderings,—depending (as they would do) largely on the context in each case, and a knowledge of the alternative verbs for which *piga* is in any particular instance purposely substituted. A few common cases can be given. *Piga* often describes (1) the proper use of a tool (in place of simple *tumia*, *endesha*, &c.), e. g. *p. bomba*, work a pump, *p. randa*, plane (wood), *p. pasi*, iron (clothes), *p. kinanda*, play an organ, *p. bunduki*, fire a gun, *p. hengele*, ring a bell, *p. chapa*, print (a book), *p. kura*, cast lots, *p. bao*, take omens. (2) construction, execution, giving form to something, e. g. *p. fundo*, tie a knot, *p. kilemba*, wear a turban, *p. mbinda (uwinda)*, adjust the loincloth, *p. mstari*, draw a line, *p. bandi*, hem. (3) of a sudden, forcible action, e. g. *p. mbio*, run, *p. kilele*, shout, *p. kofi*, give a box on the ear, *p. miayo*, yawn, *p. mbizi*, dive, *p. teke*, kick, *p. pembe*, butt, *p. mdomo*, bite (of a serpent), *p. misonyo*, whistle, *p. mikambe*, lash out with the leg (when bathing), *p. hodi*, ask admittance. (4) of producing a showy, sensational effect, *p. makuu*, play the grandee, *p. ubwana*, domineer, tyrannize, *p. umalidadi*, wear finery, and simply *p. nguo*, show off clothes, *p. kiburi*, show conceit, *p. pua*, turn up one's nose, carry one's head high, *p. umeme*, lighten (of lightning), *p. moyo konde*, take courage, *p. domo*, brag. Other examples are *p. mikono*, gesticulate. *P. mabawa*, flap the wings. *P. fatiha*, perform a religious ceremony. *P. goti*, kneel. *P. moto*, set fire to. *P. uvivu*, waste time by idling. *P. mafungu*, divide into parts. *P. marafuku*, publicly forbid. *P. shauri*, take formal counsel. *P. vita*, declare (wage) war. Ps. *pigwa*. Nt. *pigika*. Ap. *pig-ia, -iwa*, e.g. strike for (with, at, in, &c.). Also *pig-ilia, -iliwa, -ilika*,—used of special operations, e. g. *pigilia sakafu*, beat a concrete roof,—with rammers (*vipande*) till hard, lit. beat away at. Cs. *pig-isha, -ishwa*, e.g. cause to beat about, flap, wave, e.g. *pigisha tanga*, let the sail flap, *pigisha kiapo*, administer an oath, *pigisha nguo na upepo*, air clothes. Also, *pigisha chombo*, make a vessel pitch, rock, toss. *Pigisha maji*, stir up water,—with intens. force. Rp. *pigana*, e. g. hit each other, fight. Hence *pigan-isha, -ishwa*, cause to fight, set fighting, or, fight hard. Also *piganika, piganiwa*, i.e. be fought for (about, with, in, &c.). (Cf. *mpiga, mpigo, pigo, mapigano, mpiganisho*, and follg.)

Pigano, n. (*ma-*), fighting, battle, skirmish, beating each other. (Cf. prec. and *bishano, vita, shindano*.)

Pigi-pigi, n. (—), also **Pikipiki**, a stick used for knocking down fruit off a tree. Dim. *kipigi*. (Cf. for various kinds of stick *bakora*.)

Pigo, n. (*ma-*), (1) blow, stroke,

beat, e.g. *akawafundisha mapigo ya ngoma*, and he taught the proper beats of the drum. (2) calamity, plague. (Cf. *piga, mpigo*, &c.)

Pika, v. cook, prepare by the use of fire, dress (food), boil (water). Ps. *pikwa*. Nt. *pikika*. Ap. *pik-ia, -iwa*, e.g. cook for (with, in, &c.). *Pikiwa*, be cooked for, have a cook. Hence *pik-ilia, -iliwa, -ilika*, e.g. *nataka unipikilie uji*, I want you to make some gruel specially for me. Cs. *pik-isha, -ishwa*, e.g. get some one to cook, get something cooked, contract for cooking. (Cf. *mpishi, upishi, mpiko*, and ? *pishi*. For ways of cooking cf. *upish*.)

Pila, n. See *Pira*.

*****Pilau**, n. (—), a dish of boiled rice, cooked in the Indian way, with ghee, raisins, &c. (Hind., and cf. *wali*.)

Pili, n. (1) two. *Mosi na pili ndio tatu*, one and two make three. *-a pili*, the second, the next. *-a pili yake*, the next to it (him, her). *Marra ya pili*, the second time (cf. *marra mbili*, twice). *Kwa pili*, the other side, over the page. *Ya pili*, secondly, next,—after *kwanza*, first, in the first place. (Cf. *-wili, mbili*, and for numbers *hesabu, tarakimu, harufu*.) (2) name of a snake.

*****Pilipili** n. (—), pepper, seeds and pods of the plant *mpilipili*. *Pilipili manga*, common black (Arab) pepper. *Pilipili hoho*, red pepper, capsicum,—grown in Zanzibar. (Cf. Ar. *filfil*, and Hind.)

Pima, v. measure, weigh. *P. urefu*, measure the length. *P. mchele*, weigh rice. *Pima maji*, take soundings. Ps. *pimwa*. Nt. *pimika*. Ap. *pim-ia, -iwa*, e.g. *pishi ya kupimia*, a measure to measure with. *Pimiwa nguo*, have cloth measured out to one, receive a measure of cloth. Cs. *pim-isha, -ishwa*, e.g. *pimisha chakula*, superintend the measuring out of food. (Cf. *mpimo, kipimo, pima*, and syn. *kadiri, linga, enenza, hesabu*. The commonest measures of (1) length, are *shibiri, mkono*, or *thiraa, wari, pima*; (2) of capacity, *kibaba, kisaga, pishi*; (3) of weight, *wakia, rathi, pishi, frasila*.) — n. a fathom, two yards (*wari*), six feet, the stretch of a man's arms,—equal to four cubits (*mkono, thiraa*), or eight spans (*shibiri*). (Cf. *kipimo, pima*, v.)

Pinda, v. (1) bend, twist, fold, bend up, strain, put a strain on, make tense (stiff, hard); (2) hem. *P. upindi*, bend a bow. *P. upindo*, make a hem. *Jipinda*, (1) exert oneself, (2) be convulsed, i.e. *pindapinda maungo* (cf. *jinyonga*). Ps. *pindwa*. Nt. *pindika*, e.g. of a trap made by bending a tree, or a bent switch acting as a spring. Ap. *pind-ia, -iwa*, e.g. bend for (with, by, &c.). Cs. *pind-isha, -ishwa*. Rp. *pindana*, e.g. be bent together, be stiff, be tense, have cramp. *Pindana mguu*, have a club foot. (Cf. *pindua, pindamana, upindi, upindo, upindani, pindi, pindo, pindu*, and syn. *kunja, nyonga, peta, songa*.)

Pinda, n. (—, and *ma*-), an animal that has died a natural death, a carcass. (Cf. *kipinda*, and dist. *mzoga*, a dead body (of any kind), *maiti*, usually of a human body dead, *mwili*, of a body, alive or dead.)

Pindamana, v. be bent together, curved, contracted, tense, twisted. gnarled, convulsed, &c. (Cf. *pinda, pindana*, and syn. *kunjamana, petemana, kazana, shupana*.)

-pindani, a. obstinate, unyielding, stiff. (Cf. *pinda*, and *upindani*, and syn. *-gumu, -kaidi*.)

Pindi, n. (—, and *ma*-), a bend, twist, turn, curve, winding, fold, coil, ring; (2) a space or division of time, a time (of something), hour (in a general sense). E.g. *pindi za assubuhi*, morning hours. *Pindi ya chakula*, mealtime. *Pindi za mchana*, times (divisions) of the day. *Wajua pindi atakapokuja*, Do you know the time when he will arrive? *Pindi ya mua*, a ring on a sugar-cane. *Nyoka yapiga mapindi*, the snake coils itself up. *Mapindi ya mto*, windings of a river. Also as conj. when, if, supposing, although, i. e. at the time when, giving time for, allowing for. (Cf. *pinda*, v., *kipindi*, and for 'time' *saa, wakati*, and for 'bend' *kunjo, kombo, tao.*)

Pindo, n. (*ma-*), also **Upindo** (*pindo*), selvedge, border of cloth or of a garment, folded edge, hem. (Cf. *pinda*, v. and prec.)

Pindu, n. (*ma-*), turning, tumbling, somersault. E.g. *fanya* (*piga*) *pindu-pindu*, turn over and over, head over heels. (Cf. *pinda*, v. and prec., also *kichwangomba*.)

Pindua, v. turn over, give an opposite direction to, reverse position of, upset, overturn, capsize; (2) change (into something quite different), turn (into), transform. E.g. *pindua mtumbwi*, overturn a canoe. *Pindua, chombo*, wear ship, put a vessel on another tack, tack. *P. vikombe*, upset the cups. Ps. *pinduliwa. Akapinduliwa gogo*, and he was changed into a log. Nt. *pinduka*, be upset, &c., be changed (into), become, take a new direction. *Lili-popinduka jua kichwani*, when the sun passed the meridian. Hence *pinduk-ia, -iwa*, and *pinduk-iza, -izwa*, cause to fall over (on the other side). Ap. *pindu-lia, -liwa, -lika. Nikupindulie jabali*, let me roll you over the cliff. Cs. *pindu-za, -zwa*, e.g. *pinduza dau huko na huko*, turn a boat first on one side, then on the other,—to get the water out. (Rv. form of **pinda**, v. (which see).)

Pinga, v. (1) cause (be, make) an obstruction, put in the way, obstruct, stop the way, block, thwart, check, oppose, contradict; (2) bet, lay a wager. *Jipinga*, put oneself in the way, oppose. *P. mlango*, fasten (close, bar) the door. *P. shikio la chombo, pinga chombo kwa shikio*, i. e. use the rudder to check, shape the course of, a vessel. *P. njia*, block the road. Ps. *pingwa*. Nt. *pingika*. Ap. *ping-ia, -iwa*, e.g. *pingia mlango*, close the door against, or, put a bar against the door, secure the door. Cs. *pingi-sha, -shwa, pingi-za, zwa*. Rp. *pingana*, oppose each other, bet against each other. *Pingana na mtu*, oppose a person. (Cf. *pingamizi, pingo, pingu, pingua, pingani*, and the very similar *kinga*, and syn. *zuia*. For betting cf. *sharti, weka sharti*.)

Pingamisha, v. obstruct, thwart, use as an obstacle or bar,—like *pinga*, but with intens. force, of active, intentional opposition.

Pingamizi, n. (*ma-*), that which obstructs, person or thing, a difficulty, obstacle, check, stop. (Cf. *pinga*, and follg.)

-pingani, a. obstructive, contradictory, causing difficulty,—usually of persons. (Cf. *pinga*, and prec.)

Pingili, n. (—), the piece of a cane, or similar growth, between two rings or knots. (Cf. *kipingili*, and *pinga*.)

Pingo, n. (*ma-*), barrier, obstruction, bar, e.g. a door-bar. (Cf. *pinga, kipingo, pingu, kipingwa*, and for door-bar, *komeo, kiwi*.)

Pingu, n. (—, and *ma-*), (1) a fetter, and plur. fetters, i. e. two rings fastened round the leg at the ankle, and connected by an iron bar; (2) also, of a cord fastened round the ankles to assist in climbing a tree; (3) *pingu ya sikio*, a round piece or ring of wood, often ebony, worn in the lobe of the ear by women. (Cf. *jasi, kipini*, also *pingo, pinga*.)

Pingua, v. cut in pieces, cut up, cut in lengths, e.g. of sugar-cane. Ps. *pinguliwa*. Ap. *pingul-ia, -iwa*. (Cf. *pingili, pinga*, and for various kinds of cutting, *kata, pasua, chenga, chanja, tema*, &c.)

Pini, n. (—, and of size *ma-*), haft, handle,—in which a tool or instrument is inserted. (Cf. *kipini*, and for other handles, *mkono*, *utambo*.)

*Pipa, n. (*ma-*), cask, barrel, tub, butt. Dim. *kipipa*. (Hind.)

Pipya, a. irreg. form of -*pya*, new, agreeing with D 7 (*mahali*), and locatives in -*ni*,—for *papya*.

Pishi, n. (—), (1) a measure of capacity for solids, i.e. grain, &c., a dry measure, — equal to 4 *kibaba* (which see), i.e. about half a gallon. (2) it is also used as a measure of weight, corresponding generally to the above, about 6 lb. (3) the vessel used as a measure of capacity. *Kwa mizani ao kwa pishi*, by weight or measure, i.e. of capacity. (Perh. connected with Cs. form of *pika*, i.e. a conventional quantity for cooking purposes. Cf. follg.)

Pisho, n. (*ma-*), cautery, mark made by cautery. (Cf. prec. note, and *pika*, apply fire to, &c.)

Piswa, v. become silly, foolish, doting. Also as n. (*ma-*), foolishness, dotage. (Cf. *kichaa*, *pumbaa*.)

Pita, v. (1) pass, go on, go by, pass by (on, in front of, off, away, over, beyond); (2) fig. surpass, overpass, excel, exceed, outstrip, be too much for. *Pita njia*, go along a road. *Mto wapita*, the river is flowing by. *Mambo yaliyopita*, past events, the past. *Mtu wa kupita*, a passer-by, a wayfarer, a passing traveller. *Yapita cheo*, it passes bounds, is excessive. Hence *kupita cheo*, used as adv., beyond all bounds, extravagantly, abnormally. *Kupita*, as conj., more than,—in comparisons (cf. *kuliko*). *Yule mrefu kupita mimi*, he is taller than I. *Pita juu*, fly through the air. Used (like *enda*) with *zangu*, *zako*, *zake*, &c., e.g. *napita zangu*, I am going away. *Piteni zenu* (Imperat.), go away, pass on. Also in semi-Cs. sense, *njia zinazopita watu*, paths which people pass along. *Shamba linalopita maji*, a garden with a running stream. Ps. *pitwa*. Nt. *pitika*, e.g. be passed, be passable, be able to be surpassed, &c. *Njia inapitika*, the road is passable. Hence *pitikana*, be able to be passed (surpassed). *Haipitikani*, it is unsurpassable. Ap. *pitia*, *pitiwa*, e.g. (1) pass by (away from, to, &c.); (2) pass by on purpose, or by accident, and so slight, neglect, omit; (3) pass away from the mind, be forgotten. *Nimepitiwa*, I have forgotten, it has passed from my memory. Also a further deriv. *piti-lia*, *-liwa*, *-lika*, e.g. pass right by, pass quite away from, be utterly forgotten by, wholly surpass, &c., and with *mbali* (which see), e.g. *amewapitilia mbali*, he has completely outstripped them. *Nimepitiliwa*, I have quite forgotten. Also *pitiana*, e.g. of commercial or social intercourse, pass to (or from) each other, be on good terms, be in constant contact with each other, &c. Cs. *pitisha*, or more commonly *pisha*, *pishwa*, e.g. (1) cause to pass, guide, conduct; (2) let pass, make room for, allow passage to; (3) put away (aside, off), oust, neglect, reject, &c. *Pisha wakati*, spend time. *Pisha mchana* (*masika*), pass away the day (the rainy season). *Mito haipishi*, the rivers do not allow crossing,—like *haipitiki*. *Pishwa tohara*, be put through the ceremony of circumcision. Also n. *Mwenyezi Muungu atakapopisha amri yake*, when Almighty God shall ordain. Hence *pishia*, *pishiwa*, and *pishana*, pass by each other, allow each other to pass, &c. Rp. *pitana*, e.g. pass by each other, overlap. *Mila zao hazikupitana*, their customs were distinct, did not run into each other. (Cf. *pito*, *kipito*, *mpitaji*, and syn. 'go' *enda*, 'surpass' *zidi*.)

Pito, n. (*ma-*), way (means, &c.) of passing, a passage. Not often heard. Dim. *kipito*. (Cf. *pita*, and *njia*, *kijia*, *kichochoro*.)

Po is a form of the demonstrative prefix *pa*, of place,—the *o* (*a*) either denoting reference or relative distance, 'there,' (*b*) or else giving it the force of a relative pronoun, 'where.' See **Pa**, and cf. *ku, ko, mu, mo, -o*.) (1) as a demonstrative, *-po* is used of position in time, as well as place, and also of circumstances generally, and commonly occurs (*a*) in the adv. *hapo, papo*, (*b*) affixed to *ndi-* or the person-pfxs., or parts of the verb *-wa*, and its equivalents, e. g. *yupo*, he is there (here). *Ndipo alipo*, that is where he is, &c. *Alikuwapo*, he was there. *Asiopo, na lake halipo*, out of sight, out of mind. (2) as a relative, with verb-forms generally, referring (*a*) to *mahali* understood, or (*b*) of place, time, or circumstances, 'where, when, as, if, supposing, in case.' (Cf. *-o*, relative.) As a separate word, *po* only appears in such phrases as *po pote*, in whatever place, wherever it be, everywhere. (See **Pa**, and obs. *-po* in *-mojawapo*.)

Poa, v. become cool, and so (heat being a common symptom of illness) improve in health, become well, be cured. *Wali umepoa baridi*, the rice has cooled. *Amepoa ugonjwa*, he has recovered from his sickness. Ap. *poelea, poelewa*, e. g. cool off, cool down, cool itself. Cs. *poza, pozwa*, (1) cool, make cool; (2) cure, heal. *Mganga amenipoza marathi yangu*, the doctor has cured my sickness. (Cf. *pona*, and syn. *burudika*. Dist. *poza* (*posa*), cause to marry, and *pooza*, be withered.)

Podo, n. (—, or *ma-*), quiver, arrow-case,—commonly of wood. (Cf. *ala, uo*.)

Pofu, n. (—), also heard as *bofu*, scum, froth, foam, a bubble. *Pofu la bahari*, foam of the sea. *Fanya pofu*, v., foam, froth. *Hatta pofu ipande*, till scum forms on the surface. (Dist. follg.)

Pofu, and *-pofu*, a. spoiled, bereft, lacking something,—and esp. of lack of sight, blind, i. e. *pofu wa macho*. *Labuda ntakuwa pofu*, I shall perhaps become blind. (Cf. *kipofu*, and follg.)

Pofua, v. spoil, cause to fail, ruin, blight,—but esp. of sight, blind, deprive of sight. *Muungu amempofua macho asione*, God has bereft him of eyes, so that he cannot see. Ps. *pofuliwa*. Nt. *pofuka*. Ap. *pofu-lia, -liwa*. Cs. *pofusha*, intens. of *pofua*. (Cf. *pofu, kipofu*, and variants ? *tofua, tofuka*.)

Pogo, n. and adv., perh. plur. of *upogo*, lopsidedness, a one-sided, awry condition, e. g. *wana pogo za nyuso zao*, they have their faces awry. *Kwenda p.*, walk in an unequal, limping way. *Tazama p.*, squint, leer. (Cf. *upogo*, and perh. *pogoa*, and syn. *mshathali, upande, kitongo, kikombo*.)

Pogoa, v. and variants *bogoa, pagua*, lop, prune, cut away branches or leaves. Ps. *pogolewa*. Ap. *pogo-lea, -lewa*, e. g. *kisu cha kupogolea*, a pruning-knife. (Cf. *pogo, upogo, pagua*, and syn. *chenga, fyeka*.)

Poka, v. take by violence, steal away, rob (of), abduct. *Wataka poka mke wangu*, they want to carry off my wife. Ps. *pokwa*, e. g. *nimepokwa upanga*, I have been robbed of my sword. Ap. *pok-ea, -ewa* (but see **Pokea**). Rp. *pokana*, rob each other (of). (Not common in Z. Cf. *pokonya, nyang'anya*.)

Pokea, v. Ap. form of *poka*, take from some one else,—but without any idea of force or violence, or even of active seizing, as in *poka*, i. e. (1) receive, accept, take in the hand; (2) take in, welcome, entertain, receive as a guest; (3) fig. accept, assent to, agree with. E. g. *wakawapokea mizigo*, they took their loads from them, i. e. in a friendly way, they relieved them. *Ngoma za vita zikapokewa inchi yote*, the war-drums were accepted (acknowledged, attended to), through the whole country. Ps. *pokewa*. Ap. *pok-elea*,

-elewa, e. g. receive for (on behalf of, in the place of, &c.). Hence *pokeleza, -ezwa*, cause to accept. Also *pokelezana*, e. g. *pok. ng'ombe*, take turns in guarding cattle. Cs. *poke-za, -zwa*, cause to receive, gift to, put in the hands of. Hence *pokezana, pokezanya*, e. g. *pok. mizigo*, cause to carry loads by turns, take turns in carrying. (Cf. follg. and syn. *twaa, kabithi, kubali, karibisha*. For Ap. form with a limited sense cf. *amba, ambia, ona, onea, sema, semea*.)

Pokeo, n. (*ma-*), thing received, tradition. (Cf. *pokea, mapokeo*.)

Pokonya, v. take away by force, rob, plunder, abduct, ravish. Ps. *pokonywa*. (Cf. *poka*, whence perh. *pokoa*, and intens. form *-nya*. Cf. Cs. *ponya*, from *pona*. Syn. *nyang'anya*.)

-pole, a. mild, meek, gentle, sober-minded, good-humoured, amiable, kind,—opp. to *-kali*, of temper generally. *-a upole* is more common in same sense. *Pole* is used as an adv., gently, softly, quietly, slowly, &c. Often Redupl. *polepole*. Commonly used to sooth or encourage after an accident, shock, misfortune, bad news, &c.,—be calm, take it quietly, don't excite yourself, never mind (cf. *upole*). The quality implied holds a high place in native estimation, esp. as to Europeans,—contr. *ukali*, and cf. *-ema, -anana, taratibu, kiasi*.)

Poli, n. (*ma-*), forest, wilderness, uninhabited wilds. *Polini hapana nyumba wala mtu*, in a *poli* there is neither house nor inhabitant. (Cf. *pululu, nyika, mwitu*.)

Pombe, n. (—), native beer,—an intoxicant made from many kinds of grain and some fruits, e. g. bananas, by fermentation. In the earlier stage of manufacture, while sweet and unintoxicating, it is called *togwa*. (Cf. *togwa, tembo*.)

Pomboo, n. (—, and *ma-*), porpoise. *Pomboo wazama wazuka*, porpoises dive and reappear.

Pomoka, v. variant (1) for *bomoka*; (2) for *poromoka*. (Cf. *bomoa, poromoka*.)

Pomosha, v. variant (1) for *bomosha*; (2) for *poromosha*. (Cf. prec.)

Pona, v. (1) become safe, escape, be rescued (saved, delivered); (2) get a living, subsist, preserve one's life, live; and esp. (3) get well (from illness), recover health, be convalescent, regain strength. Ap. *ponea, ponewa*, e. g. (1) be saved by (with, for, at, &c.); (2) live on, be supported by, depend on for subsistence (whether food, necessaries, or occupation). *Unaponea nini?* What are you living on? *Aliponea maji siku sita*, he lived on water six days. *Cha kuponea*, subsistence, means of living. Cs. *ponya, ponywa*, e. g. save, deliver, rescue, cure, restore to health. *Uniponye wa jua, ntakuponya wa mvua*, protect me in the sun, and I will protect you in the rain. *Jiponya!* Mind yourself! Look out! (cf. *jihathari, simillah*). Also a further Cs. *pony-esha, -eshwa, ponyeka*, e. g. *haiponyeki habisa*, it is utterly incurable. (Cf. *poa, poza*, and syn. *okoa, hifathi, lisha* from *-la, pata nafuu, salimika*.)

Ponda, v. (1) crush by pounding or beating, pound to pieces, beat small, pulverize, — usually with wooden pestle and mortar (cf. *kinu, mche*). Dist. *twanga*, properly used of same process applied to cleaning grain, i. e. removing the husks, *saga*, of grinding grain to powder by millstones, pressure, attrition. Thus *twanga* is used of rice, maize, millet, &c., *ponda* of such seeds as pepper, curry (*bizari*), and also cassava, &c. (2) fig. crush, take all life and spirit away from, break down, dispirit. Ps. *pondwa*. Nt. *pondeka*, e. g. (1) be crushed, beaten down, pulverized; (2) be capable of being broken in pieces. Hence *pondekea*, e.g. *mtama umepondekea inchi*, the millet is crushed down to the ground, and also *pondekeana*, e.g. of stalks of millet crushed and bruised against each other. Ap. *pondea*, e.g. *amenipondea pilipili kinuni*, she pounded the peppercorns for me in a mortar. (Cf. *pondeo, pondo*, and *twanga, saga*.)

Pondeo, n. (*ma-*), a kind of mallet used by shoemakers. (Cf. prec. and *mnguri*.)

Pondo, n. (—, and *ma-*), a punting pole, for pushing a boat or canoe along in shallow water. *Maji ya pondo hayataki tanga*, shallow water does not require a sail.

Pongezi, n. a congratulatory address, I hope you are well, e.g. after safe return, childbirth, &c. The rejoinder is, *tu salama*, we are well. (Not usual in Z.)

Pono, n. name of a fish, said to be often in a torpid state. *Ana usingizi kama pono*, he is as sleepy as a *pono*.

Ponoa, v. strip off, e.g. of bark from a tree. (Cf. *pogoa, pagua*.)

Ponta, n. also **Punta, Pointa,** back-stitch,—in sewing. *Piga ponta*, as v., back-stitch, e.g. of a wristband or cuff.

Ponya, Ponyeka. See Pona.

Ponyoka, v. slip away, slide out, escape,—of secret, unnoticed or unexpected movement. *Mtu aliponyoka makutini akaanguka*, the man slipped off the thatch and fell. *Bilauri imeniponyoka mkononi*, the glass has slipped out of my hand. Cs. *ponyo-sha, -shwa*, e.g. cause to fall, let slip from one's hand, e.g. (prep.) *amemponyoshea kuku chembe za mtama*, she let a few grains of millet fall out of her hand for the fowl.

Ponza, v. put in danger, risk, speculate with, make a venture, do haphazard, be reckless. *Kaponza roho yake*, he just went at it, took his life in his hand. So *jiponza*. (Not often in Z. Cf. *hatirisha, bahatisha*. Dist. *ponyeza* (*ponza*), Cs. of *ponya, pona*.)

Pooza, v. become useless, withered, paralysed, impotent. *Mwenyi kupooza*, a cripple, an impotent man. Cs. *pooz-esha, -eshwa*, e.g. of the effect of illness,—cripple, disable. (Cf. follg. and syn. *chakaa, fifia*.)

Pooza, n. (*ma-*), something undeveloped, withered, dried up, arrested in growth, esp. of fruit fallen from the tree in a half-formed, withered state. Dim. *kipooza*. Also *-pooza*, a., undeveloped, withered. (Cf. *pooza*, v.)

Popo, n. (—, and of size *ma-*), a bat, a large bat. (Cf. *kipopo*, commonly used.)

Popoo, n. (*ma-*), (1) the areca nut, fruit of the *mpopoo*. Cut in thin slices, it is much used for chewing with *tambuu*, &c. in Z. See **Uraibu.** (2) a ball of iron or lead, bullet.

Popotoa, v. wrench, twist, strain, distort. E.g. *mlango ukafungwa ukapopotolewa*, the door was fastened and then wrenched open. *Popotoa mkono*, twist the hand,—so as to make the joints crack. Ps. *popotolewa*. Nt. *popotoka*, e.g. of a sprained ankle. Ap. *popoto-lea, -lewa*. Cs. *popoto-sha, -shwa*. (Cf. *potoa*, of which it seems a reduplicated form, and *pepetua*, a possible variant.)

Pora, n. (*ma-*), a young cockerel, not yet old enough to crow,—described as *pora la jimbi lianzalo kuondokea*, i.e. beginning to grow up. (Cf. *jimbi, jogoo, kuku*.)

Poroja, n. porridge, or anything of similar consistency. *Wali poroja*, rice cooked with too much water. *Poroja la chokaa*, watery mortar. Also as v. (*poroa*, or *poroja*), be watery, like gruel.

Poromoka, v. (also heard as *boromoka, boromosha*, and perh. *pomoka*), glide or slip down in a mass, or with a rush (like an avalanche, cataract, or stone-slide),—be poured out, gush out like a flood, be discharged, rush down, fall in a shower, or fit of terror, collapse. *P. mnazi*, slide down a cocoanut tree. *P. mlima*, rush down a hill. *Poromoka* is used of a banana plant bending down with its load of fruit. Ap. *poromok-ea, -ewa*. Cs. *poromo-sha, -shwa*, and *pomosha*, e. g. *p. nazi*, shower down cocoanuts from a tree, *p. mavi*, empty the bowels. *Akalipomosha sanduku*, he let the box come down with a rush. Obs. also *jiporomoa*, roll or rush down a slope. (Cf. follg. and perh. *bomoa, bomoka*, &c.)

Poromoko, n. (*ma-*), (1) place of sudden descent, precipice, steep place, face of a cliff; (2) shower, fall, discharge, rush, e. g. of stones, water, &c. *Maporomoko ya mto*, cataracts, rapids, waterfalls. (Cf. prec.)

Posa, v. and perh. *poza*, ask in marriage, become a suitor for, woo,— the person addressed being the parent or relation in the first place, e. g. *yule mume humposa baba yake*, the man proposes to the woman's father. Ps. *poswa*. Nt. *poseka*. Ap. *pos-ea, -ewa*, e. g. *mali ya kuposea*, money to arrange a marriage with, to marry on. Cs. *pos-esha, -eshwa*, e. g. *mtu wa kuposesha*, a match-making person. Rp. *posana*, agree about a marriage. — n. (*ma-*, or plur. of *uposa*, i. e. *vitu vya uposa*), marriage settlements, gifts, arrangements, &c., with a view to marriage. See also **Poso**. (Cf. follg. and *oa, oza*.)

Posha, v. give rations to, supply with daily food, serve out supplies to. Ps. *poshwa*. Ap. *posh-ea, -ewa*. Rp. *posh-eza, -ezwa*. (Cf. follg. and perh. *poka*, i. e. *pokesha*.)

Posho, n. (—, and *ma-*), rations, daily supply of food, clothing, maintenance,— e. g. such as is given to slaves, soldiers, a wife. (Cf. prec. and *sarifu, riziki, nafuu*.)

Poso, n. (*ma-*), or plur. of *uposo*, application for a bride, demand of marriage, marriage gifts or settlement, wooing. (Cf. *posa, uposo*.)

Pote, a. form of *-ote*, all, agreeing with D 7 (*mahali*), and locatives in *-ni*,—also used as adv., everywhere, in all places, and Rd. *potepote*, everywhere. (See -ote, pa, and dist. *pote*, plur. of *upote*.)

Potea, v. (1) go astray, get lost, wander, be at fault, be ruined, perish; (2) fig. fall away, deteriorate, go to ruin, become reprobate. *Potea* is the common word for material and moral loss, failure, and ruin. Frequently used with an objective pfx. as if a true Ap. form (see note), *kisu kimenipotea*, I have lost my knife, for *nimepotewa kisu* (or *na kisu*). *Akili zimempotea*, he has lost his senses. *Kupotea njia ndio kujua njia*, to lose your way is to know your way. Ps. *potewa*, e. g. incur the loss of, *kupotewa mali*, to lose money. Ap. *potelea, potelewa*,—not often used, except in the common imprecation *potelea mbali*, go and be hanged. Cs. *pote-za, -zwa*, cause to perish, throw away, ruin, corrupt, spoil. Hence *pote-zea, -zewa*, e. g. *alimpotezea maneno*, he quite refuted (thwarted, perverted) his statements. Also *potezana*. Rp. *poteana*, of several objects, get scattered, lose each other. (Cf. *-potevu, upotevu*, also *potoa, -potofu, popotoa*, and *upote*,— all indicating a verb *pota* not in use, but meaning 'be out of the straight, be twisted, askew, set cross-wise.')

Potoa, v. (1) put out of the straight, make crooked (curved, slanting, &c.), turn aside, give a twist to; (2) fig. ruin, pervert, spoil, corrupt. *P. kazi*, spoil work. *P. maneno*, pervert words. *Jipotoa*, behave extravagantly, ruin oneself, e. g. by over-dressing. Ps. *potolewa*, Nt. *potoka*, e. g. be crooked, twisted, spoiled, perverted, &c.,—also be wrong-headed, eccentric, cranky, perverse. Ap. *poto-lea, -lewa*. Cs. *potosha, -shwa*, intens., e. g. *amepotosha* *akili za mtoto asimfuate baba*, he has perverted the child's ideas, so as not to follow his father. (Cf. *potea*, note, and follg. Contr. *ongoa, nyoka*.)

-potoe, a. (*potoe* with D 4 (P), D 5 (S), D 6), out of the straight, crooked,—but usu. in the fig. sense, perverted, perverse, spoilt, headstrong, depraved. (Cf. *potoa*, and follg. The final -*e* is prob. passive, as in -*teule, mshinde*, &c.)

-potofu, a. (*potofu* with D 4 (P), D 5 (S), D 6), used generally as -*potoe*, but with act. as well as pass. force. -*potofu wa mali*, prodigal, wasteful. -*potofu wa akili*, wrongheaded. (Cf. *potoa, potea*, &c.)

Povu, -povu, povua. See pofu, -pofu, pofua.

Poza, v. Cs. of *poa*, i.e. make cool, cure. (Dist. *posa* (or *poza*), ask in marriage, and *pooza*, be withered, paralysed.) — n. plur. *mapza*, healing things, doctor's appliances, hospital stores. (Cf. *poa, pona*, and *dawa*.)

Pua, n. (—), (1) the nose,—and used to describe what resembles (or is supposed to resemble) the nose, e.g. apex of an arch. *Mwanzi wa pua*, nostril, also *tundu la pua*. *Piga pua*, snort. *Sema kipua, semea puani*, speak through the nose. *Ujinga huo wa kuacha kinywa kutia puani*, as silly as to use the nose for the mouth. (2) steel, tempered iron,—also *pua ya chuma, chuma pua*. *Tia pua kishoka*, temper the edge of an axe. (Cf. *chuma*.)

Pua, v. shell, remove from the pod,—of beans, peas, &c. (Str.). (Cf. *pura*.)

Pugi, n. a small kind of dove.

Pujua, v. (1) take the skin off, remove the outside covering, abrade, e.g. *pujua mhindi* (*embe*), e.g. of a cob of maize, or the rind of a mango, i.e. strip off with the fingers (cf. *konoa*, when an instrument is used),—not of the skin of animals. See Chuna. Also (2) fig. *jipujua*, bare oneself, cast off shame, lead a mean, beggarly life. Ps. *pujuliwa*. Nt. *pujuka*. Ap. *puju-lia, -liwa*. (Cf. follg., and *konoa, goboa*.)

-pujufu, a. shameless, beggarly, and in act. sense, wasteful, prodigal. (Cf. prec.)

Pukupuku, adv. lit. in showers, and so, in quantities, wholesale, plentifully. *Jaa pukupuku*, be full to overflowing, e.g. of a measure full till the grain runs over. *Marathi ya pukupuku*, used of a destructive epidemic, killing wholesale. (Cf. follg. and *pukute*, and syn. *farafara, furifuri*.)

Pukusa, v. (1) cause to fall in showers, cause to shower down in quantities, make shed fruit. Hence also (2) throw money about, make liberal presents; (3) make a congratulatory visit to,—with presents, &c. *Pukusa* is used of, e.g. stripping the grains off a cob of maize, leaves or fruit from a tree, giving money to a crowd, destroying lives wholesale (of an epidemic). *Twende tumpukuse*, let us go and offer our congratulations (presents) to him. But *akaupukusa mkoma mzima*, he shook all the fruit off the palm. Ps. *pukuswa*. Ap. *pukus-ia, -iwa*. Cs. *pukusisha, -shwa*. *Pukusa* also occurs as a n. of D 6, a congratulatory present, e.g. *haya pukusa zako, mwanangu*, these are presents for you, my child. (Cf. *pukupuku*, and follg.)

Pukute, n. lit. that which is showered down, or in a condition resembling such. Used of rice, when cooked so that every grain is loose and separate, i.e. *pukute ya wali*, or *wali wa pukute*. (Cf. follg.)

Pukutika, v. fall off in showers, as leaves when withered, or fruit when ripe, also rice when cooked so the grains are dry, not watery. Cs. *pukuti-sha, -shwa*, e.g. *p. umande*, wait, give time, for the dew to fall. *P. mkate*, crumble bread, let fall in crumbs. *P. jasho*, drop with sweat.

Uso wake unapukutisha jasho, sweat is dropping from his face. (Cf. *pukusa, pukute, pukupuku.*)

Puleki, n. (—), also **Puliki** and **Puluki**, a spangle, tinsel ornament.

Puliza, v. (1) blow with the mouth, puff,—and with an object, blow up, fill with air. *P. pumzi*, fill with breath. *P. kibofu*, blow up a bladder, or a football. (Perh. conn. with *pumuzi, puma*, &c., as if *pumuliza*.) (2) let go, let out, let down (or, up), lower, e.g. of a bucket in a well, a rope, fishing-line, anchor, a kite, e.g. *puliza tiara*, let the kite go up, fly the kite. Ps. *pulizwa*. Nt. *pulizika*. Ap. *puliz-ia, -iwa*, e g. (1) blow into, blow up, or (2) let down to (for, in), e.g. *amepulizia mshipi samaki baharini*, he has let down his line to a fish in the sea.

Pululu, n. (*ma-*), wilderness, uninhabited country, forest. (Cf. *poli, nyika, mwitu.*)

Puma, v. throb, pulsate, beat,—like the pulse, heart, &c., e.g. of an abscess, the head in illness. (Cf. *piga, papa, tetema, tutuma.*)

Pumba, n. (—, and *ma-*), also **Bumba**, lump, rolled-up piece, clod of earth, packet. *Kuwa mapumba*, to form lumps, stick together, congeal. Dim. *kipumba*. (Cf. *bumba, donge.*)

Pumbaa, v. be foolish, silly, weak-minded, negligent. *Pumbaa kazi*, take no pains about a job, do it carelessly, be idle. Cs. *pumbaza*, befool, make a fool of, treat as a fool, deceive, play jokes upon. *Jipumbaza*, be stupid on purpose, pretend to be a fool. Hence *pumbazwa*, and *pumbazika*, be made a fool of, be duped, e.g. *p. njia*, miss the way by carelessness. *Msiende mkapumbazike*, do not go playing the fool. (Perh. conn. with *pumba*, and follg., i.e. be lumpish, heavy.)

Pumbu, n. (*ma-*), (1) scrotum, and plur. testicles; (2) affections of the scrotum, hernia, orchitis. *Koko za* (*yai za*) *pumbu*, testicles. (Cf. *pumba*, and prec.)

Pumu, n. (*ma-*), (1) the breathing organ, lung,—esp. of a living animal; (2) any affection of the lung, chest complaint, asthma. (Cf. follg., also *kifua*, and *pafu.*)

Pumua, v. (1) draw breath, breathe, live; (2) get breath, rest, find relief, have breathing time. Cs. *pumuza*, e. g. *nimempumuza kazi*, I have caused him to rest from his labour. (Cf. *pumu*, and follg.)

Pumuzi, n. (—), and **Pumzi**, breath, breathing, respiration. *Paaza* (*pandisha, vuta*) *p.*, draw in the breath, fill the lungs. *Shusha* (*toa*) *p.*, empty the lungs. *Kokota p.* (or, *roho*), draw the breath with difficulty. (Cf. *pumu, pumua*, and follg.)

Pumzika, v. and **Pumuzika**, get breath, rest oneself, take a holiday, stop working. *P. uthia*, have a respite from annoyance. *P. kazi*, rest from work. Ap. *pumzikia*, e. g. *mahali pa kupumzikia*, a resting-place. Cs. *pumzi-sha, -shwa*, e. g. cause (invite, allow) to rest. (Cf. *pumzikio*, and prec. Also syn. *tulia, burudika.*)

Pumzikio, n. (*ma-*) and **Pumziko**, place (time, mode, &c.) of resting. (Cf. prec. and *tuo, kituo.*)

Puna, v. scrape, scrape off, peel, e.g. *p. ganda la mti*, take bark off a tree; *p. ngozi*, scrape a skin clean,—of fat, hair, &c.; *p. hari*, scrape off perspiration; *p. karatasi*, make an erasure,—in writing. Ps. *punwa*. Nt. *punika*. Ap. *pun-ia, -iwa*. Cs. *pun-isha, -ishwa*. (Cf. *kwangua, komba, paa, kuna.*)

Punda, n. (—), donkey, ass. *Punda kiongwe* a mainland (often *Nyamwezi*) donkey, commonly used for burdens in Z.,—in contrast to the large white Muscat donkey, which is much valued for riding purposes. *Punda milia*, zebra.

Punde, adv. a little, just a little,

Y

somewhat, within a little time, just now (then), presently, soon. E. g. *nikaona sijambo p.*, I felt a little better. *Mrefu p.*, a little taller. *Atakuja punde hivi*, he will come shortly. *Umefika p.*, you have arrived lately. *Punde kwa punde*, little by little. (Cf. *kidogo, kitambo*, and opp. *sana, zaidi*.)

Punga, v. (1) wave, swing, sway, move to and fro in the air, gesticulate with, fan, use or cause a rhythmical motion. Thus *p. upepo*, put the air in motion, with a fan, &c., i. e. *kwa kipepeo*. *P. mikono*, sway the arms,—gracefully in walking. *P. hewa*, cool oneself, air oneself, take a change of air,—like *badili hewa*. Hence (2) a common special meaning, of the whole ceremonial of native exorcism,—dancing, drumming, incantations, &c. E. g. *punga pepo*, exorcize a spirit, and with personal object *kupunga mtu*, put a person through the ceremony of exorcism. Ps. *pungwa*. Nt. *pungika*. Ap. *pung-ia, -iwa*, e. g. *pungia mkono* (*kitambaa, nguo*), wave the hand (handkerchief, dress) to, signal to, &c. Cs. *pung-isha, -ishwa*, e. g. *unipungishe upepo*, fan me. *Ntampungisha pepo*, I will have her exorcized. (Cf. *suka, tikisa, pepea*.)

Punga, n. plur. of **upunga** (which see).

Pungu, n. a kind of fish, also a bird of prey.

Pungua, v. grow less, diminish, abate, fail, decrease, e. g. *jua linapungua*, the sun is getting less hot. *Upepo umepungua*, the wind has dropped. *Akili zimempungua*, he is losing his mental powers. Nt. *punguka* (which see). Cs. *pungu-za, -zwa, -sha, -shwa*, make less, reduce, shorten, diminish, &c. E. g. *p. bei*, lower the price. *P. tanga*, reef a sail. *Jipunguza*, humble, depreciate oneself. (Cf. follg. and syn. for 'reduce,' *kata, fupisha, rudisha*.)

-pungufu, a. (*pungufu* with D 4 (P), D 5 (S), D 6), defective, wanting, diminished, scanty. *Mpungufu wa mali*, short of money. *Mwezi mpungufu*, an incomplete month, i.e. one of 29 days. *Mp. wa ungwana*, without a clear title to freedom. —n. (*ma-*), defect, deficiency, something wanting, flaw. (Cf. *upungufu*, and prec.)

Punguka, v. Nt. of *pungua* (which see), grow smaller, get less, diminish, abate, fail. Ap. *punguk-ia, -iwa*, e. g. *anapungukiwa mali*, his resources are failing him. (Cf. prec. and contr. *zidi, ongeza*.)

Punja, v. used in Z. only in the fig. sense, cheat, swindle. Ps. *punjwa*. Nt. *punjika*. Ap. *punj-ia, -iwa*. (Kr. gives the literal sense as 'pound.' Cf. follg., and for syn. cf. *kopa, karamkia, danganya*.)

Punje, n. (—), a grain, i. e. a single grain,—of corn, maize, &c. *Punje moja ya mtama*, a grain of millet. (Cf. prec. and *chembe*.)

Puo, n. (—), nonsense, foolish talk, silly behaviour. (Cf. *puza, upuzi*.)

Pupa, n. (—), eagerness, haste, effort, zeal, eager desire. *Fanya p. ya kwisha kazi*, be eager to finish work. *P. ya kula*, greediness, voracity. *Kula kwa p.*, to eat greedily. *Mtaka yote kwa pupa hukosa yote*, he who wants everything in a hurry loses everything. (Cf. syn. *choyo, bidii, tamaa, tadi*, and perh. *papia*.)

Pura, v. beat, beat out,—e. g. of corn, &c., i. e. thresh ; and of clothes, —clean by beating, i. e. wash in the native way. (Cf. *pua*, v., and *piga, fua*.)

Puruka, v. fly off, be scared away. Cs. *puruk-usha, -ushwa*, i. e. cause to fly off, treat with contempt, slight, make light of, be off-hand with. *Purukusha maneno*, talk heedlessly, discuss superficially. *P. sikio*, listen inattentively. *Jipurukusha*, be flighty, superficial, neglectful, inattentive.

(Seems connected with *ruka*, fly off. Cf. follg.)

Purukushani, n. negligence, superficial treatment, a hasty, careless manner. *Fanya kazi kwa purukushani*, work carelessly. (Cf. prec.)

Purura, v. rub off, strip off, e. g. of rubbing leaves off a branch, by passing it through the hand. (Cf. *para*.)

Puta, v. beat soundly, flog, thrash. Ps. *putwa*. Nt. *putika*. (Not often heard. Cf. *piga, chapa, gonga*, &c.)

Puza, v. be silly, foolish, nonsensical, esp. in talk,—gossip, flirt. *Puza kazi (maneno)*, work (talk) in a silly way. *Jipuza*, play the fool, be good for nothing. Nt. *puzika*, in same sense, e. g. *apuzika na waanake*, he is always fooling with women. Cs. *puzisha*, e. g. amuse, entertain, make sport for (or, of). Ap. *puz-ia, -iwa*. (Cf. *upuzi, -puzi, puo*, and dist. *puza, puzia, puziwa*, as forms of *puliza* (which see).)

-pwa, v. (but *kupwa* in certain tenses, like other monosyllabic verbs, see **Ku-** 1. (d)), dry, become dry, dry up, esp. of the ebb of the tide, e. g. *bahari inakupwa*, the sea is ebbing, *maji yapwa*, the tide is going out. *Maji ya kujaa na kupwa*, flow and ebb of the tide. Ap. *pwea, pwewa*, e. g. of the voice, be dry, hoarse, *sauti imenipwea, nimepwewa sauti*, I am hoarse,—and of a swelling, subside, go down. Also *pwelea, pwelewa, pweleka*, like *pwea*, but also esp. in Ps. and Nt. form of ships running aground, be high and dry, go ashore. Hence *pweleza*, e. g. (1) cause to dry up, (2) run aground. Cs. *pwe-sha, -shwa*, e. g. *Muungu amepwesha maji*, God has dried up the water, caused it to go down. Also *pwesha jipu*, reduce the swelling of an abscess. (Cf. *pwani, kipwa*, and syn. *kauka*.)

Pwaga, v. See **Pwaya**.

Pwani, n. and adv. (strictly a locative form from root *-pwa* (which see)), shore, coast, esp. the part affected by the tide, e. g. *Kilwa pwani yake hupwa sana*, at Kilwa the tide runs out a long way. *Hiyo pwani inchi nzuri*, this coast land is a fine country. *Oga pwani*, bathe on the seashore. (Cf. *-pwa*, v. and *kipwa*, also *ufuo, ufuko*.)

Pwaya, v. (1) also **Pwaga**, used of the final cleaning given to rice, &c., after pounding, removal of all husks, dust, dirt. Ps. *pwayiwa*. Nt. *pwayika*. Ap. *pway-ia, -iwa*, e. g. *nimepwayiwa mchele na watu*, I had my rice cleaned for me. Cs. *pway-isha, -ishwa*. (Cf. *twanga, ponda, kinu*.) (2) be loosely attached, move about freely, not be well fitted or fixed, e. g. of a ring on the finger. (Cf. *legea, cheza*.)

Pweke, n. and a., solitariness, alone. *Mimi ni pweke*, I am by myself,—commonly *peke yangu*. *Hii pweke ni uvundo*, this loneliness is disgusting. (Cf. *upweke, peke, pekee*.)

Pweza, n. a cuttle-fish.

-pya, a. (*mpya* with D 4 (P), D 6, *jipya* with D 5, *pipya* with D 7), new, fresh, recent, novel, modern. (Opp. to *-a kale, -a zamani, -kukuu, -zee*. Cf. for 'young in age,' *mtoto, -dogo*; for 'novel, strange,' *-geni*; for 'fresh in condition, not fully matured,' *-bichi*.)

-pyoro, a. one who cannot be trusted, one who deceives, exaggerates, &c. *Mapyoro*, deceitfulness, exaggeration, double-dealing.

R.

R is used to represent (1) the Bantu *r* sound, which in Swahili is not practically distinguished from *l*, and so not quite so distinct as the English smooth untrilled *r*. Nearly all words of African origin beginning with this sound will be found under **L**; (2) the Arabic *r* sound, which is somewhat stronger than the English *r*, but in Swahili is often assimilated to the Bantu *r*. Nearly all the words given under R will be seen to be of foreign origin.

The rolled or guttural *r* is only used in imitation (conscious or unconscious) of Arabic pronunciation, esp. of *ghain*.

Though not careful to distinguish *r* and *l*, the Swahili recognizes the difference, and preserves it as a rule in words, where needed to make the meaning clear, e. g. *hali*, condition, *hari*, sweat, and in demonstratives such as *yule*.

*Rabbi, n. lord, master,—in Z. only as a title of God,—like *Mola*. (Ar.)

*Radi, n. (—), (1) plan, design, purpose, wish, resolve, e. g. *mmekosa radi ya baba yenu*, you have failed to carry out your father's wish. (Ar. *mradi*, cf. *nia*, *kusudi*, *azima*, *shauri*.) (2) for *rathi*, see Urathi, favour, good pleasure, acquiescence, approval, pardon. *Taka (pata) radi*, ask (obtain) consent. (Ar. Cf. *rithi*, *urathi*, and *ruhusa*.) (3) also Radu, thunder-clap. *Piga radi*, thunder. (Ar. Cf. *ngurumo*.)

*Rafiki, n. (—, and *ma-*), friend,—the most common word. (Ar. Cf. *urafiki*, and syn. *mwenzi*, *mpenzi*, *sahibu*, *msiri*, *mzishi*.)

*Raha, n. rest, repose, peace, tranquillity, passive enjoyment, ideal happiness, bliss. *R. ya peponi*, heavenly happiness. *R. mstarehe*, perfect peace. (Ar. Cf. *sta-rehe*, and syn. *amani*, *ntulivu*, *furaha*, *kimya*.)

*Rahani, n. and Rehani, Rihani, pledge, mortgage, security. *Weka rahani*, deposit as a pledge (in pawn). (Ar. Cf. *amana*. Dist. *rahani*, locat. of *raha*.)

*Rahisi, a. (1) cheap, of small value (contr. *ghali*, *-a thamani*); (2) easy, without difficulties,—and so, light in weight, comfortable, soft (contr. *-zito*, *-gumu*, and syn. *-epesi*). E. g. *njia r.*, an easy road. *Kazi r.*, easy work. *Mzigo r.*, a light load. *Rahisi inavunja upishi*, cheapness spoils the cooking. (Ar.)

*Rai, v. give food to, put food in the mouth of, feed,—esp. as a sign of affection or respect. (Ar. Cf. *lisha*, Cs. of *-la*, v.)

*Rajabu, n. the seventh month of the Arabic year, regarded as esp. sacred, as the month of Mahomed's journey to Jerusalem. (Arab.)

*Rajamu, n. mark, stamp, trademark. (Ar. properly of a stone used as a mark, cf. *anwani*, *chapa*, *alama*.)

*Raka, n. (*ma-*), patch, spot. *Nguo ya rakaraka*, patched, tattered garment. *Kirakaraka*, spotted, speckled, dappled. (Ar.)

*Rakabisha, n. show vigilance (care, attention) as to, act with caution, arrange, provide, prepare. Sometimes also a Nt. *rakabika*, be done or managed with care, &c., and simple *rakabu*, in similar sense. (Ar.)

*Rali, a. (pronounced with deep guttural *r*). See Ghali. (Ar.)

*Ramani, n. and Rahmani, map, chart, plan. (Ar.)

*Ramathani, n. the Mahommedan month of fasting, when nothing is eaten or drunk between sunrise and sunset. (Ar. Cf. *mwezi*, and for fasting, *mfungo*, *funga*.)

Ramba, v. lick. See Lamba.
— n. (1) (*ma-*), a Madagascar grass-cloth, of fine plaited grass with coloured stripes; (2) a kind of knife used by shoemakers (Str.).

*Rambi-rambi, n. words or messages of condolence after a death or disaster. (Ar. See Mbirambi.)

*Ramli, n. sand. In Z. of a divining-board, covered with sand, used for foretelling the future. Hence *piga r.*, use a divining-board, take omens. *Tukaenda katika ramli*, and we resorted to divination. *Weka r.*, try divination. (Ar. Cf. B. *mchanga*.)

*Rammu, n. (with guttural *r*). See Ghammu, Hamu. (Ar.)

*Randa, n. a carpenter's plane. *Piga r.*, plane, v. (Hind.)

Randa, v. dance for joy, gambol, frisk, jump about. (Cf. *cheza, tapa.*)

***Rangi,** n. (1) colouring matter, pigment, paint; (2) colour in general, tint, hue. *Tia (paka) rangi,* colour, paint, apply paint to. *-a rangi,* coloured, painted. *-a rangirangi,* of many hues, variegated. (Hind. The only B. adjs. of colour in Swahili are *-eupe, -eusi, -ekundu,* white, black, red.)

Rarua, v. tear in pieces, tear, rend,—used regularly of a wild animal tearing its prey. Also *rarua nguo,* tear clothes. Ps. *raruliwa.* Ap. *raru-lia, -liwa.* (Cf. *pasua, papura.*)

***Rasha-rasha,** n. *Mvua ya rasha-rasha,* light drizzling rain, drizzle, showers. (Ar. Cf. *marashi, mrashi,* and follg.)

***Rashia,** v. sprinkle, besprinkle. Ps. *rashiwa.* (Ar. Cf. *marashi, mrashi,* and syn. *nyunyiza.*)

***Rasi,** n. (—) also **Ras,** (1) headland, cape, promontory; (2) capital, property, fortune,—commonly *ras il mali.* (Ar. 'head.')

***Rateli,** n. and **Rátel,** a pound-weight. See **Ratli.** (Ar.)

***Rathi,** n. (—), also sometimes **Radi,** (1) contentment, acquiescence, compliance, approval, pardon, favour, sanction; (2) apology, satisfaction offered. E. g. *kwa rathi ya Muungu,* by the favour (blessing) of God. *Alishika rathi na wosia wa baba yake,* he persevered in compliance with the charge of his father. *Taka rathi,* ask pardon, apologize. *Nimetangulia kupokea rathi zako,* I have accepted your apologies in advance. — a. contented, satisfied, willing, ready, consenting. *Ni rathi sana,* I am quite content. *Uniwie rathi,* pardon me, allow me, do not be displeased with me. Also common in the Arab. form *kunrathi,* pardon me. Rp. *rathiana,* agree together, consent, be reconciled, be of one mind. (Ar. Cf. *urathi, rithia, rithisha,* &c., and syn. *kubali, pokea, ithini,* also for Rp. *patana.* Dist. *rathi,* for *radi, mradi,* opinion, purpose, plan.)

***Ratibu,** v. arrange, put in order, settle, fix, make firm and sound. Ps. *ratibiwa.* Nt. *ratibika.* Ap. *ratib-ia, -iwa.* Cs. *ratib-isha, -ishwa,* e. g. get a matter settled, have it arranged. (Ar. Cf. *taratibu,* but *tengeneza, fanyiza* are commonly used.)

***Ratli,** n. also **Ráteli, Rátel,** a weight of about 1 lb., reckoned as equal to 16 *wakia* or ounces. (Ar. For weights, see also **Pishi, Frasila.**)

***Rayia,** n. (—), subject, dependant, tributary. (Arab. for the common *mtu, mtumwa,* dependant.)

***Reale,** n. (—), a dollar,—usually reckoned for commercial purposes as equal in value to two rupees, eight pice. The coin commonly known by the name in Z. is the Austrian Maria Theresa silver dollar, still largely used in Abyssinia, and till lately the only coin widely current in East Africa,—its actual value varying with the demand for trade purposes,—also called *Reale ya Sham,* Syrian dollar. The *reale ya mzinga* is the Spanish pillar dollar (so called from its device). The French five-franc piece is called *reale ya Fransa.* (Span. and Port.)

-refu, a. (*ndefu* with D 4 (P), D 6, *refu* with D 5 (S)), long, high, tall, deep. E. g. *mtu mrefu,* a tall man. *Mlima mrefu,* a high mountain. *Kamba ndefu,* a long rope. *Shimo refu,* a deep pit. Opp. to *-fupi.* (Cf. *urefu.*)

Regea, v. (1) also **Legea** (which see), be loose, slack. (2) Also **Rejea** (which see), return. (Ar.)

-regefu, a. See **-legefu.**

***Rehani,** n. (1) also **Rahani** (which see), pledge, pawn; (2) also **Rihani,** the herb basil (cf. *kivumbasi*);

(3) a kind of calico made at Cutch in imitation of Muscat fabric.

*Rehema, n. mercy, pity, compassion, fellow-feeling,—human and divine. Also an euphemism for death, *fikiliza rehemani*, take to mercy (rest). Cf. *marehemu*. (Ar. Cf. follg. and syn. *huruma*, perh. the same word. *Rehema* in poet. is sometimes *ruhuma*.)

*Rehemu, v. pity, have mercy on, commiserate,—and as an euphemism, end the life of, grant rest to. Ps. *rehem-iwa*, or *-ewa*, e. g. be shown mercy, die. Nt. *rehem-ika*, or *-eka*. Ap. *rehem-ia*, *-iwa*, or *-ea*, *-ewa*, like the Pr. form, show (feel) compassion to (for, by). Cs. *rehem-esha*, *-eshwa*, as Intens., show mercy to, bless, prosper. (Ar. Cf. prec. and *marehemu, huruma*.)

*Reja-reja, n. and adv., retail business, by retail. *Bei (biashara) ya reja-reja*, retail trade. Opp. to *shelabela, jumla*. (? Ar. returns, profits. Cf. *rejea*.)

*Rejea, v. (1) go back, return; (2) fig. refer (to), relate (to); (3) act. turn back, e. g. a will, for *rejeza*, e. g. *rejea wosia*, revoke. Ps. *rejewa*. Nt. *rejeka*. Cs. *rej-eza*, *-ezwa*, return, repay. Hence *rejez-ea*, *-ewa*. Also *rejezana*. Rp. *rejeana*. (Ar. Cf. syn. *rudi*, and follg.)

*Rejeo, n. usu. in plur. *marejeo*, return, requital, repayment, reference. (Ar. Cf. prec.)

*Rekebu, v. use as a vehicle, mount upon, ride, sail, &c.,—whether of animal or machine. Ps. *rekeb-iwa*. Nt. *rekebika*. Ap. *rekeb-ia*, *-iwa*. Cs. *rekeb-isha*, *-ishwa*, e. g. cause to mount up, pile up in a heap, place in position. *Rekebisha mzinga (ngazi)*, mount a cannon (fix a ladder). (Ar. Cf. *marekebu, merikebu*, and the commoner syn. B. *panda*.)

Remba, v. adorn, decorate, make beautiful (showy). Ps. *rembwa*. Nt. *rembeka*. Ap. *remb-ea*, *-ewa*. Cs. *remb-esha*, *-eshwa*. (Cf. *urembo, rembo, rembua, marembo*, and the commoner syn. *pamba*.)

Rembo, n. (*ma-*), ornament, ornamental marking (form, colour). *Marmar ya marembo*, variegated marble, i. e. with streaks, veins, &c. (Cf. prec.)

Rembua, v. Rv. of *remba*, spoil the beauty of, distort, disfigure. *Rembua macho*, show the whites of the eyes. Ps. *rembuliwa*. (Cf. prec. and *umbua*.)

*-reno, a. of Portugal, Portuguese. *Mreno*, a Portuguese. *Ureno*, Portugal. *Kireno*, the Portuguese language.

*Riba, n. interest on money or property, money-lending, usury. *Toa r.*, lend at interest, practise usury. *Mla r.*, one who takes interest, a usurer, money-lender, banker. (Ar. —sometimes, with article, *iriba*. Cf. *faida*.)

*Rihani, n. and Rehani, a sweet-scented herb, sweet basil. Two varieties are known as *r. ya kipata*, and *r. ya kiajjemi*. (Cf. *kivumbasi*.)

Rika, n. (*ma-*), age, time of life, also, a contemporary, one of the same age, equal. So *rika moja, marika mamoja*, of same age. (Cf. *marika* and *umri*.)

*Risasi, n. also Lisasi (which see), and Rusasi, lead. (Ar.)

*Ritha, n. consent, sanction, approval. Rarely used. *Kwa ritha yetu wenyewe*, by our own consent. (Ar. Cf. follg.)

*Rithi, (1) v. (the *th* pronounced as in Eng. *then*, i. e. *dh*), make content, satisfy, please, meet the wishes of. E. g. *mwenyi kumrithi mwenziwe*, one who treats his friend with kindness (courtesy, consideration). *Kama akikurithi, bassi*, if he pleases you, that is enough. Ps. *rithiwa*. Nt. *rithika*, e. g. be satisfied (contented, pleased), acquiesce, approve, consent. Ap. *rith-ia*, *-iwa*, e. g. agree with, consent to, be pleased about, approve, accept, &c. Cs. *rithi-sha, -shwa*, Intens. cause to be content, content, satisfy, please, win approval of, &c. Rp. *rithiana*, and *rathiana*, be mutually agreed, come to terms, be of one mind. (Ar. Cf. *rathi, urathi*, and syn. *pendeza, kubali*. Dist. follg.)

*Rithi, (2) v. (the *th* pronounced as in Eng. *thin*, also **Risi**, see note below), inherit, get by inheritance, be heir. *Rithi mali kwa babaye*, inherit property from his father. *Killa atakayenirithi*, all my heirs. Ps. *rithiwa*, e. g. be left as a legacy, be bequeathed, be disposed of by will. *Ameacha mtumwa huru, asiuzwe wala asirithiwe*, he has left the slave free, so that he cannot be sold or disposed of by will. Also see the Ap. Nt. *rithika*. Ap. *rith-ia, -iwa*, e. g. inherit from (by, for), &c. Cs. *rithi-sha, -shwa*, cause to inherit, instal as heir, do the duty of an executor to. In Ps. receive an inheritance, be made heir. (Ar. *warash, urish*. Cf. *warithi, mrithi, urithi*. The word has become assimilated to the quite different *rithi*, make content (which compare). Cf. syn. *acha*, bequeath, *achiwa*, inherit.)

Riza, n. also **Liza**, door chain, secured by a staple (*tumbuu*) and padlock outside the door.

*Riziki, n. (—), necessaries of life, means of subsistence, food, maintenance. (Ar. Cf. *ruzuku*, and syn. *nafuu, mafaa, chakula, maponea*.)

*Robo, n. (—), (1) a fourth part, a quarter; (2) a quarter dollar, i. e. commonly a half rupee, worth 7–8 pence; (3) any silver coin of similar appearance, e. g. an English shilling. *Robo pesa*, one pie,—of which there are three to the pice, twelve to the anna. This coin is little used in Z. *Kassa robo*, lit. less a quarter, i. e. three-quarters. *Saa tano kassa robo*, five less a quarter, i.e. a quarter to eleven (English time). (Ar. Cf. other coins, *rupia, pesa, reale*, and *themuni*.)

*Róbota, n. (—) and **Robta**, packet, parcel, bundle, bale. *Robota ya nguo*, a bale of calico. Dim. *kirobota*. (Ar. Cf. *mtumba, bahasha*.)

*Roda, n. sheave—of a pulley. (Cf. *kapi*.)

*Roho, n. (1) soul, spirit, life, vital principle,—of man or animals, regarded sometimes as wholly immaterial, e. g. *roho peke yake haina kiwiliwili*, the soul in itself has no body (cf. *kivuli cha roho*, the soul's shadow or ghost),—sometimes as having a substance of some kind, i. e. *nyama ya roho, kitu cha roho*. Cf. *killa chenyi roho*, every living thing (also cf. *uzima, uhai*). Hence (2) breath, as a sign of life, e.g. *kata roho*, die, expire, *kokota roho*, draw breath with difficulty (cf. *pumuzi*); and (3) throat, as the breath-passage, e. g. *chakula kinampalia rohoni*, the food rises up in his throat. *Kaba roho*, seize by the throat (cf. *koo*). (4) heart, as a vital organ, e. g. *roho haipigi tena*, his heart no longer beats, but also distinguished, e. g. *moyo haupigi, roho imemtoka*, the heart does not beat, his spirit is gone. (5) like *moyo*, character, individuality. *Roho yake njema*, he is good, well-principled, trustworthy. *Killa mtu ana roho yake*, every man has his individuality (cf. *nafsi, tabia*). (6) greediness, gluttony, avarice, covetousness. *Una roho*, you are greedy. *Kula kwa roho*, greedy eating. *Fanya roho*, be greedy, covetous (cf. *pupa, tamaa*). (7) sometimes for a spiritual being, spirit, with plur. *maroho* (cf. *pepo, zimwe, mzimu*). *-a roho*, of the soul, spiritual, heartfelt, &c. Also *-a kiroho*, spiritual, immaterial, abstract. (Ar. Obs. the various words compared above.)

*Rojo-rojo, n. and a., of a thick, tenacious, sticky fluid, or substance. (? Ar.)

*Roshani, n. balcony, projecting window. (Ar. window, cf. *dirisha*.)

Ruba, n. a leech. See **Mruba**.

*Rubani, n. (—, or *ma-*), pilot, steersman, guide. (Ar. Cf. *kiongozi, mshiki, msukani*.)

*Rudi, v. (1) turn (come, go) back, return, revert,—sometimes with Infin. of that from which the return is, e. g. *amerudi kutembea*, he has come back from a walk. *Maskini amerudi kuomba*, the poor man has returned from begging. (2) give back, send back, reverse, return, repay, reply to, contradict, e. g. *akawarudi salaam*, and he returned their greeting. *Muungu akurudi mema yako*, may God requite you your goodness. *Mimi siwezi kurudi liliokwisha*, I cannot reverse what is done. *Rudi neno*, contradict, deny, refuse. (3) reprove, correct, reform, punish, e. g. *rudi makosa*, correct mistakes (faults). *Rudi mtoto*, punish a child. Ps. *rudiwa*, e. g. be reversed, be returned, be punished,—*hataki kurudiwa neno lake*, he will not have his words contradicted. *Alirudiwa kwa neno la heri*, he was reformed by a word in season. Nt. *rudika*, e.g. *neno lake halirudiki*, his orders cannot be disobeyed. *Mtoto harudiki*, the child is not amenable to discipline. Ap. *rud-ia, -iwa*, e. g. return to (from, by, &c.), punish for (with, at, &c.). Cs. *rudi-sha, -shwa*, give back, send back, repay, &c. Hence *rudi-shia, -shiwa*, and *rudishana*. Rp. *rudiana*, e. g. return to each other, return all together (by common consent). (Ar. Cf. *marudi, marudio*, and syn. *rejea*, and punish, *athibu, ongoza, tisha*.)

*Rudufu, a. double, twofold, usu. in form **marudufu** (which see). (Ar. Cf. follg.)

*Rudufya, v. make double, double, redouble. (Ar. Cf. prec.)

*Rufaa, n. cargo, provisions for a voyage. *Wakapakia rufaa, killa kitu cha duniani na aina vyakula*, they put stores on board, everything in the world, and all kinds of provisions. (Ar., not common, cf. *masarifu, riziki*.)

*Rufuku, n. also **Rufaka**, prohibition, refusal. *Piga rufuku*, announce (issue) a prohibition, prohibit, forbid. (Ar. Cf. *marufuku*.) — v. prohibit, forbid,—for the common *kataza*. Ps. *rufukiwa*. Ap. *rufuk-ia, -iwa*. Cs. *rufuk-isha, -ishwa*, cause to forbid, forbid stringently. (Ar. Cf. *kataza*.)

*Ruhusa, n. (—), also **Ruksa**, leave, permission, liberty (to act). *Toa r., pa r.*, give leave. *Twaa (pokea, pewa) r.*, receive leave. *Omba r., taka r.*, ask leave. *Ruhusa ya serkali*, official warrant. (Ar. Cf. follg., and syn. *ithini, nafasi*.)

*Ruhusu, v. give leave (to), permit, allow. Ps. *ruhusiwa*. Nt. *ruhusika*. Ap. *ruhus-ia, -iwa*. Cs. *ruhus-isha, -ishwa*, e. g. give leave, get leave. (Ar. Cf. prec.)

*Rujumu, v. stone, kill by stoning. Ps. *rujumiwa*. (Ar., for common B. *piga mawe*.)

Ruka, v. (1) jump, leap, hop, spring, bound, fly, fly up, fly away, pass through the air; (2) pass over, pass beyond, overstep, transgress; (3) omit, leave out, fail to notice. *Ruka mpaka*, pass a boundary, break bounds. Used of any object moving in the air. Ps. *rukwa*, e. g. *rukwa na akili*, lose one's senses,—corresponding to the act. form *akili zinamruka*, his senses are leaving him. Ap. *ruk-ia, -iwa*, e. g. leap on, fly at, assail, attack, e. g. *chui alimrukia kuku*, a leopard pounced on the fowl. Rp. *rukiana*. Cs. *rusha, rushwa*, e. g. of a horse throwing its rider, flying a kite, letting off rockets, splashing up water, making dust fly, &c., driving away birds, &c., throwing a ball. (Cf. follg.)

Ruko, n. (*ma-*), and **Mruko**, leaping, a leap, over-stepping, trespass, omission. (Cf. prec.)

*Rum, n. Constantinople. *Sultani Rum*, the Sultan of Turkey.

Bahari Rum, the Mediterranean Sea. (Ar.)

Rungu, n. (*ma-*), also **Lungu**, club, mace, war-club, knob-kerry. (Cf. for sticks, *bakora, fimbo*.)

*****Rupia**, n. (—), (1) an Indian rupee, now worth about one shilling and fourpence. No gold coins are commonly current in Z., and all cash transactions are in rupees and pice. (Hind. Cf. *reale, pesa, robo*.) (2) a skin disease.

*****Rusasi**, n. also **Lisasi, Risasi**, lead,—the metal. (Ar.)

*****Rushwa**, n. (—), a bribe, commission. *Toa rushwa*, offer a bribe. *Penyeza r.*, give a bribe. *Ku'a r.*, to take a bribe. (Ar. Cf. *kijiri, mlungula*.)

*****Rútuba**, n. damp, moisture, dampness. (Ar. Cf. *maji, mnyefu, chepe-chepe*.)

*****Rutubika**, v. (1) be damp, wet, moist; (2) fig. be refreshed, relieved, cooled. *Roho yao wagonjwa hurutubika kidogo*, the spirits of the invalids were refreshed a little. Cs. *rutubisha*, make damp. (Ar. Cf. *lowa*, and *burudika*.)

Ruzuku, v. supply with necessaries of life, provide for, maintain, support,—used commonly of God's providential care for His creatures, i.e. bless, preserve. E.g. *mtu akimpa maskini kichache, Muungu humruzuku kingi*, if a man gives a little to the poor, God gives him abundance. *Hutaki kumruzuku mtumwa wako*, you will not give your slave daily subsistence. Ps. *ruzukiwa*. Ap. *ruzuk-ia, -iwa*. Cs. *ruzuk-isha, -ishwa*. (Ar. Cf. *riziki*.)

S.

S represents the same sound as in English, and may always be so pronounced. But it must be remembered that (1) in words of Arabic origin, *s* is used for both *Sin* and *Sad*, and is often written for the sound of *Thay*, i.e. the *th* in Eng. 'thin'; (2) a Swahili does not always clearly distinguish *s, sh*, and *z*, even when a difference of meaning in a word is involved, e.g. *sindano*, needle, and *shindano*, struggle, *shavu* and *chafu*, *shanuo* and *chanuo*. Hence somewhat different pronunciations of the same word are heard, and words not found under *S* may be looked for under *Sh, Th*, and *Z*. Obs. esp. *shindika, sindika, zindika*, and cognate words. Moreover when *s* is closely connected with a following consonant, there is a tendency to interpose a vowel sound to give it a separate syllabic force, e.g. *situka* for *stuka, sitiri* for *stiri, simillah* for *ismillah*, &c.

Saa, v. remain over, be left over, e.g. *haikusaa tende hatta moja*, not a single date remained. But the Ap. form is commonly used in this sense, i.e. *salia*, both in the simple and applied meaning,—remain over (for, to, by, in, &c.). Cs. *saza, sazwa*, leave over, cause to remain over, leave unsaid or undone, omit, e.g. *sitasaza kumweleza*, I will not fail to inform him. Hence Ap. *sazia, saziwa*, Cs. *saz-isha, -ishwa*. (Cf. *salio, sazo*, and *baki*.)

*****Saa**, n. (1) an hour, a twelfth part of the day or night; (2) time, period of time; (3) a timepiece, watch, clock. *Saa ya mkono*, a watch. The day in Z. begins at sunset, which is called *saa thenashara jioni*, i.e. twelve o'clock in the evening, about 6 p.m. all the year round, and from it the hours are reckoned on, one, two, three, &c. till 6 a.m., which is called *saa thenashara assubuhi*. The time is asked by *Saa ngapi?* How many hours? i.e. since sunset or sunrise, or *Saa gani?* What hour is it? and the reply is *saa moja, saa kwanza* (or *saa ya kwanza*), one o'clock, i.e. seven in English time, *saa mbili, saa pili* (*saa ya pili*), two o'clock, i.e. eight, *saa tatu* (*saa ya tatu*), three o'clock, and so on. *Nussu saa*, half an hour. *Robo saa*, quarter of an hour. *Saa u robo*, an hour and a quarter. *Saa mbili kassa robo*, an hour and three-quarters, lit. 2 hours less a quarter. A particular time of day is often roughly fixed by indicating the position of the sun, and the expression *jua hivi*, the sun thus. (Ar. Cf. *dakika, mchana, siku, usiku*. Dist. *saa (ma-)* for *satio*, (which see).)

Saa, int. of wonder, impatience, or simple acknowledgement of a call. *Sema saa!* Speak, will you! *Ebu saa*, in remonstrance, don't do that. *Unaumiza saa*, you hurt, I say.

*Saanda, n. See Sanda.

*Saba, n. and a., also commonly Sabaa, seven. *-a saba*, seventh. Sometimes used for *juma*, a week, e. g. *sabaa ngine*, next week. *Sabaa tatu*, three weeks. (Ar. Cf. *sabatashara, sabaini*.)

*Sababu, n. and conj., reason, cause, motive. *Toa sababu*, give a reason, assign a cause. *Hampati kwa sababu hana sababu*, he does not get him because he has no motive to. *Kwa sababu*, and simply *sababu*, because. *Sababu gani?* Why? For what reason? *Kwa sababu ya*, by reason of, on account of, for the sake of, in consequence of. *Sababu nini amekuja?* What is the reason he has come? (Ar. Cf. *ajili, maana, kwa ajili*, &c.)

*Sabaini, n. and a., also Sabuini, seventy. *-a sabaini*, seventieth. (Ar. Cf. *saba*.)

*Sabalkheri, also Subulkheri, the common Arab morning salutation, Good morning. (Ar. Cf. *assubuhi, heri*, and *masalkheri*. The common Hindoo salute is *salaam*, and the common Swahili *jambo*.)

*Sabatashara, n. and a., seventeen. *-a sabatashara*, seventeenth. (Ar. Cf. *saba, ashara*.)

*Sabiki, v. go before, lead the way. (Arab. for common *tangulia*, cf. *takadamu*.)

*Sabuini, n. and a., seventy. See Sabaini. (Ar.)

*Sabuni, n. soap. (Ar.)

*Saburi, n. patience, patient waiting, resignation. *Saburi yavuta heri*, patience brings luck. *S. ni ufunguo wa faraja*, patience is the key of comfort. — v. be patient,— also subiri (which see). (Ar. Cf. *uvumilivu, ustahimili*.)

*Sadaka, n. a religious offering, sacrifice, alms, act of charity, anything done from a religious motive. (Ar. Cf. *sadiki*, and *kafara, thabihu, zaka*.)

*Sadiki, v. believe, give credence to, accept as true (truthful). Ps. *sadikiwa*. Nt. *sadikika*. Ap. *sadik-ia, -iwa*. Cs. *sadiki-sha, -shwa*, e. g. (1) convince, win credence, justify, make out to be true; (2) intens. believe firmly, trust implicitly. — n. and a., truth, true, —but usually *kweli, hakika, amini*. (Ar. Cf. *sadaka*, and follg., also syn. *amini*.)

*-sadikifu, a. (1) prone to believe, credulous; (2) credible, trustworthy, true. (Ar. Cf. prec.)

*Safari, n. (1) a journey, voyage, expedition; (2) for *msafara*, a caravan, company of persons travelling together, an equipped party or expedition. (Such a party in E. Africa commonly includes (*a*) *wapagazi*, porters,—carrying goods and provisions; (*b*) *asikari*, an armed escort, acting also as police; (*c*) *wanyampara* (or *wasimamizi*), headmen, in charge of different detachments; (*d*) *kiongozi*, a leader, or guide,—besides the owner providing for the whole, *tajiri*.) (3) for *marra*, time, turn, instance. *S. hii nakuachilia*, this time I let you off. *S. ngine*, another time. *S. ya pili*, next time. *Funga s.*, get ready, make a start. *Safari!* Time to start! Off you go! Right away! (Ar. Cf. *safiri, msafara*.)

Safi, a. and **Swafi**, (1) clean, pure, clear, bright, lucid. *Maji (nguo, nyumba) safi*, clean water (clothes, house). Cf. *-eupe, -takatifu*. (2) honest, sincere, disinterested. *Moyo wake swafi*, his character is good. *Maneno swafi*, clear statements, straightforward account. — v. make clean. Ps. *safiwa*. Nt. *safika*. But usu. in the Cs. *safi-sha, -shwa*, clean, purify, clear up, set to rights. Ap. *saf-ia, -iwa*, e.g. *amemsafia chuo*, he has corrected the book for him. Also *saf-ilia, -iliwa*, e.g. *msasa wa kusafilia uta*, sandpaper for smoothing the bow. (Ar. Cf. follg. and *usafi, masafi*.)

*__Safidi__, v. clean, clear up, put in order, set to rights, arrange neatly, e.g. of house, effects, or person. Ps. *safidiwa*. Nt. *safidika*, e.g. *maneno yamesafidika*, the statement is clear, straightforward. Ap. *safid-ia, -iwa*. Cs. *safidi-sha, -shwa*, and intens. (Ar. Cf. prec. and *takasa, tengeneza, fanyiza*.)

*__Safina__, n. (—), a ship, a vessel, Noah's ark. (Ar. for common *jahazi, chombo*.)

*__Safiri__, v. travel, engage in a journey or expedition, sail, start. Ap. *safir-ia, -iwa, -ika*, i.e. travel for (in, by, with, &c.). Cs. *safiri-sha, -shwa*, send off, dispatch, see start, give farewell greeting to, &c. (Ar. Cf. *safari, msafara, msafiri*.)

*__Safu__, n. (—, and *ma-*), row, line, rank, series. *Panga (weka) safu* or *kwa safu*, set in rows. *Miti safu safu*, an avenue of trees. *Safu za kaida*, regular rows. (Ar. Cf. *msafa*, and *mstari*.)

*__Safura__, n. bile, biliousness, but also of disease causing a swollen or dropsical condition. (Ar.)

Saga, v. (1) grind, pulverize, triturate, crush to bits; (2) fig. grind down, oppress. Esp. of grinding grain with small native mill-stones, *mawe ya kusagia*, the upper called *mwana*, worked by a handle (*msuso*) on the lower (*mama*). *Saga meno*, grind the teeth. Ps. *sagwa*. Nt. *sagika*. Ap. *sag-ia, -iwa, -ika*. (Cf. *ponda, seta, funda*.)

Sagai, n. (—), javelin, short stabbing spear,—of the Zulus and kindred tribes. (Cf. *mkuke, fumo*.)

*__Sahani__, n. (—), dish, plate, saucer. Dim. *kisahani*. (Ar. Cf. for various dishes, &c., *chombo, chungu*, &c.)

*__Sahau__, v. forget, fail to remember or call to mind, make a silly mistake. Ps. *sahauliwa*. Nt. *sahaulika*. Ap. *sahaul-ia, -iwa*. Cs. *sahauisha, sahau-lisha, -lishwa*. (Ar. Cf. follg., and syn. *pitiwa*.)

*__-sahaulifu__, a. (1) forgetful, inattentive, absent-minded; (2) forgotten. (Cf. prec.)

*__Sahibu__, n. (—), (1) friend, acquaintance; (2) master, lord. *Walikuwa sahibu sana*, they were great friends. Also *masahibu*, friendship. *Nalikuwa na masahibu yake*, I was on familiar terms with him. (Ar. Cf. *rafiki, mwenzi*.)

*__Sahihi__, a. correct, right, free from mistakes, valid, genuine, true. *Mtu sahihi*, a man of unblemished character. *Fanya sahihi*, correct, revise, rectify. — n. attestation, guarantee, signature. *Tia sahihi*, sign, attest. — adv. rightly, truly. — v. correct, put right,—but usu. in the Cs. form *sahihi-sha, -shwa*, (1) correct, put right; (2) pass as right or valid, attest, sign. Ps. *sahihiwa*. (Ar. Cf. *usahihi*.)

*__Saidi__, n. lord, master. See **Sayidi**. (Ar.)

*__Saidia__, v. aid, help, assist, support, countenance, abet. Ps. *saidiwa*. Nt. *saidika*. Rp. *saidiana*. (Ar. Cf. *msaada*, and syn. *auni*.)

*__Saili__, v. ask, inquire (of), question. Ps. *sailiwa*. Ap. *sail-ia, -iwa*, e.g. ask about (for, in), &c. Cs. *saili-sha, -shwa*. (Ar. Cf. *swali*, and syn. *uliza, hoji*. Dist. *sali, sala*.)

*Saisi, n. (—), groom, coachman. (Ar.)

Saka, v. hunt,—of wild animals, birds, &c. (Cf. *msakaji, msako,* and syn. *winda.*)

*Sakafu, n. (—), a floor, or roof, of concrete, laid on poles in the upper stories, and rammed hard. Also of roofing generally, e. g. *sakafu ya chuma,* a roof of galvanized iron. (Ar. Cf. *sakifu.*)

*Sakama, v. (1) stick fast, be caught (held, jammed); (2) fig. be in a difficulty (perplexity, &c.). (Ar. Cf. *saki,* and syn. *kwama.*)

*Saki, v. (1) press close, fit tight (to); (2) affect deeply, come home (to), touch the feelings (of). E. g. of clothes, the stopper of a bottle. *Njaa inasaki,* hunger presses. Ps. *sakiwa.* Cs. *saki-sha, -shwa,* cause to press, make fit closely. (Ar. Cf. *sakama.*)

*Sakifu, v. make a floor or roof of concrete, provide with floor or roof, put a roof on. *Nyumba ime-sakifiwa na mbau juu,* the house was floored with planks in the upper stories. Ps. *sakifiwa.* Ap. *sakif-ia, -iwa.* Cs. *sakif-isha, -ishwa.* (Ar. Cf. *sakafu, dari, ezeka.*)

*Sala, n. (—), prayer, i. e. to God, according to Mahommedan forms and ideas, public worship, divine service, devotions, whether performed with others or alone. The five prescribed hours of prayer are (1) *alfajiri,* an hour or two before sunrise; (2) *aththuuri,* noon; (3) *alasiri,* afternoon; (4) *magaribi,* sunset; (5) *isha* or *esha,* an hour or two after sunset. (Ar. Cf. *sali, msala,* and syn. *dua, maombi.* Dist. *saili, swali.*)

*Salaam, n. (—), also Salamu, greeting, good wishes, compliments. *Salaam* is a common Arab greeting, also used by Hindoos,—in full *Salaam alek* (plur. *alekum*), peace (safety) be with you,—the reply being *wa alek (alekum) issalaam,* and with you peace,—usually accompanied by a gesture, viz. placing the hand on the heart. (Ar. Cf. *salamu, salimu, salama,* and syn. *jambo.*)

Salala, n. (—), meat from near the backbone, the chine.

*Salamu, n. (—), also Salama, and Salaam, (1) safety, security, peace, salvation, sound health; (2) greeting, good wishes, compliments. *Toa s., -pa s.,* greet. *Pana s.,* exchange greetings. *Pokea s.,* receive greetings. *Leta (peleka, chukua) s.,* convey greetings. *Salaam ya mkono,* shaking hands, offer of help. *Umsalimu ndugu yako salamu zangu,* give your brother my greetings. *Kwa salamu na amani,* in safety and peace. *Mizinga ya salaam,* a salute with cannon. *Salamu salimini,* safe and well, quite safe. A common opening of a letter is *kwa fullani salamu sana* (or, *salamu nyingi*). *Na baada ya salamu,* &c., i. e. to so and so all good wishes. And after good wishes, &c. — a. safe, secure, sound, flourishing, well. (Ar. Cf. *salimu,* and syn. *uzima, amani, wokovu.*)

*Salata, n. (—), harshness, unfeeling conduct, sarcasm. (Ar. Cf. *saliti, msalata.*)

*Sali, v. pray (to God), i. e. use the prescribed forms of Mahommedan worship, public or private,—offer prayer (divine service, worship). (Cf. *sala,* and dist. *omba,* in which the idea of earnest request, begging, is the chief one.) *Sali dua,* offer a special request to, make a petition to, God. Ap. *sal-ia, -iwa,* pray for, intercede for, &c., e. g. *mtu aliyekufa husaliwa,* prayers are said over a dead person. *Msala ni mkeka wa kusalia,* a *msala* is a praying-mat. Cs. *sali-sha, -shwa,* e. g. teach forms of prayer to, lead the prayers,—in a mosque, as is done by the *mwalimu.* Also intens. engage in worship. (Ar. Dist. *saili, sali,* petition, question, and *salia* as Ap. of *saa,* v. be left over.)

Salia, v. Ap. of (1) *sali*, v.; (2) *saa*, v.

*****Salihi**, a. good, sound, fitting, useful, proper, in good condition. *Mtu salihi*, a man of good (honourable, unblemished) character. Sometimes as a v. See **Selehi**. (Ar. Cf. *suluhisha, selehi,* and syn. *sahihi*.)

*****Salimini**, adv. in safety, safely,—used in conjunction with *salamu*, e.g. *waraka wako umenifikia salamu salimini*, your letter reached me quite safely. (Ar. Cf. follg.)

*****Salimu**, v. (1) express good wishes to, salute, greet, accost, congratulate; (2) hand over safely, deliver, rescue; (3) give up, surrender, yield, resign, e.g. *wali anakusalimu*, the governor sends his compliments to you. *Nimemsalimu wali fetha yake*, I have paid the governor his money. *Salimu roho*, give up the ghost, die. Ps. *salimiwa*. Nt. *salimika*, e.g. *salimika ajali*, meet one's fate, come to the appointed end, die. Also, be delivered, rescued, be paid off, &c. Ap. *salim-ia, -iwa*, e.g. *unisalimie baba yako*, give my kind regards to your father. Rp. *salimiana*. Cs. *salim-isha, -ishwa*, e.g. (1) cause to be safe, save, rescue; (2) give up, hand over, pay, i.e. intens. *Ntasalimisha roho yangu*, I shall die. *Mali hizi umsalimishe ndugu yangu mkononi*, pay this money into my brother's hand. *Salimisha kwa hila*, betray. (Ar. Cf. *salamu, silimu,* and syn. *toa, lipa, kabithi, ponya*.)

*****Salio**, n. usu. in plur. *masalio*, remainder, residue, remains. *Mas. ya mirathi yake*, residuary estate. (Ar. Cf. *saa*, v. and syn. *baki, sazo*.)

*****Saliti**, v. be harsh (domineering, sarcastic), bring a charge (against), attack, esp. with the tongue. (Ar. Cf. *salata, msalata*.)

*****Saluda**, n. a sweetmeat, made of saffron, sugar, and starch (Str.).

Sama, v. stick in the throat, choke. (Cf. *kwama*, and dist. *kaba*, choke by outside pressure, throttle.)

*****Samadari**, n. (—), a bedstead of foreign, non-African, make, iron or wood. Commonly of Indian beds. (? Hind. Cf. *kitanda, ulili*.)

*****Samadi**, n. (—), manure, cow-dung, dung and ashes mixed. (Ar. Cf. *mboleo*.)

*****Samaki**, n. (—), a fish (of any kind), fish (in general). Kr. gives sixty-three names of different kinds, Sacl. twice as many, and cf. Playfair's *Fishes of Zanzibar*. For some of the commonest cf. *papa, nguru, pweza, taa, changu, dagaa*. *Kambari* is the commonest fresh-water fish. *S. mbichi*, fresh fish. *S. mkavu*, dried fish. *S. ya ng'onda*, cured (sundried) fish. *S. ya chumvi*, salted fish. *Vua samaki*, fish, catch fish. *Tunga s.*, tie (hang up) fish in a row. *Bana s.*, fasten fish in a cleft stick,—to bake by a fire. Cf. *samaki akioza ni mtungo pia*, if one fish is bad, the whole lot (string) is too. (Ar.)

*****Samani**, n. (—), implement, tool, utensil, piece of furniture, movable chattel. *Samani ya chombo*, gear of a ship. (Hind. for the common *chombo*. Dist. *zamani, thamani*.)

*****Samawati**, n. (—), the heavens, the sky, sky-colour, azure. Also *rangi ya samawati* (or *samawi*), sky-blue, blue. (Ar.)

Sambamba, adv. alongside, abreast, side by side, shoulder to shoulder, in line. (Cf. *sanjari*.)

*****Sambusa**, n. (—), a small kind of cake, bun.

*****Samehe**, v. pardon, forgive, remit, pass over, e.g. of offences, debts, &c. *Nimekusamehe kosa*, I have forgiven your mistake. Ps. *samehewa*. Nt. *sameheka*. Ap. *sameh-ea, -ewa*. Cs. *sameh-esha, -eshwa*. Rp. *sameheana*. — a. forgiving, merciful. (Ar. Cf. *usamehe, msamaha, masamaha,* and syn. *achilia, ghofiri*.)

*****Samli**, n. ghee, native butter. (Cf. Ar. *samn*.

Sana, adv. very, much, in a high degree,—used as an intensive of any kind of action or quality, and translatable accordingly, e.g. *kubwa s.*, very great. *Piga s.*, flog soundly. *Sema s.*, speak loud. *Vuta s.*, pull hard. *Kimbia s.*, run fast. *Kaa s.*, remain a long time. And so on. Often with descriptive nouns, e.g. *mtu mganga sana*, a great doctor; *fundi sana*, a good workman. Sometimes doubled for emphasis *sanasana*, or combined with *mno, ajabu*, &c. Also in rejoinder, signifying appreciation, approval,—just so, certainly, I understand, quite right. (? Ar.)

*Sanaa, n. art, work of art, handicraft. (Ar.)

*Sanamaki, n. (—), senna,—the drug.

*Sanamu, n. (—, and sometimes *ma-*), image, idol, likeness, statue, picture, representation, figure. *Ibada ya sanamu*, idolatry. *Piga sanamu*, draw a picture, make a likeness. *Sanamu ya rangi*, a painting. (Ar. Cf. *taswira, mfano.*)

*Sanda, n. shroud, winding sheet, burial cloth,—commonly of thin white calico, i.e. *bafta ya kuzikia mtu*. (Ar. Cf. *mazishi.*)

*Sandali, n. (—), sandal wood,—from the tree *msandali*.

*Sandarusi, n. (—), gum copal,—fossil exudation of the tree *msandarusi*.

*Sanduku, n. (—, and of size *ma-*), chest, box, trunk, case. (Ar. Cf. *kasha.*)

*Sanjari, adv. also Shanjari, Shangari, Chinjari, in Indian file, in column, following each other, e.g. of ships in company, a convoy and consort, e.g. *tukafuata sanjari, mashua zote mbili*, and we followed in company, with both boats. (? Ar. Cf. *vinjari.*) — v. follow in line, escort, accompany,—of ships.

*Sansuri, n. a kind of sword,—also a sword-fish. (Cf. *upanga.*)

*Sarafu, n. (—), also Sarf, Sarufu, Sarifu, (1) small coin, small change; (2) more generally,—exchange, rate of exchange, e.g. *sarafu gani ya mji leo?* What is the exchange in town to-day? (3) a small metal plate or plates worn on the forehead, or neck. (Ar. Cf. *serifu.*)

*Sarifu, v. arrange, set in order, —and esp. of language, use words well (grammatically, in good style), i.e. *sarifu maneno kwa uzuri*. (Ar. Cf. *sarufi*. Dist. *serifu.*)

*Saruji, n. (—), and Seruji, (1) cement, chalk and sand mixed, Portland cement,—also called *udongo wa Ulaya*; (2) saddle, for a horse. (Ar.)

Sasa, adv. now, at this time, at present, in these days. *Sasa hivi*, directly, immediately, at once. *-a sasa, -a kisasa*, of the present day, fashionable, modern.

Sasamlanda, n. borage.

*Sataranji, n. (—), chess. (Ar.).

*Satini, n. grey long-cloth. Varieties are *s. ya Mombee, s. ya Ulaya*. (Cf. *nguo.*)

Satta, n. (*ma-*), lees of cocoanut oil, i.e. *satta la mafuta ya nazi*. (Cf. *shapo, sira.*)

*Sauti, n. (1) voice, sound, noise, —mostly of animals, birds, or instruments, not merely of sound. *Toa s.*, utter a cry. *Paaza s.*, raise the voice, speak loud. *Kwa sauti kubwa*, with a loud voice. (Ar. Cf. syn. B. *mlio*, which includes all kinds of sounds, and *uvumi, shindo, ukelele*, of loud sounds.)

*Sawa, a. (1) like, alike, equal, the same; (2) equal, fair, equitable, just, right; (3) level, smooth, even, flat, straight. *Sawa na, sawa kama*, equal to, like, just as. *Inchi sawa*, flat country, a plain. *Fanya sawa*, e.g. make equal (cf. *sawazisha*), act fairly. — n. like *usawa*, likeness, equality, flatness, &c. *Sawa kwa sawa mimi nawe*, we share equally, have half each. — adv. equally, just the same,—also *sawasawa*. (Ar.

Cf. follg., and syn. -*moja, yule yule, vile vile,* &c.)

*Sawanisha, Sawazisha, v. cause to be like, equal, even, &c., equalize, compare. Ps. *sawanishwa*. (Ar. Cf. *linganisha, pambanisha, fananisha.*)

*Sayidi, n. (—, and *ma-*), also Saidi, Seyidi, lord, master, esp. as a title, and in Z. a title of the Sultan. But also in respectful address, *Sayidi wangu* (*yangu*), Sir,—like *bwana*. (Ar.)

*Saza, v. Cs. of Saa, v. (which see). (Ar.)

*Sazo, n. (*ma-*), remainder, balance, superfluity. *Sazo la matumizi*, credit balance, excess of receipts over expenditure. (Ar. Cf. prec.)

*Sébule, n. (—), indoor reception-room, front room,—usually next the entrance, but sometimes on first floor, e.g. *akapanda darini katika sébule yake*, he went upstairs to his parlour. (? Ar. Cf. *baraza*, which is usually outside.)

*Sehemu, n. (—), part, portion, piece, share. (Ar. Cf. syn. B. *fungu*.)

Sekeneka, v. be syphilized, be infected (ruined, destroyed) by syphilis. Cs. *sekene-sha, -shwa*, infect with syphilis, ruin by disease. (Cf. follg.)

Sekeneko, n. syphilis.

*Selaha, n. (—), and Silaha, a weapon, arms (warlike, offensive). *Twaa* (*shika*) s., take up arms. (Ar.)

*Selehi, v. also Suluhi, Salihi, put in good condition, improve, make agree (with), conduce to, serve (for), be of use (to), be fitting for, reconcile, be reconciled. Ps. *selehiwa*. Nt. *selehika*. Ap. *seleh-ia, -iwa*. Rp. *selehiana*. Cs. *selehisha*, cause to agree, reconcile, make peace between, conciliate. — n. concord, peace, reconciliation, agreement. (Ar. Cf. *mselehishi, salihi, suluhi, -suluhifu*, and syn. *patanisha*.)

*Selo, n. signal of arrival or departure of a ship. (Cf. Eng. *Sail ho!*)

Sema, v. say, talk, converse, speak. *Sema sana*, speak loud. *Sema na*, talk to, converse with. But *sema* with an objective pers.-pfx. means 'speak against, abuse' (cf. *amba*, and *ambia*), e.g. *watu watamsema sana*, people will abuse him soundly. *Jisema* (and *jisemea*), pretend, profess, —to be what one is not. Ps. *semwa*. Nt. *semeka*, e.g. be said, admit of being uttered, pronounced, &c. Ap. *sem-ea, -ewa*, e.g. speak to, address, say to (contr. *ambia*, which introduces the words used). *Semea puani*, speak with a nasal twang. Hence *semeana*. Cs. *sem-esha, -eshwa, -eza, -ezwa*, and hence *semezana*, hold a conversation together, wrangle. Rp. *semana*, abuse each other.

*Semaa wa taa, an Arabic phrase sometimes heard,—hear and obey, to hear is to obey. (Cf. *tii, taa*.)

Sembuse, adv. much more, much less, not to speak of. (Also heard as *seuze*, ? a form of *usiuze*, i.e. *usiulizie*, do not ask about. Cf. *licha*.)

Seneza, v. and Seza, smooth (with an adze), flatten, take off projections, edges, blunt. Ps. *senezwa*. Nt. *senezeka*. (Cf. *sezo*. Cs. of *senea*, become smooth, blunt, &c., not common in Z.)

Seng'enge, n. (*ma-*), brass or copper wire,—made into rings or spiral twists, as bracelets and anklets. Hence of brass wire in general. (Cf. *masango*.)

Sengenya, v. calumniate, backbite, attack by secret or underhand insinuations. Ps. *sengenywa*. Rp. *sengenyana*. (Cf. syn. *singizia, amba*.)

*Senturi, n. and Santuri, musical box or similar music machine.

*Serahangi, n. (—), headman of a crew, or of part of a crew,—mate, boatswain, serang. (Hind.)

*Serakali, n. (—), and Serikali, Serkali, official executive, government, court, public authorities. *Mtu wa s.*, an official. *Fetha ya s.*, public money. (Hind.)

*Seramala, n. (—), and Semala, a carpenter. (Hind.)

*Serifu, v. spend money, pay, incur expense. Ps. *serifiwa*. Ap. *serif-ia, -iwa*, e. g. *ameserifia watu wamfuate*, he paid people to take his side. (Ar. Cf. *sarafa*, and syn. *gharimia, wakifu, lipa*.)

*Serkali, n. See Serakali.

*Seruji, n. See Saruji, saddle of a horse. (Ar.)

Seta, v. (1) crush, squash, mash, beat up,—usually of things relatively soft, e. g. *seta viazi kwa mwiko*, mash potatoes with a spoon, but also of pounding ingredients together in a mortar (cf. *mseto*). (2) jostle, press (in a crowd). Ps. *setwa*. Nt. *seteka*. Ap. *set-ea, -ewa*. Rp. *set-esha, -eshwa*, e. g. huddle together. (Cf. *twanga, ponda, saga, songa*.)

*Setiri, v. also Sitiri, and Stiri, conceal, hide, cover up, atone for. The deriv. stems commonly follow *stiri*. Thus Ps. *stiriwa*. Nt. *stirika*. Ap. *stir-ia, -iwa*. Cs. *stiri-sha, -shwa*. (Ar. Cf. *stara, msitiri*, and syn. *ficha, funika*.)

Sezo, n. (—), also Senezo, an adze. (Cf. *seneza*, and *shoka*.)

-sha (and -za) is the characteristic termination of the causal conjugation of verbs. For meanings see -za.

*Shaaban, n. eighth month of the Mahommedan year, next preceding Ramathan, and called *mwezi wa mlisho*, i. e. carnival month. (Ar. Cf. *shiba*.)

*Shaba, n. copper, brass,—also distinguished as *shaba nyekundu*, copper; *shaba nyeupe*, brass. (? Ar. mixture,—a mixed, alloyed metal.)

*Shabaha, n. (—), also Shebaha, Shabihi, (1) similarity, likeness (cf. *methali, mfano*); (2) figure, object to shoot at, target, butt (cf. *sanamu*); (3) aim (with a weapon), sight (of a gun). E. g. *twaa sh.*, take aim, aim; also *piga sh. Pata sh.*, hit the target, make a hit. Used as adv., like, the same as, e. g. *nyama shabaha* (or, *shabaha ya*) *mbwa*, an animal like a dog. (Cf. *methali, mfano, kama*.) (Ar. Cf. *shabihi*.)

*Shabbu, n. alum. (Ar.)

*Shabihi, v. and Shebihi, be like, be analogous to. (Also as n. for *shabaha*.) Rp. *shabihiana*. (Ar. for common *fanana, lingana*.)

*Shabuka, n. a snare, a trap. (Ar. 'net,' cf. *mtego*.)

*Shada, n. (—, and *ma-*), parcel, bunch, cluster,—of things fastened together, e. g. of flowers, a nosegay, also a tuft, a tassel, a rosette, a string of beads. Dim. *kishada*. (Ar.)

*Shaha, n. (*ma-*), also Shehe, Sheki, (1) head, headman, chief councillor,—used sometimes as the title of the officer ranking next to a chief, i.e. *waziri* or prime minister; (2) heart, pith,—of a cocoanut tree, the crown from which the leaves and flower spring (cf. *kilele*). (Ar. Cf. *shehe*.)

*Shahada, n. (—), (1) the Mahommedan creed, confession of faith; (2) bond, covenant, deed of ratification, e. g. *wahaandikiana shahada*, they executed a deed. Cf. *kidole cha sh.*, the fore-finger. *Maji ya shahada*, water used ceremonially at a funeral. (Ar. Cf. *shahidi, ushuhuda*.)

*Shahamu, n. (—), fat, lard, grease, i. e. animal fat. (Ar. Cf. *mafuta*, also *nona, nenepa*.)

*Shahawa, n. semen. (Ar. Cf. *mani*.)

*Shahidi, n. (*ma-*), one who attests or guarantees, a witness, an authority, a martyr. (Ar. Cf. *shahada, ushahidi, shuhudia*.)

*Shaibu, used sometimes in the (Arabic) expression *shaibu la juzi*, a very old woman. (Ar. 'greyhaired.' Cf. *kizee, kikongwe*. *Juzi* for Ar. *ajuz*, old, decrepit woman.)

*Shairi, n. (*ma-*), a line of poetry, a verse, usu. in plur. verses, poetry, song, a poem. *Tunga mashairi*, compose verses. (Ar. Cf. *mshairi*, also *utenzi*, *beti*. Dist. *shayiri*, barley.

*Shaka, n. (*ma-*), trouble, doubt, perplexity, difficulty, danger, crisis. Usu. in plur., e.g. *-wa na mashaka*, be in doubt; so *shikwa na (ona, kuta, ingia) mashaka. Tia mashaka*, cause trouble, perplex, &c. *Mashaka mengi*, a troublesome business. (Ar. Cf. *shuku*, and syn. *taabu, matata, shidda, hatari, fathaa, uthia, thiki*.)

*Shalaka, n. small hole in the gunwale of a boat for securing the loop of rope (*kishwara*) used as a rowlock. (Ar. Also (?) a knot or loop secured by a peg.)

*Shali, n. a shawl. (Ar.,—whence the Eng. word.)

*Sham, n. Syria. *Reale ya Sham*, an Austrian silver dollar. *Bahari ya Sham*, the Red Sea.

*Shamari, n. fennel. (Ar.)

*Shamasi, n. See **Shemasi**.

Shamba, n. (*ma-*), (1) a piece of ground having an owner, an estate small or large, a plantation, farm, garden, a plot of cleared or cultivated land; (2) country, as opp. to town (*mji*), and in this sense treated similarly as a proper noun, e.g. *enda shamba*, go into the country; *toka sh.*, come from the country; *shinda sh.*, live in the country. *Mtu wa shamba*, a rustic, a peasant. Cf. *kimashamba*, countrified, boorish,—of language, manners, &c.

Shambulia, v. attack, make an inroad (incursion, invasion, war) upon, rush violently on. Ps. *shambuliwa*. (Cf. follg. and syn. *pigia (letea, tolea), vita (jeuri)*.)

Shambulio, n. (*ma-*) also **Ushambulio**, sudden attack, rush, incursion. (Cf. prec.)

*Shamili, n. (*ma-*), an ear-ornament. (Ar.)

*Shamua, v. sneeze, sniff. (? Ar. smell, sniff. Cf. *chafya, enda chafya*.)

Shangaa, v. be astonished, stand and stare, be dumbfounded (with wonder, horror, &c.), be dazed. Cs. *shanga-za, -zwa*, astonish, strike with wonder, terrify, &c. (Cf. *mshangao, ajabu, toshewa, fathaika, pigwa bumbuazi*.)

Shangazi, n. (*ma-*), father's sister, paternal aunt. (Cf. *mama mdogo*.)

Shangilia, v. make rejoicings (for, at), shout or sing with joy and triumph, make demonstrations of enthusiasm, congratulate. Ps. *shangiliwa*, e.g. be received with triumph (rejoicings, congratulations). (Cf. follg. and *shangwe*, and syn. *ambia heri, pigia vigelegele, furahia*.)

Shangilio, n. (*ma-*), rejoicing, triumph, congratulation. (Cf. prec.)

Shangwe, n. rejoicing, demonstration of joy (triumph, enthusiasm). (Cf. *shangilia*.)

*Shani, n. a startling (rare, unlooked-for) thing or occurrence, a wonder, a novelty, a curiosity, an adventure, a sudden mishap, accident. E.g. *patwa na s.*, have an accident, meet with an adventure. *Nguo ya s.*, fine, new clothes, latest fashion. *Mambo hayo si shani*, that is no wonder, nothing to be surprised at. (Ar. Cf. *mwujiza, ajabu, kitisho*.)

*Shanjari, adv. See **Sanjari**.

Shanuo, n. See **Chanuo**.

Shapo, n. usu. in plur. **mashapo** (which see).

*Sharabeti, n. sherbet. (Ar.)

*Sharabu, n. (*ma-*), also **Sharwarabu, Sherabu**, moustache. (Ar.)

*Sharafa, n. *sharafa la ndevu, ndevu za sharafa*, (?) long flowing whiskers and beard. (Ar. Cf. *-sharifu*.)

*Shari, n. evil, malice, ill luck, disaster, adversity. Opp. to *heri*. *Mtu wa shari*, an evilly disposed, malicious, dangerous person. *Jahazi ya s.*, an unlucky vessel. *Hawana shari na wageni*, they do not molest strangers. *Taka s.*, defy, challenge. *Nimekuja kukutaka shari*, I have

z

come to bid you defiance. *Mtaka shari simwepi*, I do not refuse a challenge. *Mambo ya s.*, adversity. (Ar. Cf. *ukorofi, jeuri*.)

*Sharia, n. (—), also Sheria (which see). (Ar.)

*-sharifu, a. (*sharifu* with D 4 (P), D 5 (S), D 6), honourable, respectable, noble, excellent. (Ar. Cf. *usharifu*, and syn. *azizi, mashuhuri, bora*.)

*Sharika, n. (—, and *ma-*), also Shirika, partnership, action in common, common interest, communion. E. g. *ntajitia shirikani*, I will go shares. *Mali yetu ni sharika*, we are joint owners of our property. Also as adv., in common, together, in partnership. *Fanya kazi sharika*, share a job. *Tumia sh.*, use in common. (Ar. Cf. follg.)

*Shariki, v. and Shiriki, (1) share, have a share in, take part in, be partners (in), be associated (with), act together, do in common, e. g. *shariki njaa*, come in for a share of famine; *shariki katika biashara*, form a commercial partnership (company, joint-stock business). (2) be intimately connected with, be devoted to, be addicted to, e. g. *sh. kazi*, be heart and soul in a work; *sh. ulevi (uzinzi)*, be a confirmed drunkard (profligate); *sh. moyo*, give the rein to one's desires, be an utter sensualist; *sh. chuo*, be a diligent student; *sh. sanamu*, be an idolater. Also (3) in a deeper sense, of intimate communion, self-identification, communion of spirit and nature, with an object, e. g. *shiriki Muungu*, lead a wholly devoted, saintly, religious life,—also, share the divine nature (understood by Mahommedans as a wholly blasphemous claim). *Sh. shetani*, be of a diabolic temperament, a sinner of the worst kind. Ps. *sharikiwa*, be shared, &c. Nt. *sharikika*. Ap. *sharikia*, e.g. take part in, give a share to, associate with. Cs. *shariki-sha, -shwa*, e. g. cause (invite, allow, help) to share in, give a share to, &c. Rp. *sharikiana*. (Ar. Cf. prec. and *usharika, msharika, shirika*, and for sharing generally, *gawanya, eneza, twaa fungu, or sehemu*, &c.)

*Sharti, n. (—, and *ma-*), also Sharuti, Shuruti, (1) necessity, obligation (actual, practical, rather than moral), absence of choice; (2) binding contract, terms, conditions, clause of a legal document; (3) wager, bet. *S. kwenda* (or, *uende*), you must go, you have to go. *Fanya s.*, make a contract, bind oneself. *Maneno ya s.*, peremptory, uncontrovertible language. *Akataka sharti yake kuondoka*, he wanted to go in spite of everything, because he had to. *Kwa masharti*, under conditions, conditionally. *Wekana masharti, shindana (pigana) kwa masharti*, engage in betting, lay wagers. (Ar. Cf. *lazimu, farathi, juzu, mkataba*.)

*Shashi, n. a kind of muslin.

*Shasira, n. and Shazia, a long copper or brass needle, used in making mats and mattresses. (?.Ar. prick of a thorn.)

*Shati, n. an English shirt or similar short garment. (From the Eng. Cf. *koti, sitoki, fullana*.)

Shatoruma, n. shawl worn as waistband (Str.). (Cf. *mshipi, mahazamu, masombo*.)

Shaua, v. excite desire, and esp. desire which is not gratified, and so (1) make a display, show off; and (2) deceive, disappoint, delude, flatter, often as Rf. *jishaua*, e. g. (1) make a useless show, be silly (lackadaisical, frivolous, flirty), and (2) be disappointed, have a sense of failure. No deriv. stems commonly used. (Cf. follg.)

-shaufu, a. showy, pretentious, affected. (Cf. prec. and *ushaufu*.)

*Shauko, n. (—), strong desire (affection, wish, fondness, liking), sexual passion. E. g. *kuna shauku ya kitu chema au ya kitu kibaya*, i. e. *shauku* is applicable to good and bad objects. *Nina shauku naye*, I am greatly attached to him. *Shauku ya kuzungumza*, passionate fondness for amusement. *Shauku nyingi huondoa maarifa*, strong desire over-rides prudence. (Ar. Cf. *ashiki*, and syn. *habba, mapenzi, ngoa, tamaa*.)

*Shauri, n. (—, and *ma*-), (1) plan, design; (2) advice, counsel; (3) discussion, debate. E. g. *fanya shauri*, consider, deliberate, consult, hold a council, form a plan. *Toa (-pa) s.*, offer (give) advice, lay down a plan. *Uliza s.*, ask advice. *Mwenyi s., mtu wa mashauri mengi*, a wise, resourceful, clever man. *Hana shauri*, he is shiftless, helpless, sheepish. — v. ask counsel, consult. Ps. *shauriwa*. Cs. *shauri-sha, -shwa*, e. g. cause to seek advice, get advice for. Rp. *shauriana*, consult together. (Ar. Cf. *mshauri*.)

Shavu, n. (*ma*-), also Chavu, Chafu, (1) cheek, i. e. *shavu la uso*; (2) biceps, muscle of arm, i. e. *s. la mkono*; (3) calf of leg, i. e. *s. la mguu*. Also *s. la samaki*, gill of a fish; *s. la jogoo*, wattles of a cock.

*Shawishi, v. and Shaushi, persuade, coax, entice, tempt, allure. Ps. *shawishiwa*. Ap. *shaush-ia, -iwa*. (? Ar. confuse, perplex, cf. *tashwiski*, and syn. *vuta*.)

*Shayiri, n. barley. (Ar.)

*Shazasi, n. sal-ammoniac. (? Ar.)

*Shazia, n. See Shasira.

*Shebaha, Shebihi. See Shabaha.

*Shehe, n. (*ma*-), also Sheki, elder, chief, ruler, teacher, an important or powerful person. (Ar. Cf. also *shaha*, and syn. *mkubwa, mzee, mwalimu, mfalme*.)

*Shehena, n. (—), cargo, freight, load. (Ar. Cf. follg.)

*Sheheni, n. have cargo on board, be loaded up,—of a ship. Cs. *sheheneza*, cause cargo to be put on board, load up with freight. *Sh. chombo*, load a vessel. (Ar. Cf. prec.)

*Shela, n. large black veil,—usually a square of black silk, worn over the head by Arab women out of doors. Also called *shela mdeusia*, i.e. a black silk veil. Also, a sword-game, fencing (Sacl.). (? Ar. Cf. *utaji, dusumali*.)

*Shelabela, adv. in a lot, with all defects, just as they are, indiscriminately. (? Ar.)

*Shemali, n. (1) the left (hand); (2) the north (quarter); (3) north wind, mist, fog. (Ar. not usual in Z. Cf. *kushoto, kibla, kaskazi*.)

*Shemasi, n. (*wa*-), a deacon. (Ar. Cf. *kasisi*.)

*Shembea, n. a curved knife. (? Ar., or variant of *jambia* (which see), and cf. *kisu, kotama*.)

Shemegi, n. (*wa*-), also Shemeji, a relation by marriage,—usually of the first degree, i. e. wife's (or husband's) brother or sister, brother-in-law, sister-in-law.

*Sheraa, n. See Sheria. And for Sherafa, Sherabeti, see Sharafa, Sharabeti. (Ar.)

Sherehe, n. (—), and Usherehe. (1) show, pomp, display; (2) demonstrations, rejoicings, cheers, triumph. (Cf. *shangwe, kigelegele*.)

*Sheria, n. (—), also Sharia, Sheraa, law, a law, Mahommedan law, a law court, judicial proceedings. *Sh. ya chuo*, written, or statute, law. *Sh. ya inchi*, laws of the land. *Peleka sheriani*, prosecute. *Enda sheriani*, go to law, litigate. (Ar. Cf. *amri, desturi*.)

*Sherizi, n. (—), glue. (Hind. *serish*.)

*Shetani, n. (*ma*-), (1) an evil spirit, demon, devil, Satan; (2) that which suggests supernatural power, whether evil, or simply incomprehensible, e. g. (*a*) a clever dodge, great skill, conjuring; (*b*) epilepsy, fits, hysteria. (Ar. Cf. *jini, pepo*.)

*Shetri, n. poop, stern part,—of a vessel. Opp. to *gubeti, omo*, prow, bow, forepart. (Ar. Cf. *tezi*.)

*Shiba, v. (1) have enough to eat

or drink, have a full meal, be satisfied with food; (2) sometimes used fig. of being wholly filled with, and so under the influence of something, e. g. *shiba Muungu*, be wholly given up to worship and religion, be a devotee. Ap. *shib-ia, -iwa.* Cs. *shib-isha, -ishwa.* — n. (—), also **Shibe**, fullness, satiety, repletion, completion, finishing touch. E. g. *shibe ya nyama*, a full meal of meat. *Njaa si bora kuliko shiba*, hunger is not better than a good meal. *Shiba ya nguo ni kilemba*, a turban is full dress. (Ar. Cf. *shaaban*.)

***Shibiri**, n. a span, from thumb to little finger of the open hand, about 9 inches, half a cubit (*mkono, thiraa*). (Ar.)

***Shidda**, n. trouble, difficulty, want, scarceness, rarity, something hard to get. *Patwa na s., -wa na s., ingia s.*, get into trouble or distress. *Kitu hiki ni shidda kuonekana*, this article is seldom to be seen. *Kwa shidda*, with difficulty, scarcely, hardly, seldom, unlikely. (Ar. Cf. *taabu, thiki, msiba*.)

Shika, v. have in the hand, hold, hold fast, take hold of, keep hold on, seize, grasp, keep. A common word with a wide range of application, e.g. (1) get a hold on, press hard on, be on the mind, put in difficulties; (2) keep a hold on, persevere in; (3) hold to, keep to, observe, remember, attend to, obey; (4) determine, resolve, make up the mind to; (5) also as a Nt., have a hold, prevail, be urgent. E. g. *s. njia*, take to the road, start, proceed, keep to (follow) a road *S. amri*, obey an order. *S. lako*, Imperat., mind your own business. *S. kwenda*, resolve to go. *S. nyamaza*, persevere in silence. *S. mgeni*, welcome (receive, entertain) a guest. *S. bei*, hold out for a price, haggle, bargain. *Nitakayokuambia, nawe shika*, what I say to you, mind you attend to. *Masika imeshika*, the rainy season is in full force. *Njaa inashika*, famine is prevalent. *Vita inashika*, war is being waged. *Shika ras*, keep to (i. e. steer for, make for) the cape. *Shika miguu ya*, salute, pay honour to, submit to, become the slave of (cf. *shikamu*). Ps. *shikwa*, e. g. *shikwa na homa*, have an attack of fever. *S. na deni*, be pressed with debt. *Nimeshikwa kwa Sultani*, I am in difficulties with the Sultan. Nt. *shikika*, e. g. *maji hayashikiki*, water cannot be grasped in the hand. Ap. *shik-ia, -iwa*, e.g. hold by, hold on to, hold for (at, by, in), e. g. *kamba ya kushikia*, a rope to hold by. *Kushikiwa fetha*, to have money held for one, i. e. in the hands of trustees. Hence *shik-ilia, -iliwa*, e. g. hold on to (in some special way), with Cs. *shikil-iza, -izwa*, e. g. tack (in sewing), make hold fast, &c., and a further Rp. *shikilizana*, e. g. encourage each other to hold on, persevere, &c. Cs. *shik-iza, -izwa*, e. g. cause to hold, give into the hands of, make hold, make fast (firm, tight), fasten, prop, keep in place. *Shikiza nyumba*, prop up a house. *Shikiza mlango*, secure the door. *Shikiza mkono*, guide the hand, e. g. of a young scholar writing. Hence *shikiz-ia, -iwa*. Rp. *shikana*, e. g. hold each other, be friends, grapple, form connexion with. (Cf. follg. and *shikizo*, also syn. *kamata*.)

Shikamana, v. St. Rp. form of *shika*, i. e. be in a state of firmly holding together, be firm, set, hard, e. g. of mortar. *Ushikwapo shikamana*, when you are held tight, hold on tight yourself. Cs. *shikaman-isha, -ishwa*. (Cf. *shika, ma-, -mana*.)

Shikamuu (also shortened into **Shikamu, Shikam, Kamu**, and even **Kam**), a common salutation used by a slave, woman, or dependant, to a superior, i. e. 'your humble servant.' In full, *nashika miguu yako*, I hold your feet,—as a sign of inferiority and submission.

Shikio, n. (*ma-*), a thing to hold by, handle, (in a ship) rudder. *Mshiki shikio*, steersman. *Mashikio ya kikapu*, handles of a basket. (Cf. *shika*, and follg., and syn. *msukani. Sikio*, 'ear,' is sometimes pronounced *shikio*.)

Shikizo, n. (*ma-*), fastening, wedge, prop,—used for securing something firmly. (Cf. *shika, shikio*.)

*****Shilamu**, n. stem of a pipe, leading from the water-bowl to the mouthpiece. See **Kiko**.

Shimbika, v. prepare a hook for fishing, tie fast the hook and bait to the line.

Shimbiko, n. (1) a tying fast (as prec.); (2) thread used for securing the hook to the line.

Shime, n. (—), and **Sime**, a short straight sword, with a blade broadened out near the pointed end. Also used as a cry for help in danger. (Cf. *upanga*, and *kiyowe*.)

Shimo, n. (*ma-*), pit, hole, cavity, hollow, excavation,—used very generally, of small and large holes, mines, quarries, graves, pitfalls, tunnels, inside of a vessel, &c. Dim. *kishimo*. (Cf. *tundu, chimbo, pango, mvungu*.)

Shina, n. (*ma-*), root, stem of a tree,—including all parts, from the *misizi*, rootlets, to the *matawi*, branches. (Cf. *gogo*, of tree cut down, and *bua*, stem of some plants.)

Shinda, v. (1) overcome, conquer, subdue; (2) surpass, excel, be first (best), win; (3) be over, be left, remain; (4) pass time, keep on, continue, stay for a time (at), stop (in). E. g. *s. (adui) vitani*, be victorious (over enemies) in war. *S. kazi* (or, *katika kazi*), carry on work, go on working. *S. na njaa*, continue hungry, endure famine. *S. shamba*, pay a visit in (stay in) the country, at a country residence. *Amekwenda shinda*, he has gone away for a time (for the day, for a visit, for a picnic).

Maji yashinda kisimani, water is left in the well, i. e. there is still some left. *Kushinda jana*, used for 'day before yesterday,' i. e. continuing over or past yesterday. Ps. *shindwa*, e. g. *nimeshindwa*, it was too much for me, I could not do it. Nt. *shindika*, e. g. be conquered, &c., as above, but also more commonly in other and apparently different senses, perh. from another root. See **Shindika** below. Ap. *shind-ia, -iwa*. The form *shindilia* seems also different in meaning. See below and cf. *shindika*. Cs. *shind-isha, -ishwa*, and *shind-iza, -izwa*, e. g. cause to conquer, help to excel, cause to remain. Thus *shindisha nyumbani*, receive as a visitor, take in as lodger. Also apparently with a special intensive force, *maji ya kushindiza*, a flood, inundation, and a deriv. Nt. *shindizika*, of a knife or crowbar getting spoilt for use by work, blunted. Rp. *shindana*, e. g. try to overcome each other, contend, be rivals, dispute, compete. *Shindana sawasawa*, be well matched. Hence *shind-ania, -aniwa*, strive about (for, against, with, &c.), e. g. *sh. fetha*, wager, bet. *Sh. maneno*, oppose, contradict, a statement. *Sh. mtungi*, compete for (or, win by a struggle) a water-jar. Also *shind-anisha, -anishwa*, be matched, set to fight (compete, &c.). Also *shindaniana*, e. g. *sh. kima*, compete as to price, bid against each other for something. (Cf. follg. and *shindamana, shindo, mshindo, mshindi, mshinde*, &c. It seems that *shind-*, or *sind-*, has two (or three) distinct root meanings, viz. (1) surpass, (2) apply force, (3) continue. See **Shindo, Shinda, Shindika, Shindilia**, &c.)

Shinda, n. (*ma-*), remainder, residue, e. g. *shinda la mtungi* (*kinu*), what is left in the jar (mortar), a large remainder being *shinda zima* (*kuu, la kujaa*). *Gunia hii ni shinda*, this sack is partly full. *Mtungi* *u shinda ya maji*, the jar has some water in it.

Shindamana, v. be firmly pressed together, be compact, fixed fast, i.e. be in a state of being forced together. Ap. *shindaman-ia, -iwa*. Cs. *shindamani-sha, -shwa*. (Cf. *shindika, shikamana, fungamana*, and *-mana*.)

-shindani, a. rivalling, competing, opposing, contesting. (Cf. *shinda, mshindani, ushindani*.)

Shindano, n. (*ma-*), struggle, competition, race, trial of strength, &c. (Cf. *shinda*, and dist. *sindano*, needle.)

Shindika, v. (1) Nt. of **Shinda** (which see, and note), (2) also **Sindika**, apply force to,—but mostly with special senses, e.g. *shindika mafuta*, extract oil by pressure. *Sh. miwa*, crush sugar-canes. *Sh. mlango*, partly close a door, close but not fasten, set ajar, — opp. to *shindua* (*sindua*) *mlango*. Ap. *shindik-ia, -iwa*, e.g. *kinu cha kushindikia*, a crushing mill, i.e. oil-mill, sugar-mill. Cs. *shindikiza*, e.g. (1) intens. like *shindika*. (2) in special sense, attend a departing friend or guest to the door, go with him a little way, see off, give a send-off to (cf. *safirisha*, and *laki*, of going to meet an arriving friend). (Cf. follg. and *shindua*, also *shinikizo*, ? for *shindikizo*.)

Shindikizo, n. (*ma-*), and **Sinikizo**, (1) forcible pressure; (2) a pressing or crushing machine, e.g. oil-press, sugar-mill. (Cf. prec.)

Shindilia, v. press, press down, esp. of ramming a charge home, loading a gun, i.e. *sh. bunduki*. Cf. *shindilia chakula*, stuff food into the mouth. Ps. *shindiliwa*. Nt. *shindilika*. (Connected with root of *shindika*. Cf. *shindo*.)

Shindo, n. (*ma-*), used to describe a sudden, forcible, striking act, movement, effect, or sound, e.g. shock, jerk, blow, bump, outburst, rush, dash, crash, beat, bang, loud report, spasm, fit. E.g. *alisikia shindo linakuja njiani*, he heard a noise approaching in the road. *Ukatoka shindo mji wote*, the whole town was out in a moment. *Enda kwa mashindo*, trot,—of a horse. (Cf. *shinda, mshindo, kishindo, shindika*.)

Shindua, v. and **Sindua**, take off pressure, unfasten; esp. of a door, set ajar, set open. *Shindua maneno*, give vent to utterance, make an opening statement,—and so with *akili*. Ps. *shinduliwa*. Nt. *shinduka*, e.g. *maji yameshinduka*, the tide has retreated. Ap. *shindu-lia, -liwa*, e.g. open (a door) for a person. (Cf. *shinda*, and the words following it. Obs. that *shindika, shindua* seem identical with *zindika, zindua*, and their derivatives (which see),—meaning inaugurate, open, &c., and which nevertheless are commonly heard with *z* rather than *s* initial.)

Shingo, n. (*ma-*), (1) neck; (2) objects resembling a neck, e.g. an isthmus. Also fig. of hard unyielding temper, e.g. *mwenyi shingo gumu*, a stiff-necked person.

Shinikizo, n. (*ma-*), also **Sinikizo**, (1) pressing, crushing, pulping; (2) a machine or mill for such work, i.e. oil-mill, sugar-mill, &c. (Perh. for *shindikizo*. Cf. *shindika*.)

Shirika, Shiriki. See **Sharika, Shariki**.

Shisha, n. a kind of sand-glass for measuring time, used in native vessels.

Shiti, n. (*ma-*), printed calico piece-goods, prints,—sold mostly in Z. for women's dresses. (Cf. *kisuto, nguo, kanga*.)

Shoga, n. friend,—a term of endearment or familiarity between women in Z. (Cf. *jamaa, dada, somo*.)

Shogi, n. (*ma-*), also **Sogi**, a pannier, a pack-saddle, a large matting bag slung over a donkey's back, and open across the middle.

Shogoa, n. forced labour, corvée. *Tia katika shogoa*, requisition.

Shoka, n. (*ma-*), an axe. *Shoka la bapa*, an adze. Dim. *kishoka*. (Cf. *sezo*.)

Shona, v. sew, make (or, mend) by sewing. Used of shoemaking as well as tailoring, and all kinds of sewing. Ps. *shonwa*. Nt. *shoneka*. Ap. *shon-ea, -ewa*, e. g. sew for (with, in). Cs. *shon-esha, -eshwa*, e. g. employ to sew. (Cf. *mshoni, shonua*, and also *bandi, ponta, shulu*.)

Shonde, n. (*ma-*), (1) dung of animals; (2) dried cake of dung, used as fuel (Sacl.).

Shonua, v. unsew, undo sewing. Nt. *shonuka*. Ap. *shonu-lia, -liwa*. (Cf. *shona*.)

Shoti, n. gallop—of a horse. *Piga shoti, enda kwa shoti*, gallop, v. *Kumpiga shoti frasi*, to gallop a horse, to make it gallop. Also *piga shoti katika frasi*.

Shoto, n. left-hand, left-handedness. *Ana shoto*, he is left-handed. *Kushoto*, left-hand side. *-a kushoto*, on the left-hand side. Also as adj. *-shoto*, left-handed, e. g. *upande wa mkono mshoto*, on the left side. (Cf. opp. *kuume*, and Arab. *shemali*, opp. to *yamini*.)

*__Shtaka__, n. (*ma-*), also **Mshtaka**, accusation, charge, complaint, prosecution. (Ar. Cf. follg.)

*__Shtaki__, v. accuse, charge, complain of, prosecute. Ps. *shtakiwa*. Nt. *shtakika*. Ap. *shtak-ia, -iwa*, e. g. *akamshtakia baba habari za kwake*, she complained to her father about her home. Rp. *shtakiana*. Cs. *shtak-isha, -ishwa*. (Ar. Cf. *mshtaka, mshtaki*, and prec. Also *dai*.)

Shtua, v. also **Stua**, and **Situa**, (1) put out of place, move suddenly or violently, sprain, strain, e. g. *shua mguu*, sprain the ankle. (2) startle, surprise, shock. Nt. *shtuka*, be sprained, be startled (alarmed, shocked). Cs. *shtusha, shtushwa*, e. g. *shtusha mshipa*, strain a muscle (tendon). (Cf. *tegua, teguka*.)

Shua, v. let down, lower,—commonly of launching a boat or ship into the water. Ps. *shuliwa*. Nt. *shuka*, (1) go down, come down, descend, alight, disembark, land; (2) be lowered, depressed, humbled, degraded. *Shuka juu*, come downstairs. *Shuka pwani*, land on the beach, go down to the shore (coast). Hence *shukia, shukiwa*. Ap. *shu-lia, -liwa*, e. g. *vitu vya kushulia*, launching apparatus. Cs. *shusha, shushwa*, let down, throw down, put ashore, discharge (cargo, &c.). *Shusha pumuzi*, breathe out, exhale. *Jishusha moyo*, humble oneself. Hence *shush-ia, -iwa*, e. g. *shushiwa mvua*, have rain sent down on one. (Cf. *mashua*, and syn. *angua, inama*.)

*__Shubaka__, n. (*ma-*), small window, light-hole, loop-hole, port-hole, embrasure. In Z. sometimes a blind window, window-like recess in a wall (cf. *dirisha*, window; *mwangaza*, light-hole). (Ar. an aperture fitted with lattice, or trellis-work, cf. *shabuka*, net.)

Shudu, n. (*ma-*), refuse of seed after it has been crushed for oil, oil-cake.

*__Shufaka__, n. anxious care, fear, awe, pity. (Ar. not common, cf. *hofu, huruma*.)

*__Shughuli__, n. (—), also **Shuhuli**, (1) business, occupation, absence of leisure, engagements; (2) trouble, worry, anxiety. *Ana sh.*, he is busy, engaged. Opp. to *mchezo, faragha*, e. g. *hatukuja kucheza, tumekuja kwa shughuli*, we did not come to play, we are here for business. *Shughuli za inchi*, public affairs. (Ar. Cf. follg. and syn. *kazi, mambo*.)

*__Shughulika__, v. be busy (engaged, occupied), have one's hands full, be harassed, hard-worked. (Cs. *shughuli-sha, -shwa*, occupy, give trouble to, take up the time of, &c. *Jishu-*

ghulisha, trouble oneself, be nervous,—also, pretend to be busy, make excuses (for putting off, not attending to a case). (Ar. Cf. prec., and *ushuru*.)

*Shuhuda, n. (*ma-*), testimony, evidence, witness. (Ar. Cf. follg. and *shahidi, ushuhuda*.)

*Shuhudu, v. bear witness, testify, give evidence,—but usu. in the Ap. form. Ap. *shuhud-ia, -iwa, -ika*, attest, confirm, give evidence (about, for, against, &c.). Cs. *shuhud-isha, -ishwa*, e. g. call to witness. Also intens. bear emphatic witness. (Ar. Cf. prec., and *shahidi, shahada, ushuhuda*.)

*Shujaa, n. (*ma-*), a brave man, warrior, hero, champion. (Ar. Cf. *ushujaa*.)

Shuka, v. Nt. of Shua (which see).

*Shuka, n. (*ma-*), a piece of calico about two yards long, worn as a loincloth; in commerce, grey scarves. *Shuka la kitanda*, a sheet. As a measure, one fathom (*pima*). (Ar. Cf. *doti, pima*.)

Shuke, n. also Suke (which see).

*Shukrani, n. gratitude, thanksgiving, thanks. (Ar. Cf. *shukuru*.)

*Shuku, v. be doubtful, feel scruples, suspect. No deriv. stems common. Ap. *shuk-ia, -iwa*, feel doubts about, &c. (but dist. same from *shuka, shua*). — n. (—), suspicion, presentiment, doubt, scruple. (Ar. Cf. *shaka*, and syn. *tuhumu, thania*.)

*Shukuru, v. (1) thank, give thanks (to), be grateful; (2) take comfort, leave off mourning or grieving, be resigned, become contented. *Sh. Muungu* is esp. common in this latter sense, passive acquiescence in things bad and good. — n. (*ma-*), expression of gratitude, thanks. (Ar. Cf. *ahsante*.)

Shuli, n. See Tuka.

Shulu, n. a kind of sewing (? whip-stitch, herring-bone).

Shungi, n. (—, and *ma-*), (1) plait of hair, tress, crest, forelock. *Shungi mbili*, hair dressed in two large plaits or rolls. (2) used of the hair-like silky growth or beard on the ear of some kinds of grain,—maize, millet, &c. *Shungi la taa*, a flaring lamp. *Taa·inatoa shungi*, the lamp flares. (Cf. *kishungi*, also *songo, suko, sokoto, panja*.)

Shupaa, v. (1) be hard, firm, well set, compact; (2) be stiff, obstinate, unyielding, peremptory. *Shupaa kwa maneno*, affirm with urgency, insist. Cs. *shupaza*, harden, render tough, firm, strong,—also, make obstinate. Rp. *shupana*, be strong, well-compacted, stiff, unyielding, obstinate, &c. (Cf. follg., and cf. *kaza, -wa -gumu*.)

-shupafu, a. (same with D 4 (P), D 5 (S), D 6), (1) firm, compact, well-knit, tough; (2) bigoted, unyielding, &c. (Cf. prec., and syn. *-gumu*.)

Shupatu, n. (*ma-*), a narrow strip of plaited grass or leaf, used for lacing bedsteads, or sewn together for mats, bags, &c.

*Shura, n. saltpetre. (Hind.)

Shurua, n. measles.

*Shuruti, v. compel, oblige,—but seldom in simple form. Ps. *shurut-iwa*, e. g. *haikushurutiwa kutoa fetha*, there was no obligation to pay. Cs. *shuruti-sha, -shwa*, put pressure on, order peremptorily, press with argument, force, compel. Rp. *shurutiana*, make terms or conditions with each other, bind each other, wager, bet. — n. (*ma-*), also Sharuti, Sharti (which see). (Ar. Cf. *sharti*, and syn. *lazimu, juzu, bidi*.)

Shusha, v. Cs. of Shua (which see).

Shuta, v. break wind. (Cf. *shuzi*, and *jamba*.)

Shutumu, v. upbraid, reproach, revile, scold. E. g. *watu wanishutumu ubaya bilashi*, people upbraid me for wickedness without cause.

Ps. *shutumiwa.* Nt. *shutumika.* Ap. *shutum-ia, -iwa.* Cs. *shutumisha, -shwa.* Rp. *shutumiana.* — n. (*ma-*), reproach, railing, abuse. (Ar. Cf. syn. *laumu, suta, singizia.*)

Shuzi, n. (*ma-*), breaking wind. *Fathili ya punda ni mashuzi*, i. e. nothing worth having to be had from a donkey. (Cf. *shuta.*)

***Shwari**, n. a calm, calm weather. (Ar.)

Si, (1) adv. of negation, but always with a word following, which it qualifies,—never as an independent negation, no (which is *sio, sivyo*). *Si mimi*, not I. *Si mrefu*, not tall, &c. *Si* attaches itself so closely to the word qualified, as often not only to negative it, but to reverse more or less entirely its meaning. Thus *si vema* means 'badly,' as well as 'not well.' *Si lazimu kwenda*, it is necessary not to go. (And so in some verbs, e. g. *sitaki*, I want not to, I decline, *sipendi*, I dislike.) *Si* in comparisons indicates the less preferable member, 'rather than,' e. g. *jirani ya karibu si ndugu wa mbali*, a neighbour at hand is better than a brother far off. *Si* is commonly combined with (1) the Personal pronouns, e. g. *simi, siye, sinyi, sio (si wao)*; (2) the relative form of person-pfxs., e. g. *sio, sicho, sizo, sivyo*. *Sio* and *sivyo* are commonly used as an independent adv. of negation, i. e. 'no, not so' (cf. *hakuna, hapana, la*). *Si* is used with verbs to form the Negative Imperative only, e. g. *si piga (pigeni)*, do not strike. (2) as a verb-form, *si* is the negative connective corresponding to *ni*, i. e. 'is not, are not,' for all persons, Sing. and Plur., e. g. *wao si watumwa*, they are not slaves. See **Ni**.

Si-, in verbs is a pfx. of negation, in (1) 1 Person Sing. Indicative, always initial, e. g. *sioni*, I do not see, *sikuja*, I did not come. (2) all persons of the Subjunctive (Imperative) Mood, following the subjective person-pfx., e. g. *nisione*, that I may not see. *Usimpige*, do not strike him. (3) the relative form of the Negative Conjugation, e. g. *asiye*, he who is not. *Nisichokupa*, that which I did not give you. (4) sometimes with *-ja, -nge-, -ngali-*, e. g. *tusijaisha, wasingekwenda*, for the common *hatujaisha, hawangekwenda*.

Siafu, n. (—), a well-known reddish-brown kind of ant, which travels in large swarms, attacks all living creatures alike, and bites fiercely. (Cf. *chungu.*)

***Siagi**, n. butter, cream. (? Ar. *sayig*, cf. *samli, mafuta.*)

***Siara**, n. (*ma-*), and **Ziara** (which see), grave, burial place. *Masiara*, cemetery. (Ar. *zuru, ziura.* Cf. *kaburi.* See **Zuru**.)

***Sibiri**, n. for (1) *shibiri*, a span; (2) *subiri* (which see), an aloe.

***Sibu**, v. treat badly, damage, ruin, bring trouble on. (Arab. Cf. *msiba*, and *subu.*)

***Sifa**, n. (—), (1) praise, commendation, flattery, applause; (2) character, reputation, fame, characteristic. *Sifa zake njema*, he is well spoken. The following is a character of a popular chief, *Mtu mwenyi akili na huruma, asiye na choyo, msemaji sana, mwenyi ukali sana, awezaye kwenda mchana kwa usiku, asiye na kiburi na watu*, a man able, kind-hearted, not grasping, eloquent, brave and resolute, an untiring walker, and one who treats all alike with courtesy. (Ar. meaning 'quality, adjective.' Cf. *sifu*, and syn. *himidi, hamdi*, and for character, *tabia, moyo.*)

***Sifanja, Sifunja, Sifongo**, n. a sponge. (Variants of the Ar. *sifunj.*)

***Sifu**, v. praise, commend, flatter, recommend. Also *sifu mno*, flatter. *Jisifu*, brag, boast. (Cf. *jiona, jivuna, jigumba.*) Ps. *sifiwa.* Nt. *sifika.* Ap. *sif-ia, -iwa.* (Ar. Cf. *sifa, majisifu.*)

*Sifuri, n. (—), also Sifri, Sifuru, (1) brass; (2) a cipher, nought, zero. (Ar. for brass, cf. *sufuria*, and syn. *shaba*,—for zero, Ar. (?) *sifr*, empty.)

*Sihi, v. beg humbly, supplicate, beseech, intreat. Ps. *sihiwa*. Nt. *sihika*, e. g. be placable, not inexorable, open to appeal. (? Ar. cry loud, call, cf. *omba, lalama*.)

*Sihiri, v. bewitch, fascinate, throw a spell over, have power over. E. g. *mchawi aweza kutusihiri wote tukafa*, a wizard can bewitch us all to death. — n. witchcraft, e. g. *uchawi na sihiri ni kitu kimoja*, *sihiri* is the same thing as witchcraft. (Ar. for usual *loga*, cf. *pagaa, uchawi*.)

-sija, -sije-. See -ja.

*Sijafa, n. (—), wristband or cuff of a native dress, a piece turned in to receive the stitching. (Cf. *kanzu*.)

Sijambo, verb-form. See Jambo.

*Siki, n. (—), vinegar. (Hind.)

Sikia, v. (1) hear; (2) pay attention to, notice, understand, perceive; (3) heed, obey. Mostly of the sense of hearing, but also of other senses. E. g. *nasikia harufu ya samaki*, I smell fish. *Nasikia utamu wake*, I notice its taste, I taste it. *Amenisikia maneno yangu*, he has obeyed my order. Ps. *sikiwa*. Nt. *sikika*, e. g. be audible, be noticeable. Ap. *siki-lia, -liwa, -lika*, e. g. listen to (for, with, at). Hence *siki-liza, -lizwa*, usually intensive, listen,—sometimes in contrast with *sikia*, e. g. *nikamsikiliza simba nisimsikie tena*, and I listened for the lion, but did not hear it again. Also *sikiliana, sikilizana*. Cs. *siki-za, -zwa*, e. g. cause to hear, make understand, make obey,—and sometimes as *sikiliza*, listen. Hence intens. or Cs. *sikizisha* and *siki-zia, -ziwa*,—also *sikizana*, e. g. hear each other, agree together, be mutually intelligible, &c. *Ile lugha yao hatusikizani*, we do not understand each other in that language of theirs. (Cf. follg. and *msikizi, usikizi, sikio*, and syn. in general, *ona, shika, fahamu, tii*.)

-sikifu, n. and -sikilifu, attentive, teachable, docile, obedient. (Cf. *sikia, usikifu*, and syn. *-angalifu, -elekevu, -tii*.)

Sikio, n. (*ma-*), also Shikio, the ear,—organ of hearing. *Tega sikio*, listen attentively. *Tia sikioni*, remember, attend to. *Sikio halipiti kichwa*, the ear does not rise above the head. *Toga (toja) sikio*, bore holes in the outer edge of the ear, as Swahili women do, for ornaments. (Cf. *ndewe, majasi*.) (Cf. *sikia*, and prec.)

Sikitika, v. be sorry, grieve, feel regret (pity, remorse),—the common word in Z. Ap. *sikitik-ia, -iwa*, e. g. be sorry for (about, at, in). Cs. *sikiti-sha, -shwa* (for *sikitikishwa*), grieve, make sorry. (No simple *sikita* in use. Cf. follg. and *huzunika, lia*.)

Sikitiko, n. (*ma-*), sorrow, grief, object of pity, cause of sorrow, regret, &c. (Cf. prec.)

Siku, n. (—, rarely *ma-*), (1) a day, i. e. a period of 24 hours, in Z. counted from sunset to sunset, one night (*usiku*) and one day (*mchana*, period of daylight); (2) in a general sense, day, time. E. g. *siku zote*, on all days, always. *Killa siku*, every day. *Siku hizi*, nowadays, in modern times. *Siku za kale*, days of old, old times. *Siku kwa siku*, day after day, from day to day. *Siku moja, kwa siku, katika siku*, one day. *Masiku mengi*, many long days. *Siku kuu*, festival, holiday, i. e. in Z. the usual Mahommedan feasts, (1) after Ramathani; (2) *Al Haj, Idi* (or Bairam) in the third month after it; (3) *Maulidi*, the birthday of Mahomed in the sixth month. There is also a celebration of the death of Hosein in the fourth month. *Siku a mwaka*, New Year's day. See **Mchana, Usiku, Mwaka**.

*Sila, n. pail, bucket, dipper, scoop,—esp. for bailing water out of a boat, &c. (Cf. the commoner *ndoo, kata*.)

*Silaha, Silihi. See Selaha, Selehi.

*Silimu, v. become a Mahommedan, be converted, initiated. Ps. *silimiwa*. Nt. *silimika*. Cs. *silimisha, silim'-sha, -shwa*, make a Mahommedan, initiate. (Ar. Cf. *salimu, salama*.)

Simama, v. (1) stand, be standing,—i.e. of position, as opp. to sitting or lying (cf. *simika, ondoka*); (2) stand, stand up, rise,—i.e. of movement, change of posture; (3) stand, stand still, come to a stand, stop, be stationary, keep in a particular place; (4) be erect, perpendicular, high, steep, elevated; (5) cost (cf. *wakifu*), e.g. *imenisimamia fetha nyingi*, it has cost me much money. E.g. *akaondoka akasimama*, he rose and stood up. *Muungu hakusimama naye*, God did not take his side (support him). *Wali haukusimama tumboni*, the rice was not retained in the stomach. *Mlima umesimama*, the hill is steep. *Maji yamesimama*, the water is motionless, stagnant. Ap. *simam-ia, -iwa*, e.g. stand by (upon, in, for, against, &c.), oppose, obstruct, support,—but esp. common in the sense, stand over, overlook, superintend, manage, direct, administer (cf. *msimamizi*). Cs. *simam-isha, -ishwa*, e.g. (1) make stand, cause to go on with work,—also (2) cause to stop, obstruct, thwart; (3) set up, erect, make stand, cause to rise. E.g. *simamisha bei*, raise price. (Cf. *simika, simua*, and *ima*, with which *simama* is connected as a Stative form.)

Simanga, v. triumph (over), exult (against), cast in the teeth (of), reproach. Ap. *simang-ia, -iwa*. Cs. *simang-isha, -ishwa*, as intens., e.g. *Wanika walitusimangisha umasikini wetu*, the Wanika reproached us with our wretchedness. (Cf. syn. *shutumu, onea*.)

Simanzi, n. grief, sorrow, depression. (Cf. syn. *hamu, huzuni, majonzi*.)

*Simba, n. (—, and *ma-*), a lion, a lioness. Also as complimentary description of a warrior, fine child, or young man. (Ar. *sabu, sibaa*.)

Sime, n. See Shime.

Simika, v. (1) stand, be set up, be erect,—like *simama*; (2) cause to stand, set up, erect; (3) cause to prosper, support, uphold; (4) appoint, establish, arrange. E.g. *simika nyumba* (*miti, mlango*), erect a house (poles, a door). *Muungu akusimika*, God prosper you. *Mkufu hausimiki, hausimami*, a chain neither holds up nor stands up. *Nisimike mtu awe mkubwa wao*, let me set up a man to be their chief. *Simika mitego*, set traps. Ps. *simikwa*. Ap. *simik-ia, -iwa*, e.g. *wakamsimikia asikari*, and they provided him with a bodyguard. Cs. *simik-isha, -ishwa*, e.g. have a thing set, cause to set up. (Cf. *ima, simama, simua*.)

*Similla, int. Make way! Out of the road! By your leave! Often with a word following, S. *punda* (*ubau, jiwe*), make way for a donkey (plank, stone). (Ar. for *bismillah*, in the name of God. Cf. *inshallah, eewallah, wallai, allaalla*, and syn. *jihathari, jitenga*.)

Simo, verb-form, I am not in it, i.e. often, I am not responsible, it is no concern of mine,—Negat. Pfx. of 1 Pers. Sing., with *-mo*, for *humo*).

Simo, n. (—), something striking, remarkable occurrence,—not often heard in Z. E.g. *simo mpya imeingia*, a new thing has occurred. (Cf. follg. and *jambo, shani*.)

Simu, n. the telegraph, telegraphic message (news, &c.). (Perh. same as prec.)

Simua, v. place horizontal what was perpendicular, lay down. E.g.

simua mlingoti, lower a mast. (Not often in Z. Cf. *simama, simika, ima*, and syn. *shusha, weka chini, inamisha*. Rv. from *sima* not used.)

Simulia, v. also **Sumulia** (which see).

Sina, verb-form, I have not,—Negat. Pfx. *si*, and *na*, with. (Cf. *si, na*.)

Sindano, n. a needle. (Cf. *shasira*.)

Sindika, Sindua. See **Shindika, Shindua**.

Singa, v. rub with perfume, or aromatic substances, e. g. *singa mwili kwa sandali*, rub the body with sandal wood. Ps. *singwa*. (Cf. *sugua, kanda*.)

Singa, n. plur. of *usinga*, long, straight, soft hair,—of Europeans and some animals, i. e. *nyele za singa*, as opp. to *nyele za kipilipili*, the short, tufty, wiry hair of natives. *Singa za mkia wa frasi*, horse-hair from the tail. (Cf. *manyoya*, used of animal hair generally, wool, down, &c., and see **Unyele**.)

*****Singefuri**, n. cinnabar, vermilion, a red dye, anatta. (Cf. *msingefuri*.)

Singiza, v. pretend, make pretence, allege as excuse, but commonly in the Ap. *singiz-ia, -iwa*, make a fictitious, calumnious charge against, slander, insinuate. E. g. *jisingiza ugonjwa*, make a pretence of sickness. *Singizia moto*, lay the blame on the fire. Ps. *singizwa*. (Cf. follg. and syn. *amba, tukana*.)

Singizio, n. slander,—usu. in plur. *masingizio* (which see).

*****Sini**, n. China,—the country. *Wasini*, the Chinese. (Dist. *Wasini*, a town on the coast between Z. and Mombasa.)

*****Sinia**, n. (—, and *ma-*), a tray,—commonly, a circular metal tray for carrying food, &c. (Ar.)

Sinikiza, Sinikizo. See **Shindikiza**, &c.

Sinzia, v. (1) sleep, doze, be drowsy; (2) be inattentive, absent-minded, make a foolish mistake; (3) of a lamp, flicker. Ap. *sinzi-lia, -liwa*, e. g. be sleepy about, be negligent over, fail to observe or act properly. (Cf. *usingizi*.)

Sio, adv. of negation, no, not so, it is not,—negative pfx. *si* with *-o* of reference, or for *hiyo, wao*. (Cf. syn. *la, hakuna, hapana*.)

-sipo, in verbs, is a negative-relative pfx., referring to place, time, or general circumstances, i. e. where (when, in case) it is (they are) not, and so commonly 'in case . . . not, if . . . not, supposing . . . not,' e. g. *isipokuwa njema*, if it is not good. Also often supplies practically a negative form of the Pres. Partic. in *-ki-*. (Cf. *si, -po*.)

Sira, n. (*ma-*), dregs, lees. *Sira la tembo*, lees of palm wine.

*****Siri**, n. (—), a secret, hidden thing, mystery, puzzle, secrecy. *Mambo ya siri*, secrets. *Kwa siri*, secretly, privately, mysteriously. Sometimes also as a v., e. g. *alijisiri gengeni*, he secreted himself in a hollow. (Ar. Cf. *usiri*, and perh. *suria*, also syn. *fumbo, faragha*, and *setiri, ficha*. Opp. to *wazi, thahiri*. Dist. *usiri*, delay.)

Sisi, pron. of 1 Pers. Plur., we, us. *Sisi sote*, all of us. *Sisi wote*, commonly of two persons, 'both of us.' (Sometimes *siye* is used for *sisi*. Cf. *miye, weye*.)

Sisima, Sisimua, &c. See **Zizima**.

Sisimizi, n. or **Zizimizi**, a small black harmless ant. (Prob. from *zizima* (which see).)

Sita, n. and a., six. *-a sita*, sixth. (Ar. Cf. *sitashara, sittini*.)

Sita, v. (1) move in an uncertain, irregular way, hang back, dawdle, go lamely; (2) fig. be in perplexity, be undecided, be in doubt, hesitate. (Cf. *tanga, zunguka, kwama*.)

*****Sitaha**, n. and **Staha**, deck,—of a vessel. (Ar.)

*Sitahi, v. honour, respect. See **Stahi**. (Ar.)

*Sitashara, n. and a., sixteen. *-a sitashara*, sixteenth. (Ar. Cf. *sita, sittini*.)

*Sitawi, v. be in good condition, reach full development, flourish, succeed, go off well, be in full swing, be at the height. E. g. of healthy plants, of social functions, dances (*ngoma*), a feast (*karamu*), a wedding (*arusi*), or of trade (*biashara*). Cs. *sitawi-sha, -shwa*, e. g. cause to flourish, embellish, enhance, prosper, give a finish to. (? Hind., and cf. *usitawi*.)

*Sitiri, v. cover, conceal. See **Setiri**. (Ar.)

*Sitoki, n. See **Stoki**. (Eng. 'stocking.')

*Sitti, n. (—), lady,—and in address, my lady, madam. (Ar. for the common *bibi, mwana* (which see).)

*Sittini, n. and a. and **Settini**, sixty. *-a sittini*, sixtieth. (Ar. Cf. *sita, sitashara*.)

Situka, v. See **Stuka**.

Sivyo, a common form of negative adv., no, not so,—negative pfx. *si* with *-vyo* of reference. (Cf. adverbial use of *vi-* in adjectives, and *vile, hivi, ndivyo*, &c., and for negatives, *si, sio, la, hapana*.)

Siwa, n. (*ma-*), a large island,—but seldom in Z. except in reference to the Comoro Islands, e. g. *wafalme wa Masiwani*, the Sultans of Comoro. *Kisiwa* is regularly used of islands in general.

Siwa, n. used of a special kind of horn, or trumpet, of wood or ivory, which is a symbol of chieftaincy. (Cf. *panda, baragumu, pembe*.)

Siwezi, v. See **Weza**, and **Hawezi**,—also cf. *jambo, sijambo*.

Siyo, adv. of negation, like *sio, sivyo, si*, it is not, not this, no. Also for *si hiyo*.

Sizi, n. usually in the plur. *masizi*, soot, grime, e. g. from the fire, on a cooking pot, in a chimney. (Cf. *takataka*, and dist. *msizi*.)

*Soda, n. lunacy. (Ar. Cf. syn. *wazimu, kichaa*.)

Sodo, n. (—), a particular kind of napkin, used by women.

Sogea, v. come near, draw up close, approach. Ap. *soge-lea, -lewa*, and hence *sogeleana*. Cs. *soge-za, -zwa*, bring near, put ready for, &c. Hence *sogez-ea, -ewa*. Rp. *sogeana*. (Perh. conn. with *songa*, and cf. syn. *karibu, karibia*.)

*Soko, n. (*ma-*), a market, open market-place, centre of business, mart, emporium. (Ar.)

Sokota, v. twist, twine with the fingers, plait, spin. Used of thread, yarn, rope,—less properly of the hair,—also of making a cigarette. Fig. of pain, e. g. *tumbo lanisokota*, I have a twisting, griping pain, colic, in the stomach. Ps. *sokotwa*. Nt. *sokoteka*. Ap. *sokot-ea, -ewa*. Cs. *sokot-esha, -eshwa, -eza*. (Cf. follg., and *suka, songa*.)

Sokoto, n. (*ma-*), a plait, a tress, a curl. (Cf. prec., and *songo, suko, shungi*.)

*Soma, v. (1) go to school, receive teaching, study, be educated; (2) attend a service, perform devotions. Hence (3) read, i. e. attend to (listen to) a book. Ps. *somwa*. Nt. *someka*, e. g. be a subject for teaching, be decipherable. Ap. *som-ea, -ewa*, e. g. *sheki akalisomea jabali*, the chief performed a service (reading) over the stone. Cs. *som-esha, -eshwa*, e. g. send to school, educate, lead devotions, act as teacher or minister. Hence *someshea*, e. g. *unisomeshee mwanangu*, educate my son for me. (Ar. listen, i. e. the characteristic attitude of scholar, or worshipper, and hence the above meanings in Swahili. Cf. *somo*.)

Soma, n. (*ma-*), one kind of *ngoma*, or dance.

Sombea, v. move oneself by clasping or grasping, e. g. in climbing a tree, or of a cripple who cannot use his legs. (Str. and Kr. Cf. *sombo*, as that which clasps or girds.)

Sombo, n. usual in the plur. *masombo* (which see), a girdle. (Cf. follg.)

*****Somo**, n. (*ma*-), (1) that which is listened to or read, a letter, a reading; (2) a teacher, instructor, confidential adviser or friend. And so as a term of friendly address. *Njoo, somo*, come along, my friend. (Ar. Cf. *soma*, for friend, *rafiki, jamaa, mwenzi*, and *msiri*.)

Songa, v. (1) press, press together, press close, throng, meet in a mass; (2) close up by pressure, squeeze, contract, hem in ; (3) act on (form, fashion) by pressing; and (4) fig. apply pressure to, urge, press, overwhelm. E. g. *songa mbele*, press forward, *s. kamba*, of rope-making, *s. nyele*, of hair-dressing, *s. ugali*, of making porridge. *S. roho*, throttle, strangle. *Chakula chasonga*, the food chokes. *Watu wanasonga*, there is a crowd, or crush, of people. *Njia inasonga*, the road is narrow. *Nguo inasonga*, the dress is too tight. *Siku zasonga*, the days are approaching. Ps. *songwa*. Nt. *songeka*. Ap. *song-ea, -ewa*, e. g. *songea watu*, push through a crowd. Cs. *songesha, -eshwa*. Rp. *songana*. (Cf. *songo, msongo, kisongo*, and follg. *songoa, songomana, songonyoa, songomeza, sonjoa*, and perh. *sogea*, and *nyonga*.)

Songo, n. (*ma*-), a plait, coil (e. g. of a snake), tress, wreath, roll, garland. (Cf. *songa, sokoto, suko, pindi, kunjo*.)

Songoa, v. and **Sonjoa**, twist together, bind up tight, press together, e.g. *s. kamba*, of rope-making, *s. kuni*, make up faggots, *s. nguo*, wring clothes, *s. kuku*, twist a fowl's neck, &c. Ap. *songo-lea, -lewa*. (Cf. *songa*, also *choma, chomoa, chonga, chongoa*, &c.)

Songomana, v. be rolled or pressed together, e. g. of a snake wriggling and writhing, of clothes rolled up by a high wind, &c. (Cf. *songa*.)

Songomeza, v. roll or press together, e. g. of folding one's arm in a cloth, cramming food into the mouth, coiling up a rope. *Jisongomeza*, e. g. of a snake writhing. (Cf. prec., and *songa*.)

Songonyoa, v. squeeze, twist hard, wring out,—esp. of clothes, also of cleaning the teeth with a toothpick. *Tumbo lanisongonyoa*, I have colic. (Obs. *songa, songoa, songomeza, songonyoa*,—all denoting kinds of active twisting or pressure.)

Sonjoa, v. variant of songoa (which see).

Sononeka, v. (1) feel hurt, be pained, ache; (2) be grieved, vexed, troubled. Cs. *sonone-sha, -shwa*, e. g. hurt, cause pain (to), grieve, vex. (Cf. follg., and *kisonono*,—also a variant *sosoneka*.)

-sononi, a. hurt, grieved, pained. (Cf. prec.)

Sonya, v. whistle, but commonly *piga msonyo*. (Cf. *msonyo*.)

*****Soruali**, n. (—), and **Suruale**, trousers, breeches, drawers. (Ar.)

Sote, a. a form of *-ote*, used in agreement with the pers. pronoun *sisi*. *Tu sote*, we ate all together. *Twende sote*, let us all go together. *Tu wote* is commonly used of two persons, we are both ; *twende wote*, let us both go. (Cf. *-ote*, and *nyote*.)

Soza, v. reach, arrive at, meet with, approach, accost. *Soza pwani*, of a vessel, run ashore, be beached, come to land. (Not often in Z. Cf. *sogea, sogeza*, and *fika*.)

*****Sta-**, an Arab. sign of conjugation, retained in several words in Swahili. See follg.

*****Staajabu**, v. be greatly astonished, surprised, filled with wonder. — n. (*ma*-), wonder, a wonder, &c. (See **Ajabu**, and deriv. forms.)

*****Staamani**, v. have confidence, trust. See **Amini**.

Staarabu, v. get understanding,

be wise, know about things, be civilized. Also Nt. *staarabika*, in same sense. E.g. *washenzi wa papo wamestaarabika kidogo*, the natives in these parts have a touch of civilization. Cs. *staarabi-sha*, *-shwa*. (Ar. Cf. follg.)

-staarabu, a. wise, civilized. (Ar. Cf. prec.)

*Staha, n. (—), also Sitaha, deck,—of a vessel. (Ar.)

*Stahabu, v. like, prefer, be pleased (with). (Ar. Cf. *habba*.)

*Stahi, v. give honour to, show respect for, reverence. Ps. *stahiwa*. Nt. *stahika*, e.g. be a worthy, respected person. Rp. *stahiana*. (Ar. Cf. *-stahifu*, and syn. *heshimu, tukuaz*.)

*-stahifu, a. estimable, honourable, deserving respect. (Ar. Cf. *stahi*.)

*Stahiki, v. be fitting (proper, suitable, becoming), be obligatory on, be a duty, be worthy (deserving) of. Also a. deserving, honourable, respected. (Ar. Cf. *wajibu, stahili*.)

*Stahili, v. merit, deserve, be fitting, be proper, be due. E.g. *astahili kupigwa*, he deserves a beating. *Wastahili kumpenda*, you ought to like him. (Cf. *stahili salamu*, as a complimentary greeting, on some happy occasion.) Ps. *stahiliwa*. Nt. *stahilika*. Ap. *stahil-ia, -iwa*. Cs. *stahili-sha, -shwa*, e.g. make worthy, deem worth, declare deserving (suitable, good). *Jistahilisha*, think (make, pretend) oneself worthy, qualified for, &c. Also a. worthy, fitting, proper. (Ar. Cf. *astahili*, and syn. *stahiki*.)

*Stahimili, v. endure, support, persevere, put up with, be patient. Ps. *stahimiliwa*. Ap. *stahimil-ia, -iwa*. (Ar. Cf. *himili, hamali*, and syn. *vumilia, chukua, subiri*.)

*Staka, Staki. See Shtaka, Shtaki.

*Stakabathi, n. (1) earnest money, pledge (of a bargain made); (2) acknowledgement, receipt, quittance (of money paid, &c.). (Ar. Cf. *kabithi*, and syn. *wasili*.)

*Stambuli, n. Constantinople,— also called *Rum*.

*Stara, n. covering, concealment, modesty, reserve. (Ar. Cf. *setiri*.)

*Starehe, v. and Sterehe, be at rest (comfortable, undisturbed), live in peace and quietness, be still. *Starehe* (Imperat.), used commonly as a form of courtesy on meeting, or entering a room, 'keep your seat, pray do not move, do not disturb yourself.' Cs. *starehe-sha, -shwa*, make comfortable, give rest to, refresh, relieve, tranquillize. (Ar. Cf. *raha, mstarehe*, and follg., and cf. syn. *pumzisha, burudisha*.)

*-sterehefu, a. comfortable, peaceful, tranquil, calm. (Cf. prec.)

*Stima, n. a steamer. (From the English.)

*Stiri, v. cover, conceal. See Setiri.

*Stoki, n. also Sitoki, Stokini, stocking, sock. (From the Eng. 'stocking.' Cf. *koti, boi, manowari*.)

Stuka, v. sometimes Situka, (1) start, give a start or jerk, be sprained, be put out of joint; (2) be startled, taken aback, surprised, alarmed. E.g. *mguu wangu umestuka*, my foot is sprained. *Nalistuka kwa hofu*, I started in terror. Ap. *stuk-ia, -iwa*, e.g. start (be startled) at. Cs. *stusha, stushwa*, e.g. give a jerk to, sprain, startle, terrify, astonish. (*Tuka, jituka, kutuka* sometimes occur. Cf. syn. *teguka*, and *shangaa, toshewa, fathaika*.)

Subana, n. (1) a thimble (cf. *kastabani*); (2) small piece of meat, toasted on wooden skewers.

*Subaya, n. (—), outside covering of a bier, used in the better class of funerals, a pall. (Cf. *mazishi*.)

*Subiri, v. be patient (with), wait (for), endure, persevere, be resigned. E.g. *akamwambia, unisubiri, akampa saburi*, and he said to him, grant me a respite. And he did so. Ap.

subir-ia, -iwa. Cs. *subiri-sha, -shwa.* (Ar. Cf. *saburi*, and syn. *vumilia, stahimili, ngoja.* Dist. follg.)

*Subiri, n. also Shibiri, Sabiri, an aloe. (Ar.)

*Subu, v. (1) and Zubu, cast, run melted metal into a mould, i. e. *mimina madini iliyoyeyuka katika kalibu.* Ps. *subiwa.* Nt. *subika.* Ap. *sub-ia, -iwa.* Cs. *subi-sha, -shwa.* (Ar. *zab.*) (2) happen (to), take place, come to pass. (Ar., rarely used. Cf. *msiba, sibu.*)

*Subuhi, n. also Sabui, Subukhi, and (with article) *assubuhi, ussubui,* morning, the earlier part of the day. As adv., in the morning. (Ar. Cf. *assubuhi*, and contr. *jioni.*)

*Sudi, n. luck, fortune,—good or bad. (Ar. Cf. *bahati, nasibu.*)

*Sufi, n. (1) also Suf, Sufu, wool. Also of the fine soft silky cotton from the pods of the tree *msufi.* (Ar. Cf. *manyoya, pamba.*) (2) also *sufii,* a saint, holy man, devotee. (Ar. Cf. *mtawa, walii, mcha Muungu.*)

*Sufuria, n. (—, and of size, *ma-*), metal cooking pot,—of copper or iron, sometimes of very large size. (Ar. *sifr*, copper, and see Chombo, Chungu.)

Sugu, n. (—), (1) a callosity, place made hard by rubbing or use, a corn (on the foot). (2) callousness, a hard unfeeling nature. E. g. *fanya sugu kwa kazi nyingi,* get a hard lump from hard work. *Ana sugu, yu sugu,* he is callous, obstinate, stupid. (Cf. follg.)

Sugua, v. rub, scrub, scour, scrape, clean (smooth, sharpen) by rubbing. Ps. *suguliwa.* Nt. *sugulika.* Ap. *sugu-lia, -liwa,* e. g. *jiwe la kusugulia visu,* stone for cleaning and whetting knives. *Nyama ya nazi imesuguliwa,* the flesh of the cocoanut has been scraped (out). Cs. *suguli-sha, -shwa.* Rp. *suguana.* (Cf. *sugu, suguo,* and *futa, pangusa.*)

Suguo, n. (*ma-*), something to rub with, e. g. knife-board, scraper. (Cf. *sugua,* and *kinoo.*)

*Suhubu, v. make friends with, be a friend of. Rp. *suhubiana,* e. g. *si mtu wa kusuhubiana naye,* not a man to make a friend of. (Ar. Cf. *sahibu.*)

*Sujudu, v. bow down (to), prostrate oneself (before), adore, worship. Used regularly of Mahommedan ceremonial of devotion. *S. Muungu,* worship God. Ps. *sujudiwa.* Nt. *sujudika.* Ap. *sujud-ia, -iwa.* Hence *sujudiana.* Cs. *sujudi-sha, -shwa,* e. g. cause to worship, teach worship to, make bow down, turn to God. (Cf. *moskiti, mesjidi.*)

Suka, v. (1) shake, wag, move quickly to and fro, flourish, e. g. *s. mkia,* wag the tail. *S. kichwa,* shake the head. *S. maziwa,* churn milk. *Suka suka,* be violently agitated. (2) plait, twist, make by plaiting, e. g. *s. mkeka,* plait a mat,—the common occupation of all women of the poorer classes in Z. *S. ukambaa,* plait a cord. *S. nyele,* plait the hair,—regularly of the hair-plaiting, often elaborate, of Swahili women. Ps. *sukwa.* Nt. *sukika.* Ap. *suk-ia, -iwa.* Cs. *suk-isha, -ishwa.* Rp. *sukana,* e. g. *s. nyele,* each dress the other's hair. (Cf. *msuko, suko, suke, sukua,* and syn. 'shake' *tikisa, punga,* 'plait' *sokota, songa, kunja.*)

*Sukani, n. (—), rudder, helm. See Msukani. (Hind.)

*Sukari, n. (—), sugar. *Sukari guru,* half-made sugar, in large lumps and of dark colour. (Ar.)

Suke, n. (*ma-*), also Shuke, the seed-bearing head or ear of various plants, e. g. rice, millet, maize. (? Cf. *suka,* with passive ending *-e.*)

Sukua, v. untwist, loosen, slacken. Ps. *sukuliwa.* Nt. *sukulika.* Ap. *suku-lia, -liwa.* (Cf. *suka,* and dist. *sugua.* Cf. *fumua, legeza, shonua.*)

Sukuma, v. (1) push, push away (onward, back, off, &c.), move, drive, thrust; (2) urge, impel, incite, encourage. E. g. *roho yake inamsu-*

kuma mbele, his will impels him onward. *Sukuma gari*, push a cart along. Ps. *sukumiwa*. Nt. *sukumika*. Ap. *sukum-ia, -iwa*. Cs. *sukum-iza, -izwa*. Often intens., e.g. (1) give a vigorous push, or impulse to, throw, thrust away. *S. rungu*, throw a club. *S. marathi*, avert sickness. *S. pepo*, propitiate (keep off) evil spirits. *S. dau*, force the boat along. (2) rid oneself of, and hence *sukum-izia, -iziwa*, thrust on to another, e. g. blame, disaster, a load. *Wanazidi kusukumiziwa mbele*, they are impelled onward more and more. Also *sukumizana*. Rp. *sukumana*. (Cf. *songa, sogea, endesha, ondoa*.)

Sukutua, v. rinse out the mouth with water, e. g. after eating. Seldom in deriv. forms. (Cf. *piga funda*.)

*Sulibi, v. also Salibu, Sulubu, crucify,—but usu. in the Cs. form. Ps. *sulibiwa*. Nt. *sulibika*. Ap. *sulib-ia, -iwa*, e.g. *mti wa kusulubia*, i. e. a cross (*msalaba*). Cs. *sulibi-sha, -shwa*, cause to crucify (or, to be crucified), crucify. (Ar. Cf. *msalaba*.)

*Sulihi, v. See Salihi (Selehi, Suluhi). (Ar.)

Sulika. See Zulika.

*Sultani, n. (*ma-*), king, ruler, chief, head of a town or village. *Sultani Rum*, the Sultan of Turkey. (Ar. In Z. the Sultan is commonly called *sayidi*, or *bwana*.)

*Sulubika, v. (1) be strong, firm; also (2) be diligent, vigorous, energetic. (Ar. Cf. follg. Also Nt. of *sulubu*. See Sulibi.)

*Sulubu, n. and Usulubu, firmness, strength, vigour. *S. ya kazi*, energy in work, industry. (Ar. Cf. prec., and syn. *nguvu, bidii, ushupafu*.)

*Suluhi, v. See Selehi and deriv. forms. (Ar.)

*-suluhifu, a. also -selehifu, one who makes peace, reconciles, brings into order, administers, rules. (Ar. Cf. prec.)

Sululu, n. (1) a curlew; (2) a pick, pickaxe.

*Sumari, n. See Msomari, nail, and Zomari.

Sumba, v. sell off, get rid of at any price, sell under pressure,—e. g. of stolen goods. Ps. *sumbwa*. Nt. *sumbika*.

Sumbua, v. annoy, trouble, molest, vex, harass, tease, torment. Ps. *sumbuliwa*. Nt. *sumbuka*, e.g. be annoyed, troubled, &c. Hence *sumbuk-ia, -iwa*, be troubled about, anxious for,—and sometimes, be a cause of trouble to, e.g. *watoto wanamsumbukia baba*, the children's troubles fall on the father. Ap. *sumbu-lia, -liwa*, e. g. give trouble about, make a fuss about (over, to, at, &c.). Cs. *sumbu-sha, -shwa*, as Intens., e.g. of active, intentional annoyance. Rp. *sumbuana*. (Cf. follg. and *msumbuo, sumbuo*, and syn. *uthi, chokoza*.)

-sumbufu, a. (1) troublesome, causing annoyance, &c.; (2) full of trouble, troubled, annoyed. (Cf. prec., and *sumbuo, msumbuo*.)

Sumbuo, n. (*ma-*), annoyance, teasing, trouble. (Cf. *sumbua*.)

*Sumisha, v. (1) name, call by name, give a call, call out. (Ar., not usual in Z. Cf. *ita, alika*.) (2) poison, give poison to. (Ar. Cf. *sumu*.)

*Sumu, n. (—), poison. *Lisha sumu, ua kwa sumu*, and also *sumisha*, poison, give poison to. (Ar.)

*Sumughu, n. gum-arabic, sealing-wax,—used for fastening letters, &c. (Ar.)

Sumulia, v. and Simulia, narrate, relate, report, give an account, tell a story, talk, converse. *Alimsumulia habari*, he told him the news. *Anasumulia naye*, he is talking with him. Ps. *sumuliwa*. Nt. *sumulika*. Cs. *sumuli-sha, -shwa*. Rp. *sumuliana*. (Cf. *msimulizi*, and syn.

hubiri, hadithia, sema, semezana, ongea, zungumza.)

Sungura, n. (—), (1) rabbit,—represented continually in E. African beast-stories as owing ascendency to the power of outwitting all other creatures. Hence (2) an unprincipled person, a clever rogue.

*****Sunni**, n. and **Sunna**, used of what is good, commendable, meritorious, but not absolutely binding or necessary. Hence, good traditions, counsel of perfection, work of supererogation. Also, one of the Sunnite sect. Opp. to *farathi*, e. g. *kufa si sunni, ni farathi*, death is not optional, but inevitable.

*****Sunobari**, n. (—), deal, pine,—wood of the tree *msunobari*, largely imported (like *msaji*, teak) into Z. (Ar.)

Sunza, v. (1) let go grudgingly, give with reluctance—and (2) tease, provoke, annoy, e. g. by causeless delay, reluctance, &c. (Cf. syn. *sumbua.*)

*****Sura**, n. (1) form, appearance, look, expression, face, exterior, likeness. *S. ya ulimwengu*, look of the sky, weather,—or, general view, prospect. (2) a chapter of a book, i. e. esp. of the Coran. (Ar. Cf. *uso, tabia, ginsi.*)

*****Suria**, n. (*ma-*), slave concubine. (Ar. Cf. follg., and *siri.*)

*****Suriama**, n. (*ma-*), one born of a slave concubine. (Ar. Cf. prec.)

*****Suruale**, n. and **Soruali**, trousers. (Ar.)

*****Sus**, n. liquorice. (Ar.)

Suso, n. a contrivance for hanging things up in a room,—a cord, a hanging shelf, a net, a swinging stick or board.

Suta, v. reproach, make charges against, find fault with, question suspiciously, accuse. Ps. *sutwa*. Ap. *sut-ia, -iwa*. Cs. *sut-isha, -ishwa*. Rp. *sutana*. (Cf. follg., and syn. *laumu, shutumu, shtaki.*)

Suto, n. (*ma-*), reproach, charge, accusation. (Cf. prec.)

Suza, v. rinse, souse, swill,—e. g. the final stage in washing, before drying the clothes. *S. uji*, make rice gruel,—for a sick person. Ps. *suzwa*. Ap. *suz-ia, -iwa*. Cs. *suz-isha, -ishwa*.

*****Swafi**, a. pure, clean. See **Safi**. (Ar.)

*****Swahili**, n. and **Suaheli**, the Swahili coast. *Mswahili*, a Swahili. *Kiswahili*, the Swahili language. (Ar. *sahil*, coast.)

*****Swali**, n. (*ma-*), question, inquiry, interrogation, problem. (Ar. Cf. *saili*, and syn. *ulizo.*)

T.

T, as used in this Dictionary, may be pronounced as *t* in English, without serious misrepresentation of Swahili words, i. e. the words so pronounced will as a rule be readily understood. *T*, however, has to represent both sounds of *T* in Arabic, *Ta*, and *Tah* (and sometimes *Sad*), and even in Bantu words as used in Zanzibar it is possible to distinguish a smooth *t* in *tatu*, three, a sharper *t* in *tano*, five, and an emphatic or explosive *t* sound in *taka*, dirt,—this last sound being much more marked in some cognate dialects, and written as *nt* or *ht*. Hence a considerable variation in the writing of the same Swahili word by different European authorities. It must be remembered, however, that (1) these varieties of pronunciation of *t* are not so marked in Zanzibar as at Mombasa; (2) many words pronounced with *t* at Mombasa are pronounced with *ch* in Zanzibar, and so the chance of confusion of similar words is much reduced; (3) natives themselves hardly recognize varieties of the *t* sound in Zanzibar, except under the influence of Arabic pronunciation. Hence Bishop Steere appears justified in using *t* in all cases.

T is sometimes difficult to distinguish from *d* in common pronunciation.

See further under **Th**, for the sounds so represented.

Ta-, **-ta-**, (1) as a B. pfx. is the sign of the Future Tense. It cannot as a rule bear an accent, and thus when followed by a Relat. pfx. is written *taka*, without change of meaning, e. g. *nitakapokuja*, when I shall come. In the 1 Pers. Sing. *nita-* is often pronounced *nta*, and sometimes *ni* is dropped altogether, e.g. *takuja*, I will come. Obs. *ta* appears to be a formative in verbs like *ambata*, *fumbata*, *kamata*, and such verbs involve mostly the idea of holding, or grasping. (2) is often, like *sta*, the Arab. conjugational pfx., used without modifying the root meaning of the word.

***Taa**, n. (the word thus written has several widely different senses, and probably slight differences of sound when carefully pronounced. See **T**.). (1) a lamp,—of any kind, the most general word in Z. *Washa taa*, light a lamp. *Zima taa*, put out a lamp. (Perh. cf. Ar. *ddaa*, shine.) (2) obedience, allegiance, submission,—but in Z. the Africanized form *utii* is also used. (Cf. Ar. *ttaa*, and *tii*, v., and the Arab. phrase sometimes used in Swahili *semaa wa taa*, hear and obey.) (3) a large flat fish, a skate. (4) pl. of *utaa* (which see). (5) in poet. shortened for *taala*, exalted, most high. (Arab. title of God.)

***Taabika**, v. be troubled, in distress, anxious, fatigued. Cs. *taabisha*, *-ishwa*, cause trouble, &c. (Ar. Cf. follg., and *sumbua*, *uthi*.)

***Taabu**, n. trouble, distress, fatigue, annoyance. Also sometimes as v. for *taabika*, e. g. *hawataabu kitu*, they have no sort of trouble. Ps. *taabiwa*. (Ar. Cf. prec.)

***Taadabu**, **Taajabu**, v. See **Adibu**, **Ajabu**. (Ar. with *ta*,—the conjugational pfx.)

***Taala**, v. sometimes **Taa**, lit. he is exalted,—commonly used in the Arab. phrase *Allah taala*, God is exalted, God Most High,—prefixed to all letters and formal documents. (Ar.)

***Taalamu**, v. know, be learned in, be educated. Also as a. *-taalamu*, educated, scholarly, well-informed. (Ar. Cf. *elimu*, and Ar. pfx. *ta*.)

***Taali**, v. study, learn, be a student. (Ar. for common B. *soma*, *jifunza*.)

***Taarifu**, n. information, report, news, intelligence,—usually written. Also v., see **Arifu**. *Tarifu nussu ya kuonana*, news of a person is something like meeting him. (Ar. Cf. *maarifu*, *arifu*, and syn. *habari*.)

Taataa, v. move restlessly, move about, throw the hands or body about,—as in sickness, distress, &c. (Cf. *gaagaa*, *tapatapa*.)

***Taathima**, **Taathimisha**. See **Athama**, **Athimisha**. (Ar. with conjugational pfx. *ta*.)

***Taawa**, also **Taowa**. See **Tawa**. (Ar.)

***Taazia**. See **Tanzia**.

***Tabaka**, n. (—, and *ma-*), anything laid on another,—and so, lid, cover, lining (of a dress, &c.), fold, layer, row, stratum, stage, story (of a house). (Ar. Cf. *tabiki*, and syn. *bitana*, *orofa*.)

***Tabakelo**, n. (—), a snuff box, a tobacco case,—made of wood, reed, or horn. (Cf. *tumbako*.)

***Tabarudu**, v. cool, refresh, reinvigorate. Ps. *taburudiwa*. Nt. *taburudika*. (Ar. Cf. *baridi*, and *burudisha*.)

***Tabaruki**, v. and **Tabaruku**, consecrate, bless,—in a ceremonial way. (Ar. Cf. *bariki*, *mbaraka*, *mabruki*.)

***Tabassam**, v. smile. (Arab. for common B. *chekelea*.)

***Tabawali**, v. urinate. (Arab. for common B. *kojoa*, *nya*.)

***Tabia**, n. condition, state, nature. Hence (1) of persons,—character, disposition, humour, habits, attainments, gifts; (2) of things,—e.g. *tabia ya inchi*, physical features, climate, weather, &c. (Ar. Cf. syn. of character, *sifa, mathehebu, moyo, desturi*, and generally *hali, sura*.)

*Tabibia, v. treat medically, act as doctor to, attend professionally. Ps. *tabibiwa*. (Ar. Cf. *tabibu*, and syn. *uguza, alika*.)

*Tabibu, n. (*ma-*), doctor, physician, medical man. *Tabibu hazuii ajali*, doctors cannot avert doom. (Cf. common B. *mganga*, and (English) *daktari* often heard.)

*Tabiki, v. lie close to, stick to, line, cover, be attached to. Ps. *tabikiwa*. Ap. *tabik-ia, -iwa*. Hence *tabikiana*, e.g. be great friends. Cs. *tabik-isha, -ishwa*, e.g. cause to stick to, paste on, glue on, line, put a lining to. Rp. *tabikana* (*na*), e.g. adhere closely (to). (Ar. Cf. *tabaka*.)

*Tabiri, v. interpret, explain, expound, e.g. of a fortune-teller, soothsayer, prophet,—and so, foretell, predict. E.g. *tabiri mwaka kwa chuo*, foretell the (events of a) year by a book. Ps. *tabiriwa*. Nt. *tabirika*. Rp. *tabir-ia, -iwa*. Cs. *tabiri-sha, -shwa*. (Ar. *abr*, with *ta*, cf. *fasiri, bashiri*, and *hubiri*.)

*Tadariki, v. undertake, guarantee, be responsible for, come in time for. (Ar. Cf. *daraka, diriki*.)

*Tadi, v. transgress, do wrong, offend, be rude. Ap. *tad-ia, -iwa*, e.g. be rude to. — n. also Utadi, offence, rudeness, &c., e.g. *ingia kwa tadi*, enter rudely (with violence). (Ar. Cf. *jeuri, fithuli*.)

*Tafakari, v. consider, reflect, meditate. (Ar. Cf. *fikiri*,—with the Ar. pfx. *ta*.)

*Tafathali, v. please, do a kindness to, be good to. Esp. in Imperat. as a form of polite request,—be so kind as to, if you please, please do, and so of making a polite request, e.g. *akamtafathali bwana mkubwa ampige adui yake*, and he begged the governor to overcome his enemy. (Ar. Cf. *fathili, afathali, utafathali*.)

*Tafauti, n. also Tofauti, (1) difference, discrepancy, interval (of space or time); (2) excess, want; (3) blame, quarrel. *Kitu hiki kina t.*, this thing is different, not quite what I want. *Nina t. naye*, I am not quite satisfied with him. *Yuna t.*, he is not up to the mark, not trustworthy, not qualified. (Ar. *faut*, and Ar. pfx. *ta*. Cf. *hitilafu*.)

*Tafautisha, v. Cs. make a difference, cause to be different, treat differently, distinguish. Ps. *tafautishwa*. (Ar. Cf. prec., and *pambanua*.)

*Tafiti, v. be prying (inquisitive, curious). (Cf. Ar. *taftash*, and *fatiishi, utafiti, tafuta*, and syn. B. *chungulia, tazamia*.)

*Tafsiri, v. explain, interpret, expound, make intelligible, translate. — n. (*ma-*), an explanation, translation. (Ar. See Fasiri for derivatives, &c.)

Tafuna, v. chew, nibble, gnaw, masticate, eat, i.e. use the teeth and jaws upon food,—of men and animals, e.g. *t. nyama*, chew meat, *t. miwa* (*mkate*), chew sugar-cane (bread). Ps. *tafunwa*. Nt. *tafunika*. Ap. *tafun-ia, -iwa*. Cs. *tafuni-sha, -shwa*. (Perh. cf. *tafu*, for *chafu*, cheek, and for eating, *-la, mega, meza*.)

*Tafuta, v. (1) search (for), seek, look for; and also (2) search out, get by search, find, obtain. Ps. *tafutwa*. Nt. *tafutika*. Ap. *tafut-ia, -iwa*, e.g. seek out for (at, by, &c.), search into, look for. Cs. *tafut-isha, -ishwa*. Rp. *tafutana*. (Ar. Cf. *tafiti*, and note.)

Taga, v. (1) lay (an egg), of birds generally,—also *taga yai*. Ps. *tagwa*. Ap. *tag-ia, -iwa*. Cs. *tag-isha, -ishwa*. (Cf. *yai, atamia*.)

*Tagaa, v. walk fast, stride, straddle. (Cf. Ar. *taga*, and perh. *chege, tege*.)

*Tagháfali, v. (1) be taken unawares, be surprised, be off one's guard; (2) be unmindful (of), omit to notice, neglect; (3) Act. take by surprise, make a sudden attack (or, demand) on. Ps. *taghafaliwa*. Nt. *taghafalika*, e.g. be taken by surprise. Cs. *taghafal-isha, -ishwa*, intens. (Ar. Cf. *ghafala*, and cf. *gundua, stuka, zuka*.)

*Tahamaki, v. look up, observe, take notice. As an interj. *tahamaki* (Imperat.), lo and behold! (Ar. for common *angalia, tazama*.)

*Taharizi, n. (—), side piece,—of calico in making a native dress (*kanzu*), *badani* being the front and back piece. (Ar. Cf. *kanzu*.)

*Taharuki, v. also Taharaki, be in a hurry, be bustled, be excited,—from any strong emotion. Ap. *taharuk-ia, -iwa*. Cs. *taharuk-isha, -ishwa*. (Ar. Cf. *haraka*, and syn. *angaika, fathaika*.)

*Tahayari, v. become ashamed, be abashed, be shy, be humiliated. Also Nt. *tahayarika*, in same sense. Cs. *tahayar-isha, -ishwa*, make ashamed, &c. (Ar. Cf. *haya*, and syn. *aibu, fetheha*.)

*Tahidi. See Jitahidi. (Ar.)

*Tahiri, v. cleanse,—ceremonially, but esp. of circumcision as practised by Mahommedans. Ps. *tahiriwa*. Nt. *taharika*. Ap. *tahir-ia, -iwa*. Cs. *tahir-isha, -ishwa*. (Ar. Cf. *tohara*.)

*Tahlili, n. funeral song, dirge, coronach,—esp. of the monotonous recitation of the Mahommedan creed at a funeral, e.g. *mwalimu husoma tahlili na watu huitikana*, the official leads the dirge and the people respond. (Ar.)

Tai, n. (—), (1) name of a large bird of prey, eagle, vulture; (2) (also Tayi), obedient, commonly -tii (which see), and Taa.

*Taifa, n. (*ma-*), a tribe, nation. African tribes are not described by a collective word, but as a number of individuals bearing a tribal name. Thus the Yao tribe, *Wayao*; the Ganda tribe, *Waganda*. (Ar. Cf. *kabila*.)

Taja, v. name, mention by name, mention, speak of. *Taja jina*, call by name, give a name to, name. Ps. *tajwa*. Nt. *tajika*, c. g. be named, be mentionable. Ap. *taj-ia, -iwa*. Cs. *taj-isha, -ishwa*.

*Tajiri, v. get money by trading, get rich. Also Nt. *tajirika*, in same sense. Ap. *tajir-ia, -iwa*. Cs. *tajir-isha, -ishwa*, e.g. *jitajirisha*, enrich oneself. — n. (*ma-*), a merchant, wholesale trader, capitalist, man of wealth. *Tajiri na maliye, maskini na mwanawe*, a rich man and his money are like a poor man and his child. (Ar. Cf. *mtajiri, utajiri*, and syn. *mkwasi*.)

*Taka, v. feel a want of, want, desire, wish, be inclined; (2) express a want (to), ask, request; (3) be in want of, need, require; (4) (seem to want, and so) have a tendency to, incline to, be on the verge of, be going to (of an imminent result or consequence). E.g. *nataka kwenda*, I want to go,—the negative form *sitaki* being the most absolute expression of refusal, I will not. *Taka shauri*, need advice. *Kumtaka mtu pesa*, to ask a man for money. *Inataka kunya mvua*, it is going to rain. Also impersonally, e.g. *inataka unene kijinga na mtu mjinga*, you must speak to a fool in a fool's way. *Mbuzi anataka kufa*, the goat is going to die. Ps. *takwa*. Nt. *takika*. Ap. *tak-ia, -iwa*, e.g. ask of (for, from, about, at, against, &c.). Cs. rare, *takisha*. Rp. *takana*, e.g. *takana buriani*, take a final farewell of each other. (Ar. Cf. *utashi, matakwa*, and syn. *tamani, penda, hitaji, elekea*.)

Taka, n. (—), and often Taka taka (*ma-*), (1) dirt, filth, refuse, rubbish, sweepings; (2) anything of little value, i.e. trifles, odds and ends, scraps, trinkets, fancy articles, miscellany. (Cf. *uchafu, jaa, kipuzi*.)

*Takabali, v. See **Kubali**. (Ar. form with *ta*.)

*Takabari, v. be proud, give oneself airs, play the grandee. So *jitakabari*, and Cs.(intens.)*jitakabarisha*. (Ar. Cf. *kiburi*, and *ta-*.)

*Takabathi, v. receive, take in hand, take charge of, esp. of money or property. Ps. *takabathiwa*. Ap. *takabath-ia*, *-iwa*. Cs. *takabath-isha*, *-ishwa*, e. g. cause to receive, give in charge of, entrust with. (Ar. Cf. *kabithi*, and B. syn. *pokea*.)

*Takadamu, v. go before, go forward, precede, proceed, be in advance of, lead the way. (Ar. for common B. *tangulia*. Cf. *kadamu*.)

*Takana, v. Rp. of *taka*, v.

*Takarimu, n. gift, largess, bounty, hospitality, generosity. (Ar. Cf. *karimu*, *karamu*, *karama*, and for gifts generally *bakshishi*.)

Takasa, v. clean, make clean, cleanse, purify, sanctify. Includes all kinds of cleaning. Ps. *takaswa*. Nt. *takasika*. Ap. *takas-ia*, *-iwa*, e. g. *nimemtakasia shamba*, I have cleaned up his garden for him. Cs. *takas-isha*, *-ishwa*. (Cf. follg. and *utakaso*, also syn. *safisha*, *eua*, *safidi*, *tengeneza*.)

Takata, v. become clean (clear, white), be cleansed (purified, brightened). Often of weather, *kumetakata*, it has cleared up. *Uwingu umetakata*, the sky is clear. So also the Nt. *takatika*, e. g. *moyo wake umetakatika*, his mind was cleared of its passions, was calmed. (Cf. *takasa*, and follg.)

-takatifu, a. cleansed, clean, pure, sanctified, holy. (Cf. prec. and syn. *safi*, *-eupe*, which, with *-takatifu*, best lend themselves to express a high moral ideal in Swahili.)

Takato, n. (*ma-*), cleanness, purity, serenity. (Cf. *takata*, and prec.)

*Takia, n. (*ma-*), a large cushion. (Ar. Cf. *mto*.)

Tako, n. (*ma-*), (1) the seat, buttock, ham; (2) the lower part, butt-end of anything, e. g. of a gun, spear, arrow, &c. (Cf. *kitako*.)

*Taksiri, n. fault, defect, offence, crime. (Ar. Cf. *hatiya*, *thambi*, *kosa*, which are more usual.)

*Talaka, n. (—), divorce. (Ar. Cf. *taliki*.)

*Talakeki, n. (—), and **Telakeki**, a small Arab powder-horn, for carrying a fine-grained gunpowder.

*Talasimu, n. (*ma-*), talisman, charm, magic diagram. (Ar. Cf. *hirizi*, *dawa*.)

Tale, n. (*ma-*), an undeveloped, valueless cocoanut. (Cf. *nazi*, and *kitale*.)

*Tali, v. See **Taali**. (Ar.)

*Taliki, v. dismiss, divorce. Ps. *talikiwa*. (Ar. Cf. *talaka*.)

*Taliza, v. smear, plaster,—with clay or mortar, so as to give a smooth surface to the wall of a house. Ps. *talizwa*. (Cf. Ar. *tala*, and *tomea*, *paka*.)

*Tama, v. be finished, come to an end,—in Z. commonly *timia*, *isha* (which see). — a. and **Tamma**, final, decisive, finishing a matter. E. g. *shauri lake tama*, *halirudi*, his counsel is final and is never reversed. Also as adv. finally, once for all, out and out, wholly. (Ar. Cf. *timu*, *timiza*, *timamu*, and syn. *mwisho*.)

Tama, n. and **Tamma**, end, conclusion, final stage. Also in the phrase *shika tama*, meaning 'rest the head on the hand,' sit in a dejected or brooding attitude,—considered unlucky in Z. (Kr. has *tama* (1) last drop, dregs, sediment; (2) final draught (gulp, mouthful).)

*Tamaa, n. (—), longing, desire, lust, ambition, avarice, greediness. *Fanya* (*piga*, *-wa na*) *t.*, desire, be ambitious, &c. *Ni mtu wa t.*, *mwenyi t.*, *yuna t.*, he is a covetous, ambitious man. *T. ya mali*, love of money, avarice. *Kata t.*, despair. *Weka kwa t.*, keep waiting (in suspense, unsatisfied). *Shika t.*, live in hopes. (Ar. Cf. *tamani*, and syn. *roho, shauko, kutaka*.)

*Tamalaki, v. govern, rule, be master (of), possess. (Ar. for the more common form *miliki*.)

*Tamani, v. long for, desire, covet, want, lust after, like. Ps. *tamaniwa*. Nt. *tamanika*, e.g. be desired, be desirable, be attractive. Cs. *tamanisha, -ishwa*, e.g. *yatamanisha sana*, it is very alluring (seductive, attractive, desirable). — n. (—, and *ma-*), like *tamaa*, desire, longing, lust. (Ar. Cf. *tamaa*).

*Tamasha, n. (—, and *ma-*), a spectacle, show, pageant, that which excites wonder (curiosity, amusement). (Ar. Cf. *shani, ajabu, mwujiza*.)

Tamba, v. strut proudly, walk in a swaggering, conceited way, leap, dance,—e. g. of warriors returning in triumph from a victory. Also *jitamba*, e.g. *Waarabu wanatamba na kujisifu*, the Arabs are swaggering and bragging. (Cf. *tambo*, and syn. *randa* more used in Z., and *cheza*.)

Tambaa, v. creep, crawl, move slowly. *Wadudu watambaao*, insects, reptiles. *Inzi zamtambaa kichwani*, flies are crawling on his head. Ap. *tamba-lia, -liwa*, i. e. creep up to, steal upon, e. g. *akamtambalia hatta akamkaribia*, and he crawled up to him, till he got near (cf. *nyatia, nyemelea*). Cs. *tamba-za, -zwa*, e.g. *t. maneno*, speak slowly, drawl (cf. *kokoteza maneno*). (Cf. *-tambazi, ? tambaa, kitambaa*.)

Tambaa, n. (*ma-*), a piece (strip, length) of calico or similar stuff. Usually in the dim. **kitambaa** (which see). Also plur. of *utambaa*.

Tambavu, n. (*ma-*), something hung on the shoulders or over the chest, e. g. charm, amulet (to protect from danger, accident, &c.),—also, shoulder straps, bandolier. (? Cf. *ubavu*, or *tambaa*.)

-tambazi, a. creeping, crawling,— of an insect, reptile, or creeping plant. Also as n., name of a disease which spreads over the body. (Cf. *tambaa*.)

Tambi, n. macaroni, vermicelli, i. e. *tambi za maandasi*. Also plur. of *utambi* (which see). (? Cf. *tambo*.)

Tambika, v. used of performing certain ceremonies, e.g. making offerings at cross-ways in harvest time. (Perh. not in Z.)

Tambo, n. (1) a length, distance, height,—but not so general in idea as *urefu*. E. g. *pale pana tambo*, that place is a good way (piece, stretch) off. *Yule ana tambo*, that is a tall man,—also *tambo la mtu*, a tall, big man (cf. *pande la mtu*). (2) a long stride, measured step, strut, swaggering walk, e. g. *akamfuata nyuma kwa tambo*, and he marched proudly after him. (3) ? a knot (cf. *fundo*, and *tambua*). (Cf. *tamba, tambi, utambo*, and the common dim. form *kitambo*, also *mtambo*.)

Tambua, v. recognize, know again, remember, see the meaning of, discern, understand. Ps. *tambuliwa*. Nt. *tambulika*, e. g. *mtu wa kutambulika*, a well-known (remarkable, distinguished) person. Hence *tambulikana*, be recognizable, be intelligible, be knowable. *Ametambulikana kuwa mwizi*, he has been convicted of thieving. Ap. *tambu-lia, -liwa*. Cs. *tambu-lisha, -lishwa*, i. e. make known, expound, explain. Rp. *tambuana*. (Cf. *-tambuzi, utambuzi*, and syn. *fahamu, jua*, and ? root of *tambo, tambaa*, &c.)

*Tambuu, n. (—), (1) leaf of the betel-plant, *mtambuu*; (2) a mixture for chewing, of which this leaf is the chief ingredient, very popular in Z. See **Uraibu**. (Perh. a Hind. word.)

Tambuza, v. used of smith's work, —fashion by heat and hammering, beat out, forge, weld, e.g. a broken knife or hoe. Ps. *tambuzwa*. Nt. *tambuzika*. Ap. *tambuz-ia, -iwa*. Cs. *tambuz-isha, -ishwa*, e.g. have a thing welded (repaired by a smith),

&c. (Perh. cf. *tambo*, i.e. a lengthening out.)

-tambuzi, a. clever, quick, intelligent, knowing, shrewd. (Cf. *tambua*, and syn. *-juzi, -elekevu, -a akili*.)

Tam'ka, v. also Tamuka, pronounce, articulate, speak in a formal (emphatic, expressive) way. Ps. *tam'kwa*. Ap. *tam'k-ia, -iwa*. Cs. *tam'-sha, -shwa*. (Cf. follg.)

Tam'ko, n. (*ma-*), act (style, way, &c.) of speaking, articulation, pronunciation, delivery, speech. *Matam'ko ya maneno*, ways of pronouncing words. *Tam'ko la kizungu*, a European accent. (Cf. *tam'ka*.)

*Tamma, n. and a. See Tama.

*Tamu, n. (—), flavour, taste,—and esp. of pleasant taste, sweetness, pleasantness. Thus opp. to *uchungu*, e.g. *vyakula ni tamu na uchungu*, food is either sweet or bitter, pleasant or unpleasant. *Nyama za nguruwe zina tamu*, pork is nice to eat. *Ona tamu*, enjoy, find pleasure in. *Tia tamu*, make pleasant, give a relish to. (Ar. Cf. *luththa*, and follg.)

*-tamu, a. (same with D 4 (P), D 5 (S), D 6), sweet, pleasant, nice, delightful,—of all pleasures, esp. those of sense. *Sukali tamu*, sugar is sweet. *Maneno matamu*, pleasant, agreeable speech. *Maji matamu*, fresh water, as opp. to salt water. *Tamu?* Is it nice? *Tamu* is also used as adv., e.g. *kumemkalia tamu*, he has found it agreeable. (Ar. Cf. *utamu*, and opp. *-baya, -chungu, -kali, -a chumvi*, and syn. *-zuri, -ema, -a kupendeza*.)

Tamvua, n. usu. in plur. *matamvua*, ends, tips—of any kind of calico or textile fabric, and so of fringe of a cloth, lappets or hanging ends of a turban, fluff of cotton, lint. (Cf. *utamvua*.)

Tana, v. and n. See Chana.

*Tanabahi, v. give attention (to), turn the mind to, carefully notice and consider, form a conclusion (about). (Ar. *nabah*, and cf. syn. *angalia, fikiri, azimu*.)

*Tanafusi, v. breathe, draw breath, recover breath. (Ar. *nafsi*, for common *pumzika*. Cf. *nafsi, nafusi*.)

Tanda, v. spread, spread out, spread over, be spread out (over). The idea seems to be not of mere extension (*enea*) or dispersion (*tawanya*), but of something that is continuous and covers. Hence several special uses, and a large number of derivative forms. E.g. *tanda kitanda*, lace a bedstead (with cord of cocoanut fibre, making a strong springy mattress). (Dist. *tandika kitanda*, make a bed, i.e. supply with sleeping mat or coverlets.) *Uwingu umetanda, kumetanda*, the sky is overcast, it is cloudy. *Jitanda*, stretch oneself across (upon, over),—also *jitanda nguo*, cover oneself with clothes, put on an overcoat. *Tanda samaki*, catch fish in an outspread cloth, used as a net. Ps. *tandwa*. Nt. *tandika*,—most commonly in an Act. sense, spread out (over), lay out (on), cover (with), e.g. *t. mkeka kitandani* (see above), arrange a mat on a bed, make a bed,—also *tandika kitanda*. *T. punda*, harness a donkey, put saddle, &c. on, —*not* used of putting on dress. *Tandika nguo chini*, lay out clothes on the ground. *T. majamvi*, spread mats (as carpets), &c. Cf. *wengi waliotandika chini*, many were laid low, i.e. killed. *Muungu ametandika mbingu na inchi*, God spread out the heaven and earth. Hence derivs. *tandikwa*, also *tandik-ia, -iwa, tand-isha, -ishwa*, and *tandikiana*. E.g. *wakawapa nyumba wakawatandikia*, and they gave them houses, and furnished them (with mats, &c.) for them. Ap. *tand-ia, -iwa*. Cs. *tand-isha, -ishwa*. Also *tand-aza, -azwa*, like *tanda, tandika*, but of special objects, e.g. *tandaza mtama*, spread out millet on a mat to dry in the sun, also *t. nguo*. (Cf. *tandua, tandama, tandawaa, kitanda, utando, mtande, mtandio, tandiko, tando,* and also such syn. as *enea, tawanya, wamba, funika*.)

Tandama, v. St. be in an extended position, be spread out, lie stretched out, e.g. of floating on the water, as a crocodile or a log. Ap. *tandam-ia, -iwa.* Cs. *tandam-isha, -ishwa.* Rp. *tandamana*, of several objects together. (Cf. *tanda*.)

Tandawaa, v. stretch oneself at ease, recline, loll, spread oneself out on a couch. (Cf. *tanda*.)

Tandiko, n. (*ma-*), something spread out, but usu. of mats, carpets, &c., e.g. *matandiko ya chumba yaliyotandikwa chini*, the mats with which the room was furnished. Also, harness, accoutrements, but only for animals. (Cf. *tanda*.)

Tando, n. (*ma-*), something spread out, e.g. *t. la buibui*, a spider's web. *Tando*, or *tandu, la macho*, a film over the eye, causing blindness. Also (? not in Z.) tribal marks, tattooing (cf. *chale*). (Cf. *tanda*, and *utando*.)

Tandu, n. (—), or **Taandu**, a centipede.

Tandua, v. Rv. of *tanda*, e.g. take off (fold up, remove) what is laid on (spread out, &c.), and so of unfurnishing a bed or room, unharnessing an animal, &c. Ps. *tandulia*. Nt. *tanduka.* Ap. *tandu-lia, -liwa.* Cs. *tandu-za, -zwa.* (Cf. *tanda*.)

Tanga, n. (*ma-*), (1) a sail,—of a vessel, of matting or canvas, e.g. *tweka t.*, set (hoist) sail, *tua t.*, lower sail. *Kunja t.*, reef sail. *Matanga kati*, wind a beam. Obs. *tanga mbili*, of the period of shifting winds between the two monsoons, also called *malelezi* (cf. *foromali, dasi*). (2) a formal mourning,—usually in the plur. *matanga*, lasting from three or four to ten days, during which friends sleep in the mourner's house. *Kaa (weka, andika) matanga*, remain in (arrange a) mourning. *Ondoa (vunja) matanga*, go out of (end a) mourning. (Cf. *msiba* and follg.)

Tanga, v. go to and fro, go from side to side, dawdle, loiter, stroll about, wander. Also Rd. *tanga tanga*, move in a listless, objectless way. Cs. *tang-isha, -ishwa*, e.g. take for a stroll, cause to idle, &c. (Cf. *mtango, tango*, and follg., and syn. *sita, zunguka, tembea*.)

Tangaa, v. spread abroad, be in vogue, be current, become generally known, be published. E.g. *jina lake limetangaa na ulimwengu*, his name is famous throughout the world. Cs. *tanga-za, -zwa* (and perh. *tanga-isha, tangisha*), make known, publish abroad. Ap. *tanga-zia, -ziwa*, e.g. *amemtangazia aibu yake*, he made his dishonour known. Rp. *tangazana*. (Perh. cf. *tanga*, v., and *mtangazi*.)

Tangamana, Tangam'ka. See **Changamana, Changam'ka.**

Tangawizi, n. (—), ginger.

Tangi, n. (*ma-*), a large wooden chest used for carrying fresh water in a native vessel at sea, a water tank.

Tango, n. (*ma-*), (1) a vegetable like a cucumber, but with a harder rind, fruit of the *mtango*; (2) aimless wandering, idling, vagabondage, idle talk, gossip,—also perplexity, trouble. (Cf. *tanga*, v.)

Tangu, prep. since, from,—with reference to a time or, less commonly, place, regarded as a starting-point. *Tangu lini alipokuja hapa?* How long ago was it that he came here? *Tangu miaka miwili (tangu zamani)*, two years ago (a long time ago). *Tangu hapa hatta huko*, from here to there. (Cf. *toka, kutoka*, used as prep.)

Tangua, v. annul, abolish, annihilate, invalidate, bring to nought, frustrate. E.g. *t. sheria*, cancel a law; *t. ahadi*, revoke a promise; *t. ndoa*, annul a marriage; *t. usafiki*, break off friendship. Nt. *tanguka*. (A Rv. form, but no apparent connexion with *tanga*, v., and no deriv. stems in common use. Cf. follg.)

Tangulia, v. (1) go before, go first, precede, take the lead; (2) be beforehand (with), anticipate, forestall. Sometimes *tangulia mbele*, and *mbele ya*, and this is more common than construction with an objective person-pfx., i.e. *nimetangulia mbele yako*, rather than *nimekutangulia*. *Alitangulia kuniambia*, he was the first to tell me, or, he took the initiative in speaking to me. Cs. *tanguli-za*, *-zwa*, e.g. cause to go before, send on in advance, prefer, give precedence to. *Tanguliza fetha*, make a payment in advance. (No apparent connexion with *tangua*, or *tanga*. Cf. follg. and *mtangulizi*, and Ar. syn. *takadamu*.)

-tangulifu, a. (same with D 4 (P), D 5 (S), D 6), (1) in advance, before others, but commonly (2) fig. eminent, surpassing, of superior rank (quality). (Cf. prec. and *mtangulizi*.)

Tani, n. in the adverbial phrase *kwa tani*, on the back,—of position, and in *tanitani*, *kitanitani*, *matanitani*, sometimes *tana*,—in same sense. (Cf. *kichalichali*, *kingalingali*, and opp. *fudifudi*, and perh. *tanua*, spread out.)

Tano, n. and a. *-tano*, five. *-a tano*, fifth. *Jumaa tano*, Wednesday. See **Juma**. (Ar. *hamsi*, also used.)

Tanua, v. open wide, stretch apart, widen, expand, make room by. E.g. *tanua miguu*, take long strides; *t. kinwa*, open the mouth wide; *t. mashua*, push off a boat. Ps. *tanuliwa*. Nt. *tanuka*. Ap. *tanu-lia*, *-liwa*. (Cf. *tani*, and also *tanda*, *panua*.)

Tanuu, n. (—), also **Tanuru**, **Tanu**, native lime-kiln, i.e. limestone piled on a circular heap of logs and burnt. E.g. *jenga tanu ya kuoka chokaa*, make a pile of wood for burning lime. Also *choma t.*, i.e. burn lime.

Tanzi, n. (—, or *ma-*), loop, noose, slipknot, snare, trap worked by a string. E.g. *t. la ukambaa* (*la ugwe*, *la kutegea nyama*), a noose of cord (or string, for trapping animals). *T. la samaki*, a haul (catch, draught) of fish. *T. la roho*, a halter.

***Tanzia**, n. (—) and **Taazia**, news of a death, announcement of a funeral, e.g. *waraka wa tanzia* (also *barua ya msiba*), a written notification of a mourning. *Kumpa mkono wa t.*, to pay a visit of condolence to him. (Ar. Cf. *mbirambi*, *hani*.)

Tanzu, n. (*ma-*), a bough,—but in Z. usually *tawi*.

Tao, n. (*ma-*), something curved, e.g. an arch, a bend of a river, a bay or inlet, the hem round the bottom of a native dress (*kanzu*). E.g. *njia inafanya matao*, the road is winding. (Cf. *pindi*, *mzingo*, *kunjo*, *kombo*.)

Tapa, n. (*ma-*), leaf of a fan palm (*mvumo*), used by natives as an umbrella. Sometimes **Dapa**.

Tapa, v. shiver, tremble, shudder, jump about convulsively. *T. kwa baridi*, shiver with cold. *Mwili wanitapa*, my body is shuddering. *Jitapa*, jump about,—for display (cf. *randa*, *ruka*). Also *tapatapa*, of dying fish. (Cf. *kitapo*, *mtapo*, ? *tapika*.)

Tapakaa, v. be scattered about, be spread abroad, be here and there, infest, be dotted about, e.g. of the stars in the sky, of a flood, robbers, &c. (Cf. follg.)

Tapanya, v. scatter about, disperse, throw away, waste, dissipate. *T. mali*, be prodigal. Nt. *tapanyika*, e.g. of water in a flood. Rp. *tapanyikana*, of people dispersing in different directions. Cs. *tapan-isha*, *-ishwa*. (Cf. *tapakaa*, and *tawanya*.)

Tapika, v. vomit, be sick. Cs.

tapi-sha, -shwa, cause to vomit, act as an emetic. (Cf. follg.)

Tapishi, n. (*ma-*), vomit. *Tapisho*, n. (*ma-*), that which causes vomiting, an emetic. (Cf. *tapika*.)

Tapo, n. (*ma-*), a lot (troop, number) of men or animals,—esp. of a division (detachment, regiment) of fighting men. (A *tapo* would be part of a *jeshi*, or *kundi*. Cf. *kikosi*.)

*****Tarabe**, n. used to describe a door or window of wood, strong and framed, not that of a native hut. E. g. *mlango wa tarabe, tarabe ya dirisha*. (? Ar. *tarib, arb*, firm.)

*****Tarabushi**, n. and **Tarbushi**, a fez, red cap with tassel. (Ar. Cf. *kofia*.)

*****Tarafu**, n. (—), part, business, duty, work, task. (Ar. Cf. syn. *shughuli, kazi*.)

*****Taraja**, v. hope, be confident, expect. Ps. *tarajiwa*. Nt. *tarajika*. Ap. *taraj-ia, -iwa*, e. g. hope for (about, in). (Ar. Cf. *tumai, tumaini*.)

*****Tarakimu**, n. a written character, letter, numeral, figure. (Ar. Cf. *harufu, sifuri*.)

*****Tarathia**, v. try to satisfy, make apologies (to), conciliate, expostulate (with), remonstrate (with), urge objections (to). Ps. *tarathiwa*. Nt. *tarathika*. Cs. *tarath-isha, -ishwa*. (Ar., same root as *rithi, urathi*, &c.)

*****Taratibu**, n. (—), and **Utaratibu**, (1) arrangement, method, system, neatness, order; (2) quietness, slowness, gentleness. *Fanya (shika) t.*, be orderly, quiet, &c. *Kwa t.* and *taratibu* as adv., in a regular, steady, quiet, slow, easy-going way. Also as adj. and sometimes *-taratibu*, quiet, slow, regular, &c. *Uwapo mtaratibu, humshinda mwenyi nguvu*, i. e. method goes further than force, quietness than violence, &c. (Ar. Cf. *utaratibu, ratibu*, and syn. *upole, kawaida, kiasi*.)

*****Taraza**, n. (—), also **Tarizi**, a border or edging, woven on to turbans or waistcloths in Z., giving the effect of a narrow ornamental braid of silk. (Ar. Cf. *tarizi*.)

*****Tarazaki**, v. same as **Ruzuku** (which see). (Ar. Cf. *riziki*.)

*****Tari**, n. (—), a tambourine or small drum, used in various half-social, half-religious ceremonies. (Cf. *ngoma*.)

*****Tarihi**, n. (—), date, annals, chronicle, journal, history,—esp. of date of birth, e. g. *tarihi yako imo ndani ya hirizi*, your date (of birth) is inside the charm. As a specimen, *nikazaliwa katika mwezi wa Rehaji, siku ya jumaa a tatu mwezi kumi na tatu kwa saa ya sita athuuri, sene* (i. e. Ar. for *mwaka*) 1285, I was born at noon on Monday the 13th of Rehaji, 1285.

*****Tariki**, n. road, path, way. (Arab. for *njia*.)

*****Tarishi**, n. (*ma-*), a swift runner, special messenger, postman, courier, express. (Ar.)

*****Tarizi**, v. weave a border (to), make an embroidered edging (on),—i. e. usually a coloured silk braid-like border to a turban, or waistcloth, or lines of stitched work on the wrists and front of a native dress (*kanzu*). — n. like *taraza*, woven border, stitched edging. (Ar.)

Taruma, n. (*ma-*), also **Turuma, Toruma**, any piece of wood used to stiffen or strengthen a structure or framework, e. g. ledge, support, strut, spoke (of a wheel), rib (of a vessel), thwart.

Tasa, n. (—) and **Tassa**, (1) any small metal vessel, cup, jug, mug, basin, saucer, spittoon,—usually of copper, brass, or tin. (2) a game of touch (Str.).

Tasa, a. (and **Tassa**), barren, that has produced offspring once only,—of any living creature. Opp. to *-zazi*. (Cf. *utasa*.)

*****Tasbihi**, n. (—), (1) praise, ascription of praise, to God; (2)

a Mahommedan rosary, for recording praises and prayers. *Sali t.*, recite prayers by a rosary. *Vuta urathi kwa t.*, obtain grace by use of the rosary. (Ar. *sabbah*. Cf. *himidi, hemdi, sifu, sifa*.)

***Tashwishi**, n. (—), doubt, perplexity. (Ar. for the more common *mashaka, fathaa*.)

***Taslimu**, n. direct delivery, prompt (cash) payment. E. g. *nunua taslimu*, buy for ready money, i. e. *mkono kwa mkono*. (Ar. Cf. *salimu*.)

Tassa, v. not often heard in Z. Used with Negat. pfxs. only, but not changing the final *-a* to *i* in the Present, and only as a kind of auxiliary before another verb in the Infinitive. Be beforehand with, manage (to), get (to), finish (doing), what the following verb implies, e. g. *sitassa kuandika*, I have not yet written.

Tassa, n. See **Tasa**.

***Taswira**, n. (—), picture, likeness, painting, portrait. (Ar. Cf. *mfano, methali, sanamu, sura*.)

Tata, v. be in a tangle, be complicated, be in confusion, but usually in the Nt. *tatika*. Ap. *tat-ia, -iwa, -ika*, (1) make a tangle of; (2) wind up in a skein or ball; (3) puzzle, perplex, make difficulties. E. g. *tatia uzi kijitini*, wind thread on a stick. *Tatia kilemba*, arrange the folds of a turban. Also of a serpent coiling round its prey. Hence *tatiana*. Also *tat-iza, -izwa, tatiz-ia, -iwa* (Cs. *tatizana*), like *tatia*, entangle, wind, cause a complication, perplex. Rp. *tatana*, be in a tangle, be puzzled, e. g. of interlacing foliage, of confused statements. *Vyombo vinatatana katika bandari*, the dhows are all huddling together in the harbour. Hence *tatan-ia, -iwa*. Also *tatan-isha, -ishwa*. — n. usu. in plur. *matata*, tangle, mess, difficulty, perplexity, &c. E. g. *tata la uzi*, tangled thread. *Tata la maneno*, a puzzling statement. (Cf. *tatua, tatanua, tatizo, mtatio*, and dist. *tata*, plur. of *utata*.)

Tataga, v. make a crossing (with), get across, lay across. E. g. *tataga mti mtoni*, lay a tree as a bridge across a river. (Cf. *mtatago, ulalo*.)

Tatanua, v. and **Tatanyua**, (1) unravel, unwind; (2) fig. clear up a complication, disentangle, simplify, extricate, explain. Nt. *tatanuka*. (Rv. of *tatana*. See **Tata**.)

Tatizo, n. (*ma-*), entanglement, complication, difficulty. (Cf. *tata*.)

Tatu, n. and a. -tatu (*tatu* with D 4 (P), D 6 (P)), three. *-a tatu*, third. (Cf. Ar. *thelatha*, also sometimes used. Obs. the possibility in Swahili of such a word as *mtatu*, for a 'single threefold person.')

Tatua, v. also **Tataua**, Rv. of *tata*, (1) disentangle a tangle, cut a knot, solve a difficulty, e. g. *tatua tata*; but mostly (2) tear, rend, cleave, rip open or apart. E. g. *tatua nguo*, tear clothes (cf. *rarua, pasua, tumbua*). Ps. *tatuliwa*. Nt. *tatuka*, with an Ap. *tatuk-ia, -iwa*, e. g. *ametatukiwa nguo*, he has got his clothes torn for him. Hence *tatukana*. Ap. *tatu-lia, -liwa*. Cs. *tatu-lisha, -lishwa*. (Cf. *tata*; and syn. above, *rarua*, &c.)

***Taumu**, n. (*ma-*), prop, shore, support,—for a vessel ashore (Kr.). (Cf. *gadi*, and *tegemeo*.)

***Tauni**, n. (—), plague, pestilence, an epidemic. (Ar. Cf. *ugonjwa, marathi*.)

***Tausi**, n. (—), a peacock. (Ar.)

Tawa, v. (1) remain indoors, live in seclusion,—esp. for a moral or religious object, and so (2) not gad about, live a quiet, moral, religious life. Ap. *taw-ia, -iwa*. Cs. *taw-isha, -ishwa*, e. g. *kijana mwanamke akipata miaka sita hutawishwa*, a girl, when six years old, is generally confined to the house. (Cf. follg. and *mta'wa, uta'wa*, which appear the same, and of Ar. origin.)

-tawa, a. remaining indoors, choosing seclusion, devout, religious. (Cf. prec.)

Tawa, n. (—, and *ma-*), frying-pan, saucepan. (Cf. *chungu, kango.*)

Tawafa, n. (—), a candle. (Cf. syn. *meshmaa.*)

*****Tawakali**, v. put trust in, have confidence (in), rely on, take courage, hope. E.g. *tawakili kwa Muungu*, trust in God. (Ar. Cf. *wakili*, and syn. *amini, tumaini.*)

*****Tawala**, v. become governor (of), govern, rule. Ps. *tawaliwa*. Nt. *tawalika*. Ap. *tawal-ia, -iwa*. Cs. *tawal-isha, -ishwa*, and commonly *tawaza, tawazwa*, e.g. cause to rule, instal as ruler, set on the t..rone, celebrate the coronation of. (Ar. Cf. *wali, liwali*, and syn. *milikisha.*)

Tawanya, v. scatter abroad, disperse, distribute, dissipate, throw away. E.g. *tawanya mbegu (mali, adui)*, scatter seed (money, enemies). Ps. *tawanyiwa*. Nt. *tawanyika*. Ap. *tawany-ia, -iwa*. Cs. *tawany-isha, -ishwa*, intens. (Cf. follg. *mtawanya* and *tapanya.*)

Tawanyiko, n. (*ma-*), scattering, wasting, throwing away. (Cf. prec.)

*****Tawashi**, n. (*ma-*), also **Towashi**, a eunuch. (Ar. Cf. *mhassi.*)

*****Tawaza**, v. perform ceremonial ablution,—esp. as to the feet, i.e. *tawaza miguu*, as dist. from *nawa, chamba* (which see). (Ar. *wathu.* Dist. *tawaza*, Cs. of *tawala.*)

Tawi, n. (*ma-*), (1) bough, branch (of a tree); (2) stem with growing fruit or grain, bunch, cluster, ear, e.g. *t. la nazi*, bunch of cocoanuts, *t. la mzabibu (la mtende)*, bunch of grapes (dates). *Ncha (shina) ya t.*, tip (stem) of the branch (bunch). (Cf. *kitawi*, and *utawi*, with plur. *tawi*, which dist.)

Taya, n. (*ma-*), jaw, jaw-bone. *Tia hatamu tayani mwa punda*, put the bridle on the donkey's jaw.

Taya, v. reproach, rebuke, blame. Not common in Z. (Cf. *tayo*, and syn. *shutumu, laumu, suta.*)

*****Tayari**, a. ready, prepared, at hand. *Fanya (weka) t.*, make ready, prepare. — v. be ready. (Hind. Cf. *andaa.*)

*****Tayi**, a. and **Tai**, obedient. See *-tii*. (Ar.)

Tayo, n. (*ma-*), reproach, rebuke. (Cf. *taya*, and syn. *shutumu, laumu, suto.*)

Tazama, v. look (at), gaze (at), fix the eyes (on), contemplate, examine, observe, test. Ps. *tazamwa*. Nt. *tazamika*, e.g. (1) be looked at; (2) be fit to be looked at, be desirable (pleasant) to the eyes, be noteworthy. *Jitazama*, look at one's face in a glass. Ap. *tazam-ia, -iwa*, e.g. look into, examine closely, inspect, review, look with, see with. *Durabini ya kutazamia*, a telescope to look through. *T. kazi*, examine work. *Tazamiwa na mganga*, be examined by a doctor. *Jitazamia (moyo)*, examine oneself (conscience). Cs. *tazam-isha, -ishwa*, e.g. attract the eye, draw attention, be attractive (to). Also intens. gaze intently. Rp. *tazamana*. (Cf. follg. and *ona*, of perception generally, and syn. *angalia, chungulia, kagua.*)

Tazamo, n. (*ma-*), look, glance, gaze. (Cf. prec. and syn. Ar. *nathari.*)

*****Tazia**, n. condolence. See **Tanzia, Taazia**. (Ar.)

Tega, v. (1) set ready, put in position, prepare,—esp. of a trap, and so (2) snare, entrap, decoy, catch, and (3) fig. try to deceive, beguile. E.g. *t. mtego*, set a trap. *T. sikio*, listen, give ear to, prepare to hear. *T. kitendawili*, propound a riddle,—the challenge being *Kitendawili!* Here is a riddle,—and the reply *Tega*, Propound it, let us hear it. *Akajitega na uta wake*, he put himself ready with his bow. *Tega ndege kwa tanzi*, snare birds with a noose. Ps. *tegwa*. Nt. *tegeka*. Ap. *teg-ea, -ewa*. Cs. *teg-esha, -eshwa*. Rp. *tegana*. (Cf. *mtego, tego, tegua*, and syn. *nasa, guia, kamata*.)

Tegemea, v. (1) lean upon, rest on, be propped upon; (2) fig. trust (to), find protection (in), rely (upon). E. g. *alimtegemea mkono*, he leaned on his arm. *Nyumba inategemea mti*, the house is supported by a tree. Also with *kwa*, e. g. *tegemea kwa Muungu (Sultani)*, trust to Providence (the Sultan). Ps. *tegemewa*. Ap. *tegem-eza, -ezwa*, e. g. cause to rest on, prop up, support, buttress, protect, sustain. *T. chombo*, prop, or shore up, a vessel (cf. *gadimu*). *T. miguu*, rest one leg on the other. (Cf. follg. and *egemea*,—a variant with less general meaning.)

Tegemeo, n. (*ma-*), prop, buttress, support, protection. *Katika mategemeo yangu halikupati kitu*, under my protection nothing can get at you. (Cf. prec., and syn. *nguzo, hamaya, tunza*.)

Tego, n. (*ma-*), a powerful charm, capable of causing disease and death. (Cf. *tega, mtego*.)

Tegu, n. (*ma-*), a tapeworm.

Tegua, v. Rv. of *tega*, let a trap go off, remove a snare or spell, take away what was set ready or specially placed, take off the fire, put out of joint, sprain. Thus *t. mtambo*, let off a spring-trap. *T. uganga*, take off a spell,—also *.t. tego*. *T. miguu*, sprain the ankle. Ps. *teguliwa*. Nt. *teguka* (sometimes *teuka*). Ap. *tegu-lia, -liwa*. (Cf. *tega, tego, mtego*, and for 'sprain' *stuka, stusha*. Also *tekua* or *tegua* (?) for *telekua*.)

*****Teitei**, n. (*ma-*), frock, gown.

Teka, v. (1) take, take up, carry off,—of water from a well, e. g. *teka maji kisimani*, draw water at the well. But otherwise almost always implying violence, i. e. (2) plunder, ravage, ransack, capture by force, e. g. *t. mji*, plunder a town; *t. inchi*, ravage a country; *t. watu na ng'ombe*, carry off people and cattle. Ps. *tekwa*, in both senses, e. g. *kisima kilichotekwa maji*, a well from which water was drawn. *Tumetekwa*, we are prisoners of war. Ap. *tek-ea, -ewa*. Obs. *tekewa akili*, be bewildered, lose one's senses (like *potewa, rukwa na akili*). Cs. *tekana*.

Teke, n. (*ma-*), a kick. *Piga teke*, kick, v.

Teke, a. also **-teke** and **Teketeke**, (1) soft, yielding; (2) weak, feeble. *Nyama teke*, tender meat. *Mtu teke*, a soft, weak-spirited person. *Muhindi mteke*, Indian corn in a soft half-ripe state. *Tunda teke*, a soft over-ripe fruit. (Cf. (1) *-ororo, laini*, (2) *thaifu, dufu*.)

Tekea, v. and **Tekewa**. See **Teka**.

Tekelea, v. (1) arrive (at), reach, come to; (2) be accomplished, be carried through, come to its end. E. g. *wakati umetekelea*, the time has arrived. *Ahadi imetekelea*, the promise is fulfilled. Ps. *tekelewa*. Cs. *tekeleza*, fulfil, execute, carry out. (Cf. *tekeza*,—apparently from a root *teka*, syn. *fika*. Dist. *teka*, see above.)

Tekenya, v. tickle. Ps. *tekenywa*. Rp. *tekenyana*. — n. (*ma-*), a jigger,—a burrowing flea.

Teketea, v. be consumed, be destroyed, be ruined,—commonly in the literal sense and by fire, i. e. *teketea moto*, or *kwa moto*, be burnt up,—but also of the effects of a storm, *mashamba yote yameteketea*, all the plantations were ruined. Cs. *teketeza, -ezwa*, burn, destroy by fire. (Cf. *choma, angamia, potea*.)

Tekeza, v. cause to arrive, bring to an end. E. g. *t. chombo pwani*, bring a vessel to the shore. *T. roho*, die. (Cf. syn. *fikiza*, and *tekelea*. Dist. *teka*, take off.)

Tekua, v. break down, break up. See **Ekua**, which is a variant, also **Wekua**. Also for *telekua, teekua*, e.g. *tekua chungu mekoni*, take a cooking pot off the fire. See **Telekua**.

Tele, n. plenty, abundance, and a. plentiful, many, much, abundant. *Maji tele*, or *ya tele*, plenty of water. *Alimpa tele*, he gave him a quantity. (Cf. syn. *-ingi, marithawa*. Dist. *teli*.)

Telea, v. come (go) down, descend, disembark,—but in Z. only in *telem'ka* (which see). Cs. *teleza*, e.g. (1) cause to come down, cause to fall; and so (2) be slippery. Also (3) intens. slip, slide, fall by slipping. *Ameteleza kwa miguu akaanguka*, his feet slipped and he fell. *Inchi yateleza*, the ground is slippery. Hence *telezesha*, cause to slip, make slide. (Cf. *utelezi, telezi*.)

Teleka, v. (1) put on the fire,—both of cooking pot and the food in it. In full, *t. chungu motoni*, put a pot on the fire. Hence (2) cook, boil (water), prepare food. Ps. *telekwa*. Ap. *telek-ea, -ewa*, e.g. *chungu cha kutelekea maji*, a pot to boil water in. Cs. *telek-eza, -ezwa*, e.g. cause to put on the fire, get cooking done, get a meal prepared. *Tumepumzika na kut.*, we rested and got a regular meal.

Telekua, v. and **Tekua, Tegua**, take off the fire,—Rv. of *teleka*. (Cf. *epua, ipua*.)

Telemua, v. cause to go down (fall down, slip down), pull down, &c. Nt. *telemuka*, or *telem'ka*, go down, descend, slope downwards, run (slide, fall), down a steep place. (Cf. follg. and *telea*, also syn. *shuka, anguka, poromoka*.)

Telemuko, n. (*ma-*), and **Telem'ko**, act (manner, place, &c.) of going down, descent, slope, declivity, hill, fall of the ground, downward tendency. (Cf. prec. and *mshuko*.)

***Teli**, n. gold thread, gold braid. Also *teli ya thahabu*, gold thread, *teli ya fetha*, silver thread. (Hind. Cf. *uzi, zari*.)

***Telki**, n. the quick ambling step of a donkey, half walk, half run. *Enda telki*, step quickly, go at a trot or run. (Ar. Cf. common syn. B. *mbio*.)

Tema, v. (1) cut, slash, cut up, cut in strips, e.g. with a knife, sword, or tool. *T. miti* (*miwa, kuni*), cut down (small) trees (sugar-cane, firewood). *T. nakshi*, carve. *T. ulimi*, cut a tenon. (2) spit out, expectorate. *T. mate* (*kikohozi*), spit out saliva (phlegm). Ps. *temwa*. Nt. *temeka*. Ap. *tem-ea, -ewa*. Cs. *tem-esha, -eshwa*. (Cf. *kata, chonga, chanja, pasua*.)

Tembe, n. (—), a hen full-grown but not yet laying. (Cf. *kuku, koo*.)

Tembea, v. go about, take a walk, stroll, wander, take exercise, go on a tour,—usually for pleasure, not 'point to point' walking, but also of a business round. Sometimes (like *zunguka*) of a loose, unprincipled, immoral way of living. E.g. *amekwenda tembea*, he has gone for a walk. *Akili zake zatembea*, his mind is wandering. *Pa kutembea*, a pleasure-ground. Ap. *temb-elea, -elewa*, e.g. go to visit, call on, walk about in, &c. *Jitembelea*, go a stroll, go on a pleasure trip. *Fimbo ya kutembelea*, a fancy walking-stick. Rp. *tembeleana*, call on each other, be on visiting terms. Cs. *temb-eza, -ezwa*, cause to walk about,—and so, hawk about for sale, advertise, parade, make a show of, send (employ) to sell goods, show (a stranger) round a town, &c. *Chema chajiuza, kibaya chajitembeza*, a good thing sells itself, a bad thing tries to (and fails). (Cf. follg.)

Tembezi, n. usu. in plur. *matembezi*, a walk, stroll, tour, walking exercise, &c. (Cf. *tembea, utembezi*.)

Tembo, n. (1) an elephant,—the regular word in Z. but elsewhere often *ndofu*. *Mkono wa tembo*, trunk of an elephant,—also the name of a species of banana. (2) palm-wine, the fermented sap of the cocoanut tree (cf. *gema*). (3) name of a fish.

*Temsi, n. filigree work.

Tena, adv. and conj., then, secondly, further, in addition,—also, next, still, again, afterwards. A common connective of sentences, like *hatta* and *na*, denoting sequence, succession, repetition. *Nimesema tena na tena*, I have said it again and again. *Na tena?* and then? what next? *Akampiga tena*, and he beat him a second time, again. (Kr. suggests a connexion with the Ar. root of the second numeral, e.g. in *miteen*, two hundred.)

Tenda, v. do, act, practise. The most common and comprehensive word denoting action, operation, use of energy or force (cf. *tendo, kitendo, utendaji*). Often synonymous with *fanya*, e.g. *tenda kazi, fanya kazi, tenda vema, fanya vema*, but also broadly contrasted with it, as *do* with *make*, action or operation with production. See Fanya. The simple stem *tenda*, when used with a direct personal object, denotes not only direct acting upon, or treatment of, the person, but also commonly unfavourable action or bad treatment (cf. a similar use of the simple stems, *fanya, sema, amba*), in contrast to the Ap. form of the stem, implying favourable action and treatment. E.g. *akutendaye umtende*, do harm to him who does harm to you. *Sungura amenitenda leo*, the rabbit has done (what he liked to) me today. — n. *jitenda*, sometimes act as, pretend to be, make oneself. Ps. *tendwa*, e.g. *ametendwa mengi*, he has endured much ill-treatment. Nt. *tendeka*, e.g. be done, be practicable,—and hence, *tendekeza*, i.e. cause to be practicable, and *jitendekeza*, (1) get to be able to do, learn by practise, achieve; and also (2) make a display, show off an achievement.

Also *tendeana*. Ap. *tend-ea, -ewa*, e.g. do to (for, on behalf of, with, in, against),—commonly of favourable treatment (see above). Cs. *tend-esha, -eshwa, -eza, -ezwa*. Rp. *tendana*. (Cf. as above, and *utenzi*.)

Tende, n. (—), (1) fruit of the date palm *mtende*, a date,—grown in small quantities in Z., but largely imported from Arabia. Hence *rudisha tende Manga*, send dates back to Arabia,—of proverbial folly. (2) also *teende*, swelling of the limbs, elephantiasis.

Tendegu, n. (*ma-*), leg of a native bedstead. (Cf. *kitanda*.)

Tenga, v. separate, set (put, move, take) apart (aside), remove, withdraw, divide off. *Jitenga*, withdraw oneself, move out of the way. Ps. *tengwa*. Nt. *tengeka*. Ap. *tengea, -ewa*. Cs. *teng-esha, -eshwa, -eza, -ezwa*. Rp. *tengana*. (Cf. *tengo, tengano*, and syn. *ondoa, weka mbali, farikisha*, and dist. *tengea, tengeza*, follg.)

Tengea, Tengeza, v. also Tengelea, Tengeleza, Tengeleka, v. are variants of *tengenea*, &c. with same meanings.

Tengenea, v. (with variants as prec.), be settled, be arranged, be in good order, be in state of comfort (rest, well-being, &c.). E.g. *duka limetengenea*, the shop is duly furnished (stocked, fitted, ready). *Upepo umetengenea*, the wind is steady, has regularly set in. *Chombo limetengenea*, the vessel is in good order (in trim). (So *tengea, tengelea*.) Cs. *tengen-eza, -ezwa*, also *tengeza, tengeleza*, put to rights, repair, put in order, arrange, correct, settle, bring to a happy conclusion, make comfortable. E.g. *jumbe hutengeneza shughuli za inchi yake*, the chief administers the affairs of his country. *Muungu haharibu neno, illa kutengeneza neno*, God's work is not to destroy, but to set right. Hence *tengenezeka* (*tengezeka*). Also *tengenezana*. (Cf. follg. and syn. *ongoa, fanyiza*.)

Tengeneo, n. (*ma-*), arrangement, orderly disposition, administration, regulation. (Cf. prec., and syn. *daraka, maongozi*.)

Tengo, n. (*ma-*), outrigger,—of a canoe. (Cf. *galawa*.)

Tengua, v. Rv. of *tenga*, with similar meaning,—move off, put on one side. Nt. *tenguka*. (Cf. *tenga*.)

Tepetea, v. be utterly slack (idle, indolent, listless, unstrung, relaxed). (Cf. follg. and *legea*.)

-**tepetevu**, a. lazy, listless, slack, &c. (Cf. prec., and syn. -*tegefu*, -*vivu*, -*zembe*.)

Teremea, v. and **Terema**, be at ease, be free from care and anxiety, be cheerful (happy, comfortable). Nt. *teremeka* (in same sense). Cs. *terem-esha, -eshwa*. *Teremesha mgeni*, make a guest comfortable, at his ease, e. g. cheer up, gladden, relieve, put at ease. (Cf. *mteremo, mteremeshi*, and syn. *changam'ka, cheka*.)

Tesa, v. afflict, cause trouble (pain, anxiety, loss) to, persecute, harass, tease, &c. Ps. *teswa*. Nt. *teseka*. Ap. *tes-ea, -ewa*. Cs. *tese-sha, -shwa*. Rp. *tesana*, whence *tesanya* (*na*), as a Cs., i. e. set at variance (with). (Cf. *mtesi, utesi, teso*, and syn. *sumbua, uthi, chokoza*.)

Teso, n. (*ma-*), suffering, affliction, pain, trial, persecution, adversity. (Cf. *tesa, umivu, uthia*.)

Teta, v. (1) act or speak strongly, strive, insist,—but generally (2) oppose (by word or action), act or speak against, obstruct, contradict, protest, dispute, quarrel, go to law. Often with *na*, e. g. *ameteta nami*, he disputed with me. Ps. *tetewa*. Nt. *teteka*. Ap. *tet-ea, -ewa*, e. g. act (speak) for (against, in, at, &c.), defend, attack, oppose, support). Cs. *tet-esha, -eshwa*. Rp. *tetana*, e. g. quarrel, wrangle, be at enmity.

(Cf. *teto*, and syn. *bisha, zuia, shindana*.)

Tete, n. grain fully formed, but not fully ripe or hard. *Tete za mtama*, or *mtama tete*, of millet in this stage. Chicken-pox is called *tete za kwanga*, also *tete kwanga, titiwanga*.)

Tetea, v. cackle,—of a hen.

Tetema, v. tremble, shake, quake, quiver. Commonly in the Nt., i. e. *tetemeka*, e. g. *natetemeka kwa homa*, I am shivering with fever, i. e. in the cold stage of malarious fever. *Inchi inatetemeka*, the earth quakes. Cs. *tetem-esha, -eshwa*. (Cf. follg. and *tikisa, suka*.)

Tetemeko (*ma-*), also **Tetemo**, shaking, trembling, shivering. (Cf. *tetema*.)

Teteri, n. name of a small kind of dove.

Teto, n. (*ma-*), objection, argument, plea, protest. (Cf. *teta*.)

Teua, v. (1) choose, select, pick out; (2) be dainty, critical, fastidious. (*Chagua* is commonly used in Z.) Ps. *teuliwa*. Nt. *teulika*. (Cf. -*teule, mteua, mteuzi*.)

Teuka, v. be put out of place, be strained (sprained),—a variant of *teguka* (which see).

-**teule**, a. (same with D 4 (P), D 5 (S), D 6), choice, select, eligible, of best quality. (Cf. *teua, -e* being a passive termination.)

-**teuzi**, a. dainty, fastidious, critical. (Cf. *teua, mteuzi*.)

*****Tezi**, n. (—), (1) stern, poop,—of a ship (cf. *shetri*); (2) a tumour, glandular swelling, goitre, wen.

TH, as used in this book, represents the same sounds as in English, i. e. *th* both in *then* and *thin*. These sounds in Swahili words represent the four Arabic consonants *tha, thal, thad*, and *thah*,—the three latter being pronounced as *th* in *then*. To represent this latter sound, *Dh, D*, and *Z* are regularly used in much of the increasing Swahili *printed* literature, while the *th* of *thin* is written as *th* or *s*. Bishop Steere's practice is, however, here adhered to, as not only convenient, but practically sufficient, if the following rule is remembered. Always pronounce *th* as in *then*, except (1) in numerals involving the Arabic words for 2, 3, and 8, e.g. *thelatha, thenashara, themanini*, &c.; (2) *rithi*, inherit, *thubutu*, make firm, and their cognates; (3) *hadithi, thawabu, thamani, methali*, and some other words of little practical importance,—in which cases *th* is pronounced as in *thin*. Words not found under *Th* may be looked for under *Z* or *S*. When initial *th* is to be pronounced as in *thin*, *Th* is printed in italics. Obs. In a few words *Th* is used in Swahili for the Arab. consonant *Shin*, e.g. *theluji*, snow, *themanini*, eighty, &c.

*Thabihu, n. (—), a sacrifice, an offering,—both act and object. Sometimes also v. sacrifice, offer. (Ar. Cf. *mathbahu*, altar, *mathbuha*, victim, and syn. *sadaka, kafara, toleo*.)

*Thabiti, a. (1) firm, strong; (2) resolute, brave, steadfast,—of persons and things. (Ar. Cf. *thubutu, uthabiti*, and syn. *imara, -gumu, -shupafu*.)

*Thahabu, n. gold. (Ar. For metals cf. *madini*.)

*Thahiri, a. evident, plain, clear. Also as v. make clear, explain, show. (Ar. Cf. *thihirisha, uthahiri*, and syn. *wazi, baini*.)

*Thaifu, a. and -thaifu, (1) weak, feeble, infirm, powerless; (2) of a poor quality, deficient, insignificant, mean, base, despicable. E.g. *kijumba cha udongo thaifu*, a mud hovel is not stable. *Killa kitendo thaifu kiko kwake*, he is an example of every kind of baseness. (Ar. Cf. *thoofika, uthaifu*, and syn. *thalili, hafifu, -nyonge*.)

*Thalili, a. low, poor, abject, wretched. (Ar. Cf. *thaifu*, and *maskini, hohe hahe, fukara*.)

*Thalimu, a. unjust, oppressive, tyrannical, fraudulent, violent. Sometimes as v. be unjust, &c., but commonly *thulumu*. (Ar. Cf. *uthalimu, thulumu*, and syn. *jeuri, -korofi*.)

*Thama, conj. See Thamma. (Ar.)

*Thamana, n. (—), a surety, guarantee, warrant, certificate, bail. *Weka th.*, find bail, give surety. (Ar. Cf. *thamini*, and *amana*.)

*Thamani, n. (—), price, value, estimation. *-a thamani*, valuable, precious. — v. value, appraise, put a value on, price. Ps. *thamaniwa*. Nt. *thamanika*. Cs. *thaman-isha, -ishwa*. (Ar. Cf. *kadiri, kima, bei*, and dist. *zamani*, often written *thamani*, or *dh.*)

*Thambi, n. (—, and *ma-*), crime, religious offence, sin, i.e. offence of the worst class (worse than *hatiya*, and *kosa*), but from the Mahommedan point of view, i.e. formal and utilitarian rather than moral. (Ar.)

*Thamini, v. guarantee, become surety, be sponsor, give bail, go bail. *Huyu amemthamini rafikiye*, this man has gone bail for his friend. *Tumemthamini kama tutamlipa*, we have certified him that we will pay him. (Ar. Cf. *thamana*, and *amana*.)

*Thamiri, n. thought, mind, inner consciousness, conscience. *Ni thamiri yake kufanya vita*, his real intention is to make war. Also as v. think of, intend, e.g. *akamsamehe kwa yale aliyothamiria*, and he forgave him the thoughts of his heart. (Ar. Cf. *thana, nia, kusudi, wazo, moyo*.)

*Thamma, conj. (1) alike, equally, therewith, at the same time (cf. *mamoja*); (2) then, next, also, too. E.g. *thamma wamwonapo na wasipomwona*, alike whether they see him or not. *Thamma na wewe*, and you as well. (Ar.)

*Thana, n. (—), thought, idea, notion, suspicion. (Ar. Cf. follg.)

*Thani, v. think, be of opinion, fancy, suppose, suspect. Ap. *than-ia, -iwa*, think of (about, in favour of, against, &c.), suspect. E. g. *amethaniwa mwivi*, he is suspected of being a thief. (Ar. Cf. *thana*, and syn. *fikiri, waza, nia*.)

*Thara, n. usually in plur., i. e. *mathara*, hurt, harm, violence. (Ar. Cf. *thuru*, and syn. *jeuri, thulumu, hasara*.)

*Tharau, v. scorn, slight, despise, treat with contempt, insult. Ps. *tharauliwa*. Nt. *tharaulika*. Ap. *tharau-lia, -liwa*. Cs. *tharau-lisha, -lishwa*. — n. scorn, contempt, insult. E. g. *usifanye tharau yako*, do not bring contempt on yourself. (Ar. Cf. *tweza, hizi, tusha, fithulia*.)

*Tháruba, n. (—), also Thóruba, describes anything sudden and violent, e. g. (1) stroke, blow, rush,—blow of an axe, charge of an elephant, a sudden calamity. *Tháruba moja*, at a blow, in a moment, all of a sudden. (2) in arithmetic, multiplication; (3) a hurricane, storm of wind and rain, tempest. (Ar., and obs. Ar. *zaaba*, a storm, which seems confused with it. Cf. syn. *gháfula, marra moja*, and for 'storm' *tufane*.)

*Thawabu, n. (—), a reward, gift,—but esp. as from God. (Ar. Cf. for gifts generally *bakshishi*.)

**Th*elatha, n. and a., three,—but usually *tatu* in Z. (Ar. Cf. *theluth, thelitashara, thelathini*.)

*Theluji, n. (—), snow. Natives compare it with *machicha ya nazi*, grated cocoanut. (Ar.)

**Th*eluthi, n. a third (fractional) part. (Ar. Cf. *thelatha*.)

**Th*emani, n. and a., also *Th*emanya, eight,—but usually *nane* in Z. (Ar. Cf. follg. and *themuni*.)

**Th*emanini, n. and a., eighty. *-a th*., eightieth.

**Th*emantashara, n. and a., eighteen. *-a th*., eighteenth. (Ar. Cf. prec.)

**Th*emuni, n. and a. also *Th*umuni, *Th*umni, an eighth (fractional) part. *Nussu ya themuni*, a sixteenth part. Used of a quarter rupee, i. e. an eighth of a dollar,—about fourpence.

**Th*enashara, n. and a., twelve. *-a th*., twelfth. (Ar. Cf. follg. and *ashara*.)

**Th*eneen, n. and a., two,—but usually *pili, -wili*, in Z. (Ar. *ithneen*. Cf. prec.)

*Thihaka, n. (—), mockery, ridicule, scorn. (Ar. Cf. follg., and syn. *mzaha, ubishi, mcheko*.)

*Thihaki, v. ridicule, mock, deride, make fun of. E. g. *kunithihaki, kunifanya (kunifanyizia) thihaka*, to mock me. Ps. *thihakiwa*. Nt. *thihakika*. Ap. *thihak-ia, -iwa*. Cs. *thihak-isha, -ishwa*.

*Thihiri, v. make plain, be plain, —but usu. in deriv. stems. Ps. *thihiriwa*, e. g. (1) exposure for sale, show; (2) make clear, explain. Nt. *thihirika*. Ap. *thihir-ia, -iwa*. Cs. *thihir-isha, -ishwa*, make plain, explain, show clearly. (Ar. Cf. *thahiri*, and syn. *eleza, fafanua, baini*.)

-thihirifu, a. clear, evident, plain, like *thahiri*. (Cf. prec.)

*Thii, v. (1) waste away, pine, be spoiled, be consumed; (2) be hard driven, be ruined, be distressed. Ps. *thiiwa*. Nt. *thiika*. E. g. *nguo zimethiika*, the clothes are spoilt (eaten away). Cs. *thiisha, thiishwa*. E. g. *mchwa wanathiisha nyumba*, the white ants are spoiling the house. *Muungu anamthiisha*, God is sending him ruin. (Ar. Cf. *uthia, uthi*, and follg., and syn. *chakaa, angamia, fifia*.)

*Thiki, v. press hard on, put in difficulties, reduce to straits, distress. Ps. *thikiwa*. Nt. *thikika*, for which *thiki* is also used, i. e. be hard-pressed, be in difficulties, e.g. *kama umethikika na neno, unambie,* if you are in any difficulty, tell me. Ap. *thik-ia, -iwa.* Cs. *thikisha,* intens. — n. (1) narrowness, want of space, confinement; (2) being pressed, annoyance, distress, &c. (cf. *uthiki*). (Ar. Cf. syn. *temea, funga, kwama, sumbua,* &c.)

*Thikri, n. (—), name of a Dervish dance practised in Z. (Ar. 'invocation,'—the dance being accompanied by the repeated invocation *Allah hai,* God the Living One.)

*Thili, v. abase, humble, bring low, set at nought. Ps. *thiliwa.* Nt. *thilika.* Ap. *thil-ia, -iwa.* Cs. *thil-isha, -ishwa.* Rp. *thiliana.* —n. (—) and Thulli, mean condition, abasement, low state. — a. low, mean, despicable. (Ar. Cf. *-thilifu, uthilifu,* and syn. *tusha, aibisha.*)

-thilifu, a. and -tilifu, poor, mean, insignificant. Also sometimes a verb *thilifu,* reduce, make mean (poor, small), and *thilif-ika, -isha,* become poor, mean, &c. (Ar. Cf. prec.)

*Thiraa, n. (—), a cubit,—measure of length, from elbow to finger-tip, *thiraa kamili,* or to the knuckle, *thiraa konde,*—about 18 inches, half a yard (*wari*). Commonly called *mkono* (which see). (Ar. For other measures cf. *shibiri, pima.*)

*Thoofika, v. become weak (infirm, feeble), lose strength (force). Also sometimes *thoofu.* (Cs. *thoof-isha, -ishwa,* weaken. (Ar. Cf. *thaifu.*)

*Thubutu, v. (1) be firm, resolute, convinced, proved; (2) venture, dare, have the courage to. Ps. *thubutiwa.* Nt. *thubutika.* Ap. *thubut-ia, -iwa.* Cs. *thubut-isha, -ishwa,* e.g. establish, prove, make firm (strong). (Ar. Cf. *thabiti, uthabiti, mathubutu.*)

*Thuku, v. taste, try the taste of, but commonly *onja* is used. (Ar. Cf. *tamu, luththa.*)

*Thulli, n. also Uthulli, Duli, Uduli, and Thili, abject condition, misery, distress. (Ar. See Thili.)

*Thulumu, v. also Thalimu, treat unjustly, defraud, oppress. Ps. *thulumiwa.* Nt. *thulumika.* Ap. *thulum-ia, -iwa.* Rp. *thulumiana.* Cs. *thulum-isha, -ishwa.* — n. (*ma-*), injustice, fraud, oppression, violence. (Ar. Cf. *thalimu,* and syn. *jeuri, onea.*)

*Thumu, n. also Somu, garlic. (Ar. Cf. *kitunguu, somu.*)

*T*humuni, n. See T*hemuni. (Ar.)

*Thurea, n. a chandelier. (? Ar. a group of stars.)

*Thuru, v. hurt, damage, cause loss or injury to, harm,—sometimes in neut. sense, be hurt, e.g. *amechoka amethuru,* he was weary and wounded (after a fight). *Haithuru,* a common expression, meaning 'it does not matter, it is all the same, never mind' (cf. *mamoja*). Ps. *thuriwa.* Nt. *thurika.* Ap. *thur-ia, -iwa.* Hence *thuriana.* Cs. *thur-isha, -ishwa.* (Cf. *thara,* and syn. *hasiri, poteza.*)

Tia, v. (1) put, place, set; (2) apply, use, employ, bring to bear; (3) cause, effect, affect with, bring about. One of the commonest verbs in Swahili, used freely in all the above senses, translatable according to the sense of the noun with which it is associated, and often forming one verbal notion with it. Synonymous in many senses with *weka,* also very common (which compare), but (generally speaking) in *weka* the action is regarded as ending with itself (i.e. put, and leave, put and have done with it), in *tia* the action involves some further effect, or something else affected by it, i.e. put to, apply, add. E.g. *tia maji,* put water (somewhere, in something), add water, dilute. *T. dawa,* apply medicine. *T. rangi,* paint. *T. giza,* darken. *T. nguvu,* (1) apply force; (2) encourage, strengthen. *T. nanga,* cast anchor. *T. ugonjwa,* cause illness, infect with disease. *T. makali*, sharpen, make sharp. *T. mashaka* (*matata*), cause (inspire) doubts, perplex. *T. hofu*, frighten. *T. aibu*, disgrace. *T. nia* (*moyo*), apply thought, consider seriously,—so *tia moyoni* (*maanani*). *T. asikari*, employ soldiers, set a guard. *T. utumwani*, enslave. *T. chuoni*, send to school. *T. kazini*, set to a job. *T. roho*, risk one's life. *T. mfalme*, call in (appeal to, bring to bear) the chief. *Jitia uwele*, pretend illness. Ps. *tiwa*. Nt. not used. Ap. *tilia, tiliwa, tilika*, e. g. *akanitilia mwanangu ndui*, and he infected my child for me with smallpox. *Wajitiliani maneno hayo?* Why do you thrust yourself into this discussion? Hence *tililia, tililiwa*, in various special operations, e. g. *tililia uzi*, darn. Also *tiliana*, and (rarely used) *tilisha, tililisha*. Cs. never used (i. e. *tiza, tisha*). Rp. *tiana*. (*Tia* has no cognate words, and two of the commonest deriv. stems, Nt. and Cs., are never heard. Cf. generally *weka*, as above.)

*Tiabu, n. a game played by throwing up bits of stick, and watching how they fall (Str.). (For games cf. *mchezo*.)

*Tiara, n. a kite,—the child's toy. (Cf. *kishada, burutangi*.)

*Tibu, v. treat medically, give aid to, attend, treat (as a patient), cure. Ps. *tibiwa*. Nt. *tibika*. (Ar. Cf. *tabibu*, and syn. *uguza, alika, ganga*.)

*Tibu, n. perfume, scent, fragrance. Also a term of endearment, sweet. (Ar. Cf. *marashi, manukato*.)

Tibua, v. (1) stir up, make muddy; (2) excite, provoke. *Tibua maji*, stir up the mud in water. Nt. *tibuka*. (Cf. *chafua*, and follg.)

-tifu, a. loose, crumbling, dustlike, dusty,—also *tifutifu*. E. g. *mchanga mtifu*, fine sand. Also a n. *tifu* (*ma-*), e. g. *tifu la mchanga jingi*, a great cloud of sand, sand-storm, or ? mass of loose sand. *Fanya tifu*, make a dust. (Cf. follg.)

Tifua, v. cause to rise like dust, stir up, make a dust. Nt. *tifuka*. (Cf. prec.)

*Tii, v. obey, submit to, be docile (obedient, submissive). Ps. *tiiwa*, be obeyed, &c. E. g. *hatiiwi na mkewe*, he is not obeyed by his wife. Nt. *tiika*, like *tii*, i. e. be obedient. Cs. *tii-sha, -shwa*, i. e. reduce to obedience, subdue. (Ar. Cf. *taa, utii*, and follg. Only the simple *tii* is commonly used, but obs. *tisha*, v. frighten,—similar in general meaning, and perh. the same word as above. For syn. cf. *sikia, tumikia, shika miguu*.)

*-tii, a. obedient, docile, submissive. (Ar. Cf. prec. and syn. *-sikifu*.)

*Tiki, n. used of the edging of red or white silk stitched round the neck of a native dress (*kanzu*). (Ar. necklace, collar.)

*Tiki, adv. or better Diki, exactly, just, just so, in the same way, in the very way. (Cf. Ar. *diqat*.)

Tikisa, v. (1) cause to shake, wave, move to and fro; (2) make restless, agitate, excite, e. g. *tikisa mti, tunda zipate kupukutika chini*, shake a tree, so that the fruit drops off. *Tikisa inchi kwa fitina*, disturb a country by rebellion. Ps. *tikiswa*. Nt. *tikisika* (and *tikitika*, cf. *tukutika*). Ap. *tikis-ia, -iwa*. Cs. *tikis-isha, -ishwa*. Rp. *tikisana*. (Cf. syn. *tukutiza, suka, tetemesha, punga*.)

Tikiti, n. (*ma-*), a water melon, —fruit of *mtikiti*.

*Tikitiki, adv. in small pieces, to the last bit, utterly, completely, e. g. *ponda tikitiki*, crush to dust. *Oza t.*, rot away. (Ar. *daq*, fine powder, i. e. *dikidiki*.)

*Timamu, n. completion, completed state, perfected condition. — a. complete, perfect. (Ar. Cf. *timia, -timilifu, tamma*, and syn. *kamili, -zima, -ote*.)

Timazi, n. plummet, i. e. a small stone suspended by a string, used by masons. (Cf. *bildi, chubwi*.)

Timbi, n. bracelet, armlet,—the most general word. (For various kinds cf. *kekee, kikuku, banagiri, dodi, kingaja, kikoa, seng'enge.*)

*****Timia**, v. be complete, perfect, whole, finished, fulfilled, accomplished, done. E.g. *wakati umetimia*, the time is ended, is come. So of *kazi, deni*, a task, a debt, &c. *Ahadi imetimia*, the promise is carried out. Ap. *timi-lia, -liwa, -lika*, e.g. be finished for, &c., or, be finished off, become complete. Hence *timi-liza, -lizwa*. Cs. *timi-za, -zwa*, and hence *timiz-ia, -iwa*. (Ar. Cf. *-timilifu, utimizo, tamma, timamu*, and syn. *maliza, kamilika, isha, tindika.*)

*****-timilifu**, a. perfect, complete, finished, consummated. (Ar. Cf. prec. and *utimilifu.*)

Tim'ka, v. trot, run, amble,—of the running movement of an animal. Cs. *tim'sha*. (Cf. *telki, kimbia.*)

*****Timu**, v. be complete, finished,—but commonly *timia* (which see). (Ar.)

Timvi, n. and **Chimvi**, one who is considered of ill-omen, unlucky, a menace to family or neighbours,—usually a child, e.g. one born with upper front teeth or other peculiarities. (Cf. *kijego*, and perh. *kitimbi, utimbi,—b* and *v* being interchanged, cf. *jamvia, jambia.*)

-tindi, a. in an unripe stage, half-grown. Used of *mtama, muhindi*, &c. (Cf. *mtindi*, and syn. *-bichi.*)

Tindika, v. be cut off, fall short, fail, be finished, come to an end. Ap. *tindik-ia, -iwa*, e.g. be lacking to, fail to. *Tindikia kuja*, fail to come. *Nimetindikiwa maziwa*, my milk has failed me, has run short. Cs. *tindik-isha, -ishwa*. Rp. *tindi-kiana*, e.g. be cut off from each other, be separated, alienated. (? Same root as *chinja, chinjika*,—this latter retaining a specialized meaning. *Tindika* is not much heard in Z. Cf. *tindo*, and syn. *isha, katika, punguka.*)

Tindo, n. a hard chisel,—for cutting metal, &c. (Cf. prec.)

Tine, n. prepuce, when removed by circumcision. Also, a person circumcised. (Cf. *govi*, and *tahiri.*)

Tinge, n. (—), a favourite dancing game. (Cf. follg.)

Tingisha, v. like **Tikisa**, cause to shake, e.g. *tingisha inchi*, make the ground shake,—by dancing. *T. embe*, shake down mangoes,—off a tree. Nt. *tingika*. (Cf. *tinge.*)

*****Tini**, n. (—), (1) a fig, fruit of the *mtini*. (Ar.) (2) sometimes used for the 5 gal. oil-tin, in which American petroleum is often sold in Z., but this is commonly *debe*. (Eng.)

Tipitipi, n. (*ma-*), a brown bird common in Z.

Tiririka, v. glide, trickle, slide along, e.g. of the movement of a snake, of water, &c. (Cf. *churuzika.*)

Tisha, v. frighten, overawe, menace, strike with terror, e.g. *alimtisha tu, hakutaka kumua*, he only frightened him, he did not mean to kill him. Ps. *tishwa*. Nt. *tishika*. Ap. *tish-ia, -iwa*. Rp. *tishana*. (Cf. *tisho, kitisho, utisho*, and obs. similarity of some forms of *tii*, v. obey. Cf. syn. *hofisha, ogofya.*)

Tisho, n. (*ma-*), that which terrifies, a menace, a scare. (Cf. prec., and syn. *ogofya, kioja, afa.*)

*****Tissa**, n. and a. and **Tissya**, nine. *-a tissa*, ninth. (Ar. Cf. *tissatashara*, and common B. *kenda.*)

*****Tissaini**, n. and a., ninety. *-atissaini*, ninetieth. (Cf. Ar. *tissa*, and follg.)

*****Tissatashara**, n. and a., nineteen. *-a tissatashara*, nineteenth. (Ar. Cf. *tissa*, and prec. Also syn. *kumi na kenda.*)

Tita, n. (*ma-*), a bundle of firewood, a faggot. — v. (1) tie up in bundles, make faggots of, i.e. *funga* (or, *piga*) *tita*; (2) make carry (a bundle, or load). Nt. *titika*, e.g. *mtumwa ametitika mzigo na bwana wake*, the slave has been given a load to carry by his master. Cs. *titi-sha*,

-*shwa*, (1) cause to tie in bundles; (2) intens. make carry a load. (Not often used in Z. Cf. *funga, chukuza, pagaza*.)

Titi, n. (*ma-*), teat, nipple of breast. (But *enda kwa matiti* means 'trot,' v. ? Cf. *kititi*.)

Titia, v. shake, begin to sink, give way, break up,—e.g. of a rotten roof, and perh. of a rough sea. Nt. *titika*, with similar sense.

Titima, v. roll, rumble,—as thunder. Cs. *titim'sha*. (Perh. a variant of *tetema, tutuma*, which see.)

Titiwanga, n. also **Kitiwanga, Tetekwanga**, names for an eruptive fever, chicken-pox, rose-rash.

-to, a terminal suffix not commonly used in Z., but capable of being added to any appropriate noun or verb form to denote good quality, high degree, pleasing manner, i.e. excellence generally. E.g. *manukato*, sweet, high-class perfumes. *Kunyokato*, to be properly straightened. *Kazi yangu ifanyeto*, do my work well.

Toa, v. one of the commonest Swahili verbs (cf. *piga, tia, weka*), with a range of meanings so wide, and seemingly contradictory, that often the context alone defines them. The most general idea is 'put out,' and this idea is developed in two main lines,—A. put forward, offer, make prominent; B. put away, reject, totally exclude,—this latter being so marked that *toa* is regularly used to express actual negation, the negativing of an idea, and thus to supply an auxiliary of negation when combined with other verbs, e.g. *kutoa kufanya* forms the Infinitive of the Negative Conjugation, i.e. not to do, and is often shortened to *kutoa fanya*, and *kutofanya*. The following meanings and constructions may be noted among many, all traceable to the idea of *putting out*, while the examples are often capable of different and contradictory translations, e.g. A. (1) show, display, &c., *t. nuru*, shine. *T. meno*, show the teeth. *Toa taa*, display (or, remove) the lamp. *T. hadithi*, tell a story. *T. ukali*, show fierceness (bravery). *T. maua*, cause flowers to grow. (2) give, supply, produce,—in this sense regularly used for *-pa*, give (in cases where the objective pfx. is absent, and *-pa* therefore cannot be used), e.g. *t. mali*, give money. *T. gharama nyingi*, lay out large sums. *T. njia*, grant right of way. Also (3) take out, produce,—in contrast with *-pa*, e.g. *akatoa rupia akampa*, and he took out a rupee, and gave it him. (4) offer, propose, make a plan of, arrange, e.g. *toa salamu*, salute. *T. shauri*, offer advice. *T. nyumba*, design a house. *T. kazi*, supply occupation, work. *T. sharti*, propose conditions. *T. siku*, arrange a day. B. (with the idea of removal, bringing to an end, negation, more or less prominent, and often synonymous with *ondoa*). (1) take out, deliver, select, except, e.g. *t. ndani*, take from within. *T. hatarini*, save from danger. *Akamtoa na nyumba*, and he turned her out of the house. (2) give up, resign, yield, e.g. *adui wakajitoa*, the enemy surrendered. (3) force out, make come or go out, dismiss, take away. *Mtu huyu ataka kututoa roho zetu*, this man wishes to take our lives. *T. frasi shoti*, make a horse gallop, get a gallop out of him. *T. makosa*, remove blemishes, correct mistakes. *T. mimba*, produce abortion. (4) refuse, decline, fail (to do), e.g. *sababu ya kutoa kunirithisha*, because of refusing to make me heir. *Kutoa kupenda*, not to love. Ps. *tolewa*, e.g. be put out, put forward, put away, be proposed, be rejected, &c. (as above). Nt. *toka*, (1) come out, appear, be rid (of), be let out; (2) go out, go away, get out, disappear, cease (from),—in this sense syn. with *ondoka*. Used with several constructions, e.g. *toka mjini*, or *toka mji*, go out of the town. *Toka Unguja*, come from Zanzibar. *Toka utumwani*, be set free from slavery. *Toka katika chombo*, disembark from a vessel. *Natoka kumwuzia pembe*, I have just been (or, come from) selling ivory to him. *Toka* (Imperat.), Come out! But often of peremptory dismissal, Get out! Begone! Off with you! *Toka* has often a semi-transitive construction, e.g. *anatoka damu*, he is coming out with blood, i.e. he is bleeding. *Damu inamtoka*, blood is coming out of him. Thus the same thing may be described by *kutoa moshi* and *kutoka moshi*,—according to the prominence of the idea of agency, e.g. of a smoker and his pipe. Hence a Ps. form *tokwa*, e.g. *tokwa na hari* (*damu, machozi, roho*), of perspiring (bleeding, shedding tears, dying). (For *toka* as preposition, see below.) *Toka* has various deriv. stems, viz. (*a*) *tokea, tokewa*, and perh. *tokeka*, e.g. (1) come out to (for, against, in, &c., but *rarely* from, which is usually *toka* only), e.g. *akatoka mji akatokea mji mwingine*, and he left the town, and appeared at another town. *Alitokewa na malaika*, he was appeared to by an angel, i.e. an angel appeared to him; (2) result (from), be a consequence (of), *mambo mabaya yatokea na mtoto huyu*, evil consequences follow from this child; (3) *tokea* is used simply as 'appear, come on the scene, come out.' *Tokea nje*, come (appear) outside. Hence another Ap. form *toke-lea, -lewa*, e.g. *nimetokelewa na mgeni*, I had a sudden visit from a stranger,—and so *tokeleza*. (*b*) *tok-eza, -ezwa*, and hence *tokez-ea, -ewa*, also *tokezesha, -ezeshwa*, and *tokezana*, (1) cause to come out, make project (or prominent); or (2) intens. come out, ooze out, project, protrude, be prominent, e.g. *jiwe latokeza mno*, the stone projects too far. *Jino latokeza nje*, the tooth is forcing its way out. *Sindano inatokeza ncha yake, inatokea kwa pili*, the needle is getting its point through, it is appearing on the other side. *Mwana chuoni ametokeza maneno mabaya kwa watu*, the teacher has foreshadowed bad news to the people. *Muungu alimtokezea*, God appeared to him in a special way. (*c*) *tokana*, leave each other, part (from), e.g. *huyu ametokana na mkewe*, this man has parted from his wife. Ap. *tolea, tolewa, toleka, toleana*, e.g. put out for (to, from, against, with, &c.), give to, present, offer (to), spend (on),—also, take away from, remove from, save from, &c. Thus *kumtolea mali* may mean,—spend money on, or, take away money from,—a person. *Akamtolea*, with *meno*, gave him (or, showed him, or, took from him) his teeth,—with *kisimani*, took him out of the well,—with *ushairi*, recited to him a stanza. *Hatukutoleana heshima mimi naye*, we failed in courtesy to each other. (Obs. also *toeza*, cause to put forth, or intens. send out, urge forth, and perh. *toeka*, e.g. be put out, vanish, disappear, but see **Toweka, Toea**). Cs. *toza, tozwa*. Hence *tozea, tozewa*. Also *tozesha, tozeshwa*, e.g. cause to put out, force (urge, persuade, allow, &c.) to give, demand, extort, expose. Also *tozana*. *Tozea mfalme kodi*, collect taxes for the chief. *Kunitozea haki yangu*, to vindicate my rights for me. *Wahadi wa kutoza kumwuliza*, a promise not to ask him. Rp. *toana*, e.g. put each other out (or, forward), join in putting (or going) out, e.g. *walitoana katika mji kwenda vitani*, they made a general move from the town to go fighting. (Cf. *mtoza, toleo, tokeo, toka, tokea, toeka, utoko*, and generally *ondoa*.)

Toazi, n. (*ma*-), cymbal, large castanet. (For musical instruments cf. *ngoma*.)

*****Toba**, n. repentance, penitence,

regret, remorse. (Ar. Cf. *tubu*, and syn. *juto*.)

Toboa, v. bore a hole (in), make a hole (or, passage), force a way (through). Ps. *tobolewa*. Nt. *toboka*. Ap. *tobo-lea, -lewa*. Cs. (?) *tobo-sha, -shwa*. (Cf. follg., and syn. *zua, pekecha, didimia*.)

Tobwe, n. (—), (1) wood of the tree *mtobwe* (which see). Hence also (2) simpleton, fool. — n. a hole, —also *kitobwe* (a pass. noun in *-e*, from *toboa* (which see)).

Toea, v. also **Towea** (which see).

Tofaa, n. (*ma-*), fruit (like a small apple) of the tree *mtofaa*.

*__**Tofali**__, n. (*ma-*), and **Tafali**, brick, tile. (Cf. Ar. 'dry clay.')

*__**Tofauti**__, n. (*ma-*). See **Tafauti**.

Tofua, tofuka, v. perh. variants of *pofua, pofuka* (which see).

Toga, v. pierce (the ear), make incision (for ear ornament). Ps. *togwa*, e. g. *hutogwa, maana hutiwa mapete katika masikio*, the meaning of *togwa* is, having rings fixed in the ears. (Perhaps same as *toja* (which see).)

Togwa, n. (—), native beer (*pombe*) in the sweet unintoxicating stage, not fermented.

*__**Tohara**__, n. (—), (1) purity, cleanness,—esp. in a ceremonial sense, i. e. according to Mahommedan rules, e. g. of the purification of a corpse. (With reference to details, *tohara* is used as a plur. from *utohara*.) Esp. (2) circumcision. (Ar. Cf. *tahiri*, and also *ukumbi, weuo, ngariba*.)

Toja, v. make incisions (cuts, gashes, &c.), scarify, tattoo, let blood, bore the ear (for ornament). *Toja mshipa*, open a vein, bleed. (Cf. *toga*, and follg., also syn. *chanja, umika*.)

Tojo, n. (*ma-*), gash, cut, incision, tattoo,—whether for ornament, tribal mark, or medical purposes. (Cf. prec. and *nembo*.)

Toka, prep. also **Tokea**, from, out of, away from, starting from, since. E. g. *toka huko*, from yonder, from that time (place). *Toka leo*, from to-day onwards. *Toka zamani*, long since. *Tokea hapo*, or *tokeapo*, once on a time, long ago, from time immemorial. Often combined with *kwa, katika*, to define their meaning, or with locatives in *-ni*, e. g. *toka nyumbani*, from the house, *toka kwa mfalme*, from the king's presence. (Cf. *toka*, Nt. of *toa*, and follg.)

Tokea, (1) prep. See **Toka**. (2) Ap. form from **toa** (**toka**) (which see).

Tokeo, n. (*ma-*), place (time, act, mode) of going out (appearing, happening); (2) outlet, pore, e. g. *matokeo ya hari*, pores in the skin (cf. *kitundu, nyeleo*); (3) appearance, apparition, vision (cf. *njozi*); (4) occurrence, result, consequence (cf. *tukio*). (Cf. *toa, toka, tokea*.)

Tokomea, v. vanish, disappear, recede from view, extend beyond the range of the eye,—e. g. of the sea, *bahari inatokomea*. Cs. *tokom-eza, -ezwa*, e. g. reduce to nothing, annihilate. (Cf. *toweka*, and perh. *toa, toka*.)

Tokosa, v. boil, cook by boiling, —of food generally. Also of frying in fat or butter, e. g. *tokosa mkate pamoja na samli* (or, *kwa samli*), fry a cake in ghee. Of water, *pika*, or *chemsha*, is usual. Ps. *tokoswa*. Nt. *tokoseka*. Ap. *tokos-ea, -ewa*. (Cf. follg., and for cooking, *pika, upishi*.)

Tokota, v. become boiled (fried), be boiled (boiling, frying). E. g. *chungu chatokota kwa kupata moto sana*, the pot boils by getting very hot. (Cf. prec.)

Tomasa, v. press, feel, knead softly with the fingers,—of a soft yielding substance, e. g. an animal, or ripe fruit. (Cf. *papasa, bonyesha*, and *kanda*.)

Tomba, v. have sexual connexion, copulate (of animals in general, and commonly avoided as needlessly vulgar). Ps. *tombwa*. Rp. *tombana*.

Tombo, n. or **Tomboo**, a quail.

Tomea, v. used of mason's work,—bring to a surface with plaster and small stones the first rough setting of stones and mortar. Ps. *tomea*. Nt. *tomeka*. Ap. *tome-lea, -lewa*. Cs. *tomel-esha, -eshwa*. (Cf. *mtomo*, and follg. Prob. for *chomeo*, but retaining *t*, as at Mombasa, in this special sense. Cf. *choma*.)

Tomoa, v. stave in, break through, pierce,—e.g. *tomoa pipa*, stave in a barrel,—with a pole or crowbar. (Perh. same as *chomoa*.)

Tomoko, n. (*ma-*), a custard-apple, fruit of *mtomoko*, similar to the *tope-tope*.

Tomondo, n. (*ma-*), fruit of the tree *mtomondo*.

Tona, v. fall in drops, drop, drip, form a drop or dot. Also Nt. *toneka*, in same sense, and hence *tonek-ea, -ewa*, drop upon, e.g. *tonekea meza*, drop on the table. Ap. *ton-ea, -ewa*. Cs. *ton-esha, -eshwa*, cause to drip (trickle, drop),—esp. of a blow or injury to a sore place, causing it to be painful and bleed, and so fig. cause unnecessary pain, reopen old griefs. Hence Ap. *tonesh-ea, -ewa*, e.g. *umtoneshee tone la samli walini*, pour a drop of ghee over his rice. Hence *tonesheka*, and *toneshana*. Rp. *tonana*. (Cf. *tone, tonesho*, and *dondoka, donda, tiririka*.)

Tone, n. (—, and *ma-*), a drop of liquid, a dot, a blot. Dim. *kitone*. (Cf. *tona*.)

Tonesho, n. (*ma-*), causing to drip, making bleed. (Cf. *tona, tone*.)

Tonga, n. *Tonga la dafu*, a cocoanut when full of milk and in the later stage, when the nutty part is well set and tough. (Cf. *dafu*.)

Tonge, n. (—, and *ma-*), a small rounded mass, a small lump or ball, e.g. of rice or other food, as taken in the fingers and eaten by natives. Also **Donge**.

Tongo, n. plur. of *utongo*. (See also **Matongo**.)

Tongoza, v. (1) draw aside, call apart; (2) seduce. Ps. *tongozwa*. Ap. *tongoz-ea, -ewa*. Cs. *tongoz-esha, -eshwa*. Rp. *tongozana*. (Cf. *kitongo, kitongoji, utongozi*.)

Tope, n. (—, and *ma-*), also plur. of *utope*, mud, mire, dirt. *Tope nyembamba*, thin, soft mud. *Tope nene* (*nzito*), thick mud. *Watu wengi kama tope*,—descriptive of a great crowd, thick as mud. (Cf. follg.)

Topea, v. (1) sink in mud or dirt, be bogged; (2) get into difficulties, get hampered (entangled), plunge in vice. Cs. *top-eza, -ezwa*, e.g. of effect of a heavy load. *Inchi inatopeza miguu yake*, the earth makes his feet stick fast. *T. kidole katika mwili*, press the finger deep into the body. (Cf. *tope, topoa*, also syn. *zama, tota*, and perh. *bopa*.)

Tope-tope, n. (*ma-*), custard-apple, fruit of *mtopetope*.

Topoa, v. get out of a difficulty, set free from a spell or charm, extricate, counteract a poison, e.g. *topoa mtu uganga*, release a man from the power of a charm. *Dawa ya kutopoa*, antidote. Ps. *topolewa*. Nt. *topoka*, e.g. *amelala illi umtopoke ulevi*, he is asleep so that his drunkenness may leave him. (? Conn. with *tope*, and for Rv. force of *oa*, cf. *chomoa, bomoa, chongoa*, and syn. *zingua*.)

*****Torati**, n. also **Taurati**, the law of Moses, the Pentateuch. (Ar.)

Toria, n. (*ma-*), edible fruit of the tree *mtoria*. Also *kitoria*.

Toroka, v. desert, run away (from master, home, &c.), play truant. *Mtumwa amemtoroka bwana wake*, the slave has run away from his master,—also *ametoroka kwa bwana wake*. Ps. *torokwa*, be deserted, be run away from. Ap. *torok-ea*,

-*ewa*. Cs. *toro-sha, -shwa*, induce to desert, drive into running away, seduce, entice away. (Cf. *mtoro*, and syn. *kimbia*.)

Tosa, v. plunge in water, throw into the sea, cause to sink, drown. Used of launching a vessel, *waka-itosa marikebu katika bahari waka-ingia*, they launched the ship and went on board,—but commonly *shua*. (Cf. *tota*, and syn. *chovya, zamisha, didimia*. Dist. *toza*, Cs. of *toa*.)

Tosa, n. (*ma-*), fruit just ripening, nearly ripe, turning colour, beginning to be soft. *Tosa la embe, embe tosa*, a mango getting ripe. (Cf. -*ivu*, -*pevu*.)

Tosa, n. (—) and **Toza**, pipe-bowl for tobacco, short pipe, usu. of clay, with stem. (See *kiko*, which is mostly used in Z.)

Tosha, v. suffice, be sufficient (for), content, be enough (adequate, capable). *Yamtosha kazi yake*, his task is enough for him. Ap. *tosh-ea, -ewa, -eka*. Hence *toshel-ea, -ewa*, and *toshel-eza, -ezwa*, and a further deriv. form *toshelez-ea, -ewa*, e. g. *mchuzi huu utamtoshelezea wali wake*, this gravy he will find enough for his rice. *Watu wawili wata-mtoshelezea kazi yake*, two men will be enough for his job. (Cf. Ar. *kifu*, and dist. follg.)

Toshea, v. be amazed, astounded, staggered. Also Ps. *toshewa*, in same meaning,—be struck with amazement. (Cf. *sangaa, ajabu*, and dist. *toshea*, Ap. of *tosha*.)

Tota, v. sink down, sink in, be overwhelmed, be drowned. *Tota majini* (*baharini*), sink in water (the sea). *Tota macho*, have the eyes sunken, have lost the eyes (sight). *Merikebu imetota*, the ship has sunk. Ap. *tot-ea, -ewa*. Cs. *tot-esha, -eshwa* (and perh. also *tosa*, which see). *Totesha macho*, make blind (cf. *pofusha*). (Cf. *zama, didimia*.)

Toto, n. (*ma-*), same as *mtoto*, child, but commonly either (1) of size, a big, fine child; or (2) of some object resembling a child or offspring, e. g. *toto la ndizi*, the fruit bud on a banana stalk; *toto la meza*, the drawer of a table. (Cf. dim. *ki-toto*.)

Totoma, v. wander at random, get lost, be off the path. Ap. *totomea*. (Commonly *potea* in Z.)

-**tovu**, a. (?) variant of -*povu*, i. e. lacking, deprived of. (Cf. *tofua*.)

*****Towashi**, n. (*ma-*), eunuch. See **Tawashi**. (Ar.)

Towea, v. or **Toea**, use as a relish, i. e. prepare food for the table by adding sauce, curry, gravy, fish, meat, vegetables, &c. to season and flavour it,—such addition being *ki-toweo*. Ap. *towe-lea, -lewa*, e. g. *towelea wali kwa mchuzi*, i. e. flavour boiled rice with gravy. Hence *towe-leza, -lezwa*. Cs. *towesha, toweza*. (Cf. *kitoweo*, and syn. *unga*, v.)

Toweka, v. vanish, disappear, pass out of sight, die. Cs. *towe-sha, -shwa*, e. g. put out of the way, ruin. (Perh. cf. *toa*, as if *toeka*, i. e. be put away.)

Tu, adv. only, just, exactly, simply, no more, merely, barely,—always following the word it refers to, and used with nouns as well as adjs. and verbs. E. g. *mtoto tu*, a mere child, *kidogo 'tu*, just a little, *giza tu*, utter darkness. (? Cf. -*tupu*, e. g. *giza tupu*, utter darkness.)

Tu, verb-form, we are,—Pers. Pfx. of 1 Pers. Plur., e. g. *sisi tu wazima*, we are quite well.

-**tu**-, Pers. Pfx. in verbs of 1 Pers. Plur. subjective and objective, 'we, us,' and characteristic of the corresponding adjective, -*etu* (which see).

Tua, v. A. (1) put down, set down; (2) fig. cause to settle, stop, decide. E. g. *tua mzigo*, put down a load. *Tua tanga*, or *tua* alone, lower sail. *Maneno yale yalimtua asiingie*, those words stopped him, so that he did not go in, or, settled him not to go in.

B. as a Nt. (1) settle down, rest, halt, bivouac, encamp, stop for the night; (2) go down, settle down, set, e.g. *jua likatua*, the sun set; *ndege alitua*, the bird alighted. Ps. *tuliwa*. Nt. *tulika*. Ap. *tulia*, with many deriv. stems,—*tuliwa, tulika*. Also *tuli-lia, -liwa, -lika*. Hence *tulili-za, -zwa*, and *tuliliana*. Cs. *tuli-za, -zwa*, whence *tuli-zia, -ziwa*, and *tulizana*. (1) be quiet, be calm, settle down; (2) fig. become quiet (tranquil, peaceful), reform, give up bad ways, take to a quiet settled life, cease from anger (grief, excitement, passion). E. g. *tulia* (Imperat.), Be quiet! *Moyo wake umemtulia*, or, *ametuliwa moyo*, he has calmed down. *Bahari yatulia*, the sea is going down. *Uso wa kutulia*, a tranquil, peaceful expression. *Maneno haya yamekutulilia?* Have you got that matter settled? *Chakula hakimtulilii*, the food does not agree with him, i. e. he cannot digest it. *Tumetuliliwa na habari hizi*, we have been pleased with these news. *Bahari haikutulizana*, the sea was rough. *Wametulizana*, they have kept each other quiet. *Kutuliliana*, to come to an agreement or settlement among themselves. *Tuliza*, bring to rest, pacify, settle, relieve pain, comfort, bring to a better mind, effect a reform in. *Ametuliziwa moyo*, he has been tranquillized. (See **Tuesha, Tusha, Tweza**, all perh. Cs. forms connected with *tua*.) Rp. *tuana*, e. g. settle down together, all join in making a camp, set things into order, agree. (Cf. *tuo, kituo, -tulivu, tulizo, tuama*, besides *tuesha, tusha, tweza*. Obs. similar verbs *tia*, put to, *toa*, put out, *tua*, put down.)

Tua, v. rub. See **Chua**.

Tuama, v. get into a settled state, settle down, subside. E. g. of muddy water clearing itself. *Acha maji yatuame, yawe safi*, leave the water to settle and get clear. *Mambo yanatuama*, matters are settling themselves. Cs. *tuam-isha, -ishwa*. (A St. form from *tua*, cf. *-ama*.)

*****Tubu**, v. repent, be penitent, feel remorse, mend one's ways. A punished child says *nimetubu*, I am sorry, I will not do it again. Ap. *tub-ia, -iwa, -ika*, e. g. *tubia kosa*, repent of a fault; *tubia Muungu*, repent before God. Cs. *tubi-sha, -shwa*, e. g. correct, chastise, bring to a penitent state of mind. (Ar. Cf. *toba*, and syn. *juta, tulia, ongoka*.)

Tuesha, v. pay an evening visit to, call on at night, bid good-night to. Contr. *amkia*, of morning call. (Prob. specialized Cs. of *tua* (which see).)

*****Tufane**, n. storm, gale, tempest, hurricane, e. g. of rain, wind, and thunder together. (Ar. Cf. *tharuba, kimbunga, chamchela*.)

*****Tufe**, n. a ball, a game of ball. *Cheza tufe*, play at ball, e. g. cricket, tennis, golf. (Ar. 'inflated bag.' Often *mpira* in Z.)

*****Tuhumu**, v. suspect, accuse, reproach. Ps. *tuhumiwa*. Nt. *tuhumika*. Ap. *tuhum-ia, -iwa*. Rp. *tuhumiana*. Cs. *tuhumi-sha, -shwa*. — n. (1) suspicion, accusation. *Tuhumu ile imeondoka kwa kiapo*, the suspicion was allayed by ordeal.

Tui, n. (—), the creamy juice or milk got by grating the nutty part of a cocoanut (cf. *kuna, mbuzi*), mixing it with water and straining it through a sieve (*kung'uto*) or bag (*kiteo*), leaving only *machicha*, which is thrown away. *Inzi kufia tuini si hasara*, a fly does not mind dying in cocoanut cream. (*Tui* is much used in Z. for cooking. Cf. *kasimele*.)

*****Tuili**, v. be prolonged, be belated. Cs. *tuili-za, -zwa*, i. e. make late, delay, prolong. (Ar. for commoner *kawia* (which see), and *chelewa, ahiri*.)

Tuka, n. (—), post supporting the projecting eaves in front of a native house, post of a verandah. (Commonly *nguzo, kiguzo*. Kr. gives *shuli* for the projecting eaves supported by *tuka*.)

Tuka, jituka, v. See **Stuka**, of which it is perh. a variant (i. e. *stuka, situka, shituka, jituka*.)

Tukana, v. use abusive language (to), abuse, revile, insult, call names. Ps. *tukanwa*. Nt. *tukanika*. Ap. *tukan-ia, -iwa*. Cs. *tukan-isha, -ishwa*, e. g. intens. treat with scorn. *Jitukanisha kwa watu,* expose oneself to public derision, i. e. voluntarily incur abuse in public. Rp. *tukanana.* (Cf. follg., and syn. *suta, sema, amba*. *Tukana* is itself reciprocal in form only.)

Tukano, n. (*ma-*), an abusive expression, bad word, abuse. (Cf. prec., and syn. *suto, tusu*.)

Tukia, v. happen (to), occur (to), present itself, come to pass. *Jambo limenitukia leo,* a thing has happened to me to-day. *Atajitukia yuko mjini,* he will find himself in the town. Ps. *tukiwa,* e. g. *nimetukiwa na uthuru,* opportunity presented itself to me. Cs. *tuki-za, -zwa*. (Cf. follg., and syn. *tokea, kuta*. Possibly *tukia, tukiza* are variants of *tokea, tokeza,* with limited meaning, as above.)

Tukio, n. (*ma-*), occurrence, event, accident. (Cf. prec., and *tokeo*.)

-**tukufu**, a. (same with D 4 (P), D 5 (S), D 6), exalted, grand, glorious, majestic. (Cf. follg., and *utukufu,* also syn. *bora, -sharifu, -kuu*.)

Tukuka, v. become exalted, grand, glorious, &c. (Cf. prec., and *tukuza*.)

Tukusa, v. perh. a variant of *tikisa* (which see), cause to shake, make restless, agitate, &c. (Cf. also follg.)

Tukuta, v. be restless, nervous, always on the move, be tiresome, petulant. Nt. *tukutika,* e. g. move tremulously, tremble, quiver with excitement, shudder, be in a flutter. Ap. *tukut-ia, -iwa,* e. g. be annoying to. Cs. *tukut-isha,* or *-iza, -izwa*. (Cf. follg., and *tikisa, -tukutu*.)

Tukutiko, n. (*ma-*), tremor, tremulous movement, nervous trembling, fluttering excitement. E. g. *tukutiko la moyo,* fluttering of the heart, excited feeling. (Cf. follg.)

-**tukutu**, a. restless, nervous, excitable, petulant, troublesome, e. g. of children. (Cf. prec., and *tukuta, tukusa*.)

Tukuza, v. make exalted, magnify, glorify, aggrandize, place in high position, give all honour to. Ps. *tukuzwa*. Ap. *tukuz-ia, -iwa*. Cs. *tukuz-isha, -ishwa*. Rp. *tukuzana*. (Cf. *-tukufu, tukuka,* and syn. *athimisha, heshimu, kuza*.)

-**tulivu**, a. (*tulivu* with D 4 (P), D 5 (S), D 6), quiet, tranquil, peaceful, composed, gentle, docile. E. g. *maji matulivu,* standing, tranquil water. *Watu watulivu,* quiet, peaceful people. (Cf. follg., and *tua, utulivu,* also syn. *-pole, taratilu, -anana, -a amani*.)

Tulizo, n. (*ma-*), a quieting, soothing, means of soothing, relief, comfort, sedative. Dim. *kitulizo.* (Cf. *tua,* and prec.)

*****Tuluku,** v. variant of **taliki** (which see), divorce. (Ar.)

Tuma, v. employ (a person), send (a person), give work to. E. g. *tuma mtu kazi* (*kwa kazi, kufanya kazi*), set a person to work. *Tuma mtu mahali* (*mjini, Mombasa, kwenda safari*), dispatch a person to a place (to the town, to Mombasa, on an expedition). Ps. *tumwa,* i. e. be employed, be under orders, be on service (an errand, a job, a particular duty). Nt. *tumika,* e. g. (1) be engaged, be in service, be under orders, be used (in a general sense); (2) be disengaged, free to be employed, capable of service, be usable, available, &c. The Nt. applies to things as well as persons. So also *tumikana*, be capable of (free for, fit for, available for) service or use. Hence *tumik-ia, -iwa*, be used or available by, be at the service of, —and so commonly, obey, be obedient to, submit to, be servant to. *Tumikiwa*, have service done, be obeyed. Also *tumiki-sha, -shwa*, e.g. cause to obey, reduce to obedience, take as servant. Also *tumikish-ia, -iwa*. Ap. *tum-ia, -iwa, -ika*, use a person or thing, make use of, employ. E.g. *akatumia mali sana*, he spent money extravagantly. *Neno hili latumika*, this word is in use, is current. *Kisu kinatumiwa*, the knife is being used. Hence *tumil-ia, -iwa, -ika*, e.g. use for (with, in, against, &c.). *Jitumilia*, spend selfishly, waste. *Tumilia mbali*, use up, consume entirely. Also *tumiana*. Cs. *tum-isha, -ishwa, -iza, -izwa*, e.g. (1) cause to employ, make send; (2) commonly intens. give a special or urgent task to, impose a duty, give a charge to. *Zile ng'ombe ulizotumiza zimekuja*, those oxen you sent for are come. *Tutatumiza watu wa mji*, we will give work to all the people in the town. Hence *tumish-ia, -iwa*. Rp. *tumana*. (Cf. *tume, mtume, tumo, matumizi, mtumishi, mtumwa, utumwa*. Also *peleka*, which is in some senses synonymous. And dist. *chuma* and derivatives, which are sometimes pronounced, as at Mombasa, *tuma*.)

*Tumai, v. and also commonly **Tumaini**, hope, trust, expect, be confident, be trustful, rely on. *Natumai una afya*, I hope you are well. *Namtumai mtu huyu*, I trust this man. Ps. *tumaiwa, tumainiwa*. Nt. *tumainika*. Ap. *tumain-ia, -iwa, -ika*, e.g. hope in, confide in, rely on. Cs. *tumain-isha, -ishwa*, e.g. raise the hopes of. Hence *tumainish-ia, -iwa*. (Ar. Cf. follg., and syn. *taraja, amini, tegemea*.)

*Tumaini, n. (*ma-*), confidence, trust, expectation, hope. Also as a. *-tumaini*, confident, sanguine, hopeful. (Ar. Cf. prec.)

Tumba, n. (—, and *ma-*), (1) outer case, cover; (2) case, or bale, of goods. E.g. the unopened bud of a flower, *matumba mawaridi*, rosebuds. *Tumba la chuo*, cover of a book. *T. la mwezi*, the halo surrounding and encasing the moon, and *tumba la uso*, the effect produced by oiling the face. *Tumba la mchele*, a bag of rice. *Ndiye mweka wa tumba*, (of the angel of death), he it is who sets down the load. (Cf. *mtumba, kitumba*, and *mzigo*.)

*Tumbako, n. tobacco. *Vuta t.*, smoke. *Nusa t.*, take snuff. *Tafuna t.*, chew tobacco. The forms in which it is made up are known as *mkate*, cake, *ukambaa*, (ropelike) twist, *pumba*, lump. (Cf. *kiko*.)

*Tumbasi, n. (—), abscess. (? Ar., for common *jipu*.)

Tumbawe, n. (*ma-*), coral rock in the intermediate stage between coral and rock,—white and massive, but light and not fully consolidated. Used largely (from its lightness) for concrete roofs, also for cornices, being easily cut to a shape, and for lime-burning.

Tumbili, n. name of a small light-coloured monkey. Also *kitumbili*. (Cf. *kima, nyani*.)

Tumbo, n. (*ma-*), (1) stomach, belly, abdomen, womb; (2) anything resembling the stomach in shape,—a swelling, protuberance (cf. *kitumbo*); (3) or in capacity,—inside of a vessel, receptacle, hold (of a ship); (4) pain or disease in the abdominal region, colic, stomach-ache, diarrhoea, stoppage, &c. E.g. *tumbo la kuhara (la kuenenda)*, diarrhoea, looseness of the bowels; *t. la kuhara damu*, dysentery. Also of pregnancy, *yuna tumbo*, or, *tumbo kubwa*, she is pregnant. *Ndugu tumbo moja*, children of the same mother. Plur. *matumbo*, guts, entrails, bowels, i.e. contents of the lower part of the body. (Cf. *utumbo, kitumbo, tumbua, kitumbua, mtumba, mtumbwi*.)

Tumbua, v. (1) disembowel, rip up, cut open, make a hole (in), perforate; (2) lay open, display. *Tumbua ubau*, rip, or make a hole in, a plank. *Tumbua kindu*, rip a leaf into strips. *T. jipu*, lance a boil. Ps. *tumbuliwa*. Nt. *tumbuka*, e.g. (1) have a cut or hole made in it; (2) burst out, break open. *Jipu limetumbuka*, the abscess has broken. *Mahali pa chombo palipotumbuka*, the place in the dhow, which was ripped open. Hence *tumbuk-ia, -iwa*, esp. in sense (1) break out into, burst suddenly into, of a sudden rush or fall, e.g. *ametumbukia kisimani*, he has tumbled into the well; (2) get suddenly involved in, be caught or strangled in. So also Cs. *tumbukiza, -izwa*. Ap. *tumbu-lia, -liwa, -ika*, e.g. lay open for (to, at, with, against), e.g. *nimekwambia, Fanya kazi yako, nawe wanitumbulia macho*, I said to you, go on with your work, and you glare at me (cf. *kodolea macho, ngariza macho*). Hence *tumbuli-za, -zwa*, and *tumbuliz-ia, -iwa*. Cs. *tumbuza*, intens. force a way through, penetrate, come out on the other side of, e.g. *tumbuza mwitu*, pass through a forest; *t. nje ya pili*, come out on the other side; *jua limetumbuza*, the sun has burst out (cf. *penya*, and *chimbuza*). Rp. *tumbuana*. (Cf. *tumbo*, and syn. *pasua, kata, fungua, funua*.)

Tumbuika, v. be soothed by being sung to. Cs. *tumbui-za, -zwa*, soothe by singing, make a soothing sound with or without words, sing to, sing by turns. *T. kwa nyimbo* (*kwa maneno mazuri*), soothe by songs (by gentle words).

Tumbuizo, n. (*ma-*), lullaby, ditty, refrain of a song. (Cf. *utumbuizo*.)

Tume, n. (—), (1) messenger, envoy, employé, representative, servant. E.g. *wale wazee, tume za Mbega*, the old men, Mbega's envoys. Used absolutely, like *mtume*, of Mahomed, as apostle of God. Also (2) occupation, task, errand, business. *Tume zangu zimekwisha*, my duties are finished. (Cf. *tuma, mtumwa*, which is the usual term for a slave, though not limited to this meaning, and *mtumishi*, which is used of household and general service, sometimes in contrast with *mtumwa*, slave, and *tume*, implying special service.)

Tumo, n. (*ma-*), and **Mtumo**, employment, using, use, &c. (Cf. *tuma*, and dist. *chumo*, also meaning 'employment.')

*derived ***Tumu,** n. (—), (1) a fast, fasting, e.g. of Ramathani, *mwezi wa tumu*, the fasting month. (Ar. *sum*. Cf. *mfungo*.) (2) variant of **tamu** (which see), taste, tasting. (Ar.)

Tuna, v. (1) puff out, swell out; (2) show anger, be petulant (arrogant). E.g. *tuna machavu*, swell out the cheeks. *Jituna*, bluster, brag (cf. *jivuna*). Ps. *tunwa*. Nt. *tunika*. Ap. *tun-ia, -iwa*. Cs. *tuni-sha, -shwa*, e.g. (1) offend, enrage; (2) puff out, flatter.

Tunda, n. (—, and *ma-*), a fruit of any kind, a product of tree, plant, vegetable, &c. (Cf. *tundika*. There are many kinds of fruit in Z. See *nazi, chungwa, chenza, danzi, limau, ndimu, kangaja, furungu, balungi, ndizi* (many kinds), *embe, fenessi, nanasi, zambarau, pera, topetope, kunazi, duriani, chokichoki, kwaju, bunju, kungu, papai, tikitiki*, &c. Also numerous vegetables. Kr. gives *tunda*, v. get down fruit from a tree,—seldom if ever used in Z., where *angua, chuma* are common. For common vegetables cf. *mboga*.)

Tundama, v. settle down, gather, accumulate, e.g. as water at the bottom of a well or hole. Cs. *tundam-isha, -ishwa*. (Cf. *tungama, tuama, tandama*, and *-ama*.)

Tundika, v. hang up, suspend,—

but clear of walls, &c., not touching anything (contr. *angika, tungika*). E.g. *tundika bendera*, hang up a flag (cf. *tweka*). Ps. *tundikwa*. Ap. *tundik-ia, -iwa*. Cs. *tundik-isha, -ishwa*. (? Cf. *tunda*, or *tundu*.)

Tundu, n. (—, and *ma-*), hole, hollow, passage, hollow receptacle, —and hence of several objects, den or lair of a wild animal, snake, &c., nest of a bird, a cage of any kind, a basket of open wicker-work. *Tundu ya pua*, nostril. Dim. *kitundu*. *Fanya tundu*, bore a hole. *Tundu tundu*, full of holes, e. g. describing trellis-work, lattice, net-work, &c., or of moth-eaten clothes. (*Tundu* is the most general word for 'hole.' Cf. *shimo*, which is usually bigger, *kipango, kitobwe, ufa, mwanya*.)

-**tundu**, a. obstinate, perverse, naughty, self-willed, troublesome, esp. of children. *Mtoto mtundu lazima kurudi*, a naughty child must be punished.

Tunduia, v. keep a watchful eye on, look out for, spy out, lie in wait for. E. g. of a doctor, *akiugua mtoto hutaweza kumtunduia*, if the child is ill, you will not be able to attend it. Ps. *tunduiwa*. (Cf. follg., and *otea, tunza, chungulia, peleleza*.)

Tunduizi, n. one who watches, guardian, spy. (Cf. prec.)

Tunduwaa, v. be still, silent, motionless, e. g. of one amazed, deceived, fascinated, deep in thought. (Cf., for the form, *tandawaa*.)

Tunga, v. (1) put together, put in order, put in a row; (2) form by arranging, compose, bring materials or ingredients together, construct, connect, make. E. g. (1) *tunga nyama kijitini*, put bits of meat in a row on a skewer. *T. samaki*, string fish together, or, put them on a stick. *T. ushanga*, string beads. *T. maua*, tie flowers together, make a garland or nosegay. *Tunga sindano, tunga uzi* (*katika sindano*) are both used of threading a needle. (2) *T. mayayi*, form eggs,—also (Nt.) *mayayi yametunga*, the eggs are hard set,—the contents having taken form. *Mtama unatunga*, the millet (grain) is forming. *T. mimba*, conceive, form an embryo. *T. chuo* (*mashairi, nyimbo*), compose a book (poetry, songs). *T. usaha*, form matter, suppurate, e. g. of an abscess. Ps. *tungwa*. Nt. *tungika*, (1) not only as above, i. e. be put together, be formed, but (2) with the further sense, be hung up, i. e. perh. be put on a string, be suspended, be connected with, be dependent upon; and (3) sometimes Act., e. g. *tungika paa*, put up a roof, with Ps. *tungikwa* (cf. *angika, tundika*), e. g. *alitungikwa tanzi la roho*, he was hung up by a noose round the neck. *T. ngao*, hang up a shield. Hence *tungik-ia, -iwa*. Ap. *tung-ia, -iwa*, e. g. *umetungia* (*uzi*) *sindano*, you have threaded the needle. Cs. *tung-iza, -izwa, -isha*. Rp. *tungana*. (Cf. *tungama, tungamana, tunguo, mtungo, utungo, tungo*, and ? *mtungi*,—also syn. *panga*, and *tanda*.)

Tunga, n. (—), (1) a round flat basket, used for sifting husks, &c. from grain by tossing (cf. *chunga*); (2) tail-bones, or dried tail of a skate (*taa*).

Tungama, v. be in a firm, compacted state, be formed like a clot, congeal, get thick. E. g. *damu inatungama*, the blood is clotted. *Nyuki watungama*, the bees form a cluster. Also as n., an embryonic clot, an embryo, like *mimba*. (Cf. follg., and *tundama, tuama*, and -*ama*.)

Tungamana, v. hold together, be connected, agree. Cs. *tungamanisha*, e. g. *wali ametungamanisha watu maneno mamoja*, the governor got all the people to agree to one statement. (Cf. *tunga*, and *fungamana, tangamana, shikamana*.)

Tungo, n. (*ma-*), way of forming, composition, device, things in a row.

Also plur. of *utungo* (which see). (Cf. *tunga, mtungo*.)

Tungua, v. Rv. form of *tunga*, i.e. (1) unform, disconnect, take to pieces; (2) unstring, take down, let down, e.g. *t. madafu*, get down cocoanuts. *T. roho*, discourage, dishearten. (3) fig. depress, depreciate, degrade. Ps. *tunguliwa*. Nt. *tunguka*, e.g. be let down, be taken down, sink, be depressed, &c. Ap. *tungu-lia, -liwa*. Cs. *tungu-za, -zwa*. (Cf. *tunga, tungika,*—also (*angika*) *angua*, (*shuka*) *shua*, which are common in Z.)

Tunguja, n. (*ma-*), an edible fruit of the shrub *mtunguja*.

Tunu, n. something rare, choice, valuable,—a keepsake, a souvenir, an heirloom, a special present, treasure, a rare sight, a curiosity. (Cf. *tunuka, tunza*, and syn. *hedaya, kioja*.)

Tunuka, v. (1) set the heart on, treasure, prize, long for, have special affection for (i.e. perh. regard as a treasure (*tunu*), make a treasure (*tunu*) of); (2) give as a present, make a present of, e.g. *namtunuka mtu huyu*, I have set my heart on this man. Ps. *tunukwa*. Ap. *tunuk-ia, -iwa*, e.g. make a present to. *T. kofia*, give a cap to. *T. moskiti*, make a gift to a mosque. Cs. *tunuk-isha, -ishwa* (? *tunusha*, and cf. *tunza*). Rp. *tunukana*. (Cf. *tunu*, and follg.)

Tunza, v. treat with care or affection; (1) guard, protect, care for, tend, keep safe; (2) attend to, observe, examine, keep an eye on; (3) make a present to. E.g. *tunza kazi*, work with care. *T. mtoto*, mind a child. *T. akili*, keep the brain clear, use the wits. Ps. *tunzwa*. Nt. *tunzika*. Ap. *tunz-ia, -iwa*. Cs. *tunz-isha, -ishwa*. Rp. *tunzana*. — n. (—, and *ma-*), (1) care, attention, guardianship; (2) things cared for, belongings. *Akamleteo kijana na tunza zake*, and he brought him the lad and his belongings. (3) gift, present, reward. (Cf. *tunu, tunuka*, also *tuzo* (*tunzo*), and syn. *hifathi, shika, angalia*.)

Tupa, v. (1) throw, cast, fling, e.g. a spear, stone, &c.; (2) throw away, cast off, desert, abandon. *Tupa jicho*, throw a glance. Ps. *tupwa*, e.g. *nimetupwa*, I am an outcast. Nt. *tupika*. Ap. *tup-ia, -iwa*, e.g. throw at (from, with, to),—also, pass on to, refer to, e.g. *Sultani humtupia waziri maneno*, the Sultan usually refers matters to his prime minister. Hence *tupil-ia, -iwa, -ika*. Also *tupiana*. Cs. *tup-isha, -ishwa*. Rp. *tupana*. (Cf. *mtupo*, and syn. *rusha, peleka, piga*.)

Tupa, n. (—), a file,—for metal, i.e. *tupa ya chuma*. A flat file is called *tupa ya msumeno*; a rasp for wood, *tupa ya lunga*. (See **Tunga**.)

-tupu, a. (*tupu* with D 4 (P), D 5 (S), D 6, and sometimes *tupu* for all D), (1) empty, bare, void, naked; (2) mere, sheer, bare, by itself (themselves), unmixed, pure, without change or adulteration; (3) meaningless, worthless, vain, devoid of content. E.g. *mikono mitupu*, empty hands, empty-handed. *Miguu mitupu*, bare feet, barefoot. *Mtu mtupu*, just a man, a mere man, one who has nothing. *Uongo mtupu*, a sheer, downright falsehood. *Weusi watupu*, none but black people. *Maneno matupu*, idle talk, nonsense. Sometimes indecl., e.g. *vyakula vitamu tupu* (or *vitupu*), nothing but nice food. Obs. *-tupu*, includes 'unclothed, naked,' but to denote nakedness in a vulgar sense, *utupu* or *tupu* is used as an indecl. adj., e.g. *huyu ni utupu*, the person is naked. *Mtu tupu*, a naked person. A less vulgar word is *uchi*. (Cf. *utupu, uchi*.)

***Turuhani**, n. tare, allowance made in weighing for package, vehicle, &c. (? Ar. 'deduction.')

***Turuki**, n. *v.r. .s.* Turki, a

Turk, an Egyptian. Hence *Uturuki*, Turkey. *Kituruki*, Turkish language.

Turuma, n. (*ma-*). See **Taruma**.

Turupuka, v. A variant of *churupuka* (cf. *chopoa, chopoka, chupuka*. See **Chopoa**.)

Tusha, v. and **Tushua**, Cs. perh. of *tua* (cf. *tuesha, tweza*), lower, degrade, humiliate, hold in contempt, treat contemptuously. *Jituska*, disgrace oneself,—by unworthy conduct, &c. Ps. *tushwa*. Nt. *tushuka*. Ap. *tush-ia, -iwa*. (Cf. *tua*, and follg., *matusu*, also syn. *thili, tweza, aibisha, shusha*.)

Tushi, n. (*ma-*), and **Tusi, Tusu**, insulting language or conduct, abuse, ill-treatment, outrage. Also as a. *-tushi*, degraded, insulted, abased, mean, low. (Cf. prec.)

Tusi, n. (*ma-*), a litter, palanquin, sedan, sling or hammock for carrying a person. (Cf. *machela*, and *jeneza*.)

Tuta, n. (*ma-*), a raised bed for planting, a long ridge of earth with deep furrows on either side. (Also perh. *tuta*, v. pile up. Nt. *tutika*, and Rv. *tutua*, take down, lower, deceive,—but not used in Z.)

Tutuka, v. rise in little swellings (*tutu*, Kr.). (Cf. follg.)

Tutuma, v. (1) make a rumbling (muttering, grumbling, growling) sound, e. g. thunder, the bowels, &c., —perh. imitative (cf. *tetema*) or connected with (2) swell up, bubble up, boil up, and fig. be puffed up, swell up, e. g. with pride, anger, &c. Hence also a Nt. *tutum'ka*, in same sense, and Cs. *tutum'-sha, -shwa*. (Cf. *mtutumo, tutumua*, and syn. *guna, nguruma*, and *furika*.)

Tutumua, v. Rv. of *tutuma*, draw together, e. g. *jitutumua*, gather oneself up,—as for an effort. (Cf. prec. and *nyata, kunja*.)

Tuza, v. make a present (to), give as a reward (to). *Mumewe akamtuza mganga mchele*, her husband gave the doctor a present of rice.

Ps. *tuzwa*, e. g. get a present. *Akatuzwa na watu mapesa*, people gave him a reward in money. (Cf. follg., and *tunu, tunuka*, or perh. *tunza*. *Tuza* also represents sometimes *chuza*, and *tusha* (which see).)

Tuzo, n. (—), also **Tuza**, and **Tunzo**, a present,—esp. of a reward for success. (Cf. prec., and for presents generally *bakshishi, zawadi*.)

Tw- often represents the sound of *tu* before a vowel. See **Tu**.

Twaa, v. take (to oneself), take away (from another), carry away (from another), take off, receive, accept, obtain. A very common verb, syn. often with *pokea, pewa, chukua, pata, shika*. *Mimi nimetoa fetha, naye ametwaa*, I gave the money, and he received. *Alitwaa miji mingi*, he seized (got possession of) many towns. *Twaa ruhusa*, receive leave. Ps. *twawa*, e. g. *ametwawa na ghururi*, he is seized with infatuation,—but commonly in the Ap. Ps. form *twaliwa*, which thus means both (1) be taken, seized, received, or (2) be robbed of, have something taken from (or, for) one, lose. See below. Nt. *twalika*. Ap. *twa-lia, -liwa, -lika*, e. g. take (receive) from (for, with, at, &c.), rob of, relieve, rid a person of, take on behalf of, &c. Hence *twaliana*. Cs. and Rp. not used.

Twana, Twaana, Twazana, v. be like, resemble each other,—sometimes with *sura, uso*, of personal resemblance. (Cf. *fanana, lingana*.)

Twanga, v. clean grain by pounding in a mortar, pound in order to get off the husks. Ps. *twangwa*. Nt. *twangika*. Ap. *twang-ia, -iwa*. Cs. *twang-isha, -ishwa*. (Cf. *mtwango*, and cf. *kinu, ponda*.)

Tweka, v. and a variant **Twika**, hoist up, raise from the ground, lift on to a person's shoulders or head,— esp. of loads, but also *t. tanga (bendera)*, hoist a sail (a flag). Ps.

twekwa. Nt. *twekeka.* Ap. *twek-ea, -ewa.* Rp. *twekana.* (Cf. syn. *inua, pandisha, kweza.*)

Tweta, v. pant, gasp, catch the breath,—of any irregular or difficult breathing. Ap. *twetea.* (Cf. *mtweto,* and syn. *kokota roho, vuta pumuzi.*)

Twiga, n. (—), a giraffe.

Twika, v. like *tweka,* but perh. only of lifting loads on to the head or shoulder. *Jitwika,* lift on to one's own head. Cs. *twisha,* intens. of loading another person. (Cf. *tweka.*)

U.

U represents the sound of *u* in the English *rule,* or, when not accented, in *full*. *Uu* is written when the sound is very marked and sustained, as in *kukuu,* dist. *kuku.*

Before another vowel sound, *u* is commonly pronounced as a consonant, i. e. *w,* and words not found under the one may be looked for under the other.

U is used independently

A. as a verb-form, (1) you are, agreeing with the pron. of the 2 Pers. Sing., i. e. *wewe,* or (2) it is, agreeing with D 2 (S), D 4 (S), e. g. *mzigo u mzito,* the load is heavy.

B. occasionally as conj. and, e. g. *tatu u nussu,* three and a half. (Cf. Ar. *wa.*)

U- (before a vowel, **W-**) as a formative pfx. is used

A. in verbs, as (1) the pfx. of the 2 Pers. Sing., subjective only, e. g. *unapenda, wapenda* (for *uapenda*), you love. (2) the pfx., subjective and objective, agreeing with D 2 (S), D 4 (S), e. g. *mti unaota,* the tree grows. *Uimbo waupenda,* you like the song. (3) inserted before the final *a* of any verb, it forms the derived stem which may be called Reversive, as commonly *reversing* the meaning of the root, e. g. *funga,* fasten, *fungua,* unfasten, and *fufua,* raise to life, (Rd.) from *fa,* die.

B. in nouns, as the characteristic initial of a large class, like *m* and *ki,*—and in contrast with *m* and *ki,* the most general and characteristic use of *u* is to form *abstract nouns,* and any suitable root of verb, noun, or adjective may be given an abstract meaning by simply prefixing *u,* with or without a change in the final syllable. E.g. cf. *mtu,* a man (a living organized thing), *kitu,* a thing, an object (a man, only when regarded as a thing), and *utu,* humanity, human nature, and also sometimes matter, substance (though this is usually covered by *kitu*). This being so, it is impracticable to attempt a full list of actual and possible abstract nouns in *u,* and a selection is made of those most common or remarkable.

The *u* class contains, however, many nouns with concrete meanings, e. g. *ufagio,* a brush, *ufunguo,* a key, *utando, ukoko, umande,* and in a large number of *u-* nouns (1) there is no plural, or (2) the only plural in common use has the pfx. of D 5 (P), *ma-,* usually denoting concrete forms or cases of the abstract expressed by the singular; (3) the rest following the rather difficult grammatical rules for D 4 (P).

Two other meanings of *u,* as a noun-pfx., may be compared with the abstract meaning, viz. (1) *u-* to denote the inward (and relatively smaller) part of an object, its substance, or quality (cf. *ubongo, ubuyu, udevu, udole, ufupa*), and (2) *u-* to denote a country. E. g. cf. *Mzungu,* a European, *kizungu,* something European,—esp. European language, *Uzungu,* the European's country, but also the quality of being European.

Obs. further that (1) *u* initial in nouns is sometimes not formative, but part of the root; (2) *u* and *o* are often not clearly distinguished in Swahili, esp. in Arabic words, which make no distinction; (3) *u* followed by another *u* or *w* often coalesces with it, e.g. *uwambo, uambo, wambo.*

C. in adjectives, *u-* (*w-*) sometimes takes the place of *m-, mw-,* to mark agreement with (1) D 1 (S), viz. in the pronom. adj. *-angu, -ako,* &c.; (2) D 2 (S), D 4 (S), not only in the pronom. adj. but also in *-ote, -enyi, -enyewe*; (3) D 4 (S), in a few other adjs., viz. *uchungu, ume, utupu.*

The meaning of many nouns in *u-* is more fully indicated under an adjective or verb of the same root, to which reference is given. A word not found under U may be looked for under the next letter, or under W. Plurals of *u* nouns are sometimes irregular, and given in full.

Ua, n. (*maua*), a flower. *Chuma maua*, pick flowers. *Toa maua*, come into flower. (Cf. *chanua*.)

Ua, n. (*nyua*), (1) an enclosure,—commonly an open court or backyard attached to a house, and fenced with sticks, plaited leaves, or a hedge. Also (2) a fence of this kind, i. e. *ua wa nyasi* (*miti, makuti, mabua*), a fence of grass (sticks, leaves, stalks).

Ua, v. kill, destroy life. Ps. *uawa.* Ap. *ulia, uliwa. Ulia mbali*, kill outright, kill off entirely. Hence *uliana.* Rp. *uana.* (Cf. *-uaji*, and syn. *fisha, chinja, piga.*)

Ua-, for words beginning with these letters, see also under **Wa-**.

Uadui, Uahadi. See **Wadui, Wahadi.**

Uambo, n. See **Uwambo.**

Uambukizo, n. (*nyamb.* and *maamb.*), infection, infectiousness. (Cf. *ambukiza.*)

Uamini, Uaminifu, n. honesty, trustworthiness, &c. (Cf. *amini.*)

Uandamizi, Uandamano, n. (*nyand.* and *maand.*), a following, a procession. (Cf. *andamizi, andamano.*)

Uanga, n. and **Wanga** (which see).

Uangalifu, n. carefulness, attention. (Cf. follg.)

Uangalizi, n. (*ma-*), observation, taking notice, care. (Cf. *angalia.*)

Uangamizi, n. (*ma-*), ruin, collapse, description. (Cf. *angamia.*)

Uapo, n. (*nyapo*), (1) a swearing, an oath (cf. *apa*); (2) also *wapo*, a giving, a gift, e. g. *ndio uapo mnono*, that is a rich present. (Cf. *pa* v., *kipaji.*)

***Uarabu**, n. (1) country of the Arabs, Arabia,—commonly *Arabuni*, or *Manga*; (2) Arab nature. (Dist. *uharabu*).

Uashi, n. art of mason's work, building with stone, masonry, a mason's fee. (Cf. *aka, asha, m-washi.*)

***Uasi**, n. (*maasi*), rebelliousness, disobedience, rebellion, revolt, mutiny. *Fanya uasi kwa Sultani*, revolt against the Sultan. (Ar.)

Uayo, n. (*nyayo*), also **Unyago**, and **Wayo**, sole of the foot, footprint, footstep, track. (Cf. *hatua.*)

Ubaba, n. paternity, fatherhood. (Cf. *baba, umama.*)

Ubabwa, n. and **Ubwabwa**, (1) gruel, pap, e. g. rice, esp. as made for hungry children or invalids, boiled with water enough to make a paste, or (2) rice cooked plainly, without cocoanut juice. Cf. the riddle *Ubabwa wa mtoto mtamu*, a child's pap is nice,—the answer being *usingizi*, sleep. (Cf. *matabwatabwa, uji, wali.*)

***Ubadili, Ubadilifu**, n. (*ma-*), change, changeableness, exchange, interchange. (Ar. Cf. *badili.*)

***Ubahili**, n. miserliness, niggardliness. (Ar. Cf. *bahili*, and syn. *ukabithi, choyo.*)

***Ubaini, Ubainifu**, n. clearness, demonstrability, notoriety, demonstration, evidence. (Ar. Cf. *baini*, and syn. *thahiri, wazi.*)

Ubale, n. (*mbale*), strip, slice, piece, e. g. *mbale za muhogo*, cassava cut in pieces lengthways,—called also *kopa* (*ma-*) when dried. The process of cutting is *lenga* (also *kata*) *mbale*. Kr. distinguishes *ubale* (*mbale*) from *mbale* (*mibale*), somewhat larger pieces, and *bale* (*mabale*) of the largest. (Cf. *pande, mpande, kipande,* and *utamba, mbamba, bamba.*)

*Ubalehi, n. marriageable age, adult state, puberty. (Ar. Cf. *balehi,* and syn. *uzima, upevu.*)

Ubali, n. (*mbali*), distance, being distant,—seldom used, but see Mbali, and cf. *ubele*.

*Ubalozi, n. office (position, work, salary) of a consul. (Cf. *balozi.*)

Ubamba, n. (*bamba*), thin or flat piece of stone, wood, or metal,—chip, strip, flake, sheet, a flat peg. (Cf. follg. and *mbamba, bamba, -embamba.*)

Ubambo, n. (*bambo*), a thin grooved skewer, like a cheesetaster, used for testing and sampling bags of rice. (Cf. prec.)

Ubango, n. (*bango*), reed,—but in Z. *tete* is usual.

*Ubani, n. frankincense. (Hind. Cf. *udi, uvumba.*)

Ubapa, n. (*bapa*), the flat part of anything, a flat surface,—e.g. the blade of a knife, *ubapa wa kisu*. (Cf. *bapa,* and *kengee.*)

*Ubarathuli, n. foolishness, simpleness, being easily duped. Cf. *Ujinga wa kuuza si ubarathuli wa kununua,* to be outwitted in selling is better than to be duped in buying. (Ar. Cf. *barathuli,* and syn. *ujinga, uzuzu.*)

*Ubaridi, n. (1), coldness, coolness; (2) a chilling manner, dullness; (3) comfort, convalescence. (Ar. Cf. *baridi, burudisha.*)

*Ubashiri, n. (*ma-*), proclamation, prediction, announcement. (Ar. Cf. *bashiri,*—also *hubiri, tabiri.*)

*Ubathiri, Ubathirifu, n. extravagance, prodigality. (Ar. Cf. *bathiri,* and syn. *upotevu.*)

Ubati, n. (*bati*), an addition to a house,—wing, outhouse, lean-to. (Cf. *kipenu.*)

*Ubatili, n. nullity, emptiness, vanity, futility, uselessness. *Mtu wa haki haamui ubatili,* a just man does not give worthless judgement. (Ar. Cf. *batili.*)

Ubau, n. (*mbau*), board, plank, cut timber. *Pasua mbau,* saw in pieces (or, saw out) planks. (Cf. *bau.*)

Ubavu, n. (*mbavu*), a rib, side of the body, or anything corresponding to it in relative position, e.g. skirt (slope, flank) of a mountain, side, wing (of an army, &c.). *Mbavuni mwa,* at the side of, on the flanks of.

Ubawa, n. (*mbawa*), a wing feather. *Funua mbawa,* spread out the wing feathers. (Cf. *bawa,* a wing.)

*Ubawabu, n. office (work, pay) of a door-keeper (gaoler, turnkey). (Ar. Cf. *bawabu,* and syn. *ungojezi wa mlango.*)

Ubaya, n. (*ma-*), badness, wickedness, corruptness, ugliness. (Cf. *-baya,* and syn. *uovu,* contr. *uzuri, wema.*)

*Ubazazi, n. (*ma-*), occupation (condition, habits, &c.) of a shopkeeper,—bargaining, buying, and selling, &c. (Ar. Cf. *bazazi.*)

Ubele, n. position in front, a step forward, progress, promotion, advancement, success. *Pata ubele,* be promoted. (Cf. *mbele,* adv., prob. plur. of *ubele,* cf. *ubali, mbali.*)

Ubeleko, n. See Mbeleko.

Ubembe, Ubembelezi, n. (*bembe, mabembe*), flirting, coquetry, coaxing, wheedling, fondling, allurement. (Cf. *bemba, bembe.*)

*Ubeti, n. (*beti*), verse, stanza, strophe. (Ar. Cf. *beti,* and *shairi.*)

Ubichi, n. unripeness, immaturity, freshness, rawness, greenness. (Cf. *-bichi.*)

*Ubilisi, n. same as *ushetani,* devilry, madness. (Ar. Cf. *bilisi, shetani.*)

Ubinadamu, n. human nature, humanity. (Cf. *binadamu*, and syn. *utu*, *wanadamu*.)

Ubinda, n. (*mbinda*). See **Ubinja**, **Uwinda**,—different words, both of which seem to be also thus pronounced. (Cf. *binda*, *bindo*.)

Ubingwa, n. cleverness, proficiency, quality of a good workman. (Cf. *bingwa*, and syn. *ustadi*, *welekevu*.)

Ubinja, n. (*mbinja*), also **Uwinja**, **Ubinda**, a whistling noise, whistle, i. e. the act or sound of whistling. *Piga mbinja*, whistle. (Cf. *miunzi*, *msonyo*, *kibinja*, and dist. *uwinda*.)

Ubishi, n. (*mbishi*, *mabishi*), (1) joking, a joke, jest, fun (cf. *mzaha*), (2) refractoriness, contrariness, strife, opposition, obstructiveness. *Ubishi mwingi huvuta mateto*, joking carried too far leads to quarrelling. (Cf. *bisha*, also *ukaidi*, *utundu*, *ushindani*.)

Ubivu, n. ripeness, maturity, being well-cooked. (Cf. *-bivu*, *iva*.)

Ubongo, n. (*mbongo*), brain substance, brain, marrow. (Cf. *bongo*.)

Ubono, n. (*mbono*), seed of the castor-oil plant (*mbono*).

Ubora, n. excellence, pre-eminence, fine quality (of any kind). (Cf. *bora*.)

Ubovu, n. rottenness, unsoundness, corruption, badness, putrefaction. (See *-bovu*, and cf. *uozi*, *uovu*, and *ubaya*.)

Ubua, n. (*mbua*), used for *bua* (*mabua*) of the smaller kinds of grain-bearing stalk, e. g. of *mpunga*, *mwele*, and of the stalk, as substance and material. (Cf. *bua*.)

Ububu, n. dumbness. (Cf. *bubu*.)

Ubugu, n. (*mbugu*), stem of a creeping plant, used as cord. (Cf. *mbugu*, *mbungo*.)

*****Uburudisho**, n. cooling, refreshment, recreation, relief. (Ar. Cf. *baridi*, *burudisha*.)

Ubuyu, n. the pithy substance or kernel inside the nut produced by a baobab tree,—a slightly acid biscuit-like substance, when ripe, occasionally eaten. E. g. *hawakuona kitu ndani ya mabuyu illa ubuyu mtupu*, they found nothing inside the calabashes except the pith.

Ubwabwa, n. See **Ubabwa**.

Ubwana, n. (1) mastership, qualities (rights, powers) of a master; (2) an overbearing, domineering, tyrannical, masterful character. (Cf. *bwana*.)

Uchache, n. (1) fewness, scarcity, want, slightness; (2) rarity, being scarce, (and so) of value. *Uchache wa moyo*, lack of spirit, feebleness of character. (Cf. *-chache*, *haba*.)

Uchafu, n. uncleanness, filthiness, dirt. (Cf. *-chafu*, and follg.)

Uchafuko, n. (*ma-*), disorder, muddle, mess, chaos, disorganization, unsettlement, confusion. (Cf. *chafuka*.)

Uchaga, n. and **Uchala**, store-place for grain,—as used on the mainland, but *utaa* more usual in Z. (Cf. *mchago*, *utaa*.)

Uchaguo, **Uchaguzi**, n. a choosing, daintiness, fastidiousness, habit of criticism. (Cf. *chagua*, and *uteuo*.)

Uchaji, n. fear, respect, awe, reverence. (Cf. *cha* v., *kicho*, and syn. *hofu*, *woga*.)

Uchakacho, n. a rustling sound, rustle, e. g. of leaves, clothes, &c. (Also perh. *utakaso*, cf. *chakacha*.)

Uchala, n. See **Uchaga**.

Uchale, n. (*chale*), gash, cut, incision. (See **Chale**.)

Uchanga, n. (1) immaturity, unripeness, early stage of development, babyhood, littleness (see *-changa*); (2) a grain of sand. (Cf. *mchanga*.)

Uchango, n. (*chango*), (1) smaller intestine; (2) worm in the intestine. (Cf. *chango*.)

Uchawi, n. witchcraft, sorcery, black arts, magic. *Hapana maneno ya uchawi kwa watu Waswahili*, Swahilis have nothing to do with witchcraft, i.e. they leave it to the savages (*washenzi*). (Cf. *uchawi*, and see **Mganga, Uganga**.)

Uchepechepe, n. being moist, wet, watery, &c. (See **Chepechepe**, and cf. *rútuba, umaji*.)

Uchi, n. nakedness, nudity,—less vulgar than *utupu* (which see). Used also as adj. *Washenzi wa huko uchi*, the savages in that part go naked.

Uchipuko, n. (*chipuko*), shoot, sprout, blade,—of a growing plant. (Cf. *chipuka*.)

Uchochoro, n. (*ma-*), narrow passage, lane, alley, e.g. between native houses in a town. (Cf. *chochoro*, and *ujia*.)

Uchokozi, n. (*ma-*), teasing, annoyance. (Cf. *chokoza*.)

Uchomozi, n. (1) coming out, bursting out, and so (2) of the sun, getting hot, scorching. (Cf. *chomoza*.)

Uchongo, n. (1) being one-eyed (cf. *chongo*); (2) discharge from a weak or diseased eye (also *utongo*).

Uchovu, n. (1) weariness, fatigue; (2) producing weariness, tediousness, dullness. (Cf. *-chovu, choka*.)

Uchoyo, n. See **Choyo**.

Uchu, n. longing, yearning, earnest wish. (Cf. *shauko, tamaa*.)

Uchukuti, n. central part, or midrib, of cocoanut leaf. (Cf. *kuti*.)

Uchukuzi, n. getting carried, conveyance, cost of carriage, porterage. (Cf. *chukua, mchukuzi*.)

Uchumba, n. relation of lovers, of lover and sweetheart, wooing, being wooed, lover's gift. The lover supplies his bride with clothes till marriage, *nguo za uchumba*. (See **Mchumba**.)

Uchumi, (1) way of earning profits, trade, business, occupation; (2) profits, earnings, salary,—in this sense also *uchumo*. (Cf. *chuma, chumo*.)

Uchungu, n. (1) sharp pain, smart, bitterness, bitter taste; (2) fig. resentment, anger, offended feeling, grudge. *-a uchungu*, and commonly *uchungu* alone (cf. *utupu*) as adj., bitter, painful, angry, and obs. the adv. *kiuchungu*. (Cf. *-chungu, -kali, mchomo, umivu*.)

Udaku, n. (*daku*), (1) objection, demurrer, protest; (2) news got hold of secretly, gossip, rumour. Also *udakuzi*, getting hold of stories, telling tales, &c. (See **Daka, Dakizo, Dakua**, and **Dukiza**,—perh. same word.)

*****Udalali**, n. profession of salesman or auctioneer, salesman's commission or fee. (Ar. Cf. *dalali*.)

Udanganyifu, n. (*ma-*), craftiness, cunning, deceitfulness, imposture. (Cf. *danganya*, and syn. *ujanja, werevu, hila*.)

Udevu, n. (*ndevu*), a hair of the face,—of the whiskers, moustache, &c. (Cf. *ndevu, kidevu*, and *unyele*.)

*****Udi**, n. and **Uudi**, aromatic aloewood,—used for fumigation (*vukizo*). (Ar. Cf. *ubani, uvumba*.)

*****Udibaji**, n. (1) adornment, artistic form, style; (2) mere form as opp. to substance,—and so, delusion, outward show, deceit. (Ar. Cf. *dibaji*.)

*****Udobi**, n. occupation of a washerman, laundry work, payment for washing. (Hind. Cf. *dobi*, and *ufuaji, fua*.)

Udogo, n. littleness, smallness, insignificance. (Cf. *-dogo*.)

Udole, n. (*ndole*), finger, toe,—but in Z. *kidole*. *Udole* is used of the nail of a finger (in Z. *ukucha*) and claw of an animal. (Cf. *dole, kidole*.)

Udongo, n. soil, earth, clay,—including surface-soil, potter's material, red earth used in making mortar, &c.

*****Udufu**, n. poorness of quality, weakness, thinness, dullness, insipidity, worthlessness, exhaustion, good-for-nothingness. (Ar. Cf. *dufu*, and syn. *uthaifu, uhafifu*.)

Udugu, n. brotherhood, kinsmanship, being of same family or clan or tribe. (Cf. *ndugu*, and syn. *ujamaa, utani*.)

Udui, n. (*ndui*), a pimple, a vesicle. Hence *ndui*, small-pox.

Uduvi, n. also **Nduvi**, **Duvi**, shrimp, prawn. Also called *kamba* (which see). *Uduvi* is also used collectively.

Ue-, for words beginning with these letters, see also under **We-**.

*****Uele**, n. sickness, illness, esp. of a severe and crippling kind, confining the patient to bed. *U. wa macho*, ophthalmia. *U. wa viungo*, rheumatism. (Ar. Cf. *-ele*, and syn. *ugonjwa, marathi*.)

Uembe, n. See **Wembe**.

Ufa, n. (*nyufa*), a crack, split, slit, cleft, rent, tear,—or similar aperture. *Fanya (tia) ufa*, crack, v. *Usipoziba ufa, utajenga ukuta*, if you neglect a crack, you will have to build a wall.

Ufafanusi, n. (*ma-*), explanation, revelation, interpretation, telling out, publishing abroad. (Cf. *fafanua*, and syn. *elezo*.)

Ufagio, n. (*fagio*), small broom, small brush, i.e. commonly a bundle of leaf-strips tied together and used for rough sweeping, e.g. footpaths, floors, &c. (Cf. *fagia*.)

*****Ufahamu**, n. (*fahamu*), (1) recollection, memory; (2) intelligence, sense, consciousness, recognition, comprehension. *Fahamu zikamrejea*, his senses returned to him, he recovered consciousness. (Ar. Cf. *fahamu*, and syn. *akili, moyo*.)

Ufalme, n. (*falme, mafalme*,—both seldom used), (1) chieftainship, kingship, royalty; (2) sway, rule, dominion; (3) sphere of dominion, kingdom. (Cf. *mfalme*, and syn. *enzi, mamlaka, ukuu*.)

Ufanani, n. likeness, resemblance. (Cf. *fanana, mfano*.)

*****Ufasaha**, n. (*fasaha*) and **Ufasihi**, elegance, aesthetic taste, purity of style, correct form,—esp. of a literary kind. (Ar. Cf. *fasihi*, and syn. *dibaji, usahihi, uswafi*.)

*****Ufidiwa**, n. (*fidiwa*), ransoming, ransom. (Ar. See **Fidia**, and cf. *dia, ukombozi*.)

*****Ufifilisi**, n. distraining, selling up, disposing of a debtor's goods,—and more generally, financial ruin, whether self-caused (i.e. extravagance, waste) or otherwise. (Ar. Cf. *filisi*, and syn. *angamiza, poteza*.)

Ufinyanzi, n. also with final *-gi*, *-ji*, for *-zi*, art (trade, work, wages, &c.) of a potter. (Cf. *finyanga*, and *finya*.)

*****Ufisadi, Ufisiki**, n., vice, viciousness, debauchery, fornication. (Ar. Cf. *fisadi*.)

*****Ufithuli**, n. (*fithuli*), insolence, arrogance, contemptuous temper, outrage, wanton insults. (Ar. Cf. *fithulika*.)

*****Ufitina**, n., commonly **Fitina** (which see). (Ar.)

Ufito, n. (*fito*), long thin piece of wood, stick, rod, lath, or anything similar in appearance, e.g. thin bar of metal, *ufito wa chuma*, rod iron, iron bar (cf. *upao*). Often of the thin straight sticks used on native roofs to carry the thatch, laid crosswise horizontally on the rafters. (Cf. *fimbo*, and for sticks generally, *bakora*.)

Ufizi, n. (*fizi*), gum,—of the jaw.

Ufo, n. (*nyufo*), act (place, state, manner, &c.) of dying. (Cf. *-fa, kifo, -fu*, and follg., and syn. *mauti*.)

Ufu, n. state of being dead, death, deadness, numbness. (Cf. prec.)

Ufuaji, n. the act (manner, occupation) of beating, washing clothes, &c. (Cf. *fua*, and syn. *udobi*.)

Ufuasi, n. (*fuasi*, and *ma-*), following, accompanying, e.g. of musical accompaniment. (Cf. *fuata, mfuasi*.)

Ufufuko, Ufufuo, n. (*fufuko, fufuo*), restoration of life, raising from death, revival, renewing, restarting,—the neut. form in *-ko* meaning properly 'being restored to life, being renewed,' &c. (Cf. *fufua, -fa*, and syn. *huisha*.)

*Ufukara, n. utter destitution, beggary, poverty. (Ar. Cf. *fukara, fakiri, hohehahe,* and syn. *mashini.*)

Ufuko, n. (*fuko*), sandy margin of the seashore about high-water mark, i. e. *maji ya bahari yakomapo,—pwani,* including the whole shore to low-water mark. E. g. *ulichokiacha pwani kakingoje ufukoni,* the thing you left out on the shore, expect to find washed up on the sand. The Act. form *ufuo* is also used. (Cf. *fua,* used of the beating of the waves on the shore, and *ufukwe,* the fine white sand of the shore. Dist. *mfuko, kifuko, fuko,* a bag.)

Ufukwe, n. (1) the fine white sand formed by the beating of waves on the shore (cf. prec.); (2) fig. utter destitution (cf. *ufukara*).

Ufumbi, n. (*ma-*), depression between hills, valley, bottom. In Z. commonly *bonde.*

Ufundi, n. art (position, work, wages) of a *fundi,* i. e. a skilled mechanic, artisan, master workman. *Pata uf.,* become a master (after being an apprentice, *mwanafunzi*). *Piga uf.,* show off. (Cf. *fundi, fundisha.*)

Ufunga, n. (*funga*), a stone bench or seat of masonry, usually against the wall in front of the house, for the reception of visitors. (Cf. *baraza.*)

Ufungu, n. (*fungu*), (1) relationship, connexion; (2) a relative, kinsman. E. g. *ufungu wangu anakuja,* one of my family is coming. (Cf. *ukoo, ndugu, akrabba, jamaa, mtani.*)

Ufunguo, n. (*funguo*), (1) act (means, mode, &c.) of opening, commencement, exordium, preface; (2) a key,—the commonest use, e. g. *killa mlango na ufunguo wake,* every door has a key (means of opening). (Cf. *funga, fungua.*)

Ufuo, n. See Ufuko.

Ufupa, n. bony substance, cartilage, gristle. (Cf. *mfupa, kifupa, fupa.*)

Ufupi, n. shortness, brevity. (Cf. *-fupi, fupiza,* and contr. *urefu.*)

Ufupisho, n. shortening, contraction. (Cf. prec.)

Ufusio, n. sprinkling of small stones on a fresh-laid concrete floor, to bring it to a smooth surface. (Cf. *fusia, kifusi.*)

Ufuta, n. semsem,—the oil from which is called *mafuta ya uta.* (Cf. *mafuta.*)

Ufuu, n. the nutty part of a cocoa-nut inside the shell (*kifuu*), extracted by grating. Called *chicha* when mixed with water, and the oil strained out. (Cf. *nazi, chicha, tui.* Dist. *fuu,* the fruit.)

Ufuzi, n. (*fuzi, mafuzi*), a hair of the armpits, or of the pudenda.

Ufyozi, n. (1) making a contemptuous whistling noise between the teeth, so generally (2) a defiant, insolent manner of acting or speaking. (Cf. *fyoa.*)

Uga, n. (—), an open space in a town, or round a house. E. g. *akafika ugani panapo ile nyumba,* he arrived at the open place, where the house stood. (Cf. *uwanja, peupe,* and dist. *ua.*)

Ugali, n. a stiff porridge, commonly made of *mtama,* millet, mixed with water and cooked.

Uganga, n. (*ma-*), (1) art (profession, fee) of a native doctor, doctoring, healing, surgical and medical aid,—including use of charms, &c. (see Mganga). Also (2) medicine, charm. E. g. *pika (fanya, weka) uganga,* concoct (make, place in position) native medicine. *Maganga,* used of a doctor's appliances, materials, and operations generally. (Cf. *ganga,* and cont. *uchawi.*)

Ugeni, n. (1) state or condition of a stranger or foreigner, newness, strangeness; (2) state of being a guest; (3) a foreign region or country, foreign parts. *Safiri ugenini,* travel abroad, in foreign countries. (Cf. *-geni.*)

Ugeuzi, n. (*geuzi, mageuzi*), changing, changeableness, change, variation, turning round. (Cf. *geuka, geu*, and syn. *ubadili*.)

*Ughaibu, n. See Uraibu.

Ugo, n. (*nyugo*), (1) enclosure, fenced court, yard; (2) fence. In Z. commonly *ua*. (Cf. *uga, ua*.)

Ugomba, n. (*gomba*), fibre from the banana stalk (*mgomba*), very strong and fine.

Ugomvi, n. (*gomvi, magomvi*), quarrelsomeness, contentiousness, bad temper, wrangling, a quarrel. (Cf. *gomba, -gomvi, gombana*.)

Ugonjwa, n. (*gonjwa, magonjwa*), being ill, sickness, disease, ill health. *Shikwa na (patwa na, ingia) ugonjwa*, get ill. *Tia (fanya) ugonjwa*, cause sickness. *Ondoa (ponya) u.*, cure sickness. *Toka ugonjwani, poa ugonjwa*, recover from sickness. (Cf. *-gonjwa, gonjweza*, and syn. *marathi, uweli*.)

Ugono, n. (*ngono*), sleeping-time, —and so, night. (Cf. *ngono*.)

Ugua, v. (1) become sick, fall ill, be in pain, be ailing; (2) groan, wail. Ap. *ugu-lia, -liwa*, e.g. *nguo za kuugulia*, mourning dress. *Ugulia nyumba*, be ill in a house. *Unauguliwa*, you have sickness in your house. Cs. *ugu-za, -zwa*, (1) cause to be ill, produce sickness; but commonly (2) attend in sickness, as nurse, treat or doctor a sick person. (Cf. *mwuguzi, uguzi*, also *ugonjwa*, and *hawezi*.)

Ugumu, n. hardness, solidity, firmness, resolution, bravery, severity, insensibility, &c. (Cf. *-gumu*.)

Uguzi, n. (*mauguzi*), nursing the sick, care of sick people, operations (materials, means, &c.) of nursing. (Cf. *ugua*, and *mlezi*.)

Ugwe, n. (*ngwe*, and *nyugwe*), string, small cord, and anything used as such. (Cf. *kigwe, kitani, kamba*.)

*Uhaba, n. (1) fewness, scantiness, rarity; (2) being too few, deficiency, lack. (Ar. Cf. *haba*, and syn. *-chache*.)

*Uhafifu, n. lightness, cheapness, commonness, poor quality, worthlessness. (Ar. Cf. *hafifu*.)

*Uhai, n. being alive, life. (Ar. Cf. *hai, huisha*, and syn. *-zima, ishi*.)

*Uhali, n. state, condition, circumstances,—for the more common *hali* (which see), and dist. *mahali, pahali*. (Ar.)

*Uhalifu, n. (*halifu*, or *mahalifu*), disobedience, transgression, breaking rules, rebellion, naughtiness. (Ar. Cf. *halifu*, and syn. *uasi, ukaidi*.)

*Uharabu, n. destructiveness, mischievousness, vandalism. (Ar. Cf. *uharibifu, harabu, haribu*, and syn. *uvunjifu*.)

*Uharamia, n. brigandage, piracy, outlawry. (Ar. Cf. *haramia, haramu*.)

*Uharara, n. (1) warmth, heat; (2) hastiness, impetuosity, violence. (Ar. Cf. *harara, hari*.)

*Uharibifu, n. destruction, spoiling, corruption, mortality, waste. (Ar. Cf. *haribu, uharabu*, and syn. *upotevu*.)

*Uhasidi, n. and Uhusuda, envy, spite, malignity. (Ar. Cf. *hasidi*, and syn. *uwivu*.)

*Uhassi, n. castration, being a eunuch. (Ar. Cf. *hassi, maksai*.)

*Uhawara, n. being a paramour. (Ar. Cf. *hawara, hawa*, and dist. *usuria, ukahaba*.)

Uhiana, n. hardness, toughness, resistance, obstinacy, unkindness, unfairness. (Cf. *hiana*, and syn. *ugumu*.)

*Uhitaji, n. (*hitaji, mahitaji*), (1) want, need, requirement, desire; (2) indigence, necessitous condition. (Ar. Cf. *hitaji*.)

*Uhodari, n. strength, firmness, ability, resolution, courage, skill. (Cf. *hodari*, and syn. *nguvu, uwezo*.)

Uhunzi, n. work (trade, condition, wages) of a smith, metal-working. (Cf. *mhunzi*, and *mfua chuma*.)

*Uhuru, n. freedom, liberty,

emancipation. *Cheti cha uhuru,* freedom-certificate. *Mtumwa amepewa uhuru,* the slave has been emancipated. (Ar. Cf. *huru,* and *ungwana.*)

*Uhusuda, n. See Uhasidi. (Ar.)

Uiari, see Urari.

Uima, n. and adv. and Wima, uprightness (of position), upright. E. g. *watu waliosimama uima,* people who stood upright. (Cf. *ima.*)

Uimbaji, n. being a singer (minstrel, chorister), singing (as a practice or profession). (Cf. *imba,* and follg.)

Uimbo, n. (*nyimbo*), also Wimbo, a singing, a song. (Cf. *imba,* and prec.)

Uivu, n. and Uwivu, jealousy, envy. *Lia uivu,* weep for jealousy. (Cf. *-ivu,* and *husuda, hasidi.*)

Uizi, n. thieving, robbery, theft. (Cf. *iba, mwizi,* and syn. *unyang'anyi.*)

*Ujahili, n. boldness, bravery, courage. (Ar. Cf. *jahili,* and syn. *ushujaa, ukali, ugumu.*)

Ujaji, n. verbal of *-ja,* i. e. a coming, but rarely used. (Cf. *-ja, ujio, majilio,* and dist. *uchaji,* fear, *uchache,* fewness.)

Ujalifu, n. fullness, being full. (Cf. *jaa,* v. and *ujazi.*)

Ujana, n. youthfulness, youth, age of *kijana.* (See Kijana, for definition of meaning, and Mwana.)

Ujane, n. the unmarried state,—of bachelor, spinster, widow or widower. (Cf. *mjane.*)

Ujanja, n. craftiness, cunning, roguery, deceit, fraud. (Cf. *-janja,* and syn. *hila, udanganyifu, hadaa.*)

*Ujari, n. (*njari*), tiller-rope, in a native vessel, i. e. *kamba ya shikio,* or *ya msukani.* (? Ar.)

Ujazi, n. fullness, abundance, plentiful supply. (Cf. *jaa, ujalifu,* and syn. *wingi.* Dist. *jazi, ma-.*)

Ujenzi, n. (*ma-*), building operations, construction, designing, architecture. *Majenzi,* buildings,—also *majengo.* (Cf. *jenga, mjenzi.*)

*Ujeuri, n. more commonly Jeuri (*ma-*), violence, insolence, outrage, tyranny. (Ar. Cf. *jeuri,* and syn. *uthalimu, ukorofi.*)

Uji, n. gruel,—i. e. rice or other grain made into a soup or paste. Cf. *ubabwa,* and *wali* (rice so cooked that all the grains are separate and dry). *Humpa uji, halafu hukampa ubabwa,* he gives him rice-porridge, and presently gruel.

Ujia, n. (? *njia, majia*), a passage, narrow path,—used (rarely) to mark a difference from the common general term *njia,* which is perh. its plur. form. (Cf. *-ja,* and follg.)

Ujima, n. work in common, co-operation, mutual help,— e. g. in building a house, planting or harvest,—a common native practice, repaid by a beer-drinking or by similar help on occasion. (Cf. *shogoa.*)

Ujinamizi, n. bending (of the body), stooping, inclination. (Cf. *ji, inama,* and *jinamizi.*)

Ujinga, n. rawness (of a newcomer), ignorance, simplicity, folly. *Ujinga wa mtu ni werevu wake,* a man's simplicity is (often) his shrewdness. (Cf. *-jinga,* and syn. *upumbafu, ubarathuli.*)

*Ujini, n. the country or home of the genie (spirits, demons). (Ar. Cf. *jini.*)

Ujio, n. (*majio*), act (manner, time, &c.) of coming, approaching. (Cf. *-ja, ujia,* and *majilio, mjio.*)

*Ujira, n. and Ijara, hire, wages, recompense for work done. (Ar. Cf. *ajiri,* and *mshahara.*)

*Ujirani, n. (1) having neighbours, neighbours, neighbourliness, e. g. *ujirani ni fetha katika kasha,* neighbours are money in a safe. (2) neighbourhood, neighbouring district. (Cf. *jirani.*)

*Ujitahidi, n. energy, exertion, effort, personal endeavour. E. g.

ujitahidi haiondoi amri ya Muungu, effort has no power against Providence. (Ar. Cf. *jitahidi*, and syn. *utendaji, bidii*.)

Ujumbe, n. (1) office (dignity, duty, privilege, &c.) of a chief, chieftancy, supremacy, royal dignity (cf. *mjumbe*); (2) office, &c. of a messenger, ambassador (cf. *jumbe*). (Cf. *ufalme, ukuu, usultani, utume*.)

Ujume, n. the art (profession, wages, &c.) of a *mjume* (which see), high-class metal work, cutlery, &c.

*****Ujusi**, n. defilement, i. e. of a ceremonial kind, e. g. after childbirth, according to Mahommedan rules. (Ar. Cf. *unajisi, uchafu*.)

Ujuvi, n. (*ma-*), impudence, impertinence, sauciness, precocity, knowingness. (Cf. *jua*, v., and follg.)

Ujuzi, n. possession of knowledge, wisdom, sagacity, practical experience. (Cf. prec., and *jua*, v.)

*****Ukabithi**, n. economy, closefistedness, hoarding. (Ar. Cf. *kabithi*, and syn. *ubahili*.)

*****Ukadirifu**, n. estimation, valuation, assessment. (Ar. Cf. *kadiri*.)

Ukaguzi, n. inspection, examination, survey. (Cf. *kagua*.)

*****Ukahaba**, n. prostitution, fornication. (Ar. Cf. *kahaba*.)

*****Ukaimu**, n. office (dignity, work, &c.) of a vicegerent, viceroyalty. (Ar. Cf. *kaimu*.)

Ukali, n. (*ma-*), (1) a sharp, acid taste; (2) sharpness, keenness, edge; (3) strong character, firmness, resolution, spirit, bravery; (4) cruelty, severity, tyranny, fury. (Cf. *-kali, makali, uchungu, uthabiti, ugumu, ukorofi*. Dist. *ukali* as a verb-form for *ni*, i. e. is, e.g. *mtama ukali mmea*, the millet is just growing up. See Li.)

Ukalifu, n. intensity, severity, keenness, e. g. *ukalifu wa jua*, scorching heat of the sun. (Prob. same as *ukulifu* (which see), or possibly *ukali*.)

Ukambaa, n. (*kambaa*), cord, of plaited leaf-strips, like *shupatu*,—sometimes used as a whip. (Cf. *kamba*, of cocoanut fibre.)

Ukame, n. barrenness, bareness, waste condition,—of land. (Cf. *kame*, and *ukiwa*.)

*****Ukamili, Ukamilifu**, n. completeness, perfection, consummation. (Ar. Cf. *kamili*, and syn. *-timilifu, -zima*.)

*****Ukamio**, n. (*kamio*), menacing, threatening, reproaching. (Cf. *kamia*, and syn. *wogofya*.)

Ukanda, n. (*kanda*), a strip of leather, strap, thong. E. g. *ukanda wa kupigia*, a scourge. *U. wa kuvalia soruali*, a trouser-suspender. *U. wa uta*, a bow-string. (Cf. *kanda*, n.)

Ukando, n. (*kando*), side, edge, margin. (See **Kando**.)

Ukango, n. (*kango*), (1) frying; (2) frying-pan. (See **Kaango, Kaanga**.)

Ukano, n. (1) (*kano*), also **Kano** (—), and **Mkano** (*mi-*), sinew, tendon,—but in Z. commonly *mshipa* (which see); (2) verbal of *kana*, v., denial, contradiction.

Ukao, n. (*kao*), act (place, manner, &c.) of remaining (staying, residing), way of living, posture. (Cf. *kaa*, v., *kikao, makazi*, &c.)

*****Ukarimu**, n. generosity, liberality, hospitality, openhandedness. (Ar. Cf. *karimu, karamu, karama*, and syn. *upaji*.)

Ukata, n. poverty, destitution. (Cf. *mkata*.)

Ukavu, n. dryness, humour, intrepidity, nonchalance. *Ukavu wa macho*, an unconcerned, fearless, cool look. (Cf. *-kavu, kauka*.)

Ukawa, n. (*kawa*), delay. (Cf. *kawa, kawio, usiri*.)

Ukaya, n. (*kaya*), a long piece of thin blue calico or muslin, rolled up and wound round the head and under the chin, leaving two long ends, —worn by married free women of the poorer class.

Ukazi, n. act of residing (staying, remaining), right to reside, payment for lodging, &c. (Cf. *ukao, kaa*, v.)

Uke, n. (1) womanhood, female condition, status, characteristics,— but commonly for distinctness *utu uke*; (2) condition (privileges, duties) of being a wife, e.g. *uke na ume umekwisha*, we have ceased to be wife and husband; (3) for the vulgar *kuma*, vagina. (Cf. *-ke*, and contr. *-ume*.)

Ukelele, n. (*kelele*, and *ma-*), a cry, shout, exclamation, noise of voices. (Cf. *kelele*. Also *ukemi*, rarely used in Z.)

Ukengee, n. flat part of a cutting instrument, blade of knife, &c. (Cf. *kengee*, and *bapa*.)

Ukili, n. (—), a narrow length of plaited leaf-strip. Such lengths sewn together form the common mats of Zanzibar. *Suka ukili*, plait *ukili*. (See **Mwaa, Mkindu**.)

*****Ukinaifu**, n. (*kinaifu*), self-sufficiency, independence, fastidiousness, self-satisfaction, conceit. (Cf. *kinai, -kinaifu*.)

Ukindu, n. (*kindu*), material from the *mkindu*, or wild date palm, i.e. leaf used for plaiting, and fibre for string. The fruit is *kindu*. (Cf. *mkindu, mwaa, ukili*.)

Ukingo, n. (*kingo*), (1) act (means, manner, &c.) of warding off,—and so used variously of a screen in a house, an awning to keep off the sun, a fence for directing game to a trap, a barricade of trees across a road, a parapet or balustrade, &c.; (2) edge, rim, margin, verge, border, e.g. of a river, precipice, pit, &c., edge of a squared or chamfered board. (Cf. *kinga*, and *ukando*.)

Ukinzani, n. (*kinzani, ma-*), obstructiveness, contentiousness, petulance, objection, contradiction. (Cf. *kinga, kinzani*.)

*****Ukiri**, n. (1) acknowledgement, confession, justification, admission. *Jitia ukiri*, justify oneself, freely allow. (2) for *ukili*, a plait of leaf-strips. (Ar. Cf. *kiri*, and syn. *ungama*.)

Ukiwa, n. solitariness, loneliness, abandonment, desolation, state of being uninhabited. (Cf. *-kiwa*.)

Ukiziwi, n. deafness. (Cf. *kiziwi*, and *ziba*.)

Uko, verb-form, you are (it is) there, i.e. pfx. *u* agreeing with D 2 (S), D 4 (S), and with Pron. of 2 Pers. Sing. *wewe*,—and *-ko* for adv. *huko* of place or time, there, then. (Cf. *u, ko*.)

Ukoa, n. (*koa*), ring or band of metal, e.g. as used on a sword sheath, bridle, &c. (Cf. *koa*.)

Ukofi, n. See **Kofi, Ukufi**.

Ukoga, n. (*koga*), used of accretions or incrustations, such as tartar on the teeth, scum on water, scurf on the skin, &c. (Cf. *ukoko*.)

Ukohozi, n. (*ma-*), coughing, expectoration, sputum, phthisis, any chest affection causing coughing. (Cf. *kohoa, kifua*.)

Ukoka, n. a fine, creeping kind of grass, largely collected and used as fodder for horses, donkeys, and cattle in Z. (Cf. *kikoka*, and the more general term *majani*.)

Ukoko, n. used of the hard burnt caked rice at the bottom or top of a cooking pot, and perh. of other substances in similar condition. (Cf. *kikoko*.)

Ukoma, n. leprosy. (Cf. also *matana, balanga, balasi*, and perh. conn. with *koma*.)

Ukomba, n. a curved tool, used for hollowing out by cutting and scraping, e.g. for native wooden mortars, drums, measures, canoes. (Cf. *komba*, v. and follg.)

Ukombo, n. (*kombo*), curve, bend, crook. (Cf. *komba, kikombo*, and prec.)

Ukombozi, n. (1) rescue, ransoming, redemption, recovery; (2) money paid for redemption, ransom, fine. (Cf. *komboa, mkombozi.*)

Ukomo, n. (*komo*), act (manner, time, place, &c.) of coming to a stop, end, halting-place, goal, end part, limit, destruction, death. *U. wa njia* (*kisa*), end of a road (story). *U. wa bahari*, seashore. *U. wa uso*, forehead. (Cf. *koma*, v., *kikomo*, and perh. *ukoma*.)

Ukonge, n. fibre of the *mkonge*, a kind of hemp.

Ukongojo, n. (*kongojo*), and **Mkongojo**, a staff for leaning on, a prop, a crutch. (Cf. *kongoja*.)

Ukongwe, n. extreme old age. (Cf. *-kongwe*.)

Ukono, n. (*kono*), used of the tendrils, by which plants grasp or cling to anything, and of other hand-like objects. (Cf. *mkono, kikono.*)

Ukonyezo, n. (*konyezo*), (1) making a silent or secret sign, esp. with eyes or hands, a wink, a shrug; and (2) fig. hint, suggestion, warning, allusion. (Cf. *konyeza*, and *kopesa*.)

Ukoo, n. (1) relationship, kinship, affinity, ancestry, pedigree, descent, family (cf. *ujamaa, udugu, utani, akrabba, nasaba*); (2) perh. better *ukowo*, uncleanness, slovenliness, filth, dirt. (Cf. *ujusi, uchafu, taka.*)

Ukope, n. (*kope*), a hair of the eye-lash. *Hatta ukope twaonea mzito*, even an eye-lash we feel a burden. (Cf. *kope, kopesa,* and *udevu.*)

Ukopi, n. (*kopi*), (1) borrowing and not repaying, knavery, cheating, deceit, fraud (cf. *ujanja, hila, udanganyifu*); (2) thing borrowed, loan, advance (cf. *karatha, maazimo*). (Cf. *kopa, mkopi.*)

Ukorofi, n. (*korofi*), evil temper, malignity, savagery, brutality, tyranny, &c. (Cf. *-korofi.*)

Ukosefu, n. (*ma-*), failure (to obtain, reach, get), lack, want, deficiency, defect, faultiness, shortcoming. (Cf. *kosa, -kosefu.*)

Ukosekano, n. (*ma-*), like *ukosefu* (which see).

Ukosi, n. nape of the neck. (Cf. *kikosi.*)

*****Ukubali**, n. (1) acceptance, reception, consent, acquiescence; (2) acceptability, pleasingness. (Ar. Cf. *kubali, kibali.*)

Ukubwa, n. greatness, whether (1) materially,—big, bulky, huge; or (2) morally,—high, powerful, important, weighty, &c. (Cf. *-kubwa*, and *kuu.*)

Ukucha, n. (*kucha*, and *ma-*), nail (of finger or toe), claw, talon, hoof. *Piga* (*peleka*) *uk.*, scratch, lacerate, claw.

Ukufi, n. (*kufi*), as much as will lie on the flat of the hand, handful. *Punje za mtama zinazopata ukufi*, as much millet as would lie on the hand. (Cf. *kofi*, i. e. *ukufi* for *ukofi.*)

*****Ukufuru**, n. (*ma-*), unbelief, infidelity, atheism, apostacy. *Makufuru*, blasphemy, sacrilege, profane words or deeds. (Ar. Cf. *kafiri.*)

Ukulifu, n. (1) being tired, remissness, yielding; (2) oppressiveness, being overwhelming or too much, &c. (Cf. *kua, kulia, -kulifu,* and *ukalifu.*)

Ukulima, n. (*ma-*), condition (employment, operations, &c.) of a husbandman (peasant, tiller of the soil), agriculture, cultivation, peasantry. (Cf. *lima, mkulima, mlimo, kilimo.*)

Ukumbi, n. (*kumbi*), porch, vestibule, outer hall, anteroom,—inside a stone house, outside a mud house. *Ingia* (*tiwa*) *kumbini* is an euphemistic expression for being circumcised, i. e. to be excluded (for the time) from entering the house. Hence *kumbi* for *tohara*, e. g. *akamfanyia mtoto wake kumbi*, he arranged for his son to be circumcised. (Cf. *sébule.*)

Ukumbizi, n. (*kumbizi*), (1) a clearing away, sweeping up, making a clean sweep, gleaning; (2) a pushing off or away, thrusting aside. (Cf. *kumba*.)

Ukumbuko, Ukumbusho, n. a calling to mind, remembering, reminding, remembrance, memorial, souvenir. (Cf. *kumbuka, kumbukumbu*.)

Ukumbuu, n. (*kumbuu*), girdle, sash, i.e. some textile material twisted or rolled up, and worn round the waist. (Cf. *mshipi, mahazamu*.)

Ukumvi, n. (*kumvi*), empty ear or spike or head of grain-bearing plant, rice, millet, &c., without the grain, husk, bran, chaff. (Cf. *wishwa, kapi*, and *kumbi*, which is perh. from same root. Corresp. to *ganda* in 'ruit.)

Ukunde, n. (*kunde*), a bean produced in pods by the plant *mkunde*, grown for food in Z.

Ukunga, n. the trade (work, pay) of a *mkunga* (which see).

Ukungu, n. (*kungu, ma-*), (1) damp, moisture, mouldiness, mildew; (2) fog, mist, vapour,—esp. of morning and evening, and so of twilight. Hence *makungu*, of the signs of dawn, and glow after sunset. E.g. *ukungu unatanda* (*unakuja, unawamba*), the dawn is spreading. *Mkate unafanya uk.*, the bread is getting mildewed.

Ukunguru, n. also **Mkunguru** (which see).

Ukuni, n. (*kuni*), a stick of firewood. *Chanja* (*pasua*) *kuni*, cut firewood.

Ukunjufu, n. cheerfulness, gladness, good temper, geniality (of mien and manner). (Cf. *kunja, -kunjufu*.)

*****Ukurasa**, n. (*kurasa*), sheet or strip of paper, leaf or page of a book. (Ar. Cf. *karata, karatasi*.)

Ukuta, n. (*kuta*), stone wall of a house, i.e. *ukuta wa mawe*. (Dist. *boma*, which may or may not be a wall, *kiwambasa*, a partition-wall, commonly of sticks and plaster, *kitalu*, wall of a court.)

Ukuti, n. (*kuti*), a side frond of a cocoanut leaf. (Cf. *kuti, makuti*.)

Ukuu, n. greatness,—but more in a moral than material sense. (See -*kuu*, and **Kubwa**.)

Ukwaju, n. (*kwaju*), a tamarind, fruit of the *mkwaju*.

Ukwasi, n. wealth, opulence, riches. (Cf. -*kwasi* and its syn. *tajiri, mwenyi mali*.)

Ukwato, n. (*kwato*), hoof (solid, of horse), part of a cloven hoof (of cow, &c.). *Mguu wa ng'ombe una kwato mbili*, a cow's foot is cloven (in two parts).

Ukwe, n. the relationship of *wakwe*, i.e. of near connexions by marriage, e.g. father-in-law and son-in-law. (Cf. *mkwe*.)

*****Ulaanifu**, n. a cursing, a curse, being cursed. (Ar. Cf. *laana, -laanifu*, and follg.)

*****Ulaanizi**, n. a cursing, using imprecations, malediction. (Ar. Cf. prec.)

Ulafi, n. (*ma-*), over-eating, voracity, greediness, gluttony. (Cf. -*la, ulaji*, and *ulevi*.)

Ulaika, n. (*ma-*), a hair of the body, a bit of down, gossamer. (Cf. *udevu, unyele, ukope*, and dist. Ar. *malaika*, angel.)

Ulaini, Ulainifu, n. softness, smoothness, tenderness, gentleness (of accent, manner, &c.). (Ar. Cf. *laini*, and syn. *wororo, upole*.)

Ulaji, n. (*ma-*), act of eating, opportunity (means, chance) of eating, a feast. E.g. *uwape ulaji wakubwa*, give the leading people a feast. (Cf. -*la, ulafi, chukula*.)

Ulalamizi, n. (*lalamizi*), supplication, humble appeal, begging for mercy. (Cf. *lalamu*.)

Ulalo, n. (*malalo*), (1) place (time, accessories, manner) of lying down or sleeping, camping-place, bed. *Malalo*, things to sleep on, bedding (cf. *kituo, kambi*). (2) something lying or laid down, e.g. a tree or plank laid as a bridge across a stream (cf.

mtatago). (Cf. *lala, kilalo, malalo.*)

Ulambilambi, n. condition of a cocoanut, when the nutty part is just forming, still soft, and can be picked off, i. e. *ul. wa dafu*. (Cf. *lamba, dafu, nazi.* Dist. *rambirambi.*)

***Ulaya**, n. (1) native land, home,—but commonly used of foreigners, and so (2) Europe. *Ulaya Uzungu*, Europe. *U. Hindi*, India. *Ulaya wa Wareno*, Portugal. (Ar. Cf. *wilaya*, and follg.)

***Ulayiti**, n. European textile stuff, —esp. of a thin inferior kind of calico, not so stout as *Amerikani*, grey shirtings. *Kamba Ul.*, hemp rope,—not of cocoanut fibre. (Ar. Cf. prec.)

***Uledi**, n. in Z. a proper name common among slaves. (Ar., cabin boy, cook's boy.)

Ulegevu, n. and **Ulegeo**, (1) slackness, relaxed condition, exhaustion, weakness; (2) remissness, carelessness, negligence. (Cf. *legea, -legevu*, and syn. *utepetevu.*)

Ulevi, n. (*ma-*), (1) a state of drunkenness, intoxication, giddiness, staggering, reeling; (2) an intoxicant, e. g. *killa ulevi*, all kinds of intoxicants (forbidden by Mahommedan law). *Ulevi wa bahari*, sea-sickness. (Cf. *levya*, and *ulafi.*)

Ulezi, n. (*ma-*), act (trade, work, pay) of one who has the care of children, e.g. a nurse, tutor, guardian. *Malezi*, education, training. (Cf. *-lea, mlezi.*)

Ulia, v. Ap. of ua, v. (which see).

Ulili, n. (*ma-*), bedstead,—with the legs turned, not of the common Zanzibar make. (Cf. *kitanda.*)

Ulimbo, n. birdlime, gum, glue. *Ulimbo ni utomvu wa kutegea ndege, ulimbo* is a sticky stuff for catching birds with. *Penyi urembo ndipo penyi urimbo* (for *ulimbo*), finery is a snare.

Ulimbwende, n. dandyism, showy dress or manner, coxcombry. (Cf. *-limbwende, umalidali.*)

Ulimi, n. (*ndimi*), (1) the tongue, —of man and animals generally, also (2) of objects resembling it, a projection (cf. *mdomo*), e. g. 'tenon' in carpentering. *Ulimi hauna mfupa*, the tongue has no bone, i. e. nothing stable, reliable. *Kama ulimi na mate*, like tongue and spittle,—of things inseparable. *U. hauna dawa*, the tongue is incurable. *Uji wa moto haupoi kwa ncha ya ulimi*, the tip of the tongue does not cool hot rice. (Cf. *-limi.*)

Ulimwengu, n. (*ma-*), (1) the world in general, the whole creation, universe, visible things,—*killa kitu kilicho na mwanga*; (2) the sky, e. g. *ulimwengu umetakata*, the sky is clear; (3) the inhabited world, earth, globe, e. g. *ul. tunaokaa sisi*, the world we live in; (4) the present world (cf. *kuwapo ulimwenguni*, for 'to be alive'),—as opp. to the next world, which is *peponi, kuzimu, ulimwengu wa huko* (*wa baadaye, ujao*); (5) the world in a moral sense, the world as worldly, the world as transitory, unstable, evil, e. g. *mema na mabaya ndio ulimwengu*, the world is a mixture of good and evil; *mtu wa ulimwengu*, or *mlimwengu*, a worldly man; (6) the environment, each man's own surroundings (circle, circumstances). *Ametengeneza ul. wake*, he has feathered his nest. Plur. *malimwengu*, usually,—worldly affairs, worldly pleasures or interests. (Cf. Ar. *alam*, also *mlimwengu*, and syn. *dunia.*)

Ulinganifu, Ulinganyo, n. correspondence, harmony, comparison, suitableness, convenience. (Cf. *linga, -linganifu.*)

Ulingo, n. (*lingo*, and *ma-*), like *kilingo*, a platform in a plantation, for a watchman in charge of crops. (Cf. *kilindo*, and *dungu.*)

Ulinzi, n. watching, guarding, guardianship, fee for guarding. (Cf. *linda, mlinzi.*)

Ulio, n. (*lio*), something for eating from or with,—and so of a wooden platter raised on legs and used as a table. (Cf. *lia*, Ap. of *-la*, v. eat. Dist. *ulio*, verb-form, 'that which is, you who are.')

Ulipizi, n. (*ma-*), forcing payment, exaction, vengeance. (Cf. *lipa*, and syn. *kisasi*.)

Uliza, v. also **Uza**, (1) question, interrogate, inquire (of, about), ask, ask about (not 'ask for,' which is *omba, taka*), demand. E.g. *nalimwuliza hali*, I asked him about his health, how he was. *Wote kadiri aniuzaye habari*, every one who asks me for information. *Ntauza kisa hiki*, I will ask about this matter. Ps. *ulizwa* and *uzwa*, e.g. be questioned,—and so, supply an answer. *Siwezi kuulizwa uongo*, I cannot let a false answer be returned (to an inquiry). Nt. *ulizika*. Ap. *uliz-ia, -iwa, uz-ia, -iwa*, e.g. ask on behalf of, e.g. *kaniulizieni mimi sababu*, and do you demand on my behalf to have a reason given. Rp. *ulizana*. (Cf. *ulizo*, and syn. *saili, hoji, dadisi*.) (2) sell to, get to buy. See **Uza**. (It seems possible that *uliza* is a Cs. of an unused *ua*, buy, i.e. invite to buy, generalized to mean 'ask, question.' See **Uza, Uliza,** sell.)

Ulizi, n. (*ma-*), bawling, squealing, shouting, screaming, loud cry. (From the Cs. form of *lia*, with intens. force. Cf. *mlizi*, and syn. *kelele*.)

Ulozi, n. (*ma-*), witchcraft, sorcery, enchantment. (Cf. *loga, mlozi*, and syn. *upagazi, uchawi*.)

Uma, v. cause pain, hurt, bite, sting, smart, ache,—and sometimes, feel pain. E.g. *nauma meno*, I have a pain in my teeth, I have toothache, but usually *meno (kichwa, tumbo) yaniuma*, my teeth (head, stomach) hurt me. Ps. *umwa*. (Nt. *umika*, rarely used. Cf. *umika*, of medical cupping.) Ap. *umia, umiwa*, e.g. cause pain to (at, with, in, by, &c.), and also 'feel pain,' like *uma*. E.g. *nyuki ameniuma*, *nami nimeumia*, a bee stung me, and I feel it. *Nimeumia macho*, I have a pain in my eyes. *Simba alimwumia mwituni (kichwani)*, the lion bit him in the forest (on his head). Cs. *umiza, umizwa*, usually intens. and of intentional infliction of pain,—hurt, cause to feel pain. Hence *umiz-ia, -iwa*. Also *umizana*. Rp. *umana*, hurt each other,—hence *umani-sha, -shwa*, and *uman-ia, -iwa*. *Meno ya mbwa hayaumani*, a dog's teeth do not hurt each other. — n. (*uma, nyuma, mauma*), a metal spit, skewer, pointed tool, awl, punch, fork, sting (of an insect, or reptile). (Cf. *choma, washa*.)

*****Umahiri**, n. and **Umaheli**, dexterity, cleverness, good workmanship. (Ar. Cf. *mahiri*.)

Umaji, n. and **Umajimaji**, being fluid, being watery, wet, damp, moisture, humidity. (Cf. *maji*, and syn. *rutuba, uchepechepe, baridi*.)

Umalidadi, n. (1) display of dress or ornaments, fine dressing, showiness, —and so (2) over-dressing, dandyism, foppery. (Cf. *ulimbwende, urembo, fahari*.)

Umande, n. dew, damp cool air of the morning or evening, mist, fog. (Cf. *ukungu*.)

*****Umasikini**, n. poverty, wretchedness, misery. (Ar. Cf. *masikini*, and syn. *ufukara, ukata*.)

*****Umati**, n. multitude, a number of persons, people (regarded collectively). E.g. *umati wa watu, watu umati*, and *umati* alone. *Umati wa Muhamadi*, Mahomet's people, the Mahommedan world. (Ar. not often used. Cf. *watu, jamii, kundi*.)

Umba, v. give form to, shape, fashion, create, make. The word used regularly of the divine creation. *Muungu ameuumba ulimwengu*, God created the world. *Hukujiumba wee, umeumbwa na Muungu*, you did not create yourself, you were created by God. But also generally, e.g. *mfinyanzi anaumba vyungu*, the potter is making cooking-vessels. Ps. *umbwa*. Nt. *umbika*, e.g. *kuumbika kwake kuzuri*, he has a fine figure. Ap. *umb-ia, -iwa*. Cs. *umb-isha, -ishwa*. Rp. *umbana*. (Cf. *umbo, kiumbe, maumbile, umbua*, and syn. *huluku, fanya, fanyiza*.)

Umba-umba, v. See **Yumba**.

Umbo, n. (*ma-*), shape, form, natural condition (appearance, constitution). *U. la Adamu aliloumbwa mbele*, the form of Adam in which he was originally created. *U. la mtu mbali, na la nyama mbali*, men and animals have a different constitution. Also used like *hali, methali*, e.g. *najiona umbo la kuwa kiziwi*, I feel as if I were deaf. (Cf. *umba*, and syn. *asili, namna, hali, tabia*.)

Umbu, n. (*ma-*), a sister, half-sister,—i.e. *ndugu mke*, with at least one parent in common.

Umbua, v. Rv. of *umba*, take away the form of, and so (1) spoil the look of, deface, deform, disfigure; (2) depreciate, degrade, demoralize, corrupt. E.g. *asioweza kutuumba, kutuumbua hawezi*, he who cannot create cannot uncreate. Ps. *umbuliwa*. Nt. *umbuka*, e.g. *umbuka mwili*,—of the body disfigured by disease, &c. Ap. *umbu-lia, -liwa*. Rp. *umbuana*.

*****Umbuji**, n. grace, elegance, pleasing appearance, accomplishments,—of dress, manner, &c. (Ar. *bahaj*. Cf. *mbeja*.)

Ume, n. and **Uume**, (1) male nature (sex, condition, characteristics), e.g. manliness, courage, pluck,—but commonly *utu ume* for manhood generally, and *kiume* for qualities and character, i.e. manliness, e.g. *ume wa leo na kesho*, true courage lasts more than a day. (2) condition of a husband, e.g. *ume na uke umekwisha*, we have ceased to be husband and wife. (3) for the vulgar *mboo*, penis. (Cf. follg., and *uke*.)

-**ume**, a. (*ndume* with D 4 (P), D 6, and sometimes D 1 (P)), (1) of the male sex, male, masculine; (2) like a man, virile, strong, courageous, prudent; (3) of things,—strong, firm, reliable, big. *Mume* (pl. *waume*), *mtu mume* (pl. *watu waume*), *mtu wa kiume* (pl. *watu wa kiume*), and most commonly *mwanaume* (or *mwanam'me*, pl. *waanaume*) are all used of man generally, in respect of sex simply. In relation to the female sex, *mume* has the definite sense, 'husband, married man,' in contrast to *mwanaume*, which denotes an irregular connexion (cf. *mke, mwanamke*). *Mnazi mume*, the male cocoanut tree,—comparatively unfertile. *Mahindi maume*, small, inferior grains of maize. *Mkono mume*, or *wa kuume*, right hand,—also *mkono wa kulia*. *Ndugu kuumeni*, relative on the father's side. *Maume*, manly deeds, prowess, e.g. *ajetea maume*, he brags of his strength. (Cf. prec., and *mume, ndume, kuume, kiume*, also contr. -*ke, mke*, &c.)

Umeme, n. lightning. *Yapiga umeme*, it lightens. (Perh. cf. *meremeta, memeteka*.)

Umika, v. cup, apply a cupping instrument, draw blood by cupping. A horn is commonly used. E.g. *mwumishi ameniumika leo*, the cupper has cupped me to-day. *Aliumika pembe mwilini*, he applied a horn to my body. Ps. *umikwa*. Ap. *umikia, -iwa*. Cs. *umik-isha, -ishwa*, e.g. employ as cupper, cause (persuade, compel) to be cupped. (Cf. follg., and *umuka*. Blood-letting is also done by gashing with a knife. Cf. *chanja*.)

Umiko, n. also **Ndumiko**, a cupping instrument, usually a horn. (Cf. prec., and *chuku*.)

*****Umilele**, n. and **Milele**, perpetuity, eternity. Also as adv. (Ar. Cf. *milele*.)

Umio, n. (*mio*), internal throat, throat-passage,—including both alimentary and air passage. *Mio za* *mtu ni mbili*, a man has two passages in his throat. (Cf. *mio, kimio*, and *koo, roho, shingo*.)

Umito, n. heaviness, sluggishness,—commonly *uzito* in Z.

Umivu, n. (*ma-*), pain, ache, smart. (Cf. *uma*, and syn. *uchungu, uchomi*.)

Umka, v. and **Umuka**, swell up, rise up with froth or foam,—e. g. of dough when fermenting, also of breakers and foaming waves.

Umo, n. (*ma-*), hurting, bite, sting, i. e. the effect rather than the cause (cf. *uma*, n.). (*Umo* is also a verb-form, 'you are (it is) in,' i. e. prefix *u-* agreeing with Pron. of 2 Pers. Sing. *wewe*, or with D 2 (S), D 4 (S).)

Umoja, n. oneness, unity, identity, concord. (Cf. *-moja*.)

Umoto, n. and **Umotomoto**, heat, warmth, vehemence, fury, &c. (Cf. *moto, woto*.)

*****Umri**, n. time of life, age. *Umri wake apataje?* How old is he? *Ukawa mzima wa umri*, you were full-grown, come to years of discretion. Also of whole time of life, life in general, e. g. *umri wako halali yangu*, your life is at my disposal, at my mercy. (Cf. *uzima, maisha*.)

Umua, v. take by craft (from), deprive (of), steal away, e. g. honey from bees, woman from husband, &c. Ps. *umuliwa*. Nt. *umuka*. Ap. *umu-lia, -liwa*. (So Kr., but ? not used in Z., where *iba, nyang'anya, pokonya* are common. And see follg.)

Umuka, v. (1) for **Um'ka** (which see), swell up, rise; (2) Rv. of *umika*, cup, i. e. take off (the cupping instrument), or Nt. come off; (3) Nt. of *umua*. See prec.

Umuungu, n. or **Umwungu, Umungu**, deity of God, divinity, divine essence, or nature of a Personal God. (Cf. *Muungu*, and *Uungu, Wungu, Ungu*, which properly would denote deity in general,

and so as conceivably attributable to other than God Himself. But also cf. *umoto*, from *moto*, in place of *uoto*.)

Una, verb-form, 'you have, it is,' *-u* pfx. agreeing with Pron. of 2 Pers. Sing. and D 2 (S), D 4 (S),—and *na* (which see). *Unani? Una nini?* What is the matter with you?

*****Unafiki**, n. hypocrisy, dissembling, deceit. (Ar. Cf. *mnafiki*, and *mwongo*.)

*****Unajimu**, n. astronomy, astrology. (Ar. Cf. *mnajimu*, and *falaki*.)

*****Unanasi**, n. heart or inside of the pine-apple plant (*mnanasi*),—and so usually a strong fibre obtained from it, and used as sewing-thread. (Cf. *ukonge, ubugu, ununu*, &c.)

Unda, v. construct, make, build, put together, esp. of wooden structures requiring skill, e. g. ship-building, but also of other materials. *U. chombo*, build a dhow. *U. dema*, construct, repair a fish-trap. *Merikebu ile imeundwa ya thahabu*, that ship was built of gold. Ps. *undwa*. Nt. *undika*. Ap. *und-ia, -iwa*, e. g. *mti huu ukiundiwa una maisha sana*, this wood if used in ship-building is specially durable. Cs. *und-isha, -ishwa*, e. g. order a ship to be built, give (or, take) a contract for ship-building. (Cf. *mwunda, mwunzi, uunzi, kiunzi*, and in general, *fanyiza, jenga*).

Undu, n. (*nyundu*), comb of a cock (*jogoo*).

*****Uneemefu**, n. abundance, plentiful supply. (Ar. Cf. *neema, -neemefu*, and syn. *wingi, ujalifu*.)

Unenaji, n. art (power, practice) of speaking, eloquence, fluency. (Cf. *mnenaji, uneni, neno, nena*, and syn. *usemi, usemaji*.)

Unene, n. stoutness, thickness, corpulence. (Cf. *-nene, nenepa*.)

Uneni, n. power of speech, speaking, articulation. (Cf. *unenaji, nena*.)

Unga, v. (1) make a joining, join, join together, connect, make by joining, unite, form connexion (with), compound, combine; (2) hence used esp. of mixing ingredients skilfully, e. g. *u. chakula*, season food (cf. *kiungo, kitoweo, kolea*); *u. dawa*, compound medicine; *u. tambuu*, make a chewing mixture (cf. *uraibu*). Also *u. mbau*, join planks. *U. mfupa*, set a bone. *U. kamba na jiwe*, put stone and rope together, i. e. in drawing at a well. Ps. *ungwa*. Nt. *ungika*. Hence *ungikana*. Ap. *ung-ia, -iwa, -ika, -ilia, -iliwa, -ilika*. Cs. *ung-isha, -ishwa, unganya*. Rp. *ungana*. Hence *ungan-ia, -iwa, ungan-isha, -ishwa*. (Cf. *ungo, mwungo*, and generally *funga, kutanisha*.)

Unga, n. anything powdered, or ground small, esp. grain of any kind, powder, flour, meal, &c. *Unga wa msumeno*, sawdust, also—*unga wa mbau, wa mti*.

Ungama, v. acknowledge, confess, admit, allow, grant, concede. *U. uizi*, confess a robbery. *U. rupia*, admit the possession of rupees. Ps. *ungamiwa*. Nt. *ungamika*. Ap. *ungam-ia, -iwa*, e.g. *walimwungamia nyumba*, they granted him a house, i. e. agreed, allowed it. Cs. *ungamisha, -ishwa*, induce to confess, hear a confession. (Cf. *mwungamo, mwangamishi*, and syn. *kiri*.)

Ungamana, v. be joined together, united, connected, coherent, interdependent. Cs. *ungaman-isha, -ishwa*. (Cf. *unga*, and *fungamana, shikamana, -mana*.)

Ungamo, n. (*ma-*), (1) confession, concession, admission; (2) a yellow stuff, used as a dye, from the shrub *mwungamo*.

Ungara, n. brightness, lustre, light. (Cf. *ngara, ngaa, mngao*.)

Ungi, n. much, abundance, plenty, a quantity, a good deal, e. g. *ungi wa chakula*, plenty of food, or to express a 'multiple of three,' *ungi wa tatu*. (*Wingi* more common in Z. See -ingi.)

Ungo, n. (*ma-*), (1) a joining, a joint, and (of the body), a member, a part, —usually *kiungo*, but the plur. *maungo* is regularly used (*a*) of the limbs of the body collectively, and so the body as a whole, e. g. *maungo yote yanamtetemeka*, he was shaking all over. *Maungo wazi*, stripped to the skin, bare bodies; *ana maungo*, he has a fine (well-knit, well-developed, muscular) frame,—of a strong athletic man. (*b*) the back, backbone, in a similar inclusive sense, also *uti wa maungo*, i. e. the stem on which the limbs grow. E. g. *juu ya maungo ya frasi*, on horseback. *Ameshuka maungoni mwa mamaye*, he has got off his mother's back. (With this use of *maungo*, cf. *mgongo, jongo, kijongo, kibiongo*.) (2) the hymen. *Vunja ungo*, (*a*) begin to menstruate; (*b*) deflower, deprive of virginity (cf. *kisinda*); (*c*) fig. of a tree beginning to bear fruit. (3) a round flat basket used for sifting grain (cf. *tunga*). (Cf. *unga*, v., *kiungo, mwungo*.)

Ungoje, n. (*ngoje*) and **Ungojezi**, a waiting (for), being in attendance on, service, a keeping watch, wages for attendance (waiting, watching). E. g. *ungoje wa kungojea vyakula shamba*, wages for watching crops on a plantation. (Cf. *mngoje, ngoja*, and the more general *utumishi, huduma*.)

Ung'ongo, n. (*ng'ongo*), a strip of palm-leaf, esp. of the dwarf palm *mkindu*,—*ung'ongo* being one of the coarser strips next to the middle rib, used for sewing together the plaits for a mat, or basket, or for the binding round the edge. (Cf. *mwaa, utangule, uzimba, ukindu*.)

Ungu, n. (*nyungu*), a cooking pot, of the common kind, of baked clay. (Cf. *chungu*, i. e. *kiungu*, and *jungu*, i. e. *ji-ungu*.)

Ungua, v. (1) be scorched, scalded,

hardened, damaged with fire, burnt. *Nyumba imeungua moto*, the house has been (more or less) burnt, damaged by fire. Ps. *unguliwa*. Nt. *ungulika*, e.g. (1) be hardened with fire; (2) be combustible. Ap. *ungu-lia, -liwa, -lika*, e.g. apply fire to, bake (pottery). Cs. *ungu-za, -zwa*, burn, scorch, scald. (Cf. *teketea*, be burnt up, *choma*, set fire to, *waka*, be on fire.) (2) Rv. of *unga*, disjoin, disconnect, cut in two, pull apart.

Unguja, n. Zanzibar,—island and city. *Unguja ukuu*, Great Zanzibar is now a small town on the same island south of the capital. *Kiunguja*, the dialect of Swahili spoken at Zanzibar,—often carefully distinguished from the true Swahili dialect by Swahilis, but the most generally useful on the coast and in the interior.

Ungwana, n. condition (status, rank, quality) of a freeman (*mugwana*), commonly contrasted with that of a slave (*utumwa*), but also denoting a relatively high social grade,—and so, good breeding, education, accomplishments, civilization, in contrast with *ushenzi*, barbarism. Hence *kiungwana*, the speech, bearing, characteristics of a freeman (gentleman, lady). *-a kiungwana*, well-bred, educated, civilized. (Cf. *-ngwana, kiungwana*.)

Unong'onezi, n. (*nongonezi*), whispering. (Cf. *nong'ona*.)

Unono, n. (1) fatness,—of animals, (*unene*, of man), and so (2) richness, comfort, luxury. A common expression of good wishes is *ishi (lala) unono*, may you live (sleep) in comfort. (Cf. *nona, -nono*.)

Ununu, n. fibre from the inner skin of the stalk of a cocoanut leaf. (Cf. *mnazi, ukuti*.)

Ununuzi, n. buying, purchase, bargaining, bidding (for an article), custom, price. (Cf. *nunua, mnunuzi*.)

Unyaa, n. dirt, excrement. (Cf. *kinyaa, -nya*.)

Unyago, n. dancing and other ceremonies connected with the initiation of children of both sexes into tribal rights, as of adult age. Used also of other grotesque dances, i.e. mummery, acting, farce. (Cf. *kinyago*.)

Unyama, n. the nature of a beast, being like a beast, brutishness, stupidity, &c. (Cf. *nyama*.)

Unyamafu, n. silence, quiet, repose, reserve, taciturnity. (Cf. *nyamaa, -nyamafu*, and syn. *kimya*.)

Unyang'anyi, n. robbery, carrying off by force, abduction, brigandage, lawless depredation. (Cf. *nyang'anya*, and syn. *uizi*, and *uharabu*.)

Unyasi, n. (*ma-*), a blade of coarse grass, a flag-like reed.

Unyayo, n. (*nyayo*). See **Uayo**.

Unyefu, n. power of absorption, retention of moisture, dampness. (Cf. *-nya, -nyefu*.)

Unyegi, n. and **Unyeji**, itching, pruriency, heat. (Cf. *nyegi, nyea*.)

Unyele, n. (*nyele, manyele*), also *unwele, nwele*, a hair. When used alone, properly of human hair,—but *nyele za singa*, long, straight, soft hair, is used of the hair of Europeans, and of some animals when of similar kind, e.g. horse hair, mane of a lion, &c. *Nyele za kipilipili (za kusoketeka, za kusongomana)* describes the woolly, tufty, wiry hair of natives. The hairy (furry, woolly) coat of almost all animals is described as *manyoya*. (See *usinga, unyoya*, also *ulaika, udevu, ufuzi, ukope, unyushi, panja, shungi, mvi*.)

Unyeleo, n. (*nyeleo*), also *unyweleo, manyweleo*, pore,—of the skin. (Cf. *-nya, -nywa*.)

Unyenyekeo, Unyenyekevu, n. (*ma-*), humility, self-abasement, reverential awe, obsequiousness, servility, cringing. Cf. *nyenyekea, -nyenyekevu*.

Unyeo, n. itching, tickling. (Cf. *nyea, mnyeo, nyegi.*)

Unyesi, n. (*manyesi*), passing excreta, excretion, excrement, urine. (Cf. *-nya, unyaa,* and the vulgar *mavi, mkojo.*)

Unyeti, n. being tiresome, irritability, sensitiveness, causing irritation, conceit, spite, misconduct. (Cf. *nyeta.*)

Unyofu, n. (1) straightness, being straight, extension; (2) straightforwardness, honesty, uprightness. (Cf. *nyoka, -nyofu.*)

Unyonga, n. (*nyonga*), (1) hip; (2) hip complaint, lameness due to disease or injury of the hip. (Cf. *nyonga.*)

Unyonge, n. (*ma-*), condition of being mean (vile, abject, low, lowly), meanness, poverty, feebleness, insignificance. In plur. low acts, conditions, &c. (Cf. *-nyonge.*)

Unyoya, n. (*nyoya*), a fibre of wool, or animal's hair, or down, &c. of birds. (See **Nyoya, Unyele.**)

Unyozi, n. art (profession, fee, &c.) of a barber, hair-cutting, shaving. (Cf. *nyoa, kinyozi.*)

Unyushi, n. (*nyushi*), a hair of the eyebrow. (Cf. *ushi,* also *udevu, ukope,* and *unyele.*)

Unywele, n. (*nywele*). See **Unyele.**

Uo, n. (*nyuo*), cover, case, scabbard, sheath. *Uo wa kisu,* sheath of a knife. *Uo wa kitabu,* cover, binding of a book. (Cf. *chuo,* i.e. *ki-uo,* and perh. *nguo.*)

Uole, for *wole.* See **Ole.**

Uombaji, n. begging as a practice or profession, repeated or importunate requests. (Cf. follg.)

Uombi, n. (*ma-*), begging, praying, intercession, supplication, entreaty, prayer. (Cf. prec., and *omba,* and syn. *sala, dua, haja.*)

Uongo, n. (no plur.) and **Uwongo,** falseness, falsehood, a lie, lies, untruth, deception, sham, fraud, delusion, pretence. *Sema (toa) u.,* tell a lie. *Sultani akalia kwa u.,* the Sultan shed crocodile's tears. Used also as adj. (cf. *uchungu, utupu*) and adv., e.g. *kufa uongo,* to sham being dead (cf. *kifa uongo,* the sensitive plant). *Uongo si thambi, uongo ndio watu watumiao kwa biashara,* a lie is not sinful, it is a generally recognized commercial device. *Njia ya u. fupi,* lies do not go far. (Cf. *-ongo,* and contr. *kweli, hakika.*)

Uonyefu, Uonyo, n. (*onyo,* and *ma-*), warning, exhortation, remonstrance. (Cf. *onya, onyo.*)

Uovu, n. wickedness, badness, evil, corruption. (See *-ovu,* and cf. *ubaya, -baya,* and *ubovu.*)

Uozi, n. (*ma-*), act of marrying, celebration of a wedding,—esp. of the religious ceremony at a mosque, but applicable to the part of the parents, bridegroom, or celebrant. (Cf. *oa, oza,* and syn. *ndoa, harusi.*)

Upaa, n. (and **Upara**), (1) crown of the head; (2) baldness. (Cf. *kipara, kipaa,* and perh. *paa* (*ma-paa*), roof of a native house.)

Upagazi, n. (1) work (profession, pay) of a caravan-porter; (2) witchcraft, being bewitched or possessed. (Cf. *pagaa, pagao.*)

Upaja, n. (*paja*), thigh, ham. *Upaja wa tanga,* broad, bulging side of a sail. Also *paja.* (Cf. *kiweo,* of animals.)

Upaji, n. giving, free giving, liberality, open-handedness, bounty, gift. Esp. of God, as the great Giver. (Cf. *pa* v., *mpaji, kipaji.*)

Upakizi, n. (*ma-*), loading a ship, placing goods on board, freight, freightage. Also *upakio.* (Cf. *pakia,* and follg.)

Upakuzi, n. (*ma-*), ladling out, serving out, distribution, &c., esp. of food. (Cf. *pakua,* Rv., and *pakia,* Ap., and prec.)

Upamba, n. (*pamba*), (1) a small billhook, a knife with a broad, flat, thin blade, used in getting palm-wine (*tembo*),—also called *kotama* (cf. *gema*). (2) a piece of cotton wool (i.e. *pamba*), for a plug or bandage, lint, &c. in surgery, &c. *Upamba wa mafuta*, ointment spread on cotton wool or lint. (Cf. *pamba*, n.)

Upambano, n. (*ma-*), comparison, collision, quarrel. (Cf. *pambana*, *mpambano*.)

Upambo, n. decoration, adornment, furnishing a house, furniture, decorations. (Cf. *pamba*, v., and syn. *urembo*.)

Upana, n. (*ma-*), width, breadth. *Mbau zina mapana*, the planks are broad. (Cf. -*pana*, and -*nene*, *unene*.)

Upande, n. (*pande*), a piece, a portion, a certain part, a side, a direction, region, district, place. E. g. *weka u.*, put aside, on one side. *Kwenda u.*, go sideways. *Kuwa u.*, to be slanting, askew, out of the level or straight. *Pande za barra*, the mainland region. *Pande zote*, on all sides. *Upande wa chini*, lee-side,—in sailing, *u. wa juu*, weather side. Also used as a measure of cloth, i.e. a conventional piece or length, two yards. (Cf. *mpande*, *kipande*, *pande*,—forms which seem to be sometimes used in contrast, with reference to size, but not clearly differentiated.)

Upanga, n. (*panga*), (1) a sword. Also (2) a flat wooden sword-shaped instrument, used by a weaver to tighten each thread of the woof in weaving. *U. wa feleji*, a long, straight, two-edged sword. *U. wa imani*, a short sword with a kind of cross hilt. *Bapa la u.*, flat of the sword. *Makali (ya u.)*, edge. *Maungo (ya u.)*, back. *Vuta u.*, draw a sword. (Cf. *sime*, *kitara*.)

Upao, n. (*pao*), a thin stick, fastened across the rafter-poles in a native hut to carry the thatch. Used also of thin rod-iron, iron bars, *upao wa chuma*. (Cf. syn. *ufito*.)

Upapi, n. (*papi*), long, narrow strip, flat or rounded, of wood or metal, a long lath or bar, beading, edging, border. Of clothes, a gore, gusset.

Upataji, n. buying power, value, cost, price. (Cf. *pata*, *pato*.)

Upatilifu, n. reproach, blame,—whether as inflicted or incurred. (Cf. follg.)

Upatilizo, n. (*ma-*), blaming, reproaching, punishing, visiting an offence. (Cf. *pata*, and prec.)

Upato, n. (*pato*, and of size *ma-*), a round metal dish-shaped gong, with the edges turned up. Dim. *kipato*.

Upawa, n. (*pawa*), a flat, shallow ladle,—usually of a part of a cocoanut shell fixed on a short stick as handle. (Cf. *kata*, a deeper kind of ladle.)

Upekecho, n. (*pekecho*, *ma-*), (1) drilling, turning a boring tool,—but esp. (2) manner of making fire by twirling one stick pressed on another; (3) fig. annoyance, vexatious conduct. Also (4) a stick used for making fire, as above. (Cf. *pekecha*.)

Upele, n. eruption, pimples, pustules, a breaking-out on the skin. (Cf. *kipele*.)

Upembe, n. the upper corner of the triangular sail of a native vessel of the common kind (*chombo*). (Cf. *pembe*.)

Upembo, n. (*pembo*), curved end, hook, crook, a hooked stick, e. g. for pulling down fruit. (Cf. *pemba*, *pembe*, and prec. Also *kiopoo*, *mchocho*.)

Upendaji, n. habit of liking or loving something. (Cf. *penda*, and follg.)

Upendeleo, n. (*ma-*), having a special liking, bias, inclination, favour, favouritism. (Cf. prec.)

Upendelevu, n. (1) as *upendeleo*, but also admits of a pass. sense; (2) being favoured, being liked.

Upendezi, n. (*ma-*), (1) being agreeable (amiable, pleasing, lovable), pleasantness; (2) being pleased, happiness, delight. (Cf. *penda*, and prec.)

Upendo, n. (*pendo*), act (manner, &c.) of loving, liking, affection, love. (Cf. *penda*, *pendo*.)

Upendwa, n. (*ma-*), being loved, or liked. *Mapendwa*, things loved, liked. (Cf. prec., and *upenzi*.)

Upenu, n. (*penu*), space outside a native hut covered by the projecting frame and thatch of the roof, and often enclosed so as to form a small lean-to or sleeping place. Hence any similar appendage to a house. (Cf. *kipenu*.)

Upenyezi, n. (*penyezi*, and *ma-*), (1) secret, underhand, illicit action; (2) bribery, smuggling, giving commissions,—also (3) insinuation, suggestion. (Cf. *penya*.)

Upenzi, n. (*ma-*), (1) loving, liking, desiring, willing, resolving. Also (2) pass. being loved, liked, &c. (Cf. *penzi*, and *penda*.)

Upeo, n. (*peo*), limit, extremity, furthest part, boundary line, full extent or development. *Upeo wa macho*, as far as the eye can see, the limit of vision, horizon. E. g. *jangwa kubwa upeo wa macho yake*, a great waste extending as far as he could see. *Kupita upeo*, very extreme, beyond all bounds. Used as adv., to the utmost, thoroughly, as much as possible. E. g. *piga upeo*, give a sound beating to. *Furahi upeo*, be filled with joy, be enraptured. (Cf. *kipeo*, *-pevu*, *pevua*, and also *cheo*, *mpaka*.)

Upepeo, n. (*pepeo*, and *ma-*), fan, punkah, i. e. *upepeo wa kumpepelea mtu baridi*, a fan to fan a person with. (Cf. *kipepeo*, *pepo*, *upepo*, *pepea*, &c.)

Upepo, n. (*pepo*), wind, breeze, draught, fresh air,—i. e. of a light movement of air,—the plur. *pepo* being used of high winds, a gale. *U. mwanana* (*mwororo*), gentle (soft) breeze, zephyr. *Punga u.*, take fresh air, go for a change, fan oneself. *Kaa upeponi*, sit in a draught. (See **Pepo**, and **Pepea**.)

Upesi, n. and **Wepesi**, speed, quickness, velocity, lightness in movement,—but *wepesi* commonly of 'lightness' in weight. (See *-epesi*, *-pesi*.) Mostly used as adv., quickly, lightly, e. g. *njoo upesi*, come at once. *Kimbia u.*, run fast. (Cf. *haraka*, *hima*, *mbio*.)

Upeto, n. (*peto*), folding, fold, roll, something rolled up, package, bundle. (Commonly *peto*, *kipeto* (which see), and cf. generally *kikapo*, *furushi*.)

Upigano, n. (*ma-*), fighting, contest, rivalry. In plur. battle, riot, brawl. (Cf. *piga*, *pigana*, *pigo*, and *ushindani*.)

Upindani, n. (*pindani*), stiffness, obstinacy, e. g. *mmefanya u. na mimi*, you have behaved obstinately to me. (Cf. *-pindani*, *pinda*, and syn. *ukaidi*, *ugumu*, *ushindani*.)

Upindi, n. (*pindi*) and **Upinde**, a bending, a bend, a being bent, a thing bent, but commonly a bow (for shooting, the weapon) only. *Pinda u.*, bend a bow. *U. wa mvua*, a rainbow. (Cf. *pinda*, *pindi*, *kipindi*, and follg. For 'bow' cf. *uta*.)

Upindo, n. (*pindo*), (1) a bend, a fold, a turned edge; (2) of a cloth, —selvedge, hem, border, skirt; (3) a folding cloth, wrapper, e. g. for wrapping a corpse in before placing in the shroud, *saanda* (Kr.). (Cf. prec., and *kunjo*.)

Upinduzi, n. (*ma-*), upsetting, overturning, capsizing. (Cf. *pindua*, *pinda*.)

Upishi, n. (*pishi*), act (method, means, profession, &c.) of cooking, wages of a cook. *Upishi ni kuni*, no cooking without fuel. For ways of cooking cf. *tokosa*, *oka*, *kanga*, *chemsha*, *choma*. (Cf. *pika*, *mpishi*.)

Upo, n. (*nyupo*), a dipper, for baling water out of a boat, &c.,—commonly a calabash (*buyu*), or can (*kopo*). (Dist. *upawa, kata*, and the verb-form *upo*, you are (it is) here, i.e. *u-* and *-po*.)

Upofu, n. deprivation, ruin, loss, but esp. of loss of sight, blindness, i.e. *upofu wa macho*. (Cf. *pofua*, and *kipofu*.)

Upogo, n. (*pogo*), condition of being cut away, i.e. one-sided, in unequal parts, being awry, distorted, zigzag. Of the eyes,—squinting. As adv. *upogo-upogo*, from side to side, zigzag. (Cf. *pogo, pogoa*.)

Upole, n. gentleness, kindness, meekness, slowness of movement. (See *-pole*, and contr. *ukali*.)

Upondo, n. (*pondo*), also **Pondo**, sing. (which see).

Upongoo, n. (*pongoo*), central rib or stem of a cocoanut (or similar) leaf. (Cf. *kuti*.)

Uponyi, n. (*ponyi*), means of saving, way of escape, rescue, cure. (Cf. *ponya, pona, mapoza, maponyea*.)

Upooza, n. paralysis, deadness, numbness. (Cf. *pooza, mapooza*.)

Uposo, n. (*ma-*), application for a wife, proposal of marriage, present sent to bride's relations. (Cf. *posa*.)

Upote, n. (*pote*), thong, bowstring, —of sinew, i.e. *ugwe wa mikano ya ng'ombe*. (Cf. *ukanda, ugwe*.)

Upotevu, n. (1) destructiveness, waste, ruin, vandalism; (2) pass. being lost, wandering, perishing, delusion. (Cf. *potea, -potevu*.)

Upotoe, Upotofu, n. caprice, wilfulness, obstinacy. (Cf. *potoa, -potoe, -potofu*, and prec.)

Upumbafu, n. (*pumbafu*, and *ma-*), folly, stupidity, ignorance. (Cf. *-pumbafu, pumbaa*, and syn. *ujinga*.)

Upumuzi, Upumuo, n. See **Pumuzi**.

Upunga, n. (*punga*), stage in the growth of a fruit-bearing tree or plant, when the flower is full-blown and the embryo fruit beginning to form. In Z. esp. of cocoanuts (pl. *punga*, the male flowers), but also used of maize, millet, &c., and obs. *mpunga*, of rice, while still on the plant.

Upungufu, n. (*pungufu*, and *ma-*), also **Upunguo**, becoming less, abatement, decrease, deficiency, defect, privation, want, lack. (Cf. *-pungufu, punguka*, &c.)

Upupu, n. cow-itch,—the mucuna bean, covered with velvet-like glossy hairs, extremely irritating to the skin. *Up. wa bahari*, a stinging jelly-fish, medusa.

Upuzi, n. folly in talk or conduct, dissipation, gossip, nonsense, mere fun. (Cf. *puza*.)

Upweke, n. being alone, solitariness, independence, singleness, singularity. E.g. *amekufa upweke*, he died unattended. *Safari ya u. haifai*, it does not do to travel alone. (Cf. *pekee, -pweke*.)

Upya, n. (*mpya, mapya*), newness, freshness, recency, novelty, strangeness. (Cf. *-pya*, and syn. *ubichi, ugeni*.)

*****Urafiki**, n. (1) friendship, friendliness, sociability; (2) circle of friends. (Ar. Cf. *rafiki*.)

*****Uraibu**, n. and **Ughaibu**, a chewing mixture very popular in Z. and commonly called *tambuu*, from the betel leaf, in which it is wrapped and chewed. The ingredients are lime (*chokaa*), tobacco (*tumbako*), chips of areca nut (*popoo*), and often a red gum (*katu*), and cloves (*garafuu*). The gum and areca nut colour the saliva expectorated a blood-red colour, and also dye the teeth. E.g. *umeleta tambuu, haina vifaa*, you have brought the leaf (wrapper), but not the mixture for chewing. (? Ar. Cf. *tambuu*.)

*****Urari**, n. also **Uirari, Worari**, equality, proportion, evenness, balance,—a technical term used in accounts. *Urari wa hesabu*, balancing an account. *Fanya u.*, strike a balance. (? Ar. or Hind.)

*****Urasharasha**, n. sprinkling of liquid (water, rain, scent, shower, drizzling. (Ar. Cf. *mrashi, rashi,* and syn. *manyunyo.*)

*Urathi, n. feeling or making (giving) satisfaction, and so (1) contentment, satisfaction, complacency; (2) active approval, kindness, condescension, assent, authorization, sanction; (3) amends, apology, payment of claims or damages, satisfaction of demands, &c. (Ar. Cf. *rithi,* and dist. *urithi,* inheritance.)

Urefu, n. length, tallness, height, depth, distance. Also the pl. *marefu* in same sense. Further distinguished as *u. wa kwenda juu (chini),* height (depth). (Cf. *-refu,* and *ubali,* and measures of length, *wanda, shibiri, mkono, wari, pima, thiraa.*)

Urembo, n. (*rembo, ma-*), adornment, ornamentation, finery, display, esp. of dress or person, e. g. the delicate black lines sometimes painted on the face to heighten a light complexion. *Piga (fanya) u.,* make a display, dress oneself up. *U. wa Muungu,* the glorious work of God, i. e. the Universe, Cosmos. (Cf. *remba,* and syn. *pambo, uzuri, valio.* For various kinds of personal ornament see *mkufu, mtali, furungu, banagiri, kekee, kikuku, kipini, kipuli, kingaja, koa, useja, jasi, jebu, kipaji, dalia, ndonya, shamili, sarafu, azama, pete,* and for dress *nguo.*)

*Urithi, n. (*rithi*), *th* as in *thin,* —inheritance, a heritage, bequest, legacy. (Ar. Cf. *rithi,* v. inherit, *warithi, mrithi.* Dist. *urathi.*)

*Urotha, n. also Worotha, Wortha, invoice, list of goods, schedule. (? Ar.)

*Urujuani, n. purple,—the colour. (Ar.)

*Usafihi, n. See Usufii.

Usaha, n. matter (from abscess, wound, &c.), pus, discharge.

*Usahihi, n. correctness, accuracy, freedom from fault (blemish, mistake). (Ar. Cf. *safihi.*)

*Usanifu, n. technical skill, art. (Ar. Cf. *sanaa.*)

Useja, n. (*seja*), a collar of beads.

Usemaji, n. speaking as a practice or profession, eloquence, fine speech, rhetoric, fluency. (Cf. follg., and *unenaji.*)

Usemi, n. speaking, speech, talk, diction, conversation. (Cf. prec., and *sema, msemo,* and generally *uneni.*)

*Ushahidi, n. (*shahidi*), bearing witness, attestation, evidence, proof. (Ar. Cf. *shahidi, ushuhuda, shuhudia,* and syn. *mathubuti.*)

Ushanga, n. (*shanga,* and *ma-*), a bead,—and collectively, beads in general. *Shanga* in relation to beads singly, *mashanga,* collections of beads, bead articles. *Ushanga mwingi,* a quantity of beads. Beads are sold in strings(*timba, kete*), or bunches (*shada, fundo*), and hitherto have largely supplied the place of money in the interior, being imported in large variety of shape and colour to suit the peculiar taste and demand of different localities.

*Usharifu, n. nobility, excellence, respectability,—esp. of rank and character. (Ar. Cf. *sharifu.*)

*Usharika, n. (*sharika*), and Ushirika, (1) partnership, co-operation, sharing; (2) community of interests, common nature, intimate union, commission. (Ar. See Shariki.)

Ushaufu, n. delusiveness, deception, misleading display, disappointing promise. (Cf. *shaua.*)

*Ushemasi, n. office (work, salary) of a deacon, diaconate. (Ar. Cf. *shemasi.*)

Ushi, n. (*nyushi*), (1) eyebrow; (2) any ridge (projection, roughness) resembling an eyebrow, e. g. stringcourse of a wall, cornice, &c., rough surface of unplaned planks. (Cf. *unyushi.*)

Ushinda, n. (*shinda*), remainder. (Cf. *shinda, kishinda.*)

Ushindani, n. (*shindani*), rivalry, competition, emulation, contest, fighting. (Cf. *shinda, shindana,* and *upigano.*)

Ushinde, n. state of being conquered, defeat. *Asiyekiri ushinde hakuwa mshindani,* one who does not acknowledge defeat has not been a combatant. (Cf. follg., and *mshinde.*)

Ushindi, n. (*ma-*), victory, conquest, overcoming, success. (Cf. *shinda, mshindi,* and prec.)

Ushoga, n. friendship,—between women. (Cf. *shoga.*)

Ushoni, n. (*ma-*), needlework, sewing, i. e. the art, style, trade, wages, &c. of a seamstress or tailor. All sewing is done by men in Z. (Cf. *shona, mshoni.*)

*****Ushtaki**, n. accusation, prosecution, making complaint. (Ar. Cf. *shtaki, shtaka.*)

*****Ushuhuda**, n. (*shuhuda, ma-*), testimony, evidence, proof. (Cf. *ushahidi, shuhudia.*)

*****Ushujaa**, n. (*ma-*), bravery, courage, heroism. *Mashujaa,* heroic acts, exploits,—also pl. of *shujaa,* a hero, a brave man. (Ar. Cf. *shujaa.*)

*****Ushukuru**, n. (*ma-*), (1) thanksgiving, returning thanks, gratitude; (2) resignation, ceasing to feel or care, passive acquiescence. (Ar. Cf. *shukuru, shukrani.*)

Ushungi, n. (*shungi*), handkerchief, worn on the head by women out of doors. *Lazima kujifunika ushungi,* they are obliged to wear a handkerchief on their heads. (Cf. *shungi, kishungi.*)

Ushupafu, n. (1) hardness, toughness, firmness, compactness; (2) resoluteness, pertinacity, obstinacy. *U. wa mwili,* a well-knit, muscular body. *U. wa maneno,* obstructive speeches.

*****Ushuru**, n. taxation, tax, customs, duty, rate, rent, &c. *Toa u.,* pay taxes. *Toza u.,* collect taxes. (Ar. prop. a tenth, *ashr*; cf. *asharini.*)

Ushuzi, n. breaking wind. (Cf. *shuta, shuzi,* and *jamba.*)

*****Usia**, v. See **Wosia**. (Ar.)

*****Usihiri**, n. magic, sorcery, charms, spells, enchantment. (Ar. for common *uchawi, uganga, ulozi, hirizi.*)

Usikizi, n. (1) attention, hearing, listening, intelligence; (2) docility, obedience. (Cf. *sikia, msikizi.*)

Usiku, n. night, night time, i. e. the twelve hours of darkness, with which the day or diurnal period called *siku* begins, from 6 p.m. to 6 a.m., the following twelve hours of daylight being *mchana.* The pl. *siku,* and occasionally *masiku,* is not used distinctively of nights. *Siku nne mchana na usiku,* four whole days. *Usiku wa manane,* midnight, the dead of night. (See **Siku, Mchana.**)

Usimanga, n. rejoicing over another's misfortune, ill-natured triumph, mockery. (Cf. *simanga, masimango,* and syn. *thihaka.*)

Usimeme, n. firmness, stability, strength. (Cf. *simama,* and syn. *uthabiti, ushupafu, nguvu.*)

Usinga, n. (*singa*), a single hair,—of the long, straight kind, of men and certain animals. (See **Singa**.)

Usingizi, n. (*singizi*), and **Uzingizi**, sleep. *Lala usingizi,* go to sleep. *Us. mzito,* deep sleep. (Cf. *sinzia,* and perh. *zinga,* roll up, turn round, also *leppe.* Dist. *singizia, masingizio.*)

*****Usiri**, v. stay, delay, be detained, but commonly in Nt. *usirika,* be detained, delayed, be behindhand. Cs. *usir-isha, -ishwa.* — n. detention, delay, being late, lagging behind. E. g. *mwanzo huwa na usiri,* starting always seems slow to come. (Ar. Cf. *kawia, chelewa, ahiri.*)

*****Usitawi**, a flourishing condition, healthy development, full activity, success. (Cf. *sitawi.*)

Uso, n. (*nyuso*), (1) face, countenance, expression (cf. *sura*); (2) front, exterior, surface. *-pa uso,* put in countenance, relieve, comfort, assist. *Vunja uso,* disgrace, discourage. *Kunja uso*, express sorrow (anger, &c.), *kunjua uso*, of pleasure, good humour. *Uso kwa uso*, face to face. *Usoni pa*, in the presence of. *Uso wa arthi*, surface, crust of the earth.

Usoka, n. (*masoka*), brass wire,—in general, or a small piece of wire. (Cf. *masoka, masango*.)

Usononi, n. being hurt, pain. (Cf. *sononeka*.)

*Ussubuhi, n. See Assubuhi (Subuhi). (Ar.)

*Ustahifu, n. (1) respectful conduct, courtesy, deference; (2) being honoured, respected, esteemed, &c. (Ar. Cf. *stahi, -stahifu*, and follg.)

*Ustahiki, n. estimation, honour, worth. (Ar. Cf. prec.)

Usubi, n. a small biting gnat, midge, sandfly. (Cf. *imbu*.)

Usufi, n. produce of the tree *msufi*, i.e. a very soft silky cotton in a large pod.

*Usufii, n. conduct and character of a *sufii*, i.e. a Mahommedan philosopher or saint, on the higher side including piety, truthfulness, chastity, and on the lower pride, exclusiveness, solitariness. (Ar. Cf. *sufii, walii, mlawa*.)

*Usuhuba, n. friendship. (Ar. Cf. *sahibu*, for commoner *urafiki*.)

*Usukani, n. See Msukani.

*Usultani, n. office (dignity, privileges, &c.) of a sultan, chieftaincy, headship, royalty. (Ar. Cf. *sultani*.)

*Usuluhi, Usuluhifu, n. peacemaking, reconciliation, being reconciled, &c. (Ar. Cf. *suluhi*.)

Usumba, n. the fibres of the cocoanut husk, after being soaked and cleaned for use in making string, cord, &c. Also *makumbi ya usumba*. (Cf. *kumbi*.)

Usumbufu, n. (*ma-*), annoyance, vexation, worry, trouble,—whether as caused, or endured, act. or pass. (Cf. *sumbua*, and *uthia, taabu, mashaka*.)

Usuria, n. condition of being a 'suria,' domestic concubinage. (Cf. *suria*, and dist. *uhawala, ukahaba*.)

Ususi, n. plaiting, e.g. of hair, mats, &c. *Ususi wa nyele*, hairdressing, coiffure. (Cf. *msuko, suka*.)

*Uswafi, n. purity, lucidity, clearness,—esp. of elegance of style (cf. *ufasihi, usahihi*). (Ar. Cf. *safi*.)

Uta, n. (1) (*nyuta*, and *mata*), a bow, bow and arrows, i.e. the weapon complete (cf. *upindi*); (2) *mafuta ya uta*, semsem oil (i.e. *uta* for *ufuta* (?), which see). (Cf. *ute, uto*, and dist. *uti, utu*.)

Utaa, n. (*taa*), a stage, raised and covered, to put grain on for storage and drying. (Cf. *uchaga*.)

*Utabibu, n. profession (practice, fee, &c.) of a doctor, medical science, doctoring, treatment. (Ar. Cf. *tabibu*, and syn. *uganga*.)

*Utabiri, n. (*ma-*), interpretation, explanation, exposition, announcement, prediction. (Ar. Cf. *tabiri*, and syn. *ubashiri, ufasiri*.)

*Utadi, n. (*tadi*), offence, error. (Ar. Cf. *tadi*.)

*Utafathali, v. from tafathali (which see),—used as a polite formula, please, if you please, would you be so good. (Ar. Cf. *fathili, afathali*.)

Utaji, n. a piece of calico or stuff of any kind used by women and men as a covering of the head, whether to conceal the features, protect from sun, or as ornament, a veil. (Cf. *shela, dusamali*.)

*Utajiri, n. wealth, possession of capital, status of a merchant or capitalist, riches. (Ar. Cf. *tajiri*, and contr. *masikini*.)

Utakaso, n. (1) cleansing, a thing cleaned; (2) a rustling, perh. for *uchakacho*. (Cf. *mtakaso*, and *chakaza*.)

Utákatifu, n. cleanliness, purity,—material and moral,—and so, sanctity, holiness. (Cf. *-takatifu, takasa*, and syn. *weupe, uswafi*.)

Utako, n. (*tako*), breech, butt, base, lower end, bottom part. (Cf. *tako, kitako*.)

Utambaa, n. (*tambaa*), a strip of cloth, rag, bandage, duster. (See **Kitambaa**, more commonly used.)

Utambazi, n. (*tambazi*), (1) act (power, means, &c.) of creeping or crawling; (2) mark left in crawling, track, trail. (Cf. *tambaa*, v., *-tambazi*.)

Utambi, n. (*tambi*), (1) wick of a candle or lamp; (2) vermicelli, i.e. *tambi za kupika* (*za maandasi*); (3) stuff for a turban, e.g. *tengeneza* (*panza, shusha*) *u.*, arrange (put on, take off) a turban; (4) membrane enclosing the bowels. (Cf. *kitambi, tambi*.)

Utambo, n. (*tambo*), (1) strutting, swaggering, and (e.g.) of horses, prancing, high action; (2) the swinging handle of a pail, iron pot, &c. (as contr. with *mpini* (of a knife, &c.), *mkono* (of a saucepan), *shikio* (of a basket, &c.).) (Cf. *tamba, tambo*.)

Utambuzi, n. (*tambuzi*), mental quickness, intelligence, perception, facility, cleverness, skill. (Cf. *tambua, -tambuzi*, and syn. *akili, ufahamifu*.)

*****Utamu**, n. (1) flavour, taste,—in general; (2) sweet taste, sweetness, being agreeable to the sense or senses, pleasantness, charm. (Ar. Cf. *tamu*.)

Utamvua, n. (*tamvua*, and *ma-*). See **Tamvua**.

Utando, n. (*tando*) and **Utandu**. Used to describe anything spread out, extended, stretched (cf. *tanda*, v.), e.g. (1) a veil, screen, coverlet, tapestry, hangings; (2) a spider's web, *u. wa buibui*; (3) sunset glow; (4) clouded sight, whether a film over the eyes (cf. *chamba cha jicho*), or sheer drowsiness; (5) scum, crust, film, e.g. on milk, cream, or on a pot of cooked rice (cf. *ukoko*, &c.). (Cf. *tanda, tando*, syn. *ukingo, kiwambo*.)

Utani, n. kinship, clanship, membership in tribe or race. (Cf. *mtani*.)

Utapishi, n. (*ma-*), (1) causing to vomit, action of an emetic; (2) vomit. (Cf. *tapika*.)

Utari, n. (*tari*), string of an instrument, leather thong,—and perh. more generally, cord, rope. (Cf. *tari*.)

Utasa, n. and **Utassa**, barrenness, sterility,—of produce generally. *Mwaka wa utassa*, an unfruitful year. (Cf. *tassa*.)

Utashi, n. strong desire, earnest demand, importunate request, present made to back an appeal. (Cf. *taka*, v. *matakwa*. *Utashi* seems to be from a Cs. *takisha*, with intens. force.)

Utasi, n. inability or disinclination to speak, being tongue-tied.

Utata, n. (*tata*), a kind of wicker fence used for enclosing and catching fish (Kr.). Cf. similar *uzio*. (Cf. *tata*.)

Utatu, n. (1) being triple, threefoldness, trinity; (2) a third part. E.g. *kibaba cha utatu*, a third part of a *pishi*, the usual *kibaba* being *cha 'nne*, i.e. four to the *pishi*. (Cf. *kibaba*, and *tatu*.)

*****Utawa**, n. and **Utaawa, Utaowa**, (1) staying in the house, seclusion,—the usual life of Mahommedan women of the upper classes in Z.; (2) a chaste, religious, pious life and character. (Ar. Cf. *tawa*.)

Utaya, n. bone of the jaw. (Cf. *taya*.)

Ute, n. (*mate*, cf. *uta, mata*), thick, sticky, viscid fluid, e.g. saliva, mucus, lather. *Tema mate*, spit, expectorate. *Ute wa yai*, white of egg. (But cf. *uto* and *utá*, both of liquids, and dist. *uti, utu*.)

Uteketevu, n. destroying, being destroyed, destruction,—esp. as by fire, being utterly consumed. (Cf. *teketea*, and follg.)

Uteketezo, n. destruction, burning. (Cf. prec.)

Utelezi, n. (*ma-*), slipperiness,

sliding, steep descent. *Ina matelezi*, it is slippery. *U. mwingi*, very slippery. (Cf. *telea, telem'ka*.)

Utembe, n. the chewed refuse of the mixture called *tambuu* or *uraibu*, which is expectorated. It is of a blood-red colour.

Utembezi, n. (*ma-*), (1) offering for sale, advertising, exhibition of goods,—but commonly (2) walking about,—for business or pleasure, not merely for progress on a journey. Sometimes a euphemism for 'a dissipated life.' (Cf. *tembea*, and *zunguka*.)

Utembwe, n. fibre from the leafstalk of various palms, used as string. (Perh. not in Z. Cf. *ugomba*.)

Utendaji, n. activity, energy, facility in doing. (Cf. *tenda, -tendaji*, and syn. *bidii, ujitahidi*.)

Utengo, n. act (manner, place, time, &c.) of withdrawal, retirement, separation, exclusion, &c. (Cf. *tenga*.)

Utenzi, n. (*tenzi*), (1) activity, action, work, operation,—but more commonly this is *utendaji*; (2) a poem,—esp. of a religious kind, an old story told in verse. (Cf. *tenda, utendaji*, and for poetry *shairi*.)

Utepe, n. (*tepe, ma-*), a narrow strip of cloth, band, fillet, ribbon, tape, badge on the arm (of a soldier).

Utepetevu, n. languor, listlessness, indolence, lack of energy. (Cf. *-tepetevu, tepetea*, and syn. *ulegevu, uvivu*.)

Utesi, n. (*ma-*), (1) trouble, distress, annoyance, persecution; (2) strife, quarrelling, antagonism. *Utesi wa Muungu huu*, this is a visitation of God. (Cf. *tesa, teso*.)

Utete, n. (*tete*), stalk or stem of a reed or grass, used as a pipe, or musical instrument. (Cf. *tete, kitete*.)

Utetezi, n. (*ma-*), intercession, advocacy, argument or effort for or against,—and so also, opposition, obstructiveness. (Cf. *teta, tetea*, and follg.)

Uteto, n. (*ma-*), debate, argument, quarrelling, strife. (Cf. prec., and *teta*.)

Uteuzi, n. choice, choosing, criticizing, fastidious taste, daintiness,—like *uchaguzi*. (Cf. *teua, -teule*.)

***Uthabiti**, n. firmness, stability, strength, courage, resolution. (Ar. Cf. *thabiti, thabutu*.)

***Uthaifu**, n. (*thaifu*, and *ma-*), weakness, insignificance. (Ar. Cf. *thaifu, thoofika*.)

***Uthalimu**, n. (*thalimu, ma-*), injustice, tyranny, oppression, iniquity. (Ar. Cf. *thalimu, thulumu*.)

***Uthamini**, n. surety, bail, guarantee. (Ar. Cf. *thamini, thamana*.)

***Uthani**, n. See **Uzani**.

***Uthi**, v. and **Uthia**, give trouble, annoy, harass, vex, pain, grieve. Ps. *uthiwa*. Nt. *uthika*. Cs. *uthi-sha, -shwa*, intens. (Ar. Cf. follg., and *sumbua, tesa, chokoza, onea*, &c.)

***Uthia**, n. trouble, annoyance, difficulty, bother, confusion, disturbance, uproar, riot. (Ar. Cf. prec., and syn. *usumbufu, ghasia, makelele*.)

***Uthihirifu**, n. (1) making clear or evident, manifestation, demonstration; (2) clearness, plainness. (Ar. Cf. *thahiri, -thihirifu*.)

***Uthiki**, n. (1) want of room, narrowness, tightness; (2) distress, annoyance. (Ar. Cf. *thiki*.)

***Uthiko**, n. (*ma-*), trouble, annoyance, vexation. (Ar. Cf. *uthi, uthia*.)

***Uthilifu**, n. (*ma-*), being brought low, bringing low, abasement, humiliation, degradation. *Mathilifu*, troubles, disasters, adversities. (Ar. Cf. *thili, -thilifu*.)

***Uthuru**, n. (1) excuse, pretext, reason; (2) occasion, opportunity, emergency. E.g. *nalikuwa na u.*

wa kukutaka, I had a reason for asking you. *Hana ruhusa kutembea billa uthuru*, he is not allowed to go walks without occasion. *Toa u.*, offer excuse. — v. excuse, allege an excuse for, use as pretext. Ps. *uthuriwa*. Nt. *uthurika*, e. g. be excused, or excusable, have an apology made for one. Ap. *uthuria, -iwa*, e. g. allege pretext for, &c. Cs. *uthur-isha, -ishwa*. (Ar. Cf. *hoja, sababu*.)

Uti, n. (*nyuti*), of same root as *mti*, but *mti* being practically limited to the meaning 'tree,' as a whole, whether growing or as 'timber, pole,' *uti* supplies a means of rep. esenting the root in other connexions, e. g. (1) stem, trunk portion of a tree or shrub (cf. *uti wa kuti*, the central rib (wood) of the cocoanut leaf); and (2) fig. of the backbone, *uti wa maungo*, as the central support of the human frame. Also (3) the wooden part, shaft of a spear (*uti wa mkuki*), the brace of a drill (*uti wa kekee*); and (4) of a small bit of wood, a chip, splinter, e. g. matchwood. (Cf. *mti, kijiti*, ? *kiti*, and dist. *ute, uta, uto, utu*.)

Utiko, n. roof-ridge of a thatched house,—and so, ridge-tile, or anything so used. (Cf. *matiko*.)

Utimbi, Utimfi, n. mischievousness, roguery. (Cf. *kitimbi, timvi*.)

Utiriri, n. elusiveness, being provoking,—conn. with *tiririka*, glide, slip away.

Utisho, n. (*tisho*), frightening, scaring, causing abject terror. (Cf. *tisha*,—and *tiisha*, reduce to submission.)

Uto, n. (*nyuto*) or **Ute**, and perh. **Uta**, of any thick, viscid, oily fluid. E. g. *uto* (? *ute*) *wa yai*, white of egg. *Uto wa mafuta*, oil. *Uto wa lisasi*, lead in a semi-liquid (molten) state; *uto wa nyama*, dripping,— from meat, melted fat. (Cf. *utomvu*, and perh. *mto, kijuto* for *kijito*.)

*****Utohara**, n. (1) cleanness, esp. ceremonial purity; (2) circumcision. (Ar. Cf. *tohara, tahiri*, and *weno*.)

Utokezo, n. (*ma-*), (1) bringing out, displaying, utterance; (2) prominence, appearance. *U. wa maneno*, coming out with words, abrupt utterance, an aggressive speech. (Cf. *toka, tokeza, tokeo*.)

Utoko, n. mucus (Lat. e vaginâ).

Utomvu, n. thick, viscid sap or juice from a plant. (Cf. *uto, ulimbo*.)

Utongo, n. (*ma-*), a discharge from the eyes. (Cf. *chongo, matongo*.)

Utongozi, n. (*ma-*), (1) vicious propensity, lasciviousness, vicious life; (2) seduction (of women). (Cf. *tongoza, kitongo*.)

Utoro, n. (1) running away, desertion, truancy; (2) condition (life, occupation, profits) of a runaway slave; (3) robbery, brigandage. (Cf. *mtoro, toroka*.)

Utosi, n. crown of the head.

Utoto, n. state (characteristics, condition) of a child or dependent, childhood, dependence. (See **Mtoto**.)

Utu, n. human nature, humanity, manhood, membership in the human race. *Utu ume*, manhood,—as contr. with *utu uke*, womanhood. (Cf. *mtu*, and dist. *uti, uto, ute, uta*.)

Utukufu, n. exalted state or station, majesty, glory, aggrandizement. (Cf. *-tukufu, tukuza*, and syn. *athama, heshima*.)

Utukutu, n. (1) restlessness, nervousness, tremulousness; (2) playfulness, petulance, fidgeting, mischievousness, e. g. of a child. (Cf. *tikisa, tukutiza, -tukutu*.)

Utulivu, n. quietness, rest, peacefulness, gentleness, composed manner or mind. (Cf. *-tulivu, tua*, and syn. *upole, unyamafu, raha*.)

Utumbafu, n. swelling, bulging, rising up. (Cf. *tumbaa, tumba, tumbo*.)

Utumbo, n. contr. with *tumbo*

(*ma-*), as meaning (1) gut, i.e. the substance or material of the intestine; (2) the gut proper, the intestine,—*matumbo* signifying the guts generally, i.e. intestines and contents of the lower part of the body, and *tumbo*, stomach, &c. (See **Tumbo, Kitumbo,** and prec.)

Utumbuizo, n. singing a lullaby, soothing by singing, singing a refrain in a dance. (Cf. *tumbuika, tumbuizo.*)

Utume, n. being employed (sent, used), and **Utumi, Utumo,** employing (sending, using),—both meaning employment, use, service, errand, wages for service. (Cf. *tuma, tume, mtume,* and follg. For final *-e* of *utume* see *-e.* Dist. *uchumi.*)

Utumishi, n. (*tumishi,* and *ma-*), and **Utumizi,** like *utume,* i.e. being used, or using, act of service, use, employment, work (duties, pay, &c.) of a servant. E.g. *katika matumishi yangu,* in my service. *Kitu cha utumizi,* a handy article, an implement, utensil, tool. *Matumizi mengi,* many uses, much service. (Cf. *tutume, utumwa, mtumishi,* &c.)

Utumwa, n. state of being used or employed,—but esp. of slavery, forced service, being used as a tool or instrument merely. *Tia utumwani,* enslave. *Toa utumwani,* emancipate. (Cf. *tuma, mtumwa,* and prec., and contr. *uhuru, ungwana.*)

Utunda, n. (*tunda*), a string of beads, worn by women round the loins, i.e. *utunda wa ushanga.* (Cf. *kondavi.*)

Utungo, n. noun of action from *tunga* (which see) in its various meanings, like *mtungo,*—e.g. (1) composing, arranging, literary composition (novel, essay, &c.); (2) form, fashion, build, make, mould, plan; (3) idea, proposal, design, fancy; (4) invention, figment; (5) a series, succession, chain, line (of ideas, objects, &c.).

Utungu, n. same as **Uchungu,** but *utungu* is limited in Z. to the special sense, pains of childbirth, birth pangs, labour, delivery, i.e. *utungu wa kuzaa (wa uzazi).*

Utunu, n. quality of being rare, choice, valuable. (Cf. *tunu, tunuka.*)

Utupa, n. the juice of a kind of Euphorbia, *mtupa,* used as a fish-poison.

Utupu, n. (1) bareness, emptiness, simplicity, being unmixed, purity. Not common, because of the commoner meaning (2) nakedness, nudity,—in a vulgar sense, and (3) sexual organs. E.g. *wanawaume wanakwenda utupu, hawavai nguo,* the men go naked, wearing no clothes. *Utupu* is used (like *uchungu*) as an adj. preserving its special meaning. (See *-tupu,* and cf. the less vulgar *uchi.*)

Uu-, this initial sound may also be looked for under **U** and **W.**

Uuaji, n. murderousness, savagery, blood-shedding, massacre. (Cf. *ua,* v., and *-uaji.*)

*****Uudi,** n. and **Udi** (which see). (Ar.)

Uuguzi, n. (*ma-*), nursing, medical attention, care of the sick. (Cf. *ugua, mwuguzi,* and syn. *ulezi, uganga.*)

Uvimbe, n. (1) being swollen, puffed out, distention, protuberance, projection, inflation; (2) girth, circumference. (Cf. *vimba.*)

Uvivu, n. idleness, slackness, negligence, sloth, indolence. (Cf. *-vivu,* and syn. *ulegevu, utepetevu, uzembe.*)

Uvuguvugu, n. lukewarmness, tepidity, i.e. neither cold nor hot, *wala baridi wala hari.* (Cf. *-vuguvugu.*)

Uvukizo, n. (*ma-*), producing or causing smoke, burning of aromatics, fumigants, &c., fumigation. Plur. of things thus used. (Cf. *vuka, vukisa, vukizo.*)

Uvukuto, n. (1) exhalation (produced by heat), vapour, steam, smell of perspiration; (2) working bellows. (Cf. *vukuta, mvukuto, mvuke.*)

Uvulana, n. age, condition, &c., of a young unmarried man, youthfulness, bachelorhood. (Cf. *mvulana*, and syn. *ujana*.)

Uvuli, n. (*vuli*), shade, shadiness, —in general. (See **Mvuli**, and cf. *kivuli, mwavuli.*)

Uvumba, n. an odoriferous gum, used for perfume and incense. (Cf. *udi, ubani*, and *vukizo.*)

Uvumbi, n. dust, dust as a substance, a grain of dust, dust collectively (cf. *vumbi*), dustiness. *Tifua u.*, stir up dust; also *piga u.*, make a dust. (Cf. *vumbi*, a mas' of dust, and *uchanga, mchanga*, also *tifutifu.*)

Uvumi, n. (*ma-*), (1) any low indistinct sound, such as rumbling, roaring, humming, buzzing, murmuring; (2) common talk, rumour, report, gossip, fame. (Cf. *vuma, mvumo.*)

Uvumilivu, n. endurance, perseverance, patience, fortitude. (Cf. *vumilia*, and syn. *stahimili, saburi.*)

Uvundo, n. and **Uvundu**, a bad smell, stink, stench. (Cf. *harufu, vumba*, and contr. *manukato, nuka.*)

Uvungu, n. and **Uvurungu**, hollowness. *Jiwe la uvurungu*, a hollow stone. (Cf. *mvungu.*)

Uvunjifu, n. destructiveness, vandalism, destruction, devastation, broken condition, wreck. (Cf. *vunja, -vunjifu*, and syn. *uharabu, upotevu.*)

Uvunjo, n. a breaking, &c. See **Vunja, Mvunjo**.

Uvuno, n. (*ma-*), harvesting, reaping, gathering crops, getting profits. Plur. *mavuno*, crops, harvest, returns, profits. (Cf. *vuna, mavuno*, and *mavune.*)

Uvurungu, n. and **Uvungu** (which see).

Uvusho, n. act (time, place, means, fare) of carrying across, a ferry. Similarly *uvushi*. (Cf. *vuka.*)

***Uwakili**, n. condition (employment, methods, salary, &c.) of an agent or representative (*wakili*), stewardship. (Ar. Cf. *wakili.*)

***Uwali**, n. office (dignity, duties, salary, &c.) of a governor, governorship. (Ar. Cf. *wali, liwali.*)

Uwambo, n. (1) act (manner, operations, &c.) of stretching over, &c. (See **Wamba**.) (2) the laced cords of a native bedstead. (Cf. *kitanda, kiwambo.*)

Uwanda, n. (*wanda*) and **Uwanja**, an open space, i. e. (1) in towns, and so usually in Z.—public square, space before houses, or (in houses) courtyard, yard, plot of enclosed ground attached to a house; (2) in the country,—open ground, plain, wilderness. (Cf. *uwanja, kiwanja*, and syn. *ugo, ua*, and dist. *wangwa, uwanga.*)

Uwanga, n. and **Wanga** (**Uanga**) (which see).

Uwanja, n. court, enclosure, open space in front of a house or among houses. (Cf. *kiwanja*, and *uwanda*, which is the same word.)

Uwati, n. (*mbati*), (1) wall-plate. See **Mbati**. (2) an eruption on the skin.

Uwatu, n. the herb fenugreek.

***Uwazi**, n. openness, plainness, clearness, distinctness, intelligibility. (Ar. Cf. *wazi*, and syn. *uthahiri, ubaini.*)

***Uwaziri**, n. office (dignity, duties, pay) of a minister or chief secretary of a monarch. (Ar. Cf. *waziri.*)

Uwele, n. (*ma-*), the edible grain produced by the plant *mwele*, a kind of millet. (Cf. *mawele.*)

***Uwele**. See **Uele**.

Uwezo, n. and sometimes **Uweza**, **Uwezi**, (1) being able,—and so (2) strength, might, power, capacity, authority, ability, faculty. (Cf. *weza*, and syn. *nguvu, enzi, mamlaka, amri, akili.*)

Uwili, n. being twofold, duality, dualism, doubleness. (Cf. *pili, -wili*. For articles of double texture, or folded in two, extra thick, cf. *maradufu*.)

Uwima, n. See **Uima**.

Uwinda, n. (*mbinda*) and **Uwinja** (*mbinja*), also **Uinda**, **Uinja**, (1) hunting; (2) a way of wearing the loin-cloth, when engaged in hunting or hard work, viz. tucking it tightly between the legs and round the loins, and as the Banyan fashion is in Z. E. g. *ukimpenda Banyani, umpende na uinda wake*, if you love a Banyan, love his ways too; (3) a hunter's whistle or call. E. g. *piga uwinja*, (1) adjust the loin-cloth (as above), gird up the loins; (2) give a whistle. *Endeleza mbinja*, give a prolonged whistle or call. (Cf. *winda*, ?*inda*, and for whistling *msonyo*.)

Uwindaji, **Uwindi**, **Uwindo**, n. (*ma-*) and **Windo**, art (profession, method, &c.) of hunting. *Mawindo*, what is got by hunting, booty, prey. (Cf. *winda*, and prec.)

Uwingu, n. (*mbingu*), (1) the sky, cloud region, upper air, heaven; (2) cloudiness, darkness, gloom. Plur. *mbingu*, the skies, heaven,—used sometimes as sing. *Mbingu ikanena kwamba mimi bora*, Heaven said, I am best. *Mbingu sabaa*, the seven heavens. *Kumefanya uwingu mkubwa*, there came on a deep gloom. (Cf. *wingu*, a cloud, and *hewa*, *anga*.)

*****Uwitha**, n. (*mauwitha*) and **Watha**, **Witha**, sermon, solemn exhortation. (Ar. Cf. *hotuba*, *hutubu*.)

Uwivu, n. and **Uivu** (which see).

Uwongo, n. and **Uongo** (which see).

*****Uyabisi**, n. (1) dryness, drying up, hardness, stiffness; (2) disobliging conduct, rudeness, reserve. E.g. *u. wa maungo*, of rheumatism, and *u. wa tumbo*, costiveness. (Ar. Cf. *yabisi*, and *ubaridi*.)

Uyoga, n. (*nyoga*), an edible fungus, mushroom.

Uyuzi, n. for common *ujuzi*, ingenuity, cleverness, knowingness, intelligence. (Cf. *jua*, *ujuzi*, *ujuvi*.)

Uza, v. (1) sell,—the only common word. The Infin. form *kuza* is often used, making it more distinguishable from *uza*, for *uliza*, i. e. ask. *Uza* appears to be a Cs. form of a verb *ua*, buy, not used in Swahili, in which the *u* sound is light and faint, and to mean,—cause (invite, permit) to buy, effect a sale. Hence *uza* is used both (1) of persons, sell, and (2) of things, be for sale. E. g. a man may reply to, *Uza*, i. e. name a price, *Haiuzi*, it is not for sale. Hence also the peculiar form *uliza*, or *liza*, sell, i. e. another Cs. form of *ua*, from an Ap. *ulia*, e. g. *utuulize*. *Siuzi*, please let us buy. I do not sell. *Amemliza ng'ombe*, he has sold him a cow. *Nimemwuliza shamba*, I have sold him an estate. Ps. *uzwa*. Nt. *uzika*, e. g. be for sale. Ap. *uzia*, *uziwa*, and *uz-ilia*, *-iliwa*, sell to (for, in, at, with, by, &c.). No Cs. Rp. *uzana*. (Cf. *uzanya*, and *nadi*, *zabuni*, *nunua*.) (2) ask,—for *uliza* (which see).

*****Uzani**, n. weighing, weight (by measure). (Ar. Cf. *mizani*, and syn. *uzito*. For measures of weight cf. *wakia*, *ratli*, *pishi*, *frasila*.)

Uzanya, v. be for sale, be sold. (Cf. *uza*.)

Uzao, n. (*ma-*), product, production, offspring. (Cf. follg., and *mzao*, *zao*, *kizao*, *zaa*.)

Uzazi, n. (1) reproduction at any stage, production of fruit, or offspring; (2) parentage (of man or animal, male or female), begetting, procreation, childbirth, delivery, confinement; (3) reproductive power, fruitfulness, fertility, fruit-bearing; (4) produce, offspring,—but this is usually *mazao*. *Chango la uzazi*, umbilical cord. (Cf. *zaa*, *kizazi*, *mzazi*, *zao*.)

Uzee, n. being old, old age. (Cf. *mzee*, *kizee*, and perh. *zaa*.)

Uzembe, n. slackness, idleness, indifference, negligence. (Cf. -*zembe*, and syn. *uivu*, *ulegevu*.)

Uzi, n. (*nyuzi*), thread, cotton, string, fibre,—and similar objects, e. g. small sinew, ligature, a thin stripe, a fine beading.

Uzima, n. (1) life, vitality, health, vigour, soundness; (2) being full-grown, adult age, full development; (3) completeness, wholeness, totality, full dimensions, freedom from injury, (defect, harm). *Uzima* can also be used of 'life, lifetime,' but this is commonly *maisha*. ('Time of life, age' is *umri*.) *Utu uzima*, full age, manhood, years of discretion. (Cf. -*zima*, a., and see **Maisha**.)

Uzingizi, n. See **Usingizi**.

Uzingo, n. See **Uzungo**.

*****Uzini**, n. irregular sexual intercourse, adultery, fornication, immoral living. (Ar. Cf. *zini*, *zani*, and syn. *ufisadi*, *ufasiki*.)

*****Uzinifu**, n. viciousness (of temperament or life), wantonness, lasciviousness, sexual immorality. (Ar. Cf. prec.)

Uzio, n. (*nyuzio*), a fish-trap consisting of a fence of upright sticks fastened together, and used for enclosing an area, sometimes very large, on a sloping tidal shore, and preventing the escape of fish as the tide falls. (Cf. *kichaga*, *utata*, and *dema*, also *zio*.)

Uziwa, n. high sea, open unbroken expanse of water, sea as seen from the shore. (Cf. *ziwa*.)

Uzuio, n. (*ma-*), hindering, preventing, stoppage, obstructing, obstacle, hindrance, check. (Cf. *zuia*, *zuio*.)

Uzuka, n. condition of a *kizuka* (see **Kizuka** (3)), i. e. state of mourning and seclusion. *Ondoa u.*, bring mourning to an end (Kr.).

*****Uzulu**, v. remove from office, dismiss, cause to abdicate, dethrone, depose, degrade. *U. kazini* or *katika kazi*, discharge from work.

Jiuzulu, resign an office, abdicate, retire. Ps. *uzuliwa*. Ap. *uzul-ia*, *-iwa*. Cs. *uzul-isha*, *-ishwa*, intens. — n. (*ma-*), abdication, dismissal, discharge. (Ar. Cf. *ondoa*, *ondosha*, *toa*, *shusha*, *tusha*.)

Uzungo, n. and **Uzingo**, that which surrounds, goes round, is round, e. g. *uzungo wa mwezi*, a halo round the moon. (Cf. *zinga*, *mzingo*, *zunguka*, *uzungu*, &c.)

Uzungu, n. (1) Europe, the country of the foreigners, i. e. the whites (*Wazungu*); (2) strangeness, wondrousness, novelty; (3) giddiness. (Cf. -*zungu*, *mzungu*, *kizunguzungu*, *zunguka*.)

Uzuri, n. beauty,—mainly external, and appealing to the senses, and so often of things concrete, an ornament, decorative work, a work of art, a perfume, a cosmetic, &c. But also of 'excellence,' and even 'moral goodness,' considered rather as good taste than good principle (*wema*). *Fanya u.*, make a display, adorn oneself. *Tia u.*, give a finish to. A native list of points of personal beauty gives *uso mdawari*, a round face; *shingo la mwanzi*, a smooth neck; *macho ya kikombe*, large well-opened eyes; *pua ya upanga*, a thin nose (not short and broad); *mikono ya binu*, graceful, well-shaped arms; *mwili umeviringana*, a plump, well-rounded figure; *meno za pembe*, teeth like ivory. For personal ornaments see *urembo*, and cf. *pambo*. (See -*zuri*.)

Uzushi, n. and **Uzuzi**, (1) sudden appearance or bringing to light, as out of a hole,—outburst, emergence, coming in sight, bobbing up from water, &c. (2) invention, discovery, novelty, fiction, false accusation, gossip, innovation, heresy, reform. E. g. *uzushi wa lulu*, of a diver's work, bringing up pearls to the surface. *Uzushi mwingi*, a complete revolution. (Cf. *zua*, *zuka*, *mzushi*, *uzuka*.)

Uzuzu, n. condition of a newcomer, rawness, inexperience, strangeness (to country, companions, surroundings, &c.). (Cf. *mzuzu, zuzua,* and syn. *ujinga, ugeni, upya.*)

V.

V represents the same sound as in English. But it is not clearly distinguishable from *f* in some Swahili words, partly no doubt under the influence of Arabic, which has only the *f* sound. Hence words not found under **V** may be looked for under **F**. (See **F**.)

Vaa, v. put on as clothes, dress in, wear, clothe oneself, dress. *Amevaa nguo nzuri,* he is wearing a fine dress. *Hajavaa,* he is still dressing. Ps. *valiwa,* (1) of things, be worn; (2) of persons, be dressed. Nt. *vika* is used as act., clothe (with), cause to wear, dress (in), with pass. *vikwa,* be clothed (with). Ap. *valia, valiwa, valika,* e. g. (1) put on with (for, in, &c.), but esp. (2) put on something by way of addition to ordinary clothes,—and so, dress oneself up, wear fine clothes, be a dandy, —and of a soldier, put on accoutrements. E. g. *mshipi wa kuvalia nguo,* a belt to secure one's clothes with. *Amevalia leo,* he has got his best things on to-day. Also in a fig. sense, *neno hili lajivalia,* this matter stands on its merits. Hence *valiana,* e. g. collectively of many persons together. Cs. *vali-sha, -shwa,* but usually *vika,* as above, and also *visha, vishwa,* cause to wear, give clothes to, &c. Rp. *vishana.* (Cf. *vao, valio, vazi, vika, vua.*)

Valio, n. (*ma-*), extra apparel, accoutrements, ornaments, additions to usual dress. (Cf. follg.)

Vao, n. (*ma-*), style (place, act) of dressing, mode of wearing, something worn, dress, &c. (Cf. follg.)

Vazi, n. (*ma-*), article of dress, wearing apparel, dress, robes, garments, clothes. (Cf. *vaa.*)

Vema, a. and adv. for *vyema,* from *-ema,* good, i. e. rightly, well, nicely, properly, &c. Esp. as a common rejoinder of assent or approval, Certainly! Good! Very well! —like *njema, ngema, inshallah, eewallah.* (Cf. *-ema,* and *vi-.*)

Vi, verb-form, they are,—agreeing with D 3 (P), e. g. *vyakula hivi vi ghali,* this food is dear,—taking the place of *ni,* or Pres. Tense Indic. of *wa,* be.

Vi- (Vy-), as a pfx., (1) in nouns, is the Plur. pfx. of D 3 (P), and of adjs. agreeing with it; and (2) in verbs, is the pfx., subjective and objective, agreeing with the above nouns. Obs. also (3) *vivi hivi,* these very things, in this very way, just so. *Vi- (vy-),* as a pfx. of adjs., is also the commonest way of giving them an adverbial meaning. E. g. *vikubwa,* on a large scale; *vizuri,* nicely; *vibaya,* badly, and obs. *vivyo, hivi, vile, ndivyo,* and other adverbial forms. Cf. use of *ki,* e. g. *kidogo, kizungu,* &c. See **Ki-**. Obs. words beginning with *vi- (vy-)* may, as a rule, be looked for under *ki- (ch-),* or under the letter following *vi-.*

Via, v. fail of full development (completion, perfection), and so (1) be stunted, cut short, half done, unfinished, blighted, underdone, spoilt; and (2) fig. be a failure, lack life, be of a low type, be backward, stagnate. Cs. *viza, vizwa,* e. g. cut short, interrupt, break off, keep back (work, progress, growth, &c.), e. g. *ameniviza kazi,* he prevented me doing my work properly. Hence *vizia* (which see). (Perh. cf. *vilia, vizia,* and *viza,* a., and syn. *vunja, haribu, zuia, katiza.*)

Vifaa, n. plur. (sing. *kifaa* not in use), things useful, requisites, appliances, necessaries, accessories. (Cf. *faa, mafaa.*)

Vika, Vikwa, Visha, v. See **Vaa**.

Vile, a. demonstr. from *-le*, (1) agreeing with D 3 (P); (2) adv. thus, in that way, so. *Vilevile*, just the same, just so, as before, equally. (Cf. *vi-*, *vivi hivi*, *vivyo*, &c.)

Vilia, v. stop running, stagnate, e. g. of flowing blood, form clots, coagulate. Cs. *vili-za*, *-zwa*, and *viza*, *vizwa*, make stop, staunch, cut off the flow (from). (Cf. follg. and *via*.)

Vilio, n. (*ma-*), stopping short, stagnation,—but esp. of blood, coagulation, clotting, clot. (Cf. prec. Dist. *vilio*, plur. of *kilio*, and verb-form, 'those which are,' for *vilivyo*.)

Vimba, v. swell, expand, be distended (puffed out, swelled, bloated, stuffed). Ap. *vimb-ia*, *-iwa*. Cs. *vimb-isha*, *-ishwa*, e. g. *jivimbisha*, gorge oneself with food, eat gluttonously. (Cf. *uvimbe*, and *wimbi*, prob. of same root, and syn. *umka*, *fura*.)

*****Vinjari**, v. cruise about, be on the watch, search about,—but esp. of ships or boats. So *merikebu ya vinjari*, a cruiser, a ship on patrol. (? Ar. *finshari*, and cf. *sanjari*.)

Vinya, n. dandle in the arms, i. e. *vinya* (or, *vinya-vinya*) *mtoto*. (Cf. *pembeza*, *bembeza*, and dist. *finya*.)

Viringa, v. become round, form a curve or bend, be rounded (spherical). Cs. *viring-isha*, *-ishwa*, make round (curved, bent). Rp. *viringana*, be round,—like *viringa*, and hence *viringanisha*, for *viringisha*. (Cf. *mviringo*, and ? *fingirisha*.)

Visha, v. give clothes to, dress. (See Vika, Vaa.)

Vita, n. (—, but *vita* is itself often treated as D 3 (P)), (1) war, battle, fighting; (2) contest, struggle, wrangle, dispute. *Fanya* (*piga*) *vita*, make war, fight. *Leta v.*, raid, invade. *Alika v.*, issue a summons to soldiers, call to arms, muster an army,—so *kusanya v.* *Funga v.*, engage in war, commence operations. *Vita vikubwa*, a great battle. (Cf. *pigano*, *jeshi*, *asikari*, and perh. cf. *ita*, call.)

Vivi, a. only in phrase *vivi hivi*, i. e. agreeing with D 3 (P), these very, just these,—and as adv. just so, in this very way. (Cf. *vi-*, and *vivyo hivyo*.)

-vivu, a. (*vivu* with D 4 (P), D 5 (S), D 6), idle, slack, remiss, indolent, slow. (Cf. *uvivu*, and *-legefu*, *-zembe*.)

Viza, v. (1) Cs. of *via*; (2) for *viliza*, Cs. of *vilia*. — n. a spoilt thing, e. g. an addled egg, *viza la yai*, or *yai viza*. (See Via.)

Vizia, v. Ap. from *via*, i. e. spoil work for, frustrate, balk, try to prevent success or completion of (see Via). But *vizia* is commonly used in a more limited sense, waylay, be on the watch for (in a hostile sense), beleaguer, beset, keep an unfriendly eye on, molest, harass. No deriv. stems usual except Ps. *viziwa*, and Rp. *viziana*.

Vua, v. (to be distinguished from another common verb *fua*), A. take off clothes, undress, unclothe oneself, strip, both act. and neut.—with or without *nguo*. Used of any article of dress, e. g. *vua kofia*, take off a cap. Rarely of anything else, e. g. *vua macho, utazame*, open your eyes and look. Contr. *vaa*, put on clothes, dress. Ps. *vuliwa*, (1) of clothes, be taken off; (2) of persons, be undressed, stripped. Nt. *vuka*, e. g. *nguo yote imemvuka*, all his clothes have come off him,—but dist. *vuka*, cross over. Ap. *vulia*, *vuliwa*, *vulika*, e. g. take off for (from, in, with, &c.). Cs. *vuliza*, *vulizwa*, e. g. make take off clothes, force (induce, allow) to undress. Rp. *vuana*. (Cf. *vulio*.) B. fish, catch fish, try to catch fish,—with or without *samaki*. E. g. *vua baharini*, engage in sea-fishing. *Vua samaki*, catch fish. Also *vua mshipi*, fish with a line. Deriv. stems as above, e. g. *ndoana ya ku-*

vulia, a fish-hook. (Cf. *mvuvi, uvuvi, mvuo*.) C. save, preserve, get out of a difficulty,—perh. from the idea of getting across a river (see Vuka). *Avuaye ni karibu*, a preserver is at hand. *Muungu atakuvua, inshallah utavuka*, God will save you. All well, you will be safe. (Cf. *vuka, mvuko, kivuko*.)

Vuata, v. put in the mouth, hold between the teeth, e. g. a bone, tobacco, sugar, &c.

Vuaza, v. (1) make a cut in, cut, pierce; (2) fig. hurt, give pain (to). E. g. *v. mnazi*, cut the flower-stem of a cocoanut tree,—to get the sap (*tembo*). *Kisu kimenivuaza*, the knife has cut me. *Neno hili lavuaza*, this matter is painful. Ps. *vuazwa*. (Cf. syn. *kata, choma, chanja, toja*.)

-vuguvugu, a. tepid, lukewarm, neither cold nor hot. (Cf. *uvuguvugu*.)

Vuja, v. (1) allow liquid to pass in or out, leak, let in, let out; (2) of a liquid, pass in, pass out, ooze out, leak out (or, in). E. g. *mashua yavuja* (*yavuja maji*), *maji yavuja mashuani*, the boat leaks. *Nyumba yavuja*, the house lets in the rain. Ap. *vuj-ia, -iwa, -ika*, e. g. *mvua imenivujia*, the rain came in upon me. *Ukuta inavujika*, the wall is being spoilt by a leak,—by water getting in. (Cf. *chuja, chuza*.)

Vuka, A. Nt. of *vua*, (1) most commonly in the sense, get across, cross over, be ferried over, pass over, —of crossing a river or the sea in a canoe or ship; but also (2) pass through (of a forest), get to the other side (of a hill), &c.; (3) be saved, escape, be preserved, e. g. *waliosimama vitani wakavuka*, those who stood firm in the fight escaped alive. Ap. *vuk-ia, -iwa*, e. g. cross by (in, with, at, &c.), e. g. *tulivukia chini*, we crossed on our feet, by wading. *Chombo cha kuvukia*, a ferry-boat. Cs. *vuk-isha, -ishwa, vusha, vushwa*, cause (allow, induce) to cross, convey across (through, past), ferry over. Rp. *vukana*. (Cf. *vua*, C., *mvuko, kivuko, mvushi, uvushi*.) B. Nt. of *vua*, of clothes, &c., be taken off. (See **Vua**, A.) C. (in this sense also *fuka*), give out smoke or fumes, smoke, turn to smoke or vapour,— with or without *moshi*, evaporate, be vaporized. *Nyumba yao haivuki moshi*, no smoke rises from their house. Ap. *vuk-ia, -iwa*. Cs. *vuk-isha, -ishwa, -iza, -izwa*, cause to give out smoke, turn to vapour, make fumes with, smoke (i. e. apply smoke to), fumigate, cense, burn incense. E. g. *v. maiti* (*nyumba*), fumigate a corpse (a house) with incense. *V. udi*, burn aloe wood,— for fumigation. Also *v. maiti kwa uvumba*. (Cf. *vukizo, mvuke, vuke, vukizo, vukuta*, &c.,—all of which are also heard as *fukizo, mfuke*, &c.)

Vuke, n. (*ma-*), vapour, steam, a drop of condensed steam, sweat. (Cf. prec.)

Vukizo, n. (*ma-*), (1) vapour, fumes, steam, smoke; (2) anything burnt or used for fumigation, incense, &c. (Cf. prec., and *kivukizo*.)

Vukuta, v. blow with bellows, work bellows,—with or without *mfua*, bellows. (See **Mfua, Mvukuto**.)

Vukuto, n. (*ma-*), sweat, a drop of sweat, condensed vapour. Also *vukuto la jasho*. (Cf. prec., and *mvukuto, uvukuto*, also *vuka*, and follg.)

Vule, n. and **Vuli**, the season of the lesser rains in Z. (See **Mvule**.)

Vulio, n. (*ma-*), clothes laid aside or not in use, cast-off (old, rotten) clothing, the cast skin or slough of snakes, &c. (Cf. *vua*, A., and contr. *valio*.)

Vuma, v. (1) usually of any low indistinct sound, i. e. roar, growl, rumble, hum, buzz, rustle, e. g. of wind, thunder, wild beasts, insects, drum. *Baridi inavuma leo*, it is blowing hard to-day. (2) fig. rumour, talk about, spread news (of),—and also, be rumoured, be in the air, be a subject of common talk,—but thus usu. in Nt. form. Ps. *vumwa*. Nt. *vumika*, e.g. be rumoured, be talked about, become famous or notorious. *Kuvumikakwauganga*, to be famed for medical skill. Ap. *vum-ia, -iwa*, and perh. *vumilia* (which see). Cs. *vum-isha, -ishwa*, e.g. (1) cause to make a noise, sound; (2) make well-known, celebrate, advertise. Also intens. *simba akavumisha kilio kikuu*, the lion uttered a furious roar. Rp. *vumana*. (Cf. *uvumi, mvumo, vumo*.)

Vumba, n. (*ma-*), something with a bad smell, dried fish, foreshore, &c. Also the name of a famous old coast town a little north of Z. now in ruins. (Cf. *vunda, uvundo*.)

Vumbi, n. (*ma-*), dust, a mass (collection, cloud) of dust, fine powder, sediment. (Cf. *uvumbi*, and follg.)

Vumbika, v. or perh. **Fumbika** (see below),—used in a limited sense, put (cover up) in dust, ashes, leaves, embers, soil, &c., e.g. put fruit underground to ripen it, store cocoanuts for seed, put in the ground, plant a seed or seedling. Ps. *vumbikwa*. Ap. *vumbik-ia, -iwa*. Cs. *vumbikisha, -ishwa*. (Cf. *vumbi*, but rather perh. *fumba*, and so *vumbua*.)

Vumbilia, v. stir up, excite, get mixed up in, e.g. in a quarrel, brawl, war. Ps. *vumbiliwa*. Nt. *vumbilika*. (Cf. prec., and *vumbi*.)

Vumbua, v. or perh. **Fumbuka** (which see), discover, explore, open up, hunt out, invent, find out, come upon, bring to light, disclose. E.g. *vumbua inchi*, explore a country. *V. njia*, find a road. Ps. *vumbuliwa*. Nt. *vumbuka*. Ap. *vumbulia, -liwa, -lika*, e.g. *vumbulika*, be disclosed, burst out suddenly or violently, be come upon unexpectedly. Cs. *vumbusha*, e.g. intens. come on suddenly, wake up with a start. (May be compared with *fumba*, and its derivatives, or perh. *vumbi, vumbika*, and syn. *fumbua, funua*.)

Vumi, n. (*ma-*), a loud rumble, roar, hum, roll of a drum, &c. Also name of a kind of drum. (Cf. *vuma, uvumi*.)

Vumilia, v. bear, endure, persevere in, suffer, tolerate. Ps. *vumilia*. Nt. *vumilika*. Cs. *vumilisha, -ishwa*. Ap. *vumiliana*. (Perh. an Ap. from *vuma*, i.e. of a man groaning under a burden, doing hard work, &c. Cf. syn. *stahimili, chukua*.)

Vuna, v. (1) gather a crop, reap, get in harvest of any kind; (2) fig. reap profit, get an advantage, profit. Hence the expression *jivuna*, boast oneself, brag, swagger, show off, give oneself airs, be conceited (cf. *jiona, jigamba*.) Ps. *vunwa*. Nt. *vunika*. Ap. *vun-ia, -iwa*, e.g. reap for (with, at, &c.). *Nimemvunia shamba lake*, I have got in his crop for him. Cs. *vun-isha, -ishwa*, e.g. employ in reaping, contract for harvesting. (Cf. *mvuni, mavuno, majivuno, uvuno*, and syn. *chuma, faidi*.)

Vunda, v. rot, putrefy. *Nyama mbichi ao ya kuvunda*, fresh or putrid meat. (Cf. *uvundo*, and perh. *vumba*, and commoner syn. *oza*. Also dist. *funda*, v.)

Vunde, n. (*ma-*). See **Mavunde**.

-vungu, a. (same with D 4 (P), D 5 (S), D 6), hollow, having a cavity. (Cf. *mvungu, uvungu*, and syn. *-tupu*.)

Vunja, v. (1) break, break down (up, in pieces, into, through, out of, off, away), and so (2) spoil, damage, destroy; (3) put a stop to, balk, frustrate. E.g. *v. chungu*, break a cooking pot (used of the final feast or carnival before the Ramathan fast begins). *V. thamani*, destroy the value, depreciate, disgrace. *V. uso*, put to shame, bring dishonour on, insult openly. *V. mwendo*, be a drag, spoil a day's march, make delay. *V. rupia*, change a rupee,—into small coin. *V. ungo*, deflower, ravish. *V. baraza*, dismiss a meeting. *V. merikebu*, wreck a vessel. *V. nyumba*, pull down a house. *V. moyo*, discourage, dishearten. *V. adui*, defeat an enemy. *V. mwitu*, break through a forest, force one's way. Occasionally Nt., e. g. *watu wakavunja upesi*, the crowd soon broke, i. e. gave way. Ps. *vunjwa*. Nt. *vunjika*, e. g. *jahazi imevunjika*, the vessel is wrecked. Hence *vunjikana*, be breakable, be fragile. Ap. *vunj-ia, -iwa*. Cs. *vunj-isha, -ishwa* (rarely heard). Rp. *vunjana*. (Cf. *mvunjo, -vunjifu, uvunjo*, and syn. *ponda, piga, haribu, komesha*.)

Vuruga, v. also **Vuruja**, and **Vuruka**, (1) stir, stir up, stir round (about), mix by stirring,—esp. in cookery, in compounding medicines, &c., mixing ingredients for mortar, for embalming, &c. Also (2) stir the feelings of, excite, exasperate. Ps. *vurugwa*. Nt. *vurujika* (but dist. follg.). Ap. *vuruj-ia, -iwa*. Cs. *vuruj-isha, -ishwa*. (Cf. *boruga*, and syn. *changanya*.)

Vurujika, v. and **Furijika**, be in a mouldering (decaying, crumbling) condition, be completely decomposed or putrefied. E. g. *kitu hiki kinaoza, hatta kinafurujika*, this thing is decaying, and even becoming wholly decomposed.

Vurumisha, v. and **Furumiza**, **Vuvumisha**. *V. jiwe*, throw a stone. *Jivurumisha*, cast oneself headlong. (Perh. an emphatic form of *vumisha*, i. e. cause to hum. Cf. *vuma*, and syn. *rusha* from *ruka*.)

Vusha, v. Cs. of **Vuka** (which see), cross over.

Vuta, v. (1) draw, pull, drag, strain, stretch, attract, have an effect upon ; (2) change, pervert, give a new direction (meaning, aspect) to; (3) have an influence on, charm, entice, tempt, allure, lead astray. Also with various special applications, e. g. *v. makasia*, use an oar, row, and *v. mashua*, row a boat. *V. upanga*, draw a sword (cf. *chomoa*). *V. maneno*, put a strain on words, i. e. strain their meaning. *V. tumbako*, smoke a pipe. *V. maji*, bale out water. Ps. *vutwa*. Nt. *vutika*, e. g. be pulled, be capable of being stretched or altered. So also *vutikana*. Ap. *vut-ia, -iwa*, and *vut-ilia, -iliwa, -ilika*, of particular operations, e. g. in plaiting. Cs. *vut-isha, -ishwa*. Rp. *vutana*, e. g. all pull together. (Cf. *mvuto*, and syn. *kokota*, move by pulling, drag along, and dist. *futa*.)

Vuvum'ka, v. grow up fast, develop quickly, shoot up,—of vegetation and also animal life. E. g. of mangoes, children. (Cf. syn. *chipua, kua*.)

Vy-, for *vi-* before a vowel, e. g. *vyangu, vyako*, &c., and *vyote, vyeusi*.

Vya, prep., of,—form agreeing with D 3 (P). (See **Vi, -a**.)

Vyo, -vyo, (1) pron. relat. which, agreeing with D 3 (P),—only used separately in *vyo vyote*, whatever, and a few other phrases. (2) conj. 'as,' usually following *ginsi, kama, kadiri*, and other words introducing an adverbial clause,—corresponding to the use of *vi* to form adverbs from adjectives, e. g. *ginsi alivyokuwa*, as he was ; *kama alivyosema*, according to what he said ; *kadiri niwezavyo*, as far as I can. *Mimi hapa nilivyo, ni mzima*, I, as I am at present, am quite well.

W.

W represents the same sound as in English ; (1) sometimes as a distinct consonant ; (2) sometimes as a semi-vowel, not clearly distinguishable from *u*, or *uw*. Hence words not found under **W** may be looked for under **U**, or **Uw**, and some words are given under both.

W-, before a vowel, often represents the pfx. *u* (for which see **U**).

Wa, (1) prep. of,—form agreeing with D 1 (S, P), D 2 (S), D 4 (S). (See **-a**, prep.) (2) verb-form, they are, agreeing with D 1 (P), e.g. *watumwa wa rahisi*, slaves are cheap. (3) conj. Arab. and occurs sometimes, esp. in written Swahili, letters, documents, &c., and in combination, e.g. *wabadahu, wassalaam, wakatabahu*.

Wa-, as a pfx., is used :—

A. in nouns, to form plur. of D 1. It becomes *w* before vowels, except *i*, with which it coalesces to form *e*, e.g. *mwivi, wevi*, for *waivi*.

B. in adjectives, to mark agreement with plur. of D 1. It becomes *w* before vowels, except *i*, e.g. *watu wako wabaya*, your people are bad.

C. in verbs, the subjective and objective pfx. of the 3 Pers. Plur. agreeing with D 1 (P). Obs. (1) *wa-* is also one of the objective pfxs. used in agreement with *ninyi*, i.e. the pron. of the 2 Pers. Plur., e.g. *nawapa* means 'I give them,' or 'I give you' (plur.). Hence a form like *wawapenda* may mean (1) they love them ; (2) they love you (plur.) ; (3) you (*wa* for *u-a*, sing.) love them.

-wa, v. be, become, take place, exist, occur, happen. (*Kuwa* is used in certain tenses. See under **Ku**, 1 (*d*), rules for monosyllabic verb-roots.) (1) The common use of the simple verb *-wa*, in all tenses and moods, is to connect Subject and Predicate in a sentence, and to supply an auxiliary in forming compound tenses,—like the verb *To be* in English. (2) The meaning 'become' is only clear in connexion with the sign of the Pres. Tense Definite, *-na-*, e.g. *jua linakuwa kali*, the sun is becoming scorching, and the Perf. Tense *me-*, e.g. *amekuwa mgonjwa*, he has become sick, he is ill. (3) Concrete existence, i.e. being as fact, actual being or taking place, is expressed by *-wa*, e.g. *mambo haya yamekuwa*, these things have actually taken place, are facts ; and also absolute existence, so far as a Swahili conceives it, e.g. *mwenyi kuwa*, as a title of God,—the Self-existent, He who is. *Ndiye awaye*, it is he who is (exists). Obs. however, that *-wa* is rarely used at all in any sense in the Pres. Positive, and not often in the Pres. Negative, e.g. *yuwa*, he is ; *siwi*, I am not ; *hamwi*, you (plur.) are not. As a copula, it is (1) either simply omitted,—or its place is taken by (2) *ni* for all persons and numbers, or by the personal pfxs. (*ni, u, tu, wa*, &c.) used as independent forms, or (3) *li*, but only in combination with a relative pfx. (*-o, -lo, -vyo*, &c.) Simple existence is also expressed by *na* in certain combinations. (See **Na** (3) for this, and also for *-wa na*, as corresponding to the English verb 'have.') Ap. *wia, wiwa*, and *wea* (? *wewa*), (1) with the usual prepositional relations, be to (for, with, in, &c.), e.g. *uniwie rathi*, be kind to me, favour me, pardon me ; (2) with a special and definite sense, viz. be a creditor of, have a claim on, have in one's debt,—both in Act. and Pass. Thus *ananiwia* commonly means, I owe him money ; *namwia*, he owes me money. So in the Pass. form *nawiwa naye*, I am his debtor; and *awiwa nami*, he is my debtor; e.g. *wote wenyi kumwia wakutane*, let all his creditors hold a meeting; *nawiwa uzima wangu kwa Muungu*, I owe my life to God. The form *wea* (if not a different verb) is sometimes used alone for 'be good for, turn out well to, be the property of.' No Cs. in use. Rp. *wiana*, e.g. be to each other, have relations with each other, be mutually indebted or under obligations.

Waa, v. shine brightly, blaze,—e.g. of the sun or moon, but not often heard in Z. (Cf. *waka, washa, mawao*, and the common *n. 'ra*.)

Waa, n. (*ma-*), spot, patch of colour (light or dark), mark, stain, speck, blot, e.g. *kuku mwenyi mawaa*, a speckled fowl. (Perh. cf. *waa*, v. of a spot which catches the eye, and syn. *doa, kipaku.*)

*__Wabadahu__, Ar. for *wa baada ya haya*, in letters, 'and after this, and next.' (Cf. *wa*, conj.)

*__Wabba__, n. cholera. (Ar.)

*__Wadi__, Ar. (1) son of, like *bin*, and B. *wa* for *mwana wa*; (2) rarely, watercourse, bed of a torrent, ravine, i. e. *uwanja unaopita maji*.

*__Wadi__, v. keep to a time, complete a time, be up to time. Also Ap. be fully time (for), be in good time (for). (Ar. ? *wa'ad*, promise, and cf. *wahadi*.)

*__Wadui__, n. also __Uadui__, enmity, hostility. (Ar. Cf. *adui*, and syn. *ushindani, utesi*.)

__Wafi__, n. a stinging plant, a kind of nettle.

*__Wafiki__, __Wafikana__, v. suit, agree, — same as __afiki__ (which see). (Ar.)

*__Wahadi__, n. promise. See __Ahadi__. (Ar.)

*__Wahedi__, n. and a., one,—the numeral,—often used, as well as B. *mosi, -moja*. (Ar. Cf. (*wah-*) *edashara*, eleven.)

*__Wahi__, v. and __Wai__, be in time, be prompt (ready, forward) to act. E. g. *hakuwahi kufika mjini*, he had not time to get to the town (when), i. e. before he got to the town. *Akawahi kumkaribisha*, he was ready to welcome him. (Cf. *wadi*, v.)

*__Wainna__, conj. if not, otherwise. (Arab. for common B. *kama sivyo*.)

*__Wajibu__, n. what is right, fitting, proper, suitable; and so in moral sense, duty, obligation, due courtesy. *Wajibu yako*, what is expected of you, worthy of you. *Mtoto wajibu heshima na wazee wake*, a child should be respectful to his parents. Also sometimes as v., i.e. be proper, be a duty, be an obligation, with Ap. *wajibia*. (Ar. Cf. *bidi, pasa, sunna, -ema*.)

*__Wajihi__, v. appear, present oneself, — and with *kwa*, visit, meet face to face, interview, salute. *Wakawajihi kwa Seyidi*, they appeared before the Sultan. Rp. *wajihiana*, meet face to face. (Ar. Cf. common *onana, onekana, kutana*.)

__Waka__, v. (1) blaze, burn brightly, be lighted, show a flame; (2) smart, burn, hurt (as by burning), be inflamed. Ap. *wak-ia, -iwa*. Cs. *washa*, e. g. cause to burn, set fire to, light (a fire or lamp). Nt. *washika*, be lighted, burn. Hence *wash-ia, -iwa*, e.g. *uniwashie taa*, light the lamp for me,—and *washikana*, be inflammable, be capable of being lighted. (Cf. *mwako*, dist. *aka*, build.)

*__Wakala__, n. agency, appointment, commission. (Ar. Cf. *wakili*. Dist. *wakala* from *-la*, 'and they ate.')

*__Wakati__, n. (*nyakati*), time (in general), season, period of time, point of time, sufficient time, opportunity. (Ar. Cf. *saa, muda, muhulla, majira, zamani*, and B. *pindi, kipindi, kitambo*.)

__Wake__, a. (1) pron. a., his, hers, its, from *-ake*,—agreeing with D 1 (S, P), D 2 (S), D 4 (S); (2) from *-ke, mke*, females, wives. (See *-ke*.)

*__Wakfu__, n. See __Wakifu__. (Ar.)

*__Wakia__, n. an ounce (weight),— commonly reckoned in Z. as the weight of an Austrian silver dollar piece, i. e. *ni uzito wa reale*, and as 16 to the pound weight (*ratli*). (Ar. Dist. *wakia*, Ap. of *waka*.)

*__Wakifu__, v. cost, be priced at, cause expense. Ap. *wakif-ia, -iwa*, e. g. cost to (a person). — a. also __Wakfu__, and __Wakf__, set apart for religious purposes, consecrated, devoted to a holy use,—esp. of land or other gifts assigned to a mosque for its expenses, pay of the minister, &c. (Ar. Cf. *gharamia, simama*.)

*__Wakili__, n. (*ma-*), agent, steward, representative, commissioner, manager (under a proprietor). Also sometimes v., act as agent, &c., and Cs.

wakilisha, appoint as agent, commission. (Ar. Cf. *wakala*, and *mjumbe, karani*.)

Wako, (1) a. form of *-ako*, your, agreeing with D 1 (S, P), D 2 (S), D 4 (S); (2) verb-form, i. e. *wa*, pfx. agreeing with D 1 (P), and *-ko* (cf. *huko*), they are (there). (See *-ako*, **Wa, -ko**.)

*****Wala**, conj. nor. Used (1) after a negative, repeating not reversing it, and so often translatable 'or'; (2) itself repeated, *wala...wala*, neither... nor. (Ar. 'and not,' cf. *ao, ama*, and follg.)

*****Walakini**, conj. but, however, nevertheless, notwithstanding. (Ar. Cf. *wa, lakini*.)

*****Walao**, adv. even, at least, anyhow, at any rate. E. g. *humwachii walao kitu kidogo*, you do not leave him even a little. *Uganga walao wa mvua*, at least rain-medicine. (Ar.)

Wale, (1) adj. pronom. 'those, —form of *-le* agreeing with D 1 (P) (see **Yule**); (2) subjunct. mood of *-la*, v. that they may eat, let them eat. E. g. *wale wa wali wale wali*, let those (people) of the governor have a meal of rice.

Wali, n. (1) (*nyali*, seldom used), cooked rice, i. e. rice so cooked that each grain is whole and separate, though soft and thoroughly done. The staple dish of Zanzibar. *Wali ni Sultani ya chakula, watawazwa katika kiti*, cooked rice is the king of foods, it is placed on a royal throne, i. e. on a raised stool serving as a table. Rice cooked with too much water is *wali mchepechepe*, or *majimaji*. (Also cf. *poroja la wali, uji, ubabwa, matabwatabwa, mashendea*, and see **Mchele**.)

*****Wali**, n. (*ma-*), governor, the Sultan's representative in a town or district,—in Z. usually *liwali* (*ma-*), —perh. because *wali* for 'rice' is so common. (Ar. Cf. *liwali, tawala*.)

*****Walii**, n. (—), a holy one, a saint, an angel. E. g. *paka akajifanya walii sana*, a cat set up as a great saint. *Muungu akamshushia walii*, God sent down an angel to him. (Ar. Cf. *sufii, mtawa*, and *malaika*, angel.)

Walio, n. (*nyalio*), used of bits of stick put crosswise at the bottom of a cooking pot to prevent the contents from burning. Also of a kind of wattle fence for trapping fish. (Cf. *uzio, utata*, and dist. *walio* as a verb-form, 'they who are.')

*****Wallai**, a common Swahili oath, not considered profane by Mahommedans. (Ar. i. e. *wa allah hai*, by the living God. Cf. *Allah, eewallah, inshallah, bismillah*.)

Wamba, v. spread (bind, stretch, fix) over, overlay, overspread, overcast. E. g. *w. kitanda kwa mashupatu*, cover a bedstead with cords interlaced. *W. ngoma kwa ngozi*, stretch a skin tightly on a drum. *Ukungu unawamba ulimwengu*, a mist overspreads the earth. Also *umewamba mlango*, you have blocked the door,—of one who barred the way with arms and legs. (Cf. *wambo*, and *kiwambo, kiwambaza*, and perh. *ambaa*.

Wambiso, n. fastening together, holding together, attachment, clasping. (Cf. *ambisha, ambaa*.)

Wambo, n. for **Uambo**,—better **Uwambo** (which see).

*****Wamini, Waminifu**, n. faithfulness, trustworthiness, honesty, fidelity. (Ar. Cf. *amini, imani, amana, amina, -aminifu*.)

Wana, (1) verb-form, they have, i. e. *wa* pfx. agreeing with D 1 (P) and *na* (which see); (2) n. (for *waana*, plur. of *mwana*), children, or (for *uana*), youthfulness, childhood.

Wanadamu, n. (1) also **Uanadamu**, human nature, humanity (cf. *mwanadamu*, and *utu, ubinadamu*); (2) plur. of *mwanadamu*, human beings.

Wanda, v. get fat, become stout.— but in Z. commonly *nenepa, nona*. Cs. *wand-isha, -ishwa*. — n. (*nyanda*), a finger's breadth,—about 1 inch, used sometimes in measuring (cf. *chanda*). Also pl. of *uwanda* (which see).

Wanga, v. (1) count, reckon (cf. *kiwango*),—but in Z. *hesabu* is the usual word; (2) cause pain, hurt. Ps. *wangwa*, but in Z. *umiza, uma*. — n. a kind of meal made from a plant growing in streams in Zanzibar island (*Maranta arundinacea*, Sac.), arrowroot,—also used as (2) starch; (3) a sweet confection, sometimes with intoxicating ingredients; (4) name of a plant, perh. the above.

Wangafu, n. and **Uang-**, brightness, lustre, glow, transparency, power of reflecting light. (Cf. *-angafu, anga, ng'aa*, &c.)

Wangalifu, n. and **Uang-**, carefulness, attention. (Cf. *angalia*.)

Wango, n. See **Kiwango, Mwango**.

Wangwa, n. (*nyangwa*), waste, bare ground, sandy wilderness. In Z. usually *jangwa*.

Wanja, n. *W. wa manga*, antimony, used as a paint on the face. (Cf. *dalia, manjano*.)

Wano, n. (*ma-*), wooden part, or shaft, of a spear, arrow, harpoon, &c.—also called *uti*.

Wao, (1) pron. of 3 Pers. Plur., they. Denotes only persons, and sometimes animals. (2) a. pronom. their,—form of *-ao* (which see), agreeing with D 1 (S, P), D 2 (S), D 4 (S).

Wapi, (1) pron. interrog. of place, where? and colloquially, how? how so? often shortened to *-api* and *-pi*, and appended to verbs, e. g. *wendapi*, where are you going? (2) a form of *-pi*, which,—agreeing with D 1 (P).

Wapo, (1) n. (*nyapo*), for **Uapo**, from *apa*, i.e. an oath, swearing; (2) used in connexion with *-moja*, e. g. *mmojawapo*, every (any) one of them; (3) a gift, see **Uapo** (cf. *pa*, v.). (4) verb-form, 'they are here,' i.e. *wa*, pfx. of 3 Pers. Plur. and *-po*, for *hapo*.

***Waraka**, n. (*nyaraka*), a written communication, a letter (of correspondence). *Andikiana w.*, correspond (by letter). *Waraka u nussu ya kuonana*, a letter is next to seeing each other. (Ar. Cf. *barua, cheti, hati, anwani, dibaji*, and for a full account of Swahili as written in Arabic characters, Büttner, *Lehrbücher des Seminars für orientalische Sprachen*, Berlin, Band 10.)

***Wari**, n. a yard (measure), half a fathom (*pima*), equal to two *thiraa* or *mukono*. (Cf. *urefu*.)

Waria, n. a skilled workman, foreman, master-builder, contractor. Often coupled with a defining word, *seramala w.*, master carpenter,—so *mwashi w., mwunzi w.* (Cf. *mbingwa, mstadi, fundi*.)

***Waridi**, n. also **Wáradi, Wardi**, a rose. Also as adj. *hal waridi*, rosewater, essence of roses. *Maji mawaridi*, rose-water diluted for toilette and bathing. (Ar.)

***Warithi**, n. (*ma-*), an heir. (Ar. Cf. *mrithi*, which is usual, and *urithi*.)

***Wasaa**, n. room, space, freedom, means, leisure, opportunity. *Kuwa na wasaa*, to be comfortable, satisfied. *Leo sina wasaa*, I cannot do it to-day. (Ar. Cf. syn. *nafasi*.)

Washa, v. Cs. of *waka*, i. e. cause to blaze, set fire to, light, &c. See **Waka**.

***Washerati**, n. and **Uash-**. See **Asherati**. (Ar.)

***Wasi**, n. See **Uasi**. (Ar.)

***Wasia**, v. also **Wosia, Usia**, direct, commission, order, charge,—and esp. of a solemn, serious, weighty command, e. g. last directions on starting for a journey, a religious exhortation, giving the terms of a will. Thus of a dying father, *Enyi waanangu, ntawausia*, my children, I will say my last words to you. *Wakamwosia, shika vema watoto*, and they solemnly charged him, be a good guardian of the children. *Alimwasia nyumba*, he gave his house in charge to him. Ps. *wasi-*

wa. Nt. *wasika*. Ap. *wasi-lia, -liwa*, e.g. give orders about (to, &c.). Cs. *wasi-sha, -shwa*. Rp. *wasiana*. — n. (*ma-*), solemn charge, warning, exhortation, commission, last will and testament. *Ndio wasia wangu*, that is my final charge, my will. *Rejea w.*, revoke a will. (Ar. Cf. follg., and *agiza*.)

*Wasii, n. (*ma-*), executor, trustee, i.e. one named in a will, or nominated as such. (Ar. Cf. prec.)

*Wasili, v. arrive, reach, come to, get to destination, be delivered to, be received. Often followed by *kwa, katika, hatta*, and locative in *-ni*, e.g. *w. kwake* (*Unguja, hatta nyumba, kisiwani*), arrive at his house (at Zanzibar, at the house, at an island). Ps. *wasiliwa*. Ap. *wasil-ia, -iwa*. *Waraka wako umeniwasilia*, your letter has reached me. Cs. *wasilisha*, e.g. cause to arrive, send. Hence *wasil-ishia, -ishiwa*. — n. receipt, income, credit side of cash account. *Cheti cha wasili*, a receipt. Also as adj. *waraka wako wasili*, your note (is) duly received. (Ar. Cf. *fika, pata*.)

*Wasiwasi, n. doubt, perplexity, scruple, infatuation, disquiet,—esp. when caused by moral want of balance, weakness of character, yielding to temptation. *Fanya w.*, feel irresolute. *Tia w.*, confuse the mind (conscience). *Ukamwingia wasiwasi yule kijana*, the young man was filled with waverings. (Ar. Cf. syn. *mashaka*, and dist. *waziwazi*.)

*Wastani, a. middling, average, moderate, between extremes. (Ar. Cf. *kadiri, kiasi*.)

*Watha, n. also Witha, and Uwitha (which see). (Ar.)

Watu, n. (1) plur. of *mtu* (which see); (2) also Uwatu, fenugreek.

Wavu, n. (*nyavu*) a net,—used for fish, game, &c. *W. wa kulalia*, a hammock. *Tanda w., tega w.*, set a net,—to catch something. (Cf. *jarifa, juya, kimia*.)

Waya, n. (*nyaya*), an earthen dish for baking, &c. (Cf. *chungu*.)

Wayawaya, v. sway to and fro, stagger, totter, reel, e.g. of a tree loaded with fruit, a man from weakness. (Cf. *lewa, sita, yonga, yumba, ning'inia*.)

Wayo, n. (*nyayo*), and Uayo, (1) sole of the foot, footprint, track of the feet; (2) trace, vestige, symptom.

Waza, v. (1) suppose, fancy, imagine; (2) reflect, ponder, meditate, have in mind. *W. Muungu* is used of religious meditation, deep inward heart-searching (but this perh. from another Ar. word *wazaa*). Ps. *wazwa*. Nt. *wazika*. Ap. *waz-ia, -iwa*. Cs. *waz-isha, -ishwa*. Rp. *wazana*. (Cf. *fikiri, kumbuka, thani, nia, azimu*.)

*Wazi, a. sometimes -wazi, (1) open, bare, uncovered (of clear passage, free access, room inside, open book, &c.). *Mlango w.*, open door, *njia w.*, open road. *Panalia wazi*, it sounds hollow. *Kitwa kiwazi*, bare head. (2) fig. open, manifest, evident, clear, plain. (Ar. Cf. *thahiri, baini*.)

Wazimu, n. (no plur., treated as D 4), madness, mania, hallucination, desperation, infatuation. E.g. *yuna w.*, he is mad. *Fanya w.*, go mad. *Tia w.*, make mad. *Mwenyi w.*, a madman. Also as a. *yu w.*, he is mad. (Cf. *mzimu, kuzimu, zimwe*. Perh. *wazimu* is merely plur. of *mzimu*, i.e. (1) spirits, demons; (2) possession by demons, madness.)

*Waziri, n. (*ma-*), chief officer of state under a sovereign, prime minister, secretary of state. (Ar. Cf. *shehe, diwani*.)

Wazo, n. (*ma-*), thought, fancy, idea, notion, supposition, reflection. *Yu katika mawazo yake*, he is abstracted, buried in thought, absent-minded. (Cf. *waza*, and syn. *thana, nia, fikara*.)

-we, a. form of *wake*, his, hers,

its,—affixed to nouns. E.g. *mwana-we*, his son, *wenziwe*, his companions. (So *-le*, *-ze*, *-ye*.)

Wea, v. be good for, be in favour of, be useful to, turn out well for, be the property of. (Perh. an Ap. form from *-wa*, be, like *wia*. See *-wa*.)

Wee, for *wewe*, *weye*, you,—pron. of 2 Pers. Sing.

Weka, v. one of the very common Swahili words, with the general sense 'place, put, set,' and a great variety of applications, e. g. (1) put in position, set fast, place firm, e. g. *w. ulimwengu*, of the creation; *w. msinji*, lay a firm foundation; *kikao tulichomweka*, the position in which we placed him. (2) put down, put off, e. g. *w. selaha*, lay down weapons; *w. mzigo*, put down a load. (3) put aside, put away, put off, delay, adjourn. *W. hukumu*, defer judgement; *w. chakula*, put away food (till wanted), (or else, put ready, prepare). (4) reserve, store up, keep for use, e. g. *w. akiba*, lay up in store; *w. kisinda*, preserve virginity; *w. wakfu*, devote to religious purposes. (5) make place for, accommodate, have room for, contain, make comfortable, e. g. *ulimwengu wote haumweki*, the world is too small for him; *nyumba hainiweki*, my house is not comfortable. (6) entrust, deposit, commit, allot, assign, e. g. *w. fetha* (*heshima, amana*), give money (honour, a pledge). (7) set firm, establish, appoint, found, institute, e. g. *w. mfalme*, set a chief on his throne; *w. desturi*, establish a custom; *w. sheria*, lay down a law; *kiwekwacho na Muungu, mwanadamu hawezi kukiondoa*, what is appointed by God, man cannot annul. (8) a common form of pious wish or blessing is, *Muungu akuweke*, may God keep you, bless you, make you comfortable,—sometimes with *heri* added. Ps. *wekwa*. Nt. *wekeka*. Ap. *wek-ea*, *-ewa*. Hence *wekana*, e. g. *wekeana masharti*, bet together; *w. heshima*, exchange compliments. Cs. (*wek-esha*, *-eza*, seldom used). Rp. *wekana*. (Cf. *weko*, *kiweko*.)

Wekevu, n. for *welekevu*, expertness, quickness, aptness, intelligence, inclination. (Cf. *elekea*, *-ekevu*.)

Weko, n. (*ma-*), (1) place for putting something, stand, magazine, base, pedestal; (2) piece of metal used for welding. *Tia weko*, weld. (Cf. *weka*, *kiweko*.)

Wekua, v. break up, dig up, break in pieces, e. g. of a roof of concrete, or wall, with crowbars, &c. (Perh. Rv. of *weka*, or variant of *ekua*, *tekua* (which see).)

Wekundu, n. red colour, redness, ruddiness. (See *-ekundu*. The only Bantu word in Swahili for a special modification of white light (*weupe*),—*weusi* denoting its absence.)

*****Wele**, n. and **Weli**, for **Uele** (which see). (Ar.)

Welekeo, n. (1) directing, pointing, put in the way for; (2) direction, admonition, warning, hint. (Cf. *elekea*, and follg., and syn. *onyo*.)

Welekevu, n. and **Wekevu** (which see). (Cf. prec.)

Weleko, n. See **Mbeleko**.

Wema, n. goodness, excellence (of any kind). *Wema hauozi*, goodness never goes bad. (See *-ema*, for the meaning generally. Cf. *uzuri*, and contr. *ubayu*, *uovu*.)

Wembamba, n. thinness, slenderness, fineness, smallness, delicacy (of fabric, texture, grain, &c.). (Cf. *-embamba*, and *bambo*, *ubambo*.)

Wembe, n. (*nyembe*,—but *wembe* appears also to be treated as D 6, cf. dim. *kiwembe*, perh. as dist. from *kijembe*, *jembe*), a razor. (Dist. also *mwembe*, *embe*.)

Wendeleo, **Wendelezo**, and *-i*, **Wenendo**, n. going on (back), proceeding, progress, movement, and fig. conduct, behaviour, way of living. (Cf. *enenda*, *endelea*, &c.)

Wendo, n. (*nyendo*) and **Wenzo** (*nyenzo*), way of going, means of moving,—hence used of mechanical methods and instruments, lever, gear, tackle, roller. E. g. *mti hauendi illa kwa nyenzo*, a log will not move without something to move it. (Cf. *enda, mwendo.*)

Wengi, a plur. of *-ingi*, i. e. *wa-ingi*, many,—agreeing with D 1 (P). (See -ingi.)

Wengu, n. (—) or **Wengo,** the spleen.

Wenu, a. form of *-enu*, yours (plur.),—agreeing with D 1 (S, P), D 2 (S), D 4 (S). (See -enu.)

Wenzi, n. (1) *u-enzi*, friendliness, friendly association, companionship; (2) plur. of *mwenzi*, friend, companion; (3) sometimes for *jenzi* (which see), rule, power, sovereignty.

Werevu, n. cunning, shrewdness, cleverness, sagacity, worldly wisdom. (Cf. *-erevu*, and *welekevu*, *akili*, *ujanja.*)

Weu, n. (*nyeu*), clearing, open space for planting, place free from trees, forest glade. (Cf. follg., and *-eupe, weupe.*)

Weuo, n. making white, purifying, cleaning. (Cf. *eua*, and prec.)

Weupe, n. (1) whiteness, white or grey colour, a light tint in general; (2) light as opp. to shade or darkness, brightness, and esp. of the dawn, morning light; (3) cleanness; (4) fig. purity, innocence, integrity, guilelessness. (Cf. *-eupe, eua, weu*, and contr. *weusi.*)

Weusi, n. (1) blackness, black or dark colour, a dark tint in general (e. g. of blue, green, red); (2) absence of light, darkness, gloom, obscurity (not used of dirt, as such, or in fig. (moral) sense, like *weupe*; cf. *-eusi*); (3) form of a. *-eusi*,—agreeing with D 1 (P).

Wevi, n. and **Wezi,** plur. of *mwivi, mwizi*, thief, i. e. *wa-ivi*.

Wewe, pron. of 2 Pers. Sing., you,—also *weye, wee*. In sudden emphatic address often combined with *ee, ewe!* you there! I say, you! (See **Mimi.**)

Wewedeka, v. also **Weweteka, Wewezeka, Ewedeka,** talk in sleep or in delirium, or unconsciously. Cs. *wewede-sha, -shwa*. (Cf. *payuka, payo.*)

Weza, v. (1) be able, be strong, be capable, have strength. The forms of the Negative Present, *siwezi, huwezi*, &c., are regularly used in the special sense, I am sick, (ill, unwell, &c.),—so much so that *hawezi* is sometimes treated as an adj. and even a verb-root (see **Hawezi,** and generally under **Jambo**). (2) have power (means, liberty, opportunity, occasion, option, &c.), with an Infinitive following, or like the auxiliary 'can' with a verb-root form without the Infinitive sign *ku*. E. g. *aweza kwenda*, he has strength to walk, leave to go, &c. *Naweza mpiga*, I can beat him. (3) get mastery over, control, overcome, defeat, subdue,—with nouns. *Simba alimweza*, the lion overcame him. (4) be able to bear, endure, tolerate. E. g. *ukali wako hawauwezi*, they cannot endure your tyranny. Rf. *jiweza*, have power over oneself (or, in oneself, of oneself), have self-control, be temperate. Hence *jiwezea*, be able to get on (to manage, to do for oneself), be independent. Ps. *wezwa.* Nt. *wezeka*, e. g. be practicable, possible, permissible, probable,—and also commonly *wezekana*, e. g. *hawezekani*, he is invincible, beyond all control. Ap. *wez-ea, -ewa*. Cs. *weze-sha, -shwa*, e. g. empower, give authority (leave, strength, means, &c.) to. Rp. *wezana.* (Cf. *uwezo, mweza, hawezi.*)

Wia, Wiana, v. Ap. and Rp. of *wa*, v. (which see).

Wifi, n. (—), brother-in-law, sister-in-law. (Cf. *shemeji, mwamua.*)

Wika, v. crow,—of a cock. *Jogoo lawika*, the cock crows. *Likiwika lisiwike kutakucha*, whether the cock crows or not, the morning will come. (See Jogoo.)

*Wilaya, n. district, province, region, country. (Ar. Cf. Ulaya.)

-wili, a. of second numeral (*mbili* with D 4 (P), D 6 (P)), two, a pair of, together, both. *Marra mbili*, twice. *Upanga mkali kuwili*, a two-edged sword. *Walikwenda wawili*, they went together, or, they both went. *Viwili*, in a twofold way, doubly. (Cf. *pili* and *marudufu*, and perh. *mwili*.)

Wima, n. being perpendicular, uprightness, standing up. (Cf. *ima, uima*, and *simama*.)

Wimbi, n. (1) (*ma*-), a wave. *Hapana maji, yasiyo mawimbi*, no water without waves. *Killa chombo na wimbile*, every vessel has its waves to meet. *Mawimbi ya kuum'ka*, breakers. *Mawimbi ya mkoba*, rolling waves, swell, rollers. *Maw. ya kwelea*, storm waves, high seas. (2) (—) and Uwimbi, a small kind of grain (*Eleusine coracana*, Sacl.). (Cf. *kiwimbi*, and perh. *vimba*.)

Winda, v. hunt,—of game in general, animals and birds, large and small, with weapons, nets, dogs, &c. Also of pursuing a flying foe, or fugitive. (Cf. *mwinda, uwindaji, windo*, and perh. *uwinda*, and syn. *saka*.)

Winda, n. See Uwinda.

Windo, n. (1) act (art, manner, &c.) of hunting; (2) (*ma*-), what is got by hunting, booty, prey. (Cf. *winda*.)

Wingi, n. much (of), plenty, abundance, a quantity, a great deal. (Cf. *-ingi, ungi*, and syn. *tele, marithawa, neema, baraka*.)

Wingu, n. (*ma*-), cloud,—or what resembles a cloud. *W. la mvua*, rain cloud. *W. wa moshi*, cloud of smoke. Thick cloud is called *nene, zito, kubwa, jeusi*. *Wingu la giza*, a dark cloud. (Cf. *uwingu, gubari, mavunde*.)

*Wino, n. ink,—made in Z. of a gum (*gundi*), lampblack (*moshi wa taa*), and rice burnt black and powdered. *Kidau cha wino*, inkstand, inkpot.

Wishwa, n. (—, or ? *nishwa*), chaff, husks, bran. (Cf. *kumvi, kapi*.)

*Witha, n. See Uwitha. (Ar.)

Wito, n. (1) infection, infectiousness, contagion. *Pata (pewa) w.*, be infected. *Ndui ina wito sana*, small-pox is very infectious (cf. *ambukiza*). (2) casting,—of metal in a mould; also, a mould for casting (cf. *ila* and *subu*); (3)? calling, call, from *ita* (cf. *mwito*).

*Wituri, a. odd,—of numbers, i. e. not even. (Ar.)

Wivu, n. and Uivu (which see), also Uwivu.

-wivu, a. (1) and -ivu, jealous, envious (cf. prec.); (2) and most commonly -bivu, ripe, mature, fully developed. (Cf. *iva*, and n. *-ovu, -bovu*.)

Wiwa, v. Ap. Ps. of -wa, v. (See -wa.)

Wo, relative form of -o,—agreeing with D 1 (S, P), D 2 (S), D 4 (S), but used separately only in a few phrases, e. g. *wo wote*, any and all, all of whatsoever kind. (See -o.)

-wo, (1) relative as prec. used as pfx. in verbs, and generally shortened to -o, e. g. *watu walio wema*, persons who are good; (2) contracted for *wako*, and subjoined to nouns, e.g. *mwanawo*, or *mwanao*, your son.

Woga, n. (no plur.), cowardice, fear, timidity, shyness. *W. mkubwa*, panic. *Fanya (ona, ingiwa na) w.*, be frightened. (Cf. *oga, -oga, ogopa, ogofya*, and syn. *hofu*.)

Wogofya, n. (*nyogofya*, and *ma*-), causing fear, threat, menace, terrifying. (Cf. *oga, ogopa*, and syn. *kamia*.)

Wokovu, n. (no plur.), deliverance, rescue, escape, salvation. (Cf. *okoa, mwokozi*, and *ponya*.)

Wongo, n. See Uongo, -ongo.

Wonyesho, n. a showing, exhibiting, demonstrating, pointing out, &c. Also *wonyeshano*, showing to each other, mutual display, general exhibition. (Cf. *onya, onyesha, ona, onyo.*)

*****Worari**, n. See **Urari**.

*****Worotha**, n. See **Urotha**.

Wote, a. form of *-ote*, all, the whole,—agreeing with D 1 (S, P), D 2 (S), D 4 (S). *Twende wote*, let us all go,—but commonly of *two* persons, i.e. let us both go, or, go together. *Twende sote*, let us all go. *Wote wawili*, both of them, both together. (Cf. *-ote, sote.*)

Woto, n. verbal of *ota*, v. (which see) in all three senses, viz. (1) growing (as a vegetable), vegetation; (2) dreaming; (3) getting warm, basking, warmth. (Rarely found, perh. from this ambiguity of meaning.)

Y.

Y represents (1) the same sound as in English, i.e. a consonantal *i*, which in Swahili usually takes the place of *i* before another vowel, but often is not distinguishable from a slurred *i*. (2) It is used in a few words to represent a very light and evanescent sound of *i* between certain consonants, e.g. it is often written in *kunywa*, to drink,—from the root *nya*, and *kinywa*, from the same.

Y, as a formative, when inserted before the final -*a* of some verbs, gives them a Cs. meaning, e.g. *pona*, get well, *ponya*, make well, cure, save,—*ogopa*, fear, *ogofya*, make afraid.

Y-, as a pfx., is the form taken by *i*, before a vowel, and thus appears (1) in pronom. adj. agreeing with D 2 (P), D 4 (S), e.g. *miti yangu*, my trees; *nyumba yao*, their house. (2) in verbs, e.g. *miti yaota*, the trees grow; *nyumba yalijengwa*, the house was built.

Ya, prep. form of *-a*, of,—agreeing with D 2 (P), D 5 (P), D 6 (S), e.g. *nyumba ya mgeni*, the stranger's house; *makasha ya mbau*, boxes of wood. But *ya* is also the form used most generally for 'of,' whenever the reference is indefinite and general. E.g. *ya nini?* why? *ya kwamba*, that (conj.); *ya kuwa*, because, in that. Thus it is used continually with adverbs to form prepositional phrases, e.g. *mbali ya*, far from; *karibu ya*, near to; *mbele ya*, in front of; *juu ya*, above; *chini ya*, below, &c. (See -a.)

Ya, verb-form, they are,—agreeing with D 5 (P), e.g. *makasha ya tayari*, the boxes are ready,—and so in place of *ni*, or Present Tense of *wa*, v. (which see).

Ya-, pfx. corresponding to D 5 (P) in (1) pronom. adj., e.g. *makasha yangu*, for *ya-angu*, my boxes; (2) verbs, as Plur. Pfx., subjective and objective, e.g. *magari yanayachukua makasha*, the carts are carrying the boxes, or *yayachukua*, i.e. *ya-a-ya chukua*,—*ya* coalescing with *a* following, as in *yangu*, above.

*****Yaani**, conj. and **Yani**, that is, that is to say, I mean. (Ar., lit. 'it meant.')

*****Yabisi**, a. and **Yabis**, dry, hard, solid, e.g. *udongo yabisi*, hard, parched earth. *Baridi yabis*, rheumatism. Sometimes also as v., be hard, dry, with Nt. *yabisika*, in same sense, and Cs. *yabisi-sha, -shwa*, make hard. (Ar. Cf. syn. *-gumu, -shupafu.*)

Yai, n. (*mayai, mai*), an egg. *Taga yai*, lay an egg. *Atamia mayai*, sit on eggs. *Y. bichi*, fresh, uncooked egg. *Y. viza (bovu)*, bad (set, rotten) egg. *Y. la kutokosa*, boiled egg. *Y. la kukanga*, fried, poached egg.

Yake, a. pronom. form of *-ake*, his, her, its,—agreeing with D 2 (P), D 5 (P), D 6 (S).

*****Yakini**, n. truth, certainty, assurance, proof. E.g. *najua y. ya habari*, I know the truth of the story.

F f

Kwa yakini, really and truly. *Wataka yakini gani?* What sort of proof do you want? — a. true, certain, proved. — v. be sure,—but usually as follg. (Ar. Cf. follg., and syn. *hakika, kweli, thabiti.*)

*Yakinia, v. resolve on, make up one's mind to, be sure of, determine on. Ps. *yakiniwa*. Nt. *yakinika*. Cs. *yakini-sha, -shwa*, e. g. make sure, establish, confirm, prove. (Ar. Cf. prec., and syn. *hakikia, thabutisha.*)

Yako, (1) a. pronom. form of *-ako*, your, yours,—agreeing with D 2 (P), D 5 (P), D 6 (S) (see -ako) ; (2) verb-form, they are (there),—prefix *ya*, agreeing with D 5 (P), and *ko*, for *huko*.

*Yakuti, n. ruby, sapphire. (Ar. Cf. *johari.*)

Yale, a. form of *-le*,—agreeing with D 5 (P), i. e. those. (See Yule.)

Yambo, sometimes used for jambo (which see).

*Yamini, n. (1) right hand ; (2) solemn oath, sworn with right hand on the Coran. Thus 'take a solemn oath' is *twaa (piga, apa, -la) yamini*. E. g. *naweza kula yamini ya kuwa simjui*, I can solemnly swear that I do not know him. (Ar. Cf. B. syn. *mkono wa kulia*, right hand.)

*Yamkini, and Yumkini, n. possibility, e. g. *kwa yamkini*, possibly, probably. — a. possible, likely, probable, e.g. *mambo haya ni yakini*, these things are possible. — v. be possible (likely, probable). *Itayamkini kulia burre wee?* Will it be likely you should cry for nothing? *Haiyamkini*, it is out of the question. (In Ar. an impersonal form of the verb, but in Swahili treated as above, like *yakini*. Cf. *weza, wezekana.*)

Yangu, a. pronom. form of *-angu*, my, mine,—agreeing with D 2 (P), D 5 (P), D 6 (S). (See -angu.)

*Yani, conj. See Yaani. Also for *ya nini?* why?

Yao, a. pronom. form of *-ao*, their, theirs,—agreeing with D 2 (P), D 5 (P), D 6 (S). (See -ao.)

*Yasi, n. a yellow powder from India used as a cosmetic. (Cf. *dalia, liwa.*)

*Yasmini, n. a cultivated kind of jasmine. (Ar. Cf. *afu.*)

*Yatima, n. a fatherless, motherless, or orphan child. (Ar.)

Yavuyavu, n. a butcher's term for 'lungs,' or 'lights,' of an animal. (Cf. *pafu, pumu.*)

*Yaya, n. (*ma-*), a nurse, an ayah. *Killa mtoto na yaya wake*, every child with its nurse. (Hind. Cf. *mlezi.*)

Yaya, a. a peculiar form of the adj. *haya (huyu)*, used only in combination with it for emphasis, i. e. *yaya haya*, just these very things. So *lili hili, zizi hizi, vivi hivi,* &c., and cf. *yayo*.

Yayi, n. (*ma-*), egg. (See Yai.)

Yayo, a. the relative corresponding to *yaya*, a. (which see), e. g. *yayo hayo*, like *papo hapo, kuko huko*.

Ye, (1) relative pfx. of 1, 2, and 3 Sing. referring to persons and animals. Only used independently in such phrases as *ye yote*, any one whatever, whosoever ; (2) used in combination with verbs,—often heard as *-e* only. E. g. *aliye mrefu*, he who is tall. *Anayempenda*, he who loves him. (3) shortened for *yake* (which see), and subjoined to nouns and adverbs, e. g. *nyumbaye*, his house; *baadaye*, after that. (4) used in one form of the personal pronouns, except *wao*, i. e. *miye* for *mimi*, *siye* for *sisi*, &c.

Yee, for *yeye*, pron. of 3 Pers. Sing., he, she, him, her.

Yetu, Yenyewe, Yenyi, Yenu, forms of *-etu, -enyewe, -enyi, -enu*,— agreeing with D 2 (P), D 5 (P), D 6 (S).

Yeyuka, v. melt, become fluid, melt away. Cs. *yeyu-sha, -shwa*, cause to melt, melt.

Yo, (1) relative pfx., which,— agreeing with D 2 (P), D 5 (P), D 6 (S),—only used independently in *yo yote*, whatever, any whatsoever; (2) subjoined to verbs; (3) shortened for *yako*, your, yours (see -ako), subjoined to nouns, e.g. *babayo*, your father; (4) cf. form of *huyu*, used in reference, i.e. *huyo*, that person yonder. (Cf. *huyu*.)

Yoga, n. (—), mushroom. (See Uyoga.)

Yonga, v. sway, bow or bend down, stagger under a weight or from feebleness, &c. E.g. of a tree in a wind, vessel at sea, a man weak from illness, &c. Cs. *yong-esha, -eshwa*. (Cf. *wayawaya, yumba, sita, lewa*.)

Yote, a. form of *-ote*, all, the whole (which see),—agreeing with D 2 (P), D 5 (P), D 6 (S). Sometimes also used with D 1 (S), e.g. *ye yote*, whatever person; *awaye yote*, whoever he is.

Yowe, n. a loud cry, shout, scream, esp. of a call for help. *Piga y.*, give a shout. (Cf. *kelele, kilio, kiyowe*.)

Yu, verb-form, he (she) is,—used as 3 Pers. Sing. Pres. Tense of *-wa*, like other pers. pfxs. (see -wa, Ni),—the simple *a* never being used thus independently, but only in combination with a verb.

Yu-, (1) pfx. of 3 Pers. Sing., referring to a person, but in Z. not usual in verb-forms, and only before the Pres. Tense sign of monosyllabic verbs, e.g. *yuwa* (for *yu-a-wa*), he is; *yuna*, he has; *yuaja*, he comes. (It is, however, regularly used in the follg. *yuko (-po, -mo), yule, yupi*.)

Yuko, verb-form, he (she) is (there), —agreeing with D 1 (S), i.e. *yu*, pers. pfx. of 3 Pers. Sing., and *-ko*, for *huko*. So *yupo, yumo*. (Cf. prec.)

Yule, a. form of *-le*, that,—agreeing with D 1 (S). The other forms of *-le* are *wale, ule, ile, lile, kile, vile, yale, zile, pale, kule, mle*. (Cf. *huyu, -le*, and prec.)

Yumba, Yumba-yumba, v. sway, wave to and fro, stagger, e.g. of trees, a balanced pole, a drunken or feeble person. (Cf. *yonga, waya, sita, lewa*.)

*****Yumkini**, v. See Yamkini. (Ar.)

Yumo, verb-form, he (she) is within. (Cf. *yuko, yu, -mo*.)

Yuna, verb-form, he (she) has. (Cf. *yu*, and *na*.)

Yungi yungi, n. (*ma-*), name of a blue water-lily (*Nymphaea stellata*, Sacl.).

Yupi, a. form of *-pi* (which see), agreeing with D 1 (S), which person? Also for *yu wapi*, where is he (she)? (Cf. *yu, -pi*.)

Yupo, verb-form, he (she) is here. (Cf. *yuko, yu, -po*.)

Z.

Z represents the same sound as in English. But the sounds of *s* and *z* are not always easily distinguished in Swahili pronunciation, and words of Arabic origin involving the letters *Thal, Thad, Thah*, if not written with *Th*, or *Dh*, are (by some) written with Z.

Hence words not found under Z may be looked for under S, or Th.

Z-, for Zi before a vowel in verbs and pronom. adjs. See Zi.

-za, and **-sha**, are the terminations characteristic of the Cs. form of Swahili verbs—a form which under the general idea of cause includes a wide variety of meanings and applications, some of which may be distinguished as:—

A. *Causal*, and so (1) *Causal* simply, cause to (be or act), have done, get done. (2) *Compulsive*, force to (—). (3) *Permissive*, allow to (—). (4) *Attractive*, induce to (—). (5) *Passive*, let (be or act). (6) *Consequential*, lead to, end in, have the result of, be followed by being (acting, doing).

B. *Intensive*, or emphatic, i.e. be emphatically, act energetically, in the way indicated by any verb.

(For illustrations cf. any verb,

which is treated at length in its derivative forms *toa, penda, ona, funga*, &c.)

Za, prep. form of *-a* (which see), of,—agreeing with D 4 (P), D 6 (P).

Zaa, v. denotes vital reproduction, the whole process or a stage in it, of male or female, in any region of organic life,—thus, bear offspring, produce fruit, procreate, beget, have children, be pregnant, give birth to, be delivered (of a child), be fruitful (productive, fertile). Ps. *zawa*, but commonly *zaliwa*. Nt. *zalika*. Ap. *za-lia, -liwa, -lika*, e. g. bear to (for, by, at), &c. Obs. *amezaliwa mtoto*, may mean (1) a child has been born, or (2) he had a child born to him. Also *zalia* is sometimes used passively, e. g. *alizalia hapa*, he was born here, he is a native of this place (—as if for *zaliwia*). Hence *zali-sha, -shwa*, e. g. cause to bear (to be born), beget, fertilize, make productive, assist at childbirth, act as midwife, &c. Also *zaliana*, breed together, multiply. (Cf. *zao, mzao, mzazi, uzazi, kizazi, -zazi, kizalia, mzalia, ? mzee*.)

***Zabadi**, n. civet, musk,—substance taken from the civet cat, and used in perfumes. (Ar. Cf. *zabidi, ngawa, fungo*.)

***Zabibu**, n. (—), a grape, a raisin, fruit of the vine *mzabibu*. (Ar.)

***Zabidi**, v. take civet from the civet cat. (Ar. Cf. *zabadi*.)

***Zabuni**, v. buy, bid at an auction. The common word is *nunua*. (Ar. Dist. *sabuni*, soap.)

***Zaburi**, n. (—), a psalm, the psalter. (Ar. Dist. *saburi*, patience.)

***Zafarani**, n. saffron. (Ar.)

Zagaa, v. shine, glisten, give light, illuminate. Ps. *zagawa*, e. g. be lighted up, be enlightened. Cs. *zaga-za, -zwa*, cause to shine. (Cf. more usual *ng'aa, mulika*.)

***Zaidi**, adv. and **Zayidi**, more, in addition, in a greater degree or quantity. *Zaidi ya (kuliko, kama)*, more than, beside. Also as n. *zaidi ya habari*, further news. (Ar. Cf. *zidi, ziada*, and *juu*.)

***Zaka**, n. (—), tithe, offering for religious purposes. (Ar.)

Zake, Zako, a. forms of *-ake*, and *-ako*, their, theirs, your, yours,—agreeing with D 4 (P), D 6 (P).

Zama, v. (1) sink in a fluid, be immersed, dive, be drowned, sink down; (2) fig. plunge (into), be immersed (in), be overwhelmed (by). E. g. *kilimia kikizama kwa jua, huzuka kwa mvua*, if the Pleiades set in fine weather, they will rise in wet. *Zama katika elimu (katika bahari ya maneno)*, plunge into study (into the sea of words, e. g. a dictionary). Ap. *zam-ia, -iwa*, e. g. *z. lulu*, dive for pearls. Cs. *zam-isha, -ishwa*, e. g. engage as a diver, contract for diving, immerse, drown. (Cf. *mzamo, mzamishi*, and syn. *tota, didimia, zizimia*.)

***Zamani**, n. (1) time, period, e. g. *zamani moja*, at a certain time, once upon a time,—commonly in the plural. *Zamani hizi*, modern times. *Z. za kale*, ancient times. (2) ancient times, antiquity, the past. Thus often as adv. long ago, in ancient days, some time past, and sometimes of the future, e. g. *mwanamke huyu atakaa hapa zamani*, this woman will remain here for an (indefinite) time. (Ar. Cf. *wakati*, and dist. *samani, thamani*.)

***Zambarau**, n. fruit of a large tree (*mzambarau*), like a damson or sloe.

***Zamu**, n. (—), (1) properly, a six hours' spell of work, or watching; (2) period of duty or occupation, e. g. sentry, patrol, turn, innings. *Z. yangu*, it is my turn. *Ngoja z., kaa z., keti z., shika (linda) z.*, are all phrases used for keeping watch. Cf. *waliwekana zamu, wangine kulala, wangine na macho*, they arranged watches amongst themselves, some to sleep, some to remain awake. (Ar. Cf. *kesha, lindo*.)

*Zangefuri, n. and Zingefuri, cinnabar, anatta. (Ar.)

Zangu, a. form of -angu (which see), my, mine,—agreeing with D 4 (P), D 6 (P). Obs. naenda zangu, I am going away. (See Enda.)

*Zani, n. same as uzini, uzinzi (which see). (Ar.)

Zao, (1) n. (ma-), fruit, produce, product, offspring. (Cf. zaa, mzao, uzao, kizao.) (2) a. form of -ao, their, theirs,—agreeing with D 4 (P), D 6 (P). (See -ao.)

Zarambo, n. (—), a spirit distilled from palm-wine, tembo (Str.).

*Zari, n. gold thread, (braid, brocade). (? Hind.)

*Zatiti, v. put in order, put ready, arrange, prepare, provide. (Ar. for the common words tengeneza, andaa, weka tayari.)

*Zawadi, n. present, gift, keepsake,—generally of what is given on some special or extraordinary occasion, e.g. starting on or returning from a journey,—not of regular customary, expected gifts, i.e. fees, reward for service, prize, &c. (Ar. For presents generally see bakshishi.)

*Zawaridi, n. (ma-), Java sparrow,—a bird which swarms in the stone houses of Z.

*Zayidi, adv. See Zaidi. (Ar.)

-ze, (1) subjoined to a noun, shortened form for zake, his, hers, its; (2) at the end of a verb is often the subjunct. mood of Cs. form in -za.

*Zebakh, n. and Zibakh, mercury, quicksilver. (Ar.)

-zee, a. aged, old,—of animate objects,—others being described as -a zamani, -a kale, -a siku nyingi, -kukuu. (Cf. mzee, kizee, and perh. zaa.)

Zema, a. an occasional form of -ema, good, for njema, agreeing with D 4 (P), D 6 (P). (Cf. this form in the pronom. adjs. and -ote, -enyi, -enyewe.)

Zenu, Zenyewe, Zenyi, Zetu, a. forms of -enu, enyewe, enyi, etu (which see),—agreeing with D 4 (P), D 6 (P).

Zeze, n. (—), a native stringed instrument, a kind of banjo, or guitar, common in Z.

Zi, verb-form, they are,—agreeing with D 4 (P), D 6 (P), and taking the place of ni, or Pres. Tense Indic. of -wa. Nyumba hizi zi nzuri, these houses are good.

Zi- (often Z- before a vowel) is a formative (1) of pronominal adjectives, the pfx. agreeing with D 4 (P), D 6 (P); (2) of verbs, both subjective and objective pfxs. agreeing with the above; and (3) obs. zizi hizi, these very, just these.

Ziara, n. (ma-), tomb, burying-place. (Ar. 'place of visiting.' Cf. siara, zuru, and kaburi.)

*Ziba, v. fill up a hole (crevice, opening of any sort),—and so, stop up, cork, plug, dam, fill up, close, shut off. Ps. zibwa. Nt. zib-ika, -ikana. Ap. zib-ia, -iwa, e.g. fill up with (for, in, &c.). Cs. zib-isha, -ishwa. Rp. zibana, e.g. stop itself up, get stopped up, get filled up. (Cf. zibo, kizibo, zibua, and cf. fukia, funga, katiza.)

Zibo, n. (ma-), a stopper, plug, cork,—anything that stops an opening. Dim. kizibo. (Cf. prec.)

Zibua, v. Rv. of ziba, unclose an opening, remove a stopper or plug, uncork, clear a hole, open (a closed aperture). Ps. zibuliwa. Nt. zibuka. Ap. zibu-lia, -liwa. (Cf. prec. and ziba.)

*Zidi, v. (1) become more (greater, larger, taller, longer, &c.), grow, increase, multiply, be more and more. With an Infinitive following, it is very often best translated by the adv. 'more' or a comparative adverb, e.g. anazidi kwenda, he is going faster (or, further). Azidi kujua, he knows better. Habari inazidi kuenea, the news goes o.. ... Zidi also means 'come..., ... kumpiga?

Shall I beat him more? (2) be the greater, have more power (than), outstrip, gain on (in a race), be superior (to), e.g. *hao ndio watuzidio sisi*, these are the persons who surpass us (are better than us, more powerful, &c.). *Maseyidi wa Unguja waliwazidi*, the sultans of Zanzibar were their overlords. (3) get the better of, beat, overwhelm, reduce to straits. E. g. *kazi imenizidi sana*, the work is quite too much for me. This meaning is more clearly shown in the Ps. (see below). Ps. *zidiwa*, e.g. (1) be surpassed; (2) very often 'be beaten by, be put in difficulties by,' and so, be in want of help about. E. g. *nimezidiwa*, I am in a difficulty, or with *fetha*, I am in want of cash, or with *karatasi*, I have run short of paper. *Tulizidiwa na mvua*, we were quite beaten by the rain. Ap. *zid-ia, -iwa*, e.g. increase to, grow upon. Sometimes Act. *Muungu awazidie afya*, may God grant them continuance of health. Cs. *zidi-sha, -shwa*. Hence *zidi-shia, -shiwa*. (Ar. Cf. *zaidi, ziada, zidisho, mazidio*, and syn. B. *ongeza*.)

*Zidi, n. (*ma-*), Zidio (*ma-*), Zidisho (*ma-*), all used occasionally for 'increase, addition, augmentation, supplement,' &c. (Ar. Cf. prec.)

*Zifuri, n. See Sifuri. (Ar.)

Zika, v. bury, assist in burying, attend a funeral. Ps. *zikwa*. Ap. *zik-ia, -iwa*, e. g. bury in (with, for, &c.). Cs. *zisha, zishwa*, arrange (manage, provide, attend to or at) a funeral. (Cf. *mzishi, mazishi, maziko*.)

*Ziki, n. *kanzu ya ziki*, a kanzu with a collar, i. e. with white stitching round the neck, but not the usual red-silk embroidered stitching. (Cf. *kanzu*, and Ar. *zik*, collar.)

*Zikri, n. used in Z. of a kind of religious dance, like those of the dervishes, with violent jerking of the body and ejaculations of *Allah hai*. (Ar. 'meditation.')

Zile, a. form of *-le*, those,—agreeing with D 4 (P), D 6 (P). (Cf. *yule*.)

Zima, v. repress, quench, quell, extinguish, put out, rub out,—in literal and fig. sense, but with a limited range of application (the idea being not merely to restrain, put a check on (*zuia*), nor to stop access, close an avenue or passage (*ziba*), nor bring to an end, destroy (*komesha*), but rather stop by active repression, turning back on itself), e. g. of fire, *z. moto*, put out a fire,— the commonest use, but also of light, *z. taa*, and also *z. nuru*; of thirst (hunger), *z. kiu* (*njaa*); of life and consciousness, *z. roho*. *Zima maji ya chumvi*, change salt water into fresh. Also fig. *z. vita* (*ugomvi, hasira*), quell a war (quarrel, anger). Also as a Nt. *moto umezima*, the fire has gone out. *Amezima roho*, the man has fainted, become unconscious. Ps. *zimwa*. Nt. *zimika*. Ap. *zim-ia, -iwa*, e. g. put off for (by, in, with, &c.), and (like *zima*) *zimia roho*, faint. Ap. *zim-ilia, -iliwa, -iliza, -ilizwa*, e. g. *zimiliza maneno*, rub out (written) words. Cs. *zim-isha, -ishwa*, and intens. (Cf. *kuzimu, mzimu, wazimu, zimwe, zimua, zizimia*, but dist. follg. *-zima, uzima*, &c.)

-zima, a. whole, sound, unhurt, entire, alive, perfect, in good health, full grown, adult. E. g. *mimi mzima*, I am quite well. *Watu wazima*, grown-up people. *Fungu zima*, a whole heap. *Samaki mzima*, a live fish. (See Uzima, and cf. syn. *hai, kamili, -pevu*, and dist. *zima*, v.)

Zimua, v. Rv. of *zima*, with similar meaning, i.e. quench, repress, take the life or strength out of, e. g. of taking away heat, sharpness, bitter taste, newness (of liquids) by dilution or otherwise. *Z. maji ya moto*, cool hot water. *Z. tembo*, reduce the strength of fermented palm-wine. Ps. *zimuliwa*. Nt. *zimuka*. Ap. *zimu-lia, -liwa*. (Cf. *zima*, and note.)

Zimwe, n. and **Zimwi**, (1) of a quenched, extinguished, lifeless condition, e.g. *makaa ya zimwe*, dead coals, burnt-out embers. Also as a. *makaa mazimwe*. (2) condition of a hollow cocoanut, without milk or kernel (cf. *kizimbwe*), e.g. *nazi ina zimwe*, the cocoanut has nothing inside. But perh. conn. with (3) a spirit, fairy, demon, ogre, goblin, ghost (cf. *jini, pepo*, &c.). (Cf. *zima*, and note *msima, wazimu, kuzimu*, &c.,—all of the spirit world.)

Zindika, v. (1) inaugurate, dedicate, initiate, hold an opening ceremony (for), formally open; (2) protect with a charm or spell. E.g. *z. nyumba*, have a house-warming. *Z. mtoto*, put a child under a charm,—for protection. (Cf. follg., and syn. *tabaruki*, and *zinduka* in same sense, see note.)

Zindiko, n. (*ma-*), (1) opening ceremony, inauguration, &c.; (2) protecting charm, spell. (Cf. prec., and *zinduko*.)

Zindua, v. (1) open, declare open, inaugurate; (2) wake up suddenly from sleep, wake with a start (cf. *zusha, vumbusha*). Ps. *zinduliwa*. Nt. *zinduka*, i.e. (1) be opened, inaugurated, &c.; (2) wake with a start, be suddenly wakened,—and (in this sense, commonly) *zindukana*. (Cf. *zindika*, in same sense, inaugurate,—the same ceremony being at once an opening for special uses, and closing for all other uses. And obs. seeming identity with *sindika (shindika), sindua, sinduka, shinduka*.)

Zinga, v. used both act. and neut. of movement in a circle, i.e. (1) go round, go about; (2) stroll, walk, loiter, waver, gad about,—with a bad object or none; (3) turn about, waver, change, chop, veer, e.g. of winds, change of mind, &c.; (4) act., turn round, roll round, coil, wind. Ps. *zingwa*, e.g. (1) be turned round; (2) be surrounded. Ap. *zing-ia, -iwa*, and *zing-ilia, -iliwa*, e.g. *unywele ukamzingilia mguu*, the hair turned itself round his leg. Hence *zing-iliza, -ilizwa*. Cs. *zing-iza, -izwa*. Rp. *zingana*. (Cf. *mzinga, mzingo, kizingo, zingua, mazingile, mazingiwa*, and perh. *msinji*, i.e. *mzingi, usingizi*,—also prob. -*zungu, zungua, zunguka*, &c.)

Zingamana, v. be of a turning, twisting, curving kind, e.g. of a winding river. (St. Rp. of prec.)

Zingizi, n. See **Usingizi**.

Zingo, n. (*ma-*), turn, twist, bend, revolution. (Cf. *mzingo*, and *zinga*.)

Zingua, v. Rv. of *zinga*, (1) unroll, unfold, unwrap; (2) relieve of a spell or charm, disenchant, exorcize, rid of some evil thing. Ps. *zinguliwa*. Ap. *zingu-lia, -liwa*. (Cf. *zindua*, and follg.)

Zinguo, n. (*ma-*), exorcism, removal of a spell, riddance of an evil. (Cf. prec.)

*****Zini**, v. commit adultery, fornication,—of man or woman. Ps. *zinwa* (of woman). Ap. *zin-ia, -iwa*. Cs. *zin-isha, -ishwa*. — n. See **Uzini**. (Ar. Cf. *uzini, zani, -zinifu, uzinzi*, and syn. *fisidi*.)

Zio, n. (*ma-*), post used in making the sides of a native hut,—commonly *nguzo* in Z. (Cf. *uzio*.)

Zira, v. hate, have a grudge against, but in Z. *chukia* is usual.

-zito, a. (1) heavy,—in weight; (2) difficult, hard to deal with, of serious import; (3) severe, harsh, hard to bear; (4) sad, depressed, weighed down, heavy; (5) slow, sluggish, clumsy, awkward; (6) of fluids, thick; (7) pregnant. (Cf. *uzito*, and *-gumu*, and contr. *rahisi, -epesi*.)

Ziwa, n. (*ma-*), (1) lake, pond, marsh, pool; (2) breast (female), milk-producing gland, in plur.

maziwa, milk,—human or animal. (Cf. *uziwa*.)

Zizi, n. (*ma-*), (1) enclosure for keeping animals, yard, fold, pen, stable, cowshed. Dim. *kizizi* (cf. *ua, banda, kitalu,* and dist. *sizi, msizi*). (2) adj. form in the phrase *zizi hizi*, these very, just these,—agreeing with D 4 (P), D 6 (P). (Cf. *papa hapa, yaya haya,* &c. See Zi.)

Zizima, v. and **Sisima**, become cool, get cold, settle down, sink down, be calm and quiet, be composed. *Maji ya kuzizima,* very cold water, still water. *Chakula kimezizima,* the food is quite cold (cf. *poa*). Ap. *zizim-ia,-iwa,* has a somewhat specialized meaning, sink quite away, disappear completely (as a stone in water), e.g. *alizizimia, hakuzukia juu tena,* he sank, and did not come to the surface again. Cs. *zizim-isha, -ishwa,* e.g. (1) cause to be very cold; (2) cause to wholly disappear. (Cf. follg. and *zima*, also perh. *sisimizi*, and *didimia,* sink, disappear.)

-**zizima**, a. cold, still, stagnant, e.g. of water. (Cf. follg.)

Zizimua, v. Rv. of *zizima,* (1) lose the chill, get warm; (2) be stirred, excited, irritated. Nt. *zizimuka,* e.g. of nervous irritation.

Zo, (1) relat. particle, used independently only in such phrases as *zo zote,* all whatever, whatsoever,—agreeing with D 4 (P), D 6 (P); (2) relat. pfx. agreeing with the above, in combination with verbs; (3) shortened for *zako,* subjoined to nouns, e.g. *babazo,* your ancestors; (4) cf. *hizo,* form of *hizi* used in reference, those yonder, these mentioned.

Zoa, v. sweep up, gather up, gather in heaps, pick up, e.g. *z. taka* (*kifusi*), gather up mess (rubbish) for removal. Ps. *zolewa*. Nt. *zo-leka,* e.g. *chungu hazizoleki,* ants cannot be swept up and carried away. Ap. *zo-lea, -lewa,* e.g. *fagio (jamvi) la kuzolea,* a brush (mat) for clearing up rubbish. Cs. *zol-esha, -eshwa, -eza, -ezwa.* (Dist. follg.)

Zoea, v. become used (to), get accustomed (to), be familiar (with), be inured (to), practise. Ps. *zoelewa*. Nt. *zoeka,* become a customary thing. Ap. *zoe-lea, -lewa, -leka.* Hence *zoeleza*. Cs. *zoe-za, -zwa,* e.g. *jizoeza,* train oneself (to), practise. (Cf. follg., and *mazoea, mazoezi*.)

Zoea, Zoezo, n. See **Mazoea**, &c.

-**zoefu, -zoelefu**, a. accustomed (to), practised (in), familiar (with), inured (to), e.g. *mzoefu wa kazi,* an experienced workman. (Cf. prec.)

***Zomari**, n. a musical wind-instrument, a kind of pipe, flageolet, clarionet,—of wood, with a harsh, piercing tone,—like a bagpipe. (Cf. *ngoma,* for other instruments.)

Zomea, v. groan,—as an expression of grief, and also of contempt, esp. with an object expressed. E.g. *walimzomea sana,* they groaned at him contemptuously. (Cf. follg., and *ugua, fyonya*.)

Zomeo, n. (*ma-*), groan,—of sorrow or disapproval. (Cf. prec.)

Zote, a. form of -*ote,* all,—agreeing with D 4 (P), D 6 (P).

Zua, v. (1) make a hole in, perforate, bore through, make a way into, e.g. *zua tundu,* bore a hole (cf. *toboa*), *panya amezua kiwambaza,* a rat has made a hole through the wall; (2) bring to light, bring to the surface, hunt out; (3) fig. go into thoroughly, find out all about, get information, suck the brains (of), e.g. *nimemzua habari zote,* I have got out of him all he has to tell; (4) invent, discover, compose, fabricate, tell lies, make innovations, reform, revolutionize. Ps. *zuliwa,* e.g. *mti uliozuliwa tundu,* a tree with a hole bored in it. Nt. *zuka* has a special sense, emerge (as from a hole, out of water, &c.), suddenly appear, start up, bob up (cf. *mzuka, uzuka*). Ap. *zu-lia, -liwa,* e.g. invent for (against, with, &c.), e.g. tell lies about, make false excuses for, &c. Cs. *zu-sha, -shwa*, e.g. cause to emerge, bring to light, invent, reform, produce as new. (Cf. *mzushi, uzushi,* and syn. *vumbua. Zua* should perh. be treated as two words, (1) bore, (2) make new, invent, &c.

Zuia, v. (1) cause to stop, keep back, restrain, hinder, obstruct, prevent, balk, withhold, detain, cause to stop, delay; (2) resist a tendency, —and so, support, prop, strengthen. Ps. *zuiwa.* Nt. *zuika.* Ap. *zuilia, -iliwa, -ilika.* Cs. *zui-za, -zwa.* Rp. *zuiana.* (Cf. *zuio, zuizo, -zuifu,* and syn. *simamisha, komesha, pinga, ziba,* and note.)

-zuifu, a. or **-zuivu** (same with D 4 (P), D 5 (S), D 6), hindering, obstructing, delaying, &c. (Cf. follg., and *zuia.*)

Zuio, n. (*ma-*), and **Zuizo** (*ma-*), hindrance, obstruction, difficulty, support, prop, stopper. (Cf. prec.)

Zulia, n. (—, and *ma-*), a carpet.

Zuli-zuli, n. dizziness, giddiness, confusion. (Cf. *zulu.*)

Zulu, v. be giddy (dizzy), be confused in mind (bewildered, crazy). So also in Ps. *zuliwa,* be flurried, be confused, be driven mad. Nt. *zulika,* e.g. *kichwa chamzulika, akiona shimo,* his head gets dizzy if he sees a precipice. Also Ps. *amezulikwa na kichwa,* he has lost his head, turned giddy. Ap. *zul-ia, -iwa.* Cs. *zul-isha, -ishwa,* e.g. *kileo kimemzulisha kichwa,* drink has driven him crazy, turned his head. (Cf. *mazua,* and cf. *kichaa, kizunguzungu.*)

*Zumaridi, n. emerald. (Ar.)

Zumbua, v. See **Vumbua.**

-zungu, a. (1) strange, wonderful, clever, extraordinary; (2) European. (Cf. *mzungu, uzungu,* and perh. follg.)

Zungua, v. cause to go round, turn round, put round, but usually *zungusha* (see below). Nt. *zunguka,* (1) go round, be round, surround, revolve; (2) go round and round, wind about, be round about, wander about, stroll, make rounds; (2) loiter, waste time, delay,—and so, be tiresome. E.g. *njia inazunguka,* it is a circuitous path, the road winds about. *Boma lauzunguka mji,* the stockade surrounds the village. *Tumeagana, usizunguke,* we have said good-bye, so do not wait about. Hence *zunguk-ia, -iwa.* In Ps. *zungukwa,* be surrounded, be gone round, have on all sides, wear round the body. Cs. *zungu-sha, -shwa,* (1) put round, surround with, carry round; (2) cause to go round, make revolve, turn round and round, roll round; (3) keep waiting, waste the time of, cause needless annoyance. E.g. *mahali palipozungushwa boma,* a place with a palisade round it. *Wakajizungusha uwanjani,* and they formed a ring in the open space. *Zungusha maneno,* equivocate, use vague indirect statements. *Zungusha kichwa,* turn the head round. Hence *zungush-ia, -iwa,* e.g. *alimzungushia nguo,* he put clothes on him. Also *zungushana,* e.g. *tusizungushane,* do not let us keep each other waiting. (Cf. *-zungu, mzunguko, zunguko, zungusho,* and see **Zinga.**)

Zunguko, n. (*ma-*), going round, revolving, turning round, winding about, whirling,—and so of objects revolving, &c., e.g. whirlpool, eddy, roundabout speech, windings of a river, circuit, way round, wandering, &c. (Cf. follg.)

Zungumza, v. amuse oneself, converse, play, engage in any pastime. Also act. amuse, play with, and so *jizungumza,* amuse oneself, occupy one's time. (Cf. follg., and *cheza, ongea.*)

Zungumzo, n. (*ma-*), amusement, pastime, game, conversation, gossip, talk. (Cf. prec. and *maongezi, mcheza.*)

Zungusho. n. ...sing to

go round, &c., and also like *zunguko*. E. g. *mazungusho ya shamba*, fencing materials, a fence of a plantation. (Cf. *zungua*.)

*Zuri, n. and Azúr, perjury, false swearing. Also as v. commit perjury, swear falsely. (Ar.)

-zuri, a. (*nzuri* with D 4 (P), D 6, *zuri* with D 5 (S)), beautiful, good, pleasing, fine, i. e. pleasing in any way or degree to any sense or taste,—usually of externals, and so translatable in a great variety of ways, to suit the particular sense affected, and the degree in which it was affected. But also of what commends itself to the moral sense, not as good in itself so much as consonant with that sense, i. e. agreeable, amiable, worthy, excellent, praiseworthy. Thus *mtu mzuri*, a handsome person, or, an excellent, pleasant person. *Kulikuwaje huko ulikokwenda?* How did you like your visit? *Kuzuri*, very much (lit. it was nice, pleasant). (Cf. *uzuri*, and *-ema*, contr. *-baya*.)

*Zuru, v. visit, go on a visit to. Esp. of visiting a grave, e. g. *zuru kaburi*, or *katika kaburi*. *Enda kuzuru*, go to pay a call. Ps. *zuriwa*. Nt. *zurika*. Ap. *zur-ia, -iwa*, e. g. *atanizuria katika kaburi ya mtume*, he will pay a visit for me to the tomb of the apostle, i. e. Mahomet. (Ar., 'visit, go on pilgrimage to.' Cf. *ziara*, and syn. *amkia*.)

Zuruzuka, v. perh. a variant of *zunguka*, go about, wander about, loiter aimlessly, waste time, idle.

-zuzu, a. foolish, simple, inexperienced. (Cf. *mzuzu, uzuzu*, and follg., and syn. *mjinga*.)

Zuzua, v. make a fool of, play tricks on, puzzle a newcomer, treat as a simpleton. Nt. *zuzuka*, e. g. be puzzled, be at a loss, not to know what to do. (Cf. prec.)

THE END.

OXFORD
PRINTED AT THE CLARENDON PRESS
BY HORACE HART, M.A.
PRINTER TO THE UNIVERSITY

CLARENDON PRESS, OXFORD.

ENGLISH LANGUAGE & LITERATURE.

[All books are in extra foolscap octavo, bound in cloth, and are edited with Introduction, Notes, &c., unless otherwise described.]

NEW ENGLISH DICTIONARY, ON HISTORICAL PRINCIPLES: founded mainly on the materials collected by the Philological Society. Imperial 4to. Edited by Dr. MURRAY. Half-bound, 52s. 6d. each vol. Or, in half-volumes, bound with straight-grained persian leather back, cloth sides, gilt top, 1l. 7s. 6d. each.

Vol. I. A, B By Dr. MURRAY.
Vol. II. C By Dr. MURRAY.
Vol. III. { D By Dr. MURRAY.
{ E By Mr. HENRY BRADLEY.
Vol. IV. F, G By Mr. HENRY BRADLEY.
Vol. V. H–K By Dr. MURRAY.

Vol. VI. L–N By Mr. H. BRADLEY. *(In the Press.)*
Vol. VII. O, P By Dr. MURRAY. *(In the Press.)*
Vol. VIII. Q–S By Mr. W. A. CRAIGIE. *(In the Press.)*

BOSWORTH and TOLLER. Anglo-Saxon Dictionary, based on the MS. Collections of the late JOSEPH BOSWORTH, D.D. Edited and enlarged by Prof. T. N. TOLLER, M.A. *Supplement in the Press.*
Parts I–III, A–SÁR. 4to, 15s. each.
Part IV, Section I, SÁR–SWÍDRIAN. 4to, 8s. 6d.
„   „   II, SWÍÞ-SNEL–YTMEST. 4to, 18s. 6d.

BRIGHT. The Gospel of St. Luke in Anglo-Saxon. Edited from the MSS. By JAMES W. BRIGHT, Ph.D. Extra fcap. 8vo, 5s.

MAYHEW, A. L., and SKEAT, W. W. Concise Dictionary of Middle English, from A.D. 1150 to A.D. 1580. Crown 8vo, half-roan, 7s. 6d.

SKEAT, W. W. Concise Etymological Dictionary of the English Language. New Edition. Re-written and re-arranged. Crown 8vo, 5s. 6d.

SWEET, H. Student's Dictionary of Anglo-Saxon. Sm. 4to, 8s. 6d. net.

EARLE, J. Philology of the English Tongue. By J. EARLE, M.A. Fifth Edition. 8s. 6d.

—— Book for the Beginner in Anglo-Saxon. 4th Ed. 2s. 6d.

MORRIS and SKEAT. Specimens of Early English—
Part I. From Old English Homilies to King Horn (A.D. 1150 to A.D. 1300). By R. MORRIS, LL.D. Third Edition. 9s.
Part II. From Robert of Gloucester to Gower (A.D. 1298 to A.D. 1393). By R. MORRIS, LL.D., and W. W. SKEAT, Litt.D. 7s. 6d.

SKEAT, W. W. Specimens of English Literature, from the 'Ploughmans Crede' to the 'Shepheardes Calendar.' 7s. 6d.

—— Principles of English Etymology—
First Series. The Native Element. Second Edition. 8vo, 10s. 6d.
Second Series. The Foreign Element. 8vo, 10s. 6d.

—— Notes on English Etymology. Crown 8vo. 8s. 6d. *net*.

—— Primer of English Etymology. 1s. 6d.

—— Twelve Facsimiles of Old-English Manuscripts. 4to, 7s. 6d.

SWEET, H. New English Grammar, Logical and Historical—
Part I. Introduction, Phonology, and Accidence. Crown 8vo, 10s. 6d.
Part II. Syntax. Crown 8vo, 3s. 6d.

—— Short Historical English Grammar. 4s. 6d.

—— Primer of Historical English Grammar. 2s.

—— History of English Sounds from the Earliest Period. 8vo, 14s.

—— First Steps in Anglo-Saxon. 2s. 6d.

—— Anglo-Saxon Primer, with Grammar, Notes, and Glossary. Eighth Edition. 2s. 6d.

—— Anglo-Saxon Reader. In Prose and Verse. Seventh Edition, Revised and Enlarged. Crown 8vo, 9s. 6d.

—— A Second Anglo-Saxon Reader. 4s. 6d.

—— Old English Reading Primers—
Selected Homilies of Ælfric. Stiff covers, 2s.
Extracts from Alfred's Orosius. Stiff covers, 2s.

—— First Middle English Primer, with Grammar and Glossary. Second Edition. 2s. 6d.

—— Second Middle English Primer. Extracts from Chaucer, with Grammar and Glossary. 2s. 6d.

—— Primer of Spoken English. 3s. 6d.

—— Primer of Phonetics. Second Edition. 3s. 6d.

—— Manual of Current Shorthand, Orthographic and Phonetic. Crown 8vo, 4s. 6d.

TANCOCK, O. W. Elementary English Grammar and Exercise Book. Third Edition. 1s. 6d.

—— English Grammar and Reading Book for Lower Forms in Classical Schools. Fourth Edition. 3s. 6d.

A SERIES OF ENGLISH CLASSICS.

CHAUCER. Prologue; Knightes Tale; Nonne Prestes Tale. Edited by R. Morris, LL.D. New Edition, with Collations and Additional Notes, by W. W. Skeat, Litt.D. 2s. 6d.

EDITED BY W. W. SKEAT, LITT.D., ETC.

—— Prologue to the Canterbury Tales. (School Edition.) 1s.

—— Prioresses Tale; Sir Thopas; Monkes Tale; Clerkes Tale; Squieres Tale, &c. Seventh Edition. 4s. 6d.

—— Tale of the Man of Lawe; Pardoneres Tale; Second Nonnes Tale; Chanouns Yemannes Tale. New Edition, Revised. 4s. 6d.

—— Minor Poems. Crown 8vo, 10s. 6d.

CHAUCER. Legend of Good Women. Crown 8vo, 6s.
—— Hous of Fame. Crown 8vo, 2s.

LANGLAND. Vision of William concerning Piers the Plowman, by W. LANGLAND. By W. W. SKEAT, Litt.D. Sixth Edition. 4s. 6d.

HAVELOK. The Lay of Havelok the Dane. By W. W. SKEAT, Litt.D. With two Facsimiles. 4s. 6d.

GAMELYN, THE TALE OF. By W. W. SKEAT, Litt.D. 1s. 6d.

WYCLIFFE. New Testament in English according to the Version by WYCLIFFE, c. A.D. 1380. Revised by J. PURVEY, c. 1388. With Introduction, &c., by W. W. SKEAT, Litt.D. 6s.

—— Job, Psalms, Proverbs, Ecclesiastes, and Song of Solomon: according to the Wycliffite Version made by N. DE HEREFORD, c. A.D. 1381. Revised by J. PURVEY, c. A.D. 1388. By the Same. 3s. 6d.

MINOT. The Poems of Laurence Minot. By JOSEPH HALL, M.A. Second Edition. 4s. 6d.

SPENSER. The Faery Queene. Books I and II. By G. W. KITCHIN, D.D., with Glossary by A. L. MAYHEW, M.A. 2s. 6d. each.

HOOKER. Ecclesiastical Polity, I. By R. W. CHURCH, M.A. 2s.

MARLOWE. Edward II. By O. W. TANCOCK, M.A. Third Edition. Paper covers, 2s.; cloth, 3s.

MARLOWE & GREENE. MARLOWE'S Dr. Faustus, and GREENE'S Friar Bacon and Friar Bungay. By A. W. WARD, Litt.D. Fourth Edition, Revised. Crown 8vo, 6s. 6d.

SHAKESPEARE. Select Plays. Edited by W. G. CLARK, M.A., and W. ALDIS WRIGHT, D.C.L.
Merchant of Venice. 1s. Macbeth. 1s. 6d.
Richard the Second. 1s. 6d. Hamlet. 2s.

Edited by W. ALDIS WRIGHT, D.C.L.
Tempest. 1s. 6d. Coriolanus. 2s. 6d.
As You Like It. 1s. 6d. Richard the Third. 2s. 6d.
Midsummer Night's Dream. 1s. 6d. Henry the Fifth. 2s.
Twelfth Night. 1s. 6d. King John. 1s. 6d.
Julius Caesar. 2s. King Lear. 1s. 6d.
Henry the Eighth. 2s. Much Ado about Nothing. 1s. 6d.
Henry the Fourth, Part I. 2s.

SHAKESPEARE AS A DRAMATIC ARTIST. Third Edition. By R. G. MOULTON, M.A. Crown 8vo, 7s. 6d.

—— Chapters on Macbeth. Being an extract from *Shakespeare as a Dramatic Artist*. By R. G. MOULTON, M.A. Crown 8vo, 9d. net.

BACON. Advancement of Learning. By W. ALDIS WRIGHT, D.C.L. New Edition. Crown 8vo, 3s. 6d.

—— The Essays. By S. H. REYNOLDS, M.A. 8vo, 12s. 6d.

MILTON. Areopagitica. By JOHN W. HALES, M.A. 3s.

—— The Poetical Works of John Milton. Edited, after the Original Texts, by the Rev. H. C. BEECHING, M.A. Crown 8vo, with Portrait and Facsimile Title-pages. (a) Ordinary paper, cloth, 3s. 6d.; (b) India Paper, cloth extra, 8s.; and in leather bindings.

—— Poems. By R. C. BROWNE, M.A. 2 Vols. 6s. 6d.
Separately, Vol. I. 4s., Vol. II. 3s. Paper covers, Lycidas, 3d. Comus, 6d.
By OLIVER ELTON, B.A.
Lycidas, 6d. L'Allegro, 4d. Il Penseroso, 4d. Comus, 1s.

MILTON. Paradise Lost. Book I. By H. C. Beeching, M.A.
Book II. By E. K. Chambers, B.A., 1s.6d. each. (Books I and II together, 2s.6d.)

—— Samson Agonistes. By J. Churton Collins, M.A. 1s.

—— Prosody. By Robert Bridges. Also, *Classical Metres in English Verse*. By W. J. Stone. Crown 8vo, 5s. net.

BUNYAN. Pilgrim's Progress, Grace Abounding, Imprisonment of Mr. John Bunyan. Edited by E. Venables, M.A. Second Edition, Revised by Mabel Peacock. Crown 8vo, with Portrait, 3s. 6d.

—— The Holy War, and the Heavenly Footman. Edited by Mabel Peacock. 3s. 6d.

CLARENDON. History of the Rebellion. Book VI. By T. Arnold, M.A. Second Edition. Crown 8vo, 5s.

—— Selections. By G. Boyle, M.A. Crown 8vo, 7s. 6d.

DRYDEN. Select Poems. By W. D. Christie, M.A. Fifth Edition. Revised by C. H. Firth, M.A. 3s. 6d.

—— Essay of Dramatic Poesy. By T. Arnold, M.A. Second Edition. 3s. 6d.

LOCKE. Conduct of the Understanding. By T. Fowler, D.D. Third Edition. 2s. 6d.

ADDISON. Selections from Papers in the Spectator. By T. Arnold, M.A. Nineteenth Thousand. 4s. 6d.

STEELE. Selections from the Tatler, Spectator, and Guardian. By Austin Dobson. Second Edition. Crown 8vo, 7s. 6d.

SWIFT. Selections from his Works. With Life, Introductions, and Notes, by Sir Henry Craik, K.C.B. 2 Vols. Crown 8vo, 7s. 6d. each.

POPE. Essay on Man. Edited by Mark Pattison, B.D. Sixth Edition. Stiff covers. 1s. 6d.

—— Satires and Epistles. Fourth Edition. 2s.

THOMSON. The Seasons, and The Castle of Indolence. By J. Logie Robertson, M.A. 4s. 6d.

—— The Castle of Indolence. 1s. 6d.

BERKELEY. Selections. By A. C. Fraser, LL.D. Fifth Edition, Amended. Crown 8vo, 7s. 6d.

JOHNSON. Rasselas. By G. Birkbeck Hill, D.C.L. Limp, 2s.; in Parchment, 4s. 6d.

—— Rasselas; Lives of Dryden and Pope. By Alfred Milnes, M.A. 4s. 6d.

—— Lives of Dryden and Pope only. Stiff covers, 2s. 6d.

—— Life of Milton. By C. H. Firth, M.A. 1s.6d.; cloth, 2s. 6d.

—— Vanity of Human Wishes. By E. J. Payne, M.A. Paper covers, 4d.

GRAY. Selected Poems. By Edm. Gosse, M.A. Parchment, 3s.

—— The same, together with Supplementary Notes for Schools, by Foster Watson, M.A. Stiff covers, 1s. 6d.

GOLDSMITH. Selected Poems. By Austin Dobson. 3s. 6d. In Parchment, 4s. 6d.

—— The Traveller. By G. B. Hill, D.C.L. Stiff covers, 1s.

—— The Deserted Village. Paper covers, 2d.

COWPER. The Didactic Poems of 1782, with Selections from the Minor Pieces, A.D. 1779-1783. By H. T. Griffith, B.A. 3s.

—— The Task, with Tirocinium, and Selections from the Minor Poems, A.D. 1784-1799. By the Same. 3s.

BURKE. Thoughts on the Present Discontents; the two Speeches on America. By E. J. Payne, M.A. 4s. 6d.

—— Reflections on the French Revolution. 5s.

—— Four Letters on the Proposals for Peace with the Regicide Directory of France. 5s.

BURNS. Selected Poems. By J. Logie Robertson, M.A. Crown 8vo, 6s.

KEATS. The Odes of Keats. With Notes, Illustrations, Analyses, and a Memoir, by Arthur C. Downer, M.A. 3s. 6d. net.

—— Hyperion, Book I. By W. T. Arnold, B.A. 4d.

BYRON. Childe Harold. By H. F. Tozer, M.A. 3s. 6d.

SHELLEY. Adonais. By W. M. Rossetti. Crown 8vo, 5s.

SCOTT. Lady of the Lake. By W. Minto, M.A. 3s. 6d.

—— Lay of the Last Minstrel. By the Same. 1s. 6d.

—— Lay of the Last Minstrel. Introduction and Canto I. 6d.

—— Lord of the Isles. By Thomas Bayne. 2s.; cloth, 2s. 6d.

—— Marmion. By the Same. 3s. 6d.

—— Ivanhoe. By C. E. Theodosius, M.A. 2s.

—— The Talisman. By H. B. George, M.A. Stiff covers, 2s.

CAMPBELL. Gertrude of Wyoming. By H. Macaulay FitzGibbon, M.A. Second Edition. Stiff covers, 1s.

WORDSWORTH. The White Doe of Rylstone. By William Knight, LL.D. 2s. 6d.

COUCH. The Oxford Book of English Verse. 1250-1900. Chosen and Edited by A. T. Quiller-Couch. Crown 8vo, cloth, gilt top, 7s. 6d.; Fcap. 8vo, on Oxford India Paper, cloth extra, gilt top, 10s. 6d.
Also in leather bindings.

TYPICAL SELECTIONS from the best English Writers. Second Edition. In Two Volumes. 3s. 6d. each.

GEORGE and HADOW. Poems of English Country Life. Selected and Edited, with Introduction and Notes, by H. B. George, M.A. and

GEOGRAPHY, HISTORY, &c.

BARNARD. Companion to English History (Middle Ages). By F. P. BARNARD, M.A. With ninety-seven Illustrations. Crown 8vo, 8s. 6d. net.

A SCHOOL HISTORY OF ENGLAND, down to the death of Queen Victoria. With Maps, Plans and Bibliographies. By various writers. Crown 8vo, 3s. 6d.

GEORGE. Relations of Geography and History. By H. B. GEORGE, M.A. With Two Maps. Crown 8vo, 4s. 6d.

GRESWELL. History of the Dominion of Canada. By W. PARR GRESWELL, M.A. 1890. Crown 8vo, 7s. 6d.

—— Geography of the Dominion of Canada and Newfoundland. 1891. 6s.

—— Geography of Africa South of the Zambesi. 1892. 7s. 6d.

HUGHES (Alfred). Geography for Schools. Part I, Practical Geography. With Diagrams. 2s. 6d.

LUCAS. Historical Geography of the British Colonies. By C. P. LUCAS, B.A., C.B. Crown 8vo.
    Introduction. Revised by H. E. EGERTON.   [*In the Press.*
    Vol. I. The Mediterranean and Eastern Colonies (exclusive of India). With Eleven Maps. 1888. 5s.
    Vol. II. The West Indian Colonies. With Twelve Maps. 1890. 7s. 6d.
    Vol. III. West Africa. Second Edition, Revised to the end of 1899 by H. E. EGERTON. With Five Maps. 7s. 6d.
    Vol. IV. South and East Africa. Historical and Geographical. With Eleven Maps. 1898. 9s. 6d.
        Part I. Historical. 6s. 6d.   Part II. Geographical. 3s. 6d.
        Also Vol. IV, Part I, Separate Issue, with numerous Maps. 5s.
        The History of South Africa to the Jameson Raid.
    Vol. V. Canada. Part I (New France). With Maps. 6s.

MATHEMATICS & PHYSICAL SCIENCE.

ALDIS. A Text Book of Algebra (with Answers to the Examples). By W. STEADMAN ALDIS, M.A. Crown 8vo, 7s. 6d.

EMTAGE. An Introduction to the Mathematical Theory of Electricity and Magnetism. By W. T. A. EMTAGE, M.A. 2nd Ed. Cr. 8vo, 7s. 6d.

FINN. The 'Junior' Euclid. By S. W. FINN, M.A. Crown 8vo. Books I and II, 1s. 6d. Books III and IV, 2s.

FISHER. Class-Book of Chemistry. By W. W. FISHER, M.A., F.C.S. Fourth Edition. Crown 8vo, 4s. 6d.

FOCK. An Introduction to Chemical Crystallography. By ANDREAS FOCK, Ph.D. Translated and Edited by W. J. POPE. Crown 8vo, 5s.

HAMILTON and BALL. Book-keeping. By Sir R. G. C. HAMILTON, K.C.B., and JOHN BALL. New and Enlarged Edition. 2s.

—— Ruled Exercise Books, 1s. 6d.

—— —— (Preliminary Course only), 4d.

HARCOURT and MADAN. Exercises in Practical Chemistry. By A. G. VERNON HARCOURT, M.A., and H. G. MADAN, M.A. Fifth Edition.

HARGREAVES. Arithmetic. By R. HARGREAVES, M.A. Crown 8vo, 4s. 6d.

HENSLEY, L. Figures made Easy: a first Arithmetic Book. Crown 8vo, 6d. Answers, 1s.

—— The Scholar's Arithmetic. Cr. 8vo, 2s. 6d. Answers, 1s. 6d.

—— The Scholar's Algebra. An Introductory work on Algebra. Crown 8vo, 2s. 6d.

JOHNSTON. An Elementary Treatise on Analytical Geometry. By W. J. JOHNSTON, M.A. Crown 8vo, 6s.

MINCHIN. Geometry for Beginners. An easy Introduction to Geometry for Young Learners. By G. M. MINCHIN, M.A., F.R.S. 1s. 6d.

NIXON. Euclid Revised. Containing the essentials of the Elements of Plane Geometry as given by Euclid in his First Six Books. By R. C. J. NIXON, M.A. Third Edition. Crown 8vo, 6s.
Book I, 1s.   Books I, II, 1s. 6d.   Books I-IV, 3s.   Books V, VI, 3s. 6d.

—— Geometrical Exercises from Nixon's 'Euclid Revised,' with Solutions by A. LARMOR, M.A. Crown 8vo, 3s. 6d.

—— Geometry in Space. Containing parts of Euclid's Eleventh and Twelfth Books. By the Same. Crown 8vo, 3s. 6d.

—— Elementary Plane Trigonometry; that is, Plane Trigonometry without Imaginaries. By the Same. Crown 8vo, 7s. 6d.

RUSSELL. An Elementary Treatise on Pure Geometry. By J. WELLESLEY RUSSELL, M.A. Crown 8vo, 10s. 6d.

SELBY. Elementary Mechanics of Solids and Fluids. By A. L. SELBY, M.A. Crown 8vo, 7s. 6d.

WARREN. Experimental and Theoretical Course of Geometry. By A. T. WARREN, M.A. Crown 8vo. With or without Answers. 2s.

WILLIAMSON. Chemistry for Students. By A. W. WILLIAMSON, M.A., Phil. Doc., F.R.S. 8s. 6d.

WOOLLCOMBE. Practical Work in General Physics. By W. G. WOOLLCOMBE, M.A., B.Sc. Crown 8vo, 2s. each part.
Part I.   General Physics. } Second Edition Revised.
Part II. Heat.
Part III. Light and Sound.
Part IV. Magnetism and Electricity.

MISCELLANEOUS.

BALFOUR. The Educational Systems of Great Britain and Ireland. By GRAHAM BALFOUR, M.A. Second Edition, revised. 8vo, 7s. 6d. net.

BUCKMASTER. Elementary Architecture for Schools, Art Students, and General Readers. By MARTIN A. BUCKMASTER. With thirty-eight full-page Illustrations. Crown 8vo, 4s. 6d.

COOKSON. Essays on Secondary Education. By Various Contributors. Edited by CHRISTOPHER COOKSON, M.A. Crown 8vo, paper boards, 4s. 6d.

FARMER. Hymns and Chorales for Schools and Colleges. Edited by JOHN FARMER, late Organist of Balliol College, Oxford. 5s.
Hymns without the Tunes. 2s.

FOWLER. The Elements of Deductive and Inductive Logic. By T. Fowler, D.D. 7s. 6d.

The Elements of Deductive Logic, designed mainly for the use of Junior Students in the Universities. With a Collection of Examples. 3s. 6d.

The Elements of Inductive Logic, designed mainly for the use of Students in the Universities. Sixth Edition. 6s.

HULLAH, J. The Cultivation of the Speaking Voice. 2s. 6d.

SOMERVELL. Chart of the Rules of Harmony. By A. Somervell. Crown 4to, on a card. 1s. net.

—— Chart of the Rules of Counterpoint. Crown 4to, on a card. 1s. net.

TROUTBECK and DALE. A Music Primer for Schools. By J. Troutbeck, D.D., and R. F. Dale, M.A., B.Mus. Crown 8vo, 1s. 6d.

UPCOTT. An Introduction to Greek Sculpture. By L. E. Upcott, M.A. Second Edition. Crown 8vo, 4s. 6d.

HELPS TO THE STUDY OF THE BIBLE, taken from the Oxford Bible for Teachers. New, Enlarged and Illustrated Edition. Pearl 16mo, stiff covers, 1s. net. Large Paper Edition, Long Primer 8vo, cloth boards, 5s.

HELPS TO THE STUDY OF THE BOOK OF COMMON PRAYER. Being a Companion to Church Worship. By W. R. W. Stephens, D.D., late Dean of Winchester. Crown 8vo, 2s. 6d. net.

THE PARALLEL PSALTER, being the Prayer-Book Version of the Psalms, and a new Version arranged on opposite pages. With an Introduction and Glossaries by the Rev. S. R. Driver, D.D., Litt.D. 6s.

OLD TESTAMENT HISTORY FOR SCHOOLS. By T. H. Stokoe, D.D. 2s. 6d. each Part.

Part I. From the Creation to the Settlement in Palestine. Second Edition.
Part II. From the Settlement to the Disruption of the Kingdom.
Part III. From the Disruption to the Return from Captivity. (Completion.)

MANUAL OF THE FOUR GOSPELS. By T. H. Stokoe, D.D. Crown 8vo. Part I. The Gospel Narrative. 2s. Part II. The Gospel Teaching. 2s. Or, combined, 3s. 6d.

LIFE AND LETTERS OF ST. PAUL. By T. H. Stokoe, D.D. Crown 8vo. Part I. The Life. 2s. Part II. The Letters. 2s. Or, combined, 3s. 6d.

FIRST DAYS AND EARLY LETTERS OF THE CHURCH. By T. H. Stokoe, D.D. Crown 8vo. Part I. First Days of the Church. 1s. 6d. Part II. Early Letters of the Church. 2s. Or, combined, 3s.

GRADUATED LESSONS ON THE OLD TESTAMENT. By U. Z. Rule. Edited by Lt. J. M. Bebb, M.A. In three Volumes. Extra fcap. 8vo, with Maps. Each 1s. 6d. paper boards. 1s. 9d. in cloth.

NOTES ON THE GOSPEL OF ST. LUKE, FOR JUNIOR CLASSES. By Miss E. J. Moore Smith. Stiff covers, 1s. 6d.

OXFORD
AT THE CLARENDON PRESS
LONDON, EDINBURGH, AND NEW YORK
HENRY FROWDE

CPSIA information can be obtained at www.ICGtesting.com
Printed in the USA
LVOW050739020312

271200LV00025B/9/P